This envelope should contain a premium website access card. If the envelope is missing, opened, or damaged, you may not be purchasing a new book. Significant value will be lost without the premium website. Access to the website can be purchased separately by visiting http://www.ichapters.com.

Attention!
To access your Essential Textbook
Resources, please visit:
login.cengagebrain.com
Your unique access code can be found on
the back of this card.

Spreadsheet Modeling & Decision Analysis 6e

A Practical Introduction to Management Science

Cliff Ragsdale

Virginia Polytechnic Institute
and State University

In memory of those
who were killed and injured
in the noble pursuit of education
here at Virginia Tech on April 16, 2007

SOUTH-WESTERN
CENGAGE Learning™

Australia • Brazil • Japan • Korea • Mexico • Singapore • Spain • United Kingdom • United States

SOUTH-WESTERN
CENGAGE Learning™

Spreadsheet Modeling & Decision Analysis, Sixth Edition

Cliff T. Ragsdale

Vice President of Editorial, Business:
Jack W. Calhoun

Publisher: Joe Sabatino

Sr. Acquisitions Editor: Charles McCormick, Jr.

Developmental Editor: Maggie Kubale

Editorial Assistant: Nora Heink

Marketing Director: Adam Marsh

Sr. Content Project Manager: Holly Henjum

Media Editor: Chris Valentine

Print Buyer: Miranda Klapper

Sr. Marketing Communications Manager:
Libby Shipp

Production Service: MPS Limited,
a Macmillan Company

Sr. Art Director: Stacy Jenkins Shirley

Internal Designer: cMiller Design

Cover Designer: Stuart Kunkler, triARTis
Communications

Cover Image: Detail showing profile view of
the Farnese Hercules by Glykon. Image
by © Araldo de Luca/CORBIS; Δεταιλ οφ
οφφιχε © Alexander Hafemanny

Rights Acquisitions Specialist: Mardell
Glinski Schultz

Preface

Spreadsheets are one of the most popular and ubiquitous software packages on the planet. Every day, millions of business people use spreadsheet programs to build models of the decision problems they face as a regular part of their work activities. As a result, employers look for experience and ability with spreadsheets in the people they recruit.

Spreadsheets have also become the standard vehicle for introducing undergraduate and graduate students in business and engineering to the concepts and tools covered in the introductory operations research/management science (OR/MS) course. This simultaneously develops students' skills with a standard tool of today's business world and opens their eyes to how a variety of OR/MS techniques can be used in this modeling environment. Spreadsheets also capture students' interest and add a new relevance to OR/MS as they see how it can be applied with popular commercial software being used in the business world.

Spreadsheet Modeling & Decision Analysis provides an introduction to the most commonly used OR/MS techniques and shows how these tools can be implemented using Microsoft® Excel. Prior experience with Excel is certainly helpful but is not a requirement for using this text. In general, a student familiar with computers and the spreadsheet concepts presented in most introductory computer courses should have no trouble using this text. Step-by-step instructions and screenshots are provided for each example, and software tips are included throughout the text as needed.

What's New in the Sixth Edition?

The most significant change in the sixth edition of *Spreadsheet Modeling & Decision Analysis* is its extensive coverage and use of Risk Solver Platform™ for Education by Frontline Systems, Inc. Risk Solver Platform for Education is a new add-in for Excel that provides access to analytical tools for performing optimization, simulation, sensitivity analysis, and discriminant analysis, as well as the ability to create decision trees. Risk Solver Platform for Education makes it easy to run multiple parameterized optimizations and simulations and apply optimization techniques to simulation models in one integrated, coherent interface. Risk Solver Platform also offers amazing interactive simulation features in which simulation results are automatically updated in real time whenever a manual change is made to a spreadsheet. Additionally, when run in its optional Guided Mode, Risk Solver Platform provides students with more than 100 customized dialogs that provide diagnoses of various model conditions and explain the steps involved in solving problems. Risk Solver Platform offers numerous other features and will transform the way we approach OR/MS education now and in the future.

Additional changes in the revised sixth edition of *Spreadsheet Modeling & Decision Analysis* from the fifth edition include the following:

- Microsoft® Office 2010 is featured throughout.
- Data files and software to accompany the book are now available for download online.
- Chapter 1 features a new way of characterizing the quality and outcomes of decisions.

- Chapter 3 introduces Risk Solver Platform's ability to perform multiple optimizations in the context of Data Envelopment Analysis (DEA).
- Chapter 4 features new coverage of using multiple optimizations for sensitivity analysis and a new section on robust optimization.
- Chapters 8, 10, and 11 feature new coverage of Excel's AVERAGEIF( ) function.
- Chapter 12 features the interactive simulation capabilities of Risk Solver Platform, including the use of Value at Risk constraints and simulation optimization.
- Chapter 14 (formerly Chapter 15) now covers Decision Analysis featuring Risk Solver Platform's decision tree and sensitivity analysis tools.
- Chapter 15 (formerly Chapter 14) is now available exclusively online and covers project management, including Microsoft Project 2010.
- Several new and revised end-of-chapter problems have been added throughout.

Innovative Features

Aside from its strong spreadsheet orientation, the sixth edition of *Spreadsheet Modeling & Decision Analysis* contains several other unique features that distinguish it from traditional OR/MS texts.

- Algebraic formulations and spreadsheets are used side by side to help develop conceptual thinking skills.
- Step-by-step instructions and numerous annotated screenshots make examples easy to follow and understand.
- Emphasis is placed on model formulation and interpretation rather than on algorithms.
- Realistic examples motivate the discussion of each topic.
- Solutions to example problems are analyzed from a managerial perspective.
- A unique and accessible chapter covering discriminant analysis is provided.
- Sections entitled "The World of Management Science" show how each topic has been applied in a real company.

Organization

The table of contents for *Spreadsheet Modeling & Decision Analysis* is laid out in a fairly traditional format, but topics may be covered in a variety of ways. The text begins with an overview of OR/MS in Chapter 1. Chapters 2 through 8 cover various topics in deterministic modeling techniques: linear programming, sensitivity analysis, networks, integer programming, goal programming and multiple objective optimization, and nonlinear and evolutionary programming. Chapters 9 through 11 cover predictive modeling and forecasting techniques: regression analysis, discriminant analysis, and time series analysis.

Chapters 12 and 13 cover stochastic modeling techniques: simulation and queuing theory. Coverage of simulation using the inherent capabilities of Excel alone is available on the textbook's website (for more information, visit **www.cengage.com/decisionsciences/ragsdale.** Chapter 14 covers decision analysis, and Chapter 15 (available online) provides an introduction to project management.

After completing Chapter 1, a quick refresher on spreadsheet fundamentals (entering and copying formulas, basic formatting and editing, etc.) is always a good idea. Suggestions for the Excel review may be found on the website. Following this, an instructor could cover the material on optimization, forecasting, or simulation, depending on personal preferences. The chapters on queuing and project management make general references to simulation and, therefore, should follow the discussion of that topic.

Ancillary Materials

Several excellent ancillaries for the instructor accompany the revised edition of *Spreadsheet Modeling & Decision Analysis*. All instructor ancillaries are provided online at the textbook's website. Included in this convenient format are the following:

- **Instructor's Manual.** The Instructor's Manual, prepared by the author, contains solutions to all the text problems and cases.
- **Test Bank.** The Test Bank, prepared by Tom Bramorski of the University of Wisconsin-Whitewater, includes multiple-choice, true/false, and short answer problems for each text chapter. It also includes mini-projects that may be assigned as take-home assignments. The Test Bank is included as Microsoft Word files. The Test Bank also comes separately in a computerized ExamView™ format that allows instructors to use or modify the questions and create original questions.
- **PowerPoint Presentation Slides.** Microsoft PowerPoint presentation slides, prepared by the author, provide ready-made lecture material for each chapter in the book.

Instructors who adopt the text for their classes may contact their Cengage Learning Representative to request the Instructor's Resource CD (ISBN 1-111-56841-3).

Acknowledgments

I thank the following colleagues who made important contributions to the development and completion of this book. The reviewers for the sixth edition were:

Ajay K. Aggarwal, Millsaps College
Matthew D. Bailey, Bucknell University
Richard M. Bayney, University of Pennsylvania
Jason S. Bergtold, Kansas State University
Roger Blake, University of Massachusetts – Boston
Robert F. Brooker, Gannon University
Timothy W. Butler, Wayne State University
Jonathan P. Caulkins, Carnegie Mellon University
Tom Cox, University of Wisconsin – Madison
Joan M. Donohue, University of South Carolina
Sandy Edwards, Northeastern State University
Mira Ezvan, Lindenwood University
Ted Glickman, George Washington University
Deborah Hanson, University of Great Falls
David A. Larson, University of South Alabama
Leo Lopes, Monash University
Michael Martel, Ohio University
Alan Olinsky, Bryant University
Mark Polczynski, Marquette University
Eivis Qenani, Cal Poly San Luis Obispo
B. Madhu Rao, Bowling Green
M. Tony Ratcliffe, James Madison University
Cem Saydam, UNC Charlotte
Maureen Sevigny, Oregon Institute of Technology
John Seydel, Arkansas State University
John Stamey, Coastal Carolina University

William Stein, Texas A & M University
Minghe Sun, The University of Texas at San Antonio
Ahmad Syamil, Arkansas State University
Danny L. Taylor, University of Nevada
Dan Widdis, Naval Postgraduate School
Roger Woods, Michigan Technological University
Dennis Yu, Clarkson University

I also thank Tom Bramorski of the University of Wisconsin-Whitewater for preparing the test bank that accompanies this book. David Ashley also provided many of the summary articles found in "The World of Management Science" feature throughout the text and created the queuing template used in Chapter 13. Jack Yurkiewicz, Pace University, contributed several of the cases found throughout the text.

My sincere thanks goes to all students and instructors who have used previous editions of this book and provided many valuable comments and suggestions for making it better. I also thank the wonderful SMDA team at Cengage Learning: Charles McCormick, Jr., Senior Acquisitions Editor; Maggie Kubale, Developmental Editor; Holly Henjum, Senior Content Project Manager; Chris Valentine, Media Editor; and Adam Marsh, Marketing Manager. I feel very fortunate and privileged to work with each of you.

A very special word of thanks to my friend Dan Fylstra and the crew at Frontline Systems (**www.solver.com**) for conceiving and creating Risk Solver Platform and supporting me so graciously and quickly throughout my revision work on this book. In my opinion, Risk Solver Platform is the most significant development in OR/MS education since the creation of personal computers and the electronic spreadsheet. (Dan, you get my vote for a lifetime achievement award in analytical modeling and induction in the OR/MS Hall of Fame!)

Once again, I thank my dear wife, Kathy, for her unending patience, support, encouragement, and love. (You will always be the one.) This book is dedicated to our sons, Thomas, Patrick, and Daniel. I am proud of each one of you and will always be so glad that God let me be your daddy and the leader of the Ragsdale ragamuffin band.

Final Thoughts

I hope you enjoy the spreadsheet approach to teaching OR/MS as much as I do and that you find this book to be very interesting and helpful. If you find creative ways to use the techniques in this book or need help applying them, I would love to hear from you. Also, any comments, questions, suggestions, or constructive criticism you have concerning this text are always welcome.

Cliff T. Ragsdale
e-mail: crags@vt.edu

Brief Contents

Contents

Chapter 1

Introduction to Modeling and Decision Analysis

1.0 Introduction

This book is titled *Spreadsheet Modeling and Decision Analysis: A Practical Introduction to Management Science*, so let's begin by discussing exactly what this title means. By the very nature of life, all of us must continually make decisions that we hope will solve problems and lead to increased opportunities for ourselves or the organizations for which we work. But making good decisions is rarely an easy task. The problems faced by decision makers in today's competitive, fast-paced business environment are often extremely complex and can be addressed by numerous possible courses of action. Evaluating these alternatives and choosing the best course of action represents the essence of decision analysis.

During the past decade, millions of business people discovered that one of the most effective ways to analyze and evaluate decision alternatives involves using electronic spreadsheets to build computer models of the decision problems they face. A **computer model** is a set of mathematical relationships and logical assumptions implemented in a computer as a representation of some real-world object, decision problem or phenomenon. Today, electronic spreadsheets provide the most convenient and useful way for business people to implement and analyze computer models. Indeed, most business people would probably rate the electronic spreadsheet as their most important analytical tool apart from their brain! Using a **spreadsheet model** (a computer model implemented via a spreadsheet), a businessperson can analyze decision alternatives before having to choose a specific plan for implementation.

This book introduces you to a variety of techniques from the field of management science that can be applied in spreadsheet models to assist in the decision-analysis process. For our purposes, we will define **management science** as a field of study that uses computers, statistics, and mathematics to solve business problems. It involves applying the methods and tools of science to management and decision making. It is the science of making better decisions. Management science is also sometimes referred to as operations research or decision science. See Figure 1.1 for a summary of how management science has been applied successfully in a number of real-world situations.

In the not-too-distant past, management science was a highly specialized field that generally could be practiced only by those who had access to mainframe computers and who possessed an advanced knowledge of mathematics and computer programming languages. However, the proliferation of powerful PCs and the development of easy-to-use electronic spreadsheets have made the tools of management science far more practical and available to a much larger audience. Virtually everyone who uses a

FIGURE 1.1

*Examples of
successful
management
science
applications*

Over the past decade, scores of operations research and management science projects saved companies millions of dollars. Each year, the Institute for Operations Research and the Management Sciences (INFORMS) sponsors the Franz Edelman Awards competition to recognize some of the most outstanding OR/MS projects during the past year. Here are some of the "home runs" from the 2008 Edelman Awards (described in *Interfaces*, Vol. 39, No. 1, January-February, 2009).

- **Xerox** has invented, tested, and implemented an innovative group of productivity-improvement solutions, trademarked LDP Lean Document Production® solutions, for the $100 billion printing industry in the United States. These solutions have provided dramatic productivity and cost improvements for both print shops and document-manufacturing facilities. These solutions have extended the use of operations research to small- and medium-sized print shops, while increasing the scope of applications in large document-production facilities. **Benefits:** LDP solutions have generated approximately $200 million of incremental profit across the Xerox customer value chain since their initial introduction in 2000 and improved productivity by 20–40%.

- The network for transport of natural gas on the Norwegian Continental Shelf is the world's largest offshore pipeline network. The gas flowing through this network represents approximately 15% of European consumption. In a network of interconnected pipelines, system effects are prevalent, and the network must be analyzed as a whole to determine the optimal operation. The main Norwegian shipper of natural gas, **StatoilHydro**, uses a tool called GassOpt that allows users to graphically model their network and run optimizations to find the best network configuration and routing for transporting gas. **Benefits:** The company estimates that its accumulated savings related to the use of GassOpt were approximately US $2 billion as of 2008.

- In the United States, the **Federal Aviation Administration** (FAA) is responsible for providing air traffic management services and frequently faces situations where a large-scale weather system reduces airspace capacity. In June 2006, the FAA began using a tool known as Airspace Flow Programs that gave the FAA the ability to control activity in congested airspaces by issuing ground delays customized for each individual flight when large-scale thunderstorms block major flight routes. **Benefits:** During its first two years of use, the system saved aircraft operators an estimated $190 million.

- In 2006, **Netherlands Railways** introduced a new timetable designed to support the growth of passenger and freight transport on a highly used railway network and to reduce the number of train delays. Constructing a railway timetable from scratch for about 5,500 daily trains is a complex challenge. To meet this challenge, techniques were used to generate several timetables, one of which was finally selected and implemented. Additionally, because rolling stock and crew costs are the most significant expenses for a railway operator, OR (operations research) tools were used to design efficient schedules for these two resources. **Benefits:** The more efficient resource schedules and the increased number of passengers have increased annual profit by 40 million Euros (US $60 million). Moreover, the trains are transporting more passengers on the same railway infrastructure with more on-time arrivals than ever before.

spreadsheet today for model building and decision making is a practitioner of management science—whether they realize it or not.

1.1 The Modeling Approach to Decision Making

The idea of using models in problem solving and decision analysis is really not new and is certainly not tied to the use of computers. At some point, all of us have used a modeling approach to make a decision. For example, if you have ever moved into a dormitory, apartment, or house, you undoubtedly faced a decision about how to arrange the furniture in your new dwelling. There were probably a number of different arrangements to consider. One arrangement might give you the most open space but require that you build a loft. Another might give you less space but allow you to avoid the hassle and expense of building a loft. To analyze these different arrangements and make a decision, you did not build the loft. You more likely built a **mental model** of the two arrangements, picturing what each looked like in your mind's eye. Thus, a simple mental model is sometimes all that is required to analyze a problem and make a decision.

For more complex decision problems, a mental model might be impossible or insufficient, and other types of models might be required. For example, a set of drawings or blueprints for a house or building provides a **visual model** of the real-world structure. These drawings help illustrate how the various parts of the structure will fit together when it is completed. A road map is another type of visual model because it assists a driver in analyzing the various routes from one location to another.

You have probably also seen car commercials on television showing automotive engineers using **physical,** or **scale, models** to study the aerodynamics of various car designs in order to find the shape that creates the least wind resistance and maximizes fuel economy. Similarly, aeronautical engineers use scale models of airplanes to study the flight characteristics of various fuselage and wing designs. And civil engineers might use scale models of buildings and bridges to study the strengths of different construction techniques.

Another common type of model is a **mathematical model**, which uses mathematical relationships to describe or represent an object or decision problem. Throughout this book, we will study how various mathematical models can be implemented and analyzed on computers using spreadsheet software. But before we move to an in-depth discussion of spreadsheet models, let's look at some of the more general characteristics and benefits of modeling.

1.2 Characteristics and Benefits of Modeling

Although this book focuses on mathematical models implemented in computers via spreadsheets, the examples of nonmathematical models given earlier are worth discussing a bit more because they help illustrate a number of important characteristics and benefits of modeling in general. First, the models mentioned earlier are usually simplified versions of the object or decision problem they represent. To study the aerodynamics of a car design, we do not need to build the entire car complete with engine and stereo. Such components have little or no effect on aerodynamics. So, although a model is often a simplified representation of reality, the model is useful as long as it is valid. A **valid model** is one that accurately represents the relevant characteristics of the object or decision problem being studied.

Second, it is often less expensive to analyze decision problems using a model. This is especially easy to understand with respect to scale models of big-ticket items such as cars and planes. Besides the lower financial cost of building a model, the analysis of a model can help avoid costly mistakes that might result from poor decision making. For example, it is far less costly to discover a flawed wing design using a scale model of an aircraft than after the crash of a fully loaded jet liner.

Frank Brock, former executive vice president of the Brock Candy Company, related the following story about blueprints his company prepared for a new production facility. After months of careful design work, he proudly showed the plans to several of his production workers. When he asked for their comments, one worker responded, "It's a fine looking building Mr. Brock, but that sugar valve looks like it's about twenty feet away from the steam valve."

"What's wrong with that?" asked Brock.

"Well, nothing," said the worker, "except that I have to have my hands on both valves at the same time!"[1] Needless to say, it was far less expensive to discover and correct this "little" problem using a visual model before pouring the concrete and laying the pipes as originally planned.

Third, models often deliver needed information on a more timely basis. Again, it is relatively easy to see that scale models of cars or airplanes can be created and analyzed more quickly than their real-world counterparts. Timeliness is also an issue when vital data will not become available until some later point in time. In these cases, we might create a model to help predict the missing data to assist in current decision making.

Fourth, models are frequently helpful in examining things that would be impossible to do in reality. For example, human models (crash dummies) are used in crash tests to see what might happen to an actual person if a car hits a brick wall at a high speed. Likewise, models of DNA can be used to visualize how molecules fit together. Both of these are difficult, if not impossible, to do without the use of models.

Finally, and probably most importantly, models allow us to gain insight and understanding about the object or decision problem under investigation. The ultimate purpose of using models is to improve decision making. As you will see, the process of building a model can shed important light and understanding on a problem. In some cases, a decision might be made while building the model as a previously misunderstood element of the problem is discovered or eliminated. In other cases, a careful analysis of a completed model might be required to "get a handle" on a problem and gain the insights needed to make a decision. In any event, it is the insight gained from the modeling process that ultimately leads to better decision making.

1.3 Mathematical Models

As mentioned earlier, the modeling techniques in this book differ quite a bit from scale models of cars and planes or visual models of production plants. The models we will build use mathematics to describe a decision problem. We use the term "mathematics" in its broadest sense, encompassing not only the most familiar elements of math, such as algebra, but also the related topic of logic.

---

[1] Colson, Charles and Jack Eckerd, *Why America Doesn't Work* (Denver, Colorado: Word Publishing, 1991), 146–147.

Now, let's consider a simple example of a mathematical model:

$$PROFIT = REVENUE - EXPENSES \qquad 1.1$$

Equation 1.1 describes a simple relationship between revenue, expenses, and profit. It is a mathematical relationship that describes the operation of determining profit—or a mathematical model of profit. Of course, not all models are this simple, but taken piece by piece, the models we will discuss are not much more complex than this one.

Frequently, mathematical models describe functional relationships. For example, the mathematical model in equation 1.1 describes a functional relationship between revenue, expenses, and profit. Using the symbols of mathematics, this functional relationship is represented as follows:

$$PROFIT = f(REVENUE, EXPENSES) \qquad 1.2$$

In words, the previous expression means "profit is a function of revenue and expenses." We could also say that profit *depends* on (or is *dependent* on) revenue and expenses. Thus, the term PROFIT in equation 1.2 represents a **dependent variable**, whereas REVENUE and EXPENSES are **independent variables**. Frequently, compact symbols (such as A, B, and C) are used to represent variables in an equation such as 1.2. For instance, if we let Y, X_1, and X_2 represent PROFIT, REVENUE, and EXPENSES, respectively, we could rewrite equation 1.2 as follows:

$$Y = f(X_1, X_2) \qquad 1.3$$

The notation $f(\cdot)$ represents the function that defines the relationship between the dependent variable Y and the independent variables X_1 and X_2. In the case of determining PROFIT from REVENUE and EXPENSES, the mathematical form of the function $f(\cdot)$ is quite simple because we know that $f(X_1, X_2) = X_1 - X_2$. However, in many other situations we will model, the form of $f(\cdot)$ is quite complex and might involve many independent variables. But regardless of the complexity of $f(\cdot)$ or the number of independent variables involved, many of the decision problems encountered in business can be represented by models that assume the general form,

$$Y = f(X_1, X_2, \ldots, X_k) \qquad 1.4$$

In equation 1.4, the dependent variable Y represents some bottom-line performance measure of the problem we are modeling. The terms $X_1, X_2, \ldots, X_k$ represent the different independent variables that play some role or have some impact in determining the value of Y. Again, $f(\cdot)$ is the function (possibly quite complex) that specifies or describes the relationship between the dependent and independent variables.

The relationship expressed in equation 1.4 is very similar to what occurs in most spreadsheet models. Consider a simple spreadsheet model to calculate the monthly payment for a car loan, as shown in Figure 1.2.

The spreadsheet in Figure 1.2 contains a variety of **input cells** (for example purchase price, down payment, trade-in, term of loan, annual interest rate) that correspond conceptually to the independent variables $X_1, X_2, \ldots, X_k$ in equation 1.4. Similarly, a variety of mathematical operations are performed using these input cells in a manner analogous to the function $f(\cdot)$ in equation 1.4. The results of these mathematical operations determine the value of some **output cell** in the spreadsheet (for example, monthly payment) that corresponds to the dependent variable Y in equation 1.4. Thus, there is a direct correspondence between equation 1.4 and the spreadsheet in Figure 1.2. This type of correspondence exists for most of the spreadsheet models in this book.

FIGURE 1.2

Example of a simple spreadsheet model

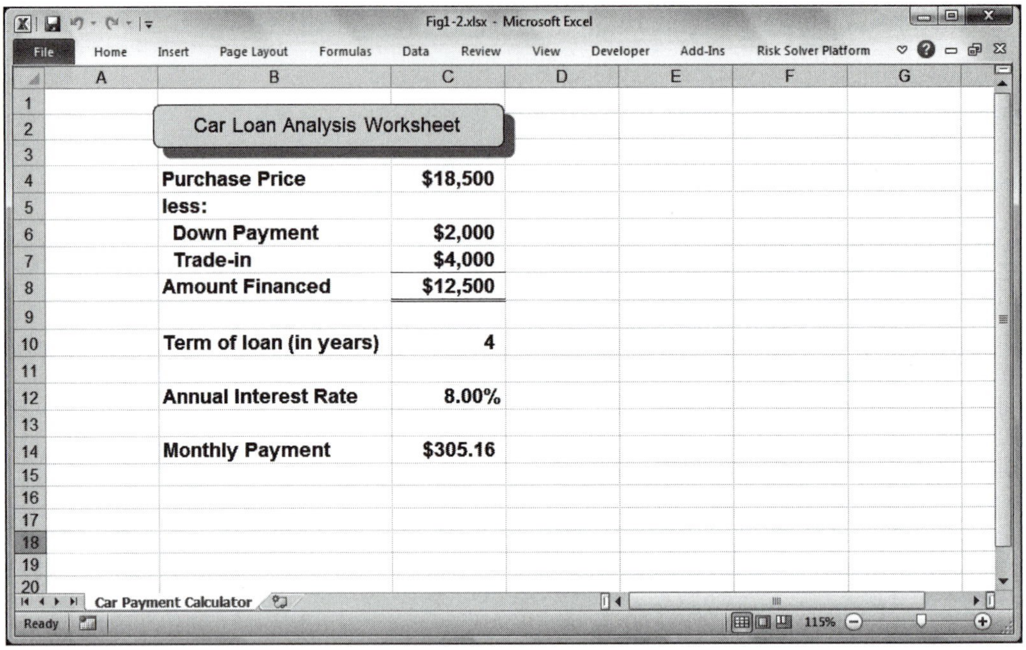

1.4 Categories of Mathematical Models

Not only does equation 1.4 describe the major elements of mathematical or spreadsheet models, but it also provides a convenient means for comparing and contrasting the three categories of modeling techniques presented in this book—Prescriptive Models, Predictive Models, and Descriptive Models. Figure 1.3 summarizes the characteristics and techniques associated with each of these categories.

In some situations, a manager might face a decision problem involving a very precise, well-defined functional relationship $f(\cdot)$ between the independent variables $X_1, X_2, \ldots, X_k$ and the dependent variable Y. If the values for the independent variables are under

FIGURE 1.3

Categories and characteristics of management science modeling techniques

| | **Model Characteristics:** | | |
Category	**Form of $f(\cdot)$**	**Values of Independent Variables**	**Management Science Techniques**
Prescriptive Models	known, well-defined	known or under decision maker's control	Linear Programming, Networks, Integer Programming, CPM, Goal Programming, EOQ, Nonlinear Programming
Predictive Models	unknown, ill-defined	known or under decision maker's control	Regression Analysis, Time Series Analysis, Discriminant Analysis
Descriptive Models	known, well-defined	unknown or uncertain	Simulation, Queuing, PERT, Inventory Models

the decision maker's control, the decision problem in these types of situations boils down to determining the values of the independent variables $X_1, X_2, \ldots, X_k$ that produce the best possible value for the dependent variable Y. These types of models are called **Prescriptive Models** because their solutions tell the decision maker what actions to take. For example, you might be interested in determining how a given sum of money should be allocated to different investments (represented by the independent variables) in order to maximize the return on a portfolio without exceeding a certain level of risk.

A second category of decision problems is one in which the objective is to predict or estimate what value the dependent variable Y will take on when the independent variables $X_1, X_2, \ldots, X_k$ take on specific values. If the function $f(\cdot)$ relating the dependent and independent variables is known, this is a very simple task—simply enter the specified values for $X_1, X_2, \ldots, X_k$ into the function $f(\cdot)$, and compute Y. In some cases, however, the functional form of $f(\cdot)$ might be unknown and must be estimated in order for the decision maker to make predictions about the dependent variable Y. These types of models are called **Predictive Models**. For example, a real estate appraiser might know that the value of a commercial property (Y) is influenced by its total square footage (X_1) and age (X_2), among other things. However, the functional relationship $f(\cdot)$ that relates these variables to one another might be unknown. By analyzing the relationship between the selling price, total square footage, and age of other commercial properties, the appraiser might be able to identify a function $f(\cdot)$ that relates these two variables in a reasonably accurate manner.

The third category of models you are likely to encounter in the business world is called **Descriptive Models**. In these situations, a manager might face a decision problem that has a very precise, well-defined functional relationship $f(\cdot)$ between the independent variables $X_1, X_2, \ldots, X_k$ and the dependent variable Y. However, there might be great uncertainty as to the exact values that will be assumed by one or more of the independent variables $X_1, X_2, \ldots, X_k$. In these types of problems, the objective is to describe the outcome or behavior of a given operation or system. For example, suppose a company is building a new manufacturing facility and has several choices about the type of machines to put in the new plant, as well as various options for arranging the machines. Management might be interested in studying how the various plant configurations would affect on-time shipments of orders (Y), given the uncertain number of orders that might be received (X_1) and the uncertain due dates (X_2) that might be required by these orders.

1.5 The Problem-Solving Process

Throughout our discussion, we have said that the ultimate goal in building models is to assist managers in making decisions that solve problems. The modeling techniques we will study represent a small but important part of the total problem-solving process. To become an effective modeler, it is important to understand how modeling fits into the entire problem-solving process.

Because a model can be used to represent a decision problem or phenomenon, we might be able to create a visual model of the phenomenon that occurs when people solve problems—what we call the problem-solving process. Although a variety of models could be equally valid, the one in Figure 1.4 summarizes the key elements of the problem-solving process and is sufficient for our purposes.

The first step of the problem-solving process, identifying the problem, is also the most important. If we do not identify the correct problem, all the work that follows will amount to nothing more than wasted effort, time, and money. Unfortunately, identifying the problem to solve is often not as easy as it seems. We know that a problem exists when there is a gap or disparity between the present situation and some desired state of affairs.

FIGURE 1.4

A visual model of the problem-solving process

However, we usually are not faced with a neat, well-defined problem. Instead, we often find ourselves facing a "mess"![2] Identifying the real problem involves gathering a lot of information and talking with many people to increase our understanding of the mess. We must then sift through all this information and try to identify the root problem or problems causing the mess. Thus, identifying the real problem (and not just the symptoms of the problem) requires insight, some imagination, time, and a good bit of detective work.

The end result of the problem-identification step is a well-defined statement of the problem. Simply defining a problem well will often make it much easier to solve. Having identified the problem, we turn our attention to creating or formulating a model of the problem. Depending on the nature of the problem, we might use a mental model, a visual model, a scale model, or a mathematical model. Although this book focuses on mathematical models, this does not mean that mathematical models are always applicable or best. In most situations, the best model is the simplest model that accurately reflects the relevant characteristic or essence of the problem being studied.

We will discuss several different management science modeling techniques in this book. It is important that you not develop too strong a preference for any one technique. Some people have a tendency to want to formulate every problem they face as a model that can be solved by their favorite management science technique. This simply will not work.

As indicated earlier in Figure 1.3, there are fundamental differences in the types of problems a manager might face. Sometimes, the values of the independent variables affecting a problem are under the manager's control; sometimes they are not. Sometimes, the form of the functional relationship $f(\cdot)$ relating the dependent and independent variables is well-defined, and sometimes it is not. These fundamental characteristics of the problem should guide your selection of an appropriate management science modeling technique. Your goal at the model-formulation stage is to select a modeling technique that fits your problem, rather than trying to fit your problem into the required format of a preselected modeling technique.

After you select an appropriate representation or formulation of your problem, the next step is to implement this formulation as a spreadsheet model. We will not dwell on the implementation process now because that is the focus of the remainder of this book. After you verify that your spreadsheet model has been implemented accurately, the next step in the problem-solving process is to use the model to analyze the problem it represents. The main focus of this step is to generate and evaluate alternatives that might lead to a solution of the problem. This often involves playing out a number of scenarios or asking several "What if?" questions. Spreadsheets are particularly helpful in analyzing mathematical models in this manner. In a well-designed spreadsheet model, it should be fairly simple to change some of the assumptions in the model to see what might happen in different situations. As we proceed, we will highlight some techniques for designing spreadsheet models that facilitate this type of "what if" analysis. "What if" analysis is also very appropriate and useful when working with nonmathematical models.

The end result of analyzing a model does not always provide a solution to the actual problem being studied. As we analyze a model by asking various "What if?" questions,

[2] This characterization is borrowed from Chapter 5, James R. Evans, *Creative Thinking in the Decision and Management Sciences* (Cincinnati, Ohio: South-Western Publishing, 1991), 89–115.

it is important to test the feasibility and quality of each potential solution. The blue-prints Frank Brock showed to his production employees represented the end result of his analysis of the problem he faced. He wisely tested the feasibility and quality of this alternative before implementing it, and discovered an important flaw in his plans. Thus, the testing process can give important new insights into the nature of a problem. The testing process is also important because it provides the opportunity to double check the validity of the model. At times, we might discover an alternative that appears to be too good to be true. This could lead us to find that some important assumption has been left out of the model. Testing the results of the model against known results (and simple common sense) helps ensure the structural integrity and validity of the model. After analyzing the model, we might discover that we need to go back and modify it.

The last step of the problem-solving process, implementation, is often the most diffi-cult. Implementation begins by deriving managerial insights from our modeling efforts, framed in the context of the real-world problem we are solving, and communicating those insights to influence actions that affect the business situation. This requires crafting a message that is understood by various stakeholders in an organization and persuading them to take a particular course of action. (See Grossman et al., 2008 for numerous helpful suggestions on this process.) By their very nature, solutions to problems involve people and change. For better or for worse, most people resist change. However, there are ways to minimize the seemingly inevitable resistance to change. For example, it is wise, if pos-sible, to involve anyone who will be affected by the decision in all steps of the problem-solving process. This not only helps develop a sense of ownership and understanding of the ultimate solution, but it also can be the source of important information throughout the problem-solving process. As the Brock Candy story illustrates, even if it is impossible to include those affected by the solution in all steps, their input should be solicited and considered before a solution is accepted for implementation. Resistance to change and new systems can also be eased by creating flexible, user-friendly interfaces for the math-ematical models that are often developed in the problem-solving process.

Throughout this book, we focus mostly on the model formulation, implementation, analysis, and testing steps of the problem-solving process, summarized previously in Figure 1.4. Again, this does not imply that these steps are more important than the oth-ers. If we do not identify the correct problem, the best we can hope for from our modeling effort is "the right answer to the wrong question," which does not solve the real problem. Similarly, even if we do identify the problem correctly and design a model that leads to a perfect solution, if we cannot implement the solution, then we still have not solved the problem. Developing the interpersonal and investigative skills required to work with people in defining the problem and implementing the solution is as important as the mathematical modeling skills you will develop by working through this book.

1.6 Anchoring and Framing Effects

At this point, some of you are probably thinking it is better to rely on subjective judgment and intuition rather than models when making decisions. Indeed, most nontrivial deci-sion problems involve some issues that are difficult or impossible to structure and ana-lyze in the form of a mathematical model. These unstructurable aspects of a decision problem may require the use of judgment and intuition. However, it is important to real-ize that human cognition is often flawed and can lead to incorrect judgments and irra-tional decisions. Errors in human judgment often arise because of what psychologists term **anchoring** and **framing** effects associated with decision problems.

Anchoring effects arise when a seemingly trivial factor serves as a starting point (or anchor) for estimations in a decision-making problem. Decision makers adjust their estimates from this anchor but nevertheless remain too close to the anchor and usually under-adjust. In a classic psychological study on this issue, one group of subjects was asked to individually estimate the value of $1 \times 2 \times 3 \times 4 \times 5 \times 6 \times 7 \times 8$ (without using a calculator). Another group of subjects was asked to estimate the value of $8 \times 7 \times 6 \times 5 \times 4 \times 3 \times 2 \times 1$. The researchers hypothesized that the first number presented (or perhaps the product of the first three or four numbers) would serve as a mental anchor. The results supported the hypothesis. The median estimate of subjects shown the numbers in ascending sequence $(1 \times 2 \times 3 \ldots)$ was 512, whereas the median estimate of subjects shown the sequence in descending order $(8 \times 7 \times 6 \ldots)$ was 2,250. Of course, the order of multiplication for these numbers is irrelevant, and the product of both series is the same: 40,320.

Framing effects refer to how a decision maker views or perceives the alternatives in a decision problem—often involving a win/loss perspective. The way a problem is framed often influences the choices made by a decision maker and can lead to irrational behavior. For example, suppose you have just been given $1,000 but must choose one of the following alternatives: (A_1) Receive an additional $500 with certainty, or ($B_1$) Flip a fair coin and receive an additional $1,000 if heads occurs or $0 additional is tails occurs. Here, alternative A_1 is a "sure win" and is the alternative most people prefer. Now suppose you have been given $2,000 and must choose one of the following alternatives: (A_2) Give back $500 immediately, or ($B_2$) Flip a fair coin and give back $0 if heads occurs or $1,000 if tails occurs. When the problem is framed this way, alternative A_2 is a "sure loss" and many people who previously preferred alternative A_1 now opt for alternative B_2 (because it holds a chance of avoiding a loss). However, Figure 1.5 shows a single decision tree for these two scenarios making it clear that, in both cases, the "A" alternative guarantees a total payoff of $1,500, whereas the "B" alternative offers a 50% chance of a $2,000 total payoff and a 50% chance of a $1,000 total payoff. (Decision trees will be covered in greater detail in a later chapter.) A purely rational decision maker should focus on the consequences of his or her choices and consistently select the same alternative, regardless of how the problem is framed.

Whether we want to admit it or not, we are all prone to make errors in estimation due to anchoring effects and may exhibit irrationality in decision making due to framing effects. As a result, it is best to use computer models to do what they are best at (that is, modeling structurable portions of a decision problem) and let the human brain do what it is best at (that is, dealing with the unstructurable portion of a decision problem).

FIGURE 1.5

Decision tree for framing effects

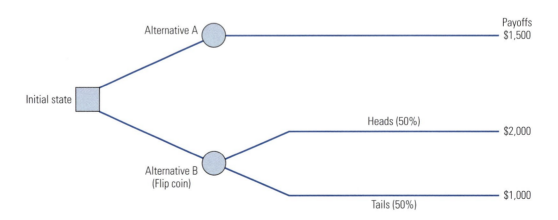

FIGURE 1.6

*A good decision
with a bad
outcome*

Andre-Francois Raffray thought he had a great deal in 1965 when he agreed to pay a 90-year-old woman named Jeanne Calment $500 a month until she died to acquire her grand apartment in Arles, northwest of Marseilles in the south of France—a town Vincent Van Gogh once roamed. Buying apartments "for life" is common in France. The elderly owner gets to enjoy a monthly income from the buyer who gambles on getting a real estate bargain—betting the owner doesn't live too long. Upon the owner's death, the buyer inherits the apartment regardless of how much was paid. But in December of 1995, Raffray died at age 77, having paid more than $180,000 for an apartment he never got to live in.

On the same day, Calment, then the world's oldest living person at 120, dined on *foie gras*, duck thighs, cheese, and chocolate cake at her nursing home near the sought-after apartment. And she does not need to worry about losing her $500 monthly income. Although the amount Raffray already paid is twice the apartment's current market value, his widow is obligated to keep sending the monthly check to Calment. If Calment also outlives her, then the Raffray children will have to pay. "In life, one sometimes makes bad deals," said Calment of the outcome of Raffray's decision. (Source: *The Savannah Morning News*, 12/29/95.)

1.7 Good Decisions vs. Good Outcomes

The goal of the modeling approach to problem solving is to help individuals make good decisions. But good decisions do not always result in good outcomes. For example, suppose the weather report on the evening news predicts a warm, dry, sunny day tomorrow. When you get up and look out the window tomorrow morning, suppose there is not a cloud in sight. If you decide to leave your umbrella at home and subsequently get soaked in an unexpected afternoon thundershower, did you make a bad decision? Certainly not. Unforeseeable circumstances beyond your control caused you to experience a bad outcome, but it would be unfair to say that you made a bad decision. Good decisions sometimes result in bad outcomes. See Figure 1.6 for the story of another good decision having a bad outcome.

The modeling techniques presented in this book can help you make good decisions but cannot guarantee that good outcomes will always occur as a result of those decisions. Figure 1.7 describes the possible combinations of good and bad decisions and good and bad outcomes. When a good or bad decision is made, luck often plays a role in determining whether a good or bad outcome occurs. However, consistently using a structured, model-based process to make decisions should produce good outcomes (and deserved success) more frequently than making decisions in a more haphazard manner.

FIGURE 1.7

*Decision quality
and outcome
quality matrix*

		Outcome Quality	
		Good	Bad
Decision Quality	Good	Deserved Success	Bad Luck
	Bad	Dumb Luck	Poetic Justice

Adapted from: J. Russo and P. Shoemaker, Winning Decisions, (NY: Doubleday, 2002).

1.8 Summary

This book introduces you to a variety of techniques from the field of management science that can be applied in spreadsheet models to assist in decision analysis and problem solving. This chapter discussed how spreadsheet models of decision problems can be used to analyze the consequences of possible courses of action before a particular alternative is selected for implementation. It described how models of decision problems differ in a number of important characteristics and how you should select a modeling technique that is most appropriate for the type of problem being faced. Finally, it discussed how spreadsheet modeling and analysis fit into the problem-solving process.

1.9 References

Edwards, J., P. Finlay, and J. Wilson. "The Role of the OR Specialist in 'Do it Yourself' Spreadsheet Development." *European Journal of Operational Research*, vol. 127, no. 1, 2000.

Forgione, G. "Corporate MS Activities: An Update." *Interfaces*, vol. 13, no. 1, 1983.

Grossman, T., J. Norback, J. Hardin, and G. Forehand. "Managerial Communication of Analytical Work." *INFORMS Transactions on Education*, vol. 8, no. 3, May 2008, pp. 125–138.

Hall, R. "What's So Scientific about MS/OR?" *Interfaces*, vol. 15, 1985.

Hastie, R. and R. M. Dawes. *Rational Choice in an Uncertain World,* Sage Publications, 2001.

Schrage, M. *Serious Play*, Harvard Business School Press, 2000.

Sonntag, C. and Grossman, T. "End-User Modeling Improves R&D Management at AgrEvo Canada, Inc." *Interfaces*, vol. 29, no. 5, 1999.

THE WORLD OF MANAGEMENT SCIENCE

"Business Analysts Trained in Management Science Can Be a Secret Weapon in a CIO's Quest for Bottom-Line Results."

Efficiency nuts. These are the people you see at cocktail parties explaining how the host could disperse that crowd around the popular shrimp dip if he would divide it into three bowls and place them around the room. As she draws the improved traffic flow on a paper napkin, you notice that her favorite word is "optimize"—a tell-tale sign she has studied the field of "operations research" or "management science" (also known as OR/MS).

OR/MS professionals are driven to solve logistics problems. This trait may not make them the most popular people at parties but is exactly what today's information systems (IS) departments need to deliver more business value. Experts say smart IS executives will learn to exploit the talents of these mathematical wizards in their quest to boost a company's bottom line.

According to Ron J. Ponder, chief information officer (CIO) at Sprint Corp. in Kansas City, Mo., and former CIO at Federal Express Corp., "If IS departments had more participation from operations research analysts, they would be building much better, richer IS solutions." As someone who has a Ph.D. in operations research and who built the renowned package-tracking systems at Federal Express, Ponder is a true believer in OR/MS. Ponder and others say analysts trained in OR/MS can turn ordinary information systems into money-saving, decision-support systems and are ideally suited to be members of the business process reengineering team. "I've always had an operations research department reporting to me, and it's been invaluable. Now I'm building one at Sprint," says Ponder.

The Beginnings

OR/MS got its start in World War II, when the military had to make important decisions about allocating scarce resources to various military operations. One of the first business applications for computers in the 1950s was to solve operations research problems for the petroleum industry. A technique called linear programming was used to figure out how to blend gasoline for the right flash point, viscosity, and octane in the most economical way. Since then, OR/MS has spread throughout business and government, from designing efficient drive-thru window operations for Burger King Corp. to creating ultra-sophisticated computerized stock trading systems.

A classic OR/MS example is the crew scheduling problem faced by all major airlines. How do you plan the itineraries of 8,000 pilots and 17,000 flight attendants when the possible combinations of planes, crews, and cities are astronomical? The OR/MS analysts at United Airlines came up with a scheduling system called Paragon that attempts to minimize the amount of paid time that crews spend waiting for flights. Their model factors in constraints such as union rules and FAA regulations and is projected to save the airline at least $1 million a year.

OR/MS and IS

Somewhere in the 1970s, the OR/MS and IS disciplines went in separate directions. "The IS profession has had less and less contact with the operations research folks . . . and IS lost a powerful intellectual driver," says Peter G. W. Keen, executive director of the International Center for Information Technologies in Washington, D.C. However, many feel that now is an ideal time for the two disciplines to rebuild some bridges.

Today's OR/MS professionals are involved in a variety of IS-related fields, including inventory management, electronic data interchange, computer-integrated manufacturing, network management, and practical applications of artificial intelligence. Furthermore, each side needs something the other side has: OR/MS analysts need corporate data to plug into their models, and the IS folks need to plug the OR/MS models into their strategic information systems. At the same time, CIOs need intelligent applications that enhance the bottom line and make them heroes with the CEO.

OR/MS analysts can develop a model of how a business process works now and simulate how it could work more efficiently in the future. Therefore, it makes sense to have an OR/MS analyst on the interdisciplinary team that tackles business process reengineering projects. In essence, OR/MS professionals add more value to the IS infrastructure by building "tools that really help decision makers analyze complex situations," says Andrew B. Whinston, director of the Center for Information Systems Management at the University of Texas at Austin.

Although IS departments typically believe their job is done if they deliver accurate and timely information, Thomas M. Cook, president of American Airlines Decision Technologies, Inc., says that adding OR/MS skills to the team can produce intelligent systems that actually recommend solutions to business problems. One

(Continued)

of the big success stories at Cook's operations research shop is a "yield management" system that decides how much to overbook and how to set prices for each seat so that a plane is filled up and profits are maximized. The yield management system deals with more than 250 decision variables and accounts for a significant amount of American Airlines' revenue.

Where to Start

So how can the CIO start down the road toward collaboration with OR/MS analysts? If the company already has a group of OR/MS professionals, the IS department can draw on their expertise as internal consultants. Otherwise, the CIO can simply hire a few OR/MS wizards, throw a problem at them, and see what happens. The payback may come surprisingly fast. As one former OR/MS professional put it: "If I couldn't save my employer the equivalent of my own salary in the first month of the year, then I wouldn't feel like I was doing my job."

Adapted from: Mitch Betts, "Efficiency Einsteins," *ComputerWorld,* March 22, 1993, p. 64.

Questions and Problems

1. What is meant by the term decision analysis?
2. Define the term computer model.
3. What is the difference between a spreadsheet model and a computer model?
4. Define the term management science.
5. What is the relationship between management science and spreadsheet modeling?
6. What kinds of spreadsheet applications would not be considered management science?
7. In what ways do spreadsheet models facilitate the decision-making process?
8. What are the benefits of using a modeling approach to decision making?
9. What is a dependent variable?
10. What is an independent variable?
11. Can a model have more than one dependent variable?
12. Can a decision problem have more than one dependent variable?
13. In what ways are prescriptive models different from descriptive models?
14. In what ways are prescriptive models different from predictive models?
15. In what ways are descriptive models different from predictive models?
16. How would you define the words description, prediction, and prescription? Carefully consider what is unique about the meaning of each word.
17. Identify one or more mental models you have used. Can any of them be expressed mathematically? If so, identify the dependent and independent variables in your model.
18. Consider the spreadsheet model shown earlier in Figure 1.2. Is this model descriptive, predictive, or prescriptive in nature, or does it not fall into any of these categories?
19. What are the steps in the problem-solving process?
20. Which step in the problem-solving process do you think is most important? Why?
21. Must a model accurately represent every detail of a decision situation to be useful? Why or why not?
22. If you were presented with several different models of a given decision problem, which would you be most inclined to use? Why?

23. Describe an example in which business or political organizations may use anchoring effects to influence decision making.
24. Describe an example in which business or political organizations may use framing effects to influence decision making.
25. Suppose sharks have been spotted along the beach where you are vacationing with a friend. You and your friend have been informed of the shark sightings and are aware of the damage a shark attack can inflict on human flesh. You both decide (individually) to go swimming anyway. You are promptly attacked by a shark while your friend has a nice time body surfing in the waves. Did you make a good or bad decision? Did your friend make a good or bad decision? Explain your answer.
26. Describe an example in which a well-known business, political, or military leader made a good decision that resulted in a bad outcome or a bad decision that resulted in a good outcome.

Patrick's Paradox

Patrick's luck had changed overnight—but not his skill at mathematical reasoning. The day after graduating from college, he used the $20 that his grandmother had given him as a graduation gift to buy a lottery ticket. He knew his chances of winning the lottery were extremely low, and it probably was not a good way to spend this money. But he also remembered from the class he took in management science that bad decisions sometimes result in good outcomes. So he said to himself, "What the heck? Maybe this bad decision will be the one with a good outcome." And with that thought, he bought his lottery ticket.

The next day Patrick pulled the crumpled lottery ticket out of the back pocket of his blue jeans and tried to compare his numbers to the winning numbers printed in the paper. When his eyes finally came into focus on the numbers they also just about popped out of his head. He had a winning ticket! In the ensuing days he learned that his share of the jackpot would give him a lump sum payout of about $500,000 after taxes. He knew what he was going to do with part of the money, buy a new car, pay off his college loans, and send his grandmother on an all expenses paid trip to Hawaii. But he also knew that he couldn't continue to hope for good outcomes to arise from more bad decisions. So he decided to take half of his winnings and invest it for his retirement.

A few days later, Patrick was sitting around with two of his fraternity buddies, Josh and Peyton, trying to figure out how much money his new retirement fund might be worth in 30 years. They were all business majors in college and remembered from their finance class that if you invest p dollars for n years at an annual interest rate of i %, then in n years you would have $p(1 + i)^n$ dollars. So they figure that if Patrick invested $250,000 for 30 years in an investment with a 10% annual return, then in 30 years he would have $4,362,351 (that is, $250,000(1 + 0.10)^{30}$).

But after thinking about it a little more, they all agreed that it would be unlikely for Patrick to find an investment that would produce a return of exactly 10% each and every year for the next 30 years. If any of this money is invested in stocks, then some years the return might be higher than 10% and some years it would probably be lower. So to help account for the potential variability in the investment returns, Patrick and his friends came up with a plan; they would assume he could find an investment that would produce an annual return of 17.5% seventy percent of the time and a return (or actually a loss) of −7.5% thirty percent of the time. Such an investment should produce an average annual return of $0.7(17.5\%) + 0.3(-7.5\%) = 10\%$. Josh felt certain that this meant Patrick could still expected his $250,000 investment to grow to $4,362,351 in 30 years (because $250,000(1 + 0.10)^{30}$ = $4,362,351).

After sitting quietly and thinking about it for a while, Peyton said that he thought Josh was wrong. The way Peyton looked at it, Patrick should see a 17.5% return in 70% of the 30 years (or 0.7(30) = 21 years) and a −7.5% return in 30% of the 30 years (or 0.3(30) = 9 years). So, according to Peyton, that would mean Patrick should have $250,000(1 + 0.175)^{21}$ $(1 − 0.075)^{9}$ = $3,664,467 after 30 years. But that's $697,884 less than what Josh says Patrick should have.

After listening to Peyton's argument, Josh said he thought Peyton was wrong because his calculation assumes that the "good" return of 17.5% would occur in each of the first 21 years and the "bad" return of −7.5% would occur in each of the last 9 years. But Peyton countered this argument by saying that the order of good and bad returns does not matter. The commutative law of arithmetic says that when you add or multiply numbers, the order doesn't matter (that is, $X + Y = Y + X$ and $X \times Y = Y \times X$). So Peyton says that because Patrick can expect 21 "good" returns and 9 "bad" returns, and it doesn't matter in what order they occur, then the expected outcome of the investment should be $3,664,467 after 30 years.

Patrick is now really confused. Both of his friends' arguments seem to make perfect sense logically, but they lead to such different answers, and they can't both be right. What really worries Patrick is that he is starting his new job as a business analyst in a couple of weeks. And if he can't reason his way to the right answer in a relatively simple problem like this, what is he going to do when he encounters the more difficult problems awaiting him the business world? Now he really wishes he had paid more attention in his management sciences class.

So what do you think? Who is right, Joshua or Peyton? And more importantly, why?

Chapter 2

Introduction to Optimization and Linear Programming

2.0 Introduction

Our world is filled with limited resources. The amount of oil we can pump out of the earth is limited. The amount of land available for garbage dumps and hazardous waste is limited and, in many areas, diminishing rapidly. On a more personal level, each of us has a limited amount of time in which to accomplish or enjoy the activities we schedule each day. Most of us have a limited amount of money to spend while pursuing these activities. Businesses also have limited resources. A manufacturing organization employs a limited number of workers. A restaurant has a limited amount of space available for seating.

Deciding how best to use the limited resources available to an individual or a business is a universal problem. In today's competitive business environment, it is increasingly important to make sure that a company's limited resources are used in the most efficient manner possible. Typically, this involves determining how to allocate the resources in such a way as to maximize profits or minimize costs. **Mathematical programming (MP)** is a field of management science that finds the optimal, or most efficient, way of using limited resources to achieve the objectives of an individual or a business. For this reason, mathematical programming is often referred to as **optimization**.

2.1 Applications of Mathematical Optimization

To help you understand the purpose of optimization and the types of problems for which it can be used, let's consider several examples of decision-making situations in which MP techniques have been applied.

Determining Product Mix. Most manufacturing companies can make a variety of products. However, each product usually requires different amounts of raw materials and labor. Similarly, the amount of profit generated by the products varies. The manager of such a company must decide how many of each product to produce in order to maximize profits or to satisfy demand at minimum cost.

Manufacturing. Printed circuit boards, like those used in most computers, often have hundreds or thousands of holes drilled in them to accommodate the different electrical components that must be plugged into them. To manufacture these boards, a computer-controlled drilling machine must be programmed to drill in a given location, then move the drill bit to the next location and drill again. This process is repeated hundreds or thousands of times to complete all the holes on a circuit board. Manufacturers of these boards would benefit from determining the drilling order that minimizes the total distance the drill bit must be moved.

Routing and Logistics. Many retail companies have warehouses around the country that are responsible for keeping stores supplied with merchandise to sell. The amount of merchandise available at the warehouses and the amount needed at each store tends to fluctuate, as does the cost of shipping or delivering merchandise from the warehouses to the retail locations. Determining the least costly method of transferring merchandise from the warehouses to the stores can save large amounts of money.

Financial Planning. The federal government requires individuals to begin withdrawing money from individual retirement accounts (IRAs) and other tax-sheltered retirement programs no later than age 70.5. There are various rules that must be followed to avoid paying penalty taxes on these withdrawals. Most individuals want to withdraw their money in a manner that minimizes the amount of taxes they must pay while still obeying the tax laws.

Optimization Is Everywhere

Going to Disney World this summer? Optimization will be your ubiquitous companion, scheduling the crews and planes, pricing the airline tickets and hotel rooms, even helping to set capacities on the theme park rides. If you use Orbitz to book your flights, an optimization engine sifts through millions of options to find the cheapest fares. If you get directions to your hotel from MapQuest, another optimization engine figures out the most direct route. If you ship souvenirs home, an optimization engine tells UPS which truck to put the packages on, exactly where on the truck the packages should go to make them fastest to load and unload, and what route the driver should follow to make his deliveries most efficiently.

(Adapted from: V. Postrel, "Operation Everything," *The Boston Globe*, June 27, 2004.)

2.2 Characteristics of Optimization Problems

These examples represent just a few areas in which MP has been used successfully. We will consider many other examples throughout this book. However, these examples give you some idea of the issues involved in optimization. For instance, each example involves one or more *decisions* that must be made: How many of each product should be produced? Which hole should be drilled next? How much of each product should be shipped from each warehouse to the various retail locations? How much money should an individual withdraw each year from various retirement accounts?

Also, in each example, restrictions, or *constraints*, are likely to be placed on the alternatives available to the decision maker. In the first example, when determining the number of products to manufacture, a production manager is probably faced with a limited amount of raw materials and a limited amount of labor. In the second example, the drill should never return to a position where a hole has already been drilled. In the third example, there is a physical limitation on the amount of merchandise a truck can carry from one warehouse to the stores on its route. In the fourth example, laws determine the minimum and maximum amounts that can be withdrawn from retirement accounts without incurring a penalty. Many other constraints can also be identified for these examples. It is not unusual for real-world optimization problems to have hundreds or thousands of constraints.

A final common element in each of the examples is the existence of some goal or *objective* that the decision maker considers when deciding which course of action is best. In the first example, the production manager can decide to produce several different product mixes given the available resources, but the manager will probably choose the mix of products that maximizes profits. In the second example, a large number of possible drilling patterns can be used, but the ideal pattern will probably involve moving the drill bit the shortest total distance. In the third example, there are numerous ways merchandise can be shipped from the warehouses to supply the stores, but the company will probably want to identify the routing that minimizes the total transportation cost. Finally, in the fourth example, individuals can withdraw money from their retirement accounts in many ways without violating tax laws, but they probably want to find the method that minimizes their tax liability.

2.3 Expressing Optimization Problems Mathematically

From the preceding discussion, we know that optimization problems involve three elements: decisions, constraints, and an objective. If we intend to build a mathematical model of an optimization problem, we will need mathematical terms or symbols to represent each of these three elements.

2.3.1 DECISIONS

The decisions in an optimization problem are often represented in a mathematical model by the symbols $X_1, X_2, \ldots, X_n$. We will refer to $X_1, X_2, \ldots, X_n$ as the **decision variables** (or simply the variables) in the model. These variables might represent the quantities of different products the production manager can choose to produce. They might represent the amount of different pieces of merchandise to ship from a warehouse to a certain store. They might represent the amount of money to be withdrawn from different retirement accounts.

The exact symbols used to represent the decision variables are not particularly important. You could use $Z_1, Z_2, \ldots, Z_n$ or symbols like Dog, Cat, and Monkey to represent the decision variables in the model. The choice of which symbols to use is largely a matter of personal preference and might vary from one problem to the next.

2.3.2 CONSTRAINTS

The constraints in an optimization problem can be represented in a mathematical model in a number of ways. Three general ways of expressing the possible constraint relationships in an optimization problem are:

A less than or equal to constraint:	$f(X_1, X_2, \ldots, X_n) \leq b$
A greater than or equal to constraint:	$f(X_1, X_2, \ldots, X_n) \geq b$
An equal to constraint:	$f(X_1, X_2, \ldots, X_n) = b$

In each case, the **constraint** is some function of the decision variables that must be less than or equal to, greater than or equal to, or equal to some specific value (represented by the letter b). We will refer to $f(X_1, X_2, \ldots, X_n)$ as the left-hand-side (LHS) of the constraint and to b as the right-hand-side (RHS) value of the constraint.

For example, we might use a less than or equal to constraint to ensure that the total labor used in producing a given number of products does not exceed the amount of available labor. We might use a greater than or equal to constraint to ensure that the total amount of money withdrawn from a person's retirement accounts is at least the minimum amount required by the IRS. You can use any number of these constraints to represent a given optimization problem depending on the requirements of the situation.

2.3.3 OBJECTIVE

The objective in an optimization problem is represented mathematically by an objective function in the general format:

$$\text{MAX (or MIN):} \qquad f(X_1, X_2, \ldots, X_n)$$

The **objective function** identifies some function of the decision variables that the decision maker wants to either MAXimize or MINimize. In our earlier examples, this function might be used to describe the total profit associated with a product mix, the total distance the drill bit must be moved, the total cost of transporting merchandise, or a retiree's total tax liability.

The mathematical formulation of an optimization problem can be described in the general format:

$$\text{MAX (or MIN):} \qquad f_0(X_1, X_2, \ldots, X_n) \qquad \textbf{2.1}$$
$$\text{Subject to:} \qquad f_1(X_1, X_2, \ldots, X_n) \leq b_1 \qquad \textbf{2.2}$$
$$f_k(X_1, X_2, \ldots, X_n) \geq b_k \qquad \textbf{2.3}$$
$$f_m(X_1, X_2, \ldots, X_n) = b_m \qquad \textbf{2.4}$$

This representation identifies the objective function (equation 2.1) that will be maximized (or minimized) and the constraints that must be satisfied (equations 2.2 through 2.4). Subscripts added to the f and b in each equation emphasize that the functions describing the objective and constraints can all be different. The goal in optimization is to find the values of the decision variables that maximize (or minimize) the objective function without violating any of the constraints.

2.4 Mathematical Programming Techniques

Our general representation of an MP model is just that—general. There are many kinds of functions you can use to represent the objective function and the constraints in an MP model. Of course, you should always use functions that accurately describe the objective and constraints of the problem you are trying to solve. Sometimes, the functions in a model are linear in nature (that is, form straight lines or flat surfaces); other times, they are nonlinear (that is, form curved lines or curved surfaces). Sometimes, the optimal values of the decision variables in a model must take on integer values (whole numbers); other times, the decision variables can assume fractional values.

Given the diversity of MP problems that can be encountered, many techniques have been developed to solve different types of MP problems. In the next several chapters, we will look at these MP techniques and develop an understanding of how they differ and when each should be used. We will begin by examining a technique called **linear programming (LP)**, which involves creating and solving optimization problems with linear objective functions and linear constraints. LP is a very powerful tool that can be applied in many business situations. It also forms a basis for several other techniques discussed later and is, therefore, a good starting point for our investigation into the field of optimization.

2.5 An Example LP Problem

We will begin our study of LP by considering a simple example. You should not interpret this to mean that LP cannot solve more complex or realistic problems. LP has been used to solve extremely complicated problems, saving companies millions of dollars. However, jumping directly into one of these complicated problems would be like starting a marathon without ever having gone out for a jog—you would get winded and could be left behind very quickly. So we'll start with something simple.

> Blue Ridge Hot Tubs manufactures and sells two models of hot tubs: the Aqua-Spa and the Hydro-Lux. Howie Jones, the owner and manager of the company, needs to decide how many of each type of hot tub to produce during his next production cycle. Howie buys prefabricated fiberglass hot tub shells from a local supplier and adds the pump and tubing to the shells to create his hot tubs. (This supplier has the capacity to deliver as many hot tub shells as Howie needs.) Howie installs the same type of pump into both hot tubs. He will have only 200 pumps available during his next production cycle. From a manufacturing standpoint, the main difference between the two models of hot tubs is the amount of tubing and labor required. Each Aqua-Spa requires 9 hours of labor and 12 feet of tubing. Each Hydro-Lux requires 6 hours of labor and 16 feet of tubing. Howie expects to have 1,566 production labor hours and 2,880 feet of tubing available during the next production cycle. Howie earns a profit of $350 on each Aqua-Spa he sells and $300 on each Hydro-Lux he sells. He is confident that he can sell all the hot tubs he produces. The question is, how many Aqua-Spas and Hydro-Luxes should Howie produce if he wants to maximize his profits during the next production cycle?

2.6 Formulating LP Models

The process of taking a practical problem—such as determining how many Aqua-Spas and Hydro-Luxes Howie should produce—and expressing it algebraically in the form of an LP model is known as **formulating** the model. Throughout the next several chapters, you will see that formulating an LP model is as much an art as a science.

2.6.1 STEPS IN FORMULATING AN LP MODEL

There are some general steps you can follow to help make sure your formulation of a particular problem is accurate. We will walk through these steps using the hot tub example.

1. **Understand the problem.** This step appears to be so obvious that it hardly seems worth mentioning. However, many people have a tendency to jump into a problem and start writing the objective function and constraints before they really understand the problem. If you do not fully understand the problem you face, it is unlikely that your formulation of the problem will be correct.

   The problem in our example is fairly easy to understand: How many Aqua-Spas and Hydro-Luxes should Howie produce to maximize his profit, while using no more than 200 pumps, 1,566 labor hours, and 2,880 feet of tubing?

2. **Identify the decision variables.** After you are sure you understand the problem, you need to identify the decision variables. That is, what are the fundamental decisions that must be made in order to solve the problem? The answers to this question often will help you identify appropriate decision variables for your model. Identifying the decision variables means determining what the symbols $X_1, X_2, \ldots, X_n$ represent in your model.

   In our example, the fundamental decision Howie faces is this: How many Aqua-Spas and Hydro-Luxes should be produced? In this problem, we will let X_1 represent the number of Aqua-Spas to produce and X_2 represent the number of Hydro-Luxes to produce.

3. **State the objective function as a linear combination of the decision variables.** After determining the decision variables you will use, the next step is to create the objective function for the model. This function expresses the mathematical relationship between the decision variables in the model to be maximized or minimized.

   In our example, Howie earns a profit of $350 on each Aqua-Spa ($X_1$) he sells and $300 on each Hydro-Lux ($X_2$) he sells. Thus, Howie's objective of maximizing the profit he earns is stated mathematically as:

$$\text{MAX:} \quad 350X_1 + 300X_2$$

   For whatever values might be assigned to X_1 and X_2, the previous function calculates the associated total profit that Howie would earn. Obviously, Howie wants to maximize this value.

4. **State the constraints as linear combinations of the decision variables.** As mentioned earlier, there are usually some limitations on the values that can be assumed by the decision variables in an LP model. These restrictions must be identified and stated in the form of constraints.

   In our example, Howie faces three major constraints. Because only 200 pumps are available, and each hot tub requires one pump, Howie cannot produce more than a total of 200 hot tubs. This restriction is stated mathematically as:

$$1X_1 + 1X_2 \leq 200$$

   This constraint indicates that each unit of X_1 produced (that is, each Aqua-Spa built) will use one of the 200 pumps available—as will each unit of X_2 produced (that is, each Hydro-Lux built). The total number of pumps used (represented by $1X_1 + 1X_2$) must be less than or equal to 200.

   Another restriction Howie faces is that he has only 1,566 labor hours available during the next production cycle. Because each Aqua-Spa he builds (each unit of X_1) requires 9 labor hours, and each Hydro-Lux (each unit of X_2) requires 6 labor hours, the constraint on the number of labor hours is stated as:

$$9X_1 + 6X_2 \leq 1,566$$

The total number of labor hours used (represented by $9X_1 + 6X_2$) must be less than or equal to the total labor hours available, which is 1,566.

The final constraint specifies that only 2,880 feet of tubing is available for the next production cycle. Each Aqua-Spa produced (each unit of X_1) requires 12 feet of tubing, and each Hydro-Lux produced (each unit of X_2) requires 16 feet of tubing. The following constraint is necessary to ensure that Howie's production plan does not use more tubing than is available:

$$12X_1 + 16X_2 \leq 2{,}880$$

The total number of feet of tubing used (represented by $12X_1 + 16X_2$) must be less than or equal to the total number of feet of tubing available, which is 2,880.

5. **Identify any upper or lower bounds on the decision variables.** Often, simple upper or lower bounds apply to the decision variables. You can view upper and lower bounds as additional constraints in the problem.

   In our example, there are simple lower bounds of zero on the variables X_1 and X_2 because it is impossible to produce a negative number of hot tubs. Therefore, the following two constraints also apply to this problem:

$$X_1 \geq 0$$
$$X_2 \geq 0$$

Constraints like these are often referred to as nonnegativity conditions and are quite common in LP problems.

2.7 Summary of the LP Model for the Example Problem

The complete LP model for Howie's decision problem can be stated as:

MAX:	$350X_1 + 300X_2$			**2.5**
Subject to:	$1X_1 +$	$1X_2 \leq$	200	**2.6**
	$9X_1 +$	$6X_2 \leq$	$1{,}566$	**2.7**
	$12X_1 +$	$16X_2 \leq$	$2{,}880$	**2.8**
	$1X_1$	$\geq$	0	**2.9**
		$1X_2 \geq$	0	**2.10**

In this model, the decision variables X_1 and X_2 represent the number of Aqua-Spas and Hydro-Luxes to produce, respectively. Our goal is to determine the values for X_1 and X_2 that maximize the objective in equation 2.5 while simultaneously satisfying all the constraints in equations 2.6 through 2.10.

2.8 The General Form of an LP Model

The technique of linear programming is so-named because the MP problems to which it applies are linear in nature. That is, it must be possible to express all the functions in an

LP model as some weighted sum (or linear combination) of the decision variables. So, an LP model takes on the general form:

$$\text{MAX (or MIN):} \quad c_1 X_1 + c_2 X_2 + \cdots + c_n X_n \qquad \textbf{2.11}$$

$$\text{Subject to:} \quad a_{11} X_1 + a_{12} X_2 + \cdots + a_{1n} X_n \leq b_1 \qquad \textbf{2.12}$$

$$a_{k1} X_1 + a_{k2} X_2 + \cdots + a_{kn} X_n \geq b_k \qquad \textbf{2.13}$$

$$a_{m1} X_1 + a_{m2} X_2 + \cdots + a_{mn} X_n = b_m \qquad \textbf{2.14}$$

Up to this point, we have suggested that the constraints in an LP model represent some type of limited resource. Although this is frequently the case, in later chapters, you will see examples of LP models in which the constraints represent things other than limited resources. The important point here is that *any* problem that can be formulated in the preceding fashion is an LP problem.

The symbols $c_1, c_2, \ldots, c_n$ in equation 2.11 are called **objective function coefficients** and might represent the marginal profits (or costs) associated with the decision variables $X_1, X_2, \ldots, X_n$, respectively. The symbol a_{ij} found throughout equations 2.12 through 2.14 represents the numeric coefficient in the *i*th constraint for variable X_j. The objective function and constraints of an LP problem represent different weighted sums of the decision variables. The b_i symbols in the constraints, once again, represent values that the corresponding linear combination of the decision variables must be less than or equal to, greater than or equal to, or equal to.

You should now see a direct connection between the LP model we formulated for Blue Ridge Hot Tubs in equations 2.5 through 2.10 and the general definition of an LP model given in equations 2.11 through 2.14. In particular, note that the various symbols used in equations 2.11 through 2.14 to represent numeric constants (that is, the c_j, a_{ij}, and b_i) were replaced by actual numeric values in equations 2.5 through 2.10. Also, note that our formulation of the LP model for Blue Ridge Hot Tubs did not require the use of equal to constraints. Different problems require different types of constraints, and you should use whatever types of constraints are necessary for the problem at hand.

2.9 Solving LP Problems: An Intuitive Approach

After an LP model has been formulated, our interest naturally turns to solving it. But before we actually solve our example problem for Blue Ridge Hot Tubs, what do you think is the optimal solution to the problem? Just by looking at the model, what values for X_1 and X_2 do you think would give Howie the largest profit?

Following one line of reasoning, it might seem that Howie should produce as many units of X_1 (Aqua-Spas) as possible because each of these generates a profit of $350, whereas each unit of X_2 (Hydro-Luxes) generates a profit of only $300. But what is the maximum number of Aqua-Spas that Howie could produce?

Howie can produce the maximum number of units of X_1 by making no units of X_2 and devoting all his resources to the production of X_1. Suppose we let $X_2 = 0$ in the model in equations 2.5 through 2.10 to indicate that no Hydro-Luxes will be produced. What then is the largest possible value of X_1? If $X_2 = 0$, then the inequality in equation 2.6 tells us:

$$X_1 \leq 200 \qquad \textbf{2.15}$$

So we know that X_1 cannot be any greater than 200 if $X_2 = 0$. However, we also have to consider the constraints in equations 2.7 and 2.8. If $X_2 = 0$, then the inequality in equation 2.7 reduces to:

$$9X_1 \leq 1{,}566 \qquad\qquad\qquad\qquad \textbf{2.16}$$

If we divide both sides of this inequality by 9, we find that the previous constraint is equivalent to:

$$X_1 \leq 174 \qquad\qquad\qquad\qquad \textbf{2.17}$$

Now consider the constraint in equation 2.8. If $X_2 = 0$, then the inequality in equation 2.8 reduces to:

$$12X_1 \leq 2{,}880 \qquad\qquad\qquad\qquad \textbf{2.18}$$

Again, if we divide both sides of this inequality by 12, we find that the previous constraint is equivalent to:

$$X_1 \leq 240 \qquad\qquad\qquad\qquad \textbf{2.19}$$

So, if $X_2 = 0$, the three constraints in our model imposing upper limits on the value of X_1 reduce to the values shown in equations 2.15, 2.17, and 2.19. The most restrictive of these constraints is equation 2.17. Therefore, the maximum number of units of X_1 that can be produced is 174. In other words, 174 is the largest value X_1 can take on and still satisfy all the constraints in the model.

If Howie builds 174 units of X_1 (Aqua-Spas) and 0 units of X_2 (Hydro-Luxes), he will have used all of the labor that is available for production ($9X_1 = 1{,}566$ if $X_1 = 174$). However, he will have 26 pumps remaining ($200 - X_1 = 26$ if $X_1 = 174$) and 792 feet of tubing remaining ($2{,}880 - 12X_1 = 792$ if $X_1 = 174$). Also, notice that the objective function value (or total profit) associated with this solution is:

$$\$350X_1 + \$300X_2 = \$350 \times 174 + \$300 \times 0 = \$60{,}900$$

From this analysis, we see that the solution $X_1 = 174$, $X_2 = 0$ is a *feasible solution* to the problem because it satisfies all the constraints of the model. But is it the *optimal solution*? In other words, is there any other possible set of values for X_1 and X_2 that also satisfies all the constraints *and* results in a higher objective function value? As you will see, the intuitive approach to solving LP problems that we have taken here cannot be trusted because there actually is a *better* solution to Howie's problem.

2.10 Solving LP Problems: A Graphical Approach

The constraints of an LP model define the set of feasible solutions—or the **feasible region**—for the problem. The difficulty in LP is determining which point or points in the feasible region correspond to the best possible value of the objective function. For simple problems with only two decision variables, it is fairly easy to sketch the feasible region for the LP model and locate the optimal feasible point graphically. Because the graphical approach can be used only if there are two decision variables, it has limited practical use. However, it is an extremely good way to develop a basic understanding of the strategy involved in solving LP problems. Therefore, we will use the graphical approach to solve the simple problem faced by Blue Ridge Hot Tubs. Chapter 3 shows how to solve this and other LP problems using a spreadsheet.

To solve an LP problem graphically, you first must plot the constraints for the problem and identify its feasible region. This is done by plotting the *boundary lines* of the constraints and identifying the points that will satisfy all the constraints. So, how do we do this for our example problem (repeated here)?

MAX:	$350X_1 + 300X_2$	**2.20**
Subject to:	$1X_1 + 1X_2 \leq 200$	**2.21**
	$9X_1 + 6X_2 \leq 1{,}566$	**2.22**
	$12X_1 + 16X_2 \leq 2{,}880$	**2.23**
	$1X_1 \geq 0$	**2.24**
	$1X_2 \geq 0$	**2.25**

2.10.1 PLOTTING THE FIRST CONSTRAINT

The boundary of the first constraint in our model, which specifies that no more than 200 pumps can be used, is represented by the straight line defined by the equation:

$$X_1 + X_2 = 200 \qquad\qquad \textbf{2.26}$$

If we can find any two points on this line, the entire line can be plotted easily by drawing a straight line through these points. If $X_2 = 0$, we can see from equation 2.26 that $X_1 = 200$. Thus, the point $(X_1, X_2) = (200, 0)$ must fall on this line. If we let $X_1 = 0$, from equation 2.26, it is easy to see that $X_2 = 200$. So, the point $(X_1, X_2) = (0, 200)$ must also fall on this line. These two points are plotted on the graph in Figure 2.1 and connected to form the straight line representing equation 2.26.

Note that the graph of the line associated with equation 2.26 actually extends beyond the X_1 and X_2 axes shown in Figure 2.1. However, we can disregard the points beyond these axes because the values assumed by X_1 and X_2 cannot be negative (because we also have the constraints given by $X_1 \geq 0$ and $X_2 \geq 0$).

The line connecting the points (0, 200) and (200, 0) in Figure 2.1 identifies the points (X_1, X_2) that satisfy the equality $X_1 + X_2 = 200$. But recall that the first constraint in the LP model is the inequality $X_1 + X_2 \leq 200$. Thus, after plotting the boundary line of a constraint, we must determine which area on the graph corresponds to feasible solutions for the original constraint. This can be done easily by picking an arbitrary point on either side of the boundary line and checking whether it satisfies the original constraint. For example, if we test the point $(X_1, X_2) = (0, 0)$, we see that this point satisfies the first constraint. Therefore, the area of the graph on the same side of the boundary line as the point (0, 0) corresponds to the feasible solutions of our first constraint. This area of feasible solutions is shaded in Figure 2.1.

2.10.2 PLOTTING THE SECOND CONSTRAINT

Some of the feasible solutions to one constraint in an LP model usually will not satisfy one or more of the other constraints in the model. For example, the point $(X_1, X_2) = (200, 0)$ satisfies the first constraint in our model, but it does not satisfy the second constraint, which requires that no more than 1,566 labor hours be used (because $9 \times 200 + 6 \times 0 = 1{,}800$). So, what values for X_1 and X_2 will simultaneously satisfy both of these constraints? To answer this question, we need to plot the second constraint on the graph as well. This is done in the same manner as before—by locating

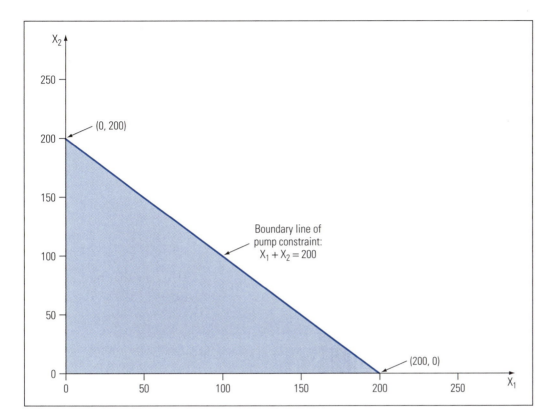

FIGURE 2.1

Graphical representation of the pump constraint

two points on the boundary line of the constraint and connecting these points with a straight line.

The boundary line for the second constraint in our model is given by:

$$9X_1 + 6X_2 = 1{,}566 \qquad \textbf{2.27}$$

If $X_1 = 0$ in equation 2.27, then $X_2 = 1{,}566/6 = 261$. So, the point $(0, 261)$ must fall on the line defined by equation 2.27. Similarly, if $X_2 = 0$ in equation 2.27, then $X_1 = 1{,}566/9 = 174$. So, the point $(174, 0)$ must also fall on this line. These two points are plotted on the graph and connected with a straight line representing equation 2.27, as shown in Figure 2.2.

The line drawn in Figure 2.2 representing equation 2.27 is the boundary line for our second constraint. To determine the area on the graph that corresponds to feasible solutions to the second constraint, we again need to test a point on either side of this line to see if it is feasible. The point $(X_1, X_2) = (0, 0)$ satisfies $9X_1 + 6X_2 \le 1{,}566$. Therefore, all points on the same side of the boundary line satisfy this constraint.

2.10.3 PLOTTING THE THIRD CONSTRAINT

To find the set of values for X_1 and X_2 that satisfies all the constraints in the model, we need to plot the third constraint. This constraint requires that no more than 2,880 feet of tubing be used in producing the hot tubs. Again, we will find two points on the graph that fall on the boundary line for this constraint and connect them with a straight line.

FIGURE 2.2

Graphical representation of the pump and labor constraints

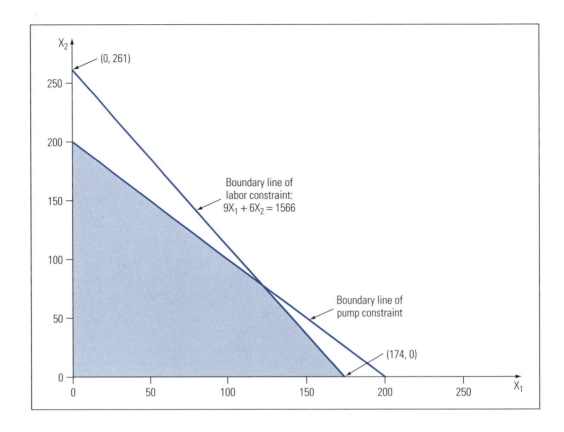

The boundary line for the third constraint in our model is:

$$12X_1 + 16X_2 = 2{,}880 \qquad \textbf{2.28}$$

If $X_1 = 0$ in equation 2.28, then $X_2 = 2{,}880/16 = 180$. So, the point (0, 180) must fall on the line defined by equation 2.28. Similarly, if $X_2 = 0$ in equation 2.28, then $X_1 = 2{,}880/12 = 240$. So, the point (240, 0) also must fall on this line. These two points are plotted on the graph and connected with a straight line representing equation 2.28, as shown in Figure 2.3.

Again, the line drawn in Figure 2.3 representing equation 2.28 is the boundary line for our third constraint. To determine the area on the graph that corresponds to feasible solutions to this constraint, we need to test a point on either side of this line to see if it is feasible. The point $(X_1, X_2) = (0, 0)$ satisfies $12X_1 + 16X_2 \leq 2{,}880$. Therefore, all points on the same side of the boundary line satisfy this constraint.

2.10.4 THE FEASIBLE REGION

It is now easy to see which points satisfy all the constraints in our model. These points correspond to the shaded area in Figure 2.3, labeled "Feasible Region." The **feasible region** is the set of points or values that the decision variables can assume and simultaneously satisfy all the constraints in the problem. Take a moment now to carefully compare the graphs in Figures 2.1, 2.2, and 2.3. In particular, notice that when we added the second constraint in Figure 2.2, some of the feasible solutions associated with the first constraint were eliminated because these solutions did not satisfy the second constraint. Similarly, when we added the third constraint in Figure 2.3, another portion of the feasible solutions for the first constraint was eliminated.

FIGURE 2.3

Graphical representation of the feasible region

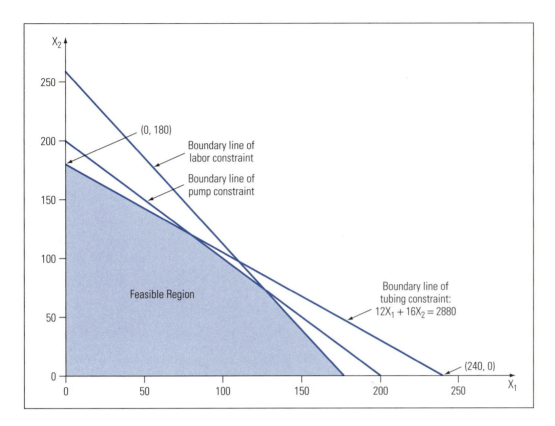

2.10.5 PLOTTING THE OBJECTIVE FUNCTION

Now that we have isolated the set of feasible solutions to our LP problem, we need to determine which of these solutions is best. That is, we must determine which point in the feasible region will maximize the value of the objective function in our model. At first glance, it might seem that trying to locate this point is like searching for a needle in a haystack. After all, as shown by the shaded region in Figure 2.3, there are an *infinite* number of feasible solutions to this problem. Fortunately, we can easily eliminate most of the feasible solutions in an LP problem from consideration. It can be shown that if an LP problem has an optimal solution with a finite objective function value, this solution will always occur at a point in the feasible region where two or more of the boundary lines of the constraints intersect. These points of intersection are sometimes called **corner points** or **extreme points** of the feasible region.

To see why the finite optimal solution to an LP problem occurs at an extreme point of the feasible region, consider the relationship between the objective function and the feasible region of our example LP model. Suppose we are interested in finding the values of X_1 and X_2 associated with a given level of profit, such as $35,000. Then, mathematically, we are interested in finding the points (X_1, X_2) for which our objective function equals $35,000, or where:

$$\$350X_1 + \$300X_2 = \$35,000 \qquad \textbf{2.29}$$

This equation defines a straight line, which we can plot on our graph. Specifically, if $X_1 = 0$ then, from equation 2.29, $X_2 = 116.67$. Similarly, if $X_2 = 0$ in equation 2.29, then $X_1 = 100$. So, the points $(X_1, X_2) = (0, 116.67)$ and $(X_1, X_2) = (100, 0)$ both fall on the line defining a profit level of $35,000. (Note that all the points on this line produce a profit level of $35,000.) This line is shown in Figure 2.4.

FIGURE 2.4

Graph showing values of X_1 and X_2 that produce an objective function value of $35,000

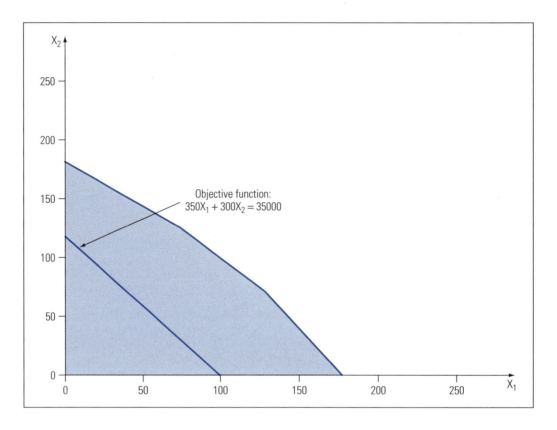

Now, suppose we are interested in finding the values of X_1 and X_2 that produce some higher level of profit, such as $52,500. Then, mathematically, we are interested in finding the points (X_1, X_2) for which our objective function equals $52,500, or where:

$$\$350X_1 + \$300X_2 = \$52,500 \qquad \textbf{2.30}$$

This equation also defines a straight line, which we could plot on our graph. If we do this, we'll find that the points $(X_1, X_2) = (0, 175)$ and $(X_1, X_2) = (150, 0)$ both fall on this line, as shown in Figure 2.5.

2.10.6 FINDING THE OPTIMAL SOLUTION USING LEVEL CURVES

The lines in Figure 2.5 representing the two objective function values are sometimes referred to as **level curves** because they represent different levels or values of the objective. Note that the two level curves in Figure 2.5 are *parallel* to one another. If we repeat this process of drawing lines associated with larger and larger values of our objective function, we will continue to observe a series of parallel lines shifting away from the origin, that is, away from the point $(0, 0)$. The very last level curve we can draw that still intersects the feasible region will determine the maximum profit we can achieve. This point of intersection, shown in Figure 2.6, represents the optimal feasible solution to the problem.

As shown in Figure 2.6, the optimal solution to our example problem occurs at the point where the largest possible level curve intersects the feasible region at a single point. This is the feasible point that produces the largest profit for Blue Ridge Hot Tubs. But how do we figure out exactly what point this is and how much profit it provides?

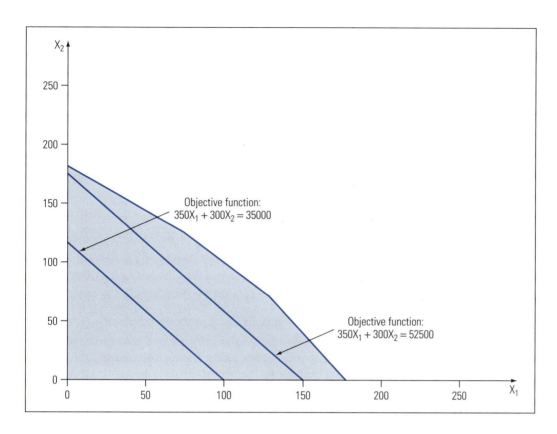

FIGURE 2.5

Parallel level curves for two different objective function values

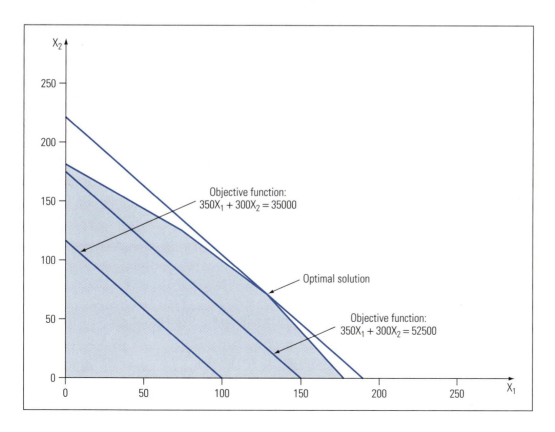

FIGURE 2.6

Graph showing optimal solution where the level curve is tangent to the feasible region

If you compare Figure 2.6 to Figure 2.3, you see that the optimal solution occurs where the boundary lines of the pump and labor constraints intersect (or are equal). Thus, the optimal solution is defined by the point (X_1, X_2) that simultaneously satisfies equations 2.26 and 2.27, which are repeated here:

$$X_1 + X_2 = 200$$
$$9X_1 + 6X_2 = 1,566$$

From the first equation, we easily conclude that $X_2 = 200 - X_1$. If we substitute this definition of X_2 into the second equation we obtain:

$$9X_1 + 6(200 - X_1) = 1,566$$

Using simple algebra, we can solve this equation to find that $X_1 = 122$. And because $X_2 = 200 - X_1$, we can conclude that $X_2 = 78$. Therefore, we have determined that the optimal solution to our example problem occurs at the point $(X_1, X_2) = (122, 78)$. This point satisfies all the constraints in our model and corresponds to the point in Figure 2.6 identified as the optimal solution.

The total profit associated with this solution is found by substituting the optimal values of $X_1 = 122$ and $X_2 = 78$ into the objective function. Thus, Blue Ridge Hot Tubs can realize a profit of \$66,100 if it produces 122 Aqua-Spas and 78 Hydro-Luxes (\$350 $\times$ 122 + \$300 $\times$ 78 = \$66,100). Any other production plan results in a lower total profit. In particular, note that the solution we found earlier using the intuitive approach (which produced a total profit of \$60,900) is inferior to the optimal solution identified here.

2.10.7 FINDING THE OPTIMAL SOLUTION BY ENUMERATING THE CORNER POINTS

Earlier, we indicated that if an LP problem has a finite optimal solution, this solution will always occur at some corner point of the feasible region. So, another way of solving an LP problem is to identify all the corner points, or extreme points, of the feasible region and calculate the value of the objective function at each of these points. The corner point with the largest objective function value is the optimal solution to the problem.

This approach is illustrated in Figure 2.7, where the X_1 and X_2 coordinates for each of the extreme points are identified along with the associated objective function values. As expected, this analysis also indicates that the point $(X_1, X_2) = (122, 78)$ is optimal.

Enumerating the corner points to identify the optimal solution is often more difficult than the level curve approach because it requires that you identify the coordinates for *all* the extreme points of the feasible region. If there are many intersecting constraints, the number of extreme points can become rather large, making this procedure very tedious. Also, a special condition exists for which this procedure will not work. This condition, known as an unbounded solution, is described shortly.

2.10.8 SUMMARY OF GRAPHICAL SOLUTION TO LP PROBLEMS

To summarize this section, a two-variable LP problem is solved graphically by performing these steps:

1. Plot the boundary line of each constraint in the model.
2. Identify the feasible region, that is, the set of points on the graph that simultaneously satisfies all the constraints.

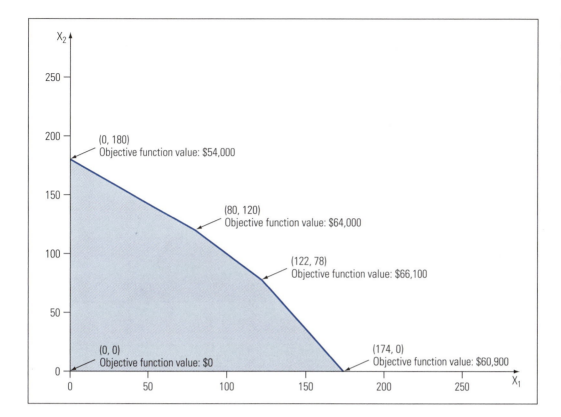

FIGURE 2.7

Objective function values at each extreme point of the feasible region

3. Locate the optimal solution by one of the following methods:
   a. Plot one or more level curves for the objective function, and determine the direction in which parallel shifts in this line produce improved objective function values. Shift the level curve in a parallel manner in the improving direction until it intersects the feasible region at a single point. Then find the coordinates for this point. This is the optimal solution.
   b. Identify the coordinates of all the extreme points of the feasible region, and calculate the objective function values associated with each point. If the feasible region is bounded, the point with the best objective function value is the optimal solution.

2.10.9 UNDERSTANDING HOW THINGS CHANGE

It is important to realize that if changes occur in any of the coefficients in the objective function or constraints of this problem, then the level curve, feasible region, and optimal solution to this problem might also change. To be an effective LP modeler, it is important for you to develop some intuition about how changes in various coefficients in the model will impact the solution to the problem. We will study this in greater detail in Chapter 4 when discussing sensitivity analysis. However, the spreadsheet shown in Figure 2.8 (and the file named Fig2-8.xlsm that accompanies this book) allows you to change any of the coefficients in this problem and instantly see its effect. You are encouraged to experiment with this file to make sure you understand the relationships between various model coefficients and their impact on this LP problem. (Case 2-1 at the end of this chapter asks some specific questions that can be answered using the spreadsheet shown in Figure 2.8.)

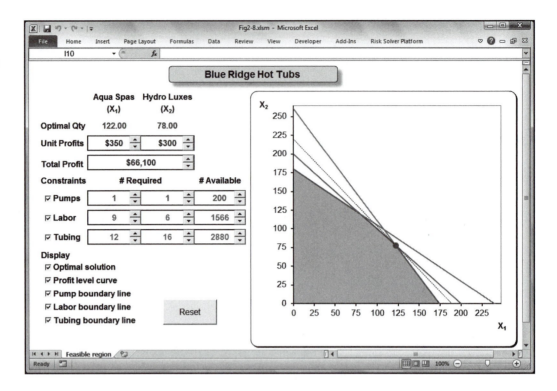

2.11 Special Conditions in LP Models

Several special conditions can arise in LP modeling: *alternate optimal solutions, redundant constraints, unbounded solutions*, and *infeasibility*. The first two conditions do not prevent you from solving an LP model and are not really problems—they are just anomalies that sometimes occur. On the other hand, the last two conditions represent real problems that prevent us from solving an LP model.

2.11.1 ALTERNATE OPTIMAL SOLUTIONS

Some LP models can actually have more than one optimal solution, or **alternate optimal solutions**. That is, there can be more than one feasible point that maximizes (or minimizes) the value of the objective function.

For example, suppose Howie can increase the price of Aqua-Spas to the point at which each unit sold generates a profit of $450 rather than $350. The revised LP model for this problem is:

$$
\begin{aligned}
\text{MAX:} \qquad & 450X_1 + 300X_2 \\
\text{Subject to:} \qquad & 1X_1 + 1X_2 \leq 200 \\
& 9X_1 + 6X_2 \leq 1{,}566 \\
& 12X_1 + 16X_2 \leq 2{,}880 \\
& 1X_1 \geq 0 \\
& 1X_2 \geq 0
\end{aligned}
$$

Because none of the constraints changed, the feasible region for this model is the same as for the earlier example. The only difference in this model is the objective function. Therefore, the level curves for the objective function are different from what we observed earlier. Several level curves for this model are plotted with its feasible region in Figure 2.9.

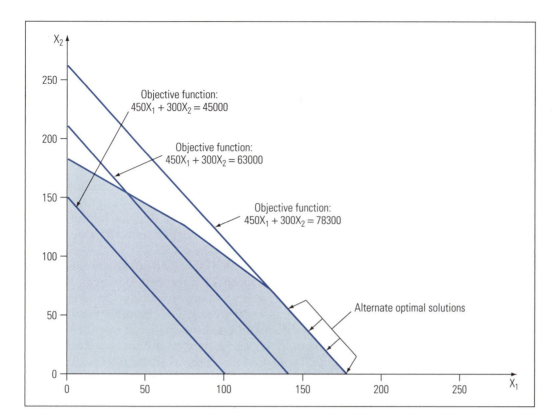

Notice that the final level curve in Figure 2.9 intersects the feasible region along an *edge* of the feasible region rather than at a single point. All the points on the line segment joining the corner point at (122, 78) to the corner point at (174, 0) produce the same optimal objective function value of $78,300 for this problem. Thus, all these points are alternate optimal solutions to the problem. If we used a computer to solve this problem, it would identify only one of the corner points of this edge as the optimal solution.

The fact that alternate optimal solutions sometimes occur is really not a problem because this anomaly does not prevent us from finding an optimal solution to the problem. In fact, in Chapter 7, "Goal Programming and Multiple Objective Optimization," you will see that alternate optimal solutions are sometimes very desirable.

2.11.2 REDUNDANT CONSTRAINTS

Redundant constraints present another special condition that sometimes occurs in an LP model. A **redundant constraint** is a constraint that plays no role in determining the feasible region of the problem. For example, in the hot tub example, suppose that 225 hot tub pumps are available instead of 200. The earlier LP model can be modified as follows to reflect this change:

$$
\begin{aligned}
\text{MAX:} \quad & 350X_1 + 300X_2 \\
\text{Subject to:} \quad & 1X_1 + 1X_2 \le 225 \\
& 9X_1 + 6X_2 \le 1{,}566 \\
& 12X_1 + 16X_2 \le 2{,}880 \\
& 1X_1 \qquad\qquad \ge 0 \\
& \qquad\quad 1X_2 \ge 0
\end{aligned}
$$

This model is identical to the original model we formulated for this problem *except* for the new upper limit on the first constraint (representing the number of pumps that can be used). The constraints and feasible region for this revised model are shown in Figure 2.10.

Notice that the pump constraint in this model no longer plays any role in defining the feasible region of the problem. That is, as long as the tubing constraint and labor constraints are satisfied (which is always the case for any feasible solution), then the pump constraint will also be satisfied. Therefore, we can remove the pump constraint from the model without changing the feasible region of the problem—the constraint is simply redundant.

The fact that the pump constraint does not play a role in defining the feasible region in Figure 2.10 implies that there will always be an excess number of pumps available. Because none of the feasible solutions identified in Figure 2.10 fall on the boundary line of the pump constraint, this constraint will always be satisfied as a strict inequality ($1X_1 + 1X_2 < 225$) and never as a strict equality ($1X_1 + 1X_2 = 225$).

Again, redundant constraints are not really a problem. They do not prevent us (or the computer) from finding the optimal solution to an LP problem. However, they do represent "excess baggage" for the computer; so if you know that a constraint is redundant, eliminating it saves the computer this excess work. On the other hand, if the model you are working with will be modified and used repeatedly, it might be best to leave any redundant constraints in the model because they might not be redundant in the future. For example, from Figure 2.3, we know that if the availability of pumps is returned to 200, then the pump constraint again plays an important role in defining the feasible region (and optimal solution) of the problem.

FIGURE 2.10

Example of a redundant constraint

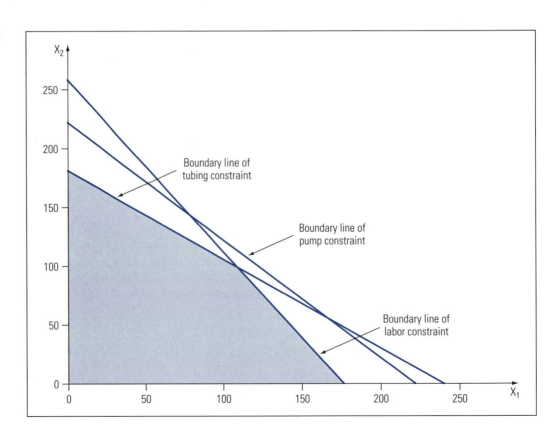

2.11.3 UNBOUNDED SOLUTIONS

When attempting to solve some LP problems, you might encounter situations in which the objective function can be made infinitely large (in the case of a maximization problem) or infinitely small (in the case of a minimization problem). As an example, consider this LP problem:

$$
\begin{aligned}
\text{MAX:} \quad & X_1 + X_2 \\
\text{Subject to:} \quad & X_1 + X_2 \geq 400 \\
& -X_1 + 2X_2 \leq 400 \\
& X_1 \geq 0 \\
& X_2 \geq 0
\end{aligned}
$$

The feasible region and some level curves for this problem are shown in Figure 2.11. From this graph, you can see that as the level curves shift farther and farther away from the origin, the objective function increases. Because the feasible region is not bounded in this direction, you can continue shifting the level curve by an infinite amount and make the objective function infinitely large.

Although it is not unusual to encounter an **unbounded** solution when solving an LP model, such a solution indicates that there is something wrong with the formulation—for example, one or more constraints were omitted from the formulation, or a less than constraint was erroneously entered as a greater than constraint.

While describing how to find the optimal solution to an LP model by enumerating corner points, we noted that this procedure will not always work if the feasible region for the problem is unbounded. Figure 2.11 provides an example of such a situation. The only extreme points for the feasible region in Figure 2.11 occur at the points (400, 0) and

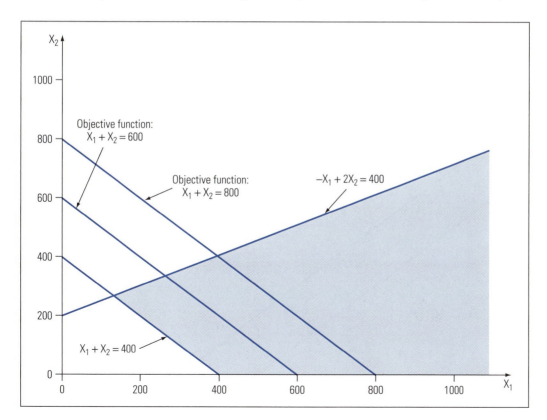

FIGURE 2.11

Example of an LP problem with an unbounded solution

(133.$\overline{3}$, 266.$\overline{6}$). The objective function value at both of these points (and at any point on the line segment joining them) is 400. By enumerating the extreme points for this problem, we might erroneously conclude that alternate optimal solutions to this problem exist that produce an optimal objective function value of 400. This is true if the problem involved *minimizing* the objective function. However, the goal here is to *maximize* the objective function value, which, as we have seen, can be done without limit. So, when trying to solve an LP problem by enumerating the extreme points of an unbounded feasible region, you must also check whether or not the objective function is unbounded.

2.11.4 INFEASIBILITY

An LP problem is **infeasible** if there is no way to simultaneously satisfy all the constraints in the problem. As an example, consider the LP model:

$$
\begin{aligned}
\text{MAX:} \quad & X_1 + X_2 \\
\text{Subject to:} \quad & X_1 + X_2 \leq 150 \\
& X_1 + X_2 \geq 200 \\
& X_1 \qquad\quad \geq \quad 0 \\
& \qquad\quad X_2 \geq \quad 0
\end{aligned}
$$

The feasible solutions for the first two constraints in this model are shown in Figure 2.12. Notice that the feasible solutions to the first constraint fall on the left side of its boundary line, whereas the feasible solutions to the second constraint fall on the right side of its boundary line. Therefore, no possible values for X_1 and X_2 exist that simultaneously satisfy both constraints in the model. In such a case, there are no feasible solutions to the problem.

FIGURE 2.12

Example of an LP problem with no feasible solution

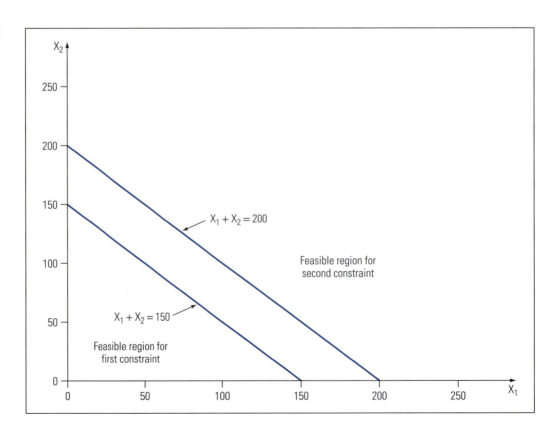

Infeasibility can occur in LP problems, perhaps due to an error in the formulation of the model—such as unintentionally making a less than or equal to constraint a greater than or equal to constraint. Or there just might not be a way to satisfy all the constraints in the model. In this case, constraints will have to be eliminated or loosened in order to obtain a feasible region (and feasible solution) for the problem.

Loosening constraints involves increasing the upper limits (or reducing the lower limits) to expand the range of feasible solutions. For example, if we loosen the first constraint in the previous model by changing the upper limit from 150 to 250, there is a feasible region for the problem. Of course, loosening constraints should not be done arbitrarily. In a real model, the value 150 would represent some actual characteristic of the decision problem (such as the number of pumps available to make hot tubs). We obviously cannot change this value to 250 unless it is appropriate to do so—that is, unless we know another 100 pumps can be obtained.

2.12 Summary

This chapter provided an introduction to an area of management science known as mathematical programming (MP), or optimization. Optimization covers a broad range of problems that share a common goal—determining the values for the decision variables in a problem that will maximize (or minimize) some objective function while satisfying various constraints. Constraints impose restrictions on the values that can be assumed by the decision variables and define the set of feasible options (or the feasible region) for the problem.

Linear programming (LP) problems represent a special category of MP problems in which the objective function and all the constraints can be expressed as linear combinations of the decision variables. Simple, two-variable LP problems can be solved graphically by identifying the feasible region and plotting level curves for the objective function. An optimal solution to an LP problem always occurs at a corner point of its feasible region (unless the objective function is unbounded).

Some anomalies can occur in optimization problems, including alternate optimal solutions, redundant constraints, unbounded solutions, and infeasibility.

2.13 References

Bazaraa, M., and J. Jarvis. *Linear Programming and Network Flows*. New York: Wiley, 1990.

Dantzig, G. *Linear Programming and Extensions*. Princeton, NJ: Princeton University Press, 1963.

Eppen, G., F. Gould, and C. Schmidt. *Introduction to Management Science*. Englewood Cliffs, NJ: Prentice Hall, 1993.

Shogan, A. *Management Science*. Englewood Cliffs, NJ: Prentice Hall, 1988.

Winston, W. *Operations Research: Applications and Algorithms*. Belmont, CA: Duxbury Press, 1997.

Questions and Problems

1. An LP model can have more than one optimal solution. Is it possible for an LP model to have exactly two optimal solutions? Why or why not?
2. In the solution to the Blue Ridge Hot Tubs problem, the optimal values for X_1 and X_2 turned out to be integers (whole numbers). Is this a general property of the solutions to LP problems? In other words, will the solution to an LP problem always consist of integers? Why or why not?

3. To determine the feasible region associated with less than or equal to constraints or greater than or equal to constraints, we graphed these constraints as if they were equal to constraints. Why is this possible?
4. Are the following objective functions for an LP model equivalent? That is, if they are both used, one at a time, to solve a problem with exactly the same constraints, will the optimal values for X_1 and X_2 be the same in both cases? Why or why not?

$$\text{MAX:} \quad 2X_1 + 3X_2$$
$$\text{MIN:} \quad -2X_1 - 3X_2$$

5. Which of the following constraints are not linear or cannot be included as a constraint in a linear programming problem?

a. $2X_1 + X_2 - 3X_3 \geq 50$
b. $2X_1 + \sqrt{X_2} \geq 60$
c. $4X_1 - \frac{1}{3}X_2 = 75$
d. $\dfrac{3X_1 + 2X_2 - 3X_3}{X_1 + X_2 + X_3} \leq 0.9$
e. $3X_1^2 + 7X_2 \leq 45$

6. Solve the following LP problem graphically by enumerating the corner points.

$$\text{MAX:} \quad 3X_1 + 4X_2$$
$$\text{Subject to:} \quad X_1 \leq 12$$
$$X_2 \leq 10$$
$$4X_1 + 6X_2 \leq 72$$
$$X_1, X_2 \geq 0$$

7. Solve the following LP problem graphically using level curves.

$$\text{MIN:} \quad 2X_1 + 3X_2$$
$$\text{Subject to:} \quad 2X_1 + 1X_2 \geq 3$$
$$4X_1 + 5X_2 \geq 20$$
$$2X_1 + 8X_2 \geq 16$$
$$5X_1 + 6X_2 \leq 60$$
$$X_1, X_2 \geq 0$$

8. Solve the following LP problem graphically using level curves.

$$\text{MAX:} \quad 2X_1 + 5X_2$$
$$\text{Subject to:} \quad 6X_1 + 5X_2 \leq 60$$
$$2X_1 + 3X_2 \leq 24$$
$$3X_1 + 6X_2 \leq 48$$
$$X_1, X_2 \geq 0$$

9. Solve the following LP problem graphically by enumerating the corner points.

$$\text{MIN:} \quad 5X_1 + 20X_2$$
$$\text{Subject to:} \quad X_1 + X_2 \geq 12$$
$$2X_1 + 5X_2 \geq 40$$

$$X_1 + X_2 \leq 15$$
$$X_1, X_2 \geq 0$$

10. Consider the following LP problem.

MAX: $3X_1 + 2X_2$
Subject to: $3X_1 + 3X_2 \leq 300$
               $6X_1 + 3X_2 \leq 480$
               $3X_1 + 3X_2 \leq 480$
               $X_1, X_2 \geq 0$

   a. Sketch the feasible region for this model.
   b. What is the optimal solution?
   c. Identify any redundant constraints in this model.

11. Solve the following LP problem graphically by enumerating the corner points.

MAX: $10X_1 + 12X_2$
Subject to: $8X_1 + 6X_2 \leq 98$
               $6X_1 + 8X_2 \leq 98$
               $X_1 + X_2 \geq 14$
               $X_1, X_2 \geq 0$

12. Solve the following LP problem using level curves.

MAX: $4X_1 + 5X_2$
Subject to: $2X_1 + 3X_2 \leq 120$
               $4X_1 + 3X_2 \leq 140$
               $X_1 + X_2 \geq 80$
               $X_1, X_2 \geq 0$

13. The Electrotech Corporation manufactures two industrial-sized electrical devices: generators and alternators. Both of these products require wiring and testing during the assembly process. Each generator requires 2 hours of wiring and 1 hour of testing and can be sold for a $250 profit. Each alternator requires 3 hours of wiring and 2 hours of testing and can be sold for a $150 profit. There are 260 hours of wiring time and 140 hours of testing time available in the next production period, and Electrotech wants to maximize profit.

   a. Formulate an LP model for this problem.
   b. Sketch the feasible region for this problem.
   c. Determine the optimal solution to this problem using level curves.

14. Refer to the previous question. Suppose that Electrotech's management decides that they need to make at least 20 generators and at least 20 alternators.

   a. Reformulate your LP model to account for this change.
   b. Sketch the feasible region for this problem.
   c. Determine the optimal solution to this problem by enumerating the corner points.
   d. Suppose that Electrotech can acquire additional wiring time at a very favorable cost. Should it do so? Why or why not?

15. The marketing manager for Mountain Mist soda needs to decide how many TV spots and magazine ads to run during the next quarter. Each TV spot costs $5,000 and is expected to increase sales by 300,000 cans. Each magazine ad costs $2,000 and

is expected to increase sales by 500,000 cans. A total of $100,000 may be spent on TV and magazine ads; however, Mountain Mist wants to spend no more than $70,000 on TV spots and no more than $50,000 on magazine ads. Mountain Mist earns a profit of $0.05 on each can it sells.

a. Formulate an LP model for this problem.
b. Sketch the feasible region for this model.
c. Find the optimal solution to the problem using level curves.

16. Blacktop Refining extracts minerals from ore mined at two different sites in Montana. Each ton of ore type 1 contains 20% copper, 20% zinc and 15% magnesium. Each ton of ore type 2 contains 30% copper, 25% zinc and 10% magnesium. Ore type 1 costs $90 per ton, while ore type 2 costs $120 per ton. Blacktop would like to buy enough ore to extract at least 8 tons of copper, 6 tons of zinc, and 5 tons of magnesium in the least costly manner.

a. Formulate an LP model for this problem.
b. Sketch the feasible region for this problem.
c. Find the optimal solution.

17. Bibbins Manufacturing produces softballs and baseballs for youth recreation leagues. Each softball costs $11 to produce and sells for $17, while each baseball costs $10.50 and sells for $15. The material and labor required to produce each item is listed here along with the availability of each resource.

Resource	Amount Required Per		Amount Available
	Softball	Baseball	
Leather	5 oz	4 oz	6,000 oz
Nylon	6 yds	3 yds	5,400 yds
Core	4 oz	2 oz	4,000 oz
Labor	2.5 min	2 min	3,500 min
Stitching	1 min	1 min	1,500 min

a. Formulate an LP model for this problem.
b. Sketch the feasible region.
c. What is the optimal solution?

18. Bill's Grill is a popular college restaurant that is famous for its hamburgers. The owner of the restaurant, Bill, mixes fresh ground beef and pork with a secret ingredient to make delicious quarter-pound hamburgers that are advertised as having no more than 25% fat. Bill can buy beef containing 80% meat and 20% fat at $0.85 per pound. He can buy pork containing 70% meat and 30% fat at $0.65 per pound. Bill wants to determine the minimum cost way to blend the beef and pork to make hamburgers that have no more than 25% fat.

a. Formulate an LP model for this problem. (*Hint*: The decision variables for this problem represent the percentage of beef and the percentage of pork to combine.)
b. Sketch the feasible region for this problem.
c. Determine the optimal solution to this problem by enumerating the corner points.

19. Zippy motorcycle manufacturing produces two popular pocket bikes (miniature motorcycles with 49cc engines): the Razor and the Zoomer. In the coming week, the manufacturer wants to produce up to 700 bikes and wants to ensure the number of Razors produced does not exceed the number of Zoomers by more than 300. Each Razor produced and sold results in a profit of $70, while each Zoomer results in a profit of $40. The bikes are identical mechanically and only differ in the appearance of the polymer-based trim around the fuel tank and seat. Each Razor's trim requires

2 pounds of polymer and 3 hours of production time, while each Zoomer requires 1 pound of polymer and 4 hours of production time. Assume that 900 pounds of polymer and 2,400 labor hours are available for production of these items in the coming week.

a. Formulate an LP model for this problem.
b. Sketch the feasible region for this problem.
c. What is the optimal solution?

20. The Quality Desk Company makes two types of computer desks from laminated particle board. The Presidential model requires 30 square feet of particle board, 1 keyboard sliding mechanism, 5 hours of labor to fabricate, and sells for $149. The Senator model requires 24 square feet of particle board, 1 keyboard sliding mechanism, 3 hours of labor to fabricate, and sells for $135. In the coming week, the company can buy up to 15,000 square feet of particle board at a price of $1.35 per square foot and up to 600 keyboard sliding mechanisms at a cost of $4.75 each. The company views manufacturing labor as a fixed cost and has 3,000 labor hours available in the coming week for the fabrication of these desks.

a. Formulate an LP model for this problem.
b. Sketch the feasible region for this problem.
c. What is the optimal solution?

21. A farmer in Georgia has a 100-acre farm on which to plant watermelons and cantaloupes. Every acre planted with watermelons requires 50 gallons of water per day and must be prepared for planting with 20 pounds of fertilizer. Every acre planted with cantaloupes requires 75 gallons of water per day and must be prepared for planting with 15 pounds of fertilizer. The farmer estimates that it will take 2 hours of labor to harvest each acre planted with watermelons and 2.5 hours to harvest each acre planted with cantaloupes. He believes that watermelons will sell for about $3 each, and cantaloupes will sell for about $1 each. Every acre planted with watermelons is expected to yield 90 salable units. Every acre planted with cantaloupes is expected to yield 300 salable units. The farmer can pump about 6,000 gallons of water per day for irrigation purposes from a shallow well. He can buy as much fertilizer as he needs at a cost of $10 per 50-pound bag. Finally, the farmer can hire laborers to harvest the fields at a rate of $5 per hour. If the farmer sells all the watermelons and cantaloupes he produces, how many acres of each crop should the farmer plant in order to maximize profits?

a. Formulate an LP model for this problem.
b. Sketch the feasible region for this model.
c. Find the optimal solution to the problem using level curves.

22. Sanderson Manufacturing produces ornate, decorative wood frame doors and windows. Each item produced goes through three manufacturing processes: cutting, sanding, and finishing. Each door produced requires 1 hour in cutting, 30 minutes in sanding, and 30 minutes in finishing. Each window requires 30 minutes in cutting, 45 minutes in sanding, and 1 hour in finishing. In the coming week Sanderson has 40 hours of cutting capacity available, 40 hours of sanding capacity, and 60 hours of finishing capacity. Assume all doors produced can be sold for a profit of $500, and all windows can be sold for a profit of $400.

a. Formulate an LP model for this problem.
b. Sketch the feasible region.
c. What is the optimal solution?

23. PC-Express is a computer retail store that sells desktops and laptops. The company earns $600 on each desktop computer it sells and $900 on each laptop. The computers PC-Express sells are actually manufactured by another company. This manufacturer has a special order to fill for another customer and cannot ship more than 80 desktops

and 75 laptops to PC-Express next month. The employees at PC-Express must spend about 2 hours installing software and checking each desktop computer they sell. They spend roughly 3 hours to complete this process for laptop computers. They expect to have about 300 hours available for this purpose during the next month. The store's management is fairly certain that they can sell all the computers they order but are unsure how many desktops and laptops they should order to maximize profits.

  a. Formulate an LP model for this problem.
  b. Sketch the feasible region for this model.
  c. Find the optimal solution to the problem by enumerating the corner points.

24. American Auto is evaluating their marketing plan for the sedans, SUVs, and trucks they produce. A TV ad featuring this SUV has been developed. The company estimates each showing of this commercial will cost $500,000 and increase sales of SUVs by 3% but reduce sales of trucks by 1% and have no effect of the sales of sedans. The company also has a print ad campaign developed that it can run in various nationally distributed magazines at a cost of $750,000 per title. It is estimated that each magazine title the ad runs in will increase the sales of sedans, SUVs, and trucks by 2%, 1%, and 4%, respectively. The company desires to increase sales of sedans, SUVs, and trucks by at least 3%, 14%, and 4%, respectively, in the least costly manner.

  a. Formulate an LP model for this problem.
  b. Sketch the feasible region.
  c. What is the optimal solution?

For The Lines They Are A-Changin' (with apologies to Bob Dylan)

CASE 2.1

The owner of Blue Ridge Hot Tubs, Howie Jones, has asked for your assistance analyzing how the feasible region and solution to his production problem might change in response to changes in various parameters in the LP model. He is hoping this might further his understanding of LP and how the constraints, objective function, and optimal solution interrelate. To assist in this process, he asked a consulting firm to develop the spreadsheet shown earlier in Figure 2.8 (and the file Fig2-8.xlsm that accompanies this book) that dynamically updates the feasible region and optimal solution as the various parameters in the model change. Unfortunately, Howie has not had much time to play around with this spreadsheet, so he has left it in your hands and asked you to use it to answer the following questions. Click the Reset button in file Fig2-8.xlsm before answering each of the following questions.

> ### Important Software Note
> The file Fig2-8.xlsm contains a macro that must be enabled for the workbook to operate correctly. To allow this (and other) macros to run in Excel, click File, Options, Trust Center, Trust Center Settings, Macro Settings; select Disable All Macros with Notification; and click OK twice. Now when Excel opens a workbook containing macros, it should display a security message indicating some active content has been disabled and will give you the opportunity to enable this content, which you should do for the Excel files accompanying this book.

1. In the optimal solution to this problem, how many pumps, hours of labor, and feet of tubing are being used?
2. If the company could increase the number of pumps available, should they? Why or why not? And if so, what is the maximum number of additional pumps they should consider acquiring and by how much would this increase profit?
3. If the company could acquire more labor hours, should they? Why or why not? If so, how much additional labor should they consider acquiring, and by how much would this increase profit?
4. If the company could acquire more tubing, should they? Why or why not? If so, how much additional tubing should they consider acquiring, and how much would this increase profit?
5. By how much would profit increase if the company could reduce the labor required to produce Aqua-Spas from 9 to 8 hours? From 8 to 7 hours? From 7 to 6 hours?
6. By how much would profit increase if the company could reduce the labor required to produce Hydro-Luxes from 6 to 5 hours? From 5 to 4 hours? From 4 to 3 hours?
7. By how much would profit increase if the company could reduce the amount of tubing required to produce Aqua-Spas from 12 to 11 feet? From 11 to 10 feet? From 10 to 9 feet?
8. By how much would profit increase if the company could reduce the amount of tubing required to produce Hydro-Luxes from 16 to 15 feet? From 15 to 14 feet? From 14 to 13 feet?
9. By how much would the unit profit on Aqua-Spas have to change before the optimal product mix changes?
10. By how much would the unit profit on Hydro-Luxes have to change before the optimal product mix changes?

Chapter 3

Modeling and Solving
LP Problems in a Spreadsheet

3.0 Introduction

Chapter 2 discussed how to formulate linear programming (LP) problems and how to solve simple, two-variable LP problems graphically. As you might expect, very few real-world LP problems involve only two decision variables. So, the graphical solution approach is of limited value in solving LP problems. However, the discussion of two-variable problems provides a basis for understanding the issues involved in all LP problems and the general strategies for solving them.

For example, every solvable LP problem has a feasible region, and an optimal solution to the problem can be found at some extreme point of this region (assuming the problem is not unbounded). This is true of all LP problems regardless of the number of decision variables. Although it is fairly easy to graph the feasible region for a two-variable LP problem, it is difficult to visualize or graph the feasible region of an LP problem with three variables because such a graph is three-dimensional. If there are more than three variables, it is virtually impossible to visualize or graph the feasible region for an LP problem because such a graph involves more than three dimensions.

Fortunately, several mathematical techniques exist to solve LP problems involving almost any number of variables without visualizing or graphing their feasible regions. These techniques are now built into spreadsheet packages in a way that makes solving LP problems a fairly simple task. So, using the appropriate computer software, you can solve almost any LP problem easily. The main challenge is ensuring that you formulate the LP problem correctly and communicate this formulation to the computer accurately. This chapter shows you how to do this using spreadsheets.

3.1 Spreadsheet Solvers

The importance of LP (and optimization in general) is underscored by the fact that all major spreadsheet packages come with built-in spreadsheet optimization tools called **solvers**. This book uses Excel to illustrate how spreadsheet solvers can solve optimization problems. However, the same concepts and techniques presented here apply to other spreadsheet packages, although certain details of implementation may differ.

You can also solve optimization problems without using a spreadsheet by using a specialized mathematical programming package. A partial list of these packages includes LINDO, CPLEX, and Xpress-MP. Typically, researchers and businesses use these packages to solve extremely large problems that do not fit conveniently in a spreadsheet.

The Spreadsheet Solver Company

Frontline Systems, Inc. created the solvers in Microsoft Excel, Lotus 1-2-3, and Corel Quattro Pro. Frontline markets enhanced versions of these solvers and other analytical tools for spreadsheets, including the Risk Solver Platform product that will be featured throughout this book. You can find out more about Frontline Systems and their products by visiting their Web site at http://www.solver.com.

3.2 Solving LP Problems in a Spreadsheet

We will demonstrate the mechanics of using the Solver in Excel by solving the problem faced by Howie Jones, described in Chapter 2. Recall that Howie owns and operates Blue Ridge Hot Tubs, a company that sells two models of hot tubs: the Aqua-Spa and the Hydro-Lux. Howie purchases prefabricated fiberglass hot tub shells and installs a common water pump and the appropriate amount of tubing into each hot tub. Every Aqua-Spa requires 9 hours of labor and 12 feet of tubing; every Hydro-Lux requires 6 hours of labor and 16 feet of tubing. Demand for these products is such that each Aqua-Spa produced can be sold to generate a profit of $350, and each Hydro-Lux produced can be sold to generate a profit of $300. The company expects to have 200 pumps, 1,566 hours of labor, and 2,880 feet of tubing available during the next production cycle. The problem is to determine the optimal number of Aqua-Spas and Hydro-Luxes to produce in order to maximize profits.

Chapter 2 developed the following LP formulation for the problem Howie faces. In this model, X_1 represents the number of Aqua-Spas to be produced, and X_2 represents the number of Hydro-Luxes to be produced.

$$
\begin{array}{llll}
\text{MAX:} & 350X_1 + 300X_2 & & \} \text{ profit} \\
\text{Subject to:} & 1X_1 + 1X_2 \leq 200 & & \} \text{ pump constraint} \\
& 9X_1 + 6X_2 \leq 1{,}566 & & \} \text{ labor constraint} \\
& 12X_1 + 16X_2 \leq 2{,}880 & & \} \text{ tubing constraint} \\
& 1X_1 \qquad\qquad \geq \quad 0 & & \} \text{ simple lower bound} \\
& \qquad\quad 1X_2 \geq \quad 0 & & \} \text{ simple lower bound}
\end{array}
$$

So, how do you solve this problem in a spreadsheet? First, you must implement, or build, this model in the spreadsheet.

3.3 The Steps in Implementing an LP Model in a Spreadsheet

The following four steps summarize what must be done to implement any LP problem in a spreadsheet.

1. **Organize the data for the model on the spreadsheet**. The data for the model consist of the coefficients in the objective function, the various coefficients in the

constraints, and the right-hand-side (RHS) values for the constraints. There is usually more than one way to organize the data for a particular problem on a spreadsheet, but you should keep in mind some general guidelines. First, the goal is to organize the data so their purpose and meaning are as clear as possible. Think of your spreadsheet as a management report that needs to communicate clearly the important factors of the problem being solved. To this end, you should spend some time organizing the data for the problem in your mind's eye—visualizing how the data can be laid out logically—before you start typing values in the spreadsheet. Descriptive labels should be placed in the spreadsheet to clearly identify the various data elements. Often, row and column structures of the data in the model can be used in the spreadsheet to facilitate model implementation. (Note that some or all of the coefficients and values for an LP model might be calculated from other data, often referred to as the primary data. It is best to maintain primary data in the spreadsheet and use appropriate formulas to calculate the coefficients and values that are needed for the LP formulation. Then, if the primary data change, appropriate changes will be made automatically in the coefficients for the LP model.)

2. **Reserve separate cells in the spreadsheet to represent each decision variable in the algebraic model.** Although you can use any empty cells in a spreadsheet to represent the decision variables, it is usually best to arrange the cells representing the decision variables in a way that parallels the structure of the data. This is often helpful in setting up formulas for the objective function and constraints. When possible, it is also a good idea to keep the cells representing decision variables in the same area of the spreadsheet. In addition, you should use descriptive labels to clearly identify the meaning of these cells.

3. **Create a formula in a cell in the spreadsheet that corresponds to the objective function in the algebraic model.** The spreadsheet formula corresponding to the objective function is created by referring to the data cells where the objective function coefficients have been entered (or calculated) and to the corresponding cells representing the decision variables.

4. **For each constraint, create a formula in a separate cell in the spreadsheet that corresponds to the left-hand-side (LHS) of the constraint.** The formula corresponding to the LHS of each constraint is created by referring to the data cells where the coefficients for these constraints have been entered (or calculated) and to the appropriate decision variable cells. Many of the constraint formulas have a similar structure. Thus, when possible, you should create constraint formulas that can be copied to implement other constraint formulas. This not only reduces the effort required to implement a model but also helps avoid hard-to-detect typing errors.

Although each of the previous steps must be performed to implement an LP model in a spreadsheet, they do not have to be performed in the order indicated. It is usually wise to perform step 1 first, followed by step 2. But the order in which steps 3 and 4 are performed often varies from problem to problem.

Also, it is often wise to use shading, background colors, and/or borders to identify the cells representing decision variables, constraints, and the objective function in a model. This allows the user of a spreadsheet to more readily distinguish between cells representing raw data (that can be changed) and other elements of the model. We have more to say about how to design and implement effective spreadsheet models for LP problems, but first, let's see how the previous steps can be used to implement a spreadsheet model using our example problem.

3.4 A Spreadsheet Model for the Blue Ridge Hot Tubs Problem

One possible spreadsheet representation for our example problem is given in Figure 3.1 (and in the file named Fig3-1.xlsm that accompanies this book). Let's walk through the creation of this model step-by-step so you can see how it relates to the algebraic formulation of the model.

FIGURE 3.1 *A spreadsheet model for the Blue Ridge Hot Tub production problem*

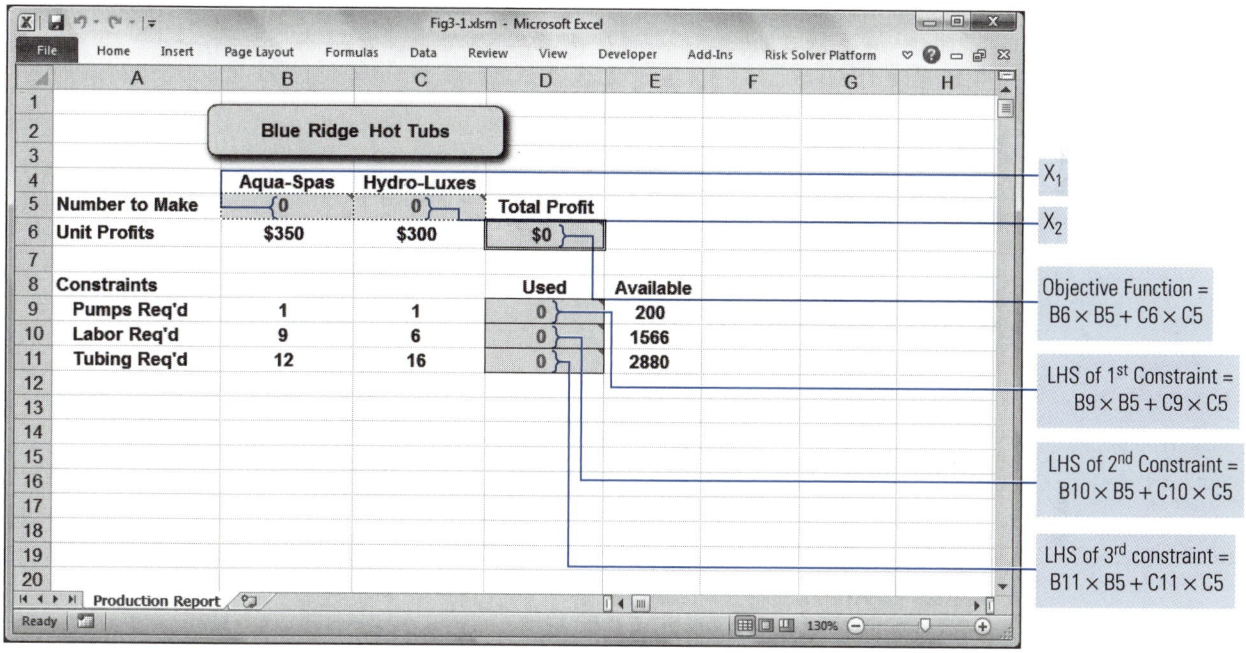

Annotations in figure:
- X_1
- X_2
- Objective Function = $B6 \times B5 + C6 \times C5$
- LHS of 1st Constraint = $B9 \times B5 + C9 \times C5$
- LHS of 2nd Constraint = $B10 \times B5 + C10 \times C5$
- LHS of 3rd constraint = $B11 \times B5 + C11 \times C5$

A Note About Macros

In most of the spreadsheet examples accompanying this book, you can click on the blue title bars at the top of the spreadsheet to toggle on and off a note that provides additional documentation about the spreadsheet model. This documentation feature is enabled through the use of macros. To enable this (and other) macros to run in Excel, click File, Options, Trust Center, Trust Center Settings, Macro Settings; select Disable All Macros with Notification; click OK; and then click OK again. If you then open a file containing macros, Excel displays a security warning indicating some active content has been disabled and should give you the opportunity to enable this content, which you should do to make use of the macro features in the spreadsheet files accompanying this book.

3.4.1 ORGANIZING THE DATA

One of the first steps in building any spreadsheet model for an LP problem is to organize the data for the model on the spreadsheet. In Figure 3.1, we enter the data for the unit profits for Aqua-Spas and Hydro-Luxes in cells B6 and C6, respectively. Next, the numbers of pumps, labor hours, and feet of tubing required to produce each type of hot tub are entered in cells B9 through C11. The values in cells B9 and C9 indicate that one pump is required to produce each type of hot tub. The values in cells B10 and C10 show that each Aqua-Spa produced requires 9 hours of labor, and each Hydro-Lux requires 6 hours. Cells B11 and C11 indicate that each Aqua-Spa produced requires 12 feet of tubing, and each Hydro-Lux requires 16 feet. The available number of pumps, labor hours, and feet of tubing are entered in cells E9 through E11. Notice that appropriate labels are also entered to identify all the data elements for the problem.

3.4.2 REPRESENTING THE DECISION VARIABLES

As indicated in Figure 3.1, cells B5 and C5 represent the decision variables X_1 and X_2 in our algebraic model. These cells are shaded and outlined with dashed borders to visually distinguish them from other elements of the model. Values of zero were placed in cells B5 and C5 because we do not know how many Aqua-Spas and Hydro-Luxes should be produced. Shortly, we will use Solver to determine the optimal values for these cells. Figure 3.2 summarizes the relationship between the decision variables in the algebraic model and the corresponding cells in the spreadsheet.

FIGURE 3.2

Summary of the relationship between the decision variables and corresponding spreadsheet cells

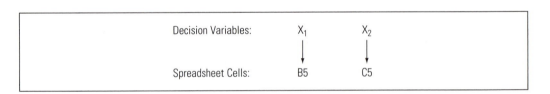

3.4.3 REPRESENTING THE OBJECTIVE FUNCTION

The next step in implementing our LP problem is to create a formula in a cell of the spreadsheet to represent the objective function. We can accomplish this in many ways. Because the objective function is $350X_1 + 300X_2$, you might be tempted to enter the formula =350*B5+300*C5 in the spreadsheet. However, if you wanted to change the coefficients in the objective function, you would have to go back and edit this formula to reflect the changes. Because the objective function coefficients are entered in cells B6 and C6, a better way of implementing the objective function is to refer to the values in cells B6 and C6 rather than entering numeric constants in the formula. The formula for the objective function is entered in cell D6 as:

Formula for cell D6:   =B6*B5+C6*C5

As shown previously in Figure 3.1, cell D6 initially returns the value 0 because cells B5 and C5 both contain zeros. Figure 3.3 summarizes the relationship between the algebraic objective function and the formula entered in cell D6. By implementing the objective function in this manner, if the profits earned on the hot tubs ever change, the spreadsheet model can be changed easily, and the problem can be re-solved to determine the impact of this change on the optimal solution. Note that cell D6 has been shaded and outlined with a double border to distinguish it from other elements of the model.

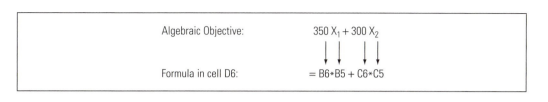

FIGURE 3.3

Summary of the relationship between the decision variables and corresponding spreadsheet cells

3.4.4 REPRESENTING THE CONSTRAINTS

The next step in building the spreadsheet model involves implementing the constraints of the LP model. Earlier we said that for each constraint in the algebraic model, you must create a formula in a cell of the spreadsheet that corresponds to the LHS of the constraint. The LHS of each constraint in our model is:

LHS of the pump constraint
$$\boxed{1X_1 + 1X_2} \leq 200$$

LHS of the labor constraint
$$\boxed{9X_1 + 6X_2} \leq 1{,}566$$

LHS of the tubing constraint
$$\boxed{12X_1 + 16X_2} \leq 2{,}880$$

We need to set up three cells in the spreadsheet to represent the LHS formulas of the three constraints. Again, this is done by referring to the data cells containing the coefficients for these constraints and to the cells representing the decision variables. The LHS of the first constraint is entered in cell D9 as:

Formula for cell D9:   =B9*B5+C9*C5

Similarly, the LHS of the second and third constraints are entered in cells D10 and D11 as:

Formula for cell D10:   =B10*B5+C10*C5
Formula for cell D11:   =B11*B5+C11*C5

These formulas calculate the number of pumps, hours of labor, and feet of tubing required to manufacture the number of hot tubs represented in cells B5 and C5. Note that cells D9 through D11 were shaded and outlined with solid borders to distinguish them from the other elements of the model.

Figure 3.4 summarizes the relationship between the LHS formulas of the constraints in the algebraic formulation of our model and their spreadsheet representations.

We know that Blue Ridge Hot Tubs has 200 pumps, 1,566 labor hours, and 2,880 feet of tubing available during its next production run. In our algebraic formulation of the LP model, these values represent the RHS values for the three constraints. Therefore, we entered the available number of pumps, hours of labor, and feet of tubing in cells E9, E10, and E11, respectively. These terms indicate the upper limits on the values cells D9, D10, and D11 can assume.

3.4.5 REPRESENTING THE BOUNDS ON THE DECISION VARIABLES

Now, what about the simple lower bounds on our decision variables represented by $X_1 \geq 0$ and $X_2 \geq 0$? These conditions are quite common in LP problems and are referred

FIGURE 3.4

Summary of the relationship between the LHS formulas of the constraints and their spreadsheet representations

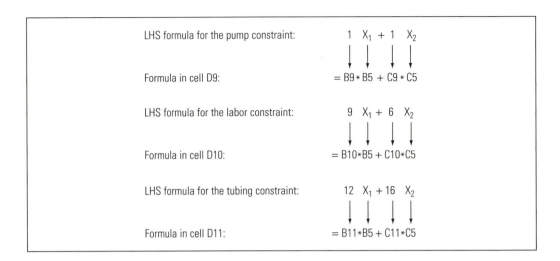

to as **nonnegativity conditions** because they indicate that the decision variables can assume only nonnegative values. These conditions might seem like constraints and can, in fact, be implemented like the other constraints. However, Solver allows you to specify simple upper and lower bounds for the decision variables by referring directly to the cells representing the decision variables. Thus, at this point, we have taken no specific action to implement these bounds in our spreadsheet.

3.5 How Solver Views the Model

After implementing our model in the spreadsheet, we can use Solver to find the optimal solution to the problem. But first, we need to define the following three components of our spreadsheet model for Solver:

- **Objective cell.** The cell in the spreadsheet that represents the *objective function* in the model (and whether its value should be maximized or minimized).
- **Variable cells.** The cells in the spreadsheet that represent the *decision variables* in the model (and any upper and lower bounds that apply to these cells).
- **Constraint cells.** The cells in the spreadsheet that represent the *LHS formulas* of the constraints in the model (and any upper and lower bounds that apply to these formulas).

These components correspond directly to the cells in the spreadsheet we established when implementing the LP model. For example, in the spreadsheet for our example problem, the objective cell is represented by cell D6, the variable cells are represented by cells B5 and C5, and the constraint cells are represented by cells D9, D10, and D11. Figure 3.5 shows these relationships. Figure 3.5 also shows a cell note documenting the purpose of cell D6. Cell notes can be a very effective way of describing details about the purpose or meaning of various cells in a model.

By comparing Figure 3.1 with Figure 3.5, you can see the direct connection between the way we formulate LP models algebraically and how Solver views the spreadsheet implementation of the model. The decision variables in the algebraic model correspond to the variable cells for Solver. The LHS formulas for the different constraints in the algebraic model correspond to the constraint cells for Solver. Finally, the objective function in the algebraic model corresponds to the objective cell for Solver. Figure 3.6 summarizes the relationships between our algebraic model and how Solver views the spreadsheet implementation of this model.

FIGURE 3.5 *Summary of Solver's view of the model*

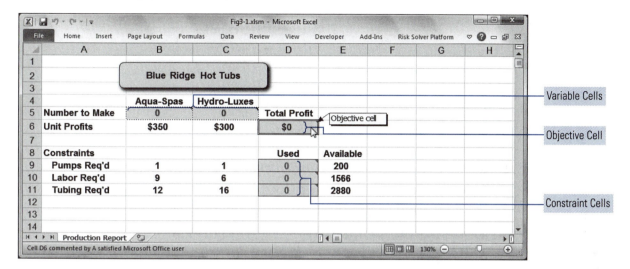

FIGURE 3.6

*Summary of
Solver terminology*

Terms used to describe LP models algebraically	Corresponding terms used by solver to describe spreadsheet LP models
objective function	objective cell
decision variables	variable (or changing) cells
LHS formulas of constraints	constraint cells

A Note About Creating Cell Comments...

It is easy to create cell comments like the one shown for cell D6 in Figure 3.5. To create a comment for a cell:

1. Click the cell to select it.
2. Choose Review, New Comment (or press Shift + F2).
3. Type the comment for the cell, and then select another cell.

The display of cell comments can be turned on or off as follows:

1. Choose Review.
2. Select the Show/Hide icon in the Comments section.

To copy a cell comment from one cell to a series of other cells:

1. Click the cell containing the comment you want to copy.
2. Choose the Copy command on the Home, Clipboard ribbon (or press Ctrl + C).
3. Select the cells you want to copy the comment to.
4. Select the Paste Special command on the Home, Clipboard, Paste ribbon (or right-click and select Paste Special).
5. Select the Comments option button.
6. Click the OK button.

Installing Risk Solver Platform for Education

This book uses Risk Solver Platform for Education—a *greatly* enhanced version of the standard Solver that ships with Excel. If you have not already done so, go to the text's Premium online content website and follow the instructions given for downloading and installing a copy of the Risk Solver Platform for Education software. (If you are running Excel in a networked environment, consult with your network administrator.) Although many of the examples in this book also work with the standard Solver that comes with Excel, Risk Solver Platform for Education includes many additional capabilities that are featured throughout this book.

3.6 Using Risk Solver Platform

After implementing an LP model in a spreadsheet, we still need to solve the problem being modeled. To do this, we must first indicate to Solver which cells in the spreadsheet represent the objective function, the decision variables, and the constraints. To invoke Solver, choose the Risk Solver Platform tab on the ribbon, as shown in Figure 3.7, to display the Risk Solver task pane.

FIGURE 3.7 *Risk Solver Platform's task pane*

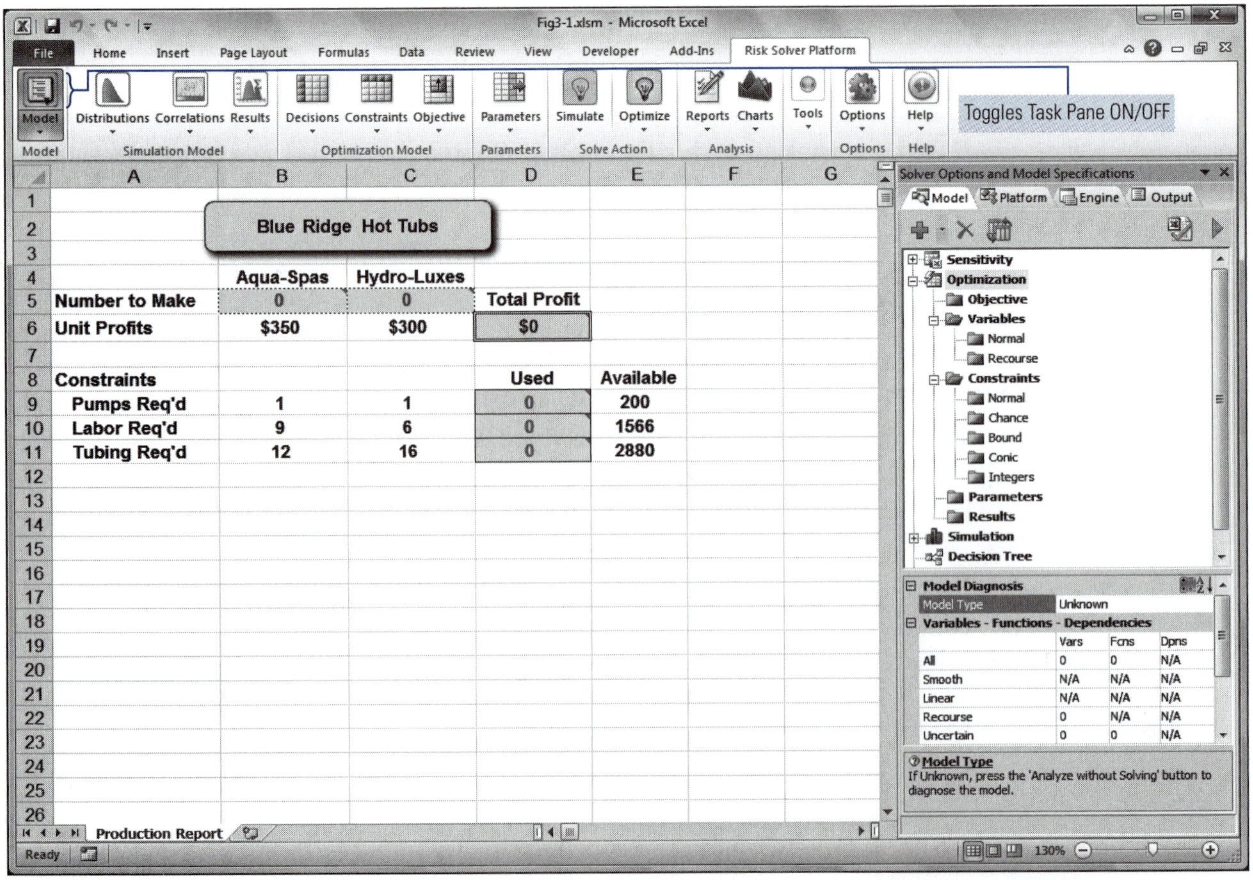

Risk Solver Platform offers a number of analytical tools (for example, Sensitivity analysis, Optimization, Simulation, Discriminant Analysis, Decision Trees) that we will discuss throughout this book. Currently we are interested in Risk Solver Platform's optimization tool, so that feature has been expanded in Figure 3.7 by double-clicking the Optimization option in Risk Solver's task pane.

S o f t w a r e   N o t e

The Risk Solver task pane shown in Figure 3.7 can be toggled on and off by clicking the Model icon on the Risk Solver Platform ribbon.

3.6.1 DEFINING THE OBJECTIVE CELL

Figure 3.8 shows how to define the Objective cell for our model. To do this, follow these steps:

1. Select cell D6 (where we implemented the formula representing the objective function for our model).
2. Click the Add Objective option from the list that appears when you click the drop-down arrow next to the green plus sign in Risk Solver's task pane.

FIGURE 3.8 *Specifying the objective cell*

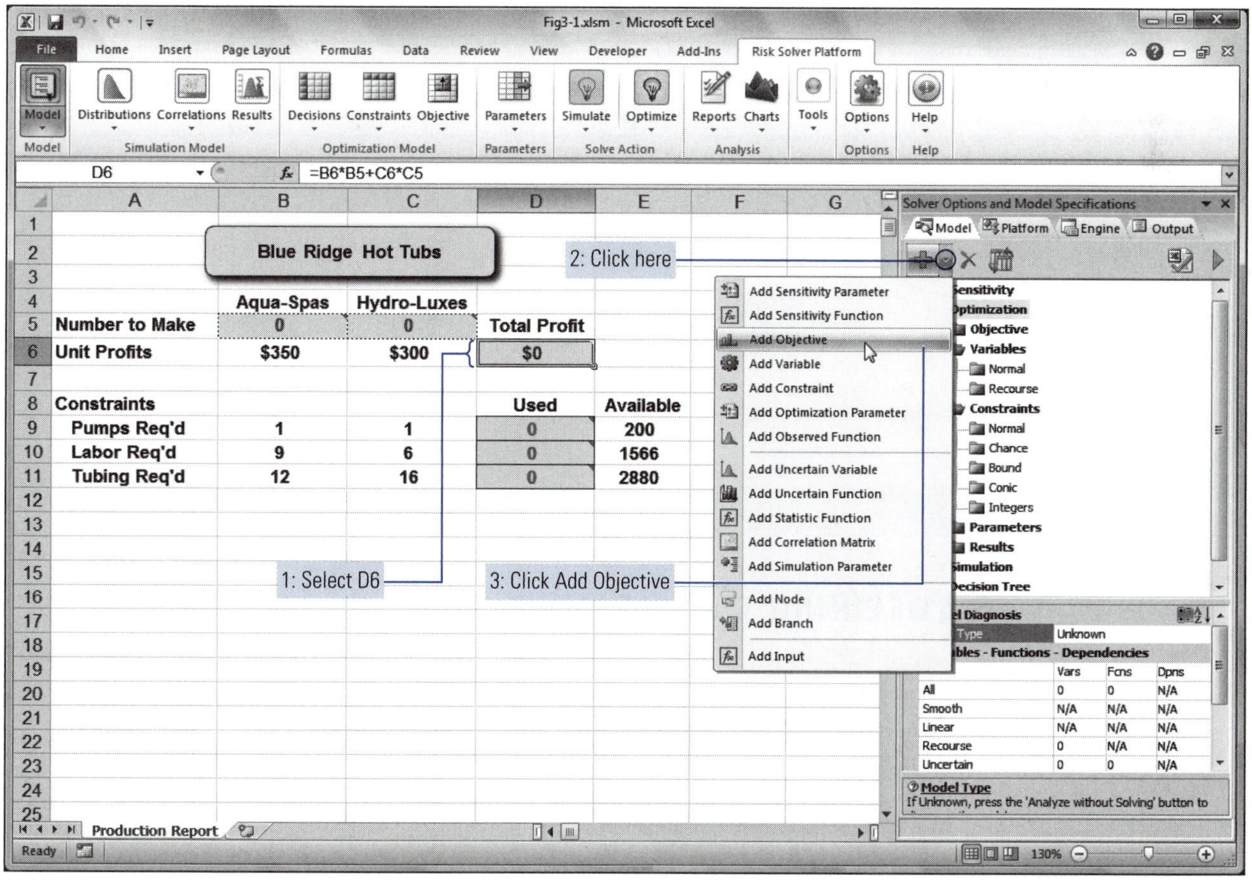

Figure 3.9 shows the result of these actions. In Risk Solver's task pane, note that cell D6 is now listed as the objective for the problem, and, by default, Solver assumes we want to maximize its value. That is the correct assumption for this problem. However, as you will see, in other situations, you might want to minimize the value of the objective function. In Figure 3.9, note that if you click on the objective cell ("$D$6") in Risk Solver's task pane, more detailed information about that selection appears at the bottom of the pane. In particular, the objective cell has a "Sense" property that you can change to indicate whether you want to maximize or minimize the value of the objective. (Alternatively, double-clicking the objective cell ("$D$6") in Risk Solver's task pane launches a dialog box that you can use to change the desired direction of optimization and other information about the objective.)

FIGURE 3.9 *Specifying the direction of optimization*

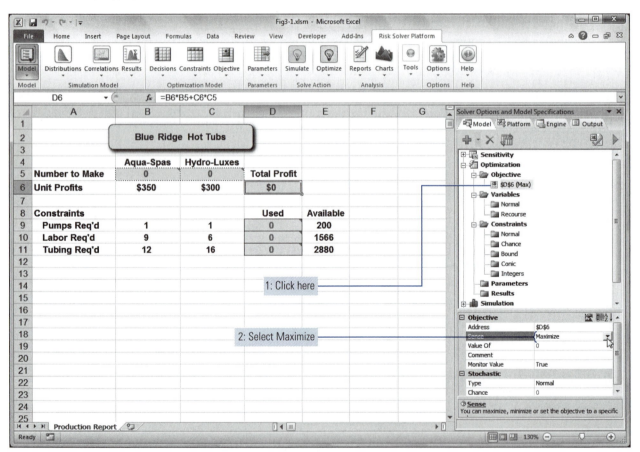

3.6.2 DEFINING THE VARIABLE CELLS

To solve our LP problem, we also need to indicate which cells represent the decision variables in the model. Figure 3.10 shows how to define the variable cells for our model. To do this, follow these steps:

1. Select cells B5 and C5.
2. Click the Add Variable option from the list that appears when you click the drop-down arrow next to the green plus sign in Risk Solver's task pane.

FIGURE 3.10   *Specifying the variable cells*

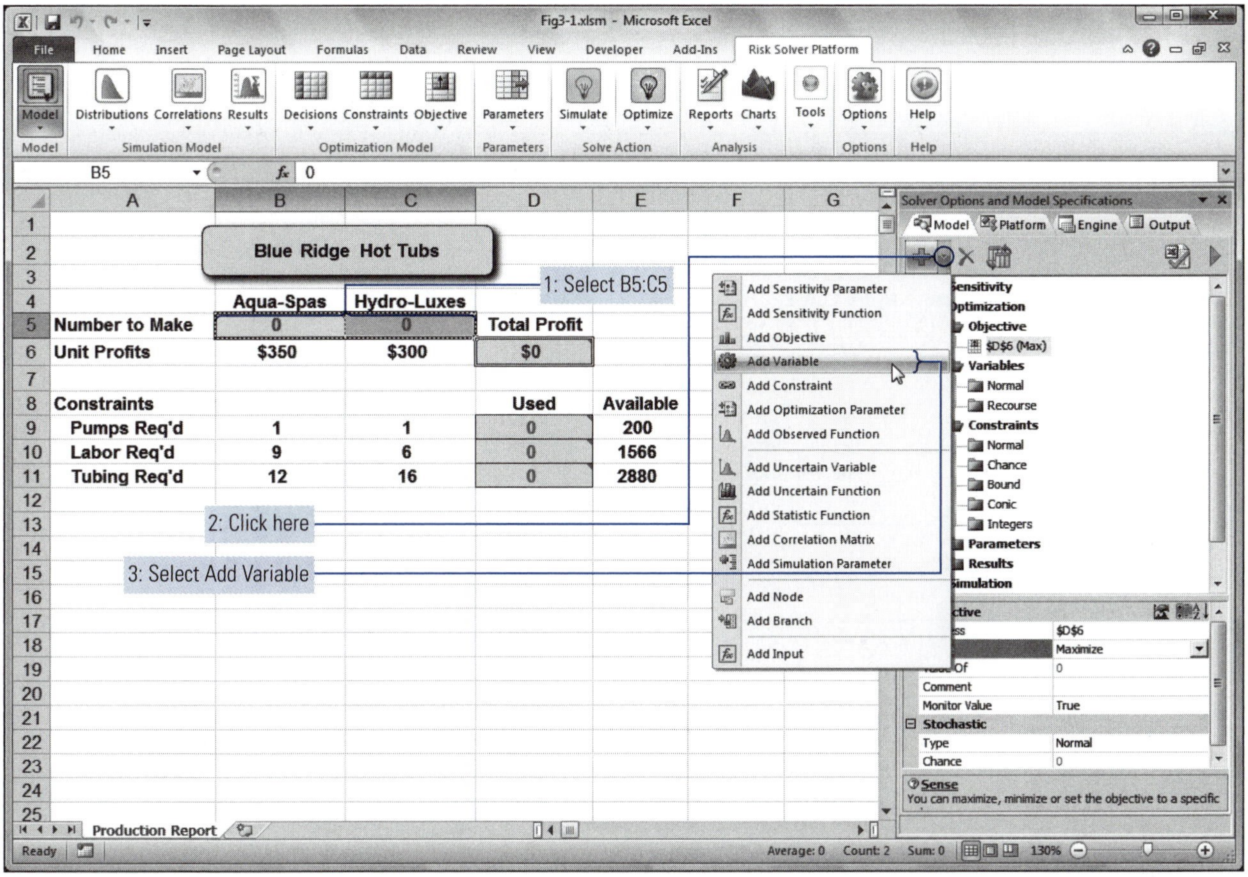

Cells B5 and C5 now represent the decision variables for the model. Solver will determine the optimal values for these cells later. If all the decision variables are not in one contiguous range, you can select all the variable cells (while pressing the Ctrl key on your keyboard) and click the Add Variable command. Alternatively, you can repeatedly go through the process of selecting individual groups of decision variable cells and clicking the Add Variable command. Whenever possible, it is best to use contiguous cells to represent the decision variables.

3.6.3 DEFINING THE CONSTRAINT CELLS

Next, we must define the constraint cells in the spreadsheet and the restrictions that apply to these cells. As mentioned earlier, the constraint cells are the cells in which we implemented the LHS formulas for each constraint in our model. Figure 3.11 shows how to define the variable cells for our model. To do this, follow these steps:

1. Select cells D9 through D11.
2. Click the Add Constraint option from the list that appears when you click the drop-down arrow next to the green plus sign in Risk Solver's task pane.

FIGURE 3.11 *Specifying the constraints cells*

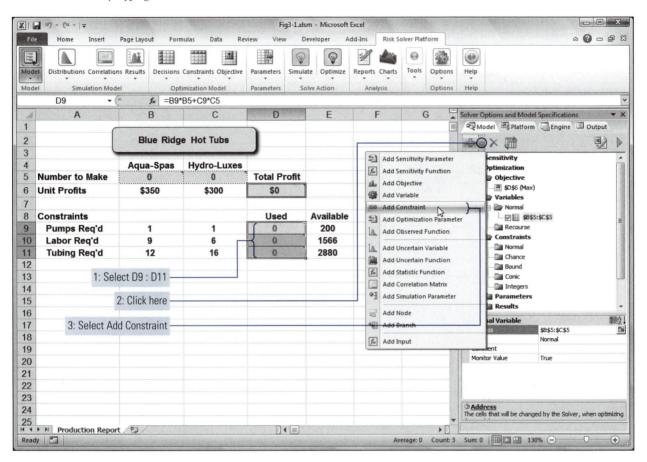

The resulting dialog is displayed in Figure 3.12. We fill out this dialog as shown to indicate that cells D9 through D11 represent constraint cells whose values must be less than or equal to the values in cells E9 through E11, respectively. If the constraint cells were not in contiguous cells in the spreadsheet, we would have to define the constraint cells repeatedly. As with the variable cells, it is usually best to choose contiguous cells in your spreadsheet to implement the LHS formulas of the constraints in a model.

If you want to define more than one constraint at the same time, as in Figure 3.12, all the constraint cells you select must be the same type (that is, they must all be ≤, ≥, or =). Therefore, where possible, it is a good idea to keep constraints of a given type grouped in contiguous cells so you can select them at the same time. For example, in our case, the three constraint cells we selected are all less than or equal to (≤) constraints. However, this consideration should not take precedence over setting up the spreadsheet in the way that communicates its purpose most clearly.

FIGURE 3.12 *Defining the constraints*

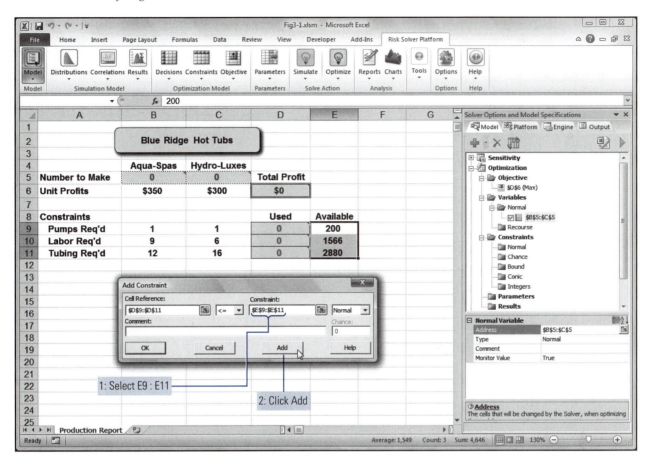

Software Note

Another way to add an objective, variables, or constraints for an optimization model using the Risk Solver task pane is to click the relevant cell(s); click the appropriate Objective, Variables, or Constraints folder icon in the Risk Solver task pane; and then click the green plus sign icon. Equivalent operations can also be carried out using icons on the Risk Solver Platform ribbon in the Optimization Model group. Alternatively, right-clicking any cell in the worksheet displays a pop-up menu that provides convenient access to the same Risk Solver Platform commands found on the ribbon. As you use Risk Solver Platform you should explore these different alternatives for defining and solving optimization problems to decide which interface features you prefer.

3.6.4 DEFINING THE NONNEGATIVITY CONDITIONS

One final specification we need to make for our model is that the decision variables must be greater than or equal to zero. As mentioned earlier, we can impose these conditions as constraints by placing appropriate restrictions on the values that can be assigned to the cells representing the decision variables (in this case, cells B5 and C5). To do this, we simply add another set of constraints to the model, as shown in Figure 3.13.

FIGURE 3.13 *Defining the nonnegativity conditions*

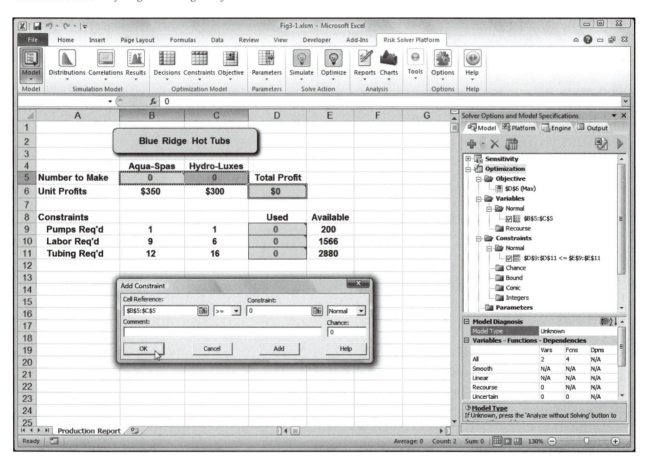

Figure 3.13 indicates that cells B5 and C5, which represent the decision variables in our model, must be greater than or equal to zero. Notice that the RHS value of this constraint is a numeric constant that is entered manually. The same type of constraints can also be used if we placed some strictly positive lower bounds on these variables (for example, if we wanted to produce at least 10 Aqua-Spas and at least 10 Hydro-Luxes). However, in that case, it would probably be best to place the minimum required production amounts on the spreadsheet so that these restrictions are clearly displayed. We can then refer to those cells in the spreadsheet when specifying the RHS values for these constraints.

Software Note

There are other ways to specify nonnegativity conditions for the decision variables. On the Engine tab in Risk Solver's task pane (see Figure 3.15), if you set the value of the Assume Non-Negative property to True, this tells Solver to assume that all the variables (or variable cells) in your model that have not been assigned explicit lower bounds should have lower bounds of zero. Additionally, on the Platform tab, you can set default values for the lower or upper bounds of the decision variables.

3.6.5 REVIEWING THE MODEL

After specifying all the elements of our model, Figure 3.14 shows the final optimization settings for our problem. It is always a good idea to review this information before solving the problem to make sure you entered all the parameters accurately and to correct any errors before proceeding. Additionally, clicking the Analyze without Solving icon causes Solver to evaluate your model and summarize its findings and conclusions. For instance, in this case, Solver determined that our model is a convex LP problem with two variables, four functions, eight dependencies (arising from two decision variables being involved in the objective function and three constraints), and two bounds. (Convexity is

FIGURE 3.14 *Summary of how Solver views the model*

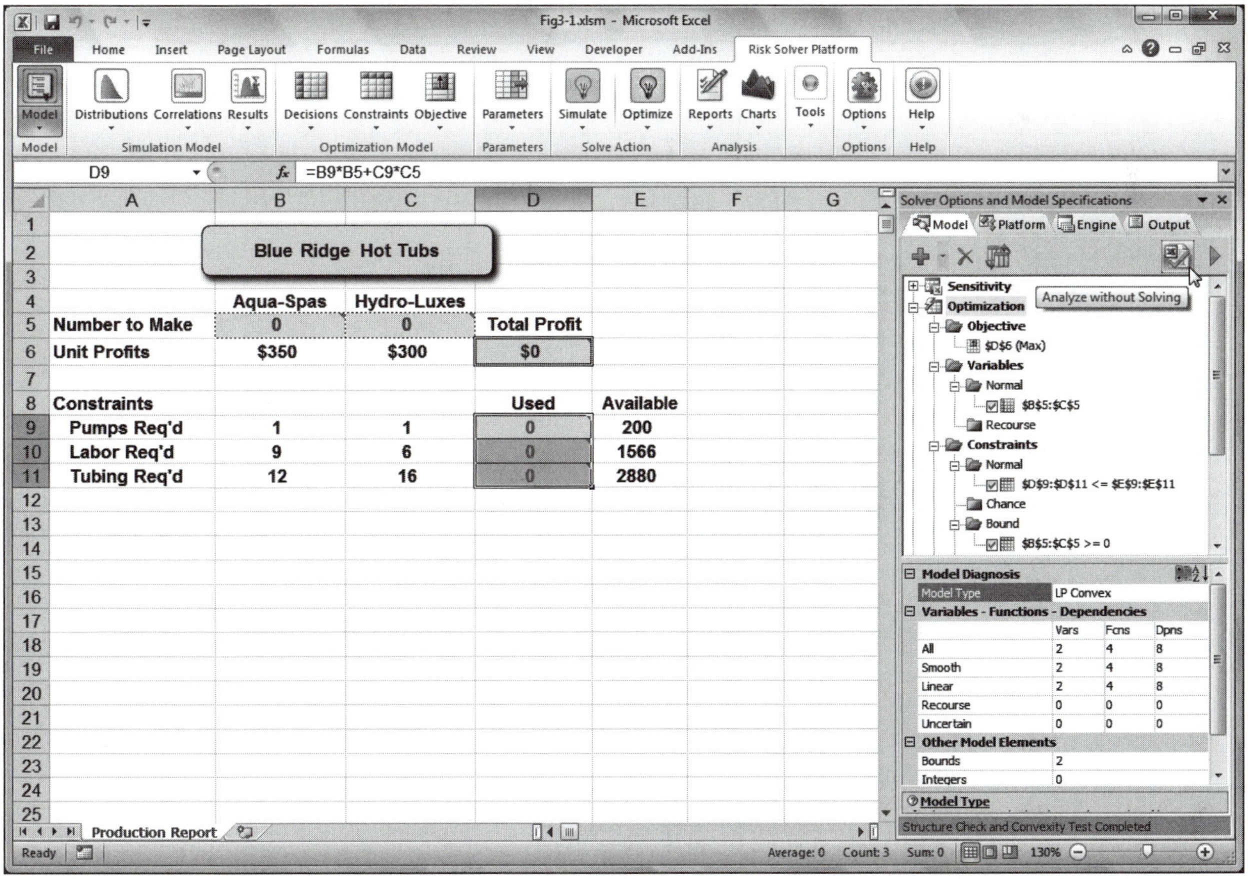

an important aspect of optimization problems that will be discussed in greater detail in Chapter 8. All LP problems are convex by definition.)

3.6.6 OTHER OPTIONS

As shown in Figure 3.15, the Engine tab in the Solver Options and Model Specification pane provides access to a number of settings for solving optimization problems. The drop-down list at the top of this pane allows you to select from a number of engines (or algorithms) for solving optimization problems. If the problem you are trying to solve is an LP problem (that is, an optimization problem with a linear objective function and linear constraints), Solver can use a special algorithm known as the **simplex method** to solve the problem. The simplex method provides an efficient way of solving LP problems and, therefore, requires less solution time. Using the simplex method also allows for expanded sensitivity information about the solution obtained. (Chapter 4 discusses this in detail.) When using Solver to solve an LP problem, it is best to select the Standard LP/Quadratic Engine as indicated in Figure 3.15.

    The Engine tab also provides a number of options that affect how Solver solves a problem. We will discuss the use of several of these options as we proceed. You can also find out more about these options by clicking the Help icon on the Risk Solver Platform ribbon.

FIGURE 3.15

The Engine tab

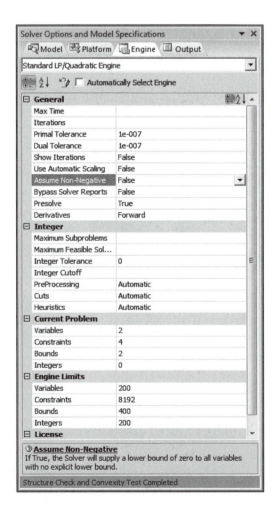

3.6.7 SOLVING THE PROBLEM

After entering all the appropriate parameters and choosing any necessary options for our model, the next step is to solve the problem. Click the Solve icon in Risk Solver's task pane to solve the problem. (Alternatively, click the Optimize icon on the Risk Solver Platform ribbon.) The Output tab in the Risk Solver task pane is activated when Solver solves the problem, providing a description of the various events occurring during the solution process. When Solver finishes, it displays a message at the bottom of Risk Solver's task pane indicating, in this case, that it found a solution, and all constraints and optimality conditions are satisfied. If Solver ever encounters a problem while performing an optimization, it will display a relevant message in this location.

FIGURE 3.16 *Solving the Blue Ridge Hot Tubs problem*

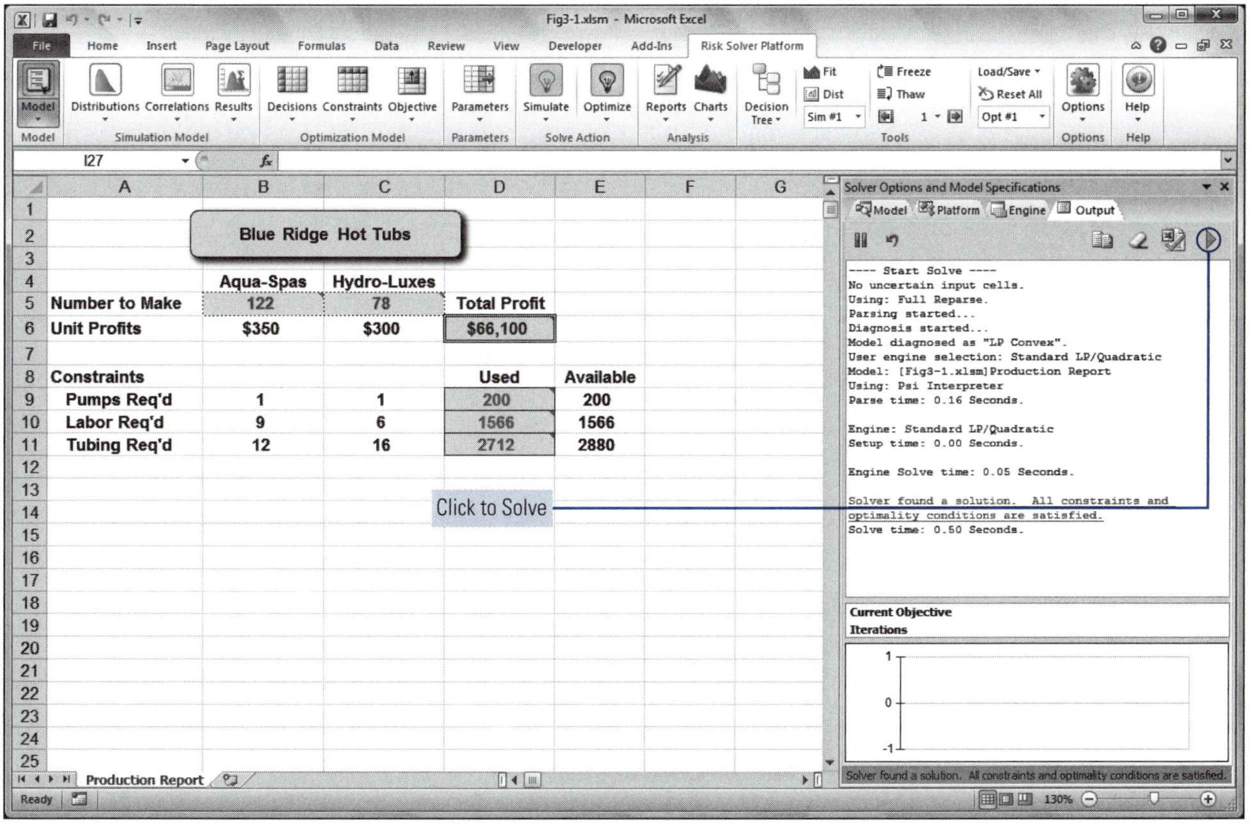

As shown in Figure 3.16, Solver determined that the optimal value for cell B5 is 122, and the optimal value for cell C5 is 78. These values correspond to the optimal values for X_1 and X_2 that we determined graphically in Chapter 2. The value of the objective cell (D6) now indicates that if Blue Ridge Hot Tubs produces and sells 122 Aqua-Spas and 78 Hydro-Luxes, the company will earn a profit of $66,100. Cells D9, D10, and D11 indicate that this solution uses all the 200 available pumps, all the 1,566 available labor hours, and 2,712 of the 2,880 feet of available tubing.

> ### Guided Mode
>
> The Risk Solver Platform includes a valuable feature called Guided Mode that provides descriptions of what Risk Solver is doing when it analyzes and solves models. This feature may be turned on or off using the Guided Mode property at the bottom of the Platform tab in the Risk Solver task pane. This book does not show any of the dialogs displayed by the Guided Mode feature. However, you are encouraged to use Guided Mode while you are learning about the Risk Solver Platform because it provides a wealth of information and instruction about the issues associated with modeling and solving the type of decision problems covered in this book.

3.7 Using Excel's Built-in Solver

As mentioned earlier, the company that makes Risk Solver Platform (Frontline Systems, Inc.) also makes the Solver that comes with Excel. Excel's built-in Solver is easy to use and is capable of solving most of the optimization problems discussed in this book. However, it lacks a number of powerful and useful features offered by Risk Solver Platform.

Figure 3.17 shows the interface of Excel's built-in Solver (accessible from the Solver command on the Data ribbon) and the settings required to use it to solve the Blue Ridge Hot Tubs problem. To use the built-in Solver, you must identify the objective cell (and the desired direction of optimization), the variables cells, and any constraints—just as we did earlier when using Risk Solver Platform. The Solver dialog in Figure 3.17 also allows you to select a solving method (analogous to selections available on the Engine tab in Risk Solver's task pane). You then click the Solve button to solve the problem.

For each of the standard optimization problems in this book, we will identify the objective cell (and whether it should be maximized or minimized), the variable cells, and the constraints. Using that information, you can use either Excel's built-in Solver or Risk Solver Platform to solve the problems.

3.8 Goals and Guidelines for Spreadsheet Design

Now that you have a basic idea of how Solver works and how to set up an LP model in a spreadsheet, we'll walk through several more examples of formulating LP models and solving them with Solver. These problems highlight the wide variety of business problems in which LP can be applied and will also show you some helpful "tricks of the trade" that should help you solve the problems at the end of this chapter. When you work through the end-of-the-chapter problems, you will better appreciate how much thought is required to find a good way to implement a given model.

As we proceed, keep in mind that you can set up these problems more than one way. Creating spreadsheet models that effectively communicate their purpose is very much an art—or at least an acquired skill. Spreadsheets are inherently free form and impose no particular structure on the way we model problems. As a result, there is no one "right" way to model a problem in a spreadsheet; however, some ways are certainly

FIGURE 3.17 *Excel's Built-In Solver*

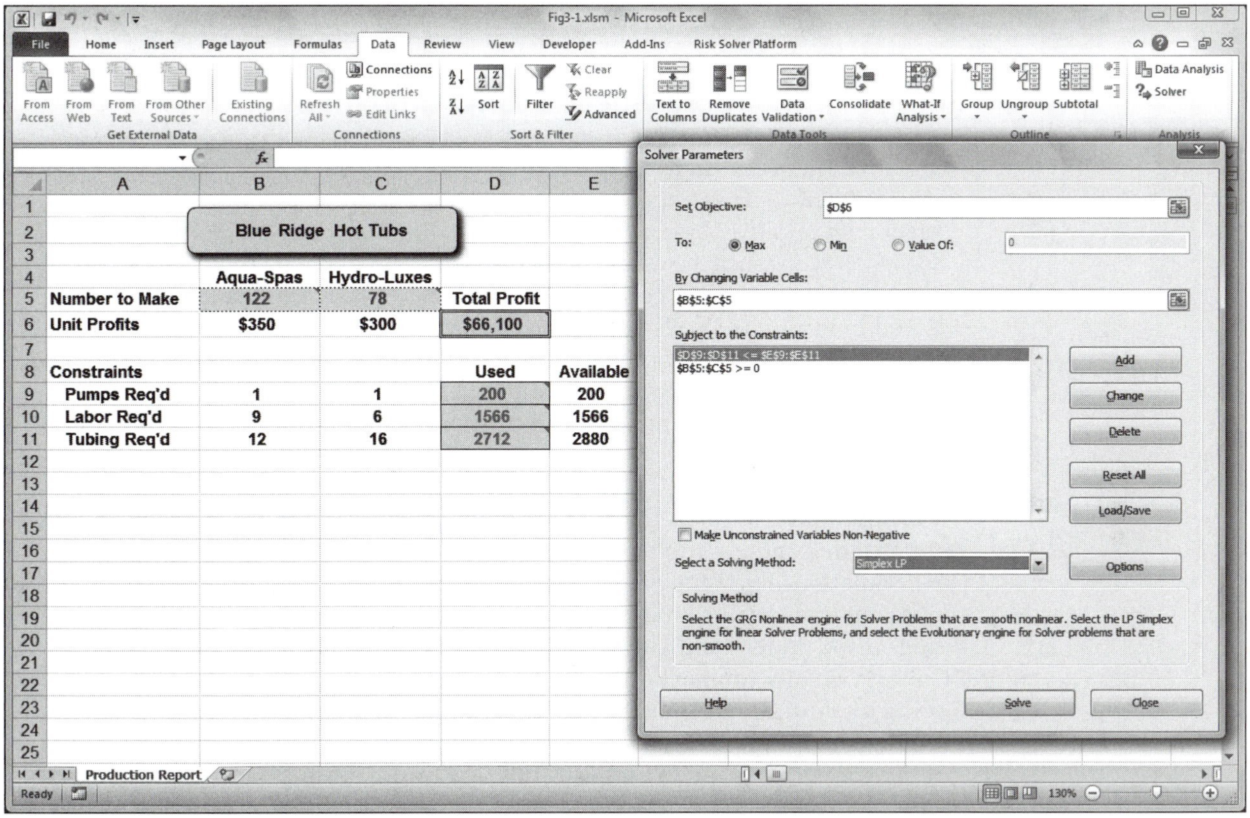

better (or more logical) than others. To achieve the end result of a logical spreadsheet design, your modeling efforts should be directed toward the following goals:

- **Communication.** A spreadsheet's primary business purpose is communicating information to managers. As such, the primary design objective in most spreadsheet modeling tasks is to communicate the relevant aspects of the problem at hand in as clear and intuitively appealing a manner as possible.

- **Reliability.** The output a spreadsheet generates should be correct and consistent. This has an obvious impact on the degree of confidence a manager places in the results of the modeling effort.

- **Auditability.** A manager should be able to retrace the steps followed to generate the different outputs from the model in order to understand the model and verify results. Models that are set up in an intuitively appealing, logical layout tend to be the most auditable.

- **Modifiability.** The data and assumptions upon which we build spreadsheet models can change frequently. A well-designed spreadsheet should be easy to change or enhance in order to meet dynamic user requirements.

In most cases, the spreadsheet design that most clearly communicates its purpose will also be the most reliable, auditable, and modifiable design. As you consider different ways of implementing a spreadsheet model for a particular problem, consider how well the modeling alternatives compare in terms of these goals. Some practical suggestions and guidelines for creating effective spreadsheet models are given in Figure 3.18.

FIGURE 3.18

Guidelines for effective spreadsheet design

Spreadsheet Design Guidelines

- **Organize the data, then build the model around the data.** After the data is arranged in a visually appealing manner, logical locations for decision variables, constraints, and the objective function tend to naturally suggest themselves. This also tends to enhance the reliability, auditability, and maintainability of the model.
- **Do not embed numeric constants in formulas.** Numeric constants should be placed in individual cells and labeled appropriately. This enhances the reliability and modifiability of the model.
- **Things which are logically related (for example, LHS and RHS of constraints) should be arranged in close physical proximity to one another and in the same columnar or row orientation.** This enhances reliability and auditability of the model.
- **A design that results in formulas that can be copied is probably better than one that does not.** A model with formulas that can copied to complete a series of calculations in a range is less prone to error (more reliable) and tends to be more understandable (auditable). Once users understand the first formula in a range, they understand all the formulas in a range.
- **Column or row totals should be in close proximity to the columns or rows being totaled.** Spreadsheet users often expect numbers at the end of a column or row to represent a total or some other summary measure involving the data in the column or row. Numbers at the ends of columns or rows that do not represent totals can be misinterpreted easily (reducing auditability).
- **The English-reading human eye scans left to right, top to bottom.** This fact should be considered and reflected in the spreadsheet design to enhance the auditability of the model.
- **Use color, shading, borders, and protection to distinguish changeable parameters from other elements of the model.** This enhances the reliability and modifiability of the model.
- **Use text boxes and cell comments to document various elements of the model.** These devices can be used to provide greater detail about a model or particular cells in a model than labels on a spreadsheet might allow.

Spreadsheet-Based LP Solvers Create New Applications for Linear Programming

In 1987, *The Wall Street Journal* reported on a then new and exciting trend in business—the availability of solvers for PCs that allowed many businesses to transfer LP models from mainframe computers. Newfoundland Energy Ltd., for example, evaluated its mix of crude oils to purchase with LP on a mainframe for 25 years.

(Continued)

Since it began using a PC for this application, the company has saved thousands of dollars per year in mainframe access time charges.

The expansion of access to LP also spawned new applications. Therese Fitzpatrick, a nursing administrator at Grant Hospital in Chicago, used spreadsheet optimization to create a staff scheduling model that was projected to save the hospital $80,000 per month in overtime and temporary hiring costs. The task of scheduling 300 nurses so that those with appropriate skills were in the right place at the right time required 20 hours per month. The LP model enabled Therese to do the job in 4 hours, even with such complicating factors as leaves, vacations, and variations in staffing requirements at different times and days of the week.

Hawley Fuel Corp., a New York wholesaler of coal, found that it could minimize its cost of purchases while still meeting customers' requirements for sulfur and ash content by optimizing a spreadsheet LP model. Charles Howard of Victoria, British Columbia, developed an LP model to increase electricity generation from a dam just by opening and closing the outlet valves at the right time.

(Source: Bulkely, William M., "The Right Mix: New Software Makes the Choice Much Easier," *The Wall Street Journal*, March 27, 1987, p. 17.)

3.9 Make vs. Buy Decisions

As mentioned at the beginning of Chapter 2, LP is particularly well-suited to problems where scarce or limited resources must be allocated or used in an optimal manner. Numerous examples of these types of problems occur in manufacturing organizations. For example, LP might be used to determine how the various components of a job should be assigned to multipurpose machines in order to minimize the time it takes to complete the job. As another example, a company might receive an order for several items that it cannot fill entirely with its own production capacity. In such a case, the company must determine which items to produce and which items to subcontract (or buy) from an outside supplier. The following is an example of this type of make vs. buy decision.

The Electro-Poly Corporation is the world's leading manufacturer of slip rings. A slip ring is an electrical coupling device that allows current to pass through a spinning or rotating connection—such as a gun turret on a ship, aircraft, or tank. The company recently received a $750,000 order for various quantities of three types of slip rings. Each slip ring requires a certain amount of time to wire and harness. The following table summarizes the requirements for the three models of slip rings.

	Model 1	Model 2	Model 3
Number Ordered	3,000	2,000	900
Hours of Wiring Required per Unit	2	1.5	3
Hours of Harnessing Required per Unit	1	2	1

Unfortunately, Electro-Poly does not have enough wiring and harnessing capacity to fill the order by its due date. The company has only 10,000 hours of wiring capacity and 5,000 hours of harnessing capacity available to devote to this order. However, the company can subcontract any portion of this order to one of its competitors. The unit costs of producing each model in-house and buying the finished products from a competitor are summarized in the following table.

	Model 1	Model 2	Model 3
Cost to Make	$50	$83	$130
Cost to Buy	$61	$97	$145

Electro-Poly wants to determine the number of slip rings to make and the number to buy to fill the customer order at the least possible cost.

3.9.1 DEFINING THE DECISION VARIABLES

To solve the Electro-Poly problem, we need six decision variables to represent the alternatives under consideration:

M_1 = number of model 1 slip rings to make in-house
M_2 = number of model 2 slip rings to make in-house
M_3 = number of model 3 slip rings to make in-house
B_1 = number of model 1 slip rings to buy from competitor
B_2 = number of model 2 slip rings to buy from competitor
B_3 = number of model 3 slip rings to buy from competitor

As mentioned in Chapter 2, we do not have to use the symbols $X_1, X_2, \ldots, X_n$ for the decision variables. If other symbols better clarify the model, you are certainly free to use them. In this case, the symbols M_i and B_i help distinguish the **M**ake in-house variables from the **B**uy from competitor variables.

3.9.2 DEFINING THE OBJECTIVE FUNCTION

The objective in this problem is to minimize the total cost of filling the order. Recall that each model 1 slip ring made in-house (each unit of M_1) costs $50; each model 2 slip ring made in-house (each unit of M_2) costs $83; and each model 3 slip ring (each unit of M_3) costs $130. Each model 1 slip ring bought from the competitor (each unit of B_1) costs $61; each model 2 slip ring bought from the competitor (each unit of B_2) costs $97; and each model 3 slip ring bought from the competitor (each unit of B_3) costs $145. Thus, the objective is stated mathematically as:

MIN: $50M_1 + 83M_2 + 130M_3 + 61B_1 + 97B_2 + 145B_3$

3.9.3 DEFINING THE CONSTRAINTS

Several constraints affect this problem. Two constraints are needed to ensure that the number of slip rings made in-house does not exceed the available capacity for wiring and harnessing. These constraints are stated as:

$2M_1 + 1.5M_2 + 3M_3 \leq 10,000$ } wiring constraint
$1M_1 + 2M_2 + 1M_3 \leq 5,000$ } harnessing constraint

Three additional constraints ensure that 3,000 model 1 slip rings, 2,000 model 2 slip rings, and 900 model 3 slip rings are available to fill the order. These constraints are stated as:

$$M_1 + B_1 = 3,000 \quad \} \text{ demand for model 1}$$
$$M_2 + B_2 = 2,000 \quad \} \text{ demand for model 2}$$
$$M_3 + B_3 = 900 \quad \} \text{ demand for model 3}$$

Finally, because none of the variables in the model can assume a value of less than zero, we also need the following nonnegativity condition:

$$M_1, M_2, M_3, B_1, B_2, B_3 \geq 0$$

3.9.4 IMPLEMENTING THE MODEL

The LP model for Electro-Poly's make vs. buy problem is summarized as:

MIN: $50M_1 + 83M_2 + 130M_3 + 61B_1 + 97B_2 + 145B_3$ } total cost

Subject to:							
M_1	$+$	B_1			$=$	3,000	} demand for model 1
M_2	$+$	B_2			$=$	2,000	} demand for model 2
M_3	$+$	B_3			$=$	900	} demand for model 3
$2M_1$	$+$	$1.5M_2$	$+$	$3M_3$	$\leq$	10,000	} wiring constraint
$1M_1$	$+$	$2M_2$	$+$	$1M_3$	$\leq$	5,000	} harnessing constraint
		$M_1, M_2, M_3, B_1, B_2, B_3$		$\geq$	0		} nonnegativity conditions

The data for this model are implemented in the spreadsheet shown in Figure 3.19 (and in the file Fig3-19.xlsm that accompanies this book). The coefficients that appear in the objective function are entered in the range B10 through D11. The coefficients for the LHS formulas for the wiring and harnessing constraints are entered in cells B17 through D18, and the corresponding RHS values are entered in cells F17 and F18. Because the LHS formulas for the demand constraints involve simply summing the decision variables, we do not need to list the coefficients for these constraints in the spreadsheet. The RHS values for the demand constraints are entered in cells B14 through D14.

Cells B6 through D7 are reserved to represent the six variables in our algebraic model. So, the objective function could be entered in cell E11 as:

Formula for cell E11: $= \text{B10*B6} + \text{C10*C6} + \text{D10*D6} + \text{B11*B7} + \text{C11*C7} + \text{D11*D7}$

In this formula, the values in the range B6 through D7 are multiplied by the corresponding values in the range B10 through D11; these individual products are then added together. Therefore, the formula is simply the sum of a collection of products—or a *sum of products*. It turns out that this formula can be implemented in an equivalent (and easier) way as:

Equivalent formula for cell E11:   =SUMPRODUCT(B10:D11,B6:D7)

The preceding formula takes the values in the range B10 through D11, multiplies them by the corresponding values in the range B6 through D7, and adds (or sums) these products. The SUMPRODUCT( ) function greatly simplifies the implementation of many formulas required in optimization problems and will be used extensively throughout this book.

Because the LHS of the demand constraint for model 1 slip rings involves adding variables M_1 and B_1, this constraint is implemented in cell B13 by adding the two cells in the spreadsheet that correspond to these variables—cells B6 and B7:

Formula for cell B13: $= \text{B6} + \text{B7}$

(Copy to C13 through D13.)

FIGURE 3.19 *Spreadsheet model for Electro-Poly's make vs. buy problem*

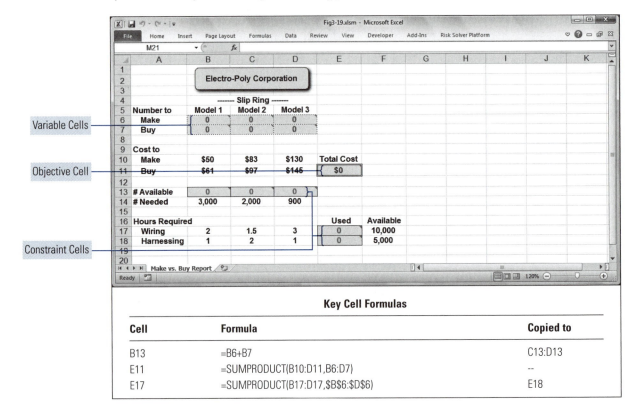

Cell	Formula	Copied to
B13	=B6+B7	C13:D13
E11	=SUMPRODUCT(B10:D11,B6:D7)	--
E17	=SUMPRODUCT(B17:D17,$B$6:$D$6)	E18

The formula in cell B13 is then copied to cells C13 and D13 to implement the LHS formulas for the constraints for model 2 and model 3 slip rings.

The coefficients for the wiring and harnessing constraints are entered in cells B17 through D18. The LHS formula for the wiring constraint is implemented in cell E17 as:

Formula for cell E17:   =SUMPRODUCT(B17:D17,$B$6:$D$6)

(Copy to cell E18.)

This formula is then copied to cell E18 to implement the LHS formula for the harnessing constraint. (In the preceding formula, the dollar signs denote absolute cell references. An **absolute cell reference** will not change if the formula containing the reference is copied to another location.)

3.9.5 SOLVING THE PROBLEM

To solve this problem, we need to specify the objective cell, variable cells, and constraint cells identified in Figure 3.19, just as we did earlier in the Blue Ridge Hot Tubs example. Figure 3.20 summarizes the Solver parameters required to solve Electro-Poly's make vs. buy problem. The optimal solution found by Solver is shown in Figure 3.21.

FIGURE 3.20

Solver settings and options for the make vs. buy problem

Solver Settings:

Objective: E11 (Min)
Variable cells: B6:D7
Constraints:
     B13:D13 = B14:D14
     E17:E18 <= F17:F18
     B6:D7 >= 0

Solver Options:
     Standard LP/Quadratic Engine (Simplex LP)

FIGURE 3.21 *Optimal solution to Electro-Poly's make vs. buy problem*

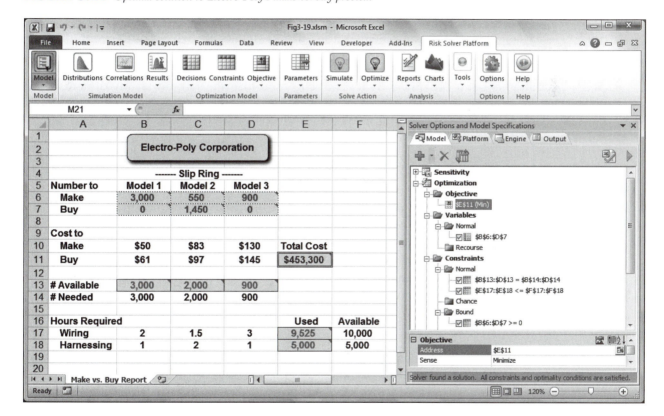

3.9.6 ANALYZING THE SOLUTION

The optimal solution shown in Figure 3.21 indicates that Electro-Poly should make (in-house) 3,000 model 1 slip rings, 550 model 2 slip rings, and 900 model 3 slip rings (that is, $M_1 = 3,000$, $M_2 = 550$, $M_3 = 900$). Additionally, it should buy 1,450 model 2 slip rings from its competitor (that is, $B_1 = 0$, $B_2 = 1,450$, $B_3 = 0$). This solution allows Electro-Poly to fill the customer order at a minimum cost of \$453,300. This solution uses 9,525 of the 10,000 hours of available wiring capacity and all 5,000 hours of the harnessing capacity.

At first glance, this solution might seem a bit surprising. Electro-Poly has to pay \$97 for each model 2 slip ring it purchases from its competitor. This represents a \$14 premium over its in-house cost of $83. On the other hand, Electro-Poly has to pay a premium of $11 over its in-house cost to purchase model 1 slip rings from its competitor. It seems as if the optimal solution would be to purchase model 1 slip rings from its competitor rather than model 2 slip rings because the additional cost premium for model 1 slip rings is smaller. However, this argument fails to consider the fact that each model 2 slip ring produced in-house uses twice as much of the company's harnessing capacity as does each model 1 slip ring. Making more model 2 slip rings in-house would deplete the company's harnessing capacity more quickly and would require buying an excessive number of model 1 slip rings from the competitor. Fortunately, the LP technique automatically considers such trade-offs in determining the optimal solution to the problem.

3.10 An Investment Problem

There are numerous problems in the area of finance for which various optimization techniques can be applied. These problems often involve attempting to maximize the return on an investment while meeting certain cash flow requirements and risk constraints. Alternatively, we may want to minimize the risk on an investment while maintaining a certain level of return. We'll consider one such problem here and discuss several other financial engineering problems throughout this text.

Brian Givens is a financial analyst for Retirement Planning Services, Inc. who specializes in designing retirement income portfolios for retirees using corporate bonds. He has just completed a consultation with a client who expects to have $750,000 in liquid assets to invest when she retires next month. Brian and his client agreed to consider upcoming bond issues from the following six companies:

Company	Return	Years to Maturity	Rating
Acme Chemical	8.65%	11	1-Excellent
DynaStar	9.50%	10	3-Good
Eagle Vision	10.00%	6	4-Fair
MicroModeling	8.75%	10	1-Excellent
OptiPro	9.25%	7	3-Good
Sabre Systems	9.00%	13	2-Very Good

The Return column in this table represents the expected annual yield on each bond, the Years to Maturity column indicates the length of time over which the bonds will be payable, and the Rating column indicates an independent underwriter's assessment of the quality or risk associated with each issue.

Brian believes that all of the companies are relatively safe investments. However, to protect his client's income, Brian and his client agreed that no more than 25% of her money should be invested in any one investment and at least half of her money should be invested in long-term bonds that mature in 10 or more years. Also, even though DynaStar, Eagle Vision, and OptiPro offer the highest returns, it was agreed that no more than 35% of the money should be invested in these bonds because they also represent the highest risks (that is, they were rated lower than "very good").

Brian needs to determine how to allocate his client's investments to maximize her income while meeting their agreed-upon investment restrictions.

3.10.1 DEFINING THE DECISION VARIABLES

In this problem, Brian must decide how much money to invest in each type of bond. Because there are six different investment alternatives, we need the following six decision variables:

$$X_1 = \text{amount of money to invest in Acme Chemical}$$
$$X_2 = \text{amount of money to invest in DynaStar}$$
$$X_3 = \text{amount of money to invest in Eagle Vision}$$
$$X_4 = \text{amount of money to invest in MicroModeling}$$
$$X_5 = \text{amount of money to invest in OptiPro}$$
$$X_6 = \text{amount of money to invest in Sabre Systems}$$

3.10.2 DEFINING THE OBJECTIVE FUNCTION

The objective in this problem is to maximize the investment income for Brian's client. Because each dollar invested in Acme Chemical (X_1) earns 8.65% annually, each dollar invested in DynaStar (X_2) earns 9.50%, and so on, the objective function for the problem is expressed as:

MAX: $.0865X_1 + .095X_2 + .10X_3 + .0875X_4 + .0925X_5 + .09X_6$ } total annual return

3.10.3 DEFINING THE CONSTRAINTS

Again, there are several constraints that apply to this problem. First, we must ensure that exactly \$750,000 is invested. This is accomplished by the following constraint:

$$X_1 + X_2 + X_3 + X_4 + X_5 + X_6 = 750{,}000$$

Next, we must ensure that no more than 25% of the total be invested in any one investment. Twenty-five percent of \$750,000 is \$187,500. Therefore, Brian can put no more than \$187,500 in any one investment. The following constraints enforce this restriction:

$$X_1 \le 187{,}500$$
$$X_2 \le 187{,}500$$
$$X_3 \le 187{,}500$$
$$X_4 \le 187{,}500$$
$$X_5 \le 187{,}500$$
$$X_6 \le 187{,}500$$

Because the bonds for Eagle Vision (X_3) and OptiPro (X_5) are the only ones that mature in fewer than 10 years, the following constraint ensures that at least half the money (\$375,000) is placed in investments maturing in 10 or more years:

$$X_1 + X_2 + X_4 + X_6 \ge 375{,}000$$

Similarly, the following constraint ensures that no more than 35% of the money (\$262,500) is placed in the bonds for DynaStar (X_2), Eagle Vision (X_3), and OptiPro (X_5):

$$X_2 + X_3 + X_5 \le 262{,}500$$

Finally, because none of the variables in the model can assume a value of less than zero, we also need the following nonnegativity condition:

$$X_1, X_2, X_3, X_4, X_5, X_6 \geq 0$$

3.10.4 IMPLEMENTING THE MODEL

The LP model for the Retirement Planning Services, Inc. investment problem is summarized as:

MAX: $.0865X_1 + .095X_2 + .10X_3 + .0875X_4 + .0925X_5 + .09X_6$ } total annual return

Subject to:

$X_1 \leq 187{,}500$		} 25% restriction per investment
$X_2 \leq 187{,}500$		} 25% restriction per investment
$X_3 \leq 187{,}500$		} 25% restriction per investment
$X_4 \leq 187{,}500$		} 25% restriction per investment
$X_5 \leq 187{,}500$		} 25% restriction per investment
$X_6 \leq 187{,}500$		} 25% restriction per investment
$X_1 + X_2 + X_3 + X_4 + X_5 + X_6 = 750{,}000$		} total amount invested
$X_1 + X_2 + X_4 + X_6 \geq 375{,}000$		} long-term investment
$X_2 + X_3 + X_5 \leq 262{,}500$		} higher-risk investment
$X_1, X_2, X_3, X_4, X_5, X_6 \geq 0$		} nonnegativity conditions

A convenient way of implementing this model is shown in Figure 3.22 (and in file Fig3-22.xlsm that accompanies this book). Each row in this spreadsheet corresponds to one of the investment alternatives. Cells C6 through C11 correspond to the decision variables for the problem ($X_1, \ldots, X_6$). The maximum value that each of these cells can take on is listed in cells D6 through D11. These values correspond to the RHS values for the first six constraints. The sum of cells C6 through C11 is computed in cell C12 as follows and will be restricted to equal the value shown in cell C13:

Formula for cell C12: =SUM(C6:C11)

The annual returns for each investment are listed in cells E6 through E11. The objective function is then implemented conveniently in cell E12 as follows:

Formula for cell E12: =SUMPRODUCT(E6:E11,$C$6:$C$11)

The values in cells G6 through G11 indicate which of these rows correspond to "long-term" investments. Note that the use of ones and zeros in this column makes it convenient to compute the sum of the cells C6, C7, C9, and C11 (representing X_1, X_2, X_4, and X_6) representing the LHS of the "long-term" investment constraint. This is done in cell G12 as follows:

Formula for cell G12: =SUMPRODUCT(G6:G11,$C$6:$C$11)

Similarly, the zeros and ones in cells I6 through I11 indicate the higher-risk investments and allow us to implement the LHS of the "higher-risk investment" constraint as follows:

Formula for cell I12: =SUMPRODUCT(I6:I11,$C$6:$C$11)

Note that the use of zeros and ones in columns G and I to compute the sums of selected decision variables is a very useful modeling technique that makes it easy for the

FIGURE 3.22 *Spreadsheet model for Retirement Planning Services, Inc. bond selection problem*

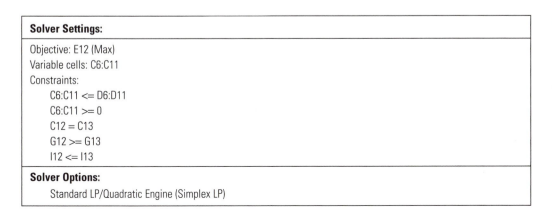

Cell	Formula	Copied to
C12	=SUM(C6:C11)	--
E12	=SUMPRODUCT(E6:E11,$C$6:$C$11)	G12 and I12

user to change the variables being included in the sums. Also note that the formula for the objective in cell E12 could be copied to cells G12 and I12 to implement LHS formulas for these constraint cells.

3.10.5 SOLVING THE PROBLEM

To solve this problem, we need to specify the objective cell, variable cells, and constraint cells identified in Figure 3.22. Figure 3.23 shows the Solver settings required to solve this problem. The optimal solution found by Solver is shown in Figure 3.24.

FIGURE 3.23

Solver settings and options for the bond selection problem

Solver Settings:

Objective: E12 (Max)
Variable cells: C6:C11
Constraints:
    C6:C11 <= D6:D11
    C6:C11 >= 0
    C12 = C13
    G12 >= G13
    I12 <= I13

Solver Options:

    Standard LP/Quadratic Engine (Simplex LP)

FIGURE 3.24 *Optimal solution to the bond selection problem*

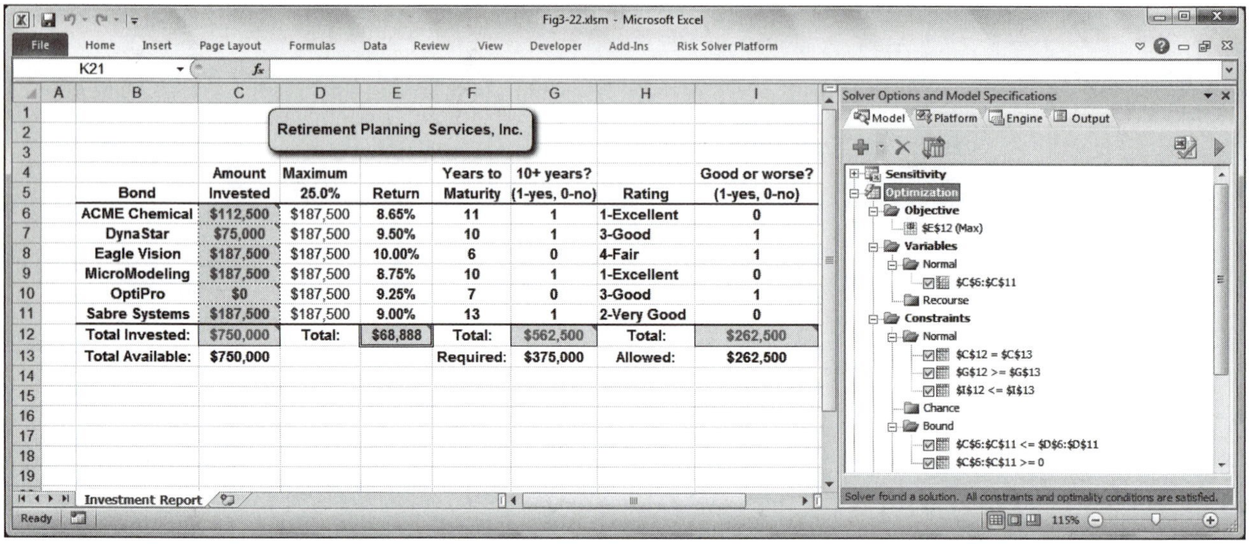

3.10.6 ANALYZING THE SOLUTION

The solution shown in Figure 3.24 indicates that the optimal investment plan places $112,500 in Acme Chemical (X_1), $75,000 in DynaStar ($X_2$), $187,500 in Eagle Vision (X_3), $187,500 in MicroModeling (X_4), $0 in OptiPro ($X_5$), and $187,500 in Sabre Systems (X_6). It is interesting to note that more money is being invested in Acme Chemical than DynaStar and OptiPro even though the return on Acme Chemical is lower than on the returns for DynaStar and OptiPro. This is because DynaStar and OptiPro are both "higher-risk" investments, and the 35% limit on "higher-risk" investments is a binding constraint (or is met as a strict equality in the optimal solution). Thus, the optimal solution could be improved if we could put more than 35% of the money into the higher-risk investments.

3.11 A Transportation Problem

Many transportation and logistics problems businesses face fall into a category of problems known as network flow problems. We will consider one such example here and study this area in more detail in Chapter 5.

Tropicsun is a leading grower and distributor of fresh citrus products with three large citrus groves scattered around central Florida in the cities of Mt. Dora, Eustis, and Clermont. Tropicsun currently has 275,000 bushels of citrus at the grove in Mt. Dora, 400,000 bushels at the grove in Eustis, and 300,000 bushels at the grove in Clermont. Tropicsun has citrus processing plants in Ocala, Orlando, and Leesburg with processing capacities to handle 200,000, 600,000, and 225,000 bushels, respectively. Tropicsun contracts with a local trucking company to transport its fruit from the groves to the processing plants. The trucking company charges a flat rate for every mile that each bushel of fruit must be transported. Each mile a bushel of fruit travels is known as a bushel-mile. The following table summarizes the distances (in miles) between the groves and processing plants:

Grove	Distances (in miles) Between Groves and Plants		
	Ocala	**Orlando**	**Leesburg**
Mt. Dora	21	50	40
Eustis	35	30	22
Clermont	55	20	25

Tropicsun wants to determine how many bushels to ship from each grove to each processing plant in order to minimize the total number of bushel-miles the fruit must be shipped.

3.11.1 DEFINING THE DECISION VARIABLES

In this situation, the problem is to determine how many bushels of fruit should be shipped from each grove to each processing plant. The problem is summarized graphically in Figure 3.25.

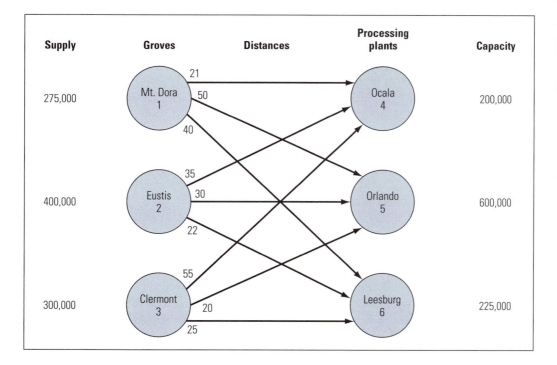

FIGURE 3.25

Diagram for the Tropicsun transportation problem

The circles (or nodes) in Figure 3.25 correspond to the different groves and processing plants in the problem. Note that a number has been assigned to each node. The arrows (or arcs) connecting the various groves and processing plants represent different shipping routes. The decision problem faced by Tropicsun is to determine how many bushels of fruit to ship on each of these routes. Thus, one decision variable is associated with each of the arcs in Figure 3.23. We can define these variables in general as:

X_{ij} = number of bushels to ship from node i to node j

Specifically, the nine decision variables are:

X_{14} = number of bushels to ship from Mt. Dora (node 1) to Ocala (node 4)

X_{15} = number of bushels to ship from Mt. Dora (node 1) to Orlando (node 5)

X_{16} = number of bushels to ship from Mt. Dora (node 1) to Leesburg (node 6)

X_{24} = number of bushels to ship from Eustis (node 2) to Ocala (node 4)

X_{25} = number of bushels to ship from Eustis (node 2) to Orlando (node 5)

X_{26} = number of bushels to ship from Eustis (node 2) to Leesburg (node 6)

X_{34} = number of bushels to ship from Clermont (node 3) to Ocala (node 4)

X_{35} = number of bushels to ship from Clermont (node 3) to Orlando (node 5)

X_{36} = number of bushels to ship from Clermont (node 3) to Leesburg (node 6)

3.11.2 DEFINING THE OBJECTIVE FUNCTION

The goal in this problem is to determine how many bushels to ship from each grove to each processing plant while minimizing the total distance (or total number of bushel-miles) the fruit must travel. The objective function for this problem is represented by:

MIN: $21X_{14} + 50X_{15} + 40X_{16} + 35X_{24} + 30X_{25} + 22X_{26} + 55X_{34} + 20X_{35} + 25X_{36}$

The term $21X_{14}$ in this function reflects the fact that each bushel shipped from Mt. Dora (node 1) to Ocala (node 4) must travel 21 miles. The remaining terms in the function express similar relationships for the other shipping routes.

3.11.3 DEFINING THE CONSTRAINTS

Two physical constraints apply to this problem. First, there is a limit on the amount of fruit that can be shipped to each processing plant. Tropicsun can ship no more than 200,000, 600,000, and 225,000 bushels to Ocala, Orlando, and Leesburg, respectively. These restrictions are reflected by the following constraints:

$X_{14} + X_{24} + X_{34} \leq 200,000$ } capacity restriction for Ocala

$X_{15} + X_{25} + X_{35} \leq 600,000$ } capacity restriction for Orlando

$X_{16} + X_{26} + X_{36} \leq 225,000$ } capacity restriction for Leesburg

The first constraint indicates that the total bushels shipped to Ocala (node 4) from Mt. Dora (node 1), Eustis (node 2), and Clermont (node 3) must be less than or equal to Ocala's capacity of 200,000 bushels. The other two constraints have similar interpretations for Orlando and Leesburg. Notice that the total processing capacity at the plants (1,025,000 bushels) exceeds the total supply of fruit at the groves (975,000 bushels). Therefore, these constraints are less than or equal to constraints because not all the available capacity will be used.

The second set of constraints ensures that the supply of fruit at each grove is shipped to a processing plant. That is, all of the 275,000, 400,000, and 300,000 bushels at Mt. Dora, Eustis, and Clermont, respectively, must be processed somewhere. This is accomplished by the following constraints:

$X_{14} + X_{15} + X_{16} = 275,000$ } supply available at Mt. Dora

$X_{24} + X_{25} + X_{26} = 400,000$ } supply available at Eustis

$X_{34} + X_{35} + X_{36} = 300,000$ } supply available at Clermont

The first constraint indicates that the total amount shipped from Mt. Dora (node 1) to the plants in Ocala (node 4), Orlando (node 5), and Leesburg (node 6) must equal the total amount available at Mt. Dora. This constraint indicates that all the fruit available at Mt. Dora must be shipped somewhere. The other two constraints play similar roles for Eustis and Clermont.

3.11. 4 IMPLEMENTING THE MODEL

The LP model for Tropicsun's fruit transportation problem is summarized as:

MIN:
$$21X_{14} + 50X_{15} + 40X_{16} +$$
$$35X_{24} + 30X_{25} + 22X_{26} +$$
$$55X_{34} + 20X_{35} + 25X_{36}$$
} total distance fruit is shipped (in bushel-miles)

Subject to:
$$X_{14} + X_{24} + X_{34} \leq 200,000$$ } capacity restriction for Ocala
$$X_{15} + X_{25} + X_{35} \leq 600,000$$ } capacity restriction for Orlando
$$X_{16} + X_{26} + X_{36} \leq 225,000$$ } capacity restriction for Leesburg
$$X_{14} + X_{15} + X_{16} = 275,000$$ } supply available at Mt. Dora
$$X_{24} + X_{25} + X_{26} = 400,000$$ } supply available at Eustis
$$X_{34} + X_{35} + X_{36} = 300,000$$ } supply available at Clermont
$$X_{ij} \geq 0, \text{ for all } i \text{ and } j$$ } nonnegativity conditions

The last constraint, as in previous models, indicates that all the decision variables must be nonnegative.

A convenient way to implement this model is shown in Figure 3.26 (and in the file Fig3-26.xlsm that accompanies this book). In this spreadsheet, the distances between each grove and plant are summarized in a tabular format in cells C7 through E9. Cells C14 through E16 are reserved for representing the number of bushels of fruit to ship from each grove to each processing plant. Notice that these nine cells correspond directly to the nine decision variables in the algebraic formulation of the model.

The LHS formulas for the three capacity constraints in the model are implemented in cells C17, D17, and E17 in the spreadsheet. To do this, the following formula is entered in cell C17 and copied to cells D17 and E17:

Formula for cell C17:   =SUM(C14:C16)
(Copy to D17 and E17.)

These cells represent the total bushels of fruit being shipped to the plants in Ocala, Orlando, and Leesburg, respectively. Cells C18 through E18 contain the RHS values for these constraint cells.

The LHS formulas for the three supply constraints in the model are implemented in cells F14, F15, and F16 as:

Formula for cell F14:   =SUM(C14:E14)
(Copy to F15 and F16.)

These cells represent the total bushels of fruit being shipped from the groves at Mt. Dora, Eustis, and Clermont, respectively. Cells G14 through G16 contain the RHS values for these constraint cells.

Finally, the objective function for this model is entered in cell E20 as:

Formula for cell E20:   =SUMPRODUCT(C7:E9,C14:E16)

FIGURE 3.26 *Spreadsheet model for Tropicsun's transportation problem*

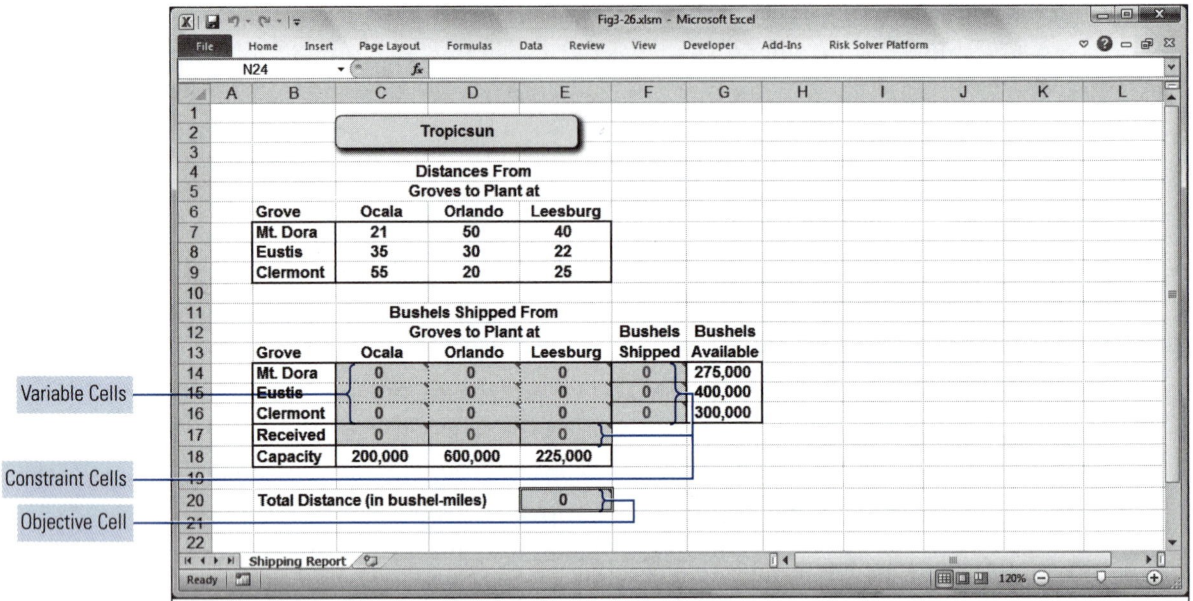

Cell	Formula	Copied to
C17	=SUM(C14:C16)	D17:E17
F14	=SUM(C14:E14)	F15:F16
E20	=SUMPRODUCT(C7:E9,C14:E16)	--

The SUMPRODUCT( ) function multiplies each element in the range C7 through E9 by the corresponding element in the range C14 through E16 and then sums the individual products.

3.11.5 HEURISTIC SOLUTION FOR THE MODEL

To appreciate what Solver is accomplishing, let's consider how we might try to solve this problem manually using a heuristic. A **heuristic** is a rule of thumb for making decisions that might work well in some instances but is not guaranteed to produce optimal solutions or decisions. One heuristic we can apply to solve Tropicsun's problem is to always ship as much as possible along the next available path with the shortest distance (or least cost). Using this heuristic, we solve the problem as follows:

1. Because the shortest available path between any grove and processing plant is between Clermont and Orlando (20 miles), we first ship as much as possible through this route. The maximum we can ship through this route is the smaller of the supply at Clermont (300,000 bushels) or the capacity at Orlando (600,000 bushels). So we would ship 300,000 bushels from Clermont to Orlando. This depletes the supply at Clermont.

2. The next shortest available route occurs between Mt. Dora and Ocala (21 miles). The maximum we can ship through this route is the smaller of the supply at Mt. Dora (275,000 bushels) or the capacity at Ocala (200,000 bushels). So we would ship 200,000 bushels from Mt. Dora to Ocala. This depletes the capacity at Ocala.

3. The next shortest available route occurs between Eustis and Leesburg (22 miles). The maximum we can ship through this route is the smaller of the supply at Eustis (400,000 bushels) or the capacity at Leesburg (225,000 bushels). So we would ship 225,000 bushels from Eustis to Leesburg. This depletes the capacity at Leesburg.
4. The next shortest available route occurs between Eustis and Orlando (30 miles). The maximum we can ship through this route is the smaller of the remaining supply at Eustis (175,000 bushels) or the remaining capacity at Orlando (300,000 bushels). So we would ship 175,000 bushels from Eustis to Orlando. This depletes the supply at Eustis.
5. The only remaining route occurs between Mt. Dora and Orlando (because the processing capacities at Ocala and Leesburg have both been depleted). This distance is 50 miles. The maximum we can ship through this route is the smaller of the remaining supply at Mt. Dora (75,000 bushels) and the remaining capacity at Orlando (125,000 bushels). So we would ship the final 75,000 bushels at Mt. Dora to Orlando. This depletes the supply at Mt. Dora.

As shown in Figure 3.27, the solution identified with this heuristic involves shipping the fruit a total of 24,150,000 bushel-miles. All the bushels available at each grove have been shipped to the processing plants and none of the capacities at the processing plants have been exceeded. Therefore, this is a *feasible* solution to the problem. And the logic used to find this solution might lead us to believe it is a reasonably good solution—but is it the *optimal* solution? Is there no other feasible solution to this problem that can make the total distance the fruit has to travel less than 24,150,000 bushel-miles?

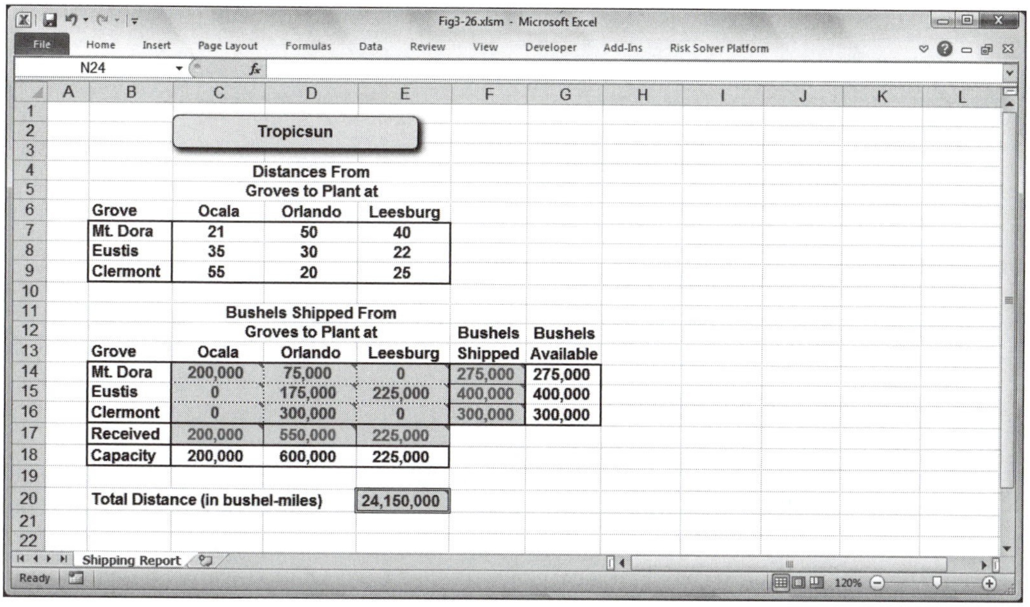

FIGURE 3.27

A heuristic solution to the transportation problem

3.11.6 SOLVING THE PROBLEM

To find the optimal solution to this model, we must indicate to Solver the objective cell, variable cells, and constraint cells identified in Figure 3.26. Figure 3.28 shows the Solver settings required to solve this problem. The optimal solution is shown in Figure 3.29.

FIGURE 3.28

Solver settings and options for the transportation problem

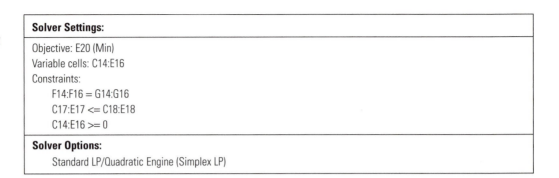

Solver Settings:
Objective: E20 (Min)
Variable cells: C14:E16
Constraints:
F14:F16 = G14:G16
C17:E17 <= C18:E18
C14:E16 >= 0
Solver Options:
Standard LP/Quadratic Engine (Simplex LP)

FIGURE 3.29 *Optimal solution to Tropicsun's transportation problem*

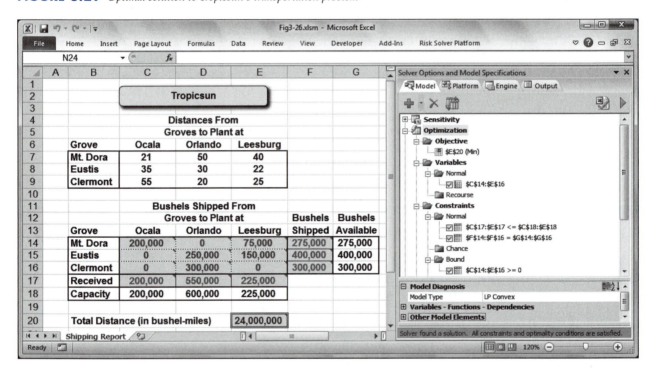

3.11.7 ANALYZING THE SOLUTION

The optimal solution in Figure 3.29 indicates that 200,000 bushels should be shipped from Mt. Dora to Ocala (X_{14} = 200,000), and 75,000 bushels should be shipped from Mt. Dora to Leesburg (X_{16} = 75,000). Of the 400,000 bushels available at the grove in Eustis, 250,000 bushels should be shipped to Orlando for processing (X_{25} = 250,000), and 150,000 bushels should be shipped to Leesburg (X_{26} = 150,000). Finally, all 300,000 bushels available in Clermont should be shipped to Orlando (X_{35} = 300,000). None of the other possible shipping routes will be used.

The solution shown in Figure 3.29 satisfies all the constraints in the model and results in a minimum shipping distance of 24,000,000 bushel-miles, which is better than the heuristic solution identified earlier. Therefore, simple heuristics can sometimes solve LP problems, but as this example illustrates, there is no guarantee that a heuristic solution is the best possible solution.

3.12 A Blending Problem

Many business problems involve determining an optimal mix of ingredients. For example, major oil companies must determine the least costly mix of different crude oils and other chemicals to blend together to produce a certain grade of gasoline. Lawn care companies must determine the least costly mix of chemicals and other products to blend together to produce different types of fertilizer. The following is another example of a common blending problem faced in the U.S. agricultural industry, which annually produces goods valued at approximately $200 billion.

Agri-Pro is a company that sells agricultural products to farmers in number of states. One service it provides to customers is custom feed mixing, whereby a farmer can order a specific amount of livestock feed and specify the amount of corn, grain, and minerals the feed should contain. This is an important service because the proper feed for various farm animals changes regularly depending on the weather, pasture conditions, and so on.

Agri-Pro stocks bulk amounts of four types of feeds that it can mix to meet a given customer's specifications. The following table summarizes the four feeds; their composition of corn, grain, and minerals; and the cost per pound for each type.

Nutrient	Percent of Nutrient in			
	Feed 1	Feed 2	Feed 3	Feed 4
Corn	30%	5%	20%	10%
Grain	10%	30%	15%	10%
Minerals	20%	20%	20%	30%
Cost per Pound	$0.25	$0.30	$0.32	$0.15

On average, U.S. citizens consume almost 70 pounds of poultry per year. To remain competitive, chicken growers must ensure that they feed the required nutrients to their flocks in the most cost-effective manner. Agri-Pro has just received an order from a local chicken farmer for 8,000 pounds of feed. The farmer wants this feed to contain at least 20% corn, 15% grain, and 15% minerals. What should Agri-Pro do to fill this order at minimum cost?

3.12.1 DEFINING THE DECISION VARIABLES

In this problem, Agri-Pro must determine how much of the various feeds to blend together to meet the customer's requirements at minimum cost. An algebraic formulation of this problem might use the following four decision variables:

$$X_1 = \text{pounds of feed 1 to use in the mix}$$
$$X_2 = \text{pounds of feed 2 to use in the mix}$$
$$X_3 = \text{pounds of feed 3 to use in the mix}$$
$$X_4 = \text{pounds of feed 4 to use in the mix}$$

3.12.2 DEFINING THE OBJECTIVE FUNCTION

The objective in this problem is to fill the customer's order at the lowest possible cost. Because each pound of feed 1, 2, 3, and 4 costs $0.25, $0.30, $0.32, and $0.15, respectively, the objective function is represented by:

$$\text{MIN:} \qquad .25X_1 + .30X_2 + .32X_3 + .15X_4$$

3.12.3 DEFINING THE CONSTRAINTS

Four constraints must be met to fulfill the customer's requirements. First, the customer wants a total of 8,000 pounds of feed. This is expressed by the constraint:

$$X_1 + X_2 + X_3 + X_4 = 8,000$$

The customer also wants the order to consist of at least 20% corn. Because each pound of feed 1, 2, 3, and 4 consists of 30%, 5%, 20%, and 10% corn, respectively, the total amount of corn in the mix is represented by:

$$.30X_1 + .05X_2 + .20X_3 + .10X_4$$

To ensure that *corn* constitutes at least 20% of the 8,000 pounds of feed, we set up the following constraint:

$$\frac{.30X_1 + .05X_2 + .20X_3 + .10X_4}{8,000} \geq .20$$

Similarly, to ensure that *grain* constitutes at least 15% of the 8,000 pounds of feed, we use the constraint:

$$\frac{.10X_1 + .30X_2 + .15X_3 + .10X_4}{8,000} \geq .15$$

Finally, to ensure that *minerals* constitute at least 15% of the 8,000 pounds of feed, we use the constraint:

$$\frac{.20X_1 + .20X_2 + .20X_3 + .30X_4}{8,000} \geq .15$$

3.12.4 SOME OBSERVATIONS ABOUT CONSTRAINTS, REPORTING, AND SCALING

We need to make some important observations about the constraints for this model. First, these constraints look somewhat different from the usual linear sum of products. However, these constraints are equivalent to a sum of products. For example, the constraint for the required percentage of corn can be expressed as:

$$\frac{.30X_1 + .05X_2 + .20X_3 + .10X_4}{8,000} \geq .20$$

or as:

$$\frac{.30X_1}{8,000} + \frac{.050X_2}{8,000} + \frac{.20X_3}{8,000} + \frac{.10X_4}{8,000} \geq .20$$

or, if you multiply both sides of the inequality by 8,000, as:

$$.30X_1 + .05X_2 + .20X_3 + .10X_4 \geq 1,600$$

All these constraints define exactly the same set of feasible values for $X_1, \ldots, X_4$. Theoretically, we should be able to implement and use *any* of these constraints to solve the problem. However, we need to consider a number of practical issues in determining which form of the constraint to implement.

Notice that the LHS formulas for the first and second versions of the constraint represent the *proportion* of corn in the 8,000 pound order, whereas the LHS in the third version of the constraint represents the *total pounds* of corn in the 8,000 pound order.

Because we must implement the LHS formula of one of these constraints in the spreadsheet, we need to decide which number to display in the spreadsheet—the *proportion* (or percentage) of corn in the order or the *total pounds of corn* in the order. If we know one of these values, we can easily set up a formula to calculate the other value. But, when more than one way to implement a constraint exists (as is usually the case), we need to consider what the value of the LHS portion of the constraint means to the user of the spreadsheet so that the results of the model can be reported as clearly as possible.

Another issue to consider involves *scaling* the model so that it can be solved accurately. For example, suppose we decide to implement the LHS formula for the first or second version of the corn constraint given earlier so that the *proportion* of corn in the 8,000 pound feed order appears in the spreadsheet. The coefficients for the variables in these constraints are *very* small values. In either case, the coefficient for X_2 is 0.05/8,000 or 0.000006250.

As Solver tries to solve an LP problem, it must perform intermediate calculations that make the various coefficients in the model larger or smaller. As numbers become extremely large or small, computers often run into storage or representation problems that force them to use approximations of the actual numbers. This opens the door for problems to occur in the accuracy of the results and, in some cases, can prevent the computer from solving the problem at all. So, if some coefficients in the initial model are extremely large or extremely small, it is a good idea to rescale the problem so that all the coefficients are of similar magnitudes.

3.12.5 RE-SCALING THE MODEL

To illustrate how a problem is rescaled, consider the following equivalent formulation of the Agri-Pro problem:

$$X_1 = \text{amount of feed 1 } \textit{in thousands of pounds} \text{ to use in the mix}$$
$$X_2 = \text{amount of feed 2 } \textit{in thousands of pounds} \text{ to use in the mix}$$
$$X_3 = \text{amount of feed 3 } \textit{in thousands of pounds} \text{ to use in the mix}$$
$$X_4 = \text{amount of feed 4 } \textit{in thousands of pounds} \text{ to use in the mix}$$

The objective function and constraints are represented by:

MIN: $250X_1 + 300X_2 + 320X_3 + 150X_4$ } total cost

Subject to: $X_1 + X_2 + X_3 + X_4 = 8$ } pounds of feed required

$$\frac{.30X_1 + .05X_2 + .20X_3 + .10X_4}{8} \geq 0.20 \quad \text{\} min \% of corn required}$$

$$\frac{.10X_1 + .30X_2 + .15X_3 + .10X_4}{8} \geq 0.15 \quad \text{\} min \% of grain required}$$

$$\frac{.20X_1 + .20X_2 + .20X_3 + .30X_4}{8} \geq 0.15 \quad \text{\} min \% of minerals required}$$

$$X_1, X_2, X_3, X_4 \geq 0 \quad \text{\} nonnegativity conditions}$$

Each unit of X_1, X_2, X_3, and X_4 now represents 1,000 pounds of feed 1, 2, 3, and 4, respectively. So the objective now reflects the fact that each unit (or each 1,000 pounds) of X_1, X_2, X_3, and X_4 costs $250, $300, $320, and $150, respectively. The constraints have also been adjusted to reflect that the variables now represent thousands of pounds of the different feeds. Notice that the smallest coefficient in the constraints is now 0.05/8 = 0.00625, and the largest coefficient is 8 (that is, the RHS value for the first constraint). In our original formulation, the smallest coefficient was 0.00000625, and the largest coefficient was 8,000. By rescaling the problem, we dramatically reduced the range between the smallest and largest coefficients in the model.

Using Automatic Scaling

The Engine tab in the Risk Solver task pane offers a Use Automatic Scaling option. If you use this option, Solver attempts to rescale the data in your model before solving the problem. Although this option is very effective, you should not rely solely on it to solve all scaling problems that might occur in your model.

Scaling and Linear Models

When using Solver's LP optimizers, several internal tests are automatically performed to verify that the model is truly linear in the objective and constraints. If Solver's tests indicate that a model is not linear, a message appears indicating that the conditions for linearity are not satisfied. The internal tests Solver applies are nearly 100% accurate but sometimes indicate that a model is not linear when, in fact, it is. This is most likely to occur when a model is poorly scaled. If you encounter this message and you are certain that your model is linear, re-solving the problem might result in Solver identifying the optimal solution. If this does not work, try reformulating your model so that it is more evenly scaled.

3.12.6 IMPLEMENTING THE MODEL

One way to implement this model in a spreadsheet is shown in Figure 3.30 (and in the file Fig3-30.xlsm that accompanies this book). In this spreadsheet, cells B5 through E5 contain the costs of the different types of feeds. The percentage of the different nutrients found in each type of feed is listed in cells B10 through E12.

Cell G6 contains the total amount of feed (in 1,000s of pounds) required for the order, and the minimum percentage of the three types of nutrients required by the customer order are entered in cells G10 through G12. Notice that the values in column G correspond to the RHS values for the various constraints in the model.

In this spreadsheet, cells B6, C6, D6, and E6 are reserved to represent the decision variables X_1, X_2, X_3, and X_4. These cells will ultimately indicate how much of each type of feed should be mixed together to fill the order. The objective function for the problem is implemented in cell F5 using the formula:

Formula for cell F5:   =SUMPRODUCT(B5:E5,B6:E6)

The LHS formula for the first constraint involves calculating the sum of the decision variables. This relationship is implemented in cell F6 as:

Formula for cell F6:   =SUM(B6:E6)

The RHS for this constraint is in cell G6. The LHS formulas for the other three constraints are implemented in cells F10, F11, and F12. Specifically, the LHS formula for the second constraint (representing the proportion of corn in the mix) is implemented in cell F10 as:

FIGURE 3.30 *Spreadsheet model for Agri-Pro's blending problem*

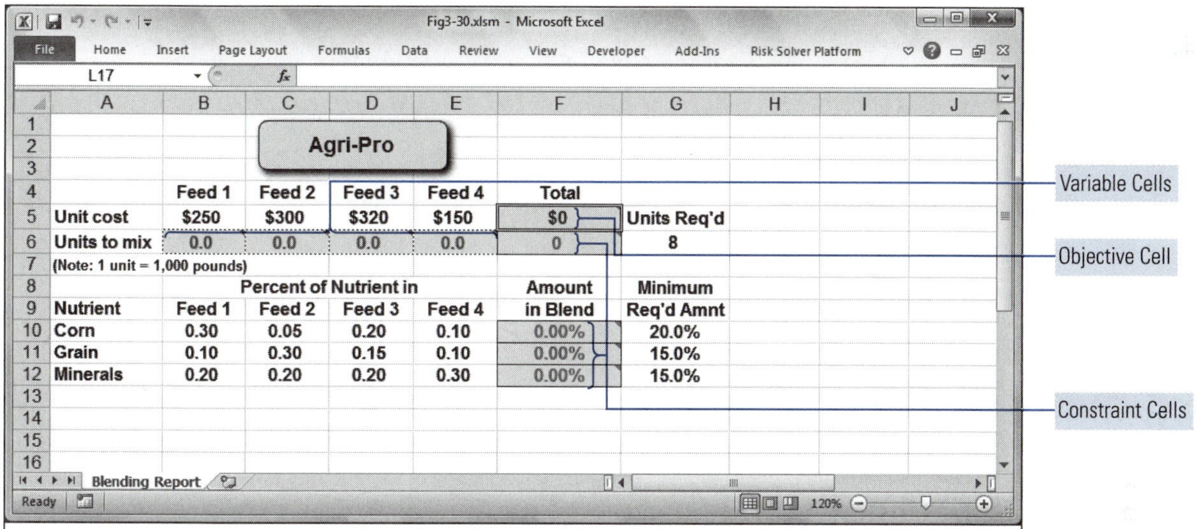

	Feed 1	Feed 2	Feed 3	Feed 4	Total	
5 Unit cost	$250	$300	$320	$150	$0	Units Req'd
6 Units to mix	0.0	0.0	0.0	0.0	0	8
7 (Note: 1 unit = 1,000 pounds)						

	Percent of Nutrient in				Amount	Minimum
9 Nutrient	Feed 1	Feed 2	Feed 3	Feed 4	in Blend	Req'd Amnt
10 Corn	0.30	0.05	0.20	0.10	0.00%	20.0%
11 Grain	0.10	0.30	0.15	0.10	0.00%	15.0%
12 Minerals	0.20	0.20	0.20	0.30	0.00%	15.0%

Key Cell Formulas

Cell	Formula	Copied to
F5	=SUMPRODUCT(B5:E5,B6:E6)	--
F6	=SUM(B6:E6)	--
F10	=SUMPRODUCT(B10:E10,$B$6:$E$6)/$G$6	F11:F12

Formula for cell F10:   =SUMPRODUCT(B10:E10,$B$6:$E$6)/$G$6
(Copy to F11 through F12.)

This formula is then copied to cells F11 and F12 to implement the LHS formulas for the remaining two constraints. Again, cells G10 through G12 contain the RHS values for these constraints.

Notice that this model is implemented in a user-friendly way. Each constraint cell has a logical interpretation that communicates important information. For any given values for the variable cells (B6 through E6) totaling 8 (in thousands), the constraint cells (F10 through F12) indicate the *actual* percentage of corn, grain, and minerals in the mix.

3.12.7 SOLVING THE PROBLEM

Figure 3.31 shows the Solver parameters required to solve this problem. The optimal solution is shown in Figure 3.32.

3.12.8 ANALYZING THE SOLUTION

The optimal solution shown in Figure 3.32 indicates that the 8,000 pound feed order is produced at the lowest possible cost by mixing 4,500 pounds of feed 1 ($X_1 = 4.5$) with 2,000 pounds of feed 2 ($X_2 = 2$) and 1,500 pounds of feed 4 ($X_4 = 1.5$). Cell F6 indicates this produces exactly 8,000 pounds of feed. Cells F10 through F12 indicate this mix contains 20% corn, 15% grain, and 21.88% minerals. The total cost of producing this mix is $1,950, as indicated by cell F5.

FIGURE 3.31

Solver settings and options for the blending problem

Solver Settings:

Objective: F5 (Min)
Variable cells: B6:E6
Constraints:
    F10:F12 >= G10:G12
    F6 = G6
    B6:E6 >= 0

Solver Options: Standard LP/Quadratic Engine (Simplex LP)

FIGURE 3.32 *Optimal solution to Agri-Pro's blending problem*

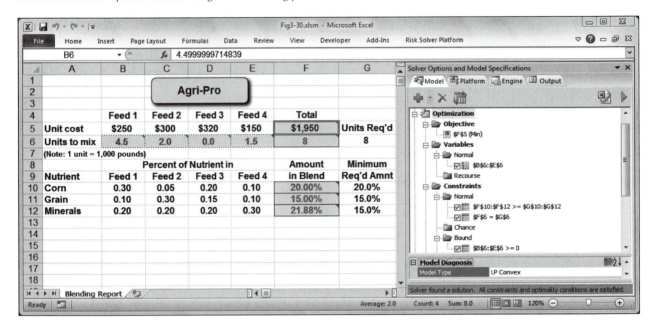

Have You Seen LP at Your Grocery Store?

The next time you are at your local grocery store, make a special trip down the aisle where the pet food is located. On the back of just about any bag of dog or cat food, you should see the following sort of label (taken directly from the author's dog's favorite brand of food):

This product contains:

- At least 21% crude protein
- At least 8% crude fat
- At most 4.5% crude fiber
- At most 12% moisture

(Continued)

In making such statements, the manufacturer guarantees that these nutritional requirements are met by the product. Various ingredients (such as corn, soybeans, meat and bone meal, animal fat, wheat, and rice) are blended to make the product. Most companies are interested in determining the blend of ingredients that satisfies these requirements in the least costly way. Not surprisingly, almost all of the major pet food manufacturing companies use LP extensively in their production process to solve this type of blending problem.

3.13 A Production and Inventory Planning Problem

One of the most fundamental problems facing manufacturing companies is that of planning their production and inventory levels. This process considers demand forecasts and resource constraints for the next several time periods and determines production and inventory levels for each of these time periods to meet the anticipated demand in the most economical way. As the following example illustrates, the multiperiod nature of these problems can be handled very conveniently in a spreadsheet to greatly simplify the production planning process.

The Upton Corporation manufactures heavy duty air compressors for the home and light industrial markets. Upton is presently trying to plan its production and inventory levels for the next six months. Because of seasonal fluctuations in utility and raw material costs, the per unit cost of producing air compressors varies from month to month—as does the demand for air compressors. Production capacity also varies from month to month due to differences in the number of working days, vacations, and scheduled maintenance and training. The following table summarizes the monthly production costs, demands, and production capacity that Upton's management expects to face over the next six months.

	Month					
	1	2	3	4	5	6
Unit Production Cost	$ 240	$ 250	$ 265	$ 285	$ 280	$ 260
Units Demanded	1,000	4,500	6,000	5,500	3,500	4,000
Maximum Production	4,000	3,500	4,000	4,500	4,000	3,500

Given the size of Upton's warehouse, a maximum of 6,000 units can be held in inventory at the end of any month. The owner of the company likes to keep at least 1,500 units in inventory as safety stock to meet unexpected demand contingencies. To maintain a stable workforce, the company wants to produce no less than one-half of its maximum production capacity each month. Upton's controller estimates that the cost of carrying a unit in any given month is approximately equal to 1.5% of the unit production cost in the same month. Upton estimates the number of units carried in inventory each month by averaging the beginning and ending inventory for each month.

There are 2,750 units currently in inventory. Upton wants to identify the production and inventory plan for the next six months that will meet the expected demand each month while minimizing production and inventory costs.

3.13.1 DEFINING THE DECISION VARIABLES

The basic decision Upton's management team faces is how many units to manufacture in each of the next six months. We will represent these decision variables as follows:

$$P_1 = \text{number of units to produce in month 1}$$
$$P_2 = \text{number of units to produce in month 2}$$
$$P_3 = \text{number of units to produce in month 3}$$
$$P_4 = \text{number of units to produce in month 4}$$
$$P_5 = \text{number of units to produce in month 5}$$
$$P_6 = \text{number of units to produce in month 6}$$

3.13.2 DEFINING THE OBJECTIVE FUNCTION

The objective in this problem is to minimize the total production and inventory costs. The total production cost is computed easily as:

$$\text{Production Cost} = 240P_1 + 250P_2 + 265P_3 + 285P_4 + 280P_5 + 260P_6$$

The inventory cost is a bit trickier to compute. The cost of holding a unit in inventory each month is 1.5% of the production cost in the same month. So, the unit inventory cost is \$3.60 in month 1 (that is, 1.5% $\times$ \$240 = \$3.60), \$3.75 in month 2 (that is, 1.5% $\times$ \$250 = \$3.75), and so on. The number of units held each month is to be computed as the average of the beginning and ending inventory for the month. Of course, the beginning inventory in any given month is equal to the ending inventory from the previous month. So if we let B_i represent the beginning inventory for month i, the total inventory cost is given by:

$$\text{Inventory Cost} = 3.6(B_1 + B_2)/2 + 3.75(B_2 + B_3)/2 + 3.98(B_3 + B_4)/2$$
$$+ 4.28(B_4 + B_5)/2 + 4.20(B_5 + B_6)/2 + 3.9(B_6 + B_7)/2$$

Note that the first term in the previous formula computes the inventory cost for month 1 using B_1 as the beginning inventory for month 1 and B_2 as the ending inventory for month 1. Thus, the objective function for this problem is given as:

MIN: $240P_1 + 250P_2 + 265P_3 + 285P_4 + 280P_5 + 260P_6$
$+ 3.6(B_1 + B_2)/2 + 3.75(B_2 + B_3)/2 + 3.98(B_3 + B_4)/2$ } total cost
$+ 4.28(B_4 + B_5)/2 + 4.20(B_5 + B_6)/2 + 3.9(B_6 + B_7)/2$

3.13.3 DEFINING THE CONSTRAINTS

There are two sets of constraints that apply to this problem. First, the number of units produced each month cannot exceed the maximum production levels stated in the problem. However, we must also make sure that the number of units produced each month is no less than one-half of the maximum production capacity for the month. These conditions can be expressed concisely as follows:

$$2{,}000 \leq P_1 \leq 4{,}000 \quad \text{} \text{production level for month 1}$$
$$1{,}750 \leq P_2 \leq 3{,}500 \quad \text{} \text{production level for month 2}$$

$$2,000 \le P_3 \le 4,000 \quad \text{\} production level for month 3}$$
$$2,250 \le P_4 \le 4,500 \quad \text{\} production level for month 4}$$
$$2,000 \le P_5 \le 4,000 \quad \text{\} production level for month 5}$$
$$1,750 \le P_6 \le 3,500 \quad \text{\} production level for month 6}$$

These restrictions simply place the appropriate lower and upper limits on the values that each of the decision variables may assume. Similarly, we must ensure that the ending inventory each month falls between the minimum and maximum allowable inventory levels of 1,500 and 6,000, respectively. In general, the ending inventory for any month is computed as:

$$\text{Ending Inventory} = \text{Beginning Inventory} + \text{Units Produced} - \text{Units Sold}$$

Thus, the following restrictions indicate that the ending inventory in each of the next six months (after meeting the demand for the month) must fall between 1,500 and 6,000.

$$1,500 \le B_1 + P_1 - 1,000 \le 6,000 \quad \text{\} ending inventory for month 1}$$
$$1,500 \le B_2 + P_2 - 4,500 \le 6,000 \quad \text{\} ending inventory for month 2}$$
$$1,500 \le B_3 + P_3 - 6,000 \le 6,000 \quad \text{\} ending inventory for month 3}$$
$$1,500 \le B_4 + P_4 - 5,500 \le 6,000 \quad \text{\} ending inventory for month 4}$$
$$1,500 \le B_5 + P_5 - 3,500 \le 6,000 \quad \text{\} ending inventory for month 5}$$
$$1,500 \le B_6 + P_6 - 4,000 \le 6,000 \quad \text{\} ending inventory for month 6}$$

Finally, to ensure that the beginning balance in one month equals the ending balance from the previous month, we have the following additional restrictions:

$$B_2 = B_1 + P_1 - 1,000$$
$$B_3 = B_2 + P_2 - 4,500$$
$$B_4 = B_3 + P_3 - 6,000$$
$$B_5 = B_4 + P_4 - 5,500$$
$$B_6 = B_5 + P_5 - 3,500$$
$$B_7 = B_6 + P_6 - 4,000$$

3.13.4 IMPLEMENTING THE MODEL

The LP problem for Upton's production and inventory planning problem may be summarized as:

MIN:
$$240P_1 + 250P_2 + 265P_3 + 285P_4 + 280P_5 + 260P_6$$
$$+ 3.6(B_1 + B_2)/2 + 3.75(B_2 + B_3)/2 + 3.98(B_3 + B_4)/2 \quad \text{total cost}$$
$$+ 4.28(B_4 + B_5)/2 + 4.20(B_5 + B_6)/2 + 3.9(B_6 + B_7)/2$$

Subject to:
$$2,000 \le P_1 \le 4,000 \quad \text{\} production level for month 1}$$
$$1,750 \le P_2 \le 3,500 \quad \text{\} production level for month 2}$$
$$2,000 \le P_3 \le 4,000 \quad \text{\} production level for month 3}$$
$$2,250 \le P_4 \le 4,500 \quad \text{\} production level for month 4}$$
$$2,000 \le P_5 \le 4,000 \quad \text{\} production level for month 5}$$
$$1,750 \le P_6 \le 3,500 \quad \text{\} production level for month 6}$$

$$1,500 \leq B_1 + P_1 - 1,000 \leq 6,000 \qquad \} \text{ ending inventory for month 1}$$
$$1,500 \leq B_2 + P_2 - 4,500 \leq 6,000 \qquad \} \text{ ending inventory for month 2}$$
$$1,500 \leq B_3 + P_3 - 6,000 \leq 6,000 \qquad \} \text{ ending inventory for month 3}$$
$$1,500 \leq B_4 + P_4 - 5,500 \leq 6,000 \qquad \} \text{ ending inventory for month 4}$$
$$1,500 \leq B_5 + P_5 - 3,500 \leq 6,000 \qquad \} \text{ ending inventory for month 5}$$
$$1,500 \leq B_6 + P_6 - 4,000 \leq 6,000 \qquad \} \text{ ending inventory for month 6}$$

where:

$$B_2 = B_1 + P_1 - 1,000$$
$$B_3 = B_2 + P_2 - 4,500$$
$$B_4 = B_3 + P_3 - 6,000$$
$$B_5 = B_4 + P_4 - 5,500$$
$$B_6 = B_5 + P_5 - 3,500$$
$$B_7 = B_6 + P_6 - 4,000$$

A convenient way of implementing this model is shown in Figure 3.33 (and file Fig3-33.xlsm that accompanies this book). Cells C7 through H7 in this spreadsheet represent the number of air compressors to produce in each month and therefore correspond to the decision variables (P_1 through P_6) in our model. We will place appropriate upper and lower bounds on these cells to enforce the restrictions represented by the first six constraints in our model. The estimated demands for each time period are listed just below the decision variables in cells C8 through H8.

With the beginning inventory level of 2,750 entered in cell C6, the ending inventory for month 1 is computed in cell C9 as follows:

Formula for cell C9:   =C6+C7−C8

(Copy to cells D9 through H9.)

This formula can be copied to cells D9 through H9 to compute the ending inventory levels for each of the remaining months. We will place appropriate lower and upper limits on these cells to enforce the restrictions indicated by the second set of six constraints in our model.

To ensure that the beginning inventory in month 2 equals the ending inventory from month 1, we place the following formula in cell D6:

Formula for cell D6:   =C9

(Copy to cells E6 through H6.)

This formula can be copied to cells E6 through H6 to ensure that the beginning inventory levels in each month equal the ending inventory levels from the previous month. It is important to note that because the beginning inventory levels can be calculated directly from the ending inventory levels, there is no need to specify these cells as constraint cells to Solver.

With the monthly unit production costs entered in cell C17 through H17, the monthly unit carrying costs are computed in cells C18 through H18 as follows:

Formula for cell C18:   =$B$18*C17

(Copy to cells D18 through H18.)

The total monthly production and inventory costs are then computed in rows 20 and 21 as follows:

FIGURE 3.33 *Spreadsheet model for Upton's production problem*

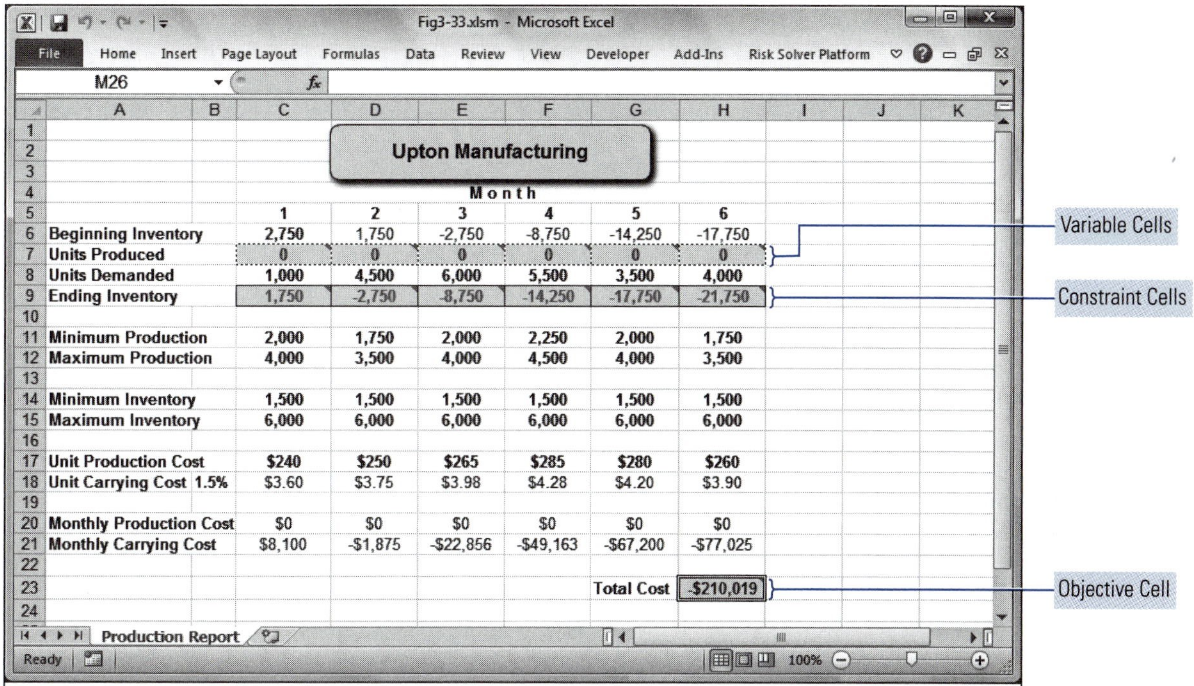

		C	D	E	F	G	H
				Month			
		1	2	3	4	5	6
Beginning Inventory		2,750	1,750	-2,750	-8,750	-14,250	-17,750
Units Produced		0	0	0	0	0	0
Units Demanded		1,000	4,500	6,000	5,500	3,500	4,000
Ending Inventory		1,750	-2,750	-8,750	-14,250	-17,750	-21,750
Minimum Production		2,000	1,750	2,000	2,250	2,000	1,750
Maximum Production		4,000	3,500	4,000	4,500	4,000	3,500
Minimum Inventory		1,500	1,500	1,500	1,500	1,500	1,500
Maximum Inventory		6,000	6,000	6,000	6,000	6,000	6,000
Unit Production Cost		$240	$250	$265	$285	$280	$260
Unit Carrying Cost	1.5%	$3.60	$3.75	$3.98	$4.28	$4.20	$3.90
Monthly Production Cost		$0	$0	$0	$0	$0	$0
Monthly Carrying Cost		$8,100	-$1,875	-$22,856	-$49,163	-$67,200	-$77,025
						Total Cost	-$210,019

Key Cell Formulas

Cell	Formula	Copied to
C9	=C6+C7-C8	D9:H9
D6	=C9	E6:H6
C18	=$B$18*C17	D18:H18
C20	=C17*C7	D20:H20
C21	=C18*(C6+C9)/2	D21:H21
H23	=SUM(C20:H21)	--

Formula for cell C20: =C17*C7
(Copy to cells D20 through H20.)

Formula for cell C21: =C18*(C6+C9)/2
(Copy to cells D21 through H21.)

Finally, the objective function representing the total production and inventory costs for the problem is implemented in cell H23 as follows:

Formula for cell H23: =SUM(C20:H21)

3.13.5 SOLVING THE PROBLEM

Figure 3.34 shows the Solver settings required to solve this problem. The optimal solution is shown in Figure 3.35.

FIGURE 3.34

Solver settings and options for the production problem

Solver Settings:

Objective: H23 (Min)
Variable cells: C7:H7
Constraints:
C9:H9 <= C15:H15
C9:H9 >= C14:H14
C7:H7 <= C12:H12
C7:H7 >= C11:H11

Solver Options:

Standard LP/Quadratic Engine (Simplex LP)

FIGURE 3.35 *Optimal solution to Upton's production problem*

	A	C	D	E	F	G	H
1							
2			Upton Manufacturing				
3							
4				Month			
5		1	2	3	4	5	6
6	Beginning Inventory	2,750	5,750	4,750	2,750	1,500	2,000
7	Units Produced	4,000	3,500	4,000	4,250	4,000	3,500
8	Units Demanded	1,000	4,500	6,000	5,500	3,500	4,000
9	Ending Inventory	5,750	4,750	2,750	1,500	2,000	1,500
10							
11	Minimum Production	2,000	1,750	2,000	2,250	2,000	1,750
12	Maximum Production	4,000	3,500	4,000	4,500	4,000	3,500
13							
14	Minimum Inventory	1,500	1,500	1,500	1,500	1,500	1,500
15	Maximum Inventory	6,000	6,000	6,000	6,000	6,000	6,000
16							
17	Unit Production Cost	$240	$250	$265	$285	$280	$260
18	Unit Carrying Cost 1.5%	$3.60	$3.75	$3.98	$4.28	$4.20	$3.90
19							
20	Monthly Production Cost	$960,000	$875,000	$1,060,000	$1,211,250	$1,120,000	$910,000
21	Monthly Carrying Cost	$15,300	$19,688	$14,906	$9,084	$7,350	$6,825
22							
23						Total Cost	$6,209,403
24							

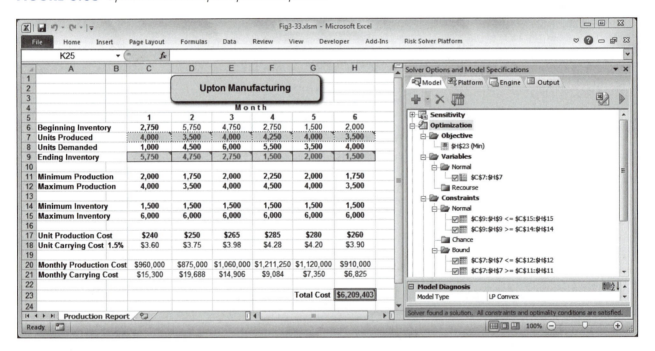

3.13.6 ANALYZING THE SOLUTION

The optimal solution shown in Figure 3.35 indicates Upton should produce 4,000 units in period 1, 3,500 units in period 2, 4,000 units in period 3, 4,250 units in period 4, 4,000 units in period 5, and 3,500 units in period 6. Although the demand for air compressors in month 1 can be met by the beginning inventory, production in month 1 is required to build inventory for future months in which demand exceeds the available production capacity. Notice that this production schedule calls for the company to operate at full production capacity in all months except month 4. Month 4 is expected to have the highest per unit production cost. Therefore, it is more economical to produce extra units in prior months and hold them in inventory for sale in month 4.

It is important to note that although the solution to this problem provides a production plan for the next six months, it does not bind Upton's management team to implement this particular solution throughout the next six months. At an operational level, the management team is most concerned with the decision that must be made now, namely the number of units to schedule for production in month 1. At the end of month 1, Upton's management should update the inventory, demand, and cost estimates, and re-solve the problem to identify the production plan for the next six months (presently months 2 through 7). At the end of month 2, this process should be repeated again. Thus, multiperiod planning models such as this should be used repeatedly on a periodic basis as part of a rolling planning process.

3.14 A Multiperiod Cash Flow Problem

Numerous business problems involve decisions that have a ripple effect on future decisions. In the previous example, we saw how the manufacturing plans for one time period can impact the amount of resources available and the inventory carried in subsequent time periods. Similarly, many financial decisions involve multiple time periods because the amount of money invested or spent at one point in time directly affects the amount of money available in subsequent time periods. In these types of multiperiod problems, it can be difficult to account for the consequences of a current decision on future time periods without an LP model. The formulation of such a model is illustrated next in an example from the world of finance.

Taco-Viva is a small but growing restaurant chain specializing in Mexican fast food. The management of the company has decided to build a new location in Wilmington, North Carolina, and wants to establish a construction fund (or sinking fund) to pay for the new facility. Construction of the restaurant is expected to take six months and cost $800,000. Taco-Viva's contract with the construction company requires it to make payments of $250,000 at the end of the second and fourth months, and a final payment of $300,000 at the end of the sixth month when the restaurant is completed. The company can use four investment opportunities to establish the construction fund; these investments are summarized in the following table:

Investment	Available in Month	Months to Maturity	Yield at Maturity
A	1, 2, 3, 4, 5, 6	1	1.8%
B	1, 3, 5	2	3.5%
C	1, 4	3	5.8%
D	1	6	11.0%

The table indicates that investment A will be available at the beginning of each of the next six months, and funds invested in this manner mature in one month with a yield of 1.8%. Funds can be placed in investment C only at the beginning of months 1 and/or 4, and mature at the end of three months with a yield of 5.8%.

The management of Taco-Viva needs to determine the investment plan that allows them to meet the required schedule of payments while placing the least amount of money in the construction fund.

This is a multiperiod problem because a six-month planning horizon must be considered. That is, Taco-Viva must plan which investment alternatives to use at various times during the next six months.

3.14.1 DEFINING THE DECISION VARIABLES

The basic decision faced by the management of Taco-Viva is how much money to place in each investment vehicle during each time period when the investment opportunities are available. To model this problem, we need different variables to represent each investment/time period combination. This can be done as:

$A_1, A_2, A_3, A_4, A_5, A_6$ = the amount of money (in \$1,000s) placed in investment A at the beginning of months 1, 2, 3, 4, 5, and 6, respectively

B_1, B_3, B_5 = the amount of money (in \$1,000s) placed in investment B at the beginning of months 1, 3, and 5, respectively

C_1, C_4 = the amount of money (in \$1,000s) placed in investment C at the beginning of months 1 and 4, respectively

D_1 = the amount of money (in \$1,000s) placed in investment D at the beginning of month 1

Notice that all variables are expressed in units of thousands of dollars to maintain a reasonable scale for this problem. So, keep in mind that when referring to the amount of money represented by our variables, we mean the amount in thousands of dollars.

3.14.2 DEFINING THE OBJECTIVE FUNCTION

Taco-Viva's management wants to minimize the amount of money it must initially place in the construction fund in order to cover the payments that will be due under the contract. At the beginning of month 1, the company wants to invest some amount of money that, along with its investment earnings, will cover the required payments without an additional infusion of cash from the company. Because A_1, B_1, C_1, and D_1 represent the initial amounts invested by the company in month 1, the objective function for the problem is:

MIN: $A_1 + B_1 + C_1 + D_1$ } total cash invested at the beginning of month 1

3.14.3 DEFINING THE CONSTRAINTS

To formulate the cash-flow constraints for this problem, it is important to clearly identify (1) when the different investments can be made, (2) when the different investments will mature, and (3) how much money will be available when each investment matures. Figure 3.36 summarizes this information.

The negative values, represented by −1 in Figure 3.34, indicate when dollars can flow *into* each investment. The positive values indicate how much these same dollars will be worth when the investment matures, or when dollars flow *out* of each investment. The double-headed arrow symbols indicate time periods in which funds remain in a particular investment. For example, the third row of the table in Figure 3.36 indicates that every dollar placed in investment C at the beginning of month 1 will be worth \$1.058 when this investment matures three months later—at the *beginning* of month 4. (Note that the beginning of month 4 occurs at virtually the same instant as the *end* of month 3. Thus, there is no practical difference between the beginning of one time period and the end of the previous time period.)

Investment	\multicolumn{7}{c}{Cash Inflow/Outflow at the Beginning of Month}
	1	2	3	4	5	6	7
A_1	−1	1.018					
B_1	−1	← →	1.035				
C_1	−1	← →	← →	1.058			
D_1	−1	← →	← →	← →	← →	← →	1.11
A_2		−1	1.018				
A_3			−1	1.018			
B_3			−1	← →	1.035		
A_4				−1	1.018		
C_4				−1	← →	← →	1.058
A_5					−1	1.018	
B_5					−1	← →	1.035
A_6						−1	1.018
Req'd Payments (in $1,000s)	$0	$0	$250	$0	$250	$0	$300

FIGURE 3.36

Cash-flow summary table for Taco-Viva's investment opportunities

Assuming that the company invests the amounts represented by A_1, B_1, C_1, and D_1 at the beginning of month 1, how much money will be available to reinvest or make the required payments at the beginning of months 2, 3, 4, 5, 6, and 7? The answer to this question allows us to generate the set of cash-flow constraints needed for this problem.

As indicated by the second column of Figure 3.36, the only funds maturing at the beginning of month 2 are those placed in investment A at the beginning of month 1 (A_1). The value of the funds maturing at the beginning of month 2 is $1.018A_1$. Because no payments are required at the beginning of month 2, all the maturing funds must be reinvested. But the only new investment opportunity available at the beginning of month 2 is investment A (A_2). Thus, the amount of money placed in investment A at the beginning of month 2 must be $1.018A_1$. This is expressed by the constraint:

$$1.018A_1 = A_2 + 0 \qquad \} \text{ cash flow for month 2}$$

This constraint indicates that the total amount of money maturing at the beginning of month 2 ($1.018A_1$) must equal the amount of money reinvested at the beginning of month 2 (A_2) plus any payment due in month 2 ($0).

Now, consider the cash flows that will occur during month 3. At the beginning of month 3, any funds that were placed in investment B at the beginning of month 1 (B_1) will mature and be worth a total of $1.035B_1$. Similarly, any funds placed in investment A at the beginning of month 2 (A_2) will mature and be worth a total of $1.018A_2$. Because a payment of $250,000 is due at the beginning of month 3, we must ensure that the funds maturing at the beginning of month 3 are sufficient to cover this payment and that any remaining funds are placed in the investment opportunities available at the beginning of month 3 (A_3 and B_3). This requirement can be stated algebraically as:

$$1.035B_1 + 1.018A_2 = A_3 + B_3 + 250 \qquad \} \text{ cash flow for month 3}$$

This constraint indicates that the total amount of money maturing at the beginning of month 3 ($1.035B_1 + 1.018A_2$) must equal the amount of money reinvested at the beginning of month 3 ($A_3 + B_3$) plus the payment due at the beginning of month 3 ($250,000).

The same logic we applied to generate the cash-flow constraints for months 2 and 3 can also be used to generate cash-flow constraints for the remaining months. Doing so produces a cash-flow constraint for each month that takes on the general form:

$$\begin{pmatrix} \text{Total \$ amount} \\ \text{maturing at the} \\ \text{beginning of} \\ \text{the month} \end{pmatrix} = \begin{pmatrix} \text{Total \$ amount} \\ \text{reinvested at the} \\ \text{beginning of} \\ \text{the month} \end{pmatrix} + \begin{pmatrix} \text{Payment} \\ \text{due at the} \\ \text{beginning of} \\ \text{the month} \end{pmatrix}$$

Using this general definition of the cash flow relationships, the constraints for the remaining months are represented by:

$$1.058C_1 + 1.018A_3 = A_4 + C_4 \qquad \} \text{ cash flow for month 4}$$
$$1.035B_3 + 1.018A_4 = A_5 + B_5 + 250 \qquad \} \text{ cash flow for month 5}$$
$$1.018A_5 = A_6 \qquad \} \text{ cash flow for month 6}$$
$$1.11D_1 + 1.058C_4 + 1.035B_5 + 1.018A_6 = 300 \qquad \} \text{ cash flow for month 7}$$

To implement these constraints in the spreadsheet, we must express them in a slightly different (but algebraically equivalent) manner. Specifically, to conform to our general definition of an equality constraint ($f(X_1, X_2, \ldots, X_n) = b$) we need to rewrite the cash-flow constraints so that all the *variables* in each constraint appear on the LHS of the equal sign, and a numeric constant appears on the RHS of the equal sign. This can be done as:

$$1.018A_1 - 1A_2 = 0 \qquad \} \text{ cash flow for month 2}$$
$$1.035B_1 + 1.018A_2 - 1A_3 - 1B_3 = 250 \qquad \} \text{ cash flow for month 3}$$
$$1.058C_1 + 1.018A_3 - 1A_4 - 1C_4 = 0 \qquad \} \text{ cash flow for month 4}$$
$$1.035B_3 + 1.018A_4 - 1A_5 - 1B_5 = 250 \qquad \} \text{ cash flow for month 5}$$
$$1.018A_5 - 1A_6 = 0 \qquad \} \text{ cash flow for month 6}$$
$$1.11D_1 + 1.058C_4 + 1.035B_5 + 1.018A_6 = 300 \qquad \} \text{ cash flow for month 7}$$

There are two important points to note about this alternate expression of the constraints. First, each constraint takes on the following general form, which is algebraically equivalent to our previous general definition for the cash-flow constraints:

$$\begin{pmatrix} \text{Total \$ amount} \\ \text{maturing at the} \\ \text{beginning of} \\ \text{the month} \end{pmatrix} - \begin{pmatrix} \text{Total \$ amount} \\ \text{reinvested at the} \\ \text{beginning of} \\ \text{the month} \end{pmatrix} = \begin{pmatrix} \text{Payment} \\ \text{due at the} \\ \text{beginning of} \\ \text{the month} \end{pmatrix}$$

Although the constraints look slightly different in this form, they enforce the same relationships among the variables as expressed by the earlier constraints.

Second, the LHS coefficients in the alternate expression of the constraints correspond directly to the values listed in the cash-flow summary table in Figure 3.36. That is, the coefficients in the constraint for month 2 correspond to the values in the column for month 2 in Figure 3.36; the coefficients for month 3 correspond to the values in the column for month 3; and so on. This relationship is true for all the constraints and will be very helpful in implementing this model in the spreadsheet.

3.14.4 IMPLEMENTING THE MODEL

The LP model for Taco-Viva's construction fund problem is summarized as:

MIN: $A_1 + B_1 + C_1 + D_1$ } cash invested at beginning of month 1

Subject to:

$$1.018A_1 - 1A_2 \qquad\qquad = \quad 0 \ \} \text{ cash flow for month 2}$$
$$1.035B_1 + 1.018A_2 - 1A_3 - 1B_3 \quad = 250 \ \} \text{ cash flow for month 3}$$
$$1.058C_1 + 1.018A_3 - 1A_4 - 1C_4 \quad = \quad 0 \ \} \text{ cash flow for month 4}$$
$$1.035B_3 + 1.018A_4 - 1A_5 - 1B_5 \quad = 250 \ \} \text{ cash flow for month 5}$$
$$1.018A_5 - 1A_6 \qquad\qquad = \quad 0 \ \} \text{ cash flow for month 6}$$
$$1.11D_1 + 1.058C_4 + 1.035B_5 + 1.018A_6 = 300 \ \} \text{ cash flow for month 7}$$
$$A_i, B_i, C_i, D_i, \geq 0, \text{ for all } i \qquad\qquad \} \text{ nonnegativity conditions}$$

One approach to implementing this model is shown in Figure 3.37 (and in file Fig3-37.xlsm that accompanies this book). The first three columns of this spreadsheet summarize the different investment options that are available and the months in which money may flow into and out of these investments. Cells D6 through D17 represent the decision variables in our model and indicate the amount of money (in $1,000s) to be placed in each of the possible investments.

FIGURE 3.37 *Spreadsheet model for Taco-Viva's construction fund problem*

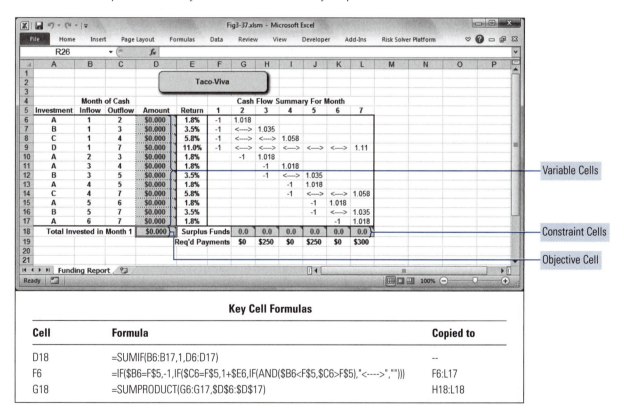

Key Cell Formulas

Cell	Formula	Copied to
D18	=SUMIF(B6:B17,1,D6:D17)	--
F6	=IF($B6=F$5,-1,IF($C6=F$5,1+$E6,IF(AND($B6<F$5,$C6>F$5),"<---->","")))	F6:L17
G18	=SUMPRODUCT(G6:G17,$D$6:$D$17)	H18:L18

The objective function for this problem requires that we compute the total amount of money being invested in month 1. This was done in cell D18 as follows:

$$\text{Formula for cell D18:} \qquad =\text{SUMIF(B6:B17,1,D6:D17)}$$

This SUMIF( ) function compares the values in cells B6 through B17 to the value 1 (its second argument). If any of the values in B6 through B17 equal 1, it sums the corresponding values in cells D6 through D17. In this case, the values in cells B6 through B9 all equal 1; therefore, the function returns the sum of the values in cells D6 through D9. Note that although we could have implemented the objective using the formula SUM(D6:D9), the previous SUMIF( ) formula makes for a more modifiable and reliable model. If any of the values in column B are changed to or from 1, the SUMIF( ) function continues to represent the appropriate objective function, whereas the SUM( ) function would not.

Our next job is to implement the cash inflow/outflow table described earlier in Figure 3.36. Recall that each row in Figure 3.36 corresponds to the cash flows associated with a particular investment alternative. This table can be implemented in our spreadsheet using the following formula:

Formula for cell F6: =IF($B6=F$5,-1,IF($C6=F$5,1+$E6,IF(AND($B6<F$5,$C6>F$5)," <--->","")))
(Copy to cells F6 through L17.)

This formula first checks to see if the "month of cash inflow" value in column B matches the month indicator value in row 5. If so, the formula returns the value -1. Otherwise, it goes on to check to see if the "month of cash outflow" value in column C matches the month indicator value in row 5. If so, the formula returns a value equal to 1 plus the return for the investment (from column E). If neither of the first two conditions is met, the formula next checks whether the current month indicator in row 5 is larger than the "month of cash inflow" value (column B) and smaller than the "month of cash outflow" value (column C). If so, the formula returns the characters "<---->" to indicate periods in which funds neither flow into or out of a particular investment. Finally, if none of the previous three conditions are met, the formula simply returns an empty (or null) string (""). Although this formula looks a bit intimidating, it is simply a set of three nested IF functions. More importantly, it automatically updates the cash flow summary if any of the values in columns B, C, or E are changed, increasing the reliability and modifiability of the model.

Earlier, we noted that the values listed in columns 2 through 7 of the cash inflow/outflow table correspond directly to the coefficients appearing in the various cash-flow constraints. This property allows us to implement the cash-flow constraints in the spreadsheet conveniently. For example, the LHS formula for the cash-flow constraint for month 2 is implemented in cell G18 through the formula:

Formula in cell G18:   =SUMPRODUCT(G6:G17,$D$6:$D$17)
(Copy to H18 through L18.)

This formula multiplies each entry in the range G6 through G17 by the corresponding entry in the range D6 through D17 and then sums these individual products. This formula is copied to cells H18 through L18. (Notice that the SUMPRODUCT( ) formula treats cells containing labels and null strings as if they contained the value zero.) Take a moment now to verify that the formulas in cells G18 through L18 correspond to the LHS formulas of the cash-flow constraints in our model. Cells G19 through L19 list the RHS values for the cash-flow constraints.

3.14.5 SOLVING THE PROBLEM

To find the optimal solution to this model, we must indicate to Solver the objective cell, variable cells, and constraint cells identified in Figure 3.37. Figure 3.38 shows the Solver settings required to solve this problem. The optimal solution is shown in Figure 3.39.

FIGURE 3.38

Solver settings and options for the construction fund problem

Solver Settings:
Objective: D18 (Min)
Variable cells: D6:D17
Constraints:
G18:L18 = G19:L19
D6:D17 >= 0
Solver Options:
Standard LP/Quadratic Engine (Simplex LP)

FIGURE 3.39 *Optimal solution to Taco-Viva's construction fund problem*

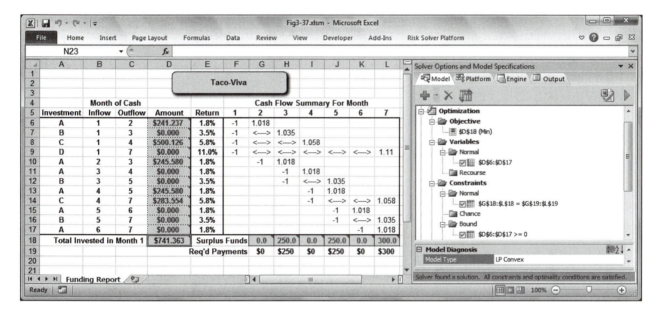

3.14.6 ANALYZING THE SOLUTION

The value of the objective cell (D18) in Figure 3.39 indicates that a total of $741,363 must be invested to meet the payments on Taco-Viva's construction project. Cells D6 and D8 indicate that approximately $241,237 should be placed in investment A at the beginning of month 1 ($A_1 = 241.237$) and approximately $500,126 should be placed in investment C ($C_1 = 500.126$).

At the beginning of month 2, the funds placed in investment A at the beginning of month 1 will mature and be worth $245,580 ($241,237 \times 1.018 = 245,580$). The value in cell D10 indicates these funds should be placed back into investment A at the beginning of month 2 ($A_2 = 245.580$).

At the beginning of month 3, the first $250,000 payment is due. At that time, the funds placed in investment A at the beginning of month 2 will mature and be worth $250,000 ($1.018 \times 245,580 = 250,000$)—allowing us to make this payment.

At the beginning of month 4, the funds placed in investment C at the beginning of month 1 will mature and be worth $529,134. Our solution indicates that $245,580 of this amount should be placed in investment A ($A_4 = 245.580$), and the rest should be reinvested in investment C ($C_4 = 283.554$).

If you trace through the cash flows for the remaining months, you will discover that our model is doing exactly what it was designed to do. The amount of money scheduled to mature at the beginning of each month is exactly equal to the amount of money scheduled to be reinvested after required payments are made. Thus, out of an infinite number of possible investment schedules, our LP model found the one schedule that requires the least amount of money up front.

3.14.7 MODIFYING THE TACO-VIVA PROBLEM TO ACCOUNT FOR RISK (OPTIONAL)

In investment problems like this, it is not uncommon for decision makers to place limits on the amount of risk they are willing to assume. For instance, suppose the chief financial officer (CFO) for Taco-Viva assigned the following risk ratings to each of the possible investments on a scale from 1 to 10 (where 1 represents the least risk, and 10 the greatest risk). We will also assume that the CFO wants to determine an investment plan where the weighted average risk level does not exceed 5.

Investment	Risk Rating
A	1
B	3
C	8
D	6

We will need to formulate an additional constraint for each time period to ensure the weighted average risk level never exceeds 5. To see how this can be done, let's start with month 1.

In month 1, funds can be invested in A_1, B_1, C_1, and/or D_1, and each investment is associated with a different degree of risk. To calculate the weighted average risk during month 1, we must multiply the risk factors for each investment by the proportion of money in that investment. This is represented by:

$$\text{Weighted average risk in month 1} = \frac{1A_1 + 3B_1 + 8C_1 + 6D_1}{A_1 + B_1 + C_1 + D_1}$$

We can ensure that the weighted average risk in month 1 does not exceed the value 5 by including the following constraint in our LP model:

$$\frac{1A_1 + 3B_1 + 8C_1 + 6D_1}{A_1 + B_1 + C_1 + D_1} \leq 5 \quad \} \text{ risk constraint for month 1}$$

Now, consider month 2. According to the column for month 2 in our cash inflow/outflow table, the company can have funds invested in B_1, C_1, D_1, and/or A_2 during this month. Thus, the weighted average risk that occurs in month 2 is defined by:

$$\text{Weighted average risk in month 2} = \frac{3B_1 + 8C_1 + 6D_1 + 1A_2}{B_1 + C_1 + D_1 + A_2}$$

Again, the following constraint ensures that this quantity never exceeds 5:

$$\frac{3B_1 + 8C_1 + 6D_1 + 1A_2}{B_1 + C_1 + D_1 + A_2} \leq 5 \quad \} \text{ risk constraint for month 2}$$

The risk constraints for months 3 through 6 are generated in a similar manner, and appear as:

$$\frac{8C_1 + 6D_1 + 1A_3 + 3B_3}{C_1 + D_1 + A_3 + B_3} \leq 5 \quad \} \text{ risk constraint for month 3}$$

$$\frac{6D_1 + 3B_3 + 1A_4 + 8C_4}{D_1 + B_3 + A_4 + C_4} \leq 5 \quad \} \text{ risk constraint for month 4}$$

$$\frac{6D_1 + 8C_4 + 1A_5 + 3B_5}{D_1 + C_4 + A_5 + B_5} \leq 5 \quad \} \text{ risk constraint for month 5}$$

$$\frac{6D_1 + 8C_4 + 3B_5 + 1A_6}{D_1 + C_4 + B_5 + A_6} \leq 5 \quad \} \text{ risk constraint for month 6}$$

Although the risk constraints listed here have a very clear meaning, it is easier to implement these constraints in the spreadsheet if we state them in a different (but algebraically equivalent) manner. In particular, it is helpful to eliminate the fractions on the LHS of the inequalities by multiplying each constraint through by its denominator and re-collecting the variables on the LHS of the inequality. The following steps show how to rewrite the risk constraint for month 1:

1. Multiply both sides of the inequality by the denominator:

$$(A_1 + B_1 + C_1 + D_1) \frac{1A_1 + 3B_1 + 8C_1 + 6D_1}{A_1 + B_1 + C_1 + D_1} \leq (A_1 + B_1 + C_1 + D_1)5$$

to obtain:

$$1A_1 + 3B_1 + 8C_1 + 6D_1 \leq 5A_1 + 5B_1 + 5C_1 + 5D_1$$

2. Re-collect the variables on the LHS of the inequality sign:

$$(1 - 5)A_1 + (3 - 5)B_1 + (8 - 5)C_1 + (6 - 5)D_1 \leq 0$$

to obtain:

$$-4A_1 - 2B_1 + 3C_1 + 1D_1 \leq 0$$

Thus, the following two constraints are algebraically equivalent:

$$\frac{1A_1 + 3B_1 + 8C_1 + 6D_1}{A_1 + B_1 + C_1 + D_1} \leq 5 \quad \} \text{ risk constraint for month 1}$$

$$-4A_1 - 2B_1 + 3C_1 + 1D_1 \leq 0 \quad \} \text{ risk constraint for month 1}$$

The set of values for A_1, B_1, C_1, and D_1 that satisfies the first of these constraints also satisfies the second constraint (that is, these constraints have exactly the same set of feasible values). So, it does not matter which of these constraints we use to find the optimal solution to the problem.

The remaining risk constraints are simplified in the same way, producing the following constraints:

$-2B_1$	$+$	$3C_1$	$+$	$1D_1$	$-$	$4A_2$		≤ 0	$\}$ risk constraint for month 2
		$3C_1$	$+$	$1D_1$	$-$	$4A_3$	$- 2B_3$	≤ 0	$\}$ risk constraint for month 3
		$1D_1$	$-$	$2B_3$	$-$	$4A_4$	$+ 3C_4$	≤ 0	$\}$ risk constraint for month 4
		$1D_1$	$+$	$3C_4$	$-$	$4A_5$	$- 2B_5$	≤ 0	$\}$ risk constraint for month 5
		$1D_1$	$+$	$3C_4$	$-$	$2B_5$	$- 4A_6$	≤ 0	$\}$ risk constraint for month 6

Notice that the coefficient for each variable in these constraints is simply the risk factor for the particular investment minus the maximum allowable weighted average risk value of 5. That is, all A_i variables have coefficients of $1 - 5 = -4$; all B_i variables have coefficients of $3 - 5 = -2$; all C_i variables have coefficients of $8 - 5 = 3$; and all D_i variables have coefficients of $6 - 5 = 1$. This observation will help us implement these constraints efficiently.

3.14.8 IMPLEMENTING THE RISK CONSTRAINTS

Figure 3.40 (and file Fig3-40.xlsm that accompanies this book) illustrates an easy way to implement the risk constraints for this model. Earlier we noted that the coefficient for each variable in each risk constraint is simply the risk factor for the particular investment minus the maximum allowable weighted average risk value. Thus, the strategy in Figure 3.40 is to generate these values in the appropriate columns and rows of the spreadsheet so that the SUMPRODUCT( ) function can implement the LHS formulas for the risk constraints.

FIGURE 3.40 *Spreadsheet model for Taco-Viva's revised construction fund problem*

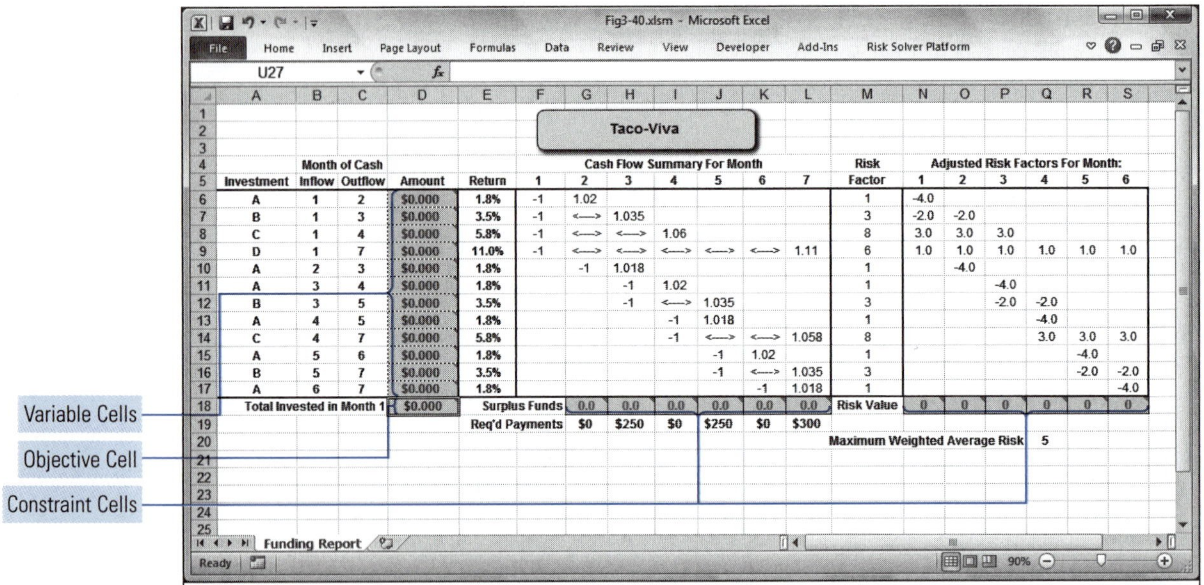

Key Cell Formulas

Cell	Formula	Copied to
D18	=SUMIF(B6:B17,1,D6:D17)	--
F6	=IF($B6=F$5,-1,IF($C6=F$5,1+$E6,IF(AND($B6<F$5,$C6>F$5),"<---->","")))	F6:L17
G18	=SUMPRODUCT(G6:G17,$D$6:$D$17)	H18:L18 and N18:S18
N6	=IF(OR(F6=-1,LEFT(F6)="<"),$M6-$Q$20,"")	N6:S17

Recall that the risk constraint for each month involves only the variables representing investments that actually held funds during that month. For any given month, the investments that actually held funds during that month have the value −1 or contain a text entry starting with the "<" symbol (the first character of the "<---->" entries) in the corresponding column of the cash inflow/outflow summary table. For example, during month 2, funds can be invested in B_1, C_1, D_1, and/or A_2. The corresponding cells for month 2 in Figure 3.40 (cells G7, G8, G9, and G10, respectively) each contain either the value -1 or a text entry starting with the "<" symbol. Therefore, to generate the appropriate coefficients for the risk constraints, we can instruct the spreadsheet to scan the cash inflow/outflow summary for cells containing the value -1 or text entries starting with the "<" symbol, and return the correct risk constraint coefficients in the appropriate cells. To do this we enter the following formula in cell N6:

> Formula in cell N6:   =IF(OR(F6=−1,LEFT(F6)="<"),$M6-$Q$20,"")
> (Copy to N6 through S17.)

To generate the appropriate value in cell N6, the previous formula checks if cell F6 is equal to -1 or contains a text entry that starts with the "<" symbol. If either of these conditions is true, the function takes the risk factor for the investment from cell M6 and subtracts the maximum allowable risk factor found in cell Q20; otherwise, the function returns a null string (with a value of zero). This formula is copied to the remaining cells in the range N6 through S17, as shown in Figure 3.40.

The values in cells N6 through S17 in Figure 3.40 correspond to the coefficients in the LHS formulas for each of the risk constraints formulated earlier. Thus, the LHS formula for the risk constraint for month 1 is implemented in cell N18 as:

> Formula in cell N18:   =SUMPRODUCT(N6:N17,$D$6:$D$17)
> (Copy to O18 through S18.)

The LHS formulas for the remaining risk constraints are implemented by copying this formula to cells O18 through S18. We will tell Solver that these constraint cells must be less than or equal to zero.

3.14. 9 SOLVING THE PROBLEM

To find the optimal solution to this model, we must communicate the appropriate information about the new risk constraints to Solver. Figure 3.41 shows the Solver parameters required to solve this problem. The optimal solution is shown in Figure 3.42.

FIGURE 3.41

Solver settings and options for the revised construction fund problem

Solver Settings:
Objective: D18 (Min)
Variable cells: D6:D17
Constraints:
G18:L18 = G19:L19
N18:S18 <= 0
D6:D17 >= 0
Solver Options:
Standard LP/Quadratic Engine (Simplex LP)

3.14.10 ANALYZING THE SOLUTION

The optimal solution to the revised Taco-Viva problem with risk constraints is quite different from the solution obtained earlier. In particular, the new solution requires that funds be placed in investment A in every time period. This is not too surprising given

FIGURE 3.42 *Optimal solution to Taco-Viva's revised construction fund problem*

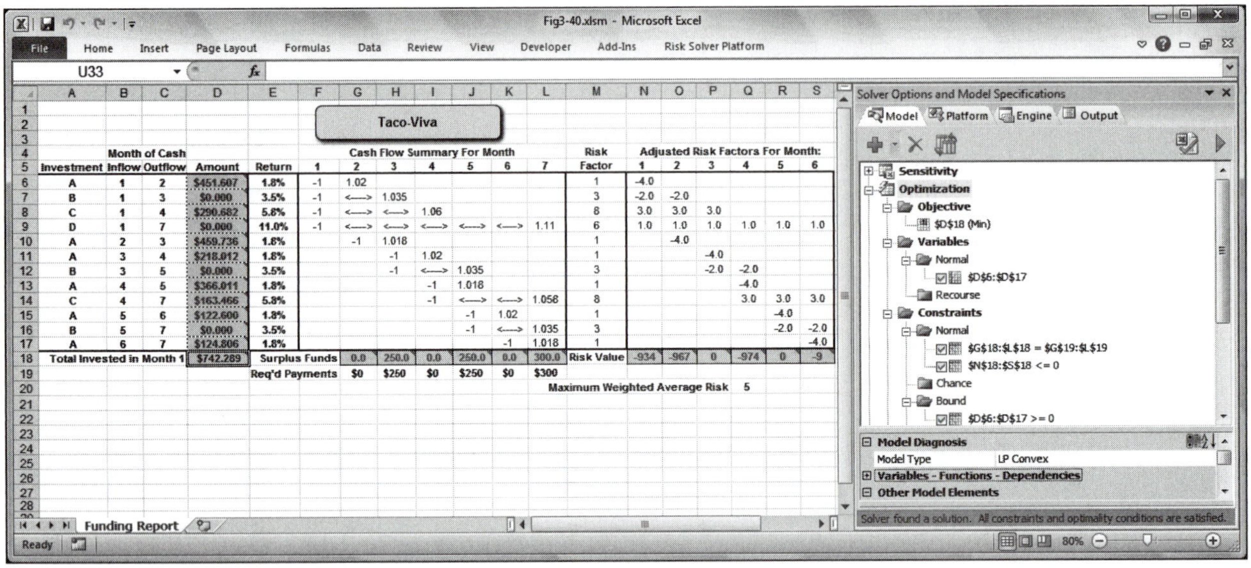

that investment A has the lowest risk rating. What may be somewhat surprising is that of the remaining investments, B and D are never used. Although these investments have lower risk ratings than investment C, the combination of funds placed in investment A and C allows for the least amount of money to be invested in month 1 while meeting the scheduled payments and keeping the weighted average risk at or below the specified level.

3.15 Data Envelopment Analysis

Managers are often interested in determining how efficiently various units within a company operate. Similarly, investment analysts may be interested in comparing the efficiency of several competing companies within an industry. Data Envelopment Analysis (DEA) is an LP-based methodology for performing this type of analysis. DEA determines how efficiently an operating unit (or company) converts inputs to outputs when compared with other units. We will consider how DEA may be applied via the following example.

> Mike Lister is a district manager for the Steak & Burger fast-food restaurant chain. The region Mike manages contains 12 company-owned units. Mike is in the process of evaluating the performance of these units during the past year to make recommendations on how much of an annual bonus to pay each unit's manager. He wants to base this decision, in part, on how efficiently each unit has been operated. Mike has collected the data shown in the following table on each of the 12 units. The outputs he has chosen include each unit's net profit (in $100,000s), average customer satisfaction rating, and average monthly cleanliness score. The inputs include total labor hours (in 100,000s) and total operating costs (in $1,000,000s). He wants to apply DEA to this data to determine an efficiency score of each unit.

Unit	Outputs			Inputs	
	Profit	Satisfaction	Cleanliness	Labor Hours	Operating Costs
1	5.98	7.7	92	4.74	6.75
2	7.18	9.7	99	6.38	7.42
3	4.97	9.3	98	5.04	6.35
4	5.32	7.7	87	3.61	6.34
5	3.39	7.8	94	3.45	4.43
6	4.95	7.9	88	5.25	6.31
7	2.89	8.6	90	2.36	3.23
8	6.40	9.1	100	7.09	8.69
9	6.01	7.3	89	6.49	7.28
10	6.94	8.8	89	7.36	9.07
11	5.86	8.2	93	5.46	6.69
12	8.35	9.6	97	6.58	8.75

3.15.1 DEFINING THE DECISION VARIABLES

Using DEA, the efficiency of an arbitrary unit i is defined as follows:

$$\text{Efficiency of unit } i = \frac{\text{Weighted sum of unit } i\text{'s outputs}}{\text{Weighted sum of unit } i\text{'s input}} = \frac{\sum_{j=1}^{n_O} O_{ij} w_j}{\sum_{j=1}^{n_I} I_{ij} v_j}$$

Here, O_{ij} represents the value of unit i on *output* j, I_{ij} represents the value of unit i on *input* j, w_j is a nonnegative weight assigned to output j, v_j is a nonnegative weight assigned to input j, n_O is the number of output variables, and n_I is the number of input variables. The problem in DEA is to determine values for the weights w_j and v_j. Thus, w_j and v_j represent the decision variables in a DEA problem.

3.15.2 DEFINING THE OBJECTIVE

A separate LP problem is solved for each unit in a DEA problem. However, for each unit, the objective is the same: to maximize the weighted sum of that unit's outputs. For an arbitrary unit i, the objective is stated as:

$$\text{MAX: } \sum_{j=1}^{n_O} O_{ij} w_j$$

Thus, as each LP problem is solved, the unit under investigation is given the opportunity to select the best possible weights for itself (or the weights that maximize the weighted sum of its output), subject to the following constraints.

3.15.3 DEFINING THE CONSTRAINTS

It is impossible for any unit to be more than 100% efficient. So as each LP is solved, the unit under investigation cannot select weights for itself that would cause the efficiency for any unit (including itself) to be greater than 100%. Thus, for each individual unit, we require the weighted sum of the unit's outputs to be less than or equal to the weighted sum of its inputs (so the ratio of weighted outputs to weighted inputs does not exceed 100%).

$$\sum_{j=1}^{n_o} O_{kj}w_j \le \sum_{j=1}^{n_I} I_{kj}v_j, \quad \text{for } k = 1 \text{ to the number of units}$$

or equivalently,

$$\sum_{j=1}^{n_o} O_{kj}w_j - \sum_{j=1}^{n_I} I_{kj}v_j \le 0, \quad \text{for } k = 1 \text{ to the number of units}$$

To prevent unbounded solutions, we also require the sum of the weighted inputs for the unit under investigation (unit i) to equal one.

$$\sum_{j=1}^{n_I} I_{ij}v_j = 1$$

Because the sum of weighted inputs for the unit under investigation must equal one, and its sum of the weighted outputs (being maximized) cannot exceed this value, the maximum efficiency score for the unit under investigation is also one (or 100%). Thus, units that are efficient will have a DEA efficiency score of 100%.

Important Point

When applying DEA, it is assumed that for output variables "more is better" (for example, profit) and for input variables "less is better" (for example, costs). Any output or input variables that do not naturally conform to these rules should be transformed before applying DEA. For example, the percentage of defective products produced is not a good choice for an output because fewer defects is actually a good thing. However, the percentage of nondefective products produced would be an acceptable choice for an output because "more is better" in that case.

3.15.4 IMPLEMENTING THE MODEL

To evaluate the efficiency of unit 1 in our example problem, we would solve the following LP problem,

MAX: $5.98w_1 + 7.7w_2 + 92w_3$ } weighted output for unit 1

Subject to: $5.98w_1 + 7.7w_2 + 92w_3 - 4.74v_1 - 6.75v_2 \le 0$ } efficiency constraint for unit 1

$7.18w_1 + 9.7w_2 + 99w_3 - 6.38v_1 - 7.42v_2 \le 0$ } efficiency constraint for unit 2

and so on to . . .

$8.35w_1 + 9.6w_2 + 97w_3 - 6.58v_1 - 8.75v_2 \le 0$ } efficiency constraint for unit 12

$4.74v_1 + 6.75v_2 = 1$ } input constraint for unit 1

$w_1, w_2, w_3, v_1, v_2 \ge 0$ } nonnegativity conditions

A convenient way to implement this model is shown in Figure 3.43 (and in the file Fig3-43.xlsm that accompanies this book).

FIGURE 3.43 *Spreadsheet model for the Steak & Burger DEA problem*

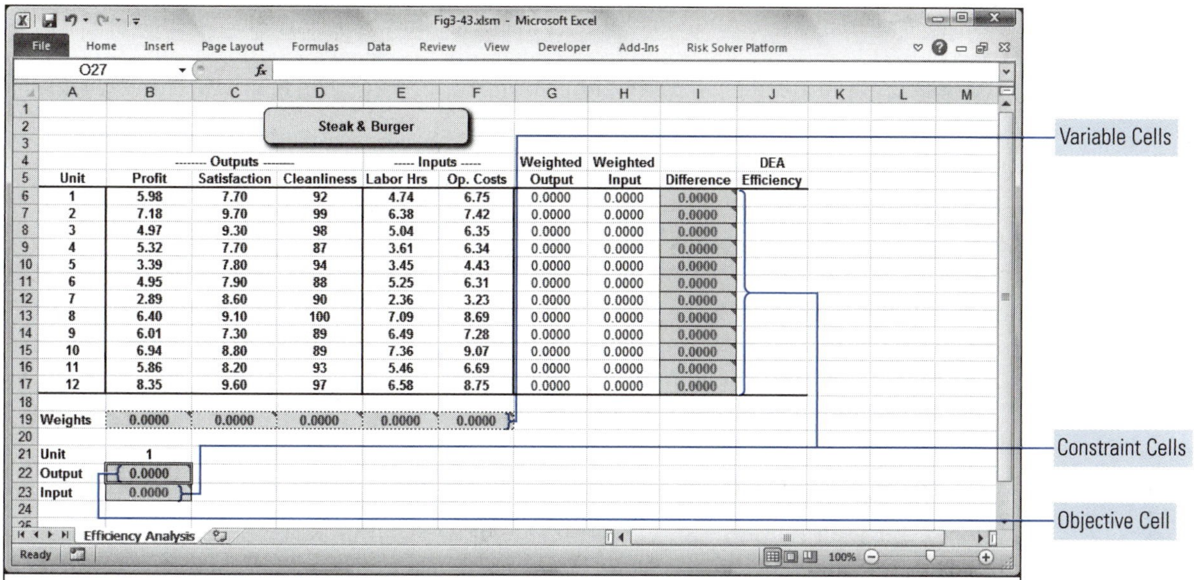

Unit	Profit	Satisfaction	Cleanliness	Labor Hrs	Op. Costs	Weighted Output	Weighted Input	Difference	DEA Efficiency
	Outputs			Inputs					
1	5.98	7.70	92	4.74	6.75	0.0000	0.0000	0.0000	
2	7.18	9.70	99	6.38	7.42	0.0000	0.0000	0.0000	
3	4.97	9.30	98	5.04	6.35	0.0000	0.0000	0.0000	
4	5.32	7.70	87	3.61	6.34	0.0000	0.0000	0.0000	
5	3.39	7.80	94	3.45	4.43	0.0000	0.0000	0.0000	
6	4.95	7.90	88	5.25	6.31	0.0000	0.0000	0.0000	
7	2.89	8.60	90	2.36	3.23	0.0000	0.0000	0.0000	
8	6.40	9.10	100	7.09	8.69	0.0000	0.0000	0.0000	
9	6.01	7.30	89	6.49	7.28	0.0000	0.0000	0.0000	
10	6.94	8.80	89	7.36	9.07	0.0000	0.0000	0.0000	
11	5.86	8.20	93	5.46	6.69	0.0000	0.0000	0.0000	
12	8.35	9.60	97	6.58	8.75	0.0000	0.0000	0.0000	
Weights	0.0000	0.0000	0.0000	0.0000	0.0000				
Unit	1								
Output	0.0000								
Input	0.0000								

Key Cell Formulas

Cell	Formula	Copied to
G6	=SUMPRODUCT(B6:D6,$B$19:$D$19)	G7:G17
H6	=SUMPRODUCT(E6:F6,$E$19:$F$19)	H7:H17
I6	=G6-H6	I7:I17
B22	=INDEX(G6:G17,B21,1)	--
B23	=INDEX(H6:H17,B21,1)	--

In Figure 3.43, cells B19 through F19 are reserved to represent the weights for each of the input and output variables. The weighted output for each unit is computed in column G as follows:

Formula for cell G6: =SUMPRODUCT(B6:D6,$B$19:$D$19)
(Copy to G7 through G17.)

Similarly, the weighted input for each unit is computed in column H as:

Formula for cell H6: =SUMPRODUCT(E6:F6,$E$19:$F$19)
(Copy to H7 through H17.)

The differences between the weighted outputs and weighted inputs are computed in column I. We will instruct Solver to constrain these values to be less than or equal to 0.

Formula for cell I6: =G6-H6
(Copy to I7 through I17.)

The weighted output for unit 1 (computed in cell G6) implements the appropriate objective function and could be used as the objective cell for Solver in this problem. Similarly, the weighted input for unit 1 is computed in cell H6 and could be constrained to equal 1 (as specified by the input constraint for unit 1 earlier). However, because we need to solve a separate LP problem for each of the 12 units, it will be more convenient to handle the objective function and input constraint in a slightly different manner. To this end, we reserve cell B21 to indicate the unit number currently under investigation. Cell B22 contains a formula that returns the weighted output for this unit from the list of weighted outputs in column G.

Formula for cell B22:   =INDEX(G6:G17,B21,1)

In general, the function INDEX(*range,row number,column number*) returns the value in the specified *row number* and *column number* of the given *range*. Because cell B21 contains the number 1, the previous formula returns the value in the first row and first column of the range G6:G17—or the value in cell G6. Thus, as long as the value of cell B21 represents a valid unit number from 1 to 12, the value in cell B22 will represent the appropriate objective function for the DEA model for that unit. Similarly, the input constraint requiring the weighted inputs for the unit in question to equal 1 can be implemented in cell B23 as follows:

Formula for cell B23:   =INDEX(H6:H17,B21,1)

So, for whatever unit number is listed in cell B21, cell B22 represents the appropriate objective function to be maximized, and cell B23 represents the weighted input that must be constrained to equal 1. This arrangement greatly simplifies the process of solving the required series of DEA models.

3.15.5 SOLVING THE PROBLEM

To solve this problem, we specify the objective cell, variable cells, and constraints specified in Figure 3.44. Note that exactly the same Solver settings would be used to find the optimal DEA weights for any other unit. The optimal solution for unit 1 is shown in Figure 3.45. Notice that unit 1 achieves an efficiency score of 0.9667 and is therefore slightly inefficient.

To complete the analysis for the remaining units, Mike could change the value in cell B21 manually to 2, 3, ..., 12 and use Solver to reoptimize the worksheet for each unit and record their efficiency scores in column J. However, if there were 120 units rather than 12, this manual approach would become quite cumbersome. Fortunately, Risk Solver Platform provides a much easier way to automate this process.

FIGURE 3.44

Solver settings and options for the DEA problem

Solver Settings:
Objective: B22 (Max)
Variable cells: B19:F19
Constraints:
I6:I17 <= 0
B23 = 1
B19:F19 >= 0
Solver Options:
Standard LP/Quadratic Engine (Simplex LP)

FIGURE 3.45 *Optimal DEA solution for unit 1*

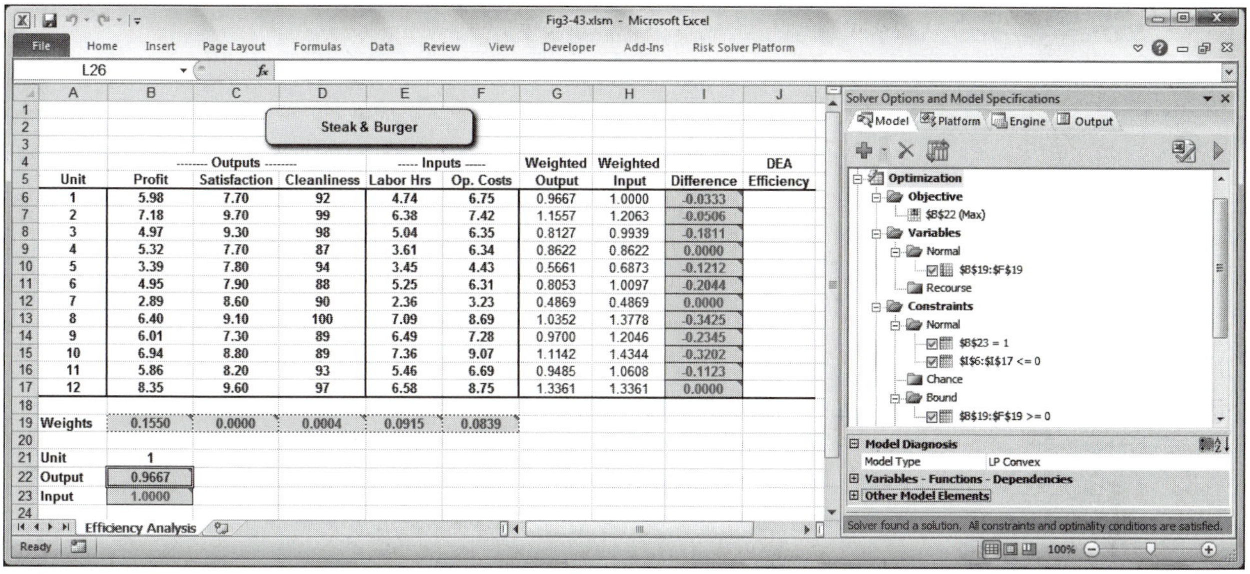

	Outputs		Inputs		Weighted	Weighted		DEA
Unit	Profit	Satisfaction	Cleanliness	Labor Hrs	Op. Costs	Output	Input	Difference	Efficiency
1	5.98	7.70	92	4.74	6.75	0.9667	1.0000	-0.0333	
2	7.18	9.70	99	6.38	7.42	1.1557	1.2063	-0.0506	
3	4.97	9.30	98	5.04	6.35	0.8127	0.9939	-0.1811	
4	5.32	7.70	87	3.61	6.34	0.8622	0.8622	0.0000	
5	3.39	7.80	94	3.45	4.43	0.5661	0.6873	-0.1212	
6	4.95	7.90	88	5.25	6.31	0.8053	1.0097	-0.2044	
7	2.89	8.60	90	2.36	3.23	0.4869	0.4869	0.0000	
8	6.40	9.10	100	7.09	8.69	1.0352	1.3778	-0.3425	
9	6.01	7.30	89	6.49	7.28	0.9700	1.2046	-0.2345	
10	6.94	8.80	89	7.36	9.07	1.1142	1.4344	-0.3202	
11	5.86	8.20	93	5.46	6.69	0.9485	1.0608	-0.1123	
12	8.35	9.60	97	6.58	8.75	1.3361	1.3361	0.0000	
Weights	0.1550	0.0000	0.0004	0.0915	0.0839				
Unit	1								
Output	0.9667								
Input	1.0000								

Figure 3.46 shows a slightly modified version of the spreadsheet for this problem where two key changes have been made. First, the following formula was inserted in cell B21:

Formula for cell B21: =PsiCurrentOpt( )

The PsiCurrentOpt( ) function is not a built-in Excel function but, instead, is part of Risk Solver Platform. As it turns out, we can instruct Risk Solver to perform multiple parameterized optimizations, changing one or more parameters in each optimization run. (Though not used in this example, the PsiOptParam( ) function can be used to change the value of a parameter in a problem as each optimization run is performed.) In this case, the PsiCurrentOpt( ) function entered in cell B21 returns the current optimization number as Risk Solver performs several optimization runs. So if we instruct Risk Solver to perform 12 optimization runs (one for each of the 12 units in our data set), the value in cell B21 will take on the values 1, 2, 3, …, 12 as each of 12 separate optimization runs are carried out.

The second change to the model in Figure 3.46 is the addition of the following formula in column J:

Formula for cell J6: =PsiOptValue($B$22,A6)

(Copy to J7 through J17.)

The PsiOptValue( ) is another custom function that comes with Risk Solver Platform in support of multiple parameterized optimizations. When Risk Solver Platform performs multiple parameterized optimizations, it will compute and store in the computer's memory an optimal solution associated with each of the runs. However, it can only display these solutions on the screen one at a time. The PSIOptValue( ) function allows you to gain access to the values associated with any of the solutions stored in the computer's memory. So the function PSIOptValue($B$22, A6) returns the value associated with a particular cell (in this case, indicated by cell

FIGURE 3.46 *Modifying the model for multiple optimization*

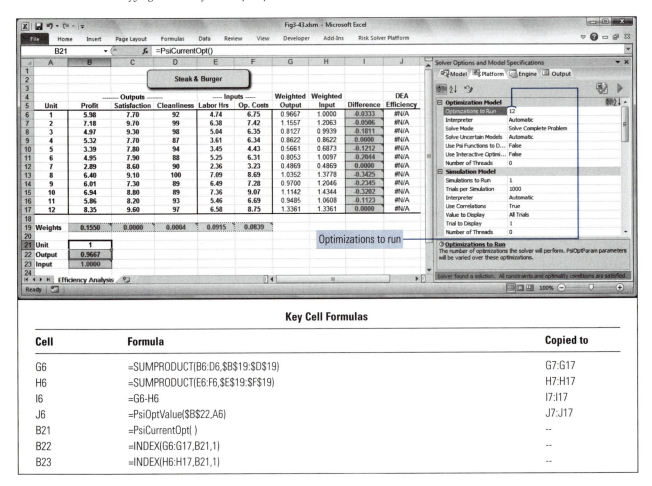

Key Cell Formulas

Cell	Formula	Copied to
G6	=SUMPRODUCT(B6:D6,$B$19:$D$19)	G7:G17
H6	=SUMPRODUCT(E6:F6,$E$19:$F$19)	H7:H17
I6	=G6-H6	I7:I17
J6	=PsiOptValue($B$22,A6)	J7:J17
B21	=PsiCurrentOpt( )	--
B22	=INDEX(G6:G17,B21,1)	--
B23	=INDEX(H6:H17,B21,1)	--

$B$22) for a particular optimization run (in this case, indicated by the value in cell A6). Initially, the values of the PSIOptValue( ) function in column J return error values of "#N/A" because we have not yet asked Solver to perform the multiple optimization runs.

The Solver settings (that is, objective cell, variables cells, and constraint cells) required for this problem are exactly the same as in Figures 3.44 and 3.45. However, in Figure 3.46 note that on the Platform tab in the Risk Solver task pane, the value for the setting "Optimizations to Run" has been changed to 12. Now when Solver solves the problem, it will run a total of 12 optimizations, changing the value in cell B21 from 1 to 12 (via the PSIOptParam( ) function in cell B21), and the resulting optimal objective value for each run will be displayed in column J (via the PSIOptValue( ) functions in column J). Figure 3.47 shows the resulting display.

In Figure 3.47, note that 12 optimizations have been run, and we can inspect any of the 12 solutions by choosing the optimization of interest using the displayed drop-down list on the Risk Solver Platform ribbon. Figure 3.47 currently displays the solution associated with optimization run 10. However, note that the values in column J correspond to the optimal objective values for each of the individual optimization runs.

FIGURE 3.47 *DEA efficiency scores for all the units*

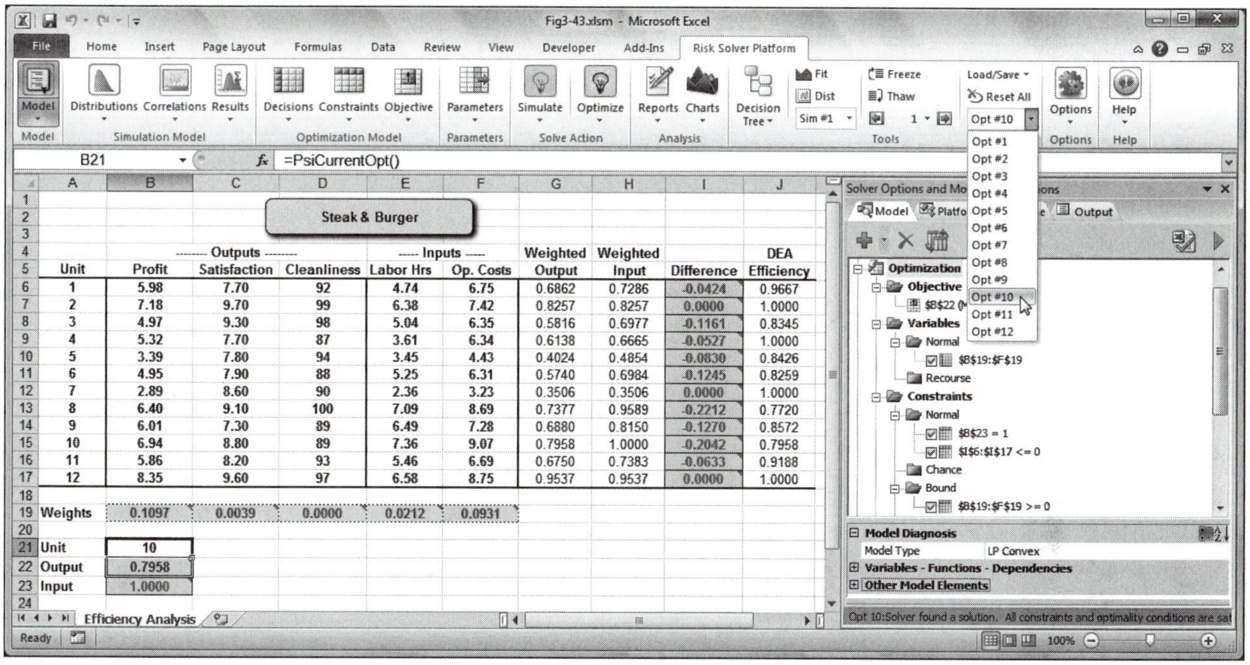

Software Note

By default, when running multiple parameterized optimizations, Risk Solver keeps track of (or monitors) the optimal values of the objective function, decision variables, and any cells referenced by a PSIOptValue( ) function. On the Model tab in the Risk Solver task pane, you will see a Monitor Value property for various model elements. If this property is set to True, Risk Solver will track (or monitor) the resulting values in the associated cells across multiple optimizations.

3.15.6 ANALYZING THE SOLUTION

The solution shown in Figure 3.47 indicates that units 2, 4, 7, and 12 are operating at 100% efficiency (in the DEA sense), while the remaining units are operating less efficiently. Note that an efficiency rating of 100% does not necessarily mean that a unit is operating in the best possible way. It simply means that no linear combination of the other units in the study results in a composite unit that produces at least as much output using the same or less input. On the other hand, for units that are DEA *inefficient*, there is a linear combination of efficient units that results in a composite unit that produces at least as much output using the same or less input than the inefficient unit. The idea in DEA is that an inefficient unit should be able to operate as efficiently as this hypothetical composite unit formed from a linear combination of the efficient units.

For instance, unit 1 has an efficiency score of 96.67% and is, therefore, somewhat inefficient. Figure 3.48 (and file Fig3-48.xlsm that accompanies this book) shows that a weighted average of 26.38% of unit 4, plus 28.15% of unit 7, plus 45.07% of unit 12 produces a hypothetical composite unit with outputs greater than or equal to those of unit 1 and requiring less input than unit 1. The assumption in DEA is that unit 1 should have been able to achieve this same level of performance.

FIGURE 3.48

Example of a composite unit that is more efficient than unit 1

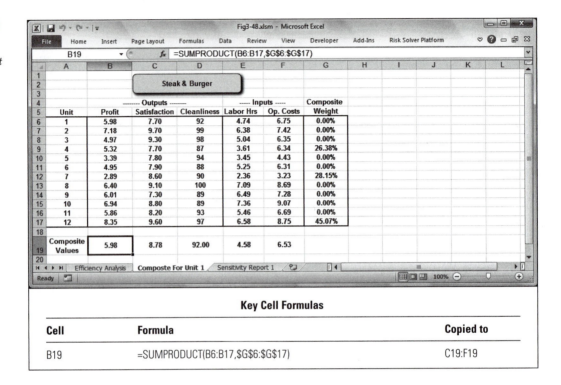

average of 26.38% of unit 4, plus 28.15% of unit 7, plus 45.07% of unit 12 produces a hy-

| | | | | Key Cell Formulas | | | |

Key Cell Formulas

Cell	Formula	Copied to
B19	=SUMPRODUCT(B6:B17,$G$6:$G$17)	C19:F19

For any inefficient unit, you can determine the linear combination of efficient units that results in a more efficient composite unit as follows:

1. Solve the DEA problem for the unit in question.
2. On the Risk Solver ribbon, select Reports, Optimization, Sensitivity.

In the resulting sensitivity report, the absolute value of the Shadow Prices for the "Difference" constraints are the weights that should create a composite unit that is more efficient than the unit in question. The sensitivity report for unit 1 is shown in Figure 3.49. (All the information given on the sensitivity report is covered in detail in Chapter 4.)

3.16 Summary

This chapter described how to formulate an LP problem algebraically, implement it in a spreadsheet, and solve it using Solver. The decision variables in the algebraic formulation of a model correspond to the variable cells in the spreadsheet. The LHS formulas for each constraint in an LP model must be implemented in different cells in the spreadsheet. Also, a cell in the spreadsheet must represent the objective function in the LP model. Thus, there is a direct relationship between the various components of an algebraic formulation of an LP problem and its implementation in a spreadsheet.

FIGURE 3.49 *Sensitivity report for unit 1*

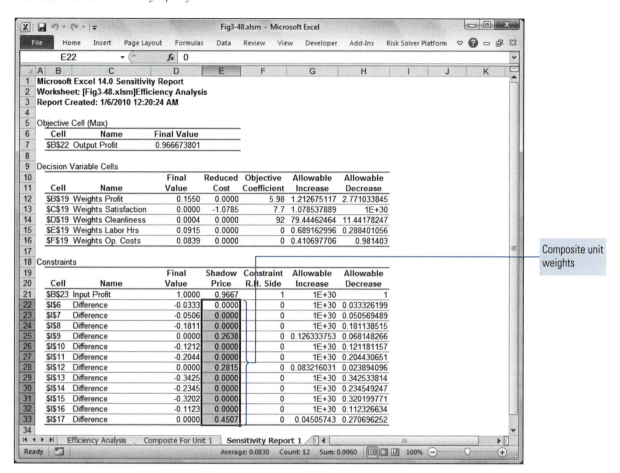

There are many ways a given LP problem can be implemented in a spreadsheet. The process of building spreadsheet models is more an art than a science. A good spreadsheet implementation represents the problem in a way that clearly communicates its purpose, is reliable, auditable, and modifiable.

3.17 References

Charnes, C., et al. *Data Envelopment Analysis: Theory, Methodology, and Application*, New York: Kluwer Academic Publishers, 1996.

Hilal, S., and W. Erickson. "Matching Supplies to Save Lives: Linear Programming the Production of Heart Valves." *Interfaces*, vol. 11, no. 6, 1981.

Lanzenauer, C., et al. "RRSP Flood: LP to the Rescue." *Interfaces*, vol. 17, no. 4, 1987.

McKay, A. "Linear Programming Applications on Microcomputers." *Journal of the Operational Research Society*, vol. 36, July 1985.

Roush, W., et al. "Using Chance-Constrained Programming for Animal Feed Formulation at Agway." *Interfaces*, vol. 24, no. 2, 1994.

Shogan, A. *Management Science*. Englewood Cliffs, NJ: Prentice Hall, 1988.

Subramanian, R., et al., "Coldstart: Fleet Assignment at Delta Airlines," *Interfaces*, vol. 24, no. 1, 1994.

Williams, H. *Model Building in Mathematical Programming*. New York: Wiley, 1990.

THE WORLD OF MANAGEMENT SCIENCE

Optimizing Production, Inventory, and Distribution at Kellogg

The Kellogg Company (http://www.Kellogs.com) is the largest cereal producer in the world and a leading producer of convenience foods. In 1999, Kellogg's world-wide sales totaled nearly $7 billion. Kellogg operates 5 plants in the United States and Canada and has 7 core distribution centers and roughly 15 co-packers that contract to produce or pack some of Kellogg's products. In the cereal business alone, Kellogg must coordinate the production of 80 products while inventorying and distributing more than 600 stock keeping units with roughly 90 production lines and 180 packaging lines. Optimizing this many decision variables is obviously a daunting challenge.

Since 1990, Kellogg has been using a large-scale, multiperiod linear program, called the Kellogg Planning System (KPS), to guide production and distribution decisions. Most large companies like Kellogg employ some sort of enterprise resource planning (ERP). Kellogg's ERP system is a largely custom, home-grown product, and KPS is custom developed tool to complement the ERP system.

An operational-level version of KPS is used at a weekly level of detail to help determine where products are produced and how finished products and in-process products are shipped between plants and distribution centers. A tactical-level version of KPS is used at a monthly level of detail to help establish plant budgets and make capacity and consolidation decisions. Kellogg attributes annual savings of $40–$45 million to the use of the KPS system.

Source: Brown, G., J. Keegan, B. Vigus, and K. Wood, "The Kellogg Company Optimizes Production, Inventory, and Distribution," *Interfaces*, vol. 35, no. 6, 2001.

Questions and Problems

1. In creating the spreadsheet models for the problems in this chapter, cells in the spreadsheets had to be reserved to represent each of the decision variables in the algebraic models. We reserved these cells in the spreadsheets by entering values of zero in them. Why didn't we place some other value or formula in these cells? Would doing so have made any difference?
2. Four goals should be considered when trying to design an effective spreadsheet model: communication, reliability, auditability, and maintainability. We also noted that a spreadsheet design that results in formulas that can be copied is usually more effective than other designs. Briefly describe how using formulas that can be copied supports the four spreadsheet modeling goals.
3. Refer to question 13 at the end of Chapter 2. Implement a spreadsheet model for this problem and solve it using Solver.
4. Refer to question 14 at the end of Chapter 2. Implement a spreadsheet model for this problem and solve it using Solver.
5. Refer to question 17 at the end of Chapter 2. Implement a spreadsheet model for this problem and solve it using Solver.

6. Refer to question 18 at the end of Chapter 2. Implement a spreadsheet model for this problem and solve it using Solver.
7. Refer to question 19 at the end of Chapter 2. Implement a spreadsheet model for this problem and solve it using Solver.
8. Refer to question 20 at the end of Chapter 2. Implement a spreadsheet model for this problem and solve it using Solver.
9. Refer to question 21 at the end of Chapter 2. Implement a spreadsheet model for this problem and solve it using Solver.
10. Refer to question 22 at the end of Chapter 2. Implement a spreadsheet model for this problem and solve it using Solver.
11. Refer to question 23 at the end of Chapter 2. Implement a spreadsheet model for this problem and solve it using Solver.
12. Refer to question 24 at the end of Chapter 2. Implement a spreadsheet model for this problem and solve it using Solver.
13. A furniture manufacturer produces two types of tables (country and contemporary) using three types of machines. The time required to produce the tables on each machine is given in the following table.

Machine	Country	Contemporary	Total Machine Time Available per Week
Router	1.5	2.0	1,000
Sander	3.0	4.5	2,000
Polisher	2.5	1.5	1,500

Country tables sell for $350 and contemporary tables sell for $450. Management has determined that at least 20% of the tables made should be country and at least 30% should be contemporary. How many of each type of table should the company produce if it wants to maximize its revenue?
   a. Formulate an LP model for this problem.
   b. Create a spreadsheet model for this problem and solve it using Solver.
   c. What is the optimal solution?
   d. How will your spreadsheet model differ if there are 25 types of tables and 15 machine processes involved in manufacturing them?
14. Incline Electronics produces three different products in a plant that is open 40 hours per week. Each product requires the following processing times (in hours) on each of three machines.

	Product 1	Product 2	Product 3
Machine 1	2	2	1
Machine 2	3	4	6
Machine 3	4	6	5

Each machine must be run by one of 19 cross-trained workers who are each available 35 hours per week. The plant has 10 type 1 machines available, 6 type 2 machines available, and 8 type 3 machines available. Products 1, 2, and 3 contribute $90, $120, and $150, respectively, in marginal profit per unit produced.
   a. Formulate an LP model for this problem.
   b. Implement your model in a spreadsheet and solve it.
   c. What is the optimal solution?
   d. How many workers should be assigned to each type of machine?

15. Tuckered Outfitters plans to market a custom brand of packaged trail mix. The ingredients for the trail mix will include Raisins, Grain, Chocolate Chips, Peanuts, and Almonds costing, respectively, $2.50, $1.50, $2.00, $3.50, and $3.00 per pound. The vitamin, mineral, and protein content of each of the ingredients (in grams per pound) is summarized in the following table along with the calories per pound of ingredient:

	Raisins	Grain	Chocolate	Peanuts	Almonds
Vitamins	20	10	10	30	20
Minerals	7	4	5	9	3
Protein	4	2	1	10	1
Calories	450	160	500	300	500

The company would like to identify the least costly mix of these ingredients that provides at least 40 grams of vitamins, 15 grams of minerals, 10 grams of protein, and 600 calories per 2-pound package. Additionally, they want each ingredient to account for at least 5% and no more than 50% of the weight of the package.

a. Formulate a LP model for this problem.

b. Implement your model in a spreadsheet and solve it.

c. What is the optimal mix, and how much is the total ingredient cost per package?

16. Aire-Co produces home dehumidifiers at two different plants in Atlanta and Phoenix. The per-unit cost of production in Atlanta and Phoenix is $400 and $360, respectively. Each plant can produce a maximum of 300 units per month. Inventory holding costs are assessed at $30 per unit in beginning inventory each month. Aire-Co estimates the demand for its product to be 300, 400, and 500 units, respectively, over the next three months. Aire-Co wants to be able to meet this demand at minimum cost.

a. Formulate an LP model for this problem.

b. Implement your model in a spreadsheet and solve it.

c. What is the optimal solution?

d. How does the solution change if each plant is required to produce at least 50 units per month?

e. How does the solution change if each plant is required to produce at least 100 units per month?

17. The Molokai Nut Company (MNC) makes four different products from macadamia nuts grown in the Hawaiian Islands: chocolate-coated whole nuts (Whole), chocolate-coated nut clusters (Cluster), chocolate-coated nut crunch bars (Crunch), and plain roasted nuts (Roasted). The company is barely able to keep up with the increasing demand for these products. However, increasing raw material prices and foreign competition are forcing MNC to watch its margins to ensure it is operating in the most efficient manner possible. To meet marketing demands for the coming week, MNC needs to produce at least 1,000 pounds of the Whole product, between 400 and 500 pounds of the Cluster product, no more than 150 pounds of the Crunch product, and no more than 200 pounds of Roasted product. Each pound of the Whole, Cluster, Crunch, and Roasted product contains, respectively, 60%, 40%, 20%, and 100% macadamia nuts with the remaining weight made up of chocolate coating. The company has 1,100 pounds of nuts and 800 pounds of chocolate available for use in the next week. The various products are made using four different machines that hull the nuts, roast the nuts, coat the nuts in chocolate (if needed), and package the products. The following table summaries the time required by each product on each machine. Each machine has 60 hours of time available in the coming week.

Machine	Minutes Required per Pound			
	Whole	Cluster	Crunch	Roasted
Hulling	1.00	1.00	1.00	1.00
Roasting	2.00	1.50	1.00	1.75
Coating	1.00	0.70	0.20	0.00
Packaging	2.50	1.60	1.25	1.00

The selling price and variable cost associated with each pound of product is summarized in the following table:

	Per Pound Revenue and Costs			
	Whole	Cluster	Crunch	Roasted
Selling Price	$5.00	$4.00	$3.20	$4.50
Variable Cost	$3.15	$2.60	$2.16	$3.10

a. Formulate an LP model for this problem.
b. Create a spreadsheet model for this problem and solve it using Solver.
c. What is the optimal solution?

18. A company is trying to determine how to allocate its $145,000 advertising budget for a new product. The company is considering newspaper ads and television commercials as its primary means for advertising. The following table summarizes the costs of advertising in these different media and the number of new customers reached by increasing amounts of advertising.

Media & # of Ads	# of New Customers Reached	Cost per Ad
Newspaper: 1–10	900	$1,000
Newspaper: 11–20	700	$900
Newspaper: 21–30	400	$800
Television: 1–5	10,000	$12,000
Television: 6–10	7,500	$10,000
Television: 11–15	5,000	$8,000

For instance, each of the first 10 ads the company places in newspapers will cost $1,000 and is expected to reach 900 new customers. Each of the next 10 newspaper ads will cost $900 and is expected to reach 700 new customers. Note that the number of new customers reached by increasing amounts of advertising decreases as the advertising saturates the market. Assume the company will purchase no more than 30 newspaper ads and no more than 15 television ads.

a. Formulate an LP model for this problem to maximize the number of new customers reached by advertising.
b. Implement your model in a spreadsheet and solve it.
c. What is the optimal solution?
d. Suppose the number of new customers reached by 11–20 newspaper ads is 400, and the number of new customers reached by 21–30 newspaper ads is 700. Make these changes in your spreadsheet, and reoptimize the problem. What is the new optimal solution? What (if anything) is wrong with this solution and why?

19. The Shop at Home Network sells various household goods during live television broadcasts. The company owns several warehouses to hold many of the goods it

sells but also leases extra warehouse space when needed. During the next five months, the company expects it will need to lease the following amounts of extra warehouse space:

Month	1	2	3	4	5
Square Feet Needed	20,000	30,000	40,000	35,000	50,000

At the beginning of any month, the company can lease extra space for one or more months at the following costs:

Lease Term (months)	1	2	3	4	5
Cost per Sq. Ft. Leased	$55	$95	$130	$155	$185

So, for instance, at the start of month 1, the company can lease as much space as it wants for four months at a cost of $155 per square foot. Similarly, at the start of month 3, the company can lease any amount of space for two months at a cost of $95 per square foot. The company wants to determine the least costly way of meeting their warehousing needs over the coming five months.

a. Formulate an LP model for this problem.
b. Create a spreadsheet model for this problem, and solve it using Solver.
c. What is the optimal solution?
d. How much would it cost the company to meet its space needs if in each month it leases for one month exactly the amount of space required for the month?

20. A bank has $650,000 in assets to allocate among investments in bonds, home mortgages, car loans, and personal loans. Bonds are expected to produce a return of 10%, mortgages 8.5%, car loans 9.5%, and personal loans 12.5%. To make sure the portfolio is not too risky, the bank wants to restrict personal loans to no more than the 25% of the total portfolio. The bank also wants to ensure that more money is invested in mortgages than personal loans. The bank also wants to invest more in bonds than personal loans.

a. Formulate an LP model for this problem with the objective of maximizing the expected return on the portfolio.
b. Implement your model in a spreadsheet, and solve it.
c. What it the optimal solution?

21. Valu-Com Electronics manufactures five different models of telecommunications interface cards for PCs and laptops. As summarized in the following table, each of these devices requires differing amounts of printed circuit board, resistors, memory chips, and assembly.

	Per Unit Requirements				
	HyperLink	FastLink	SpeedLink	MicroLink	EtherLink
Printed Circuit Board (square inches)	20	15	10	8	5
Resistors	28	24	18	12	16
Memory Chips	8	8	4	4	6
Assembly Labor (in hours)	0.75	0.6	0.5	0.65	1

The unit wholesale price and manufacturing cost for each model are as follows.

Per Unit Revenues and Costs

	HyperLink	FastLink	SpeedLink	MicroLink	EtherLink
Wholesale Price	$189	$149	$129	$169	$139
Manufacturing Cost	$136	$101	$ 96	$137	$101

In its next production period, Valu-Com has 80,000 square inches of PC board, 100,000 resistors, 30,000 memory chips, and 5,000 hours of assembly time available. The company can sell all the product it can manufacture, but the marketing department wants to be sure the company produces at least 500 units of each product and at least twice as many FastLink cards as HyperLink cards while maximizing profit.
a. Formulate an LP model for this problem.
b. Create a spreadsheet model for this problem, and solve it using Solver.
c. What is the optimal solution?
d. Could Valu-Com make more money if it schedules assembly workers to work overtime?

22. A trust officer at the Blacksburg National Bank needs to determine how to invest $100,000 in the following collection of bonds to maximize the annual return.

Bond	Annual Return	Maturity	Risk	Tax-Free
A	9.5%	Long	High	Yes
B	8.0%	Short	Low	Yes
C	9.0%	Long	Low	No
D	9.0%	Long	High	Yes
E	9.0%	Short	High	No

The officer wants to invest at least 50% of the money in short-term issues and no more than 50% in high-risk issues. At least 30% of the funds should go in tax-free investments, and at least 40% of the total annual return should be tax free.
a. Formulate an LP model for this problem.
b. Create a spreadsheet model for this problem, and solve it using Solver.
c. What is the optimal solution?

23. The Weedwacker Company manufactures two types of lawn trimmers: an electric model and a gas model. The company has contracted to supply a national discount retail chain with a total of 30,000 electric trimmers and 15,000 gas trimmers. However, Weedwacker's production capability is limited in three departments: production, assembly, and packaging. The following table summarizes the hours of processing time available and the processing time required by each department, for both types of trimmers:

Hours Required per Trimmer

	Electric	Gas	Hours Available
Production	0.20	0.40	10,000
Assembly	0.30	0.50	15,000
Packaging	0.10	0.10	5,000

The company makes its electric trimmer in-house for $55 and its gas trimmer for $85. Alternatively, it can buy electric and gas trimmers from another source for $67 and $95, respectively. How many gas and electric trimmers should Weedwacker make, and how many should it buy from its competitor in order to fulfill its contract in the least costly manner?

   a. Formulate an LP model for this problem.
   b. Create a spreadsheet model for this problem, and solve it using Solver.
   c. What is the optimal solution?

24. A manufacturer of prefabricated homes has decided to subcontract four components of the homes. Several companies are interested in receiving this business, but none can handle more than one subcontract. The bids made by the companies for the various subcontracts are summarized in the following table.

**Bids by Companies
(in \$1,000s) for Various Subcontracts**

	Company			
Component	A	B	C	D
1	185	225	193	207
2	200	190	175	225
3	330	320	315	300
4	375	389	425	445

Assuming all the companies can perform each subcontract equally well, to which company should each subcontract be assigned if the home manufacturer wants to minimize payments to the subcontractors?
   a. Formulate an LP model for this problem.
   b. Create a spreadsheet model for this problem, and solve it using Solver.
   c. What is the optimal solution?

25. Tarmac Chemical Corporation produces a special chemical compound—called CHEMIX—that is used extensively in high school chemistry classes. This compound must contain at least 20% sulfur, at least 30% iron oxide, and at least 30% but no more than 45% potassium. Tarmac's marketing department has estimated that it will need at least 600 pounds of this compound to meet the expected demand during the coming school session. Tarmac can buy three compounds to mix together to produce CHEMIX. The makeup of these compounds is shown in the following table.

Compound	Sulfur	Iron Oxide	Potassium
1	20%	60%	20%
2	40%	30%	30%
3	10%	40%	50%

Compounds 1, 2, and 3 cost \$5.00, \$5.25, and \$5.50 per pound, respectively. Tarmac wants to use an LP model to determine the least costly way of producing enough CHEMIX to meet the demand expected for the coming year.
   a. Formulate an LP model for this problem.
   b. Create a spreadsheet model for this problem, and solve it using Solver.
   c. What is the optimal solution?

26. Holiday Fruit Company buys oranges and processes them into gift fruit baskets and fresh juice. The company grades the fruit it buys on a scale from 1 (lowest quality) to 5 (highest quality). The following table summarizes Holiday's current inventory of fruit.

Grade	Supply (1000s of lbs)
1	90
2	225
3	300
4	100
5	75

Each pound of oranges devoted to fruit baskets results in a marginal profit of $2.50, whereas each pound devoted to fresh juice results in a marginal profit of $1.75. Holiday wants the fruit in its baskets to have an average quality grade of at least 3.75 and its fresh juice to have an average quality grade of at least 2.50.

a. Formulate an optimization model for this problem.
b. Implement your model in a spreadsheet, and solve it.
c. What is the optimal solution?

27. Riverside Oil Company in eastern Kentucky produces regular and supreme gasoline. Each barrel of regular sells for $21 and must have an octane rating of at least 90. Each barrel of supreme sells for $25 and must have an octane rating of at least 97. Each of these types of gasoline are manufactured by mixing different quantities of the following three inputs:

Input	Cost per Barrel	Octane Rating	Barrels Available (in 1000s)
1	$17.25	100	150
2	$15.75	87	350
3	$17.75	110	300

Riverside has orders for 300,000 barrels of regular and 450,000 barrels of supreme. How should the company allocate the available inputs to the production of regular and supreme gasoline to maximize profits?

a. Formulate an LP model for this problem.
b. Create a spreadsheet model for this problem, and solve it using Solver.
c. What is the optimal solution?

28. Maintenance at a major theme park in central Florida is an ongoing process that occurs 24 hours a day. Because it is a long drive from most residential areas to the park, employees do not like to work shifts of fewer than eight hours. These eight-hour shifts start every four hours throughout the day. The number of maintenance workers needed at different times throughout the day varies. The following table summarizes the minimum number of employees needed in each four-hour time period.

Time Period	Minimum Employees Needed
12 a.m. to 4 a.m.	90
4 a.m. to 8 a.m.	215
8 a.m. to 12 p.m.	250
12 p.m. to 4 p.m.	165
4 p.m. to 8 p.m.	300
8 p.m. to 12 a.m.	125

The maintenance supervisor wants to determine the minimum number of employees to schedule that meets the minimum staffing requirements.

a. Formulate an LP model for this problem.
b. Create a spreadsheet model for this problem, and solve it using Solver.
c. What is the optimal solution?

29. Radmore Memorial Hospital has a problem in its fluids analysis lab. The lab has available three machines that analyze various fluid samples. Recently, the demand for analyzing blood samples has increased so much that the lab director is having difficulty getting all the samples analyzed quickly enough and still completing the other fluid work that comes into the lab. The lab works with five types of blood specimens. Any machine can be used to process any of the specimens. However, the amount of time required by each machine varies depending on the type of specimen being analyzed. These times are summarized in the following table.

**Required Specimen
Processing Time in Minutes**

	Specimen Type				
Machine	1	2	3	4	5
A	3	4	4	5	3
B	5	3	5	4	5
C	2	5	3	3	4

Each machine can be used a total of eight hours a day. Blood samples collected on a given day arrive at the lab and are stored overnight and processed the next day. So, at the beginning of each day, the lab director must determine how to allocate the various samples to the machines for analysis. This morning, the lab has 80 type-1 specimens, 75 type-2 specimens, 80 type-3 specimens, 120 type-4 specimens, and 60 type-5 specimens awaiting processing. The lab director wants to know how many of each type of specimen should be analyzed on each machine in order to minimize the total time the machines are devoted to analyzing blood samples.

a. Formulate an LP model for this problem.

b. Create a spreadsheet model for this problem, and solve it using Solver.

c. What is the optimal solution?

d. How much processing time will be available on each machine if this solution is implemented?

e. How would the model and solution change if the lab director wanted to balance the use of each machine so that each machine were used approximately the same amount of time?

30. Virginia Tech operates its own power generating plant. The electricity generated by this plant supplies power to the university and to local businesses and residences in the Blacksburg area. The plant burns three types of coal, which produce steam that drives the turbines that generate the electricity. The Environmental Protection Agency (EPA) requires that for each ton of coal burned, the emissions from the coal furnace smoke stacks contain no more than 2,500 parts per million (ppm) of sulfur and no more than 2.8 kilograms (kg) of coal dust. The following table summarizes the amounts of sulfur, coal dust, and steam that result from burning a ton of each type of coal.

Coal	Sulfur (in ppm)	Coal Dust (in kg)	Pounds of Steam Produced
1	1,100	1.7	24,000
2	3,500	3.2	36,000
3	1,300	2.4	28,000

The three types of coal can be mixed and burned in any combination. The resulting emission of sulfur or coal dust and the pounds of steam produced by any mixture are given as the weighted average of the values shown in the table for each type of coal. For example, if the coals are mixed to produce a blend that consists of 35% of coal 1, 40% of coal 2, and 25% of coal 3, the sulfur emission (in ppm) resulting from burning one ton of this blend is:

$$0.35 \times 1,100 + 0.40 \times 3,500 + 0.25 \times 1,300 = 2,110$$

The manager of this facility wants to determine the blend of coal that will produce the maximum pounds of steam per ton without violating the EPA requirements.

a. Formulate an LP model for this problem.

b. Create a spreadsheet model for this problem, and solve it using Solver.

c. What is the optimal solution?

d. If the furnace can burn up to 30 tons of coal per hour, what is the maximum amount of steam that can be produced per hour?

31. Kentwood Electronics manufactures three components for stereo systems: CD players, amplifiers, and stereo tuners. The wholesale price and manufacturing cost of each item are shown in the following table.

Component	Wholesale Price	Manufacturing Cost
CD Player	$150	$75
Amplifier	$85	$35
Stereo Tuner	$70	$30

Each CD player produced requires 3 hours of assembly; each amplifier requires 2 hours of assembly; and each tuner requires 1 hour of assembly. The marketing department has indicated that it can sell no more than 150,000 CD players, 100,000 amplifiers, and 90,000 stereo tuners. However, the demand is expected to be at least 50,000 units of each item, and Kentwood wants to meet this demand. If Kentwood has 400,000 hours of assembly time available, how many CD players, amplifiers, and stereo tuners should it produce in order to maximize profits while meeting the minimum demand figures?

a. Formulate an LP model for this problem.

b. Create a spreadsheet model for this problem, and solve it using Solver.

c. What is the optimal solution?

32. The Rent-A-Dent car rental company allows its customers to pick up a rental car at one location and return it to any of its locations. Currently, two locations (1 and 2) have 16 and 18 surplus cars, respectively, and four locations (3, 4, 5, and 6) each need 10 cars. The costs of getting the surplus cars from locations 1 and 2 to the other locations are summarized in the following table.

	Costs of Transporting Cars Between Locations			
	Location 3	**Location 4**	**Location 5**	**Location 6**
Location 1	$54	$17	$23	$30
Location 2	$24	$18	$19	$31

Because 34 surplus cars are available at locations 1 and 2, and 40 cars are needed at locations 3, 4, 5, and 6, some locations will not receive as many cars as they need. However, management wants to make sure that all the surplus cars are sent where they are needed and that each location needing cars receives at least five.

a. Formulate an LP model for this problem.

b. Create a spreadsheet model for this problem, and solve it using Solver.

c. What is the optimal solution?

33. The Sentry Lock Corporation manufactures a popular commercial security lock at plants in Macon, Louisville, Detroit, and Phoenix. The per-unit cost of production at each plant is $35.50, $37.50, $39.00, and $36.25, respectively, while the annual production capacity at each plant is 18,000, 15,000, 25,000, and 20,000, respectively. Sentry's locks are sold to retailers through wholesale distributors in seven cities across the United States. The unit cost of shipping from each plant to each distributor is summarized in the following table along with the forecasted demand from each distributor for the coming year.

Plants	Unit Shipping Cost to Distributor in						
	Tacoma	San Diego	Dallas	Denver	St. Louis	Tampa	Baltimore
Macon	$2.50	$2.75	$1.75	$2.00	$2.10	$1.80	$1.65
Louisville	$1.85	$1.90	$1.50	$1.60	$1.00	$1.90	$1.85
Detroit	$2.30	$2.25	$1.85	$1.25	$1.50	$2.25	$2.00
Phoenix	$1.90	$0.90	$1.60	$1.75	$2.00	$2.50	$2.65
Demand	8,500	14,500	13,500	12,600	18,000	15,000	9,000

Sentry wants to determine the least expensive way of manufacturing and shipping locks from its plants to the distributors. Because the total demand from distributors exceeds the total production capacity for all the plants, Sentry realizes it will not be able to satisfy all the demand for its product but wants to make sure each distributor will have the opportunity to fill at least 80% of the orders received.

a. Create a spreadsheet model for this problem, and solve it.

b. What is the optimal solution?

34. A paper recycling company converts newspaper, mixed paper, white office paper, and cardboard into pulp for newsprint, packaging paper, and print stock quality paper. The following table summarizes the yield for each kind of pulp recovered from each ton of recycled material.

	Recycling Yield		
	Newsprint	Packaging	Print Stock
Newspaper	85%	80%	—
Mixed Paper	90%	80%	70%
White Office Paper	90%	85%	80%
Cardboard	80%	70%	—

For instance, a ton of newspaper can be recycled using a technique that yields 0.85 tons of newsprint pulp. Alternatively, a ton of newspaper can be recycled using a technique that yields 0.80 tons of packaging paper. Similarly, a ton of cardboard can be recycled to yield 0.80 tons of newsprint or 0.70 tons of packaging paper pulp. Note that newspaper and cardboard cannot be converted to print stock pulp using the techniques available to the recycler.

The cost of processing each ton of raw material into the various types of pulp is summarized in the following table along with the amount of each of the four raw materials that can be purchased and their costs.

	Processing Costs per Ton			Purchase Cost Per Ton	Tons Available
	Newsprint	Packaging	Print Stock		
Newspaper	$6.50	$11.00	—	$15	600
Mixed Paper	$9.75	$12.25	$9.50	$16	500
White Office Paper	$4.75	$7.75	$8.50	$19	300
Cardboard	$7.50	$8.50	—	$17	400

The recycler wants to determine the least costly way of producing 500 tons of newsprint pulp, 600 tons of packaging paper pulp, and 300 tons of print stock quality pulp.

a. Create a spreadsheet model for this problem, and solve it.

b. What is the optimal solution?

35. A winery has the following capacity to produce an exclusive dinner wine at either of its two vineyards at the indicated costs:

Vineyard	Capacity	Cost per Bottle
1	3,500 bottles	$23
2	3,100 bottles	$25

Four Italian restaurants around the country are interested in purchasing this wine. Because the wine is exclusive, they all want to buy as much as they need but will take whatever they can get. The maximum amounts required by the restaurants and the prices they are willing to pay are summarized in the following table.

Restaurant	Maximum Demand	Price
1	1,800 bottles	$69
2	2,300 bottles	$67
3	1,250 bottles	$70
4	1,750 bottles	$66

The costs of shipping a bottle from the vineyards to the restaurants are summarized in the following table.

	Restaurant			
Vineyard	1	2	3	4
1	$7	$8	$13	$9
2	$12	$6	$8	$7

The winery needs to determine the production and shipping plan that allows it to maximize its profits on this wine.
   a. Formulate an LP model for this problem.
   b. Create a spreadsheet model for this problem, and solve it using Solver.
   c. What is the optimal solution?
36. The Pitts Barbecue Company makes three kinds of barbecue sauce: Extra Hot, Hot, and Mild. Pitts' vice president of marketing estimates that the company can sell 8,000 cases of its Extra Hot sauce plus 10 extra cases for every dollar it spends promoting this sauce; 10,000 cases of Hot sauce plus 8 extra cases for every dollar spent promoting this sauce; and 12,000 cases of its Mild sauce plus 5 extra cases for every dollar spent promoting this sauce. Although each barbecue sauce sells for $10 per case, the cost of producing the different types of sauce varies. It costs the company $6 to produce a case of Extra Hot sauce, $5.50 to produce a case of Hot sauce, and $5.25 to produce a case of Mild sauce. The president of the company wants to make sure the company manufactures at least the minimum amounts of each sauce that the marketing vice president thinks the company can sell. A budget of $25,000 total has been approved for promoting these items of which at least $5,000 must be spent advertising each item. How many cases of each type of sauce should be made, and how do you suggest that the company allocate the promotional budget to maximize profits?
   a. Formulate an LP model for this problem.
   b. Create a spreadsheet model for this problem, and solve it using Solver.
   c. What is the optimal solution?
37. Acme Manufacturing makes a variety of household appliances at a single manufacturing facility. The expected demand for one of these appliances during the next four months is shown in the following table along with the expected production costs and the expected capacity for producing these items.

	Month			
	1	**2**	**3**	**4**
Demand	420	580	310	540
Production Cost	$49.00	$45.00	$46.00	$47.00
Production Capacity	500	520	450	550

Acme estimates it costs $1.50 per month for each unit of this appliance carried in inventory (estimated by averaging the beginning and ending inventory levels each month). Currently, Acme has 120 units in inventory on hand for this product. To maintain a level workforce, the company wants to produce at least 400 units per month. The company also wants to maintain a safety stock of at least 50 units per month. Acme wants to determine how many of each appliance to manufacture during each of the next four months to meet the expected demand at the lowest possible total cost.

a. Formulate an LP model for this problem.
b. Create a spreadsheet model for this problem, and solve it using Solver.
c. What is the optimal solution?
d. How much money could Acme save if they were willing to drop the restriction about producing at least 400 units per month?

38. Paul Bergey is in charge of loading cargo ships for International Cargo Company (ICC) at the port in Newport News, Virginia. Paul is preparing a loading plan for an ICC freighter destined for Ghana. An agricultural commodities dealer wants to transport the following products aboard this ship.

Commodity	Amount Available (tons)	Volume per Ton (cubic feet)	Profit per Ton ($)
1	4,800	40	70
2	2,500	25	50
3	1,200	60	60
4	1,700	55	80

Paul can elect to load any and/or all of the available commodities. However, the ship has three cargo holds with the following capacity restrictions:

Cargo Hold	Weight Capacity (tons)	Volume Capacity (cubic feet)
Forward	3,000	145,000
Center	6,000	180,000
Rear	4,000	155,000

More than one type of commodity can be placed in the same cargo hold. However, because of balance considerations, the weight in the forward cargo hold must be within 10% of the weight in the rear cargo hold, and the center cargo hold must be between 40% to 60% of the total weight on board.

a. Formulate an LP model for this problem.
b. Create a spreadsheet model for this problem, and solve it using Solver.
c. What is the optimal solution?

39. The Pelletier Corporation has just discovered that it will not have enough warehouse space for the next five months. The additional warehouse space requirements for this period are listed in the following table.

Month	1	2	3	4	5
Additional Space Needed (in 1,000 sq ft)	25	10	20	10	5

To cover its space requirements, the firm plans to lease additional warehouse space on a short-term basis. Over the next five months, a local warehouse has agreed to lease Pelletier any amount of space for any number of months according to the following cost schedule.

Length of Lease (in months)	1	2	3	4	5
Cost per 1,000 square feet	$300	$525	$775	$850	$975

This schedule of leasing options is available to Pelletier at the beginning of each of the next five months. For example, the company could elect to lease 5,000 square feet for four months beginning in month 1 (at a cost of $850 × 5) and lease 10,000 square feet for two months beginning in month 3 (at a cost of $525 × 10).

a. Formulate an LP model for this problem.
b. Create a spreadsheet model for this problem, and solve it using Solver.
c. What is the optimal solution?

40. Carter Enterprises is involved in the soybean business in South Carolina, Alabama, and Georgia. The president of the company, Earl Carter, goes to a commodity sale once a month where he buys and sells soybeans in bulk. Carter uses a local warehouse for storing his soybean inventory. This warehouse charges $10 per average ton of soybeans stored per month (based on the average of the beginning and ending inventory each month). The warehouse guarantees Carter the capacity to store up to 400 tons of soybeans at the end of each month. Carter has estimated what he believes the price per ton of soybeans will be during each of the next six months. These prices are summarized in the following table.

Month	1	2	3	4	5	6
Price per Ton	$135	$110	$150	$175	$130	$145

Assume Carter currently has 70 tons of soybeans stored in the warehouse. How many tons of soybeans should Carter buy and sell during each of the next six months to maximize his profit trading soybeans?

a. Formulate an LP model for this problem.
b. Create a spreadsheet model for this problem, and solve it using Solver.
c. What is the optimal solution?

41. Jack Potts recently won $1,000,000 in Las Vegas and is trying to determine how to invest his winnings. He has narrowed his decision down to five investments, which are summarized in the following table.

	Summary of Cash Inflows and Outflows (at beginning of years)			
	1	2	3	4
A	−1	0.50	0.80	
B		−1	⟷	1.25
C	−1	⟷	⟷	1.35
D			−1	1.13
E	−1	⟷	1.27	

If Jack invests $1 in investment A at the beginning of year 1, he will receive $0.50 at the beginning of year 2 and another $0.80 at the beginning of year 3. Alternatively, he can invest $1 in investment B at the beginning of year 2 and receive $1.25 at the beginning of year 4. Entries of "⟷" in the table indicate times when no cash inflows or outflows can occur. At the beginning of any year, Jack can place money in a money market account that is expected to yield 8% per year. He wants to keep at least $50,000 in the money market account at all times and doesn't want to place any more than $500,000 in any single investment. How would you advise Jack to invest his winnings if he wants to maximize the amount of money he'll have at the beginning of year 4?

a. Formulate an LP model for this problem.
b. Create a spreadsheet model for this problem, and solve it using Solver.
c. What is the optimal solution?

42. Fred and Sally Merrit recently inherited a substantial amount of money from a deceased relative. They want to use part of this money to establish an account to pay for their daughter's college education. Their daughter, Lisa, will be starting college five years from now. The Merrits estimate that her first year college expenses will amount to $12,000 and increase $2,000 per year during each of the remaining three years of her education. The following investments are available to the Merrits:

Investment	Available	Matures	Return at Maturity
A	Every year	1 year	6%
B	1, 3, 5, 7	2 years	14%
C	1, 4	3 years	18%
D	1	7 years	65%

The Merrits want to determine an investment plan that will provide the necessary funds to cover Lisa's anticipated college expenses with the smallest initial investment.

a. Formulate an LP model for this problem.
b. Create a spreadsheet model for this problem, and solve it using Solver.
c. What is the optimal solution?

43. Refer to the previous question. Suppose the investments available to the Merrits have the following levels of risk associated with them.

Investment	A	B	C	D
Risk Factor	1	3	6	8

If the Merrits want the weighted average risk level of their investments to not exceed 4, how much money will they need to set aside for Lisa's education, and how should they invest it?

a. Formulate an LP model for this problem.
b. Create a spreadsheet model for this problem, and solve it using Solver.
c. What is the optimal solution?

44. WinterWearhouse operates a clothing store specializing in ski apparel. Given the seasonal nature of their business, there is often somewhat of an imbalance between when bills must be paid for inventory purchased and when the goods are actually sold and cash is received. Over the next six months, the company expects cash receipts and requirements for bill paying as follows:

	Month					
	1	2	3	4	5	6
Cash Receipts	$100,000	$225,000	$275,000	$350,000	$475,000	$625,000
Bills Due	$400,000	$500,000	$600,000	$300,000	$200,000	$100,000

The company likes to maintain a cash balance of at least $20,000 and currently has $100,000 cash on hand. The company can borrow money from a local bank for the following term/rate structure: 1 month at 1%, 2 months at 1.75%, 3 months at 2.49%, 4 months at 3.22%, and 5 months at 3.94%. When needed, money is borrowed at the end of a month and repaid, with interest, at the end of the month in which the obligation is due. For instance, if the company borrows $10,000 for 2 months in month 3, they would have to pay back $10,175 at the end of month 5.

a. Create a spreadsheet model for this problem, and solve it.
b. What is the optimal solution?
c. Suppose its bank limits WinterWearhouse to borrowing no more than $100,000 at each level in the term/rate structure. How would this restriction change the optimal solution?

45. The accounting firm of Coopers & Andersen is conducting a benchmarking survey to assess the satisfaction level of their clients versus clients served by competing accounting firms. The clients are divided into four groups:

> Group 1: Large clients of Coopers & Andersen
> Group 2: Small clients of Coopers & Andersen
> Group 3: Large clients of other accounting firms
> Group 4: Small clients of other accounting firms

A total of 4,000 companies are being surveyed either by telephone or via a two-way web cam interviews. The costs associated with surveying the different types of companies are summarized in the following table:

	Survey Costs	
Group	**Telephone**	**Web Cam**
1	$18	$40
2	$14	$35
3	$25	$60
4	$20	$45

Coopers & Andersen wants the survey to carry out the survey in the least costly way that meets the following conditions:

- At least 10% but not more than 50% of the total companies surveyed should come from each group.
- At least 50% of the companies surveyed should be clients of Coopers & Andersen.
- At least 25% of the surveys should be done via web cam.
- At least 50% of the large clients of Coopers & Anderson who are surveyed should be done via web cam.
- A maximum of 40% of those surveyed may be small companies.
- A maximum of 25% of the small companies surveyed should be done via web cam.

a. Formulate an LP model for this problem.
b. Create a spreadsheet model for this problem, and solve it using Solver.
c. What is the optimal solution?

46. The CFO for Eagle's Beach Wear and Gift Shop is in the process of planning for the company's cash flows for the next six months. The following table summarizes the expected accounts receivables and planned payments for each of these months (in $100,000s).

	January	February	March	April	May	June
Accounts Receivable Balances Due	1.50	1.00	1.40	2.30	2.00	1.00
Planned Payments (net of discounts)	1.80	1.60	2.20	1.20	0.80	1.20

The company currently has a beginning cash balance of $40,000 and desires to maintain a balance of at least $25,000 in cash at the end of each month. To accomplish this, the company has a number of ways of obtaining short-term funds:

1. *Delay Payments.* In any month, the company's suppliers permit it to delay any or all payments for one month. However, for this consideration, the company forfeits a 2% discount that normally applies when payments are made on time. (Loss of this 2% discount is, in effect, a financing cost.)
2. *Borrow Against Accounts Receivables.* In any month, the company's bank will loan it up to 75% of the accounts receivable balances due that month. These loans must be repaid in the following month and incur an interest charge of 1.5%.
3. *Short-Term Loan.* At the beginning of January, the company's bank will also give it a 6-month loan to be repaid in a lump sum at the end of June. Interest on this loan is 1% per month and is payable at the end of each month.

Assume the company earns 0.5% interest each month on cash held at the beginning of the month. Create a spreadsheet model the company can use to determine the least costly cash management plan (that is, minimal net financing costs) for this six-month period. What is the optimal solution?

47. The DotCom Corporation is implementing a pension plan for its employees. The company intends to start funding the plan with a deposit of $50,000 on January 1, 2008. It plans to invest an additional $12,000 one year later and continue making additional investments (increasing by $2,000 per year) on January 1 of each year from 2010 through 2022. To fund these payments, the company plans to purchase a number of bonds. Bond 1 costs $970 per unit and will pay a $65 coupon on January 1 of each year from 2009 through 2012 plus a final payment of $1,065 on January 1, 2013. Bond 2 costs $980 and will pay a $73 coupon on January 1 of each year from 2009 through 2018 plus a final payment of $1,073 on January 1, 2019. Bond 3 costs $1,025 and will pay a $85 coupon on January 1 of each year from 2009 through 2021 plus a final payment of $1,085 on January 1, 2022. The company's cash holdings earn an interest rate of 4.5%. Assume the company wants to purchase bonds on January 1, 2008 and cannot buy them in fractional units. How much should the company invest in the various bonds and cash account to fund this plan through January 1, 2022 in the least costly way?
    a. Create a spreadsheet model for this problem, and solve it.
    b. What is the optimal solution?

48. A natural gas trading company wants to develop an optimal trading plan for the next 10 days. The following table summarizes the estimated prices (per thousand cubic feet [cf]) at which the company can buy and sell natural gas during this time. The company may buy gas at the "Ask" price and sell gas at the "Bid" price.

Day	1	2	3	4	5	6	7	8	9	10
Bid	$3.06	$4.01	$6.03	$4.06	$4.01	$5.02	$5.10	$4.08	$3.01	$4.01
Ask	$3.22	$4.10	$6.13	$4.19	$4.05	$5.12	$5.28	$4.23	$3.15	$4.18

The company currently has 150,000 cf of gas in storage and has a maximum storage capacity of 500,000 cf. To maintain the required pressure in the gas transmission pipeline system, the company can inject no more than 200,000 cf into the storage facility each day and can extract no more than 180,000 cf per day. Assume extractions occur in the morning, and injections occur in the evening. The owner of the storage facility charges a storage fee of 5% of the market (bid) value of the average daily gas inventory. (The average daily inventory is computed as the average of each day's beginning and ending inventory.)

a. Create a spreadsheet model for this problem, and solve it.
b. What is the optimal solution?
c. Assuming price forecasts for natural gas change on a daily basis, how would you suggest the company in this problem actually use your model?

49. The Embassy Lodge hotel chain wants to compare its brand efficiency to that of its major competitors using DEA. Embassy collected the following data reported in industry trade publications. Embassy views customers' perceptions of satisfaction and value (scored from 0 to 100 where 100 is best) to be outputs produced as a function of the following inputs: price, convenience, room comfort, climate control, service, and food quality. (All inputs are expressed on scales where less is better.)

Brand	Satis-faction	Value	Price	Conven-ience	Room Comfort	Climate Control	Service	Food Quality
Embassy Lodge	85	82	70.00	2.3	1.8	2.7	1.5	3.3
Sheritown Inn	96	93	70.00	1.5	1.1	0.2	0.5	0.5
Hynton Hotel	78	87	75.00	2.2	2.4	2.6	2.5	3.2
Vacation Inn	87	88	75.00	1.8	1.6	1.5	1.8	2.3
Merrylot	89	94	80.00	0.5	1.4	0.4	0.9	2.6
FairPrice Inn	93	93	80.00	1.3	0.9	0.2	0.6	2.8
Nights Inn	92	91	85.00	1.4	1.3	0.6	1.4	2.1
Western Hotels	97	92	90.00	0.3	1.7	1.7	1.7	1.8

a. Compute the DEA efficiency for each brand.
b. Which brands are efficient?
c. Is Embassy Lodge efficient? If not, what input and output values should they aspire to in order to become efficient?

50. Fidelity Savings & Loans (FS&L) operates a number of banking facilities throughout the Southeastern United States. The officers of FS&L want to analyze the efficiency of the various branch offices using DEA. The following data has been selected to represent appropriate input and output measures of each banking facility.

Branch	R.O.A.	New Loans	Satisfaction	Labor Hrs	Op. Costs
1	5.32	770	92	3.73	6.34
2	3.39	780	94	3.49	4.43
3	4.95	790	93	5.98	6.31
4	6.01	730	82	6.49	7.28
5	6.40	910	98	7.09	8.69
6	2.89	860	90	3.46	3.23
7	6.94	880	89	7.36	9.07
8	7.18	970	99	6.38	7.42
9	5.98	770	94	4.74	6.75
10	4.97	930	91	5.04	6.35

a. Identify the inputs and outputs for FS&L. Are they all measured on the appropriate scale for use with DEA?
b. Compute the DEA efficiency of each branch office.
c. Which offices are DEA efficient?
d. What input and output levels should branch 5 aspire to in order to become efficient?

CASE 3.1

Putting the Link in the Supply Chain

Rick Eldridge is the new vice president for operations at the The Golfer's Link (TGL), a company specializing in the production of quality, discount sets of golf clubs. Rick was hired primarily because of his expertise in supply chain management (SCM). SCM is the integrated planning and control of all resources in the logistics process from the acquisition of raw materials to the delivery of finished products to the end user. While SCM seeks to optimize all activities in the supply chain, including transactions between firms, Rick's first priority is ensuring that all aspects of production and distribution within TGL are operating optimally.

TGL produces three different lines of golf clubs for men, women, and junior golfers at manufacturing plants in Daytona Beach, FL; Memphis, TN; and Tempe, AZ. The plant in Tempe produces all three line of clubs while the one in Daytona only produces Men's and Women's lines, and the plant in Memphis only produces the Women's and Junior's lines. Each line of clubs requires varying amounts of three raw materials that are sometimes in short supply: titanium, aluminum, and a distinctive rock maple wood that TGL uses in all of its drivers. The manufacturing process for each line of clubs at each plant is identical. Thus, the amount of each of these materials required in each set of the different lines of clubs is summarized in the following table.

Resources Required per Club Set (in lbs)

	Men's	Women's	Juniors'
Titanium	2.9	2.7	2.5
Aluminum	4.5	4	5
Rock Maple	5.4	5	4.8

The estimated amount of each of these key resources available at each plant during the coming month is given as:

Estimated Resource Availability (in lbs)

	Daytona	Memphis	Tempe
Titanium	4500	8500	14500
Aluminum	6000	12000	19000
Rock Maple	9500	16000	18000

TGL's reputation for quality and affordability ensures that they can sell all the clubs the company can make. The Men's, Women's, and Junior's lines generate wholesale revenues of $225, $195, and $165, respectively, regardless of where they are produced. Club sets are shipped from the production plants to distribution centers in Sacramento, CA; Denver, CO; and Pittsburgh, PA. Each month, the different distributions centers order the number of club sets in each of the three lines that they would like to receive. TGL's contract with this distributor requires the company to fill at least 90% (but no more than 100%) of all distributor orders. Rick recently received the following distributor orders for the coming month:

	Number of Club Sets Ordered		
	Men's	**Women's**	**Juniors'**
Sacramento	700	900	900
Denver	550	1,000	1,500
Pittsburgh	900	1,200	1,100

The cost of shipping a set of clubs to each distribution point from each production facility is summarized in the following table. Note again that Daytona does not produce Junior's club sets, and Memphis does not produce Men's club sets.

	Shipping Costs						
	Men's		**Women's**			**Juniors'**	
To/From	**Daytona**	**Tempe**	**Daytona**	**Memphis**	**Tempe**	**Memphis**	**Tempe**
Sacramento	$51	$10	$49	$33	$9	$31	$8
Denver	$28	$43	$27	$22	$42	$21	$40
Pittsburgh	$36	$56	$34	$13	$54	$12	$52

Rick has asked you to determine an optimal production and shipping plan for the coming month.

1. Create a spreadsheet model for this problem, and solve it. What is the optimal solution?
2. If Rick wanted to improve this solution, what additional resources would be needed, and where would they be needed? Explain.
3. What would TGL's optimal profit be if the company was not required to supply at least 90% of each distributor's order?
4. Suppose TGL's agreement included the option of paying a $10,000 penalty if the company cannot supply at least 90% of each the distributor's order but instead supply at least 80% of each distributor's order. Comment on the pros and cons of TGL exercising this option.

Foreign Exchange Trading at Baldwin Enterprises

CASE 3.2

Baldwin Enterprises is a large manufacturing company with operations and sales divisions located in the United States and several other countries. The CFO of the organization, Wes Hamrick, is concerned about the amount of money Baldwin has been paying in transaction costs in the foreign exchange markets and has asked you to help optimize Baldwin's foreign exchange treasury functions.

With operations in several countries, Baldwin maintains cash assets in several different currencies: U.S. dollars (USD), the European Union's euro (EUR), Great Britain's pound (GBP), Hong Kong dollars (HKD), and Japanese yen (JPY). To meet the different cash flow requirements associated with the company's operations around the world, Baldwin must often move funds from one location (and currency) to another. For instance, to pay an unexpected maintenance expense at their facility in Japan, Baldwin may need to convert some of its holdings in U.S. dollars to Japanese yen.

The foreign exchange (FX) market is a network of financial institutions and brokers in which individuals, businesses, banks, and governments buy and sell the currencies of different countries. They do so in order to finance international trade, invest or do business abroad, or speculate on currency price changes. The FX market operates 24 hours a day and represents the largest and most liquid marketplace in the global economy. On average, the equivalent of about $1.5 trillion in different currencies is traded daily in the FX market around the world. The liquidity of the market provides businesses with access to international markets for goods and services by providing foreign currency necessary for transactions worldwide (see http://www.ny.frb.org/fxc).

The FX market operates in much the same way as a stock or commodity market where there is a bid price and ask price for each commodity (or, in this case, currency). A bid price is the price at with the market is willing to buy a particular currency, and the ask price is the price at which the market is willing to sell a currency. The ask prices are typically slightly higher than the bid prices for the same currency—representing the transaction cost or the profit earned by the organizations that keep the market liquid.

The following table summarizes the current FX rates for the currencies Baldwin currently holds. The entries in this table represent the conversion rates from the row currencies to the column currencies.

Convert/To	USD	EUR	GBP	HKD	JPY
USD	1	1.01864	0.6409	7.7985	118.55
EUR	0.9724	1	0.6295	7.6552	116.41
GBP	1.5593	1.5881	1	12.154	184.97
HKD	0.12812	0.1304	0.0821	1	15.1005
JPY	0.00843	0.00856	0.0054	0.0658	1

For example, the table indicates that 1 British pound (GBP) can be exchanged (or sold) for 1.5593 U.S. dollars (USD). Thus, $1.5593 is the bid price, in U.S. dollars, for 1 British pound. Alternatively, the table indicates 1 U.S. dollar (USD) can be exchanged (sold) for 0.6409 British pounds (GBP). So, it takes about 1.5603 U.S. dollars (or 1/0.6409) to buy 1 British pound (or the ask price, in U.S. dollars, for 1 British pound is roughly $1.5603).

Notice that if you took 1 British pound, converted it to 1.5593 U.S. dollars, and then converted those 1.5593 dollars back to British pounds, you would end up with only 0.999355 British pounds (that is, $1 \times 1.5593 \times 0.6409 = 0.999355$). The money you lose in this exchange is the transaction cost.

Baldwin's current portfolio of cash holdings includes 2 million USD, 5 million EUR, 1 million GBP, 3 million HKD, and 30 million JPY. This portfolio is equivalent to $9,058,560 USD under the current exchange rates (given earlier). Wes has asked you to design a currency-trading plan that would increase Baldwin's euro and yen holdings to 8 million EUR and 54 JPY, respectively, while maintaining the equivalent of at least $250,000 USD in each currency. Baldwin measures transaction costs as the change in the USD equivalent value of the portfolio.

1. Create a spreadsheet model for this problem, and solve it.
2. What is the optimal trading plan?
3. What is the optimal transaction cost (in equivalent USD)?
4. Suppose another executive thinks that holding $250,000 USD in each currency is excessive and wants to lower the amount to $50,000 USD in each currency. Does this help to lower the transaction cost? Why or why not?
5. Suppose the exchange rate for converting USD to GBP increased from 0.6409 to 0.6414. What happen to the optimal solution in this case?

The Wolverine Retirement Fund

CASE 3.3

Kelly Jones is a financial analyst for Wolverine Manufacturing, a company that produces engine bearings for the automotive industry. Wolverine is in the process of hammering out a new labor agreement with its unionized workforce. One of the major concerns of the labor union is the funding of Wolverine's retirement plan for its hourly employees. The union believes the company has not been contributing enough money to this fund to cover the benefits it will need to pay to retiring employees. Because of this, the union wants the company to contribute approximately $1.5 million dollars in additional money to this fund over the next 20 years. These extra contributions would begin with an extra payment of $20,000 at the end of 1 year with annual payments increasing by 12.35% per year for the next 19 years.

The union has asked the company to set up a sinking fund to cover the extra annual payments to the retirement fund. The Wolverines' CFO and the union's chief negotiator have agreed that AAA-rated bonds recently issued by three different companies may be used to establish this fund. The following table summarizes the provisions of these bonds.

Company	Maturity	Coupon Payment	Price	Par Value
AC&C	15 years	$80	$847.88	$1,000
IBN	10 years	$90	$938.55	$1,000
MicroHard	20 years	$85	$872.30	$1,000

According to this table, Wolverine may buy bonds issued by AC&C for $847.88 per bond. Each AC&C bond will pay the bondholder $80 per year for the next 15 years, plus an extra payment of $1,000 (the par value) in the fifteenth year. Similar interpretations apply to the information for the IBN and MicroHard bonds. A money market fund yielding 5% may be used to hold any coupon payments that are not needed to meet the company's required retirement fund payment in any given year.

Wolverine's CFO has asked Kelly to determine how much money the company would have to invest and which bonds the company should buy in order to meet the labor union's demands.

1. If you were Kelly, what would you tell the CFO?
2. Suppose the union insists on including one of the following stipulations in the agreement:
   a. No more than half of the total number of bonds purchased may be purchased from a single company.
   b. At least 10% of the total number of bonds must be purchased from each of the companies.
Which stipulation should Wolverine agree to?

Saving the Manatees

CASE 3.4

"So how am I going to spend this money," thought Tom Wieboldt as he sat staring at the pictures and posters of manatees around his office. An avid environmentalist, Tom is the president of "Friends of the Manatees," a nonprofit organization trying to help pass legislation to protect manatees.

Manatees are large, gray-brown aquatic mammals with bodies that taper to a flat, paddle-shaped tail. These gentle and slow-moving creatures grow to an average adult length of 10 feet and weigh an average of 1,000 pounds. Manatees are found in shallow, slow-moving rivers, estuaries, saltwater bays, canals, and coastal areas. In the United States, manatees are concentrated in Florida in the winter but can be found in summer months as far west as Alabama and as far north as Virginia and the Carolinas. They have no natural enemies, but loss of habitat is the most serious threat facing manatees today. Most human-related manatee deaths occur from collisions with motor boats.

Tom's organization has been supporting a bill before the Florida legislature to restrict the use of motor boats in areas known to be inhabited by manatees. This bill is scheduled to come up for a vote in the legislature. Tom recently received a phone call from a national environmental protection organization indicating that they are going to donate $300,000 to Friends of the Manatees to help increase public awareness about the plight of the manatees and to encourage voters to urge their representatives in the state legislature to vote for this bill. Tom intends to use this money to purchase various types of advertising media to "get the message out" during the four weeks immediately preceding the vote.

Tom is considering several different advertising alternatives: newspapers, TV, radio, billboards, and magazines. A marketing consultant provided Tom with the following data on the costs and effectiveness of the various types of media being considered.

Advertising Medium	Unit Cost	Unit Impact Rating
Half-page, daily paper	$800	55
Full-page, daily paper	$1,400	75
Half-page, Sunday paper	$1,200	65
Full-page, Sunday paper	$1,800	80
Daytime TV spot	$2,500	85
Evening TV spot	$3,500	100
Highway billboards	$750	35
15-second radio spot	$150	45
30-second radio spot	$300	55
Half-page, magazine	$500	50
Full-page, magazine	$900	60

According to the marketing consultant, the most effective type of advertising for this type of problem would be short TV ads during the evening prime-time hours. Thus, this type of advertising was given a "unit impact rating" of 100. The other types of advertising were then given unit impact ratings that reflect their expected effectiveness relative to an evening TV ad. For instance, a half-page magazine ad is expected to provide half the effectiveness of an evening TV ad and is therefore given an impact rating of 50.

Tom wants to allocate the $300,000 to these different advertising alternatives in a way that will maximize the impact achieved. However, he realizes it is important to spread his message via several different advertising channels as not everyone listens to the radio and not everyone watches TV in the evenings.

The two most widely read newspapers in the state of Florida are the *Orlando Sentinel* and the Miami Herald. During the four weeks prior to the vote, Tom wants to have half-page ads in the daily (Monday-Saturday) versions of each of these papers at least three times per week. He also wants to have one full-page ad in the daily version of each paper the week before the vote, and he is willing to run more full-page ads if this would be helpful. He also wants to run full-page ads in the Sunday editions of each paper the Sunday before the vote. Tom never wants to run a full-page and half-page ad in a paper on the same day. So the maximum number of full-page ads and half-page ads that can be run in the daily papers should be 48 (that is, 4 weeks × 6 days per week × 2 papers = 48). Similarly, the maximum number of full and half-page ads that can be run in the Sunday papers is 8.

Tom wants to have at least one and no more than three daytime TV ads every day during the four-week period. He also wants to have at least one ad on TV every night but no more than two per night.

There are 10 billboard locations throughout the state that are available for use during the four weeks before the vote. Tom definitely wants to have at least 1 billboard in each of the cities of Orlando, Tampa, and Miami.

Tom believes that the ability to show pictures of the cute, pudgy, lovable manatees in the print media offers a distinct advantage over radio ads. However, the radio ads are relatively inexpensive and may reach some people that the other ads will not reach. Thus, Tom wants to have at least two 15-second ads and at least two 30-second ads on the radio each day. However, he wants to limit the number of radio ads to five 15-second ads and five 30-second ads per day.

There are three different weekly magazines in which Tom can run ads. Tom wants to run full-page ads in each of the magazines at some point during the four-week period. However, he never wants to run full-page ads and half-page ads in the same magazine in a given week. Thus, the total number of full-page ads and half-page magazine ads selected should not exceed 12 (that is, 4 weeks × 3 magazines × 1 ad per magazine per week = 12 ads).

Although Tom has some ideas about the minimum and maximum number of ads to run in the various types of media, he's not sure how much money this will take. And if he can afford to meet all the minimums, he's really confused about the best way to spend the remaining funds. So again Tom asks himself, "How am I going to spend this money?"

1. Create a spreadsheet model for this problem, and solve it. What is the optimal solution?
2. Of the constraints Tom placed on this problem, which are "binding" or preventing the objective function from being improved further?
3. Suppose Tom was willing to increase the allowable number of evening TV ads. How much would this improve the solution?
4. Suppose Tom was willing to double the allowable number of radio ads aired each day. How much would this improve the solution?

Chapter 4

Sensitivity Analysis and the Simplex Method

4.0 Introduction

In Chapters 2 and 3, we studied how to formulate and solve LP models for a variety of decision problems. However, formulating and solving an LP model does not necessarily mean that the original decision problem has been solved. After solving a model, a number of questions often arise about the optimal solution to the LP model. In particular, we might be interested in how sensitive the optimal solution is to changes in various coefficients of the LP model.

Businesses rarely know with certainty what costs will be incurred or the exact amount of resources that will be consumed or available in a given situation or time period. Thus, optimal solutions obtained using models that assume all relevant factors are known with certainty might be viewed with skepticism by management. Sensitivity analysis can help overcome this skepticism and provide a better picture of how the solution to a problem will change if different factors in the model change. Sensitivity analysis also can help answer a number of practical managerial questions that might arise about the solution to an LP problem.

4.1 The Purpose of Sensitivity Analysis

As noted in Chapter 2, any problem that can be stated in the following form is an LP problem:

$$\text{MAX (or MIN):} \quad c_1X_1 + c_2X_2 + \cdots + c_nX_n$$

$$\text{Subject to:} \quad a_{11}X_1 + a_{12}X_2 + \cdots + a_{1n}X_n \leq b_1$$

$$\vdots$$

$$a_{k1}X_1 + a_{k2}X_2 + \cdots + a_{kn}X_n \geq b_k$$

$$\vdots$$

$$a_{m1}X_1 + a_{m2}X_2 + \cdots + a_{mn}X_n = b_m$$

All the coefficients in this model (the c_j, a_{ij}, and b_i) represent numeric constants. So, when we formulate and solve an LP problem, we implicitly assume that we can specify the exact values for these coefficients. However, in the real world, these coefficients might change from day to day or minute to minute. For example, the price a company charges for its products can change on a daily, weekly, or monthly basis. Similarly, if a skilled machinist calls in sick, a manufacturer might have less capacity to produce items on a given machine than was originally planned.

Realizing that such uncertainties exist, a manager should consider how sensitive an LP model's solution is to changes or estimation errors that might occur in (1) the objective function coefficients (the c_j), (2) the constraint coefficients (the a_{ij}), and (3) the RHS values for the constraints (the b_i). A manager also might ask a number of "What if?" questions about these values. For example, what if the cost of a product increases by 7%? What if a reduction in setup time allows for additional capacity on a given machine? What if a worker's suggestion results in a product requiring only two hours of labor rather than three? Sensitivity analysis addresses these issues by assessing the sensitivity of the solution to uncertainty or estimation errors in the model coefficients, as well as the solution's sensitivity to changes in model coefficients that might occur because of human intervention.

4.2 Approaches to Sensitivity Analysis

You can perform sensitivity analysis on an LP model in a number of ways. If you want to determine the effect of some change in the model, the most direct approach is to simply change the model and re-solve it. This approach is suitable if the model does not take an excessive amount of time to change or solve. In addition, if you are interested in studying the consequences of *simultaneously* changing several coefficients in the model, this might be the only practical approach to sensitivity analysis.

Solver also provides some sensitivity information after solving an LP problem. As mentioned in Chapter 3, one of the benefits of using the simplex method to solve LP problems is its speed—it is considerably faster than the other optimization techniques. However, another advantage of using the simplex method is that it provides more sensitivity analysis information than the other techniques. In particular, the simplex method provides us with information about the following:

- The range of values the objective function coefficients can assume without changing the optimal solution
- The impact on the optimal objective function value of increases or decreases in the availability of various constrained resources
- The impact on the optimal objective function value of forcing changes in the values of certain decision variables away from their optimal values
- The impact that changes in constraint coefficients will have on the optimal solution to the problem

4.3 An Example Problem

We will again use the Blue Ridge Hot Tubs problem to illustrate the types of sensitivity analysis information available using Solver. The LP formulation of the problem is repeated here, where X_1 represents the number of Aqua-Spas, and X_2 represents the number of Hydro-Luxes to be produced:

$$
\begin{array}{llll}
\text{MAX:} & 350X_1 + 300X_2 & & \} \text{ profit} \\
\text{Subject to:} & 1X_1 + 1X_2 \leq 200 & & \} \text{ pump constraint} \\
& 9X_1 + 6X_2 \leq 1{,}566 & & \} \text{ labor constraint} \\
& 12X_1 + 16X_2 \leq 2{,}880 & & \} \text{ tubing constraint} \\
& X_1, X_2 \geq 0 & & \} \text{ nonnegativity conditions}
\end{array}
$$

FIGURE 4.1 *Spreadsheet model for the Blue Ridge Hot Tubs product mix problem*

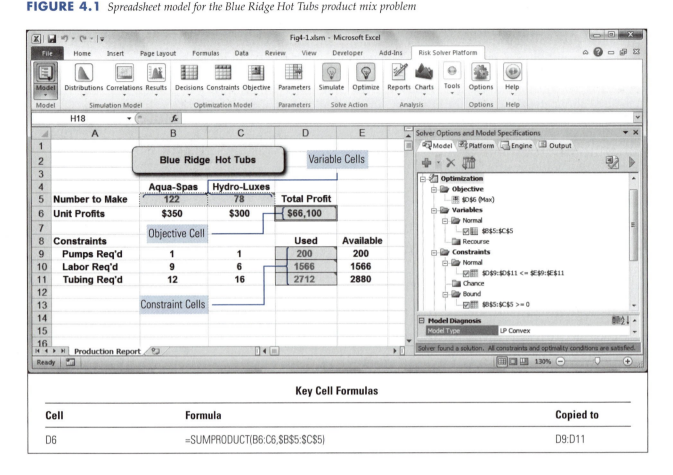

	Key Cell Formulas	
Cell	**Formula**	**Copied to**
D6	=SUMPRODUCT(B6:C6,$B$5:$C$5)	D9:D11

This model is implemented in the spreadsheet shown in Figure 4.1 (and file Fig4-1xlsm that accompanies this book). (See Chapter 3 for details on the procedure used to create and solve this spreadsheet model.) After solving the LP problem, a number of reports are available about its solution via the Reports icon on the Risk Solver Platform ribbon.

> ### Software Note
>
> When solving an LP problem, be sure to use Solver's Standard LP/Quadratic Engine. This allows for the maximum amount of sensitivity analysis information in the reports discussed throughout this chapter.

4.4 The Answer Report

Figure 4.2 shows the Answer Report for the Blue Ridge Hot Tubs problem. To create this report, first solve the LP problem in the usual way, and then click Reports, Optimization, Answer on the Risk Solver Platform ribbon. This report summarizes the solution to the problem and is fairly self-explanatory. The first section of the report summarizes the

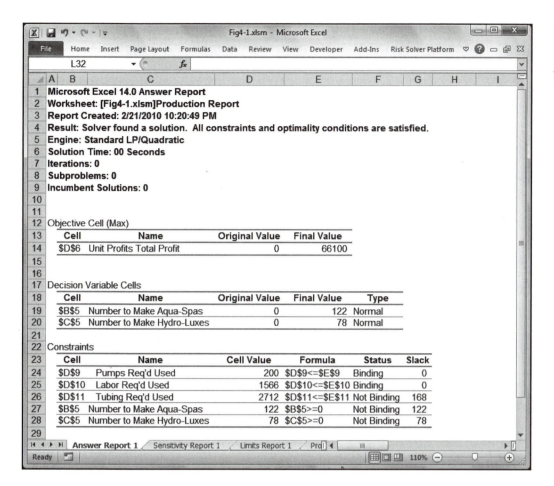

FIGURE 4.2

Answer Report for the hot tub problem

original and final (optimal) value of the objective cell. The next section summarizes the original and final (optimal) values of the decision variable cells.

The final section of this report provides information about the constraints. In particular, the Cell Value column shows the final (optimal) value assumed by each constraint cell. Note that these values correspond to the final value assumed by the LHS formula of each constraint. The Formula column indicates the upper or lower bounds that apply to each constraint cell. The Status column indicates which constraints are binding and which are nonbinding. A constraint is **binding** if it is satisfied as a strict equality in the optimal solution; otherwise, it is **nonbinding**. Notice that the constraints for the number of pumps and amount of labor used are both binding, meaning that *all* the available pumps and labor hours will be used if this solution is implemented. Therefore, these constraints are preventing Blue Ridge Hot Tubs from achieving a higher level of profit.

Finally, the values in the Slack column indicate the difference between the LHS and RHS of each constraint. By definition, binding constraints have zero slack, and nonbinding constraints have some positive level of slack. The values in the Slack column indicate that if this solution is implemented, all the available pumps and labor hours will be used, but 168 feet of tubing will be left over. The slack values for the nonnegativity conditions indicate the amounts by which the decision variables exceed their respective lower bounds of zero.

The Answer Report does not provide any information that could not be derived from the solution shown in the spreadsheet model. However, the format of this report gives a convenient summary of the solution that can be incorporated easily into a word-processing document as part of a written report to management.

Report Headings

When creating the reports described in this chapter, Solver will try to use various text entries from the original spreadsheet to generate meaningful headings and labels in the reports. Given the various ways in which a model can be implemented, Solver might not always produce meaningful headings. However, you can change any text entry to make the report more meaningful or descriptive.

4.5 The Sensitivity Report

Figure 4.3 shows the Sensitivity Report for the Blue Ridge Hot Tubs problem. This report summarizes information about the variable cells and constraints for our model. This information is useful in evaluating how sensitive the optimal solution is to changes in various coefficients in the model.

FIGURE 4.3

Sensitivity Report for the hot tub problem

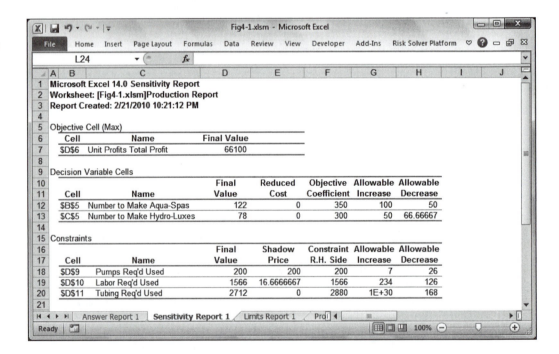

4.5.1 CHANGES IN THE OBJECTIVE FUNCTION COEFFICIENTS

Chapter 2 introduced the level-curve approach to solving a graphical LP problem and showed how to use this approach to solve the Blue Ridge Hot Tubs problem. This graphical solution is repeated in Figure 4.4 (and file Fig4-4.xlsm that accompanies this book).

FIGURE 4.4 *Graph of original feasible region and optimal solution*

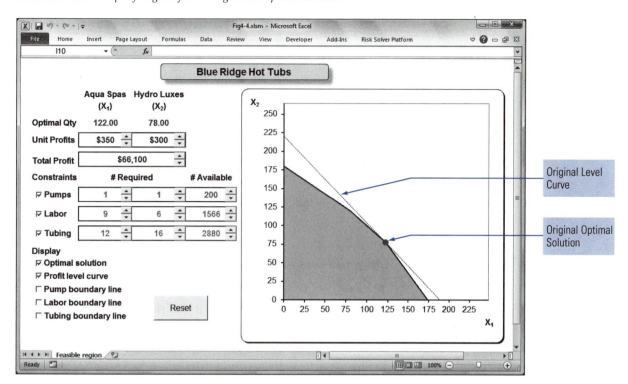

The slope of the original level curve in Figure 4.4 is determined by the coefficients in the objective function of the model (the values 350 and 300). In Figure 4.5, we can see that if the slope of the level curve were different, the extreme point represented by $X_1 = 80$, $X_2 = 120$ would be the optimal solution. Of course, the only way to change the level curve for the objective function is to change the coefficients in the objective function. So, if the objective function coefficients are at all uncertain, we might be interested in determining how much these values could change before the optimal solution would change.

For example, if the owner of Blue Ridge Hot Tubs does not have complete control over the costs of producing hot tubs (which is likely because he purchases the fiberglass hot tub shells from another company), the profit figures in the objective function of our LP model might not be the exact profits earned on hot tubs produced in the future. So before the manager decides to produce 122 Aqua-Spas and 78 Hydro-Luxes, he might want to determine how sensitive this solution is to the profit figures in the objective. That is, the manager might want to determine how much the profit figures could change before the optimal solution of $X_1 = 122$, $X_2 = 78$ would change. This information is provided in the Sensitivity Report shown in Figure 4.3.

The original objective function coefficients associated with the variable cells are listed in the Objective Coefficient column in Figure 4.3. The next two columns show the allowable increases and decreases in these values. For example, the objective function value associated with Aqua-Spas (or variable X_1) can increase by as much as $100 or decrease by as much as $50 without changing the optimal solution, assuming all other coefficients remain constant. (You can verify this by changing the profit coefficient for Aqua-Spas to any value in the range from $300 to $450 and re-solving the model.) Similarly, the objective function value associated with Hydro-Luxes (or variable X_2) can increase by $50 or decrease by approximately $66.67 without changing the optimal values

FIGURE 4.5 *How a change in an objective function coefficient can change the slope of the level curve and the optimal solution*

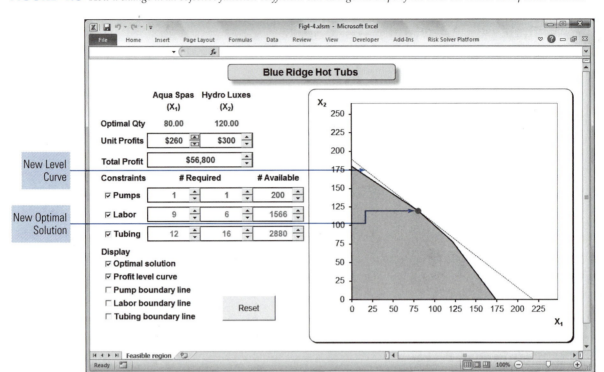

of the decision variables, assuming all other coefficients remain constant. (Again, you can verify this by re-solving the model with different profit values for Hydro-Luxes.)

> ### Software Note
>
> When setting up a spreadsheet model for an LP problem for which you intend to generate a Sensitivity Report, it is a good idea to make sure the cells corresponding to RHS values of constraints contain constants or formulas that do not involve the decision variables. Thus, any RHS formula related directly or indirectly to the decision variables should be moved algebraically to the LHS of the constraint before implementing your model. This will help to reduce problems in interpreting Solver's Sensitivity Report.

4.5.2 A NOTE ABOUT CONSTANCY

The phrase "assuming all other coefficients remain constant" in the previous paragraph underscores the fact that the allowable increases and decreases shown in the Sensitivity Report apply only if *all* the other coefficients in the LP model do not change. The objective coefficient for Aqua-Spas can assume any value from $300 to $450 without changing the optimal solution—*but this is guaranteed to be true only if all the other coefficients in the model remain constant (including the objective function coefficient for X_2).* Similarly, the objective function coefficient for X_2 can assume any value between $233.33 and $350 without changing the optimal solution—*but this is guaranteed to be true only if all the other coefficients* *in the model remain constant (including the objective function coefficient for* X_1*).* Later in this chapter, you will see how to determine whether the current solution remains optimal if changes are made in two or more objective coefficients at the same time.

4.5.3 ALTERNATE OPTIMAL SOLUTIONS

Sometimes, the allowable increase or allowable decrease for the objective function coefficient for one or more variables will equal zero. In the absence of degeneracy (to be described later), this indicates that alternate optimal solutions exist. You can usually get Solver to produce an alternate optimal solution (when they exist) by (1) adding a constraint to your model that holds the objective function at the current optimal value, and then (2) attempting to maximize or minimize the value of one of the decision variables that had an objective function coefficient with an allowable increase or decrease of zero. This approach sometimes involves some trial and error in step 2 but should cause Solver to produce an alternate optimal solution to your problem.

4.5.4 CHANGES IN THE RHS VALUES

As noted earlier, constraints that have zero slack in the optimal solution to an LP problem are called binding constraints. Binding constraints prevent us from further improving (that is, maximizing or minimizing) the objective function. For example, the Answer Report in Figure 4.2 indicates that the constraints for the number of pumps and hours of labor available are binding, whereas the constraint on the amount of tubing available is nonbinding. This is also evident in Figure 4.3 by comparing the Final Value column with the Constraint R.H. Side column. The values in the Final Value column represent the LHS values of each constraint at the optimal solution. A constraint is binding if its Final Value is equal to its Constraint R.H. Side value.

After solving an LP problem, you might want to determine how much better or worse the solution would be if we had more or less of a given resource. For example, Howie Jones might wonder how much more profit could be earned if additional pumps or labor hours were available. The Shadow Price column in Figure 4.3 provides the answers to such questions.

The **shadow price** for a constraint indicates the amount by which the objective function value changes given a unit *increase* in the RHS value of the constraint, assuming all other coefficients remain constant. If a shadow price is positive, a unit increase in the RHS value of the associated constraint results in an increase in the optimal objective function value. If a shadow price is negative, a unit increase in the RHS value of the associated constraint results in a decrease in the optimal objective function value. To analyze the effects of decreases in the RHS values, you reverse the sign on the shadow price. That is, the negated shadow price for a constraint indicates the amount by which the optimal objective function value changes given a unit *decrease* in the RHS value of the constraint, assuming all other coefficients remain constant. The shadow price values apply provided that the increase or decrease in the RHS value falls within the allowable increase or allowable decrease limits in the Sensitivity Report for each constraint.

For example, Figure 4.3 indicates that the shadow price for the labor constraint is 16.67. Therefore, if the number of available labor hours increased by any amount in the range from 0 to 234 hours, the optimal objective function value changes (increases) by $16.67 for each additional labor hour. If the number of available labor hours decreased by any amount in the range from 0 to 126 hours, the optimal objective function value changes (decreases) by −$16.67 for each lost labor hour. A similar interpretation holds for the shadow price for the constraint on the number of pumps. (It is coincidental that the shadow price for the pump constraint (200) is the same as that constraint's RHS and Final Values.)

4.5.5 SHADOW PRICES FOR NONBINDING CONSTRAINTS

Now, let's consider the shadow price for the nonbinding tubing constraint. The tubing constraint has a shadow price of zero with an allowable increase of infinity and an allowable decrease of 168. Therefore, if the RHS value for the tubing constraint increases by *any* amount, the objective function value does not change (or changes by zero). This result is not surprising. Because the optimal solution to this problem leaves 168 feet of tubing unused, *additional* tubing will not produce a better solution. Furthermore, because the optimal solution includes 168 feet of unused tubing, we can reduce the RHS value of this constraint by 168 without affecting the optimal solution.

As this example illustrates, the shadow price of a nonbinding constraint is always zero. There is always some amount by which the RHS value of a nonbinding constraint can be changed without affecting the optimal solution.

4.5.6 A NOTE ABOUT SHADOW PRICES

One important point needs to be made concerning shadow prices. To illustrate this point, let's suppose that the RHS value of the labor constraint for our example problem increases by 162 hours (from 1,566 to 1,728) due to the addition of new workers. Because this increase is within the allowable increase listed for the labor constraint, you might expect that the optimal objective function value would increase by $16.67 \times 162 = $2,700$. That is, the new optimal objective function value would be approximately $68,800 ($66,100 + $16.67 \times 162 = $68,800$). Figure 4.6 shows the re-solved model after increasing the RHS value for the labor constraint by 162 labor hours to 1,728.

FIGURE 4.6 *Solution to the revised hot tub problem with 162 additional labor hours*

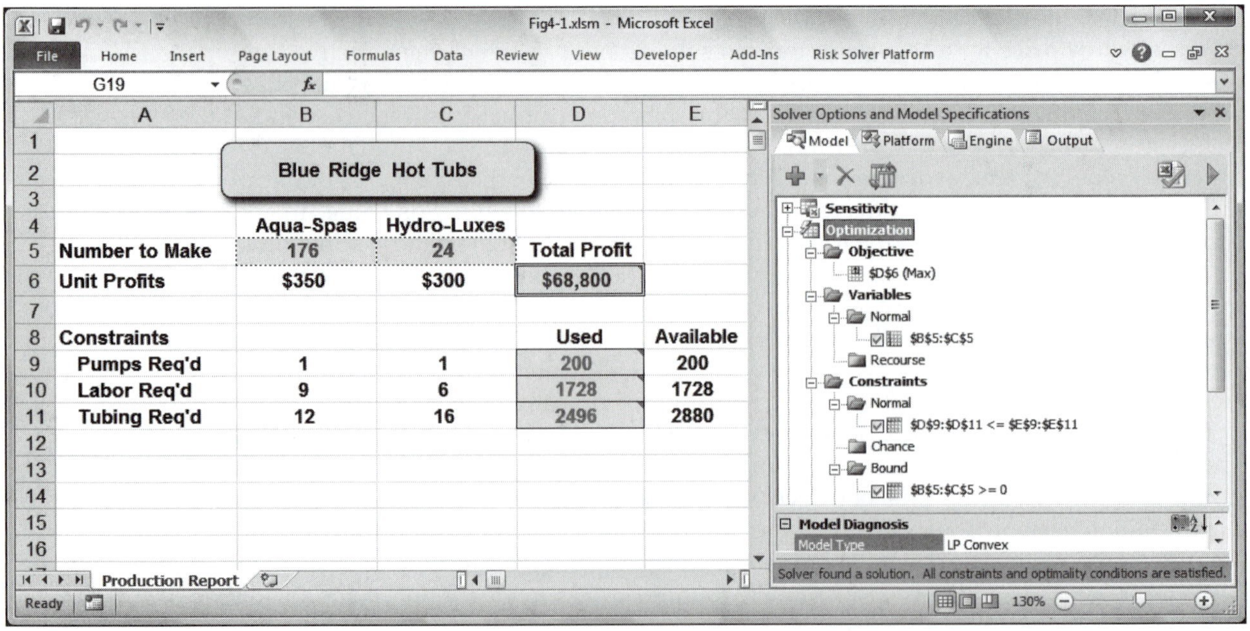

In Figure 4.6, the new optimal objective function value is $68,800, as expected. But this solution involves producing 176 Aqua-Spas and 24 Hydro-Luxes. That is, the optimal solution to the revised problem is *different* from the solution to the original problem shown in Figure 4.1. This is not surprising because changing the RHS of a constraint also changes the feasible region for the problem. The effect of increasing the RHS of the labor constraint is shown graphically in Figure 4.7.

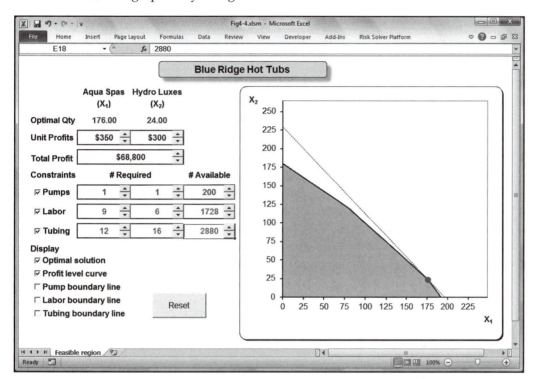

FIGURE 4.7

How a change in the RHS value of the labor constraint changes the feasible region and optimal solution

So, although shadow prices indicate how the objective function value changes if a given RHS value changes, they *do not* tell you which values the decision variables need to assume in order to achieve this new objective function value. Determining the new optimal values for the decision variables requires that you make the appropriate changes in the RHS value and re-solve the model.

Another Interpretation
of Shadow Prices

Unfortunately, there is no one universally accepted way of reporting shadow prices for constraints. In some software packages, the signs of the shadow prices do not conform to the convention used by Solver. Regardless of which software package you use, there is another way to look at shadow prices that should always lead to a proper interpretation. The absolute value of the shadow price always indicates the amount by which the objective function will be *improved* if the corresponding constraint is *loosened*. A less than or equal to constraint is loosened by *increasing* its RHS value, whereas a greater than or equal to constraint is loosened by *decreasing* its RHS value. (The absolute value of the shadow price can also be interpreted as the amount by which the objective will be made *worse* if the corresponding constraint is *tightened*.)

4.5.7 SHADOW PRICES AND THE VALUE OF ADDITIONAL RESOURCES

In the previous example, an additional 162 hours of labor allowed us to increase profits by $2,700. A question might then arise as to how much we should be willing to pay to acquire these additional 162 hours of labor. The answer to this question is, "It depends. . . ."

If labor is a *variable* cost that was subtracted (along with other variable costs) from the selling price of the hot tubs to determine the marginal profits associated with each type of tub, we should be willing to pay up to $2,700 *above and beyond* what we would ordinarily pay to acquire 162 hours of labor. In this case, notice that both the original and revised profit figures of $66,100 and $68,800, respectively, represent the profit earned *after* the normal labor charge has been paid. Therefore, we could pay a premium of up to $2,700 to acquire the additional 162 hours of labor (or an extra $16.67 per additional labor hour) and still earn at least as much profit as we would have without the additional 162 hours of labor. Thus, if the normal labor rate is $12 per hour, we could pay up to $28.67 per hour to acquire each of the additional 162 hours of labor.

On the other hand, if labor is a sunk cost, which must be paid regardless of how many hot tubs are produced, it would not (or should not) have been subtracted from the selling price of the hot tubs in determining the marginal profit coefficients for each tub produced. In this case, we should be willing to pay a maximum of $16.67 per hour to acquire each of the additional 162 hours of labor.

4.5.8 OTHER USES OF SHADOW PRICES

Because shadow prices represent the marginal values of the resources in an LP problem, they can help us answer a number of other managerial questions that might arise. For example, suppose Blue Ridge Hot Tubs is considering introducing a new model of hot tub called the Typhoon-Lagoon. Suppose that each unit of this new model requires 1 pump, 8 hours of labor, and 13 feet of tubing, and can be sold to generate a marginal profit of $320. Would production of this new model be profitable?

Because Blue Ridge Hot Tubs has limited resources, the production of any Typhoon-Lagoons would consume some of the resources currently devoted to the production of Aqua-Spas and Hydro-Luxes. So, producing Typhoon-Lagoons will reduce the number of pumps, labor hours, and tubing available for producing the other types of hot tubs. The shadow prices in Figure 4.3 indicate that each pump taken away from production of the current products will reduce profits by $200. Similarly, each labor hour taken away from the production of the current products will reduce profits by $16.67. The shadow price for the tubing constraint indicates that the supply of tubing can be reduced without adversely affecting profits.

Because each Typhoon-Lagoon requires 1 pump, 8 hours of labor, and 13 feet of tubing, the diversion of resources required to produce one unit of this new model would cause a reduction in profit of $200 × 1 + $16.67 × 8 + $0 × 13 = $333.33. This reduction would be partially offset by the $320 increase in profit generated by each Typhoon-Lagoon. The net effect of producing each Typhoon-Lagoon would be a $13.33 reduction in profit ($320 − $333.33 = −$13.33). Therefore, the production of Typhoon-Lagoons would not be profitable (although the company might choose to produce a small number of Typhoon-Lagoons to enhance its product line for marketing purposes).

Another way to determine whether or not Typhoon-Lagoons should be produced is to add this alternative to our model and solve the resulting LP problem. The LP model for this revised problem is represented as follows, where X_1, X_2, and X_3 represent the number of Aqua-Spas, Hydro-Luxes, and Typhoon-Lagoons to be produced, respectively:

$$
\begin{array}{lll}
\text{MAX:} & 350X_1 + 300X_2 + 320X_3 & \} \text{ profit} \\
\text{Subject to:} & 1X_1 + 1X_2 + 1X_3 \le 200 & \} \text{ pump constraint} \\
& 9X_1 + 6X_2 + 8X_3 \le 1{,}566 & \} \text{ labor constraint} \\
& 12X_1 + 16X_2 + 13X_3 \le 2{,}880 & \} \text{ tubing constraint} \\
& X_1, X_2, X_3 \ge 0 & \} \text{ nonnegativity conditions}
\end{array}
$$

This model is implemented and solved in the spreadsheet, as shown in Figure 4.8 (and file Fig4-8.xlsm that accompanies this book). Notice that the optimal solution to this problem involves producing 122 Aqua-Spas ($X_1 = 122$), 78 Hydro-Luxes ($X_2 = 78$), and no Typhoon-Lagoons ($X_3 = 0$). So, as expected, the optimal solution does not involve producing Typhoon-Lagoons. Figure 4.9 shows the Sensitivity Report for our revised model.

FIGURE 4.8 *Spreadsheet model for the revised product mix problem with three hot tub models*

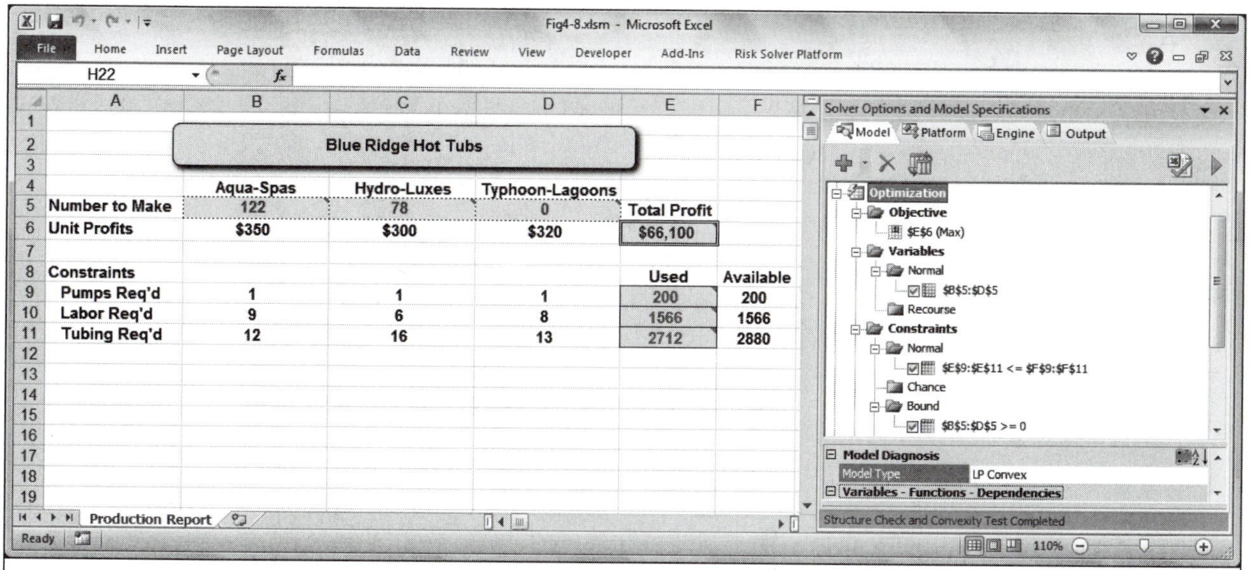

Key Cell Formulas		
Cell	**Formula**	**Copied to**
E6	=SUMPRODUCT(B6:D6,$B$5:$D$5)	E9:E11

4.5.9 THE MEANING OF THE REDUCED COSTS

The Sensitivity Report in Figure 4.9 for our revised model is identical to the sensitivity report for our original model *except* that it includes an additional row in the Adjustable Cells section. This row reports sensitivity information on the number of Typhoon-Lagoons to produce. Notice that the Reduced Cost column indicates that the reduced cost value for Typhoon-Lagoons is −13.33. This is the same number that we calculated in the previous section when determining whether or not it would be profitable to produce Typhoon-Lagoons.

FIGURE 4.9

*Sensitivity Report
for the revised
product mix
problem with three
hot tub models*

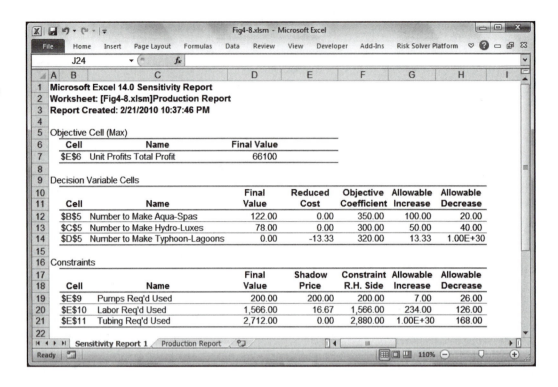

The reduced cost for each variable is equal to the per-unit amount the product contributes to profits minus the per-unit value of the resources it consumes (where the consumed resources are priced at their shadow prices). For example, the reduced cost of each variable in this problem is calculated as:

Reduced cost of Aqua-Spas $= 350 - 200 \times 1 - 16.67 \times 9 - 0 \times 12 = 0$

Reduced cost of Hydro-Luxes $= 300 - 200 \times 1 - 16.67 \times 6 - 0 \times 16 = 0$

Reduced cost of Typhoon-Lagoons $= 320 - 200 \times 1 - 16.67 \times 8 - 0 \times 13 = -13.33$

The allowable increase in the objective function coefficient for Typhoon-Lagoons equals 13.33. This means that the current solution will remain optimal provided that the marginal profit on Typhoon-Lagoons is less than or equal to $320 + $13.33 = $333.33 (because this would keep its reduced cost less than or equal to zero). However, if the marginal profit for Typhoon-Lagoons is more than $333.33, producing this product would be profitable and the optimal solution to the problem would change.

It is interesting to note that the shadow prices (marginal values) of the resources equate exactly with the marginal profits of the products that, at optimality, assume values between their simple lower and upper bounds. This will always be the case. In the optimal solution to an LP problem, the variables that assume values *between* their simple lower and upper bounds always have reduced cost values of zero. (In our example problem, all the variables have implicit simple upper bounds of positive infinity.) The variables with optimal values equal to their simple lower bounds have reduced cost values that are less than or equal to zero for maximization problems, or greater than or equal to zero for minimization problems. Variables with optimal values equal to their simple upper bounds have reduced cost values that are greater than or equal to zero for maximization problems, or less than or equal to zero for minimization problems. Figure 4.10 summarizes these relationships.

FIGURE 4.10

Summary of optimal reduced cost values

Type of Problem	Optimal Value of Decision Variable	Optimal Value of Reduced Cost
Maximization	at simple lower bound	≤ 0
	between lower and upper bounds	$= 0$
	at simple upper bound	≥ 0
Minimization	at simple lower bound	≥ 0
	between lower and upper bounds	$= 0$
	at simple upper bound	≤ 0

Generally, at optimality, a variable assumes its largest possible value (or is set equal to its simple upper bound) if this variable helps improve the objective function value. In a maximization problem, the variable's reduced cost must be nonnegative to indicate that if the variable's value increased, the objective value would increase (improve). In a minimization problem, the variable's reduced cost must be nonpositive to indicate that if the variable's value increased, the objective value would decrease (improve).

Similar arguments can be made for the optimal reduced costs of variables at their lower bounds. At optimality, a variable assumes its smallest (lower bound) value if it cannot be used to improve the objective value. In a maximization problem, the variable's reduced cost must be nonpositive to indicate that if the variable's value increased, the objective value would decrease (worsen). In a minimization problem, the variable's reduced cost must be nonnegative to indicate that if the variable's value increased, the objective value would increase (worsen).

Key Points

Our discussion of Solver's Sensitivity Report highlights some key points concerning shadow prices and their relationship to reduced costs. These key points are summarized as:

- The shadow prices of resources equate the marginal value of the resources consumed with the marginal benefit of the goods being produced.
- Resources in excess supply have a shadow price (or marginal value) of zero.
- The reduced cost of a product is the difference between its marginal profit and the marginal value of the resources it consumes.
- Products whose marginal profits are less than the marginal value of the goods required for their production will not be produced in an optimal solution.

4.5.10 ANALYZING CHANGES IN CONSTRAINT COEFFICIENTS

Given what we know about reduced costs and shadow prices, we can now analyze how changes in some constraint coefficients affect the optimal solution to an LP problem. For example, it is unprofitable for Blue Ridge Hot Tubs to manufacture Typhoon-Lagoons assuming that each unit requires eight hours of labor. However, what would happen if the product could be produced in only seven hours? The reduced cost value for Typhoon-Lagoons is calculated as:

$$\$320 - \$200 \times 1 - \$16.67 \times 7 - \$0 \times 13 = \$3.31$$

Because this new reduced cost value is positive, producing Typhoon-Lagoons would be profitable in this scenario, and the solution shown in Figure 4.8 would no longer be optimal. We could also reach this conclusion by changing the labor requirement for Typhoon-Lagoons in our spreadsheet model and re-solving the problem. In fact, we have to do this to determine the new optimal solution if each Typhoon-Lagoon requires only seven hours of labor.

As another example, suppose that we wanted to know the maximum amount of labor that is required to assemble a Typhoon-Lagoon while keeping its production economically justifiable. The production of Typhoon-Lagoons would be profitable provided that the reduced cost for the product is greater than or equal to zero. If L_3 represents the amount of labor required to produce a Typhoon-Lagoon, we want to find the maximum value of L_3 that keeps the reduced cost for Typhoon-Lagoons greater than or equal to zero. That is, we want to find the maximum value of L_3 that satisfies the inequality:

$$\$320 - \$200 \times 1 - \$16.67 \times L_3 - \$0 \times 13 \geq 0$$

If we solve this inequality for L_3, we obtain:

$$L_3 \leq \frac{120}{16.67} = 7.20$$

Thus, the production of Typhoon-Lagoons would be economically justified provided that the labor required to produce them does not exceed 7.20 hours per unit. Similar types of questions can be answered using knowledge of the basic relationships among reduced costs, shadow prices, and optimality conditions.

4.5.11 SIMULTANEOUS CHANGES IN OBJECTIVE FUNCTION COEFFICIENTS

Earlier, we noted that the values in the Allowable Increase and Allowable Decrease columns in the Sensitivity Report for the objective function coefficients indicate the maximum amounts by which each objective coefficient can change without altering the optimal solution—*assuming all other coefficients in the model remain constant*. A technique known as *The 100% Rule* determines whether the current solution remains optimal when more than one objective function coefficient changes. The following two situations could arise when applying this rule:

Case 1. All variables whose objective function coefficients change have nonzero reduced costs.

Case 2. At least one variable whose objective function coefficient changes has a reduced cost of zero.

In case 1, the current solution remains optimal provided that the objective function coefficient of each changed variable remains within the limits indicated in the Allowable Increase and Allowable Decrease columns of the Sensitivity Report.

Case 2 is a bit trickier. In case 2, we must perform the following analysis where:

c_j = the original objective function coefficient for variable X_j
Δc_j = the planned change in c_j
I_j = the allowable increase in c_j given in the Sensitivity Report
D_j = the allowable decrease in c_j given in the Sensitivity Report

$$r_j = \begin{cases} \dfrac{\Delta c_j}{I_j}, & \text{if } \Delta c_j \geq 0 \\[2ex] \dfrac{-\Delta c_j}{D_j}, & \text{if } \Delta c_j < 0 \end{cases}$$

Notice that r_j measures the ratio of the planned change in c_j to the maximum allowable change for which the current solution remains optimal. If only one objective function coefficient changed, the current solution remains optimal provided that $r_j \leq 1$ (or, if r_j is expressed as a percentage, it must be less than or equal to 100%). Similarly, if more than one objective function coefficient changes, the current solution will remain optimal provided that $\Sigma r_j \leq 1$. (Note that if $\Sigma r_j > 1$, the current solution might remain optimal, but this is not guaranteed.)

4.5.12 A WARNING ABOUT DEGENERACY

The solution to an LP problem sometimes exhibits a mathematical anomaly known as **degeneracy**. The solution to an LP problem is degenerate if the RHS values of any of the constraints have an allowable increase or allowable decrease of zero. The presence of degeneracy impacts our interpretation of the values on the Sensitivity Report in a number of important ways:

1. When the solution is degenerate, the methods mentioned earlier for detecting alternate optimal solutions cannot be relied upon.
2. When a solution is degenerate, the reduced costs for the variable cells may not be unique. Additionally, in this case, the objective function coefficients for variable cells must change by at least as much as (and possibly more than) their respective reduced costs before the optimal solution would change.
3. When the solution is degenerate, the allowable increases and decreases for the objective function coefficients still hold, and, in fact, the coefficients may have to be changed substantially beyond the allowable increase and decrease limits before the optimal solution changes.
4. When the solution is degenerate, the given shadow prices and their ranges may still be interpreted in the usual way, but they may not be unique. That is, a different set of shadow prices and ranges may also apply to the problem (even if the optimal solution is unique).

So before interpreting the results on a Sensitivity Report, you should always first check to see if the solution is degenerate because this has important ramifications on how the numbers on the report should be interpreted. A complete description of the degeneracy anomaly goes beyond the intended scope of this book. However, degeneracy is sometimes caused by having redundant constraints in an LP model. *Extreme caution* (and perhaps consultation with an expert in mathematical programming) is in order if important business decisions are being made based on the Sensitivity Report for a degenerate LP problem.

4.6 The Limits Report

The Limits Report for the original Blue Ridge Hot Tubs problem is shown in Figure 4.11. This report lists the optimal value of the set cell. It then summarizes the optimal values for each variable cell and indicates what values the set cell assumes if each variable cell is set to its upper or lower limits. The values in the Lower Limits column indicate the smallest value each variable cell can assume while the values of all other variable cells remain constant and all the constraints are satisfied. The values in the Upper Limits column indicate the largest value each variable cell can assume while the values of all other variable cells remain constant and all the constraints are satisfied.

FIGURE 4.11

Limits Report for the original Blue Ridge Hot Tubs problem

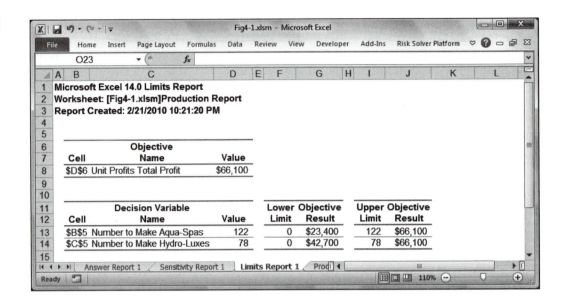

4.7 Ad Hoc Sensitivity Analysis

Although the standard sensitivity reports Solver prepares can be quite useful, they cannot possibly anticipate and provide answers to every question that might arise about the solution to an LP problem and the effects that changes to model parameters might have on the optimal solution. However, Risk Solver Platform provides a number of powerful features that we can use to address *ad hoc* sensitivity analysis questions when they arise. In this section, we will consider two such ad hoc techniques: Spider Tables/Plots and Solver Tables. A Spider Table/Plot summarizes the optimal value for one output cell as individual changes are made to various input cells. A Solver Table summarizes the optimal value for multiple output cells as changes are made to a single input cell. As illustrated in the following example, these tools can be helpful in developing an understanding of how changes in various model parameters affect the optimal solution to a problem.

4.7.1 CREATING SPIDER TABLES AND PLOTS

Recall that the optimal solution to the original Blue Ridge Hot Tubs problem involves producing 122 Aqua-Spas and 78 Hydro-Luxes for a total profit of $66,100. However, this solution assumes there will be exactly 200 pumps, 1,566 labor hours, and 2,880 feet of tubing available. In reality, pumps and tubing are sometimes defective, and workers sometimes call in sick. So, the owner of the company may wonder how sensitive the total profit is to changes in these parameters. Although Solver's Sensitivity Report provides some information about this issue, a Spider Table and Plot is sometimes more helpful in communicating this information to management.

Again, a Spider Table summarizes the optimal value for one output cell as individual changes are made to various model input cells (or parameters). In this case, the output cell of interest is cell D6 representing total profit. The parameters of interest are cells E9, E10, and E 11 representing, respectively, the availability of pumps, labor, and tubing. Figure 4.12 (and file Fig4-12.xlsm that accompanies this book) shows how to set up a Spider Table for this problem.

FIGURE 4.12 *Set up for creating a Spider Table and Plot*

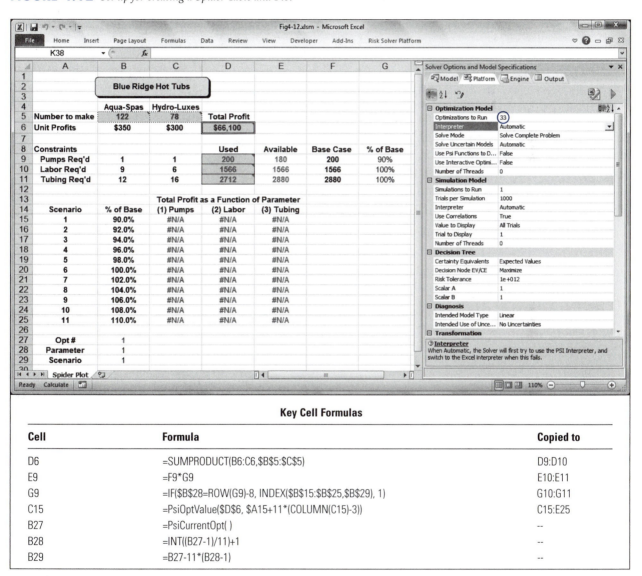

Key Cell Formulas		
Cell	**Formula**	**Copied to**
D6	=SUMPRODUCT(B6:C6,$B$5:$C$5)	D9:D10
E9	=F9*G9	E10:E11
G9	=IF($B$28=ROW(G9)-8, INDEX($B$15:$B$25,$B$29), 1)	G10:G11
C15	=PsiOptValue($D$6, $A15+11*(COLUMN(C15)-3))	C15:E25
B27	=PsiCurrentOpt( )	--
B28	=INT((B27-1)/11)+1	--
B29	=B27-11*(B28-1)	--

The strategy in Figure 4.12 is to individually vary the availability of pumps, labor, and tubing between 90% and 110% of their original (or base case) values in 2% increments, as indicated by cells B15 through B25. The base case values for each of our three parameters are listed in cells F9 through F11. For each of these three parameters, we will create and optimize 11 different scenarios (while holding the other two parameters at their base case values) and record the corresponding optimal value for the objective function (cell D6). Therefore, we will use Risk Solver to solve a total of 33 (that is, 3 × 11) variations of our Blue Ridge Hot Tubs problem. In the first 11 runs, we will change the first parameter (the number of pumps available) between 90% and 110% of its base case value. In the next 11 runs (runs 12 to 22), we will change the second parameter (the amount of labor available) between 90% and 110% of its base case value. Finally, in the last 11 runs (runs 23 to 33), we will change the third parameter (the amount of tubing available) between 90% and 110% of its base case value.

Cell B27 contains the following formula that will return an integer from 1 to 33 indicating which optimization is currently being performed:

Formula or cell B27:   =PsiCurrentOpt( )

As the 33 optimizations are carried out, cell B28 computes which of the three parameters in our model is currently being adjusted as follows:

Formula or cell B28:   =INT((B27-1)/11) + 1

The INT( ) function returns the integer portion of its argument. Thus, when B27 take on integer values from 1 to 11, cell B28 returns the value 1 (associated with the first parameter); when B27 takes on values from 12 to 22, cell B28 returns the value 2; and when B27 takes on values from 23 to 33, cell B28 returns a value of 3.

For a given parameter value in cell B28, cell B29 computes which of the 11 scenarios is represented by each of the 33 optimization runs as follows:

Formula or cell B29:   =B27-11*(B28-1)

For each optimization run, the formulas in cells G9 through G10 return the appropriate percentages of the base case values for each of the three parameters.

Formula or cell G9:   =IF($B$28=ROW(G9)-8, INDEX($B$15:$B$25,$B$29), 1)
(Copy to G10:G11.)

In this formula, the IF( ) function first checks to see if the current parameter value in cell B28 (that is, 1, 2, or 3) corresponds to the parameter of the row in question. Note that for cell G9, ROW(G9)-8=9-8=1; for cell G10, ROW(G10)-8=10-8=2; and for cell G11, ROW(G11)-8=11-8=3. If so, the INDEX( ) function returns the percentage value from the list of values in cells B15 through B25 that corresponds to the current scenario value in cell B29; otherwise, the value 1 (or 100%) is returned.

Cells E9 through E11 then simply multiply the base case values in F9 through F11 by the adjustment values in cells G9 through G11 to provide the appropriate LHS values for the constraints needed for each of the 33 optimization runs.

Formula or cell E9:   =F9*G9
(Copy to E10:E11.)

As Risk Solver performs each of the 33 optimizations, it tracks (or monitors) the optimal values of the objective and the decision variables for each solution. We can extract any of these values to our spreadsheet via the function PsiOptValue(X, Y), which, in general, returns the optimal value for monitored cell X for optimization number Y. The optimal objective value for each optimization is extracted to cells C15 through E25 as follows:

Formula or cell C15:   =PsiOptValue($D$6, $A15+11*(COLUMN(C15)-3))
(Copy to C15:E25.)

Note that the second argument in this PsiOptValue( ) simply computes the appropriate optimization number (from 1 to 33) for each of the cells in the range from C15 through E25. (It returns the appropriate value from A15 through A25 plus 0, 11, or 22 if the formula is in column C, D, or E, respectively.)

To solve this problem, we use the same settings for the objective cell, variable cells, and constraint cells as before. However, to make Risk Solver run the multiple optimizations needed for this problem, we must set the Optimizations to Run property to 33 on the Platform tab in the Risk Solver task pane as shown earlier in Figure 4.12. We then click the Run icon (the green arrow) in the Risk Solver task pane to produce the results shown in Figure 4.13.

FIGURE 4.13 *A Spider Table and Plot showing the relationship between profit and the availability of pumps, labor, and tubing*

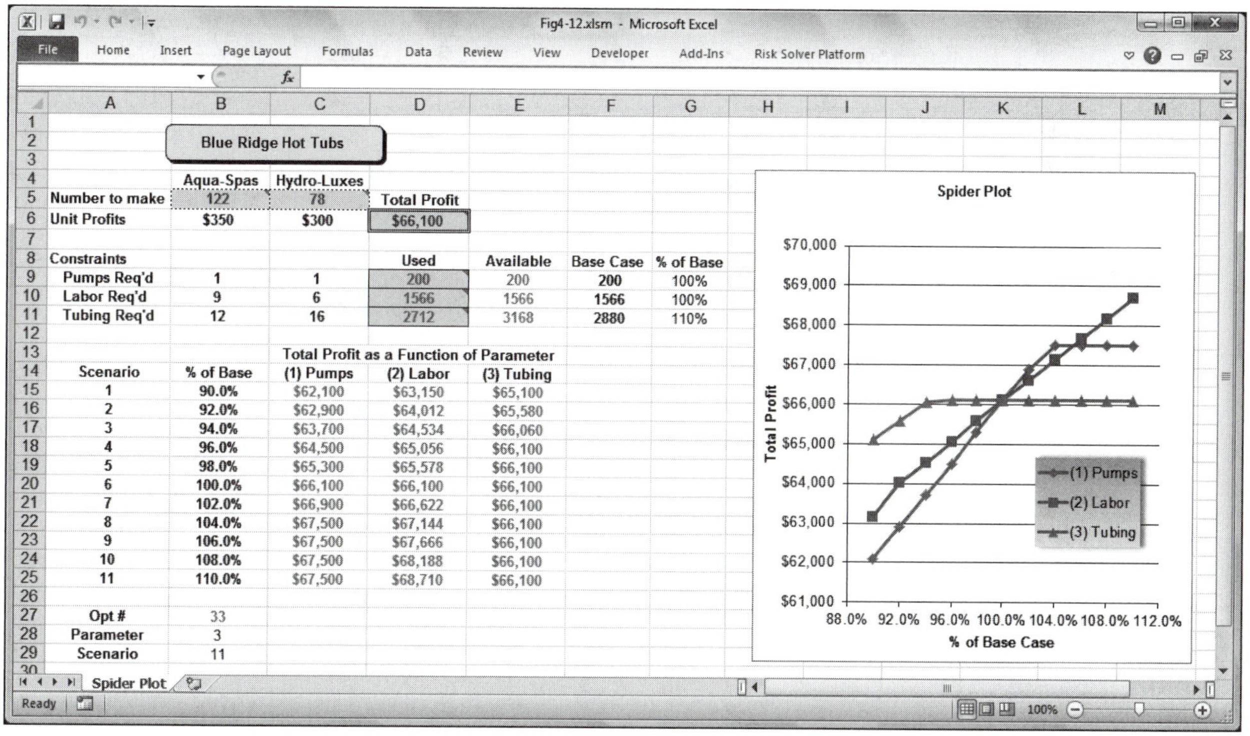

	A	B	C	D	E	F	G
2		Blue Ridge Hot Tubs					
4		Aqua-Spas	Hydro-Luxes				
5	Number to make	122	78	Total Profit			
6	Unit Profits	$350	$300	$66,100			
8	Constraints			Used	Available	Base Case	% of Base
9	Pumps Req'd	1	1	200	200	200	100%
10	Labor Req'd	9	6	1566	1566	1566	100%
11	Tubing Req'd	12	16	2712	3168	2880	110%
13			Total Profit as a Function of Parameter				
14	Scenario	% of Base	(1) Pumps	(2) Labor	(3) Tubing		
15	1	90.0%	$62,100	$63,150	$65,100		
16	2	92.0%	$62,900	$64,012	$65,580		
17	3	94.0%	$63,700	$64,534	$66,060		
18	4	96.0%	$64,500	$65,056	$66,100		
19	5	98.0%	$65,300	$65,578	$66,100		
20	6	100.0%	$66,100	$66,100	$66,100		
21	7	102.0%	$66,900	$66,622	$66,100		
22	8	104.0%	$67,500	$67,144	$66,100		
23	9	106.0%	$67,500	$67,666	$66,100		
24	10	108.0%	$67,500	$68,188	$66,100		
25	11	110.0%	$67,500	$68,710	$66,100		
27	Opt #	33					
28	Parameter	3					
29	Scenario	11					

In Figure 4.13, cells C15 through E25 show the optimal objective function values for each of our 33 optimization runs. As indicated, we can also graph this data to create an aptly named Spider Plot. The center point in the graph corresponds to the optimal solution to the original model with 100% of the pumps, labor, and tubing available. Each of the points in the graph shows the impact on total profit of varying the original resource levels by the indicated percentage.

It is clear from Figure 4.13 that total profit is relatively insensitive to modest decreases or large increases in the availability of tubing. This is consistent with the sensitivity information regarding tubing shown earlier in Figure 4.9. The optimal solution to the original problem involved using all the pumps and all the labor hours but only 2,712 feet of the 2,880 available feet of tubing. As a result, we could achieve the same level of profit even if the availability of tubing was reduced by 168 feet (or to about 94.2% of its original value). Similarly, because we are not using all of the available tubing, acquiring more tubing would only increase the surplus and not allow for any improvement in profit. Thus, our analysis suggests that the availability of tubing probably should not be a top concern in this problem. On the other hand, the Spider Plot suggests that changes in the availability of pumps and labor have a more pronounced impact on profit and the optimal solution to the problem.

Creating a Spider Plot

To create a Spider Plot like the one shown in Figure 4.13, follow these steps:

1. Select cells B14 through E25.
2. Click Insert, Scatter, and Scatter with Straight Lines and Markers.

These steps will create a basic Spider Plot on your worksheet. You can then click the chart and use the Chart Tools ribbon to format and customize various elements of the chart.

4.7.2 CREATING A SOLVER TABLE

The Spider Plot in Figure 4.13 suggests that the total profit earned is most sensitive to changes in the available supply of pumps. We can create a Solver Table to study in greater detail the impact of changes in the available number of pumps. Recall that a Solver Table summarizes the optimal value of multiple output cells as changes are made to a single input cell. In this case, the single input we want to change is cell E9 representing the number of pumps available. We might want to track what happens to several output cells, including the optimal number of Aqua-Spas and Hydro-Luxes (cells B5 and C5), the total profit (cell D6), and the total amount of pumps, labor, and tubing used (cells D9, D10, and D11). Figure 4.14 (and file Fig4-14.xlsm that accompanies this book) shows how to set up the Solver Table for this problem.

In this problem, we want to perform 11 optimizations, varying the number of pumps available in each run. Cells B15 through B25 contain the different possible numbers of available pumps that we want to use in cell E9 in each of the optimizations. The following formula in cell E9 accomplishes this:

Formula for cell E9:   =PsiOptParam(B15:B25)

This formula instructs Risk Solver to use the values from cells B15 through B25 sequentially in E9 as it performs each of the 11 optimizations.

Cells C15 through H25 contain PsiOptValue( ) functions that report the optimal values of various output cells we want to track. Thus, cells C15 through H15 each contain a formula referring to one of our output cells.

Formula for cell C15:   =PsiOptValue($B$5, A15)
(Copy to C16:C25.)

Formula for cell D15:   =PsiOptValue($C$5, A15)
(Copy to D16:D25.)

Formula for cell E15:   =PsiOptValue($D$6, A15)
(Copy to E16:E25.)

FIGURE 4.14 *Set up for creating a Solver Table*

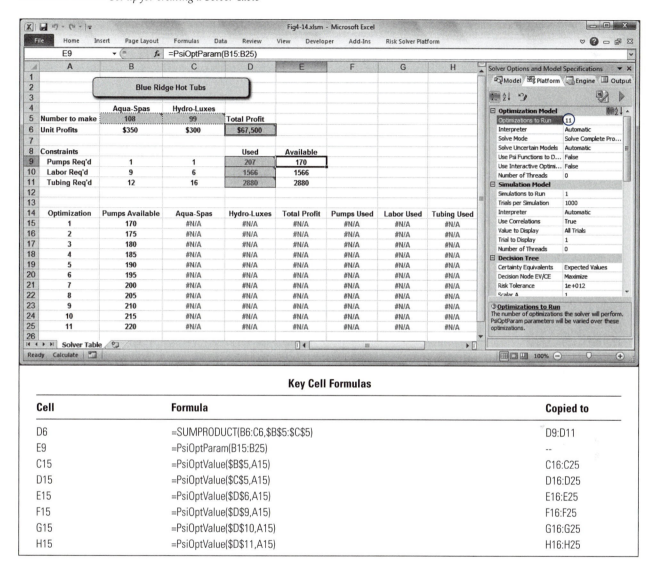

Key Cell Formulas

Cell	Formula	Copied to
D6	=SUMPRODUCT(B6:C6,$B$5:$C$5)	D9:D11
E9	=PsiOptParam(B15:B25)	--
C15	=PsiOptValue($B$5,A15)	C16:C25
D15	=PsiOptValue($C$5,A15)	D16:D25
E15	=PsiOptValue($D$6,A15)	E16:E25
F15	=PsiOptValue($D$9,A15)	F16:F25
G15	=PsiOptValue($D$10,A15)	G16:G25
H15	=PsiOptValue($D$11,A15)	H16:H25

Formula for cell F15:   =PsiOptValue($D$9, A15)
(Copy to F16:F25.)

Formula for cell G15:   =PsiOptValue($D$10, A15)
(Copy to G16:G25.)

Formula for cell H15:   =PsiOptValue($D$11, A15)
(Copy to H16:H25.)

To complete the Solver Table, we instruct Risk Solver to perform 11 optimizations as shown in Figure 4.14 on the Platform tab in the Risk Solver task pane and then click the Run icon. The resulting Solver Table is shown in Figure 4.15.

FIGURE 4.15 *Solver Table showing changes in the optimal solution, profit, and resource usage and the number of pumps changed*

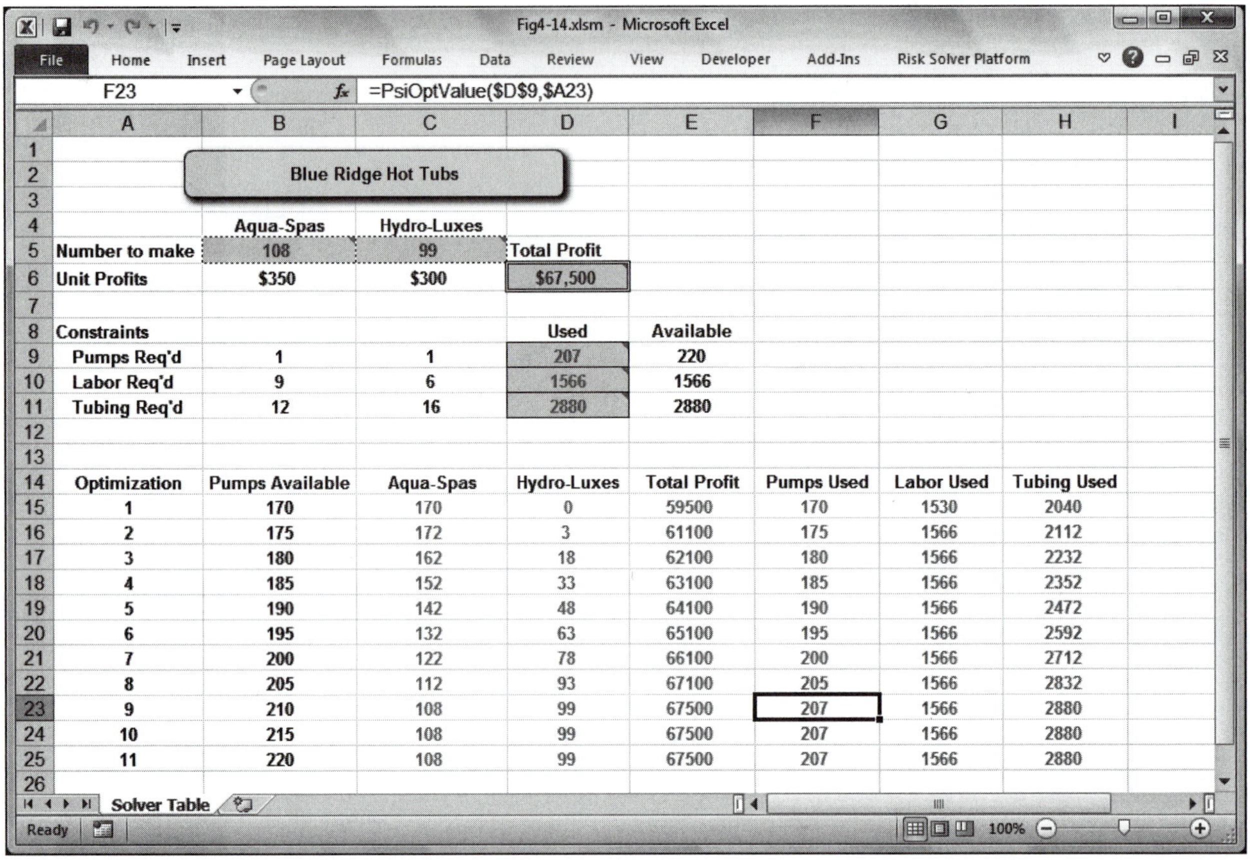

Fig4-14.xlsm - Microsoft Excel

F23 =PsiOptValue($D$9,$A23)

Blue Ridge Hot Tubs

	Aqua-Spas	Hydro-Luxes	
Number to make	108	99	Total Profit
Unit Profits	$350	$300	$67,500

Constraints			Used	Available
Pumps Req'd	1	1	207	220
Labor Req'd	9	6	1566	1566
Tubing Req'd	12	16	2880	2880

Optimization	Pumps Available	Aqua-Spas	Hydro-Luxes	Total Profit	Pumps Used	Labor Used	Tubing Used
1	170	170	0	59500	170	1530	2040
2	175	172	3	61100	175	1566	2112
3	180	162	18	62100	180	1566	2232
4	185	152	33	63100	185	1566	2352
5	190	142	48	64100	190	1566	2472
6	195	132	63	65100	195	1566	2592
7	200	122	78	66100	200	1566	2712
8	205	112	93	67100	205	1566	2832
9	210	108	99	67500	207	1566	2880
10	215	108	99	67500	207	1566	2880
11	220	108	99	67500	207	1566	2880

Solver Table

A number of interesting insights emerge from Figure 4.15. First, compare columns B and F: As the number of available pumps increases from 170 up to 205, they are always all used. With about 175 pumps, we also begin to use all the available labor. However, when the number of available pumps increases to 210 or more, only 207 pumps can be used because we run out of both tubing and labor at that point. This suggests that the company should not be interested in getting more than 7 additional pumps unless it can also increase the amount of tubing and/or labor available.

Also note that the addition or subtraction of 5 pumps from the initial supply of 200 causes the optimal objective function value (column E) to change by $1,000. This suggests that if the company has 200 pumps, the marginal value of each pump is about $200 (that is, $1000/5=$200). Of course, this is equivalent to the **shadow price** of pumps shown earlier in Figure 4.9.

Finally, it is interesting to note that when the availability of pumps is between 175 and 205, each increase of 5 pumps causes the optimal number of Aqua-Spas to decrease by 10 and the optimal number of Hydro-Luxes to increase by 15. Thus, one advantage of the Solver Table over the Sensitivity Report is that it tells you not only how much the optimal value of the objective function changes as the number of pumps change but also how the optimal solution changes.

4.7.3 COMMENTS

Additional Solver Tables and Spider Tables/Plots could be constructed to analyze every element of the model, including objective function and constraint coefficients. However, these techniques are considered "computationally expensive" because they require the LP model to be solved repeatedly. For small problems like Blue Ridge Hot Tubs, this is not really a problem. But as problem size and complexity increases, this approach to sensitivity analysis can become impractical.

4.8 Robust Optimization

As we have seen, an optimal solution to an LP problem will occur on the boundary of its feasible region. While these boundaries can be determined very precisely for a given set of data, any uncertainties or changes in the data will result in uncertainties or changes in the boundaries of the feasible region. Thus, the optimal solution to an LP problem can be somewhat fragile and could actually become infeasible (and a costly mistake) if any of the coefficients in an LP model are incorrect or differ from the real-world phenomena being modeled. In recent years, this reality has led a number of researchers and practitioners to consider (and often prefer) robust solutions to optimization problems. A **robust solution** to an LP problem is a solution in the *interior* of the feasible region (rather than on the boundary of the feasible region) that has a reasonably good objective function value. Clearly, such a solution will not maximize (or minimize) the objective function value (except in trivial cases), so it is not an optimal solution in the traditional sense of the word. However, a robust solution will generally remain feasible if modest perturbations or changes occur to the coefficients in the model.

Risk Solver Platform offers a number of powerful tools for identifying robust solutions to optimization problems. For LP problems, we can easily accommodate uncertainties in constraint coefficients using uncertainty set (USet) chance constraints. To illustrate this, recall that the original Blue Ridge Hot Tubs problem assumed each Aqua-Spa required 1 pump, 9 hours of labor, and 12 feet of tubing, while each Hydro-Lux required 1 pump, 6 hours of labor, and 16 feet of tubing. The optimal solution to this problem was to make 122 Aqua-Spas and 78 Hydro-Luxes (see Figure 4.1). Clearly, each hot tub will require 1 pump, so there is really no uncertainty about that constraint. However, the actual amount of labor and tubing might vary a bit from the values assumed earlier. So, suppose the amount of labor required per hot tub might vary from their originally assumed values by 15 minutes (or .25 hours), and the amount of tubing required might vary by 6 inches (or 0.5 feet). That is, the amount of labor required per Aqua-Spa is uncertain but can reasonably be expected to vary uniformly between 8.75 and 9.25 hours, and the labor required per Hydro-Lux is expected to vary uniformly from 5.75 to 6.25 hours. Similarly, the amount of tubing required per Aqua-Spa is uncertain but can reasonably be expected to vary uniformly between 11.5 and 12.5 feet, and the tubing required per Hydro-Lux is expected to vary uniformly from 15.5 to 16.5 feet. Figure 4.16 (and the file Fig4-16.xlsm that accompanies this book) shows a revised version of the Blue Ridge Hot Tubs problem that accounts for these uncertainties in the labor and tubing constraints.

In Figure 4.16, note that the previous numeric constants in cells B10 through C11 have been replaced by the following random number generators:

Formula for cell B10:   =PsiUniform(8.75, 9.25)
Formula for cell C10:   =PsiUniform(5.75, 6.25)

FIGURE 4.16 *A robust optimization spreadsheet for the Blue Ridge Hot Tubs problem*

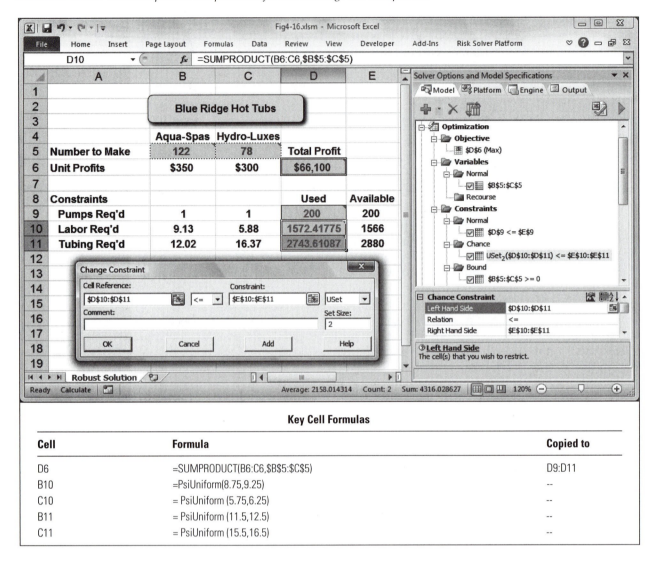

Formula for cell B11:   =PsiUniform(11.5, 12.5)

Formula for cell C11:   =PsiUniform(15.5, 16.5)

The PsiUniform(Lower, Upper) function is a Risk Solver Platform function that returns a random value from a uniform distribution between a specified lower and upper limit each time the spreadsheet is recalculated. Because the numbers are randomly generated (or randomly sampled) the actual numbers on your computer's screen will likely differ from those in Figure 4.16. (You will learn much more about using random number generators in Chapter 12.) Also notice that the optimal solution of 122 Aqua-Spas and 78 Hydro-Luxes actually violates the labor constraint in the random scenario shown in Figure 4.16. So, as stated earlier, the optimal solution to an LP problem can actually end up being infeasible if uncertainty exists about the values of one or more model coefficients that we simply ignore or assume away. The spreadsheet in Figure 4.16 does not ignore the uncertainties in the labor and tubing coefficients but, instead, models them explicitly.

In Figure 4.16, notice that the constraint on the number of pumps used was defined in the usual way and appears as a "normal" constraint in the Risk Solver task pane Model tab. When defining the labor and tubing constraints, we must select the USet constraint type and specify a value for the Set Size. (Notice that these constraints appear as Chance constraints in the Risk Solver task pane Model tab.) The Set Size is sometimes referred to as the budget of uncertainty for the constraint. There is no prescribed way of determining the Set Size value. Generally speaking, as the Set Size value increases, the solution obtained becomes more conservative (or more robust).

FIGURE 4.17 *A conservative robust solution to the Blue Ridge Hot Tubs problem*

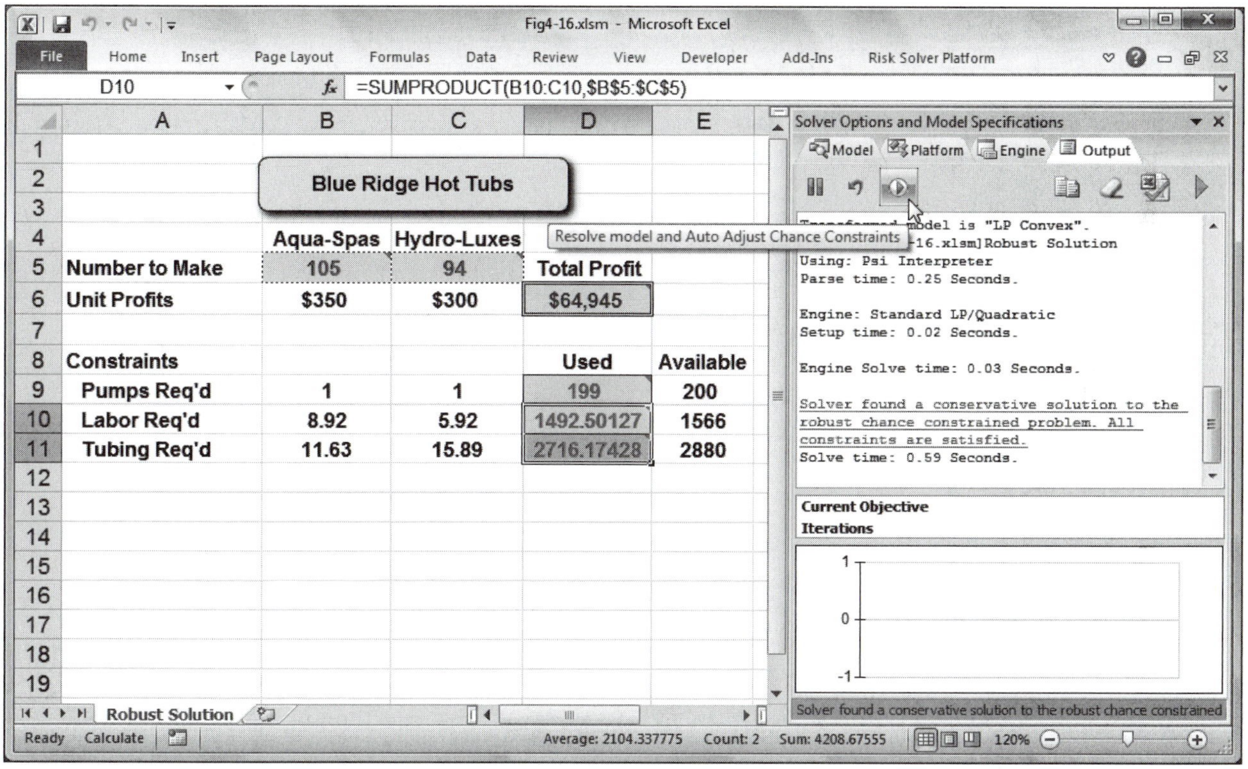

When we solve this problem, Risk Solver actually formulates a larger LP problem with several different coefficient values for the USet constraints. It then solves this problem to obtain a solution that satisfies all of these possible constraint configurations. Figure 4.17 shows the first solution Risk Solver found for this problem. This solution involves producing about 105 Aqua-Spas and 94 Hydro-Luxes for a profit of $64,945. If you evaluate this solution under our original deterministic assumptions—where Aqua-Spas require 9 hours of labor and 12 feet of tubing and Hydro-Luxes require 6 hours of labor and 16 feet of tubing—you will see that this solution uses about 1,509 of the available 1,566 hours of labor and about 2,764 feet of the available 2,880 feet of tubing. So as indicated on the Output tab in the Risk Solver task pane, this is a "conservative solution" that does not make use of all the available resources. If you click the smaller green arrow on the Output tab, Risk Solver will display a less conservative solution to the problem as shown in Figure 4.18

FIGURE 4.18 *A less conservative robust solution to the Blue Ridge Hot Tubs problem*

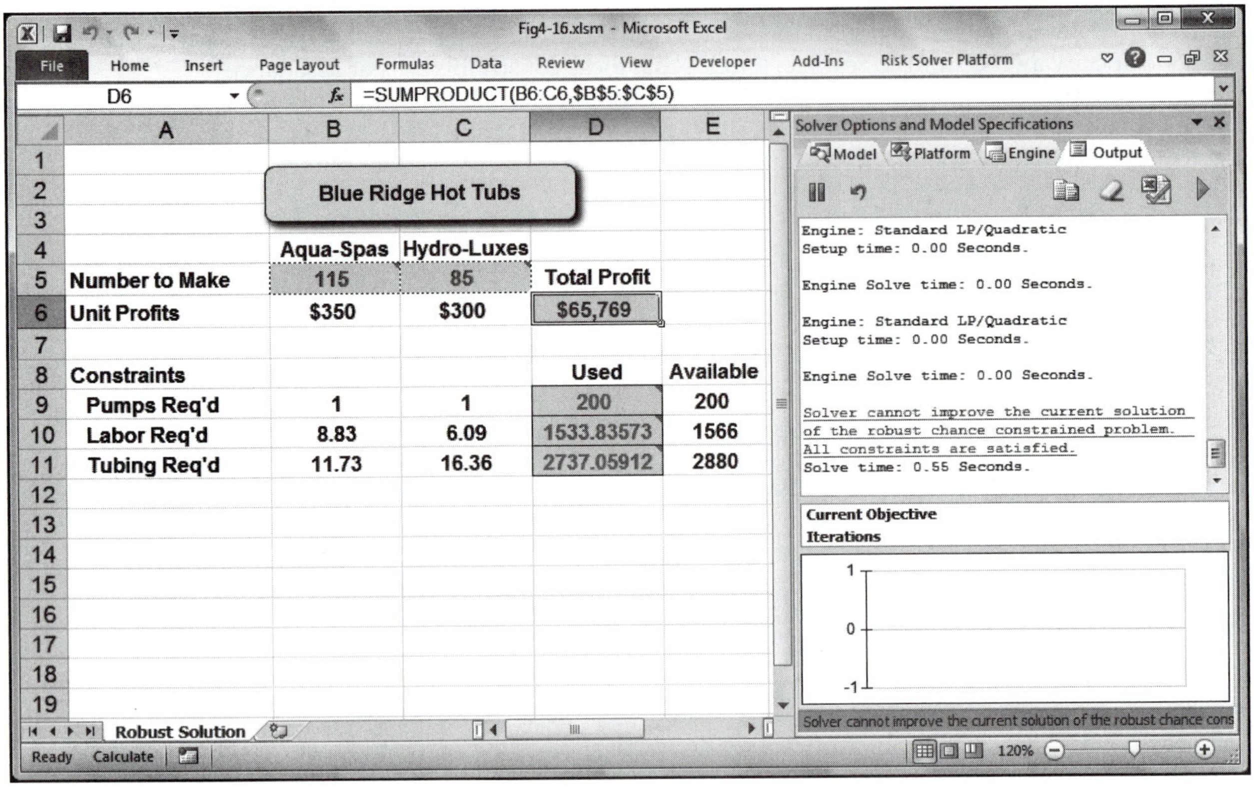

The solution in Figure 4.18 involves producing about 115 Aqua-Spas and 85 Hydro-Luxes for a profit of $65,769. If you evaluate this solution under our original deterministic assumptions (with 9 hours of labor and 12 feet of tubing for Aqua-Spas, and 6 hours of labor and 16 feet of tubing for Hydro-Luxes), you will see that this solution uses about 1,545 of the available 1,566 hours of labor and about 2,740 feet of the available 2,880 feet of tubing. This solution is better than the previous one shown in Figure 4.17 from a profit perspective but takes us much closer to the boundary of the labor constraint.

As you can see, robust optimization is a very powerful technique but requires a bit of trial and error on the part of the decision maker in terms of specifying the set size and evaluating the trade-offs between satisfying the constraints by a comfortable margin (to allow for uncertainties) and sacrificing objective function value. A complete discussion of robust optimization is beyond the scope of this book, but you can read the *Risk Solver Platform User Manual* for more information and additional reference resources. We will also explore the idea of optimization under uncertainty in Chapter 12.

4.9 The Simplex Method

We have repeatedly mentioned that the simplex method is the preferred method for solving LP problems. This section provides an overview of the simplex method and shows how it relates to some of the items that appear on the Answer Report and the Sensitivity Report.

4.9.1 CREATING EQUALITY CONSTRAINTS USING SLACK VARIABLES

Because our original formulation of the LP model for the Blue Ridge Hot Tubs problem has only *two* decision variables (X_1 and X_2), you might be surprised to learn that Solver actually used *five* variables to solve this problem. As you saw in Chapter 2 when we plotted the boundary lines for the constraints in an LP problem, it is easier to work with equal to conditions rather than less than or equal to, or greater than or equal to conditions. Similarly, the simplex method requires that *all* constraints in an LP model be expressed as equalities.

To solve an LP problem using the simplex method, Solver temporarily turns all inequality constraints into equality constraints by adding one new variable to each less than or equal to constraint and subtracting one new variable from each greater than or equal to constraint. The new variables used to create equality constraints are called **slack variables**.

For example, consider the less than or equal to constraint:

$$a_{k1}X_1 + a_{k2}X_2 + \dots + a_{kn}X_n \leq b_k$$

Solver can turn this constraint into an equal to constraint by adding the nonnegative slack variable S_k to the LHS of the constraint:

$$a_{k1}X_1 + a_{k2}X_2 + \dots + a_{kn}X_n + S_k = b_k$$

The variable S_k represents the amount by which $a_{k1}X_1 + a_{k2}X_2 + \dots + a_{kn}X_n$ is less than b_k. Now consider the greater than or equal to constraint:

$$a_{k1}X_1 + a_{k2}X_2 + \dots + a_{kn}X_n \geq b_k$$

Solver can turn this constraint into an equal to constraint by subtracting the nonnegative slack variable S_k from the LHS of the constraint:

$$a_{k1}X_1 + a_{k2}X_2 + \dots + a_{kn}X_n - S_k = b_k$$

In this case, the variable S_k represents the amount by which $a_{k1}X_1 + a_{k2}X_2 + \dots + a_{kn}X_n$ exceeds b_k.

To solve the original Blue Ridge Hot Tubs problem using the simplex method, Solver actually solved the following modified problem involving *five* variables:

MAX:	$350X_1 +$	$300X_2$					} profit
Subject to:	$1X_1 +$	$1X_2 +$	S_1	$=$	200		} pump constraint
	$9X_1 +$	$6X_2 +$	S_2	$=$	$1{,}566$		} labor constraint
	$12X_1 +$	$16X_2 +$	S_3	$=$	$2{,}880$		} tubing constraint
		X_1, X_2, S_1, S_2, S_3		$\geq$	0		} nonnegativity conditions

We will refer to X_1 and X_2 as the **structural variables** in the model to distinguish them from the slack variables.

Recall that we did not set up slack variables in the spreadsheet or include them in the formulas in the constraint cells. Solver automatically sets up the slack variables it needs to solve a particular problem. The only time Solver even mentions these variables is when it creates an Answer Report like the one shown in Figure 4.2. The values in the Slack column in the Answer Report correspond to the optimal values of the slack variables.

4.9.2 BASIC FEASIBLE SOLUTIONS

After all the inequality constraints in an LP problem have been converted into equalities (by adding or subtracting appropriate slack variables), the constraints in the LP model represent a system (or collection) of linear equations. If there are a total of n variables in a system of m equations, one strategy for finding a solution to the system of equations is to select any m variables and try to find values for them that solve the system, assuming all other variables are set equal to their lower bounds (which are usually zero). This strategy requires more variables than constraints in the system of equations—or that $n \geq m$.

The m variables selected to solve the system of equations in an LP model are sometimes called **basic variables**, while the remaining variables are called **nonbasic variables**. If a solution to the system of equations can be obtained using a given set of basic variables (while the nonbasic variables are all set equal to zero), that solution is called a **basic feasible solution**. Every basic feasible solution corresponds to one of the extreme points of the feasible region for the LP problem, and we know that the optimal solution to the LP problem also occurs at an extreme point. So, the challenge in LP is to find the set of basic variables (and their optimal values) that produce the basic feasible solution corresponding to the optimal extreme point of the feasible region.

Because our modified problem involves three constraints and five variables, we could select 3 basic variables in 10 different ways to form possible basic feasible solutions for the problem. Figure 4.19 summarizes the results for these 10 options.

The first five solutions in Figure 4.19 are feasible and, therefore, represent basic feasible solutions to this problem. The remaining solutions are infeasible because they violate the nonnegativity conditions. The best feasible alternative shown in Figure 4.19 corresponds

FIGURE 4.19

Possible basic feasible solutions for the original Blue Ridge Hot Tubs problem

	Basic Variables	Nonbasic Variables	Solution	Objective Value
1	S_1, S_2, S_3	X_1, X_2	$X_1=0, X_2=0,$ $S_1=200, S_2=1566, S_3=2880$	0
2	X_1, S_1, S_3	X_2, S_2	$X_1=174, X_2=0,$ $S_1=26, S_2=0, S_3=792$	60,900
3	X_1, X_2, S_3	S_1, S_2	$X_1=122, X_2=78,$ $S_1=0, S_2=0, S_3=168$	66,100
4	X_1, X_2, S_2	S_1, S_3	$X_1=80, X_2=120,$ $S_1=0, S_2=126, S_3=0$	64,000
5	X_2, S_1, S_2	X_1, S_3	$X_1=0, X_2=180,$ $S_1=20, S_2=486, S_3=0$	54,000
6*	X_1, X_2, S_1	S_2, S_3	$X_1=108, X_2=99,$ $S_1=-7, S_2=0, S_3=0$	67,500
7*	X_1, S_1, S_2	X_2, S_3	$X_1=240, X_2=0,$ $S_1=-40, S_2=-594, S_3=0$	84,000
8*	X_1, S_2, S_3	X_2, S_1	$X_1=200, X_2=0,$ $S_1=0, S_2=-234, S_3=480$	70,000
9*	X_2, S_2, S_3	X_1, S_1	$X_1=0, X_2=200,$ $S_1=0, S_2=366, S_3=-320$	60,000
10*	X_2, S_1, S_3	X_1, S_2	$X_1=0, X_2=261,$ $S_1=-61, S_2=0, S_3=-1296$	78,300

Note: * denotes infeasible solutions

to the optimal solution to the problem. In particular, if X_1, X_2, and S_3 are selected as basic variables, and S_1 and S_2 are nonbasic and assigned their lower bound values (zero), we try to find values for X_1, X_2, and S_3 that satisfy the following constraints:

$$
\begin{aligned}
1X_1 + 1X_2 \qquad\quad &= 200 &\quad &\text{\} pump constraint} \\
9X_1 + 6X_2 \qquad\quad &= 1{,}566 &\quad &\text{\} labor constraint} \\
12X_1 + 16X_2 + S_3 &= 2{,}880 &\quad &\text{\} tubing constraint}
\end{aligned}
$$

Notice that S_1 and S_2 in the modified equal to constraints are not included in the preceding constraint equations because we are assuming that the values of these nonbasic variables are equal to zero (their lower bounds). Using linear algebra, the simplex method determines that the values $X_1 = 122$, $X_2 = 78$, and $S_3 = 168$ satisfy the equations given previously. So, a basic feasible solution to this problem is $X_1 = 122$, $X_2 = 78$, $S_1 = 0$, $S_2 = 0$, $S_3 = 168$. As indicated in Figure 4.19, this solution produces an objective function value of \$66,100. (Notice that the optimal values for the slack variables S_1, S_2, and S_3 also correspond to the values shown earlier in the Answer Report in Figure 4.2 in the Slack column for constraint cells D9, D10, and D11.) Figure 4.20 shows the relationships between the basic feasible solutions listed in Figure 4.16 and the extreme points of the feasible region for this problem.

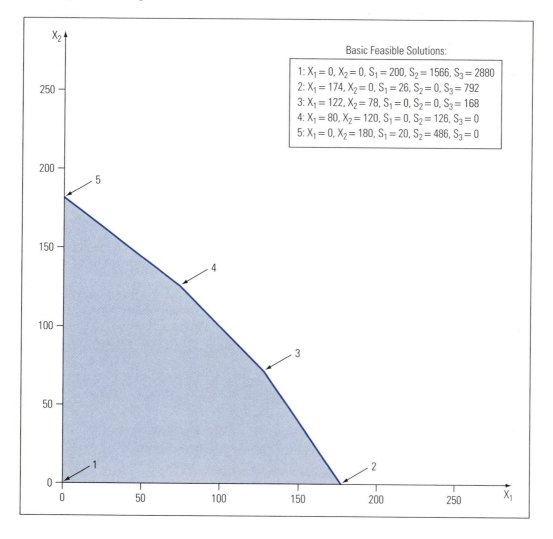

FIGURE 4.20

Illustration of the relationship between basic feasible solutions and extreme points

Basic Feasible Solutions:

1: $X_1 = 0$, $X_2 = 0$, $S_1 = 200$, $S_2 = 1566$, $S_3 = 2880$
2: $X_1 = 174$, $X_2 = 0$, $S_1 = 26$, $S_2 = 0$, $S_3 = 792$
3: $X_1 = 122$, $X_2 = 78$, $S_1 = 0$, $S_2 = 0$, $S_3 = 168$
4: $X_1 = 80$, $X_2 = 120$, $S_1 = 0$, $S_2 = 126$, $S_3 = 0$
5: $X_1 = 0$, $X_2 = 180$, $S_1 = 20$, $S_2 = 486$, $S_3 = 0$

4.9.3 FINDING THE BEST SOLUTION

The simplex method operates by first identifying any basic feasible solution (or extreme point) for an LP problem, and then moving to an adjacent extreme point, if such a move improves the value of the objective function. When no adjacent extreme point has a better objective function value, the current extreme point is optimal, and the simplex method terminates.

The process of moving from one extreme point to an adjacent one is accomplished by switching one of the basic variables with one of the nonbasic variables to create a new basic feasible solution that corresponds to the adjacent extreme point. For example, in Figure 4.20, moving from the first basic feasible solution (point 1) to the second basic feasible solution (point 2) involves making X_1 a basic variable and S_2 a nonbasic variable. Similarly, we can move from point 2 to point 3 by switching basic variables with nonbasic variables. So, starting at point 1 in Figure 4.20, the simplex method could move to point 2 and then to the optimal solution at point 3. Alternatively, the simplex method could move from point 1 through points 5 and 4 to reach the optimal solution at point 3. Thus, although there is no guarantee that the simplex method will take the shortest route to the optimal solution of an LP problem, it will find the optimal solution eventually.

To determine whether switching a basic and nonbasic variable will result in a better solution, the simplex method calculates the reduced cost for each nonbasic variable to determine if the objective function could be improved if any of these variables are substituted for one of the basic variables. (Note that unbounded solutions are detected easily in the simplex method by the existence of a nonbasic variable that could improve the objective value by an infinite amount if it were made basic.) This process continues until no further improvement in the objective function value is possible.

4.10 Summary

This chapter described the methods for assessing how sensitive an LP model is to various changes that might occur in the model or its optimal solution. The impact of changes in an LP model can be analyzed easily by re-solving the model. Solver also provides a significant amount of sensitivity information automatically. For LP problems, the maximum amount of sensitivity information is obtained by solving the problem using the simplex method. Before using the information on the Sensitivity Report, you should always first check for the presence of degeneracy because this can have a significant impact on how to interpret the numbers on this report.

The simplex method considers only the extreme points of the feasible region and is an efficient way of solving LP problems. In this method, slack variables are first introduced to convert all constraints to equal to constraints. The simplex method systematically moves to better and better corner point solutions until no adjacent extreme point provides an improved objective function value.

4.11 References

Bazaraa, M., and J. Jarvis. *Linear Programming and Network Flows*. New York: Wiley, 1990.

Eppen, G., F. Gould and C. Schmidt. *Introductory Management Science*, 4th ed., Englewoods Cliffs, NJ: Prentice-Hall, 1993.

Shogan, A. *Management Science*. Englewood Cliffs, NJ: Prentice Hall, 1988.

Wagner, H., and D. Rubin. "Shadow Prices: Tips and Traps for Managers and Instructors," *Interfaces*, vol. 20, no. 4, 1990.

Winston, W. *Operations Research: Applications and Algorithms*. Belmont, CA: Duxbury Press, 1994.

THE WORLD OF MANAGEMENT SCIENCE

Fuel Management and Allocation Model Helps National Airlines Adapt to Cost and Supply Changes

Fuel is a major component in the cost structure of an airline. Price and availability of fuel can vary from one air terminal to the next, and it is sometimes advantageous for an aircraft to carry more than the necessary minimum for the next leg of its route. Fuel loaded for the purpose of taking advantage of price or availability at a specific location is said to be tankered. A disadvantage of tankering is that fuel consumption increases when an aircraft is carrying more weight.

The use of LP to determine when and where to fuel aircraft saved National Airlines several million dollars during the first two years of implementation. In particular, National Airlines saw its average fuel costs drop 11.75% during a period when the average fuel cost for all domestic trunk airlines increased by 2.87%.

The objective function in the Fuel Management and Allocation Model consists of fuel costs and increases in operating costs from tankering. The constraints in the model address availability, minimum reserves, and aircraft capacities.

A particularly useful feature of the Fuel Management and Allocation Model is a series of reports that assist management in modifying the fuel-loading plan when sudden changes occur in availability or price. Shadow prices, along with the associated range of applicability, provide information about supply changes. Information about changes in price per gallon comes from the allowable increase and decrease for objective function coefficients.

For example, the availability report might indicate that the optimal quantity to purchase at Los Angeles from Shell West is 2,718,013 gallons; but if its supply decreases and fuel must be purchased from the next most attractive vendor, total cost would increase at the rate of $0.0478 per gallon (the shadow price). This fuel would be replaced by a prior purchase of up to 159,293 gallons from Shell East at New Orleans, tankered to Los Angeles.

The price report shows, for example, that vendor substitutions should be made if the current price of Shell West at Los Angeles, $0.3074, increases to $0.32583 or decreases to $0.27036. The report also indicates what that substitution should be.

Source: Darnell, D. Wayne and Carolyn Loflin, "National Airlines Fuel Management and Allocation Model," *Interfaces*, vol. 7, no. 2, February 1977, pp 1–16.

Questions and Problems

1. Howie Jones used the following information to calculate the profit coefficients for Aqua-Spas and Hydro-Luxes: pumps cost $225 each, labor costs $12 per hour, and tubing costs $2 per foot. In addition to pumps, labor, and tubing, the production of Aqua-Spas and Hydro-Luxes consumes, respectively, $243 and $246 per unit in other resources that are not in short supply. Using this information, Howie calculated the marginal profits on Aqua-Spas and Hydro-Luxes as shown in the following table.

	Aqua-Spas	Hydro-Luxes
Selling Price	$950	$875
Pump Cost	−$225	−$225
Labor Cost	−$108	−$72
Tubing Cost	−$24	−$32
Other Variable Costs	−$243	−$246
Marginal Profit	$350	$300

Howie's accountant reviewed these calculations and thinks Howie made a mistake. For accounting purposes, factory overhead is assigned to products at a rate of $16 per labor hour. Howie's accountant argues that because Aqua-Spas require nine labor hours, the profit margin on this product should be $144 less. Similarly, because Hydro-Luxes require six labor hours, the profit margin on this product should be $96 less. Who is right and why?

2. A variable that assumes an optimal value between its lower- and upper bounds has a reduced cost value of zero. Why must this be true? (Hint: What if such a variable's reduced cost value is not zero? What does this imply about the value of the objective function?)

3. Implement the following LP problem in a spreadsheet. Use Solver to solve the problem and create a Sensitivity Report. Use this information to answer the following questions:

$$\begin{aligned}
\text{MAX:} \quad & 4X_1 + 2X_2 \\
\text{Subject to:} \quad & 2X_1 + 4X_2 \le 20 \\
& 3X_1 + 5X_2 \le 15 \\
& X_1, X_2 \ge 0
\end{aligned}$$

   a. What range of values can the objective function coefficient for variable X_1 assume without changing the optimal solution?
   b. Is the optimal solution to this problem unique, or are there alternate optimal solutions?
   c. How much does the objective function coefficient for variable X_2 have to increase before it enters the optimal solution at a strictly positive level?
   d. What is the optimal objective function value if X_2 equals 1?
   e. What is the optimal objective function value if the RHS value for the second constraint changes from 15 to 25?
   f. Is the current solution still optimal if the coefficient for X_2 in the second constraint changes from 5 to 1? Explain.

4. Implement the following LP model in a spreadsheet. Use Solver to solve the problem and create a Sensitivity Report. Use this information to answer the following questions:

$$\begin{aligned}
\text{MAX:} \quad & 2X_1 + 4X_2 \\
\text{Subject to:} \quad & -X_1 + 2X_2 \leq 8 \\
& X_1 + 2X_2 \leq 12 \\
& X_1 + X_2 \geq 2 \\
& X_1, X_2 \geq 0
\end{aligned}$$

a. Which of the constraints are binding at the optimal solution?
b. Is the optimal solution to this problem unique, or is there an alternate optimal solution?
c. What is the optimal solution to this problem if the value of the objective function coefficient for variable X_1 is zero?
d. How much can the objective function coefficient for variable X_2 decrease before changing the optimal solution?
e. Given the objective in this problem, if management could increase the RHS value for any of the constraints for identical costs, which would you choose to increase and why?

5. Implement the following LP model in a spreadsheet. Use Solver to solve the problem and create a Sensitivity Report. Use this information to answer the following questions:

$$\begin{aligned}
\text{MIN:} \quad & 5X_1 + 3X_2 + 4X_3 \\
\text{Subject to:} \quad & X_1 + X_2 + 2X_3 \geq 2 \\
& 5X_1 + 3X_2 + 2X_3 \geq 1 \\
& X_1, X_2, X_3 \geq 0
\end{aligned}$$

a. What is the smallest value the objective function coefficient for X_3 can assume without changing the optimal solution?
b. What is the optimal objective function value if the objective function coefficient for X_3 changes to –1? (*Hint:* The answer to this question is not given in the Sensitivity Report. Consider what the new objective function is relative to the constraints.)
c. What is the optimal objective function value if the RHS value of the first constraint increases to 7?
d. What is the optimal objective function value if the RHS value of the first constraint decreases by 1?
e. Will the current solution remain optimal if the objective function coefficients for X_1 and X_3 both decrease by 1?

6. The CitruSun Corporation ships frozen orange juice concentrate from processing plants in Eustis and Clermont to distributors in Miami, Orlando, and Tallahassee. Each plant can produce 20 tons of concentrate each week. The company has just received orders of 10 tons from Miami for the coming week, 15 tons for Orlando, and 10 tons for Tallahassee. The cost per ton for supplying each of the distributors from each of the processing plants is shown in the following table.

	Miami	Orlando	Tallahassee
Eustis	$260	$220	$290
Clermont	$230	$240	$310

The company wants to determine the least costly plan for filling their orders for the coming week.
a. Formulate an LP model for this problem.
b. Implement the model in a spreadsheet and solve it.

c. What is the optimal solution?

d. Is the optimal solution degenerate?

e. Is the optimal solution unique? If not, identify an alternate optimal solution for the problem.

f. How would the solution change if the plant in Clermont is forced to shut for one day resulting in a loss of 4 tons of production capacity?

g. What would the optimal objective function value be if the processing capacity in Eustis was reduced by 5 tons?

h. Interpret the reduced cost for shipping from Eustis to Miami.

7. Use Solver to create Answer and Sensitivity Reports for question 13 at the end of Chapter 2, and answer the following questions:

a. How much excess wiring and testing capacity exists in the optimal solution?

b. What is the company's total profit if it has 10 additional hours of wiring capacity?

c. By how much does the profit on alternators need to increase before their production is justified?

d. Does the optimal solution change if the marginal profit on generators decreases by $50 and the marginal profit on alternators increases by $75?

e. Suppose the marginal profit on generators decreases by $25. What is the maximum profit that can be earned on alternators without changing the optimal solution?

f. Suppose the amount of wiring required on alternators is reduced to 1.5 hours. Does this change the optimal solution? Why or why not?

8. Use Solver to create Answer and Sensitivity Reports for question 19 at the end of Chapter 2, and answer the following questions:

a. If the profit on Razors decreased to $35, would the optimal solution change?

b. If the profit on Zoomers decreased to $35, would the optimal solution change?

c. Interpret the shadow price for the supply of polymer.

d. Why is the shadow price $0 for the constraint limiting the production of pocket bikes to no more than 700 units?

e. Suppose the company could obtain 300 additional labor hours in production? What would the new optimal level of profit be?

9. Use Solver to create Answer and Sensitivity Reports for question 21 at the end of Chapter 2, and answer the following questions:

a. How much can the price of watermelons drop before it is no longer optimal to plant any watermelons?

b. How much does the price of cantaloupes have to increase before it is optimal to only grow cantaloupes?

c. Suppose the price of watermelons drops by $60 per acre, and the price of cantaloupes increases by $50 per acre. Is the current solution still optimal?

d. Suppose the farmer can lease up to 20 acres of land from a neighboring farm to plant additional crops. How many acres should the farmer lease, and what is the maximum amount he should pay to lease each acre?

10. Use Solver to create Answer and Sensitivity Reports for question 22 at the end of Chapter 2, and answer the following questions:

a. If the profit on doors increased to $700, would the optimal solution change?

b. If the profit on windows decreased to $200, would the optimal solution change?

c. Explain the shadow price for the finishing process.

d. If 20 additional hours of cutting capacity became available, how much additional profit could the company earn?

e. Suppose another company wanted to use 15 hours of Sanderson's sanding capacity and was willing to pay $400 per hour to acquire it. Should Sanderson agree to this? How (if at all) would your answer change if the company instead wanted 25 hours of sanding capacity?

11. Create a Sensitivity Report for Electro-Poly's make vs. buy problem in Section 3.9 of Chapter 3, and answer the following questions.
    a. Is the solution degenerate?
    b. How much can the cost of making model 1 slip rings increase before it becomes more economical to buy some of them?
    c. Suppose the cost of buying model 2 slip rings decreased by $9 per unit. Would the optimal solution change?
    d. Assume workers in the wiring area normally make $12 per hour and get 50% more when they work overtime. Should Electro-Poly schedule these employees to work overtime to complete this job? If so, how much money would this save?
    e. Assume workers in the harnessing area normally make $12 per hour and get 50% more when they work overtime. Should Electro-Poly schedule these employees to work overtime to complete this job? If so, how much money would this save?
    f. Create a Spider Plot that shows the effect of varying each of the wiring and harnessing requirements (in cells B17 thru D18) to 90% of their current levels in 1% increments. If Electro-Ploy wanted to invest in training or new technology to reduce one of these values, which one offers the greatest potential for cost savings?

12. Use Solver to create a Sensitivity Report for question 13 at the end of Chapter 3, and answer the following questions:
    a. If the company could get 50 more units of routing capacity, should they do it? If so, how much should they be willing to pay for it?
    b. If the company could get 50 more units of sanding capacity, should they do it? If so, how much should they be willing to pay for it?
    c. Suppose the polishing time on country tables could be reduced from 2.5 to 2 units per table. How much should the company be willing to pay to achieve this improvement in efficiency?
    d. Contemporary tables sell for $450. By how much would the selling price have to decrease before we would no longer be willing to produce contemporary tables? Does this make sense? Explain.

13. Use Solver to create a Sensitivity Report for question 14 at the end of Chapter 3, and answer the following questions:
    a. Is the solution degenerate?
    b. Explain the value of the shadow price associated with Machine 1.
    c. If the plant could hire another cross-trained worker, would you recommend the company do so? Why?
    d. Suppose the marginal profit for each product was computed using estimated costs. If you could get more accurate profit estimates for these products, which one(s) would be of greatest interest to your? Why?

14. Use Solver to create a Sensitivity Report for question 15 at the end of Chapter 3, and answer the following questions:
    a. Is the solution degenerate?
    b. Would the solution change if the price of raisins was $2.80 per pound?
    c. Would the solution change if the price of peanuts was $3.25 per pound?
    d. If you could relax one of the nutritional constraints, which one would you choose? Why?

15. Use Solver to create a Sensitivity Report for question 21 at the end of Chapter 3, and answer the following questions:
    a. Which of the constraints in the problem are binding?
    b. If the company was going to eliminate one of its products, which should it be?

c. If the company could buy 1,000 additional memory chips at the usual cost, should they do it? If so, how much would profits increase?
d. Suppose the manufacturing costs used in this analysis were estimated hastily and are known to be somewhat imprecise. Which products would you be most concerned about having more precise cost estimates for before implementing this solution?
e. Create a Spider Plot showing the sensitivity of the total profit to the selling price of each product (adjusting the original values by 90%, 92%, ..., 110%). According to this graph, total profit is most sensitive to which product?

16. Use Solver to create a Sensitivity Report for question 23 at the end of Chapter 3, and answer the following questions:
    a. How much would electric trimmers have to cost in order for the company to consider purchasing these items rather than making them?
    b. If the cost to make gas trimmers increased to $90 per unit, how would the optimal solution change?
    c. How much should the company be willing to pay to acquire additional capacity in the assembly area? Explain.
    d. How much should the company be willing to pay to acquire additional capacity in the production area? Explain.
    e. Prepare a Spider Plot showing the sensitivity of the total cost to changes in costs to make and the costs to buy (adjusting the original values by of 90%, 92%, ..., 110%). Which of these costs is the total cost most sensitive to?
    f. Suppose the hours of production capacity available are uncertain and could vary from 9,500 to 10,500. How does the optimal solution change for every 100-hour change in production capacity within this range?

17. Use Solver to create a Sensitivity Report for question 25 at the end of Chapter 3, and answer the following questions.
    a. Suppose the cost of the first two compounds increases by $1.00 per pound, and the cost of the third compound increases by $0.50 per pound. Does the optimal solution change?
    b. How does the solution change if the maximum amount of potassium allowed decreases from 45% to 40%?
    c. How much does the cost of the mix increase if the specifications for CHEMIX change to require at least 31% sulfur? (*Hint*: Remember that the shadow price indicates the impact on the objective function if the RHS value of the associated constraint increases by 1.)

18. Use Solver to create a Sensitivity Report for question 26 at the end of Chapter 3, and answer the following questions.
    a. What is the maximum level profit that can be achieved for this problem?
    b. Are there alternate optimal solutions to this problem? If so, identify the solution that allows the most grade 5 oranges to be used in fruit baskets while still achieving the maximum profit identified in part a.
    c. If Holiday could acquire 1,000 more pounds of grade 4 oranges at a cost of $2.65 per pound, should the company do so? Why?
    d. Create a Spider Table and Plot showing the change in the total profit obtained by changing the required grade of fruit baskets and juice from 90% to 110% in 1% increments. If the department of agriculture wants to increase the required rating of one of these products, which product should the company lobby for?

19. Use Solver to create a Sensitivity Report for question 27 at the end of Chapter 3, and answer the following questions:
    a. Are there alternate optimal solutions to this problem? Explain.

b. What is the highest possible octane rating for regular gasoline, assuming the company wants to maximize its profits? What is the octane rating for supreme gasoline at this solution?

c. What is the highest possible octane rating for supreme gasoline, assuming the company wants to maximize its profits? What is the octane rating for regular gasoline at this solution?

d. Which of the two profit-maximizing solutions identified in parts b and c would you recommend the company implement? Why?

e. If the company could buy another 150 barrels of input 2 at a cost of $17 per barrel, should the company do it? Why?

20. Use Solver to create a Sensitivity Report for question 31 at the end of Chapter 3, and answer the following questions:

a. What total profit level is realized if 100 extra hours of labor are available?

b. Assume a marginal labor cost of $11 per hour in determining the unit profits of each of the three products. How much should management pay to acquire 100 additional labor hours?

c. Interpret the reduced cost value for tuners. Why are more tuners not being produced?

21. Use Solver to create a Sensitivity Report for question 32 at the end of Chapter 3, and answer the following questions:

a. Is the optimal solution unique? How can you tell?

b. Which location is receiving the fewest cars?

c. Suppose a particular car at location 1 must be sent to location 3 in order to meet a customer's request. How much does this increase costs for the company?

d. Suppose location 6 must have at least eight cars shipped to it. What impact does this have on the optimal objective function value?

22. Refer to the previous question. Suppose location 1 has 15 cars available rather than 16. Create a Sensitivity Report for this problem, and answer the following questions:

a. Is the optimal solution unique? How can you tell?

b. According to the Sensitivity Report, by how much should the total cost increase if we force a car to be shipped from location 1 to location 3?

c. Add a constraint to the model to force one car to be shipped from location 1 to location 3. By how much did the total cost increase?

23. Use Solver to create a Sensitivity Report for question 33 at the end of Chapter 3, and answer the following questions:

a. Is the solution unique?

b. If Sentry wants to increase its production capacity in order to meet more of the demand for its product, which plant should the company use? Explain.

c. If the cost of shipping from Phoenix to Tacoma increased to $1.98 per unit, would the solution change? Explain.

d. Could the company make more money if it relaxed the restriction that each distributor must receive at least 80% of the predicted demand? Explain.

e. How much extra should the company charge the distributor in Tacoma if this distributor insisted on receiving 8,500 units?

24. Use Solver to create a Sensitivity Report for question 34 at the end of Chapter 3, and answer the following questions.

a. Is the solution degenerate?

b. Is the solution unique?

c. How much should the recycler be willing to pay to acquire more cardboard?

d. If the recycler could buy 50 more tons of newspaper at a cost of $18 per ton, should the company do it? Why or why not?

e. What is the recycler's marginal cost of producing each of the three different types of pulp?
f. By how much would the cost of converting white office paper into newsprint have to drop before it would become economical to use white office paper for this purpose?
g. By how much would the yield of newsprint pulp per ton of cardboard have to increase before it would become economical to use cardboard for this purpose?

25. Use Solver to create a Sensitivity Report for question 38 at the end of Chapter 3, and answer the following questions.
   a. Is the solution degenerate?
   b. Is the solution unique?
   c. How much can the profit per ton on commodity 1 decrease before the optimal solution would change?
   d. Create a Spider Table and Plot showing the change in the total profit obtained by changing the profit per ton on each commodity from 95% to 105% in 1% increments. If the shipping company wanted to increase the price of transporting one of the commodities, which one would have the greatest influence on total profits?

26. Use Solver to create a Sensitivity Report for question 39 at the end of Chapter 3, and answer the following questions.
   a. Is the solution degenerate?
   b. Is the solution unique?
   c. Use a Solver Table to determine the maximum price the Pelletier Corporation should be willing to pay for a two-month lease.
   d. Suppose the company is not certain that it will need exactly 20,000 sq. ft. in month 3 and believes that the actual amount needed may be as low as 15,000 sq ft or as high as 25,000 sq. ft. Use a Solver Table to determine if this would have any impact on the leasing arrangements the company selects in months 1 and 2.

27. Refer to question 48 in Chapter 3, and create a Solver table to answer the following questions.
   a. Suppose the gas producer is in need of an extra 50,000 cf of storage capacity for the next 10 days and wants to buy this capacity from the gas trading firm. What is the least amount of money the gas trading company should demand to provide this capacity?
   b. How much should the gas trading company be willing to pay to increase its available storage capacity by 500,000 cf?

28. Consider the following LP problem:

$$\text{MIN:} \quad 4X_1 + 2X_2$$
$$\text{Subject to:} \quad 2X_1 + 4X_2 \le 20$$
$$3X_1 + 5X_2 \le 15$$
$$X_1, X_2 \ge 0$$

   a. Use slack variables to rewrite this problem so that all its constraints are equal-to constraints.
   b. Identify the different sets of basic variables that might be used to obtain a solution to the problem.
   c. Of the possible sets of basic variables, which lead to feasible solutions, and what are the values for all the variables at each of these solutions?
   d. Graph the feasible region for this problem, and indicate which basic feasible solution corresponds to each of the extreme points of the feasible region.

e. What is the value of the objective function at each of the basic feasible solutions?
f. What is the optimal solution to the problem?
g. Which constraints are binding at the optimal solution?

29. Consider the following LP problem:

$$\text{MAX:} \qquad 2X_1 + 4X_2$$
$$\text{Subject to:} \qquad -X_1 + 2X_2 \leq 8$$
$$X_1 + 2X_2 \leq 12$$
$$X_1 + X_2 \geq 2$$
$$X_1, X_2 \geq 0$$

a. Use slack variables to rewrite this problem so that all its constraints are equal-to constraints.
b. Identify the different sets of basic variables that might be used to obtain a solution to the problem.
c. Of the possible sets of basic variables, which lead to feasible solutions, and what are the values for all the variables at each of these solutions?
d. Graph the feasible region for this problem, and indicate which basic feasible solution corresponds to each of the extreme points of the feasible region.
e. What is the value of the objective function at each of the basic feasible solutions?
f. What is the optimal solution to the problem?
g. Which constraints are binding at the optimal solution?

30. Consider the following LP problem:

$$\text{MIN:} \qquad 5X_1 + 3X_2 + 4X_3$$
$$\text{Subject to:} \qquad X_1 + X_2 + 2X_3 \geq 2$$
$$5X_1 + 3X_2 + 2X_3 \geq 1$$
$$X_1, X_2, X_3 \geq 0$$

a. Use slack variables to rewrite this problem so that all its constraints are equal-to constraints.
b. Identify the different sets of basic variables that might be used to obtain a solution to the problem.
c. Of the possible sets of basic variables, which lead to feasible solutions, and what are the values for all the variables at each of these solutions?
d. What is the value of the objective function at each of the basic feasible solutions?
e. What is the optimal solution to the problem?
f. Which constraints are binding at the optimal solution?

31. Consider the following constraint, where S is a slack variable:

$$2X_1 + 4X_2 + S = 16$$

a. What was the original constraint before the slack variable was included?
b. What value of S is associated with each of the following points:

i) $X_1 = 2, X_2 = 2$
ii) $X_1 = 8, X_2 = 0$
iii) $X_1 = 1, X_2 = 3$
iv) $X_1 = 4, X_2 = 1$

32. Consider the following constraint, where S is a slack variable:

$$3X_1 + 4X_2 - S = 12$$

a. What was the original constraint before the slack variable was included?
b. What value of S is associated with each of the following points:

    i) $X_1 = 5, X_2 = 0$
    ii) $X_1 = 2, X_2 = 2$
    iii) $X_1 = 7, X_2 = 1$
    iv) $X_1 = 4, X_2 = 0$

CASE 4.1 — A Nut Case

The Molokai Nut Company (MNC) makes four different products from macadamia nuts grown in the Hawaiian Islands: chocolate-coated whole nuts (Whole), chocolate-coated nut clusters (Cluster), chocolate-coated nut crunch bars (Crunch), and plain roasted nuts (Roasted). The company is barely able to keep up with the increasing demand for these products. However, increasing raw material prices and foreign competition are forcing MNC to watch its margins to ensure it is operating in the most efficient manner possible. To meet marketing demands for the coming week, MNC needs to produce at least 1,000 pounds of the Whole product, between 400 and 500 pounds of the Cluster product, no more than 150 pounds of the Crunch product, and no more than 200 pounds of the Roasted product.

Each pound of the Whole, Cluster, Crunch, and Roasted product contains, respectively, 60%, 40%, 20%, and 100% macadamia nuts with the remaining weight made up of chocolate coating. The company has 1,100 pounds of nuts and 800 pounds of chocolate available for use in the next week. The various products are made using four different machines that hull the nuts, roast the nuts, coat the nuts in chocolate (if needed), and package the products. The following table summarizes the time required by each product on each machine. Each machine has 60 hours of time available in the coming week.

	Minutes Required per Pound			
Machine	**Whole**	**Cluster**	**Crunch**	**Roasted**
Hulling	1.00	1.00	1.00	1.00
Roasting	2.00	1.50	1.00	1.75
Coating	1.00	0.70	0.20	0.00
Packaging	2.50	1.60	1.25	1.00

The controller recently presented management with the following financial summary of MNC's average weekly operations over the past quarter. From this report, the controller is arguing that the company should cease producing its Cluster and Crunch products.

	Product				
	Whole	**Cluster**	**Crunch**	**Roasted**	**Total**
Sales Revenue	$5,304	$1,800	$510	$925	$8,539
Variable Costs					
Direct materials	$1,331	$560	$144	$320	$2,355
Direct labor	$1,092	$400	$96	$130	$1,718

(continued)

Manufacturing overhead	$333	$140	$36	$90	$599
Selling & Administrative	$540	$180	$62	$120	$902
Allocated Fixed Costs					
Manufacturing overhead	$688	$331	$99	$132	$1,250
Selling & Administrative	$578	$278	$83	$111	$1,050
Net Profit	$742	−$88	−$11	$22	$665
Units Sold	1040	500	150	200	1890
Net Profit Per Unit	$0.71	−$0.18	−$0.07	$0.11	$0.35

1. Do you agree with the controller's recommendation? Why or why not?
2. Formulate an LP model for this problem.
3. Create a spreadsheet model for this problem, and solve it using Solver.
4. What is the optimal solution?
5. Create a Sensitivity Report for this solution, and answer the following questions.
6. Is the solution degenerate?
7. Is the solution unique?
8. If MNC wanted to decrease the production on any product, which one would you recommend and why?
9. If MNC wanted to increase the production of any product, which one would you recommend and why?
10. Which resources are preventing MNS from making more money? If the company could acquire more of this resource, how much should be acquired and how much should the company be willing to pay to acquire it?
11. How much should MNC be willing to pay to acquire more chocolate?
12. If the marketing department wanted to decrease the price of the Whole product by $0.25, would the optimal solution change?
13. Create a Spider Plot showing the impact on net profit of changing each product's required time in the roasting process from between 70% to 130% of their original values in 5% increments. Interpret the information in the resulting chart.
14. Create a Spider Plot showing the impact on net profit of changing the availability of nuts and chocolate from between 70% to 100% of their original values in 5% increments. Interpret the information in the resulting chart.

Parket Sisters

CASE 4.2

(Contributed by Jack Yurkiewicz, Lubin School of Business, Pace University, New York.)

Computers and word processors notwithstanding, the art of writing by hand recently entered a boom era. People are buying fountain pens again, and mechanical pencils are becoming more popular than ever. Joe Script, the president and CEO of Parket Sisters, a small but growing pen and pencil manufacturer, wants to establish a better foothold in the market. The writing market is divided into two main sectors. One, dominated by Mont Blanc, Cross, Parker Brothers, Waterman, Schaffer, and a few others, caters to people who want writing instruments. The product lines from these companies consist of pens and pencils of elaborate design, lifetime warranty, and high price. At the other end of the market are manufacturers such as BIC, Pentel, and many companies from the Far East, offering good quality items, low price, few trims, and limited diversity. These pens and pencils are meant to be used for a limited time and disposed of when the ink in a ballpoint pen runs out or when the lead in a mechanical pencil won't retract or extend. In short, these items are not meant for repair.

Joe thinks that there must be a middle ground, and that is where he wants to position his company. Parket Sisters makes high-quality items, with limited trim and diversity, but also offers lifetime warranties. Furthermore, its pens and pencils are ergonomically efficient. Joe knows that some people want the status of the Mont Blanc Meisterstuck pen, for example, but he has never met a person who said that writing with such a pen is enjoyable. The pen is too large and clumsy for smooth writing. Parket Sisters' products, on the other hand, have a reputation for working well, are easy to hold and use, and cause limited "writer's fatigue."

Parket Sisters makes only three items—a ballpoint pen, a mechanical pencil, and a fountain pen. All are available in just one color, black, and are sold mostly in specialty stores and from better catalog companies. The per-unit profit of the items is $3.00 for the ballpoint pen, $3.00 for the mechanical pencil, and $5.00 for the fountain pen. These values take into account labor, the cost of materials, packing, quality control, and so on.

The company is trying to plan its production mix for each week. Joe believes that the company can sell any number of pens and pencils it produces, but production is currently limited by the available resources. Because of a recent strike and certain cash-flow problems, the suppliers of these resources are selling them to Parket Sisters in limited amounts. In particular, Joe can count on getting at most 1,000 ounces of plastic, 1,200 ounces of chrome, and 2,000 ounces of stainless steel each week from his suppliers, and these figures are not likely to change in the near future. Because of Joe's excellent reputation, the suppliers will sell Joe any amount (up to his limit) of the resources he needs when he requires them. That is, the suppliers do not require Joe to buy some fixed quantities of resources in advance of his production of pens and pencils; therefore, these resources can be considered variable costs rather than fixed costs for the pens and pencils.

Each ballpoint pen requires 1.2 ounces of plastic, 0.8 ounces of chrome, and 2 ounces of stainless steel. Each mechanical pencil requires 1.7 ounces of plastic, no chrome, and 3 ounces of stainless steel. Each fountain pen requires 1.2 ounces of plastic, 2.3 ounces of chrome, and 4.5 ounces of stainless steel. Joe believes LP could help him decide what his weekly product mix should consist of.

Getting his notes and notebooks, Joe grapples with the LP formulation. In addition to the constraints of the available resources, he recognizes that the model should include many other constraints (such as labor time availability and materials for packing). However, Joe wants to keep his model simple. He knows that eventually he will have to take other constraints into account, but as a first-pass model, he will restrict the constraints to just the three resources: plastic, chrome, and stainless steel.

With only these three constraints, Joe can formulate the problem easily as:

$$\text{MAX:} \quad 3.0X_1 + 3.0X_2 + 5.0X_3$$

$$\text{Subject to:} \quad 1.2X_1 + 1.7X_2 + 1.2X_3 \leq 1000$$
$$0.8X_1 + 0X_2 + 2.3X_3 \leq 1200$$
$$2.0X_1 + 3.0X_2 + 4.5X_3 \leq 2000$$
$$X_1, X_2, X_3 \geq 0$$

where:

$$X_1 = \text{the number of ballpoint pens}$$
$$X_2 = \text{the number of mechanical pencils}$$
$$X_3 = \text{the number of fountain pens}$$

Joe's knowledge of Excel and the Solver feature is limited so he asks you to enter and solve the problem for him, and then answer the following questions. (Assume each question is independent unless otherwise stated.)

1. What should the weekly product mix consist of, and what is the weekly net profit?
2. Is the optimal solution to question 1 degenerate? Explain your response.
3. Is the optimal solution from question 1 unique, or are there alternate answers to this question? Explain your response.
4. What is the marginal value of one more unit of chrome? Of plastic?
5. A local distributor has offered to sell Parket Sisters an additional 500 ounces of stainless steel for $0.60 per ounce more than it ordinarily pays. Should the company buy the steel at this price? Explain your response.
6. If Parket Sisters buys the additional 500 ounces of stainless steel noted in question 5, what is the new optimal product mix, and what is the new optimal profit? Explain your response.
7. Suppose that the distributor offers to sell Parket Sisters some additional plastic at a price of only $1.00 over its usual cost of $5.00 per ounce. However, the distributor will sell the plastic only in lot sizes of 500 ounces. Should Parket Sisters buy one such lot? Explain your response.
8. The distributor is willing to sell the plastic in lots of just 100 ounces instead of the usual 500-ounce lots, still at $1.00 over Parket Sisters' cost of $5.00 per ounce. How many lots (if any) should Parket Sisters buy? What is the optimal product mix if the company buys these lots, and what is the optimal profit?
9. Parket Sisters has an opportunity to sell some of its plastic for $6.50 per ounce to another company. The other company (which does not produce pens and pencils and, therefore, is not a competitor) wants to buy 300 ounces of plastic from Parket Sisters. Should Parket Sisters sell the plastic to the other company? What happens to Parket Sisters' product mix and overall profit if it does sell the plastic? Be as specific as possible.
10. The chrome supplier might have to fulfill an emergency order and would be able to send only 1,000 ounces of chrome this week instead of the usual 1,200 ounces. If Parket Sisters receives only 1,000 ounces of chrome, what is the optimal product mix and optimal profit? Be as specific as possible.
11. The R&D department at Parket Sisters has been redesigning the mechanical pencil to make it more profitable. The new design requires 1.1 ounces of plastic, 2.0 ounces of chrome, and 2.0 ounces of stainless steel. If the company can sell one of these pencils at a net profit of $3.00, should it approve the new design? Explain your response.
12. If the per-unit profit on ballpoint pens decreases to $2.50, what is the optimal product mix and what is the company's total profit?
13. The marketing department suggested introducing a new felt tip pen that requires 1.8 ounces of plastic, 0.5 ounces of chrome, and 1.3 ounces of stainless steel. What profit must this product generate in order to make it worthwhile to produce?
14. What must the minimum per-unit profit of mechanical pencils be in order to make them worthwhile to produce?
15. Management believes that the company should produce at least 20 mechanical pencils per week to round out its product line. What effect would this have on overall profit? Give a numerical answer.
16. If the profit on a fountain pen is $6.75 instead of $5.00, what is the optimal product mix and optimal profit?

Kamm Industries

If your home or office is carpeted, there's a good chance that carpet came from Dalton, Georgia—also known as the "Carpet Capital of the World." Manufacturers in the Dalton area produce more than 70% of the total output of the $9 billion worldwide carpet industry. Competition in this industry is intense and forces producers to strive for maximum efficiency and economies of scale. It also forces producers to continually evaluate investments in new technology.

Kamm Industries is one of the leading carpet producers in the Dalton area. Its owner, Geoff Kamm, has asked for your assistance in planning the production schedule for the next quarter (13 weeks). The company has orders for 15 different types of carpets that the company can either produce on 2 types of looms: Dobbie looms and Pantera looms. Pantera looms produce standard tufted carpeting. Dobbie looms can also produce standard tufted carpeting but also allow the incorporation of designs (such as flowers or corporate logos) into the carpeting. The following table summarizes the orders for each type of carpet that must be produced in the coming quarter along with their production rates and costs on each type of loom, and the cost of subcontracting each order. Note that the first 4 orders involved special production requirements that can only be achieved on a Dobbie loom or via subcontracting. Assume that any portion of an order may be subcontracted.

	Demand	Dobbie		Pantera		Subcontract
Carpet	Yds	Yd/Hr	Cost/Yd	Yd/Hr	Cost/Yd	Cost/Yd
1	14,000	4.510	$2.66	na	na	$2.77
2	52,000	4.796	2.55	na	na	2.73
3	44,000	4.629	2.64	na	na	2.85
4	20,000	4.256	2.56	na	na	2.73
5	77,500	5.145	1.61	5.428	$1.60	1.76
6	109,500	3.806	1.62	3.935	1.61	1.76
7	120,000	4.168	1.64	4.316	1.61	1.76
8	60,000	5.251	1.48	5.356	1.47	1.59
9	7,500	5.223	1.50	5.277	1.50	1.71
10	69,500	5.216	1.44	5.419	1.42	1.63
11	68,500	3.744	1.64	3.835	1.64	1.80
12	83,000	4.157	1.57	4.291	1.56	1.78
13	10,000	4.422	1.49	4.558	1.48	1.63
14	381,000	5.281	1.31	5.353	1.30	1.44
15	64,000	4.222	1.51	4.288	1.50	1.69

Kamm currently owns and operates 15 Dobbie looms and 80 Pantera looms. To maximize efficiency and keep pace with demand, the company operates 24 hours a day, 7 days a week. Each machine is down for routine maintenance for approximately 2 hours per week. Create a spreadsheet model for this problem that can be used to determine the optimal production plan, and answer the following questions.

1. What is the optimal production plan and associated cost?
2. Is the solution degenerate?
3. Is the solution unique?
4. What would happen to the total cost if one of the Dobbie machines broke and could not be used at all during the quarter?
5. What would happen to the total cost if an additional Dobbie machine was purchased and available for the quarter?

6. What would happen to the total cost if one of the Pantera machines broke and could not be used at all during the quarter?

7. What would happen to the total cost if an additional Pantera machine was purchased and available for the quarter?

8. Explain the shadow prices and the values in the Allowable Increase column of the Sensitivity Report for the products that are being outsourced.

9. How much money does it cost to produce carpet order 2? How much would the total cost decrease if that order were eliminated? Explain.

10. If the carpets in orders 5 through 15 all sell for the same amount, which type of carpet should Kamm encourage its sales force to sell more of? Why?

11. If the cost of buying the carpet in order 1 increased to $2.80 per yard, would the optimal solution change? Why?

12. If the cost of buying the carpet in order 15 decreased to $1.65 per yard, would the optimal solution change? Why?

Chapter 5

Network Modeling

5.0 Introduction

A number of practical decision problems in business fall into a category known as **network flow problems**. These problems share a common characteristic—they can be described or displayed in a graphical form known as a **network**. This chapter focuses on several types of network flow problems: transshipment problems, shortest path problems, maximal flow problems, transportation/assignment problems, and generalized network flow problems. Although specialized solution procedures exist for solving network flow problems, we will consider how to formulate and solve these problems as LP problems. We will also consider a different type of network problem known as the **minimum spanning tree problem**.

5.1 The Transshipment Problem

Let's begin our study of network flow problems by considering the transshipment problem. As you will see, most of the other types of network flow problems all can be viewed as simple variations of the transshipment problem. So, after you understand how to formulate and solve transshipment problems, the other types of problems will be easy to solve. The following example illustrates the transshipment problem.

> The Bavarian Motor Company (BMC) manufactures expensive luxury cars in Hamburg, Germany, and exports cars to sell in the United States. The exported cars are shipped from Hamburg to ports in Newark, New Jersey, and Jacksonville, Florida. From these ports, the cars are transported by rail or truck to distributors located in Boston, Massachusetts; Columbus, Ohio; Atlanta, Georgia; Richmond, Virginia; and Mobile, Alabama. Figure 5.1 shows the possible shipping routes available to the company along with the transportation cost for shipping each car along the indicated path.
>
> Currently, 200 cars are available at the port in Newark, and 300 are available in Jacksonville. The numbers of cars needed by the distributors in Boston, Columbus, Atlanta, Richmond, and Mobile are 100, 60, 170, 80, and 70, respectively. BMC wants to determine the least costly way of transporting cars from the ports in Newark and Jacksonville to the cities where they are needed.

5.1.1 CHARACTERISTICS OF NETWORK FLOW PROBLEMS

Figure 5.1 illustrates a number of characteristics common to all network flow problems. All network flow problems can be represented as a collection of nodes connected by

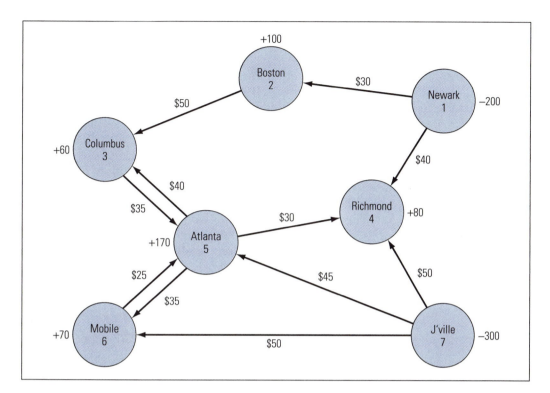

FIGURE 5.1

Network representation of the BMC transshipment problem

arcs. The circles in Figure 5.1 are called **nodes** in the terminology of network flow problems, and the lines connecting the nodes are called **arcs**. The arcs in a network indicate the valid paths, routes, or connections between the nodes in a network flow problem. When the lines connecting the nodes in a network are arrows that indicate a direction, the arcs in the network are called **directed arcs**. This chapter discusses directed arcs primarily but, for convenience, refers to them as arcs.

The notion of **supply nodes** (or sending nodes) and **demand nodes** (or receiving nodes) is another common element of network flow problems illustrated in Figure 5.1. The nodes representing the port cities of Newark and Jacksonville are both supply nodes because each has a supply of cars to send to other nodes in the network. Richmond represents a demand node because it demands to receive cars from the other nodes. All the other nodes in this network are transshipment nodes. **Transshipment nodes** can both send to and receive from other nodes in the network. For example, the node representing Atlanta in Figure 5.1 is a transshipment node because it can *receive* cars from Jacksonville, Mobile, and Columbus, and it can also send cars to Columbus, Mobile, and Richmond.

The net supply or demand for each node in the network is indicated, respectively, by a negative or positive number next to each node. We use a **positive number** to represent the needed net flow into (that is, the demand at) a given node, and a **negative number** to represent the available net flow out of (that is, the supply at) a node. For example, the value +80 next to the node for Richmond indicates that the number of cars needs to increase by 80—or that Richmond has a *demand* for 80 cars. The value −200 next to the node for Newark indicates that the number of cars there can be reduced by 200—or that Newark has a *supply* of 200 cars. A transshipment node can have either a net supply or demand but not both. In this particular problem, all the transshipment nodes have demands. For example, the node representing Mobile in Figure 5.1 has a demand for 70 cars.

5.1.2 THE DECISION VARIABLES FOR NETWORK FLOW PROBLEMS

The goal in a network flow model is to determine how many items should be moved (or flow) across each of the arcs. In our example, BMC needs to determine the least costly method of transporting cars along the various arcs shown in Figure 5.1 to distribute cars where they are needed. Thus, each of the arcs in a network flow model represents a decision variable. Determining the optimal flow for each arc is the equivalent of determining the optimal value for the corresponding decision variable.

It is customary to use numbers to identify each node in a network flow problem. In Figure 5.1, the number 1 identifies the node for Newark, 2 identifies the node for Boston, and so on. You can assign numbers to the nodes in any manner, but it is best to use a series of consecutive integers. The node numbers provide a convenient way to identify the decision variables needed to formulate the LP model for the problem. For each arc in a network flow model, you need to define one decision variable as:

X_{ij} = the number of items shipped (or flowing) *from* node *i* *to* node *j*

The network in Figure 5.1 for our example problem contains 11 arcs. Therefore, the LP formulation of this model requires the following 11 decision variables:

X_{12} = the number of cars shipped *from* node 1 (Newark) *to* node 2 (Boston)

X_{14} = the number of cars shipped *from* node 1 (Newark) *to* node 4 (Richmond)

X_{23} = the number of cars shipped *from* node 2 (Boston) *to* node 3 (Columbus)

X_{35} = the number of cars shipped *from* node 3 (Columbus) *to* node 5 (Atlanta)

X_{53} = the number of cars shipped *from* node 5 (Atlanta) *to* node 3 (Columbus)

X_{54} = the number of cars shipped *from* node 5 (Atlanta) *to* node 4 (Richmond)

X_{56} = the number of cars shipped *from* node 5 (Atlanta) *to* node 6 (Mobile)

X_{65} = the number of cars shipped *from* node 6 (Mobile) *to* node 5 (Atlanta)

X_{74} = the number of cars shipped *from* node 7 (Jacksonville) *to* node 4 (Richmond)

X_{75} = the number of cars shipped *from* node 7 (Jacksonville) *to* node 5 (Atlanta)

X_{76} = the number of cars shipped *from* node 7 (Jacksonville) *to* node 6 (Mobile)

5.1.3 THE OBJECTIVE FUNCTION FOR NETWORK FLOW PROBLEMS

Each unit that flows from node *i* to node *j* in a network flow problem usually incurs some cost, c_{ij}. This cost might represent a monetary payment, a distance, or some other type of penalty. The objective in most network flow problems is to minimize the total cost, distance, or penalty that must be incurred to solve the problem. Such problems are known as **minimum cost network flow problems**.

In our example problem, different monetary costs must be paid for each car shipped across a given arc. For example, it costs $30 to ship each car from node 1 (Newark) to node 2 (Boston). Because X_{12} represents the number of cars shipped from Newark to Boston, the total cost incurred by cars shipped along this path is determined by $30X_{12}$. Similar calculations can be done for the other arcs in the network. Because BMC is interested in minimizing the total shipping costs, the objective function for this problem is expressed as:

$$\text{MIN:} \quad +30X_{12} + 40X_{14} + 50X_{23} + 35X_{35} + 40X_{53} + 30X_{54}$$
$$+ 35X_{56} + 25X_{65} + 50X_{74} + 45X_{75} + 50X_{76}$$

5.1.4 THE CONSTRAINTS FOR NETWORK FLOW PROBLEMS

Just as the number of arcs in the network determines the number of variables in the LP formulation of a network flow problem, the number of nodes determines the number of constraints. In particular, there must be one constraint for each node. A simple set of rules, known as the **balance-of-flow rules**, applies to constructing the constraints for minimum cost network flow problems. These rules are summarized as follows:

For Minimum Cost Network Flow Problems Where:	Apply This Balance-of-Flow Rule at Each Node:
Total Supply > Total Demand	Inflow − Outflow ≥ Supply or Demand
Total Supply = Total Demand	Inflow − Outflow = Supply or Demand
Total Supply < Total Demand	Inflow − Outflow ≤ Supply or Demand

It should be noted that if the total supply in a network flow problem is less than the total demand, then it will be impossible to satisfy all the demand. The balance-of-flow rule listed for this case assumes that you want to determine the least costly way of distributing the available supply—knowing that it is impossible to satisfy all the demand. If you want to meet as much of the demand as possible, add an artificial supply node to the network with an arbitrarily large supply (so that total supply ≥ total demand) and connect it to each demand node with an arbitrarily large cost of flow. The optimal solution to the resulting problem (ignoring flows on the artificial arcs) meets as much of the demand as possible in the least costly manner.

So to apply the correct balance-of-flow rule, we must first compare the total supply in the network to the total demand. In our example problem, there is a total supply of 500 cars and a total demand for 480 cars. Because the total supply exceeds the total demand, we will use the first balance-of-flow rule to formulate our example problem. That is, at each node, we will create a constraint of the form:

$$\text{Inflow} - \text{Outflow} \geq \text{Supply or Demand}$$

For example, consider node 1 (Newark) in Figure 5.1. No arcs flow into this node, but two arcs (represented by X_{12} and X_{14}) flow out of the node. According to the balance-of-flow rule, the constraint for this node is:

$$\text{Constraint for node 1: } -X_{12} - X_{14} \geq -200$$

Notice that the supply at this node is represented by -200 following the convention we established earlier. If we multiply both sides of this inequality by -1, we see that it is equivalent to $+X_{12} + X_{14} \leq +200$. (Note that multiplying an inequality by -1 reverses the direction of the inequality.) This constraint indicates that the total number of cars flowing out of Newark must not exceed 200. So, if we include either form of this constraint in the model, we can ensure that no more than 200 cars will be shipped from Newark.

Now consider the constraint for node 2 (Boston) in Figure 5.1. Because Boston has a demand for 100 cars, the balance-of-flow rule requires that the total number of cars coming into Boston from Newark (via X_{12}) minus the total number of cars being shipped out of Boston to Columbus (via X_{23}) must leave at least 100 cars in Boston. This condition is imposed by the constraint:

$$\text{Constraint for node 2: } +X_{12} - X_{23} \geq +100$$

Note that this constraint makes it possible to leave more than the required number of cars in Boston (for example, 200 cars could be shipped into Boston and only 50 shipped out, leaving 150 cars in Boston). However, because our objective is to minimize costs, we can be sure that an excess number of cars will never be shipped to any city because that would result in unnecessary costs being incurred.

Using the balance-of-flow rule, the constraints for each of the remaining nodes in our example problem are represented as:

Constraint for node 3:	$+X_{23} + X_{53} - X_{35} \geq +60$
Constraint for node 4:	$+X_{14} + X_{54} + X_{74} \geq +80$
Constraint for node 5:	$+X_{35} + X_{65} + X_{75} - X_{53} - X_{54} - X_{56} \geq +170$
Constraint for node 6:	$+X_{56} + X_{76} - X_{65} \geq +70$
Constraint for node 7:	$-X_{74} - X_{75} - X_{76} \geq -300$

Again, each constraint indicates that the flow into a given node minus the flow out of that same node must be greater than or equal to the supply or demand at the node. So, if you draw a graph of a network flow problem like the one in Figure 5.1, it is easy to write out the constraints for the problem by following the balance-of-flow rule. Of course, we also need to specify the following nonnegativity condition for all the decision variables because negative flows should not occur on arcs:

$$X_{ij} \geq 0 \text{ for all } i \text{ and } j$$

5.1.5 IMPLEMENTING THE MODEL IN A SPREADSHEET

The formulation for the BMC transshipment problem is summarized as:

MIN: $+30X_{12} + 40X_{14} + 50X_{23} + 35X_{35} + 40X_{53}$
$+30X_{54} + 35X_{56} + 25X_{65} + 50X_{74} + 45X_{75}$ $\left.\right\}$ total shipping cost
$+50X_{76}$

Subject to:

$-X_{12} - X_{14} \geq -200$	} flow constraint for node 1
$+X_{12} - X_{23} \geq +100$	} flow constraint for node 2
$+X_{23} + X_{53} - X_{35} \geq +60$	} flow constraint for node 3
$+X_{14} + X_{54} + X_{74} \geq +80$	} flow constraint for node 4
$+X_{35} + X_{65} + X_{75} - X_{53} - X_{54} - X_{56} \geq +170$	} flow constraint for node 5
$+X_{56} + X_{76} - X_{65} \geq +70$	} flow constraint for node 6
$-X_{74} - X_{75} - X_{76} \geq -300$	} flow constraint for node 7
$X_{ij} \geq 0 \text{ for all } i \text{ and } j$	} nonnegativity conditions

A convenient way of implementing this type of problem is shown in Figure 5.2 (and in the file Fig5-2.xlsm that accompanies this book). In this spreadsheet, cells B6 through B16 are used to represent the decision variables for our model (or the number of cars that should flow between each of the cities listed). The unit cost of transporting cars between each city is listed in column G. The objective function for the model is then implemented in cell G18 as follows:

Formula for cell G18:   =SUMPRODUCT(B6:B16,G6:G16)

To implement the LHS formulas for the constraints in this model, we need to compute the total inflow minus the total outflow for each node. This is done in cells K6 through K12 as follows:

Formula for cell K6:   =SUMIF($E$6:$E$16,I6,$B$6:$B$16)−
(Copy to cells K7 through K12.)   SUMIF($C$6:$C$16,I6,$B$6:$B$16)

FIGURE 5.2 *Spreadsheet implementation of the BMC transshipment problem*

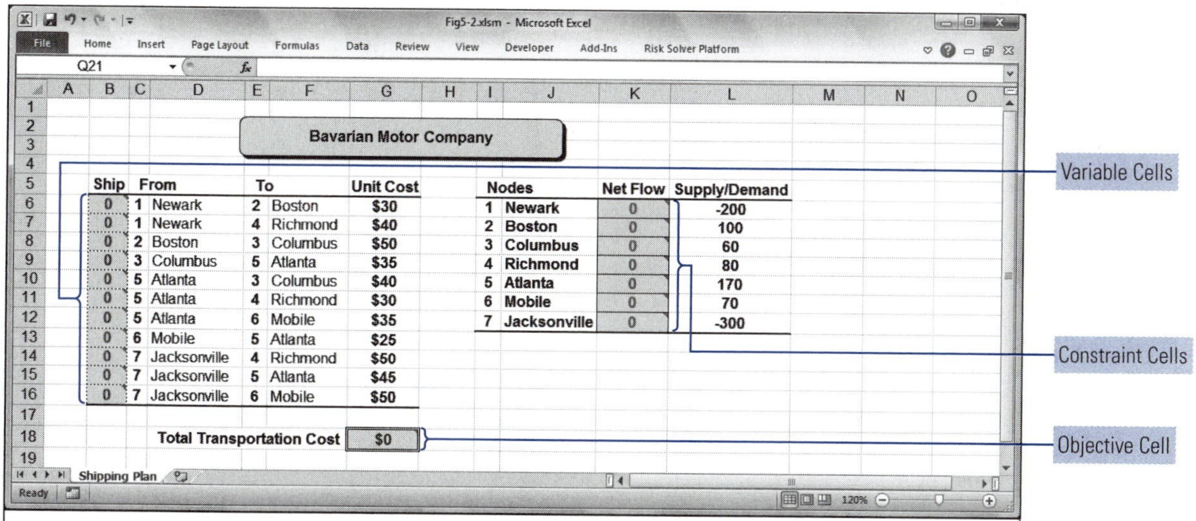

Cell	Formula	Copied to
D6	=VLOOKUP(C6,$I$6:$J$12,2)	D7:D16 and F6:F16
G18	=SUMPRODUCT(B6:B16,G6:G16)	--
K6	=SUMIF($E$6:$E$16,I6,$B$6:$B$16) -SUMIF($C$6:$C$16,I6,$B$6:$B$16)	K7:K12

Key Cell Formulas

The first SUMIF( ) function in this formula compares the values in the range E6 through E16 to the value in I6 and, if a match occurs, sums the corresponding value in the range B6 through B16. Of course, this gives us the total number of cars flowing *into* Newark (which in this case will always be zero because none of the values in E6 through E16 match the value in I6). The next SUMIF( ) function compares the values in the range C6 through C16 to the value in I6 and, if a match occurs, sums the corresponding values in the range B6 through B16. This gives us the total number of cars flowing *out of* Newark (which in this case will always equal the values in cells B6 and B7 because these are the only arcs flowing out of Newark). Copying this formula to cells K7 though K12 allows us to easily calculate the total inflow minus the total outflow for each of the nodes in our problem. The RHS values for these constraint cells are shown in cells L6 though L12.

Figure 5.3 shows the Solver parameters and options required to solve this problem. The optimal solution to the problem is shown in Figure 5.4.

5.1.6 ANALYZING THE SOLUTION

Figure 5.4 shows the optimal solution for BMC's transshipment problem. The solution indicates that 120 cars should be shipped from Newark to Boston ($X_{12} = 120$), 80 cars from Newark to Richmond ($X_{14} = 80$), 20 cars from Boston to Columbus ($X_{23} = 20$), 40 cars from Atlanta to Columbus ($X_{53} = 40$), 210 cars from Jacksonville to Atlanta ($X_{75} = 210$), and 70 cars from Jacksonville to Mobile ($X_{76} = 70$). Cell G18 indicates that the total cost associated with this shipping plan is $22,350. The values of the constraint cells in K6 and K12 indicate, respectively, that all 200 cars available at Newark are being shipped, and only 280 of

FIGURE 5.3

Solver settings and options for the BMC transshipment problem

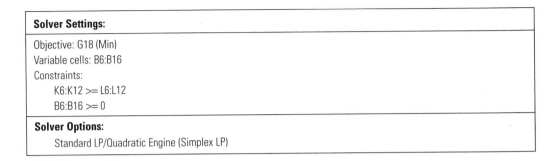

Solver Settings:
Objective: G18 (Min)
Variable cells: B6:B16
Constraints:
K6:K12 >= L6:L12
B6:B16 >= 0
Solver Options:
Standard LP/Quadratic Engine (Simplex LP)

FIGURE 5.4 *Optimal solution to the BMC transshipment problem*

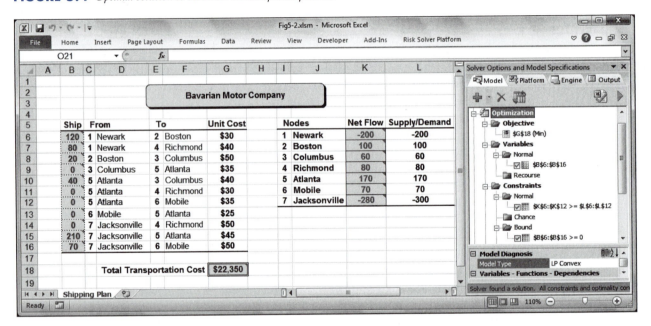

the 300 cars available at Jacksonville are being shipped. A comparison of the remaining constraint cells in K7 through K11 with their RHS values in L7 through L11 reveals that the demand at each of these cities is being met by the net flow of cars through each city.

This solution is summarized graphically, as shown in Figure 5.5. The values in the boxes next to each arc indicate the optimal flows for the arcs. The optimal flow for all the other arcs in the problem, which are not shown in Figure 5.5, is 0. Notice that the amount flowing into each node minus the amount flowing out of each node is equal to the supply or demand at the node. For example, 210 cars are being shipped from Jacksonville to Atlanta. Atlanta will keep 170 of the cars (to satisfy the demand at this node) and send the extra 40 to Columbus.

5.2 The Shortest Path Problem

In many decision problems, we need to determine the shortest (or least costly) route or path through a network from a starting node to an ending node. For example, many cities are developing computerized models of their highways and streets to help

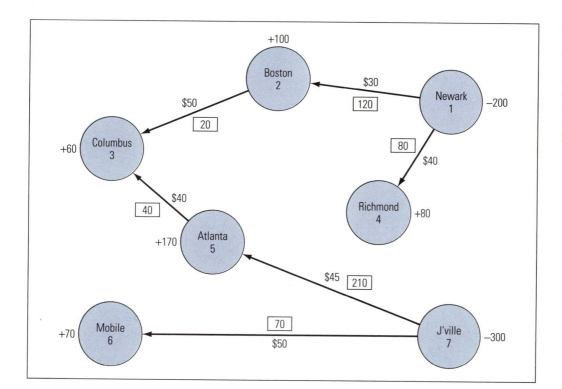

FIGURE 5.5

Network representation of the optimal solution for the BMC transshipment problem

emergency vehicles identify the quickest route to a given location. Each street intersection represents a potential node in a network, and the streets connecting the intersections represent arcs. Depending on the day of the week and the time of day, the time required to travel various streets can increase or decrease due to changes in traffic patterns. Road construction and maintenance also affect traffic flow patterns. So, the quickest route (or shortest path) for getting from one point in the city to another can change frequently. In emergency situations, lives or property can be lost or saved depending on how quickly emergency vehicles arrive where they are needed. The ability to quickly determine the shortest path to the location of an emergency situation is extremely useful in these situations. The following example illustrates another application of the shortest path problem.

The American Car Association (ACA) provides a variety of travel-related services to its members, including information on vacation destinations, discount hotel reservations, emergency road assistance, and travel route planning. This last service, travel route planning, is one of its most popular services. When members of the ACA are planning to take a driving trip, they call the organization's toll-free 800 number and indicate what cities they will be traveling from and to. The ACA then determines an optimal route for traveling between these cities. The ACA's computer databases of major highways and interstates are kept up-to-date with information on construction delays and detours and estimated travel times along various segments of roadways.

Members of the ACA often have different objectives in planning driving trips. Some are interested in identifying routes that minimize travel times. Others, with more leisure time on their hands, want to identify the most scenic route to their desired destination. The ACA wants to develop an automated system for identifying an optimal travel plan for its members.

FIGURE 5.6

Network of possible routes for the ACA's shortest path problem

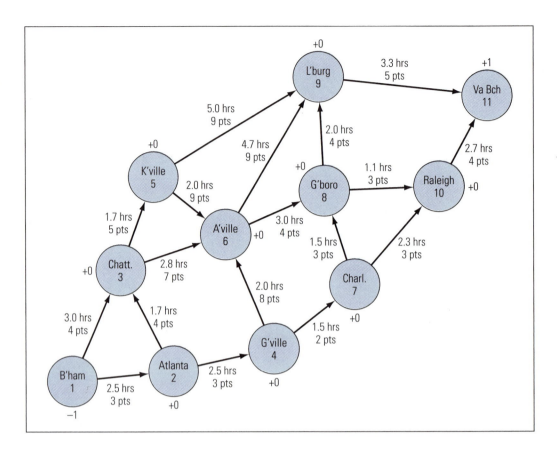

To see how the ACA could benefit by solving shortest path problems, consider the simplified network shown in Figure 5.6 for a travel member who wants to drive from Birmingham, Alabama, to Virginia Beach, Virginia. The nodes in this graph represent different cities, and the arcs indicate the possible travel routes between the cities. For each arc, Figure 5.6 lists both the estimated driving time to travel the road represented by each arc and the number of points that route has received on the ACA's system for rating the scenic quality of the various routes.

Solving this problem as a network flow model requires the various nodes to have some supply or demand. In Figure 5.6, node 1 (Birmingham) has a supply of 1, node 11 (Virginia Beach) has a demand of 1, and all other nodes have a demand (or supply) of 0. If we view this model as a transshipment problem, we want to find either the quickest way or the most scenic way of shipping 1 unit of flow from node 1 to node 11. The route this unit of supply takes corresponds to either the shortest path or the most scenic path through the network, depending on which objective is being pursued.

5.2.1 AN LP MODEL FOR THE EXAMPLE PROBLEM

Using the balance-of-flow rule, the LP model to minimize the driving time in this problem is represented as:

MIN: $+2.5X_{12} + 3X_{13} + 1.7X_{23} + 2.5X_{24} + 1.7X_{35} + 2.8X_{36} + 2X_{46} + 1.5X_{47} + 2X_{56} + 5X_{59}$
$+ 3X_{68} + 4.7X_{69} + 1.5X_{78} + 2.3X_{7,10} + 2X_{89} + 1.1X_{8,10} + 3.3X_{9,11} + 2.7X_{10,11}$

Subject to:

$$
\begin{array}{llll}
-X_{12} - X_{13} & & = -1 & \text{\} flow constraint for node 1} \\
+X_{12} - X_{23} - X_{24} & & = 0 & \text{\} flow constraint for node 2} \\
+X_{13} + X_{23} - X_{35} - X_{36} & & = 0 & \text{\} flow constraint for node 3} \\
+X_{24} - X_{46} - X_{47} & & = 0 & \text{\} flow constraint for node 4} \\
+X_{35} - X_{56} - X_{59} & & = 0 & \text{\} flow constraint for node 5} \\
+X_{36} + X_{46} + X_{56} - X_{68} - X_{69} & & = 0 & \text{\} flow constraint for node 6} \\
+X_{47} - X_{78} - X_{7,10} & & = 0 & \text{\} flow constraint for node 7} \\
+X_{68} + X_{78} - X_{89} - X_{8,10} & & = 0 & \text{\} flow constraint for node 8} \\
+X_{59} + X_{69} + X_{89} - X_{9,11} & & = 0 & \text{\} flow constraint for node 9} \\
+X_{7,10} + X_{8,10} - X_{10,11} & & = 0 & \text{\} flow constraint for node 10} \\
+X_{9,11} + X_{10,11} & & = +1 & \text{\} flow constraint for node 11} \\
X_{ij} \geq 0 \text{ for all } i \text{ and } j & & & \text{\} nonnegativity conditions}
\end{array}
$$

Because the total supply equals the total demand in this problem, the constraints should be stated as equalities. The first constraint in this model ensures that the 1 unit of supply available at node 1 is shipped to node 2 or node 3. The next nine constraints indicate that anything flowing to nodes 2 though node 10 must also flow out of these nodes because each has a demand of 0. For example, if the unit of supply leaves node 1 for node 2 (via X_{12}), the second constraint ensures that it will leave node 2 for node 3 or node 4 (via X_{23} or X_{24}). The last constraint indicates that the unit must ultimately flow to node 11. Thus, the solution to this problem indicates the quickest route for getting from node 1 (Birmingham) to node 11 (Virginia Beach).

5.2.2 THE SPREADSHEET MODEL AND SOLUTION

The optimal solution to this problem shown in Figure 5.7 (and in the file Fig5-7.xlsm that accompanies this book) was obtained using the Solver parameters and options shown in Figure 5.8. Notice that this model includes calculations of both the total expected driving time (cell G26) and total scenic rating points (cell H26) associated with any solution. Either of these cells can be chosen as the objective function according to the client's desires. However, the solution shown in Figure 5.7 minimizes the expected driving time.

The optimal solution shown in Figure 5.7 indicates that the quickest travel plan involves driving from node 1 (Birmingham) to node 2 (Atlanta), then to node 4 (Greenville), then to node 7 (Charlotte), then to node 10 (Raleigh), and finally to node 11 (Virginia Beach). The total expected driving time along this route is 11.5 hours. Also note that this route receives a rating of 15 points on the ACA's scenic rating scale.

Using this spreadsheet, we can also determine the most scenic route by instructing Solver to maximize the value in cell H26. Figure 5.9 shows the optimal solution obtained in this case. This travel plan involves driving from Birmingham to Atlanta, to Chattanooga, to Knoxville, to Asheville, to Lynchburg, and, finally, to Virginia Beach. This itinerary receives a rating of 35 points on the ACA's scenic rating scale but takes almost 16 hours of driving time.

5.2.3 NETWORK FLOW MODELS AND INTEGER SOLUTIONS

Up to this point, each of the network flow models we have solved generated integer solutions. If you use the simplex method to solve any minimum cost network flow model

FIGURE 5.7 *Spreadsheet model and solution showing the route that minimizes estimated driving time for the ACA's shortest path problem*

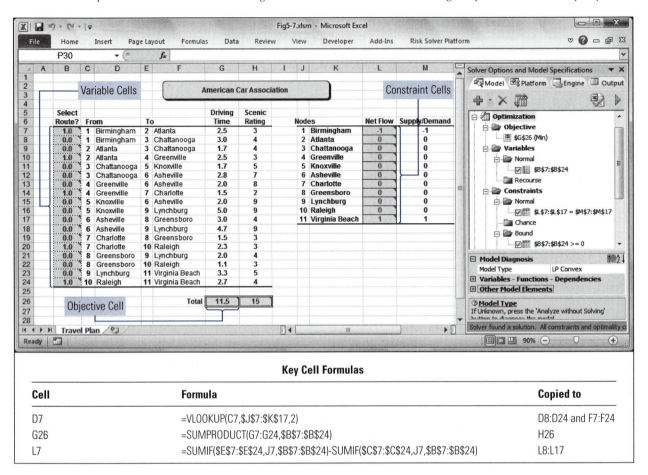

Key Cell Formulas

Cell	Formula	Copied to
D7	=VLOOKUP(C7,$J$7:$K$17,2)	D8:D24 and F7:F24
G26	=SUMPRODUCT(G7:G24,$B$7:$B$24)	H26
L7	=SUMIF($E$7:$E$24,J7,$B$7:$B$24)-SUMIF($C$7:$C$24,J7,$B$7:$B$24)	L8:L17

FIGURE 5.8

Solver settings and options for the ACA's shortest path problem

Solver Settings:

Objective: G26 (Min)
Variable cells: B7:B24
Constraints:
    L7:L17 = M7:M17
    B7:B24 >= 0

Solver Options:
Standard LP/Quadratic Engine (Simplex LP)

having integer constraint RHS values, then the optimal solution automatically assumes integer values. This property is helpful because the items flowing through most network flow models represent discrete units (such as cars or people).

Sometimes, it is tempting to place additional constraints (or side constraints) on a network model. For example, in the ACA problem, suppose that the customer wants to get to Virginia Beach in the most scenic way possible within 14 hours of driving time. We can easily add a constraint to the model to keep the total driving time G26 less than

FIGURE 5.9 *Solution showing the most scenic route*

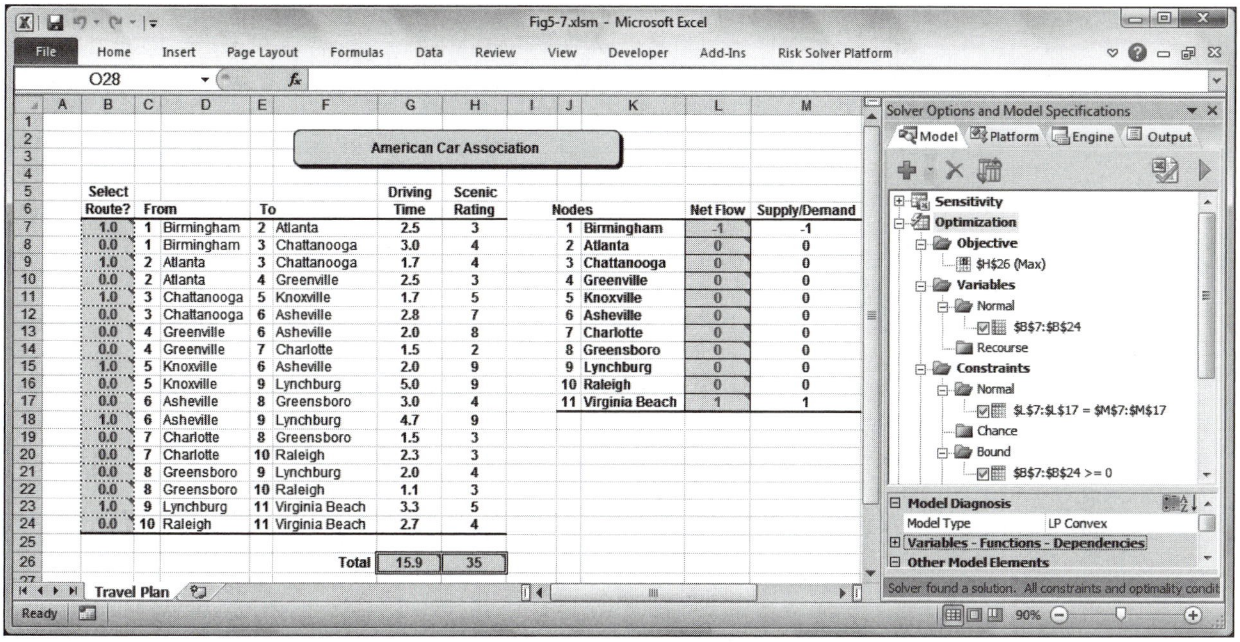

or equal to 14 hours. If we then re-solve the model to maximize the scenic rating in cell H26, we obtain the solution shown in Figure 5.10.

Unfortunately, this solution is useless because it produces fractional results. Thus, if we add **side constraints** to network flow problems that do not obey the balance-of-flow rule, we can no longer ensure that the solution to the LP formulation of the problems

FIGURE 5.10 *Example of a non-integer solution to a network problem with side constraints*

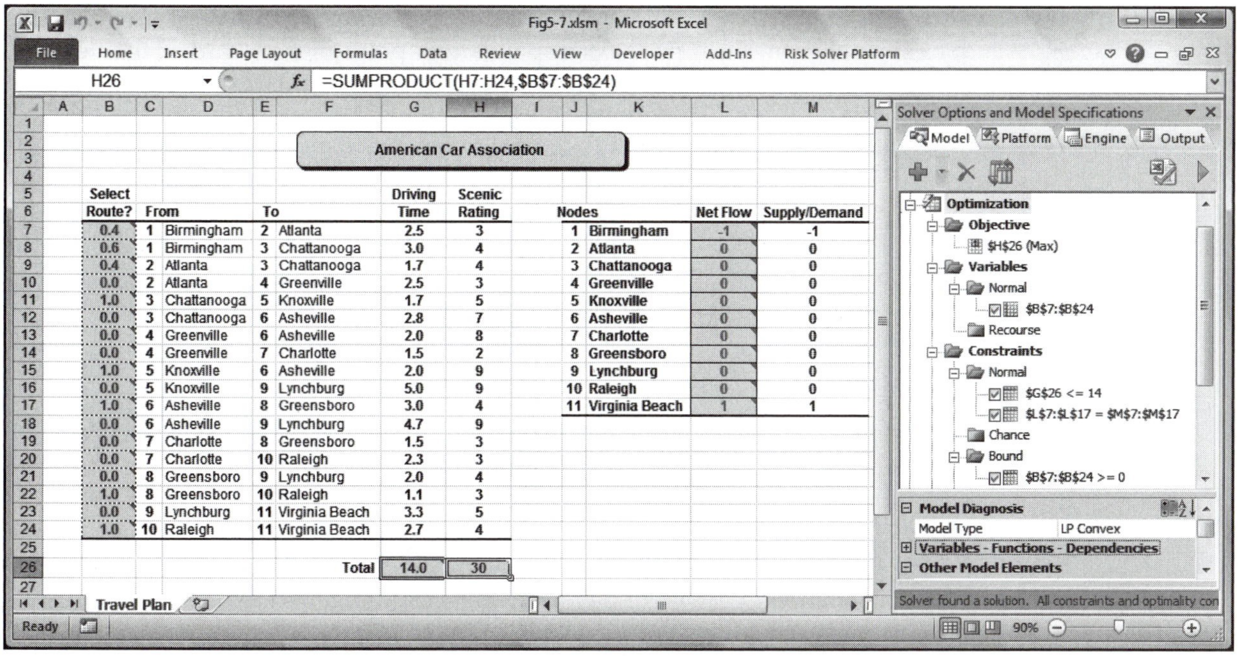

will be integral. If integer solutions are needed for such problems, the integer programming techniques discussed in Chapter 6 must be applied.

5.3 The Equipment Replacement Problem

The equipment replacement problem is a common type of business problem that can be modeled as a shortest path problem. This type of problem involves determining the least costly schedule for replacing equipment over a specified length of time. Consider the following example.

> Jose Maderos is the owner of Compu-Train, a small company that provides hands-on software education and training for businesses in and around Boulder, Colorado. Jose leases the computer equipment used in his business, and he likes to keep the equipment up-to-date so that it will run the latest, state-of-the-art software in an efficient manner. Because of this, Jose wants to replace his equipment at least every two years.
>
> Jose is currently trying to decide between two different lease contracts his equipment supplier has proposed. Under both contracts, Jose would be required to pay $62,000 initially to obtain the equipment he needs. However, the two contracts differ in terms of the amount Jose would have to pay in subsequent years to replace his equipment. Under the first contract, the price to acquire new equipment would increase by 6% per year, but he would be given a trade-in credit of 60% for any equipment that is one year old and 15% for any equipment that is two years old. Under the second contract, the price to acquire new equipment would increase by just 2% per year, but he would be given a trade-in credit of only 30% for any equipment that is one year old and 10% for any equipment that is two years old.
>
> Jose realizes that no matter what he does, he will have to pay $62,000 to obtain the equipment initially. However, he wants to determine which contract would allow him to minimize the remaining leasing costs over the next five years and when he should replace his equipment under the selected contract.

Each of the two contracts Jose is considering can be modeled as a shortest path problem. Figure 5.11 shows how this would be accomplished for the first contract under consideration. Each node corresponds to a point in time during the next five years when Jose can replace his equipment. Each arc in this network represents a choice available to Jose. For example, the arc from node 1 to node 2 indicates that Jose can keep the equipment he initially acquires for one year and then replace it (at the beginning of year 2) for a net cost of $28,520 ($62,000 × 1.06 − 0.6 × $62,000 = $28,520). Alternatively, the arc from node 1 to node 3 indicates that Jose can keep his initial equipment for two years and replace it at the beginning of year 3 for a net cost of $60,363 ($62,000 × 1.06² − 0.15 × $62,000 = $60,363).

The arc from node 2 to node 3 indicates that if Jose replaces his initial equipment at the beginning of year 2, he can keep the new equipment for one year and replace it at the beginning of year 3 at a net cost of $30,231 ($62,000 × 1.06^2 − 0.60 × ($62,000 × 1.06) = $30,231). The remaining arcs and costs in the network can be interpreted in the same way. Jose's decision problem is to determine the least costly (or shortest) way of getting from node 1 to node 5 in this network.

5.3.1 THE SPREADSHEET MODEL AND SOLUTION

The LP formulation of Jose's decision problem can be generated from the graph in Figure 5.11 using the balance-of-flow rule in the same manner as the previous network

FIGURE 5.11

Network representation of Compu-Train's first contract alternative for their equipment replacement problem

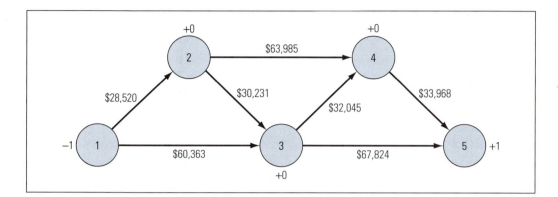

flow problems. The spreadsheet model for this problem was implemented as shown in Figure 5.12 (and in the file Fig5-12.xlsm that accompanies this book) and solved using the settings shown in Figure 5.13. To assist Jose in comparing the two different alternatives he faces, notice that an area of the spreadsheet in Figure 5.12 has been reserved to represent assumptions about the annual increase in leasing costs (cell G5), and the

FIGURE 5.12 *Spreadsheet model and solution for Compu-Train's first lease contract alternative*

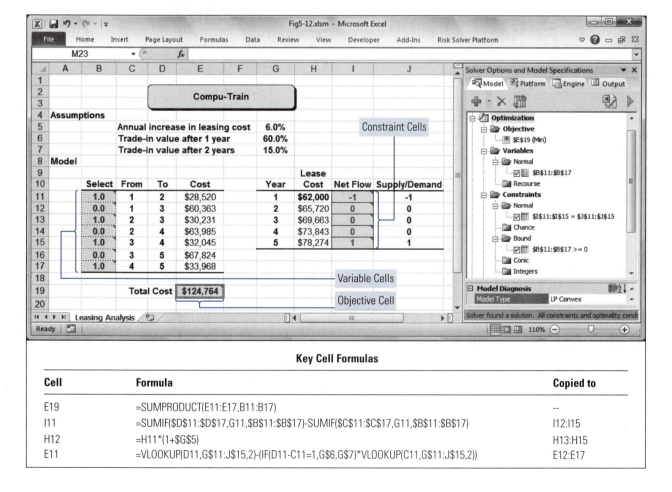

Key Cell Formulas

Cell	Formula	Copied to
E19	=SUMPRODUCT(E11:E17,B11:B17)	--
I11	=SUMIF($D$11:$D$17,G11,$B$11:$B$17)-SUMIF($C$11:$C$17,G11,$B$11:$B$17)	I12:I15
H12	=H11*(1+$G$5)	H13:H15
E11	=VLOOKUP(D11,G$11:J$15,2)-(IF(D11-C11=1,G$6,G$7)*VLOOKUP(C11,G$11:J$15,2))	E12:E17

FIGURE 5.13

Solver settings and options for Compu-Train's equipment replacement problem

Solver Settings:

Objective: E19 (Min)
Variable cells: B11:B17
Constraints:
I11:I15 = J11:J15
B11:B17 >= 0

Solver Options:

Standard LP/Quadratic Engine (Simplex LP)

trade-in values for one- and two-year old equipment (cells G6 and G7). The rest of the spreadsheet model uses these assumed values to compute the various costs. This enables us to change any of the assumptions and re-solve the model very easily.

The optimal solution to this problem shows that under the provisions of the first contract, Jose should replace his equipment at the beginning of each year at a total cost of $124,764. This amount is in addition to the $62,000 he has to pay upfront at the beginning of year 1.

To determine the optimal replacement strategy and costs associated with the second contract, Jose could simply change the assumptions at the top of the spreadsheet and re-solve the model. The results of this are shown in Figure 5.14.

The optimal solution to this problem shows that under the provisions of the second contract, Jose should replace his equipment at the beginning of years 3 and 5 at a total cost of $118,965. Again, this amount is in addition to the $62,000 he has to pay upfront at the beginning of year 1. Although the total costs under the second contract are lower than under the first, under the second contract Jose would be working with older equipment during years 2 and 4. Thus, although the solution to these two models makes the

FIGURE 5.14 *Solution for Compu-Train's second lease contract alternative*

Select	From	To	Cost	Year	Lease Cost	Net Flow	Supply/Demand
0.0	1	2	$44,640	1	$62,000	-1	-1
1.0	1	3	$58,305	2	$63,240	0	0
0.0	2	3	$45,533	3	$64,505	0	0
0.0	2	4	$59,471	4	$65,795	0	0
0.0	3	4	$46,443	5	$67,111	1	1
1.0	3	5	$60,660				
0.0	4	5	$47,372				

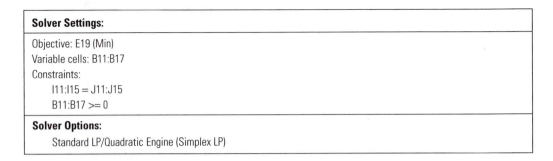

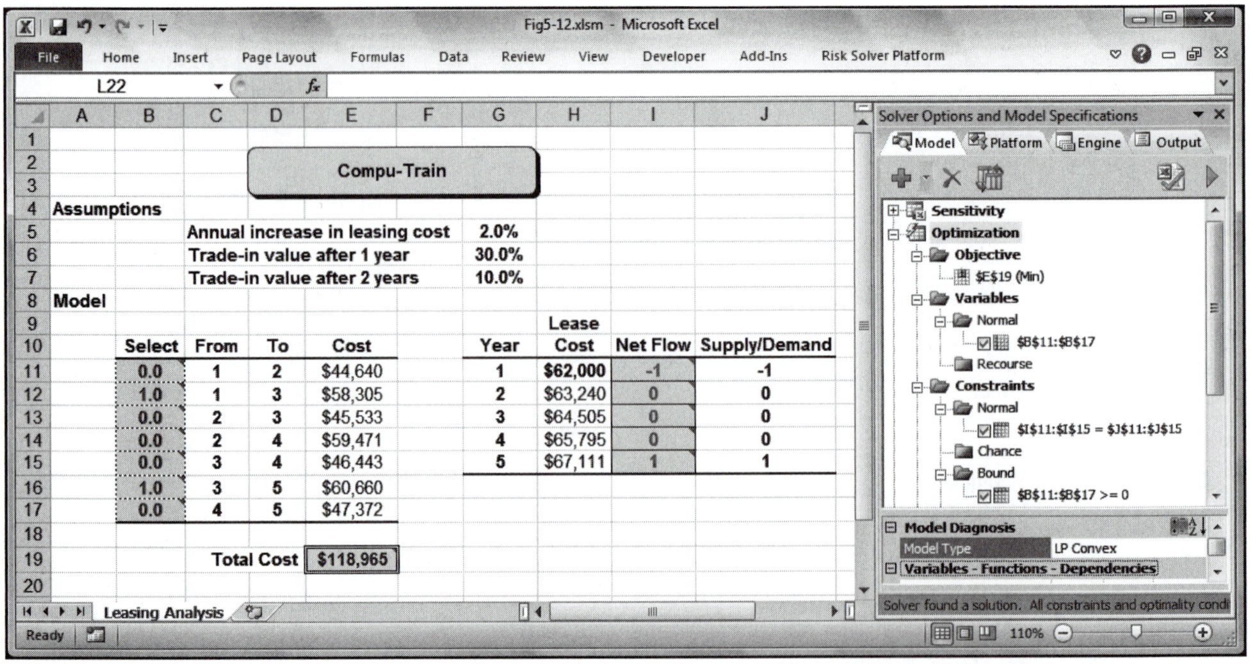

financial consequences of the two different alternatives clear, Jose still must decide for himself whether the benefits of the financial cost savings under the second contract outweigh the nonfinancial costs associated with using slightly out-of-date equipment during years 2 and 4. Of course, regardless of which contract Jose decides to go with, he will get to reconsider whether or not to upgrade his equipment at the beginning of each of the next four years.

Summary of Shortest Path Problems

You can model any shortest path problem as a transshipment problem by assigning a supply of 1 to the starting node, a demand of 1 to the ending node, and a demand of 0 to all other nodes in the network. Because the examples presented here involved only a small number of paths through each of the networks, it might have been easier to solve these problems simply by enumerating the paths and calculating the total distance of each one. However, in a problem with many nodes and arcs, an automated LP model is far easier than a manual solution approach.

5.4 Transportation/Assignment Problems

Chapter 3 presented an example of another type of network flow problem known as the transportation/assignment problem. The example involved the Tropicsun Company—a grower and distributor of fresh citrus products. The company wanted to determine the least expensive way of transporting freshly picked fruit from three citrus groves to three processing plants. The network representation of the problem is repeated in Figure 5.15.

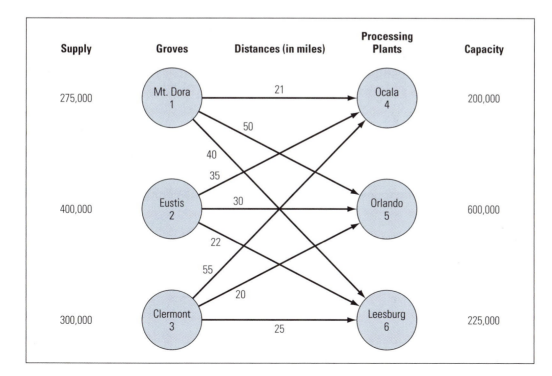

FIGURE 5.15

Network representation of Tropicsun's transportation/ assignment problem

The network shown in Figure 5.15 differs from the earlier network flow problems in this chapter because it contains no transshipment nodes. Each node in Figure 5.15 is either a sending node or a receiving node. The lack of transshipment nodes is the key feature that distinguishes transportation/assignment problems from other types of network flow problems. As you saw in Chapter 3, this property allows you to set up and solve transportation/assignment problems conveniently in a matrix format in the spreadsheet. Although it is possible to solve transportation/assignment problems in the same way in which we solved transshipment problems, it is much easier to implement and solve these problems using the matrix approach described in Chapter 3.

Sometimes, transportation/assignment problems are **sparse** or not fully interconnected (meaning not all the supply nodes have arcs connecting them to all the demand nodes). These "missing" arcs can be handled conveniently in the matrix approach to implementation by assigning arbitrarily large costs to the variable cells representing these arcs so that flow on these arcs becomes prohibitively expensive. However, as the number of missing arcs increases, the matrix approach to implementation becomes less and less computationally efficient compared to the procedure described in this chapter.

5.5 Generalized Network Flow Problems

In all of the network problems we have considered so far, the amount of flow that exited an arc was always the same as the amount that entered the arc. For example, if we put 40 cars on a train in Jacksonville and sent them to Atlanta, the same 40 cars came off the train in Atlanta. However, there are numerous examples of network flow problems in which a gain or loss occurs on flows across arcs. For instance, if oil or gas is shipped through a leaky pipeline, the amount of oil or gas arriving at the intended destination will be less than the amount originally placed in the pipeline. Similar loss-of-flow examples occur as a result of evaporation of liquids, spoilage of foods and other perishable items, or imperfections in raw materials entering production processes that result in a certain amount of scrap. Many financial cash flow problems can be modeled as network flow problems in which flow gains (or increases) occur in the form of interest or dividends as money flows through various investments. The following example illustrates the modeling changes required to accommodate these types of problems.

Nancy Grant is the owner of Coal Bank Hollow Recycling, a company that specializes in collecting and recycling paper products. Nancy's company uses two different recycling processes to convert newspaper, mixed paper, white office paper, and cardboard into paper pulp. The amount of paper pulp extracted from the recyclable materials and the cost of extracting the pulp differs depending on which recycling process is used. The following table summarizes the recycling processes:

Material	Recycling Process 1		Recycling Process 2	
	Cost per Ton	Yield	Cost per Ton	Yield
Newspaper	$13	90%	$12	85%
Mixed Paper	$11	80%	$13	85%
White Office Paper	$9	95%	$10	90%
Cardboard	$13	75%	$14	85%

For instance, every ton of newspaper subjected to recycling process 1 costs $13 and yields 0.9 tons of paper pulp. The paper pulp produced by the two different recycling processes goes through other operations to be transformed into pulp for newsprint, packaging paper, or print stock quality paper. The yields associated with transforming the recycled pulp into pulp for the final products are summarized in the following table:

Pulp Source	Newsprint Pulp		Packaging Paper Pulp		Print Stock Pulp	
	Cost per Ton	Yield	Cost per Ton	Yield	Cost per Ton	Yield
Recycling Process 1	$5	95%	$6	90%	$8	90%
Recycling Process 2	$6	90%	$8	95%	$7	95%

For instance, a ton of pulp exiting recycling process 2 can be transformed into 0.95 tons of packaging paper at a cost of $8.

Nancy currently has 70 tons of newspaper, 50 tons of mixed paper, 30 tons of white office paper, and 40 tons of cardboard. She has a contract to produce 60 tons of newsprint pulp, 40 tons of packaging paper pulp, and 50 tons of print stock pulp, and she wants to determine the most efficient way to meet this obligation.

Figure 5.16 shows how Nancy's recycling problem can be viewed as a generalized network flow problem. The arcs in this graph indicate the possible flow of recycling material through the production process. On each arc, we have listed both the cost of flow along the arc and the reduction factor that applies to flow along the arc. For instance, the arc from node 1 to node 5 indicates that each ton of newspaper going to recycling process 1 costs $13 and yields 0.90 tons of paper pulp.

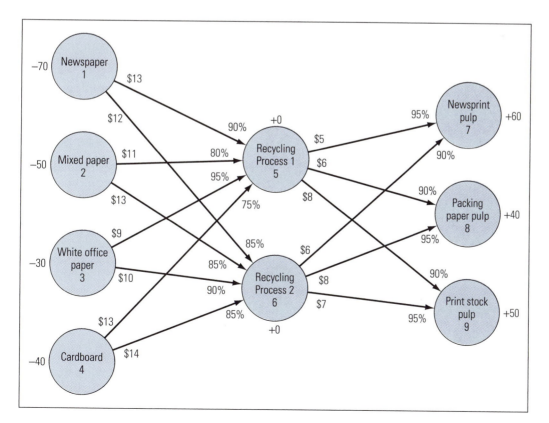

FIGURE 5.16

Graphical representation of Coal Bank Hollow Recycling's generalized network flow problem

5.5.1 FORMULATING AN LP MODEL
FOR THE RECYCLING PROBLEM

To formulate the LP model for this problem algebraically, we defined the decision variable X_{ij} to represent the tons of product flowing from node i to node j. The objective is then stated in the usual way as follows:

$$\text{MIN:} \quad 13X_{15} + 12X_{16} + 11X_{25} + 13X_{26} + 9X_{35} + 10X_{36} + 13X_{45} + 14X_{46} + 5X_{57}$$
$$+ 6X_{58} + 8X_{59} + 6X_{67} + 8X_{68} + 7X_{69}$$

The constraints for this problem may be generated using the balance-of-flow rule for each node. The constraints for the first four nodes (representing the supply of newspaper, mixed paper, white office paper, and cardboard, respectively) are given by:

$$-X_{15} - X_{16} \geq -70 \qquad \} \text{ flow constraint for node 1}$$
$$-X_{25} - X_{26} \geq -50 \qquad \} \text{ flow constraint for node 2}$$
$$-X_{35} - X_{36} \geq -30 \qquad \} \text{ flow constraint for node 3}$$
$$-X_{45} - X_{46} \geq -40 \qquad \} \text{ flow constraint for node 4}$$

These constraints simply indicate that the amount of product flowing out of each of these nodes may not exceed the supply available at each node. (Recall that the constraint given for node 1 is equivalent to $+X_{15} +X_{16} \leq +70$.)

Applying the balance-of-flow rule at nodes 5 and 6 (representing the two recycling processes), we obtain:

$$+0.9X_{15} + 0.8X_{25} + 0.95X_{35} + 0.75X_{45} - X_{57} - X_{58} - X_{59} \geq 0 \} \text{ flow constraint for node 5}$$
$$+0.85X_{16} + 0.85X_{26} + 0.9X_{36} + 0.85X_{46} - X_{67} - X_{68} - X_{69} \geq 0 \} \text{ flow constraint for node 6}$$

To better understand the logic of these constraints, we will rewrite them in the following algebraically equivalent manner:

$$+0.9X_{15} + 0.8X_{25} + 0.95X_{35} + 0.75X_{45} \geq +X_{57} + X_{58} + X_{59} \qquad \} \text{ equivalent flow constraint for node 5}$$

$$+0.85X_{16} + 0.85X_{26} + 0.9X_{36} + 0.85X_{46} \geq +X_{67} + X_{68} + X_{69} \qquad \} \text{ equivalent flow constraint for node 6}$$

Notice that the constraint for node 5 requires that the amount being shipped from node 5 (given by $X_{57} +X_{58} +X_{59}$) cannot exceed the net amount that would be available at node 5 (given by $0.9X_{15} +0.8X_{25} +0.95X_{35} +0.75X_{45}$). Thus, here the yield factors come into play in determining the amount of product that would be available from the recycling processes. A similar interpretation applies to the constraint for node 6.

Finally, applying the balance-of-flow rule to nodes 7, 8, and 9, we obtain the constraints:

$$+0.95X_{57} + 0.90X_{67} \geq 60 \qquad \} \text{ flow constraint for node 7}$$
$$+0.9X_{58} + 0.95X_{68} \geq 40 \qquad \} \text{ flow constraint for node 8}$$
$$+0.9X_{59} + 0.95X_{69} \geq 50 \qquad \} \text{ flow constraint for node 9}$$

The constraint for node 7 ensures that the final amount of product flowing to node 7 $(0.95X_{57} +0.90X_{67})$ is sufficient to meet the demand for pulp at this node. Again, similar interpretations apply to the constraints for nodes 8 and 9.

5.5.2 IMPLEMENTING THE MODEL

The model for Coal Bank Hollow Recycling's generalized network flow problem is summarized as:

MIN: $13X_{15} + 12X_{16} + 11X_{25} + 13X_{26} + 9X_{35} + 10X_{36} + 13X_{45} + 14X_{46} + 5X_{57}$
   $+ 6X_{58} + 8X_{59} + 6X_{67} + 8X_{68} + 7X_{69}$

Subject to:

$-X_{15} - X_{16} \geq -70$	} flow constraint for node 1
$-X_{25} - X_{26} \geq -50$	} flow constraint for node 2
$-X_{35} - X_{36} \geq -30$	} flow constraint for node 3
$-X_{45} - X_{46} \geq -40$	} flow constraint for node 4
$+0.9X_{15} + 0.8X_{25} + 0.95X_{35} + 0.75X_{45} - X_{57} - X_{58} - X_{59} \geq 0$	} flow constraint for node 5
$+0.85X_{16} + 0.85X_{26} + 0.9X_{36} + 0.85X_{46} - X_{67} - X_{68} - X_{69} \geq 0$	} flow constraint for node 6
$+0.95X_{57} + 0.90X_{67} \geq 60$	} flow constraint for node 7
$+0.9X_{58} + 0.95X_{68} \geq 40$	} flow constraint for node 8
$+0.9X_{59} + 0.95X_{69} \geq 50$	} flow constraint for node 9
$X_{ij} \geq 0$ for all i and j	} nonnegativity conditions

In all the other network flow models we have seen up to this point, all the coefficients in all the constraints were implicitly always +1 or –1. This is not true in the preceding model. Thus, we must give special attention to the coefficients in the constraints as we implement this model in the spreadsheet. One approach to implementing this problem is shown in Figure 5.17 (and the file Fig5-17.xlsm that accompanies this book).

The spreadsheet in Figure 5.17 is very similar to those of the other network flow problems we have solved. Cells A6 through A19 represent the decision variables (arcs) for our model, and the corresponding unit cost associated with each variable is listed in the range from H6 through H19. The objective function is implemented in cell H21 as:

   Formula for cell H21:   =SUMPRODUCT(H6:H19,A6:A19)

To implement the LHS formulas for our constraints, we can no longer simply sum the variables flowing into each node and subtract the variables flowing out of the nodes. Instead, we need to first multiply the variables flowing into a node by the appropriate yield factor. With the yield factors entered in column D, the yield-adjusted flow for each arc is computed in column E as follows:

   Formula for cell E6:   =A6*D6
   (Copy to cells E7 through E19.)

Now, to implement the LHS formulas for each node in cells L6 through L14, we will sum the yield-adjusted flows into each node and subtract the raw flow out of each node. This may be done as follows:

   Formula for cell L6:   =SUMIF($F$6:$F$19,J6,$E$6:$E$19)–
   (Copy to cells L7 through L14.)   SUMIF($B$6:$B$19,J6,$A$6:$A$19)

Notice that the first SUMIF( ) function in this formula sums the appropriate yield-adjusted flows in column E, while the second SUMIF( ) sums the appropriate raw flow values from column A. Thus, although this formula is very similar to the ones used in earlier models, there is a critical difference here that must be carefully noted and understood. The RHS values for these constraint cells are listed in cells M6 through M14.

FIGURE 5.17 *Spreadsheet model for Coal Bank Hollow Recycling's generalized network flow problem*

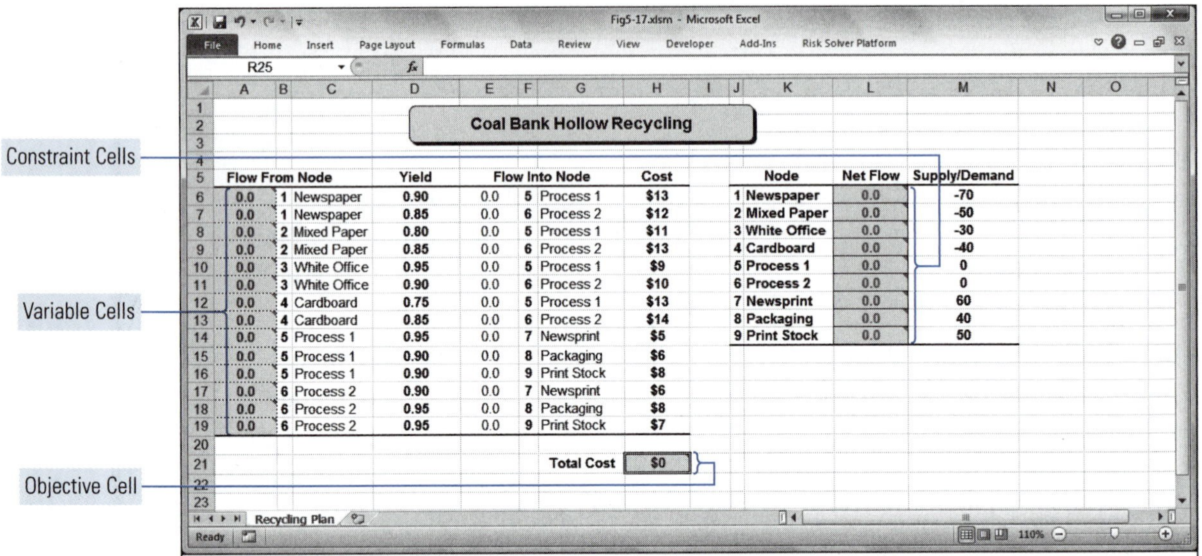

Constraint Cells

Variable Cells

Objective Cell

Key Cell Formulas

Cell	Formula	Copied to
C6	=VLOOKUP(B6,$J$6:$K$14,2)	C7:C19 and G6:G19
E6	=D6*A6	E7:E19
H21	=SUMPRODUCT(H6:H19,A6:A19)	--
L6	=SUMIF($F$6:$F$19,J6,$E$6:$E$19)	L7:L14
	-SUMIF($B$6:$B$19,J6,$A$6:$A$19)	

5.5.3 ANALYZING THE SOLUTION

The Solver parameters used to solve this problem are shown in Figure 5.18, and the optimal solution is shown in Figure 5.19.

In this solution, 43.4 tons of newspaper, 50 tons of mixed paper, and 30 tons of white office paper are assigned to recycling process 1 (that is, $X_{15} = 43.4$, $X_{25} = 50$, $X_{35} = 30$). This recycling process then yields a total of 107.6 tons of pulp (that is, $0.9 \times 43.3 + 0.8 \times 50 + 0.95 \times 30 = 107.6$) of which 63.2 tons are allocated to the production of newsprint pulp ($X_{57} = 63.2$), and 44.4 tons are allocated to the production of pulp for packaging paper ($X_{58} = 44.4$). This allows us to meet the demand for 60 tons of newsprint pulp ($0.95 \times 63.2 = 60$) and 40 tons of packaging paper ($0.90 \times 44.4 = 40$).

FIGURE 5.18

Solver options and settings for the recycling problem

Solver Settings:
Objective: H21 (Min)
Variable cells: A6:A19
Constraints:
L6:L14 >= M6:M14
A6:A19 >= 0
Solver Options:
Standard LP/Quadratic Engine (Simplex LP)

FIGURE 5.19 *Optimal solution to Coal Bank Hollow Recycling's generalized network flow problem*

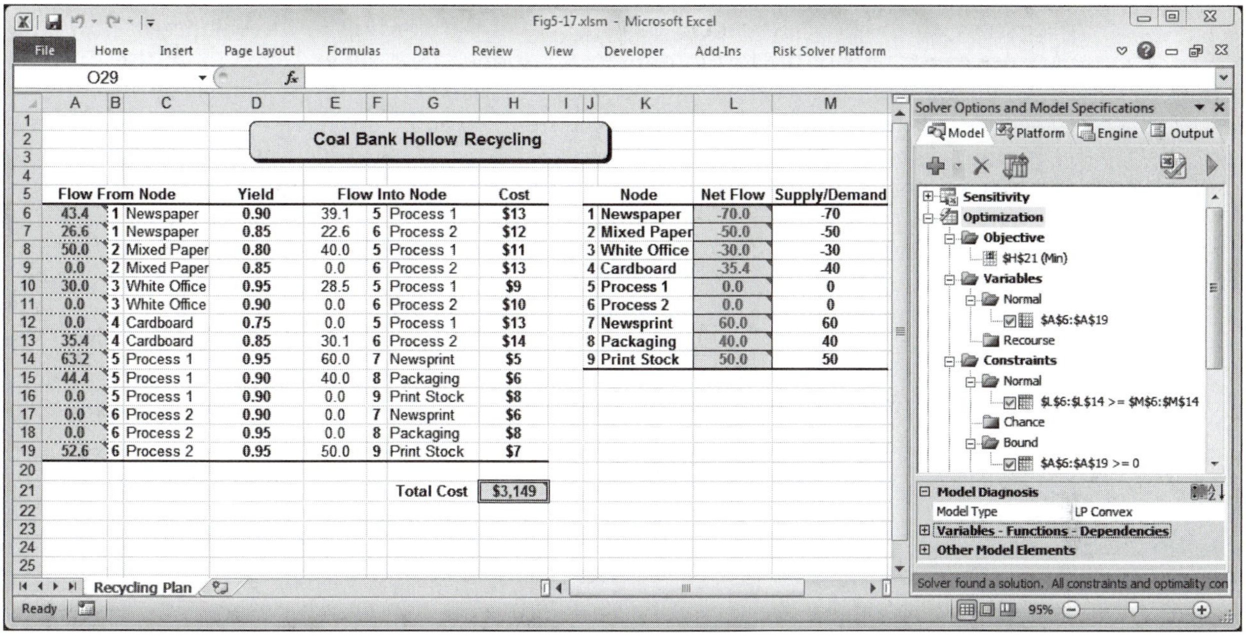

Coal Bank Hollow Recycling

Flow	From Node	Yield	Flow	Into Node	Cost
43.4	1 Newspaper	0.90	39.1	5 Process 1	$13
26.6	1 Newspaper	0.85	22.6	6 Process 2	$12
50.0	2 Mixed Paper	0.80	40.0	5 Process 1	$11
0.0	2 Mixed Paper	0.85	0.0	6 Process 2	$13
30.0	3 White Office	0.95	28.5	5 Process 1	$9
0.0	3 White Office	0.90	0.0	6 Process 2	$10
0.0	4 Cardboard	0.75	0.0	5 Process 1	$13
35.4	4 Cardboard	0.85	30.1	6 Process 2	$14
63.2	5 Process 1	0.95	60.0	7 Newsprint	$5
44.4	5 Process 1	0.90	40.0	8 Packaging	$6
0.0	5 Process 1	0.90	0.0	9 Print Stock	$8
0.0	6 Process 2	0.90	0.0	7 Newsprint	$6
0.0	6 Process 2	0.95	0.0	8 Packaging	$8
52.6	6 Process 2	0.95	50.0	9 Print Stock	$7
				Total Cost	$3,149

Node	Net Flow	Supply/Demand
1 Newspaper	-70.0	-70
2 Mixed Paper	-50.0	-50
3 White Office	-30.0	-30
4 Cardboard	-35.4	-40
5 Process 1	0.0	0
6 Process 2	0.0	0
7 Newsprint	60.0	60
8 Packaging	40.0	40
9 Print Stock	50.0	50

The remaining 26.6 tons of newspaper are combined with 35.4 tons of cardboard in recycling process 2 (that is, $X_{16} = 26.6$, $X_{46} = 35.4$). This results in a yield of 52.6 tons of pulp (that is, $0.85 \times 26.6 + 0.85 \times 35.4 = 52.6$), which is all devoted to the production of 50 tons of print stock quality pulp ($0.95 \times 52.6 = 50$).

It is important for Nancy to note that this production plan calls for the use of all her supply of newspaper, mixed paper, and white office paper, but it leaves about 4.6 tons of cardboard left over. Thus, she should be able to lower her total costs further by acquiring more newspaper, mixed paper, or white office paper. It would be wise for her to see if she could trade her surplus cardboard to another recycler for the material that she is running short on.

5.5.4 GENERALIZED NETWORK FLOW PROBLEMS AND FEASIBILITY

In generalized network flow problems, the gains and/or losses associated with flows across each arc *effectively* increase and/or decrease the supply available in the network. For example, consider what happens in Figure 5.16 if the supply of newspaper is reduced to 55 tons. Although it *appears* that the total supply in the network (175 tons) still exceeds the total demand (150 tons), if we try to solve the modified problem, Solver will tell us that the problem has no feasible solution. (You may verify this on your own.) So we are not able to satisfy all of the demand due to the loss of material that occurs in the production process.

The point being made here is that with generalized network flow problems, you cannot always tell before solving the problem if the total supply is adequate to meet the total demand. As a result, you cannot always know which balance-of-flow rule to apply. When the issue is unclear, it is safest (see question 3 at the end of this chapter for more on this issue) to first assume that all the demand can be met and (according to the balance-of-flow rule) use constraints of the form: Inflow − Outflow ≥ Supply or Demand. If the resulting problem is infeasible (and there are no errors in the model!), then we know all the demand cannot be satisfied and (according to the balance-of-flow rule) use constraints of the form: Inflow − Outflow ≤ Supply or Demand. In this case, the solution will identify the least costly way of distributing the available supply.

As an example of this approach, Figures 5.20 and 5.21 show, respectively, the Solver parameters and optimal solution for this revised recycling problem with 55 tons of newspaper. Note that this solution uses all of the available supply of each of the recycling materials. Although the solution satisfies all the demand for newsprint pulp and packaging paper pulp, it falls almost 15 tons short of the total demand for print stock pulp. The recycling company would need to consult with its customer about whether this shortage should be subcontracted or backlogged.

When the total supply cannot meet the total demand, another possible managerial objective is to meet as much of the demand as possible at minimum cost. This is done easily by adding an artificial supply node to the network with an arbitrarily large amount of supply (so that total supply > total demand) and connecting it directly to

FIGURE 5.20

Solver parameters for modified recycling problem

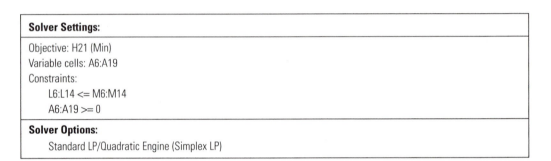

Solver Settings:
Objective: H21 (Min)
Variable cells: A6:A19
Constraints:
L6:L14 <= M6:M14
A6:A19 >= 0
Solver Options:
Standard LP/Quadratic Engine (Simplex LP)

FIGURE 5.21   *Optimal solution to modified recycling problem*

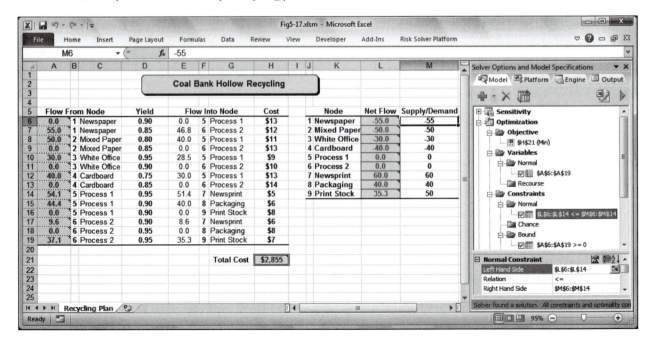

each of the demand nodes with an arbitrarily large cost on flows over those arcs. Flows over the artificial arcs will be minimized because they incur a large cost penalty. This, in turn, causes as much of the demand as possible to be met by the real (non-artificial) supply nodes in the network.

As an example of this approach, Figures 5.22 and 5.23 (and the file Fig5-23.xlsm that accompanies this book) show, respectively, the Solver parameters and optimal solution for this revised recycling problem with 55 tons of newspaper and an artificial supply

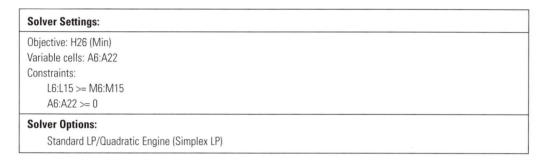

FIGURE 5.22

Solver settings and options for modified recycling problem with an artificial supply node

Solver Settings:

Objective: H26 (Min)
Variable cells: A6:A22
Constraints:
　　L6:L15 >= M6:M15
　　A6:A22 >= 0

Solver Options:
　　Standard LP/Quadratic Engine (Simplex LP)

FIGURE 5.23 *Spreadsheet model and optimal solution to modified recycling problem with an artificial supply node*

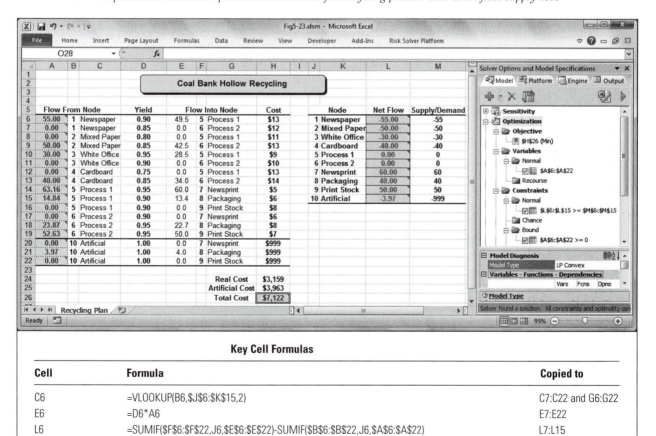

Key Cell Formulas

Cell	Formula	Copied to
C6	=VLOOKUP(B6,$J$6:$K$15,2)	C7:C22 and G6:G22
E6	=D6*A6	E7:E22
L6	=SUMIF($F$6:$F$22,J6,$E$6:$E$22)-SUMIF($B$6:$B$22,J6,$A$6:$A$22)	L7:L15
H24	=SUMPRODUCT(H6:H19,A6:A19)	--
H25	=SUMPRODUCT(H20:H22,A20:A22)	--
H26	=H24+H25	--

node. Note an artificial node (node 10) was added to this problem with an arbitrarily large amount of supply. Additionally, three new arcs were added to connect this new supply node to nodes 7, 8, and 9, which represent, respectively, the demand nodes for newspaper pulp, packaging paper pulp, and print stock pulp. Thus, any demand that cannot be met by the flow of real materials can now be met (in a virtual sense) by the artificial supply. Arbitrarily large costs of $999 are assigned to flows on these artificial arcs in cells H20 through H22. The total cost to be minimized in cell H26 is made up of the real cost of materials flowing through the network (cell H24) and the cost of using the artificial supply (cell H25). Note that the optimal solution shown in Figure 5.23 has a real cost of $3,159 and falls almost 4 tons short of meeting the total demand for packaging paper pulp. This solution meets as much of the total demand as possible in the least costly manner and might be preferred by management (and the company's customer) over the solution shown in Figure 5.21.

Important Modeling Point

For generalized network flow problems, the gains and/or losses associated with flows across each arc *effectively* increase and/or decrease the supply available in the network. As a result, it is sometimes difficult to tell in advance whether the total supply is actually adequate to meet the total demand in a generalized network flow problem. When in doubt, it is best to assume the total supply is capable of satisfying the total demand and use Solver to prove (or refute) this assumption.

5.6 Maximal Flow Problems

The maximal flow problem (or max flow problem) is a type of network flow problem in which the goal is to determine the maximum amount of flow that can occur in the network. In a maximal flow problem, the amount of flow that can occur over each arc is limited by some capacity restriction. This type of network might be used to model the flow of oil in a pipeline (in which the amount of oil that can flow through a pipe in a unit of time is limited by the diameter of the pipe). Traffic engineers also use this type of network to determine the maximum number of cars that can travel through a collection of streets with different capacities imposed by the number of lanes in the streets and speed limits. The following example illustrates a max flow problem.

5.6.1 AN EXAMPLE OF A MAXIMAL FLOW PROBLEM

The Northwest Petroleum Company operates an oil field and refinery in Alaska. The crude obtained from the oil field is pumped through the network of pumping substations shown in Figure 5.24 to the company's refinery located 500 miles from the oil field. The amount of oil that can flow through each of the pipelines, represented by the arcs in the network, varies due to differing pipe diameters. The numbers next to the arcs in the network indicate the maximum amount of oil that can flow through the various pipelines (measured in thousands of barrels per hour). The company wants to determine the maximum number of barrels per hour that can flow from the oil field to the refinery.

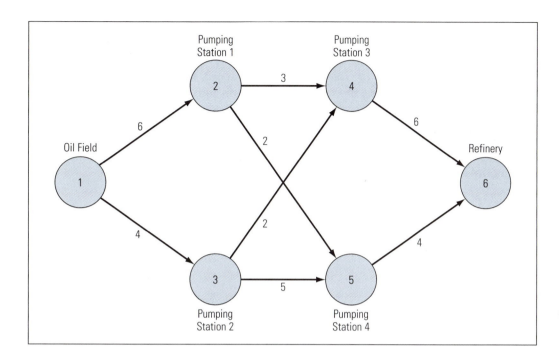

FIGURE 5.24

Network representation of Northwest Petroleum's oil refinery operation

The max flow problem appears to be very different from the network flow models described earlier because it does not include specific supplies or demands for the nodes. However, you can solve the max flow problem in the same way as a transshipment problem if you add a return arc from the ending node to the starting node, assign a demand of 0 to all the nodes in the network, and attempt to maximize the flow over the return arc. Figure 5.25 shows these modifications to the problem.

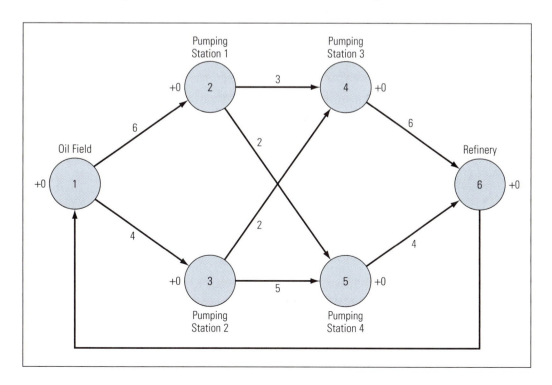

FIGURE 5.25

Network structure of Northwest Petroleum's max flow problem

To understand the network in Figure 5.25, suppose that k units are shipped from node 6 to node 1 (where k represents some integer). Because node 6 has a supply of 0, it can send k units to node 1 only if these units can be returned through the network to node 6 (to balance the flow at node 6). The capacities on the arcs limit how many units can be returned to node 6. Therefore, the maximum flow through the network corresponds to the largest number of units that can be shipped from node 6 to node 1 and then returned through the network to node 6 (to balance the flow at this node). We can solve an LP model to determine the maximal flow by maximizing the flow from node 6 to node 1, given appropriate upper bounds on each arc and the usual balance-of-flow constraints. This model is represented as:

$$\text{MAX:} \quad X_{61}$$

Subject to:
$$+X_{61} - X_{12} - X_{13} = 0$$
$$+X_{12} - X_{24} - X_{25} = 0$$
$$+X_{13} - X_{34} - X_{35} = 0$$
$$+X_{24} + X_{34} - X_{46} = 0$$
$$+X_{25} + X_{35} - X_{56} = 0$$
$$+X_{46} + X_{56} - X_{61} = 0$$

with the following bounds on the decision variables:

$$0 \le X_{12} \le 6 \qquad 0 \le X_{25} \le 2 \qquad 0 \le X_{46} \le 6$$
$$0 \le X_{13} \le 4 \qquad 0 \le X_{34} \le 2 \qquad 0 \le X_{56} \le 4$$
$$0 \le X_{24} \le 3 \qquad 0 \le X_{35} \le 5 \qquad 0 \le X_{61} \le \infty$$

5.6.2 THE SPREADSHEET MODEL AND SOLUTION

This model is implemented in the spreadsheet shown in Figure 5.26 (and in the file Fig5-26.xlsm that accompanies this book). This spreadsheet model differs from the earlier network models in a few minor, but important, ways. First, column G in Figure 5.26 represents the upper bounds for each arc. Second, the objective function (or set cell) is represented by cell B16, which contains the formula:

Formula in cell B16:   =B14

Cell B14 represents the flow from node 6 to node 1 (or X_{61}). This cell corresponds to the variable we want to maximize in the objective function of the LP model. The Solver parameters and options shown in Figure 5.27 are used to obtain the optimal solution shown in Figure 5.26.

Because the arcs leading to node 6 (X_{46} and X_{56}) have a total capacity for 10 units of flow, it might be surprising to learn that only 9 units can flow through the network. However, the optimal solution shown in Figure 5.26 indicates that the maximal flow through the network is just 9 units.

The optimal flows identified in Figure 5.26 for each arc are shown in the boxes next to the capacities for each arc in Figure 5.28. In Figure 5.28, the arc from node 5 to node 6 is at its full capacity of 4 units, whereas the arc from node 4 to node 6 is 1 unit below its full capacity of 6 units. Although the arc from node 4 to node 6 can carry 1 additional unit of flow, it is prevented from doing so because all the arcs flowing to node 4 (X_{24} and X_{34}) are at full capacity.

A graph like Figure 5.28, which summarizes the optimal flows in a max flow problem, is helpful in identifying where increases in flow capacity would be most

FIGURE 5.26 *Spreadsheet model and solution to Northwest Petroleum's max flow problem*

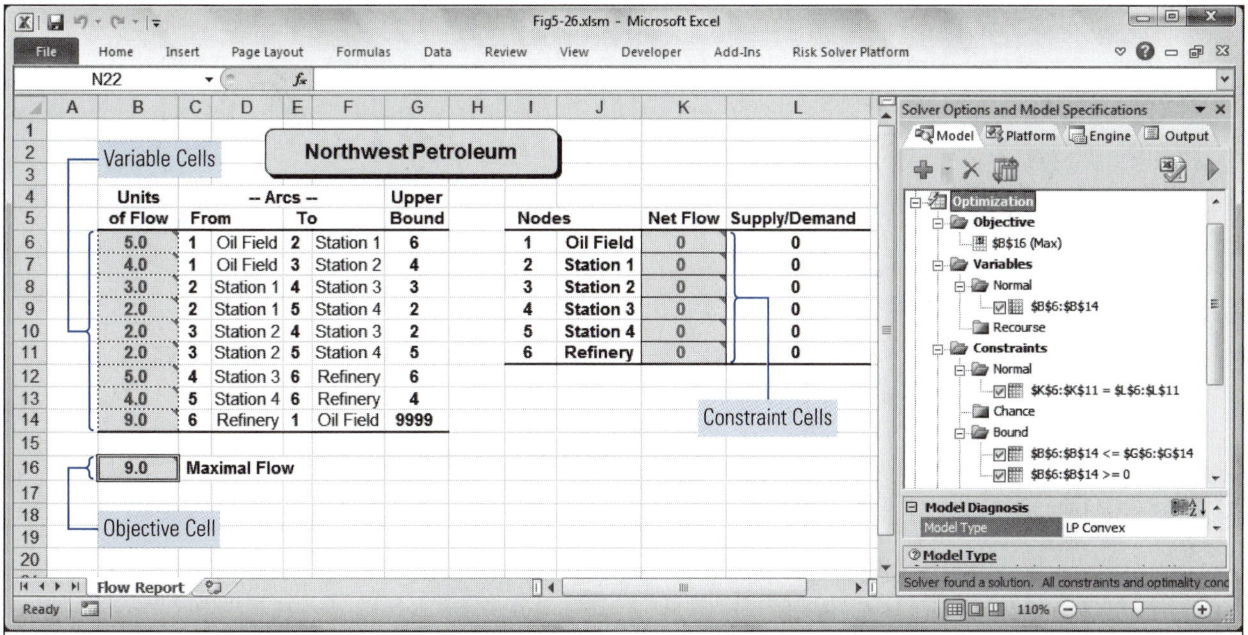

Key Cell Formulas

Cell	Formula	Copied to
B16	=B14	--
D6	=VLOOKUP(C6,$I$6:$J$11,2)	D7:D14 and F6:F14
K6	=SUMIF($E$6:$E$14,I6,$B$6:$B$14)-SUMIF($C$6:$C$14,I6,$B$6:$B$14)	K7:K11

FIGURE 5.27

Solver settings and options for Northwest Petroleum's max flow problem

Solver Settings:

Objective: B16 (Max)
Variable cells: B6:B14
Constraints:
    B6:B14 <= G6:G14
    K6:K11 = L6:L11
    B6:B14 >= 0

Solver Options:
    Standard LP/Quadratic Engine (Simplex LP)

effective. For example, from this graph, we can see that even though X_{24} and X_{34} are both at full capacity, increasing their capacity will not necessarily increase the flow through the network. Increasing the capacity of X_{24} would allow for an increased flow through the network because an additional unit could then flow from node 1 to node 2 to node 4 to node 6. However, increasing the capacity of X_{34} would not allow for an increase in the total flow because the arc from node 1 to node 3 is already at full capacity.

FIGURE 5.28

*Network
representation of
the solution to
Northwest
Petroleum's max
flow problem*

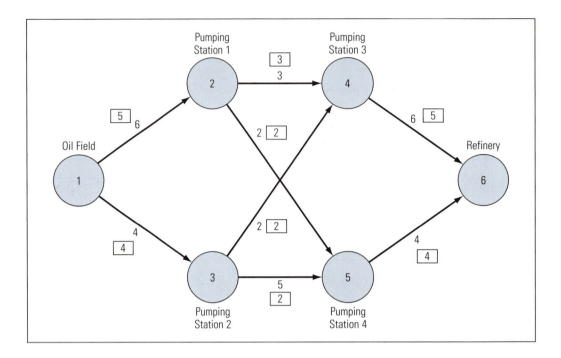

5.7 Special Modeling Considerations

A number of special conditions can arise in network flow problems that require a bit of creativity to model accurately. For example, it is easy to impose minimum or maximum flow restrictions on individual arcs in the networks by placing appropriate lower and upper bounds on the corresponding decision variables. However, in some network flow problems, minimum or maximum flow requirements may apply to the *total* flow emanating from a given node. For example, consider the network flow problem shown in Figure 5.29.

FIGURE 5.29

*Example network
flow problem*

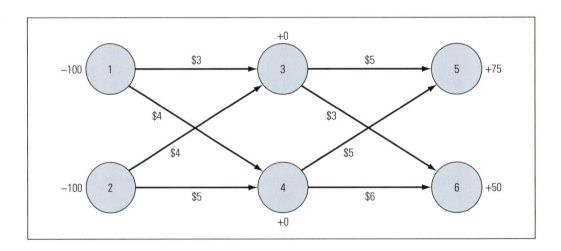

Now suppose that the total flow into node 3 must be at least 50, and the total flow into node 4 must be at least 60. We could easily enforce these conditions with the following constraints:

$$X_{13} + X_{23} \geq 50$$
$$X_{14} + X_{24} \geq 60$$

Unfortunately, these constraints do not conform to the balance-of-flow rule and would require us to impose *side constraints* on the model. An alternative approach to modeling this problem is shown in Figure 5.30.

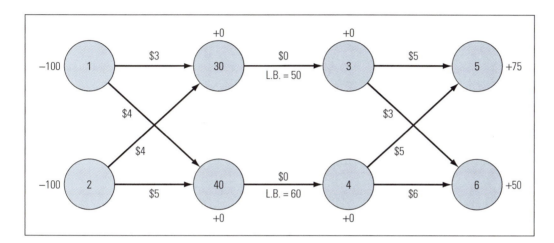

FIGURE 5.30

Revised network flow problem with lower bounds on the total flow into nodes 3 and 4

Two additional nodes and arcs were inserted in Figure 5.30. Note that the arc from node 30 to node 3 has a lower bound (L.B.) of 50. This will ensure that at least 50 units flow into node 3. Node 3 must then distribute this flow to nodes 5 and 6. Similarly, the arc connecting node 40 to node 4 ensures that at least 60 units will flow into node 4. The additional nodes and arcs added to Figure 5.30 are sometimes referred to as **dummy/artificial nodes** and **dummy/artificial arcs**.

As another example, consider the network in the upper portion of Figure 5.31 in which the flow between two nodes can occur at two different costs. One arc has a cost of $6 per unit of flow and an upper bound (U.B., in the figure) of 35. The other arc has a cost of $8 per unit of flow with no upper bound on the amount of flow allowed. Note that the minimum cost solution is to send 35 units of flow from node 1 to node 2 across the $6 arc, and 15 units from node 1 to node 2 across the $8 arc.

To model this problem mathematically, we would like to have two arcs called X_{12} because both arcs go from node 1 to node 2. However, if both arcs are called X_{12}, there is no way to distinguish one from the other! A solution to this dilemma is shown in the lower portion of Figure 5.31 in which we inserted a dummy node and a dummy arc. Thus, there are now two distinct arcs flowing into node 2: X_{12} and $X_{10,2}$. Flow from node 1 to node 2 across the $8 arc now must first go through node 10.

As a final example, note that upper bounds (or capacity restrictions) on the arcs in a network flow may *effectively* limit the amount of supply that can be sent through the network to meet the demand. As a result, in a network flow problem with flow restrictions (upper bounds) on the arcs, it is sometimes difficult to tell in advance whether the total demand can be met—even if the total supply available exceeds the total demand. This again creates a potential problem in knowing which balance-of-flow rule to use. Consider the example in Figure 5.32.

FIGURE 5.31

Alternative networks allowing two different types of flow between two nodes

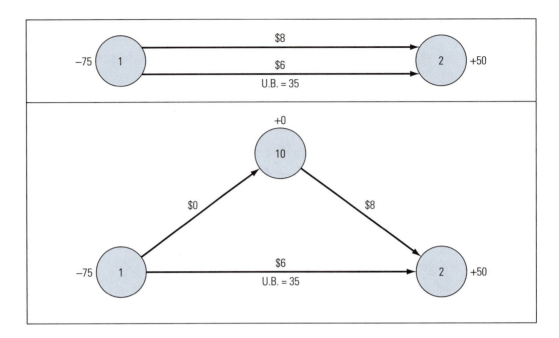

FIGURE 5.32

Example of using a dummy demand node

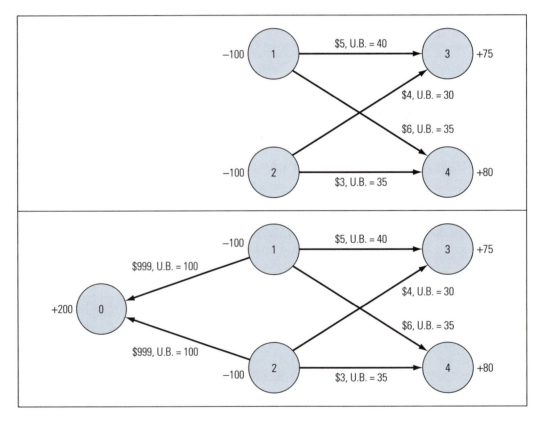

The upper portion of Figure 5.32 shows a network with a total supply of 200 and a total demand of 155. Because the total supply appears to exceed the total demand, we are inclined to apply the balance-of-flow rule that would generate constraints of the form: Inflow − Outflow ≥ Supply or Demand. This balance-of-flow rule requires the total inflow to nodes 3 and 4 to be greater than or equal to their demands of 75 and 80, respectively. However, the upper bounds on the arcs leading into node 3 limit the total flow into this node to 70 units. Similarly, the total flow into node 4 is limited to 70. As a result, there is no feasible solution to the problem. In this case, we cannot resolve the infeasibility by reversing the constraints to be of the form: Inflow − Outflow ≤ Supply or Demand. Although this allows for less than the total amount demanded to be sent to nodes 3 and 4, it now *requires* all the supply to be sent out of nodes 1 and 2. Clearly, some of the 200 units of supply available from nodes 1 and 2 will have nowhere to go if the total flow into nodes 3 and 4 cannot exceed 140 units (as required by the upper bounds on the arcs).

A solution to this predicament is shown in the bottom half of Figure 5.32. Here, we added a dummy demand node (node 0) that is connected directly to nodes 1 and 2 with arcs that impose very large costs on flows to the dummy node. Note that the demand at this dummy node is equal to the total supply in the network. Now, the total demand exceeds the total supply so the balance-of-flow rule mandates we use constraints of the form: Inflow − Outflow ≤ Supply or Demand. Again, this allows for less than the total amount demanded to be sent to nodes 0, 3, and 4 but *requires* all the supply to be sent out of nodes 1 and 2. Due to the large costs associated with flows from nodes 1 and 2 to the dummy demand node, Solver will ensure that as much of the supply as possible is first sent to nodes 3 and 4. Any remaining supply at nodes 1 and 2 would then be sent to the dummy node. Of course, flows to the dummy node actually represent excess supply or inventory at nodes 1 and 2 that would not actually be shipped anywhere or incur any costs. But using a dummy node in this manner allows us to model and solve the problem accurately.

Dummy nodes and arcs can be helpful in modeling a variety of situations that naturally occur in network problems. The techniques illustrated here are two "tricks of the trade" in network modeling and may prove useful in some of the problems at the end of this chapter.

5.8 Minimal Spanning Tree Problems

Another type of network problem is known as the minimal spanning tree problem. This type of problem cannot be solved as an LP problem but is solved easily using a simple manual algorithm.

For a network with n nodes, a **spanning tree** is a set of $n − 1$ arcs that connects all the nodes and contains no loops. A minimum spanning tree problem involves determining the set of arcs that connects all the nodes in a network while minimizing the total length (or cost) of the selected arcs. Consider the following example.

Jon Fleming is responsible for setting up a local area network (LAN) in the design engineering department of Windstar Aerospace Company. A LAN consists of a number of individual computers connected to a centralized computer or file server. Each computer in the LAN can access information from the file server and communicate with the other computers in the LAN.

Installing a LAN involves connecting all the computers together with communications cables. Not every computer has to be connected directly to the file server, but there must be some link between each computer in the network. Figure 5.33 summarizes all the possible connections that Jon could make. Each node in this figure represents one of the computers to be included in the LAN. Each line connecting the nodes represents a possible connection between pairs of computers. The dollar amount on each line represents the cost of making the connection.

FIGURE 5.33

Network representation of Windstar Aerospace's minimal spanning tree problem

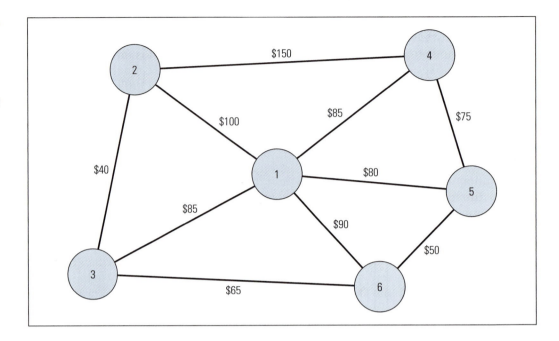

The arcs in Figure 5.33 have no specific directional orientation, indicating that information can move in either direction across the arcs. Also note that the communication links represented by the arcs do not exist yet. Jon's challenge is to determine which links to establish. Because the network involves $n = 6$ nodes, a spanning tree for this problem consists of $n - 1 = 5$ arcs that results in a path existing between any pair of nodes. The objective is to find the minimal (least costly) spanning tree for this problem.

5.8.1 AN ALGORITHM FOR THE MINIMAL SPANNING TREE PROBLEM

You can apply a simple algorithm to solve minimal spanning tree problems. Following are the steps to this algorithm:

1. Select any node. Call this the current subnetwork.
2. Add to the current subnetwork the cheapest arc that connects any node within the current subnetwork to any node not in the current subnetwork. (Ties for the cheapest arc can be broken arbitrarily.) Call this the current subnetwork.
3. If all the nodes are in the subnetwork, stop; this is the optimal solution. Otherwise, return to step 2.

5.8.2 SOLVING THE EXAMPLE PROBLEM

You can program this algorithm easily or, for simple problems, execute it manually. The following steps illustrate how to execute the algorithm manually for the example problem shown in Figure 5.33.

Step 1. If we select node 1 in Figure 5.33, then node 1 is the current subnetwork.

Step 2. The cheapest arc connecting the current subnetwork to a node not in the current subnetwork is the $80 arc connecting nodes 1 and 5. This arc and node 5 are added to the current subnetwork.

Step 3. Four nodes (nodes 2, 3, 4, and 6) remain unconnected—therefore, return to step 2.

Step 2. The cheapest arc connecting the current subnetwork to a node not in the current subnetwork is the $50 arc connecting nodes 5 and 6. This arc and node 6 are added to the current subnetwork.

Step 3. Three nodes (nodes 2, 3, and 4) remain unconnected—therefore, return to step 2.

Step 2. The cheapest arc connecting the current subnetwork to a node not in the current subnetwork is the $65 arc connecting nodes 6 and 3. This arc and node 3 are added to the current subnetwork.

Step 3. Two nodes (nodes 2 and 4) remain unconnected—therefore, return to step 2.

Step 2. The cheapest arc connecting the current subnetwork to a node not in the current subnetwork is the $40 arc connecting nodes 3 and 2. This arc and node 2 are added to the current subnetwork.

Step 3. One node (node 4) remains unconnected—therefore, return to step 2.

Step 2. The cheapest arc connecting the current subnetwork to a node not in the current subnetwork is the $75 arc connecting nodes 5 and 4. This arc and node 4 are added to the current subnetwork.

Step 3. All the nodes are now connected. Stop; the current subnetwork is optimal.

Figure 5.34 shows the optimal (minimal) spanning tree generated by this algorithm. The algorithm described here produces the optimal (minimal) spanning tree regardless of which node is selected initially in step 1. You can verify this by solving the example problem again starting with a different node in step 1.

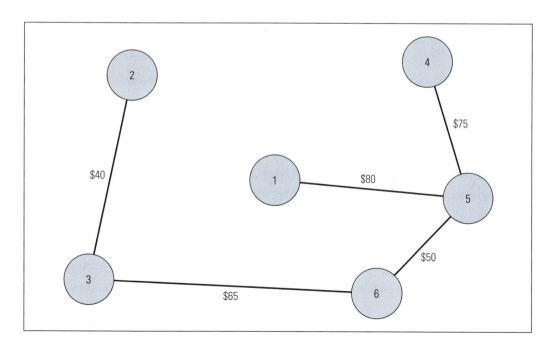

FIGURE 5.34

Optimal solution to Windstar Aerospace's minimal spanning tree problem

5.9 Summary

This chapter presented several business problems modeled as network flow problems, including transshipment problems, shortest path problems, maximal flow problems, transportation/assignment problems, and generalized network flow models. It also introduced the minimal spanning tree problem and presented a simple algorithm for solving this type of problem manually.

Although special algorithms exist for solving network flow problems, you can also formulate and solve them as LP problems. The constraints in an LP formulation of a network flow problem have a special structure that enables you to implement and solve these models easily in a spreadsheet. Although there might be more efficient ways of solving network flow problems, the methods discussed in this chapter are often the most practical. For extremely complex network flow problems, you might need to use a specialized algorithm. Unfortunately, you are unlikely to find this type of software at your local software store. However, various network optimization packages can be found in the technical/scientific directories on the Internet.

5.10 References

Glassey, R., and V. Gupta. "A Linear Programming Analysis of Paper Recycling," *Studies in Mathematical Programming*. New York: North–Holland, 1978.

Glover, F,. and D. Klingman. "Network Applications in Industry and Government," *AIIE Transactions*, vol. 9, no. 4, 1977.

Glover, F., D. Klingman, and N. Phillips. *Network Models and Their Applications in Practice*. New York: Wiley, 1992.

Hansen, P., and R. Wendell. "A Note on Airline Commuting," *Interfaces*, vol. 11, no. 12, 1982.

Phillips, D., and A. Diaz. *Fundamentals of Network Analysis*. Englewood Cliffs, NJ: Prentice Hall, 1981.

Vemuganti, R., et al. "Network Models for Fleet Management," *Decision Sciences*, vol. 20, Winter 1989.

THE WORLD OF MANAGEMENT SCIENCE

Yellow Freight System Boosts Profits and Quality with Network Optimization

One of the largest motor carriers in the United States, Yellow Freight System, Inc. of Overland Park, Kansas, uses network modeling and optimization to assist management in load planning, routing empty trucks, routing trailers, dropping or adding direct service routes, and strategic planning of terminal size and location. The system, called SYSNET, operates on a network of Sun workstations optimizing over a million network flow variables. The company also uses a tactical planning room equipped with graphical display tools that allow planning meetings to be conducted interactively with the system.

The company competes in the less-than-truckload (LTL) segment of the trucking market. That is, they contract for shipments of any size, regardless of whether the shipment fills the trailer. To operate efficiently, Yellow Freight must consolidate and transfer shipments at 23 break-bulk terminals located throughout the United States. At these terminals, shipments might be reloaded into different trailers depending

(Continued)

on the final destination. Each break-bulk terminal serves several end-of-line terminals in a hub-and-spoke network. Normally, shipments are sent by truck to the break-bulk dedicated to the origination point. Local managers occasionally try to save costs by loading direct, which means bypassing a break-bulk and sending a truckload of consolidated shipments directly to the final destination. Before SYSNET, these decisions were made in the field without accurate information on how they would affect costs and reliability in the entire system.

Since its implementation in 1989, SYSNET has scored high with upper management. Often, the first response to a new proposal is, "Has it been run through SYSNET?" The benefits attributed to the new system include the following:

- An increase of 11.6% in freight loaded directly, saving $4.7 million annually
- Better routing of trailers, saving $1 million annually
- Savings of $1.42 million annually by increasing the average number of pounds loaded per trailer
- Reduction in claims for damaged merchandise
- A 27% reduction in the number of late deliveries
- Tactical planning projects with SYSNET in 1990 that identified $10 million in annual savings

Equally important has been the effect on the management philosophy and culture at Yellow Freight. Management now has greater control over network operations; tradition, intuition, and "gut feel" have been replaced with formal analytical tools; and Yellow Freight is better able to act as a partner with customers in total quality management and just-in-time inventory systems.

Source: Braklow, John W., William W. Graham, Stephen M. Hassler, Ken E. Peck and Warren B. Powell, "Interactive Optimization Improves Service and Performance for Yellow Freight System," *Interfaces*, 22:1, January–February 1992, pgs. 147–172.

Questions and Problems

1. This chapter followed the convention of using negative numbers to represent the supply at a node and positive numbers to represent the demand at a node. Another convention is just the opposite—using positive numbers to represent supply and negative numbers to represent demand. How would the balance-of-flow rule presented in this chapter need to be changed to accommodate this alternate convention?
2. To use the balance-of-flow rule presented in this chapter, constraints for supply nodes must have negative RHS values. Some LP software packages cannot solve problems in which the constraints have negative RHS values. How should the balance-of-flow rules be modified to produce LP models that can be solved with such software packages?
3. Consider the revised Coal Bank Hollow recycling problem discussed in Section 5.5.4 of this chapter. We said that it is safest to assume the supply in a generalized network flow problem is capable of meeting the demand (until Solver proves otherwise).
   a. Solve the problem in Figure 5.17 (and file Fig5-17.xlsm on your data disk) assuming 80 tons of newspaper is available and that the supply is *not* adequate to meet the demand. How much of each of the raw recycling materials is used? How much demand for each product is met? What is the cost of this solution?

b. Solve the problem again assuming that the supply is adequate to meet the demand. How much of each of the raw recycling materials is used? How much demand for each product is met? What is the cost of this solution?

c. Which one is better? Why?

d. Suppose there are 55 tons of newspaper available. Figure 5.21 shows the least cost solution for distributing the supply in this case. In that solution, the demand for newsprint pulp and packaging pulp is met, but we are almost 15 tons short on print stock pulp. How much can this shortage be reduced (without creating shortages of the other products), and how much extra would it cost to do so?

4. Consider the generalized transportation problem shown in Figure 5.35. How can this problem be transformed into an equivalent transportation problem? Draw the network for the equivalent problem.

5. Draw the network representation of the following network flow problem.

$$\text{MIN:} \qquad +7X_{12} + 6X_{14} + 3X_{23} + 4X_{24} + 5X_{32} + 9X_{43} + 8X_{52} + 5X_{54}$$

Subject to:
$$-X_{12} - X_{14} = -5$$
$$+X_{12} + X_{52} + X_{32} - X_{23} - X_{24} = +4$$
$$-X_{32} + X_{23} + X_{43} = +8$$
$$+X_{14} + X_{24} + X_{54} - X_{43} = +0$$
$$-X_{52} - X_{54} = -7$$
$$X_{ij} \geq 0 \text{ for all } i \text{ and } j$$

FIGURE 5.35

Graph of a generalized network flow problem

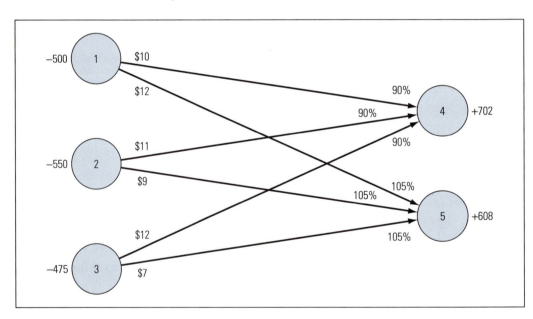

6. Draw the network representation of the following network flow problem. What kind of network flow problem is this?

$$\text{MIN:} \qquad +2X_{13} + 6X_{14} + 5X_{15} + 4X_{23} + 3X_{24} + 7X_{25}$$

Subject to:
$$-X_{13} - X_{14} - X_{15} = -8$$
$$-X_{23} - X_{24} - X_{25} = -7$$
$$+X_{13} + X_{23} \qquad\quad = +5$$
$$+X_{14} + X_{24} \qquad\quad = +5$$

$$+X_{15} + X_{25} \qquad = +5$$
$$X_{ij} \geq 0 \text{ for all } i \text{ and } j$$

7. Refer to the equipment replacement problem discussed in Section 5.3 of this chapter. In addition to the lease costs described for the problem, suppose that it costs Compu-Train $2,000 extra in labor costs whenever the company replaces its existing computers with new ones. What effect does this have on the formulation and solution of the problem? Which of the two leasing contracts is optimal in this case?

8. Suppose the X's in the following table indicate locations where fire sprinkler heads need to be installed in an existing building. The **S** indicates the location of the water source to supply these sprinklers. Assume pipe can only be run vertically or horizontally (not diagonally) between the water source and the sprinkler heads.

	1	2	3	4	5	6	7
1		X					
2	X	X	X		X	X	X
3	X		X		X	X	X
4	X	X	X			X	X
5	X	X	X		X		X
6							
7	X						
8				S			X

a. Create a spanning tree showing how water can be brought to all the sprinkler heads using a minimal amount of pipe.

b. Suppose that it takes 10 feet of pipe to connect each cell in the table to each adjacent cell. How much pipe does your solution require?

9. SunNet is a residential Internet Service Provider (ISP) in the central Florida area. Presently, the company operates one centralized facility that all of its clients call into for Internet access. To improve service, the company is planning to open three satellite offices in the cities of Pine Hills, Eustis, and Sanford. The company has identified five different regions to be serviced by these three offices. The following table summarizes the number of customers in each region, the service capacity at each office, and the average monthly per customer cost of providing service to each region from each office. Table entries of "n.a." indicate infeasible region to service center combinations. SunNet would like to determine how many customers from each region to assign to each service center in order to minimize cost.

Region	Pine Hills	Eustis	Sanford	Customers
1	$6.50	$7.50	n.a.	30,000
2	$7.00	$8.00	n.a.	40,000
3	$8.25	$7.25	$6.75	25,000
4	n.a.	$7.75	$7.00	35,000
5	n.a.	$7.50	$6.75	33,000
Capacity	60,000	70,000	40,000	

a. Draw a network flow model to represent this problem.

b. Implement your model in Excel and solve it.

c. What is the optimal solution?

10. Acme Manufacturing makes a variety of household appliances at a single manufacturing facility. The expected demand for one of these appliances during the next four

months is shown in the following table along with the expected production costs and the expected capacity for producing these items.

	Month			
	1	2	3	4
Demand	420	580	310	540
Production Cost	$49.00	$45.00	$46.00	$47.00
Production Capacity	500	520	450	550

Acme estimates it costs $1.50 per month for each unit of this appliance carried in inventory at the end of each month. Currently, Acme has 120 units in inventory on hand for this product. To maintain a level workforce, the company wants to produce at least 400 units per month. They also want to maintain a safety stock of at least 50 units per month. Acme wants to determine how many of each appliance to manufacture during each of the next four months to meet the expected demand at the lowest possible total cost.

a. Draw a network flow model for this problem.
b. Create a spreadsheet model for this problem, and solve it using Solver.
c. What is the optimal solution?
d. How much money could Acme save if the company were willing to drop the restriction about producing at least 400 units per month?

11. Sunrise Swimwear manufactures ladies swimwear in January through June of each year that is sold through retail outlets in March through August. The following table summarizes the monthly production capacity and retail demand (in 1000s), and inventory carrying costs (per 1000):

Month	Capacity	Demand	Production Cost per 1000	Carrying Cost	
				First Month	Other Months
January	16	—	$7,100	$110	$55
February	18	—	$7,700	$110	$55
March	20	14	$7,600	$120	$55
April	28	20	$7,800	$135	$55
May	29	26	$7,900	$150	$55
June	36	33	$7,400	$155	$55
July	—	28	—	—	—
August	—	10	—	—	—

a. Draw a network flow representation of this problem.
b. Implement a spreadsheet model for this problem.
c. What is the optimal solution?

12. Jacobs Manufacturing produces a popular custom accessory for pick-up trucks at plants in Huntington, West Virginia, and Bakersfield, California, and ships them to distributors in Dallas, Texas; Chicago, Illinois; Denver, Colorado; and Atlanta, Georgia. The plants in Huntington and Bakersfield have, respectively, the capacity to produce 3,000 and 4,000 units per month. For the month of October, costs of shipping a carton of 10 units from each plant to each distributor are summarized in the following table:

	Shipping Cost per Container			
	Dallas	Chicago	Denver	Atlanta
Huntington	$19	$15	$14	$12
Bakersfield	$16	$18	$11	$13

Jacobs has been notified that these shipping rates will each increase by $1.50 on November 1. Each distributor has ordered 1,500 units of Jacobs' product for October and 2,000 units for November. In any month, Jacobs can send each distributor up to 500 units more than they have ordered if Jacobs provides a $2 per unit discount on the excess (which the distributor must hold in inventory from one month to the next). In October, the per-unit cost of production in Huntington and Bakersfield is $12 and $16, respectively. In November, Jacobs expects the cost of production at both plants to be $14 per unit. The company wants to develop a production and distribution plan for the months of October and November that would allow the company to meet the expected demand from each distributor at the minimum cost.

a. Draw a network flow model for this problem.
b. Implement your model in a spreadsheet and solve it.
c. What is the optimal solution?

13. A construction company wants to determine the optimal replacement policy for the earth mover it owns. The company has a policy of not keeping an earth mover for more than five years and has estimated the annual operating costs and trade-in values for earth movers during each of the five years they might be kept as shown in the following table:

	Age in Years				
	0-1	1-2	2-3	3-4	4-5
Operating Cost	$8,000	$9,100	$10,700	$9,200	$11,000
Trade-in Value	$14,000	$9,000	$6,000	$3,500	$2,000

Assume that new earth movers currently cost $25,000 and are increasing in cost by 4.5% per year. The company wants to determine when it should plan on replacing its current, two-year-old earth mover. Use a five-year planning horizon.

a. Draw the network representation of this problem.
b. Write out the LP formulation of this problem.
c. Solve the problem using Solver. Interpret your solution.

14. The Ortega Food Company needs to ship 100 cases of hot tamales from its warehouse in San Diego to a distributor in New York City at minimum cost. The costs associated with shipping 100 cases between various cities are listed in the following table:

	To					
From	Los Angeles	Denver	St. Louis	Memphis	Chicago	New York
San Diego	5	13	—	45	—	105
Los Angeles	—	27	19	50	—	95
Denver	—	—	14	30	32	—
St. Louis	—	14	—	35	24	—
Memphis	—	—	35	—	18	25
Chicago	—	—	24	18	—	17

a. Draw the network representation of this problem.
b. Write out the LP formulation of this problem.
c. Solve the problem using Solver. Interpret your solution.

15. A cotton grower in south Georgia produces cotton on farms in Statesboro and Brooklet, ships it to cotton gins in Claxton and Millen where it is processed, and then sends it to distribution centers in Savannah, Perry, and Valdosta where it is sold to customers for $60 per ton. Any surplus cotton is sold to a government warehouse in Hinesville

for $25 per ton. The cost of growing and harvesting a ton of cotton at the farms in Statesboro and Brooklet is $20 and $22, respectively. There are presently 700 and 500 tons of cotton available in Statesboro and Brooklet, respectively. The cost of transporting the cotton from the farms to the gins and the government warehouse is shown in the following table:

	Claxton	Millen	Hinesville
Statesboro	$4.00	$3.00	$4.50
Brooklet	$3.5	$3.00	$3.50

The gin in Claxton has the capacity to process 700 tons of cotton at a cost of $10 per ton. The gin in Millen can process 600 tons at a cost of $11 per ton. Each gin must use at least one half of its available capacity. The cost of shipping a ton of cotton from each gin to each distribution center is summarized in the following table:

	Savannah	Perry	Valdosta
Claxton	$10	$16	$15
Millen	$12	$18	$17

Assume the demand for cotton in Savannah, Perry, and Valdosta is 400, 300, and 450 tons, respectively.
a. Draw a network flow model to represent this problem.
b. Implement your model in Excel and solve it.
c. What is the optimal solution?

16. The blood bank wants to determine the least expensive way to transport available blood donations from Pittsburgh and Staunton to hospitals in Charleston, Roanoke, Richmond, Norfolk, and Suffolk. The supply and demand for donated blood is shown in Figure 5.36 along with the unit cost of shipping along each possible arc.
a. Create a spreadsheet model for this problem.
b. What is the optimal solution?
c. Suppose that no more than 1,000 units of blood can be transported over any one arc. What is the optimal solution to this revised problem?

17. A furniture manufacturer has warehouses in cities represented by nodes 1, 2, and 3 in Figure 5.37. The values on the arcs indicate the per-unit shipping costs required to transport living room suites between the various cities. The supply of living room suites at each warehouse is indicated by the negative number next to nodes 1, 2, and

FIGURE 5.36

Network flow model for the blood bank problem

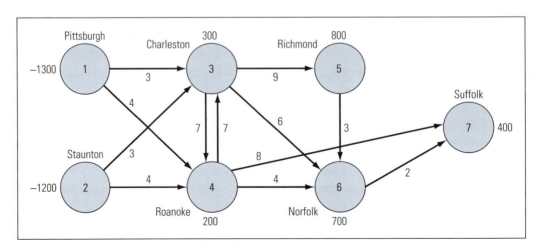

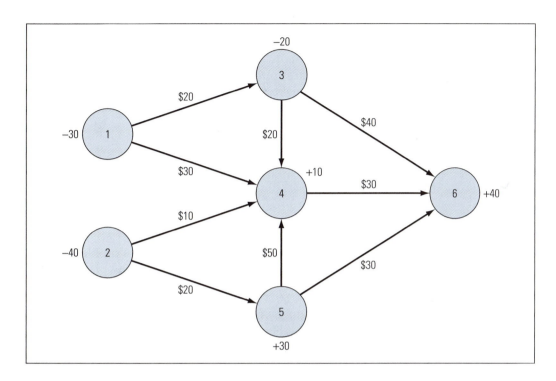

FIGURE 5.37

Network flow model for the furniture manufacturing problem

3. The demand for living room suites is indicated by the positive number next to the remaining nodes.
   a. Identify the supply, demand, and transshipment nodes in this problem.
   b. Use Solver to determine the least costly shipping plan for this problem.
18. The graph in Figure 5.38 represents various flows that can occur through a sewage treatment plant with the numbers on the arcs representing the maximum

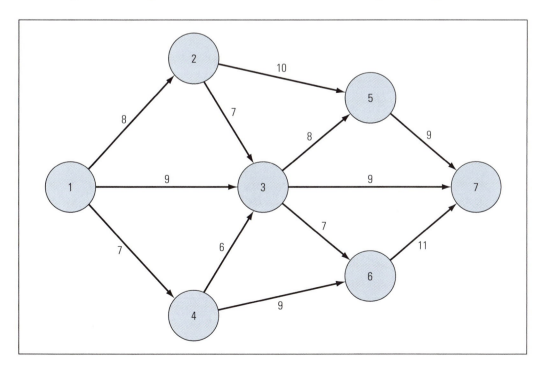

FIGURE 5.38

Network flow model for the sewage treatment plant

flow (in tons of sewage per hour) that can be accommodated. Formulate an LP model to determine the maximum tons of sewage per hour that can be processed by this plant.

19. A company has three warehouses that supply four stores with a given product. Each warehouse has 30 units of the product. Stores 1, 2, 3, and 4 require 20, 25, 30, and 35 units of the product, respectively. The per-unit shipping costs from each warehouse to each store are given in the following table:

| | Store | | | |
Warehouse	1	2	3	4
1	5	4	6	5
2	3	6	4	4
3	4	3	3	2

   a. Draw the network representation of this problem. What kind of problem is this?
   b. Formulate an LP model to determine the least expensive shipping plan to fill the demands at the stores.
   c. Solve the problem using Solver.
   d. Suppose that shipments are not allowed between warehouse 1 and store 2 or between warehouse 2 and store 3. What is the easiest way to modify the spreadsheet so that you can solve this modified problem? What is the optimal solution to the modified problem?

20. A used-car broker needs to transport his inventory of cars from locations 1 and 2 in Figure 5.39 to used-car auctions being held at locations 4 and 5. The costs of transporting cars along each of the routes are indicated on the arcs. The trucks used to carry the cars can hold a maximum of 10 cars. Therefore, the maximum number of cars that can flow over any arc is 10.
   a. Formulate an LP model to determine the least costly method of distributing the cars from locations 1 and 2 so that 20 cars will be available for sale at location 4, and 10 cars will be available for sale at location 5.
   b. Use Solver to find the optimal solution to this problem.

FIGURE 5.39

Network flow model for the used car problem

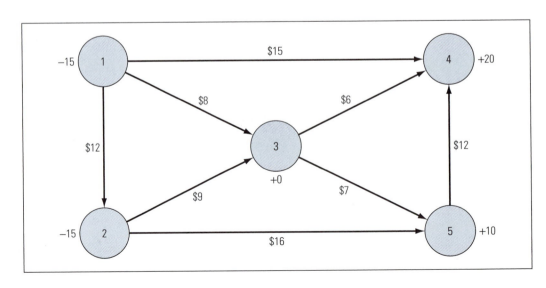

21. An information systems consultant who lives in Dallas must spend the majority of the month of March onsite with a client in San Diego. Her travel schedule for the month is as follows:

Leave Dallas	Leave San Diego
Monday, March 2	Friday, March 6
Monday, March 9	Thursday, March 12
Tuesday, March 17	Friday, March 20
Monday, March 23	Wednesday, March 25

The usual round-trip ticket price between Dallas and San Diego is $750. However, the airline offers a 25% discount if the dates on a round-trip ticket cover less than 7 nights and include a weekend. A 35% discount is offered for round-trip tickets covering 10 or more nights, and a 45% discount is available for round-trip tickets covering 20 or more nights. The consultant can purchase 4 round-trip tickets in any manner that allows her to leave Dallas and San Diego on the days indicated.
   a. Draw a network flow model for this problem.
   b. Implement the problem in a spreadsheet and solve it.
   c. What is the optimal solution? How much does this save for 4 full-cost, round-trip tickets?

22. The Conch Oil Company needs to transport 30 million barrels of crude oil from a port in Doha, Qatar in the Persian Gulf to three refineries throughout Europe. The refineries are in Rotterdam, Netherlands; Toulon, France; and Palermo, Italy, and they require 6 million, 15 million, and 9 million barrels, respectively. The oil can be transported to the refineries in three different ways. First, oil may be shipped from Qatar to Rotterdam, Toulon, and Palermo on supertankers traveling around Africa at costs of $1.20, $1.40, and $1.35 per barrel, respectively. Conch is contractually obligated to send at least 25% of its oil via these supertankers. Alternatively, oil can be shipped from Doha to Suez, Egypt at a cost of $0.35 per barrel, then through the Suez Canal to Port Said at a cost of $0.20 per barrel, then from Port Said to Rotterdam, Toulon, and Palermo at per-barrel costs of $0.27, $0.23, and $0.19, respectively. Finally, up to 15 million barrels of the oil shipped from Doha to Suez can then be sent via pipeline to Damietta, Egypt at $0.16 per barrel. From Damietta, it can be shipped to Rotterdam, Toulon, and Palermo at costs of $0.25, $0.20, and $0.15, respectively.
   a. Draw a network flow model for this problem.
   b. Implement your model in a spreadsheet and solve it.
   c. What is the optimal solution?

23. Omega Airlines has several nonstop flights between Atlanta and Los Angeles every day. The schedules of these flights are shown in the following table.

Flight	Departs Atlanta	Arrives in L.A.	Flight	Departs L.A.	Arrive in Atlanta
1	6 am	8 am	1	5 am	9 am
2	8 am	10 am	2	6 am	10 am
3	10 am	Noon	3	9 am	1 pm
4	Noon	2 pm	4	Noon	4 pm
5	4 pm	6 pm	5	2 pm	6 pm
6	6 pm	8 pm	6	5 pm	9 pm
7	7 pm	9 pm	7	7 pm	11 pm

Omega wants to determine the optimal way of assigning flight crews to these different flights. The company wants to ensure that the crews always return to the city from which they left each day. FAA regulations require at least one hour of rest for flight crews between flights. However, flight crews become irritated if they are forced to wait for extremely long periods of time between flights, so Omega wants to find an assignment of flight schedules that minimizes these waiting periods.

   a. Draw a network flow model for this problem.

   b. Implement the problem in a spreadsheet and solve it.

   c. What is the optimal solution? What is the longest period of time a flight crew has to wait between flights according to your solution?

   d. Are there alternate optimal solutions to this problem? If so, do any alternate optimal solutions result in a smaller maximum waiting period between flights?

24. A residential moving company needs to move a family from city 1 to city 12 in Figure 5.40 where the numbers on the arcs represent the driving distance in miles between cities.

   a. Create a spreadsheet model for this problem.

   b. What is the optimal solution?

   c. Suppose the moving company gets paid by the mile and, as a result, wants to determine the longest path from city 1 to city 12. What is the optimal solution?

   d. Now suppose travel is permissible in either direction between cities 6 and 9. Describe the optimal solution to this problem.

25. Joe Jones wants to establish a construction fund (or sinking fund) to pay for a new bowling alley he is having built. Construction of the bowling alley is expected to take six months and cost $300,000. Joe's contract with the construction company requires

FIGURE 5.40

Network flow model for the moving company problem

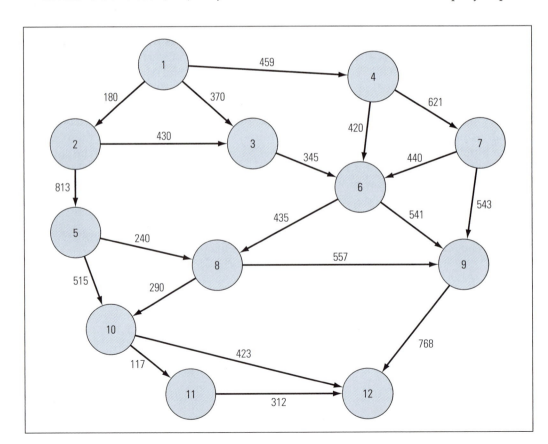

him to make payments of $50,000 at the end of the second and fourth months, and a final payment of $200,000 at the end of the sixth month when the bowling alley is completed. Joe has identified four investments that he can use to establish the construction fund; these investments are summarized in the following table:

Investment	Available in Month	Months to Maturity	Yield at Maturity
A	1, 2, 3, 4, 5, 6	1	1.2%
B	1, 3, 5	2	3.5%
C	1, 4	3	5.8%
D	1	6	11.0%

The table indicates that investment A will be available at the beginning of each of the next six months, and funds invested in this manner mature in one month with a yield of 1.2%. Similarly, funds can be placed in investment C only at the beginning of months 1 and/or 4, and they mature at the end of three months with a yield of 5.8%. Joe wants to minimize the amount of money he must invest in month 1 to meet the required payments for this project.
a. Draw a network flow model for this problem.
b. Create a spreadsheet model for this problem and solve it.
c. What is the optimal solution?
26. Telephone calls for the YakLine, a discount long distance carrier, are routed through a variety of switching devices that interconnect various network hubs in different cities. The maximum number of calls that can be handled by each segment of their network is shown in the following table:

Network Segments	Calls (in 1,000s)
Washington, DC to Chicago	800
Washington, DC to Kansas City	650
Washington, DC to Dallas	700
Chicago to Dallas	725
Chicago to Denver	700
Kansas City to Denver	750
Kansas City to Dallas	625
Denver to San Francisco	900
Dallas to San Francisco	725

YakLine wants to determine the maximum number of calls that can go from its East Coast operations hub in Washington, DC to its West Coast operations hub in San Francisco.
a. Draw a network flow model for this problem.
b. Create a spreadsheet model for this problem and solve it.
c. What is the optimal solution?
27. Union Express has 60 tons of cargo that need to be shipped from Boston to Dallas. The shipping capacity on each of the routes Union Express planes fly each night is shown in the following table:

Nightly Flight Segments	Capacity (in tons)
Boston to Baltimore	30
Boston to Pittsburgh	25
Boston to Cincinnati	35
Baltimore to Atlanta	10
Baltimore to Cincinnati	5

Pittsburgh to Atlanta	15
Pittsburgh to Chicago	20
Cincinnati to Chicago	15
Cincinnati to Memphis	5
Atlanta to Memphis	25
Atlanta to Dallas	10
Chicago to Memphis	20
Chicago to Dallas	15
Memphis to Dallas	30
Memphis to Chicago	15

Will Union Express be able to move all 60 tons from Boston to Dallas in one night?

a. Draw a network flow model for this problem.

b. Create a spreadsheet model for the problem and solve it.

c. What is the maximum flow for this network?

28. E-mail messages sent over the Internet are broken up into electronic packets that may take a variety of different paths to reach their destination where the original message is reassembled. Suppose the nodes in the graph shown in Figure 5.41 represents a series of computer hubs on the Internet, and the arcs represent connections between them. Suppose the values on the arcs represent the number of packets per minute (in 1,000,000s) that can be transmitted over each arc.

a. Implement a network flow model to determine the maximum number of packets that can flow from node 1 to node 12 in one minute.

b. What is the maximum flow?

FIGURE 5.41

Network hubs and interconnections for the e-mail problem

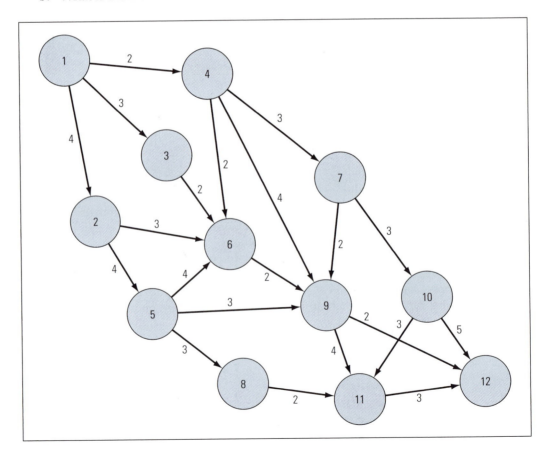

29. The Britts & Straggon company manufactures small engines at three different plants. From the plants, the engines are transported to two different warehouse facilities before being distributed to three wholesale distributors. The per-unit manufacturing cost at each plant is shown in the following table in addition to the minimum required and maximum available daily production capacities.

Plant	Manufacturing Cost	Minimum Required Production	Maximum Production Capacity
1	$13	150	400
2	$15	150	300
3	$12	150	600

The unit cost of transporting engines from each plant to each warehouse is shown in the following table:

Plant	Warehouse 1	Warehouse 2
1	$4	$5
2	$6	$4
3	$3	$5

The unit cost of shipping engines from each warehouse to each distributor is shown in the following table along with the daily demand for each distributor.

Warehouse	Distributor 1	Distributor 2	Distributor 3
1	$6	$4	$3
2	$3	$5	$2
Demand	300	600	100

Each warehouse can process up to 500 engines per day.
a. Draw a network flow model to represent this problem.
b. Implement your model in Excel and solve it.
c. What is the optimal solution?

30. A new airport being built will have three terminals and two baggage pickup areas. An automated baggage delivery system has been designed to transport the baggage from each terminal to the two baggage pickup areas. This system is depicted graphically in Figure 5.42, where nodes 1, 2, and 3 represent the terminals, and nodes 7 and 8 represent the baggage pickup areas. The maximum number of bags per minute that can be handled by each part of the system is indicated by the value on each arc in the network.
a. Formulate an LP model to determine the maximum number of bags per minute that can be delivered by this system.
b. Use Solver to find the optimal solution to this problem.

31. Bull Dog Express runs a small airline that offers commuter flights between several cities in Georgia. The airline flies into and out of small airports only. These airports have limits on the number of flights Bull Dog Express can make each day. The airline can make five round-trip flights daily between Savannah and Macon, four round-trip flights daily between Macon and Albany, two round-trip flights daily between Macon and Atlanta, two round-trip flights daily between Macon and Athens, two round-trip flights daily between Athens and Atlanta, and two round-trip flights daily from Albany to Atlanta. The airline wants to determine the maximum number of times connecting flights from Savannah to Atlanta can be offered in a single day.
a. Draw the network representation of this problem.
b. Formulate an LP model for this problem. What kind of problem is this?
c. Use Solver to determine the optimal solution to this problem.

FIGURE 5.42

Network flow model for the airport terminal problem

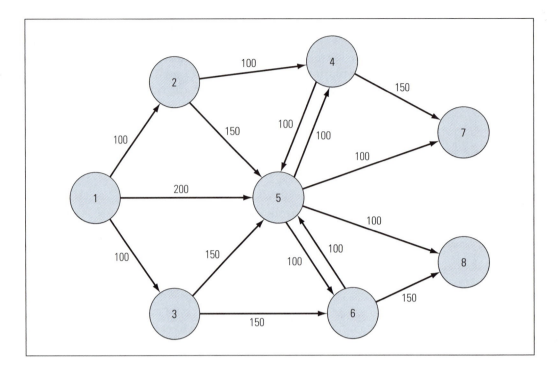

32. The U.S. Department of Transportation (DOT) is planning to build a new interstate to run from Detroit, Michigan, to Charleston, South Carolina. A number of different routes have been proposed and are summarized in Figure 5.43, where node 1 represents Detroit, and node 12 represents Charleston. The numbers on the arcs indicate the estimated construction costs of the various links (in millions of dollars). It is estimated that all of the routes will require approximately the same total driving time to make the trip from Detroit to Charleston. Thus, the DOT is interested in identifying the least costly alternative.
    a. Formulate an LP model to determine the least costly construction plan.
    b. Use Solver to determine the optimal solution to this problem.
33. A building contractor is designing the ductwork for the heating and air conditioning system in a new, single-story medical building. Figure 5.44 summarizes the possible connections between the primary air handling unit (node 1) and the various air outlets to be placed in the building (nodes 2 through 9). The arcs in the network represent possible ductwork connections, and the values on the arcs represent the feet of ductwork required.
    Starting at node 1, use the minimal spanning tree algorithm to determine how much ductwork should be installed to provide air access to each vent while requiring the least amount of ductwork.
34. The manager of catering services for the Roanoker Hotel has a problem. The banquet hall at the hotel is booked each evening during the coming week for groups who have reserved the following numbers of tables:

Day	Monday	Tuesday	Wednesday	Thursday	Friday
Tables Reserved	400	300	250	400	350

The hotel has 500 tablecloths that can be used for these banquets. However, the tablecloths used at each banquet will have to be cleaned before they can be used

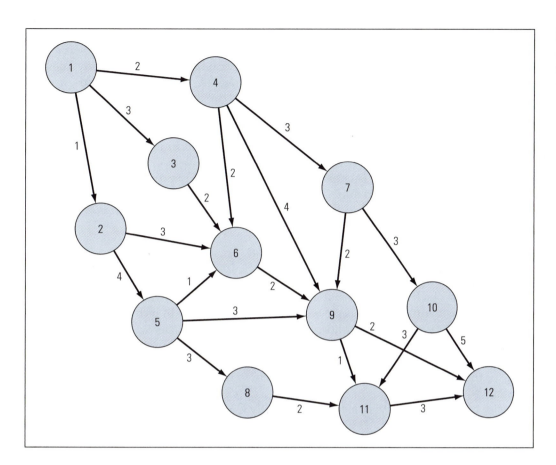

FIGURE 5.43

Possible routes for the interstate construction problem

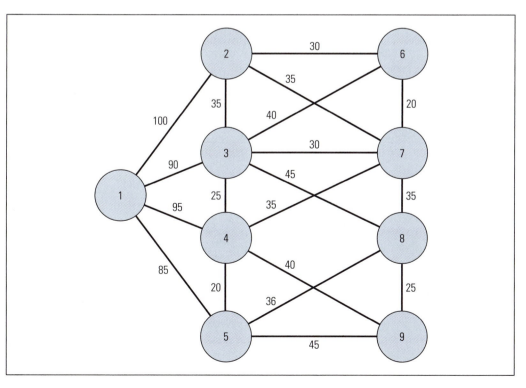

FIGURE 5.44

Network representation of the ductwork problem

again. A local cleaning service will pick up the soiled tablecloths each evening after the banquet and offers overnight cleaning for $2 per tablecloth, or 2-day service for $1 per tablecloth (that is, a tablecloth picked up Monday night can be ready Tuesday for $2 or ready for use Wednesday for $1). There are no tablecloth losses, and all tablecloths must be cleaned. Due to the cleaner's capacity restrictions, the overnight service can be performed only on up to 250 tablecloths, and overnight service is not available on tablecloths picked up Friday night. All cloths used on Friday must be ready for use again by Monday. The hotel wants to determine the least costly plan for having its tablecloths cleaned.

a. Draw a network flow model for this problem. (*Hint*: Express the supplies and de-mands as minimum required and maximum allowable flows over selected arcs.)
b. Create a spreadsheet model for this problem and solve it. What is the optimal solution?

CASE 5.1   Hamilton & Jacobs

Hamilton & Jacobs (H&J) is a global investment company, providing start-up capital to promising new ventures around the world. Due to the nature of its business, H&J holds funds in a variety of countries and converts between currencies as needs arise in different parts of the world. Several months ago, the company moved $16 million into Japanese yen (JPY) when one U.S. dollar (USD) was worth 75 yen. Since that time, the value of the dollar has fallen sharply, where it now requires almost 110 yen to purchase 1 dollar.

Besides its holdings of yen, H&J also currently owns 6 million European euros and 30 million Swiss francs (CHF). H&J's chief economic forecaster is predicting that all of the currencies it is presently holding will continue to gain strength against the dollar for the rest of the year. As a result, the company would like to convert all its surplus currency holdings back to U.S. dollars until the economic picture improves.

The bank H&J uses for currency conversions charges different transaction fees for converting between various currencies. The following table summarizes the transaction fess (expressed as a percentage of the amount converted) for U.S. dollars (USD), Aus-tralian dollars (AUD), British pounds (GBP), European euros (EURO), Indian rupees (INR), Japanese yen (JPY), Singapore dollars (SGD), and Swiss francs (CHF).

Transaction Fee Table

From/To	USD	AUD	GBP	EUR	INR	JPY	SGD	CHF
USD	—	0.10%	0.50%	0.40%	0.40%	0.40%	0.25%	0.50%
AUD	0.10%	—	0.70%	0.50%	0.30%	0.30%	0.75%	0.75%
GBP	0.50%	0.70%	—	0.70%	0.70%	0.40%	0.45%	0.50%
EUR	0.40%	0.50%	0.70%	—	0.05%	0.10%	0.10%	0.10%
INR	0.40%	0.30%	0.70%	0.05%	—	0.20%	0.10%	0.10%
JPY	0.40%	0.30%	0.40%	0.10%	0.20%	—	0.05%	0.50%
SGD	0.25%	0.75%	0.45%	0.10%	0.10%	0.05%	—	0.50%
CHF	0.50%	0.75%	0.50%	0.10%	0.10%	0.50%	0.50%	—

Because it costs differing amounts to convert between various currencies, H&J determined that converting existing holdings directly into U.S. dollars may not be the best strategy. Instead, it might be less expensive to convert existing holdings to an intermediate currency before converting the result back to U.S. dollars. The follow-ing table summarizes the current exchange rates for converting from one currency to another.

Exchange Rate Table

From/To	USD	AUD	GBP	EUR	INR	JPY	SGD	CHF
USD	1	1.29249	0.55337	0.80425	43.5000	109.920	1.64790	1.24870
AUD	0.77370	1	0.42815	0.62225	33.6560	85.0451	1.27498	0.96612
GBP	1.80710	2.33566	1	1.45335	78.6088	198.636	2.97792	2.25652
EUR	1.24340	1.60708	0.68806	1	54.0879	136.675	2.04900	1.55263
INR	0.02299	0.02971	0.01272	0.01849	1	2.5269	0.03788	0.02871
JPY	0.00910	0.01176	0.00503	0.00732	0.39574	1	0.01499	0.01136
SGD	0.60683	0.78433	0.33581	0.48804	26.3972	66.7031	1	0.75775
CHF	0.80083	1.03507	0.44316	0.64407	34.8362	88.0275	1.31969	1

The exchange rate table indicates, for instance, that one Japanese yen can be converted into 0.00910 U.S. dollars. So 100,000 yen would produce $910 USD. However, the bank's 0.40% fee for this transaction would reduce the net amount received to $910 × (1 − 0.004) = $906.36. So H&J wants your assistance in determining the best way to convert all of its non-U.S. currency holdings back into U.S. dollars.

1. Draw a network flow diagram for this problem.
2. Create a spreadsheet model for this problem and solve it.
3. What is the optimal solution?
4. If H&J converted each non-U.S. currency it owns directly into U.S. dollars, how many U.S. dollars would it have?
5. Suppose H&J wants to perform the same conversion but also leave $5 million in Australian dollars. What is the optimal solution in this case?

Old Dominion Energy

CASE 5.2

The United States is the biggest consumer of natural gas and the second largest natural gas producer in the world. According to the U.S. Energy Information Administration (EIA), the United States consumed 22.7 trillion cubic feet of natural gas in 2001. Stemming from phased deregulation, the transportation and delivery of natural gas from wellheads has grown since the 1980s, and there are now more than 278,000 miles of gas pipeline nationwide. With more electric power companies turning to natural gas as a cleaner-burning fuel, natural gas is expected to grow even more quickly over the next 20 years.

To ensure an adequate supply of natural gas, gas storage facilities have been built in numerous places along the pipeline. Energy companies can buy gas when prices are low and store it in these facilities for use or sale at a later date. Because energy consumption is influenced greatly by the weather (which is not entirely predictable), imbalances often arise in the supply and demand for gas in different parts of the country. Gas traders constantly monitor these market conditions and look for opportunities to sell gas from storage facilities when the price offered at a certain location is high enough. This decision is complicated by the fact that it costs different amounts of money to transport gas through different segments of the nationwide pipeline, and the capacity available in different parts of the pipeline is constantly changing. Thus, when a trader sees an opportunity to sell at a favorable price, he or she must quickly see how much capacity is available in the network and create deals with individual pipeline operators for the necessary capacity to move gas from storage to the buyer.

Bruce McDaniel is a gas trader for Old Dominion Energy (ODE), Inc. The network in Figure 5.45 represents a portion of the gas pipeline where ODE does business. The values next to each arc in this network are of the form (x,y) where x is the cost per thousand

FIGURE 5.45

Gas pipeline network for Old Dominion Energy

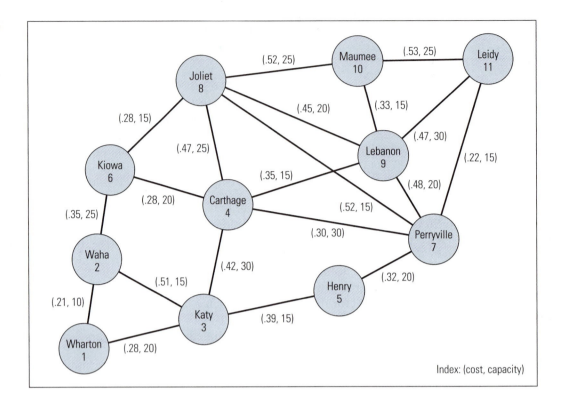

Index: (cost, capacity)

cubic feet (cf) of transporting gas along the arc, and y is the available transmission capacity of the arc in thousands of cubic feet. Note that the arcs in this network are bidirectional (that is, gas can flow in either direction at the prices and capacities listed).

Bruce currently has 100,000 cf of gas in storage at Katy. Industrial customers in Joliet are offering $4.35 per thousand cf for up to 35,000 cf of gas. Buyers in Leidy are offering $4.63 per thousand cf for up to 60,000 cf of gas. Create a spreadsheet model to help Bruce answer the following questions.

1. Given the available capacity in the network, how much gas can be shipped from Katy to Leidy? From Katy to Joliet?
2. How much gas should Bruce offer to sell to Joliet and Leidy if he wants to maximize profits?
3. Is Bruce able to meet all the demand from both customers? If not, why not?
4. If Bruce wanted to try to pay more to obtain additional capacity on some of the pipelines, which ones should he investigate and why?

CASE 5.3   U.S. Express

U.S. Express is an overnight package delivery company based in Atlanta, Georgia. Jet fuel is one of the largest operating costs incurred by the company, and the company wants your assistance in managing this cost. The price of jet fuel varies considerably at different airports around the country. As a result, it seems that it might be wise to "fill up" on jet fuel at airports where it is least expensive. However, the amount of fuel an airliner burns depends, in part, on the weight of the plane—and excess fuel makes an airplane heavier and, therefore, less fuel-efficient. Similarly, more fuel is burned on flights from the East Coast to the West Coast (going against the jet stream) than from the West Coast to the East Coast (going with the jet stream).

The following table summarizes the flight schedule (or rotation) flown nightly by one of the company's planes. For each flight segment, the table summarizes the minimum required and maximum allowable amount of fuel on board at takeoff and the cost of fuel at each point of departure. The final column provides a linear function relating fuel consumption to the amount of fuel on board at takeoff.

Segment	Depart	Arrive	Minimum Fuel Level at Takeoff (in 1000s)	Maximum Fuel Level at Takeoff (in 1000s)	Cost per Gallon	Fuel Used in Flight with G Gallons (in 1000s) on Board at Takeoff
1	Atlanta	San Francisco	21	31	$0.92	$3.20 + 0.45 \times G$
2	San Francisco	Los Angeles	7	20	$0.85	$2.25 + 0.65 \times G$
3	Los Angeles	Chicago	18	31	$0.87	$1.80 + 0.35 \times G$
4	Chicago	Atlanta	16	31	$1.02	$2.20 + 0.60 \times G$

For instance, if the plane leaves Atlanta for San Francisco with 25,000 gallons on board, it should arrive in San Francisco with approximately $25 - (3.2 + 0.45 \times 25) = 10.55$ thousand gallons of fuel.

The company has many other planes that fly different schedules each night, so the potential cost savings from efficient fuel purchasing is quite significant. But before turning you loose on all of their flight schedules, the company wants you to create a spreadsheet model to determine the most economical fuel purchasing plan for the previous schedule. (*Hint*: Keep in mind that the most fuel you would purchase at any departure point is the maximum allowable fuel level for takeoff at that point. Also, assume that whatever fuel is on board when the plane returns to Atlanta at the end of the rotation will still be on board when the plane leaves Atlanta the next evening.)

1. Draw the network diagram for this problem.
2. Implement the model for this problem in your spreadsheet and solve it.
3. How much fuel should U.S. Express purchase at each departure point, and what is the cost of this purchasing plan?

The Major Electric Corporation

CASE 5.4

Henry Lee is the Vice President of Purchasing for the consumer electronics division of the Major Electric Corporation (MEC). The company recently introduced a new type of video camcorder that has taken the market by storm. Although Henry is pleased with the strong demand for this product in the marketplace, it has been a challenge to keep up with MEC's distributors' orders of this camcorder. His current challenge is how to meet requests from MEC's major distributors in Pittsburgh, Denver, Baltimore, and Houston who have placed orders of 10,000, 20,000, 30,000, and 25,000 units, respectively, for delivery in two months (there is a one-month manufacturing and one-month shipping lead time for this product).

MEC has contracts with companies in Hong Kong, Korea, and Singapore who manufacture camcorders for the company under the MEC label. These contracts require MEC to order a specified minimum number of units each month at a guaranteed per unit cost. The contracts also specify the maximum number of units that may be ordered at this price. The following table summarizes these contracts:

	Monthly Purchasing Contract Provisions		
Supplier	Unit Cost	Minimum Required	Maximum Allowed
Hong Kong	$375	20,000	30,000
Korea	$390	25,000	40,000
Singapore	$365	15,000	30,000

MEC also has a standing contract with a shipping company to transport product from each of these suppliers to ports in San Francisco and San Diego. The cost of shipping from each supplier to each port is given in the following table along with the minimum required and maximum allowable number of shipping cartons each month:

	Monthly Shipping Contract Provisions					
	San Francisco Requirements			San Diego Shipping Requirements		
Supplier	Cost per Container	Minimum Containers	Maximum Containers	Cost per Container	Minimum Containers	Maximum Containers
Hong Kong	$2,000	5	20	$2,300	5	20
Korea	$1,800	10	30	$2,100	10	30
Singapore	$2,400	5	25	$2,200	5	15

Under the terms of this contract, MEC guarantees it will send at least 20 but no more than 65 shipping containers to San Francisco each month, and at least 30 but no more than 70 shipping containers to San Diego each month.

Each shipping container can hold 1,000 video cameras and will ultimately be trucked from the seaports on to the distributors. Again, MEC has a standing contract with a trucking company to provide trucking services each month. The cost of trucking a shipping container from each port to each distributor is summarized in the following table:

	Unit Shipping Cost per Container			
	Pittsburgh	Denver	Baltimore	Houston
San Francisco	$1,100	$850	$1,200	$1,000
San Diego	$1,200	$1,000	$1,100	$900

As with the other contracts, to obtain the prices just given, MEC is required to use a certain minimum amount of trucking capacity on each route each month and may not exceed certain maximum shipping amounts without incurring cost penalties. These minimum and maximum shipping restrictions are summarized in the following table:

	Minimum Required and Maximum Allowable Number of Shipping Containers per Month							
	Pittsburgh		Denver		Baltimore		Houston	
	Min	Max	Min	Max	Min	Max	Min	Max
San Francisco	3	7	6	12	10	18	5	15
San Diego	4	6	5	14	5	20	10	20

Henry is left with the task of sorting through all this information to determine the least purchasing and distribution plan to fill the distributor's requests. But because he and his wife have tickets to the symphony for this evening, he has asked you to take a look at this problem and give him your recommendations at 9:00 tomorrow morning.

1. Create a network flow model for this problem. (*Hint*: Consider inserting intermediate nodes in your network to assist in meeting the minimum monthly purchase restrictions for each supplier and the minimum monthly shipping requirements for each port.)
2. Implement a spreadsheet model for this problem and solve it.
3. What is the optimal solution?

Chapter 6

Integer Linear Programming

6.0 Introduction

When some or all of the decision variables in an LP problem are restricted to assuming only integer values, the resulting problem is referred to as an **integer linear programming** (ILP) problem. Many practical business problems need integer solutions. For example, when scheduling workers, a company needs to determine the optimal number of employees to assign to each shift. If we formulate this problem as an LP problem, its optimal solution could involve allocating fractional numbers of workers (for example, 7.33 workers) to different shifts, but this is not an integer feasible solution. Similarly, if an airline is trying to decide how many 767s, 757s, and A-300s to purchase for its fleet, it must obtain an integer solution because the airline cannot buy fractions of planes.

This chapter discusses how to solve optimization problems in which certain decision variables must assume only integer values. This chapter also shows how the use of integer variables allows us to build more accurate models for a number of business problems.

6.1 Integrality Conditions

To illustrate some of the issues involved in an ILP problem, let's consider again the decision problem faced by Howie Jones, the owner of Blue Ridge Hot Tubs, described in Chapters 2, 3, and 4. This company sells two models of hot tubs, the Aqua-Spa and the Hydro-Lux, which it produces by purchasing prefabricated fiberglass hot tub shells and installing a common water pump and an appropriate amount of tubing. Each Aqua-Spa produced requires 1 pump, 9 hours of labor, and 12 feet of tubing, and contributes $350 to profits. Each Hydro-Lux produced requires 1 pump, 6 hours of labor, and 16 feet of tubing, and contributes $300 to profits. Assuming the company has 200 pumps, 1,566 labor hours, and 2,880 feet of tubing available, we created the following LP formulation for this problem where X_1 and X_2 represent the number of Aqua-Spas and Hydro-Luxes to produce:

$$
\begin{array}{lll}
\text{MAX:} & 350X_1 + 300X_2 & \} \text{ profit} \\
\text{Subject to:} & 1X_1 + 1X_2 \leq 200 & \} \text{ pump constraint} \\
& 9X_1 + 6X_2 \leq 1{,}566 & \} \text{ labor constraint} \\
& 12X_1 + 16X_2 \leq 2{,}880 & \} \text{ tubing constraint} \\
& X_1, X_2 \geq 0 & \} \text{ nonnegativity conditions}
\end{array}
$$

Blue Ridge Hot Tubs is undoubtedly interested in obtaining the best possible *integer solution* to this problem because hot tubs can be sold only as discrete units. Thus, we can be sure the company wants to find the *optimal integer solution* to this problem. So, in addition to the constraints stated previously, we add the following integrality condition to the formulation of the problem:

$$X_1 \text{ and } X_2 \text{ must be integers}$$

An **integrality condition** indicates that some (or all) of the variables in the formulation must assume only **integer values**. We refer to such variables as the integer variables in a problem. In contrast, variables that are not required to assume strictly integer values are referred to as **continuous variables**. Although it is easy to state integrality conditions for a problem, such conditions often make a problem more difficult (and sometimes impossible) to solve.

6.2 Relaxation

One approach to finding the optimal integer solution to a problem is to relax, or ignore, the integrality conditions and solve the problem as if it were a standard LP problem where all the variables are assumed to be continuous. This model is sometimes referred to as the **LP relaxation** of the original ILP problem. Consider the following ILP problem:

$$
\begin{aligned}
\text{MAX:} \quad & 2X_1 + 3X_2 \\
\text{Subject to:} \quad & X_1 + 3X_2 \le 8.25 \\
& 2.5X_1 + X_2 \le 8.75 \\
& X_1, X_2 \ge 0 \\
& X_1, X_2 \text{ must be integers}
\end{aligned}
$$

The LP relaxation for this problem is represented by:

$$
\begin{aligned}
\text{MAX:} \quad & 2X_1 + 3X_2 \\
\text{Subject to:} \quad & X_1 + 3X_2 \le 8.25 \\
& 2.5X_1 + X_2 \le 8.75 \\
& X_1, X_2 \ge 0
\end{aligned}
$$

The only difference between the ILP and its LP relaxation is that all integrality conditions imposed by the ILP are dropped in the relaxation. However, as illustrated in Figure 6.1, this change has a significant impact on the feasible regions for the two problems.

As shown in Figure 6.1, the feasible region for the ILP consists of only 11 discrete points. On the other hand, the feasible region for its LP relaxation consists of an infinite number of points represented by the shaded area. This figure illustrates an important point about the relationship between the feasible region of an ILP and its LP relaxation. The feasible region of the LP relaxation of an ILP problem *always* encompasses *all* the feasible integer solutions to the original ILP problem. Although the relaxed feasible region might include additional noninteger solutions, it will *not* include any integer solutions that are not feasible solutions to the original ILP.

6.3 Solving the Relaxed Problem

The LP relaxation of an ILP problem is often easy to solve using the simplex method. As explained in Chapter 2, an optimal solution to an LP problem occurs at one of the corner points of its feasible region (assuming that the problem has a bounded optimal solution). Thus, if we are extremely lucky, the optimal solution to the LP relaxation of an ILP

FIGURE 6.1

Integer feasible region versus LP feasible region

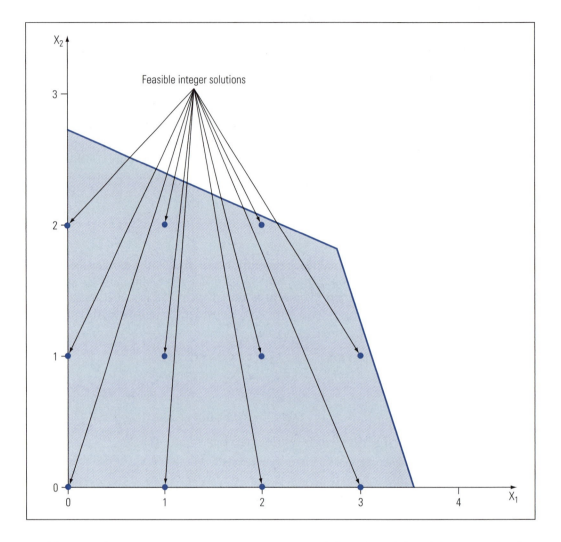

problem might occur at an integer corner point of the relaxed feasible region. In this case, we find the optimal integer solution to the ILP problem simply by solving its LP relaxation. This is exactly what happened in Chapters 2 and 3 when we originally solved the relaxed LP model for the hot tub problem. Figure 6.2 (and the file Fig6-2.xlsm that accompanies this book) shows the solution to this problem.

The optimal solution to the relaxed LP formulation of the hot tub problem assigns integer values to the decision variables ($X_1 = 122$ and $X_2 = 78$). So in this case, the relaxed LP problem happens to have an integer-valued optimal solution. However, as you might expect, this will not always be the case.

Suppose, for example, that Blue Ridge Hot Tubs has only 1,520 hours of labor and 2,650 feet of tubing available during its next production cycle. The company might be interested in solving the following ILP problem:

$$
\begin{aligned}
\text{MAX:} \quad & 350X_1 + 300X_2 && \text{\} profit} \\
\text{Subject to:} \quad & 1X_1 + 1X_2 \leq 200 && \text{\} pump constraint} \\
& 9X_1 + 6X_2 \leq 1{,}520 && \text{\} labor constraint} \\
& 12X_1 + 16X_2 \leq 2{,}650 && \text{\} tubing constraint} \\
& X_1, X_2 \geq 0 && \text{\} nonnegativity conditions} \\
& X_1, X_2 \text{ must be integers} && \text{\} integrality conditions}
\end{aligned}
$$

FIGURE 6.2 *Integer solution obtained as optimal solution to the Blue Ridge Hot Tubs LP problem*

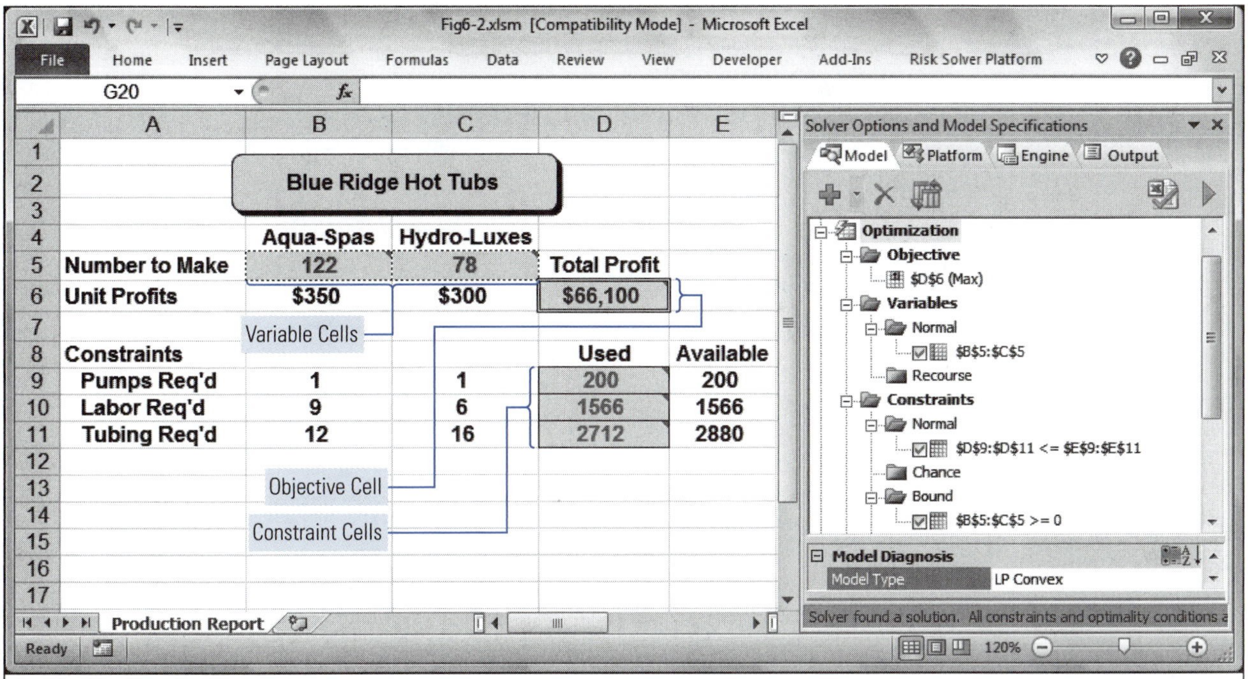

Key Cell Formulas		
Cell	Formula	Copied to
D6	=B6*$B$5+C6*$C$5	D9:D11

If we relax the integrality conditions and solve the resulting LP problem, we obtain the solution shown in Figure 6.3. This solution indicates that producing 116.9444 Aqua-Spas and 77.9167 Hydro-Luxes will generate a maximum profit of $64,306. But this solution violates the integrality conditions stated in the original problem. As a general rule, the optimal solution to the LP relaxation of an ILP problem is not guaranteed to produce an integer solution. In such cases, other techniques must be applied to find the optimal integer solution for the problem being solved. (There are some exceptions to this rule. In particular, the network flow problems discussed in Chapter 5 often can be viewed as ILP problems. For reasons that go beyond the scope of this text, the LP relaxation of network flow problems will always have integer solutions if the supplies and/or demands at each node are integers and the problem is solved using the simplex method.)

6.4 Bounds

Before discussing how to solve ILP problems, an important point must be made about the relationship between the optimal solution to an ILP problem and the optimal solution to its LP relaxation: The objective function value for the optimal solution to the ILP problem can *never* be better than the objective function value for the optimal solution to its LP relaxation. For example, the solution shown in Figure 6.3 indicates that if the company could produce (and sell) fractional numbers of hot tubs, it could make a maximum profit of $64,306

FIGURE 6.3 *Noninteger solution obtained as the optimal solution to the revised Blue Ridge Hot Tubs LP problem*

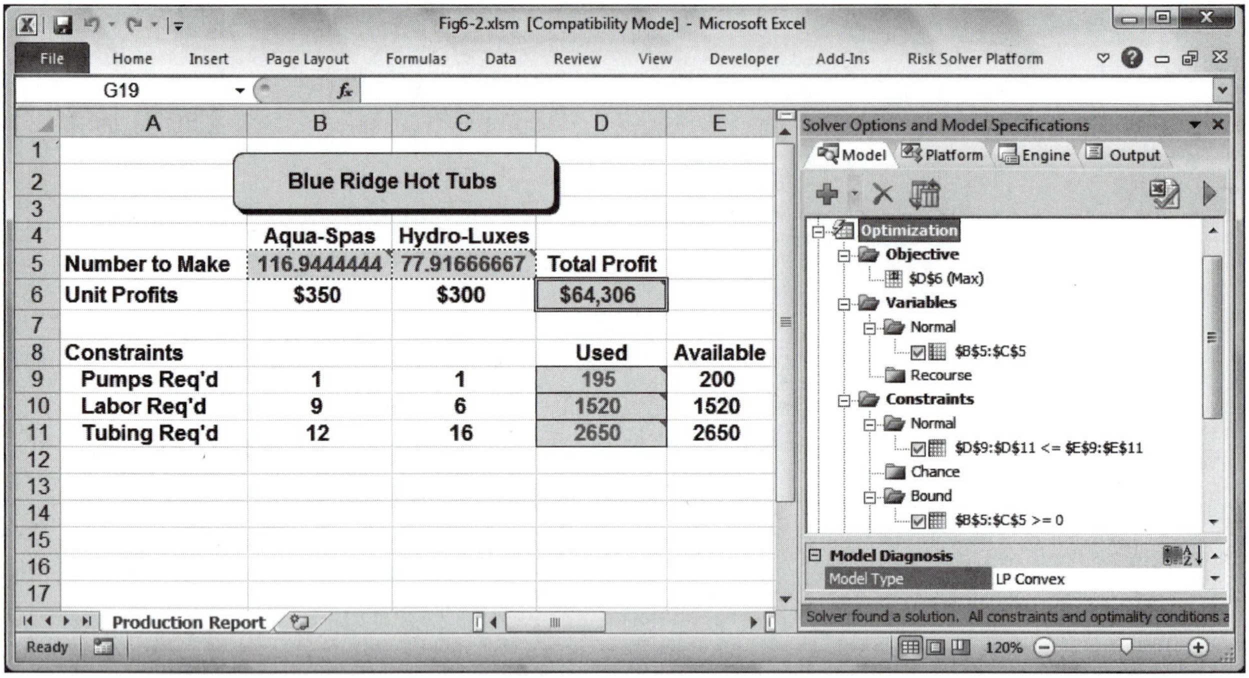

by producing 116.9444 Aqua-Spas and 77.9167 Hydro-Luxes. No other feasible solution (integer or otherwise) could result in a better value of the objective function. If a better feasible solution existed, the optimization procedure would have identified this better solution as optimal because our aim was to maximize the value of the objective function.

Although solving the LP relaxation of the revised hot tub problem might not provide the optimal integer solution to our original ILP problem, it does indicate that the objective function value of the optimal integer solution cannot possibly be greater than $64,306. This information can be important in helping us evaluate the quality of integer solutions we might discover during our search for the optimal solution.

Key Concept

For *maximization* problems, the objective function value at the optimal solution to the LP relaxation represents an *upper bound* on the optimal objective function value of the original ILP problem. For *minimization* problems, the objective function value at the optimal solution to the LP relaxation represents a *lower bound* on the optimal objective function value of the original ILP problem.

6.5 Rounding

As mentioned earlier, the solution to the LP relaxation of an ILP problem might satisfy the ILP problem's integrality conditions and, therefore, represent the optimal integer solution to the problem. But what should we do if this is not the case (as usually happens)? One frequently used technique involves rounding the relaxed LP solution.

When the solution to the LP relaxation of an ILP problem does not result in an integer solution, it is tempting to think that simply rounding this solution will generate the optimal integer solution. Unfortunately, this is not the case. For example, if the values for the decision variables shown in Figure 6.3 are manually rounded up to their closest integer values, as shown in Figure 6.4, the resulting solution is infeasible. The company cannot manufacture 117 Aqua-Spas and 78 Hydro-Luxes because this would involve using more labor and tubing than are available.

Because rounding up does not always work, perhaps we should round down, or truncate, the values for the decision variables identified in the LP relaxation. As shown in Figure 6.5, this results in a feasible solution where 116 Aqua-Spas and 77 Hydro-Luxes are manufactured for a total profit of $63,700. However, this approach presents two possible problems. First, rounding down could also result in an infeasible solution, as shown in Figure 6.6.

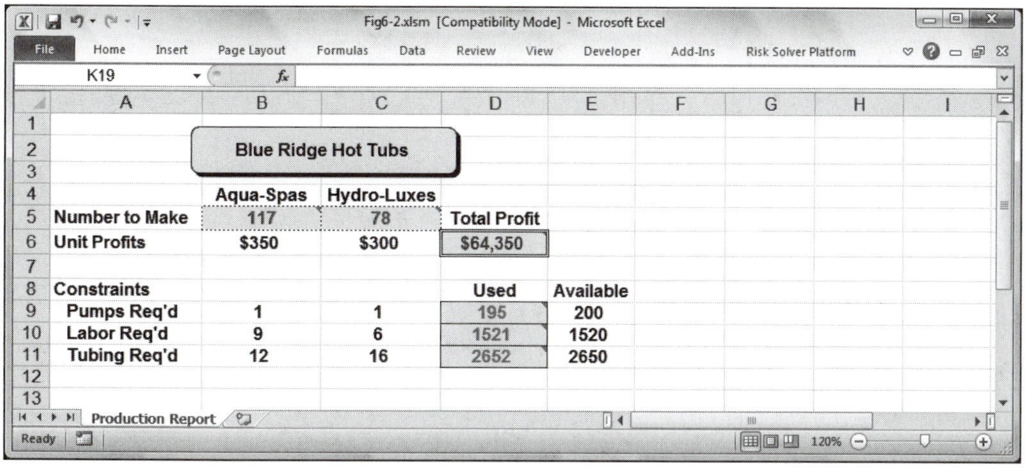

FIGURE 6.4

Infeasible integer solution obtained by rounding up

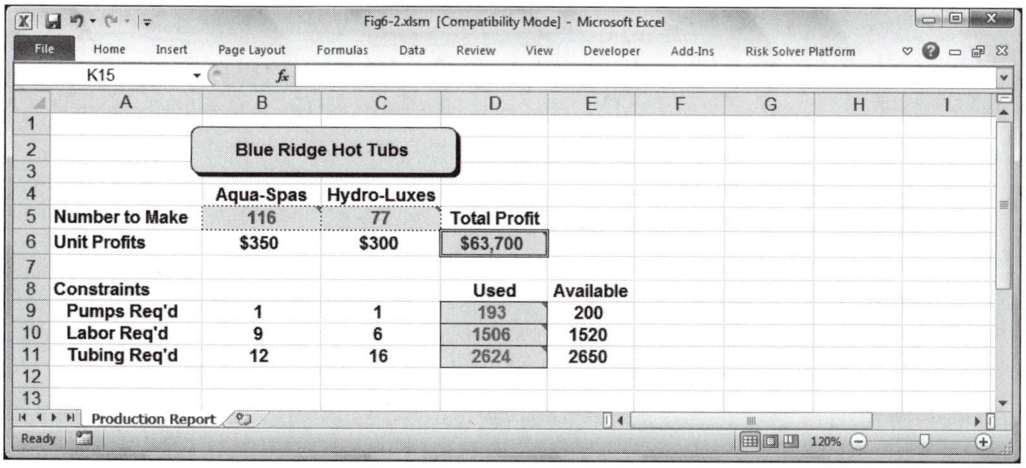

FIGURE 6.5

Feasible integer solution obtained by rounding down

Another problem with rounding down is that even if it results in a feasible integer solution to the problem, there is no guarantee that it is the *optimal* integer solution. For example, the integer solution obtained by rounding down shown in Figure 6.5 produced a total profit of $63,700. However, as shown in Figure 6.7, a better integer solution exists for this problem. If the company produces 118 Aqua-Spas and 76 Hydro-Luxes, it can achieve a

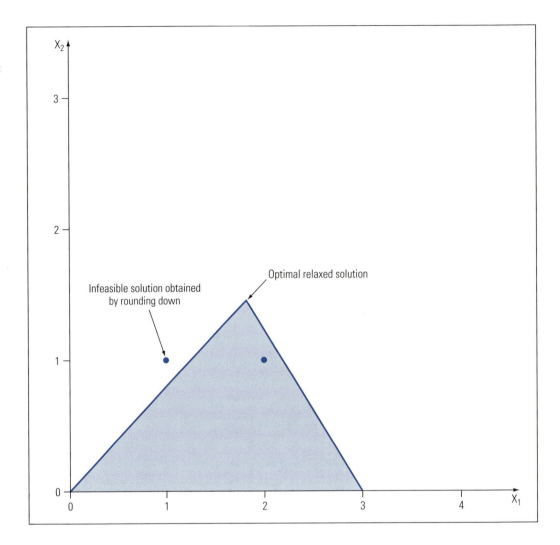

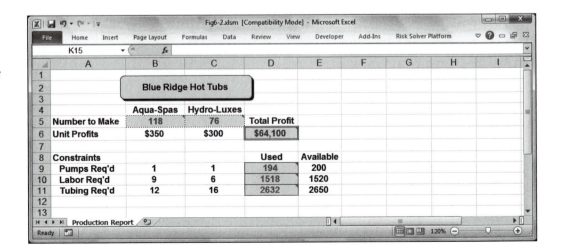

total profit of $64,100 (which is the optimal integer solution to this problem). Simply rounding the solution to the LP relaxation of an ILP problem is not guaranteed to provide the optimal integer solution. Although the integer solution obtained in this problem by rounding is very close to the optimal integer solution, rounding does not always work this well.

As we have seen, the solution to the LP relaxation of an ILP is not guaranteed to produce an integer solution, and rounding the solution to the LP relaxation is not guaranteed to produce the optimal integer solution. Therefore, we need another way to find the optimal integer solution to an ILP problem. Various procedures have been developed for this purpose. The most effective and widely used of these procedures is the **branch-and-bound (B&B) algorithm**. The B&B algorithm theoretically allows us to solve any ILP problem by solving a series of LP problems called candidate problems. For those who are interested, a discussion of how the B&B algorithm works is given at the end of this chapter.

6.6 Stopping Rules

Finding the optimal solution for simple ILP problems can sometimes require the evaluation of hundreds of candidate problems. More complex problems can require the evaluation of thousands of candidate problems, which can be a very time-consuming task even for the fastest computers. For this reason, many ILP packages allow you to specify a suboptimality tolerance of X% (where X is some numeric value), which tells the B&B algorithm to stop when it finds an integer solution that is no more than X% worse than the optimal integer solution. This is another area where obtaining upper or lower bounds on the optimal integer solution can be helpful.

As noted earlier, if we relax all the integrality conditions in an ILP with a maximization objective and solve the resulting LP problem, the objective function value at the optimal solution to the relaxed problem provides an upper bound on the optimal integer solution. For example, when we relaxed the integrality conditions for the revised Blue Ridge Hot Tubs problem and solved it as an LP, we obtained the solution shown earlier in Figure 6.3, which has an objective function value of $64,306. Thus, we know that the optimal integer solution to this problem cannot have an objective function value greater than $64,306. Now, suppose the owner of Blue Ridge Hot Tubs is willing to settle for any integer solution to its problem that is no more than 5% below the optimal integer solution. It is easy to determine that 95% of $64,306 is $61,090 ($0.95 \times \$64,306 = \$61,090$). Therefore, any integer solution with an objective function value of at least $61,090 can be no worse than 5% below the optimal integer solution.

Specifying suboptimality tolerances can be helpful if you are willing to settle for a good but suboptimal solution to a difficult ILP problem. However, most B&B packages employ some sort of default suboptimality tolerance and, therefore, might produce a suboptimal solution to the ILP problem without indicating that a better solution might exist. (We will look at an example where this occurs shortly.) It is important to be aware of suboptimality tolerances because they can determine whether or not the true optimal solution to an ILP problem is found.

6.7 Solving ILP Problems Using Solver

Now that you have some understanding of the effort required to solve ILP problems, you can appreciate how using Solver simplifies this process. This section shows how to use Solver with the revised Blue Ridge Hot Tubs problem.

Figure 6.8 shows the Solver settings required to solve the revised Blue Ridge Hot Tubs problem as a standard LP problem. However, none of these parameters indicate that the cells representing the decision variables (cells B5 and C5) must assume integer values. To communicate this to Solver, we need to add constraints to the problem as shown in Figure 6.9. In Figure 6.9, cells B5 through C5 are specified as the cell references for the additional constraints. Because we want these cells to assume only integer values, we

FIGURE 6.8 *Solver parameters for the relaxed Blue Ridge Hot Tubs problem*

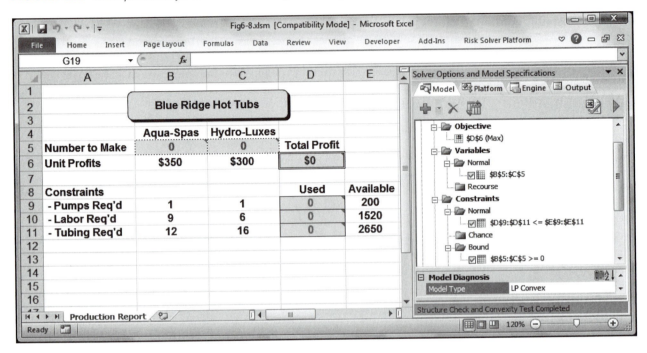

FIGURE 6.9 *Selecting integer constraints*

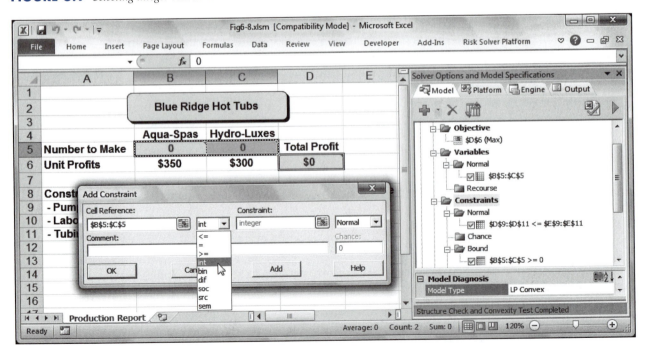

need to select the "int" option from the drop-down menu, as shown in Figure 6.9, and click OK.

Figure 6.10 shows the Solver setting and optimal solution with cells B5 and C5 constrained to assume only integer values. The message at the bottom of the Risk Solver Task Pane indicates that Solver found a solution "within tolerance" that satisfies all constraints. Thus, we might suspect that the optimal integer solution to this problem involves producing 117 Aqua-Spas and 77 Hydro-Luxes for a total profit of $64,050. However, if you refer back to Figure 6.7, you will recall that an even better integer solution to this problem can be obtained by producing 118 Aqua-Spas and 76 Hydro-Luxes for a total profit of $64,100. So why did Solver select an integer solution with a total profit of $64,050 when a better integer solution exists? The answer lies in Solver's suboptimality tolerance factor.

FIGURE 6.10 *Solver parameters and optimal solution to the revised Blue Ridge Hot Tubs problem with integer constraints*

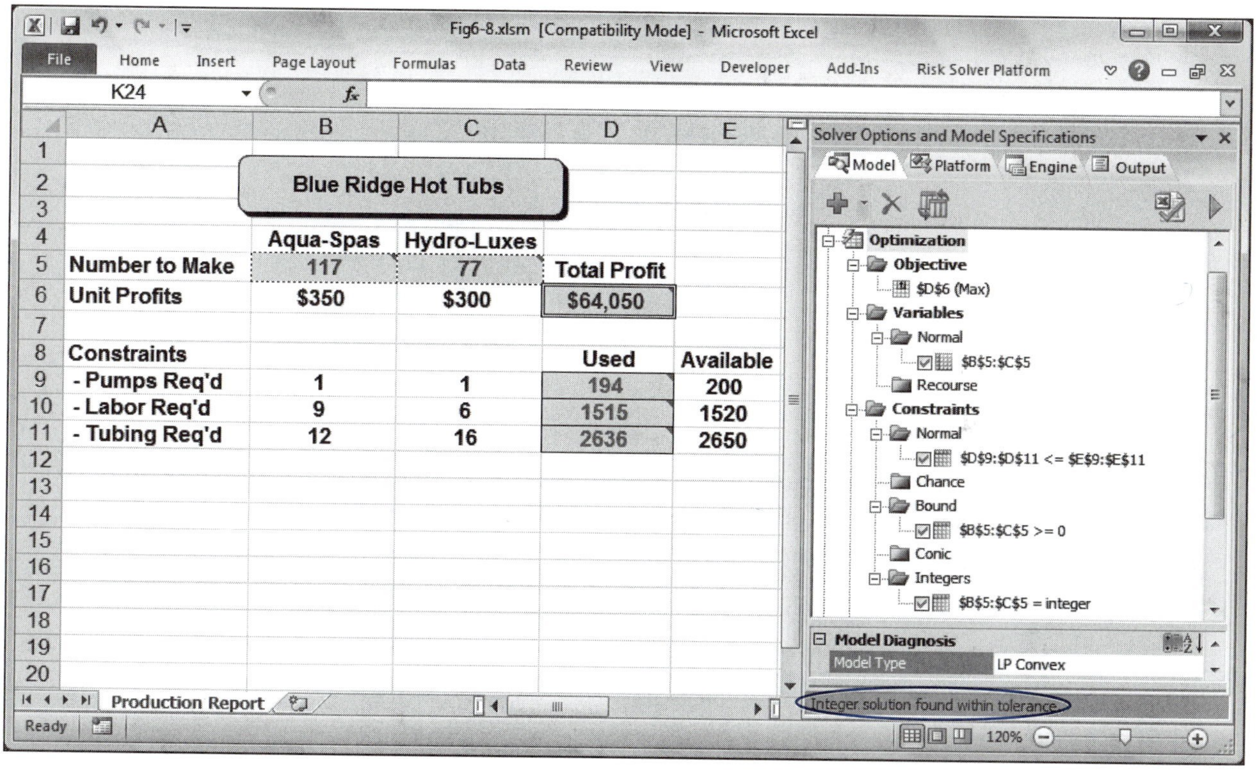

By default, Solver uses a suboptimality tolerance factor of 5%. So, when Solver found the integer solution with the objective function value of $64,050 shown in Figure 6.10, it determined that this solution was within 5% of the optimal integer solution and abandoned its search. (Again, note the message in Figure 6.10, "Integer solution found within tolerance.") To ensure that Solver finds the best possible solution to an ILP problem, we must change its suboptimality tolerance factor by clicking the Engine tab in the Risk Solver Task Pane and then changing the Integer Tolerance value as shown in Figure 6.11.

As shown in Figure 6.11, you can set a number of options to control Solver's operations. The Integer Tolerance option represents Solver's suboptimality tolerance value. To make sure Solver finds the best possible solution to an ILP problem, we must change this setting from its default value of 0.05 to 0. If we do this and re-solve the current problem, we obtain the solution shown in Figure 6.12. This solution is the best possible integer solution to the problem.

FIGURE 6.11

Changing the suboptimality tolerance factor

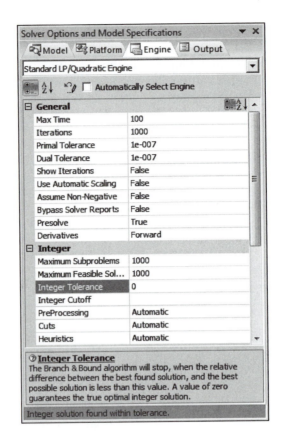

FIGURE 6.12 *Optimal integer solution to the revised Blue Ridge Hot Tubs problem*

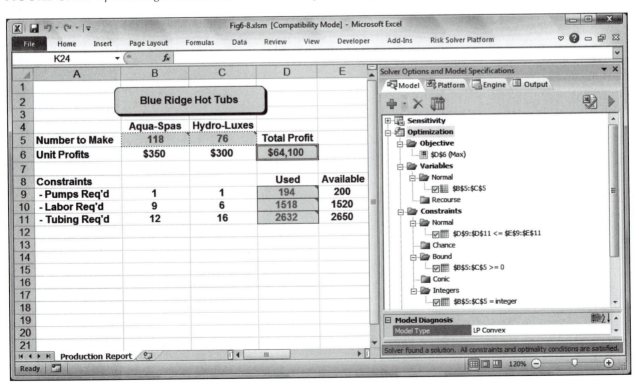

6.8 Other ILP Problems

Many decision problems encountered in business can be modeled as ILPs. As we have seen from the Blue Ridge Hot Tubs example, some problems that are initially formulated as LP problems might turn into ILP formulations if they require integer solutions. However, the importance of ILP extends beyond simply allowing us to obtain integer solutions to LP problems.

The ability to constrain certain variables to assume only integer values enables us to model a number of important conditions more accurately. For example, up to this point, we have not considered the impact of quantity discounts, setup or lump-sum costs, or batch size restrictions on a given decision problem. Without ILP techniques, we could not model these decision issues. We now consider several examples that illustrate the expanded modeling capabilities available through the use of integer variables.

6.9 An Employee Scheduling Problem

Anyone responsible for creating work schedules for a number of employees can appreciate the difficulties in this task. It can be very difficult to develop a feasible schedule, much less an optimal schedule. Trying to ensure that a sufficient number of workers is available when needed is a complicated task when you must consider multiple shifts, rest breaks, and lunch or dinner breaks. However, some sophisticated LP models have been devised to solve these problems. Although a discussion of these models is beyond the scope of this text, we will consider a simple example of an employee-scheduling problem to give you an idea of how LP models are applied in this area.

Air-Express is an express shipping service that guarantees overnight delivery of packages anywhere in the continental United States. The company has various operations centers, called hubs, at airports in major cities across the country. Packages are received at hubs from other locations and then shipped to intermediate hubs or to their final destinations.

The manager of the Air-Express hub in Baltimore, Maryland, is concerned about labor costs at the hub and is interested in determining the most effective way to schedule workers. The hub operates seven days a week, and the number of packages it handles each day varies from one day to the next. Using historical data on the average number of packages received each day, the manager estimates the number of workers needed to handle the packages as shown in the following table:

Day of Week	Workers Required
Sunday	18
Monday	27
Tuesday	22
Wednesday	26
Thursday	25
Friday	21
Saturday	19

The package handlers working for Air-Express are unionized and are guaranteed a five-day work week with two consecutive days off. The base wage for the handlers is $655 per week. Because most workers prefer to have Saturday or Sunday off, the union has negotiated bonuses of $25 per day for its members who work on these days. The possible shifts and salaries for package handlers are given in the following table:

Shift	Days Off	Wage
1	Sunday and Monday	$680
2	Monday and Tuesday	$705
3	Tuesday and Wednesday	$705
4	Wednesday and Thursday	$705
5	Thursday and Friday	$705
6	Friday and Saturday	$680
7	Saturday and Sunday	$655

The manager wants to keep the total wage expense for the hub as low as possible. With this in mind, how many package handlers should be assigned to each shift if the manager wants to have a sufficient number of workers available each day?

6.9.1 DEFINING THE DECISION VARIABLES

In this problem, the manager must decide how many workers to assign to each shift. Because there are seven possible shifts, we need the following seven decision variables:

$$X_1 = \text{the number of workers assigned to shift 1}$$
$$X_2 = \text{the number of workers assigned to shift 2}$$
$$X_3 = \text{the number of workers assigned to shift 3}$$
$$X_4 = \text{the number of workers assigned to shift 4}$$
$$X_5 = \text{the number of workers assigned to shift 5}$$
$$X_6 = \text{the number of workers assigned to shift 6}$$
$$X_7 = \text{the number of workers assigned to shift 7}$$

6.9.2 DEFINING THE OBJECTIVE FUNCTION

The objective in this problem is to minimize the total wages paid. Each worker on shifts 1 and 6 is paid $680 per week, and each worker on shift 7 is paid $655. All other workers are paid $705 per week. Thus, the objective of minimizing the total wage expense is expressed as:

MIN: $680X_1 + 705X_2 + 705X_3 + 705X_4 + 705X_5 + 680X_6 + 655X_7$ } total wage expense

6.9.3 DEFINING THE CONSTRAINTS

The constraints for this problem must ensure that at least 18 workers are scheduled for Sunday, at least 27 are scheduled for Monday, and so on. We need one constraint for each day of the week.

To make sure that at least 18 workers are available on Sunday, we must determine which decision variables represent shifts that are scheduled to work on Sunday. Because shifts 1 and 7 are the only shifts that have Sunday scheduled as a day off, the remaining shifts, 2 through 6, all are scheduled to work on Sunday. The following constraint ensures that at least 18 workers are available on Sunday:

$0X_1 + 1X_2 + 1X_3 + 1X_4 + 1X_5 + 1X_6 + 0X_7 \geq 18$ } workers required on Sunday

Because workers on shifts 1 and 2 have Monday off, the constraint for Monday should ensure that the sum of the variables representing the number of workers on the remaining shifts, 3 through 7, is at least 27. This constraint is expressed as:

$$0X_1 + 0X_2 + 1X_3 + 1X_4 + 1X_5 + 1X_6 + 1X_7 \geq 27 \qquad \} \text{ workers required on Monday}$$

Constraints for the remaining days of the week are generated easily by applying the same logic used in generating the previous two constraints. The resulting constraints are stated as:

$$1X_1 + 0X_2 + 0X_3 + 1X_4 + 1X_5 + 1X_6 + 1X_7 \geq 22 \qquad \} \text{ workers required on Tuesday}$$
$$1X_1 + 1X_2 + 0X_3 + 0X_4 + 1X_5 + 1X_6 + 1X_7 \geq 26 \qquad \} \text{ workers required on Wednesday}$$
$$1X_1 + 1X_2 + 1X_3 + 0X_4 + 0X_5 + 1X_6 + 1X_7 \geq 25 \qquad \} \text{ workers required on Thursday}$$
$$1X_1 + 1X_2 + 1X_3 + 1X_4 + 0X_5 + 0X_6 + 1X_7 \geq 21 \qquad \} \text{ workers required on Friday}$$
$$1X_1 + 1X_2 + 1X_3 + 1X_4 + 1X_5 + 0X_6 + 0X_7 \geq 19 \qquad \} \text{ workers required on Saturday}$$

Finally, all our decision variables must assume nonnegative integer values. These conditions are stated as:

$$X_1, X_2, X_3, X_4, X_5, X_6, X_7 \geq 0$$

All X_i must be integers

6.9.4 A NOTE ABOUT THE CONSTRAINTS

At this point, you might wonder why the constraints for each day are greater than or equal to rather than equal to constraints. For example, if Air-Express needs only 19 people on Saturday, why do we have a constraint that allows *more* than 19 people to be scheduled? The answer to this question relates to feasibility. Suppose we restate the problem so that all the constraints are equal to constraints. There are two possible outcomes for this problem: (1) it might have a feasible optimal solution, or (2) it might not have a feasible solution.

In the first case, if the formulation using equal to constraints has a feasible optimal solution, this same solution also must be a feasible solution to our formulation using greater than or equal to constraints. Because both formulations have the same objective function, the solution to our original formulation could not be worse (in terms of the optimal objective function value) than a formulation using equal to constraints.

In the second case, if the formulation using equal to constraints has no feasible solution, there is no schedule where the *exact* number of employees required can be scheduled each day. To find a feasible solution in this case, we would need to make the constraints less restrictive by allowing for more than the required number of employees to be scheduled (that is, using greater than or equal to constraints).

Therefore, using greater than or equal to constraints does not preclude a solution where the exact number of workers needed is scheduled for each shift, if such a schedule is feasible and optimal. If such a schedule is not feasible or not optimal, the formulation using greater than or equal to constraints also guarantees that a feasible optimal solution to the problem will be obtained.

6.9.5 IMPLEMENTING THE MODEL

The LP model for the Air-Express scheduling problem is summarized as:

MIN: $680X_1 + 705X_2 + 705X_3 + 705X_4 + 705X_5 + 680X_6 + 655X_7$ } total wage expense

Subject to:

$$0X_1 + 1X_2 + 1X_3 + 1X_4 + 1X_5 + 1X_6 + 0X_7 \geq 18 \quad \} \text{ workers required on Sunday}$$
$$0X_1 + 0X_2 + 1X_3 + 1X_4 + 1X_5 + 1X_6 + 1X_7 \geq 27 \quad \} \text{ workers required on Monday}$$
$$1X_1 + 0X_2 + 0X_3 + 1X_4 + 1X_5 + 1X_6 + 1X_7 \geq 22 \quad \} \text{ workers required on Tuesday}$$
$$1X_1 + 1X_2 + 0X_3 + 0X_4 + 1X_5 + 1X_6 + 1X_7 \geq 26 \quad \} \text{ workers required on Wednesday}$$
$$1X_1 + 1X_2 + 1X_3 + 0X_4 + 0X_5 + 1X_6 + 1X_7 \geq 25 \quad \} \text{ workers required on Thursday}$$
$$1X_1 + 1X_2 + 1X_3 + 1X_4 + 0X_5 + 0X_6 + 1X_7 \geq 21 \quad \} \text{ workers required on Friday}$$
$$1X_1 + 1X_2 + 1X_3 + 1X_4 + 1X_5 + 0X_6 + 0X_7 \geq 19 \quad \} \text{ workers required on Saturday}$$
$$X_1, X_2, X_3, X_4, X_5, X_6, X_7 \geq 0$$

All X_i must be integers

A convenient way of implementing this model is shown in Figure 6.13 (and in the file Fig6-13.xlsm that accompanies this book). Each row in the table shown in this spreadsheet corresponds to one of the seven shifts in the problem. For each day of the week, entries have been made to indicate which shifts are scheduled to be on or off. For example, shift 1 is scheduled off Sunday and Monday, and works on the remaining days of the week. Notice that the values for each day of the week in Figure 6.13 correspond directly to the coefficients in the constraint in our LP model for the same day of the week. The required number of workers for each day is listed in cells B13 through H13 and corresponds to the RHS values of each constraint. The wages to be paid to each worker on the various shifts are listed in cells J5 through J11 and correspond to the objective function coefficients in our model.

Cells I5 through I11 indicate the number of workers assigned to each shift and correspond to the decision variables X_1 through X_7 in our algebraic formulation of the LP

FIGURE 6.13 *Spreadsheet model for the Air-Express employee-scheduling problem*

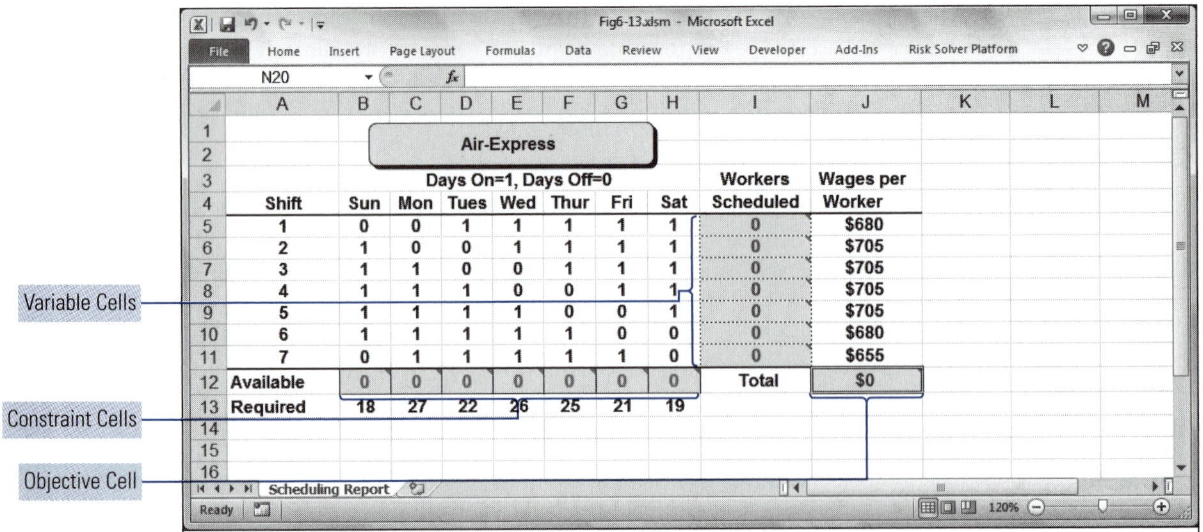

Cell	Formula	Copied to
B12	=SUMPRODUCT(B5:B11,$I$5:$I$11)	C12:H12 and J12

model. The LHS formula for each constraint is implemented easily using the SUMPRODUCT( ) function. For example, the formula in cell B12 implements the LHS of the constraint for the number of workers needed on Sunday as:

> Formula for cell B12:   =SUMPRODUCT(B5:B11,$I$5:$I$11)
>
> (Copy to C12 through H12 and J12.)

This formula is then copied to cells C12 through H12 to implement the LHS formulas of the remaining constraints. With the coefficients for the objective function entered in cells J5 through J11, the previous formula is also copied to cell J12 to implement the objective function for this model.

6.9.6 SOLVING THE MODEL

Figure 6.14 shows the Solver parameters required to solve this problem. The optimal solution is shown in Figure 6.15.

Solver Settings:
Objective: J12 (Min)
Variable cells: I5:I11
Constraints:
B12:H12 >= B13:H13
I5:I11 = integer
I5:I11 >= 0
Solver Options:
Standard LP/Quadratic Engine (Simplex LP)
Integer Tolerance = 0

FIGURE 6.14

Solver settings and options for the Air-Express scheduling problem

FIGURE 6.15 *Optimal solution to the Air-Express employee-scheduling problem*

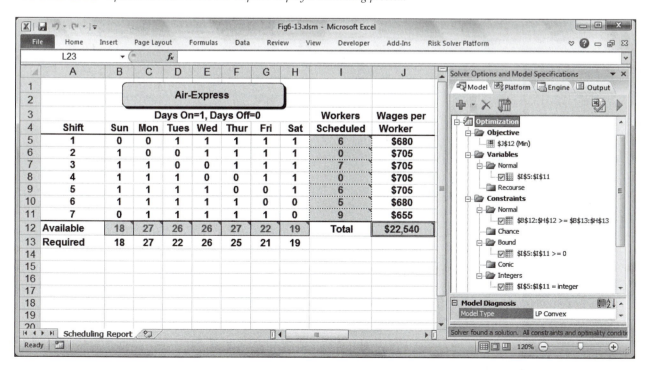

6.9.7 ANALYZING THE SOLUTION

The solution shown in Figure 6.15 ensures that the available number of employees is at least as great as the required number of employees for each day. The minimum total wage expense associated with this solution is $22,540. (There are alternate optimal solutions to this problem.)

6.10 Binary Variables

As mentioned earlier, some LP problems naturally evolve into ILP problems when we realize that we need to obtain integer solutions. For example, in the Air-Express problem discussed in the previous section, we needed to determine the number of workers to assign to each of seven shifts. Because workers are discrete units, we needed to impose integrality conditions on the decision variables in this model representing the number of workers scheduled for each shift. To do so, we changed the continuous variables in the model into **general integer variables**, or variables that could assume any integer value (provided that the constraints of the problem are not violated). In many other situations, we might want to use **binary integer variables** (or binary variables), which can assume *only two* integer values: 0 and 1. Binary variables can be useful in a number of practical modeling situations, as illustrated in the following examples.

6.11 A Capital Budgeting Problem

In a capital budgeting problem, a decision maker is presented with several potential projects or investment alternatives and must determine which projects or investments to choose. The projects or investments typically require different amounts of various resources (for example, money, equipment, personnel) and generate different cash flows to the company. The cash flows for each project or investment are converted to a net present value (NPV). The problem is to determine which set of projects or investments to select in order to achieve the maximum possible NPV. Consider the following example:

In his position as vice president of research and development (R&D) for CRT Technologies, Mark Schwartz is responsible for evaluating and choosing which R&D projects to support. The company received 18 R&D proposals from its scientists and engineers, and identified 6 projects as being consistent with the company's mission. However, the company does not have the funds available to undertake all 6 projects. Mark must determine which of the projects to select. The funding requirements for each project are summarized in the following table along with the NPV the company expects each project to generate.

Project	Expected NPV (in $1,000s)	Capital (in $1,000s) Required in				
		Year 1	Year 2	Year 3	Year 4	Year 5
1	$141	$ 75	$25	$20	$15	$10
2	$187	$ 90	$35	$ 0	$ 0	$30
3	$121	$ 60	$15	$15	$15	$15
4	$ 83	$ 30	$20	$10	$ 5	$ 5
5	$265	$100	$25	$20	$20	$20
6	$127	$ 50	$20	$10	$30	$40

The company currently has \$250,000 available to invest in new projects. It has budgeted \$75,000 for continued support for these projects in year 2 and \$50,000 per year for years 3, 4, and 5. Surplus funds in any year are reappropriated for other uses within the company and may not be carried over to future years.

6.11.1 DEFINING THE DECISION VARIABLES

Mark must decide which of the six projects to select. Thus, we need six variables to represent the alternatives under consideration. We will let $X_1, X_2, \ldots, X_6$ represent the six decision variables for this problem and assume they operate as:

$$X_i = \begin{cases} 1, \text{ if project } i \text{ is selected} \\ 0, \text{ otherwise} \end{cases} \quad i = 1, 2, \ldots, 6$$

Each decision variable in this problem is a binary variable that assumes the value 1 if the associated project is selected, or the value 0 if the associated project is not selected. In essence, each variable acts like an "on/off switch" to indicate whether or not a given project has been selected.

6.11.2 DEFINING THE OBJECTIVE FUNCTION

The objective in this problem is to maximize the total NPV of the selected projects. This is stated mathematically as:

$$\text{MAX:} \quad 141X_1 + 187X_2 + 121X_3 + 83X_4 + 265X_5 + 127X_6$$

Notice that this objective function simply sums the NPV figures for the selected projects.

6.11.3 DEFINING THE CONSTRAINTS

We need one capital constraint for each year to ensure that the selected projects do not require more capital than is available. This set of constraints is represented by:

$$75X_1 + 90X_2 + 60X_3 + 30X_4 + 100X_5 + 50X_6 \leq 250 \quad \text{\} year 1 capital constraint}$$
$$25X_1 + 35X_2 + 15X_3 + 20X_4 + 25X_5 + 20X_6 \leq 75 \quad \text{\} year 2 capital constraint}$$
$$20X_1 + 0X_2 + 15X_3 + 10X_4 + 20X_5 + 10X_6 \leq 50 \quad \text{\} year 3 capital constraint}$$
$$15X_1 + 0X_2 + 15X_3 + 5X_4 + 20X_5 + 30X_6 \leq 50 \quad \text{\} year 4 capital constraint}$$
$$10X_1 + 30X_2 + 15X_3 + 5X_4 + 20X_5 + 40X_6 \leq 50 \quad \text{\} year 5 capital constraint}$$

6.11.4 SETTING UP THE BINARY VARIABLES

In our formulation of this problem, we assume that each decision variable is a binary variable. We must include this assumption in the formal statement of our model by adding the constraints:

$$\text{All } X_i \text{ must be binary}$$

6.11.5 IMPLEMENTING THE MODEL

The ILP model for the CRT Technologies project selection problem is summarized as:

MAX: $141X_1 + 187X_2 + 121X_3 + 83X_4 + 265X_5 + 127X_6$

Subject to:
$$75X_1 + 90X_2 + 60X_3 + 30X_4 + 100X_5 + 50X_6 \leq 250$$
$$25X_1 + 35X_2 + 15X_3 + 20X_4 + 25X_5 + 20X_6 \leq 75$$
$$20X_1 + 0X_2 + 15X_3 + 10X_4 + 20X_5 + 10X_6 \leq 50$$
$$15X_1 + 0X_2 + 15X_3 + 5X_4 + 20X_5 + 30X_6 \leq 50$$
$$10X_1 + 30X_2 + 15X_3 + 5X_4 + 20X_5 + 40X_6 \leq 50$$

All X_i must be binary

This model is implemented in the spreadsheet shown in Figure 6.16 (and in the file Fig6-16.xlsm that accompanies this book). In this spreadsheet, the data for each project are listed in separate rows.

Cells B6 through B11 contain values of 0 to indicate that they are reserved for representing the six variables in our algebraic model. The LHS formula for the capital constraint is entered in cell D12 and then copied to cells E12 through H12, as:

Formula for cell D12:   =SUMPRODUCT(D6:D11,$B$6:$B$11)
(Copy to E12 through H12.)

The RHS values for the constraints are listed in cells D13 through H13. Finally, the objective function of the model is implemented in cell D15 as:

Formula for cell D15:   =SUMPRODUCT(C6:C11,$B$6:$B$11)

FIGURE 6.16 *Spreadsheet model for the CRT Technologies project selection problem*

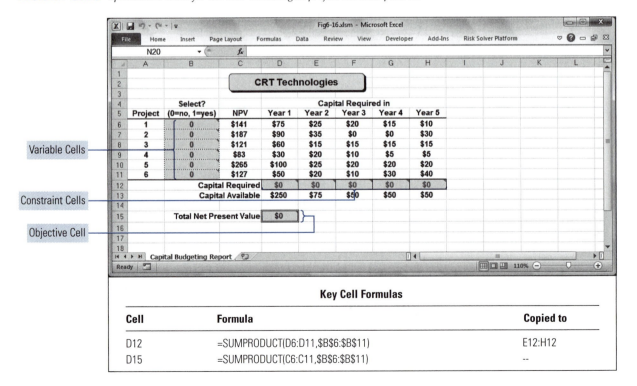

					Key Cell Formulas		

Cell	Formula	Copied to
D12	=SUMPRODUCT(D6:D11,$B$6:$B$11)	E12:H12
D15	=SUMPRODUCT(C6:C11,$B$6:$B$11)	--

6.11.6 SOLVING THE MODEL

To solve this model, we must tell Solver where we have implemented our objective function, decision variables, and constraints. The Solver settings and options shown in Figure 6.17 indicate that the objective function is implemented in cell D15 and that the decision variables are represented by cells B6 through B11. Also, notice that only two sets of constraints are specified for this problem.

The first set of constraints ensures that cells B6 through B11 will operate as binary variables. We implement these constraints by referring to the cells in the spreadsheet that represent our decision variables and selecting the "bin" (for binary) option in the Add Constraint dialog (see Figure 6.9). The last set of constraints indicates that the values in cells D12 through H12 must be less than or equal to the values in cells D13 through H13 when the problem is solved. These conditions correspond to the capital constraints in the problem.

Solver Settings:

Objective: D15 (Max)
Variable cells: B6:B11
Constraints:
  B6:B11 = binary
  D12:H12 <= D13:H13

Solver Options:
  Standard LP/Quadratic Engine (Simplex LP)
  Integer Tolerance = 0

FIGURE 6.17

Solver settings and options for the CRT Technologies project selection problem

---

Because this model contains six decision variables and each variable can assume only one of two values, at most $2^6 = 64$ possible integer solutions exist for this problem. Some of these integer solutions will not fall in the feasible region, so we might suspect that this problem will not be too difficult to solve optimally. If we set the Integer Tolerance factor to 0 and solve the problem, we obtain the solution shown in Figure 6.18.

6.11.7 COMPARING THE OPTIMAL SOLUTION TO A HEURISTIC SOLUTION

The optimal solution shown in Figure 6.18 indicates that if CRT Technologies selects projects 1, 4, and 5, it can achieve a total NPV of $489,000. Although this solution does not use all of the capital available in each year, it is still the best possible integer solution to the problem.

Another approach to solving this problem is to create a ranked list of the projects in decreasing order by NPV and then select projects from this list, in order, until the capital is depleted. As shown in Figure 6.19, if we apply this heuristic to the current problem, we would select projects 5 and 2, but we could not select any more projects due to a lack of capital in year 5. This solution would generate a total NPV of $452,000. Again, we can see the potential benefit of optimization techniques over heuristic solution techniques.

FIGURE 6.18 *Optimal integer solution to the CRT Technologies project selection problem*

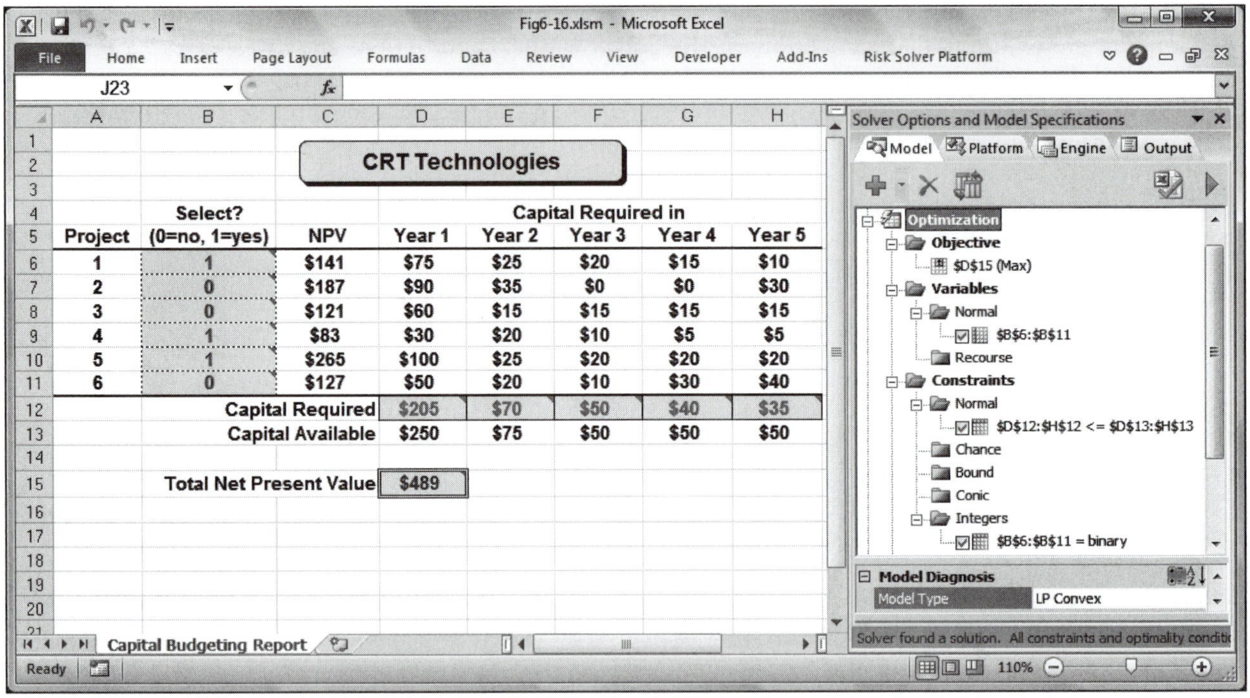

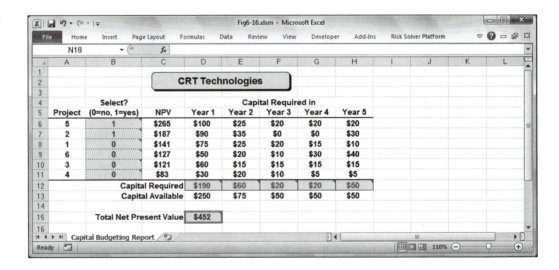

FIGURE 6.19

A suboptimal heuristic solution to the CRT Technologies project selection problem

6.12 Binary Variables and Logical Conditions

Binary variables can be used to model a number of logical conditions that might apply in a variety of problems. For example, in the CRT Technologies problem, several of the projects under consideration (for example, projects 1, 3, and 6) might represent alternative approaches for producing a certain part for a product. The company might want to limit the solution to include *no more than one* of these three alternatives. The following type of constraint accomplishes this restriction:

$$X_1 + X_3 + X_6 \leq 1$$

Because X_1, X_3, and X_6 represent binary variables, no more than one of them can assume the value 1 and still satisfy the previous constraint. If we want to ensure that the solution includes *exactly one* of these alternatives, we could include the following constraint in our model:

$$X_1 + X_3 + X_6 = 1$$

As an example of another type of logical condition, suppose that project 4 involves a cellular communications technology that will not be available to the company unless it undertakes project 5. In other words, the company cannot select project 4 unless it also selects project 5. This type of relationship can be imposed on the solution with the constraint:

$$X_4 - X_5 \leq 0$$

The four possible combinations of values for X_4 and X_5 and their relationships to the previous constraint are summarized in the following table.

Value of			
X_4	X_5	Meaning	Feasible?
0	0	Do not select either project	Yes
1	1	Select both projects	Yes
0	1	Select 5, but not 4	Yes
1	0	Select 4, but not 5	No

As indicated in this table, the previous constraint prohibits any solution in which project 4 is selected and project 5 is not selected.

As these examples illustrate, you can model certain logical conditions using binary variables. Several problems at the end of this chapter allow you to use binary variables (and your own creativity) to formulate models for decision problems that involve these types of logical conditions.

6.13 The Fixed-Charge Problem

In most of the LP problems discussed in earlier chapters, we formulated objective functions to maximize profits or minimize costs. In each of these cases, we associated a per-unit cost or per-unit profit with each decision variable to create the objective function. However, in some situations, the decision to produce a product results in a lump-sum cost, or fixed-charge, in addition to a per-unit cost or profit. These types of problems are known as **fixed-charge** or fixed-cost problems. The following are some examples of fixed-costs:

- The cost to lease, rent, or purchase a piece of equipment or a vehicle that will be required if a particular action is taken
- The setup cost required to prepare a machine or production line to produce a different type of product
- The cost to construct a new production line or facility that will be required if a particular decision is made
- The cost of hiring additional personnel that will be required if a particular decision is made

In each of these examples, the fixed costs are *new* costs that will be incurred if a particular action or decision is made. In this respect, fixed costs are different from **sunk costs**, which are costs that will be incurred regardless of what decision is made. Sunk costs are irrelevant for decision-making purposes because, by definition, decisions do not influence these costs. On the other hand, fixed costs are important factors in decision making because the decision determines whether or not these costs will be incurred. The following example illustrates the formulation and solution of a fixed-charge problem.

Remington Manufacturing is planning its next production cycle. The company can produce three products, each of which must undergo machining, grinding, and assembly operations. The following table summarizes the hours of machining, grinding, and assembly required by each unit of each product, and the total hours of capacity available for each operation.

Operation	Hours Required By			Total Hours Available
	Product 1	Product 2	Product 3	
Machining	2	3	6	600
Grinding	6	3	4	300
Assembly	5	6	2	400

The cost accounting department has estimated that each unit of product 1 manufactured and sold will contribute $48 to profit, and each unit of products 2 and 3 contributes $55 and $50, respectively. However, manufacturing a unit of product 1 requires a setup operation on the production line that costs $1,000. Similar setups are required for products 2 and 3 at costs of $800 and $900, respectively. The marketing department believes it can sell all the products produced. Therefore, the management of Remington wants to determine the most profitable mix of products to produce.

6.13.1 DEFINING THE DECISION VARIABLES

Although only three products are under consideration in this problem, we need six variables to formulate the problem accurately. We can define these variables as:

$$X_i = \text{the amount of product } i \text{ to be produced, } i = 1, 2, 3$$

$$Y_i = \begin{cases} 1, \text{ if } X_i > 0 \\ 0, \text{ if } X_i = 0 \end{cases}, \ i = 1, 2, 3$$

We need three variables, X_1, X_2, and X_3, to correspond to the units of products 1, 2, and 3 produced. Each of the X_i variables has a corresponding binary variable, Y_i, that will equal 1 if X_i assumes any positive value, or will equal 0 if X_i is 0. For now, do not be concerned about how this relationship between the X_i and Y_i is enforced. We will explore that soon.

6.13.2 DEFINING THE OBJECTIVE FUNCTION

Given our definition of the decision variables, the objective function for our model is stated as:

$$\text{MAX:} \quad 48X_1 + 55X_2 + 50X_3 - 1000Y_1 - 800Y_2 - 900Y_3$$

The first three terms in this function calculate the marginal profit generated by the number of products 1, 2, and 3 sold. The last three terms in this function subtract the fixed costs for the products produced. For example, if X_1 assumes a positive value, we know from our definition of the Y_i variables that Y_1 should equal 1. And if $Y_1 = 1$, the value of the objective function will be reduced by \$1,000 to reflect payment of the setup cost. On the other hand, if $X_1 = 0$, we know that $Y_1 = 0$. Therefore, if no units of X_1 are produced, the setup cost for product 1 will not be incurred in the objective. Similar relationships exist between X_2 and Y_2 and between X_3 and Y_3.

6.13.3 DEFINING THE CONSTRAINTS

Several sets of constraints apply to this problem. Capacity constraints are needed to ensure that the number of machining, grinding, and assembly hours used does not exceed the number of hours available for each of these resources. These constraints are stated as:

$$2X_1 + 3X_2 + 6X_3 \leq 600 \quad \} \text{ machining constraint}$$
$$6X_1 + 3X_2 + 4X_3 \leq 300 \quad \} \text{ grinding constraint}$$
$$5X_1 + 6X_2 + 2X_3 \leq 400 \quad \} \text{ assembly constraint}$$

We also need to include integer and nonnegativity conditions on the X_i variables as:

$$X_i \geq 0 \text{ and integer, } i = 1, 2, 3$$

The following constraint on the Y_i variables is needed to ensure that they operate as binary variables:

$$\text{All } Y_i \text{ must be binary}$$

As mentioned earlier, we must ensure that the required relationship between the X_i and Y_i variables is enforced. In particular, the value of the Y_i variables can be determined from the X_i variables. Therefore, we need constraints to establish this *link* between the value of the Y_i variables and the X_i variables. These linking constraints are represented by:

$$X_1 \leq M_1Y_1$$
$$X_2 \leq M_2Y_2$$
$$X_3 \leq M_3Y_3$$

In each of these constraints, the M_i is a numeric constant that represents an upper bound on the optimal value of the X_i. Let's assume that all the M_i are arbitrarily large numbers, for example, $M_i = 10,000$. Then each constraint sets up a link between the value of the X_i and the Y_i. For example, if any X_i variables in the previous constraints assume a value greater than 0, the corresponding Y_i variable must assume the value 1 or the constraint will be violated. On the other hand, if any of the X_i variables are equal to 0, the corresponding Y_i variables could equal 0 or 1 and still satisfy the constraint. However, if we consider the objective function to this problem, we know that when given a choice, Solver will always set the Y_i equal to 0 (rather than 1) because this results in a better objective function value. Therefore, we can conclude that if any X_i variables are equal to 0, Solver will set the corresponding Y_i variable equal to 0 because this is feasible and results in a better objective function value.

6.13.4 DETERMINING VALUES FOR "BIG M"

The M_i values used in the linking constraints are sometimes referred to as "Big M" values because they can be assigned arbitrarily large values. However, for reasons that go beyond the scope of this text, these types of problems are much easier to solve if the M_i values are kept as small as possible. As indicated earlier, the M_i values impose upper bounds on the values of the X_i. So, if a problem indicates that a company could manufacture and sell no more than 60 units of X_1, for example, we could let $M_1 = 60$. However, even if upper bounds for the X_i are not explicitly indicated, it is sometimes easy to derive implicit upper bounds for these variables.

Let's consider the variable X_1 in the Remington problem. What is the maximum number of units of X_1 that can be produced in this problem? Referring back to our capacity constraints, if the company produces 0 units of X_2 and X_3, it would run out of machining capacity after producing $600/2 = 300$ units of X_1. Similarly, it would run out of grinding capacity after producing $300/6 = 50$ units of X_1, and it would run out of assembly capacity after producing $400/5 = 80$ units of X_1. Therefore, the maximum number of units of X_1 the company can produce is 50. Using similar logic, we can determine that the maximum units of X_2 the company can produce is MIN(600/3, 300/3, 400/6) = 66.67, and the maximum units of X_3 is MIN(600/6, 300/4, 400/2) = 75. Thus, for this problem, reasonable upper bounds for X_1, X_2, and X_3 are represented by $M_1 = 50$, $M_2 = 66.67$, and $M_3 = 75$, respectively. (Note that the method illustrated here for obtaining reasonable values for the M_i does not apply if any of the coefficients in the machining, grinding, or assembly constraints are negative. Why is this?) When possible, you should determine reasonable values for the M_i in this type of problem. However, if this is not possible, you can assign arbitrarily large values to the M_i.

6.13.5 IMPLEMENTING THE MODEL

Using the values for the M_i calculated earlier, our ILP formulation of Remington's production planning model is summarized as:

MAX: $48X_1 + 55X_2 + 50X_3 - 1000Y_1 - 800Y_2 - 900Y_3$

Subject to: $2X_1 + 3X_2 + 6X_3 \leq 600$ } machining constraint

$6X_1 + 3X_2 + 4X_3 \leq 300$ } grinding constraint

$5X_1 + 6X_2 + 2X_3 \leq 400$ } assembly constraint

$X_1 - 50Y_1 \leq 0$ } linking constraint

$X_2 - 67Y_2 \leq 0$ } linking constraint

$X_3 - 75Y_3 \leq 0$ } linking constraint

All Y_i must be binary   } binary constraints

All X_i must be integer   } integrality conditions

$X_i \geq 0, i = 1, 2, 3$ } nonnegativity conditions

This model expresses the linking constraints in a slightly different (but algebraically equivalent) manner in order to follow our convention of having all the variables on the LHS of the inequality and a constant on the RHS. This model is implemented in the spreadsheet shown in Figure 6.20 (and in the file Fig6-20.xlsm that accompanies this book).

In the spreadsheet in Figure 6.20, cells B5, C5, and D5 represent the variables X_1, X_2, and X_3, and cells B15, C15, and D15 represent Y_1, Y_2, and Y_3. The coefficients for the

FIGURE 6.20 *Spreadsheet model for Remington's fixed-charge problem*

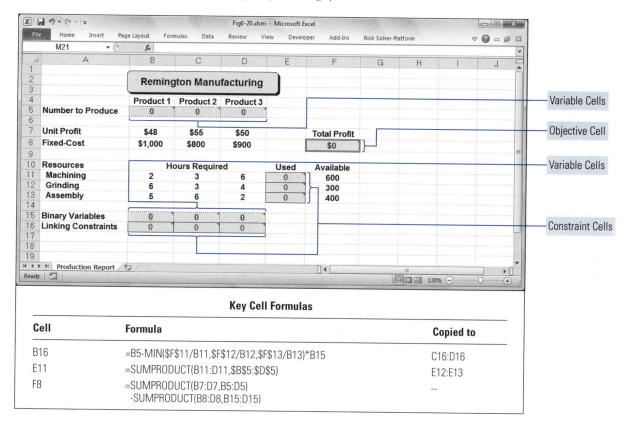

Key Cell Formulas

Cell	Formula	Copied to
B16	=B5-MIN($F$11/B11,$F$12/B12,$F$13/B13)*B15	C16:D16
E11	=SUMPRODUCT(B11:D11,$B$5:$D$5)	E12:E13
F8	=SUMPRODUCT(B7:D7,B5:D5) -SUMPRODUCT(B8:D8,B15:D15)	--

objective function are in cells B7 through D8. The objective function is implemented in cell F8 with the formula:

$$\text{Formula for cell F8: } =\text{SUMPRODUCT(B7:D7,B5:D5)} - \text{SUMPRODUCT(B8:D8,B15:D15)}$$

Cells B11 through D13 contain the coefficients for the machining, grinding, and assembly constraints. The LHS formulas for these constraints are implemented in cells E11 through E13, and cells F11 through F13 contain the RHS values for these constraints. Finally, the LHS formulas for the linking constraints are entered in cells B16 through D16 as:

Formula for cell B16:   =B5 − MIN($F$11/B11,$F$12/B12,$F$13/B13)*B15

(Copy to cells C16 through D16.)

Instead of entering the values for M_i in these constraints, we implemented formulas that would automatically calculate correct M_i values if the user of this spreadsheet changed any of the coefficients or RHS values in the capacity constraints.

6.13.6 SOLVING THE MODEL

The required Solver settings and options for this problem are shown in Figure 6.21. Notice that the ranges B5 through D5 and B15 through D15, which correspond to the X_i and Y_i

FIGURE 6.21

Solver settings and options for Remington's fixed-charge problem

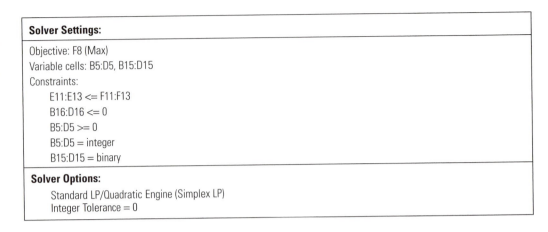

Solver Settings:

Objective: F8 (Max)
Variable cells: B5:D5, B15:D15
Constraints:
    E11:E13 <= F11:F13
    B16:D16 <= 0
    B5:D5 >= 0
    B5:D5 = integer
    B15:D15 = binary

Solver Options:
    Standard LP/Quadratic Engine (Simplex LP)
    Integer Tolerance = 0

variables, are both listed as ranges of cells that Solver can change. Also, notice the necessary binary constraint is imposed on cells B15 through D15.

Because so few integer variables exist in this problem, we should be able to obtain an optimal integer solution easily. If we set the Integer Tolerance to 0, we obtain the optimal solution to this problem shown in Figure 6.22.

6.13.7 ANALYZING THE SOLUTION

The solution shown in Figure 6.22 indicates that the company should produce 0 units of product 1, 56 units of product 2, and 32 units of product 3 ($X_1 = 0$, $X_2 = 56$, and $X_3 = 32$).

FIGURE 6.22 *Optimal integer solution to Remington's fixed-charge problem*

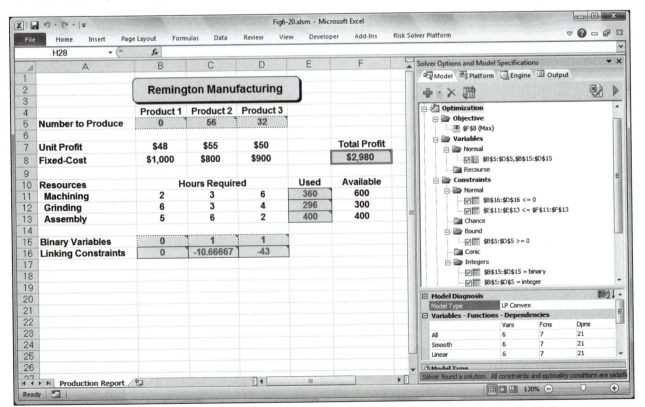

Solver assigned values of 0, 1, and 1, respectively, to cells B15, C15, and D15 ($Y_1 = 0$, $Y_2 = 1$, and $Y_3 = 1$). Thus, Solver maintained the proper relationship between the X_i and Y_i because the linking constraints were specified for this problem.

The values in B16, C16, and D16 indicate the amounts by which the values for X_1, X_2, and X_3 (in cells B5, C5, and D5) fall below the upper bounds imposed by their respective linking constraints. Thus, the optimal value of X_2 is approximately 10.67 units below its upper bound of 66.67, and the optimal value of X_3 is 43 units below its upper bound of 75. Because the optimal value of Y_1 is zero, the linking constraint for X_1 and Y_1 imposes an upper bound of 0 on X_1. Thus, the value in cell B16 indicates that the optimal value of X_1 is 0 units below its upper bound of 0.

6.13.8 A COMMENT ON IF( ) FUNCTIONS

In Figure 6.22, it is important to note that we are treating cells B15, C15, and D15, which represent the binary variables Y_1, Y_2, and Y_3, just like any other cells representing decision variables. We simply entered values of 0 into these cells to indicate that they represent decision variables. We then let Solver determine what values should be placed in these cells so that all the constraints are satisfied, and the objective function is maximized. Some people try to make Solver's job (or their own life) "easier" by using an alternate approach with IF( ) functions in the objective to turn on or off the fixed costs depending on the values of cells B5, C5, and D5, which correspond to the variables X_1, X_2, and X_3. For example, consider the model in Figure 6.23 (and Fig6-23.xlsm in the files accompanying this book) where we have eliminated the binary variables and linking

FIGURE 6.23 *An alternate implementation of Remington's fixed-charge problem with IF( ) functions replacing the binary variables and linking constraints*

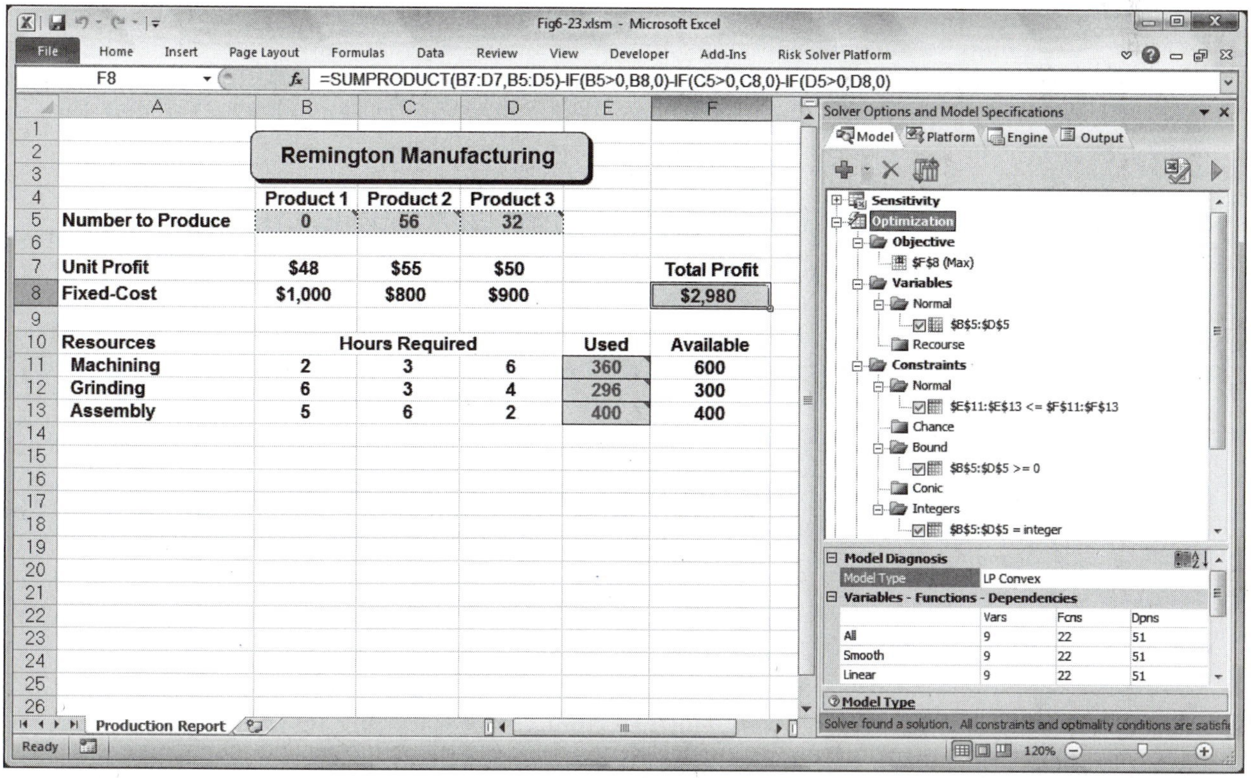

constraints and replaced them with IF( ) functions in the objective (cell F8) to model the fixed costs in this problem as follows:

Formula for cell F8: =SUMPRODUCT(B7:D7,B5:D5)-IF(B5>0,B8,0)–
IF(C5>0,C8,0)-IF(D5>0,D8,0)

Although this approach seems to make sense, it can produce unwanted results. Using IF( ) functions in this way introduces discontinuities in the spreadsheet model that makes it more difficult for Solver (particularly Excel's built-in Solver) to find the optimal solution. One of the rather amazing features of Risk Solver Platform is its ability to automatically transform a model containing certain types of IF( ) functions into an equivalent integer programming model without IF( ) functions.

When you solve this problem, the diagnostic information on the Output tab in the Risk Solver task pane (not shown) indicates that this model is diagnosed as a non-smooth problem, and Solver automatically transforms it into a "LP Convex" problem. Note that this transformation is not made on your worksheet but instead refers to how Risk Solver is handling the model internally. Now, although the solution shown in Figure 6.23 matches the optimal solution shown in Figure 6.22, note that the number of variables (Vars), functions (Fcns), and dependencies (Dpns) listed in the bottom of the Risk Solver task pane in Figure 6.23 are significantly higher than those listed in Figure 6.22. That is, Risk Solver's automatic transformation of the model in Figure 6.23 with IF( ) functions resulted in a problem with 9 variables, 22 functions, and 51 dependencies, whereas our original model in Figure 6.22 using binary variables and linking constraints has only 6 variables, 7 functions, and 21 dependencies. Thus, while the same solution was obtained using IF( ) functions, it required Risk Solver to formulate and solve a significantly more complicated model. In this case, the added complexity was not an issue. However, it is easy to see how the complications caused by IF( ) functions could become problematic as problem size increases. Additionally, Risk Solver cannot always successfully transform a model containing IF( ) functions. Thus, for a variety of reasons, it is best to avoid IF( ) functions when possible and not rely on Risk Solver's ability to automatically transform some models containing them. (If desired, you can disable this type of automatic transformation in Risk Solver by setting the Nonsmooth Model Transformation property to Never on the Platform tab in the task pane.)

6.14 Minimum Order/Purchase Size

Many investment, production, and distribution problems have minimum purchase amounts or minimum production lot size requirements that must be met. For example, a particular investment opportunity might require a minimum investment of \$25,000. Or, a supplier of a given part used in a production process might require a minimum order of 10 units. Similarly, many manufacturing companies have a policy of not producing any units of a given item unless a certain minimum lot size will be produced.

To see how these types of minimum order/purchase requirements can be modeled, suppose that in the previous problem, Remington Manufacturing did not want to produce any units of product 3 (X_3) unless it produced at least 40 units of this product. This type of restriction is modeled as:

$$X_3 \leq M_3 Y_3$$
$$X_3 \geq 40 Y_3$$

The first constraint is the same type of linking constraint described earlier, in which M_3 represents an upper bound on X_3 (or an arbitrarily large number), and Y_3 represents a binary variable. If X_3 assumes any positive value, Y_3 must equal 1 (if $X_3 > 0$, then $Y_3 = 1$). However, according to the second constraint, if Y_3 equals 1, then X_3 must be greater than or equal to 40 (if $Y_3 = 1$, then $X_3 \geq 40$). On the other hand, if X_3 equals 0, Y_3 must also equal 0 in order to satisfy both constraints. Together, these two constraints ensure that if X_3 assumes any positive value, that value must be at least 40. This example illustrates how binary variables can be used to model a practical condition that is likely to occur in a variety of decision problems.

6.15 Quantity Discounts

In all the LP problems considered to this point, we have assumed that the profit or cost coefficients in the objective function were constant. For example, consider our revised Blue Ridge Hot Tubs problem, which is represented by:

MAX:	$350X_1 + 300X_2$		} profit
Subject to:	$1X_1 + 1X_2 \leq 200$		} pump constraint
	$9X_1 + 6X_2 \leq 1{,}520$		} labor constraint
	$12X_1 + 16X_2 \leq 2{,}650$		} tubing constraint
	$X_1, X_2 \geq 0$		} nonnegativity conditions
	X_1, X_2 must be integers		} integrality conditions

This model assumes that *every* additional Aqua-Spa (X_1) manufactured and sold results in a \$350 increase in profit. It also assumes that every additional Hydro-Lux (X_2) manufactured and sold results in a \$300 increase in profit. However, as the production of these products increases, quantity discounts might be obtained on component parts that would cause the profit margin on these items to increase.

For example, suppose that if the company produces more than 75 Aqua-Spas, it will be able to obtain quantity discounts and other economies of scale that would increase the profit margin to \$375 per unit for each unit produced in excess of 75. Similarly, suppose that if the company produces more than 50 Hydro-Luxes, it will be able to increase its profit margin to \$325 for each unit produced in excess of 50. That is, each of the first 75 units of X_1 and the first 50 units of X_2 would produce profits of \$350 and \$300 per unit, respectively, and each additional unit of X_1 and X_2 would produce profits of \$375 and \$325 per unit, respectively. How do we model this type of problem?

6.15.1 FORMULATING THE MODEL

To accommodate the different profit rates that can be generated by producing Aqua-Spas and Hydro-Luxes, we need to define new variables for the problem, where:

X_{11} = the number of Aqua-Spas produced at \$350 profit per unit
X_{12} = the number of Aqua-Spas produced at \$375 profit per unit
X_{21} = the number of Hydro-Luxes produced at \$300 profit per unit
X_{22} = the number of Hydro-Luxes produced at \$325 profit per unit

Using these variables, we can begin to reformulate our problem as:

MAX:	$350X_{11} + 375X_{12} + 300X_{21} + 325X_{22}$	
Subject to:	$1X_{11} + 1X_{12} + 1X_{21} + 1X_{22} \leq 200$	} pump constraint
	$9X_{11} + 9X_{12} + 6X_{21} + 6X_{22} \leq 1{,}520$	} labor constraint

$$12X_{11} + 12X_{12} + 16X_{21} + 16X_{22} \leq 2{,}650 \qquad \text{} \text{tubing constraint}$$
$$\text{All } X_{ij} \geq 0 \qquad\qquad\qquad\qquad\qquad\qquad \text{} \text{simple lower bounds}$$
$$\text{All } X_{ij} \text{ must be integers} \qquad\qquad\qquad \text{} \text{integrality conditions}$$

This formulation is not complete. Notice that the variable X_{12} would always be preferred over X_{11} because X_{12} requires exactly the same resources as X_{11} and generates a larger per-unit profit. The same relationship holds between X_{22} and X_{21}. Thus, the optimal solution to the problem is $X_{11} = 0$, $X_{12} = 118$, $X_{21} = 0$, and $X_{22} = 76$. However, this solution is not allowable because we cannot produce any units of X_{12} until we have produced 75 units of X_{11}; and we cannot produce any units of X_{22} until we have produced 50 units of X_{21}. Therefore, we must identify some additional constraints to ensure that these conditions are met.

6.15.2 THE MISSING CONSTRAINTS

To ensure that the model does not allow any units of X_{12} to be produced unless we have produced 75 units of X_{11}, consider the constraints:

$$X_{12} \leq M_{12}Y_1$$
$$X_{11} \geq 75Y_1$$

In the first constraint, M_{12} represents some arbitrarily large numeric constant, and Y_1 represents a binary variable. The first constraint requires that $Y_1 = 1$ if any units of X_{12} are produced (if $X_{12} > 0$, then $Y_1 = 1$). However, if $Y_1 = 1$, then the second constraint would require X_{11} to be at least 75. According to the second constraint, the only way that fewer than 75 units of X_{11} can be produced is if $Y_1 = 0$, which, by the first constraint, implies $X_{12} = 0$. These two constraints do not allow any units of X_{12} to be produced unless at least 75 units of X_{11} have been produced. The following constraints ensure that the model does not allow any units of X_{22} to be produced unless we have produced 50 units of X_{21}:

$$X_{22} \leq M_{22}Y_2$$
$$X_{21} \geq 50Y_2$$

If we include these new constraints in our previous formulation (along with the constraints necessary to make Y_1 and Y_2 operate as binary variables), we would have an accurate formulation of the decision problem. The optimal solution to this problem is $X_{11} = 75$, $X_{12} = 43$, $X_{21} = 50$, $X_{22} = 26$.

6.16 A Contract Award Problem

Other conditions often arise in decision problems that can be modeled effectively using binary variables. The following example, which involves awarding contracts, illustrates some of these conditions.

B&G Construction is a commercial building company located in Tampa, Florida. The company has recently signed contracts to construct four buildings in different locations throughout southern Florida. Each building project requires large amounts of cement to be delivered to the building sites. At B&G's request, three cement companies have submitted bids for supplying the cement for these jobs. The following table summarizes the prices the three companies charge per delivered ton of cement and the maximum amount of cement that each company can provide.

	Cost per Delivered Ton of Cement				
	Project 1	**Project 2**	**Project 3**	**Project 4**	**Max. Supply**
Company 1	$120	$115	$130	$125	525
Company 2	$100	$150	$110	$105	450
Company 3	$140	$ 95	$145	$165	550
Total Tons Needed	450	275	300	350	

For example, company 1 can supply a maximum of 525 tons of cement, and each ton delivered to projects 1, 2, 3, and 4 will cost $120, $115, $130, and $125, respectively. The costs vary primarily because of the different distances between the cement plants and the construction sites. The numbers in the last row of the table indicate the total amount of cement (in tons) required for each project.

In addition to the maximum supplies listed, each cement company placed special conditions on its bid. Specifically, company 1 indicated that it will not supply orders of less than 150 tons for any of the construction projects. Company 2 indicated that it can supply more than 200 tons to no more than one of the projects. Company 3 indicated that it will accept only orders that total 200 tons, 400 tons, or 550 tons.

B&G can contract with more than one supplier to meet the cement requirements for a given project. The problem is to determine what amounts to purchase from each supplier to meet the demands for each project at the least total cost.

This problem seems like a transportation problem in which we want to determine how much cement should be shipped from each cement company to each construction project in order to meet the demands of the projects at a minimum cost. However, the special conditions imposed by each supplier require side constraints, which are not usually found in a standard transportation problem. First, we'll discuss the formulation of the objective function and the transportation constraints. Then, we'll consider how to implement the side constraints required by the special conditions in the problem.

6.16.1 FORMULATING THE MODEL: THE OBJECTIVE FUNCTION AND TRANSPORTATION CONSTRAINTS

To begin formulating this problem, we need to define our decision variables as:

X_{ij} = tons of cement purchased from company i for construction project j

The objective function to minimize total cost is represented by:

$$\text{MIN:} \quad 120X_{11} + 115X_{12} + 130X_{13} + 125X_{14}$$
$$+100X_{21} + 150X_{22} + 110X_{23} + 105X_{24}$$
$$+140X_{31} + 95X_{32} + 145X_{33} + 165X_{34}$$

To ensure that the maximum supply of cement from each company is not exceeded, we need the following constraints:

$$X_{11} + X_{12} + X_{13} + X_{14} \leq 525 \quad \} \text{ supply from company 1}$$
$$X_{21} + X_{22} + X_{23} + X_{24} \leq 450 \quad \} \text{ supply from company 2}$$
$$X_{31} + X_{32} + X_{33} + X_{34} \leq 550 \quad \} \text{ supply from company 3}$$

To ensure that the requirement for cement at each construction project is met, we need the following constraints:

$$X_{11} + X_{21} + X_{31} = 450 \qquad \} \text{ demand for cement at project 1}$$
$$X_{12} + X_{22} + X_{32} = 275 \qquad \} \text{ demand for cement at project 2}$$
$$X_{13} + X_{23} + X_{33} = 300 \qquad \} \text{ demand for cement at project 3}$$
$$X_{14} + X_{24} + X_{34} = 350 \qquad \} \text{ demand for cement at project 4}$$

6.16.2 IMPLEMENTING THE TRANSPORTATION CONSTRAINTS

The objective function and the constraints of this problem are implemented in the spreadsheet model shown in Figure 6.24 (and in the file Fig6-24.xlsm that accompanies this book).

In this spreadsheet, the costs per delivered ton of cement are shown in cells B6 through E8. Cells B12 through E14 represent the decision variables in the model. The objective function is entered in cell G17 as:

Formula for cell G17:   =SUMPRODUCT(B6:E8,B12:E14)

The LHS formulas of the supply constraints are entered in cells F12 through F14 as:

Formula for cell F12:   =SUM(B12:E12)

(Copy to F13 through F14.)

FIGURE 6.24 *Spreadsheet model for the transportation portion of B&G's contract award problem*

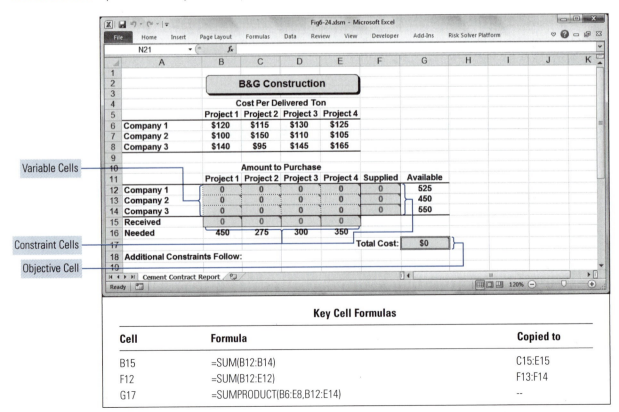

Cells G12 through G14 contain the RHS values for these constraints. The LHS formulas for the demand constraints are entered in cells B15 through E15 as:

Formula for cell B15:   =SUM(B12:B14)

(Copy to C15 through E15.)

Cells B16 through E16 contain the RHS values for these constraints.

6.16.3 FORMULATING THE MODEL: THE SIDE CONSTRAINTS

Company 1 indicated that it will not accept orders for less than 150 tons for any of the construction projects. This minimum-size order restriction is modeled by the following eight constraints, where the Y_{ij} represent binary variables:

$$X_{11} \leq 525Y_{11} \quad \text{(implement as } X_{11} - 525Y_{11} \leq 0\text{)}$$
$$X_{12} \leq 525Y_{12} \quad \text{(implement as } X_{12} - 525Y_{12} \leq 0\text{)}$$
$$X_{13} \leq 525Y_{13} \quad \text{(implement as } X_{13} - 525Y_{13} \leq 0\text{)}$$
$$X_{14} \leq 525Y_{14} \quad \text{(implement as } X_{14} - 525Y_{14} \leq 0\text{)}$$
$$X_{11} \geq 150Y_{11} \quad \text{(implement as } X_{11} - 150Y_{11} \geq 0\text{)}$$
$$X_{12} \geq 150Y_{12} \quad \text{(implement as } X_{12} - 150Y_{12} \geq 0\text{)}$$
$$X_{13} \geq 150Y_{13} \quad \text{(implement as } X_{13} - 150Y_{13} \geq 0\text{)}$$
$$X_{14} \geq 150Y_{14} \quad \text{(implement as } X_{14} - 150Y_{14} \geq 0\text{)}$$

Each constraint has an algebraically equivalent constraint, which will ultimately be used in implementing the constraint in the spreadsheet. The first four constraints represent linking constraints that ensure if X_{11}, X_{12}, X_{13}, or X_{14} is greater than 0, then its associated binary variable (Y_{11}, Y_{12}, Y_{13}, or Y_{14}) must equal 1. (These constraints also indicate that 525 is the maximum value that can be assumed by X_{11}, X_{12}, X_{13}, and X_{14}.) The next four constraints ensure that if X_{11}, X_{12}, X_{13}, or X_{14} is greater than 0, it must be at least 150. We include these constraints in the formulation of this model to ensure that any order given to company 1 is for at least 150 tons of cement.

Company 2 indicated that it can supply more than 200 tons to no more than one of the projects. This type of restriction is represented by the following set of constraints where, again, the Y_{ij} represent binary variables:

$$X_{21} \leq 200 + 250Y_{21} \quad \text{(implement as } X_{21} - 200 - 250Y_{21} \leq 0\text{)}$$
$$X_{22} \leq 200 + 250Y_{22} \quad \text{(implement as } X_{22} - 200 - 250Y_{22} \leq 0\text{)}$$
$$X_{23} \leq 200 + 250Y_{23} \quad \text{(implement as } X_{23} - 200 - 250Y_{23} \leq 0\text{)}$$
$$X_{24} \leq 200 + 250Y_{24} \quad \text{(implement as } X_{24} - 200 - 250Y_{24} \leq 0\text{)}$$
$$Y_{21} + Y_{22} + Y_{23} + Y_{24} \leq 1 \quad \text{(implement as is)}$$

The first constraint indicates that the amount supplied from company 2 for project 1 must be less than 200 if $Y_{21} = 0$, or less than 450 (the maximum supply from company 2) if $Y_{21} = 1$. The next three constraints have similar interpretations for the amount supplied from company 2 to projects 2, 3, and 4, respectively. The last constraint indicates that at most, one of Y_{21}, Y_{22}, Y_{23}, and Y_{24} can equal 1. Therefore, only one of the projects can receive more than 200 tons of cement from company 2.

The final set of constraints for this problem addresses company 3's stipulation that it will accept only orders totaling 200, 400, or 550 tons. This type of condition is modeled using binary Y_{ij} variables as:

$$X_{31} + X_{32} + X_{33} + X_{34} = 200Y_{31} + 400Y_{32} + 550Y_{33}$$

$$\text{(implement as } X_{31} + X_{32} + X_{33} + X_{34} - 200Y_{31} - 400Y_{32} - 550Y_{33} = 0)$$

$$Y_{31} + Y_{32} + Y_{33} \leq 1 \quad \text{(implement as is)}$$

These constraints allow for the total amount ordered from company 3 to assume four distinct values. If $Y_{31} = Y_{32} = Y_{33} = 0$, then no cement will be ordered from company 3. If $Y_{31} = 1$, then 200 tons must be ordered. If $Y_{32} = 1$ then 400 tons must be ordered. Finally, if $Y_{33} = 1$, then 550 tons must be ordered from company 3. These two constraints enforce the special condition imposed by company 3.

6.16.4 IMPLEMENTING THE SIDE CONSTRAINTS

Although the side constraints in this problem allow us to impose important restrictions on the feasible solutions that can be considered, these constraints serve more of a "mechanical" purpose—to make the model work—but are not of primary interest to management. Thus, it is often convenient to implement side constraints in an out-of-the-way area of the spreadsheet so that they do not detract from the primary purpose of the spreadsheet, in this case, to determine how much cement to order from each potential supplier. Figure 6.25 shows how the side constraints for the current problem can be implemented in a spreadsheet.

To implement the side constraints for company 1, we enter the batch-size restriction of 150 in cell B20, and reserve cells B21 through E21 to represent the binary variables Y_{11}, Y_{12}, Y_{13}, and Y_{14}. The LHS formulas for the linking constraints for company 1 are implemented in cells B22 through E22 as:

> Formula for cell B22:   =B12–$G$12*B21
>
> (Copy to C22 through E22.)

Cell F22 contains a reminder for us to tell Solver that these cells must be less than or equal to 0. The LHS formulas for the batch-size constraints for company 1 are implemented in cells B23 through E23 as:

> Formula for cell B23:   =B12–$B$20*B21
>
> (Copy to C23 through E23.)

Cell F23 contains a reminder for us to tell Solver that these cells must be greater than or equal to 0.

To implement the side constraints for company 2, we enter the maximum supply value of 200 in cell B25, and reserve cells B26 through E26 to represent the binary variables Y_{21}, Y_{22}, Y_{23}, and Y_{24}. The LHS formulas for the maximum supply constraints are implemented in cells B27 through E27 as:

> Formula for cell B27:   =B13–$B$25–($G$13–$B$25)*B26
>
> (Copy to C27 through E27.)

Cell F27 reminds us to tell Solver that these cells must be less than or equal to 0. As discussed earlier, to ensure that no more than one order from company 2 exceeds

FIGURE 6.25 *Spreadsheet model for the side constraints in B&G's contract award problem*

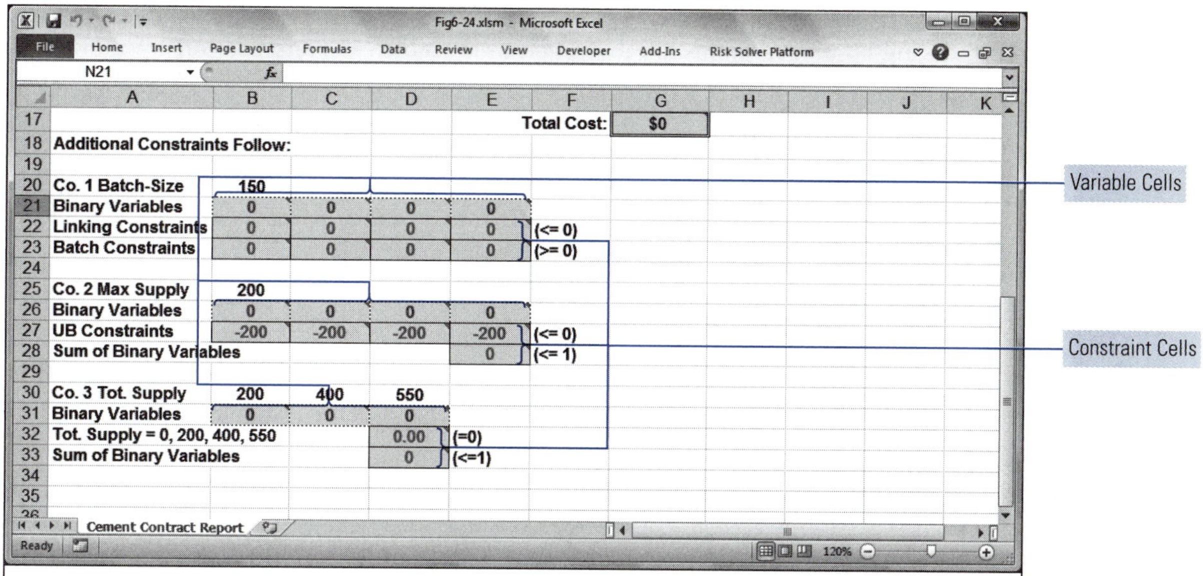

Cell	Formula	Copied to
	Key Cell Formulas	
B22	=B12-$G$12*B21	C22:E22
B23	=B12-$B$20*B21	C23:E23
B27	=B13-$B$25-($G$13-$B$25)*B26	C27:E27
E28	=SUM(B26:E26)	--
D32	=SUM(B14:E14)-SUMPRODUCT(B30:D30,B31:D31)	--
D33	=SUM(B31:D31)	--

200 tons, the sum of the binary variables for company 2 cannot exceed 1. The LHS formula for this constraint is entered in cell E28 as:

Formula for cell E28:   =SUM(B26:E26)

Cell F28 reminds us to tell Solver that this cell must be less than or equal to 1.

To implement the side constraints for company 3, the three possible total order amounts are entered in cells B30 through D30. Cells B31 through D31 are reserved to represent the binary variables Y_{31}, Y_{32}, and Y_{33}. The LHS formula for company 3's total supply side constraint is entered in cell D32 as:

Formula for cell D32:   =SUM(B14:E14)–SUMPRODUCT(B30:D30,B31:D31)

Cell E32 reminds us to tell Solver that cell D32 must equal 0. Finally, to ensure that no more than one of the binary variables for company 3 is set equal to 1, we enter the sum of these variables in cell D33 as:

Formula for cell D33:   =SUM(B31:D31)

Cell E33 reminds us to tell Solver that this cell must be less than or equal to 1.

6.16.5 SOLVING THE MODEL

The Solver parameters required for this problem in Figure 6.26. Note that all of the cells representing binary variables are identified as variable cells and are constrained to assume only integer values of 0 or 1.

FIGURE 6.26

Solver settings and options for B&G's contract award problem

Solver Settings:
Objective: G17 (Min)
Variable cells: B12:E14, B21:E21, B26:E26, B31:D31
Constraints:
B12:E14 ≥ 0
B21:E21 = binary
B26:E26 = binary
B31:D31 = binary
F12:F14 ≤ G12:G14
B15:E15 = B16:E16
B22:E22 ≤ 0
B23:E23 ≥ 0
B27:E27 ≤ 0
E28 ≤ 1
D32 = 0
D33 ≤ 1
Solver Options:
Standard LP/Quadratic Engine (Simplex LP)
Integer Tolerance = 0

6.16.6 ANALYZING THE SOLUTION

An optimal solution to this problem is shown in Figure 6.27 (there are alternate optimal solutions to this problem). In this solution, the amounts of cement required by each construction project are met exactly. Also, each condition imposed by the side constraints for each company is met. Specifically, the orders awarded to company 1 are for at least 150 tons; only one of the orders awarded to company 2 exceeds 200 tons; and the sum of the orders awarded to company 3 is exactly equal to 400 tons.

6.17 The Branch-and-Bound Algorithm (Optional)

As mentioned earlier, a special procedure, known as the branch-and-bound (B&B) algorithm is required to solve ILPs. Although we can easily indicate the presence of integer variables in a model, it usually requires quite a bit of effort on Solver's part to actually solve an ILP problem using the B&B algorithm. To better appreciate and understand what is involved in the B&B algorithm, let's consider how it works.

The B&B algorithm starts by relaxing all the integrality conditions in an ILP and solving the resulting LP problem. As noted earlier, if we are lucky, the optimal solution to

FIGURE 6.27 *Optimal solution to B&G's contract award problem*

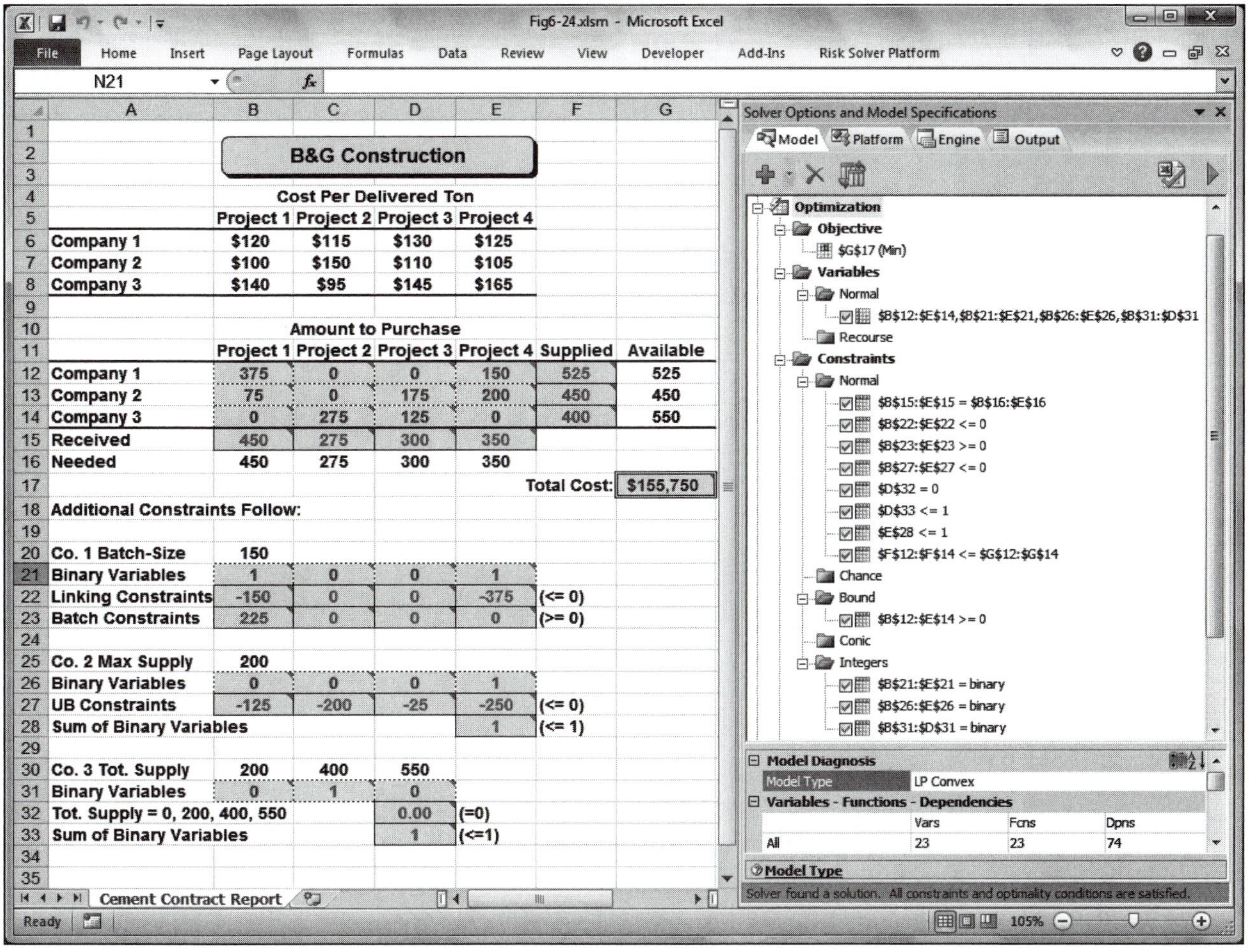

the relaxed LP problem might happen to satisfy the original integrality conditions. If this occurs, then we are done—the optimal solution to the LP relaxation is also the optimal solution to the ILP. However, it is more likely that the optimal solution to the LP will violate one or more of the original integrality conditions. For example, consider the problem whose integer and relaxed feasible regions were shown in Figure 6.1 and are repeated in Figure 6.28:

$$\text{MAX:} \qquad 2X_1 + 3X_2$$
$$\text{Subject to:} \qquad X_1 + 3X_2 \le 8.25$$
$$2.5X_1 + X_2 \le 8.75$$
$$X_1, X_2 \ge 0$$
$$X_1, X_2 \text{ must be integers}$$

If we relax the integrality conditions in this problem and solve the resulting LP problem, we obtain the solution $X_1 = 2.769$, $X_2 = 1.826$ shown in Figure 6.28. This solution clearly violates the integrality conditions stated in the original problem. Part

FIGURE 6.28

Solution to LP relaxation at noninteger corner point

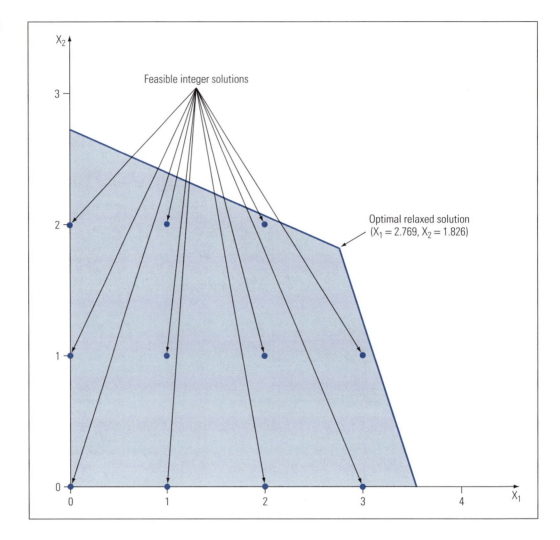

of the difficulty here is that none of the corner points of the relaxed feasible region are integer feasible (other than the origin). We know that the optimal solution to an LP problem will occur at a corner point of its feasible region but, in this case, none of those corner points (except the origin) correspond to integer solutions. Thus, we need to modify the problem so that the integer feasible solutions to the problem occur at corner points of the relaxed feasible region. This is accomplished by branching.

6.17.1 BRANCHING

Any integer variable in an ILP that assumes a fractional value in the optimal solution to the relaxed problem can be designated as a **branching variable**. For example, the variables X_1 and X_2 in the previous problem should assume only integer values but were assigned the values $X_1 = 2.769$ and $X_2 = 1.826$ in the optimal solution to the LP relaxation of the problem. Either of these variables could be selected as branching variables.

Let's arbitrarily choose X_1 as our branching variable. Because the current value of X_1 is not integer feasible, we want to eliminate this solution from further consideration. Many other solutions in this same vicinity of the relaxed feasible region can be eliminated as well. That is, X_1 must assume a value less than or equal to 2 ($X_1 \leq 2$) or greater than or equal to 3 ($X_1 \geq 3$) in the optimal integer solution to the ILP. Therefore, all other possible solutions where X_1 assumes values between 2 and 3 (such as the current solution where $X_1 = 2.769$) can be eliminated from consideration. By branching on X_1, our original ILP problem can be subdivided into the following two candidate problems:

Problem I: MAX: $2X_1 + 3X_2$
              Subject to: $X_1 + 3X_2 \leq 8.25$
                            $2.5X_1 + X_2 \leq 8.75$
                            $X_1 \leq 2$
                            $X_1, X_2 \geq 0$
                            X_1, X_2 must be integers

Problem II: MAX: $2X_1 + 3X_2$
              Subject to: $X_1 + 3X_2 \leq 8.25$
                            $2.5X_1 + X_2 \leq 8.75$
                            $X_1 \geq 3$
                            $X_1, X_2 \geq 0$
                            X_1, X_2 must be integers

The integer and relaxed feasible regions for each candidate problem are shown in Figure 6.29. Notice that a portion of the relaxed feasible region shown in Figure 6.28 has been eliminated in Figure 6.29, but none of the feasible integer solutions shown in Figure 6.28 have been eliminated. This is a general property of the branching operation in the B&B algorithm. Also notice that several feasible integer solutions now occur on the boundary lines of the feasible regions shown in Figure 6.29. More importantly, one of these feasible integer solutions occurs at an extreme point of the relaxed feasible region for Problem I (at the point $X_1 = 2$, $X_2 = 0$). If we relax the integrality conditions in Problem I and solve the resulting LP, we could obtain an integer solution because one of the corner points of the relaxed feasible region corresponds to such a point. (However, this integer feasible extreme point still might not be the optimal solution to the relaxed LP problem.)

6.17.2 BOUNDING

The next step in the B&B algorithm is to select one of the existing candidate problems for further analysis. Let's arbitrarily select Problem I. If we relax the integrality conditions in Problem I and solve the resulting LP, we obtain the solution $X_1 = 2$, $X_2 = 2.083$ and an objective function value of 10.25. This value represents an upper bound on the best possible integer solution that can be obtained from Problem I. That is, because the relaxed solution to Problem I is not integer feasible, we have not yet found the best possible integer solution for this problem. However, we do know that the objective function value of the best possible integer solution that can be obtained from Problem I can be no greater than 10.25. As you will see, this information can be useful in re-

FIGURE 6.29

*Feasible solutions
to the candidate
problems after the
first branch*

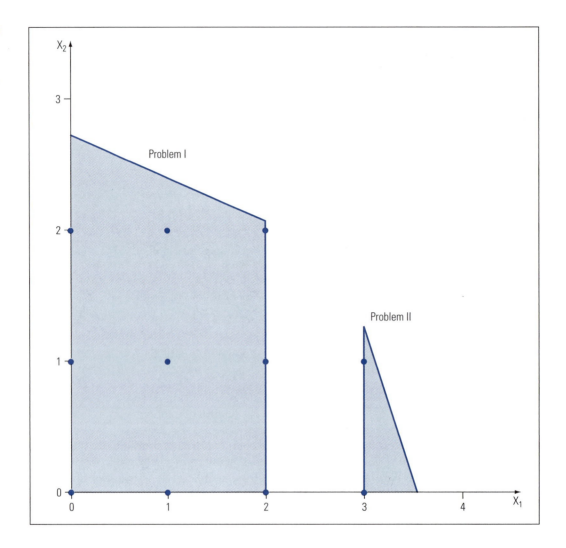

ducing the amount of work required to locate the optimal integer solution to an ILP problem.

6.17.3 BRANCHING AGAIN

Because the relaxed solution to Problem I is not entirely integer feasible, the B&B algorithm proceeds by selecting X_2 as a branching variable and creating two additional candidate problems from Problem I. These problems are represented as:

Problem III: MAX: $2X_1 + 3X_2$

Subject to: $X_1 + 3X_2 \leq 8.25$

$2.5X_1 + X_2 \leq 8.75$

$X_1 \leq 2$

$X_2 \leq 2$

$X_1, X_2 \geq 0$

X_1, X_2 must be integers

Problem IV: MAX: $2X_1 + 3X_2$
                Subject to: $X_1 + 3X_2 \leq 8.25$
                               $2.5X_1 + X_2 \leq 8.75$
                               $X_1 \leq 2$
                               $X_2 \geq 3$
                               $X_1, X_2 \geq 0$
                               X_1, X_2 must be integers

Problem III is created by adding the constraint $X_2 \leq 2$ to Problem I. Problem IV is created by adding the constraint $X_2 \geq 3$ to Problem I. Thus, our previous solution to Problem I (where $X_2 = 2.083$) will be eliminated from consideration as a possible solution to the LP relaxations of Problems III and IV.

Problem IV is infeasible because there are no feasible solutions where $X_2 \geq 3$. The integer and relaxed feasible regions for Problems II and III are summarized in Figure 6.30.

All of the corner points to the relaxed feasible region of Problem III correspond to integer feasible solutions. Thus, if we relax the integrality conditions in Problem III and

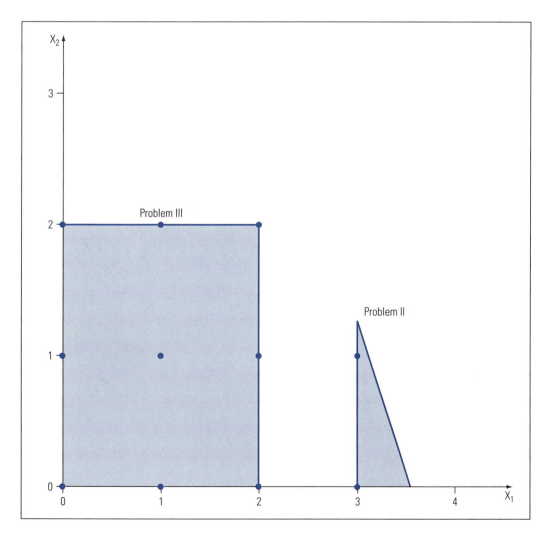

FIGURE 6.30

Feasible solutions to the candidate problems after the second branch

solve the resulting LP problem, we must obtain an integer feasible solution. The solution to Problem III is represented by $X_1 = 2$, $X_2 = 2$ and has an objective function value of 10.

6.17.4 BOUNDING AGAIN

Although we have obtained an integer feasible solution to our problem, we won't know if it is the *optimal* integer solution until we evaluate the remaining candidate problem (that is, Problem II). If we relax the integrality conditions in Problem II and solve the resulting LP problem, we obtain the solution $X_1 = 3$, $X_2 = 1.25$ with an objective function value of 9.75.

Because the solution to Problem II is not integer feasible, we might be inclined to branch on X_2 in a further attempt to determine the best possible integer solution for Problem II. However, this is not necessary. Earlier we noted that for *maximization* ILP problems, the objective function value at the optimal solution to the LP relaxation of the problem represents an *upper bound* on the optimal objective function value of the original ILP problem. This means that even though we do not yet know the optimal integer solution to Problem II, we do know that its objective function value cannot be greater than 9.75. And because 9.75 is worse than the objective function value for the integer solution obtained from Problem III, we cannot find a better integer solution by continuing to branch Problem II. Therefore, Problem II can be eliminated from further consideration. Because we have no more candidate problems to consider, we can conclude that the optimal integer solution to our problem is $X_1 = 2$, $X_2 = 2$ with an optimal objective function value of 10.

6.17. 5 SUMMARY OF B&B EXAMPLE

The steps involved in the solution to our example problem can be represented graphically in the form of a *branch-and-bound tree*, as shown in Figure 6.31. Although

FIGURE 6.31

Branch-and-bound tree for the example problem

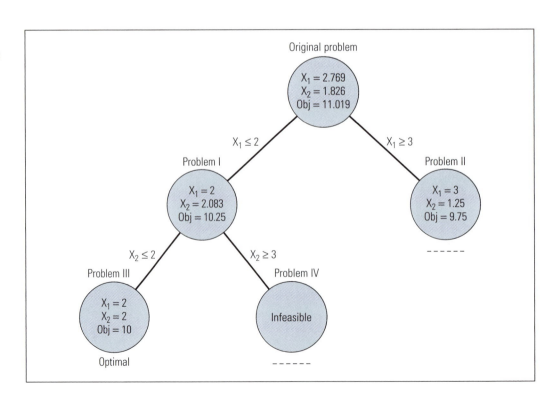

Figure 6.28 indicates that 11 integer solutions exist for this problem, we do not have to locate all of them in order to prove that the integer solution we found is the optimal solution. The bounding operation of the B&B algorithm eliminated the need to explicitly enumerate all the integer feasible solutions and select the best of those as the optimal solution.

If the relaxed solution to Problem II was greater than 10 (say 12.5), then the B&B algorithm would have continued branching from this problem in an attempt to find a better integer solution (an integer solution with an objective function value greater than 10). Similarly, if Problem IV had a feasible noninteger solution, we would have needed to perform further branching from that problem if its relaxed objective value was better than that of the best known integer feasible solution. Thus, the first integer solution obtained using B&B will not always be the optimal integer solution. A more detailed description of the operations of the B&B algorithm is given in Figure 6.32.

FIGURE 6.32

Detailed description of the B&B algorithm for solving ILP problems

THE BRANCH-AND-BOUND ALGORITHM

1. Relax all the integrality conditions in ILP and solve the resulting LP problem. If the optimal solution to the relaxed LP problem happens to satisfy the original integrality conditions, stop—this is the optimal integer solution. Otherwise, proceed to step 2.
2. If the problem being solved is a maximization problem let $Z_{best} = -$infinity. If it is a minimization problem, let $Z_{best} = +$infinity. (In general Z_{best} represents the objective function value of the best known integer solution as the algorithm proceeds.)
3. Let X_j represent one of the variables that violated the integrality conditions in the solution to the problem that was solved most recently and let b_j represent its noninteger value. Let INT(b_j) represent the largest integer that is less than b_j. Create two new candidate problems: one by appending the constraint $X_j \leq$ INT(b_j) to the most recently solved LP problem, and the other by appending the constraint $X_j \geq$ INT(b_j) + 1 to the most recently solved LP problem. Place both of these new LP problems in a list of candidate problems to be solved.
4. If the list of candidate problems is empty, proceed to step 9. Otherwise, remove a candidate problem from the list, relax any integrality conditions in the problem, and solve it.
5. If there is not a solution to the current candidate problem (that is, it is infeasible), proceed to step 4. Otherwise, let Z_{cp} denote the optimal objective function value for the current candidate problem.
6. If Z_{cp} is not better than Z_{best} (for a maximization problem $Z_{cp} \leq Z_{best}$ or for a minimization problem $Z_{cp} \geq Z_{best}$), proceed to step 4.
7. If the solution to the current candidate problem *does not* satisfy the original integrality conditions, proceed to step 3.
8. If the solution to the current candidate problem *does* satisfy the original integrality conditions, a better integer solution has been found. Thus, let $Z_{best} = Z_{cp}$ and save the solution obtained for this candidate problem. Then go back to step 4.
9. Stop. The optimal solution has been found and has an objective function value given by the current value of Z_{best}.

6.18 Summary

This chapter discussed the issues involved in formulating and solving ILP problems. In some cases, acceptable integer solutions to ILP problems can be obtained by rounding the solution to the LP relaxation of the problem. However, this procedure can lead to suboptimal solutions, which might still be viable if you can show that the solution obtained by rounding is within an acceptable distance from the optimal integer solution. This approach might be the only practical way to obtain integer solutions for some ILP problems.

The B&B algorithm is a powerful technique for solving ILP problems. A great deal of skill and creativity are involved in formulating ILPs so that they can be solved efficiently using the B&B technique. Binary variables can be useful in overcoming a number of the simplifying assumptions often made in the formulation of LP models. Here again, quite a bit of creativity might be required on the part of the model builder to identify the constraints to implement various logical conditions in a given problem.

6.19 References

Bean, J., et al. "Selecting Tenants in a Shopping Mall. *Interfaces*, vol. 18, no. 2, 1988.

Blake, J., and J. Donald. "Mount Sinai Hospital Uses Integer Programming to Allocate Operating Room Time." *Interfaces*, vol. 32, no. 2, 2002.

Calloway, R., M. Cummins, and J. Freeland. "Solving Spreadsheet-Based Integer Programming Models: An Example From the Telecommunications Industry." *Decision Sciences*, vol. 21, 1990.

Nauss, R., and R. Markland. "Theory and Application of an Optimizing Procedure for the Lock Box Location Analysis." *Management Science*, vol. 27, no. 8, 1981.

Nemhauser, G., and L. Wolsey. *Integer and Combinatorial Optimization*. New York: Wiley, 1988.

Peiser, R., and S. Andrus. "Phasing of Income-Producing Real Estate." *Interfaces*, vol. 13, no. 1, 1983.

Schindler, S., and T. Semmel, "Station Staffing at Pan American World Airways." *Interfaces*, vol. 23, no. 3, 1993.

Stowe, J. "An Integer Programming Solution for the Optimal Credit Investigation/Credit Granting Sequence." *Financial Management*, vol. 14, Summer 1985.

Tavakoli, A., and C. Lightner. "Implementing a Mathematical Model for Locating EMS Vehicles in Fayetteville, NC." *Computers & Operations Research*, vol 31, 2004.

THE WORLD OF MANAGEMENT SCIENCE

Who Eats the Float?—Maryland National Improves Check Clearing Operations and Cuts Costs

Maryland National Bank (MNB) of Baltimore typically processes about 500,000 checks worth over $250,000,000 each day. Those checks not drawn on MNB or a local bank must be cleared via the Federal Reserve System, a private clearing bank, or a "direct send" by courier service to the bank on which they were drawn.

Because funds are not available until the check clears, banks try to maximize the availability of current funds by reducing the float—the time interval required for a check to clear. Banks publish an availability schedule listing the number of days before funds from a deposited check are available to the customer. If clearing time is longer than the schedule, the bank must "eat the float." If the check is cleared through the Federal Reserve, and clearing takes longer than the Federal Reserve availability schedule, then the Federal Reserve "eats the float." If clearing time is

(Continued)

actually less than the local bank's availability schedule, the customer "eats the float." The cost of float is related to the daily cost of capital.

MNB uses a system based on binary integer LP to decide the timing and method to be used for each bundle of checks of a certain type (called a cash letter). Total clearing costs (the objective function) include float costs, clearing charges from the Federal Reserve or private clearing banks, and transportation costs for direct sends. Constraints ensure that exactly one method is chosen for each check type and that a method can be used only at a time that method is available. Use of this system saves the bank $100,000 annually.

Source: Markland, Robert E., and Robert M. Nauss, "Improving Transit Check Clearing Operations at Maryland National Bank," *Interfaces*, vol. 13, no. 1, February 1983, pp. 1–9.

Questions and Problems

1. As shown in Figure 6.1, the feasible region for an ILP consists of a relatively small, *finite* number of points, whereas the feasible region of its LP relaxation consists of an *infinite* number of points. Why, then, are ILPs so much harder to solve than LPs?
2. Identify reasonable values for M_{12} and M_{22} in the example on quantity discounts presented in Section 6.15.2 of this chapter.
3. The following questions refer to the CRT Technologies project selection example presented in this chapter. Formulate a constraint to implement the conditions described in each of the following statements.
   a. Out of projects 1, 2, 4, and 6, CRT's management wants to select exactly two projects.
   b. Project 2 can be selected only if project 3 is selected and vice versa.
   c. Project 5 cannot be undertaken unless both projects 3 and 4 are also undertaken.
   d. If projects 2 and 4 are undertaken, then project 5 must also be undertaken.
4. In the CRT Technologies project selection example in this chapter, the problem indicates that surplus funds in any year are reappropriated and cannot be carried over to the next year. Suppose this is no longer the case, and surplus funds may be carried over to future years.
   a. Modify the spreadsheet model given for this problem to reflect this change in assumptions.
   b. What is the optimal solution to the revised problem?
5. The following questions refers to the Blue Ridge Hot Tubs example discussed in this chapter.
   a. Suppose Howie Jones has to purchase a single piece of equipment for $1,000 in order to produce any Aqua-Spas or Hydro-Luxes. How will this affect the formulation of the model of his decision problem?
   b. Suppose Howie must buy one piece of equipment that costs $900 in order to produce any Aqua-Spas and a different piece of equipment that costs $800 in order to produce any Hydro-Luxes. How will this affect the formulation of the model for his problem?
6. Eric Brown is responsible for upgrading the wireless network for his employer. He has identified seven possible locations to install new nodes for the network. Each node can provide service to different regions within the corporate campus. The cost of installing each node and the regions that can be served by each node are summarized here:

Node 1: Regions 1, 2, 5; Cost: $700
Node 2: Regions 3, 6, 7; Cost $600

Node 3: Regions 2, 3, 7, 9; Cost $900
Node 4: Regions 1, 3, 6, 10; Cost $1,250
Node 5: Regions 2, 4, 6, 8; Cost $850
Node 6: Regions 4, 5, 8, 10; Cost $1,000
Node 7: Regions 1, 5, 7, 8, 9; Cost $1,100

a. Formulate an ILP for this problem.
b. Implement your model in a spreadsheet and solve it.
c. What is the optimal solution?

7. Garden City Beach is a popular summer vacation destination for thousands of people. Each summer, the city hires temporary lifeguards to ensure the safety of the vacationing public. Garden City's lifeguards are assigned to work five consecutive days each week and then have two days off. However, the city's insurance company requires them to have at least the following number of lifeguards on duty each day of the week:

	Minimum Number of Lifeguards Required Each Day						
	Sunday	**Monday**	**Tuesday**	**Wednesday**	**Thursday**	**Friday**	**Saturday**
Lifeguards	18	17	16	16	16	14	19

The city manager would like to determine the minimum number of lifeguards that will have to be hired.

a. Formulate an ILP for this problem.
b. Implement your model in a spreadsheet and solve it.
c. What is the optimal solution?
d. Several lifeguards have expressed a preference to be off on Saturdays and Sundays. What is the maximum number of lifeguards that can be off on the weekend without increasing the total number of life guards required?

8. Snookers Restaurant is open from 8:00 am to 10:00 pm daily. Besides the hours they are open for business, workers are needed an hour before opening and an hour after closing for setup and cleanup activities. The restaurant operates with both full-time and part-time workers on the following shifts:

Shift	Daily Pay Rate
7:00 am–11:00 am	$32
7:00 am– 3:00 pm	$80
11:00 am– 3:00 pm	$32
11:00 am– 7:00 pm	$80
3:00 pm– 7:00 pm	$32
3:00 pm–11:00 pm	$80
7:00 pm–11:00 pm	$32

The following numbers of workers are needed during each of the indicated time blocks.

Hours	Workers Needed
7:00 am–11:00 am	11
11:00 am– 1:00 pm	24
1:00 pm– 3:00 pm	16
3:00 pm– 5:00 pm	10
5:00 pm– 7:00 pm	22
7:00 pm– 9:00 pm	17
9:00 pm–11:00 pm	6

At least one full-time worker must be available during the hour before opening and after closing. Additionally, at least 30% of the employees should be full-time (8-hour) workers during the restaurant's busy periods from 11:00 am − 1:00 pm and 5:00 pm − 7:00 pm.

a. Formulate an ILP for this problem with the objective of minimizing total daily labor costs.

b. Implement your model in a spreadsheet and solve it.

c. What is the optimal solution?

9. A power company is considering how to increase its generating capacity to meet expected demand in its growing service area. Currently, the company has 750 megawatts (MW) of generating capacity but projects it will need the following minimum generating capacities in each of the next five years:

	Year				
	1	2	3	4	5
Minimum Capacity in Megawatts (MW)	780	860	950	1,060	1,180

The company can increase its generating capacity by purchasing four different types of generators: 10 MW, 25 MW, 50 MW, and/or 100 MW. The cost of acquiring and installing each of the four types of generators in each of the next five years is summarized in the following table:

	Cost of Generator (in $1,000s) in Year				
Generator Size	**1**	**2**	**3**	**4**	**5**
10 MW	$300	$250	$200	$170	$145
25 MW	$460	$375	$350	$280	$235
50 MW	$670	$558	$465	$380	$320
100 MW	$950	$790	$670	$550	$460

a. Formulate a mathematical programming model to determine the least costly way of expanding the company's generating assets to the minimum required levels.

b. Implement your model in a spreadsheet and solve it.

c. What is the optimal solution?

10. Health Care Systems of Florida (HCSF) is planning to build a number of new emergency-care clinics in central Florida. HCSF management has divided a map of the area into seven regions. They want to locate the emergency centers so that all seven regions will be conveniently served by at least one facility. Five possible sites are available for constructing the new facilities. The regions that can be served conveniently by each site are indicated by an X in the following table:

	Possible Building Sites				
Region	**Sanford**	**Altamonte**	**Apopka**	**Casselberry**	**Maitland**
1	X		X		
2	X	X		X	X
3		X		X	
4			X		X
5	X	X			
6			X		X
7				X	X
Cost ($1,000s)	$450	$650	$550	$500	$525

   a. Formulate an ILP problem to determine which sites should be selected in order to provide convenient service to all locations in the least costly manner.

   b. Implement your model in a spreadsheet and solve it.

   c. What is the optimal solution?

11. Kentwood Electronics manufactures three components for stereo systems: CD players, tape decks, and stereo tuners. The wholesale price and manufacturing cost of each item are given in the following table:

Component	Wholesale Price	Manufacturing Cost
CD Player	$150	$75
Tape Deck	$ 85	$35
Stereo Tuner	$ 70	$30

Each CD player produced requires three hours of assembly; each tape deck requires two hours of assembly; and each tuner requires one hour of assembly. However, the company manufactures these products only in batches of 150—partial batches are not allowed. The marketing department believes it can sell no more than 150,000 CD players, 100,000 tape decks, and 90,000 stereo tuners. It expects a demand for at least 50,000 units of each item and wants to be able to meet this demand. If Kentwood has 400,000 hours of assembly time available, how many batches of CD players, tape decks, and stereo tuners should it produce in order to maximize profits while meeting the minimum demand figures supplied by marketing?

   a. Formulate an ILP model for this problem. (Hint: Let your decision variables represent the number of batches of each item to produce.)

   b. Create a spreadsheet model for this problem and solve it.

   c. What is the optimal solution?

12. Radford Castings can produce brake shoes on six different machines. The following table summarizes the manufacturing costs associated with producing the brake shoes on each machine along with the available capacity on each machine. If the company has received an order for 1,800 brake shoes, how should it schedule these machines?

Machine	Fixed Cost	Variable Cost	Capacity
1	$1,000	$21	500
2	$ 950	$23	600
3	$ 875	$25	750
4	$ 850	$24	400
5	$ 800	$20	600
6	$ 700	$26	800

   a. Formulate an ILP model for this problem.

   b. Create a spreadsheet model for this problem and solve it.

   c. What is the optimal solution?

13. The teenage daughter of a recently deceased movie star inherited a number of items from her famous father's estate. Rather than convert these assets to cash immediately, her financial advisor has recommended that she let some of these assets appreciate in value before disposing of them. An appraiser has given the following estimates of the assets' worth (in $1,000s) for each of the next five years.

	Year 1	Year 2	Year 3	Year 4	Year 5
Car	$ 35	$ 37	$ 39	$ 42	$ 45
Piano	$ 16	$ 17	$ 18	$ 19	$ 20

Necklace	$125	$130	$136	$139	$144
Desk	$ 25	$ 27	$ 29	$ 30	$ 33
Golf Clubs	$ 40	$ 43	$ 46	$ 50	$ 52
Humidor	$ 5	$ 7	$ 8	$ 10	$ 11

Knowing this teenager's propensity to spend money, her financial advisor would like to develop a plan to dispose of these assets that will maximize the amount of money received and ensure that at least $30,000 of new funds become available each year to pay her college tuition.

a. Formulate an ILP model for this problem.
b. Create a spreadsheet model for this problem and solve it.
c. What is the optimal solution?

14. A developer of video game software has seven proposals for new games. Unfortunately, the company cannot develop all the proposals because its budget for new projects is limited to $950,000, and it has only 20 programmers to assign to new projects. The financial requirements, returns, and the number of programmers required by each project are summarized in the following table. Projects 2 and 6 require specialized programming knowledge that only one of the programmers has. Both of these projects cannot be selected because the programmer with the necessary skills can be assigned to only one of the projects. (Note: All dollar amounts represent thousands.)

Project	Programmers Required	Capital Required	Estimated NPV
1	7	$250	$650
2	6	$175	$550
3	9	$300	$600
4	5	$150	$450
5	6	$145	$375
6	4	$160	$525
7	8	$325	$750

a. Formulate an ILP model for this problem.
b. Create a spreadsheet model for this problem and solve it.
c. What is the optimal solution?

15. Tropicsun is a leading grower and distributor of fresh citrus products with three large citrus groves scattered around central Florida in the cities of Mt. Dora, Eustis, and Clermont. Tropicsun currently has 275,000 bushels of citrus at the grove in Mt. Dora, 400,000 bushels at the grove in Eustis, and 300,000 at the grove in Clermont. Tropicsun has citrus processing plants in Ocala, Orlando, and Leesburg with processing capacities to handle 200,000, 600,000, and 225,000 bushels, respectively. Tropicsun contracts with a local trucking company to transport its fruit from the groves to the processing plants. The trucking company charges a flat rate of $8 per mile regardless of how many bushels of fruit are transported. The following table summarizes the distances (in miles) between each grove and processing plant:

Distances (in Miles) Between Groves and Plants

	Processing Plant		
Grove	Ocala	Orlando	Leesburg
Mt. Dora	21	50	40
Eustis	35	30	22
Clermont	55	20	25

Tropicsun wants to determine how many bushels to ship from each grove to each processing plant in order to minimize the total transportation cost.

a. Formulate an ILP model for this problem.
b. Create a spreadsheet model for this problem and solve it.
c. What is the optimal solution?

16. A real estate developer is planning to build an apartment building specifically for graduate students on a parcel of land adjacent to a major university. Four types of apartments can be included in the building: efficiencies, and one-, two-, or three-bedroom units. Each efficiency requires 500 square feet; each one-bedroom apartment requires 700 square feet; each two-bedroom apartment requires 800 square feet; and each three-bedroom unit requires 1,000 square feet. The developer believes that the building should include no more than 15 one-bedroom units, 22 two-bedroom units, and 10 three-bedroom units. Local zoning ordinances do not allow the developer to build more than 40 units in this particular building location and restrict the building to a maximum of 40,000 square feet. The developer has already agreed to lease 5 one-bedroom units and 8 two-bedroom units to a local rental agency that is a "silent partner" in this endeavor. Market studies indicate that efficiencies can be rented for $350 per month, one-bedrooms for $450 per month, two-bedrooms for $550 per month, and three-bedrooms for $750 per month. How many rental units of each type should the developer include in the building plans in order to maximize the potential rental income from the building?

a. Formulate an LP model for this problem.
b. Create a spreadsheet model for this problem and solve it using Solver.
c. What is the optimal solution?
d. Which constraint in this model limits the builder's potential rental income from increasing any further?

17. Bellows Lumber Yard, Inc. stocks standard length, 25-foot boards, which it cuts to custom lengths to fill individual customer orders. An order has just come in for 5,000 7-foot boards, 1,200 9-foot boards, and 300 11-foot boards. The lumber yard manager has identified six ways to cut the 25-foot boards to fill this order. The six cutting patterns are summarized in the following table.

	Number of Boards Produced		
Cutting Pattern	7 ft	9 ft	11 ft
1	3	0	0
2	2	1	0
3	2	0	1
4	1	2	0
5	0	1	1
6	0	0	2

One possibility (cutting pattern 1) is to cut a 25-foot board into three 7-foot boards, and not to cut any 9- or 11-foot boards. Note that cutting pattern 1 uses a total of 21 feet of board and leaves a 4-foot piece of scrap. Another possibility (cutting pattern 4) is to cut a 25-foot board into one 7-foot board and two 9-foot boards (using all 25 feet of the board). The remaining cutting patterns have similar interpretations. The lumber yard manager wants to fill this order using the fewest number of 25-foot boards as possible. To do this, the manager needs to determine how many 25-foot boards to run through each cutting pattern.

a. Formulate an LP model for this problem.
b. Create a spreadsheet model for this problem and solve it using Solver.

c. What is the optimal solution?

d. Suppose the manager wants to minimize waste. Would the solution change?

18. Howie's Carpet World has just received an order for carpets for a new office building. The order is for 4,000 yards of carpet 4-feet wide, 20,000 yards of carpet 9-feet wide, and 9,000 yards of carpet 12-feet wide. Howie can order two kinds of carpet rolls, which he will then have to cut to fill this order. One type of roll is 14-feet wide, 100-yards long, and costs $1,000 per roll; the other is 18-feet wide, 100-yards long, and costs $1,400 per roll. Howie needs to determine how many of the two types of carpet rolls to order and how they should be cut. He wants to do this in the least costly way possible.

a. Formulate an LP model for this problem.

b. Create a spreadsheet model for this problem and solve it using Solver.

c. What is the optimal solution?

d. Suppose Howie wants to minimize waste. Would the solution change?

19. A manufacturer is considering alternatives for building new plants in order to be located closer to three of its primary customers with whom it intends to develop long-term, sole-supplier relationships. The net cost of manufacturing and transporting each unit of the product to its customers will vary depending on where the plant is built and the production capacity of the plant. These costs are summarized in the following table:

| | Net Cost per Unit to Supply Customer | | |
Plant	X	Y	Z
1	35	30	45
2	45	40	50
3	70	65	50
4	20	45	25
5	65	45	45

The annual demand for products from customers X, Y, and Z is expected to be 40,000, 25,000, and 35,000 units, respectively. The annual production capacity and construction costs for each plant are given in the following table:

Plant	Production Capacity	Construction Cost (in $1,000s)
1	40,000	$1,325
2	30,000	$1,100
3	50,000	$1,500
4	20,000	$1,200
5	40,000	$1,400

The company wants to determine which plant to build in order to satisfy customer demand at a minimum total cost.

a. Formulate an ILP model for this problem.

b. Create a spreadsheet model for this problem and solve it.

c. What is the optimal solution?

20. Refer to the previous question. Suppose plants 1 and 2 represent different building alternatives for the same site (that is, only one of these plants can be built). Similarly, suppose plants 4 and 5 represent different building alternatives for another site.

a. What additional constraints are required to model these new conditions?

b. Revise the spreadsheet to reflect these additional constraints and solve the resulting problem.

c. What is the optimal solution?

21. A company manufactures three products: A, B, and C. The company currently has an order for 3 units of product A, 7 units of product B, and 4 units of product C. There is no inventory for any of these products. All three products require special processing that can be done on one of two machines. The cost of producing each product on each machine is summarized in the following table:

Cost of Producing a Unit of Product

Machine	A	B	C
1	$13	$ 9	$10
2	$11	$12	$ 8

The time required to produce each product on each machine is summarized in the following table:

Time (Hours) Needed to Produce a Unit of Product

Machine	A	B	C
1	0.4	1.1	0.9
2	0.5	1.2	1.3

Assume machine 1 can be used for eight hours and machine 2 can be used for six hours. Each machine must undergo a special setup operation to prepare it to produce each product. After completing this setup for a product, any number of that product type can be produced. The setup costs for producing each product on each machine are summarized in the following table:

Setup Costs for Producing

Machine	A	B	C
1	$55	$93	$60
2	$65	$58	$75

   a. Formulate an ILP model to determine how many units of each product to produce on each machine in order to meet demand at a minimum cost.
   b. Implement your model in a spreadsheet and solve it.
   c. What is the optimal solution?
22. Clampett Oil purchases crude oil products from suppliers in Texas (TX), Oklahoma (OK), Pennsylvania (PA), and Alabama (AL), from which it refines four end-products: gasoline, kerosene, heating oil, and asphalt. Because of differences in the quality and chemical characteristics of the oil from the different suppliers, the amount of each end-product that can be refined from a barrel of crude oil varies depending on the source of the crude. Additionally, the amount of crude available from each source varies, as does the cost of a barrel of crude from each supplier. These values are summarized in the following table. For example, the first line of this table indicates that a barrel of crude oil from Texas can be refined into 2 barrels of gasoline, 2.8 barrels of kerosene, 1.7 barrels of heating oil, or 2.4 barrels of asphalt. Each supplier requires a minimum purchase of at least 500 barrels.

Raw Material Characteristics

Crude Oils	Barrels Available	Possible Production Per Barrel				Cost Per Barrel	Trucking Cost
		Gas	Kero.	Heat	Asphalt		
TX	1,500	2.00	2.80	1.70	2.40	$22	$1,500
OK	2,000	1.80	2.30	1.75	1.90	$21	$1,700
PA	1,500	2.30	2.20	1.60	2.60	$22	$1,500
AL	1,800	2.10	2.60	1.90	2.40	$23	$1,400

The company owns a tanker truck that picks up whatever crude oil it purchases. This truck can hold 2,000 barrels of crude. The cost of sending the truck to pick up oil from the various locations is shown in the column labeled "Trucking Cost." The company's plans for its next production cycle specify 750 barrels of gasoline, 800 barrels of kerosene, 1,000 barrels of heating oil, and 300 barrels of asphalt to be produced.

a. Formulate an ILP model that can be solved to determine the purchasing plan that will allow the company to implement its production plan at the least cost.

b. Implement this model in a spreadsheet and solve it.

c. What is the optimal solution?

23. The Clampett Oil Company has a tanker truck that it uses to deliver fuel to customers. The tanker has five different storage compartments with capacities to hold 2,500, 2,000, 1,500, 1,800 and 2,300 gallons, respectively. The company has an order to deliver 2,700 gallons of diesel fuel; 3,500 gallons of regular unleaded gasoline; and 4,200 gallons of premium unleaded gasoline. If each storage compartment can hold only one type of fuel, how should Clampett Oil load the tanker? If it is impossible to load the truck with the full order, the company wants to minimize the total number of gallons by which the order is short. (*Hint*: Consider using slack variables to represent shortage amounts.)

a. Formulate an ILP model for this problem.

b. Implement this model in a spreadsheet and solve it.

c. What is the optimal solution?

24. Dan Boyd is a financial planner trying to determine how to invest $100,000 for one of his clients. The cash flows for the five investments under consideration are summarized in the following table:

Summary of Cash In-Flows and Out-Flows
(at Beginning of Year)

	A	B	C	D	E
Year 1	−1.00	0.00	−1.00	0.00	−1.00
Year 2	+0.45	−1.00	0.00	0.00	0.00
Year 3	+1.05	0.00	0.00	−1.00	1.25
Year 4	0.00	+1.30	+1.65	+1.30	0.00

For example, if Dan invests $1 in investment A at the beginning of year 1, he will receive $0.45 at the beginning of year 2 and another $1.05 at the beginning of year 3. Alternatively, he can invest $1 in investment B at the beginning of year 2 and receive $1.30 at the beginning of year 4. Entries of "0.00" in the preceding table indicate times when no cash in-flows or out-flows can occur. The minimum required investment for each of the possible investments is $50,000. Also, at the beginning of each year, Dan may also place any or all of the available money in a money market account that is expected to yield 5% per year. How should Dan plan his investments if he wants to maximize the amount of money available to his client at the end of year 4?

a. Formulate an ILP model for this problem.

b. Create a spreadsheet model for this problem and solve it using Solver.

c. What is the optimal solution?

25. The Mega-Bucks Corporation is planning its production schedule for the next four weeks and is forecasting the following demand for compound X—a key raw material used in its production process:

Forecasted Demand of Compound X

Week	1	2	3	4
Demand	400 lbs	150 lbs	200 lbs	350 lbs

The company currently has no compound X on hand. The supplier of this product delivers only in batch sizes that are multiples of 100 pounds (0, 100, 200, 300, and so on). The price of this material is $125 per 100 pounds. Deliveries can be arranged weekly, but there is a delivery charge of $50. Mega-Bucks estimates that it costs $15 for each 100 pounds of compound X held in inventory from one week to the next. Assuming Mega-Bucks does not want more than 50 pounds of compound X in inventory at the end of week 4, how much should it order each week so that the demand for this product will be met in the least costly manner?

a. Formulate an ILP model for this problem.

b. Create a spreadsheet model for this problem and solve it using Solver.

c. What is the optimal solution?

26. An automobile manufacturer is considering mechanical design changes in one of its top-selling cars to reduce the weight of the car by at least 400 pounds to improve its fuel efficiency. Design engineers have identified 10 changes that could be made in the car to make it lighter (for example, using composite body pieces rather than metal). The weight saved by each design change and the estimated costs of implementing each change are summarized in the following table:

	Design Change									
	1	**2**	**3**	**4**	**5**	**6**	**7**	**8**	**9**	**10**
Weight Saved (lbs)	50	75	25	150	60	95	200	40	80	30
Cost (in $1,000s)	$150	$350	$50	$450	$90	$35	$650	$75	$110	$30

Changes 4 and 7 represent alternate ways of modifying the engine block and, therefore, only one of these options could be selected. The company wants to determine which changes to make in order to reduce the total weight of the car by at least 400 pounds in the least costly manner.

a. Formulate an ILP model for this problem.

b. Create a spreadsheet model for this problem and solve it.

c. What is the optimal solution?

27. Darten Restaurants owns and operates several different restaurant chains, including Red Snapper and the Olive Grove. The company is considering opening a number of new units in Ohio. There are 10 different sites available for the company to build new restaurants, and the company can build either type of restaurant at a given site. The following table summarizes the estimated NPV of the cash flows (in millions) resulting from locating each type of restaurant at each of the sites and also indicates which sites are within 15 miles of each other.

Site	Red Snapper NPV	Olive Grove NPV	Other Sites within 15 Miles
1	$11.8	$16.2	2, 3, 4
2	13.3	13.8	1, 3, 5
3	19.0	14.6	1, 2, 4, 5
4	17.8	12.4	1, 3
5	10.0	13.7	2, 3, 9
6	16.1	19.0	7
7	13.3	10.8	6, 8
8	18.8	15.2	7
9	17.2	15.9	5, 10
10	14.4	16.8	9

a. Suppose the company does not want to build two units from the same chain within 15 miles of each other (for example, it does not want to build two Red Snappers within 15 miles of each other nor is it willing to build two Olive Groves within 15 miles of each other). Create a spreadsheet model to determine which (if any) restaurant it should build at each site in order to maximize total NPV.

b. What is the optimal solution?

c. Now additionally suppose the company does not want to build a Red Snapper unless it also builds an Olive Grove at another site within 15 miles. Modify your spreadsheet model to determine which (if any) restaurant it should build at each site in order to maximize total NPV.

d. What is the optimal solution?

28. Paul Bergey is in charge of loading cargo ships for International Cargo Company (ICC) at the port in Newport News, Virginia. Paul is preparing a loading plan for an ICC freighter destined for Ghana. An agricultural commodities dealer would like to transport the following products aboard this ship:

Commodity	Amount Available (tons)	Volume per Ton (cubic feet)	Profit per Ton ($)
1	4,800	40	70
2	2,500	25	50
3	1,200	60	60
4	1,700	55	80

Paul can elect to load any and/or all of the available commodities. However, the ship has three cargo holds with the following capacity restrictions:

Cargo Hold	Weight Capacity (tons)	Volume Capacity (cubic feet)
Forward	3,000	145,000
Center	6,000	180,000
Rear	4,000	155,000

Only one type of commodity can be placed into any cargo hold. However, because of balance considerations, the weight in the forward cargo hold must be within 10% of the weight in the rear cargo hold, and the center cargo hold must be between 40% and 60% of the total weight on board.

a. Formulate an ILP model for this problem.

b. Create a spreadsheet model for this problem and solve it using Solver.

c. What is the optimal solution?

29. KPS Communications is planning to bring wireless Internet access to the town of Ames, Iowa. Using a geographic information system, KPS has divided Ames into the following 5 by 5 grid. The values in each block of the grid indicate the expected annual revenue (in $1,000s) KPS will receive if wireless Internet service is provided to the geographic area represented by each block.

Expected Annual Revenue by Area (in $1,000s)

$34	$43	$62	$42	$34
$64	$43	$71	$48	$65
$57	$57	$51	$61	$30
$32	$38	$70	$56	$40
$68	$73	$30	$56	$44

KPS can build wireless towers in any block in the grid at a cost of $150,000 per tower. Each tower can provide wireless service to the block it is in and to all adjacent blocks. (Blocks are considered to be adjacent if they share a side. Blocks touching only at corner points are not considered adjacent.) KPS would like to determine how many towers to build and where to build them in order to maximize profits in the first year of operations. (Note: If a block can receive wireless service from two different towers, the revenue for that block should only be counted once.)

a. Create a spreadsheet model for this problem and solve it.
b. What is the optimal solution and how much money will KPS make in the first year?
c. Suppose KPS is required to provide wireless service to all of the blocks. What is the optimal solution, and how much money will KPS make in the first year?

30. The emergency services coordinator for Clarke County is interested in locating the county's two ambulances to maximize the number of residents that can be reached within four minutes in emergency situations. The county is divided into five regions, and the average times required to travel from one region to the next are summarized in the following table:

	To Region				
From Region	1	2	3	4	5
1	0	4	6	3	2
2	4	0	2	3	6
3	6	2	0	5	3
4	3	3	5	0	7
5	2	6	3	7	0

The population in regions 1, 2, 3, 4, and 5 are estimated as 45,000, 65,000, 28,000, 52,000, and 43,000, respectively. In which two regions should the ambulances be placed?

a. Formulate an ILP model for this problem.
b. Implement your model in a spreadsheet and solve it.
c. What is the optimal solution?

31. Ken Stark is an operations analyst for an insurance company in Muncie, Indiana. Over the next 6 weeks, the company needs to send 2,028,415 pieces of marketing literature to customers in the following 16 states:

State	Mailing Pieces
AZ	82,380
CA	212,954
CT	63,796
GA	136,562
IL	296,479
MA	99,070
ME	38,848
MN	86,207
MT	33,309
NC	170,997
NJ	104,974
NV	29,608
OH	260,858
OR	63,605
TX	214,076
VA	134,692
TOTAL	**2,028,415**

In order to coordinate with other marketing efforts, all the mailings for a given state must go out the same week (that is, if Ken decides to schedule mailings for Georgia in week 2, then all of the 136,562 pieces of mail for Georgia must be sent that week). Ken would like to balance the workload in each week as much as possible and, in particular, would like to minimize the maximum amount of mail to be processed in any given week during the 6-week period.

a. Create a spreadsheet model to determine which states should be processed each week in order to achieve Ken's objective.

b. What is the optimal solution?

32. The CoolAire Company manufactures air conditioners that are sold to five different retail customers across the United States. The company is evaluating its manufacturing and logistics strategy to ensure that it is operating in the most efficient manner possible. The company can produce air conditioners at six plants across the country and stock these units in any of four different warehouses. The cost of manufacturing and shipping a unit between each plant and warehouse is summarized in the following table along with the monthly capacity and fixed cost of operating each plant:

	Warehouse 1	Warehouse 2	Warehouse 3	Warehouse 4	Fixed Cost	Capacity
Plant 1	$700	$1,000	$900	$1,200	$55,000	300
Plant 2	$800	$ 500	$600	$ 700	$40,000	200
Plant 3	$850	$ 600	$700	$ 500	$45,000	300
Plant 4	$600	$ 800	$500	$ 600	$50,000	250
Plant 5	$500	$ 600	$450	$ 700	$42,000	350
Plant 6	$700	$ 600	$750	$ 500	$40,000	400

Similarly, the per-unit cost of shipping units from each warehouse to each customer is given in the following table, along with the monthly fixed cost of operating each warehouse:

	Customer 1	Customer 2	Customer 3	Customer 4	Customer 5	Fixed Cost
Warehouse 1	$40	$80	$60	$90	$50	$40,000
Warehouse 2	$60	$50	$75	$40	$35	$50,000
Warehouse 3	$55	$40	$65	$60	$80	$35,000
Warehouse 4	$80	$30	$80	$50	$60	$60,000

The monthly demand from each customer is summarized below.

	Customer 1	Customer 2	Customer 3	Customer 4	Customer 5
Demand	200	300	200	150	250

CoolAire would like to determine which plants and warehouses it should operate to meet demand in the most cost-effective manner.
a. Create a spreadsheet model for this problem and solve it.
b. Which plants and warehouses should CoolAire operate?
c. What is the optimal shipping plan?

33. A blood bank wants to determine the least expensive way to transport available blood donations from Pittsburgh and Staunton to hospitals in Charleston, Roanoke, Richmond, Norfolk, and Suffolk. Figure 6.33 shows the possible shipping paths between cities along with the per-unit cost of shipping along each possible arc. Additionally, the courier service used by the blood bank charges a flat rate of $125 any time it makes a trip across any of these arcs, regardless of how many units of blood is transported. The van used by the courier service can carry a maximum of 800 units of blood.

Assume Pittsburgh has 600 units of blood type O positive (O+) and 800 units of blood type AB available. Assume Staunton has 500 units of O+ and 600 units of AB available. The following table summarizes the number of units of each blood type needed at the various hospitals:

	Units Needed	
Hospital	O+	AB
Charleston	100	200
Roanoke	100	100
Richmond	500	300
Norfolk	200	500
Suffolk	150	250

FIGURE 6.33

Possible shipping routes for the blood bank problem

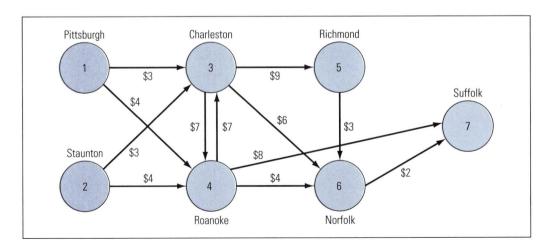

a. Create a spreadsheet model for this problem.
b. What is the optimal solution?
c. Suppose that the courier services switches to a new type of van that can carry no more than 1,000 units of blood between any two cities. What is the optimal solution to this revised problem?

34. CaroliNet is an Internet Service Provider (ISP) for residential consumers in the state of North Carolina. The company is planning to expand and offer Internet service in South Carolina as well. The company wants to establish a set of hubs throughout the state in such a way as to ensure that all residents of the state can access at least one of their hubs via a local phone call. Local phone service is available between all adjacent counties throughout the state. Figure 6.34 (and the file Fig6-34.xlsm that accompanies this book) show an Excel spreadsheet with a matrix indicating county adjacencies throughout the state. That is, values of 1 in the matrix indicate counties that are adjacent to one another while values of 0 indicate counties that are not adjacent to one another. (Note that a county is also considered to be adjacent to itself.)
   a. Assume CaroliNet wants to minimize the number of hubs they must install. In what counties should the hubs be installed?
   b. Suppose CaroliNet is willing to install hubs in exactly 10 different counties. In what counties should the hubs be installed if the company wants to maximize its service coverage?

FIGURE 6.34 *County adjacency matrix for the CaroliNet ISP location problem*

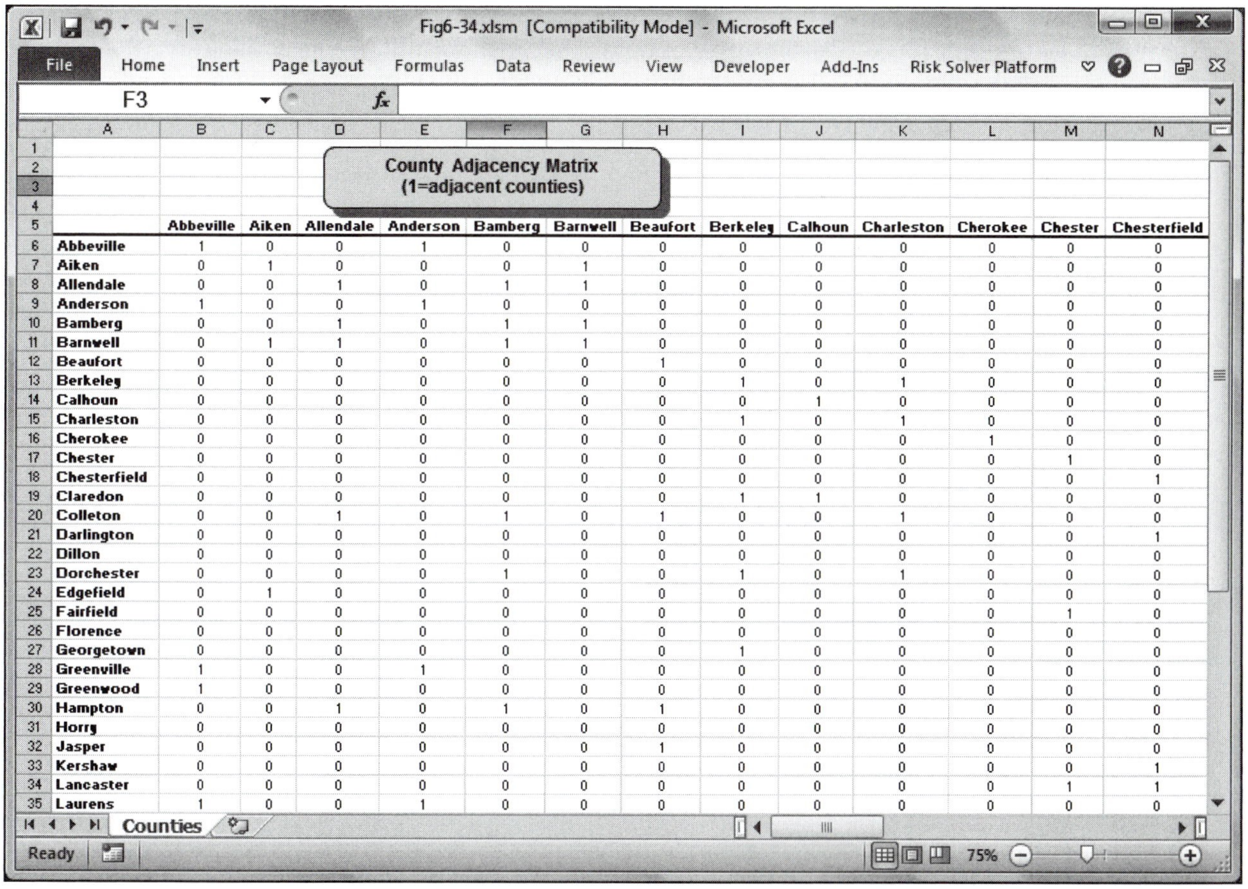

	Abbeville	Aiken	Allendale	Anderson	Bamberg	Barnwell	Beaufort	Berkeley	Calhoun	Charleston	Cherokee	Chester	Chesterfield
Abbeville	1	0	0	1	0	0	0	0	0	0	0	0	0
Aiken	0	1	0	0	0	1	0	0	0	0	0	0	0
Allendale	0	0	1	0	1	1	0	0	0	0	0	0	0
Anderson	1	0	0	1	0	0	0	0	0	0	0	0	0
Bamberg	0	0	1	0	1	1	0	0	0	0	0	0	0
Barnwell	0	1	1	0	1	1	0	0	0	0	0	0	0
Beaufort	0	0	0	0	0	0	1	0	0	0	0	0	0
Berkeley	0	0	0	0	0	0	0	1	0	1	0	0	0
Calhoun	0	0	0	0	0	0	0	0	1	0	0	0	0
Charleston	0	0	0	0	0	0	0	1	0	1	0	0	0
Cherokee	0	0	0	0	0	0	0	0	0	0	1	0	0
Chester	0	0	0	0	0	0	0	0	0	0	0	1	0
Chesterfield	0	0	0	0	0	0	0	0	0	0	0	0	1
Claredon	0	0	0	0	0	0	0	1	1	0	0	0	0
Colleton	0	0	1	0	1	0	1	0	0	1	0	0	0
Darlington	0	0	0	0	0	0	0	0	0	0	0	0	1
Dillon	0	0	0	0	0	0	0	0	0	0	0	0	0
Dorchester	0	0	0	0	1	0	0	1	0	1	0	0	0
Edgefield	0	1	0	0	0	0	0	0	0	0	0	0	0
Fairfield	0	0	0	0	0	0	0	0	0	0	0	1	0
Florence	0	0	0	0	0	0	0	0	0	0	0	0	0
Georgetown	0	0	0	0	0	0	0	1	0	0	0	0	0
Greenville	1	0	0	1	0	0	0	0	0	0	0	0	0
Greenwood	1	0	0	0	0	0	0	0	0	0	0	0	0
Hampton	0	0	1	0	1	0	1	0	0	0	0	0	0
Horry	0	0	0	0	0	0	0	0	0	0	0	0	0
Jasper	0	0	0	0	0	0	1	0	0	0	0	0	0
Kershaw	0	0	0	0	0	0	0	0	0	0	0	0	1
Lancaster	0	0	0	0	0	0	0	0	0	0	0	1	1
Laurens	1	0	0	1	0	0	0	0	0	0	0	0	0

35. Solve the following problem manually using the B&B algorithm. You can use the computer to solve the individual problems generated. Create a branch-and-bound tree to display the steps you complete.

$$\text{MAX:} \qquad 6X_1 + 8X_2$$

$$\text{Subject to:} \qquad 6X_1 + 3X_2 \leq 18$$

$$2X_1 + 3X_2 \leq 9$$

$$X_1, X_2 \geq 0$$
$$X_1, X_2 \text{ must be integers}$$

36. During the execution of the B&B algorithm, many candidate problems are likely to be generated and awaiting further analysis. In the B&B example in this chapter, we chose the next candidate problem to analyze in a rather arbitrary way. What other, more structured ways might we use to select the next candidate problem? What are the pros and cons of these techniques?

CASE 6.1 # Optimizing a Timber Harvest

The state of Virginia is one of the largest producers of wood furniture in the United States, with the furniture industry accounting for 50% of value added to wood materials. Over the past 40 years, the inventory volume of wood in Virginia's forests has increased by 81%. Today, 15.4 million acres, which is well over half of the state, are covered in forest. Private owners hold 77% of this land. When making decisions about which trees to harvest, forestry professionals consider many factors and must follow numerous laws and regulations.

Figure 6.35 depicts a tract of forested land that has been sectioned off into 12 harvestable areas, indicated by dashed lines. Area 2 provides the only access to the forest via a paved road, so any timber cut must ultimately be transported out of the forest through area 2. Currently, there are no roads through this forest. So to harvest the timber,

FIGURE 6.35

Forest diagram for the timber harvesting problem

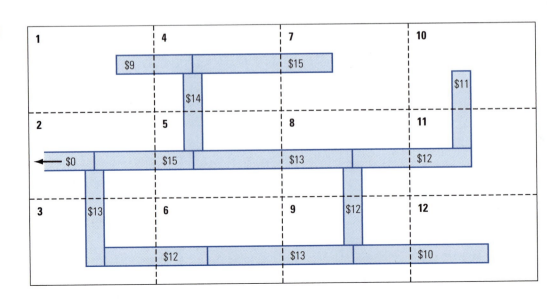

forest roads will need to be built. The allowable routes for these roads are also shown in Figure 6.35 and are determined largely on the geography of the land and location of streams and wildlife habitats.

Not all areas of the forest have to be harvested. However, to harvest any area, a forest road must be built to that area. The cost of building each section of forest road (in $1,000s) is indicated in the figure. Finally, the net value of the harvestable timber in each area is estimated as follows:

	Harvested Value (in $1,000s)											
Area	1	2	3	4	5	6	7	8	9	10	11	12
Value	$15	$7	$10	$12	$8	$17	$14	$18	$13	$12	$10	$11

Which areas should be harvested, and what roads should be built to make the most profitable use of this forest?
1. Create a spreadsheet model for this problem.
2. What is the optimal solution?
3. Suppose the cost of building the road connecting areas 4 and 5 dropped to $12,000. What impact does this have on the optimal solution?

Power Dispatching at Old Dominion

CASE 6.2

The demand for electricity varies greatly during the day. Because large amounts of electricity cannot be stored economically, electric power companies cannot manufacture electricity and hold it in inventory until it is needed. Instead, power companies must balance the production of power with the demand for power in real time. One of the greatest uncertainties in forecasting the demand for electricity is the weather. Most power companies employ meteorologists who constantly monitor weather patterns and update computer models that predict the demand for power over a rolling, seven-day planning horizon. This forecasted seven-day window of demand is referred to as the company's load profile and is typically updated on an every hour basis.

Every power company has a base-load demand that is relatively constant. To satisfy this base-load demand, a power company uses its most economical, low-cost power generating assets and keeps them running continuously. To meet additional demands for power above the base load, a power company must dispatch (or turn on) other generators. These other generators are sometimes called "peakers" as they help the power company meet the highest demands or peak loads. It costs different amounts of money to bring different types of peakers online. And because different peakers use different types of fuel (for example, coal, gas, bio-mass) their operating costs per megawatt (MW) generated also differ. Thus, dispatchers for a power company continually have to decide which generator to bring online or turn off to meet their load profile in the least costly manner.

The Old Dominion Power (ODP) Company provides electrical power throughout Virginia and the Carolinas. Suppose ODP's peak-load profile (that is, the estimated load above base load) in MWs is currently estimated as follows:

	Day						
	1	2	3	4	5	6	7
Load (in MWs)	4,300	3,700	3,900	4,000	4,700	4,800	3,600

ODP currently has three peaking generators offline that are available to help meet this load. The generators have the following operating characteristics:

Generator Location	Startup Cost	Cost per Day	Maximum MW Capacity per Day
New River	$ 800	$200 + $5 per MW	2,100
Galax	$1,000	$300 + $4 per MW	1,900
James River	$ 700	$250 + $7 per MW	3,000

To get an offline generator up and running, a startup cost must be paid. After a generator is running, it can continue to run indefinitely without having to pay this startup cost again. However, if the generator is turned off at any point, the setup cost must be paid again to get it back up and running. Each day that a generator runs, there is both a fixed and variable cost that must be paid. For example, any day that the New River generator is online, it incurs a fixed cost of $200 plus $5 per MW generated. So even if this generator is not producing any MWs, it still costs $200 per day to keep it running (so as to avoid a restart). When they are running, each generator can supply up to the maximum daily MWs listed in the final column of the table.

1. Formulate a mathematical programming model for ODP's power dispatching problem.
2. Implement your model in a spreadsheet and solve it.
3. What is the optimal solution?
4. Suppose ODP can sometimes buy power from a competitor. How much should ODP be willing to pay to acquire 300 MW of power on day 1? Explain your answer.
5. What concerns, if any, would you have about implementing this plan?

CASE 6.3

The MasterDebt Lockbox Problem

MasterDebt is a national credit card company with thousands of card holders located across the United States. Every day throughout the month, MasterDebt sends out statements to different customers summarizing their charges for the previous month. Customers then have 30 days to remit a payment for their bills. MasterDebt includes a pre-addressed envelope with each statement for customers to use in making their payments.

One of the critical problems facing MasterDebt involves determining what address to put on the pre-addressed envelopes sent to various parts of the country. The amount of time that elapses between when a customer writes his check and when MasterDebt receives the cash for the check is referred to as **float**. Checks can spend several days floating in the mail and in processing before being cashed. This float time represents lost revenue to MasterDebt because if they could receive and cash these checks immediately, they could earn additional interest on these funds.

To reduce the interest being lost from floating checks, MasterDebt would like to implement a lockbox system to speed the processing of checks. Under such a system, MasterDebt might have all its customers on the West Coast send their payments to a bank in Sacramento, which, for a fee, processes the checks and deposits the proceeds in a MasterDebt account. Similarly, MasterDebt might arrange for a similar service with a bank on the East Coast for its customers there. Such lockbox systems are a common method companies use to improve their cash flows.

MasterDebt has identified six different cities as possible lockbox sites. The annual fixed cost of operating a lockbox in each of the possible locations is given in the following table.

Annual Lockbox Operating Costs (in $1,000s)

Sacramento	Denver	Chicago	Dallas	New York	Atlanta
$25	$30	$35	$35	$30	$35

An analysis was done to determine the average number of days a check floats when sent from seven different regions of the country to each of these six cities. The results of this analysis are summarized in the following table. This table indicates, for instance, that a check sent from the central region of the country to New York spends an average of three days in the mail and in processing before MasterDebt actually receives the cash for the check.

Average Days of Float between Regions and Possible Lockbox Locations

	Sacramento	Denver	Chicago	Dallas	New York	Atlanta
Central	4	2	2	2	3	3
Mid-Atlantic	6	4	3	4	2	2
Midwest	3	2	3	2	5	4
Northeast	6	4	2	5	2	3
Northwest	2	3	5	4	6	7
Southeast	7	4	3	2	4	2
Southwest	2	3	6	2	7	6

Further analysis was done to determine the average amount of payments being sent from each region of the country. These results are given next:

Average Daily Payments (in $1,000s) by Region

	Payments
Central	$45
Mid-Atlantic	$65
Midwest	$50
Northeast	$90
Northwest	$70
Southeast	$80
Southwest	$60

Thus, if payments from the Central Region are sent to New York, on any given day, there is an average of $135,000 in undeposited checks from the Central Region. Because MasterDebt can earn 15% on cash deposits, it would be losing $20,250 per year in potential interest on these checks alone.

1. Which of the six potential lockbox locations should MasterDebt use, and to which lockbox location should each region be assigned?
2. How would your solution change if a maximum of four regions could be assigned to any lockbox location?

Removing Snow in Montreal   CASE 6.4

Based on: Campbell, J., and Langevin, A. "The Snow Disposal Assignment Problem." *Journal of the Operational Research Society*, 1995, pp. 919–929.

Snow removal and disposal are important and expensive activities in Montreal and many northern cities. While snow can be cleared from streets and sidewalks by plowing and shoveling, in prolonged subfreezing temperatures, the resulting banks of accumulated snow can impede pedestrian and vehicular traffic and must be removed.

To allow timely removal and disposal of snow, a city is divided up into several sectors, and snow removal operations are carried out concurrently in each sector. In Montreal, accumulated snow is loaded onto trucks and hauled away to disposal sites (for example, rivers, quarries, sewer chutes, surface holding areas). For contractual reasons, each sector may be assigned to only a *single* disposal site. (However, each disposal site may receive snow from multiple sectors.) The different types of disposal sites can accommodate different amounts of snow due to either the physical size of the disposal facility or environmental restrictions on the amount of snow (often contaminated by salt and de-icing chemicals) that can be dumped into rivers. The annual capacities for five different snow disposal sites are given in the following table (in 1,000s of cubic meters):

	Disposal Site				
	1	**2**	**3**	**4**	**5**
Capacity	350	250	500	400	200

The cost of removing and disposing of snow depends mainly on the distance it must be trucked. For planning purposes, the city of Montreal uses the straight-line distance between the center of each sector to each of the various disposal sites as an approximation of the cost involved in transporting snow between these locations. The following table summarizes these distances (in kilometers) for 10 sectors in the city.

	Disposal Site				
Sector	**1**	**2**	**3**	**4**	**5**
1	3.4	1.4	4.9	7.4	9.3
2	2.4	2.1	8.3	9.1	8.8
3	1.4	2.9	3.7	9.4	8.6
4	2.6	3.6	4.5	8.2	8.9
5	1.5	3.1	2.1	7.9	8.8
6	4.2	4.9	6.5	7.7	6.1
7	4.8	6.2	9.9	6.2	5.7
8	5.4	6.0	5.2	7.6	4.9
9	3.1	4.1	6.6	7.5	7.2
10	3.2	6.5	7.1	6.0	8.3

Using historical snowfall data, the city is able to estimate the annual volume of snow requiring removal in each sector as four times the length of streets in the sectors in meters (that is, it is assumed each linear meter of street generates four cubic meters of snow to remove over an entire year). The following table estimates the snow removal requirements (in 1,000s of cubic meters) for each sector in the coming year:

Estimated Annual Snow Removal Requirements									
1	**2**	**3**	**4**	**5**	**6**	**7**	**8**	**9**	**10**
153	152	154	138	127	129	111	110	130	135

1. Create a spreadsheet that Montreal could use to determine the most efficient snow removal plan for the coming year. Assume it costs $0.10 to transport 1 cubic meter of snow 1 kilometer.
2. What is the optimal solution?
3. How much will it cost Montreal to implement your snow disposal plan?
4. Ignoring the capacity restrictions at the disposal sites, how many different assignments of sectors to disposal sites are possible?
5. Suppose Montreal can increase the capacity of a single disposal site by 100,000 cubic meters. Which disposal site's capacity (if any) should be increased, and how much should the city be willing to pay to obtain this extra disposal capacity?

Chapter 7

Goal Programming and Multiple Objective Optimization

7.0 Introduction

Chapter 6 discussed the modeling techniques that apply to optimization problems that require integer solutions. This chapter presents two other modeling techniques that are sometimes helpful in solving optimization problems. The first technique—goal programming—involves solving problems containing not one specific objective function but rather a collection of goals that we would like to achieve. As you will see, a goal can be viewed as a constraint with a flexible, or soft, RHS value.

The second technique—multiple objective optimization—is closely related to goal programming and applies to problems containing more than one objective function. In business and government, different groups of people frequently pursue different objectives. Therefore, it is quite possible that a variety of objective functions can be proposed for the same optimization problem.

Both techniques require an *iterative solution procedure* in which the decision maker investigates a variety of solutions to find one that is most satisfactory. Thus, unlike the LP and ILP procedures presented earlier, we cannot formulate a multiple objective or goal programming problem and solve one optimization problem to identify the optimal solution. In these problems, we might need to solve several variations of the problem before we find an acceptable solution.

We will begin with the topic of goal programming. Then, we will investigate multiple objective optimization and see how the concepts and techniques of goal programming can be applied to these problems as well.

7.1 Goal Programming

The optimization techniques presented in the preceding chapters have always assumed that the constraints in the model are **hard constraints**, or constraints that *cannot* be violated. For example, labor constraints indicated that the amount of labor used to produce a variety of products could not exceed some fixed amount (such as 1,566 hours). As another example, monetary constraints indicated that the amount of money invested in a number of projects could not exceed some budgeted amount (such as $850,000).

Hard constraints are appropriate in many situations; however, these constraints might be too restrictive in other situations. For example, when you buy a new car, you probably have in mind a maximum purchase price that you do not want to exceed. We might call this your goal. However, you will probably find a way to spend more than this amount if it is impossible to acquire the car you really want for your goal amount. So, the goal you have in mind is *not* a hard constraint that cannot be violated. We might view it more accurately as a **soft constraint**—representing a target you would like to achieve.

Numerous managerial decision-making problems can be modeled more accurately using goals rather than hard constraints. Often, such problems do not have one explicit objective function to be maximized or minimized over a constraint set but, instead, can be stated as a collection of goals that might also include hard constraints. These types of problems are known as **goal programming** (GP) problems.

Balancing Objectives for Enlightened Self-Interest

As he stood on a wooded hillside watching water cascade over what was once a coal mine, Roger Holnback, executive director of the Western Virginia Land Trust, described what that section of land could have looked like if a typical subdivision was being built in the area. "They'd figure out a way to use this bottom land for development," he said, pointing out how neatly a row of houses could fit in below the hill. "They maximize the lots they build to whatever the zoning says."

But because of an agreement between developers Bill Ellenbogen and Steve Bodtke and the Western Virginia Land Trust and New River Land Trust, nearly half of a 225-acre subdivision on Coal Bank Ridge will be preserved through a conservation easement. "Our goal was to do a nice development while protecting the surrounding areas," Ellenbogen said. Conservation easements are agreements between landowners and land trusts to restrict development while allowing the owner to keep the property and continue to use it. The trusts monitor use of the land to make sure it complies with the conditions of the easement.

Ellenbogen doesn't try to hide the fact that he's a businessman, and as a developer he needs to make a profit. But making a profit and preserving the scenic views and rural character of the area are not mutually exclusive goals. "We think it adds tremendous value," he said. "People live in this community because of the beauty of the land. If you destroy that beauty, people won't want to live here. I call it enlightened self-interest."

"The question is, 'How can I make money and still have a livable community?'" Holnback said. "It's a simple concept."

Adapted from: "Developers See Conservation as Smart Business," *The Roanoke Times*, Dec. 20, 2003.

7.2 A Goal Programming Example

The technique of linear programming can help a decision maker analyze and solve a GP problem. The following example illustrates the concepts and modeling techniques used in GP problems.

Davis McKeown is the owner of a resort hotel and convention center in Myrtle Beach, South Carolina. Although his business is profitable, it is also highly seasonal; the summer months are the most profitable time of year. To increase profits during the rest of the year, Davis wants to expand his convention business, but he needs to expand his conference facilities to do so. Davis hired a marketing research firm to determine the number and sizes of conference rooms that would be required by the conventions he wants to attract. The results of this study indicated that Davis's facilities should include at least 5 small (400 square foot) conference rooms, 10 medium (750 square foot) conference rooms, and 15 large (1,050 square foot) conference rooms. Additionally, the marketing research firm indicated that if the expansion consisted of a total of 25,000 square feet, Davis would have the largest convention center among his competitors—which would be desirable for advertising purposes. While discussing his expansion plans with an architect, Davis learned that he can expect to pay $18,000 for each small conference room in the expansion, $33,000 for each medium conference room, and $45,150 for each large conference room. Davis wants to limit his expenditures on the convention center expansion to approximately $1,000,000.

7.2.1 DEFINING THE DECISION VARIABLES

In this problem, the fundamental decision facing the hotel owner is how many small, medium, and large conference rooms to include in the conference center expansion. These quantities are represented by X_1, X_2, and X_3, respectively.

7.2.2 DEFINING THE GOALS

This problem is somewhat different from the problems presented earlier in this book. Rather than one specific objective, this problem involves a number of goals, which are stated (in no particular order) as:

Goal 1: The expansion should include approximately 5 small conference rooms.
Goal 2: The expansion should include approximately 10 medium conference rooms.
Goal 3: The expansion should include approximately 15 large conference rooms.
Goal 4: The expansion should consist of approximately 25,000 square feet.
Goal 5: The expansion should cost approximately $1,000,000.

Notice that the word "approximately" appears in each goal. This word underscores the fact that these are soft goals rather than hard constraints. For example, if the first four goals could be achieved at a cost of $1,001,000, it is very likely that the hotel owner would not mind paying an extra $1,000 to achieve such a solution. However, we must determine if we can find a solution that exactly meets all of the goals in this problem and, if not, what trade-offs can be made among the goals to determine an acceptable solution. We can formulate an LP model for this GP problem to help us make this determination.

7.2.3 DEFINING THE GOAL CONSTRAINTS

The first step in formulating an LP model for a GP problem is to create a goal constraint for each goal in the problem. A **goal constraint** allows us to determine how close a given solution comes to achieving the goal. To understand how these constraints should be formulated, let's begin with the three goal constraints associated with the number of small, medium, and large conference rooms in the expansion.

If we wanted to make sure that *exactly* 5 small, 10 medium, and 15 large conference rooms were included in the planned expansion, we would include the following hard constraints in our GP model:

$$X_1 = 5$$
$$X_2 = 10$$
$$X_3 = 15$$

However, the goals stated that the expansion should include *approximately* 5 small conference rooms, *approximately* 10 medium conference rooms, and *approximately* 15 large conference rooms. If it is impossible to achieve all the goals, the hotel owner might consider a solution involving only 14 large conference rooms. The hard constraints would not allow for such a solution; they are too restrictive. However, we can modify them easily to allow for departures from the stated goals, as:

$$X_1 + d_1^- - d_1^+ = 5 \qquad \} \text{ small rooms}$$
$$X_2 + d_2^- - d_2^+ = 10 \qquad \} \text{ medium rooms}$$
$$X_3 + d_3^- - d_3^+ = 15 \qquad \} \text{ large rooms}$$
$$\text{where } d_i^-, d_i^+ \geq 0 \text{ for all } i$$

The RHS value of each goal constraint (the values 5, 10, and 15 in the previous constraints) is the **target value** for the goal because it represents the level of achievement that the decision maker wants to obtain for the goal. The variables d_i^- and d_i^+ are called **deviational variables** because they represent the amount by which each goal deviates from its target value. The d_i^- represent the amount by which each goal's target value is *underachieved*, and the d_i^+ represents the amount by which each goal's target value is *overachieved*.

To illustrate how deviational variables work, suppose that we have a solution where $X_1 = 3$, $X_2 = 13$, and $X_3 = 15$. To satisfy the first goal constraint listed previously, its deviational variables would assume the values $d_1^- = 2$ and $d_1^+ = 0$ to reflect that the goal of having 5 small conference rooms is *underachieved* by 2. Similarly, in order to satisfy the second goal constraint, its deviational variables would assume the values $d_2^- = 0$ and $d_2^+ = 3$ to reflect that the goal of having 10 medium conference rooms is *overachieved* by 3. Finally, in order to satisfy the third goal constraint, its deviational variables would assume the values $d_3^- = 0$ and $d_3^+ = 0$ to reflect that the goal of having 15 medium conference rooms is *exactly* achieved.

We can formulate the goal constraints for the remaining goals in the problem in a similar manner. Because each small, medium, and large conference room requires 400, 750, and 1,050 square feet, respectively, and the hotel owner wants the total square footage of the expansion to be 25,000, the constraint representing this goal is:

$$400X_1 + 750X_2 + 1,050X_3 + d_4^- - d_4^+ = 25,000 \qquad \} \text{ square footage}$$

Because each small, medium, and large conference room results in building costs of $18,000, $33,000, and $45,150, respectively, and the hotel owner wants to keep the cost of the expansion at approximately $1,000,000, the constraint representing this goal is:

$$18,000X_1 + 33,000X_2 + 45,150X_3 + d_5^- - d_5^+ = 1,000,000 \qquad \} \text{ building cost}$$

The deviational variables in each of these goal constraints represent the amounts by which the actual values obtained for the goals deviate from their respective target values.

7.2.4 DEFINING THE HARD CONSTRAINTS

As noted earlier, not all of the constraints in a GP problem have to be goal constraints. A GP problem can also include one or more hard constraints typically found in LP problems. In our example, if $1,000,000 was the absolute maximum amount that the hotel owner was willing to spend on the expansion, this could be included in the model as a hard constraint. (As you'll see, it is also possible to change a soft constraint into a hard constraint during the analysis of a GP problem.)

7.2.5 GP OBJECTIVE FUNCTIONS

Although it is fairly easy to formulate the constraints for a GP problem, identifying an appropriate objective function can be quite tricky and usually requires some mental effort. Before formulating the objective function for our sample problem, let's consider some of the issues and options involved in this process.

The objective in a GP problem is to determine a solution that achieves all the goals as closely as possible. The *ideal* solution to any GP problem is one in which each goal is achieved exactly at the level specified by its target value. (In such an ideal solution, all the deviational variables in all the goal constraints would equal 0.) Often, it is not possible to achieve the ideal solution because some goals might conflict with others. In such a case, we want to find a solution that deviates as little as possible from the ideal solution. One possible objective for our example GP problem is:

Minimize the sum of the deviations: MIN: $\sum_i (d_i^- + d_i^+)$

With this objective, we attempt to find a solution to the problem where all the deviational variables are 0—or where all the goals are met exactly. But if such a solution is not possible, will this objective always produce a desirable solution? The answer is, "Probably not."

The previous objective has a number of shortcomings. First, the deviational variables measure entirely different things. In our example problem, $d_1^-, d_1^+, d_2^-, d_2^+, d_3^-$, and d_3^+ all measure rooms of one size or another, whereas d_4^- and d_4^+ are measures of square footage, and d_5^- and d_5^+ are financial measures of building costs. One obvious criticism of the previous objective is that it is unclear how to interpret any numerical value the objective assumes (7 rooms + 1,500 dollars = 1,507 units of what?).

One solution to this problem is to modify the objective function so that it measures the sum of *percentage deviations* from the various goals. This is accomplished as follows, where t_i represents the target value for goal i:

Minimize the sum of the percentage deviations: MIN: $\sum_i \frac{1}{t_i}(d_i^- + d_i^+)$

In our example problem, suppose we arrive at a solution where the first goal is underachieved by 1 room ($d_1^- = 1$), the fifth goal is overachieved by \$20,000 ($d_5^+ = 20,000$), and all other goals are achieved exactly (all other d_i^- and d_i^+ equal 0). Using the sum of percentage deviations objective, the optimal objective function value is:

$$\frac{1}{t_1}d_1^- + \frac{1}{t_5}d_5^+ = \frac{1}{5} \times 1 + \frac{1}{1,000,000} \times 20,000 = 20\% + 2\% = 22\%$$

Note that the percentage deviation objective can be used only if all the target values for all the goals are nonzero; otherwise, a division by zero error will occur.

Another potential criticism of the previous objective functions concerns how they evaluate deviations. In the previous example, where the objective function value is 22%, the objective function implicitly assumes that having 4 small conference rooms (rather than 5) is 10 times worse than being \$20,000 over the desired building cost budget. That is, the budget overrun of \$20,000 would have to increase 10 times to \$200,000 before the percentage deviation on this goal equaled the 20% deviation caused by being one room below the goal of having 5 small conference rooms. Is having one fewer conference room really as undesirable as having to pay \$200,000 more than budgeted? Only the decision maker in this problem can answer this question. It would be nice to provide the decision maker a way to evaluate and change the implicit trade-offs among the goals if he or she wanted to do so.

Both of the previous objective functions view a deviation from any goal in any direction as being equally undesirable. For example, according to both of the previous objective functions, a solution resulting in a building cost of \$900,000 (if $X_5 = 900,000$ and

d_5^- = 100,000) is as undesirable as a solution with a building cost of $1,100,000 (if X_5 = 1,100,000 and d_5^+ = 100,000). But, the hotel owner probably would prefer to pay $900,000 for the expansion rather than $1,100,000. So, while overachieving the building cost goal is an undesirable occurrence, underachieving this goal is probably desirable or at least neutral. On the other hand, underachieving the goal related to the number of small conference rooms might be viewed as undesirable, whereas overachieving this goal might be viewed as desirable or possibly neutral. Again, it would be nice to provide the decision maker a way to represent which deviations are desirable and undesirable in the objective function.

One solution to the previous criticisms is to allow the decision maker to assign weights to the deviational variables in the objective function of a GP problem to better reflect the importance and desirability of deviations from the various goals. So, a more useful type of objective function for a GP problem is:

$$\text{Minimize the weighted sum of the deviations: MIN: } \sum_i (w_i^- d_i^- + w_i^+ d_i^+)$$

or

$$\text{Minimize the weighted sum of the percentage deviations: MIN: } \sum_i \frac{1}{t_i}(w_i^- d_i^- + w_i^+ d_i^+)$$

In these weighted objective functions, the w_i^- and w_i^+ represent numeric constants that can be assigned values to weight the various deviational variables in the problem. A variable that represents a highly undesirable deviation from a particular goal is assigned a relatively large weight—making it highly undesirable for that variable to assume a value larger than 0. A variable that represents a neutral or desirable deviation from a particular goal is assigned a weight of 0 or some value lower than 0 to reflect that it is acceptable or even desirable for the variable to assume a value greater than 0.

Unfortunately, no standard procedure is available for assigning values to the w_i^- and w_i^+ in a way that guarantees you will find the most desirable solution to a GP problem. Rather, you need to follow an iterative procedure in which you try a particular set of weights, solve the problem, analyze the solution, and then refine the weights and solve the problem again. You might need to repeat this process many times to find a solution that is the most desirable to the decision maker.

7.2.6 DEFINING THE OBJECTIVE

In our example problem, assume that the decision maker considers it undesirable to underachieve any of the first three goals related to the number of small, medium, and large conference rooms but is indifferent about overachieving these goals. Also assume that the decision maker considers it undesirable to underachieve the goal of adding 25,000 square feet but equally undesirable to overachieve this goal. Finally, assume that the decision maker finds it undesirable to spend more than $1,000,000 but is indifferent about spending less than this amount. In this case, if we want to minimize the weighted percentage deviation for our example problem, we use the following objective:

$$\text{MIN:} \quad \frac{w_1^-}{5}d_1^- + \frac{w_2^-}{10}d_2^- + \frac{w_3^-}{15}d_3^- + \frac{w_4^-}{25,000}d_4^- + \frac{w_4^+}{25,000}d_4^+ + \frac{w_5^+}{1,000,000}d_5^+$$

Notice that this objective omits (or assigns weights of 0 to) the deviational variables about which the decision maker is indifferent. Thus, this objective would not penalize a solution where, for example, 7 small conference rooms were selected (and therefore d_1^+ = 2) because we assume that the decision maker would not view this as an undesirable deviation from the goal of having 5 small conference rooms. On the other hand, this objective would penalize a solution where 3 small conference rooms were selected (and therefore $d_1^- = 2$) because this represents an undesirable deviation from the goal of having 5 small conference rooms. To begin our analysis of this problem, we will assume that $w_1^- = w_2^- = w_3^- = w_4^- = w_4^+ = w_5^+ = 1$ and all other weights are 0.

7.2.7 IMPLEMENTING THE MODEL

To summarize, the LP model for our example GP problem is:

$$\text{MIN:} \quad \frac{w_1^-}{5} d_1^- + \frac{w_2^-}{10} d_2^- + \frac{w_3^-}{15} d_3^- + \frac{w_4^-}{25,000} d_4^- + \frac{w_4^+}{25,000} d_4^+ + \frac{w_5^+}{1,000,000} d_5^+$$

Subject to:

$$X_1 + d_1^- - d_1^+ = 5 \quad \text{} \text{small rooms}$$
$$X_2 + d_2^- - d_2^+ = 10 \quad \text{} \text{medium rooms}$$
$$X_3 + d_3^- - d_3^+ = 15 \quad \text{} \text{large rooms}$$
$$400X_1 + 750X_3 + 1,050X_3 + d_4^- - d_4^+ = 25,000 \quad \text{} \text{square footage}$$
$$18,000X_1 + 33,000X_2 + 45,150X_3 + d_5^- - d_5^+ = 1,000,000 \quad \text{} \text{building cost}$$
$$d_i^-, d_i^+ \geq 0 \text{ for all } i \quad \text{} \text{nonnegativity conditions}$$
$$X_i \geq 0 \text{ for all } i \quad \text{} \text{nonnegativity conditions}$$

X_i must be integers

Because this is an ILP model, it can be implemented in a spreadsheet in the usual way. One approach for doing this is shown in Figure 7.1 (and in the file Fig7-1.xlsm that accompanies this book).

The first section of the spreadsheet lists basic data about the square footage and costs of the different conference rooms. The next section represents the decision variables, deviational variables, and goal constraints for the problem. Specifically, cells B9 through D9 correspond to X_1, X_2, and X_3—the number of small, medium, and large conference rooms to be included in the expansion. Cells E9 and F9 contain the following formulas, which calculate the total square footage and total building cost for any combination of small, medium, and large conference rooms:

Formula for cell E9:   =SUMPRODUCT(B9:D9,B5:D5)

Formula for cell F9:   =SUMPRODUCT(B9:D9,B6:D6)

Cells B10 through F11 correspond to the deviational variables in our algebraic model. These cells indicate the amount by which each goal is underachieved or overachieved. The LHS formulas for the goal constraints are implemented in cells B12 through F12. Specifically, in cell B12, we enter the following formula and then copy it to cells C12 through F12:

Formula for cell B12:   =B9+B10−B11

(Copy to C12 through F12.)

The target (or RHS) values for the goal constraints are listed in cells B13 through F13.

To implement the objective function, we first implemented formulas to convert the values of the deviational variables into percent format by dividing each deviational variable represented in cells B10 through F11 by the appropriate target value. This is done as follows:

Formula for cell B16:   =B10/B$13

(Copy to B16 through F17.)

Next, weights for each of the deviational variables are entered in cells B20 through F20. Because solving a GP problem is an iterative process in which you will probably need to change the weights for the objective, it is best to place the weights in a separate location on the spreadsheet.

FIGURE 7.1 *Spreadsheet implementation of the GP model*

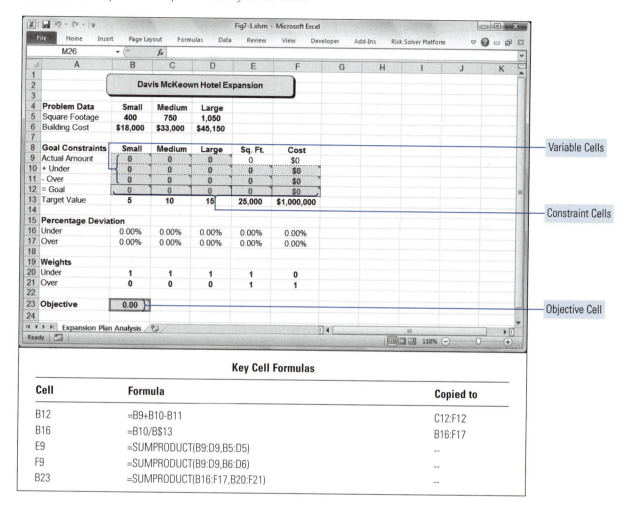

Key Cell Formulas

Cell	Formula	Copied to
B12	=B9+B10-B11	C12:F12
B16	=B10/B$13	B16:F17
E9	=SUMPRODUCT(B9:D9,B5:D5)	--
F9	=SUMPRODUCT(B9:D9,B6:D6)	--
B23	=SUMPRODUCT(B16:F17,B20:F21)	--

Finally, cell B23 contains the following formula, which implements the objective function for the problem:

Formula for cell B23:   =SUMPRODUCT(B16:F17,B20:F21)

7.2.8 SOLVING THE MODEL

The model can be solved using the Solver settings and options shown in Figure 7.2. The solution obtained using these settings is shown in Figure 7.3.

7.2.9 ANALYZING THE SOLUTION

As shown in Figure 7.3, this solution includes exactly 5 small, 10 medium, and 15 large rooms in the expansion. Thus, there is no deviation at all from the target values for the first three goals, which would please the decision maker. However, considering the fourth and fifth goals, the current solution overachieves the targeted square footage level by 250 square feet (or 1%) and is over the building cost goal by $97,250 (or 9.73%).

FIGURE 7.2

Solver settings and options for the GP model

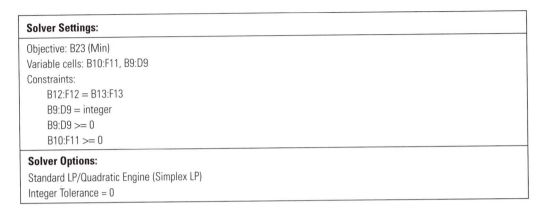

Solver Settings:
Objective: B23 (Min)
Variable cells: B10:F11, B9:D9
Constraints:
B12:F12 = B13:F13
B9:D9 = integer
B9:D9 >= 0
B10:F11 >= 0
Solver Options:
Standard LP/Quadratic Engine (Simplex LP)
Integer Tolerance = 0

FIGURE 7.3 *First solution to the GP model*

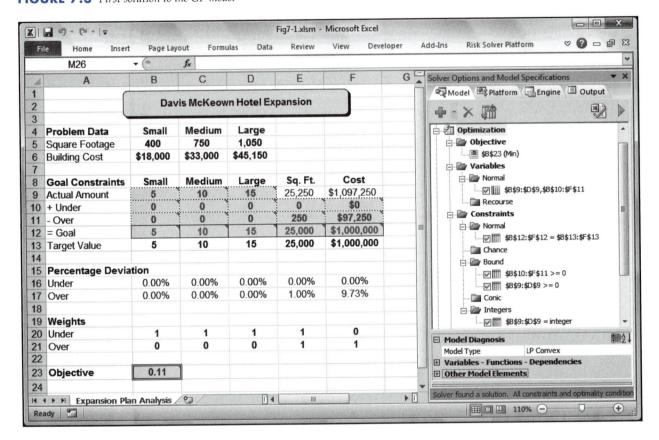

7.2.10 REVISING THE MODEL

Although the decision maker might not mind being 1% over the square footage goal, exceeding the building cost goal by almost $100,000 most likely would be a concern. The decision maker might want to find another solution that comes closer to achieving the building cost goal. This can be done by adjusting the weights in the problem so that a larger penalty is assigned to overachieving the building cost goal. That is, we can increase the value in cell F21 representing w_5^+. Again, there is no way to tell exactly how much larger this value should be. As a rule of thumb, we might change its value by one order of magnitude, or from 1 to 10. If we make this change in the spreadsheet and resolve the problem, we obtain the solution shown in Figure 7.4.

FIGURE 7.4 *Second solution to the GP model*

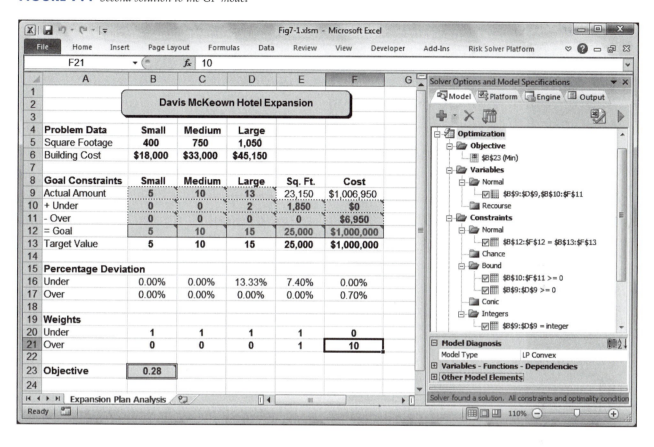

In Figure 7.4, notice that increasing the penalty for overachieving the building cost goal from 1 to 10 reduced the overachievement of this goal from $97,250 to $6,950. We are now within 1% of the target value for the building cost goal. However, in order to obtain this improved level of achievement on the building cost goal, we had to give up two large conference rooms, resulting in a 13.33% underachievement for this goal. If the decision maker considers this unacceptable, we can increase the penalty on this deviational variable from 1 to 10 and re-solve the problem. Figure 7.5 shows the resulting solution.

7.2.11 TRADE-OFFS: THE NATURE OF GP

In Figure 7.5, the target number of large conference rooms is met exactly, but the desired number of medium rooms is now underachieved by 3. Depending on the preferences of the decision maker, we could continue to fine-tune the weights in the problem until we reach a solution that is most satisfactory to the decision maker. The nature of GP involves making trade-offs among the various goals until a solution is found that gives the decision maker the greatest level of satisfaction. Thus, unlike the other applications of LP presented earlier, the use of LP in GP does not indicate immediately the best possible solution to the problem (unless the decision maker initially specifies an appropriately weighted objective function). Rather, it provides a method by which a decision maker can explore a variety of possible solutions and try to find the solution that comes closest to satisfying the goals under consideration. Figure 7.6 provides a summary of the steps involved in solving a GP problem.

FIGURE 7.5 *Third solution to the GP model*

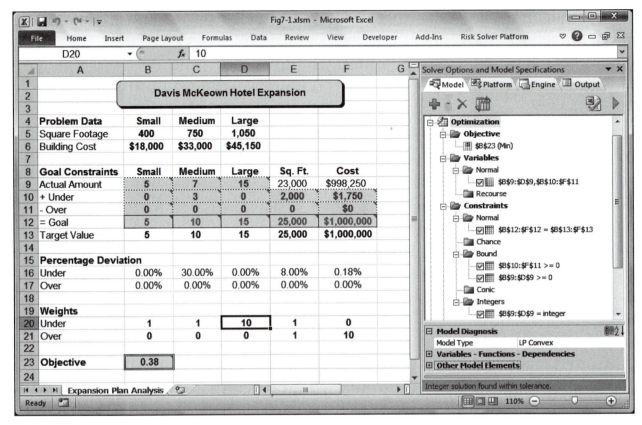

FIGURE 7.6

Summary of the steps involved in formulating and solving a GP problem

Summary of Goal Programming

1. Identify the decision variables in the problem.
2. Identify any hard constraints in the problem and formulate them in the usual way.
3. State the goals of the problem along with their target values.
4. Create constraints using the decision variables that would achieve the goals exactly.
5. Transform the above constraints into goal constraints by including deviational variables.
6. Determine which deviational variables represent undesirable deviations from the goals.
7. Formulate an objective that penalizes the undesirable deviations.
8. Identify appropriate weights for the objective.
9. Solve the problem.
10. Inspect the solution to the problem. If the solution is unacceptable, return to step 8 and revise the weights as needed.

7.3 Comments about Goal Programming

Some additional comments should be made before we leave the topic of GP. First, it is important to note that different GP solutions cannot be compared simply on the basis of their optimal objective function values. The user changes the weights in the objective functions from iteration to iteration; therefore, comparing their values is not appropriate because they measure different things. The objective function in a GP problem serves more of a mechanical purpose, allowing us to explore possible solutions. Thus, we should compare the solutions that are produced—not the objective function values.

Second, in some GP problems, one or more goals might be viewed as being infinitely more important than the other goals. In this case, we could assign arbitrarily large weights to deviations from these goals to ensure that undesirable deviations from them never occur. This is sometimes referred to as *preemptive* GP because certain goals preempt others in order of importance. If the target values for these goals can be achieved, the use of preemptive weights effectively makes these goals hard constraints that should never be violated.

Third, we can place hard constraints on the amount by which we can deviate from a goal. For example, suppose that the owner of the hotel in our example problem wants to eliminate from consideration any solution that exceeds the target building cost by more than $50,000. We could easily build this requirement into our model with the hard constraint:

$$d_5^+ \le 50{,}000$$

Fourth, the concept of deviational variables is not limited to GP. These types of variables can be used in other problems that are quite different from GP problems. So, understanding deviational variables can prove useful in other types of mathematical programming situations.

Finally, another type of objective function, called the MINIMAX objective, is sometimes helpful in GP when you want to minimize the maximum deviation from any goal. To implement the MINIMAX objective, we must create one additional constraint for each deviational variable as follows, where Q is the MINIMAX variable:

$$d_1^- \le Q$$
$$d_1^+ \le Q$$
$$d_2^- \le Q$$

and so on ...

The objective is to minimize the value of Q, stated as:

$$\text{MIN: } Q$$

Because the variable Q must be greater than or equal to the values of all the deviational variables and because we are trying to minimize it, Q will always be set equal to the maximum value of the deviational variables. At the same time, this objective function tries to find a solution where the maximum deviational variable (and the value of Q) is as small as possible. Therefore, this technique allows us to minimize the maximum deviation from all the goals. As we will see shortly, this type of objective is especially valuable if a GP problem involves hard constraints.

7.4 Multiple Objective Optimization

We now consider how to solve LP problems involving multiple objective functions. These problems are called **multiple objective linear programming** (MOLP) problems.

Most of the LP and ILP problems discussed in previous chapters involved one objective function. These objective functions typically sought to maximize profits or minimize costs. However, another objective function could be formulated for most of these problems. For example, if a production process creates a toxic pollutant that is dangerous to the environment, a company might want to minimize this toxic by-product. But this objective is likely to be in direct conflict with the company's other objective of maximizing profits. Increasing profit will likely always result in the creation of additional toxic waste. Figure 7.7 shows a hypothetical example of the potential trade-offs between profit and the production of toxic waste. Each point on the curve in this graph corresponds to a possible level of profit and the minimum amount of toxic waste that must be produced to achieve this level of profit. Clearly, reaching higher levels of profit (which is desirable) is associated with incurring greater levels of toxic waste production (which is undesirable). So the decision maker must decide what level of trade-off between profit and toxic waste is most desirable.

Another important MOLP issue to note in Figure 7.7 is the concept of dominated and nondominated solutions. Accepting a solution that offers the combination of profit and toxic waste indicated by point A is clearly undesirable. There is another alternative (that is, point B on the graph) that offers less toxic waste production for the same level of profit. Also, there is another alternative (that is, point C on the graph) that offers more profit for the same level of toxic waste. So points B and C would both be preferable to (or dominate) point A. Indeed, all the points along the curve connecting point B to point C dominate point A. In MOLP, a decision alternative is **dominated** if there is another alternative that produces a better value for at least one objective without worsening the value of the other objectives. Clearly, rational decision makers should want to consider only decision alternatives that are nondominated. The technique for MOLP presented in this chapter guarantees that the solutions presented to the decision maker are nondominated.

FIGURE 7.7

Illustration of trade-offs between objectives and dominated decision solution alternatives

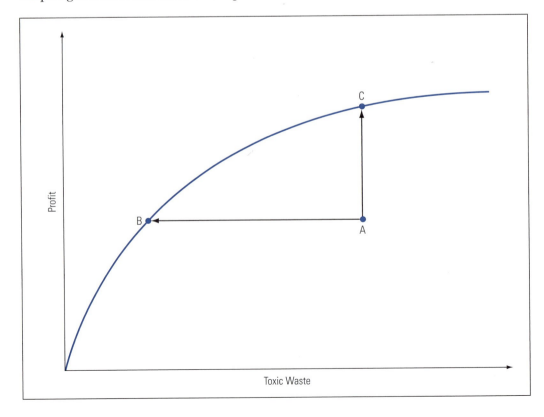

Fortunately, MOLP problems can be viewed as special types of GP problems where, as part of solving the problem, we must also determine target values for each goal or objective. Analyzing these problems effectively also requires that we use the MINIMAX objective described earlier.

7.5 An MOLP Example

The following example illustrates the issues involved in an MOLP problem. Although this example involves only three objectives, the concepts and techniques presented apply to problems involving any number of objectives.

Lee Blackstone is the owner of the Blackstone Mining Company, which operates two different coal mines in Wythe and Giles counties in southwest Virginia. Due to increased commercial and residential development in the primary areas served by these mines, Lee is anticipating an increase in demand for coal in the coming year. Specifically, her projections indicate a 48-ton increase in the demand for high-grade coal, a 28-ton increase in the demand for medium-grade coal, and a 100-ton increase in the demand for low-grade coal. To handle this increase in demand, Lee must schedule extra shifts of workers at the mines. It costs $40,000 per month to run an extra shift of workers at the Wythe county mine, and $32,000 per month at the Giles mine. Only one additional shift can be scheduled each month at each mine. The amount of coal that can be produced in a month's time at each mine by a shift of workers is summarized in the following table.

Type of Coal	Wythe Mine	Giles Mine
High grade	12 tons	4 tons
Medium grade	4 tons	4 tons
Low grade	10 tons	20 tons

Unfortunately, the methods used to extract coal from these mines produce toxic water that enters the local groundwater aquifers. At the Wythe mine, running an extra shift will generate approximately 800 gallons of toxic water per month, whereas the mine in Giles county will generate about 1,250 gallons of toxic water. Although these amounts are within EPA guidelines, Lee is concerned about the environment and doesn't want to create any more pollution than is absolutely necessary. Additionally, although the company follows all OSHA safety guidelines, company records indicate that approximately 0.20 life-threatening accidents occur per shift each month at the Wythe mine, whereas 0.45 accidents occur per shift each month at the Giles mine. Lee knows that mining is a hazardous occupation, but she cares about the health and welfare of her workers and wants to keep the number of life-threatening accidents to a minimum.

7.5.1 DEFINING THE DECISION VARIABLES

In this problem, Lee has to determine the number of months to schedule an extra shift at each of the company's mines. Thus, we can define the decision variables as:

X_1 = number of months to schedule an extra shift at the Wythe county mine

X_2 = number of months to schedule an extra shift at the Giles county mine

7.5.2 DEFINING THE OBJECTIVES

This problem is different from the other types of LP problems we have considered in that three different objective functions are possible. Lee might be interested in minimizing costs, minimizing the production of toxic wastewater, or minimizing the expected number of life-threatening accidents. These three different objectives would be formulated as follows:

Minimize:	$\$40X_1 + \$32X_2$	} production costs (in \$1,000s)
Minimize:	$800X_1 + 1{,}250X_2$	} toxic water produced (in gallons)
Minimize:	$0.20X_1 + 0.45X_2$	} life-threatening accidents

In an LP model, Lee would be forced to decide which of these three objectives is most important or most appropriate and use that single objective in the model. However, in an MOLP model, Lee can consider how all of these objectives (and any others she might want to formulate) can be incorporated into the analysis and solution of the problem.

7.5.3 DEFINING THE CONSTRAINTS

The constraints for this problem are formulated in the same way as for any LP problem. The following three constraints ensure that required amounts of high-grade, medium-grade, and low-grade coal are produced.

$12X_1 + 4X_2 \geq 48$	} high-grade coal required
$4X_1 + 4X_2 \geq 28$	} medium-grade coal required
$10X_1 + 20X_2 \geq 100$	} low-grade coal required

7.5.4 IMPLEMENTING THE MODEL

To summarize, the MOLP formulation of this problem is represented as:

Minimize:	$\$40X_1 + \$32X_2$	} production costs (in \$1,000s)
Minimize:	$800X_1 + 1{,}250X_2$	} toxic water produced (in gallons)
Minimize:	$0.20X_1 + 0.45X_2$	} life-threatening accidents
Subject to:	$12X_1 + 4X_2 \geq 48$	} high-grade coal required
	$4X_1 + 4X_2 \geq 28$	} medium-grade coal required
	$10X_1 + 20X_2 \geq 100$	} low-grade coal required
	$X_1, X_2 \geq 0$	} nonnegativity conditions

This model is implemented in a spreadsheet in the usual way except that three different cells represent the three objective functions. One approach to implementing this model is shown in Figure 7.8 (and in the file Fig7-8.xlsm that accompanies this book).

In Figure 7.8, cells B5 and C5 represent the decision variables X_1 and X_2, respectively. The coefficients for the various objective functions are entered in cells B8 through C10. Next, the coefficients for the constraints are entered in cells B13 through C15. The objectives are then implemented in cells D8 through D10 as follows,

Formula for cell D8:   =SUMPRODUCT(B8:C8,$B$5:$C$5)

(Copy to D9 through D10.)

FIGURE 7.8 *Spreadsheet implementation of the MOLP problem*

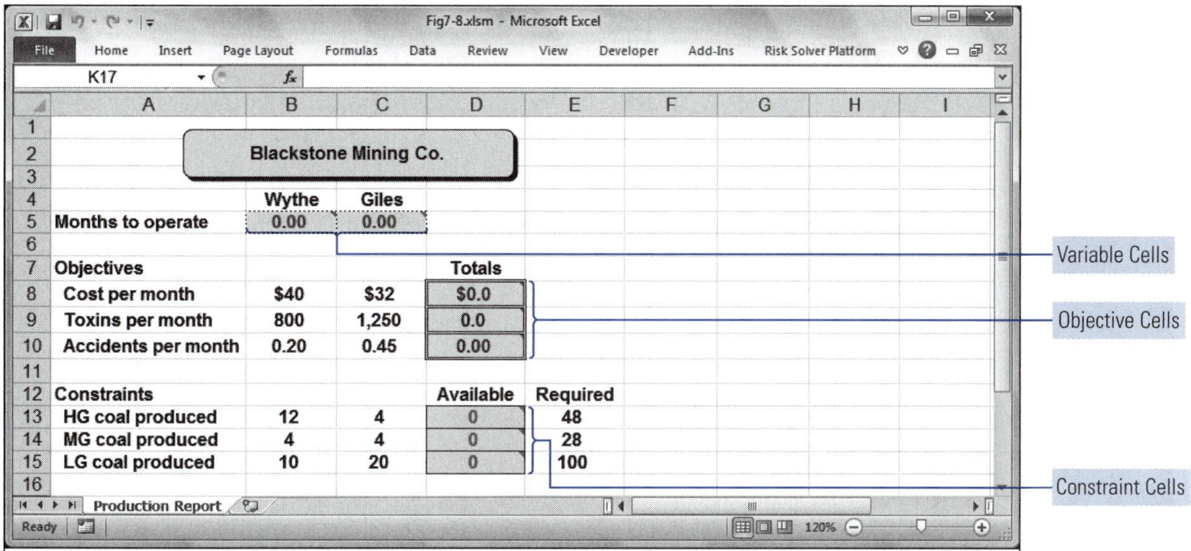

	Key Cell Formulas	
Cell	**Formula**	**Copied to**
D8	=SUMPRODUCT(B8:C8,$B$5:$C$5)	D9:D10 and D13:D15

Next, the coefficients for the constraints are entered in cells B13 through C15. The LHS formulas for the constraints are then entered in cells D13 through D15.

Formula for cell D13:   =SUMPRODUCT(B13:C13,$B$5:$C$5)

(Copy to D14 through D15.)

The RHS values for these constraints are given by cells E13 through E15.

7.5.5 DETERMINING TARGET VALUES FOR THE OBJECTIVES

An LP problem can have only one objective function, so how can we include three objectives in our spreadsheet model? If these objectives had target values, we could treat them the same way as the goals in our example earlier in this chapter. That is, the objectives in this problem can be stated as the following goals if we have appropriate values for t_1, t_2, and t_3:

Goal 1: The total production cost should be approximately t_1.
Goal 2: The gallons of toxic water produced should be approximately t_2.
Goal 3: The number of life-threatening accidents should be approximately t_3.

Unfortunately, the problem did not provide explicit values for t_1, t_2, and t_3. However, if we solve our model to find the solution that minimizes the first objective (total production cost), the optimal value of this objective function would be a reasonable value to use as t_1 in the first goal. Similarly, if we solve the problem two more times, minimizing the second and third objectives, respectively, the optimal objective function values for these solutions would provide reasonable values to use as t_2 and t_3 in the second and third goals. We could then view our MOLP problem in the format of a GP problem.

Figure 7.9 shows the Solver settings and options required to determine the minimum production cost that could be realized in this problem. Note that this involves minimizing the value of cell D8. Figure 7.10 shows the optimal solution obtained by solving this LP problem. Notice that the best possible (minimum) production cost for this problem is $244 (in $1,000s), and this solution can be obtained by running an extra shift at the Wythe county mine for 2.5 months and at the Giles county mine for 4.5 months. Thus, a reasonable value for t_1 is $244. It is impossible to obtain a solution to this problem with a production cost lower than this amount.

FIGURE 7.9

Solver settings and options to minimize production costs

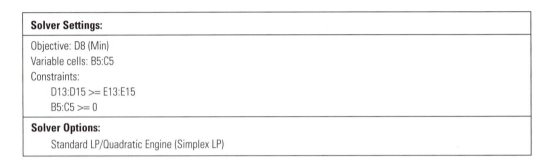

Solver Settings:

Objective: D8 (Min)
Variable cells: B5:C5
Constraints:
  D13:D15 >= E13:E15
  B5:C5 >= 0

Solver Options:
  Standard LP/Quadratic Engine (Simplex LP)

FIGURE 7.10 *Optimal solution when minimizing production costs*

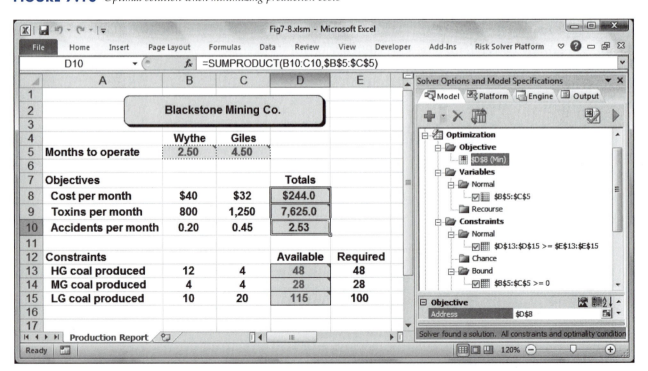

FIGURE 7.11 *Optimal solution when minimizing the amount of toxic water generated*

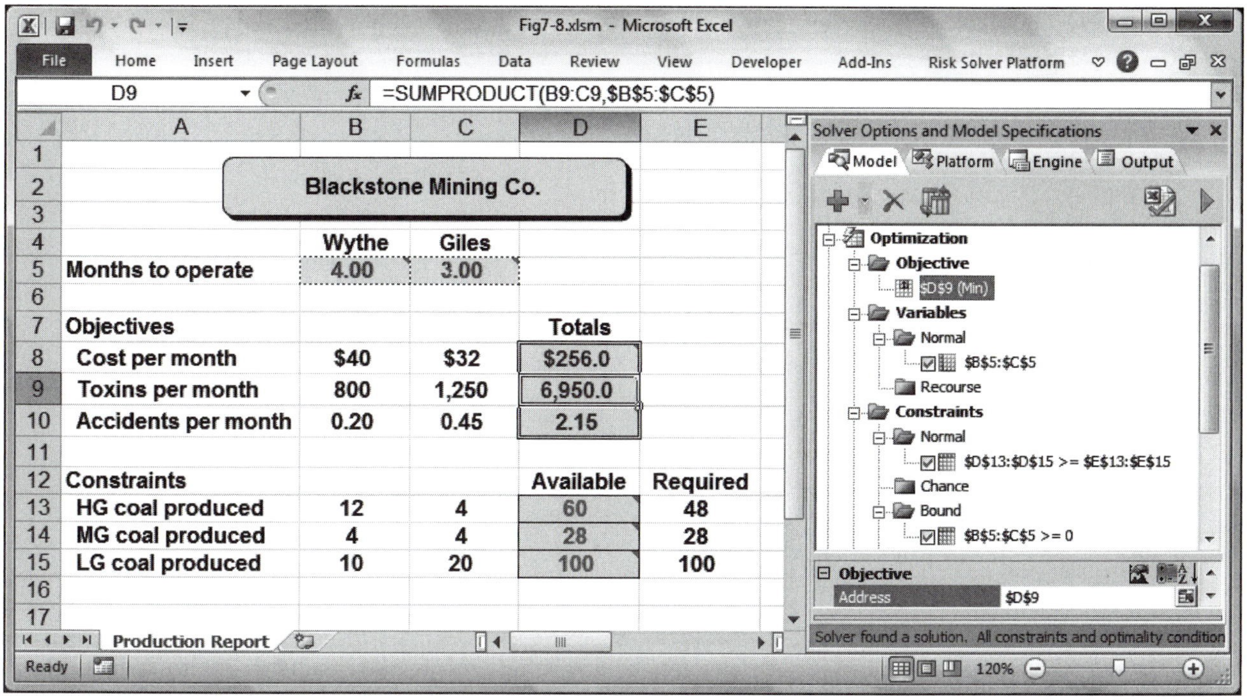

Figure 7.11 shows the solution obtained if we minimize the generation of toxic groundwater pollutants (obtained by minimizing the value in cell D9). This production schedule requires that we run an extra shift at the Wythe county mine for 4.0 months and at the Giles county mine for 3.0 months and generates a total of 6,950 gallons of toxic water. Thus, a reasonable value for t_2 is 6,950. It is impossible to obtain a solution to this problem that produces less toxic water.

Finally, Figure 7.12 shows the solution obtained if we minimize the expected number of life-threatening accidents (obtained by minimizing the value in cell D10). This production schedule requires that we run an extra shift at the Wythe county mine for 10.0 months and not run any extra shifts at the Giles mine. A total of 2 life-threatening accidents can be expected with this schedule. Thus, a reasonable value for t_3 is 2. It is impossible to obtain a solution to this problem with a lower number of expected life-threatening accidents.

7.5.6 SUMMARIZING THE TARGET SOLUTIONS

Figure 7.13 summarizes the solutions shown in Figures 7.10, 7.11, and 7.12 and shows where each of the solutions occurs in terms of the feasible region for this problem.

Two important points should be observed here. First, Figure 7.13 clearly shows that the objectives in this problem conflict with one another. Solution 1 has the lowest production cost ($244,000) but also has the highest expected number of accidents (2.53). Conversely, solution 3 has the lowest expected number of accidents (2.0) but generates the highest production costs ($400,000) and also the highest creation of toxic water (8,000 gallons). This is not surprising but does underscore the fact that this problem involves trade-offs among the three objectives. No single feasible point

FIGURE 7.12 *Optimal solution when minimizing the expected number of life-threatening accidents*

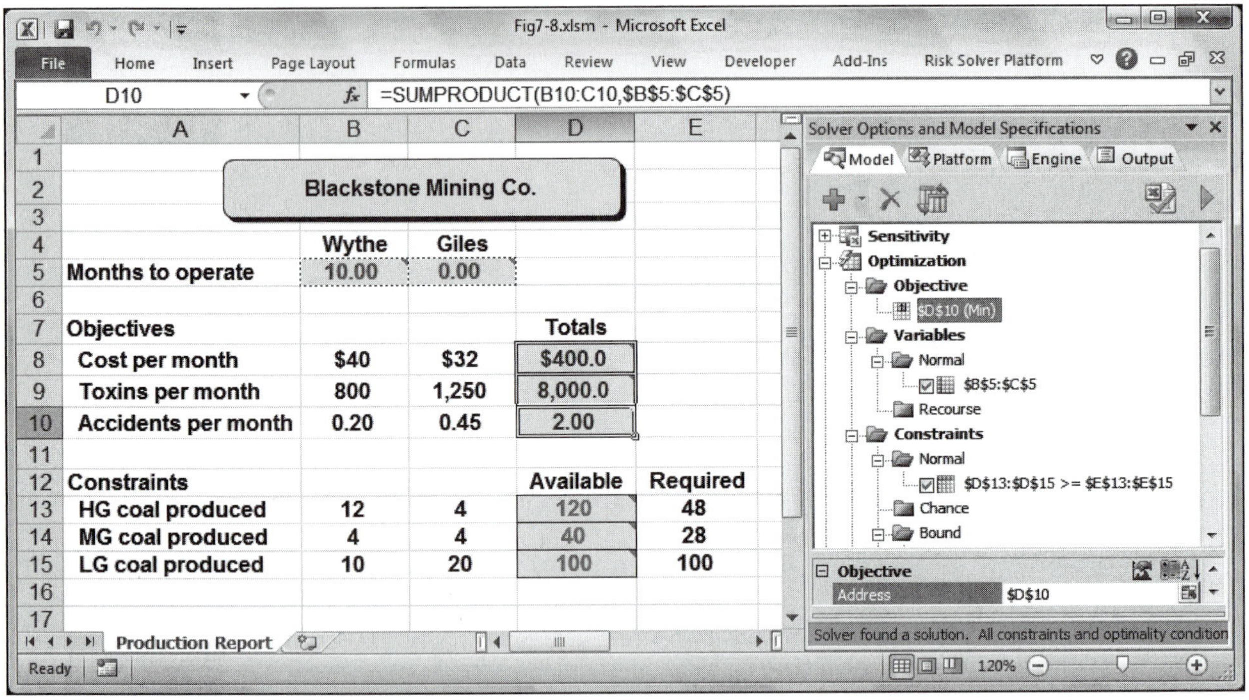

simultaneously optimizes all of the objective functions. To improve the value of one objective, we must sacrifice the value of the others. This characteristic is common to most MOLP problems. Thus, the purpose of MOLP (and of GP) is to study the trade-offs among the objectives in order to find a solution that is the most desirable to the decision maker.

Second, the graph in Figure 7.13 shows the solutions only at three corner points of the feasible region for this problem. Because we have already determined the levels of cost, toxic water production, and expected accident rates offered by these three solutions, if none of these solutions are acceptable, the decision maker may wish to explore some of the other *non-corner point* feasible solutions shown in Figure 7.13. As we will see, this poses a tricky problem.

7.5.7 DETERMINING A GP OBJECTIVE

Now that we have target values for the three objectives in our problem, we can formulate a weighted GP objective to allow the decision maker to explore possible solutions. Earlier in this chapter, we discussed several GP objectives and illustrated the use of an objective that minimized the weighted percentage deviation from the goals' target values. Let's consider how to formulate this same type of objective for the current problem.

We can restate the objectives of this problem as the following goals:

Goal 1: The total production cost should be approximately $244.
Goal 2: The gallons of toxic water produced should be approximately 6,950.
Goal 3: The number of life-threatening accidents should be approximately 2.0.

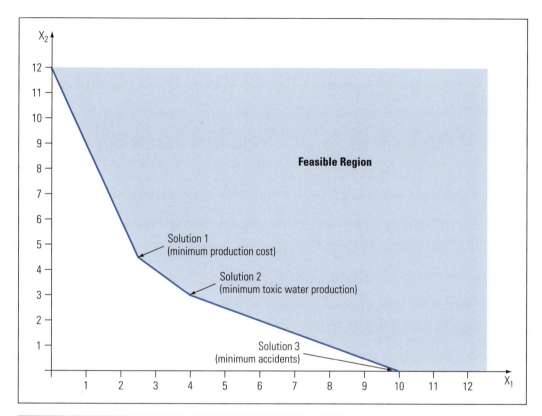

Solution	Months of Operation at Wythe Mine (X_1)	Months of Operation at Giles Mine (X_2)	Production Cost	Gallons of Toxic Pollutants Produced	Expected Number of Life Threatening Accidents
1	2.5	4.5	$244	7,625	2.53
2	4.0	3.0	$256	6,950	2.15
3	10.0	0.0	$400	8,000	2.00

We now know that the actual total production cost can never be smaller than its target (optimum) value of $244, so the percentage deviation from this goal may be computed as:

$$\frac{\text{actual value} - \text{target value}}{\text{target value}} = \frac{(40X_1 + 32X_2) - 244}{244}$$

Similarly, the actual amount of toxic water generated can never be less than its target (optimum) value of 6,950, so the percentage deviation from this goal is calculated as:

$$\frac{\text{actual value} - \text{target value}}{\text{target value}} = \frac{(800X_1 + 1,250X_2) - 6,950}{6,950}$$

Finally, the actual expected number of life-threatening accidents can never be less than its target (optimum) value of 2, so the percentage deviation from this goal is calculated as:

$$\frac{\text{actual value} - \text{target value}}{\text{target value}} = \frac{(0.20X_1 + 0.45X_2) - 2}{2}$$

These percentage deviation calculations are all linear functions of the decision variables. Thus, if we form an objective function as a weighted combination of these percentage deviation functions, we obtain the following linear objective function:

$$\text{MIN: } w_1\left(\frac{(40X_1 + 32X_2) - 244}{244}\right) + w_2\left(\frac{(800X_1 + 1{,}250X_2) - 6{,}950}{6{,}950}\right) + w_3\left(\frac{(0.20X_1 + 0.45X_2) - 2}{2}\right)$$

Recall from Chapter 2 that the optimal solution to an LP problem (that is, an optimization problem with linear constraints and a linear objective function) *always* occurs at an extreme (corner) point of the feasible region. So, if we use the preceding objective to solve our example problem as a GP problem, we will *always* obtain one of the four extreme points shown in Figure 7.13 as the optimal solution to the problem, regardless of the weights assigned to w_1, w_2, and w_3. Thus, to explore the nonextreme feasible solutions to this GP problem (or any other GP problem with hard constraints), we need to use a different type of objective function.

7.5.8 THE MINIMAX OBJECTIVE

As it turns out, the MINIMAX objective, described earlier, can be used to explore the points on the edge of the feasible region—in addition to corner points. To illustrate this, let's attempt to minimize the maximum weighted percentage deviation from the target values for the goals in our example problem using the objective:

$$\text{MIN: the maximum of } w_1\left(\frac{(40X_1 + 32X_2) - 244}{244}\right), \; w_2\left(\frac{(800X_1 + 1{,}250X_2) - 6{,}950}{6{,}950}\right),$$
$$\text{and } w_3\left(\frac{(0.20X_1 + 0.45X_2) - 2}{2}\right)$$

We implement this objective by establishing a MINIMAX variable Q that we minimize with the objective:

$$\text{MIN: Q}$$

subject to the additional constraints:

$$w_1\left(\frac{(40X_1 + 32X_2) - 244}{244}\right) \leq Q$$
$$w_2\left(\frac{(800X_1 + 1{,}250X_2) - 6{,}950}{6{,}950}\right) \leq Q$$
$$w_3\left(\frac{(0.20X_1 + 0.45X_2) - 2}{2}\right) \leq Q$$

The first constraint indicates that the weighted percentage deviation from the target production cost must be less than or equal to Q. The second constraint indicates that the weighted percentage deviation from the target level of toxic water production must also be less than or equal to Q. The third constraint indicates that the weighted percentage deviation from the target expected number of life-threatening accidents must also be less than or equal to Q. Thus, as we minimize Q, we are also minimizing the weighted percentage deviations from the target values for each of our goals. In this way, the maximum weighted deviation from any of the goals is minimized—or we have MINImized the MAXimum deviation (hence the term MINIMAX).

7.5.9 IMPLEMENTING THE REVISED MODEL

The revised GP model of our investment problem is summarized as:

MIN: Q
Subject to:

$$12X_1 + \quad 4X_2 \geq \quad 48 \qquad \text{\} high-grade coal required}$$
$$4X_1 + \quad 4X_2 \geq \quad 28 \qquad \text{\} medium-grade coal required}$$
$$10X_1 + \quad 20X_2 \geq \quad 100 \qquad \text{\} low-grade coal required}$$
$$w_1(40X_1 + \quad 32X_2 - \quad 244)/244 \leq Q \qquad \text{\} goal 1 MINIMAX constraint}$$
$$w_2(800X_1 + 1{,}250X_2 - 6{,}950)/6{,}950 \leq Q \qquad \text{\} goal 2 MINIMAX constraint}$$
$$w_3(0.20X_1 + 0.45X_2 - 2)/2 \leq Q \qquad \text{\} goal 3 MINIMAX constraint}$$
$$X_1, X_2 \geq 0 \qquad \text{\} nonnegativity conditions}$$

w_1, w_2, w_3 are positive constants

The spreadsheet shown earlier in Figure 7.8 can be modified easily to implement this new model. The revised spreadsheet is shown in Figure 7.14 (and in the file Fig7-14.xlsm that accompanies this book).

In Figure 7.14, cells E8 through E10 contain the target values for the goals. The percentage deviations from each goal are calculated in cells F8 through F10 as follows:

Formula for cell F8: $=(D8-E8)/E8$

(Copy to cells F9 through F10.)

FIGURE 7.14 *Spreadsheet implementation of the GP model to analyze the MOLP problem*

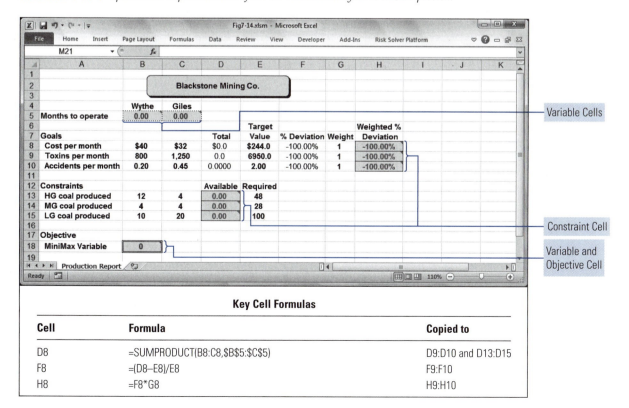

Cell	Formula	Copied to
D8	=SUMPRODUCT(B8:C8,$B$5:$C$5)	D9:D10 and D13:D15
F8	=(D8–E8)/E8	F9:F10
H8	=F8*G8	H9:H10

Arbitrary weights for the deviations from the goals were entered in cells G8 through G10. Cells H8 through H10 contain the following formulas, which calculate the weighted percentage deviation from the goals:

Formula for cell H8:   =F8*G8

(Copy to cells H9 through H10.)

The formulas in cells H8 through H10 are equivalent to the LHS formulas of the MINIMAX constraints for each of the goals in our model. Finally, cell B18 is reserved to represent the MINIMAX variable Q. Notice that this cell is a variable cell (because it represents the variable Q) *and* also represents the objective to be minimized.

7.5.10 SOLVING THE MODEL

The Solver settings and options shown in Figure 7.15 were used to solve the model shown in Figure 7.14. The solution obtained for this model is shown in Figure 7.16.

Notice that the solution shown in Figure 7.16 ($X_1 = 4.23$, $X_2 = 2.88$) *does not* occur at an extreme point of the feasible region shown earlier in Figure 7.13. Also notice that this solution is within approximately 7.2% of achieving the target solution for goals 1 and 3 and is less than 1% from the target value for goal 2. Thus, the decision maker in this problem might find this solution more appealing than the other solutions occurring at the extreme points of the feasible region. Using other weights would produce different solutions. Figure 7.17 shows a number of representative solutions indicated on the original feasible region for this problem.

Figure 7.17 illustrates that as the relative weight on the first goal (w_1) increases, the solution is driven closer to achieving the target value for this goal (which occurs at the point $X_1 = 2.5$, $X_2 = 4.5$, as shown in Figure 7.13). As the relative weight on the second goal (w_2) increases, the solution is driven closer to achieving the target value for this goal (which occurs at the point $X_1 = 4.0$, $X_2 = 3.0$). Finally, as the relative weight on the third goal (w_3) increases, the solution is driven closer to achieving the target value for this goal (which occurs at the point $X_1 = 10.0$, $X_2 = 0.0$). Thus, by adjusting the weights, the decision maker can explore a variety of solutions that do not necessarily occur at the corner points of the original feasible region to the problem.

FIGURE 7.15

Solver settings and options for the GP implementation of the MOLP problem

Solver Settings:
Objective: B18 (Min)
Variable cells: B18, B5:C5
Constraints:
H8:H10 <= B18
D13:D15 >= E13:E15
B5:C5 >= 0
Solver Options:
Standard LP/Quadratic Engine (Simplex LP)

FIGURE 7.16   *Solution to the MOLP problem obtained through GP*

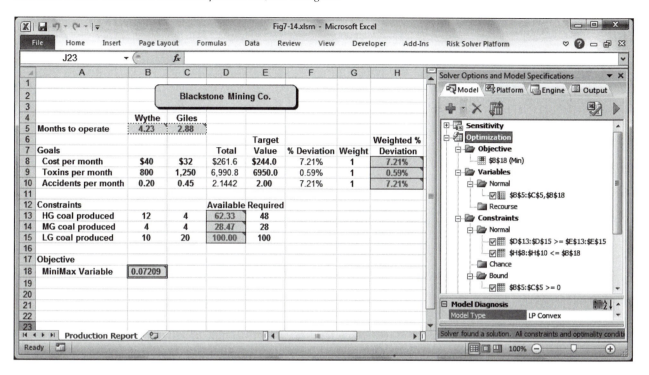

FIGURE 7.17

Graph of other solutions obtained using the MINIMAX objective

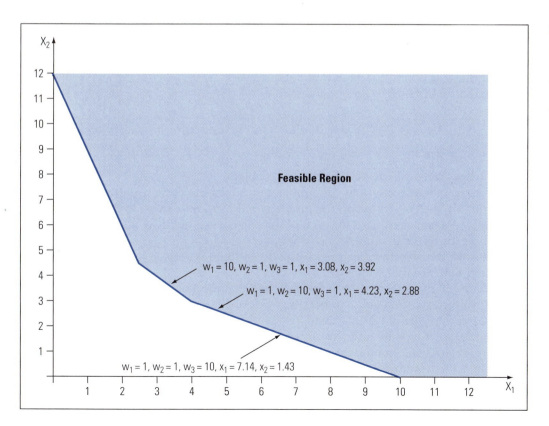

7.6 Comments on MOLP

Figure 7.18 provides a summary of the steps involved in solving an MOLP problem. Although the MOLP example in this chapter was somewhat simple, the same basic process applies in virtually any MOLP problem, regardless of the number of objectives or the complexity of the problem.

One advantage of using the MINIMAX objective to analyze MOLP problems is that the solutions generated are always *Pareto optimal*. That is, given any solution generated using this approach, we can be certain that no other feasible solution allows an increase in any objective without decreasing at least one other objective. (There are one or two exceptions to this statement, but they go beyond the scope of this text.)

Although the MINIMAX objective is helpful in the analysis of MOLPs, its usefulness is not limited to these problems. Like deviational variables, the MINIMAX technique can prove useful in other types of mathematical programming situations.

In the example MOLP problem presented here, all of the goals were derived from minimization objectives. Because of this, we knew that the actual value for any goal could never be less than its derived target value, and we used the following formula to calculate the percentage deviation for each goal constraint:

$$\frac{\text{actual value} - \text{target value}}{\text{target value}}$$

For goals derived from maximization objectives, we know that the actual value of the goal can never be greater than its derived target value, and the percentage deviation for such goals should be calculated as:

$$\frac{\text{target value} - \text{actual value}}{\text{target value}}$$

If the target value of a goal is zero, it is not possible to use weighted percentage deviations in the solution to the MOLP because division by zero is not permissible. In this case, you can simply use weighted deviations.

FIGURE 7.18

Summary of the steps involved in formulating and solving an MOLP problem

Summary of Multiple Objective Optimization

1. Identify the decision variables in the problem.
2. Identify the objectives in the problem and formulate them in the usual way.
3. Identify the constraints in the problem and formulate them in the usual way.
4. Solve the problem once for each of the objectives identified in step 2 to determine the optimal value of each objective.
5. Restate the objectives as goals using the optimal objective values identified in step 4 as the target values.
6. For each goal, create a deviation function that measures the amount by which any given solution fails to meet the goal (either as an absolute or a percentage).
7. For each of the deviation functions identified in step 6, assign a weight to the deviation function and create a constraint that requires the value of the weighted deviation function to be less than the MINIMAX variable Q.
8. Solve the resulting problem with the objective of minimizing Q.
9. Inspect the solution to the problem. If the solution is unacceptable, adjust the weights in step 7 and return to step 8.

7.7 Summary

This chapter presented two separate but closely related issues in optimization—GP and MOLP. GP provides a way of analyzing potential solutions to a decision problem that involves soft constraints. Soft constraints can be stated as goals with target values. These goals can be translated into constraints through the use of deviational variables, which measure the amount by which a given solution deviates from a particular goal. The objective in GP problems is to minimize some weighted function of the deviational variables. By adjusting the weights on the deviational variables, a variety of potential solutions can be analyzed.

MOLP provides a way to analyze LP problems involving multiple objectives that conflict with one another. Although an MOLP problem is somewhat different from a standard GP problem, the objectives can be restated as goals after identifying appropriate target values for the objectives. The MINIMAX objective is helpful in analyzing the possible solutions to an MOLP problem.

Solving a GP or MOLP problem is not as simple as solving a single LP problem. Rather, a sequence of problems must be solved to allow the decision maker to analyze the trade-offs among the various goals and objectives at different possible solutions. Thus, both of these procedures are highly iterative and interactive.

7.8 References

Gass, S. "A Process for Determining Priorities and Weights for Large-Scale Linear Goal Programs." *Journal of the Operational Research Society*, vol. 37, August 1986.

Ignizio, J. "A Review of Goal Programming: A Tool for Multiobjective Analysis." *Journal of the Operational Research Society*, vol. 29, no. 11, 1978.

Steuer, R. *Multiple Criteria Optimization: Theory, Computation, and Application.* New York: Wiley, 1986.

Taylor, B., and A. Keown. "A Goal Programming Application of Capital Project Selection in the Production Area." *AIIE Transactions*, vol. 10, no. 1, 1978.

THE WORLD OF MANAGEMENT SCIENCE

Truck Transport Corporation Controls Costs and Disruptions While Relocating a Terminal

The Truck Transport Corporation, having decided to move its East St. Louis terminal, knew that relationships with customers and suppliers (independent truckers) were critical factors for continued profitable operations. Therefore, when evaluating five potential new sites, management considered driver and customer preferences as well as costs in making its final selection.

At Truck Transport Corporation, the traditional approach to evaluating a new site is to include the candidate site in a transportation LP model with the 4 other terminals and 12 major customers, and find the solution that minimizes total transportation costs. This minimum cost solution is then compared with those for the other candidates to choose the most efficient site. An assignment problem is solved

(Continued)

to assign independent truckers to terminals to minimize travel costs from the truckers' homes.

Some of the drivers, however, have strong preferences not to be assigned to particular terminals, usually on the basis of personal relationships with terminal managers. Some customers also have similar preferences. In a competitive market, failure to consider these preferences might cause the drivers or customers to do business elsewhere.

The linear GP model used to evaluate the sites combined the transportation problem and the trucker assignment problem. The constraints defined the following deviational variables, in declining order of priority: shortages in number of trips to major customers, shortages in number of trips assigned to each driver, number of driver preferences violated, number of customer preferences violated, increase in transportation costs from drivers' homes, and increase in transportation costs to the customers.

The model was validated by evaluating the East St. Louis site and comparing results to historical costs. The site ultimately selected fully satisfied the requirements for number of shipments and preferences. Total transportation costs for all drivers were projected to increase only $3,200, and customer transportation costs were projected to increase $1,400. The East St. Louis terminal was moved with no changes in the usual patterns of driver turnover or business with customers, and no complaints from drivers about decreased profitability because of the new site.

Source: Schneiderjans, Marc J., N. K. Kwak, and Mark C. Helmer, "An Application of Goal Programming to Resolve a Site Location Problem." *Interfaces*, vol. 12, no. 3, June 1982, pp. 65–70.

Questions and Problems

1. What is the difference between an objective function and a goal?
2. Is there an optimal solution to a GP or MOLP problem? Explain.
3. Read the feature at the end of Section 7.1 in this chapter titled "Balancing Objectives for Enlightened Self-Interest." What objectives were the real estate developers in this article considering in their plans for the Coal Bank Ridge development? Describe how the objectives you identify might conflict or support each other.
4. In 2005, hurricane Katrina decimated the gulf coast of the United States between Mobile, Alabama and New Orleans, Louisiana. The aftermath of this storm left the city of New Orleans flooded, both with water and human victims of the storm. Responding to this disaster was a logistical nightmare and presented governmental decision makers with an extremely difficult challenge.
   a. Identify several key objectives that the decision makers who managed this problem must have consider simultaneously.
   b. Identify the key resources that the decision makers needed to allocate.
   c. How do the objectives and the resources interrelate?
   d. Do the objectives you identified conflict or compete with one another in terms of resource usage?
   e. How might the techniques presented in this chapter have helped decision makers determine how to allocate resources to achieve the objectives?

5. Refer to the MOLP example presented in this chapter.
   a. What weights could be used to generate the solution at $X_1 = 2.5$, $X_2 = 4.5$?
   b. What weights could be used to generate the solution at $X_1 = 4.0$, $X_2 = 3.0$?
   c. What weights could be used to generate the solution at $X_1 = 10.0$, $X_2 = 0.0$?
   d. What weights could be used to generate solutions along the edge of the feasible region that runs from the point $X_1 = 0$, $X_2 = 12.0$ to the point $X_1 = 2.5$, $X_2 = 4.5$?
6. Suppose that the first goal in a GP problem is to make $2X_1 + 5X_2$ approximately equal to 25.
   a. Using the deviational variables d_1^- and d_1^+, what constraint can be used to express this goal?
   b. If we obtain a solution where $X_1 = 4$ and $X_2 = 3$, what values do the deviational variables assume?
   c. Consider a solution where $X_1 = 4$, $X_2 = 3$, $d_1^- = 6$, and $d_1^+ = 4$. Can this solution ever be optimal? Why or why not?
7. Consider the following MOLP:

$$
\begin{aligned}
\text{MAX:} \quad & 4X_1 + 2X_2 \\
\text{MIN:} \quad & X_1 + 3X_2 \\
\text{Subject to:} \quad & 2X_1 + X_2 \le 18 \\
& X_1 + 4X_2 \le 12 \\
& X_1 + X_2 \ge 4 \\
& X_1, X_2 \ge 0
\end{aligned}
$$

   a. Graph the feasible region for this problem.
   b. Calculate the value of each objective at each extreme point.
   c. What feasible points in this problem are Pareto optimal?
8. It has been suggested that one way to solve MOLP problems is to create a composite objective function as a linear combination of all the objectives in the problem. For example, in the previous problem, we might weight the first objective by 0.75 and the second by 0.25 to obtain the composite objective, MAX: $2.75X_1 + 0.75X_2$. (Note that the second objective in the previous problem is equivalent to MAX: $-X_1 - 3X_2$.) We then use this as the objective in an LP model to generate possible solutions. What problem, if any, do you see with this approach?
9. Refer to the MOLP problem presented in this chapter. The solutions shown in Figures 7.9, 7.10, and 7.11 each result in more than the required amount of one or more types of coal being produced, as summarized in the following table.

Solution Shown in:	High-Grade Coal	Excess Production of Medium-Grade Coal	Low-Grade Coal
Figure 7.9	0 tons	0 tons	15 tons
Figure 7.10	12 tons	0 tons	0 tons
Figure 7.11	72 tons	12 tons	0 tons

   a. Formulate an LP model that could be solved to find the solution that minimizes the maximum amount of excess coal produced. (*Hint*: Use a MINIMAX objective rather than a MAX( ) function.)
   b. Implement your model in a spreadsheet and solve it.
   c. What is the optimal solution?
   d. Revise your model to find the solution that minimizes the maximum percentage of excess coal produced. What is the optimal solution?

10. The CFO for the Shelton Corporation has $1.2 million to allocate to the following budget requests from five departments:

Dept 1	Dept 2	Dept 3	Dept 4	Dept 5
$450,000	$310,000	$275,000	$187,500	$135,000

Because the total budget requests exceed the available $1.2 million, not all the requests can be satisfied. Suppose the CFO considers the requests for departments 2 and 3 to be twice as important as those from departments 4 and 5, and the request from department 1 to be twice as important as those from departments 2 and 3. Further suppose the CFO want to make sure each department receives at least 70% of the requested amount.
   a. Formulate a GP model for this problem.
   b. Implement your model and solve it. What is the optimal solution?
   c. Suppose the CFO is willing to allocated more than $1.2 million to these budgets but regards exceeding the $1.2 million figure as being twice as undesirable as not meeting the budget request of department 1. What is the optimal solution?
   d. Suppose the CFO regards all deviations from the original budget amounts (including the $1.2 million available) to be equally undesirable. What solution minimizes the maximum percentage deviation from the budgeted amounts?

11. The Reeves Corporation wants to assign each of their 13 corporate clients to exactly one of their three salespersons. The estimated annual sales potential (in $1,000,000s) for each of the clients is summarized in the following table:

Client	A	B	C	D	E	F	G	H	I	J	K	L	M
Est. Sales	$67	$84	$52	$70	$74	$62	$94	$63	$73	$109	$77	$36	$114

Reeves wants each salesperson to be assigned to at least three customers and no more than six customers. The company wants to assign customers to the sales force in such a way that the estimated annual sales potential for each salesperson's set of customers is as equal as possible.
   a. Formulate a GP model for this problem. (*Hint*: There should be a goal for the estimated annual sales potential for each salesperson.)
   b. Assume the company wants to minimize the sum of the absolute deviations from each goal. Implement your model in a spreadsheet and solve it.

12. Blue Ridge Hot Tubs manufactures and sells two models of hot tubs: the Aqua-Spa and the Hydro-Lux. Howie Jones, the owner and manager of the company, needs to decide how many of each type of hot tub to produce during his next production cycle. Howie buys prefabricated fiberglass hot tub shells from a local supplier and adds the pump and tubing to the shells to create his hot tubs. (This supplier has the capacity to deliver as many hot tub shells as Howie needs.) Howie installs the same type of pump into both hot tubs. He will have only 200 pumps available during his next production cycle. From a manufacturing standpoint, the main difference between the two models of hot tubs is the amount of tubing and labor required. Each Aqua-Spa requires 9 hours of labor and 12 feet of tubing. Each Hydro-Lux requires 6 hours of labor and 16 feet of tubing. Howie expects to have 1,566 production labor hours and 2,880 feet of tubing available during the next production cycle. Howie earns a profit of $350 on each Aqua-Spa he sells and $300 on each Hydro-Lux he sells. He is confident that he can sell all the hot tubs he produces. The production of each Aqua-Spa generates 15 pounds of a toxic resin, whereas each Hydro-Lux

produces 10 pounds of toxic resin. Howie has identified two different objectives that could apply to his problem: He can maximize profit, or he can minimize the production of toxic resin. Suppose Howie considers the maximization of profit as half as important as the minimization of toxic resin.

a. Formulate an MOLP model for Howie's decision problem.
b. Implement your model in a spreadsheet and solve it.
c. What is the solution to Howie's MOLP problem?
d. The feasible region for this problem was shown in Figure 2.7. Identify on this graph the Pareto optimal solutions for Howie's MOLP problem.

13. The owner of the Weiner-Meyer meat processing plant wants to determine the best blend of meats to use in the next production run of hamburgers. Three sources of meat can be used. The following table summarizes relevant characteristics of these meats:

	Meat 1	Meat 2	Meat 3
Cost per pound	$0.75	$0.87	$0.98
% Fat	15%	10%	5%
% Protein	70%	75%	80%
% Water	12%	10%	8%
% Filler	3%	5%	7%

A local elementary school has ordered 500 pounds of meat for $1.10 per pound. The only requirement is that the meat consist of at least 75% protein and at most 10% each of water and filler. Ordinarily, the owner would produce the blend of meats that achieved this objective in the least costly manner. However, with the concern of too much fat in school lunches, the owner also wants to produce a blend that minimizes the fat content of the meat produced.

a. Formulate an MOLP for this problem.
b. Implement your formulation in a spreadsheet, and individually optimize the two objectives under consideration.
c. How much profit must be forfeited in order to fill this order using the mix that minimizes the fat content?
d. Solve this problem with the objective of minimizing the maximum percentage deviation from the target values of the goals. What solution do you obtain?
e. Assume the owner considers minimizing the fat content twice as important as maximizing profit. What solution does this imply?

14. A new Italian restaurant called the Olive Grove is opening in a number of locations in the Memphis area. The marketing manager for these stores has a budget of $150,000 to use in advertising and promotions for the new stores. The manager can run magazine ads at a cost of $2,000 each that result in 250,000 exposures each. TV ads result in approximately 1,200,000 exposures each but cost $12,000 each. The manager wants to run at least 5 TV ads and 10 magazine ads, while maximizing the number of exposures generated by the advertising campaign. But the manager also wants to spend no more than $120,000 on magazine and TV advertising so that the remaining $30,000 could be used for other promotional purposes. However, the manager would spend more than $120,000 on advertising if it resulted in a substantial increase in advertising coverage.

a. Formulate a GP model for this problem assuming the marketing manager has the following goals:

Goal 1: Exposures should be maximized.
Goal 2: No more than $120,000 should be spent on advertising.

(Note that you will have to determine an appropriate target value for the first goal.) Assume the marketing manager wants to minimize the maximum percentage deviation from either goal.

b. Implement your model in a spreadsheet and solve it.

c. What is the solution you obtain?

d. What changes do you make to your model if the manager wants to spend less on advertising than your solution suggests?

15. The city of Abingdon is determining its tax rate structure for the coming year. The city needs to generate $6 million in tax revenue via taxes of property, sales, prepared food, and utilities. The following table summarizes how much tax revenue would be generated from each segment of the population by the 1% increase in each tax category. (For instance, a 2% tax on prepared food would generate $240,000 in tax revenue from upper-income residents.)

Revenues (in $1,000s) per 1% Tax Rate

Income Group	Sales	Property	Food	Utility
Low	$200	$ 600	$ 50	$ 80
Middle	$250	$ 800	$100	$100
Upper	$400	$1200	$120	$120

City commissioners have specified that the tax rate for each revenue category must be between 1% and 3%, and the tax rate on prepared food cannot exceed half the sales tax rate. Ideally, the commissioners have a goal of making up the $6 million tax budget with $1.5 million from low-income residents, $2.1 million from middle-income residents, and $2.4 million from high-income residents. If that is not possible, the commissioners would like a solution that minimizes the maximum percentage deviation from these tax revenue goals for each income group.

a. Create a spreadsheet model for this problem.

b. What is the optimal solution?

16. The Royal Seas Company runs a three-night cruise to the Caribbean from Port Canaveral. The company wants to run TV ads promoting its cruises to high-income men, high-income women, and retirees. The company has decided to consider airing ads during prime time, afternoon soap operas, and during the evening news. The number of exposures (in millions) expected to be generated by each type of ad in each of the company's target audiences is summarized in the following table:

	Prime Time	Soap Operas	Evening News
High-income men	6	3	6
High-income women	3	4	4
Retirees	4	7	3

Ads during prime time, the afternoon soaps, and the news hour cost $120,000, $85,000, and $100,000, respectively. Royal Seas wants to achieve the following goals:

Goal 1: Spend approximately $900,000 of TV advertising.
Goal 2: Generate approximately 45 million exposures among high-income men.
Goal 3: Generate approximately 60 million exposures among high-income women.
Goal 4: Generate approximately 50 million exposures among retirees.

a. Formulate a GP model for this problem. Assume overachievement of the first goal is equally as undesirable as underachievement of the remaining goals on a percentage deviation basis.

b. Implement your model in a spreadsheet and solve it.

c. What is the optimal solution?

d. What solution allows the company to spend as close to $900,000 as possible without exceeding this amount?

e. Assume that the company can spend no more than $900,000. What solution minimizes the maximum percentage underachievement of all the goals?

f. Which of the two preceding solutions would you most prefer? Why?

17. Virginia Tech operates its own power-generating plant. The electricity generated by this plant supplies power to the university and to local businesses and residences in the Blacksburg area. The plant burns three types of coal, which produce steam that drives the turbines that generate the electricity. The Environmental Protection Agency (EPA) requires that for each ton of coal burned, the emissions from the coal furnace smoke stacks contain no more than 2,500 parts per million (ppm) of sulfur and no more than 2.8 kilograms (kg) of coal dust. However, the managers of the plant are concerned about the environment and want to keep these emissions to a minimum. The following table summarizes the amounts of sulfur, coal dust, and steam that result from burning a ton of each type of coal.

Coal	Sulfur (in ppm)	Coal Dust (in kg)	Pounds of Steam Produced
1	1,100	1.7	24,000
2	3,500	3.2	36,000
3	1,300	2.4	28,000

The three types of coal can be mixed and burned in any combination. The resulting emission of sulfur or coal dust and the pounds of steam produced by any mixture are given as the weighted average of the values shown in the table for each type of coal. For example, if the coals are mixed to produce a blend that consisted of 35% of coal 1, 40% of coal 2, and 25% of coal 3, the sulfur emission (in ppm) resulting from burning 1 ton of this blend is:

$$0.35 \times 1,100 + 0.40 \times 3,500 + 0.25 \times 1,300 = 2,110$$

The manager of this facility wants to select a blend of coal to burn while considering the following objectives:

Objective 1: Maximize the pounds of steam produced.
Objective 2: Minimize sulfur emissions.
Objective 3: Minimize coal dust emissions.

a. Formulate an MOLP model for this problem, and implement your model in a spreadsheet.

b. Determine the best possible value for each objective in the problem.

c. Determine the solution that minimizes the maximum percentage deviation from the optimal objective function values. What solution do you obtain?

d. Suppose management considers maximizing the amount of steam produced five times as important as achieving the best possible values for the other objectives. What solution does this suggest?

18. The Waygate Corporation makes five different types of metal casing for personal computers. The company is in the process of replacing its machinery with three different new models of metal stamping machines: the Robo-I, Robo-II, and Robo-III. The unit costs of each machine are $18,500, $25,000, and $35,000, respectively. Each

machine can be programmed to produce any of the five casings. After the machine is programmed, it produces each type of casing at the following rates:

	Casings per Hour				
	Type 1	Type 2	Type 3	Type 4	Type 5
Robo-I	100	130	140	210	80
Robo-II	265	235	170	220	120
Robo-III	200	160	260	180	220

The company has the following goals:

Goal 1: To spend no more than approximately $400,000 on the purchase of new machines

Goal 2: To have the ability to produce approximately 3,200 units of type 1 casings per hour

Goal 3: To have the ability to produce approximately 2,500 units of type 2 casings per hour

Goal 4: To have the ability to produce approximately 3,500 units of type 3 casings per hour

Goal 5: To have the ability to produce approximately 3,000 units of type 4 casings per hour

Goal 6: To have the ability to produce approximately 2,500 units of type 5 casings per hour

a. Formulate a GP model for this problem. Assume all percentage deviations from all goals are equally undesirable.

b. Implement your model in a spreadsheet and solve it.

c. What is the optimal solution?

d. What is the solution that minimizes the maximum percentage deviation from all the goals?

e. Assume that the company can spend no more than $400,000. What is the solution that minimizes the maximum percentage deviation from all the remaining goals?

19. The central Florida high school basketball tournament pits teams from four different counties against one another. The average distance (in miles) between tournament locations in each country is given in the following table.

	Average Distance (in miles) Between Counties			
	Orange	Seminole	Osceola	Volusia
Orange	—	30	45	60
Seminole	30	—	50	20
Osceola	45	50	—	75
Volusia	60	20	75	—

Games are officiated by certified refereeing crews from each county. Orange, Seminole, Osceola, and Volusia counties have 40, 22, 20, and 26 certified crews, respectively. During the tournament, officiating crews cannot work games in their home counties and are paid $0.23 per mile in travel costs (in addition to a $50 per-game officiating fee). (Assume each officiating crew travels to games in a single vehicle.) Additionally, crews from one county cannot work more than 50% of the games in any other single county. It is anticipated that Orange, Seminole, Osceola, and Volusia counties will host 28, 24, 16, and 20 games, respectively.

a. Create a spreadsheet model to determine the least costly plan for allocating officiating crews from the various counties.

   b. What is the optimal solution and associated travel cost for the referees?

   c. Suppose it is desired to spend no more than $700 on referee travel expenses for these games. Is that possible? If not, determine the solution that minimizes the maximum percentage deviation from the 50% officiating requirement for each county while requiring no more than $700 in travel costs.

20. The Chick'n-Pick'n fast-food chain is considering how to expand its operations. Three types of retail outlets are possible: a lunch counter operation designed for office buildings in downtown areas, an eat-in operation designed for shopping malls, and a stand-alone building with drive-through and sit-down facilities. The following table summarizes the number of jobs, startup costs, and annual returns associated with each type of operation:

	Lunch Counter	Mall	Stand-alone
Jobs	9	17	35
Costs	$150,000	$275,000	$450,000
Returns	$ 85,000	$125,000	$175,000

The company has $2,000,000 available to pay startup costs for new operations in the coming year. Additionally, there are five possible sites for lunch counter operations, seven possible mall locations, and three possible stand-alone locations. The company wants to plan its expansion in a way that maximizes annual returns and the number of jobs created.

   a. Formulate an MOLP for this problem.

   b. Determine the best possible value for each objective in the problem.

   c. Implement your model in a spreadsheet, and solve it to determine the solution that minimizes the maximum percentage deviation from the optimal objective function values. What solution do you obtain?

   d. Suppose management considers maximizing returns three times as important as maximizing the number of jobs created. What solution does this suggest?

21. A private foundation has offered $3 million to allocate to cities to help fund programs that aid the homeless. Grant proposals were received from cities A, B, and C seeking assistance of $750,000, $1.2 million, and $2.5 million, respectively. In the grant proposals, cities were requested to quantify the number of assistance units that would be provided using the funds (an assistance unit is a night on a bed in a shelter or a free meal). Cities A, B, and C reported they could provide 485,000, 850,000, and 1.5 million assistance units, respectively, with the funds requested during the coming year. The directors of the foundation have two objectives. They want to maximize the number of assistance units obtained with the $3 million. However, they also want to help each of the cities by funding as much of their individual requests as possible (this might be done by maximizing the minimum percentage of funding received by any city).

   a. Formulate an MOLP for this problem.

   b. Determine the best possible value for each objective in the problem.

   c. Implement your model in a spreadsheet, and solve it to determine the solution that minimizes the maximum percentage deviation from the optimal objective function values. What solution do you obtain?

22. The marketing manager for Glissen Paint is working on the weekly sales and marketing plan for the firm's industrial and contractor sales staff. Glissen's sales representatives contact two types of customers: existing customers and new customers. Each contact with an existing customer normally takes 3 hours of the salesperson's time (including travel time) and results in an average sale of $425.

Contacts with new customers generally take a bit longer, on average 4 hours, and result in an average sale of $350. The company's salespeople are required to work 40 hours a week but often work more to achieve their sales quotas (on which their bonuses are based). The company has a policy limiting the number of hours a salesperson can work to 50 hours per week. The sales manager wants to set customer contact quotas for the salespeople that will achieve the following goals (listed in order of importance):

Goal 1: Each salesperson should achieve an average weekly sales level of $6,000.
Goal 2: Each salesperson should contact at least 10 existing customers per week.
Goal 3: Each salesperson should contact at least 5 new customers per week.
Goal 4: Each salesperson should limit overtime to no more than 5 hours per week.

a. Formulate this problem as a GP with an objective of minimizing the sum of the weighted undesirable percentage deviation from the goals.
b. Implement your model in a spreadsheet and solve it by assuming equal weights on each goal. What solution do you obtain?

23. A paper recycling company converts newspaper, mixed paper, white office paper, and cardboard into pulp for newsprint, packaging paper, and print-stock quality paper. The recycler is currently trying to determine the best way of filling an order for 500 tons of newsprint pulp, 600 tons of packaging paper pulp, and 300 tons of print-stock quality pulp. The following table summarizes the yield for each kind of pulp recovered from each ton of recycled material.

	Recycling Yield		
	Newsprint	**Packaging**	**Print Stock**
Newspaper	85%	80%	—
Mixed Paper	90%	80%	70%
White Office Paper	90%	85%	80%
Cardboard	80%	70%	—

For instance, a ton of newspaper can be recycled using a technique that yields 0.85 tons of newsprint pulp. Alternatively, a ton of newspaper can be recycled using a technique that yields 0.80 tons of packaging paper. Similarly, a ton of cardboard can be recycled to yield 0.80 tons of newsprint or 0.70 tons of packaging paper pulp. Note that newspaper and cardboard cannot be converted to print-stock pulp using the techniques available to the recycler. As each material is recycled, it also produces a toxic sludge that the recycler must dispose of. The amount of toxic sludge (in pounds) created by processing a ton of each of the raw materials into each of the types of pulp is summarized in the following table. For instance, each ton of newspaper that is processed into newspaper pulp creates 125 pounds of sludge.

	Sludge (lbs)		
	Newsprint	**Packaging**	**Print Stock**
Newspaper	125	100	0
Mixed Paper	50	100	150
White Office Paper	50	75	100
Cardboard	100	150	0

The cost of processing each ton of raw material into the various types of pulp is summarized in the following table along with the amount of each of the four raw materials that can be purchased and their costs.

	Processing Costs per Ton			Purchase Cost Per Ton	Tons Available
	Newsprint	**Packaging**	**Print Stock**		
Newspaper	$6.50	$11.00	—	$15	600
Mixed Paper	$9.75	$12.25	$9.50	$16	500
White Office Paper	$4.75	$ 7.75	$8.50	$19	300
Cardboard	$7.50	$ 8.50	—	$17	400

These processing costs include the cost of disposing of sludge. However, the managers of the recycling facility would prefer to minimize the amount of sludge created as well as the total cost of filling the order.

a. Formulate an MOLP model for this problem, and implement your model in a spreadsheet.

b. Determine the best possible value for each objective in the problem.

c. Determine the solution that minimizes the maximum percentage deviation from the optimal objective function values. What solution do you obtain?

d. Suppose management considers minimizing costs to be twice as important as minimizing the amount of sludge produced. What solution does this suggest?

24. A trust officer at Pond Island Bank needs to determine what percentage of the bank's investable funds to place in each of following investments.

Investment	Yield	Maturity	Risk
A	11.0%	8	5
B	8.0%	1	2
C	8.5%	7	1
D	10.0%	6	5
E	9.0%	2	3

The Yield column represents each investment's annual yield. The Maturity column indicates the number of years funds must be placed in each investment. The Risk column indicates an independent financial analyst's assessment of each investment's risk. In general, the trust officer wants to maximize the weighted average yield on the funds placed in these investments while minimizing the weighted average maturity and the weighted average risk.

a. Formulate an MOLP model for this problem, and implement your model in a spreadsheet.

b. Determine the best possible value for each objective in the problem.

c. Determine the solution that minimizes the maximum percentage deviation from the optimal objective function values. What solution do you obtain?

d. Suppose management considers minimizing the average maturity to be twice as important as minimizing average risk, and maximizing average yield to be twice as important as minimizing average maturity. What solution does this suggest?

25. A major city in the northeast wants to establish a central transportation station from which visitors can ride buses to four historic landmarks. The city is arranged in a grid, or block, structure with equally spaced streets running north and south and equally spaced avenues running east and west. The coordinates of any corner of any block in

the city can be identified by the street and avenue numbers intersecting at that particular corner. The following table gives the coordinates for the four historic landmarks:

Landmark	Street	Avenue
1	7	3
2	3	1
3	1	6
4	6	9

The transportation planners want to build the transportation station at the location in the city that minimizes the total travel distance (measured rectangularly) to each landmark. For example, if they built the station at 6th Street and 2nd Avenue, the total distance to each landmark will be:

Landmark	Distance
1	$|7-6| + |3-2| = 1 + 1 = 2$
2	$|3-6| + |1-2| = 3 + 1 = 4$
3	$|1-6| + |6-2| = 5 + 4 = 9$
4	$|6-6| + |9-2| = 0 + 7 = 7$
	Total Distance $= 22$

a. Plot the locations of the various historical landmarks on a graph where the X-axis represents avenue numbers (starting at 0), and the Y-axis represents street numbers (starting at 0).

b. Formulate an LP model to determine the corner at which the central transportation station should be located. *Hint*: Let the decision variables represent the street location (X_1) and avenue location (X_2) of the station and use deviational variables to measure the absolute street distance and absolute avenue distance from each landmark to X_1 and X_2. Minimize the sum of the deviational variables.

26. KPS Communications is planning to bring wireless Internet access to the town of Ames, Iowa. Using a geographic information system, KPS has divided Ames into the following 5 by 5 grid. The values in each block of the grid indicate the expected annual revenue (in $1,000s) KPS will receive if wireless Internet service is provided to the geographic area represented by each block.

Expected Annual Revenue by Area (in $1,000s)

$34	$43	$62	$42	$34
$64	$43	$71	$48	$65
$57	$57	$51	$61	$30
$32	$38	$70	$56	$40
$68	$73	$30	$56	$44

KPS can build wireless towers in any block in the grid at a cost of $150,000 per tower. Each tower can provide wireless service to the block it is in and to all adjacent blocks. (Blocks are considered to be adjacent if they share a side. Blocks touching only at corner point are not considered adjacent.) KPS wants to determine how many towers to build and where to build them in order to maximize profits in the first year of operations. (Note: If a block can receive wireless service from two different towers, the revenue for that block should only be counted once.)

a. Create a spreadsheet model for this problem and solve it.

b. What is the optimal solution, and how much money will KPS make in the first year?

c. In order to be the dominant player in this market, KPS is also considering providing wireless access to all of Ames—even if it is less profitable to do so in the short term. Modify your model as necessary to determine the tower location plan that maximizes the wireless coverage in Ames. What is the optimal solution, and how much profit will it provide?

d. Clearly, there is a trade-off between the objective in part b of maximizing profit and the objective in part c of maximizing wireless coverage. Determine the solution that minimizes the maximum percentage deviation from the optimal objective function values from parts b and c.

e. Suppose KPS considers maximizing profit to be twice as important as maximizing coverage. What solution does this suggest?

27. A car dealer specializing in late model used cars collected the following data on the selling price and mileage of five cars of the same make and model year at an auto auction:

Mileage	Price
43,890	$12,500
35,750	$13,350
27,300	$14,600
15,500	$15,750
8,900	$17,500

Because there seems to be a strong relationship between mileage and price, the dealer wants to use this information to predict this type of car's market value on the basis of its mileage. The dealer thinks that the car's selling price can be predicted as:

$$\text{Estimated price} = A + B \times \text{mileage}$$

A and B represent numeric constants (which might be positive or negative). Using the data collected at last week's auction, the dealer wants to determine appropriate values for A and B that minimize the following quantity:

$$\text{MIN:} \quad |A + B \times 43,890 - 12,500| + |A + B \times 35,750 - 13,350| +$$
$$|A + B \times 27,300 - 14,600| + |A + B \times 15,500 - 15,750| +$$
$$|A + B \times 8,900 - 17,500|$$

Notice that this objective seeks to find values of A and B that minimize the sum of the absolute value of the deviations between the actual prices of the cars and the estimated prices.

a. Create an LP model using deviational variables whose solution provides the best values for A and B using the stated criteria. That is, what values of A and B minimize the sum of the absolute deviations between the actual and estimated selling prices?

b. Implement your model in a spreadsheet and solve it.

c. Using the values of A and B determined by your solution, what should the estimated selling price be for each car?

28. Refer to the previous question. Suppose that the car dealer wanted to find values for A and B that minimized the maximum absolute deviation between the actual and estimated selling price for each car. What values of A and B achieve this objective?

29. A job in a machine shop must undergo five operations—A, B, C, D, and E. Each operation can be performed on either of two machines. The following table summarizes the time required for each machine to perform each operation:

	A	B	C	D	E
Machine 1	7	8	4	4	9
Machine 2	5	3	9	6	8

Formulate a model that can be solved to determine the job routing that minimizes the maximum amount of time used on either machine. That is, if t_i is the total time used on machine i, find the solution that minimizes the maximum of t_1 and t_2.

CASE 7.1   # Removing Snow in Montreal

Based on: James Campbell and Andre Langevin, "The Snow Disposal Assignment Problem," *Journal of the Operational Research Society*, 1995, pp. 919–929.

Snow removal and disposal are important and expensive activities in Montreal and many northern cities. Although snow can be cleared from streets and sidewalks by plowing and shoveling, in prolonged subfreezing temperatures, the resulting banks of accumulated snow can impede pedestrian and vehicular traffic and must be removed.

To allow timely removal and disposal of snow, a city is divided up into several sectors, and snow removal operations are carried out concurrently in each sector. In Montreal, accumulated snow is loaded into trucks and hauled away to disposal sites (for example, rivers, quarries, sewer chutes, surface holding areas). The different types of disposal sites can accommodate different amounts of snow due to the physical size of the disposal facility. The annual capacities for five different snow disposal sites are given in the following table (in 1,000s of cubic meters):

	Disposal Site				
	1	2	3	4	5
Capacity	350	250	500	400	200

The snow transported to various disposal sites is often contaminated by salt and de-icing chemicals. When the snow melts, these contaminants ultimately wind up in lakes, rivers, and the local water supply. The different disposal sites are equipped to remove different amounts of contaminants from the snow they receive. The percentage of contaminants that can be removed from the snow delivered to each disposal site is given in the following table. The amount of contaminant contained in removed snow is relatively constant across sectors.

	Disposal Site				
	1	2	3	4	5
Contaminant Removed	30%	40%	20%	70%	50%

The cost of removing and disposing of snow depends mainly on the distance it must be trucked. For planning purposes, the City of Montreal uses the straight-line distance from the center of each sector to each of the various disposal sites as an approximation of the cost involved in transporting snow between these locations. The following table summarizes these distances (in kilometers) for 10 sectors in the city.

	Disposal Site				
Sector	**1**	**2**	**3**	**4**	**5**
1	3.4	1.4	4.9	7.4	9.3
2	2.4	2.1	8.3	9.1	8.8
3	1.4	2.9	3.7	9.4	8.6
4	2.6	3.6	4.5	8.2	8.9
5	1.5	3.1	2.1	7.9	8.8
6	4.2	4.9	6.5	7.7	6.1
7	4.8	6.2	9.9	6.2	5.7
8	5.4	6.0	5.2	7.6	4.9
9	3.1	4.1	6.6	7.5	7.2
10	3.2	6.5	7.1	6.0	8.3

Using historical snowfall data, the city is able to estimate the annual volume of snow requiring removal in each sector as four times the length of streets in the sectors in meters (that is, it is assumed each linear meter of street generates 4 cubic meters of snow to remove over an entire year). The following table estimates the snow removal requirements (in 1000s of cubic meters) for each sector in the coming year:

Estimated Annual Snow Removal Requirements

1	2	3	4	5	6	7	8	9	10
153	152	154	138	127	129	111	110	130	135

1. If Montreal wants to pursue the objective of minimizing the distance the snow must be moved (and therefore the cost of removing snow), how much snow should it plan to move from each sector to each disposal site?
2. If it costs $35 to move 1,000 cubic meters of snow 1 kilometer, how much should Montreal plan on spending on the transportation for the removal of snow?
3. If Montreal wants to pursue the objective of maximizing the amount of contaminant that is removed from transported snow, how much snow should it plan to move from each sector to each disposal site, and what transportation cost is associated with this solution?
4. Suppose Montreal wants to minimize the maximum percentage deviation from the optimal value for each of the two objectives mentioned earlier. What is the optimal solution, and how far is each objective function from its optimal value?
5. Suppose the removal of contaminants is regarded as five times more important than transportation cost minimization. What solution minimizes the maximum weighted percentage deviation for each objective? How far is each objective from its optimal value?
6. What other suggestions might you have for Montreal as it attempts to deal with these two conflicting objectives?

Planning Diets for the Food Stamp Program

Based on: S. Taj, "A Mathematical Model for Planning Policies for Food Stamps." *Applications of Management Science*, Vol. 7, 25–48, 1993.

The United States Department of Agriculture (USDA) is responsible for managing and administering the national food stamp program. This program provides vouchers to low-income families that can be used in place of cash to purchase food at grocery stores. In determining the cash value of the vouchers issued, the USDA must consider how much it costs to obtain a nutritional, well-balanced diet for men and women in various age groups. As a first step in this process, the USDA identified and analyzed 31 different food groups and determined the contributions a serving from each group makes to 24 different nutritional categories. A partial listing of this information is given in Figure 7.19 (and in the file Fig7-19.xlsm that accompanies this book).

The last two rows in this spreadsheet indicate the minimum and/or maximum nutrients required per week for men between the ages of 20 and 50. (Maximum values of 9999 indicate that no maximum value applies to that particular nutritional requirement.)

The USDA uses this information to design a diet (or weekly consumption plan) that meets the indicated nutritional requirements. The last two columns in Figure 7.19 represent two different objectives that can be pursued in creating a diet. First, we may want to identify the diet that meets the nutritional requirements at a minimum cost. Although such a diet might be very economical, it might also be very unsatisfactory to the tastes of the people who are expected to eat it. To help address this issue, the USDA conducted a survey to assess people's preferences for different food groups. The last column in Figure 7.19 summarizes these preferences ratings, with higher scores indicating more desirable foods, and lower scores indicating less desirable foods. Thus, another objective that

FIGURE 7.19 *Data for the USDA diet-planning problem*

	Food	Weekly Units	Carbo-hydrates	Total Fat	Saturated Fat	Monosat. Fats	Polysat. Fat	Choles-terol	Sugar	Cost per unit	Pref. Rating
8	6 Other fruit	0	71.40	1.60	0.30	0.30	0.40	0.00	32.00	$0.961	14.88
9	7 Whole-grain/high-fiber breakfast cereals	0	323.60	21.90	4.60	6.90	8.90	0.00	140.00	$2.770	8.22
10	8 Other cereals	0	382.30	6.20	2.50	1.10	1.80	0.00	392.00	$3.327	9.43
11	9 Whole-grain/high-fiber flour, meal, rice	0	328.50	17.90	2.70	4.30	8.80	0.00	8.00	$0.966	4.4
12	10 Other flour, meal, rice, pasta	0	346.00	6.20	1.20	2.30	11.00	52.00	52.00	$0.720	0.28
13	11 Whole grain/high fiber bread	0	217.10	14.90	2.60	3.70	6.40	1.00	4.00	$1.553	5.52
14	12 Other breads	0	225.10	18.60	4.30	7.10	5.20	7.00	16.00	$1.111	4.9
15	13 Bakery products	0	300.40	69.10	21.50	27.20	14.30	112.00	392.00	$2.460	9.03
16	14 Grain mixtures	0	196.80	25.10	9.50	8.60	4.80	61.00	24.00	$1.556	25.67
17	15 Milk, yogurt	0	32.00	14.80	9.30	4.10	0.60	60.00	4.00	$0.362	17.34
18	16 Cheese	0	10.50	134.40	85.15	38.30	4.00	413.00	0.00	$2.811	22.72
19	17 Cream, mixtures mostly milk	0	107.30	60.50	41.80	13.50	2.00	137.00	256.00	$1.223	17.1
20	18 Lower-cost red meats, variety meats	0	1.30	84.90	33.60	37.10	4.50	284.00	0.00	$1.918	44.58
21	19 Higher-cost red meats, variety meats	0	0.60	74.00	28.30	32.50	5.90	278.00	0.00	$2.801	89.24
22	20 Poultry	0	0.40	42.10	12.00	16.90	9.20	271.00	0.00	$1.281	57.53
23	21 Fish, shellfish	0	2.40	12.70	2.70	4.30	3.80	172.00	4.00	$3.471	78.18
24	22 Bacon, sausage, luncheon meats	0	7.60	170.40	63.00	79.10	18.40	287.00	16.00	$2.481	17.83
25	23 Eggs	0	4.90	40.10	12.40	15.24	5.50	1698.00	0.00	$0.838	9.35
26	24 Dry beans, peas, lentils	0	235.60	5.00	1.30	1.00	1.80	5.00	44.00	$1.309	13.08
27	25 Mixtures, mostly meat, poultry, fish, egg	0	58.40	37.70	11.70	14.70	8.00	101.00	20.00	$1.967	46.2
28	26 Nuts, peanut butter	0	88.60	221.70	37.80	102.00	71.10	0.00	56.00	$2.504	21.26
29	27 Fats, oils	0	14.80	370.00	90.40	137.20	125.80	152.00	24.00	$1.198	3.17
30	28 Sugar, sweets	0	406.90	7.30	4.00	2.33	0.50	3.00	1576.00	$1.111	2.39
31	29 Seasonings	0	36.30	5.50	1.80	1.70	1.20	0.00	4.00	$2.077	5.8
32	30 Soft drinks, punches, ades	0	58.40	0.00	0.00	0.00	0.00	0.00	116.00	$0.249	47.42
33	31 Coffee, tea	0	87.70	1.70	0.60	0.10	0.50	0.00	4.00	$6.018	7.7
34	Weekly Total	0	0	0	0	0	0	0	0	$0.000	0
35	Weekly Lower Limit		0.00	0.00	0.00	0.00	0.00	0.00	0.00		
36	Weekly Upper Limit		9999	676.67	225.56	9999	9999	2100	2436		

could be pursued would be that of determining the diet that meets the nutritional requirements and produces the highest total preference rating. However, this solution is likely to be quite expensive. Assume that the USDA has asked you to help them analyze this situation using MOLP.

1. Find the weekly diet that meets the nutritional requirements in the least costly manner. What is the lowest possible minimum cost? What preference rating does this solution have?
2. Find the weekly diet that meets the nutritional requirements with the highest preference rating. What preference rating does this solution have? What cost is associated with this solution?
3. Find the solution that minimizes the maximum percentage deviation from the optimum values for each individual objective. What cost and preference rating is associated with this solution?
4. Suppose that deviations from the optimal cost value are weighted twice as heavily as those from the optimal preference value. Find the solution that minimizes the maximum weighted percentage deviations. What cost and preference rating is associated with this solution?
5. What other factors or constraints might you want to include in this analysis if you had to eat the resulting diet?

Sales Territory Planning at Caro-Life

CASE 7.3

Caro-Life is a financial services firm that specializes in selling life, auto, and home insurance to residential consumers in the state of North Carolina. The company is planning to expand and offer its services in South Carolina as well. The company wants to open a set of 10 offices throughout the state in such a way to ensure that all residents of the state can access at least 1 office in either their county of residence or an adjacent county. The set of counties adjacent to the county containing each office will be regarded as the sales territory for that office. (Note that a county is considered to be adjacent to itself.) Figure 7.20 (and the file Fig7-20.xlsm that accompanies this book) shows a portion of an Excel spreadsheet with a matrix indicating county adjacencies throughout the state and the estimated population and geographic size (in square miles) for each potential sales territory. (Values of 1 in the matrix indicate counties that are adjacent to one another.)

Sales of insurance products in a given area tend to be highly correlated with the number of people living in the area. As a result, agents assigned to the various offices want their sales territories to contain as many people as possible (to maximize sales potential). On the other hand, territories containing large amounts of people may also be comprised of a large geographic area that may require lots of travel on the part of the agents. So the goal of having a territory with lots of people is sometimes in conflict with having a territory that is compact in size. It is important for Caro-Life to design its sales territories in as equitable a manner as possible (that is, where the territories are similar in terms of geographic size and sales potential).

1. Assume Caro-Life wants to maximize the average sales potential of its 10 offices. Where should it locate offices, and what is the population and geographic area associated with each office?
2. Assume Caro-Life wants to minimize the average geographic area covered by each of its 10 offices. Where should it locate offices, and what is the population and geographic area associated with each office?

FIGURE 7.20 *Data for the Caro-Life sales territory-planning problem*

	Abbeville	Aiken	Allendale	Anderson	Bamberg	Barnwell	Beaufort	Berkeley	Calhoun	Charleston	Cherokee	Chester
28 Georgetown	0	0	0	0	0	0	0	1	0	0	0	0
29 Greenville	1	0	0	1	0	0	0	0	0	0	0	0
30 Greenwood	1	0	0	0	0	0	0	0	0	0	0	0
31 Hampton	0	0	1	0	1	0	1	0	0	0	0	0
32 Horry	0	0	0	0	0	0	0	0	0	0	0	0
33 Jasper	0	0	0	0	0	0	1	0	0	0	0	0
34 Kershaw	0	0	0	0	0	0	0	0	0	0	0	0
35 Lancaster	0	0	0	0	0	0	0	0	0	0	0	1
36 Laurens	1	0	0	1	0	0	0	0	0	0	0	0
37 Lee	0	0	0	0	0	0	0	0	0	0	0	0
38 Lexington	0	1	0	0	0	0	0	0	1	0	0	0
39 Marion	0	0	0	0	0	0	0	0	0	0	0	0
40 Marlboro	0	0	0	0	0	0	0	0	0	0	0	0
41 McCormick	1	0	0	0	0	0	0	0	0	0	0	0
42 Newberry	0	0	0	0	0	0	0	0	0	0	0	0
43 Oconee	0	0	0	1	1	0	0	0	0	0	0	0
44 Orangeburg	0	1	0	0	1	1	0	1	1	0	0	0
45 Pickens	0	0	0	1	0	0	0	0	0	0	0	0
46 Richland	0	0	0	0	0	0	0	0	1	0	0	0
47 Saluda	0	1	0	0	0	0	0	0	0	0	0	0
48 Spartanburg	0	0	0	0	0	0	0	0	0	0	1	0
49 Sumter	0	0	0	0	0	0	0	0	1	0	0	0
50 Union	0	0	0	0	0	0	0	0	0	0	1	1
51 Williamsburg	0	0	0	0	0	0	0	1	0	0	0	0
52 York	0	0	0	0	0	0	0	0	0	0	1	1
53												
54 Population	732400	533200	112300	830100	368900	289500	208700	812600	809400	635400	529300	335800
55 Sq. Miles	3666.59	4381.67	2966.42	3853.36	5272.3	3529.08	2857.77	6053.86	4216.38	3648.24	2400.47	3012.91

3. Determine the solution that minimizes the maximum percentage deviation from the optimal objective function values identified in questions 1 and 2. According to this solution, where should Caro-Life locate its offices, and what is the population and geographic area associated with each office?

4. Suppose Caro-Life considers maximizing average sales potential of its territories to be twice as important as minimizing the average geographic size of its territories. Find the solution that minimizes the maximum weighted percentage deviations. According to this solution, where should Caro-Life locate its offices, and what is the population and geographic area associated with each office?

5. What other issues would you suggest Caro-Life take into account in modeling this decision problem?

Chapter 8

Nonlinear Programming and Evolutionary Optimization

8.0 Introduction

Up to this point in our study of optimization, we have considered only mathematical programming models in which the objective function and constraints are *linear* functions of the decision variables. In many decision problems, the use of such linear functions is appropriate. Other types of optimization problems involve objective functions and constraints that *cannot* be modeled adequately using linear functions of the decision variables. These types of problems are called **nonlinear programming** (NLP) problems.

The process of formulating an NLP problem is virtually the same as formulating an LP problem. In each case, you must identify the appropriate decision variables and formulate an appropriate objective function and constraints using these variables. As you will see, the process of implementing and solving NLP problems in a spreadsheet is also similar to that for LP problems. However, the mechanics (that is, mathematical procedures) involved in solving NLP problems are very different. Although optimization software such as Solver makes this difference somewhat transparent to the user of such systems, it is important to understand these differences so you can understand the difficulties you might encounter when solving an NLP problem. This chapter discusses some of the unique features and challenges involved in solving NLP problems and presents several examples of managerial decision-making problems that can be modeled as NLP problems.

8.1 The Nature of NLP Problems

The main difference between an LP and NLP problem is that NLPs can have a nonlinear objective function and/or one or more nonlinear constraints. To understand the differences and difficulties nonlinearities introduce to an optimization problem, consider the various hypothetical NLP problems shown in Figure 8.1.

The first graph in Figure 8.1, labeled (a), illustrates a problem with a linear objective function and a *nonlinear* feasible region. Note that the boundary lines of the feasible region for this problem are not all straight lines. At least one of the constraints in this problem must be nonlinear to cause the curve in the boundary line of the feasible region. This curve causes the unique optimal solution to this problem to occur at a solution that is not a corner point of the feasible region.

The second graph in Figure 8.1, labeled (b), shows a problem with a *nonlinear* objective function and a linear constraint set. As indicated in this graph, if an NLP problem

FIGURE 8.1

Examples of NLP problems with optimal solutions not at a corner point of the feasible region

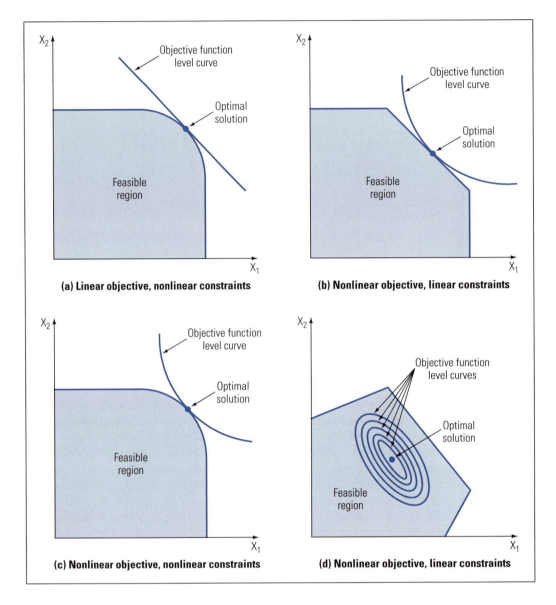

(a) Linear objective, nonlinear constraints

(b) Nonlinear objective, linear constraints

(c) Nonlinear objective, nonlinear constraints

(d) Nonlinear objective, linear constraints

has a nonlinear objective function, the level curves associated with the objective are also nonlinear. So from this graph, we observe that a nonlinear objective can cause the optimal solution to the NLP problem to occur at a solution that is not a corner point of the feasible region—even if all the constraints are linear.

The third graph in Figure 8.1, labeled (c), shows a problem with a *nonlinear* objective and a *nonlinear* constraint set. Here again, we see that the optimal solution to this NLP problem occurs at a solution that is not a corner point of the feasible region.

Finally, the fourth graph in Figure 8.1, labeled (d), shows another problem with a *nonlinear* objective and a *linear* constraint set. The optimal solution to this problem occurs at a point in the interior of the feasible region.

These graphs illustrate the major difference between LP and NLP problems—an optimal solution to an LP problem always occurs at a corner point of its feasible region, but this is not true of NLP problems. The optimal solution to some NLP problems might not occur on the boundary of the feasible region at all but at some point in the interior of the feasible region. Therefore, the strategy of searching the corner points of the feasible region employed by the simplex method to solve LP problems will not work with NLP problems. We need another strategy to solve NLP problems.

8.2 Solution Strategies for NLP Problems

The solution procedure Solver uses to solve NLP problems is called the **generalized reduced gradient** (GRG) algorithm. The mathematics involved in this procedure are rather complex and go beyond the scope and purpose of this text. However, the following discussion should give you a very basic (if somewhat imprecise) understanding of the ideas behind the GRG and other NLP solution algorithms.

NLP algorithms begin at any feasible solution to the NLP problem. This initial feasible solution is called the **starting point**. The algorithm then attempts to move from the starting point in a direction through the feasible region that causes the objective function value to improve. Some amount of movement (or a **step size**) in the selected feasible direction is then taken resulting in a new, and better, feasible solution to the problem. The algorithm next attempts to identify another feasible direction in which to move to obtain further improvements in the objective function value. If such a direction exists, the algorithm determines a new step size and moves in that direction to a new and better feasible solution. This process continues until the algorithm reaches a point at which there is no feasible direction in which to move that results in an improvement in the objective function. When no further possibility for improvement exists (or the potential for further improvement becomes arbitrarily small), the algorithm terminates.

Figure 8.2 shows a graphical example of how a crude NLP algorithm might work. In this graph, an initial feasible solution occurs at the origin (point A). The fastest rate of

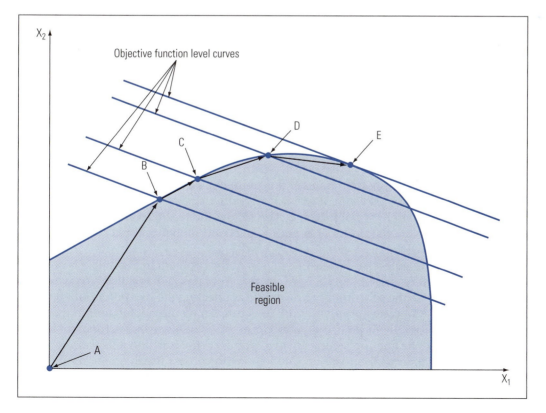

FIGURE 8.2

Example of an NLP solution strategy

improvement in the objective function value occurs by moving from point A in the direction that is perpendicular to (or forms a 90-degree angle with) the level curves of the objective function. Feasible movement in this direction is possible from point A to point B where a boundary of the feasible region is encountered. From point B, moving along the edge of the feasible region to point C further improves the objective function value. At point C, the boundary of the feasible region begins to curve; therefore, continued movement in the direction from point B to point C is no longer feasible. From point C, a new direction through the interior of the feasible region allows movement to point D. This process continues from point D until the solution becomes arbitrarily close (or converges) to point E—the optimal solution.

In moving from point A in Figure 8.2, we selected the direction that resulted in the fastest rate of improvement in the objective function. In retrospect, we can see that it would have been better to move from point A in the direction of point E. This direction does not result in the fastest rate of improvement in the objective as we move from point A, but it would have taken us to the optimal solution in a more direct fashion. Thus, it is not always best to move in the direction producing the fastest rate of improvement in the objective, nor is it always best to move as far as possible in that direction. The GRG algorithm used by Solver takes these issues into consideration as it determines the direction and step size of the movements to make. Thus, although the GRG algorithm usually cannot move directly from a starting point to an optimal solution, it does choose the path it takes in a more refined manner than outlined in Figure 8.2.

8.3 Local vs. Global Optimal Solutions

NLP solution algorithms terminate whenever they detect that no feasible direction exists in which it can move to produce a better objective function value (or when the amount of potential improvement becomes arbitrarily small). In such a situation, the current solution is a **local optimal solution**—a solution that is better than any other feasible solution in its immediate, or local, vicinity. However, a given local optimal solution might not be the best possible, or **global optimal**, solution to a problem. Another local optimal solution in some other area of the feasible region could be the best possible solution to the problem. This type of anomaly is illustrated in Figure 8.3.

If an NLP algorithm starts at point A in Figure 8.3, it could move immediately to point B and then along the feasible direction from B to C. Because no feasible point in the vicinity of C produces a better objective function value, point C is a local optimal solution, and the algorithm terminates at this point. However, this is clearly *not* the best possible solution to this problem. If an NLP algorithm starts at point D in Figure 8.3, it could move immediately to point E, and then follow the feasible direction from E to F and from F to G. Note that point G is both a local and global optimal solution to this problem.

It is important to note that the feasible region of the problem in Figure 8.3 is nonconvex, while those in Figures 8.1 and 8.2 are convex. A set points X is called a convex set if for *any* two points in the set a straight line drawn connecting the two points falls entirely within X. (A line connecting points B and E in Figure 8.3 would not fall within the feasible region. Therefore the feasible region in Figure 8.3 is nonconvex.) A function is convex (or concave) if the line connecting any two points on the function falls entirely above (or below) the function. Optimization problems with convex feasible regions and convex (or concave) objective functions are considerably easier to solve to global optimality than those that do not exhibit these properties.

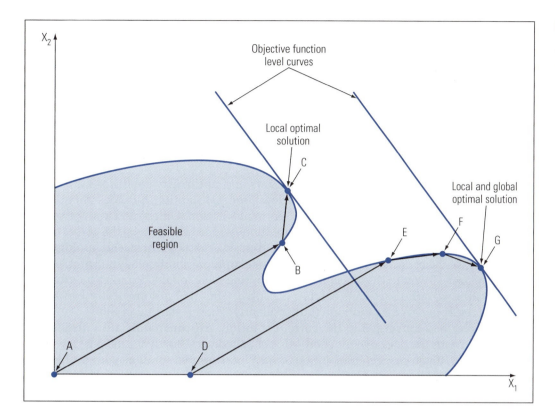

FIGURE 8.3

*Local vs. global
optimal solutions*

Figure 8.3 highlights two important points about the GRG and all other NLP algorithms:

- NLP algorithms can terminate at a local optimal solution that might not be the global optimal solution to the problem.
- The local optimal solution at which an NLP algorithm terminates depends on the initial starting point.

The possibility of terminating at a local optimal solution is undesirable—but we have encountered this type of difficulty before. In our study of integer programming, we noted that suboptimal solutions to ILPs might be acceptable if they are within some allowable tolerance of the global optimal solution. Unfortunately, with NLP problems, it is difficult to determine how much worse a given local optimal solution is than the global optimal solution because most optimization packages do not provide a way of obtaining bounds on the optimal objective function values for these problems. However, many NLP problems have a single local optimal solution that, by definition, must also be the global optimal solution. So in many problems, NLP algorithms will locate the global optimal solution, but as a general rule, we will not know whether the solution obtained is a global optimal solution. However, in Risk Solver Platform, some information about this issue can be obtained by running the convexity tester (by choosing Optimize, Analyze Without Solving, or by clicking the X-Checkbox icon on the Model tab in the task pane). The result of convexity testing may be Proven Convex, Proven Nonconvex, or Nothing Proven. If you see Model Type - NLP Convex in the Model Diagnosis area of the task pane Model tab, then you know that a local optimal solution is also a global optimal solution. If you see NLP NonCvx or just NLP, then you have to assume that you have only a local optimal solution. In the nonconvex case, it is usually a good idea to try starting NLP algorithms from different points to determine if the problem has different local optimal solutions. This procedure often reveals the global optimal solution. (Two questions at the end of this chapter illustrate this process.)

"Optimal" Solutions

When solving an NLP problem, Solver normally stops when the first of three numerical tests is satisfied, causing one of the following three completion messages to appear:

1. **"Solver found a solution. All constraints and optimality conditions are satisfied."**   This means Solver found a local optimal solution, but does not guarantee that the solution is the global optimal solution. Unless you know that a problem has only one local optimal solution (which must also be the global optimal solution), you should run Solver from several different starting points to increase the chances that you find the global optimal solution to your problem. The easiest way to do this is to set the Engine tab Global Optimization group MultiStart option to True before you solve. This will automatically run the Solver from several randomly (but efficiently) chosen starting points.
2. **"Solver has converged to the current solution. All constraints are satisfied."** This means the objective function value changed very slowly for the past few iterations. If you suspect the solution is not a local optimal solution, your problem may be poorly scaled. The convergence option in the Solver Options dialog box can be reduced to avoid convergence at suboptimal solutions.
3. **"Solver cannot improve the current solution. All constraints are satisfied."** This rare message means that your model is degenerate, and the Solver is cycling. Degeneracy can often be eliminated by removing redundant constraints in a model.

Starting Points

Solver sometimes has trouble solving an NLP problem if it starts at the null starting point, where all the decision variables are set equal to 0—even if this solution is feasible. Therefore, when solving an NLP problem, it is best to specify a non-null starting solution whenever possible.

We will now consider several examples of NLP problems. These examples illustrate some of the differences between LP and NLP problems and provide insight into the broad range of problems that cannot be modeled adequately using LP.

8.4 Economic Order Quantity Models

The economic order quantity (EOQ) problem is one of the most common business problems for which nonlinear optimization can be used. This problem is encountered when a manager must determine the optimal number of units of a product to purchase whenever an order is placed. The basic model for an EOQ problem makes the following assumptions:

- Demand for (or use of) the product is fairly constant throughout the year.
- Each new order is delivered in full when the inventory level reaches 0.

Figure 8.4 illustrates the type of inventory patterns observed for a product when the preceding conditions are met. In each graph, the inventory levels are depleted at a constant rate, representing constant demand. Also, the inventory levels are replenished instantly whenever the inventory levels reach 0.

The key issue in an EOQ problem is to determine the optimal quantity to order whenever an order is placed for an item. The trade-offs in this decision are evident in Figure 8.4. The graphs indicate two ways of obtaining 150 units of a product during the year. In the first graph, an order for 50 units is received whenever the inventory level drops to 0. This requires that three purchase orders be issued during the year and

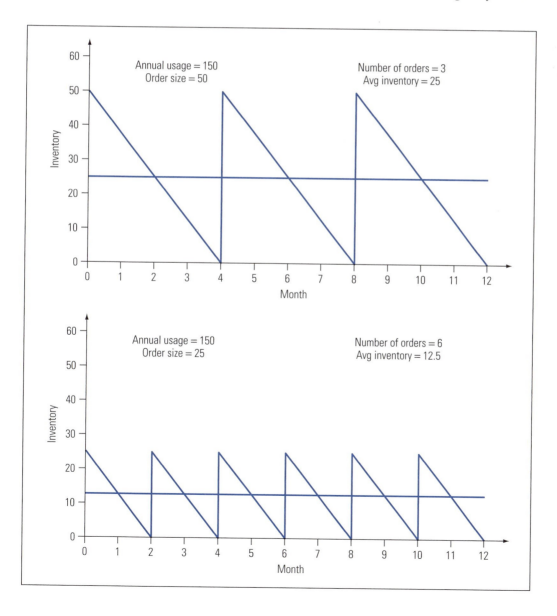

FIGURE 8.4

Inventory profiles of products for which the EOQ assumptions are met

results in an average inventory level of 25 units. In the second graph, an order for 25 units is received whenever the inventory level drops to 0. This requires that six purchase orders be issued throughout the year and results in an average inventory level of 12.5 units. Thus, the first ordering strategy results in fewer purchase orders (and lower ordering costs) but higher inventory levels (and higher carrying costs). The second ordering strategy results in more purchase orders (and higher ordering costs) but lower levels of inventory (and lower carrying costs).

In the basic EOQ model, the total annual cost of stocking a product is computed as the sum of the actual purchase cost of the product, plus the fixed cost of placing orders, plus the cost of holding (or carrying) the product in inventory. Figure 8.5 shows the relationships among order quantity, carrying cost, ordering cost, and total cost. Notice that as the order quantity increases, ordering costs decrease, and carrying costs increase. The goal in this type of problem is to find the EOQ that minimizes the total cost.

The total annual cost of acquiring products that meet the stated assumptions is represented by:

$$\text{Total annual cost} = DC + \frac{D}{Q}S + \frac{Q}{2}Ci$$

where:

D = annual demand for the item

C = unit purchase cost for the item

S = fixed cost of placing an order

i = cost of holding one unit in inventory for a year (expressed as a percentage of C)

Q = order quantity, or quantity ordered each time an order is placed

FIGURE 8.5

Relationships among order quantity, carrying cost, ordering cost, and total cost

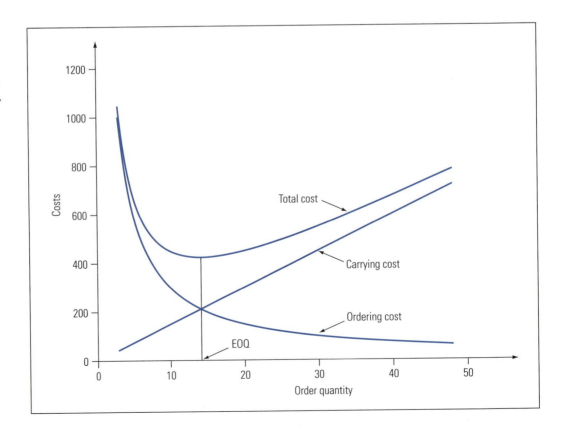

The first term in this formula (DC) represents the cost of purchasing a year's worth of the product. The second term $\frac{D}{Q}S$ represents the annual ordering costs. Specifically, $\frac{D}{Q}$ represents the number of orders placed during a year. Multiplying this quantity by S represents the cost of placing these orders. The third term $\frac{Q}{2}Ci$ represents the annual cost of holding inventory. On average, $\frac{Q}{2}$ units are held in inventory throughout the year (refer to Figure 8.4). Multiplying this term by Ci represents the cost of holding these units. The following example illustrates the use of the EOQ model.

> Alan Wang is responsible for purchasing the paper used in all the copy machines and laser printers at the corporate headquarters of MetroBank. Alan projects that in the coming year, he will need to purchase a total of 24,000 boxes of paper, which will be used at a fairly steady rate throughout the year. Each box of paper costs $35. Alan estimates that it costs $50 each time an order is placed (this includes the cost of placing the order plus the related costs in shipping and receiving). MetroBank assigns a cost of 18% to funds allocated to supplies and inventories because such funds are the lifeline of the bank and could be lent out to credit card customers who are willing to pay this rate on money borrowed from the bank. Alan has been placing paper orders once a quarter, but he wants to determine if another ordering pattern would be better. He wants to determine the most economical order quantity to use in purchasing the paper.

8.4.1 IMPLEMENTING THE MODEL

To solve this problem, we first need to create a spreadsheet model of the total cost formula described earlier, substituting the data for Alan's problem for the parameters D, C, S, and i. This spreadsheet implementation is shown in Figure 8.6 (and in the file Fig8-6.xlsm that accompanies this book).

In Figure 8.6, cell D4 represents the annual demand (D), cell D5 represents the per-unit cost (C), cell D6 represents the cost of placing an order (S), cell D7 represents the inventory holding cost (i) expressed as a percentage of an item's value, and cell D9 represents the order quantity (Q). The data corresponding to Alan's decision problem have been entered into the appropriate cells in this model. Because Alan places orders once a quarter (or four times a year), the order quantity in cell D9 is set at 24,000 ÷ 4 = 6,000.

We calculate each of the three pieces of our total cost function in cells D11, D12, and D13. Cell D11 contains the cost of purchasing a year's worth of paper, cell D12 represents the cost associated with placing orders, and cell D13 is the inventory holding cost that would be incurred. The sum of these costs is calculated in cell D14.

> Formula for cell D11: =D5*D4
>
> Formula for cell D12: =D4/D9*D6
>
> Formula for cell D13: =D9/2*D7*D5
>
> Formula for cell D14: =SUM(D11:D13)

8.4.2 SOLVING THE MODEL

The goal in this problem is to determine the order quantity (the value of Q) that minimizes the total cost. That is, we want Solver to determine the value for cell D9 that minimizes the value in cell D14. Figure 8.7 shows the Solver parameters and options required to solve this problem. Note that a constraint has been placed on cell D9 to prevent the order quantity from becoming 0 or negative. This constraint requires that at least one order must be placed during the year.

FIGURE 8.6 *Spreadsheet implementation of MetroBank's paper purchasing problem*

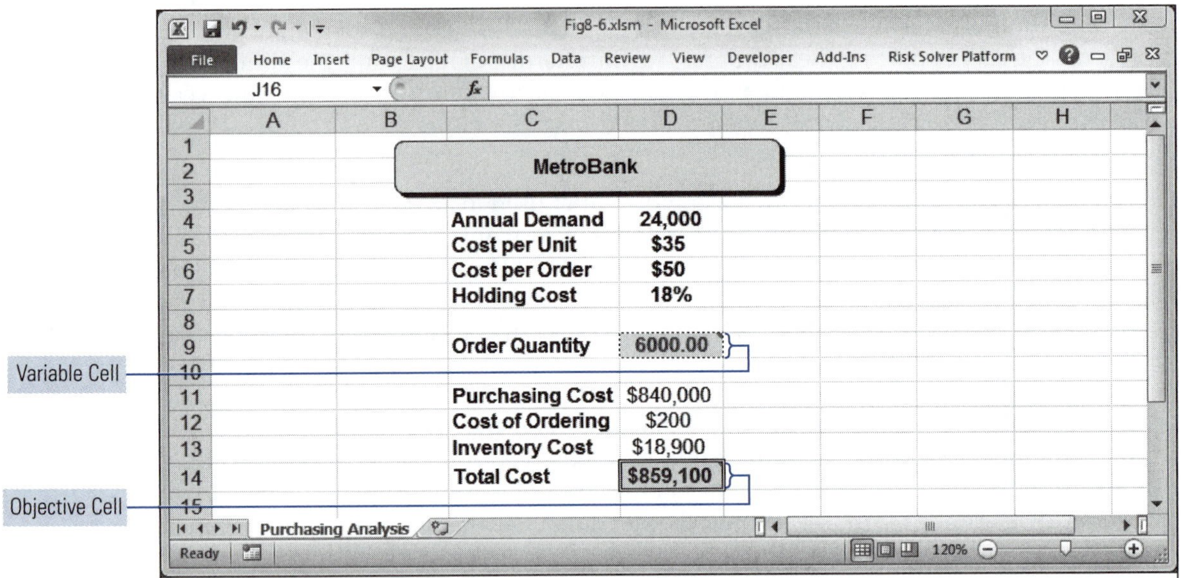

Key Cell Formulas

Cell	Formula	Copied to
D11	=D5*D4	--
D12	=D4/D9*D6	--
D13	=D9/2*D5*D7	--
D14	=SUM(D11:D13)	--

FIGURE 8.7

Solver parameters for MetroBank's paper purchasing problem

Solver Settings:

Objective: D14 (Min)
Variable cells: D9
Constraints:
    B9:D9 >= 1

Solver Options:
    Standard GRG Nonlinear Engine

The Assume Linear Model Option

When solving an NLP problem, it is important *not* to select the Standard LP Engine option. When this option is selected, Solver conducts a number of internal tests to verify that the model is truly linear in the objective and constraints. If this option is selected and Solver's tests indicate that the model is *not* linear, a message appears indicating that the conditions for linearity are not satisfied.

8.4.3 ANALYZING THE SOLUTION

The optimal solution to this problem is shown in Figure 8.8. This solution indicates that the optimal number of boxes for Alan to order at any time is approximately 617. Because the total cost curve in the basic EOQ model has one minimum point, we can be sure that this local optimal solution is also the global optimal solution for this problem. Notice this solution occurs where the total ordering costs are in balance with the total holding costs. Using this order quantity, costs are reduced by approximately $15,211 from the earlier level shown in Figure 8.7 when an order quantity of 6,000 was used.

If Alan orders 617 boxes, he needs to place approximately 39 orders during the year (24,000 ÷ 617 = 38.89), or 1.333 orders per week (52 ÷ 39 = 1.333). As a practical matter, it might be easier for Alan to arrange for weekly deliveries of approximately 461 boxes. This would increase the total cost by only $167 to $844,055 but probably would be easier to manage and still save the bank more than $15,000 per year.

8.4.4 COMMENTS ON THE EOQ MODEL

There is another way to determine the optimal order quantity using the simple EOQ model. Using calculus, it can be shown that the optimal value of Q is represented by:

$$Q^* = \sqrt{\frac{2DS}{Ci}}$$

If we apply this formula to our example problem, we obtain:

$$Q^* = \sqrt{\frac{2 \times 24{,}000 \times 50}{35 \times 0.18}} = \sqrt{\frac{2{,}400{,}000}{6.3}} = 617.214$$

FIGURE 8.8 *Optimal solution to MetroBank's paper purchasing problem*

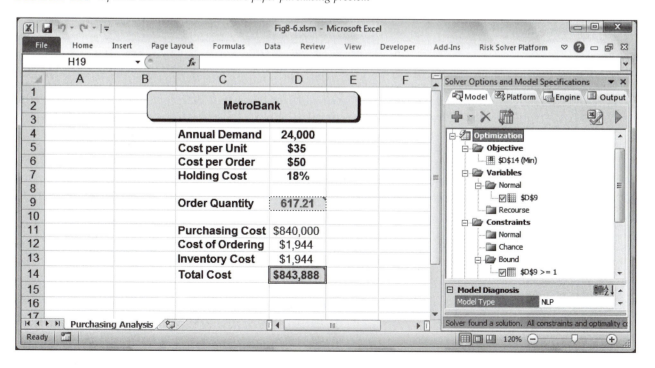

The value obtained using calculus is almost the same value obtained using Solver (refer to cell D9 in Figure 8.8). The slight difference in the results might be due to rounding or to Solver stopping just short of converging on the exact solution.

Although the previous EOQ formula has its uses, we often must impose financial or storage space restrictions when determining optimal order quantities. The previous formula does not explicitly allow for such restrictions, but it is easy to impose these types of restrictions using Solver. In some of the problems at the end of this chapter, we will consider how the EOQ model can be adjusted to accommodate these types of restrictions, as well as quantity discounts. A complete discussion of the proper use and role of EOQ models in inventory control is beyond the scope of this text but can be found in other texts devoted to production and operations management.

8.5 Location Problems

A number of decision problems involve determining the location of facilities or service centers. Examples might include determining the optimal location of manufacturing plants, warehouses, fire stations, or ambulance centers. The objective in these types of problems is often to determine a location that minimizes the distance between two or more service points. You might recall from basic algebra that the straight-line (or Euclidean) distance between two points (X_1, Y_1) and (X_2, Y_2) on a standard X-Y graph is defined as:

$$\text{Distance} = \sqrt{(X_1 - X_2)^2 + (Y_1 - Y_2)^2}$$

This type of calculation is likely to be involved in any problem in which the decision variables represent possible locations. The distance measure might occur in the objective function (for example, we might want to minimize the distance between two or more points), or it might occur in a constraint (for example, we might want to ensure that some minimum distance exists between two or more locations). Problems involving this type of distance measure are nonlinear. The following example illustrates the use of distance measures in a location problem.

> The Rappaport Communications Company provides cellular telephone services in several Midwestern states. The company is planning to expand its customer base by offering cellular service in northeastern Ohio to the cities of Cleveland, Akron, Canton, and Youngstown. The company will install the hardware necessary to service customers in each city on preexisting communications towers in each city. The locations of these towers are summarized in Figure 8.9.
>
> However, the company also needs to construct a new communications tower somewhere between these cities to handle intercity calls. This tower will also allow cellular calls to be routed onto the satellite system for worldwide calling service. The tower the company is planning to build can cover areas within a 40-mile radius. Thus, the tower needs to be located within 40 miles of each of these cities.

It is important to note that we could have overlaid the X- and Y-axes on the map in Figure 8.9 in more than one way. The origin in Figure 8.9 could be located anywhere on the map without affecting the analysis. To establish the X-Y coordinates, we need an absolute reference point for the origin, but virtually any point on the map could be selected as the origin. Also we can express the scaling of the X-axis and Y-axis in a number of ways: meters, miles, inches, feet, and so on. For our purposes, we will assume that each unit along the X- and Y-axes represents 1 mile.

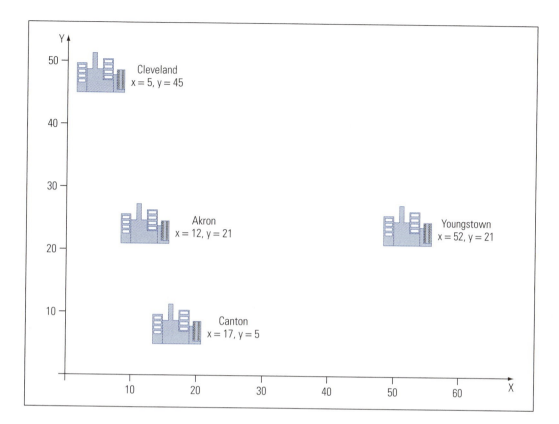

FIGURE 8.9

*Map of Rappaport
Communication's
tower location
problem*

8.5.1 DEFINING THE DECISION VARIABLES

In Figure 8.9, definite X-Y coordinates have been established to describe the locations of the cities. These points are fixed and are not under the decision maker's control. However, the coordinates of the new communications tower have not been established. We will assume that Rappaport wants to determine the tower location that minimizes the total distance between the new tower and those in each of the four cities. (Note that this is equivalent to minimizing the average distance as well.) Thus, the coordinates of the new tower represent the decision variables in this problem, which are defined as:

X_1 = location of the new tower with respect to the X-axis

Y_1 = location of the new tower with respect to the Y-axis

8.5.2 DEFINING THE OBJECTIVE

The objective in this problem is to minimize the total distance from the new tower to each of the existing towers, defined as:

$$\text{MIN: } \sqrt{(5 - X_1)^2 + (45 - Y_1)^2} + \sqrt{(12 - X_1)^2 + (21 - Y_1)^2}$$
$$+ \sqrt{(17 - X_1)^2 + (5 - Y_1)^2} + \sqrt{(52 - X_1)^2 + (21 - Y_1)^2}$$

The first term in the objective calculates the distance from the tower in Cleveland, at X-Y coordinates (5, 45), to the location of the new tower, whose location is defined by the values X_1 and Y_1. The remaining terms perform similar calculations for the towers in Akron, Canton, and Youngstown.

8.5.3 DEFINING THE CONSTRAINTS

The problem statement noted that the new tower has a 40-mile transmission radius and therefore must be located within 40 miles of each of the existing towers. The following constraints ensure that the distance from each of the existing towers to the new tower is no larger than 40 miles.

$$\sqrt{(5 - X_1)^2 + (45 - Y_1)^2} \leq 40 \qquad \} \text{ Cleveland distance constraint}$$

$$\sqrt{(12 - X_1)^2 + (21 - Y_1)^2} \leq 40 \qquad \} \text{ Akron distance constraint}$$

$$\sqrt{(17 - X_1)^2 + (5 - Y_1)^2} \leq 40 \qquad \} \text{ Canton distance constraint}$$

$$\sqrt{(52 - X_1)^2 + (21 - Y_1)^2} \leq 40 \qquad \} \text{ Youngstown distance constraint}$$

Graphically, these constraints would be drawn as four circles, each with a 40-mile radius, and each centered at one of the of the four existing tower locations. The intersection of these circles would represent the feasible region for the problem.

8.5.4 IMPLEMENTING THE MODEL

In summary, the problem Rappaport Communications wants to solve is:

$$\text{MIN: } \sqrt{(5 - X_1)^2 + (45 - Y_1)^2} + \sqrt{(12 - X_1)^2 + (21 - Y_1)^2}$$
$$+ \sqrt{(17 - X_1)^2 + (5 - Y_1)^2} + \sqrt{(52 - X_1)^2 + (21 - Y_1)^2}$$

Subject to:

$$\sqrt{(5 - X_1)^2 + (45 - Y_1)^2} \leq 40 \qquad \} \text{ Cleveland distance constraint}$$

$$\sqrt{(12 - X_1)^2 + (21 - Y_1)^2} \leq 40 \qquad \} \text{ Akron distance constraint}$$

$$\sqrt{(17 - X_1)^2 + (5 - Y_1)^2} \leq 40 \qquad \} \text{ Canton distance constraint}$$

$$\sqrt{(52 - X_1)^2 + (21 - Y_1)^2} \leq 40 \qquad \} \text{ Youngstown distance constraint}$$

Note that both the objective and constraints for this problem are nonlinear. One approach to implementing the model for this problem in a spreadsheet is shown in Figure 8.10 (and in the file Fig8-10.xlsm that accompanies this book).

In this spreadsheet, cells C6 and D6 are used to represent the decision variables X_1 and Y_1, which correspond to the X-Y coordinates of the location of the new tower. The locations of the existing towers are listed in terms of their X-Y coordinates in rows 7 through 10 of columns C and D. Reasonable starting values for X_1 and Y_1 in this problem would be the average values of the X and Y coordinates of the existing tower locations. These averages were computed and entered in cells C6 and D6.

Column E calculates the distance from each existing tower to the selected location for the new tower. Specifically, cell E7 contains the following formula, which is copied to cells E8 through E10:

Formula for cell E7:   =SQRT((C7-$C$6)^2+(D7-$D$6)^2)

(Copy to E8 through E10.)

These cells represent the LHS formulas for the problem. The RHS values for these constraints are given in cells F7 through F10. The objective function for the problem is then implemented easily in cell E11 with the formula:

Formula for cell E11:   =SUM(E7:E10)

FIGURE 8.10 *Spreadsheet implementation of the tower location problem*

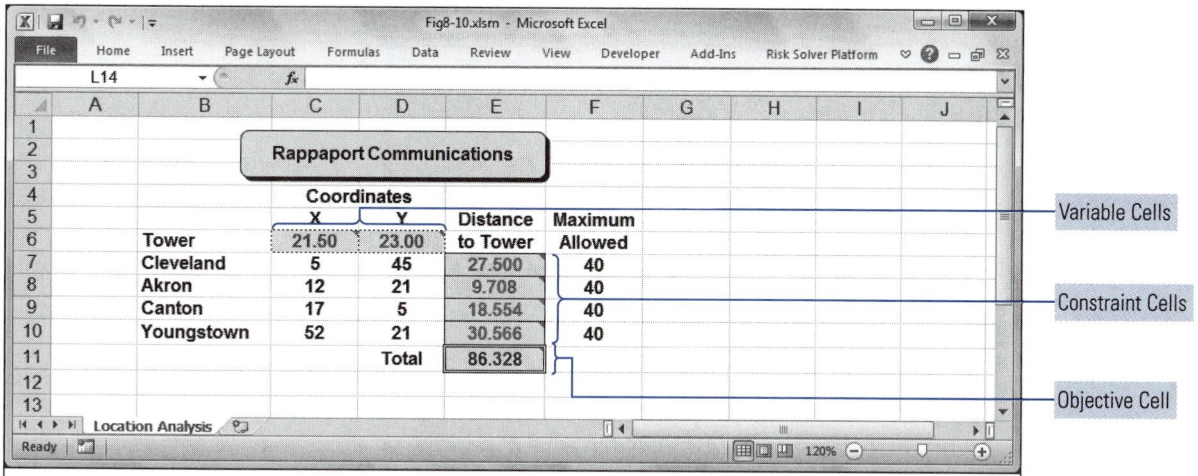

Key Cell Formulas

Cell	Formula	Copied to
E7	=SQRT((C7-$C$6)^2+(D7-$D$6)^2)	E8:E10
E11	=SUM(E7:E10)	--

8.5.5 SOLVING THE MODEL AND ANALYZING THE SOLUTION

Figure 8.11 shows the Solver settings and options used to solve this problem, and Figure 8.12 shows the optimal solution.

The solution in Figure 8.12 indicates that if the new tower is located at the coordinates $X_1 = 12.0$ and $Y_1 = 21.0$, the total distance between the towers is 81.761 miles (so the average distance is 20.4 miles). If you try re-solving this problem from a variety of starting points, you can verify that this is the global optimal solution to the problem. Interestingly, the coordinates of this location for the new tower are virtually identical to the coordinates of the existing tower in Akron. So, the solution to this problem may not involve building a new tower at all, but, instead, Rappaport may want to investigate the feasibility of upgrading or retrofitting the existing Akron tower to play the role of the "new" tower.

FIGURE 8.11

Solver parameters for the tower location problem

Solver Settings:

Objective: E11 (Min)
Variable cells: C6:D6
Constraints:
    E7:E10 <= F7:F10

Solver Options:
    Standard GRG Nonlinear Engine

FIGURE 8.12 *Optimal solution to the tower location problem*

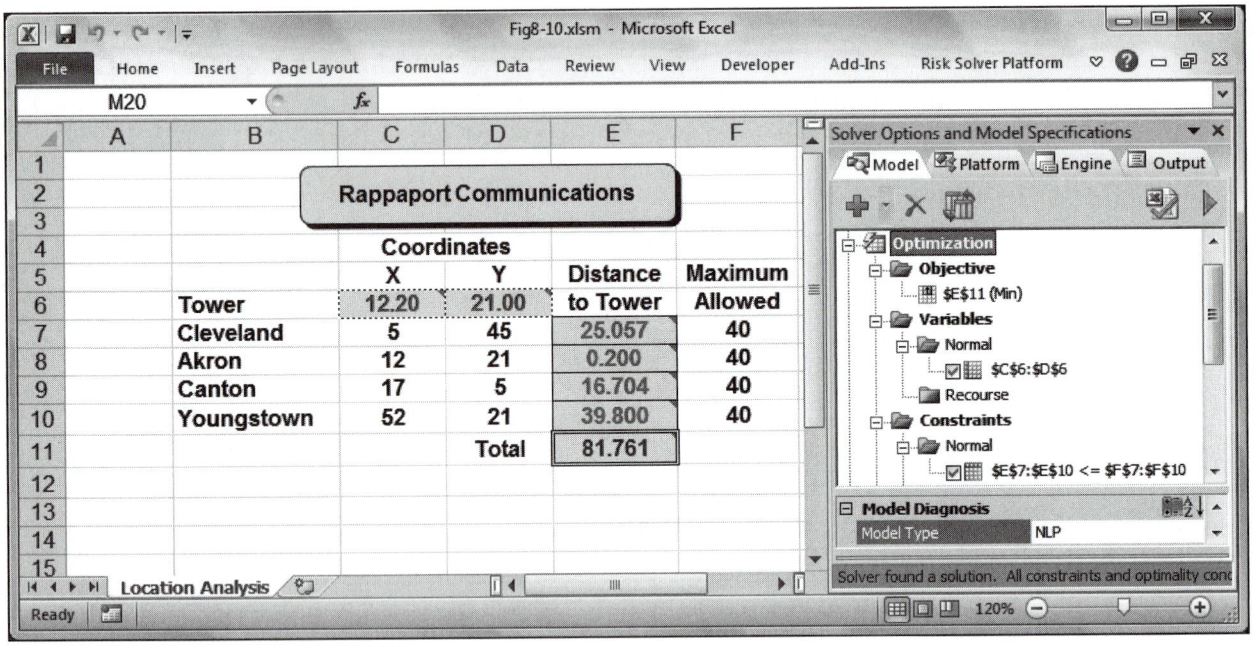

8.5.6 ANOTHER SOLUTION TO THE PROBLEM

The solution shown in Figure 8.12 positions the new tower at essentially the same location as the existing tower in Akron. So, instead of building a new tower, perhaps the company should consider upgrading the tower at Akron with the equipment needed for handling intercity calls. On the other hand, the distance from Akron to the tower in Youngstown is almost 40 miles—the limit of the broadcast radius of the new equipment. Thus, Rappaport may prefer a solution that provides more of a safety margin on their broadcast range, to help ensure quality and reliability during inclement weather.

Another objective that could be applied to this problem would attempt to minimize the maximum distance from the new tower to each of the existing towers. Figure 8.13 (and the file Fig8-13.xlsm that accompanies this book) shows the solution to this new problem.

To obtain this solution, we implemented a new objective function in cell E12 to compute the maximum of the distances in column E as follows:

Formula for cell E12:   =MAX(E7:E10)

We then instructed Solver to minimize E12 to obtain the solution shown. This solution positions the new tower at the X-Y coordinates (26.84, 29.75). Although the total distance associated with this solution increased to 97.137 (or an average of 24.28 miles), the maximum distance was reduced to about 26.6 miles. Thus, Rappaport might prefer this solution to the alternative shown in Figure 8.12.

8.5.7 SOME COMMENTS ABOUT THE SOLUTION TO LOCATION PROBLEMS

When solving location problems, it is possible that the location indicated by the optimal solution may simply not work. For instance, the land at the optimal location might not be for sale, the "land" at this location might be a lake, the land might be zoned for residential

FIGURE 8.13 *Another solution to the tower location problem minimizing the maximum distance*

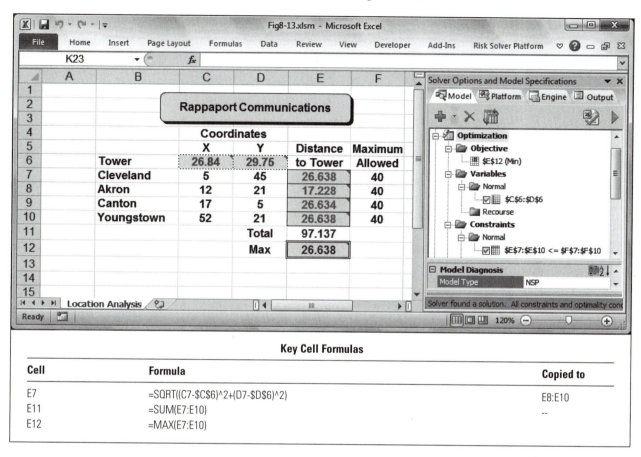

Cell	Formula	Copied to
	Key Cell Formulas	
E7	=SQRT((C7-$C$6)^2+(D7-$D$6)^2)	E8:E10
E11	=SUM(E7:E10)	--
E12	=MAX(E7:E10)	

purposes only, and so on. However, solutions to location problems often give decision makers a good idea about where to start looking for suitable property to acquire for the problem at hand. It might also be possible to add constraints to location problems that eliminate certain areas from consideration if they are inappropriate or unavailable.

8.6 Nonlinear Network Flow Problem

In Chapter 5, we looked at several different types of network flow problems with linear objective functions and linear constraint sets. We noted that the constraints in network flow models have a special structure in which the flow into a node must be balanced with the flow out of the same node. Numerous decision problems exist in which the balance-of-flow restrictions must be maintained while optimizing a nonlinear objective function. We present one such example here.

> SafetyTrans is a trucking company that specializes in transporting extremely valuable and extremely hazardous materials. Due to the nature of its business, the company places great importance on maintaining a clean driving safety record. This not only helps keep their reputation up but also helps keep their insurance premiums down. The company is also conscious of the fact that when carrying hazardous materials, the environmental consequences of even a minor accident could be disastrous.

Whereas most trucking companies are interested in identifying routes that provide for the quickest or least costly transportation, SafetyTrans likes to ensure that it selects routes that are the least likely to result in an accident. The company is currently trying to identify the safest routes for carrying a load of hazardous materials from Los Angeles, California to Amarillo, Texas. The network in Figure 8.14 summarizes the routes under consideration. The numbers on each arc represent the probability of having an accident on each potential leg of the journey. SafetyTrans maintains a national database of such probabilities developed from data they receive from the National Highway Safety Administration and the various Departments of Transportation in each state.

8.6.1 DEFINING THE DECISION VARIABLES

The problem summarized in Figure 8.14 is very similar to the shortest path problem described in Chapter 5. As in the shortest path problem, here we will need one variable for each of the arcs (or routes) in the problem. Each decision variable will indicate whether or not a particular route is used. We will define these variables as follows:

$$Y_{ij} = \begin{cases} 1, \text{ if the route from node } i \text{ to node } j \text{ is selected} \\ 0, \text{ otherwise} \end{cases}$$

8.6.2 DEFINING THE OBJECTIVE

The objective in this problem is to find the route that minimizes the probability of having an accident, or equivalently, the route that maximizes the probability of not having an accident. Let P_{ij} = the probability of having an accident while traveling from node i to node j. Then, the probability of *not* having an accident while traveling from node i to node j is $1-P_{ij}$. For example, the probability of not having an accident while traveling

FIGURE 8.14

Network representation of the SafetyTrans routing problem

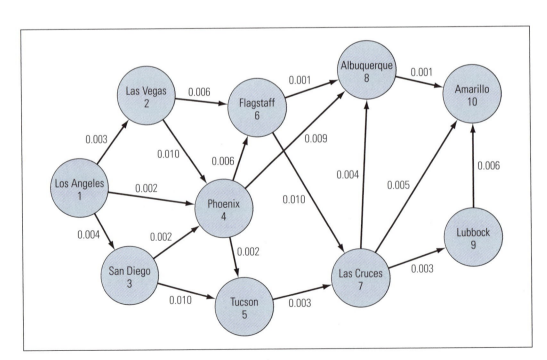

from Los Angeles to Las Vegas is $1 - P_{12} = 1 - 0.003 = 0.997$. The objective of maximizing the probability of not having an accident is given by:

$$\text{MAX: } (1 - P_{12}Y_{12})(1 - P_{13}Y_{13})(1 - P_{14}Y_{14})(1 - P_{24}Y_{24})(1 - P_{26}Y_{26}) \ldots (1 - P_{9,10}Y_{9,10})$$

The first term in this objective returns the value 1 if $Y_{12} = 0$ and the value $1 - P_{12}$ if $Y_{12} = 1$. Thus, if we take the route from Los Angeles to Las Vegas ($Y_{12} = 1$), the value 0.997 is multiplied by the remaining terms in the objective function. If we do not take the route from Los Angeles to Las Vegas ($Y_{12} = 0$), the value 1 is multiplied by the remaining terms in the objective function. (Of course, multiplying by 1 has no effect.) The remaining terms in the objective have similar interpretations. So, this objective function computes the probabilities of not having accidents on whichever routes are selected and then computes the products of these values. The result is the overall probability of not having an accident on any set of selected routes. This is the value SafetyTrans wants to maximize.

8.6.3 DEFINING THE CONSTRAINTS

To solve a shortest path network flow problem, we assign the starting node a supply value of -1, assign the ending node a demand value of $+1$, and apply the balance-of-flow rule covered in Chapter 5. This results in the following set of constraints for our example problem.

$$
\begin{array}{lcl}
-Y_{12} - Y_{13} - Y_{14} & = -1 & \} \text{ balance-of-flow constraint for node 1} \\
+Y_{12} - Y_{24} - Y_{26} & = 0 & \} \text{ balance-of-flow constraint for node 2} \\
+Y_{13} - Y_{34} - Y_{35} & = 0 & \} \text{ balance-of-flow constraint for node 3} \\
+Y_{14} + Y_{24} + Y_{34} - Y_{45} - Y_{46} - Y_{48} & = 0 & \} \text{ balance-of-flow constraint for node 4} \\
+Y_{35} + Y_{45} - Y_{57} & = 0 & \} \text{ balance-of-flow constraint for node 5} \\
+Y_{26} + Y_{46} - Y_{67} - Y_{68} & = 0 & \} \text{ balance-of-flow constraint for node 6} \\
+Y_{57} + Y_{67} - Y_{78} - Y_{79} - Y_{7,10} & = 0 & \} \text{ balance-of-flow constraint for node 7} \\
+Y_{48} + Y_{68} + Y_{78} - Y_{8,10} & = 0 & \} \text{ balance-of-flow constraint for node 8} \\
+Y_{79} - Y_{9,10} & = 0 & \} \text{ balance-of-flow constraint for node 9} \\
+Y_{7,10} + Y_{8,10} + Y_{9,10} & = 1 & \} \text{ balance-of-flow constraint for node 10}
\end{array}
$$

The first constraint ensures that one unit flows out of node 1 to nodes 2, 3, or 4. The last constraint ensures that one unit flows into node 10 from nodes 7, 8, or 9. The remaining constraints ensure that any flow into nodes 2 through 9 is balanced by an equal amount of flow out of those nodes.

8.6.4 IMPLEMENTING THE MODEL

In summary, the problem SafetyTrans wants to solve is:

$$\text{MAX: } \quad (1 - 0.003Y_{12})(1 - 0.004Y_{13})(1 - 0.002Y_{14})(1 - 0.010Y_{24})$$
$$(1 - 0.006Y_{26}) \ldots (1 - 0.006Y_{9,10})$$

Subject to:

$$
\begin{array}{lcl}
-Y_{12} - Y_{13} - Y_{14} & = -1 & \} \text{ balance-of-flow constraint for node 1} \\
+Y_{12} - Y_{24} - Y_{26} & = 0 & \} \text{ balance-of-flow constraint for node 2} \\
+Y_{13} - Y_{34} - Y_{35} & = 0 & \} \text{ balance-of-flow constraint for node 3} \\
+Y_{14} + Y_{24} + Y_{34} - Y_{45} - Y_{46} - Y_{48} & = 0 & \} \text{ balance-of-flow constraint for node 4}
\end{array}
$$

$$+Y_{35} \; +Y_{45} \; -Y_{57} \qquad\qquad = \; 0 \qquad \} \text{ balance-of-flow constraint for node 5}$$

$$+Y_{26} \; +Y_{46} \; -Y_{67} -Y_{68} \qquad = \; 0 \qquad \} \text{ balance-of-flow constraint for node 6}$$

$$+Y_{57} \; +Y_{67} \; -Y_{78} -Y_{79} -Y_{7,10} \quad = \; 0 \qquad \} \text{ balance-of-flow constraint for node 7}$$

$$+Y_{48} \; +Y_{68} \; +Y_{78} -Y_{8,10} \qquad = \; 0 \qquad \} \text{ balance-of-flow constraint for node 8}$$

$$+Y_{79} \; -Y_{9,10} \qquad\qquad\qquad = \; 0 \qquad \} \text{ balance-of-flow constraint for node 9}$$

$$+Y_{7,10} +Y_{8,10} +Y_{9,10} \qquad\qquad = \; 1 \qquad \} \text{ balance-of-flow constraint for node 10}$$

All Y_{ij} binary

One approach to implementing this model is shown in Figure 8.15. In this spreadsheet, cells A6 through A23 represent our decision variables.

The LHS formulas for the constraints in this problem are implemented in cells K6 through K15 using the same technique as described in Chapter 5. The RHS for the constraints are given in cells L6 through L15. Specifically, we enter the following formula in cells K6 and copy down the rest of the column:

Formula for cell K6:   =SUMIF($D$6:$D$23,I6,$A$6:$A$23)
(Copy to cells K7 through K15.)   −SUMIF($B$6:$B$23,I6,$A$6:$A$23)

FIGURE 8.15 *Spreadsheet implementation of the SafetyTrans routing problem*

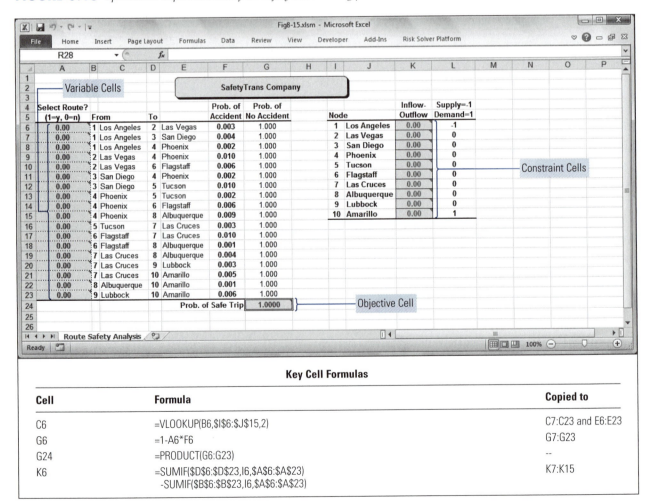

Key Cell Formulas

Cell	Formula	Copied to
C6	=VLOOKUP(B6,$I$6:$J$15,2)	C7:C23 and E6:E23
G6	=1−A6*F6	G7:G23
G24	=PRODUCT(G6:G23)	--
K6	=SUMIF($D$6:$D$23,I6,$A$6:$A$23) -SUMIF($B$6:$B$23,I6,$A$6:$A$23)	K7:K15

The probabilities of having an accident on each of the routes are listed in cells F6 through F23. Each of the terms for the objective function were then implemented in cells G6 through G23 as follows:

Formula for cell G6: $=1-A6*F6$

(Copy to cells G7 through G23.)

Note that the formula in G6 corresponds exactly to the first term in the objective $(1 - Y_{12}P_{12})$ as described earlier. Next, the product of the values in cells G6 through G23 is calculated in cell G24 as:

Formula for cell G24: $=PRODUCT(G6:G23)$

Figure 8.16 shows the Solver settings and options used to solve this problem. The optimal solution is shown in Figure 8.17.

Solver Settings:

Objective: G24 (Max)
Variable cells: A6:A23
Constraints:
    K6:K15 = L6:L15
    A6:A23 = binary

Solver Options:
    Standard GRG Nonlinear Engine
    Integer Tolerance = 0

FIGURE 8.16

Solver parameters for the SafetyTrans problem

FIGURE 8.17 *Optimal solution to the SafetyTrans problem*

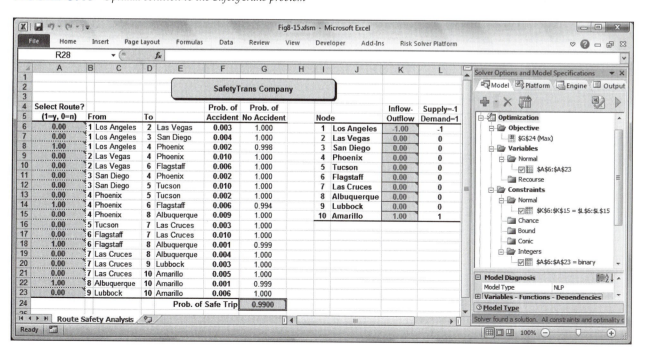

8.6.5 SOLVING THE MODEL AND ANALYZING THE SOLUTION

The solution to this problem indicates $Y_{14} = Y_{46} = Y_{68} = Y_{8,10} = 1$, and all other $Y_{ij} = 0$. Thus, the optimal (safest) route is to travel from Los Angeles to Phoenix to Flagstaff to Albuquerque to Amarillo. Following this route, there is a 0.99 probability of not having an accident. Solving this problem from numerous starting points indicates that this is the global optimal solution to the problem.

If you solve this model again minimizing the objective, you will discover that the least safe route has a 0.9626 probability of not having an accident. This may lead some to conclude that it doesn't make much difference which route is taken because the differences in the best-case and worst-case probabilities seem minimal. However, if it costs $30,000,000 to clean up an accident involving hazardous waste, the expected cost of taking the safest route is $(1 - 0.99) \times \$30,000,000 = \$300,000$, and the expected cost of taking the least safe route is $(1 - 0.9626) \times \$30,000,000 = \$1,122,000$. So although the differences in probabilities may appear small, the differences in the potential outcomes can be quite significant. Of course, this doesn't even consider the potential loss of life and environmental damage that no amount of money can fix.

There are a number of other areas to which this type of nonlinear network flow model can be applied. Analysts are often interested in determining the "weakest link" in a telecommunications network or production system. The same type of problem described here could be solved to determine the least reliable path through these types of networks.

8.7 Project Selection Problems

In Chapter 6, we looked at a project selection example in which we wanted to select the combination of projects that produced the greatest net present value (NPV) subject to various resource restrictions. In these types of problems, there is often some uncertainty about whether a selected project can actually be completed successfully, and this success might be influenced by the amount of resources devoted to the project. The following example illustrates how NLP techniques can be used to help model this uncertainty in a selected project's potential for success.

The directors of the TMC Corporation are trying to determine how to allocate their R&D budget for the coming year. Six different projects are under consideration. The directors believe that the success of each project depends in part on the number of engineers assigned. Each project proposal includes an estimate of the probability of success as a function of the number of engineers assigned. Each probability function is of the form:

$$P_i = \text{probability of success for project } i \text{ if assigned } X_i \text{ engineers} = \frac{X_i}{X_i + \varepsilon_i}$$

where ε_i is a positive constant for project i that determines the shape of its probability function.

The probability functions for several of the projects are shown in Figure 8.18. The following table summarizes the initial startup funds required for each project and the estimated NPV the project will generate if it is successful.

Project	1	2	3	4	5	6
Startup Costs	$325	$200	$490	$125	$710	$240
Net Present Value	$750	$120	$900	$400	$1,110	$800
Probability Parameter ε_i	3.1	2.5	4.5	5.6	8.2	8.5

(Note: All monetary values are in $1,000s.)

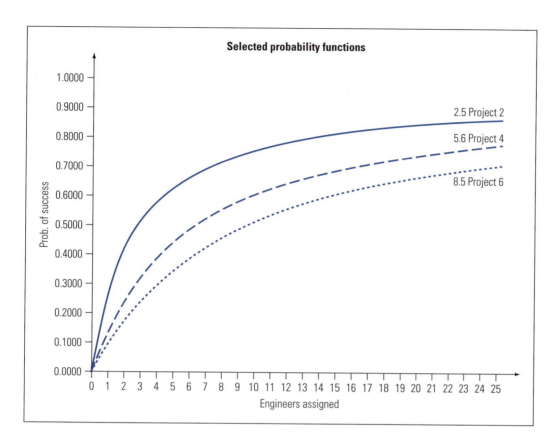

FIGURE 8.18

Graph showing the probability of success for selected projects in the TMC problem

TMC's directors have agreed to hire up to 25 engineers to assign to these projects and are willing to allocate $1.7 million of the R&D budget to cover the startup costs for selected projects. They want to determine the project selection and resource allocation strategy that will maximize the expected NPV.

8.7.1 DEFINING THE DECISION VARIABLES

TMC's directors must make two separate but related decisions. First, they must determine which projects to select. We will use the following binary variables to model these decisions:

$$Y_i = \begin{cases} 1, \text{ if project } i \text{ is selected} \\ 0, \text{ otherwise} \end{cases}, i = 1, 2, 3, \ldots, 6$$

Second, the directors must determine the number of engineers to assign to each project. We will model these decisions with the following variables:

X_i = the number of engineers to assign to project i, $i = 1, 2, 3, \ldots, 6$

8.7.2 DEFINING THE OBJECTIVE FUNCTION

TMC's directors want to maximize the expected NPV of their decision, so our objective function must correspond to this quantity. This requires that we multiply each project's expected return by the probability of the project being successful. This is accomplished as follows:

$$\text{MAX:} \quad \frac{750X_1}{(X_1 + 3.1)} + \frac{120X_2}{(X_2 + 2.5)} + \frac{900X_3}{(X_3 + 4.5)} + \frac{400X_4}{(X_4 + 5.6)} + \frac{1{,}100X_5}{(X_5 + 8.2)} + \frac{800X_6}{(X_6 + 8.5)}$$

8.7.3 DEFINING THE CONSTRAINTS

Several constraints apply to this problem. We must ensure that the projects selected require no more than $1.7 million in startup funds. This is accomplished as follows:

$$325Y_1 + 200Y_2 + 490Y_3 + 125Y_4 + 710Y_5 + 240Y_6 \leq 1{,}700 \qquad \text{\} constraint on startup funds}$$

Next, we must ensure that no more than 25 engineers are assigned to selected projects. This is accomplished by the following constraint:

$$X_1 + X_2 + X_3 + X_4 + X_5 + X_6 \leq 25 \qquad \text{\} constraint on engineers}$$

Finally, we need to make sure that engineers are assigned only to the projects that have been selected. This requires the use of linking constraints that were first presented in Chapter 6 when discussing the fixed-charge problem. The linking constraints for this problem could be stated as:

$$X_i - 25Y_i \leq 0, \quad i = 1, 2, 3, \ldots, 6 \qquad \text{\} linking constraints}$$

These linking constraints ensure that an X_i variable can be greater than 0 if and only if its associated Y_i variable is 1.

Instead of using the previous constraint on the number of engineers and the associated six linking constraints, we could have used the following single nonlinear constraint:

$$X_1Y_1 + X_2Y_2 + X_3Y_3 + X_4Y_4 + X_5Y_5 + X_6Y_6 \leq 25 \qquad \text{\} constraint on engineers}$$

This would sum the number of engineers assigned to selected projects. (Note that if we used this constraint, we would also need to multiply each term in the objective function by its associated Y_i variable. Do you see why?) Using this single nonlinear constraint might appear to be easier than the previous seven constraints. However, when you have a choice between using linear constraints and nonlinear constraints, it is almost always better to use the linear constraints.

8.7.4 IMPLEMENTING THE MODEL

The model for TMC's project selection problem is summarized as:

$$\text{MAX:} \quad \frac{750X_1}{(X_1 + 3.1)} + \frac{120X_2}{(X_2 + 2.5)} + \frac{900X_3}{(X_3 + 4.5)} + \frac{400X_4}{(X_4 + 5.6)} + \frac{1{,}100X_5}{(X_5 + 8.2)} + \frac{800X_6}{(X_6 + 8.5)}$$

Subject to:

$$325Y_1 + 200Y_2 + 490Y_3 + 125Y_4 + 710Y_5 + 240Y_6 \leq 1{,}700 \qquad \text{\} constraint on startup funds}$$

$$X_1 + X_2 + X_3 + X_4 + X_5 + X_6 \leq 25 \qquad \text{\} constraint on engineers}$$

$$X_i - 25Y_i \leq 0, i = 1, 2, 3, \ldots, 6 \qquad \text{\} linking constraints}$$

$$X_i \geq 0 \text{ and integer}$$

$$Y_i \text{ binary}$$

Notice that this problem has a nonlinear objective function and linear constraints. One approach to implementing this model is shown in Figure 8.19 (and in the file Fig8-19.xlsm that accompanies this book). In this spreadsheet, cells B7 through B12 are used to represent our binary Y_i variables indicating whether or not each project is selected. Cells C7 through C12 represent the X_i variables indicating the number of engineers assigned to each project.

We implemented the linking constraints for this problem by entering the LHS formulas in cells D7 through D12 as follows:

Formula for cell D7: $\quad$ =C7 − B7*$C$14

(Copy to cells D8 through D12.)

We will constrain these values to be less than or equal to zero. The LHS for the constraint on the number of engineers assigned to projects is implemented in cell C13 as follows:

Formula for cell C13: $\quad$ =SUM(C7:C12)

The RHS value for this constraint is given in cell C14. Similarly, the LHS for the constraint of the total startup funds is implemented in cell I13 with its RHS value listed in I14.

Formula for cell I13: $\quad$ =SUMPRODUCT(B7:B12,I7:I12)

To implement the objective function, we first calculate the probability of success for each project. This is done in column F as follows:

Formula for cell F7: $\quad$ =C7/(C7+E7)

(Copy to cells F8 through F12.)

FIGURE 8.19 *Spreadsheet implementation of TMC's project selection problem*

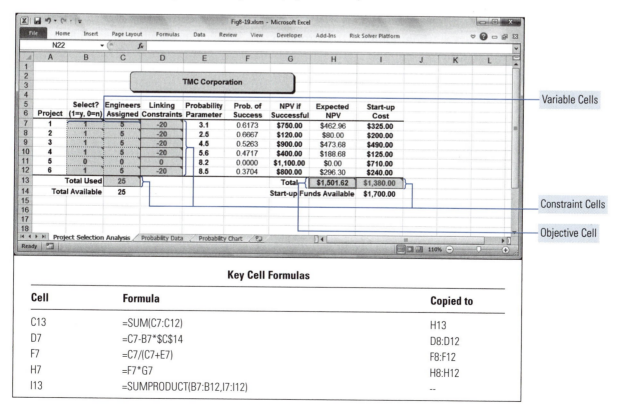

Key Cell Formulas

Cell	Formula	Copied to
C13	=SUM(C7:C12)	H13
D7	=C7-B7*$C$14	D8:D12
F7	=C7/(C7+E7)	F8:F12
H7	=F7*G7	H8:H12
I13	=SUMPRODUCT(B7:B12,I7:I12)	--

Next, the expected NPV value for each project is computed by multiplying the probability of success for each project by the NPV it should generate if the project is successful. This is done in column H as follows:

Formula for cell H7:   =F7*G7

(Copy to cells H8 through H12.)

Finally, we compute the sum of the expected NPVs for selected projects in cell H13:

Formula for cell H13:   =SUM(H7:H12)

The Solver settings and options used to solve this problem are shown in Figure 8.20.

FIGURE 8.20

Solver parameters for TMC's project selection problem

Solver Settings:
Objective: H13 (Max)
Variable cells: B7:C12
Constraints:
C13 <= C14
I13 <= I14
D7:D12 <= 0
C7:C12 >= 0
B7:B12 = binary
C7:C12 = integer
Solver Options:
Standard GRG Nonlinear Engine
Integer Tolerance = 0

8.7.5 SOLVING THE MODEL

An arbitrary starting point for this problem was selected as shown in Figure 8.19. From this arbitrary starting point, Solver located the solution shown in Figure 8.21, which has an expected NPV of approximately $1.716 million. In this solution, notice that the probability of success for project 4 is only 0.2632. Thus, project 4 is almost three times as likely to fail as succeed if it is assigned only two engineers. As a result, we might want to add a constraint to this problem to ensure that if a project is selected, it must have at least a 50% chance of succeeding. An exercise at the end of this chapter asks you to do that.

8.8 Optimizing Existing Financial Spreadsheet Models

So far in our discussion of optimization, we have always constructed an algebraic model of a decision problem and then implemented this model in a spreadsheet for solution and analysis. However, we can apply optimization techniques to virtually any existing spreadsheet model. Many existing spreadsheets involve financial calculations that are inherently nonlinear. The following is an example of how optimization can be applied to an existing spreadsheet.

Thom Pearman's life is changing dramatically. He and his wife recently bought a new home and are expecting their second child in a few months. These new responsibilities have prompted Thom to think about some serious issues, including life insurance. Ten years ago, Thom purchased an insurance policy that provides a

FIGURE 8.21 *First solution to the TMC project selection problem*

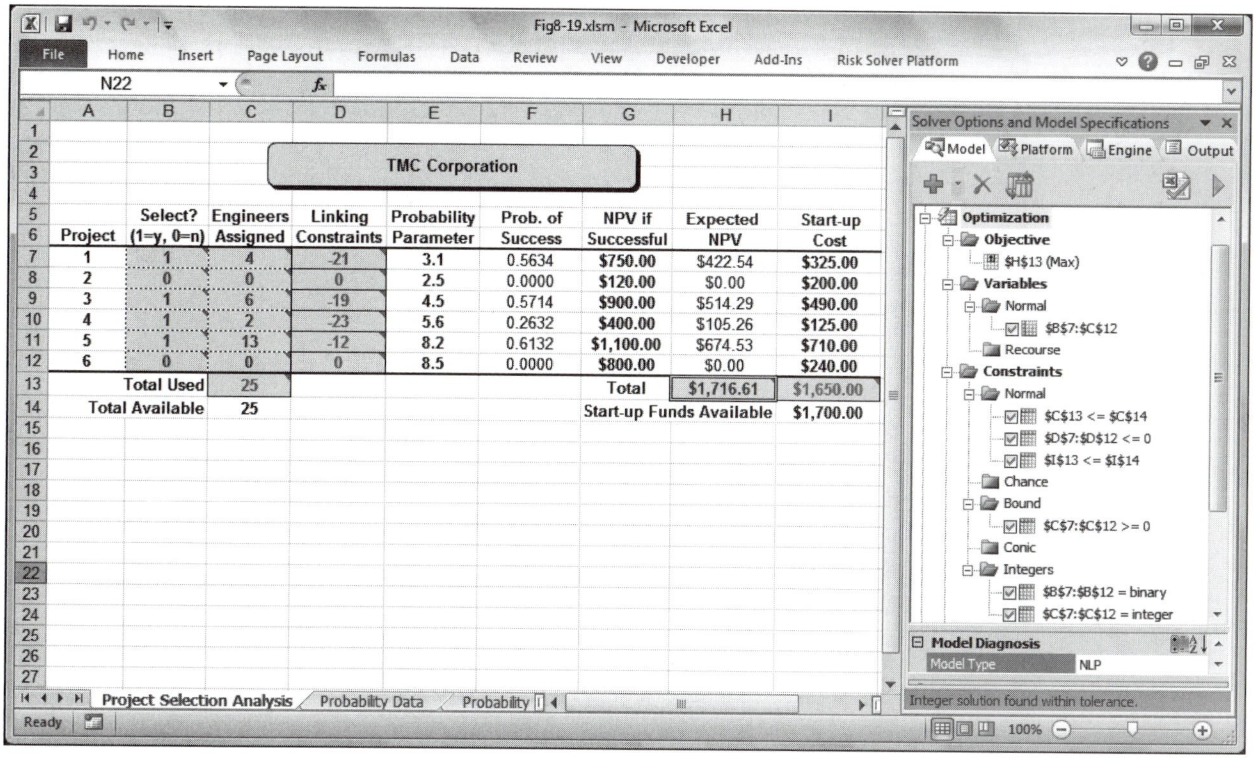

death benefit of $40,000. This policy is paid for in full and will remain in force for the rest of Thom's life. Alternatively, Thom can surrender this policy and receive an immediate payoff of approximately $6,000 from the insurance company.

Ten years ago, the $40,000 death benefit provided by the insurance policy seemed more than adequate. However, Thom now feels that he needs more coverage to care for his wife and children adequately in the event of his untimely death. Thom is investigating a different kind of insurance that would provide a death benefit of $350,000 but would also require ongoing annual payments to keep the coverage in force. He received the following estimates of the annual premiums for this new policy in each of the next 10 years:

Year	1	2	3	4	5	6	7	8	9	10
Premium	$423	$457	$489	$516	$530	$558	$595	$618	$660	$716

To pay the premiums for this new policy, one alternative Thom is considering involves surrendering his existing policy and investing the $6,000 he would receive to generate the after-tax income needed to pay the premiums on his new policy. However, to see if this is possible, he wants to determine the minimum rate of return he would have to earn on his investment to generate after-tax investment earnings that would cover the premium payments for the new policy. Thom likes the idea of keeping the $6,000 in case of an emergency and does not want to use it to pay premiums. Thom's marginal tax rate is 28%.

8.8.1 IMPLEMENTING THE MODEL

A spreadsheet model for Thom's decision problem is shown in Figure 8.22 (and in the file Fig8-22.xlsm that accompanies this book). The strategy in this spreadsheet is to determine how much money would be invested at the beginning of each year, how much money would be earned during the year after taxes, and how much would be left at the end of the year after paying taxes and the insurance premium due for that year.

As shown in Figure 8.22, cells D4 and D5 contain the assumptions about the initial amount invested and Thom's marginal tax rate. Cell D6 represents the expected annual return (which is compounded quarterly). The annual return of 15% was entered in this cell simply for planning purposes. This is the value that we will attempt to minimize when we optimize the spreadsheet.

The beginning balance for the first year (cell B10) is equal to the initial amount of money invested. The beginning balance for each of the following years is the ending balance from the previous year. The formula in cell C10 calculates the amount earned for the year given the interest rate in cell D6. This same formula applies to cells C11 through C19.

$$\text{Formula for cell C10:} \qquad =B10*(1+\$D\$6/4)^4-B10$$

(Copy to cells C11through C19.)

Because Thom pays 28% in taxes, the values in the Earnings After Taxes column are 72% of the investment earnings listed in column C ($100\% - 28\% = 72\%$). The values in

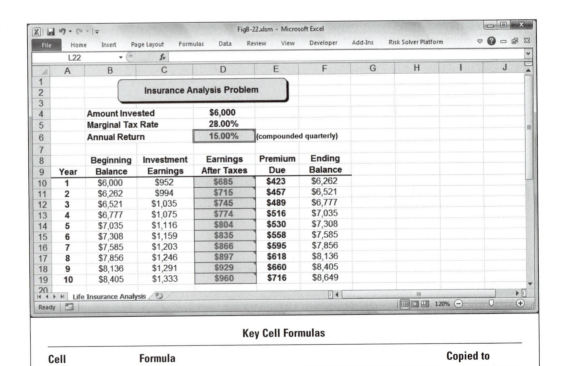

FIGURE 8.22

Spreadsheet implementation of Thom's insurance funding problem

Cell	Formula	Copied to
B10	=B4	--
B11	=F10	B12:B19
C10	=B10*(1+$D$6/4)^4-B10	C11:C19
D10	=(1-$D$5)*C10	D11:D19
F10	=B10+D10-E10	F11:F19

the Ending Balance column are the beginning balances plus the earnings after taxes minus the premium due for the year.

8.8.2 OPTIMIZING THE SPREADSHEET MODEL

Three elements are involved in any optimization problem: one or more decision variables, an objective function, and constraints. The objective in the current problem is to determine the minimum annual return that will generate after-tax earnings to pay the premiums each year. Thus, the decision variable in this model is the interest rate in cell D6. The value in cell D6 also represents the objective in the problem because we want to minimize its value. For constraints, the after-tax earnings each year should be greater than or equal to the premium due for the year. Thus, we require that the values in cells D10 through D19 be greater than or equal to the values in cells E10 through E19. Figure 8.23 shows the Solver settings and options required to solve this problem, and Figure 8.24 shows the optimal solution.

Solver Settings:

Objective: D6 (Min)
Variable cells: D6
Constraints:
    D10:D19 >= E10:E19

Solver Options:
    Standard GRG Nonlinear Engine

FIGURE 8.23

Solver parameters for the insurance funding problem

FIGURE 8.24 *Optimal solution to the insurance funding problem*

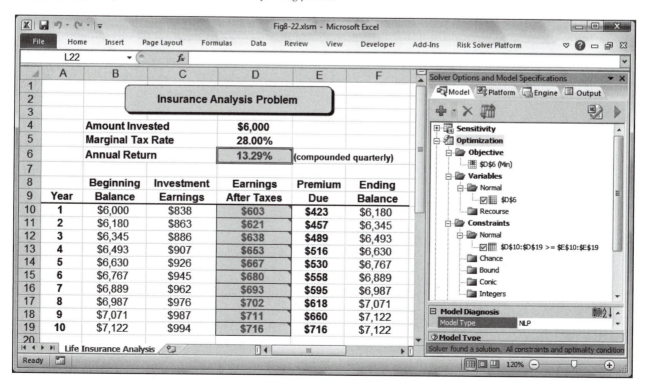

8.8.3 ANALYZING THE SOLUTION

The solution shown in Figure 8.24 indicates that Thom needs to obtain an annual return of at least 13.29% in order for the after-tax earnings from his investment of $6,000 to pay the premiums on his new policy for the next 10 years. This rate of return causes his after-tax earnings in year 10 to equal exactly the premium payment of $716 due that year. Thus, in order for Thom's plan to succeed, he needs to identify an investment that is capable of producing at least a 13.29% annual return each year for the next 10 years. Thom might want to use the technique described in Section 8.9 to help design such an investment.

8.8.4 COMMENTS ON OPTIMIZING EXISTING SPREADSHEETS

One difficulty in optimizing an existing spreadsheet model is determining whether the underlying algebraic model is linear or nonlinear. This is important in determining whether a global optimal solution to the problem has been obtained. As mentioned earlier, if we instruct Solver to assume that the model is linear, it conducts a series of numerical tests to determine whether this assumption is appropriate. If Solver detects that the model is not linear, a message is displayed to that effect, and we need to re-solve the model as an NLP. So when applying optimization techniques to an existing spreadsheet model, it is a good idea to instruct Solver to assume that the model is linear. If Solver can find a solution under this assumption, we can be confident that it is the global optimal solution. If Solver detects that the model is nonlinear, we must be aware that any solution obtained might represent a local optimal solution as opposed to the global optimal solution. In this case, we might re-solve the model several times from different starting points to see if better local optimal solutions exist for the problem. (Note that if a problem is poorly scaled, Solver's linearity tests will sometimes indicate that the model is not linear when, in fact, it is.)

As you develop your skills and intuition about spreadsheet optimization, you might be inclined to skip the step of writing out algebraic formulations of your models. For straightforward problems, this might be appropriate. However, in more complex problems, this can lead to undesirable results. For example, in Chapter 6, we noted how it can be tempting to implement the binary variables in a fixed-charge problem using an IF( ) function in a spreadsheet. Unfortunately, this causes Solver to view the problem as an NLP rather than as a mixed-integer LP problem. So, how you implement the model for a problem can impact whether Solver finds the global optimal solution. As the model builder, you must understand what kind of model you have and implement it in the most appropriate way. Writing out the algebraic formulation of the model often helps to ensure that you thoroughly understand the model you are attempting to solve.

8.9 The Portfolio Selection Problem

One of the most famous applications of NLP involves determining the optimal mix of investments to hold in a portfolio in order to minimize the risk of the portfolio while achieving a desired level of return. One way to measure the risk inherent in an individual investment is the variance (or, alternatively, the standard deviation) of the returns it has generated over a period of time. One of the key objectives in portfolio selection is to smooth out the variation in the return on a portfolio by choosing investments whose returns tend to vary in opposite directions. That is, we might want to choose investments that have a negative covariance or negative correlation so that when one investment generates a lower-than-average return, another investment in our portfolio offsets this with a higher-than-average return. This tends to make the variance of the return of the portfolio smaller than that of any individual investment. The following example illustrates a portfolio selection problem.

Ray Dodson is an independent financial advisor. He recently met with a new client, Paula Ribben, who wanted Ray's advice on how best to diversify a portion of her investments. Paula has invested a good portion of her retirement savings in the stock of International Business Corporation (IBC). During the past 12 years, this stock has produced an average annual return of 7.64% with a variance of approximately 0.0026. Paula wants to earn more on her investments, but is very cautious and doesn't like to take risks. Paula has asked Ray to recommend a portfolio of investments that would provide at least a 12% average return with as little additional risk as possible. After some research, Ray identified two additional stocks, from the National Motor Corporation (NMC) and the National Broadcasting System (NBS), that he believes could help meet Paula's investment objectives. Ray's initial research is summarized in Figure 8.25.

As indicated in Figure 8.25, shares of NMC have produced an average rate of return of 13.43% over the past 12 years, while those of NBS have generated an average return of 14.93%. Ray used the COVAR( ) function in Excel to create the covariance matrix in this spreadsheet. The numbers along the main diagonal in this matrix correspond to the variances of the returns for each stock. For example, the covariance matrix indicates

FIGURE 8.25

Data for the portfolio selection problem

	A	B	C	D	E	F	G	H	I
1									
2				Portfolio Data					
3									
4			Annual Return				Covariance Matrix		
5	Year	IBC	NMC	NBS			IBC	NMC	NBS
6	1	11.2%	8.0%	10.9%		IBC	0.00258	-0.00025	0.00440
7	2	10.8%	9.2%	22.0%		NMC	-0.00025	0.00276	-0.00542
8	3	11.6%	6.6%	37.9%		NBS	0.00440	-0.00542	0.03677
9	4	-1.6%	18.5%	-11.8%					
10	5	-4.1%	7.4%	12.9%					
11	6	8.6%	13.0%	-7.5%					
12	7	6.8%	22.0%	9.3%					
13	8	11.9%	14.0%	48.7%					
14	9	12.0%	20.5%	-1.9%					
15	10	8.3%	14.0%	19.1%					
16	11	6.0%	19.0%	-3.4%					
17	12	10.2%	9.0%	43.0%					
18	Average	7.64%	13.43%	14.93%					
19									

Portfolio Data

Key Cell Formulas

Cell	Formula	Copied to
B18	=AVERAGE(B6:B17)	C18:D18
G6	=COVAR(B6:B17,$B$6:$B$17)	H6:I6
G7	=COVAR(B6:B17,$C$6:$C$17)	H7:I7
G8	=COVAR(B6:B17,$D$6:$D$17)	H8:I8

that the variances in the annual returns for IBC, NMC, and NBS are 0.00258, 0.00276, and 0.03677, respectively. The entries off the main diagonal represent covariances between different pairs of stocks. For example, the covariance between IBC and NMC is approximately -0.00025, the covariance between IBC and NBS is approximately 0.00440, and the covariance between NMC and NBS is approximately -0.00542.

Ray wants to determine what percentage of Paula's funds should be allocated to each of the stocks in order to achieve an overall expected return of 12% while minimizing the variance of the total return on the portfolio.

8.9.1 DEFINING THE DECISION VARIABLES

In this problem, we must determine what percentage of the total funds invested should go toward the purchase of each of the three stocks. Thus, to formulate the model for this problem, we need the following three decision variables:

$$p_1 = \text{proportion of total funds invested in IBC}$$
$$p_2 = \text{proportion of total funds invested in NMC}$$
$$p_3 = \text{proportion of total funds invested in NBS}$$

Because these variables represent proportions, we also need to ensure that they assume values no less than 0 and that they sum to 1 (or 100%). We will handle these conditions when we identify the constraints for the problem.

8.9.2 DEFINING THE OBJECTIVE

The objective in this problem is to minimize the risk of the portfolio as measured by its variance. In general, the variance of a portfolio consisting of n investments is defined in most finance texts as:

$$\text{Portfolio variance} = \sum_{i=1}^{n} \sigma_i^2 p_i^2 + 2 \sum_{i=1}^{n-1} \sum_{j=i+1}^{n} \sigma_{ij} p_i p_j$$

where:

$$p_i = \text{the percentage of the portfolio invested in investment } i$$
$$\sigma_i^2 = \text{the variance of investment } i$$
$$\sigma_{ij} = \sigma_{ji} = \text{the covariance between investments } i \text{ and } j$$

If you are familiar with matrix multiplication, you might realize that the portfolio variance can also be expressed in matrix terms as:

$$\text{Portfolio variance} = \mathbf{p}^T \mathbf{C} \mathbf{p}$$

where:

$$\mathbf{p}^T = (p_1, p_2, \ldots, p_n)$$

$$\mathbf{C} = \text{the } n \times n \text{ covariance matrix} = \begin{bmatrix} \sigma_1^2 & \sigma_{12} & \cdots & \sigma_{1n} \\ \sigma_{21} & \sigma_2^2 & \cdots & \sigma_{2n} \\ \vdots & \vdots & \ddots & \vdots \\ \sigma_{n1} & \sigma_{n2} & \cdots & \sigma_n^2 \end{bmatrix}$$

Notice that if 100% of the funds available are placed in a single investment i, then the portfolio variance reduces to σ_i^2— the variance for that single investment.

In our example problem, we have:

$$\sigma_i^2 = 0.00258, \quad \sigma_2^2 = 0.00276, \quad \sigma_3^2 = 0.03677$$
$$\sigma_{12} = -0.00025, \quad \sigma_{13} = 0.00440, \quad \sigma_{23} = -0.00542$$

So, using the preceding formula, the objective for our problem is stated as:

MIN: $\quad 0.00258\, p_1^2 + 0.00276\, p_2^2 + 0.03677\, p_3^2$
$$+ 2(-0.00025\, p_1 p_2 + 0.0044\, p_1 p_3 - 0.00542\, p_2 p_3)$$

This objective function is not a linear combination of the decision variables, so we must solve this problem as an NLP. However, it can be shown that the solution produced when using this objective for a portfolio selection is a global optimal solution. (This problem is actually an example of a quadratic programming [QP] problem.)

8.9.3 DEFINING THE CONSTRAINTS

Only two main constraints apply to this problem. As mentioned earlier, because only three investments are under consideration for this portfolio, and our decision variables represent the percentage of funds invested in each of these investments, we must ensure that our decision variables sum to 100%. This can be accomplished easily as:

$$p_1 + p_2 + p_3 = 1$$

We also need a constraint to ensure that the expected return of the entire portfolio achieves or exceeds the desired return of 12%. This condition is expressed as:

$$0.0764 p_1 + 0.1343 p_2 + 0.1493 p_3 \geq 0.12$$

The LHS of this constraint represents a weighted average of the expected returns from the individual investments. This constraint indicates that the weighted average expected return on the portfolio must be at least 12%.

Finally, because the decision variables must represent proportions, we should also include the following upper and lower bounds:

$$p_1, p_2, p_3 \geq 0$$
$$p_1, p_2, p_3 \leq 1$$

The last condition, requiring each p_i to be less than or equal to 1, is mathematically redundant because the p_i must also be nonnegative and sum to 1. However, we will include this restriction for completeness.

8.9.4 IMPLEMENTING THE MODEL

In summary, the algebraic model for this problem is given as:

MIN: $\quad 0.00258\, p_1^2 + 0.00276\, p_2^2 + 0.03677\, p_3^2$
$$+ 2(-0.00025\, p_1 p_2 + 0.0044\, p_1 p_3 - 0.00542\, p_2 p_3)$$

Subject to:
$$p_1 + p_2 + p_3 = 1$$
$$0.0764 p_1 + 0.1343 p_2 + 0.1493 p_3 \geq 0.12$$
$$p_1, p_2, p_3 \geq 0$$
$$p_1, p_2, p_3 \leq 1$$

FIGURE 8.26 *Spreadsheet implementation for the portfolio selection problem*

		Annual Return				Covariance Matrix				
	Year	IBC	NMC	NBS		IBC	NMC	NBS		
	1	11.2%	8.0%	10.9%	IBC	0.00258	-0.00025	0.00440		
	2	10.8%	9.2%	22.0%	NMC	-0.00025	0.00276	-0.00542		
	3	11.6%	6.6%	37.9%	NBS	0.00440	-0.00542	0.03677		
	4	-1.6%	18.5%	-11.8%						
	5	-4.1%	7.4%	12.9%		IBC	NMC	NBS	Total	
	6	8.6%	13.0%	-7.5%	Portfolio	100.0%	0.0%	0.0%	100%	
	7	6.8%	22.0%	9.3%						
	8	11.9%	14.0%	48.7%	Expected Return		7.64%			
	9	12.0%	20.5%	-1.9%	Required Return		12.00%			
	10	8.3%	14.0%	19.1%						
	11	6.0%	19.0%	-3.4%	Portfolio Variance		0.00258			
	12	10.2%	9.0%	43.0%						
	Average	7.64%	13.43%	14.93%						

Portfolio Selection Problem

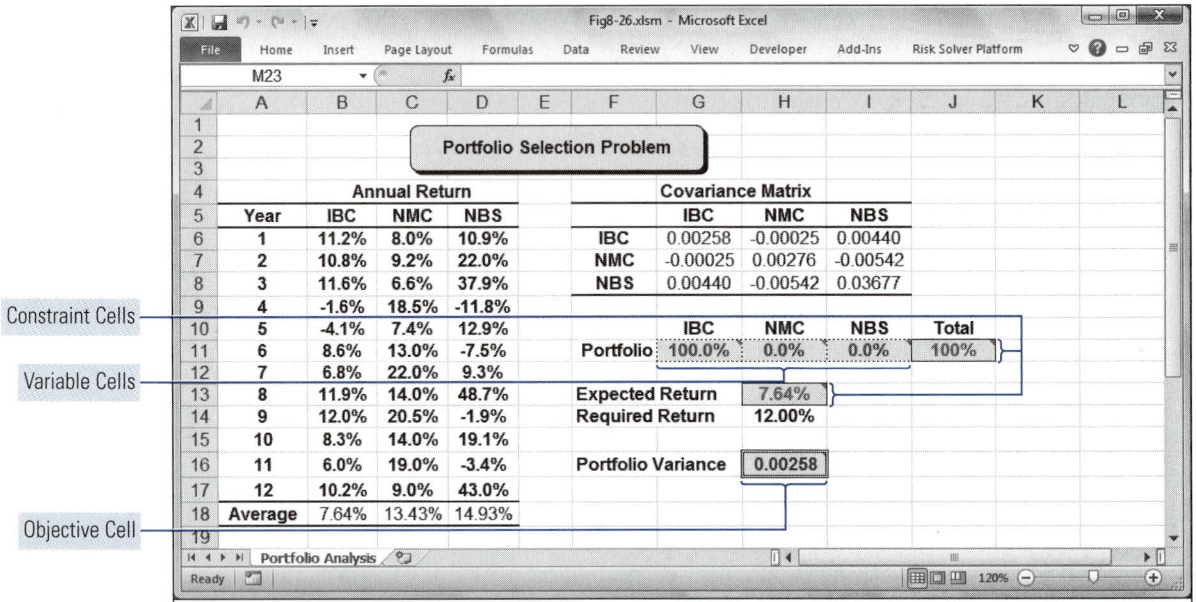

Constraint Cells
Variable Cells
Objective Cell

Key Cell Formulas

Cell	Formula	Copied to
J11	=SUM(G11:I11)	--
H13	=SUMPRODUCT(B18:D18,G11:I11)	--
H16	=SUMPRODUCT(MMULT(G11:I11,G6:I8),G11:I11)	--

One approach to implementing this model in a spreadsheet is shown in Figure 8.26 (and in the file Fig8-26.xlsm that accompanies this book). In this spreadsheet, cells G11, H11, and I11 represent the decision variables p_1, p_2, and p_3, respectively. The initial values in these cells reflect the investor's current portfolio, which consists entirely of stock in IBC.

We can implement the objective function for this problem in a number of ways. The standard approach is to implement a formula that corresponds exactly to the algebraic form of the objective function. This is represented by:

Formula for cell H16:   =G6*G11^2+H7*H11^2+I8*I11^2+2* (H6*G11*H11+I6*G11*I11+H8*H11*I11)

Entering this formula is tedious and prone to error, and would be even more so if this example involved more than three stocks. The following is an alternative, and easier, way of expressing this objective:

Alternative formula for cell H16: =SUMPRODUCT(MMULT(G11:I11,G6:I8),G11:I11)

This alternative formula uses matrix multiplication (the MMULT( ) function) to compute the portfolio variance. Although both formulas generate the same result, the second formula is much easier to enter and can accommodate any number of investments. Notice that the value 0.00258 in cell H16 in Figure 8.26 indicates that when 100% of the funds are invested in IBC stock, the variance of the portfolio is the same as the variance of the IBC stock.

The LHS formulas of the two main constraints are implemented in cells J11 and H13 as:

Formula for cell J11:   =SUM(G11:I11)

Formula for cell H13:   =SUMPRODUCT(B18:D18,G11:I11)

Figure 8.27 shows the Solver settings and options used to solve this problem, and Figure 8.28 shows the optimal solution.

8.9.5 ANALYZING THE SOLUTION

In contrast to the original solution shown in Figure 8.26, the optimal solution shown in Figure 8.28 indicates that a better solution would result by placing 27.2% of the investor's money in IBC, 63.4% in NMC, and 9.4% in NBS. Cell H13 indicates that this mix of investments would achieve the desired 12% expected rate of return, and cell H16 indicates that the variance for this portfolio would be only 0.00112.

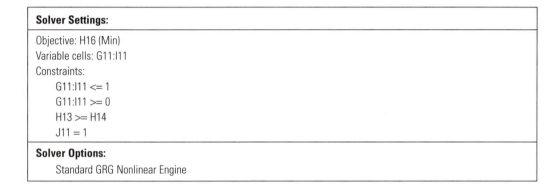

FIGURE 8.27

Solver parameters for the portfolio selection problem

FIGURE 8.28 *Optimal solution to the portfolio selection problem*

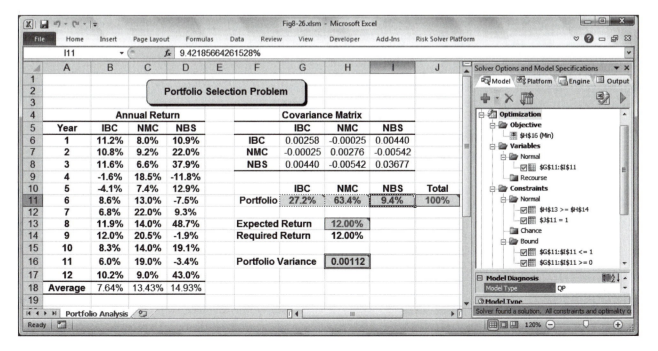

The solution to this problem indicates that a portfolio exists that produces a *higher* expected return for Paula with *less* risk than was involved in her original portfolio. Paula's original investment would be called inefficient in the terms of portfolio theory. Portfolio theory stipulates that for each possible level of investment return, there is a portfolio that minimizes risk, and accepting any greater level of risk at that level of return is inefficient. Alternatively, for each level of investment risk, there is a portfolio that maximizes the return, and accepting any lower level of return at this level of risk is also inefficient.

The optimal trade-off between risk and return for a given portfolio problem can be summarized by a graph of the **efficient frontier**, which plots the minimal portfolio risk associated with each possible level of return. Figure 8.29 (and the file Fig8-29.xlsm that accompanies this book) shows the efficient frontier for our example problem. This graph plots the minimal level of risk associated with 15 different portfolios where the required rate is varied in equal steps between 7.64% and 14.93% (representing, respectively, the

FIGURE 8.29 *Efficient frontier for the portfolio selection problem*

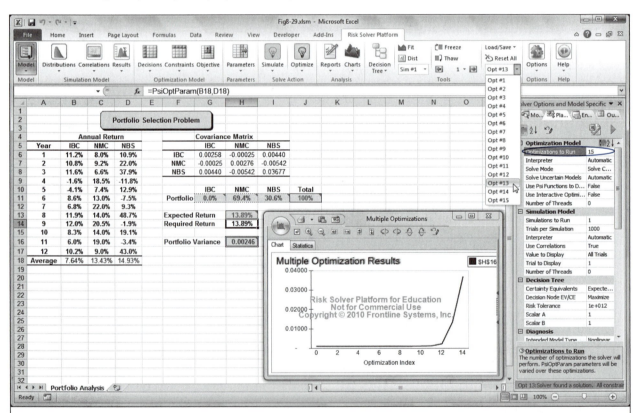

Cell	Formula	Copied to
J11	=SUM(G11:I11)	--
H13	=SUMPRODUCT(B18:D18,G11:I11)	--
H14	=PsiOptParam(B18, D18)	--
H16	=SUMPRODUCT(MMULT(G11:I11,G6:I8),G11:I11)	--

minimum and maximum possible rates of return). To create this graph, we first placed the following formula in cell H14:

Formula for cell H14:   =PsiOptParam(B18, D18)

This causes the required return value in cell H14 to be varied from 7.64% (cell B18) to 14.93% (cell D18) in equal steps as Solver runs the number of optimizations indicated by the Optimizations to Run setting on the Platform tab in the Solver task pane (which was set to 15 for this example). After Solver performs the optimizations, you can easily construct a graph like the one shown in Figure 8.29 by following these steps:

1. Click the Charts icon on the Risk Solver Platform tab.
2. Select Multiple Optimizations, Monitored Cells.
3. Expand the Objective option, select $H$16, and click the > button.
4. Click OK.

The resulting graph in Figure 8.29 shows how the optimal portfolio variance increases for each of the 15 optimizations as the required expected return increased in equal increments from 7.64% to 14.93%. This graph is helpful not only in identifying the maximum level of risk that should be accepted for each possible level of return but also in identifying where further increases in expected returns incur much greater amounts of risk. In this case, there is a fairly significant increase in the portfolio variance (risk) between the 13th and 14th optimization run. The drop-down list in Figure 8.29 allows us to select and inspect the details of each optimization run.

Whether you attempt to minimize risk subject to a certain required rate of return or maximize the return subject to a given level of risk, the solutions obtained may still be inefficient. For instance, in the solution to our example problem, there may be a different portfolio that produces a higher return for the same level of risk. We could check for this by solving the problem again—maximizing the expected return while holding the minimal level of risk constant.

8.9.6 HANDLING CONFLICTING OBJECTIVES IN PORTFOLIO PROBLEMS

As we have seen, there are two different conflicting objectives that can be applied to portfolio selection problems: minimizing risk (portfolio variance) and maximizing expected returns. One way of dealing with these conflicting objectives is to solve the following problem:

MAX: $(1 - \mathbf{r}) \times$ (Expected Portfolio Return) $- \mathbf{r} \times$ (Portfolio Variance)

Subject to: $\sum p_i = 1$

$p_i \geq 0$ for all i

Here, the p_i again represent the percentages of money we should invest in each stock in the portfolio, and $\mathbf{r}$ is a constant between 0 and 1 representing the investor's aversion to risk (or the **risk aversion value**). When $\mathbf{r} = 1$ (indicating maximum risk aversion), the objective function attempts to minimize the portfolio variance. Such a solution is shown in Figure 8.30 (and in the file Fig8-30.xlsm that accompanies this book) in which we have implemented the expected return in cell H13, the portfolio variance in cell H14, the risk aversion factor in cell H15, and the objective function in cell H16. This solution places 36% of the investor's money in IBC, 57% in NMC, and 7.1% in NBS. This results in a

FIGURE 8.30 *Solution showing the least risky portfolio*

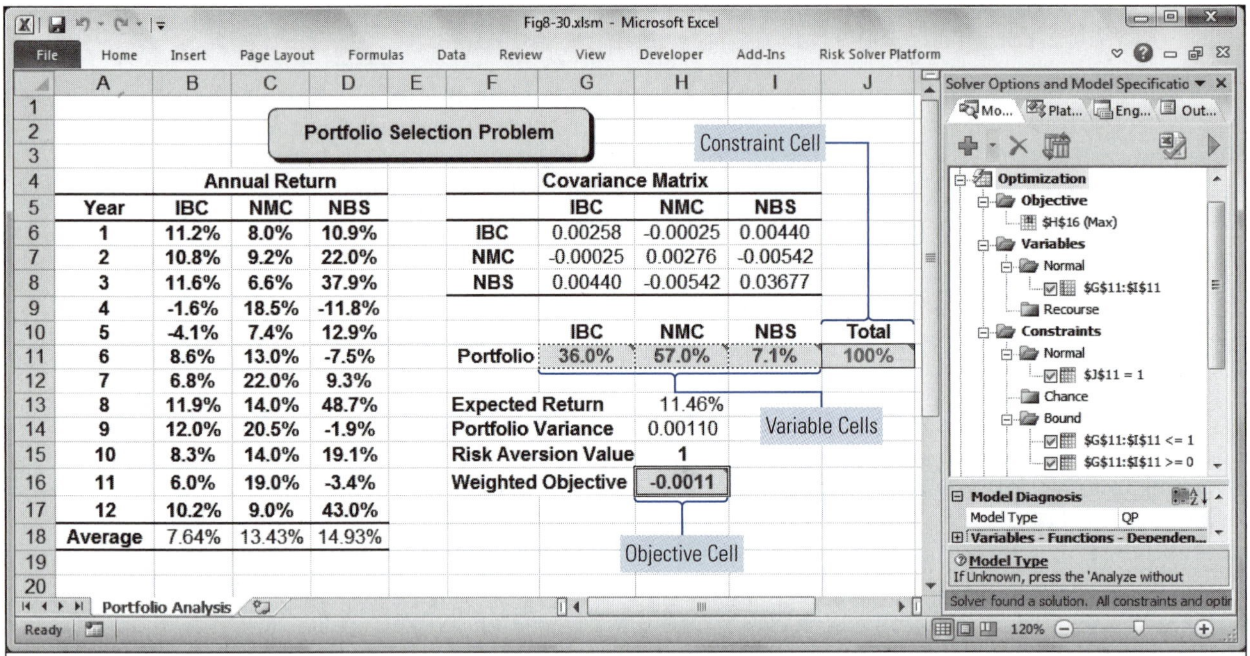

	A	B	C	D	E	F	G	H	I	J
4		Annual Return					Covariance Matrix			
5	Year	IBC	NMC	NBS			IBC	NMC	NBS	
6	1	11.2%	8.0%	10.9%		IBC	0.00258	-0.00025	0.00440	
7	2	10.8%	9.2%	22.0%		NMC	-0.00025	0.00276	-0.00542	
8	3	11.6%	6.6%	37.9%		NBS	0.00440	-0.00542	0.03677	
9	4	-1.6%	18.5%	-11.8%						
10	5	-4.1%	7.4%	12.9%			IBC	NMC	NBS	Total
11	6	8.6%	13.0%	-7.5%		Portfolio	36.0%	57.0%	7.1%	100%
12	7	6.8%	22.0%	9.3%						
13	8	11.9%	14.0%	48.7%		Expected Return		11.46%		
14	9	12.0%	20.5%	-1.9%		Portfolio Variance		0.00110		
15	10	8.3%	14.0%	19.1%		Risk Aversion Value		1		
16	11	6.0%	19.0%	-3.4%		Weighted Objective		-0.0011		
17	12	10.2%	9.0%	43.0%						
18	Average	7.64%	13.43%	14.93%						

Key Cell Formulas

Cell	Formula	Copied to
J11	=SUM(G11:I11)	--
H13	=SUMPRODUCT(B18:D18,G11:I11)	--
H14	=SUMPRODUCT(MMULT(G11:I11,G6:I8),G11:I11)	--
H16	=(1-H15)*H13-H15*H14	--

portfolio variance of 0.0011. This is the smallest possible portfolio variance for this collection of stocks.

Conversely, when **r** = 0 (indicating a total disregard of risk), the objective attempts to maximize the expected portfolio return. This solution is shown in Figure 8.31. This solution places 100% of the investor's money in NBS because this produces the largest return for the portfolio.

For values of **r** between 0 and 1, Solver will always attempt to keep the expected return as large as possible and the portfolio variance as small as possible (because the objective function in this problem is being maximized). As the value of the parameter **r** increases, more and more weight is placed on the importance of making the portfolio variance as small as possible (or minimizing risk). Thus, a risk-averse investor should prefer solutions with relatively large values of **r**. By solving a series of problems, each time adjusting the value of **r**, an investor can select a portfolio that provides the greatest utility, or the optimum balance of risk and return for their own attitudes toward risk and return. Alternatively, if an investor feels minimizing risk is twice as important as maximizing returns, we can solve the problem with **r** = 0.667 (and (1 − **r**) = 0.333) to reflect the investor's attitude toward risk and return. An **r** value of 0.99275 will produce the same solution shown earlier in Figure 8.28.

FIGURE 8.31 *Solution showing the maximum return portfolio*

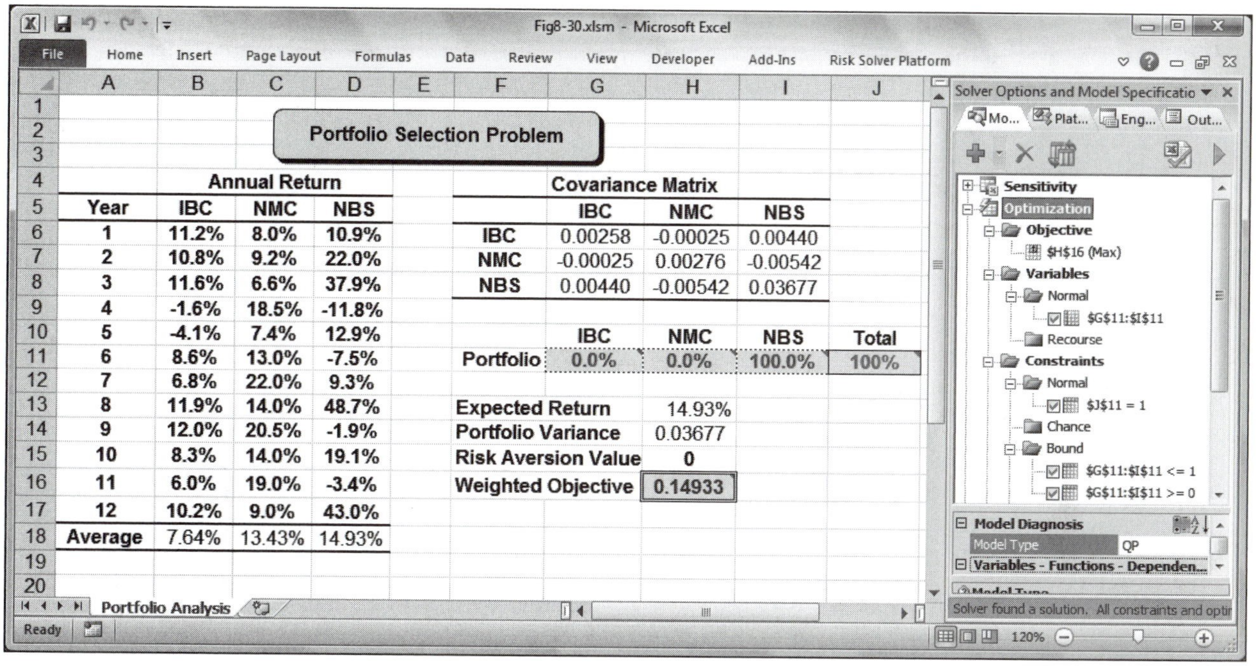

8.10 Sensitivity Analysis

In Chapter 4, we analyzed how sensitive the optimal solution to an LP model is to changes in various coefficients in the model. We noted that one advantage of using the simplex method to solve LP problems is that it provides expanded sensitivity information. A certain amount of sensitivity information is also available when using nonlinear optimization methods to solve linear or nonlinear problems.

To understand the sensitivity information available from nonlinear optimization, we will compare it to what we learned in Chapter 4 about the sensitivity information that results from using the simplex method. In Chapter 4, we solved the following modified version of the Blue Ridge Hot Tubs problem, where a third type of hot tub—the Typhoon-Lagoon—was included in the model:

$$
\begin{aligned}
\text{MAX:} \quad & 350X_1 + 300X_2 + 320X_3 && \} \text{ profit} \\
\text{Subject to:} \quad & 1X_1 + 1X_2 + 1X_3 \leq 200 && \} \text{ pump constraint} \\
& 9X_1 + 6X_2 + 8X_3 \leq 1{,}566 && \} \text{ labor constraint} \\
& 12X_1 + 16X_2 + 13X_3 \leq 2{,}880 && \} \text{ tubing constraint} \\
& X_1, X_2, X_3 \geq 0 && \} \text{ nonnegativity conditions}
\end{aligned}
$$

The spreadsheet implementation of this problem is shown in Figure 8.32 (and in the file Fig8-32.xlsm that accompanies this book). Figure 8.33 shows the Sensitivity Report generated for this problem after solving it using the simplex method. Figure 8.34 shows the Sensitivity Report for this problem after solving it using Solver's nonlinear optimizer.

FIGURE 8.32 *Spreadsheet model for the revised Blue Ridge Hot Tubs problem*

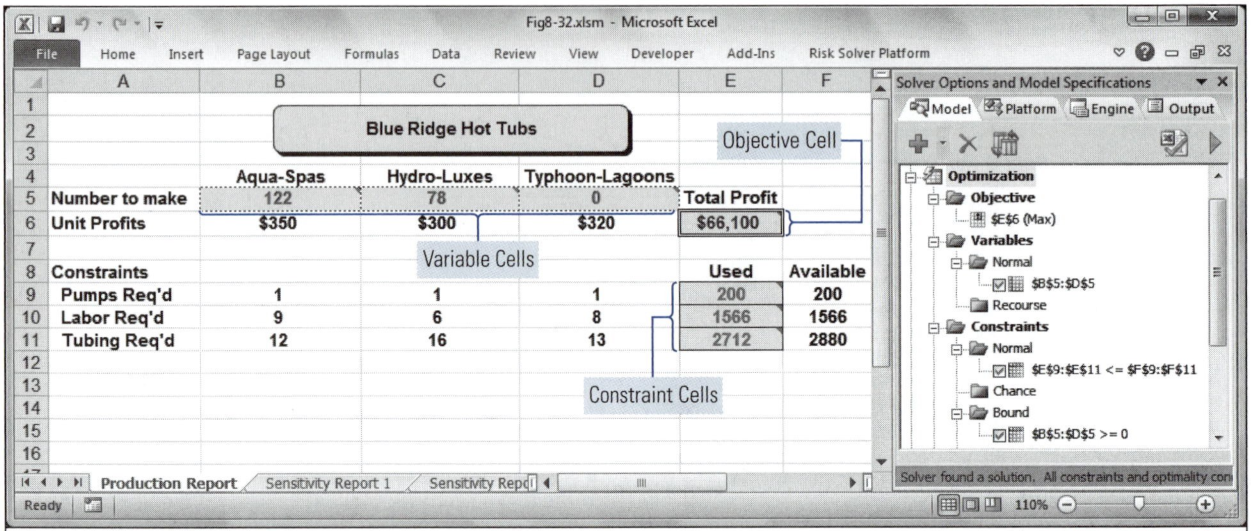

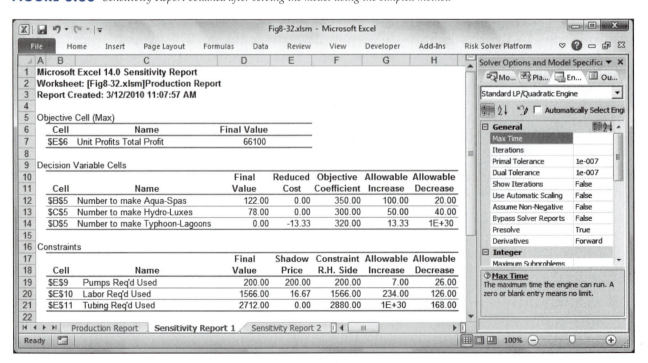

Key Cell Formulas

Cell	Formula	Copied to
E6	=SUMPRODUCT(B6:D6,$B$5:$D$5)	E9:E11

FIGURE 8.33 *Sensitivity Report obtained after solving the model using the simplex method*

Microsoft Excel 14.0 Sensitivity Report
Worksheet: [Fig8-32.xlsm]Production Report
Report Created: 3/12/2010 11:07:57 AM

Objective Cell (Max)

Cell	Name	Final Value
$E$6	Unit Profits Total Profit	66100

Decision Variable Cells

Cell	Name	Final Value	Reduced Cost	Objective Coefficient	Allowable Increase	Allowable Decrease
$B$5	Number to make Aqua-Spas	122.00	0.00	350.00	100.00	20.00
$C$5	Number to make Hydro-Luxes	78.00	0.00	300.00	50.00	40.00
$D$5	Number to make Typhoon-Lagoons	0.00	-13.33	320.00	13.33	1E+30

Constraints

Cell	Name	Final Value	Shadow Price	Constraint R.H. Side	Allowable Increase	Allowable Decrease
$E$9	Pumps Req'd Used	200.00	200.00	200.00	7.00	26.00
$E$10	Labor Req'd Used	1566.00	16.67	1566.00	234.00	126.00
$E$11	Tubing Req'd Used	2712.00	0.00	2880.00	1E+30	168.00

FIGURE 8.34 *Sensitivity Report obtained after solving the model using Solver's nonlinear GRG optimizer*

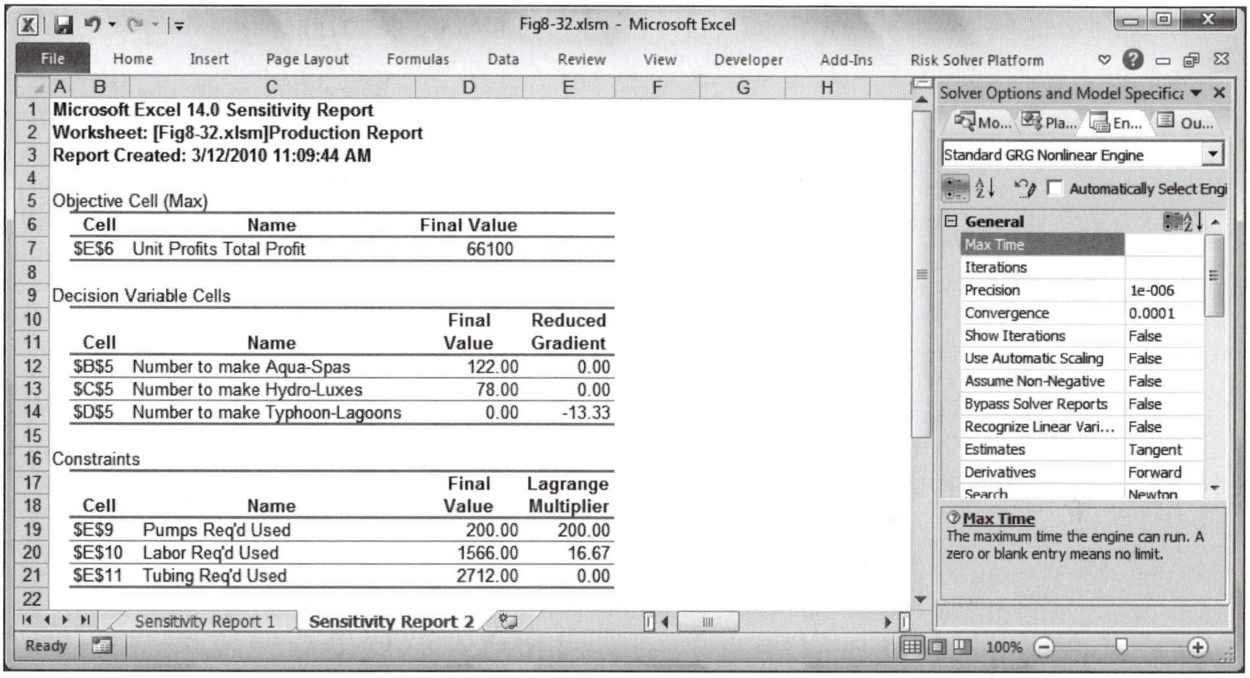

In comparing Figures 8.33 and 8.34, notice that the same optimal solution is obtained regardless of whether the problem is solved using the simplex method or the nonlinear optimizer. Both reports indicate that 122 Aqua-Spas, 78 Hydro-Luxes, and 0 Typhoon-Lagoons should be produced. Both reports also indicate that this solution requires 200 pumps, 1,566 labor hours, and 2,712 feet of tubing. The fact that the two optimization techniques found the same optimal solution is not surprising because this problem is known to have a unique optimal solution. However, if an LP problem has alternative optimal solutions, the simplex method and the nonlinear optimizer will not necessarily identify the same optimal solution.

Another similarity between the two Sensitivity Reports is apparent if we compare the values in the Reduced Cost and Shadow Price columns in Figure 8.33 with the values in the Reduced Gradient and Lagrange Multiplier columns in Figure 8.34. The reduced cost for each variable in Figure 8.33 is the same as the reduced gradient for each variable in Figure 8.34. Similarly, the shadow price for each constraint in Figure 8.33 is the same as the Lagrange multiplier for each constraint in Figure 8.34. This is not simply a coincidence.

8.10.1 LAGRANGE MULTIPLIERS

In Chapter 4, we saw that the shadow price of a constraint represents the marginal value of an additional unit of the resource represented by the constraint—or the amount by which the objective function would improve if the RHS of the constraint is loosened by one unit. This same interpretation applies in a more approximate sense to Lagrange multipliers. The main difference between shadow prices and Lagrange multipliers involves the range of RHS values over which the shadow price or Lagrange multiplier remains valid.

As discussed in Chapter 4 (and shown previously in Figure 8.33), after solving an LP problem using the simplex method, we can identify the allowable increase and decrease in a constraint's RHS value over which the shadow price of the constraint remains valid. We can do this because the objective function and constraints in an LP problem are all linear, making the impact of changes in a constraint's RHS value on the objective function value relatively easy to compute. However, in NLP problems, we have no general way to determine such ranges for the RHS values of the constraints. So, when using Solver's nonlinear optimizer to solve an optimization problem, we cannot easily determine the range of RHS values over which a constraint's Lagrange multiplier will remain valid. The Lagrange multipliers can be used only to estimate the approximate impact on the objective function of changing a constraint's RHS value by small amounts.

8.10.2 REDUCED GRADIENTS

In Chapter 4, we saw that the reduced cost of a variable that assumes its simple lower (or upper) bound in the optimal solution generally represents the amount by which the objective function would be reduced (or improved) if this variable were allowed to increase by one unit. Again, this same interpretation applies in a more approximate sense to reduced gradient values. In particular, nonzero reduced gradient values indicate the approximate impact on the objective function value of very small changes in the value of a given variable. For example, in Chapter 4, we saw that forcing the production of one Typhoon-Lagoon resulted in a $13.33 reduction in total profit for the problem shown in Figure 8.32. This is reflected by the reduced cost value for Typhoon-Lagoons in Figure 8.33 and the reduced gradient value for Typhoon-Lagoons in Figure 8.34.

Although we used an LP model to discuss the meaning of reduced gradients and Lagrange multipliers, their interpretation is the same for nonlinear problems. As stated earlier, an LP problem can be viewed as a special type of NLP problem where the objective function and constraints are linear.

8.11 Solver Options for Solving NLPs

Although we can represent an LP problem by a highly structured and relatively simple objective function and set of constraints, the objective function and constraints in an NLP problem can be virtually *any* mathematical function. Thus, it is not uncommon to encounter difficulties while trying to solve NLP problems.

Solver provides several options for controlling how it solves NLPs. These options—Estimates, Derivatives, and Search—are located in the Engine tab in the Solver task pane, as shown in Figure 8.35. The default settings for these options work well for many problems. However, if you have difficulty solving an NLP, you might try changing these options to force Solver to use a different search strategy. A complete description of these options would require an in-depth understanding of calculus, which is not assumed in this book. The following descriptions provide a nontechnical overview of these options.

As Solver searches for an optimal solution to an NLP, it terminates if the relative change in the objective function value for several iterations is smaller than the convergence factor. If you think Solver is stopping too quickly as it converges on an optimal solution, you should reduce the Convergence setting shown in Figure 8.35.

The Estimates option determines how Solver estimates the values of the decision variables while searching for improved solutions. The default setting, Tangent, estimates values using a linear extrapolation technique, whereas the alternate setting, Quadratic, uses a nonlinear extrapolation technique.

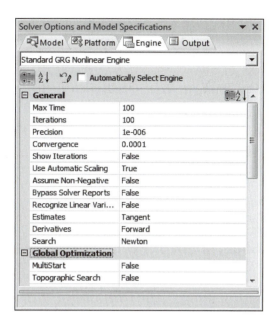

FIGURE 8.35

Solver options for NLP problems

The Derivatives option determines how Solver estimates derivatives. When using the default setting, Forward, Solver obtains estimates of first derivatives at a point by perturbing the point once in a forward direction and computing the rise over the run. With the Central setting, Solver obtains estimates of first derivatives by perturbing away from a point in both a backward and forward direction and computing the rise over the run between the two points. The Central setting requires twice as many recalculations as the Forward option but can improve the estimates of the derivatives, yielding better search directions and often fewer iterations. However, the difference in accuracy is usually not worth the extra effort, hence the default is Forward.

The Search option determines how Solver chooses a search direction along which to seek a feasible point with an improved objective value. The default setting, Newton, causes Solver to use the Broyden-Fletcher-Goldfarb-Shanno Quasi-Newton method to identify search directions. The Conjugate setting instructs Solver to use the conjugate gradient method. The details of these techniques go beyond the scope of this text but can be found in most texts devoted to NLP.

As mentioned earlier, the local optimal solution at which an NLP algorithm terminates often depends on the initial starting point. Note that the MultiStart option in Figure 8.35, if set to True, causes Solver to apply methods to attempt to find a global, rather than a local, optimal solution. Additionally, scaling problems often affect how easily Solver can solve a problem. Thus, selecting the Use Automatic Scaling option is also a possible remedy to try if Solver encounters difficulty in solving an NLP.

8.12 Evolutionary Algorithms

In recent years, one of the most interesting and exciting developments in the field of optimization has centered on research into the area of evolutionary (or genetic) algorithms. Inspired by ideas from Darwin's theory of evolution, researchers interested in mathematical optimization have devised heuristic search techniques that mimic processes in biological reproduction and apply the principle of "survival of the fittest" to create general-purpose optimization engines.

In a nutshell, genetic algorithms (GAs) start with a set of chromosomes (numeric vectors) representing possible solutions to an optimization problem. The individual components (numeric values) within a chromosome are referred to as genes. New chromosomes are created by crossover and mutation. **Crossover** is the probabilistic exchange of values between solution vectors. **Mutation** is the random replacement of values in a solution vector. Chromosomes are then evaluated according to a fitness (or objective) function with the fittest surviving into the next generation. The result is a gene pool that evolves over time to produce better and better solutions to a problem.

Figure 8.36 gives an example of how one iteration through the evolutionary process might work on a simple problem involving four decision variables. In this case, we arbitrarily started with a population of 7 possible solution vectors (chromosomes). (In reality, most GAs use a population size of 50 to 100 chromosomes.) Each chromosome is evaluated according to some fitness (objective) function for the problem.

Next, we apply the crossover and mutation operators to generate new possible solutions to the problem. The second table in Figure 8.36 shows the results of this process. Note that the values for X_3 and X_4 in chromosomes 1 and 2 have been exchanged, as have

FIGURE 8.36

Example of one iteration through an evolutionary algorithm

INITIAL POPULATION

Chromosome	X_1	X_2	X_3	X_4	Fitness
1	7.84	24.39	28.95	6.62	282.08
2	10.26	16.36	31.26	3.55	293.38
3	3.88	23.03	25.92	6.76	223.31
4	9.51	19.51	26.23	2.64	331.28
5	5.96	19.52	33.83	6.89	453.57
6	4.77	18.31	26.21	5.59	229.49
7	8.72	22.12	29.85	2.30	409.68

CROSSOVER & MUTATION

Chromosome	X_1	X_2	X_3	X_4	Fitness
1	7.84	24.39	31.26	3.55	334.28
2	10.26	16.36	28.95	6.62	227.04
3	3.88	19.75	25.92	6.76	301.44
4	9.51	19.51	32.23	2.64	495.52
5	4.77	18.31	33.83	6.89	332.38
6	5.96	19.52	26.21	5.59	444.21
7	8.72	22.12	29.85	4.60	478.93

Crossover

Mutation

Crossover

NEW POPULATION

Chromosome	X_1	X_2	X_3	X_4	Fitness
1	7.84	24.39	31.26	3.55	334.28
2	10.26	16.36	31.26	3.55	293.38
3	3.88	19.75	25.92	6.76	301.44
4	9.51	19.51	32.23	2.64	495.52
5	5.96	19.52	33.83	6.89	453.57
6	5.96	19.52	26.21	5.59	444.21
7	8.72	22.12	29.85	4.60	478.93

the values for X_1 and X_2 in chromosomes 5 and 6. This represents the crossover operation. Also note that the values of X_2, X_3, and X_4 in chromosomes 3, 4, and 7, respectively, have been changed randomly—representing mutation. The fitness of each new chromosome is then calculated and compared against the fitness of the corresponding chromosome in the original population with the most-fit chromosome surviving into the next population. Various procedures can be used to implement the crossover, mutation, and survival of the fittest. This simple example is intended to give you a basic understanding of how a GA might work.

To a certain extent, Solver's evolutionary algorithm picks up where its nonlinear GRG algorithm leaves off. As we have seen, for nonlinear problems, the solution Solver generates depends on the starting point and may be a local rather than global optimum solution. Also, Solver tends to have difficulty solving problems with discontinuities and unsmooth landscapes, which are typical of spreadsheet models employing logical IF( ) and/or lookup tables. Although the evolutionary algorithm cannot completely avoid the possibility of becoming trapped at a local optimal solution, its use of a randomized initial gene pool and probabilistic crossover and mutation operators make this occurrence less likely. Moreover, the evolutionary algorithm can operate on virtually any spreadsheet model—even those containing IF( ) functions, lookup tables, and custom macro functions. We will now consider a few examples of problems where Solver's evolutionary algorithm can be applied.

8.13 Forming Fair Teams

A variety of problems exist where the goal is to form fair/balanced teams from a group of people. This can happen in amateur golf tournaments where the goal is to form teams with similar handicaps, and in civic organizations that sponsor networking events where there is a desire to ensure diversity in seating arrangements for tables. Another such problem is illustrated next.

> Steve Sorensen is the director of the MBA program at Claytor College. Each year, he forms project teams for the incoming class of full-time MBA students. Students work in the same team for each of their classes during their first semester in order to get to know one another and learn how to deal with people that they might not have otherwise chosen to work with. There are 34 students in the next incoming class that Steve would like to organize into 7 teams. He would like to assign students to teams so that the average GMAT score for each team is as similar as possible.

8.13.1 A SPREADSHEET MODEL FOR THE PROBLEM

Figure 8.37 shows a spreadsheet containing GMAT scores for the 34 new MBA students for Claytor College. (Note that rows 17 to 26 of this table have been hidden to save space.) Cells D5 through D38 represent decision variables indicating to which of the 7 teams each student is assigned. Arbitrary values have been assigned to these cells at present. We will instruct Solver to assign integer values from 1 to 7 to each of these cells. Cells G5 through G11 compute the average GMAT score for students assigned to each team as follows,

Formula for cell G5:   =AVERAGEIF($D$5:$D$38,F5,$C$5:$C$38)
(Copy to cells G6 through G11.)

FIGURE 8.37 *Spreadsheet model for the MBA team assignment problem*

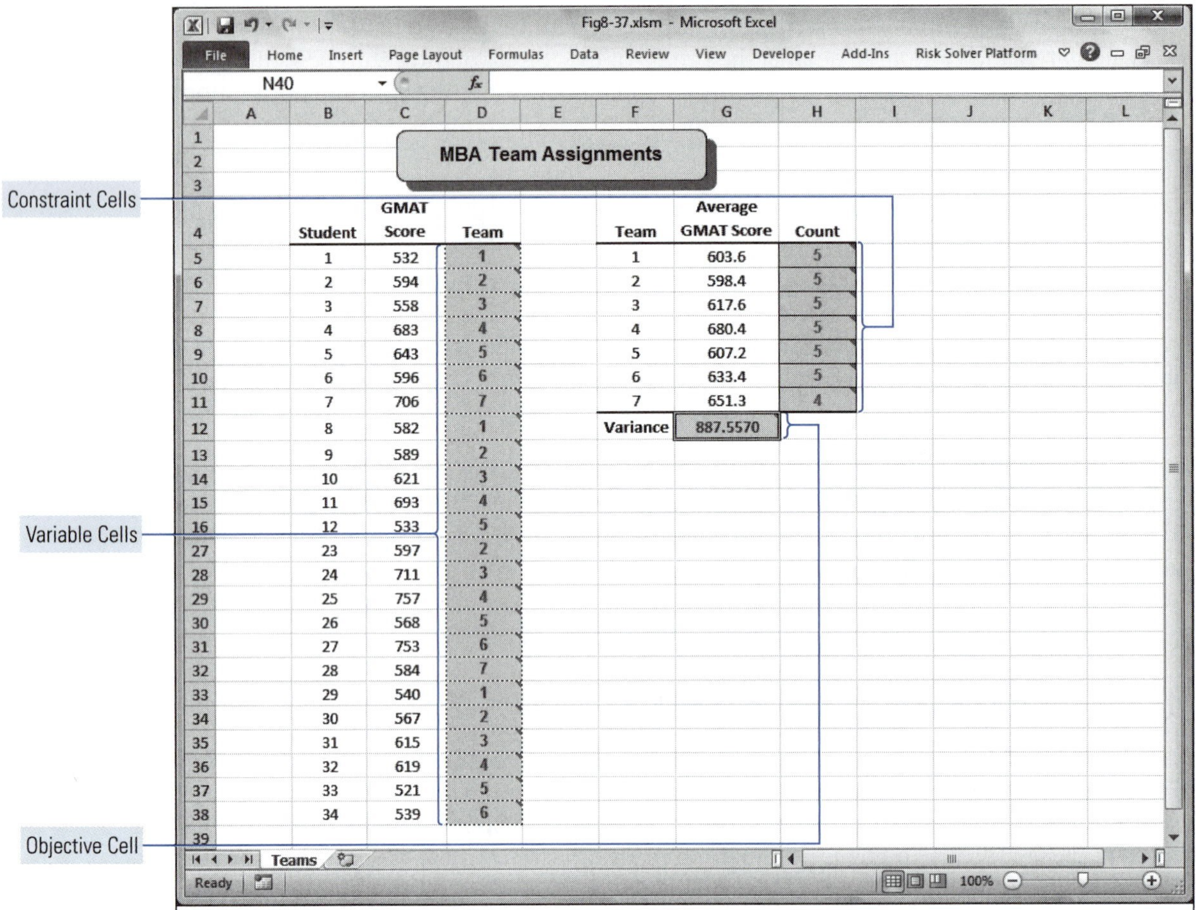

Constraint Cells

Variable Cells

Objective Cell

Cell	Formula	Copied to
	Key Cell Formulas	
G5	= AVERAGEIF($D$5:$D$38,F5,$C$5:$C$38)	G6:G11
H5	= COUNTIF($D$5:$D$38,F5)	H6:H11
G12	= IFERROR(VAR(G5:G11),999999999)	--

The AVERAGEIF( ) function works in much the same way as the SUMIF( ) function covered earlier in this chapter (and in Chapter 5). In cell G5, the AVERAGEIF($D$5:$D$38, F5, $C$5:$C$38) function for team 1 compares the team assignment values in cells D5 through D38 to the value of 1 in cell F5 and, when matches occur, averages the corresponding GMAT values in cells C5 through C38.

Cell G12 computes the variance of the average GMAT scores and will serve as our objective function to be minimized for this problem.

Formula for cell G12:   =IFERROR(VAR(G5:G11),999999999)

The IFERROR( ) function returns an arbitrarily large value of 999999999 if an error is ever encountered in computing the variance of G5 through G11. So if Solver happens to assign values to the decision cells that produce an error value in other computations, the objective value for such a solution will be a very large (poor) value rather than being an error value. (For instance, if Solver does not assign any students to a particular group, the AVERAGEIF( ) function for that group will return a division by zero error. [Only Chuck Norris can divide by zero.])

To keep an approximately equal number of students assigned to each team, we will allow a maximum of five students per team. The number of students assigned to each team is computed in cells H5 through H11 as follows:

Formula for cell H5:   =COUNTIF($D$5:$D$38, F5)

(Copy to cells H6 through H11.)

8.13.2 SOLVING THE MODEL

In this problem, we want to use Solver to determine values for the team assignment in cells D5 through D38 that minimize the variance of the team GMAT scores in cell G12 while assigning no more than five students to each team.

Unfortunately, the AVERAGEIF( ) and COUNTIF( ) functions used in this model create discontinuities that cause Solver's GRG algorithm to be fairly ineffective on this problem. Indeed, if you attempt to use Solver's GRG algorithm on this problem, it goes no further than the initial solution shown in Figure 8.37. However, if we solve the problem using Solver's evolutionary algorithm, using the settings shown in Figure 8.38, we obtain the solution shown in Figure 8.39.

Solver Settings:
Objective: G12 (Min)
Variable cells: D5:D38
Constraints:
H5:H11 <= 5
D5:D38 <= 7
D5:D38 >= 1
D5:D38 = integer
Solver Options:
Standard Evolutionary Engine

FIGURE 8.38

Solver settings and options for the MBA team assignment problem

8.13.3 ANALYZING THE SOLUTION

The optimal team assignments shown in Figure 8.39 have reduced the variance of the average team GMAT scores significantly, from 887.5 to 0.7332. It is important to remember that Solver's evolutionary algorithm is a heuristic that might or might not find the global optimal solution. Often, when Solver stops and reports that it cannot improve on the current solution, restarting Solver will result in a different (and potentially better) solution.

FIGURE 8.39 *Optimal solution for the MBA team assignment problem*

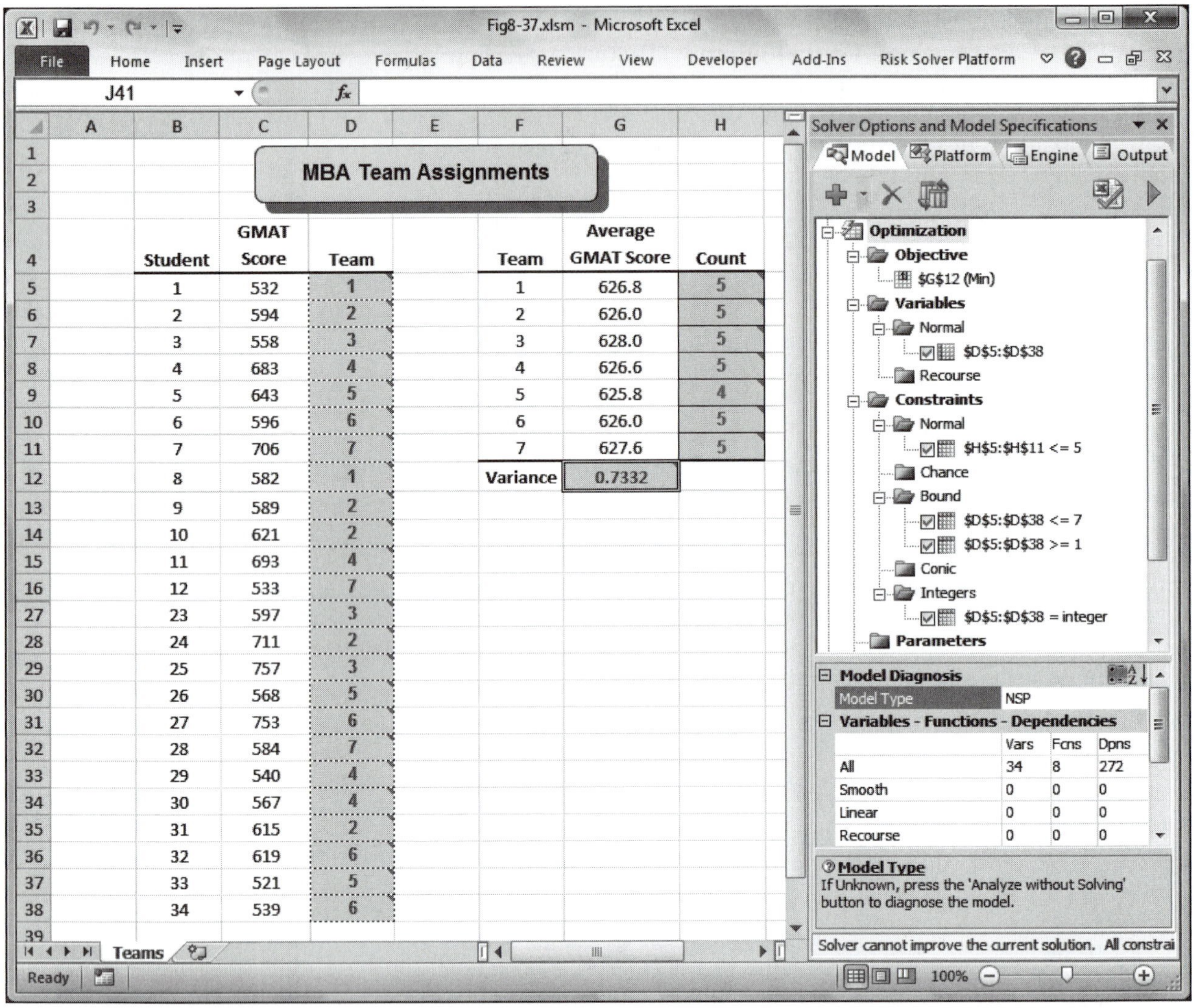

8.14 The Traveling Salesperson Problem

The Traveling Salesperson Problem (TSP) is one of the most famous problems in the field of management science. This problem can be described succinctly as follows:

> A salesperson wants to find the least costly (or shortest) route for visiting clients in n different cities, visiting each city exactly once before returning home.

Although this problem is very simple to state, it becomes extremely difficult to solve as the number of cities increases. In general, for an n-city TSP, there are $(n - 1)!$ possible routes (or tours) the salesman can take (where $(n - 1)! = (n - 1) \times (n - 2) \times (n - 3) \times \ldots \times 2 \times 1$). The following table shows the value of $(n - 1)!$ for several different values of n:

n	(n − 1)!
3	2
5	24
9	40,320
13	479,001,600
17	20,922,789,888,000
20	121,645,100,408,832,000

Thus, for a 3-city TSP, there are only two distinct routes for the salesperson (that is, $1 \rightarrow 2 \rightarrow 3 \rightarrow 1$ and $1 \rightarrow 3 \rightarrow 2 \rightarrow 1$, assuming the salesperson starts in city 1). However, with just 17 cities, the number of possible routes increases to almost 21 *trillion*. Because TSPs are so difficult, heuristic solution techniques (like genetic algorithms) are often used to solve these problems.

Although it is unlikely that many traveling salespersons really care about solving this type of problem, there are numerous other examples of practical business problems that can be described in the general form of a TSP. One such example is described next.

> The Wolverine Manufacturing Company owns and operates a number of computer-controlled machines that can be programmed to perform precise drilling and machining operations. The company is currently programming their drilling machine for a job that requires nine holes to be drilled in precise locations on a flat fiberglass panel that is used in the production of a popular automobile. After each hole is drilled, the machine will automatically retract the drill bit, and move it to the next location until all the holes have been drilled. Because the machine will be required to repeat this process for millions of panels, Wolverine is interested in making sure that it programs the machine to drill the series of holes in the most efficient manner. In particular, they want to minimize the total distance the drill bit must be moved in order to complete the nine drilling operations.

If you imagine the drill bit in this problem representing a salesperson, and each of the required hole locations as representing cities the drill bit must visit, it is easy to see that this is a TSP.

8.14.1 A SPREADSHEET MODEL FOR THE PROBLEM

To solve Wolverines' TSP, the company first must determine the straight-line distance between each pair of required hole locations. A matrix showing the distance (in inches) between each pair of required hole locations is shown in Figure 8.40 (and the file Fig8-40.xlsm that accompanies this book). Note that we are using the integers from 0 to 8 to identify the nine holes in this problem. The reason for numbering the holes starting at zero (rather than one) will become apparent shortly.

An arbitrary tour for the drill bit ($0 \rightarrow 1 \rightarrow 2 \rightarrow 3 \rightarrow 4 \rightarrow 5 \rightarrow 6 \rightarrow 7 \rightarrow 8 \rightarrow 0$) is shown in cells E18 through F26. The distance between each of the required hole locations in this tour is shown in cells G18 through G26 using the following formula,

> Formula for cell G18:   =INDEX($C$6:$K$14,E18+1,F18+1)
> (Copy to cells G19 through G26.)

In general, the function INDEX(*range, row number, column number*) returns the value in the specified *row number* and *column number* of the given *range*. Because cell E18 contains the number 0, and F18 contains the number 1, the previous formula returns the value in the first row (E18 + 1) and second column (F18 + 1) of the range C6:K14—or the value in cell D6.

FIGURE 8.40 *Spreadsheet model for Wolverine's TSP*

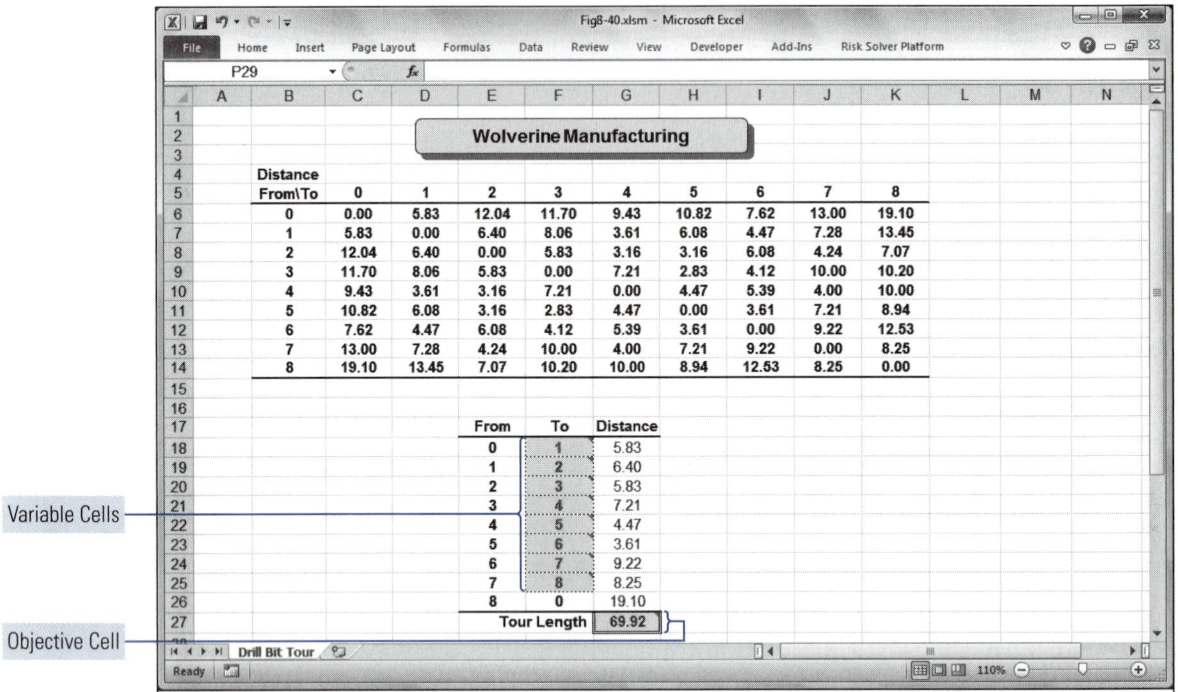

The following is the data embedded in the spreadsheet image:

Wolverine Manufacturing

Distance
From\To:

From\To	0	1	2	3	4	5	6	7	8
0	0.00	5.83	12.04	11.70	9.43	10.82	7.62	13.00	19.10
1	5.83	0.00	6.40	8.06	3.61	6.08	4.47	7.28	13.45
2	12.04	6.40	0.00	5.83	3.16	3.16	6.08	4.24	7.07
3	11.70	8.06	5.83	0.00	7.21	2.83	4.12	10.00	10.20
4	9.43	3.61	3.16	7.21	0.00	4.47	5.39	4.00	10.00
5	10.82	6.08	3.16	2.83	4.47	0.00	3.61	7.21	8.94
6	7.62	4.47	6.08	4.12	5.39	3.61	0.00	9.22	12.53
7	13.00	7.28	4.24	10.00	4.00	7.21	9.22	0.00	8.25
8	19.10	13.45	7.07	10.20	10.00	8.94	12.53	8.25	0.00

From	To	Distance
0	1	5.83
1	2	6.40
2	3	5.83
3	4	7.21
4	5	4.47
5	6	3.61
6	7	9.22
7	8	8.25
8	0	19.10
	Tour Length	69.92

Variable Cells (label pointing to From/To columns)
Objective Cell (label pointing to Tour Length)

Key Cell Formulas

Cell	Formula	Copied to
E19	=F18	E20:F26
G18	=INDEX($C$6:$K$14,E18+1,F18+1)	G19:G26
G27	=SUM(G18:G26)	--

Of course, any hole location that the drill bit moves *to* becomes the next location that it will move *from*. Thus, the following formula was entered in cells E19 through E26 to ensure this occurs.

$$\text{Formula for cell E19:} \quad =F18$$

(Copy to cells E20 through E26.)

The number 0 was entered in cell F26 to ensure that the drill bit's last move is always back to its starting position. Because the solution to a TSP requires n cities to be visited exactly once, the length of the optimal tour will not change regardless of which city is selected as the starting point. (There may be alternate optimal tours, but they will all have the same objective function value.) So by selecting a starting point for a TSP, we reduce the number of possible solutions in the TSP from $n!$ to $(n - 1)!$, which, as shown earlier, becomes quite significant as n increases.

The objective in this problem is to minimize the total distance the drill bill has to travel. Thus, our objective (or fitness) function should compute the total distance associated with the current tour. This is calculated in cell G27 as follows:

$$\text{Formula for cell G27:} \quad =SUM(G18:G26)$$

If we start at hole position zero, any permutation of the set of integers from 1 to 8 in cells F18 through F25 represents a feasible tour for the drill bit. (A **permutation** is simply a rearrangement of the elements of a set.) Fortunately, Solver allows for permutations via a special type of constraint for changing cells known as the *alldifferent* constraint. The **alldifferent** constraint can be applied to a contiguous range of N changing cells and instructs Solver to only use a permutation of the set of integers from 1 to N in those cells. The alldifferent constraint used in combination with Solver's evolutionary optimizer allows us to model and solve a number of very challenging but practical business problems involving the optimal sequencing of jobs or activities. Several such problems are found in the questions and cases at the end of this chapter.

Solver's alldifferent Constraint

Solver's alldifferent constraint (selected via the "dif" option in Solver's Add Constraint dialog) can be applied to a contiguous range of n changing cells and instructs Solver to only use a permutation of the set of integers from 1 to n in those cells. Currently, you may not place any other bounds or restrictions on the cells covered by an alldifferent constraint. Thus, if you need to determine the optimal permutation of a set of integers from, for example, 21 to 28, you can:

1. Apply the alldifferent constraint to a set of eight changing cells (so Solver will generate permutations of 1 to 8 in these cells).
2. Place formulas in another set of eight cells that add 20 to the values Solver generates for the alldifferent changing cells.

8.14.2 SOLVING THE MODEL

Figure 8.41 shows the Solver settings and options used to solve this problem. The alldifferent constraint type is selected by choosing the "dif" option when adding constraints for the variable cells. The solution obtained is shown in Figure 8.42.

8.15.3 ANALYZING THE SOLUTION

The solution shown in Figure 8.42 represents a 33.5% reduction in the total distance the drill bit needs to travel. If this drilling operation is going to be repeated on millions

Solver Settings:

Objective: G27 (Min)
Variable cells: F18:F25
Constraints:
    F18:F25 = alldifferent

Solver Options:
    Standard Evolutionary Engine

FIGURE 8.41

Solver parameters for Wolverine's TSP

FIGURE 8.42   *A solution for Wolverine's TSP*

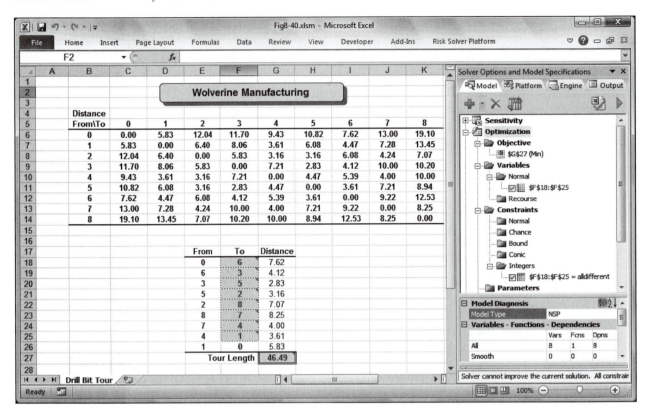

of parts, the reduction in processing time and machine wear and tear associated with implementing the optimal tour would likely be quite significant for this company.

It is important to remember that Solver's evolutionary algorithm randomly generates the initial population of solutions and uses probabilistic crossover and mutation operations. So if you solve this problem, you may not obtain the same solution shown in Figure 8.42 (or you may obtain an alternate optimal solution). Indeed, with large TSP type problems, if you run Solver's evolutionary optimizer several times, it will likely locate better and better solutions to the problem until the global optimal solution is found. Such is the nature of heuristic optimization techniques! As stated earlier, the evolutionary algorithm is one of the most exciting developments in the field of optimization in recent years. Solver's evolutionary search capabilities will undoubtedly continue to be refined and improved in future software releases.

8.15 Summary

This chapter introduced some of the basic concepts involved in nonlinear programming and discussed several applications. The steps involved in formulating and solving an NLP problem are not very different from those required to solve an LP problem—the decision variables are identified, and an objective function and any constraints are stated in terms of the decision variables. Because the objective function and constraints in an NLP problem might be nonlinear, the calculations involved in solving NLP problems are different from those included in the simplex method, which is used most often to solve LP problems. NLP problems sometimes have several local optimal solutions. Thus, finding the global optimal solution to a difficult NLP problem might require re-solving the model several times using different initial starting points.

Evolutionary (or genetic) algorithms use random search techniques and the principle of survival of the fittest to solve difficult optimization problems for which linear and nonlinear optimization techniques are not suitable. Research into genetic algorithms is ongoing, but this promises to become a very useful and powerful optimization tool for business.

8.16 References

Bazaraa, M., and C. Shetty. *Nonlinear Programming: Theory and Algorithms*. New York: Wiley, 1993.

DeWitt, C., et al. "OMEGA: An Improved Gasoline Blending System for Texaco." *Interfaces*, vol. 19, no. 1, 1985.

Fylstra, D., et al. "The Design, Use, and Impact of Microsoft's Excel Solver." Interfaces, vol. 28, no. 5, 1998.

Holland, J. H., "Genetic Algorithms." *Scientific American*, vol. 267, no. 1, pp. 66–72.

Kolesar, P., and E. Blum. "Square Roots Law for Fire Engine Response Distances." *Management Science*, vol. 19, 1973.

Lasdon, L., and S. Smith. "Solving Sparse Nonlinear Programs Using GRG." *ORSA Journal on Computing*, vol. 4, no. 1, 1992.

Markowitz, H. *Portfolio Selection, Efficient Diversification of Investments*. New York: Wiley, 1959.

Reeves, C. R. "Genetic Algorithms for the Operations Researcher." *INFORMS Journal on Computing*, vol. 9, no. 3, Summer 1997, pp. 231–265.

Taylor, B., L. Moore, and E. Clayton. "R&D Project Selection and Manpower Allocation with Integer Nonlinear Programming." *Management Science*, vol. 28, no. 10, 1982.

Vollman, T., W. Berry, and C. Whybark. *Manufacturing Planning and Control Systems*. Homewood, IL: Irwin, 1987.

THE WORLD OF MANAGEMENT SCIENCE

Water Spilled Is Energy Lost: Pacific Gas and Electric Uses Nonlinear Optimization to Manage Power Generation

The power produced by a hydroelectric generator is a nonlinear function of the flow rate of water through the turbine and the pressure. Pressure, or head, is determined by the difference in water level upstream from the generator.

Pacific Gas and Electric Company (PG&E), the world's largest privately held utility, generates power from fossil fuels, nuclear energy, wind, solar energy, and geothermal steam, as well as hydropower. Its Sierra, Nevada Hydro System is a complex network of 15 river basins, 143 reservoirs, and 67 power plants. Stream flow peaks markedly in the spring from snow melting in the mountains, whereas demand for electric power peaks in the summer.

Water spilled from a dam cannot be used to generate power at that dam, although it can increase the head at a dam downstream and contribute to power generation there. If the water spills at a time when all of the downstream reservoirs are full, it will spill from all the dams, and its energy will be lost forever. Hydrologists at PG&E attempt to maximize the useful generation of electricity by strategically timing controlled spills to manage the levels of all reservoirs in the system

(Continued)

and minimize wasted flow. If done effectively, this reduces the company's reliance on fossil fuel and reduces the cost of electricity to its customers.

This problem was modeled as a nonlinear program with a nonlinear objective function and linear constraints. Because many of the constraints are network flow constraints, using a network flow algorithm along with the linear terms of the objective function produced a good starting point for the NLP algorithm. A good starting point can be a critical factor in the successful use of NLP.

PG&E management confirms that the optimization system saves between $10 and $45 million annually compared to manual systems, and the California Public Utilities Commission has recommended its use to others.

Source: Ikura, Yoshiro, George Gross, and Gene Sand Hall. "PG&E's State-of-the-Art Scheduling Tool for Hydro Systems." *Interfaces*, vol. 16, no. 1, January-February 1986, pp 65–82.

Questions and Problems

1. Can the GRG algorithm be used to solve LP problems? If so, will it always identify a corner point of the feasible region as the optimal solution (as does the simplex method)?

2. In describing the NLP solution strategy summarized in Figure 8.2, we noted that the *fastest* improvement in the objective function is obtained by moving from point A in a direction that is perpendicular to the level curve of the objective function. However, there are other directions that also result in improvements to the objective.
   a. How would you describe or define the set of all directions that results in improvement to the objective?
   b. How would your answer change if the level curve of the objective function at point A was nonlinear?

3. Consider an optimization problem with two variables and the constraints $X_1 \leq 5$, $X_2 \leq 5$ where both X_1 and X_2 are nonnegative.
   a. Sketch the feasible region for this problem.
   b. Sketch level curves of a nonlinear objective for this problem that would have exactly one local optimal solution that is also the global optimal solution.
   c. Redraw the feasible region and sketch level curves of a nonlinear objective for this problem that would have a local optimal solution that is not the global optimal solution.

4. Consider the following function:

$$Y = -0.865 + 8.454X - 1.696X^2 + 0.132X^3 - 0.00331X^4$$

   a. Plot this function on an X-Y graph for positive values of X from 1 to 20.
   b. How many local maximum solutions are there?
   c. How many local minimum solutions are there?
   d. Use Solver to find the maximum value of Y using a starting value of $X = 2$. What value of Y do you obtain?
   e. Use Solver to find the maximum value of Y using a starting value of $X = 14$. What value of Y do you obtain?

5. Consider the following function:

$$Y = 37.684 - 15.315X + 3.095X^2 - 0.218X^3 + 0.005X^4$$

   a. Plot this function on an X-Y graph for positive values of X from 1 to 20.
   b. How many local maximum solutions are there?
   c. How many local minimum solutions are there?
   d. Use Solver to find the minimum value of Y using a starting value of $X = 3$. What value of Y do you obtain?
   e. Use Solver to find the minimum value of Y using a starting value of $X = 18$. What value of Y do you obtain?

6. Refer to TMC's project selection problem presented in this chapter. In the solution shown in Figure 8.21, notice that the probability of success for project 4 is only 0.3488. Thus, project 4 is almost twice as likely to fail as succeed if it is assigned only three engineers. As a result, management might want to add a constraint to this problem to ensure that if a project is selected, it must have at least a 50% chance of succeeding.
   a. Reformulate TMC's problem so that if a project is selected, it must have at least a 50% chance of succeeding.
   b. Implement your model in a spreadsheet.
   c. What is the optimal solution?

7. The PENTEL Corporation manufactures three different types of computer chips. Each type of chip requires different amounts of processing time in three different departments as summarized in the following table.

	Processing Hours Req'd per 100 Chips			
	Chip A	**Chip B**	**Chip C**	**Hours Available**
Dept 1	3	2	4	10,000
Dept 2	2	4	3	9,000
Dept 3	3	4	2	11,000

The total profit for each type of chip may be described as follows:

Chip A profit $= -0.35A^2 + 8.3A + 540$

Chip B profit $= -0.60B^2 + 9.45B + 1,108$

Chip C profit $= -0.47C^2 + 11.0C + 850$

where A, B, and C represent the number of chips produced in 100s.
   a. Formulate an NLP model for this problem.
   b. Implement your model in a spreadsheet and solve it.
   c. What is the optimal solution?

8. A car dealership needs to determine how to allocate its $20,000 advertising budget. They have estimated the expected profit from each dollar (X) spent in four different advertising media as follows:

Medium	**Expected Profit**
Newspaper	$100X^{0.7}$
Radio	$125X^{0.65}$
TV	$180X^{0.6}$
Direct Mail	$250X^{0.5}$

If the company wants to spend at least $500 on each medium, how should it allocate its advertising budget in order to maximize profit?

9. The XYZ Company produces two products. The total profit achieved from these products is described by the following equation:

$$\text{Total profit} = -0.2X_1^2 - 0.4X_2^2 + 8X_1 + 12X_2 + 1{,}500$$

where: X_1 = thousands of units of product 1

X_2 = thousands of units of product 2

Every 1,000 units of X_1 requires one hour of time in the shipping department, and every 1,000 units of X_2 requires 30 minutes in the shipping department. Each unit of each product requires 2 pounds of a special ingredient, of which 64,000 pounds are available. Additionally, 80 hours of shipping labor are available. Demand for X_1 and X_2 is unlimited.

a. Formulate an NLP model for this problem.
b. Implement your model in a spreadsheet and solve it.
c. What is the optimal solution?

10. A traveler was recently stranded in her car in a snowy blizzard in Wyoming. Unable to drive any farther, the stranded motorist used her cell phone to dial 911 to call for help. Because the caller was unsure of her exact location, it was impossible for the emergency operator to dispatch a rescue squad. Rescue personnel brought in telecommunications experts who determined that the stranded motorist's cell phone call could be picked up by three different communications towers in the area. Based on the strength of the signal being received at each tower, they were able to estimate the distance from each tower to the caller's location. The following table summarizes the location (X-Y coordinates) of each tower and the tower's *estimated* straight-line (or Euclidean) distance to the caller.

Tower	X-Position	Y-Position	Estimated Distance
1	17	34	29.5
2	12	5	4.0
3	3	23	17.5

The caller's cell phone battery is quickly discharging, and it is unlikely the motorist will survive much longer in the subfreezing temperatures. However, the emergency operator has a copy of Excel on her computer and believes it may be possible, with your help, to use Solver to determine the approximate location of the stranded motorist.

a. Formulate an NLP for this problem.
b. Implement your model in a spreadsheet and solve it.
c. To approximately what location should the rescue personnel be dispatched to look for the motorist?

11. Refer to the insurance problem faced by Thom Pearman discussed in Section 8.8 of this chapter. Let b*i* represent the balance in his investment at the beginning of year *i*, and let *r* represent the annual interest rate.

a. What is the objective function for this problem? Is it linear or nonlinear?
b. Write out the first two constraints for this problem algebraically. Are they linear or nonlinear?

12. In the insurance problem discussed in Section 8.8 of this chapter, suppose that Thom is confident that he can invest his money to earn a 15% annual rate of return compounded quarterly. Assuming a fixed 15% return, suppose he now wants to determine the minimum amount of money he must invest in order for his after-tax earnings to cover the planned premium payments.

a. Make whatever changes are necessary to the spreadsheet, and answer Thom's question.
b. Is the model you solved linear or nonlinear? How can you tell?

13. The yield of a bond is the interest rate that makes the present value of its cash flows equal to its selling price. Assume a bond can be purchased for $975 and generates the following cash flows:

Years from now	1	2	3	4	5
Cash Flow	$100	$120	$90	$100	$1,200

Use Solver to determine the yield for this bond. (*Hint*: In Excel, use the NPV() function to compute the present value of the cash flows.) What is the yield on this bond?

14. Suppose a gift shop in Myrtle Beach has an annual demand for 15,000 units for a souvenir kitchen magnet that it buys for $0.50 per unit. Assume it costs $10 to place an order, and the inventory carrying cost is 25% of the item's unit cost. Use Solver to determine the optimal order quantity if the company wants to minimize the total cost of procuring this item.

   a. What is the optimal order quantity?

   b. What is the total cost associated with this order quantity?

   c. What are the annual order and annual inventory holding costs for this solution?

15. Vijay Bashwani is organizing a charity golf tournament where teams of four players will play in a captain's choice format. The handicaps of the 40 players who have registered for the tournament are summarized in the following table. Vijay needs to create 10 teams of four players each in such a way that the total handicap of each team is as equal as possible. He would like to do this by minimizing the variance of the total handicaps of all the teams.

Player Handicaps			
0	3	6	9
0	3	6	9
0	3	6	10
0	4	6	10
0	4	7	11
1	4	7	11
1	4	7	11
1	5	8	12
2	5	8	13
2	5	8	13

   a. Create a spreadsheet model for this problem and solve it.

   b. What are the optimal team assignments?

16. SuperCity is a large retailer of electronics and appliances. The store sells three different models of TVs that are ordered from different manufacturers. The demands, costs, and storage requirements for each model are summarized in the following table:

	Model 1	Model 2	Model 3
Annual Demand	800	500	1,500
Unit Cost	$300	$1,100	$600
Storage Space Req'd	9 sq ft	25 sq ft	16 sq ft

It costs $60 to do the administrative work associated with preparing, processing, and receiving orders, and SuperCity assumes a 25% annual carrying cost for all items it holds in inventory. There are 3,000 square feet of total warehouse space available for storing these items, and the store never wants to have more than

$45,000 invested in inventory for these items. The manager of this store wants to determine the optimal order quantity for each model of TV.

a. Formulate an NLP model for this problem.
b. Implement your model in a spreadsheet and solve it.
c. What are the optimal order quantities?
d. How many orders of each type of TV will be placed each year?
e. Assuming demand is constant throughout the year, how often should orders be placed?

17. The Radford hardware store expects to sell 1,500 electric garbage disposal units in the coming year. Demand for this product is fairly stable over the year. It costs $20 to place an order for these units, and the company assumes a 20% annual holding cost on inventory. The following price structure applies to Radford's purchases of this product:

	Order Quantity		
	0 to 499	**500 to 999**	**1,000 and up**
Price per Unit	$35	$33	$31

So if Radford orders 135 units, it pays $35 per unit; if 650, it pays $33 per unit; and if 1,200, it pays $31 per unit.

a. What is the most economical order quantity and total cost of this solution? (*Hint*: Solve a separate EOQ problem for each of the order quantity ranges given, and select the solution that yields the lowest total cost.)
b. Suppose the discount policy changed so that Radford had to pay $35 for the first 499 units ordered, $33 for the next 500 units ordered, and $31 for any additional units. What is the most economical order quantity, and what is the total cost of this solution?

18. A long-distance telephone company is trying to determine the optimal pricing structure for its daytime and evening long-distance calling rates. It estimates the demand for phone lines as follows:

Daytime Lines (in 1,000s) Demanded per Minute $= 600 - 5,000P_d + 1,000P_e$

Evening Lines (in 1,000s) Demanded per Minute $= 400 + 3,000P_d - 9,500P_e$

where P_d represents the price per minute during the day, and P_e represents the price per minute during the evening. Assume it costs $100 per minute to provide every 1,000 lines in long-distance capacity. The company will have to maintain the maximum number of lines demanded throughout the day, even if the demand is greater during the day than during the evening.

a. What prices should the telephone company charge if it wants to maximize profit?
b. How many long-distance lines does the company need to maintain?

19. Howie Jones, owner of Blue Ridge Hot Tubs, is facing a new problem. Although sale of the two hot tubs manufactured by his company (Aqua-Spas and Hydro-Luxes) have been brisk, the company is not earning the level of profits that Howie wants to achieve. Having established a reputation for high quality and reliability, Howie believes he can increase profits by increasing the prices of the hot tubs. However, he is concerned that a price increase might have a detrimental effect on demand, so Howie has engaged a marketing research firm to estimate the level of demand for Aqua-Spas and Hydro-Luxes at various prices. The marketing research firm used the technique of regression analysis (discussed in Chapter 9) to develop a model of the relationship between the prices and demand for the hot tubs. After analyzing the situation, the marketing research firm concluded that a reasonable price range for the hot tubs is

between $1,000 and $1,500, and that within this range, Howie can expect the demand for hot tubs in the next quarter to vary with price in the following way:

Demand for Aqua-Spas	$= 300 - 0.175 \times$ price of Aqua-Spas
Demand for Hydro-Luxes	$= 325 - 0.15 \times$ price of Hydro-Luxes

Howie determined that the costs of manufacturing Aqua-Spas and Hydro-Luxes are $850 and $700 per unit, respectively. Ideally, he wants to produce enough hot tubs to meet demand exactly and carry no inventory. Each Aqua-Spa requires 1 pump, 9 hours of labor, and 12 feet of tubing; each Hydro-Lux requires 1 pump, 6 hours of labor, and 16 feet of tubing. Howie's suppliers have committed to supplying him with 200 pumps and 2,800 feet of tubing. Also, 1,566 hours of labor are available for production. Howie wants to determine how much to charge for each type of hot tub and how many of each type to produce.

a. Formulate an NLP model for this problem.
b. Implement your model in a spreadsheet and solve it.
c. What is the optimal solution?
d. Which of the resource constraints are binding at the optimal solution?
e. What values would you expect the Lagrange multipliers to take on for these constraints? (Create a Sensitivity Report for this problem to verify your answer.)

20. Carnival Confections, Inc. produces two popular southern food items, pork rinds and fried peanuts, which it sells at a local recreation area on weekends. The owners of the business have estimated their profit function on these items to be:

$$0.6p - 0.002p^2 + 0.5f - 0.0009f^2 - 0.001pf$$

Note that p is the number of packages of pork rinds produced, and f is the number of packages of fried peanuts produced. Both of these items require deep frying. The company's fryer has the capacity to produce a total of 600 packages of pork rinds and/or fried peanuts. One minute of labor is required to dry and package the pork rinds, and 30 seconds are required to dry and package the peanuts. The company devotes a total of 16 hours of labor to producing these products each week.

a. Formulate an NLP model for this problem.
b. Implement your model in a spreadsheet.
c. What is the optimal solution?

21. A new mother wants to establish a college education fund for her newborn child. She wants this fund to be worth $100,000 in 18 years.

a. If she invests $75 per month, what is the minimum rate of return she would need to earn on her investment? Assume monthly compounding. (Hint: Consider using the future value function FV( ) in your spreadsheet.)
b. Suppose the mother knows of an investment that will guarantee a 12% annual return compounded monthly. What is the minimum amount she should invest each month to achieve her goal?

22. The Arctic Oil Company has recently drilled two new wells in a remote area of Alaska. The company is planning to install a pipeline to carry the oil from the two new wells to a transportation and refining (T&R) center. The locations of the oil wells and the T&R center are summarized in the following table. Assume a unit change in either coordinate represents 1 mile.

	X-Coordinate	Y-Coordinate
Oil Well 1	50	150
Oil Well 2	30	40
T&R center	230	70

Installing the pipeline is a very expensive undertaking, and the company wants to minimize the amount of pipeline required. Because the shortest distance between two points is a straight line, one of the analysts assigned to the project believes that a separate pipe should be run from each well to the T&R center. Another alternative is to run separate pipes from each well to some intermediate substation where the two lines are joined into a single pipeline that continues on to the T&R center. Arctic Oil's management wants to determine which alternative is best. Furthermore, if using the intermediate substation is best, management wants to determine where this station should be located.

a. Create a spreadsheet model to determine how many miles of pipeline Arctic Oil must install if it runs separate pipelines from each oil well to the T&R center. How much pipe will be needed?

b. If Arctic Oil wants to build a substation, where should it be built? How much pipe is needed in this solution?

c. Which alternative is best?

d. Suppose the substation cannot be built within a 10-mile radius of the coordinates $X = 80, Y = 95$. (Assume the pipeline can run through this area, but the substation cannot be built in the area.) What is the optimal location of the substation now, and how much pipe will be needed?

23. The Rugger Corporation is a Seattle-based R&D company that recently developed a new type of fiber substrate that is waterproof and resists dirt. Several carpet manufacturers in northeast Georgia want to use Rugger as their sole supplier for this new fiber. The locations of the carpet manufacturers are summarized in the following table.

Carpet Mill Locations	X-Coordinate	Y-Coordinate
Dalton	9	43
Rome	2	28
Canton	51	36
Kennesaw	19	4

Rugger expects to make 130, 75, 90, and 80 deliveries to the carpet producers in Dalton, Rome, Canton, and Kennesaw, respectively. The company wants to build its new plant in the location that would minimize the annual shipping miles. However, Rugger also wants to be within 50 miles of each of the new customers so that it will be easy to provide on-site technical support for any production problems that may occur.

a. Formulate an NLP model for this problem.

b. Implement your model in a spreadsheet and solve it.

c. What is the optimal location for the new plant? How many annual shipping miles are associated with this solution?

d. Suppose the company wants to identify the location that minimizes the average distance to each of its customers. Where is this location, and how many annual shipping miles would Rugger incur if the new plant locates there?

e. Suppose the company wants to identify the location that minimizes maximum distance to any of its customers. Where is this location, and how many annual shipping miles would Rugger incur if the new plant locates there?

24. An air-ambulance service in Colorado is interested in keeping its helicopter in a central location that would minimize the flight distance to four major ski resorts. An X-Y

grid was laid over a map of the area to determine the following latitude and longitude coordinates for the four resorts:

Resort	Longitude	Latitude
Bumpyride	35	57
Keyrock	46	48
Asprin	37	93
Goldenrod	22	67

a. Formulate an NLP model to determine where the ambulance service should be located in order to minimize the total distance to each resort.
b. Implement your model in a spreadsheet and solve it. Where should the ambulance service be located?
c. What other factors might affect the decision, and how might you incorporate them in your model? (Consider, for example, differences in the average number of skiers and accidents at the different resorts, and the topography of the area.)

25. The Heat-Aire Company has two plants that produce identical heat pump units. However, production costs at the two differ due to the technology and labor used at each plant. The total costs of production at the plants depend on the quantity produced and are described as:

Total cost at plant 1: $2X_1^2 - 1X_1 + 15$
Total cost at plant 2: $X_2^2 + 0.3X_2 + 10$

Note that X_1 is the number of heat pumps produced at plant 1, and X_2 is the number of heat pumps produced at plant 2. Neither plant can make more than 600 heat pumps. Heat pumps can be shipped from either plant to satisfy demand from four different customers. The unit shipping costs and demands for each customer are summarized in the following table.

	Customer 1	Customer 2	Customer 3	Customer 4
Plant 1	$23	$30	$32	$26
Plant 2	$33	$27	$25	$24
Demand	300	250	150	400

What is the optimal production and shipping plan if management wants to meet customer demand at the lowest total cost?
a. Formulate an NLP model for this problem.
b. Implement your model in a spreadsheet and solve it.
c. What is the optimal solution?

26. Beth Dale is the director of development for a nonprofit organization that depends largely on charitable gifts for its operations. Beth needs to assign four different staff people to make trips to call on four possible donors. Only one staff person can call on each donor, and each staff person can make only one call. Beth estimates the probability of each staff person successfully obtaining the donation from each potential giver as follows:

	Donor			
Staff	1	2	3	4
Sam	0.95	0.91	0.90	0.88
Billie	0.92	0.95	0.95	0.82

(Continued)

	Donor			
Staff	1	2	3	4
Sally	0.95	0.93	0.93	0.85
Fred	0.94	0.87	0.92	0.86

a. Formulate an NLP model to determine the assignment of staff persons to donors that maximizes the probability of receiving all donations.

b. Implement your model in a spreadsheet and solve it. What is the optimal solution?

c. Suppose it is estimated that the donations possible from donors 1, 2, 3, and 4 are for $1 million, $2 million, $0.5 million, and $0.75 million, respectively. How should Beth assign her staff if she wants to maximize the expected value of the donations received?

d. All staffers will have the least luck soliciting funds from donor number 4, so no one really wants to be assigned to this donor. Indeed, each staffer will regret not being assigned to the donor with whom they have the highest probability of success. Suppose we define the amount of this regret for each staffer by their maximum probability of success minus the probability of success for their actual assignment. What assignment of staffers to donors will minimize the maximum regret suffered by any staffer?

27. Water is delivered throughout New York City using eight main waterlines that are connected at six pumping stations as shown in Figure 8.43. The numbers on each of the arcs indicates the maximum allowable flow of water through each waterline (in 1,000s of gallons per minute).

FIGURE 8.43

Main waterlines and pumping stations in New York

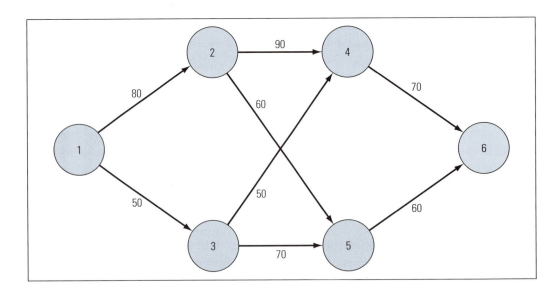

Because the city's waterlines are aging, breaks have been occurring more frequently and are related to the increasing demands being placed on the system. Civil engineers have estimated the probability of a waterline break occurring as follows:

Probability of failure on the line from station i to station j = $1 - \text{EXP}\left(-a_{ij}F_{ij}/1{,}000\right)$

where F_{ij} is the flow (in 1,000s of gallons per minute) on the line from station i to station j, and the values for the parameters a_{ij} are given as follows:

From Station	To Station	a_{ij}
1	2	0.10
1	3	0.17
2	4	0.19
2	5	0.15
3	4	0.14
3	5	0.16
4	6	0.11
5	6	0.09

Engineers can use control valves to limit how much water flows through each waterline. During peak demand times, a total of 110,000 gallons of water per minute needs to flow through this system.

a. Create a spreadsheet model to determine the flow pattern that meets the required demand for water in the most reliable way.

b. How much water should flow through each waterline?

c. What is the probability that no waterline will fail while operating in this way?

28. The Wiggly Piggly Grocery Company owns and operates numerous grocery stores throughout the state of Florida. It is developing plans to consolidate warehouse operations so that there will be 3 different warehouses that supply stores in 10 different regions of the state. The company plans to sell all its existing warehouses and build new, state-of-the-art warehouses. Each warehouse can supply multiple regions; however, all stores in a particular region will be assigned to only 1 warehouse. The locations of the different regions are summarized in the following table.

Region	Location X	Y
1 Panama City	1.0	14.0
2 Tallahassee	6.1	15.0
3 Jacksonville	13.0	15.0
4 Ocala	12.0	11.0
5 Orlando	13.5	9.0
6 Tampa	11.0	7.5
7 Ft. Pierce	17.0	6.0
8 Ft. Myers	12.5	3.5
9 West Palm	17.5	4.0
10 Miami	17.0	1.0

a. Create a spreadsheet model to determine approximately where Wiggly Piggly should locate its new warehouses and which regions should be assigned to each of the new warehouses. Assume the company wants to build its warehouses in locations that minimize the distances to each of the regions it serves.

b. What is the optimal solution?

29. An investor wants to determine the safest way to structure a portfolio from several investments. Investment A produces an average annual return of 14% with a variance of 0.025. Investment B produces an average rate of return of 9% with a variance of 0.015. Investment C produces an average rate of return of 8% with a variance of 0.010. Investments A and B have a covariance of 0.00028, and investments

A and C have a covariance of -0.006. Investments B and C have a covariance of 0.00125.

    a. Suppose the investor wants to achieve at least a 12% return. What is the least risky way of achieving this goal?

    b. Suppose the investor regards risk minimization as being five times more important than maximizing return. What portfolio would be most appropriate for the investor?

30. Betsy Moore wants to invest in the stocks of companies A, B, C, and D, whose annual returns for the past 13 years are as follows.

| Year | **Annual Return** | | | |
	A	**B**	**C**	**D**
1	8.0%	12.0%	10.9%	11.2%
2	9.2%	8.5%	22.0%	10.8%
3	7.7%	13.0%	19.0%	9.7%
4	6.6%	−2.6%	37.9%	11.6%
5	18.5%	7.8%	−11.8%	−1.6%
6	7.4%	3.2%	12.9%	−4.1%
7	13.0%	9.8%	−7.5%	8.6%
8	22.0%	13.5%	9.3%	6.8%
9	14.0%	6.5%	48.7%	11.9%
10	20.5%	−3.5%	−1.9%	12.0%
11	14.0%	17.5%	19.1%	8.3%
12	19.0%	14.5%	−3.4%	6.0%
13	9.0%	18.9%	43.0%	10.2%

    a. Suppose Betsy is completely risk averse. What percentage of her portfolio should be invested in each stock, and what would the expected risk and return be on the resulting portfolio?

    b. Suppose Betsy is completely insensitive to risk and wants the maximum possible return. What percentage of her portfolio should be invested in each stock, and what would the expected risk and return be on the resulting portfolio?

    c. Suppose Betsy has determined her risk aversion value is $r = 0.95$. What percentage of her portfolio should be invested in each stock, and what is the expected risk and return on the resulting portfolio?

31. Sometimes, the historical data on returns and variances may be poor predictors of how investments will perform in the future. In this case, the *scenario approach* to portfolio optimization may be used. Using this technique, we identify several different scenarios describing the returns that might occur for each investment during the next year and estimate the probability associated with each scenario. A common set of investment proportions (or weights) is used to compute the portfolio return r_i for each scenario. The expected return and variance on the portfolio are then estimated as:

$$\text{Expected Portfolio Return} = EPR = \sum_i r_i s_i$$

$$\text{Variance of Portfolio Return} = VPR = \sum_i (r_i - EPR)^2 s_i$$

where r_i is the portfolio return for a given set of investment proportions under scenario i, and s_i is the probability that scenario i will occur. We can use Solver to find the set of investment proportions that generate a desired EPR while minimizing the

VPR. Given the following scenarios, find the investment proportions that generate an *EPR* of 12% while minimizing the *VPR.*

			Returns		
Scenario	Windsor	Flagship	Templeman	T-Bills	Probability
1	0.14	−0.09	0.10	0.07	0.10
2	−0.11	0.12	0.14	0.06	0.10
3	0.09	0.15	−0.11	0.08	0.10
4	0.25	0.18	0.33	0.07	0.30
5	0.18	0.16	0.15	0.06	0.40

32. Barbara Roberts recently received $30,000 as a small inheritance from a distant relative. She wants to invest the money so as to earn $900 to buy a notebook computer next year when she enters graduate school one year from now. (Barbara plans to use her inheritance to pay the tuition for her graduate studies.) She wants to create a portfolio using three stocks, whose annual percentage returns are summarized in the following table:

Year	Amalgamated Industries	Babbage Computers	Consolidated Foods
1996	−3.3	5.92	−2.4
1997	−4.7	−3.8	28.1
1998	11.9	−7	−7.2
1999	9.7	6.6	−2.3
2000	8.6	−4.2	20.4
2001	9.4	11.2	17.4
2002	5.3	3.2	−11.8
2003	−4.9	16.1	−6.6
2004	8.5	10.8	−13.4
2005	−8.3	−8.3	10.9

Barbara wants to diversify her potential holdings by investing at least $500, but no more than $20,000, in any one stock. Barbara wants to minimize the total variance (which also involves the covariance between the various pairs of stock) of the portfolio.

a. Formulate and solve a nonlinear programming model to determine how much money Barbara should invest in each stock in order to meet her financial goals. What is the optimal solution?

b. Will Barbara have enough money to buy a notebook computer next year?

33. A mortgage company owns the following 10 mortgages. Investors will purchase packages of mortgages worth at least $1 million. What is the maximum number of such packages that can be created from this set of mortgages?

					Mortgage					
	1	2	3	4	5	6	7	8	9	10
Amount (in $1,000s)	$900	$860	$780	$525	$240	$185	$165	$164	$135	$125

a. Create a spreadsheet model for this problem, and use Solver's evolutionary algorithm to solve it.

b. What is the optimal solution?

34. A small printing shop has 10 jobs it must schedule. The processing times and due dates for each job are summarized in the following table.

Job	Processing Time (Days)	Due Date
1	10	12
2	11	35
3	7	20
4	5	27
5	3	23
6	7	36
7	5	40
8	5	40
9	12	55
10	11	47

   a. Suppose the jobs are scheduled in ascending order by processing time. How many jobs will be late? By how many totals days will the jobs be late? What is the maximum amount by which any job is late?

   b. Suppose the jobs are scheduled in ascending order by due date. How many jobs will be late? By how many totals days will the jobs be late? What is the maximum amount by which any job is late?

   c. Use Solver's evolutionary algorithm to determine the schedule that minimizes the number of jobs that are late. What is the solution? (Note that you may want to run Solver several times.)

   d. Use Solver's evolutionary algorithm to determine the schedule that minimizes the total number of days by which the jobs are late. What is the solution?

   e. Use Solver's evolutionary algorithm to determine the schedule that minimizes the maximum number of days by which any job is late. What is the solution?

35. The Major Motors Corporation manufactures heavy trucks at a plant in Dublin, Virginia. The factory's stock of spare and custom parts is stored in a huge shelving system that is several stories high and runs the length of several football fields. An automated "cherry picking" vehicle runs back and forth along a shelving unit and is able to simultaneously raise or lower to any height to pick needed stock items from the various bins in the shelving unit. Each bin in the shelving unit is of equal size and is identified by a specific row and column number. Typically, each run the cherry picker makes involves visiting several different bins to retrieve various parts. To help minimize operating costs, the company wants to develop a system to determine the most efficient way for the cherry picker to visit each required bin site before returning to its initial position. As an example, suppose the cherry picker needs to retrieve 10 parts stored in the following bin locations.

Part	Row	Column
1	3	27
2	14	22
3	1	13
4	20	3
5	20	16
6	28	12
7	30	31
8	11	19
9	7	3
10	10	25

Assume the cherry picker must start and finish at row 0 and column 0.
   a. Use a spreadsheet to compute the straight-line distance between each pair of bin locations.
   b. Use Solver's evolutionary algorithm to determine the shortest tour for the cherry picker to follow.
   c. What is the best tour you can find?
36. A regional quality inspector for Green Roof Inns has 16 properties she must visit next month. The driving time from one property to the next is proportional to the straight-line distance between the properties. The X and Y coordinates for each property are given in the following table.

Property

	1	2	3	4	5	6	7	8	9	10	11	12	13	14	15	16
X	190	179	170	463	153	968	648	702	811	305	512	481	763	858	517	439
Y	158	797	290	394	853	12	64	592	550	538	66	131	289	529	910	460

Assume the inspector's home is located at X coordinate 509 and Y coordinate 414.
   a. Create a distance matrix that computes the straight-line distance between each pair of properties (including the inspector's home). Round these distances to two decimal places.
   b. Suppose the inspector starts at her home and visits each property in numerical order before returning home. How far would she have traveled?
   c. Suppose the inspector wants to start from her home and visit each property before returning home and wants to do so traveling the least distance possible. Which route should she take, and how far will she travel?
   d. Suppose the inspector wants to visit all 16 properties over a four-week period visiting exactly 4 properties each week. Each week, she will leave from her home on Monday morning and return to her home on Friday evening. Which properties should she visit each week, and in what order should she visit them if she wants to minimize the total distance she must travel?
37. Companies are often interested in segmenting their customers to better target specific product offerings to meet specific customer needs. The file CustomerData.xls that accompanies this book contains data on 198 customers for an online retailer. Specifically, this file lists demographic data for each customer's income level (X_1) and number of dependents (X_2) as well as buying behavior data, including the number of purchases made last year (X_3) and the average value of each purchase (X_4). Suppose you have been asked to cluster each of these customers to one of three groups. After your group assignments are made, you can compute the average values on each of the four variables within each group. These four average values for each group would represent the typical (or average) customer found in each respective group. Obviously, you want to group similar customers together. To do so, you could generalize the straight-line distance measure to four dimensions to calculate each customer's distance to his or her assigned group.
   a. Use Solver to make group assignments that minimize the sum of the distance from each customer to his or her assigned group.
   b. How would you describe the differences in the three groups or clusters you identify?
38. Max Gooding is tired of losing money in his office's weekly football pool and has decided to try to do something about it. Figure 8.44 (and file Fig8-44.xls that accompanies this book) contains a listing of the teams in the Imaginary Football League (IFL) along with the outcomes of all the games played in the league last season.
   For instance, cell F5 indicates the Minnesota Raiders beat the Atlanta Eagles by two points last year, whereas cell F6 indicates that Atlanta beat the Los Angeles Pirates

FIGURE 8.44 *Spreadsheet for the Imaginary Football League (IFL)*

Imaginary Football League

Team No.	Team Name	Visiting Team	Home Team	Margin of Home Team Victory (or Loss)
1	Atlanta Eagles	16	1	-2
2	Buffalo Wings	13	1	3
3	Chicago Grizzlies	18	1	-22
4	Cincinnati Tigers	14	1	16
5	Cleveland Reds	25	1	2
6	Dallas Cowpokes	15	2	3
7	Denver Bravos	23	2	17
8	Detroit Leopards	3	2	14
9	Green Bay Pickers	11	2	35
10	Houston Greasers	4	2	11
11	Indianapolis Ponies	17	2	4
12	Kansas City Indians	16	3	3
13	Los Angeles Pirates	19	3	2
14	Los Angeles Goats	20	3	5
15	Miami Tarpons	28	3	-14
16	Minnesota Raiders	9	3	9
17	New England Volunteers	8	3	9
18	New Orleans Sinners	10	4	-24
19	New York Midgets	28	4	-8
20	New York Rockets	26	4	-7
21	Philadelphia Hawks	6	5	-13
22	Phoenix Sparrows	4	5	1
23	Pittsburgh Robbers	20	5	-4
24	San Diego Checkers	23	5	2
25	San Francisco 39ers	28	6	-3
26	Seattle Sea Lions	21	6	-25
27	Tampa Bay Raiders	19	6	4
28	Washington Pigskins	4	6	11

by three points. Max believes it may be possible to use the evolutionary algorithm in Solver to estimate the margin of victory in a match-up between any two teams. Using last season's data, Max wants to identify ratings or weights for each team such that the estimated margin of victory for any match-up would be:

$$\begin{matrix}\text{Estimated Margin}\\\text{of Victory}\end{matrix} = \begin{pmatrix}\text{Home Team}\\\text{Rating}\end{pmatrix} + \begin{pmatrix}\text{Home Field}\\\text{Advantage}\end{pmatrix} - \begin{pmatrix}\text{Visiting Team}\\\text{Rating}\end{pmatrix}$$

With this information, Max could estimate the margin of victory in a match-up between any two teams. He wants to do this in a way that minimizes the sum of the squared differences between the actual and estimated margins of victory for each of the games last year. (Assume each team's rating should be between 0 and 100, and the home field advantage should be between 0 and 20.)

a. Create a Solver model that achieves Max's objective.
b. If Max used this model to predict the winner in each of last year's games, how many times would he have correctly picked the winning team?
c. Suppose Max wants to maximize the chance of picking the winning teams. Resolve the problem to achieve this objective.
d. If Max used your model from part c to predict the winner in each of last year's games, how many times would he have correctly picked the winning team?

Tour de Europe

The summer before completing his MBA, Noah Franklin finally decided to take the trip to Europe that he had always dreamed about. However, given his limited bank account, he knows he will have to plan and budget wisely in order to go everywhere and see everything he wants to see. With some quick detective work on the Internet, Noah quickly found inexpensive sleeping quarters in each of the 10 cities he is interested in visiting. He also discovered there are several low-cost airlines providing no-frills transportation between various European cities. Figure 8.45 summarizes the possible airline flights between 10 different European cities with flight costs indicated on the arcs.

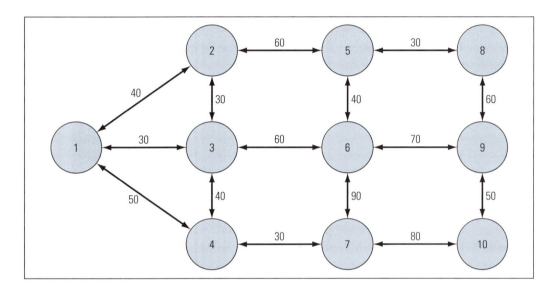

FIGURE 8.45

Possible flights for the Tour De Europe problem

Noah would really like to visit each of the 10 cities. Because his round-trip flight from the United States arrives at and, following his vacation, departs from city 1, his tour of Europe needs to begin and end in city 1:

1. Construct a spreadsheet model Noah could use to determine the least costly way to visit all 10 European cities exactly once. What is the optimal itinerary for this problem, and how much airfare would Noah have to pay?
2. Suppose the solution to the previous problem requires more money for airfare than Noah can afford. Construct a spreadsheet model Noah could use to determine the least costly way to visit cities 6, 8, and 10, starting and finishing from city 1. What is the optimal itinerary for this problem, and how much airfare would Noah have to pay?

Electing the Next President

"So it's come down to this," thought Roger Mellichamp as he looked around at the empty Styrofoam coffee cups and papers littering his office. When he accepted the job of campaign manager for his long-time friend's run for the White House, he knew there would be long hours, lots of traveling, and constant media pressure. But the thing he most wanted to avoid was a close race with a final showdown just before the election. Roger knew that making decisions under those circumstances would be agonizing because the success of the campaign and, in many ways, the future of the country would hinge on those very decisions. Unfortunately, that's just where things stand.

With only two weeks before the U.S. presidential election, Roger's friend and the incumbent president are running neck-and-neck in the polls. So, Roger's plans for the final two weeks of the campaign will be critical, and he wants to make sure he uses the candidate's time and the campaign's remaining money in the most effective way. Although the outcome of the election has been pretty much decided in most states, the electoral votes from the states of Florida, Georgia, California, Texas, Illinois, New York, Virginia, and Michigan are still up for grabs by either candidate. Roger knows they must win as many of these states as possible if his friend is to become the next president.

Several weeks ago, it became evident that the race was going to be close. So, Roger hired a statistical consultant to estimate the percentage of votes the campaign will receive in each of the states based on the amount of money the campaign spends and the number of times the candidate visits each state during the final two weeks before the election. The results of the consultant's analysis provided the following function:

$$\text{Percentage of votes state } k = 1 - \text{EXP}(-a V_k - b D_k)$$

where:

V_k = the number of times the candidate visits state k in the last two weeks of the campaign

D_k = the dollars (in \$1,000,000s) the campaign spends on advertising in state k in the last two weeks of the campaign

The following table summarizes the consultant's estimates of the parameters a and b for each state, along with the number of electoral votes at stake in each state:

State	a	b	Electoral Votes
Florida	0.085	0.31	25
Georgia	0.117	0.27	13
California	0.098	0.21	54
Texas	0.125	0.28	32
Illinois	0.128	0.26	22
New York	0.105	0.22	33
Virginia	0.134	0.24	13
Michigan	0.095	0.38	18

Roger believes the candidate can make 21 campaign stops in the next two weeks, and there is \$15 million left in the campaign budget available for advertising. He wants to spend at least \$500,000 in each of these states in the next two weeks. He also wants the candidate to make at least 1, but no more than 5, campaign stops in each of these states. Within these constraints, Roger wants to allocate these resources to maximize the number of electoral votes his candidate can receive. Assume a candidate needs 51% of the vote to win in each state.

1. Formulate an NLP model for this problem.
2. Implement your model in a spreadsheet and solve it.
3. How much money should Roger spend in each state?
4. How many campaign stops should the candidate make in each state?
5. What is the expected number of electoral votes generated by this solution?

Making Windows at Wella

Wella Corporation is a privately held manufacturer of doors and windows with annual sales in excess of $900 million. Some of the company's products are "standard size" and sold through wholesale and retail building material centers. However, much of their business involves manufacturing custom windows that can vary in size from 12 inches to 84 inches in quarter-inch increments.

The company has 2 plants located in Iowa and Pennsylvania. Each plant has 5 production lines devoted to custom window manufacturing. Each of these production lines operates 8 hours a day, 5 days a week and produces 50 windows per hour.

Sash and frame parts for the windows are cut from standard size "stock" pieces of lumber 16 feet in length. These stock pieces are purchased from a supplier who takes various pieces of lumber of various lengths, cuts out the defects (knot holes, cracks, and so on) and finger joins the pieces together to create the 16-foot stock pieces that are basically free of defects.

Wella cuts all the sash and frame parts for a particular window and then immediately passes that set of parts to the next operation in the production process for further assembly (that is, it does not carry inventories of parts of various length). However, the parts for any particular window may be cut in any order.

The demand for custom windows varies such that no two days (or even hours) of production are ever the same. Currently, line workers take a 16-foot piece of stock and start cutting parts for a window in the same order as they are listed on the bill of materials (BOM) until the remaining piece of stock is too short to cut the next required part.

As a simplified example, suppose the first window being produced has a BOM listing two 3-foot parts and two 4-foot parts (in that order). (Note that most of Wella's windows actually require 8 or 9 parts.) Those parts might be cut from a 16-foot stock piece and leave a 2-foot piece of scrap.

Now suppose the next window has a BOM that requires two 3-foot pieces and two 1-foot pieces (in that order). Because the 3-foot pieces can't be cut from the 2-foot scrap left over from the first piece of stock, Wella would start cutting a new piece of stock. It seems to make more sense to use the 2-foot piece of scrap from the first piece of stock to cut the two 1-foot pieces required by the second window. However, reordering the pieces for the second window to eliminate the 2-foot piece of scrap could actually lead to the creation of a 3-foot piece of scrap later in the production process. (Any pieces of "scrap" at the end of one stock piece that cannot be used in the next job are indeed scrapped as moving these scrap pieces into and out of inventory becomes a logistical nightmare.)

Being able to "look ahead" to see the downstream impacts of reordering decisions is beyond the capability of most humans, especially when this must be repeated over and over on an ongoing basis. As a result, Wella wants to develop a system to optimize the production on each line on an hour-by-hour basis.

The file WellaData.xls contains data for a half-hour of production on one of Wella's lines. (This line produces windows that require 8 sash/frame parts per window.) Assume Wella wants to produce the windows in the order indicated, but the parts for each window can be produced in any order. Wella wants to determine the optimal part-cutting sequence that would allow the company to minimize the amount of scrap (and the number of stock pieces required to fill all the orders).

1. How many possible solutions are there to this problem?
2. Design a spreadsheet model for this problem. How many pieces of stock would have to be cut to produce the windows in this half-hour of production if Wella processes the windows and parts in the order given (in WellaData.xls)? How much scrap is generated by this solution?

3. Use Solver to optimize the problem. How many pieces of stock would have to be cut to produce the windows in this half-hour of production if Wella processes the windows and parts in the order Solver identifies? How much scrap is generated by this solution?

4. Assume that Wella pays $4 for each 16-foot piece of stock. If the results identified in the previous question are representative of the results that could be obtained on all of Wella's production lines, how much money could Wella save over the course of a year?

5. What other suggestions/issues (if any) do you think Wella should consider before implementing your solution on their factory floor?

CASE 8.4   Newspaper Advertising Insert Scheduling

Advertising is the primary source of revenue for newspaper companies. Over the past 10 to15 years, the newspaper industry has been adjusting to changes in the mix of services that produce this revenue. The two main categories of services are run on press (ROP) advertising and preprinted insert advertising. ROP advertising is printed in the newspaper during the live press run each night, whereas preprinted inserts are produced (usually at a commercial printing facility) before the nightly production run and inserted into or delivered with the newspaper. Preprinted inserts offer several advantages for advertisers. Different sizes and quality of paper stock can be used to make ads unique and more colorful than possible on a newspaper printing press. Also, advertisers can tightly control quality for preprinted inserts unlike newspaper quality that varies widely.

Although revenue has been increasing in both categories of advertising, revenue from preprinted inserts has been growing at a higher rate than ROP advertising. For many newspaper companies, this shift in revenue mix has created scheduling challenges in the production area. With inserts, advertisers can select the zones to which specific sets of advertisements are distributed. A *zone* is a distinct geographical area where all the papers delivered in the area receive the same set of advertising inserts. The challenge for newspaper companies is to schedule the production run to process the correct combination of inserts for all the different zones and complete the run early enough to get the papers to the circulation department (and readers) on time. For many papers, the problem is exacerbated by advertisers' desires to "micro-zone" or have more zones of smaller size, increasing the specificity with which different groups of consumers can be targeted.

Art Carter is the production manager for a medium-sized newspaper company. Each night, he and his employees must design a schedule for combining the appropriate advertising inserts for 36 different delivery zones into the newspaper. Art's company owns four inserting machines that can each be loaded with the inserts for a particular zone. Two of the inserting machines operate at a rate of 12,000 papers per hour, whereas the other two machines operate at a rate of 11,000 per hour. The equipment inserts the loaded set of inserts into newspapers coming off the production press until all the papers for a particular zone are completed.

When the inserts for a particular zone are completed, the inserting machine is stopped and reloaded with the inserts for the next zone. This reloading (or changeover) process takes different amounts of time depending on how much work is required to load the machine with the next zone's set of inserts. The zones can be processed in any order and on any of the four inserting machines. However, all the advertising for a particular zone must be processed on the same inserting machine (that is, the inserts for a single zone are not distributed across multiple inserting machines).

The file NewspaperData.xls that accompanies this book contains sample data for a typical night's inserting workload for this company. In particular, this file contains the quantity of newspapers being produced for each of the 36 delivery zones and the estimated changeover times required to switch from one zone's set of inserts to another zone. Art has asked you to develop a model to design an optimal production schedule for the inserting equipment. In particular, he wants to determine which zones should be assigned to each of the four machines and the optimal order for processing the jobs assigned to each machine. His objective is to minimize the amount of time is takes (start to finish) to complete all the newspapers.

Chapter 9

Regression Analysis

9.0 Introduction

Regression analysis is a modeling technique for analyzing the relationship between a *continuous* (real-valued) dependent variable Y and one or more independent variables $X_1, X_2, \ldots, X_k$. The goal in regression analysis is to identify a function that describes, as closely as possible, the relationship between these variables so that we can predict what value the dependent variable will assume given specific values for the independent variables. This chapter shows how to estimate these functions and how to use them to make predictions in a business environment.

9.1 An Example

As a simple example of how regression analysis might be used, consider the relationship between sales for a company and the amount of money it spends on advertising. Few would question that the level of sales for a company will depend on or be influenced by advertising. Thus, we could view sales as the dependent variable Y and advertising as the independent variable X_1. Although some relationship exists between sales and advertising, we might not know the exact functional form of this relationship. Indeed, there probably is not an exact functional relationship between these variables.

We expect that sales for a company depend to some degree on the amount of money the company spends on advertising. But many other factors might also affect a company's sales, such as general economic conditions, the level of competition in the marketplace, product quality, and so on. Nevertheless, we might be interested in studying the relationship between the dependent variable sales (Y) and the independent variable advertising (X_1) and predicting the average level of sales expected for a given level of advertising. Regression analysis provides the tool for making such predictions.

In order to identify a function that describes the relationship between advertising and sales for a company, we first need to collect sample data to analyze. Suppose that we obtain the data shown in Figure 9.1 (and in the file Fig9-1.xlsm that accompanies this book) for a company on the level of sales observed for various levels of advertising expenditures in 10 different test markets around the country. We will assume that the different test markets are similar in terms of size and other demographic and economic characteristics. The main difference in each market is the level of advertising expenditure.

The data from Figure 9.1 are displayed graphically in Figure 9.2. This graph suggests a strong linear relationship between advertising expenditures and sales. Note that as advertising expenditures increase, sales increase proportionately. However, the relationship between advertising and sales is not perfect. For example, advertising expenditures of

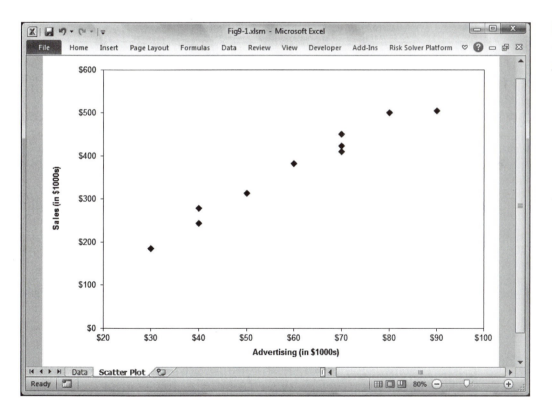

FIGURE 9.1

Sample data for advertising expenditures and observed sales

Obs	Advertising (in $1000s)	Actual Sales (in $1000s)
1	30	184.4
2	40	279.1
3	40	244.0
4	50	314.2
5	60	382.2
6	70	450.2
7	70	423.6
8	70	410.2
9	80	500.4
10	90	505.3

FIGURE 9.2

Scatter diagram for sales and advertising data

$70,000 were used in three different test markets and resulted in three different levels of sales. Thus, the level of sales that occurs for a given level of advertising is subject to random fluctuation.

The random fluctuation, or scattering, of the points in Figure 9.2 suggests that some of the variation in sales is not accounted for by advertising expenditures. Because of the scattering of points, this type of graph is called a **scatter diagram** or **scatter plot**. So although there is not a perfect *functional* relationship between sales and advertising (where each level of advertising yields one unique level of sales), there does seem to be a *statistical* relationship between these variables (where each level of sales is associated with a range or distribution of possible sales values).

Creating a Scatter Plot

To create a scatter plot like the one shown in Figure 9.2, follow these steps:

1. Select cells B4 through C13 shown in Figure 9.1.
2. Click the Insert tab.
3. Click Scatter on the Charts menu.
4. Click Scatter with only Markers.

Excel's Chart Tool command then appears at the top of the screen, allowing you to make several selections concerning the type of chart you want and how it should be labeled and formatted. After Excel creates a basic chart, you can customize it in many ways. Double-click a chart element to display a dialog box with options for modifying the appearance of the element.

9.2 Regression Models

We will formalize the somewhat imprecise nature of a statistical relationship by adding an *error term* to what is otherwise a functional relationship. That is, in regression analysis, we consider models of the form:

$$Y = f(X_1, X_2, \ldots, X_k) + \varepsilon \qquad \qquad \textbf{9.1}$$

where ε represents a random disturbance, or error, term. Equation 9.1 is a **regression model**. The number of independent variables in a regression model differs from one application to another. Similarly, the form of $f(\cdot)$ varies from simple linear functions to more complex polynomial and nonlinear forms. In any case, the model in equation 9.1 conveys the two essential elements of a statistical relationship:

- A tendency for the dependent variable Y to vary with the independent variable(s) in a systematic way, as expressed by $f(X_1, X_2, \ldots, X_k)$ in equation 9.1
- An element of *unsystematic* or random variation in the dependent variable, as expressed by ε in equation 9.1

The regression model in equation 9.1 indicates that for any values assumed by the independent variables $X_1, \ldots, X_k$, there is a probability distribution that describes the possible values that can be assumed by the dependent variable Y. This is portrayed graphically in Figure 9.3 for the case of a single independent variable. The curve drawn in Figure 9.3 represents the regression line (or regression function). It denotes the *systematic* variation between the dependent and independent variables (represented by $f(X_1, X_2, \ldots, X_k)$ in equation 9.1). The probability distributions in Figure 9.3 denote the *unsystematic* variation in the dependent variable Y at different levels of the independent variable. This represents random variation in the dependent variable (represented by ε in equation 9.1) that cannot be accounted for by the independent variable.

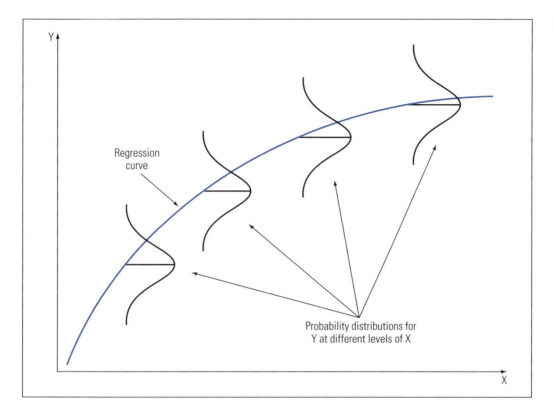

Notice that the regression function in Figure 9.3 passes through the mean, or average, value for each probability distribution. Therefore, the regression function indicates what value, on average, the dependent variable is expected to assume at various levels of the independent variable. If we want to predict what value the dependent variable Y would assume at some level of the independent variable, the best estimate we could make is given by the regression function. That is, our best estimate of the value that Y will assume at a given level of the independent variable X_1 is the mean (or average) of the distribution of values for Y at that level of X_1.

The actual value assumed by the dependent variable is likely to be somewhat different from our estimate because there is some random, unsystematic variation in the dependent variable that cannot be accounted for by our regression function. If we could repeatedly sample and observe actual values of Y at a given level of X_1, sometimes the actual value of Y would be higher than our estimated (mean) value, and sometimes it would be lower. So, the difference between the actual value of Y and our predicted value of Y would, on average, tend toward 0. For this reason, we can assume that the error term ε in equation 9.1 has an average, or expected, value of 0 if the probability distributions for the dependent variable Y at the various levels of the independent variable are normally distributed (bell-shaped) as shown in Figure 9.3.

9.3 Simple Linear Regression Analysis

As mentioned earlier, the function $f(\cdot)$ in equation 9.1 can assume many forms. However, the scatter plot in Figure 9.2 suggests that a strong linear relationship exists between the independent variable in our example (advertising expenditures) and the dependent variable (sales). That is, we could draw a straight line through the data in Figure 9.2 that would fit the data fairly well. So, the formula of a straight line might account for the systematic variation between advertising and sales. Therefore, the following simple linear regression model might be an appropriate choice for describing the relationship between advertising and sales:

$$Y_i = \beta_0 + \beta_1 X_{1_i} + \varepsilon_i \qquad\qquad 9.2$$

In equation 9.2, Y_i denotes the *actual* sales value for the ith observation, X_{1_i} denotes the advertising expenditures associated with Y_i, and ε_i is an error term indicating that when X_{1_i} dollars are spent on advertising, sales might not always equal $\beta_0 + \beta_1 X_{1_i}$. The parameter β_0 represents a constant value (sometimes referred to as the Y-intercept because it represents the point where the line goes through the Y-axis), and β_1 represents the slope of the line (that is, the amount by which the line rises or falls per unit increase in X_1). Assuming that a straight line accounts for the systematic variation between Y and X_1, the error terms ε_i represent the amounts by which the actual levels of sales are scattered around the regression line. Again, if the errors are scattered randomly around the regression line, they should average out to 0 or have an expected value of 0.

The model in equation 9.2 is a simple model because it contains only one independent variable. It is linear because none of the parameters (β_0 and β_1) appear as an exponent in the model or are multiplied or divided by one another.

Conceptually, it is important to understand that we are assuming that a large population of Y values occurs at each level of X_1. The parameters β_0 and β_1 represent, respectively, the intercept and slope of the *true* regression line relating these populations. For this reason, β_0 and β_1 are sometimes referred to as **population parameters**. We usually never know the exact numeric values for the population parameters in a given regression problem (we know that these values exist, but we don't know what they are). In order to determine the numeric values of the population parameters, we would have to look at the entire population of Y at each level of X_1—usually an impossible task. However, by taking a sample of Y values at selected levels of X_1, we can estimate the values of the population parameters. We will identify the estimated values of β_0 and β_1 as b_0 and b_1, respectively. The remaining problem is to determine the best values of b_0 and b_1 from our sample data.

9.4 Defining "Best Fit"

An infinite number of values could be assigned to b_0 and b_1. So, searching for the exact values for b_0 and b_1 to produce the line that best fits our sample data might seem like searching for a needle in a haystack—and it is certainly not something we want to do manually. To have the computer estimate the values for b_0 and b_1 that produce the line that best fits our data, we must give it some guidance and define what we mean by the best fit.

We will use the symbol $\hat{Y}_i$ to denote our estimated, or fitted, value of Y_i, which is defined as:

$$\hat{Y}_i = b_0 + b_1 X_{1_i} \qquad\qquad 9.3$$

We want to the find values for b_0 and b_1 that make all the *estimated* sales values ($\hat{Y}_i$) as close as possible to the corresponding *actual* sales values (Y_i). For example, the data shown earlier in Figure 9.1 indicate that we spent \$30,000 on advertising ($X_{1_1} = 30$) and observed sales of \$184,400 ($Y_1 = 184.4$). So in equation 9.3, if we let $X_{1_i} = 30$, we want $\hat{Y}_i$

to assume a value that is as close as possible to 184.4. Similarly, in the three instances in Figure 9.1 where \$70,000 was spent on advertising ($X_{1_6} = X_{1_7} = X_{1_8} = 70$), we observed sales of \$450,200, \$423,600, and \$410,200 ($Y_6 = 450.2$, $Y_7 = 423.6$, $Y_8 = 410.2$). So in equation 9.3, if we let $X_{1_i} = 70$, we want $\hat{Y}_i$ to assume a value that is as close as possible to 450.2, 423.6, and 410.2.

If we could find values for b_0 and b_1 so that all the estimated sales values were exactly the same as all the actual sales values ($\hat{Y}_i = Y_i$ for all observations i), we would have the equation of the straight line that passes through each data point—in other words, the line would fit our data perfectly. This is impossible for the data in Figure 9.2 because a straight line could not be drawn to pass through each data point in the graph. In most regression problems, it is impossible to find a function that fits the data perfectly because most data sets contain some amount of unsystematic variation.

Although we are unlikely to find values for b_0 and b_1 that will allow us to fit our data perfectly, we will try to find values that make the differences between the estimated values for the dependent variable and the corresponding actual values for the dependent variable ($Y_i - \hat{Y}_i$) as small as possible. We refer to the difference $Y_i - \hat{Y}_i$ as the **estimation error** for observation i because it measures how far away the estimated value $\hat{Y}_i$ is from the actual value Y_i. The estimation errors in a regression problem are also referred to as **residuals**.

Although different criteria can be used to determine the best values for b_0 and b_1, the most widely used method determines the values that minimize the sum of squared estimation errors—or **error sum of squares** (ESS) for short. That is, we will attempt to find values for b_0 and b_1 that minimize:

$$\text{ESS} = \sum_{i=1}^{n} (Y_i - \hat{Y}_i)^2 = \sum_{i=1}^{n} (Y_i - (b_0 + b_1 X_{1_i}))^2 \qquad \textbf{9.4}$$

Several observations should be made concerning ESS. Because each estimation error is squared, the value of ESS will always be nonnegative and, therefore, the smallest value ESS can assume is 0. The only way for ESS to equal 0 is for all the individual estimation errors to be 0 ($Y_i - \hat{Y}_i = 0$ for all observations), in which case the estimated regression line would fit our data perfectly. Thus, minimizing ESS seems to be a good objective to use in searching for the best values of b_0 and b_1. Because regression analysis finds the values of the parameter estimates that minimize the sum of squared estimation errors, it is sometimes referred to as the **method of least squares**.

9.5 Solving the Problem Using Solver

We can calculate the optimal parameter estimates for a linear regression model in a number of ways. As in earlier chapters, we can use Solver to find the values for b_0 and b_1 that minimize the ESS quantity in equation 9.4.

The problem of finding the optimal values for b_0 and b_1 in equation 9.4 is an unconstrained nonlinear optimization problem. Consider the spreadsheet in Figure 9.4 (and file Fig9-4.xlsm that accompanies this book).

In Figure 9.4, cells C15 and C16 represent the values for b_0 and b_1, respectively. These cells are labeled Intercept and Slope because b_0 represents the intercept in equation 9.3, and b_1 represents the slope. Values of 70 and 5 were entered for these cells as rough guesses of their optimal values.

To use Solver to calculate the optimal values of b_0 and b_1, we need to implement a formula in the spreadsheet that corresponds to the ESS calculation in equation 9.4. This formula represents the objective function to be minimized. To calculate the ESS, we first need

FIGURE 9.4 *Using Solver to solve the regression problem*

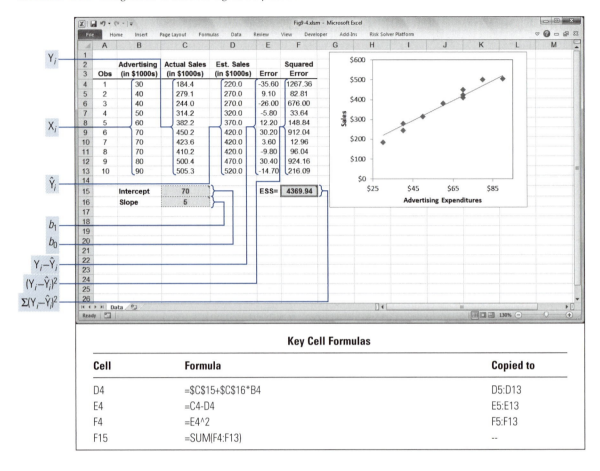

Key Cell Formulas

Cell	Formula	Copied to
D4	=$C$15+$C$16*B4	D5:D13
E4	=C4-D4	E5:E13
F4	=E4^2	F5:F13
F15	=SUM(F4:F13)	--

to calculate the sales values estimated by the regression function in equation 9.3 for each observation in our sample. These estimated sales values ($\hat{Y}_i$) were created in column D as:

Formula for cell D4: =$C$15+$C$16*B4
(Copy to D5 through D13.)

The estimation errors ($Y_i - \hat{Y}_i$) were calculated in column E as:

Formula for cell E4: =C4−D4
(Copy to E5 through E13.)

The squared estimation errors (($Y_i - \hat{Y}_i)^2$) were calculated in column F as:

Formula for cell F4: =E4^2
(Copy to F5 through F13.)

Finally, the sum of the squared estimation errors (ESS) was calculated in cell F15 as:

Formula for cell F15: =SUM(F4:F13)

Note that the formula in cell F15 corresponds exactly to equation 9.4.

The graph in Figure 9.4 plots the line connecting the estimated sales values against the actual sales values. The intercept and slope of this line are determined by the values in C15 and

FIGURE 9.5

Solver settings and options for the regression problem

Solver Settings:
Objective: F15 (Min)
Variable cells: C15:C16
Constraints:
None
Solver Options:
Standard GRG Nonlinear Engine

FIGURE 9.6 *Optimal solution to the regression problem*

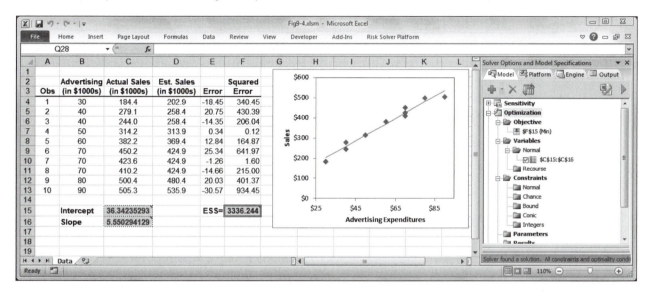

C16. Although this line seems to fit our data fairly well, we do not know if this is the line that minimizes the ESS value. However, we can use the Solver settings and options shown in Figure 9.5 to determine the values for C15 and C16 that minimize the ESS value in F15.

Figure 9.6 shows the optimal solution to this problem. In this spreadsheet, the intercept and slope of the line that best fits our data are $b_0 = 36.34235$ and $b_1 = 5.550294$, respectively. The ESS value of 3,336.244 associated with these optimal parameter estimates is better (or smaller) than the ESS value for the parameter estimates shown in Figure 9.4. No other values for b_0 and b_1 would result in an ESS value smaller than the one shown in Figure 9.6. Thus, the equation of the straight line that best fits our data according to the least squares criterion is represented by:

$$\hat{Y}_i = 36.34235 + 5.550294X_{1i} \qquad \qquad \textbf{9.5}$$

9.6 Solving the Problem Using the Regression Tool

In addition to Solver, Excel provides another tool for solving regression problems that is easier to use and provides more information about a regression problem. We will demonstrate the use of this regression tool by referring back to the original data for the current problem in Figure 9.1 (repeated in the file Fig9-7.xlsm that accompanies this book). Before you can use the regression tool in Excel, you need to make sure that the Analysis ToolPak add-in is available. You can do this by completing the following steps:

1. Click File, Options, Add-Ins.
2. Locate and activate the Analysis ToolPak add-in. (If Analysis ToolPak is not listed among your available add-ins, you will need to install it from your Microsoft Office CD.)

After ensuring that the Analysis ToolPak is available, you can access the regression tool by completing the following steps:

1. Click the Data tab.
2. Click Data Analysis in the Analysis menu.
3. Select Regression, and click OK.

After you choose the Regression command, the Regression dialog box appears, as shown in Figure 9.7. This dialog box presents many options and selections; at this point, we will focus on only three options: the Input Y Range, the Input X Range, and the Output Range. The Input Y Range corresponds to the range in the spreadsheet containing the sample observations for the *dependent* variable (C4 through C13 for the example in Figure 9.1). The Input X Range corresponds to the range in the spreadsheet containing the sample observations for the *independent* variable (B4 through B13 for the current example). You also need to specify the Output Range where you want the regression results to be reported. In Figure 9.7, you'll see that the New Worksheet Ply option has been selected to indicate that the regression results should be placed on a new sheet named "Results." With the dialog box selections complete, you can click the OK button, and Excel will calculate the least squares values for b_0 and b_1 (along with other summary statistics).

Figure 9.8 shows the Results sheet for our example. For now, we will focus on only a few values in Figure 9.8. Note that the value labeled "Intercept" in cell B17 represents the optimal value for b_0 ($b_0 = 36.342$). The value representing the coefficient for "X Variable 1" in cell B18 represents the optimal value for b_1 ($b_1 = 5.550$). Thus, the estimated regression function is represented by:

$$\hat{Y}_i = b_0 + b_1 X_{1_i} = 36.342 + 5.550 X_{1_i} \qquad \textbf{9.6}$$

Equation 9.6 is essentially the same result we obtained earlier using Solver (refer to equation 9.5). Thus, we can calculate the parameter estimates for a regression function using either Solver or the regression tool shown earlier in Figure 9.7. The advantage of the

FIGURE 9.7

Regression dialog box

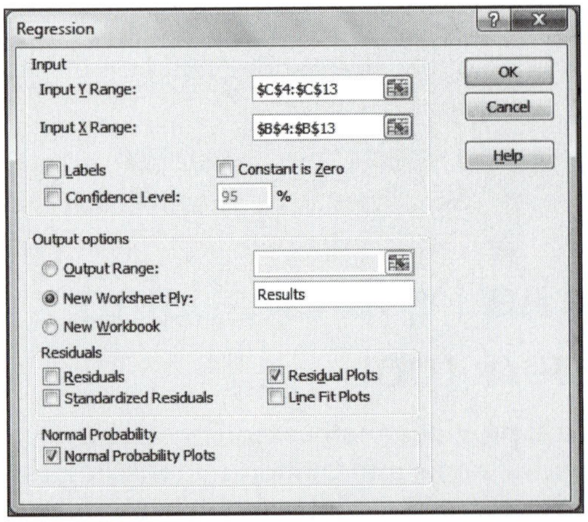

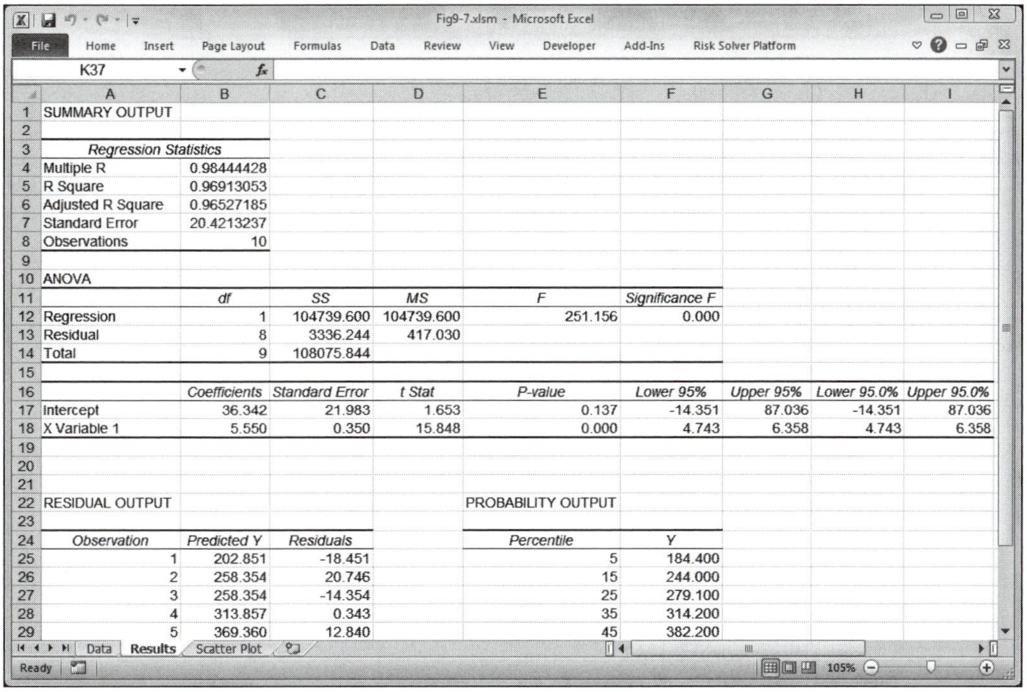

	A	B	C	D	E	F	G	H	I
1	SUMMARY OUTPUT								
2									
3	*Regression Statistics*								
4	Multiple R	0.98444428							
5	R Square	0.96913053							
6	Adjusted R Square	0.96527185							
7	Standard Error	20.4213237							
8	Observations	10							
9									
10	ANOVA								
11		*df*	*SS*	*MS*	*F*	*Significance F*			
12	Regression	1	104739.600	104739.600	251.156	0.000			
13	Residual	8	3336.244	417.030					
14	Total	9	108075.844						
15									
16		*Coefficients*	*Standard Error*	*t Stat*	*P-value*	*Lower 95%*	*Upper 95%*	*Lower 95.0%*	*Upper 95.0%*
17	Intercept	36.342	21.983	1.653	0.137	-14.351	87.036	-14.351	87.036
18	X Variable 1	5.550	0.350	15.848	0.000	4.743	6.358	4.743	6.358
19									
20									
21									
22	RESIDUAL OUTPUT				PROBABILITY OUTPUT				
23									
24	*Observation*	*Predicted Y*	*Residuals*		*Percentile*	*Y*			
25	1	202.851	-18.451		5	184.400			
26	2	258.354	20.746		15	244.000			
27	3	258.354	-14.354		25	279.100			
28	4	313.857	0.343		35	314.200			
29	5	369.360	12.840		45	382.200			

FIGURE 9.8

Results for the regression calculations

regression tool is that it does not require us to set up any special formulas or cells in the spreadsheet, and it produces additional statistical results about the problem under study.

9.7 Evaluating the Fit

Our goal in the example problem is to identify the equation of a straight line that fits our data well. Having calculated the estimated regression line (using either Solver or the regression tool), we might be interested in determining how well the line fits our data. Using equation 9.6, we can compute the estimated or expected level of sales ($\hat{Y}_i$) for each observation in our sample. The $\hat{Y}_i$ values could be calculated in column D of Figure 9.9 as follows:

Formula for cell D4: =36.342+5.550*B4
(Copy to D5 through D13.)

However, we can also use the TREND( ) function in Excel to compute the $\hat{Y}_i$ values in column D as follows:

Alternate formula for cell D4: =TREND($C$4:$C$13,$B$4:$B$13,B4)
(Copy to D5 through D13.)

This TREND( ) function computes the least squares linear regression line using a Y-range of C4 through C13 and an X-range of B4 through B13. It then uses this regression function to estimate the value of Y using the value of X given in cell B4. Thus, using the TREND( ) function, we don't have to worry about typing the wrong values for the estimated intercept or slope. Notice that the resulting estimated sales values shown in column D in Figure 9.9 match the predicted Y values shown toward the bottom on column B in Figure 9.8.

FIGURE 9.9

Estimated sales values at each level of advertising

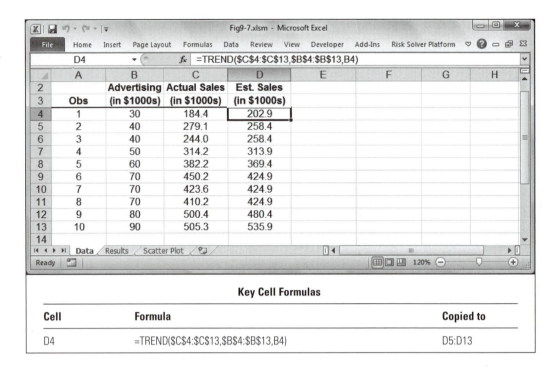

Key Cell Formulas

Cell	Formula	Copied to
D4	=TREND($C$4:$C$13,$B$4:$B$13,B4)	D5:D13

The TREND( ) Function

The TREND( ) function can be used to calculate the estimated values for linear regression models. The format of the TREND( ) function is as follows:

TREND(Y-range, X-range, X-value for prediction)

where Y-range is the range in the spreadsheet containing the dependent Y variable, X-range is the range in the spreadsheet containing the independent X variable(s), and X-value for prediction is a cell (or cells) containing the values for the independent X variable(s) for which we want an estimated value of Y. The TREND( ) function has an advantage over the regression tool in that it is dynamically updated whenever any inputs to the function change. However, it does not provide the statistical information provided by the regression tool. It is best to use these two different approaches to doing regression in conjunction with one another.

Figure 9.10 shows a graph of the estimated regression function along with the actual sales data. This function represents the expected amount of sales that would occur for each value of the independent variable (that is, each value in column D of Figure 9.9 falls on this line). To insert this estimated trend line on the existing scatter plot:

1. Right-click on any of the data points in the scatter plot to select the series of data.
2. Select Add Trendline.
3. Click Linear.
4. Select the Display Equation on Chart and Display R-Squared Value on Chart options.
5. Click Close.

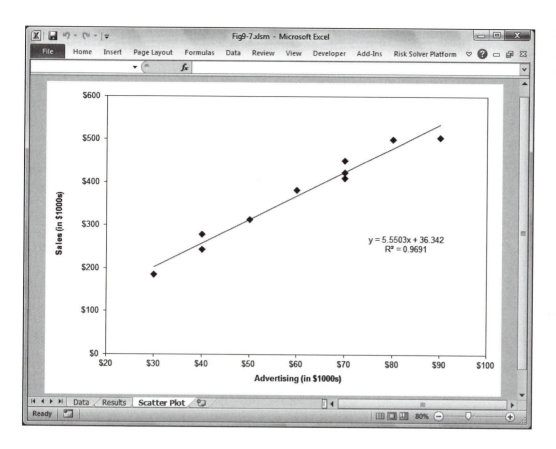

FIGURE 9.10

*Graph of the
regression line
through the actual
sales data*

From this graph, we see that the regression function seems to fit the data reasonably well in this example. In particular, it seems that the actual sales values fluctuate around this line in a fairly unsystematic, or random, pattern. Thus, it appears that we have achieved our goal of identifying a function that accounts for most, if not all, of the systematic variation between the dependent and independent variables.

9.8 The R^2 Statistic

In Figure 9.8, the value labeled "R Square" in cell B5 (or "R^2" in Figure 9.10) provides a goodness-of-fit measure. This value represents the **R^2 statistic** (also referred to as the **coefficient of determination**). This statistic ranges in value from 0 to 1 ($0 \leq R^2 \leq 1$) and indicates the proportion of the total variation in the dependent variable Y around its mean (average) that is accounted for by the independent variable(s) in the estimated regression function.

The total variation in the dependent variable Y around its mean is described by a measure known as the **total sum of squares** (TSS), which is defined as:

$$TSS = \sum_{i=1}^{n} (Y_i - \bar{Y})^2 \qquad \textbf{9.7}$$

The TSS equals the sum of the squared differences between each observation Y_i in the sample and the average value of Y, denoted in equation 9.7 by $\bar{Y}$. The difference between each observed value of Y_i and the average value $\bar{Y}$ can be decomposed into two parts as:

$$Y_i - \bar{Y}_i = (Y_i - \hat{Y}_i) + (\hat{Y}_i - \bar{Y}) \qquad \textbf{9.8}$$

Figure 9.11 illustrates this decomposition for a hypothetical data point. The value $Y_i - \hat{Y}_i$ in equation 9.8 represents the estimation error, or the amount of the total deviation between Y_i and $\bar{Y}$ that is not accounted for by the regression function. The value $\hat{Y}_i - \bar{Y}$ in equation 9.8 represents the amount of the total deviation in Y_i from $\bar{Y}$ that is accounted for by the regression function.

The decomposition of the individual deviation in equation 9.8 also applies to the TSS in equation 9.7. That is, the TSS can be decomposed into the following two parts:

$$\sum_{i=1}^{n}(Y_i - \bar{Y})^2 = \sum_{i=1}^{n}(Y_i - \hat{Y}_i)^2 + \sum_{i=1}^{n}(\hat{Y}_i - \bar{Y})^2 \qquad 9.9$$

$$\text{TSS} \quad = \quad \text{ESS} \quad + \quad \text{RSS}$$

ESS is the quantity that is minimized in least squares regression. ESS represents the amount of variation in Y around its mean that the regression function cannot account for, or the amount of variation in the dependent variable that is unexplained by the regression function. Therefore, the **regression sum of squares** (RSS) represents the amount of variation in Y around its mean that the regression function can account for, or the amount of variation in the dependent variable that is explained by the regression function. In Figure 9.8, cells C12, C13, and C14 contain the values for RSS, ESS, and TSS, respectively.

Now consider the following definitions of the R^2 statistic:

$$R^2 = \frac{\text{RSS}}{\text{TSS}} = 1 - \frac{\text{ESS}}{\text{TSS}} \qquad 9.10$$

From the previous definition of TSS in equation 9.9, we can see that if ESS = 0 (which can occur only if the regression function fits the data perfectly), then TSS = RSS, and,

FIGURE 9.11

Decomposition of the total deviation into error and regression components

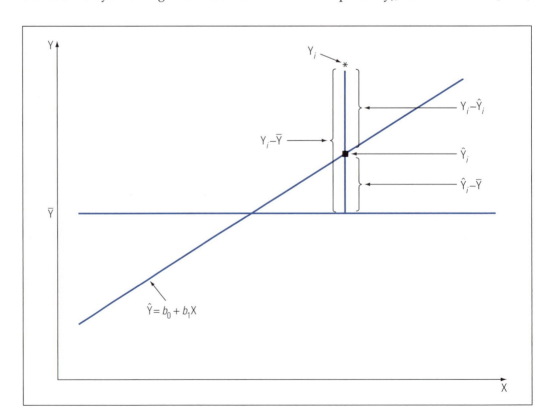

therefore, $R^2 = 1$. On the other hand, if RSS = 0 (which means that the regression function was unable to explain any of the variation in the behavior of the dependent variable Y), then TSS = ESS, and $R^2 = 0$. So, the closer the R^2 statistic is to the value 1, the better the estimated regression function fits the data.

From cell B5 in Figure 9.8, we observe that the value of the R^2 statistic is approximately 0.969. This indicates that approximately 96.9% of the total variation in our dependent variable around its mean has been accounted for by the independent variable in our estimated regression function. Because this value is fairly close to the maximum possible R^2 value (1), this statistic indicates that the regression function we have estimated fits our data well. This is confirmed by the graph in Figure 9.10.

The **multiple R** statistic shown in cell B4 of the regression output in Figure 9.8 represents the strength of the linear relationship between actual and estimated values for the dependent variable. As with the R^2 statistic, the multiple R statistic varies between 0 and 1 with values near 1 indicating a good fit. When a regression model includes only one independent variable, the multiple R statistic is equivalent to the square root of the R^2 statistic. We'll focus on the R^2 statistic because its interpretation is more apparent than that of the multiple R statistic.

9.9 Making Predictions

Using the estimated regression in equation 9.6, we can make predictions about the level of sales expected for different levels of advertising expenditures. For example, suppose the company wants to estimate the level of sales that would occur if $65,000 was spent on advertising in a given market. Assuming the market in question is similar to those used in estimating the regression function, the expected sales level is estimated as:

$$\text{Estimated Sales} = b_0 + b_1 \times 65 = 36.342 + 5.550 \times 65 = 397.092$$

(in $1,000s)

So, if the company spends $65,000 on advertising (in a market similar to those used to estimate the regression function), we would expect (on average) to observe sales of approximately $397,092. The *actual* level of sales is likely to differ somewhat from this value due to other random factors influencing sales.

9.9.1 THE STANDARD ERROR

A measure of the accuracy of the prediction obtained from a regression model is given by the standard deviation of the estimation errors—also known as the standard error, S_e. If we let n denote the number of observations in the data set, and k denote the number of independent variables in the regression model, the formula for the standard error is represented by:

$$S_e = \sqrt{\frac{\sum_{i=1}^{n} (Y_i - \hat{Y}_i)^2}{n - k - 1}}$$

9.11

The **standard error** measures the amount of scatter, or variation, in the actual data around the fitted regression function. Cell B7 in Figure 9.8 indicates that the standard error for our example problem is $S_e = 20.421$.

The standard error is useful in evaluating the level of uncertainty in predictions we make with a regression model. As a *very* rough rule of thumb, there is approximately a 68% chance of the actual level of sales falling within ± 1 standard error of the predicted value $\hat{Y}_i$. Alternatively, the chance of the actual level of sales falling within ± 2 standard errors of the predicted value $\hat{Y}_i$ is approximately 95%. In our example, if the company spends \$65,000 on advertising, we could be roughly 95% confident that the actual level of sales observed would fall somewhere in the range from \$356,250 to \$437,934 ($\hat{Y}_i \pm 2S_e$).

9.9.2 PREDICTION INTERVALS FOR NEW VALUES OF Y

To calculate a more accurate confidence interval for a prediction, or **prediction interval**, of a new value of Y when $X_1 = X_{1_h}$, we first calculate the estimated value $\hat{Y}_h$ as:

$$\hat{Y}_h = b_0 + b_1 X_{1_h} \qquad \textbf{9.12}$$

A $(1 - \alpha)$% prediction interval for a new value of Y when $X_1 = X_{1_h}$ is represented by:

$$\hat{Y}_h \pm t_{(1-\alpha/2;n-2)} S_p \qquad \textbf{9.13}$$

where $t_{(1-\alpha/2;n-2)}$ represents the $1 - \alpha/2$ percentile of a t-distribution with $n - 2$ degrees of freedom, and S_p represents the standard prediction error defined by:

$$S_p = S_e \sqrt{1 + \frac{1}{n} + \frac{(X_{1_h} - \bar{X})^2}{\sum\limits_{i=1}^{n} (X_{1_i} - \bar{X})^2}} \qquad \textbf{9.14}$$

The rule of thumb presented earlier is a generalization of equation 9.13. Notice that S_p is always larger than S_e because the term under the square root symbol is always greater than 1. Also notice that the magnitude of the difference between S_p and S_e increases as the difference between X_{1_h} and $\bar{X}$ increases. Thus, the prediction intervals generated by the rule of thumb tend to underestimate the true amount of uncertainty involved in making predictions. This is illustrated in Figure 9.12.

FIGURE 9.12

Comparison of prediction intervals obtained using the rule of thumb and the more accurate statistical calculation

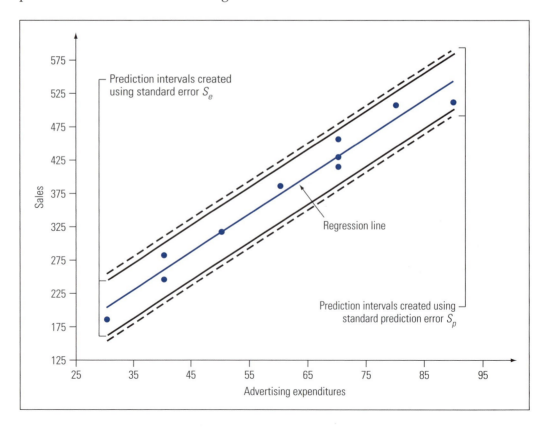

As shown in Figure 9.12, for this example problem, there is not a lot of difference between the prediction intervals created using the rule of thumb and the more accurate prediction interval given in equation 9.13. In a situation requiring a precise prediction interval, the various quantities needed to construct the prediction interval in equation 9.13 can be computed easily in Excel. Figure 9.13 provides an example of a 95% prediction interval for a new value of sales when $65,000 is spent on advertising.

To create this prediction interval, we first use the TREND( ) function to calculate the estimated sales level ($\hat{Y}_h$) when advertising equals $65,000 ($X_{1_h} = 65$). The value 65 is entered in cell B17 to represent X_{1_h} and the estimated sales level ($\hat{Y}_h$) is calculated in cell D17 as:

Formula for cell D17: =TREND($C$4:$C$13,$B$4:$B$13,B17)

The expected level of sales when $65,000 is spent on advertising is approximately $397,100. The standard error (S_e) shown in cell B19 is extracted from the Results sheet shown in Figure 9.8 as:

Formula for cell B19: =Results!B7

Fig9-7.xlsm - Microsoft Excel

D17 =TREND($C$4:$C$13,$B$4:$B$13,B17)

	A	B	C	D	E	F
2		Advertising	Actual Sales	Est. Sales		
3	Obs	(in $1000s)	(in $1000s)	(in $1000s)		
4	1	30	184.4	202.9		
5	2	40	279.1	258.4		
6	3	40	244.0	258.4		
7	4	50	314.2	313.9		
8	5	60	382.2	369.4		
9	6	70	450.2	424.9		
10	7	70	423.6	424.9		
11	8	70	410.2	424.9		
12	9	80	500.4	480.4		
13	10	90	505.3	535.9		
14						
15					95% Prediction Interval	
16					Lower Limit	Upper Limit
17	Prediction	65	?	397.1	347.557	446.666
18						
19	Se	20.4213				
20	Sp	21.48953				
21	t	2.30600				
22						

Data / Results / Scatter Plot

Key Cell Formulas

Cell	Formula	Copied to
D17	=TREND($C$4:$C$13,$B$4:$B$13,B17)	--
B19	=Results!B7	--
B20	=B19*SQRT(1+1/10+(B17-AVERAGE(B4:B13))^2/(10*VARP(B4:B13)))	--
B21	=TINV(1-0.95,8)	--
E17	=D17-B21*B20	--
F17	=D17+B21*B20	--

FIGURE 9.13

Example of calculating a prediction interval

The standard prediction error (S_p) is calculated in cell B20 as:

Formula for cell B20:   =B19*SQRT(1+1/10+

(B17−AVERAGE(B4:B13)) ^2/(10*VARP(B4:B13)))

The value 10 appearing in the preceding formula corresponds to the sample size n in equation 9.14. The appropriate t-value for a 95% confidence (or prediction) interval is calculated in cell B21 as:

Formula for cell B21:   =TINV(1−0.95,8)

The first argument in the preceding formula corresponds to 1 minus the desired confidence level (or $\alpha = 0.05$). The second argument corresponds to $n - 2$ ($10 - 2 = 8$). Cells E17 and F17 calculate the lower and upper limits of the prediction interval as:

Formula for cell E17:   =D17−B21*B20

Formula for cell F17:   =D17+B21*B20

The results indicate that when $65,000 is spent on advertising, we expect to observe sales of approximately $397,100 but realize that the actual sales level is likely to deviate somewhat from this value. However, we can be 95% confident that the actual sales value observed will fall somewhere in the range from $347,556 to $446,666. (Notice that this prediction interval is somewhat wider than the range from $356,250 to $437,934 generated earlier using the rule of thumb.)

9.9.3 CONFIDENCE INTERVALS FOR MEAN VALUES OF Y

At times, you might want to construct a confidence interval for the average, or mean, value of Y when $X_1 = X_{1_h}$. This involves a slightly different procedure from constructing a prediction interval for a new individual value of Y when $X_1 = X_{1_h}$. A $(1 - \alpha)$% confidence interval for the average value of Y when $X_1 = X_{1_h}$ is represented by:

$$\hat{Y}_h \pm t_{(1-\alpha/2;n-2)}S_a \qquad \text{9.15}$$

where $\hat{Y}_h$ is defined by equation 9.12, $t_{(1-\alpha/2;n-2)}$ represents the $1 - \alpha/2$ percentile of a t-distribution with $n - 2$ degrees of freedom, and S_a is represented by:

$$S_a = S_e \sqrt{\frac{1}{n} + \frac{(X_{1_h} - \bar{X})^2}{\sum_{i=1}^{n}(X_{1_i} - \bar{X})^2}} \qquad \text{9.16}$$

Comparing the definition of S_a in equation 9.16 with that of S_p in equation 9.14 reveals that S_a will always be smaller than S_p. Therefore, the confidence interval for the average value of Y when $X_1 = X_{1_h}$ will be tighter (or cover a smaller range) than the prediction interval for a new value of Y when $X_1 = X_{1_h}$. This type of confidence interval can be implemented in a similar way to that described earlier for prediction intervals.

9.9.4 EXTRAPOLATION

Predictions made using an estimated regression function might have little or no validity for values of the independent variable that are substantially different from those represented in the sample. For example, the advertising expenditures represented earlier in the sample in Figure 9.1 range from $30,000 to $90,000. Thus, we cannot assume that our model will give accurate estimates of sales levels at advertising expenditures significantly above or below this range of values because the relationship between sales and advertising might be quite different outside this range.

9.10 Statistical Tests for Population Parameters

Recall that the parameter β_1 shown earlier in equation 9.2 represents the slope of the *true* regression line (or the amount by which the dependent variable Y is expected to change given a unit change in X_1). If no linear relationship exists between the dependent and independent variables, the true value of β_1 for the model in equation 9.2 should be 0. As mentioned earlier, we cannot calculate or observe the true value of β_1 but instead must estimate its value using the sample statistic b_1. However, because the value of b_1 is based on a sample rather than on the entire population of possible values, its value is probably not exactly equal to the true (but unknown) value of β_1. Thus, we might want to determine how different the true value of β_1 is from its estimated value b_1. The regression results in Figure 9.8 provide a variety of information addressing this issue.

Cell B18 in Figure 9.8, shown earlier, indicates that the estimated value of β_1 is $b_1 = 5.550$. Cells F18 and G18 give the lower and upper limits of a 95% confidence interval for the true value of β_1. That is, we can be 95% confident that $4.74 \leq \beta_1 \leq 6.35$. This indicates that for every \$1,000 increase in advertising, we would expect to see an increase in sales of approximately \$4,740 to \$6,350. Notice that this confidence interval does not include the value 0. Thus, we can be at least 95% confident that a linear relationship exists between advertising and sales ($\beta_1 \neq 0$). (If we want an interval other than a 95% confidence interval, we can use the Confidence Level option in the Regression dialog box, shown in Figure 9.7, to specify a different interval.)

The *t*-statistic and *p*-value listed in cells D18 and E18 in Figure 9.8 provide another way of testing whether $\beta_1 = 0$. According to statistical theory, if $\beta_1 = 0$, then the ratio of b_1 to its standard error should follow a *t*-distribution with $n - 2$ degrees of freedom. Thus, the *t*-statistic for testing if $\beta_1 = 0$ in cell D18 is:

$$t\text{-statistic in cell D18} = \frac{b_1}{\text{standard error of } b_1} = \frac{5.550}{0.35022} = 15.848$$

The *p*-value in cell E18 indicates the probability of obtaining an outcome that is more extreme than the observed test statistic value if $\beta_1 = 0$. In this case, the *p*-value is 0, indicating that there is virtually no chance that we will obtain an outcome as large as the observed value for b_1 if the true value of β_1 is 0. Therefore, we conclude that the true value of β_1 is not equal to 0. This is the same conclusion implied earlier by the confidence interval for β_1.

The *t*-statistic, *p*-value, and confidence interval for the intercept β_0 are listed in Figure 9.8 in row 17 and would be interpreted in the same way as demonstrated for β_1. Notice that the confidence interval for β_0 straddles the value 0, so we cannot be certain that the intercept is significantly different from 0. The *p*-value for β_0 indicates that we have a 13.7% chance of obtaining an outcome more extreme than the observed value of b_0 if the true value of β_0 is 0. Both of these results indicate a fair chance that $\beta_0 = 0$.

9.10.1 ANALYSIS OF VARIANCE

The **analysis of variance** (ANOVA) results, shown earlier in Figure 9.8, provide another way of testing whether or not $\beta_1 = 0$. The values in the MS column in the ANOVA table represent values known as the **mean squared regression** (MSR) and **mean squared error** (MSE), respectively. These values are computed by dividing the RSS and ESS values in C12 and C13 by the corresponding degrees of freedom values in cells B12 and B13.

If $\beta_1 = 0$, then the ratio of MSR to MSE follows an F-distribution. The statistic labeled "F" in cell E12 is:

$$\text{F-statistic in cell E12} = \frac{\text{MSR}}{\text{MSE}} = \frac{104,739.6}{417.03} = 251.156$$

The value in F12 labeled "Significance F" is similar to the p-values described earlier, and indicates the probability of obtaining a value in excess of the observed value for the F-statistic if $\beta_1 = 0$. In this case, the significance of F is 0, indicating that there is virtually no chance that we would have obtained the observed value for b_1 if the true value of β_1 is 0. Therefore, we conclude that the true value of β_1 is not equal to 0. This is the same conclusion implied earlier by our previous analysis.

The F-statistic might seem a bit redundant, given that we can use the t-statistic to test whether or not $\beta_1 = 0$. However, the F-statistic serves a different purpose, which becomes apparent in multiple regression models with more than one independent variable. The F-statistic tests whether or not *all* of the β_i for *all* of the independent variables in a regression model are all simultaneously equal to 0. A simple linear regression model contains only one independent variable. In this case, the tests involving the F-statistic and the t-statistic are equivalent.

9.10.2 ASSUMPTIONS FOR THE STATISTICAL TESTS

The methods for constructing confidence intervals are based on important assumptions concerning the simple linear regression model presented earlier in equation 9.2. Throughout this discussion, we assumed that the error terms ε_i are independent, normally distributed random variables with expected (or mean) values of 0 and constant variances. Thus, the statistical procedures for constructing intervals and performing t-tests apply only when these assumptions are true for a given set of data. As long as these assumptions are not seriously violated, the procedures described offer good approximations of the desired confidence intervals and t-tests. Various diagnostic checks can be performed on the residuals $(Y_i - \hat{Y}_i)$ to see whether or not our assumptions concerning the properties of the error terms are valid. These diagnostics are discussed in-depth in most statistics books but are not repeated in this text. Excel also provides basic diagnostics that can be helpful in determining whether assumptions about the error terms are violated.

The Regression dialog box (shown in Figure 9.7) provides two options for producing graphs that highlight serious violations of the error term assumptions. These options are Residual Plots and Normal Probability Plots. Figure 9.14 shows the graphs produced by these two options for our example problem.

The first graph in Figure 9.14 results from the Residual Plots option. This graph plots the residuals (or estimation errors) versus each independent variable in the regression model. Our example problem involves one independent variable—therefore, we have one residual plot. If the assumptions underlying the regression model are met, the residuals should fall within a horizontal band centered on zero and should display no systematic tendency to be positive or negative. The residual plot in Figure 9.14 indicates that the residuals for our example problem fall randomly within a range from -30 to $+30$. Thus, no serious problems are indicated by this graph.

The second graph in Figure 9.14 results from the Normal Probability Plot option. If the error terms in equation 9.2 are normally distributed random variables, the dependent variable in equation 9.2 is a normally distributed random variable prior to sampling. Thus, one way to evaluate whether we can assume that the error terms are normally distributed is to determine if we can assume that the dependent variable is normally distributed. The normal probability plot provides an easy way to evaluate whether the

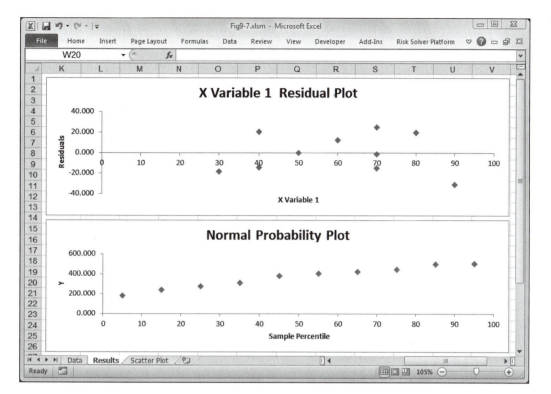

FIGURE 9.14

Residual plot and normal probability plot for the example problem

sample values on the dependent variable are consistent with the normality assumption. A plot with an approximately linear rate of increase (such as the one in Figure 9.14) supports the assumption of normality.

If the residual plot shows a systematic tendency for the residuals to be positive or negative, this indicates that the function chosen to model the systematic variation between the dependent and independent variables is inadequate and that another functional form would be more appropriate. An example of this type of residual plot is given in the first graph in Figure 9.15.

If the residual plot indicates that the magnitude of the residuals is increasing (or decreasing) as the value of the independent variable increases, we would question the validity of the assumption of constant error variances. An example of this type of residual plot is given in the second graph in Figure 9.15. (Note that checking for increasing or decreasing magnitude in the residuals requires multiple observations on Y at the same value of X and at various levels of X.) In some cases, a simple transformation of the dependent variable can correct the problem of nonconstant error variances. Such transformations are discussed in more advanced texts on regression analysis.

Regardless of the form of the distribution of the error terms, least squares regression can always be used to fit regression curves to data in order to predict the value the dependent variable will assume for a given level of the independent variables. Many decision makers never bother to look at residual plots or to construct confidence intervals for parameters in the regression models for the predictions they make. However, the accuracy of predictions made using regression models depends on how well the regression function fits the data. At the very least, we should always check to see how well a regression function fits a given data set. We can do so using residual plots, graphs of the actual data versus the estimated values, and the R^2 statistic.

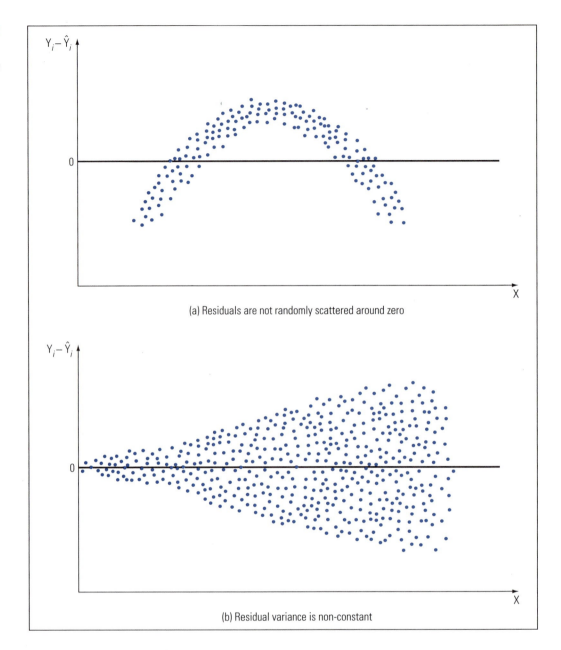

(a) Residuals are not randomly scattered around zero

(b) Residual variance is non-constant

9.11 Introduction to Multiple Regression

We have seen that regression analysis involves identifying a function that relates the *systematic* changes in a continuous dependent variable to the values of one or more independent variables. That is, our goal in regression analysis is to identify an appropriate representation of the function $f(\bullet)$ in:

$$Y = f(X_1, X_2, \ldots, X_k) + \varepsilon \qquad \textbf{9.17}$$

The previous sections in this chapter introduced some of the basic concepts of regression analysis by considering a special case of equation 9.17 that involves a *single* independent variable. Although such a model might be appropriate in some situations, a businessperson is far more likely to encounter situations involving more than one (or multiple) independent variable. We'll now consider how *multiple* regression analysis can be applied to these situations.

For the most part, multiple regression analysis is a direct extension of simple linear regression analysis. Although volumes have been written on this topic, we'll focus our attention on the multiple linear regression function represented by:

$$\hat{Y}_i = b_0 + b_1 X_{1_i} + b_2 X_{2_i} + \cdots + b_k X_{k_i} \qquad \textbf{9.18}$$

The regression function in equation 9.18 is similar to the simple linear regression function except that it allows for more than one (or "k") independent variables. Here again, $\hat{Y}_i$ represents the estimated value for the ith observation in our sample whose actual value is Y_i. The symbols $X_{1_i}, X_{2_i}, \ldots, X_{k_i}$ represent the observed values of the independent variables associated with observation i. Assuming that each of these variables vary in a linear fashion with the dependent variable Y, the function in equation 9.18 might be applied appropriately to a variety of problems.

We can easily visualize the equation of a straight line in our earlier discussion of regression analysis. In multiple regression analysis, the concepts are similar, but the results are more difficult to visualize. Figure 9.16 shows an example of the type of regression surface we might fit using equation 9.18 if the regression function involves only two independent variables. With two independent variables, we fit a *plane* to our data. With three or more independent variables, we fit a *hyperplane* to our data. It is difficult

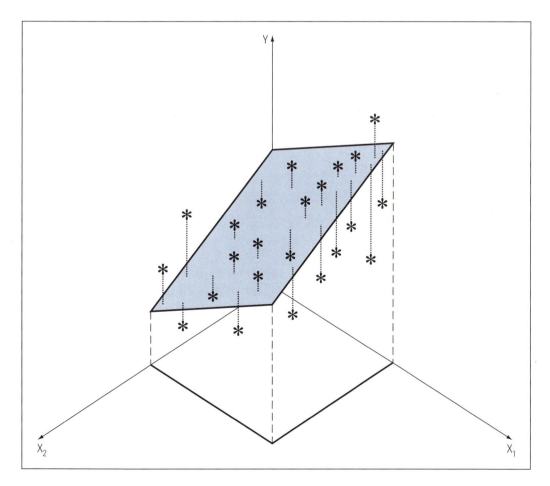

FIGURE 9.16

Example of a regression surface for two independent variables

to visualize or draw graphs in more than three dimensions, so we cannot actually see what a hyperplane looks like. However, just as a **plane** is a generalization of a straight line into three dimensions, a **hyperplane** is a generalization of a plane into more than three dimensions.

Regardless of the number of independent variables, the goal in multiple regression analysis is the same as the goal in a problem with a single independent variable. That is, we want to find the values for $b_0, b_1, \ldots, b_k$ in equation 9.18 that minimize the sum of squared estimation errors represented by:

$$\text{ESS} = \sum_{i=1}^{n} (Y_i - \hat{Y}_i)^2$$

We can use the method of least squares to determine the values for $b_0, b_1, \ldots, b_k$ that minimize ESS. This should allow us to identify the regression function that best fits our data.

9.12 A Multiple Regression Example

The following example illustrates how to perform multiple linear regression.

A real estate appraiser is interested in developing a regression model to help predict the fair market value of houses in a particular town. She visited the county courthouse and collected the data shown in Figure 9.17 (and in the file Fig9-17.xlsm that accompanies this book). The appraiser wants to determine if the selling price of the houses can be accounted for by the total square footage of living area, the size of the garage (as measured by the number of cars that can fit in the garage), and the number of bedrooms in each house. (Note that a garage size of 0 indicates that the house has no garage.)

In this example, the dependent variable Y represents the selling price of a house, and the independent variables X_1, X_2, and X_3 represent the total square footage, the size of the garage, and the number of bedrooms, respectively. To determine if the multiple linear regression function in equation 9.18 is appropriate for these data, we should first construct

FIGURE 9.17

Data for the real estate appraisal problem

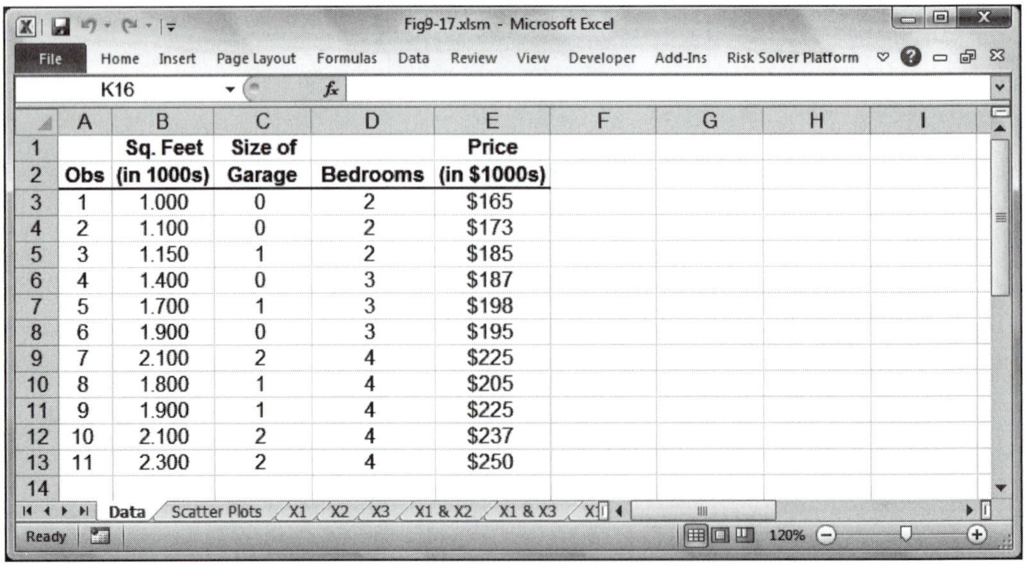

Obs	Sq. Feet (in 1000s)	Size of Garage	Bedrooms	Price (in $1000s)
1	1.000	0	2	$165
2	1.100	0	2	$173
3	1.150	1	2	$185
4	1.400	0	3	$187
5	1.700	1	3	$198
6	1.900	0	3	$195
7	2.100	2	4	$225
8	1.800	1	4	$205
9	1.900	1	4	$225
10	2.100	2	4	$237
11	2.300	2	4	$250

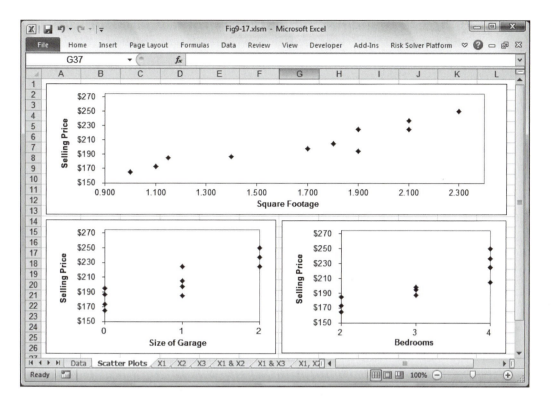

FIGURE 9.18

*Scatter plots of the
real estate
appraisal problem*

scatter plots between the dependent variable (selling price) and each independent variable, as shown in Figure 9.18. These graphs seem to indicate a linear relationship between each independent variable and the dependent variable. Thus, we have reason to believe that a multiple linear regression function would be appropriate for these data.

9.13 Selecting the Model

In our discussion of modeling and problem-solving in Chapter 1, we noted that the best model is often the simplest model that accurately reflects the relevant characteristics of the problem being studied. This is particularly true in multiple regression models. The fact that a particular problem might involve numerous independent variables does not necessarily mean that all of the variables should be included in the regression function. If the data used to build a regression model represent a sample from a larger population of data, it is possible to overanalyze or *overfit* the data in the sample. That is, if we look too closely at a sample of data, we are likely to discover characteristics of the sample that are not representative (or which do not generalize) to the population from which the sample was drawn. This can lead to erroneous conclusions about the population being sampled. To avoid the problem of overfitting when building a multiple regression model, we should attempt to identify the *simplest* regression function that adequately accounts for the behavior of the dependent variable we are studying.

9.13.1 MODELS WITH ONE INDEPENDENT VARIABLE

With this idea of simplicity in mind, the real estate appraiser in our example problem might begin her analysis by trying to estimate the selling prices of the houses in the sample using a simple regression function with only one independent variable. The appraiser might first try to fit each of the following three simple linear regression functions to the data:

$$\hat{Y}_i = b_0 + b_1 X_{1_i} \qquad\qquad\qquad \textbf{9.19}$$
$$\hat{Y}_i = b_0 + b_2 X_{2_i} \qquad\qquad\qquad \textbf{9.20}$$
$$\hat{Y}_i = b_0 + b_3 X_{3_i} \qquad\qquad\qquad \textbf{9.21}$$

In equations 9.19 through 9.21, $\hat{Y}_i$ represents the estimated or fitted selling price for the ith observation in the sample, and X_{1_i}, X_{2_i}, and X_{3_i} represent the total square footage, size of garage, and number of bedrooms for this same observation i, respectively.

To obtain the optimal values for the b_i in each regression function, the appraiser must perform three separate regressions. She would do so in the same way as described earlier in our example involving the prediction of sales from advertising expenditures. Figure 9.19 summarizes the results of these three regression functions.

FIGURE 9.19

Regression results for the three simple linear regression models

Independent Variable in the Model	R^2	Adjusted-R^2	S_e	Parameter Estimates
X_1	0.870	0.855	10.299	$b_0 = 109.503$, $b_1 = 56.394$
X_2	0.759	0.731	14.030	$b_0 = 178.290$, $b_2 = 28.382$
X_3	0.793	0.770	12.982	$b_0 = 116.250$, $b_3 = 27.607$

The values of the R^2 statistic in Figure 9.19 indicate the proportion of the total variation in the dependent variable around its mean accounted for by each of the three simple linear regression functions. (We will comment on the adjusted-R^2 and S_e values shortly.) The model that uses X_1 (square footage) as the independent variable accounts for 87% of the variation in Y (selling price). The model using X_2 (garage size) accounts for roughly 76% of the variation in Y, and the model that uses X_3 (number of bedrooms) as the independent variable accounts for about 79% of the variation in the selling price.

If the appraiser wants to use only one of the available independent variables in a simple linear regression model to predict the selling price of a house, it seems that X_1 would be the best choice because, according to the R^2 statistics, it accounts for more of the variation in selling price than either of the other two variables. In particular, X_1 accounts for about 87% of the variation in the dependent variable. This leaves approximately 13% of the variation in Y unaccounted for. Thus, the best linear regression function with one independent variable is represented by:

$$\hat{Y}_i = b_0 + b_1 X_{1_i} = 109.503 + 56.394\, X_{1_i} \qquad\qquad \textbf{9.22}$$

9.13.2 MODELS WITH TWO INDEPENDENT VARIABLES

Next, the appraiser might want to determine if one of the other two variables could be combined with X_1 in a *multiple* regression model to account for a significant portion of the remaining 13% variation in Y that was not accounted for by X_1. To do this, the appraiser could fit each of the following multiple regression functions to the data:

$$\hat{Y}_i = b_0 + b_1 X_{1_i} + b_2 X_{2_i} \qquad\qquad\qquad \textbf{9.23}$$
$$\hat{Y}_i = b_0 + b_1 X_{1_i} + b_3 X_{3_i} \qquad\qquad\qquad \textbf{9.24}$$

To determine the optimal values for the b_i in the regression model in equation 9.23, we would use the settings shown in the Regression dialog box in Figure 9.20. The Input X-Range in this dialog box is the range in Figure 9.17 that corresponds to the values for X_1 (total square footage) and X_2 (garage size). After we click the OK button, Excel performs the appropriate calculations and displays the regression results shown in Figure 9.21.

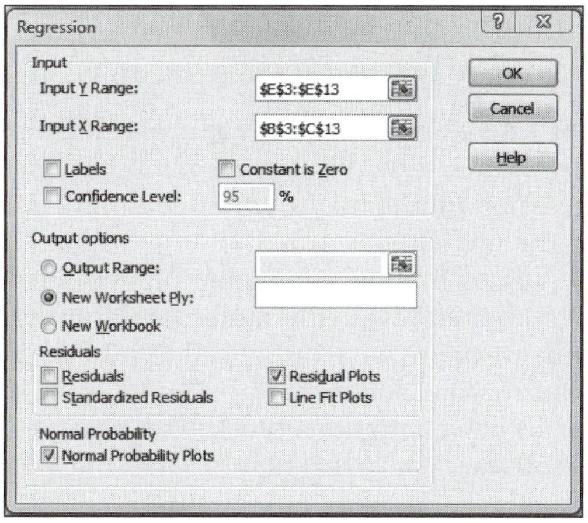

FIGURE 9.20 *Regression dialog box settings for the multiple regression model using square footage and garage size as independent variables*

FIGURE 9.21 *Results of the multiple regression model using square footage and garage size as independent variables*

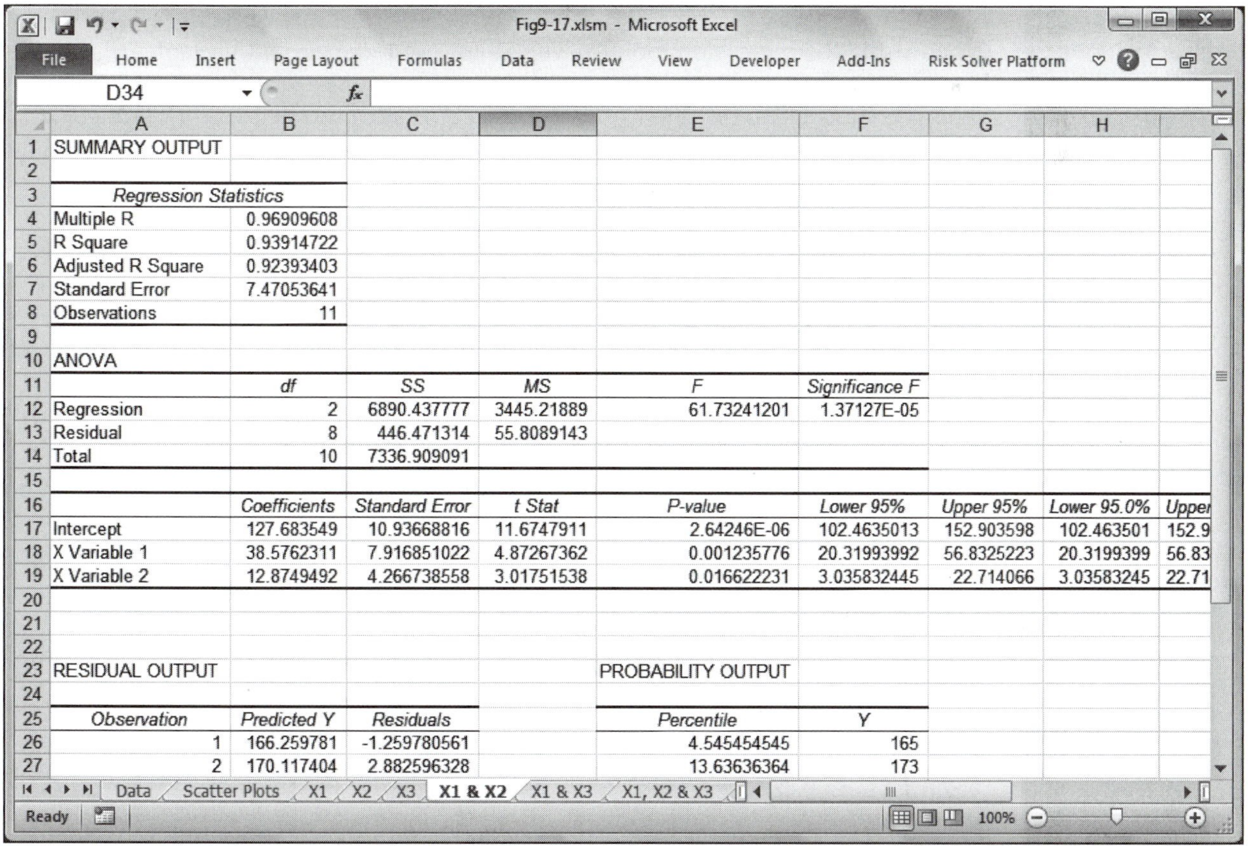

	A	B	C	D	E	F	G	H	
1	SUMMARY OUTPUT								
2									
3	*Regression Statistics*								
4	Multiple R	0.96909608							
5	R Square	0.93914722							
6	Adjusted R Square	0.92393403							
7	Standard Error	7.47053641							
8	Observations	11							
9									
10	ANOVA								
11		*df*	*SS*	*MS*	*F*	*Significance F*			
12	Regression	2	6890.437777	3445.21889	61.73241201	1.37127E-05			
13	Residual	8	446.471314	55.8089143					
14	Total	10	7336.909091						
15									
16		*Coefficients*	*Standard Error*	*t Stat*	*P-value*	*Lower 95%*	*Upper 95%*	*Lower 95.0%*	*Upper*
17	Intercept	127.683549	10.93668816	11.6747911	2.64246E-06	102.4635013	152.903598	102.463501	152.9
18	X Variable 1	38.5762311	7.916851022	4.87267362	0.001235776	20.31993992	56.8325223	20.3199399	56.83
19	X Variable 2	12.8749492	4.266738558	3.01751538	0.016622231	3.035832445	22.714066	3.03583245	22.71
20									
21									
22									
23	RESIDUAL OUTPUT				PROBABILITY OUTPUT				
24									
25	*Observation*	*Predicted Y*	*Residuals*		*Percentile*	Y			
26	1	166.259781	-1.259780561		4.545454545	165			
27	2	170.117404	2.882596328		13.63636364	173			

Figure 9.21 lists *three* numbers in the Coefficients column. These numbers correspond to the parameter estimates b_0, b_1, and b_2. Note that the value listed for X Variable 1 is the coefficient for the first variable in the X-Range (which, in some cases, might be X_2 or X_3, depending on how the data are arranged in the spreadsheet). The value for X Variable 2 corresponds to the second variable in the X-Range (which might be X_3 or X_1, depending on the arrangement of the data).

From the regression results in Figure 9.21, we know that when using X_1 (square footage) and X_2 (garage size) as independent variables, the estimated regression function is:

$$\hat{Y}_i = b_0 + b_1X_{1_i} + b_2X_{2_i} = 127.684 + 38.576X_{1_i} + 12.875X_{2_i} \qquad \textbf{9.25}$$

Notice that adding the second independent variable caused the values of b_0 and b_1 to change from their earlier values shown in equation 9.22. Thus, the values assumed by the parameters in a regression model might vary depending on the number (and combination) of variables in the model.

We could obtain the values for the parameters in the second multiple regression model (shown earlier in equation 9.24) in the same way. Note, however, that before issuing the Regression command again, we would need to rearrange the data in the spreadsheet so that the values for X_1 (total square footage) and X_3 (number of bedrooms) are located next to each other in one contiguous block. The regression tool in Excel (and in most other spreadsheet software packages) requires that the X-Range be represented by one contiguous block of cells.

Keep the X-Range Contiguous

When using the regression tool, the values for the independent variables *must* be listed in *adjacent* columns in the spreadsheet and cannot be separated by any intervening columns. That is, the Input X Range option in the Regression dialog box must always specify a contiguous block of numbers.

Figure 9.22 compares the regression results for the model in equation 9.24 and the results for the model in equation 9.23 versus the earlier results of the best simple linear regression model in equation 9.22, where X_1 was the only independent variable in the model.

These results indicate that when using X_1 (square footage) and X_3 (number of bedrooms) as independent variables, the estimated regression function is:

$$\hat{Y}_i = b_0 + b_1X_{1_i} + b_3X_{3_i} = 108.311 + 44.313X_{1_i} + 6.743X_{3_i} \qquad \textbf{9.26}$$

FIGURE 9.22

Comparison of regression results for models with two independent variables versus the best model with one independent variable

Independent Variables in the Model	R^2	Adjusted-R^2	S_e	Parameter Estimates
X_1	0.870	0.855	10.299	$b_0 = 109.503$, $b_1 = 56.394$
X_1 and X_2	0.939	0.924	7.471	$b_0 = 127.684$, $b_1 = 38.576$, $b_2 = 12.875$
X_1 and X_3	0.877	0.847	10.609	$b_0 = 108.311$, $b_1 = 44.313$, $b_3 = 6.743$

The appraiser was hoping that the inclusion of a second independent variable in the models in equation 9.23 and equation 9.24 might help to explain a significant portion of the remaining 13% of the variation in the dependent that was not accounted for by the simple linear regression function in equation 9.22. How can we tell if this happened?

9.13.3 INFLATING R^2

Figure 9.22 indicates that adding either X_2 or X_3 to the simple linear regression model caused the R^2 statistic to increase. This should not be surprising. As it turns out, the value of R^2 can never decrease as a result of adding an independent variable to a regression function. The reason for this is easy to see. From equation 9.10, recall that $R^2 = 1 - ESS/TSS$. Thus, the only way R^2 could decrease as the result of adding an independent variable (X_n) to the model would be if ESS *increased*. However, because the method of least squares attempts to minimize ESS, a new independent variable cannot cause ESS to increase because this variable could simply be ignored by setting $b_n = 0$. In other words, if adding the new independent variable does not help to reduce ESS, least squares regression would simply ignore the new variable.

When you add *any* independent variable to a regression function, the value of the R^2 statistic can never decrease and will usually increase at least a little. Therefore, we can make the R^2 statistic arbitrarily large simply by including enough independent variables in the regression function—regardless of whether or not the new independent variables are related at all to the dependent variable. For example, the real estate appraiser could probably increase the value R^2 to some degree by including another independent variable in the model that represents the height of the mailbox at each house—which probably has little to do with the selling price of a house. This results in a model that overfits our data and may not generalize well to other data not included in the sample being analyzed.

9.13.4 THE ADJUSTED-R^2 STATISTIC

The value of the R^2 statistic can be inflated artificially by including independent variables in a regression function that have little or no logical connection with the dependent variable. Thus, another goodness-of-fit measure, known as the **adjusted-R^2 statistic** (denoted by R_a^2), has been suggested that accounts for the number of independent variables included in a regression model. The adjusted-R^2 statistic is defined as:

$$R_a^2 = 1 - \left(\frac{ESS}{TSS}\right)\left(\frac{n-1}{n-k-1}\right) \qquad \textbf{9.27}$$

where n represents the number of observations in the sample, and k represents the number of independent variables in the model. As variables are added to a regression model, the ratio of ESS to TSS in equation 9.27 will decrease (because ESS decreases, and TSS remains constant), but the ratio of $n-1$ to $n-k-1$ will increase (because $n-1$ remains constant, and $n-k-1$ decreases). Thus, if we add a variable to the model that does not reduce ESS enough to compensate for the increase in k, the adjusted-R^2 value will decrease.

The adjusted-R^2 value can be used as a rule of thumb to help us decide if an additional independent variable enhances the predictive ability of a model or if it simply inflates the R^2 statistic artificially. However, using the adjusted-R^2 statistic in this way is not foolproof and requires a good bit of judgment on the part of the person performing the analysis.

9.13.5 THE BEST MODEL WITH TWO INDEPENDENT VARIABLES

As shown in Figure 9.22, when X_2 (garage size) is introduced to the model, the adjusted-R^2 *increases* from 0.855 to 0.924. We can conclude from this increase that the addition of X_2 to the regression model helps to account for a significant portion of the remaining variation in Y that was not accounted for by X_1. On the other hand, when X_3 is introduced as an independent variable in the regression model, the adjusted-R^2 statistic in Figure 9.22 *decreases* (from 0.855 to 0.847). This indicates that adding this variable to the model does not help account for a significant portion of the remaining variation in Y if X_1 is already in the model. The best model with two independent variables is given in equation 9.25, which uses X_1 (total square footage) and X_2 (garage size) as predictors of selling price. According to the R^2 statistic in Figure 9.22, this model accounts for about 94% of the total variation in Y around its mean. This model leaves roughly 6% of the variation in Y unaccounted for.

9.13.6 MULTICOLLINEARITY

We should not be too surprised that no significant improvement was observed when X_3 (number of bedrooms) was added to the model containing X_1 (total square footage) because both of these variables represent similar factors. That is, the number of bedrooms in a house is closely related (or correlated) to the total square footage in the house. Thus, if we have already used total square footage to help explain variations in the selling prices of houses (as in the first regression function), adding information about the number of bedrooms is somewhat redundant. Our analysis confirms this.

The term **multicollinearity** is used to describe the situation when the independent variables in a regression model are correlated among themselves. Multicollinearity tends to increase the uncertainty associated with the parameters estimates (b_i) in a regression model and should be avoided whenever possible. Specialized procedures for detecting and correcting multicollinearity can be found in advanced texts on regression analysis.

9.13.7 THE MODEL WITH THREE INDEPENDENT VARIABLES

As a final test, the appraiser might want to see if X_3 (number of bedrooms) helps to explain a significant portion of the remaining 6% variation in Y that was not accounted for by the model using X_1 and X_2 as independent variables. This involves fitting the following multiple regression function to the data:

$$\hat{Y}_i = b_0 + b_1 X_{1_i} + b_2 X_{2_i} + b_3 X_{3_i} \qquad \textbf{9.28}$$

Figure 9.23 shows the regression results for this model. The results of this model are also summarized for comparison purposes in Figure 9.24, along with the earlier results for the best model with one independent variable and the best model with two independent variables.

Figure 9.24 indicates that when X_3 is added to the model that contains X_1 and X_2, the R^2 statistic increases slightly (from 0.939 to 0.943). However, the adjusted-R^2 drops from 0.924 to 0.918. Thus, it does not appear that adding information about X_3 (number of bedrooms) helps to explain selling prices in any significant way when X_1 (total square footage) and X_2 (size of garage) are already in the model.

FIGURE 9.23 *Results of regression model using all three independent variables*

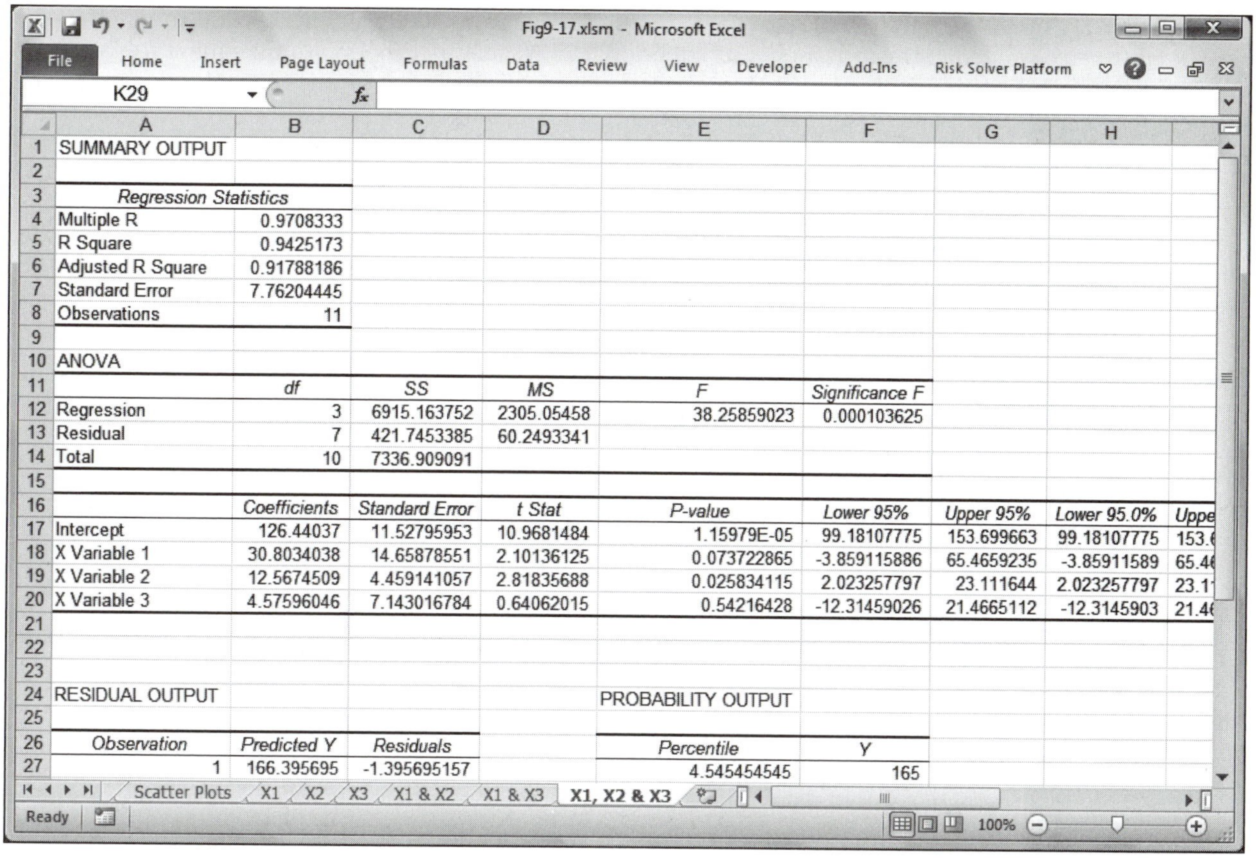

	A	B	C	D	E	F	G	H
1	SUMMARY OUTPUT							
2								
3	*Regression Statistics*							
4	Multiple R	0.9708333						
5	R Square	0.9425173						
6	Adjusted R Square	0.91788186						
7	Standard Error	7.76204445						
8	Observations	11						
9								
10	ANOVA							
11		*df*	*SS*	*MS*	*F*	*Significance F*		
12	Regression	3	6915.163752	2305.05458	38.25859023	0.000103625		
13	Residual	7	421.7453385	60.2493341				
14	Total	10	7336.909091					
15								
16		*Coefficients*	*Standard Error*	*t Stat*	*P-value*	*Lower 95%*	*Upper 95%*	*Lower 95.0%* Uppe
17	Intercept	126.44037	11.52795953	10.9681484	1.15979E-05	99.18107775	153.699663	99.18107775 153.6
18	X Variable 1	30.8034038	14.65878551	2.10136125	0.073722865	-3.859115886	65.4659235	-3.85911589 65.46
19	X Variable 2	12.5674509	4.459141057	2.81835688	0.025834115	2.023257797	23.111644	2.023257797 23.11
20	X Variable 3	4.57596046	7.143016784	0.64062015	0.54216428	-12.31459026	21.4665112	-12.3145903 21.46
21								
22								
23								
24	RESIDUAL OUTPUT				PROBABILITY OUTPUT			
25								
26	*Observation*	*Predicted Y*	*Residuals*		*Percentile*	*Y*		
27	1	166.395695	-1.395695157		4.545454545	165		

FIGURE 9.24

Comparison of regression results for the model with three independent variables versus the best models with one and two independent variables

Independent Variables in the Model	R^2	Adjusted-R^2	S_e	Parameter Estimates
X_1	0.870	0.855	10.299	$b_0 = 109.503$, $b_1 = 56.394$
X_1 and X_2	0.939	0.924	7.471	$b_0 = 127.684$, $b_1 = 38.576$, $b_2 = 12.875$
X_1, X_2, and X_3	0.943	0.918	7.762	$b_0 = 126.44$, $b_1 = 30.803$, $b_2 = 12.567$, $b_3 = 4.576$

It is also interesting to note that the best model with two independent variables also has the smallest standard error S_e. This means that the confidence intervals around any predictions made with this model will be narrower (or more precise) than those of the other models. It can be shown that the model with the highest adjusted-R^2 always has the smallest standard error. For this reason, the adjusted-R^2 statistic is sometimes the sole criterion used to select which multiple regression model to use in a given problem. However, other procedures for selecting regression models exist and are discussed in advanced texts on regression analysis.

9.14 Making Predictions

On the basis of this analysis, the appraiser most likely would choose to use the estimated regression model in equation 9.25, which includes X_1 (total square footage) and X_2 (garage size) as independent variables. For a house with X_{1_i} total square feet and space for X_{2_i} cars in its garage, the estimated selling price $\hat{Y}_i$ is:

$$\hat{Y}_i = 127.684 + 38.576X_{1_i} + 12.875X_{2_i}$$

For example, the expected selling price (or average market value) of a house with 2,100 square feet and a two-car garage is estimated as:

$$\hat{Y}_i = 127.684 + 38.576 \times 2.1 + 12.875 \times 2 = 234.444$$

or approximately \$234,444. Note that in making this prediction, we expressed the square footage of the house in the same units in which X_1 (total square footage variable) was expressed in the sample used to estimate the model. This should be done for all independent variables when making predictions.

The standard error of the estimation errors for this model is 7.471. Therefore, we should not be surprised to see prices for houses with 2,100 square feet and two-car garages varying within roughly ± 2 standard errors (or $\pm\$14,942$) of our estimate. That is, we expect prices on this type of house to be as low as \$219,502 or as high as \$249,386 depending on other factors not included in our analysis (such as age or condition of the roof, presence of a swimming pool, and so on).

As demonstrated earlier in the case of simple linear regression models, more accurate techniques exist for constructing prediction intervals using multiple regression models. In the case of a multiple regression model, the techniques used to construct prediction intervals require a basic knowledge of matrix algebra, which is not assumed in this text. The interested reader should consult advanced texts on multiple regression analysis for a description of how to construct more accurate prediction intervals using multiple regression models. Keep in mind that the simple rule of thumb described earlier gives an underestimated (narrower) approximation of the more accurate prediction interval.

9.15 Binary Independent Variables

As just mentioned, the appraiser might want to include other independent variables in her analysis. Some of these, such as age of the roof, could be measured numerically and be included as an independent variable. But how would we create variables to represent the presence of a swimming pool or the condition of the roof?

The presence of a swimming pool can be included in the analysis with a binary independent variable coded as:

$$X_{p_i} = \begin{cases} 1, & \text{if house } i \text{ has a pool} \\ 0, & \text{otherwise} \end{cases}$$

The condition of the roof could also be modeled with binary variables. Here, however, we might need more than one binary variable to model all the possible conditions. If some qualitative variable can assume p possible values, we need $p - 1$ binary variables to model the possible outcomes. For example, suppose that the condition of the roof could be rated as good, average, or poor. There are three possible values for the variable representing the condition of the roof; therefore, we need two binary variables to model these outcomes. These binary variables are coded as:

$$X_{r_i} = \begin{cases} 1, \text{ if the roof of house } i \text{ is in good condition} \\ 0, \text{ otherwise} \end{cases}$$

$$X_{r+1_i} = \begin{cases} 1, \text{ if the roof of house } i \text{ is in average condition} \\ 0, \text{ otherwise} \end{cases}$$

It might appear that we left out a coding for a roof in poor condition. However, note that this condition is implied when $X_{r_i} = 0$ and $X_{r+1_i} = 0$. That is, if the roof is *not* in good condition (as implied by $X_{r_i} = 0$) *and* the roof is *not* in average condition (as implied by $X_{r+1_i} = 0$), then the roof must be in poor condition. Thus, we need only two binary variables to represent three possible roof conditions. For reasons that go beyond the scope of this text, the computer could not perform the least squares calculations if we included a third binary variable to indicate houses with roofs in poor condition. Also, it would be inappropriate to model the condition of the roof with a single variable coded as 1 for good, 2 for average, and 3 for poor because this implies that the average condition is twice as bad as the good condition, and that the poor condition is three times as bad as the good condition and one and a half times as bad as the average condition.

As this example illustrates, we can use binary variables as independent variables in regression analysis to model a variety of conditions that are likely to occur. In each case, the binary variables would be placed in the X-Range of the spreadsheet and appropriate b_i values would be calculated by the regression tool.

9.16 Statistical Tests for the Population Parameters

Statistical tests for the population parameters in a multiple regression model are performed in much the same way as for the simple regression model. As described earlier, the F-statistic tests whether or not *all* of the β_i for *all* of the independent variables are *all* simultaneously equal to 0 (that is, $\beta_1 = \beta_2 = \ldots = \beta_k = 0$). The value in the regression results labeled Significance of F indicates the probability of this condition being true for the data under consideration.

In the case of a multiple regression model, the *t*-statistics for each independent variable require a slightly different interpretation due to the possible presence of multicollinearity. Each *t*-statistic can be used to test whether or not the associated population parameter $\beta_i = 0$ *given all the other independent variables in the model*. For example, consider the *t*-statistics and *p*-values associated with the variable X_1 shown in Figures 9.21 and 9.23. The *p*-value for X_1 in cell E18 of Figure 9.21 indicates only a 0.123% chance that $\beta_1 = 0$ when X_2 is the only other independent variable in the model. The *p*-value for X_1 in cell E18 of Figure 9.23 indicates a 7.37% chance that $\beta_1 = 0$ when X_2 *and* X_3 are also in the model. This illustrates one of the potential problems caused by multicollinearity. Because X_1 and X_3 are highly correlated, it is less certain that X_1 plays a significant (nonzero) role in accounting for the behavior of the dependent variable Y when X_3 is also in the model.

In Figure 9.23, the *p*-value associated with X_3 indicates a 54.2% chance that $\beta_3 = 0$ given the other variables in the model. Thus, if we had started our analysis by including all three independent variables in the model, the *p*-value for X_3 in Figure 9.23 suggests that it might be wise to drop X_3 from the model because there is a fairly good chance that it contributes 0 ($\beta_3 = 0$) to explaining the behavior of the dependent variable, given the other variables in the model. In this case, if we drop X_3 from the model, we end up with the same model selected using the adjusted-R^2 criterion.

The statistical tests considered here are valid only when the underlying errors around the regression function are normally distributed random variables with constant means and variances. The graphical diagnostics described earlier apply equally to the case of multiple regression. However, the various statistics presented give reasonably accurate results if the assumptions about the distribution of the error terms are not violated too seriously. Furthermore, the R^2 and adjusted-R^2 statistics are purely descriptive in nature and do not depend in any way on the assumptions about the distribution of the error terms.

9.17 Polynomial Regression

When introducing the multiple linear regression function in equation 9.18 earlier, we noted that this type of model might be appropriate when the independent variables vary in a linear fashion with the dependent variable. Business problems exist where there is *not* a linear relationship between the dependent and independent variables. For example, suppose that the real estate appraiser in our earlier example had collected the data in Figure 9.25 (and in the file Fig9-25.xlsm that accompanies this book) showing the total square footage and selling price for a number of houses. Figure 9.26 shows a scatter plot of these data.

Figure 9.26 indicates a very strong relationship between total square footage and the selling price of the houses in this sample. However, this relationship is *not* linear. Rather, more of a *curvilinear* relationship exists between these variables. Does this mean that linear regression analysis cannot be used with these data? Not at all.

The data in Figure 9.25 (plotted in Figure 9.26) indicate a *quadratic* relationship between square footage and selling price. So, to account adequately for the variation in the selling price of houses, we need to use the following type of regression function:

$$\hat{Y}_i = b_0 + b_1 X_{1_i} + b_2 X_{1_i}^2 \qquad \textbf{9.29}$$

where $\hat{Y}_i$ represents the estimated selling price of the ith house in our sample, and X_{1_i} represents the total square footage in the house. Notice that the second independent variable in equation 9.29 is the first independent variable squared (X_1^2).

FIGURE 9.25

Data for nonlinear regression example

Obs	Sq. Feet (in 1000s)	Price (in $1000s)
1	1.000	$169
2	1.100	$173
3	1.200	$176
4	1.400	$178
5	1.600	$186
6	1.800	$197
7	1.900	$203
8	1.900	$208
9	2.100	$229
10	2.100	$237
11	2.200	$260

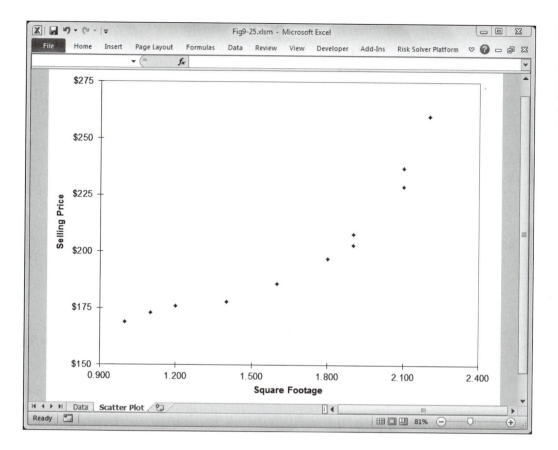

FIGURE 9.26

Scatter plot of data showing relationship between total square footage and selling price

9.17.1 EXPRESSING NONLINEAR RELATIONSHIPS USING LINEAR MODELS

Equation 9.29 is not a linear function because it contains the nonlinear variable X_1^2. It *is* linear with respect to the parameters the computer must estimate—namely, b_0, b_1, and b_2. That is, none of the parameters in the regression function appear as an exponent or are multiplied together. Thus, we can use least squares regression to estimate the optimal values for b_0, b_1, and b_2. Note that if we define a new independent variable as $X_{2_i} = X_{1_i}^2$, then the regression function in equation 9.29 is equivalent to:

$$\hat{Y}_i = b_0 + b_1 X_{1_i} + b_2 X_{2_i} \qquad \textbf{9.30}$$

Equation 9.30 is equivalent to the multiple linear regression function in equation 9.29. As long as a regression function is linear with respect to its parameters, we can use Excel's regression analysis tool use to find the least squares estimates for the parameters.

To fit the regression function in equation 9.30 to our data, we must create a second independent variable to represent the values of X_{2_i}, as shown in Figure 9.27 (and the file Fig9-27.xlsm that accompanies this book).

Because the X-Range for the Regression command must be represented as one contiguous block, we inserted a new column between the square footage and selling price columns and placed the values of X_{2_i} in this column. Note that $X_{2_i} = X_{1_i}^2$ in column C in Figure 9.27:

Formula for cell C3:   =B3^2

(Copy to C4 through C13.)

FIGURE 9.27

Modification of data to include squared independent variable

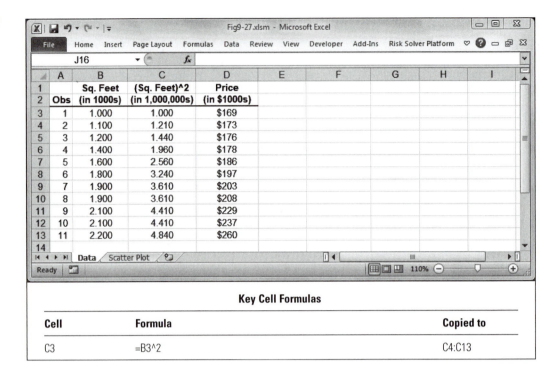

Key Cell Formulas

Cell	Formula	Copied to
C3	=B3^2	C4:C13

The regression results are generated with a Y-Range of D3:D13 and an X-Range of B3:C13. Figure 9.28 shows the regression results.

In Figure 9.28, the estimated regression function is represented by:

$$\hat{Y}_i = b_0 + b_1X_{1_i} + b_2X_{2_i} = 294.9714 - 203.3812X_{1_i} + 83.4063X_{2_i} \qquad \textbf{9.31}$$

FIGURE 9.28 *Regression results for nonlinear example problem*

	A	B	C	D	E	F	G	H	I
1	SUMMARY OUTPUT								
2									
3	*Regression Statistics*								
4	Multiple R	0.984952458							
5	R Square	0.970131344							
6	Adjusted R Square	0.96266418							
7	Standard Error	5.736768013							
8	Observations	11							
9									
10	ANOVA								
11		*df*	*SS*	*MS*	*F*	*Significance F*			
12	Regression	2	8551.443215	4275.721607	129.9196508	7.95908E-07			
13	Residual	8	263.2840579	32.91050723					
14	Total	10	8814.727273						
15									
16		*Coefficients*	*Standard Error*	*t Stat*	*P-value*	*Lower 95%*	*Upper 95%*	*Lower 95.0%*	*Upper 95.0%*
17	Intercept	294.9714091	34.23724921	8.615511351	2.55154E-05	216.0201709	373.9226474	216.0201709	373.9226474
18	X Variable 1	-203.381237	45.08699888	-4.51086215	0.001973565	-307.3520424	-99.4104307	-307.352042	-99.4104307
19	X Variable 2	83.40635268	14.04028535	5.940502675	0.000345639	51.0293966	115.7833088	51.0293966	115.7833088
20									

According to the R^2 statistic, this function accounts for 97.0% of the total variation in selling prices, so we expect that this function fits our data well. We can verify this by plotting the prices that would be estimated by the regression function in equation 9.31 for each observation in our sample against the actual selling prices.

To calculate the estimated selling prices, we applied the formula in equation 9.31 to each observation in the sample, as shown in Figure 9.29 where the following formula was entered in cell E3, and then copied to cells E4 through E20:

> Formula for cell E3:   =TREND($D$3:$D$13,$B$3:$C$13,B3:C3)
>
> (Copy to E4 through E13.)

Figure 9.30 shows a curve representing the estimated prices calculated in column E of Figure 9.29. This curve was added to our previous scatter plot as follows:

1. Right-click on any of the data points in the scatter plot to select the series of data.
2. Click Add Trendline.
3. Click Polynomial, and use an Order value of 2.
4. Select Display Equation on Chart and Display R-squared Value on Chart.
5. Click Close.

This graph indicates that our regression model accounts for the nonlinear, quadratic relationship between the square footage and selling price of a house in a reasonably accurate manner.

Figure 9.31 shows the result obtained by fitting a third-order polynomial model to our data of the form:

$$\hat{Y}_i = b_0 + b_1 X_{1_i} + b_2 X_{1_i}^2 + b_3 X_{1_i}^3 \qquad \textbf{9.32}$$

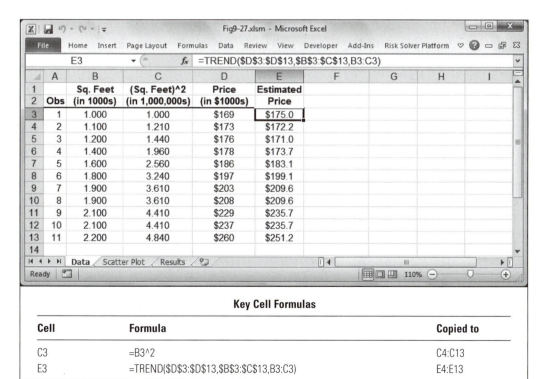

FIGURE 9.29

Estimated selling prices using a second order polynomial model

Key Cell Formulas

Cell	Formula	Copied to
C3	=B3^2	C4:C13
E3	=TREND($D$3:$D$13,$B$3:$C$13,B3:C3)	E4:E13

FIGURE 9.30

Plot of estimated regression function versus actual data

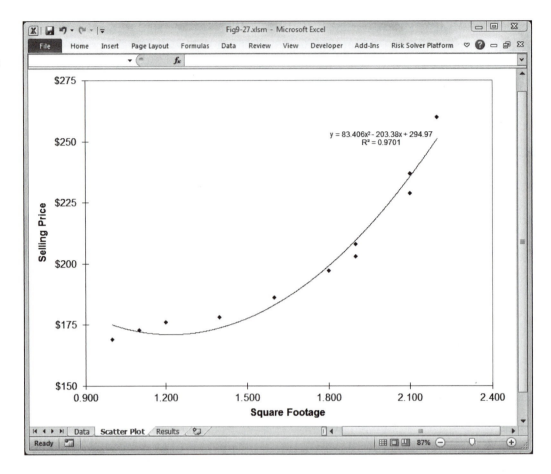

This model appears to provide an even better fit than the model shown in Figure 9.30. As you might imagine, we could continue to add higher order terms to the model and further increase the value of the R^2 statistic. Here again, the adjusted-R^2 statistic could help us select a model that provides a good fit to our data without overfitting the data.

9.17.2 SUMMARY OF NONLINEAR REGRESSION

This brief example of a polynomial regression problem highlights the fact that regression analysis can be used not only in fitting straight lines or hyperplanes to linear data but also in fitting other types of curved surfaces to nonlinear data. An in-depth discussion of nonlinear regression is beyond the intended scope of this book, but a wealth of information is available on this topic in numerous texts devoted solely to regression analysis.

This example should help you appreciate the importance of preparing scatter plots of each independent variable against the dependent variable in a regression problem to see if the relationship between the variables is linear or nonlinear. Relatively simple nonlinear relationships, such as the one described in the previous example, can often be accounted for by including squared or cubed terms in the model. In more complicated cases, sophisticated transformations of the dependent or independent variables might be required.

FIGURE 9.31

Plot of estimated regression function using a third order polynomial model

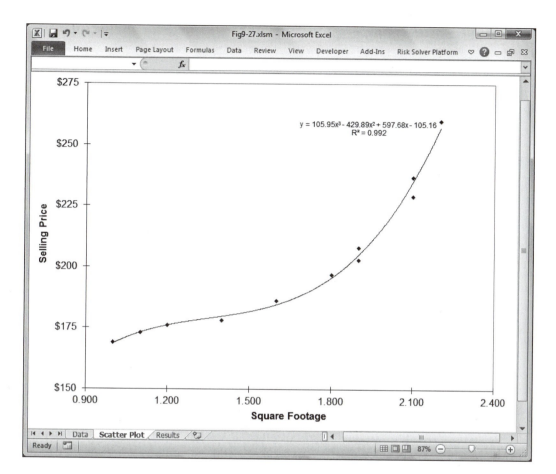

9.18 Summary

Regression analysis is a statistical technique that can be used to identify and analyze the relationship between one or more independent variables and a continuous dependent variable. This chapter presented an overview of some key issues involved in performing regression analysis and demonstrated some of the tools and methods available in Excel to assist managers in performing regression analysis.

The goal in regression analysis is to identify a function of the independent variables that adequately accounts for the behavior of the dependent variable. The method of least squares provides a way to determine the best values for the parameters in a regression model for a given sample of data. After identifying such a function, it can be used to predict what value the dependent variable will assume given specific values for the independent variables. Various statistical techniques are available for evaluating how well a given regression function fits a data set and for determining which independent variables are most helpful in explaining the behavior of the dependent variable. Although regression functions can assume a variety of forms, this chapter focused on linear regression models where a linear combination of the independent variables is used to model the dependent variable. Simple transformations of the independent variables can allow this type of model to fit both linear and nonlinear data sets.

9.19 References

Montgomery D., and E. Peck. *Introduction to Linear Regression Analysis.* New York: Wiley, 1991.
Neter, J., W. Wasserman, and M. Kutner. *Applied Linear Statistical Models.* Homewood, IL: Irwin, 1990.
Younger, M. *A First Course in Linear Regression.* Boston: Duxbury Press, 1985.

THE WORLD OF MANAGEMENT SCIENCE

Better Predictions Create Cost Savings for Ohio National Bank

The Ohio National Bank in Columbus must process checks for clearing in a timely manner in order to minimize float. This had been difficult because of wide and seemingly unpredictable variations in the volume of checks received.

As checks pass through the processing center, they are encoded with the dollar amount in magnetic ink at the bottom of the check. This operation requires a staff of clerks, whose work schedules must be planned so that staffing is adequate during peak times. Because the bank could not accurately predict these peaks, deadlines often were missed, and the clerks often were required to work overtime.

The variations in check volume seemed to be caused by changes in business activity brought about by the calendar—that is, volume was influenced by certain months, days of the week, days of the month, and proximity to certain holidays. A linear regression model was developed to predict staffing needs using a set of binary (dummy) independent variables representing these calendar effects. The regression study was very successful. The resulting model had a coefficient of determination (R^2) of 0.94 and a mean absolute percentage error of 6%. The bank then used these predictions as input to an LP shift-scheduling model that minimized the number of clerks needed to cover the predicted check volumes.

The planning process required data on check volumes and productivity estimates from the line supervisors in the encoding department. Initial reluctance of the supervisors to supply this information presented an obstacle to the implementation of the system. Eventually, this was overcome by taking time to explain the reasons for the data collection to the supervisors.

The new system provides estimated savings of $700,000 in float costs and $300,000 in labor costs. The close-out time of 10 pm is now met 98% of the time; previously, it was rarely met. Management has performed sensitivity analysis with the model to study the effects of productivity improvements associated with employing experienced full-time encoding clerks instead of part-time clerks.

Source: Krajewski, L. J., and L. P. Ritzman, "Shift Scheduling in Banking Operations: A Case Application." *Interfaces*, vol. 10, no. 2, April 1980, pp 1–6.

Questions and Problems

1. Members of the Roanoke Health and Fitness Club pay an annual membership fee of $250 plus $3 each time they use the facility. Let X denote the number of times a person visits the club during the year. Let Y denote the total annual cost for membership in the club.
   a. What is the mathematical relationship between X and Y?
   b. Is this a functional or statistical relationship? Explain your answer.
2. In comparing two different regression models that were developed using the same data, we might say that the model with the higher R^2 value will provide the most accurate predictions. Is this true? Why or why not?
3. Show how R_a^2 and S_e are related algebraically (identify the function $f(\cdot)$ such that $R_a^2 = f(S_e)$).
4. Least squares regression finds the estimated values for the parameters in a regression model to minimize $\text{ESS} = \sum_{i=1}^{n} (Y_i - \hat{Y}_i)^2$. Why is it necessary to square the estimation errors? What problem might be encountered if we attempt to minimize just the sum of the estimation errors?
5. Suppose you are interested in creating a prediction interval for Y at a particular value of X_1 (denoted by X_{1_h}) using a simple linear regression model, and data has not yet been collected. For a given sample size n, how you would attempt to collect the sample data to make the most accurate prediction? (*Hint*: Consider equation 9.14.)
6. An accounting firm that specializes in auditing mining companies collected the data found in the file Dat9-6.xlsx that accompanies this book describing the long-term assets and long-term debt of its 12 clients.
   a. Prepare a scatter plot of the data. Does there appear to be a linear relationship between these variables?
   b. Develop a simple linear regression model that can be used to predict long-term debt from long-term assets. What is the estimated regression equation?
   c. Interpret the value of R^2.
   d. Suppose that the accounting firm has a client with total assets of $50,000,000. Construct an approximate 95% confidence interval for the amount of long-term debt the firm expects this client to have.
7. The IRS wants to develop a method for detecting whether or not individuals have overstated their deductions for charitable contributions on their tax returns. To assist in this effort, the IRS supplied data found in the file Dat9-7.xlsx that accompanies this book listing the adjusted gross income (AGI) and charitable contributions for 11 taxpayers whose returns were audited and found to be correct.
   a. Prepare a scatter plot of the data. Does there appear to be a linear relationship between these variables?
   b. Develop a simple linear regression model that can be used to predict the level of charitable contributions from a return's AGI. What is the estimated regression equation?
   c. Interpret the value of R^2.
   d. How might the IRS use the regression results to identify returns with unusually high charitable contributions?
8. Roger Gallagher owns a used car lot that deals solely in used Corvettes. He wants to develop a regression model to help predict the price he can expect to receive for the cars he owns. He collected the data found in the file Dat9-8.xlsx that accompanies this book describing the mileage, model year, presence of a T-top, and selling price

of a number of cars he has sold in recent months. Let Y represent the selling price, X_1 the mileage, X_2 the model year, and X_3 the presence (or absence) of a T-top.

a. If Roger wants to use a simple linear regression function to estimate the selling price of a car, which X variable do you recommend he use?

b. Determine the parameter estimates for the regression function represented by:

$$\hat{Y}_i = b_0 + b_1X_{1_i} + b_2X_{2_i}$$

What is the estimated regression function? Does X_2 help to explain the selling price of the cars if X_1 is also in the model? What might be the reason for this?

c. Set up a binary variable (X_{3_i}) to indicate whether or not each car in the sample has a T-top. Determine the parameter estimates for the regression function represented by:

$$\hat{Y}_i = b_0 + b_1X_{1_i} + b_3X_{3_i}$$

Does X_3 help to explain the selling price of the cars if X_1 is also in the model? Explain.

d. According to the previous model, on average, how much does a T-top add to the value of a car?

e. Determine the parameter estimates for the regression function represented by:

$$\hat{Y}_i = b_0 + b_1X_{1_i} + b_2X_{2_i} + b_3X_{3_i}$$

What is the estimated regression function?

f. Of all the regression functions considered here, which do you recommend Roger use?

9. Refer to question 8. Prepare scatter plots of the values of X_1 and X_2 against Y.

a. Do these relationships seem to be linear or nonlinear?

b. Determine the parameter estimates for the regression function represented by:

$$\hat{Y}_i = b_0 + b_1X_{1_i} + b_2X_{2_i} + b_3X_{3_i} + b_4X_{4_i}$$

where $X_{4_i} = X_{2_i}^2$. What is the estimated regression function?

c. Consider the p-values for each β_i in this model. Do these values indicate that any of the independent variables should be dropped from the model?

10. Golden Years Easy Retirement Homes owns several adult care facilities throughout the southeast United States. A budget analyst for Golden Years has collected the data found in the file Dat9-10.xlsx that accompanies this book describing for each facility: the number of beds (X_1), the annual number of medical in-patient days (X_2), the total annual patient days (X_3), and whether or not the facility is in a rural location (X_4). The analyst would like to build a multiple regression model to estimate the annual nursing salaries (Y) that should be expected for each facility.

a. Prepare scatter plots showing the relationship between the nursing salaries and each of the independent variables. What sort of relationship does each plot suggest?

b. If the budget analyst wanted to build a regression model using only one independent variable to predict the nursing salaries, what variable should be used?

c. If the budget analyst wanted to build a regression model using only two independent variables to predict the nursing salaries, what variables should be used?

d. If the budget analyst wanted to build a regression model using three independent variables to predict the nursing salaries, what variables should be used?

e. What set of independent variables results in the highest value for the adjusted R^2 statistic?

f. Suppose the personnel director chooses to use the regression function with all independent variables X_1, X_2, and X_3. What is the estimated regression function?

g. In your spreadsheet, calculate an estimated annual nursing salary for each facility using the regression function identified in part f. Based on this analysis, which facilities, if any, should the budget analyst be concerned about? Explain your answer.

11. The O-rings in the booster rockets on the space shuttle are designed to expand when heated to seal different chambers of the rocket so that solid rocket fuel is not ignited prematurely. According to engineering specifications, the O-rings expand by some amount, say at least 5%, in order to ensure a safe launch. Hypothetical data on the amount of O-ring expansion and the atmospheric temperature in Fahrenheit at the time of several different launches are given in the file Dat9-11.xlsx that accompanies this book.
   a. Prepare a scatter plot of the data. Does there appear to be a linear relationship between these variables?
   b. Obtain a simple linear regression model to estimate the amount of O-ring expansion as a function of atmospheric temperature. What is the estimated regression function?
   c. Interpret the R^2 statistic for the model you obtained.
   d. Suppose that NASA officials are considering launching a space shuttle when the temperature is 29 degrees. What amount of O-ring expansion should they expect at this temperature according to your model?
   e. On the basis of your analysis of these data, would you recommend that the shuttle be launched if the temperature is 29 degrees? Why or why not?

12. An analyst for Phidelity Investments wants to develop a regression model to predict the annual rate of return for a stock based on the price-earnings (PE) ratio of the stock and a measure of the stock's risk. The data found in the file Dat9-12.xlsx were collected for a random sample of stocks.
   a. Prepare scatter plots for each independent variable versus the dependent variable. What types of model do these scatter plots suggest might be appropriate for the data?
   b. Let Y = Return, X_1 = PE Ratio, and X_2 = Risk. Obtain the regression results for the following regression model:

   $$\hat{Y}_i = b_0 + b_1 X_{1_i} + b_2 X_{2_i}$$

   Interpret the value of R2 for this model.
   c. Obtain the regression results for the following regression model:

   $$\hat{Y}_i = b_0 + b_1 X_{1_i} + b_2 X_{2_i} + b_3 X_{3_i} + b_4 X_{4_i}$$

   where $X_{3_i} = X_{1_i}^2$ and $X_{4_i} = X_{2_i}^2$. Interpret the value of R^2 for this model.
   d. Which of the previous two models would you recommend that the analyst use?

13. Oriented Strand Board (OSB) is manufactured by gluing wood chips together to form panels. Several panels are then bonded together to form a board. One of the factors influencing the strength of the final board is the amount of glue used in the production process. An OSB manufacturer conducted a test to determine the breaking point of a board based on the amount of glue used in the production process. In each test, a board was manufactured using a given amount of glue. Weight was then applied to determine the point at which the board would fail (or break). This test was performed 27 times using various amounts of glue. The data obtained from this testing may be found in the file Dat9-13.xlsx that accompanies this book.
   a. Prepare a scatter plot of this data.
   b. What type of regression function would you use to fit this data?
   c. Estimate the parameters of the regression function. What is the estimated regression function?

    d. Interpret the value of the R^2 statistic.

    e. Suppose the company wants to manufacture boards that will withstand up to 110 lbs. of pressure per square inch. How much glue should they use?

14. When interest rates decline, Patriot Bank has found they get inundated with requests to refinance home mortgages. To better plan its staffing needs in the mortgage processing area of its operations, Patriot wants to develop a regression model to help predict the total number of mortgage applications (Y) each month as a function of the prime interest rate (X_1). The bank collected the data shown in the file Dat9-14.xlsx that accompanies this book representing the average prime interest rate and total number of mortgage applications in 20 different months.

    a. Prepare a scatter plot of these data.

    b. Fit the following regression model to the data:

$$\hat{Y}_i = b_0 + b_1 X_{1_i}$$

    Plot the number of monthly mortgage applications that are estimated by this model along with the actual values in the sample. How well does this model fit the data?

    c. Using the previous model, develop a 95% prediction interval for the number of mortgage applications Patriot could expect to receive in a month where the interest rate is 6%. Interpret this interval.

    d. Fit the following regression model to the data:

$$\hat{Y}_i = b_0 + b_1 X_{1_i} + b_2 X_{2_i}$$

    where $X_{2_i} = X_{1_i}^2$. Plot the number of monthly mortgage applications that are estimated by this model along with the actual values in the sample. How well does this model fit the data?

    e. Using the previous model, develop a 95% prediction interval for the number of mortgage applications Patriot could expect to receive in a month where the interest rate is 6%. Interpret this interval.

    f. Which model would you suggest Patriot Bank use and why?

15. Creative Confectioners is planning to introduce a new brownie. A small-scale "taste test" was conducted to assess consumer's preferences (Y) with regard to moisture content (X_1) and sweetness (X_2). Data from the taste test may be found in the file Dat9-15.xlsx that accompanies this book.

    a. Prepare a scatter plot of moisture content versus preference. What type of relationship does your plot suggest?

    b. Prepare a scatter plot of sweetness versus preference. What type of relationship does your plot suggest?

    c. Estimate the parameters for the following regression function:

$$\hat{Y}_i = b_0 + b_1 X_{1_i} + b_2 X_{1_i}^2 + b_3 X_{2_i} + b_4 X_{2_i}^2$$

    What is the estimated regression function?

    d. Using the estimated regression function in part c, what is the expected preference rating of a brownie recipe with a moisture content of 7 and a sweetness rating of 9.5?

16. *AutoReports* is a consumer magazine that reports on the cost of maintaining various types of automobiles. The magazine collected the data found in the file Dat9-16.xlsx that accompanies this book describing the annual maintenance cost of a certain type of luxury imported automobile along with the age of the car (in years).

    a. Prepare a scatter plot of these data.

    b. Let Y = Maintenance Cost and X = Age. Fit the following regression model to the data:

$$\hat{Y}_i = b_0 + b_1 X_{1_i}$$

Plot the maintenance costs that are estimated by this model along with the actual costs in the sample. How well does this model fit the data?

c. Fit the following regression model to the data:

$$\hat{Y}_i = b_0 + b_1X_{1_i} + b_2X_{2_i}$$

where $X_{2_i} = X_{1_i}^2$. Plot the maintenance costs that are estimated by this model along with the actual costs in the sample. How well does this model fit the data?

d. Fit the following regression model to this data:

$$\hat{Y}_i = b_0 + b_1X_{1_i} + b_2X_{2_i} + b_3X_{3_i}$$

where $X_{2_i} = X_{1_i}^2$ and $X_{3_i} = X_{1_i}^3$. Plot the maintenance costs that are estimated by this model along with the actual costs in the sample. How well does this model fit the data?

17. Duque Power Company wants to develop a regression model to help predict its daily peak power demand. This prediction is useful in determining how much generating capacity needs to be available (or purchased from competitors) on a daily basis. The daily peak power demand is influenced primarily by the weather and the day of the week. The file Dat9-17.xlsx that accompanies this book contains data summarizing Duque's daily peak demand and maximum daily temperature during the month of July last year.

a. Build a simple linear regression model to predict peak power demand using maximum daily temperature. What is the estimated regression equation?

b. Prepare a line chart plotting the actual peak demand data against the values predicted by this regression equation. How well does the model fit the data?

c. Interpret the R^2 statistic for this model.

d. Build a multiple linear regression model to predict peak power demand using maximum daily temperature and the day of the week as independent variables. (Note: This model will have seven independent variables.) What is the estimated regression equation?

e. Prepare a line chart plotting the actual peak demand data against the values predicted by this regression equation. How well does the model fit the data?

f. Interpret the R^2 statistic for this model.

g. Using the model you developed in part d, what is the estimated peak power demand Duque should expect on a Wednesday in July when the daily high temperature is forecasted to be 94?

h. Compute a 95% prediction interval for the estimate in the previous question. Explain the managerial implications of this interval for Duque.

18. An appraiser collected the data found in file Dat9-18.xlsx that accompanies this book describing the auction selling price, diameter (in inches), and item type of several pieces of early 20th century metal tableware manufactured by a famous artisan. The item type variable is coded as follows: B = bowl, C = casserole pan, D = dish, T = tray, and P = plate. The appraiser wants to build a multiple regression model for this data to predict average selling prices of similar items.

a. Construct a multiple regression model for this problem. (*Hint*: Create binary independent variables to represent the item type data.) What is the estimated regression function?

b. Interpret the value of the R^2 statistic for this model.

c. Construct an approximate 95% prediction interval for the expected selling price of an 18-inch diameter casserole pan. Interpret this interval.

d. What other variables not included in the model might help explain the remaining variation in auction selling prices for these items?

19. Chris Smith is a sports car enthusiast with a particular love for Mini Coopers. He downloaded data from eBay on completed auctions of Mini Coopers and used it to create the data set in file Dat9-19.xlsx showing the selling prices, age, mileage, and location of Mini Cooper automobiles. He would like to use this data to build a regression model to predict the estimated selling price of Mini Coopers.
    a. Prepare scatter plots showing the relationship between selling price and each of the independent variables. What sort of relationship does each plot suggest?
    b. Using only the variables in this data set, what regression model has the highest R^2 value? What is the model, and what is its R^2 value?
    c. Using only the variables in this data set, what regression model has the highest adjusted R^2 value? What is the model, and what is its adjusted R^2 value?
    d. Which of the cars in this data set appear to be the best bargains relative to their estimated prices using the model identified in part c?
    e. What other variables, if available, might help Chris to build a more accurate regression model for this problem?

20. Hydroxyethyl cellulose (HEC) is a gelling and thickening agent created from a molecular combination of cellulose, ethylene oxide (EO), and nitric acid. It is designed to mix with a water-based solution to increase the viscosity of the mixture. This added viscosity acts as a suspension polymer that, for example, allows the herbs in a salad dressing to stay in the solution and not settle to the bottom of the bottle. Gaston Moat is a manufacturing engineer for the Atlas Corporation, which is one of the major manufacturers of HEC in the United States. He has collected the data given in file Dat9-20.xlsx from several production lots of HEC. For each production lot, he recorded the viscosity of the HEC (Y) produced along with the viscosity of the of the cellulose material used (X_1), the square root of the viscosity of the cellulose material used (X_2), the length of the cellulose fibers used (X_3), the amount (in pounds) of cellulose used (X_4), and amount (in pounds) of EO used, the temperature of the nitric acid used (X_5), and the ratio of cellulose to EO used (X_6). Atlas' customers often specify the average viscosity level needed for a particular HEC application. Gaston would like to build a multiple regression function to better understand how the various inputs in the production process relate to viscosity of the final HEC product.
    a. Prepare scatter plots showing the relationship between HEC viscosity and each of the independent variables. What sort of relationship does each plot suggest?
    b. Using the variables in this data set, what regression model has the highest R^2 value? What is the model, and what is its R^2 value?
    c. Using the variables in this data set, what regression model has the highest adjusted R^2 value? What is the model, and what is its adjusted R^2 value?
    d. Suppose a customer wants a batch of HEC with an average viscosity level of 7,000. Gaston plans to fill this order using a batch of cellulose with a viscosity of level of 20,300, an average fiber length of 30, and a nitric temperature of 50. How much EO should he plan to use in this batch to achieve the desired HEC average viscosity level?

21. The personnel director for a small manufacturing company has collected the data found in the file Dat9-21.xlsx that accompanies this book describing the salary (Y) earned by each machinist in the factory along with the average performance rating (X_1) over the past three years, the years of service (X_2), and the number of different machines each employee is certified to operate (X_3).

    The personnel director wants to build a regression model to estimate the average salary an employee should expect to receive based on his or her performance, years of service, and certifications.

a. Prepare three scatter plots showing the relationship between the salaries and each of the independent variables. What sort of relationship does each plot suggest?

b. If the personnel director wanted to build a regression model using only one independent variable to predict the salaries, what variable should be used?

c. If the personnel director wanted to build a regression model using only two independent variables to predict the salaries, what two variables should be used?

d. Compare the adjusted-R^2 statistics obtained in parts b and c with that of a regression model using all three independent variables. Which model would you recommend the personnel director use?

e. Suppose the personnel director chooses to use the regression function with all three independent variables. What is the estimated regression function?

f. Suppose the company considers an employee's salary to be "fair" if it is within 1.5 standard errors of the value estimated by the regression function in part e. What salary range would be appropriate for an employee with 12 years of service, who has received average reviews of 4.5, and is certified to operate 4 pieces of machinery?

22. Caveat Emptor, Inc. is a home inspection service that provides prospective homebuyers with a thorough assessment of the major systems in a house prior to the execution of the purchase contract. Prospective homebuyers often ask the company for an estimate of the average monthly heating cost of the home during the winter. To answer this question, the company wants to build a regression model to help predict the average monthly heating cost (Y) as a function of the average outside temperature in winter (X_1), the amount of attic insulation in the house (X_2), the age of the furnace in the house (X_3), and the size of the house measured in square feet (X_4). Data on these variables for a number of homes was collected and may be found in the file Dat9-22.xlsx that accompanies this book.

a. Prepare scatter plots showing the relationship between the average heating cost and each of the potential independent variables. What sort of relationship does each plot suggest?

b. If the company wanted to build a regression model using only one independent variable to predict the average heating cost of these houses, what variable should be used?

c. If the company wanted to build a regression model using only two independent variables to predict the average heating cost of these houses, what variables should be used?

d. If the company wanted to build a regression model using only three independent variables to predict the average heating cost of these houses, what variables should be used?

e. Suppose the company chooses to use the regression function with all four independent variables. What is the estimated regression function?

f. Suppose the company decides to use the model with the highest adjusted R^2 statistic. Develop a 95% prediction interval for the average monthly heating cost of a house with 4 inches of attic insulation, a 5-year-old furnace, 2,500 square feet, and in a location with an average outside winter temperature of 40 degrees. Interpret this interval.

23. Throughout our discussion of regression analysis, we used the Regression command to obtain the parameter estimates that minimize the sum of squared estimation errors. Suppose that we want to obtain parameter estimates that minimize the sum of the absolute value of the estimation errors, or:

$$\text{MIN:} \sum_{i=1}^{n} |Y_i - \hat{Y}_i|$$

a. Use Solver to obtain the parameter estimates for a simple linear regression function that minimizes the sum of the absolute value of the estimation errors for the data in question 9.

b. What advantages, if any, do you see in using this alternate objective to solve a regression problem?

c. What disadvantages, if any, do you see in using this alternate objective to solve a regression problem?

24. Throughout our discussion of regression analysis, we used the Regression command to obtain the parameter estimates that minimize the sum of squared estimation errors. Suppose that we want to obtain parameter estimates that minimize the absolute value of the maximum estimation error, or:

$$\text{MIN: MAX} (|Y_1 - \hat{Y}_1|, |Y_2 - \hat{Y}_2|, \ldots, |Y_n - \hat{Y}_n|)$$

a. Use Solver to obtain the parameter estimates for a simple linear regression function that minimizes the absolute value of the maximum estimation error for the data in question 9.

b. What advantages, if any, do you see in using this alternate objective to solve a regression problem?

c. What disadvantages, if any, do you see in using this alternate objective to solve a regression problem?

CASE 9.1 Diamonds Are Forever

(Inspired from actual events related by former Virginia Tech MBA student Brian Ellyson.)

With Christmas coming, Ryan Bellison was searching for the perfect gift for his wife. After several years of marriage, Ryan leaned back in his chair at the office and tried to think of the one thing his wife had wanted during the years they pinched pennies to get through graduate school. Then he remembered the way her eyes lit up last week when they walked by the jewelry store windows at the mall and she saw the diamond earrings. He knew he wanted to see that same look on her face Christmas morning. And so his hunt began for the perfect set of diamond earrings.

Ryan's first order of business was to educate himself about the things to look for when buying diamonds. After perusing the web, he learned about the "4Cs" of diamonds: cut, color, clarity, and carat (see http://www.adiamondisforever.com). He knew his wife wanted round cut earrings mounted in white gold settings, so he immediately narrowed his focus to evaluating color, clarity, and carat for that style of earring.

After a bit of searching, Ryan located a number of possible earring sets that he would consider purchasing. But he knew the pricing of diamonds varied considerably, and he wanted to make sure he didn't get ripped off. To assist in his decision making, Ryan decided to use regression analysis to develop a model to predict the retail price of different sets of round cut earrings based on their color, clarity, and carat scores. He assembled the data in the file Diamonds.xlsx that accompanies this book for this purpose. Use this data to answer the following questions for Ryan.

1. Prepare scatter plots showing the relationship between the earring prices (Y) and each of the potential independent variables. What sort of relationship does each plot suggest?

2. Let X_1, X_2, and X_3 represent diamond color, clarity, and carats, respectively. If Ryan wanted to build a linear regression model to estimate earring prices using these variables, which variables would you recommend he use? Why?

3. Suppose Ryan decides to use clarity (X_2) and carats (X_3) as independent variables in a regression model to predict earring prices. What is the estimated regression equation? What is the value of the R^2 and adjusted-R^2 statistics?

4. Use the regression equation identified in the previous question to create estimated prices for each of the earring sets in Ryan's sample. Which sets of earrings appear to be overpriced, and which appear to be bargains? Based on this analysis, which set of earrings would you suggest Ryan purchase?

5. Ryan now remembers that it sometimes helps to perform a square root transformation on the dependent variable in a regression problem. Modify your spreadsheet to include a new dependent variable that is the square root on the earring prices (use Excel's SQRT( ) function). If Ryan wanted to build a linear regression model to estimate the square root of earring prices using the same independent variables as before, which variables would you recommend he use? Why?

6. Suppose Ryan decides to use clarity (X_2) and carats (X_3) as independent variables in a regression model to predict the square root of the earring prices. What is the estimated regression equation? What is the value of the R^2 and adjusted-R^2 statistics?

7. Use the regression equation identified in the previous question to create estimated prices for each of the earring sets in Ryan's sample. (Remember, your model estimates the square root of the earring prices. So you must square the model's estimates to convert them to actually price estimates.) Which sets of earring appears to be overpriced, and which appear to be bargains? Based on this analysis, which set of earrings would you suggest Ryan purchase?

8. Ryan now also remembers that it sometimes helps to include interaction terms in a regression model—where you create a new independent variable as the product of two of the original variables. Modify your spreadsheet to include three new independent variables X_4, X_5, and X_6 representing interaction terms where $X_4 = X_1 \times X_2$, $X_5 = X_1 \times X_3$, and $X_6 = X_2 \times X_3$. There are now six potential independent variables. If Ryan wanted to build a linear regression model to estimate the square root of earring prices using some combination of these six independent variables, which variables would you recommend he use? Why?

9. Suppose Ryan decides to use color (X_1), carats (X_3), and the interaction terms X_4 and X_5 as independent variables in a regression model to predict the square root of the earring prices. What is the estimated regression equation? What is the value of the R^2 and adjusted-R^2 statistics?

10. Use the regression equation identified in the previous question to create estimated prices for each of the earring sets in Ryan's sample. (Remember, your model estimates the square root of the earring prices. So you must square the model's estimates to convert them to actually price estimates.) Which sets of earring appear to be overpriced, and which appear to be bargains? Based on this analysis, which set of earrings would you suggest Ryan purchase?

Fiasco in Florida   CASE 9.2

The 2000 U.S. presidential election was one of the most controversial in history with the final outcome ultimately being decided in a court of law rather than in the voting booth. At issue were the election results in Palm Beach, Florida. Palm Beach County used a so-called "butterfly" ballot where the candidates' names were arranged to the left and right of a center row of holes. Voters were to specify their preference by "punching" the appropriate hole next to the desired candidate. According to several news accounts, many voters in Palm Beach, Florida, claimed they were confused by the ballot structure and may have inadvertently voted for Pat Buchanan when in fact they intended to vote for Al Gore. This allegedly contributed to Gore not obtaining enough votes to overtake George W. Bush's slim margin of victory in Florida and ultimately cost Gore the election.

The file Votes.xlsx that accompanies this book contains the original vote totals by Florida county for Gore, Bush, and Buchanan as of November 8, 2000. (These data reflect the results prior to the hand recount that was done due to other problems with the election in Florida, for example, the "hanging chad" problem.) Use the data in this file to answer the following questions.

1. What was George W. Bush's margin of victory in Florida?
2. Prepare a scatter plot showing the relationship between the number of votes received by Gore (X-axis) and Buchanan (Y-axis) in each county. Does there appear to be any outliers? If so, for what counties?
3. Estimate the parameters for a simple linear regression model for predicting the number of votes for Buchanan in each county (excluding Palm Beach County) as a function of the number of votes for Gore. What is the estimated regression equation?
4. Interpret the value for R^2 obtained using the equation from question 3.
5. Using the regression results from question 3, develop a 99% prediction interval for the number of votes you expect Buchanan to receive in Palm Beach County. What are the upper- and lower limits of that interval? How does this compare with the actual number of votes reported for Buchanan in Palm Beach County?
6. Prepare a scatter plot showing the relationship between the number of votes received by Bush (X-axis) and Buchanan (Y-axis) in each county. Does there appear to be any outliers? If so, for what counties?
7. Estimate the parameters for a simple linear regression model for predicting the number of votes for Buchanan in each county (excluding Palm Beach County) as a function of the number of votes for Bush. What is the estimated regression equation?
8. Interpret the value for R^2 obtained using the equation from question 7.
9. Using the regression results from question 7, develop a 99% prediction interval for the number of votes you expect Buchanan to receive in Palm Beach County. What are the upper- and lower limits of that interval? How does this compare with the actual number of votes reported for Buchanan in Palm Beach County?
10. What do these results suggest? What assumptions are being made by using regression analysis in this way?

CASE 9.3   The Georgia Public Service Commission

(Inspired by discussions with Mr. Nolan E. Ragsdale of Banks County, Georgia.)

Nolan Banks is an auditor for the Public Service Commission for the state of Georgia. The Public Service Commission is a government agency responsible for ensuring that utility companies throughout the state manage their operations efficiently so that they can provide quality services to the public at fair prices.

Georgia is the largest state east of the Mississippi River, and various communities and regions throughout the state have different companies that provide water, power, and phone service. These companies have a monopoly in the areas they serve and, therefore, could take unfair advantage of the public. One of Nolan's jobs is to visit the companies and audit their financial records to detect whether or not any abuse is occurring.

A major problem Nolan faces in his job is determining whether the expenses reported by the utility companies are reasonable. For example, when he reviews a financial report for a local phone company, he might see line maintenance costs of $1,345,948, and he needs to determine if this amount is reasonable. This determination is complicated by the fact that the companies differ in size—so he cannot compare the costs of one company directly to another. Similarly, he cannot come up with a simple ratio to determine costs (such as 2% for the ratio of line maintenance costs to total revenue) because a single ratio might not be appropriate for companies of different sizes.

To help solve this problem, Nolan wants you to build a regression model to estimate what level of line maintenance expense would be expected for companies of different sizes. One measure of size for a phone company is the number of customers it has. Nolan collected the data in the file PhoneService.xlsx that accompanies this book representing the number of customers and line maintenance expenses of 12 companies he audited in the past year and determined were being run in a reasonably efficient manner.

1. Enter the data in a spreadsheet.
2. Create a scatter diagram of these data.
3. Use regression to estimate the parameters for the following linear equation for the data.

$$\hat{Y} = b_0 + b_1 X_1$$

What is the estimated regression equation?
4. Interpret the value for R^2 obtained using the equation from question 3.
5. According to the equation in question 3, what level of line maintenance expense would be expected for a phone company with 75,000 customers? Show how you arrive at this value.
6. Suppose that a phone company with 75,000 customers reports a line maintenance expense of $1,500,000. Based on the results of the linear model, should Nolan view this amount as reasonable or excessive?
7. In your spreadsheet, calculate the estimated line maintenance expense that would be predicted by the regression function for each company in the sample. Plot the predicted values you calculate on your graph (connected with a line) along with the original data. Does it appear that a linear regression model is appropriate?
8. Use regression to estimate the parameters for the following quadratic equation for the data:

$$\hat{Y} = b_0 + b_1 X_1 + b_2 X_1^2$$

To do this, you must insert a new column in your spreadsheet next to the original X values. In this new column, calculate the values X_1^2. What is the new estimated regression equation for this model?
9. Interpret the value for R^2 obtained using the equation in question 8.
10. What is the value for the adjusted-R^2 statistic? What does this statistic tell you?
11. What level of line maintenance expense would be expected for a phone company with 75,000 customers according to this new estimated regression function? Show how you arrive at this value.
12. In your spreadsheet, calculate the estimated line maintenance expense that would be predicted by the quadratic regression function for each company in the sample. Plot these values on your graph (connected with a line) along with the original data and the original regression line.
13. Suppose that a phone company with 75,000 customers reports a line maintenance expense of $1,500,000. Based on the results of the quadratic model, should Nolan view this amount as reasonable or excessive?
14. Which of the two regression functions would you suggest Nolan use for prediction purposes?

Chapter 10

Discriminant Analysis

10.0 Introduction

Discriminant analysis (DA) is a statistical technique that uses the information available in a set of independent variables to predict the value of a *discrete*, or *categorical*, dependent variable. Typically, the dependent variable in a DA problem is coded as a series of integer values representing various groups to which the observations in a sample belong. The goal of DA is to develop a rule for predicting to what group a new observation is most likely to belong based on the values the independent variables assume. To gain an understanding of the purpose and value of DA, consider the following business situations where DA could be useful.

- **Credit scoring.** The credit manager of a mortgage company classifies the loans it has made into two groups: those resulting in default and those that are current. For each loan, the manager has data describing the income, assets, liabilities, credit history, and employment history of the person who received the loan. The manager wants to use this information to develop a rule for predicting whether or not a new loan applicant will default if granted a loan.
- **Insurance rating.** An automotive insurance company uses claims data from the past five years to classify its current policyholders into three categories: high risk, moderate risk, and low risk. The company has data describing each policyholder's age, marital status, number of children, educational level, employment record, and number of traffic citations received during the past five years. The company wants to analyze how the three groups differ with regard to these characteristics and use this information to predict into which risk category a new insurance applicant is likely to fall.

DA differs from most other predictive statistical methods (for example, regression analysis) because the dependent variable is *discrete*, or *categorical*, rather than *continuous*. For instance, in the first example given previously, the credit manager wants to predict whether a loan applicant will (1) default or (2) repay the loan. Similarly, in the second example, the company wants to predict into which risk category a new client is most likely to fall: (1) high risk, (2) moderate risk, or (3) low risk. In each example, we can arbitrarily assign a number (1, 2, 3, . . .) to each group represented in the problem, and our goal is to predict to which group (1, 2, 3, . . .) a new observation is most likely to belong.

It might seem that we could handle these types of problems with least squares regression by using the independent variables to predict the value of a discrete dependent variable coded to indicate the group membership (1, 2, 3, . . .) of each observation in the sample. This is true for problems involving only two groups, such as the credit-scoring example given earlier. However, the regression approach does not work in problems involving more than two groups, such as the insurance-rating example. Because many DA problems involve the analysis of only two groups, we will split our discussion of DA into two parts. The first introduces the concepts of DA and covers the regression approach to the two-group problem. The second presents the more general k-group problem in DA (where $k \geq 2$).

10.1 The Two-Group DA Problem

The following personnel selection example illustrates the regression approach to two-group DA. Later, we will extend this example to illustrate the more general k-group approach to DA.

> In her role as personnel director for ACME Manufacturing, Marie Becker is responsible for interviewing and hiring new hourly employees for the factory. As part of the preemployment screening process, each prospective hourly employee is required to take an exam that measures mechanical and verbal aptitudes. Marie has access to historical data on the test scores received by all of ACME's current employees. As part of an annual performance evaluation, each factory employee is rated as performing at either a satisfactory or unsatisfactory level. Marie also has access to these data. Marie wants to analyze the data about current employees to see if there are differences between the preemployment test scores for the satisfactory and unsatisfactory workers. If so, she wants to use this information to develop a rule for predicting whether or not a new potential employee will be a satisfactory or unsatisfactory worker on the basis of the test scores.

This example is somewhat oversimplified because it involves only two independent, or explanatory, variables—the mechanical and verbal aptitude test scores. The personnel director probably has access to many more variables that are likely to be important determinants of satisfactory and unsatisfactory job performance. However, this example is restricted to two independent variables for convenience in illustrating how DA works. The approach to DA described here can be applied to problems involving any number of independent variables.

The two groups of interest in this example—satisfactory and unsatisfactory employees—will be labeled group 1 and group 2, respectively. The mechanical and verbal aptitude test scores for the current ACME employees are listed in Figure 10.1 (and in the file Fig10-1.xlsm that accompanies this book) in the Mechanical and Verbal columns. We will refer to this group of observations as the "training sample" because we will use this data set to train or develop a rule for classifying new job applicants. The Group column in the spreadsheet contains the value 1 for observations representing satisfactory employees, and the value 2 for unsatisfactory employees.

10.1.1 GROUP LOCATIONS AND CENTROIDS

Because this data set includes only two independent variables, we can display these data graphically, as shown in Figure 10.2. The ovals drawn in Figure 10.2 outline the typical observations for group 1 and group 2. The points in Figure 10.2 labeled "C_1" and "C_2" represent the centroids for group 1 and group 2, respectively. A group's **centroid** is the set of averages for the independent variables for the group. The centroid indicates where a group is centered, or located. The coordinates of the group centroids are calculated in Figure 10.1 in the rows labeled "Group Averages" as:

Formula for cell C24:   =AVERAGEIF($B$4:$B$23,$B24,C$4:C$23)

(Copy to C24 through D25.)

FIGURE 10.1 *Data for current ACME employees*

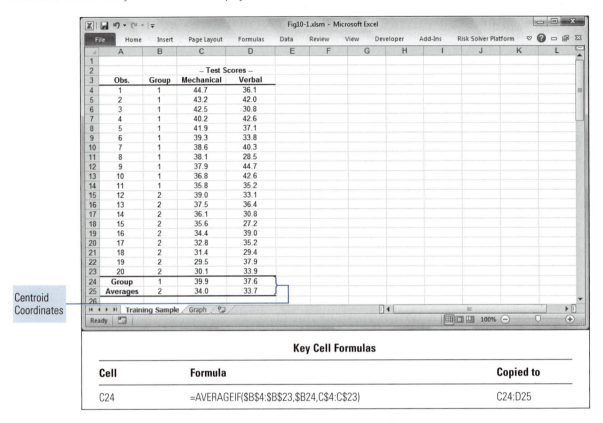

Obs.	Group	Mechanical	Verbal
1	1	44.7	36.1
2	1	43.2	42.0
3	1	42.5	30.8
4	1	40.2	42.6
5	1	41.9	37.1
6	1	39.3	33.8
7	1	38.6	40.3
8	1	38.1	28.5
9	1	37.9	44.7
10	1	36.8	42.6
11	1	35.8	35.2
12	2	39.0	33.1
13	2	37.5	36.4
14	2	36.1	30.8
15	2	35.6	27.2
16	2	34.4	39.0
17	2	32.8	35.2
18	2	31.4	29.4
19	2	29.5	37.9
20	2	30.1	33.9
Group	1	39.9	37.6
Averages	2	34.0	33.7

Centroid Coordinates

Key Cell Formulas

Cell	Formula	Copied to
C24	=AVERAGEIF($B$4:$B$23,$B24,C$4:C$23)	C24:D25

FIGURE 10.2

Graph of data for current employees

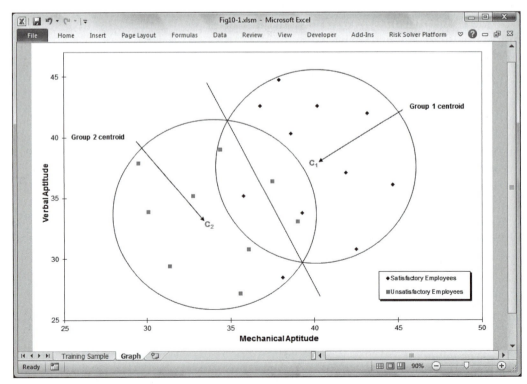

The AVERAGEIF( ) function in cell C24 compares the values in the range B4 through B23 to the value in B24 and, if a match occurs, averages the corresponding value in the range C4 through C23. Thus, the number displayed by the formula in cell C24 represents the average mechanical aptitude test score for employees in group 1. The values computed in cells C25, D24, and D25 have similar interpretations for their respective groups and test scores. Note that the centroid for group 1 is (39.9, 37.6), and the centroid for group 2 is (34.0, 33.7).

We might expect that the more the centroids for the groups in a DA problem differ, the easier it is to distinguish between the groups. In general, this is true. For example, because the group centroids in Figure 10.2 are well separated, it is easy to see that the unsatisfactory employees tend to have lower mechanical and verbal aptitudes than the satisfactory employees. However, if the two groups' centroids were both located at the same point, it would be difficult to tell which group an observation belonged to based on only its location because all observations would be scattered around the same centroid point.

Although the groups in Figure 10.2 are well separated, the two groups overlap. This overlapping area makes it difficult to establish a rule or boundary line for separating the satisfactory employees from the unsatisfactory ones. One such boundary line has been drawn arbitrarily in Figure 10.2. DA provides an objective means for determining the best straight line for separating or distinguishing between groups.

10.1.2 CALCULATING DISCRIMINANT SCORES

Viewing the data in Figure 10.1 from a regression perspective, we want to model the behavior of the group variable using the mechanical and verbal aptitude test scores. In the following regression equation, the dependent variable $\hat{Y}$ represents the estimated value of the Group variable, and X_1 and X_2 correspond to values for the independent variables representing the mechanical and verbal test scores, respectively:

$$\hat{Y}_i = b_0 + b_1 X_{1_i} + b_2 X_{2_i} \qquad \text{10.1}$$

Note that we can expand equation 10.1 easily to include any number of independent variables. But regardless of the number of independent variables in a problem, the purpose of the regression equation is to combine the information available in the variables into a single-valued estimate of the group variable. This estimated value of the Group variable is referred to as a **discriminant score** and is denoted by $\hat{Y}$. But what are the values of b_0, b_1, and b_2 that will result in the best discriminant scores for our data? We can use the regression tool in Excel to estimate these values.

The Regression dialog box in Figure 10.3 shows the settings required for the current problem. Notice that the Input Y Range entry corresponds to the group values shown in Figure 10.1, and the Input X Range entry corresponds to the values of the mechanical and verbal aptitude test scores. Figure 10.4 shows the regression results.

The estimated value for b_0 is represented by the Intercept value in cell B17 of Figure 10.4, and the estimated values for b_1 and b_2 are shown in cells B18 and B19, respectively. Thus, our estimated regression function is:

$$\hat{Y}_i = 5.373 - 0.0791 X_{1_i} - 0.0272 X_{2_i} \qquad \text{10.2}$$

FIGURE 10.3

Regression dialog box for the personnel selection example

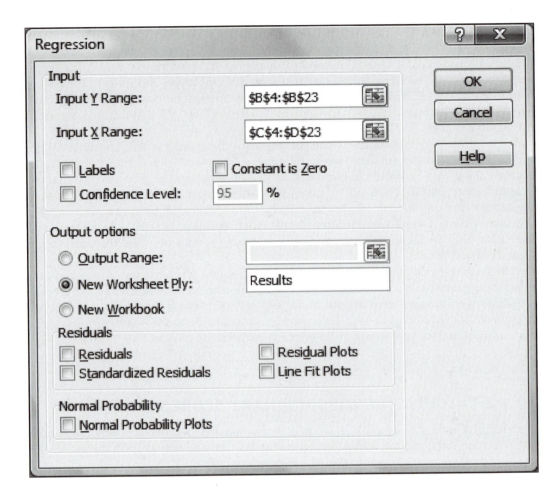

FIGURE 10.4

Regression results for the personnel selection example

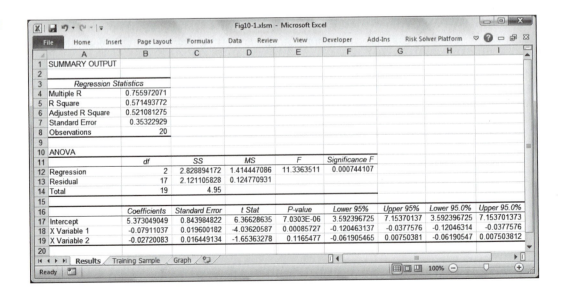

Non-Normality Note

Note that because the dependent variable in a two-group DA problem assumes only two possible values, it cannot be a normally distributed variable. Thus, virtually all of the statistical results in the regression output for a two-group DA problem are not subject to their usual interpretation. Even the R^2 statistic is not a particularly meaningful goodness-of-fit measure for these types of problems. Later, we'll discuss another way to assess how well a given regression function performs on a DA problem.

Equation 10.2 is applied to the data in our example to generate the discriminant score values for each observation. These values are listed in the Discriminant Score column in Figure 10.5 (and in the file Fig10-5.xlsm that accompanies this book).

For example, the discriminant score for the first observation could be calculated in cell E4 as:

Formula for cell E4: $=5.373 - 0.0791{*}C4 - 0.0272{*}D4$ **10.3**

(Copy to E5 through E23.)

FIGURE 10.5

Discriminant scores for the personnel selection example

Obs.	Group	Test Scores — Mechanical	Verbal	Discriminant Score	Predicted Group	
1	1	44.7	36.1	0.855	1	
2	1	43.2	42.0	0.813	1	
3	1	42.5	30.8	1.173	1	
4	1	40.2	42.6	1.034	1	
5	1	41.9	37.1	1.049	1	
6	1	39.3	33.8	1.345	1	
7	1	38.6	40.3	1.223	1	
8	1	38.1	28.5	1.584	2	**
9	1	37.9	44.7	1.159	1	
10	1	36.8	42.6	1.303	1	
11	1	35.8	35.2	1.583	2	**
12	2	39.0	33.1	1.387	1	**
13	2	37.5	36.4	1.416	1	**
14	2	36.1	30.8	1.679	2	
15	2	35.6	27.2	1.817	2	
16	2	34.4	39.0	1.591	2	
17	2	32.8	35.2	1.821	2	
18	2	31.4	29.4	2.089	2	
19	2	29.5	37.9	2.008	2	
20	2	30.1	33.9	2.070	2	
Group	1	39.9	37.6	1.193		
Averages	2	34.0	33.7	1.764		
			Cutoff Value	1.479		

Sheet tabs: Training Sample / Graph / Results / Distributions / Classification Sample

Key Cell Formulas

Cell	Formula	Copied to
E4	=TREND($B$4:$B$23,$C$4:$D$23,C4:D4)	E5:E23
C24	=AVERAGEIF($B$4:$B$23,$B24,C$4:C$23)	C24:E25
E26	=(E24+E25)/2	--
F4	=IF(E4<=$E$26,1,2)	F5:F23
G4	=IF(F4<>B4,"**","")	G5:G23

Alternatively, we could calculate the discriminant scores using the TREND( ) function as follows:

Alternate formula for cell E4:   =TREND($B$4:$B$23,$C$4:$D$23,C4:D4)   **10.3a**
(Copy to E5 through E23.)

Using either equation 10.3 or 10.3a in cell E4 should give approximately the same result, though those obtained using the TREND( ) function should be more accurate (due to less rounding error).

The formula in cell E4 is copied to cells E5 through E23 to calculate the discriminant scores for each of the remaining observations. Cells E24 and E25 calculate the average discriminant score for each group using the following AVERAGEIF( ) function:

Formula for cell E24:   =AVERAGEIF($B$4:$B$23,$B24,E$4:E$23)
(Copy to E25.)

We will refer to these average discriminant scores for groups 1 and 2 as $\hat{\bar{Y}}_1$ and $\hat{\bar{Y}}_2$, respectively.

10.1.3 THE CLASSIFICATION RULE

Because the discriminant scores are not equal to our group values of 1 and 2, we need a method for translating these scores into group membership predictions. The following classification rule can be used for this purpose:

Classification Rule: If an observation's discriminant score is less than or equal to some cut-off value, then assign it to group 1; otherwise, assign it to group 2.

The remaining problem is to determine an appropriate cut-off value. We can do so in a number of ways. One possibility is to select the cut-off value that minimizes the *number* of misclassifications in the training sample. However, this approach might not be best if our goal is to classify *new* observations correctly. Consider the situation that would occur if the independent variables were normally distributed with equal variances and covariances equal to 0. The resulting distributions of discriminant scores would be similar to those shown in Figure 10.6.

Notice that the distributions of discriminant scores for group 1 and group 2 are centered at $\hat{\bar{Y}}_1$ and $\hat{\bar{Y}}_2$, respectively. The area in Figure 10.6 where the tails of the distributions overlap corresponds to observations that are most likely to be classified incorrectly. Generally, DA attempts to minimize this area of overlap. With these data conditions, it is easy to see that the midpoint between the average discriminant score for each group is likely to be the best choice for a cut-off value because this point minimizes the *probability* of misclassification for future observations. Even if the independent variables violate the normality assumption, this midpoint value often provides good classification results for new observations. The cut-off value listed in cell E26 of Figure 10.5 shown earlier is the average of the estimates of $\hat{\bar{Y}}_1$ and $\hat{\bar{Y}}_2$:

$$\text{Cut-off value} = \frac{\hat{\bar{Y}}_1 + \hat{\bar{Y}}_2}{2} + \frac{1.193 + 1.764}{2} = 1.479 \qquad \textbf{10.4}$$

Note, however, that the midpoint cut-off value is not always optimal and, in some cases, might lead to poor classification results.

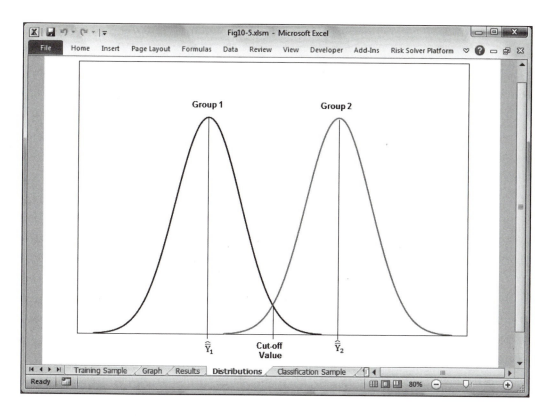

FIGURE 10.6

Possible distributions of discriminant scores

10.1.4 REFINING THE CUT-OFF VALUE

Because the tails of the distributions in Figure 10.6 overlap, we can be fairly certain that some observations will be classified incorrectly using the classification rule stated earlier. For example, our classification rule might predict that certain job applicants will be satisfactory employees when, in fact, they will be unsatisfactory. Hiring such employees could be a costly mistake. Alternatively, our classification rule might predict incorrectly that certain applicants will be unsatisfactory when, in fact, they would be very good employees. Not hiring these applicants would represent a lost opportunity (or opportunity cost) for the company. However, these *costs of misclassification* are not taken into account by the midpoint cut-off value in equation 10.4.

To illustrate another potential problem with the midpoint cut-off value, suppose that the personnel director knows from experience that the majority of applicants to the company are unqualified and would be unsatisfactory workers. In this case, the population of unqualified (potentially unsatisfactory) applicants is larger than the population of qualified (potentially satisfactory) applicants. Thus, a higher probability exists that a given applicant will be an unsatisfactory worker rather than a satisfactory worker. It would be helpful if we could incorporate these preexisting, or prior, probabilities in our classification rule. However, the midpoint cut-off value in equation 10.4 assumes that new observations are equally likely to come from either group.

We can use an alternative method for specifying what cut-off value to use in our classification rule. This method considers the costs of misclassification and prior probabilities. Suppose we define the costs of misclassification and prior probabilities as:

$C(1\,|\,2)$ = the cost of classifying an observation into group 1 when it belongs to group 2
$C(2\,|\,1)$ = the cost of classifying an observation into group 2 when it belongs to group 1

p_1 = the prior probability that a new observation belongs to group 1

p_2 = the prior probability that a new observation belongs to group 2

A general method for determining the cut-off value for the classification rule is represented by:

$$\text{Cut-off value} = \frac{\hat{Y}_1 + \hat{Y}_2}{2} + \frac{S_{\hat{Y}_p}^2}{\hat{Y}_1 - \hat{Y}_2} \times \text{LN}\left(\frac{p_2 C(1\,|\,2)}{p_1 C(2\,|\,1)}\right) \qquad \textbf{10.5}$$

where LN($\cdot$) represents the natural logarithm, and

$$S_{\hat{Y}_p}^2 = \frac{(n_1 - 1)\, S_{\hat{Y}_1}^2 + (n_2 - 1) S_{\hat{Y}_2}^2}{n_1 + n_2 - 2}$$

where n_i represents the number of observations in group i, and $S_{\hat{Y}_i}^2$ represents the sample variance of the discriminant scores for group i. Notice that if the costs of misclassification are equal ($C(1\,|\,2) = C(2\,|\,1)$), and the prior probabilities are equal ($p_1 = p_2$), the cut-off value in equation 10.5 reduces to the midpoint cut-off value in equation 10.4 because LN(1) = 0.

To illustrate this refined cut-off value, suppose that the personnel director in our example believes there is a 40% chance that a given applicant would be a satisfactory employee ($p_1 = 0.40$) and a 60% chance that a given applicant would be an unsatisfactory employee ($p_2 = 0.60$). Furthermore, suppose that the company considers it twice as costly to hire a person who turns out to be an unsatisfactory worker as it is to not hire a person who would have been a satisfactory worker. This implies that $C(1\,|\,2) = 2 \times C(2\,|\,1)$.

To calculate the refined cut-off value obtained using equation 10.5, we first calculate $S_{\hat{Y}_1}^2$ and $S_{\hat{Y}_2}^2$ using Excel's VAR( ) function to obtain:

$$S_{\hat{Y}_1}^2 = \text{VAR(E4:E14)} = 0.0648$$
$$S_{\hat{Y}_2}^2 = \text{VAR(E15:E23)} = 0.0705$$

Because $n_1 = 11$ and $n_2 = 9$, $S_{\hat{Y}_p}^2$ is computed as:

$$S_{\hat{Y}_p}^2 = \frac{(11 - 1)(0.0648) + (9 - 1)(0.0705)}{(11 + 9 - 2)} = 0.06733$$

We can then use equation 10.5 to compute the refined cut-off value as:

$$\text{Refined cut-off value} = \frac{1.193 + 1.764}{2} + \frac{0.06733}{1.193 - 1.764} \text{LN}\left(\frac{2(0.6)}{(0.4)}\right) = 1.349$$

This refined cut-off value reduces the chance of an observation from group 2 being misclassified into group 1 (which is the more costly mistake) and increases the chance of an observation from group 1 being misclassified into group 2 (which is the less costly mistake).

10.1.5 CLASSIFICATION ACCURACY

Our ultimate goal in DA is to predict to which group a new observation (or job applicant) belongs. Because we already know which group each observation in our training sample belongs to, it might seem pointless to try to classify these observations. Yet, by doing so we can get some idea of how accurate our classification rule is likely to be with other new observations whose true group memberships are unknown. For our example, if we use the midpoint cut-off value technique, our classification rule is:

Classification Rule: If an observation's discriminant score is less than or equal to 1.479, then assign it to group 1; otherwise, assign it to group 2.

The Predicted Group column in Figure 10.5 contains the results of applying this classification rule. This rule is implemented by placing the following formula in cell F4 and copying it to cells F5 through F23:

Formula for cell F4:   =IF(E4<=$E$26,1,2)
(Copy to F5 through F23.)

Comparing the values in the Predicted Group column to the values in the Group column indicates that a number of observations in the training sample were misclassified using the preceding classification rule. Misclassified observations can be identified easily by implementing the following formula in cell G4 and copying it to cells G5 through G23:

Formula for cell G4:   =IF(F4<>B4,"**"," ")
(Copy to G5 through G23.)

This marks the misclassified observations with asterisks (**) in Figure 10.5. Figure 10.7 summarizes these classification results.

		Predicted Group		
		1	2	Total
Actual	1	9	2	11
Group	2	2	7	9
	Total	11	9	20

FIGURE 10.7

Summary of classification results on the training sample for the two groups

Figure 10.7 shows that 9 of the 11 observations (81.8%) that belong to group 1 were classified correctly in this group, and the other 2 observations (18.2%) belonging to group 1 were misclassified into group 2. Similarly, 7 of the 9 observations (77.8%) that belong to group 2 were classified correctly in this group, and the other 2 observations (22.2%) belonging to group 2 were misclassified into group 1. Overall, 16 out of 20 observations (80.0%) in our training sample were classified correctly, and a total of 4 observations (20.0%) were misclassified. The matrix shown in Figure 10.7 is sometimes referred to as a **confusion matrix** because it indicates how much confusion exists regarding the group memberships of the observations in the training sample.

From these results, we might expect that our classification rule will provide correct classifications approximately 80% of the time if we use it to predict the group membership of new applicants. Actually, the figure of 80% is probably somewhat favorably biased. That is, the observations in our training sample influenced the development of the classification rule; therefore, we expect that this rule might be successful in classifying these same observations. However, we should not expect the procedure to duplicate this level of accuracy when classifying new observations that did not influence the development of the classification rule.

10.1.6 CLASSIFYING NEW EMPLOYEES

As mentioned previously, the ultimate goal in DA is to predict into which group a new observation (or potential employee) is most likely to fall. In our example, this involves

FIGURE 10.8

Predicted group memberships of the new job applicants

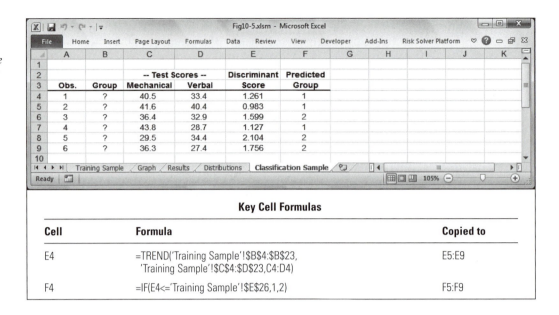

		-- Test Scores --		Discriminant	Predicted
Obs.	Group	Mechanical	Verbal	Score	Group
1	?	40.5	33.4	1.261	1
2	?	41.6	40.4	0.983	1
3	?	36.4	32.9	1.599	2
4	?	43.8	28.7	1.127	1
5	?	29.5	34.4	2.104	2
6	?	36.3	27.4	1.756	2

Key Cell Formulas

Cell	Formula	Copied to
E4	=TREND('Training Sample'!$B$4:$B$23, 'Training Sample'!$C$4:$D$23,C4:D4)	E5:E9
F4	=IF(E4<='Training Sample'!$E$26,1,2)	F5:F9

predicting whether or not a new job applicant will be a satisfactory or unsatisfactory employee. Figure 10.8 shows a new worksheet named Classification Sample. This worksheet is similar to the one in Figure 10.1, but here all the observations represent new job applicants being considered for employment. Because we do not know whether these applicants will be satisfactory or unsatisfactory employees, question marks (?) have been entered in the Group column. The values in the Mechanical and Verbal columns represent the applicants' scores on the two aptitude tests.

We can use the regression results and classification rule developed for our training sample to calculate discriminant scores and predict whether each new observation (or applicant) would fall into group 1 or group 2. To calculate these scores, the following formula is implemented in cell E4 and copied to cells E5 through E9:

> Formula for cell E4:   =TREND('Training Sample'!$B$4:$B$23,'Training
> (Copy to E5 through E9.)   Sample'!$C$4:$D$23,C4:D4)

The classification rule is implemented by entering the following formula in cell F4 and copying it to cells F5 through F9:

> Formula for cell F4:   =IF(E4<='Training Sample'!$E$26,1,2)
> (Copy to F5 through F9.)

The Predicted Group column shows an *estimate*, or *forecast*, of which group each new job applicant would fall into if hired. For example, we are predicting that the applicants listed as observations 1, 2, and 4 in Figure 10.8 would be satisfactory employees (belonging to group 1), and the other applicants would be unsatisfactory (belonging to group 2).

Only time will tell how accurate these predictions are for the applicants hired, and we will never know if the predictions are correct for applicants that are not hired. But the DA technique has provided the personnel director with an objective way of incorporating the mechanical and verbal aptitude test scores in the hiring decision. As with any statistical tool, these results should be used in conjunction with other information available and with the decision maker's professional judgment of each applicant's potential value to the company.

10.2 The *k*-Group DA Problem

It might seem as if the regression approach for two-group DA could be extended easily to problems with more than two groups. For example, suppose that we have a problem with three groups (labeled A, B, and C) and one independent variable X. We could set up a dependent variable Y and assign it a value of 1, 2, or 3 to indicate observations belonging to group A, B, or C, respectively. We might attempt to model the behavior of this dependent variable as:

$$\hat{Y}_i = b_0 + b_1X_i \qquad\qquad \textbf{10.6}$$

We could then apply regression analysis to estimate values for b_0 and b_1 so that we could calculate the discriminant scores $\hat{Y}_i$. Figure 10.9 (and file Fig10-9.xlsm that accompanies this book) displays hypothetical data for such a problem.

Having obtained the discriminant scores, we might use the following rule to classify observations:

If the Discriminant Score Is	Assign Observation to Group
$\hat{Y} < 1.5$	A
$1.5 \le \hat{Y} \le 2.5$	B
$\hat{Y} > 2.5$	C

Although such an approach might seem reasonable, it has a major flaw. Note that the linear relationship between the dependent and independent variables in Figure 10.9 is due solely to the manner in which the dependent variable numbers were assigned to the groups. That is, if we assign the number 2 to group A and the number 1 to group B, the linear relationship between the variables is destroyed, as illustrated in Figure 10.10.

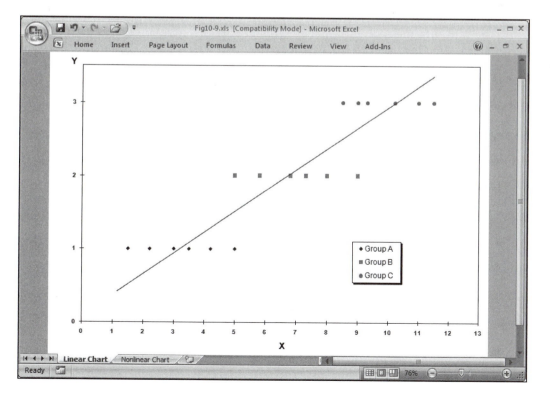

FIGURE 10.9

Graph of three-group example with one independent variable showing a linear relationship

FIGURE 10.10

Graph of three-group example with one independent variable showing a nonlinear relationship

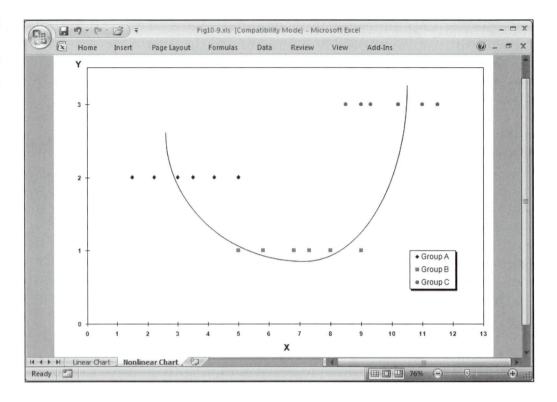

In general, the regression function in equation 10.6 cannot be used for DA problems with more than two groups because the relationship between the dependent and independent variables might not be linear. Even if we could make the relationship linear with some appropriate coding for the dependent variable, it can be very difficult to discern what this coding should be if the problem involves more than one independent variable. In this section, we will discuss another approach to DA that can be used when the problem involves more than two groups.

10.2.1 MULTIPLE DISCRIMINANT ANALYSIS

To distinguish this approach from the two-group regression approach, we refer to it as **multiple discriminant analysis** (MDA). The following modified personnel selection example illustrates the MDA approach.

> Suppose that instead of being rated as either satisfactory or unsatisfactory in their annual performance reviews, the employees for ACME Manufacturing are rated as performing in either a superior, average, or inferior manner. Marie wants to analyze the differences in preemployment screening test scores for these three groups of employees and develop a rule for predicting to which group a new potential employee would belong. Her plan is to hire any applicant classified in the superior group and reject applicants in the inferior group. Applicants in the average group will be screened more closely with additional interviews and reference checking before Marie makes a hiring decision.

In this example, the personnel director is interested in discriminating among *three* groups: (1) superior employees, (2) average employees, and (3) inferior employees. We cannot apply the regression-based technique described earlier to this example because it involves more than two groups. We are using three groups in this example for convenience in illustrating the MDA approach. This approach can be applied to problems involving any number of groups. The MDA approach also can accommodate more than two independent variables.

The data for this example are displayed in Figure 10.11 (and in the file Fig10-11.xlsm that accompanies this book). The Training Sample worksheet contains data for the company's current employees, whom the personnel director has classified into one of the three groups: (1) superior, (2) average, and (3) inferior. These group assignments are indicated by the numbers in the Group column. Each employee's mechanical and verbal scores on the aptitude test are displayed in the adjacent columns.

Although the MDA approach is different from the regression technique described earlier for the two-group example, the basic idea is the same. Figure 10.12 shows the plot of all the scores on the aptitude tests for each group along with the centroids. Note that most of the observations in each group cluster around the group's centroid. If we don't already know to which group an observation belongs, we could classify the observation based on its proximity to the centroids. That is, to determine to which group a new observation belongs, we could plot it on this graph and visually judge the distance between it and each of the centroids. A logical classification rule is to assign observations to the group represented by the closest centroid. This is the approach taken in MDA, although at a somewhat more sophisticated level.

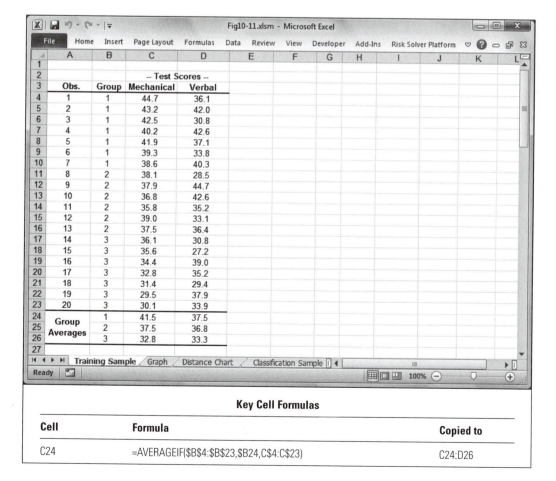

FIGURE 10.11

Data for current employees classified into three groups

Obs.	Group	Mechanical	Verbal
		-- Test Scores --	
1	1	44.7	36.1
2	1	43.2	42.0
3	1	42.5	30.8
4	1	40.2	42.6
5	1	41.9	37.1
6	1	39.3	33.8
7	1	38.6	40.3
8	2	38.1	28.5
9	2	37.9	44.7
10	2	36.8	42.6
11	2	35.8	35.2
12	2	39.0	33.1
13	2	37.5	36.4
14	3	36.1	30.8
15	3	35.6	27.2
16	3	34.4	39.0
17	3	32.8	35.2
18	3	31.4	29.4
19	3	29.5	37.9
20	3	30.1	33.9
Group Averages	1	41.5	37.5
	2	37.5	36.8
	3	32.8	33.3

Key Cell Formulas

Cell	Formula	Copied to
C24	=AVERAGEIF($B$4:$B$23,$B24,C$4:C$23)	C24:D26

FIGURE 10.12

Graph of data for the three-group example

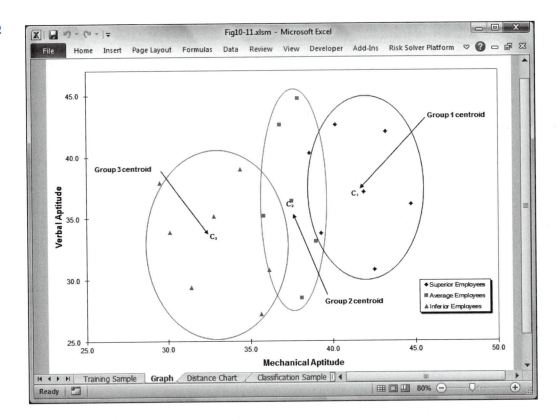

10.2.2 DISTANCE MEASURES

The problem with the visual approach is that some observations might be "too close to call," appearing to be equally close to several centroids. For example, in Figure 10.12, several points fall midway between two of the centroids and might be difficult to classify visually. Also, if the problem involves more than two independent variables, the graph displaying the data must be drawn in three or more dimensions, making a visual inspection of the data difficult or impossible. Rather than just "eyeballing" it, we need a more formal measure of the distance between each observation and each centroid.

You might recall from high school algebra (or Chapter 8) that the Euclidean (straight-line) distance between two points (A_1, B_1) and (A_2, B_2) in two dimensions can be measured by:

$$\text{Distance} = \sqrt{(A_1 - A_2)^2 + (B_1 - B_2)^2} \qquad \textbf{10.7}$$

For example, the distance between two arbitrary points $(3, 7)$ and $(9, 5)$ is:

$$\sqrt{(3 - 9)^2 + (7 - 5)^2} = \sqrt{40} = 6.324$$

This distance formula generalizes easily to any number of dimensions. We can use this formula in MDA to measure the distance from a given observation to the centroid of each group, and then assign the observation to the group it is closest to. From a statistical viewpoint, this distance measure in equation 10.7 is somewhat weak because it ignores the variances of the independent variables. To see this, suppose that X_1 represents one of the independent variables, and X_2 represents the other. If X_2 has a much larger variance than X_1, the effects of *small but important* differences in X_1 could be masked or dwarfed in equation 10.7 by *large but unimportant* differences in X_2. Figure 10.13 illustrates this problem, where the ellipses represent regions containing 99% of the values belonging to each group.

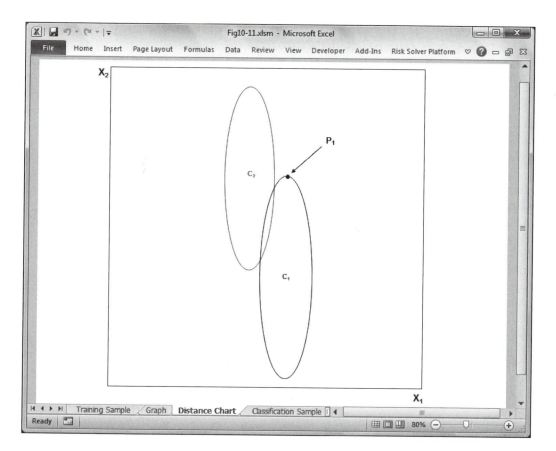

FIGURE 10.13

Regions containing 99% of the observations in each group

Consider the observation labeled P_1 in Figure 10.13. This observation appears to be closest to C_2, and, indeed, if we used the standard distance measure in equation 10.7, we would assign it to group 2 because its distance from C_1 with respect to the X_2-axis is relatively large. However, it is extremely unlikely that this observation belongs to group 2 because its location with respect to the X_1-axis exceeds the typical values for group 2. Thus, it would be helpful to refine our distance measure in equation 10.7 to account for possible differences in the variances of the independent variables.

If we let D_{ij} represent the distance from observation i to the centroid for group j, we can define this distance as:

$$D_{ij} = \sqrt{\sum_k \frac{(X_{ik} - \bar{X}_{jk})^2}{S_{jk}^2}} \qquad \textbf{10.8}$$

where X_{ik} represents the value of observation i on the kth independent variable, $\bar{X}_{jk}$ represents the average value of group j on the kth independent variable, and S_{jk}^2 represents the sample variance of group j on the kth independent variable.

10.2.3 MDA CLASSIFICATION

There are numerous variations on the distance measure in equation 10.8. One of the most popular variations—known as the **Mahalanobis distance measure**—refines the calculation in equation 10.8 to account for differences in the covariances between the independent variables. Risk Solver Platform includes a tool for performing MDA in Excel using

Mahalanobis distance measures. This tool calculates the Mahalanobis distance from each observation to the centroid for each of the possible groups. It then assigns each observation to the group it is closest to based on these distance measures. (Alternatively, for each observation, it can calculate the probability of the observation belonging to each of the possible groups and assign the observation to the group with the highest probability.)

To open the Discriminant Analysis dialog box shown in Figure 10.14, follow these steps:

1. Click the Risk Solver Platform tab.
2. Click Reports, Discriminant Analysis.

Risk Solver Platform's Discriminant Analysis dialog box is similar to that of the regression tool in Excel. We must indicate the Grouping Variable Range (representing the dependent Y variable) and the Predictor Variable Range (representing the independent X variables) for the training sample, as well as the Predictor Variable Range for the classification sample. In the Covariance Matrices section of this dialog box, you may choose to use either pooled or unpooled estimates of the covariance matrix. The Pooled Estimates option should be used if there is reason to believe that the variances and covariances of the predictor (X-Range) variables are the same in each group. (Using the Pooled Estimates option should produce the same results as the regression approach to DA for two-group problems.) Figure 10.15 displays the first portion of the report from the Discriminant Analysis tool for our example problem.

As shown in Figure 10.15, the Discriminant Analysis tool first computes the centroids and relative frequencies for each group. Next, the Mahalanobis distance from each observation in the training sample to the centroid of each group is computed. These distances

FIGURE 10.14 *Discriminant Analysis dialog box*

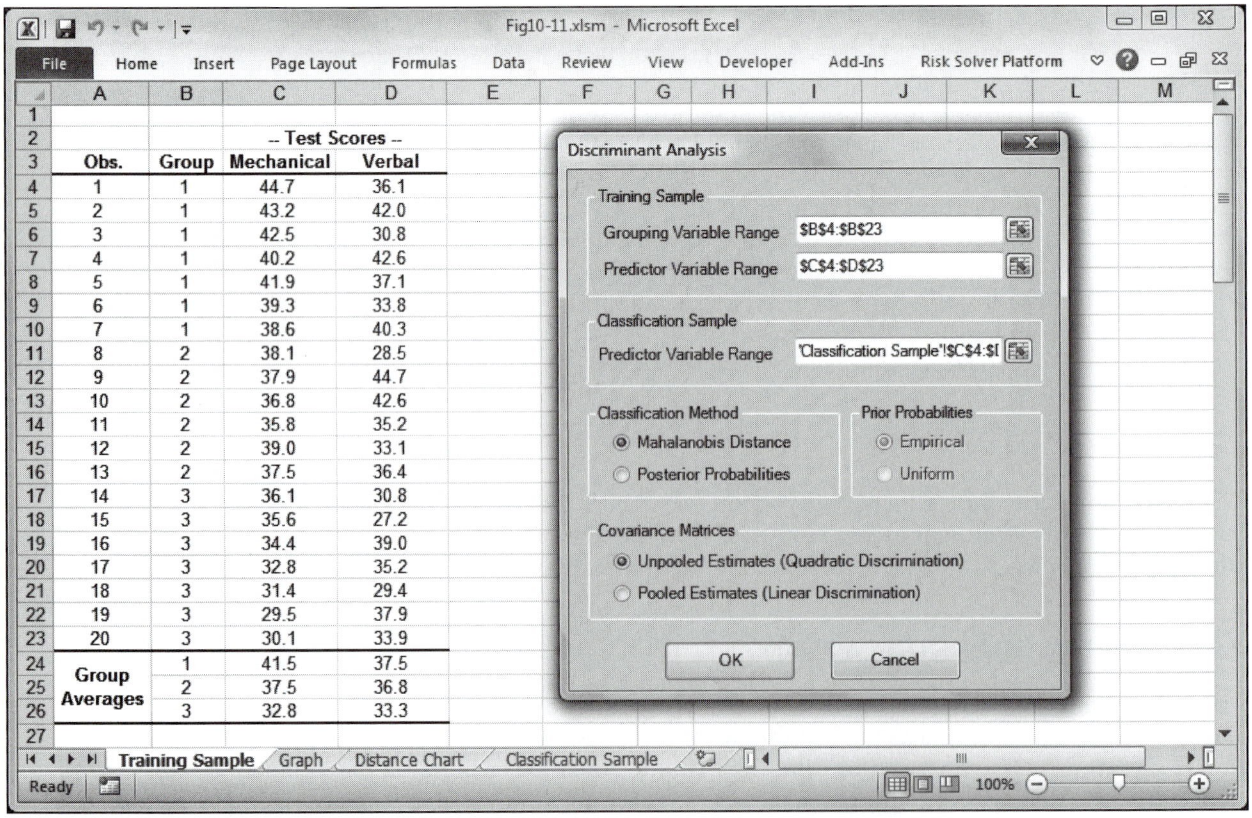

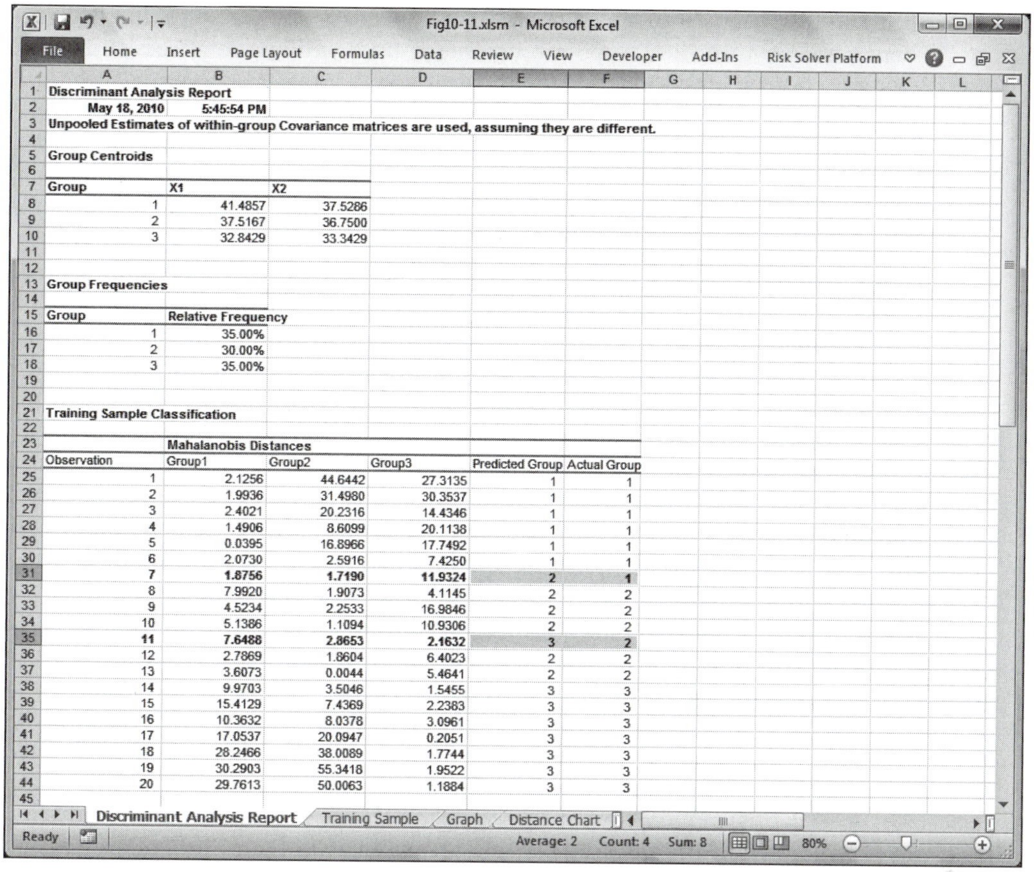
Discriminant Analysis Report

May 18, 2010 5:45:54 PM

Unpooled Estimates of within-group Covariance matrices are used, assuming they are different.

Group Centroids

Group	X1	X2
1	41.4857	37.5286
2	37.5167	36.7500
3	32.8429	33.3429

Group Frequencies

Group	Relative Frequency
1	35.00%
2	30.00%
3	35.00%

Training Sample Classification

	Mahalanobis Distances				
Observation	Group1	Group2	Group3	Predicted Group	Actual Group
1	2.1256	44.6442	27.3135	1	1
2	1.9936	31.4980	30.3537	1	1
3	2.4021	20.2316	14.4346	1	1
4	1.4906	8.6099	20.1138	1	1
5	0.0395	16.8966	17.7492	1	1
6	2.0730	2.5916	7.4250	1	1
7	**1.8756**	**1.7190**	**11.9324**	**2**	**1**
8	7.9920	1.9073	4.1145	2	2
9	4.5234	2.2533	16.9846	2	2
10	5.1386	1.1094	10.9306	2	2
11	**7.6488**	**2.8653**	**2.1632**	**3**	**2**
12	2.7869	1.8604	6.4023	2	2
13	3.6073	0.0044	5.4641	2	2
14	9.9703	3.5046	1.5455	3	3
15	15.4129	7.4369	2.2383	3	3
16	10.3632	8.0378	3.0961	3	3
17	17.0537	20.0947	0.2051	3	3
18	28.2466	38.0089	1.7744	3	3
19	30.2903	55.3418	1.9522	3	3
20	29.7613	50.0063	1.1884	3	3

FIGURE 10.15

Discriminant Analysis results

are displayed in cells B25 through D44. The column labeled Predicted Group indicates which group each observation is closest to based on these distance measures, whereas the adjacent column, labeled, Actual Group, indicates which group each observation in the training sample actually belongs to. Note that 2 of the 20 observations in the training sample for this example have been misclassified using the Mahalanobis distances.

Figure 10.16 displays the remainder of the Discriminant Analysis tool's report. In rows 49 through 53, a confusion matrix is shown summarizing the results from the

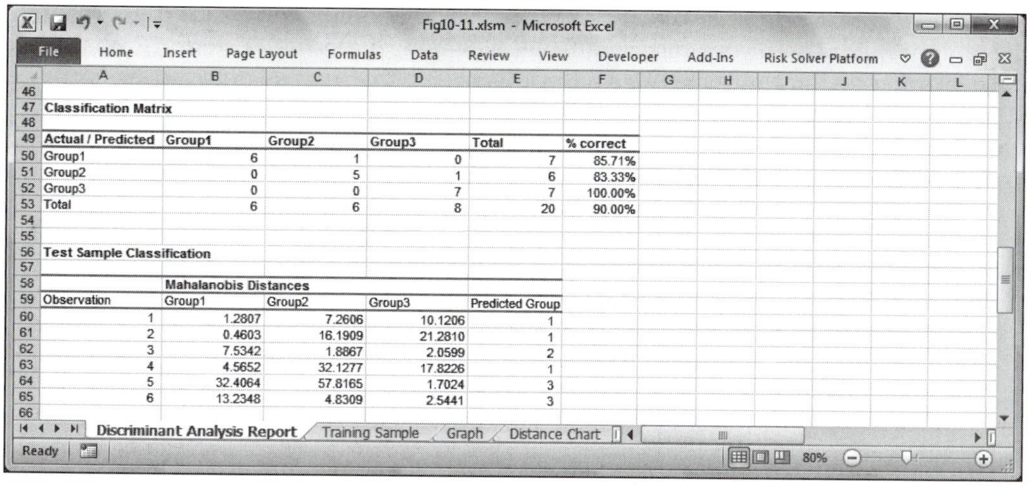
Classification Matrix

Actual / Predicted	Group1	Group2	Group3	Total	% correct
Group1	6	1	0	7	85.71%
Group2	0	5	1	6	83.33%
Group3	0	0	7	7	100.00%
Total	6	6	8	20	90.00%

Test Sample Classification

	Mahalanobis Distances			
Observation	Group1	Group2	Group3	Predicted Group
1	1.2807	7.2606	10.1206	1
2	0.4603	16.1909	21.2810	1
3	7.5342	1.8867	2.0599	2
4	4.5652	32.1277	17.8226	1
5	32.4064	57.8165	1.7024	3
6	13.2348	4.8309	2.5441	3

FIGURE 10.16

Discriminant Analysis results continued

training sample. This matrix indicates that 6 of the 7 observations that actually belong to group 1 were correctly classified as coming from group 1, while one observation from group 1 was erroneously classified as coming from group 2 (see observation number 7 in Figure 10.15). Similarly, 5 of the 6 observations belonging to group 2 were correctly classified, while 1 observation from group 2 was misclassified into group 3 (see observation number 11 in Figure 10.15). Finally, all 7 observations from group 3 in the training sample were correctly classified. Thus, cell F53 indicates that 90% (or a total of 18 out of 20) of the observations were correctly classified.

Rows 58 through 65 of Figure 10.16 show the classification results for the same six new applicants that were classified using the two-group approach to DA in Figure 10.8. It is interesting to compare the results of these analyses. Recall that the personnel director's plan is to classify applicants into three groups and hire any applicant in the superior group (group 1), reject any applicant in the inferior group (group 3), and conduct a follow-up interview and check the references on applicants in the average group (group 2). In Figure 10.16, note that applicants 1, 2, and 4, who were classified earlier as satisfactory, are now identified as superior candidates. Applicants 5 and 6, who were classified earlier as unsatisfactory, are now identified as inferior candidates. However, applicant 3, who was classified earlier as unsatisfactory, is now identified as average and requires additional screening by the personnel director before a hiring decision is made.

As mentioned earlier, Risk Solver Platform's Discriminant Analysis tool can also calculate the probability of each observation belonging to each of the possible groups and assign the observation to the group with the highest probability. To do this, you would choose the Posterior Probabilities classification method on the Discriminant Analysis dialog box shown earlier in Figure 10.14. Selecting the Posterior Probabilities classification method then enables you to select either the Empirical or Uniform option in the Prior Probabilities section of the dialog box. You should select the Empirical option if the relative group frequencies in the training sample are representative of the relative group frequencies in the population from which the training sample was drawn. Alternatively, you may select the Uniform option if the relative group frequencies in the training sample are not equal, but the group frequencies are approximately equal in the population from which the sample was drawn (as may happen if, for example, it is easier to collect data from one group than another group).

When using the Posterior Probabilities classification method, it is important to remember that the calculated probabilities assume that the data arise from a multivariate normal distribution. If that assumption is true, then the probabilities are accurate and the classifications made with this approach are theoretically optimal. However, if the data under consideration is not from a multivariate normal distribution, the probabilities might not be accurate, and classifications arising from the Posterior Probabilities classification method must be viewed as a heuristic that may or may not be optimal. Likewise, when using the Mahalanobis distance measure approach to classification, if the data is from a multivariate normal distribution, then the minimum distance classification rule is theoretically optimal; otherwise, it must be viewed as a heuristic.

10.3 Summary

DA is a statistical technique that can be used to develop a rule for predicting in which of two or more groups an observation belongs. DA is similar to regression analysis in that it uses a set of independent variables to predict the value of a dependent variable. However, in DA, the dependent variable is coded in a discrete, or categorical, manner to represent the different groups under consideration.

This chapter presented two approaches to DA. When the problem involves only two groups, regression analysis can be used to develop a classification rule. However, when the problem involves more than two groups, the regression approach is no longer appropriate, and the more general *k*-group approach to DA is required. The *k*-group DA approach can be used with problems involving two or more groups.

DA is a powerful technique with a deep and rich theoretical basis. Our discussion of DA has only scratched the surface, but it should give you a good understanding of the issues involved in DA and some of the methods for solving classification problems. Other techniques exist for performing DA and MDA, and these might be more appropriate for a particular data set than the procedures described in this chapter.

10.4 References

Altman, E. I., R. B. Avery, R. A. Eisenbeis, and J. F. Sinkey. *Application of Classification Techniques in Business, Banking and Finance.* Greenwich, CT: JAI Press, 1981.

Booth, D. E., A. Pervaiz, S. N. Ahkam, and B. Osyk. "A Robust Multivariate Procedure for the Identification of Problem Savings and Loan Institutions." *Decision Sciences,* 20, 1989, pp. 320–333.

Campbell, T. S., and J. K. Dietrich. "The Determinants of Default on Insured Conventional Residential Mortgage Loans." *Journal of Finance,* 1983, 38, pp. 1569–1581.

Flury, B., and H. Riedwyl. *Multivariate Statistics: A Practical Approach.* New York: Chapman and Hall, 1988.

Hand, D. J. *Discrimination and Classification.* New York: Wiley, 1981.

Labe, R. "Database Marketing Increases Prospecting Effectiveness at Merrill Lynch." *Interfaces,* vol. 24, no. 5, 1994.

Morrison, D. F. *Multivariate Statistical Methods,* Third Edition. New York: McGraw-Hill, 1990.

Welker, R. B. "Discriminant and Classification Analysis as an Aid to Employee Selection." *Accounting Review,* 49, 1974, pp. 514–523.

THE WORLD OF MANAGEMENT SCIENCE

La Quinta Motor Inns Predicts Successful Sites with Discriminant Analysis

Management at La Quinta Motor Inns wanted a fast, reliable method for predicting whether potential sites for new inns would be successful. One of the first issues to be resolved in designing a regression model was to define a measure of success that would be useful in making predictions. After considering several alternatives, operating margin—defined as profit plus depreciation and interest expenses as a percentage of total revenue—was chosen. Total revenue and total profit were unsuitable measures because they are too highly correlated with the size of the inn. Occupancy was also considered unsuitable because it is too sensitive to the economic cycle.

Data were collected on all 151 existing inns operated by La Quinta at the time of the study. The regression model was developed using 57 inns, and the other 94 were set aside for validation. During the selection of independent variables, care was taken to measure collinearity and keep it under control. A coefficient of determination (R^2) of 0.51 was obtained for a model showing that operating margin is positively influenced by the price of the inn (a measure of the competitive room rate of the market area) and the location of nearby colleges. Negative influences

(Continued)

were distance to the nearest La Quinta Inn (a reverse measure of market penetration) and median income in the market area (suggesting an industrial economic base). After careful analysis, one outlier was deleted from the data, substantially improving the model.

The regression model itself was not the tool that management had in mind, however. Management needed a criterion to use for either choosing or rejecting potential sites. After specifying an acceptable risk of choosing a bad site, classification tables were used to develop a decision rule for discriminating between "good" sites and "bad" sites. The cut-off value was a predicted operating margin of 35%.

The model was then tested on the 94 inns set aside for validation, and the error rates were as expected. Set up as a spreadsheet, the model is now used to screen potential sites for possible development, with the final decision made by the president of the company.

Source: Sheryl E. Kimes and James A. Fitzsimmons. "Selecting Profitable Hotel Sites at La Quinta Motor Inns." *Interfaces*, vol. 20, no. 2, March–April 1990, pp. 12–20.

Questions and Problems

1. What is a centroid?
2. It can be argued that regression analysis and DA both use a set of independent variables to predict the value of a dependent variable. What, then, is the difference between regression analysis and DA?
3. In discussing the approach to DA using distance measures, we calculated the distance from an observation to the centroid of each group. We then assigned the observation to the group it was closest to based on the distance measures. Can you think of another way distance measures might be used to classify observations? What classification rule is used under this method?
4. This chapter noted that the R^2 statistic cannot be relied upon as a goodness-of-fit measure in the regression approach to two-group DA. What was the value of the R^2 statistic for the two-group DA example in this chapter? How does it compare with the percentage of correctly classified observations in this same example?
5. The director of the MBA program at Salterdine University wants to use DA to determine which applicants to admit to the MBA program. The director believes that an applicant's undergraduate grade point average (GPA) and score on the GMAT exam are helpful in predicting which applicants will be good students. To assist in this endeavor, the director asked a committee of faculty members to classify 30 of the current students in the MBA program into two groups: (1) good students and (2) weak students. The file Dat10-5.xls that accompanies this book summarizes these ratings, along with the GPA and GMAT scores for the 30 students.
   a. What are the coordinates of the centroids for the good students and the weak students?
   b. Use the regression approach to two-group DA to develop a classification rule for predicting to which group a new student will belong. State your classification rule.
   c. Create a confusion matrix that summarizes the accuracy of your classification rule on the current students. Overall, how accurate does your classification rule appear to be?

d. Suppose that the MBA director receives applications for admission to the MBA program from the following individuals. According to DA, which of these individuals do you expect to be good students and which do you expect to be weak?

Name	GPA	GMAT
Mike Dimoupolous	3.02	450
Scott Frazier	2.97	587
Paula Curry	3.95	551
Terry Freeman	2.45	484
Dana Simmons	3.26	524

6. Refer to question 5. The MBA director could make two types of admission mistakes using DA. One mistake is to classify a student into the weak category (and, therefore, not admit the student) when, in fact, the student belongs in the good category. We will call this a type I error. The other type of error (which we will call a type II error) is to classify a student into the good category (and, therefore, admit the student) when, in fact, the student is a weak student. Suppose that the MBA director considers a type I error to be twice as costly as a type II error. How does the classification rule change to accommodate these unequal costs of misclassification? What is the new classification rule?

7. Refer to question 5 and answer the following questions:

   a. Use the Mahalanobis distance measure approach to DA to classify each of the current students.

   b. Create a confusion matrix that summarizes the accuracy of the distance measure approach on the data for the current students. Overall, how accurate does the distance measure approach to DA appear to be on these data?

   c. Classify each of the five new applicants from question 5 using the distance measure approach. Whom do you expect to be good students and whom do you expect to be weak?

   d. If the two approaches to DA reach the same conclusion about a given applicant, what effect should this have on the MBA director's opinion of that applicant? What action might the director take if the two approaches to DA suggest conflicting classifications?

8. The Royalty Gold Corporation prospects for undiscovered gold deposits around the world. The company is currently investigating a possible site on the island of Milos off the coast of Greece in the Mediterranean. When prospecting, the company drills to collect soil and rock samples and then analyzes the chemical properties of the samples to help determine whether or not the site is likely to contain significant gold deposits. Gold is made up of various elements, including calavarite, sylvanite, and petzite. Sites with higher concentrations of these elements are more likely to contain significant gold deposits. The company has collected the data found in the file Dat10-8.xls that accompanies this book representing the average levels of calavarite, sylvanite, and petzite in samples collected from previous various sites examined in previous prospecting expeditions. These data are grouped according to whether or not significant gold deposits were found at the location (1=significant, 2=insignificant).

   a. What are the coordinates of the centroids for the two groups?

   b. Use the regression approach to two-group DA to develop a classification rule for predicting whether or not a given site will contain a significant amount of gold. State your classification rule.

   c. Create a confusion matrix that summarizes the accuracy of your classification rule on the given data. Overall, how accurate is your classification rule?

d.   Suppose the company analyzes five sites on Milos that produce the following average levels of calavarite, sylvanite, and petzite. Which of these sites, if any, would you recommend for further analysis?

Site	Calavarite	Sylvanite	Petzite
1	0.058	0.041	0.037
2	0.045	0.023	0.039
3	0.052	0.023	0.044
4	0.043	0.042	0.056
5	0.050	0.032	0.038

9. Refer to the previous question. Suppose that Royalty Gold classifies potential sites into three categories: 1-High Profit, 2-Medium Profit, and 3-Low Profit. Suppose the first 10 sites in the data given previously represent high-profit sites, the next 10 observations represent medium-profit sites, and the final 10 observations represent low-profit sites. Perform discriminant analysis on these three groups using a pooled covariance matrix, and answer the following questions.
   a.   What are the coordinates of the centroids for the three groups?
   b.   Create a confusion matrix that summarizes the accuracy of your classification rule on the given data. Overall, how accurate is your classification rule?
   c.   Suppose the company analyzes five sites on Milos that produce the average levels of calavarite, sylvanite, and petzite given in question 8 part d. Indicate whether each site would be a high-, medium-, or low-profit site according to your discriminant results.

10. The manager of the commercial loan department for a bank wants to develop a rule to use in determining whether or not to approve various requests for loans. The manager believes that three key characteristics of a company's performance are important in making this decision: liquidity, profitability, and activity. The manager measures liquidity as the ratio of current assets to current liabilities. Profitability is measured as the ratio of net profit to sales. Activity is measured as the ratio of sales to fixed assets. The manager has collected the data found in the file Dat10-10.xls that accompanies this book containing a sample of 18 loans that the bank has made in the past five years. These loans have been classified into two groups: (1) those that were acceptable and (2) those that should have been rejected.
   a.   What are the coordinates of the centroids for the two groups?
   b.   Use the regression approach to two-group DA to develop a classification rule for predicting whether or not a given loan applicant will repay the loan, if approved. State your classification rule.
   c.   Create a confusion matrix that summarizes the accuracy of your classification rule on the data for the current loans. Overall, how accurate does your classification rule seem?
   d.   Suppose that the manager receives loan applications from companies with the following financial information. According to DA, which of these companies do you expect to be acceptable credit risks?

Company	Liquidity	Profitability	Activity
A	0.78	0.27	1.58
B	0.91	0.23	1.67
C	0.68	0.33	1.43
D	0.78	0.23	1.23
E	0.67	0.26	1.78

11. Refer to question 10. Suppose that the manager wants to classify loan applicants into one of three groups: (1) acceptable loan applications, (2) loan applications requiring further scrutiny, and (3) unacceptable loan applications. Assume that the first six observations given in question 10 correspond to group 1, the next six correspond to group 2, and the final six correspond to group 3.
    a. Use the distance measure approach to DA to classify each loan.
    b. Create a confusion matrix that summarizes the accuracy of the distance measure approach on the data for the current loans. Overall, how accurate does the distance measure approach to DA appear to be on these data?
    c. Classify each of the five new applicants from question 10 part d using the distance measure approach. Into which of the three groups do you expect each loan applicant to fall?
12. Consider the two-group personnel selection example discussed in this chapter. Some might argue that the best classification rule for this problem is the one that minimizes the number of misclassifications in the analysis sample. Formulate a mixed-integer programming model that could be solved to determine the linear classification rule that minimizes the number of misclassifications in the analysis sample. (*Hint*: Create one constraint for each observation. Include a unique binary variable in each constraint to indicate whether or not the observation is misclassified.)

Detecting Management Fraud

CASE 10.1

In the wake of the Enron scandal in 2002, two public accounting firms, Oscar Anderson (OA) and Trice-Milkhouse-Loopers (TML) merged (forming OATML) and are reviewing their methods for detecting management fraud during audits. The two firms had each developed their own set of questions that auditors could use in assessing management fraud.

To avoid a repeat of the problems faced by Enron's auditors, OATML wants to develop an automated decision tool to assist auditors in predicting whether or not their clients are engaged in fraudulent management practices. This tool would basically ask an auditor all the OA or TML fraud-detection questions and then automatically render a decision about whether or not the client company is engaging in fraudulent activities. The decision problem OATML faces is really two-fold: (1) Which of the two sets of fraud detection questions are best at detecting fraud? and, (2) What's the best way to translate the answers to these questions into a prediction or classification about management fraud?

To assist in answering these questions, the company has compiled an Excel spreadsheet (Fraud.xls) that contains both the OA and TML fraud-detection questions and answers to both sets of questions based on 382 audits previously conducted by the two companies (see sheets OA and TML, respectively). (Note: For all data, 1=yes, 0=no.) For each audit, the last variable in the spreadsheet indicates whether or not the respective companies were engaged in fraudulent activities (that is, 77 audits uncovered fraudulent activities, 305 did not).

You have been asked to perform the following analysis and provide a recommendation as to what combination of fraud questions OATML should adopt.

1. For the OA fraud questions, identify the 16 variables that have the strongest correlation (in absolute value) with whether or not a company was involved in fraudulent activities (use Excel's CORREL(), ABS(), and RANK() functions). Using the regression approach to two-group discriminant analysis, use these 16 variables to develop a rule for predicting whether or not a company is involved in fraud.
    a. What is your decision rule?

b. Develop a confusion matrix showing how accurate this decision rule is for the given data.

2. For the TML fraud questions, identify the 16 variables that have the strongest correlation (in absolute value) with whether or not a company was involved in fraudulent activities (use Excel's CORREL(), ABS(), and RANK() functions). Using the regression approach to two-group discriminant analysis, use these 16 variables to develop a rule for predicting whether or not a company is involved in fraud.
   a. What is your decision rule?
   b. Develop a confusion matrix showing how accurate this decision rule is for the given data.

3. Suppose OATML wants to use both fraud-detection instruments and combine their individual results to create a composite prediction. Let D1 represent the discriminant score for a given company using the OA fraud detection instrument, and D2 represent the same company's discriminant score using the TML instrument. The composite score for the company might then be defined as $C = w_1 D_1 + (1-w_1)D_2$, where $0 \le w_1 \le 1$. A decision rule could then be created where we classify the company as nonfraudulent if C is less than or equal to some cut-off value and is otherwise considered fraudulent. Use Solver's evolutionary optimizer to find the optimal value of w_1 and the cut-off value that minimizes the number of classification errors for the data given.

4. Of the two fraud-detection instruments, which would you recommend OATML implement?

5. What others techniques can you think of for combining OA's and TML's fraud-detection questionnaires that might be beneficial to OATML?

CASE 10.2   CapitalUno Credit Cards

CapitalUno (CU) is one of the largest credit card issuers in the United States. CU uses television commercials and direct mail as its primary means of offering cards to potential customers. CU spends millions of dollars each year on the postage and printing costs associated with its direct mail marketing efforts. Throughout the industry, the response rate to direct mail solicitations is notoriously low. As a result, CU could drastically reduce the cost and increase the effectiveness of its direct mail marketing efforts if it could do a better job of predicting who will and will not respond to its credit card solicitations.

Firms in the financial services industry often share information with each other about the demographic and financial attributes of their customers. Using this information, CU created and maintains a massive database for its direct mail activities. Each record in the database contains detailed data about each household in their coverage area. Thus, in addition to the family name and address at each household, CU has information about the number of people in each household, the family income level, the number of cars the family owns, and the number of bank credit cards held by each family. CU wants to use this information to develop a predictive model for whether or not a household will respond positively to a direct mail solicitation.

As an experiment, CU sent credit cards offers to 20 households. The data found in the file CapitalUno.xls summarizes the demographics and response to the solicitation for each household. A response value of 1 indicates the household did not respond, whereas a 2 indicates the acceptance of the credit card offer.

1. Calculate the centroids for each group in the analysis sample. What do these values indicate?

2. Use the regression approach to two-group DA to develop a rule for predicting whether or not a household will respond to a credit card solicitation. State the classification rule you identify.
3. Use the classification rule you identify in question 2 to classify each observation in the analysis sample. Create a confusion matrix summarizing the classification results. Overall, how accurate does this classification rule seem to be?
4. Suppose that the CU also gave you the following data on six additional households. Based on the classification rule you developed using regression, which (if any) of the six new households would you expect to accept a credit card solicitation?

Obs	Response	Family Size	Family Income ($1,000s)	Number of Cars	Number of Credit Cards
1	?	3	44.6	2	3
2	?	4	62.7	2	3
3	?	3	50.4	2	2
4	?	3	41.0	1	3
5	?	5	51.9	2	4

5. CU also wants you to analyze the data using the Mahalanobis distance measure approach discussed in this chapter. Carry out this analysis. Which of the two methods would you recommend that the CU use?
6. What other independent variables do you think might be relevant to this problem?

Predicting Bank Failure

CASE 10.3

Based on K.Y. Tam and M.Y. Kiang. "Managerial Applications of Neural Networks: The Case of Bank Failure Prediction." *Management Science*, 1992, vol. 38, no. 7, pp. 926–947.

The number of bankruptcies in the banking industry in the 1990s reached an historic high unparalleled since the Great Depression. In 1984, fewer than 50 bankruptcy cases were filed with the Federal Deposit Insurance Corporation (FDIC), whereas in 1991, more than 400 were filed. To monitor the member banks and to assure their proper compliance with federal regulations, the FDIC commits substantial efforts to both on-site examinations and off-site surveillance activities. To facilitate this process, the FDIC is developing an early warning system that will alert the agency to banks that might be approaching or entering financial distress. Using the technique of DA, you will help the FDIC develop such an early warning system.

Specifically, the FDIC wants to develop a procedure to help predict if a bank will enter financial distress in the coming year. The following financial ratios are helpful in making such predictions:

$$\text{Ratio 1} = \frac{\text{Total Captial}}{\text{Total Assets}}$$

$$\text{Ratio 2} = \frac{\text{Total Expenses}}{\text{Total Assets}}$$

$$\text{Ratio 3} = \frac{\text{Total Loans and Leases}}{\text{Total Deposits}}$$

The FDIC supplied you with data on these ratios collected one year ago for a sample of banks. It also indicated which banks are currently in financial distress. These data are

summarized in the file BankData.xls that accompanies this book (where Group 1 =
financially distressed banks, Group 2 = financially strong banks).

1. Calculate the centroids for each group in the analysis sample. What do these values
   indicate?
2. Use the regression approach to two-group DA to develop a rule for predicting
   whether or not a bank will enter financial distress. State the classification rule you
   identify.
3. Use the classification rule you identify in question 2 to classify each observation in
   the analysis sample. Create a confusion matrix summarizing the classification results. Overall, how accurate does this classification rule seem to be?
4. Suppose that the FDIC also gave you the following data on six new banks. Based on
   the classification rule you developed using regression, which (if any) of the six new
   banks would you expect to enter financial distress?

Obs	Group	Ratio 1	Ratio 2	Ratio 3
1	?	3.3	0.13	0.63
2	?	9.2	0.08	0.26
3	?	9.3	0.09	0.59
4	?	3.2	0.16	0.57
5	?	11.4	0.09	0.69
6	?	8.1	0.14	0.72

5. The FDIC also wants you to analyze the data using the Mahalanobis distance measure approach discussed in this chapter. Carry out this analysis. Which of the two
   methods would you recommend that the FDIC use?

Chapter 11

Time Series Forecasting

11.0 Introduction

A **time series** is a set of observations on a quantitative variable collected over time. For example, every night the evening news reports the closing value of the Dow Jones Industrial Average. These closing values represent a series of values for a quantitative variable over time—or a time series. Most businesses keep track of a number of time series variables. Examples might include daily, weekly, monthly, or quarterly figures on sales, costs, profits, inventory, back orders, customer counts, and so on.

Businesses often are interested in forecasting future values of a time series variable. For example, if we could accurately predict future closing values of the Dow Jones Industrial Average, we could become very wealthy investing in the stock market by "buying low and selling high." In constructing business plans, most companies make some attempt to forecast the expected levels of sales, costs, profits, inventory, back orders, customer counts, and so on. These types of forecasts often are required inputs to the other types of modeling techniques discussed throughout this text.

In Chapter 9, we investigated how to build and use regression models to predict the behavior of a dependent variable using one or more independent variables that are believed to be related to the dependent variable in a *causal* fashion. That is, when building a regression model, we often select independent variables that are believed to cause the observed behavior of the dependent variable. Although we can sometimes use this same approach to build a causal regression model for a time series variable, we cannot always do so.

For example, if we do not know which causal independent variables are influencing a particular time series variable, we cannot build a regression model. And even if we do have some idea which causal variables are affecting a time series, there might not be any data available for those variables. If data on the causal variables are available, the best regression function estimated from these data might not fit the data well. Finally, even if the estimated regression function fits the data well, we might have to forecast the values of the causal independent variables in order to estimate future values of the dependent (time series) variable. Forecasting the causal independent variables might be more difficult than forecasting the original time series variable.

On the Importance of Forecasting...

"You do not plan to ship goods across the ocean, or to assemble merchandise for sale, or to borrow money without first trying to determine what the future may hold in store. Ensuring that the materials you order are delivered on time, seeing to it that the items you plan to sell are produced on schedule, and getting your sales facilities in place all must be planned before that moment when the customers show up and lay their money on the counter. The successful business executive is a forecaster first: purchasing, producing, marketing, pricing, and organizing all follow." —Peter Bernstein. *Against the Gods: The Remarkable Story of Risk*. New York: John Wiley & Sons, 1996, pp. 21–22.

11.1 Time Series Methods

In many business planning situations, it is difficult, undesirable, or even impossible to forecast time series data using a causal regression model. However, if we can discover some sort of systematic variation in the past behavior of the time series variable, we can attempt to construct a model of this behavior to help us forecast its future behavior. For example, we might find a long-term upward (or downward) trend in the time series that might be expected to continue in the future. Or, we might discover some predictable seasonal fluctuations in the data that could help us make estimates about the future. As you may have surmised, time series forecasting is based largely on the maxim that history tends to repeat itself.

Techniques that analyze the past behavior of a time series variable to predict the future are sometimes referred to as **extrapolation** models. The general form of an extrapolation model is:

$$\hat{Y}_{t+1} = f(Y_t, Y_{t-1}, Y_{t-2}, \ldots) \tag{11.1}$$

where $\hat{Y}_{t+1}$ represents the *predicted* value for the time series variable in time period $t + 1$, Y_t represents the *actual* value of the time series variable in time period t, Y_{t-1} represents the *actual* value of the time series variable in time period $t - 1$, and so on. The goal of an extrapolation model is to identify a function $f(\ )$ for equation 11.1 that produces accurate forecasts of future values of the time series variable.

This chapter presents a variety of methods for analyzing time series data. We'll first discuss several techniques that are appropriate for **stationary** time series, where there is no significant upward or downward trend in the data over time. Then, we'll discuss techniques for handling **nonstationary** time series, where there is some upward or downward trend in the data over time. We'll also discuss techniques for modeling **seasonal** patterns in both stationary and nonstationary time series data.

11.2 Measuring Accuracy

Many methods are available for modeling time series data. In most cases, it is impossible to know in advance which method will be the most effective for a given set of data. Thus, a common approach to time series analysis involves trying several modeling techniques on a given data set and evaluating how well they explain the past behavior of the time series variable. We can evaluate these techniques by constructing line graphs that show the actual data versus the values predicted by the various modeling techniques. More formal quantitative measures of the accuracy (or "goodness of fit") of time series modeling techniques also exist. Four common accuracy measures are the **mean absolute deviation** (MAD), the **mean absolute percent error** (MAPE), the **mean square error** (MSE), and the **root mean square error** (RMSE). These quantities are defined as follows:

$$MAD = \frac{1}{n}\sum_i \left|Y_i - \hat{Y}_i\right|$$

$$MAPE = \frac{100}{n}\sum_i \left|\frac{Y_i - \hat{Y}_i}{Y_i}\right|$$

$$MSE = \frac{1}{n}\sum_i (Y_i - \hat{Y}_i)^2$$

$$RMSE = \sqrt{MSE}$$

In each of these formulas, Y_i represents the *actual* value for the ith observation in the time series, and $\hat{Y}_i$ is the *forecasted* or predicted value for this observation. These quantities measure the differences between the actual values in the time series and the predicted, or fitted, values generated by the forecasting technique. The MSE and RMSE measures are closely related to the sum of square estimation errors criterion introduced in our discussion of regression analysis. Although all of these measures are commonly used in time series modeling, we will focus on the MSE measure because it is somewhat easier to calculate.

11.3 Stationary Models

The following example will be used to demonstrate several of the most common time series techniques for stationary data.

Electra-City is a retail store that sells audio and video equipment for the home and car. Each month, the manager of the store must order merchandise from a distant warehouse. Currently, the manager is trying to estimate how many digital video recorders (DVRs) the store is likely to sell in the next month. To assist in this process, he has collected the data shown in Figure 11.1 (and in the file Fig11-1.xlsm that accompanies this book) on the number of DVRs sold in each of the previous 24 months. He wants to use these data in making his prediction.

After collecting the data for a time series variable, the next step in building a time series model is to inspect the data plotted over time. Figure 11.1 includes a plot of the DVR data. Notice that this plot does not suggest a strong upward or downward trend in the data. This plot suggests that the number of DVRs sold each month fell somewhere between 30 and 40 units over the past two years with no continuing pattern or regularity from month to month. Thus, we expect that one of the extrapolation techniques discussed in the following sections would be an appropriate method for modeling these data.

FIGURE 11.1 *Historical DVR sales data for the Electra-City forecasting problem*

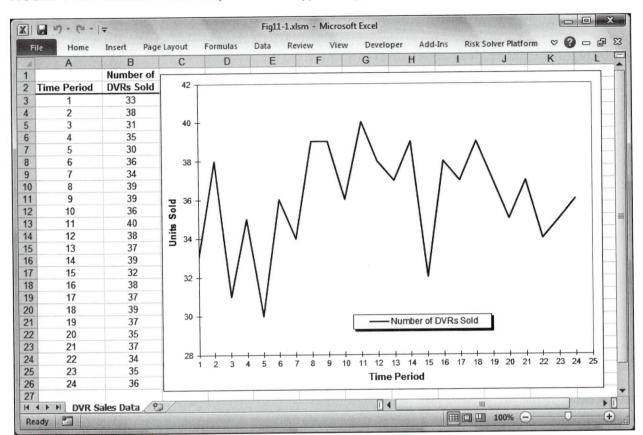

Creating a Line Graph

To create a scatter plot like the one shown in Figure 11.1:

1. Select cells A1 through B26.
2. Click Insert.
3. Click the Scatter Chart option.
4. Click Scatter with Straight Lines and Markers.

After Excel creates a basic chart, you can customize it in many ways. Right-clicking a chart element displays a dialog box with options for modifying the appearance of the element.

11.4 Moving Averages

The **moving average** technique is probably the easiest extrapolation method for stationary data to use and understand. With this technique, the predicted value of the time series in period $t + 1$ (denoted by $\hat{Y}_{t+1}$) is simply the average of the k previous observations in the series;

that is:

$$\hat{Y}_{t+1} = \frac{Y_t + Y_{t-1} + Y_{t-k+1}}{k}$$ **11.2**

The value k in equation 11.2 determines how many previous observations will be included in the moving average. No general method exists for determining what value of k will be best for a particular time series. Therefore, we must try several values of k to see which gives the best results. This is illustrated in Figure 11.2 (and in the file Fig11-2.xlsm that accompanies this book) where the monthly number of DVRs sold for Electra-City is fit using moving average models with k values of 2 and 4.

We generated the moving average forecasts in Figure 11.2 using the AVERAGE( ) function. For example, the two-month moving average forecasts are generated by implementing the following formula in cell C5 and copying it to cells C6 through C26:

Formula for cell C5:   =AVERAGE(B3:B4)

(Copy to C6 through C26.)

The four-month moving average forecasts are generated by implementing the following formula in cell D7 and copying it to cells D8 through D26:

Formula for cell D7:   =AVERAGE(B3:B6)

(Copy to D8 through D26.)

The actual DVR sales data are plotted in Figure 11.2 along with the predicted values from the two moving average models. This graph shows that the predicted values tend to be less volatile, or smoother, than the actual data. This should not be surprising because

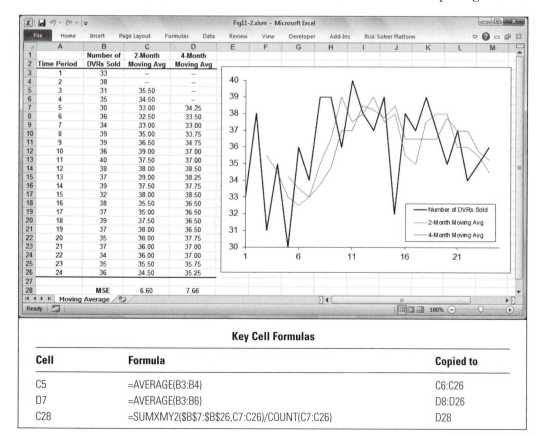

FIGURE 11.2

Moving average forecasts for the DVR sales data

Key Cell Formulas

Cell	Formula	Copied to
C5	=AVERAGE(B3:B4)	C6:C26
D7	=AVERAGE(B3:B6)	D8:D26
C28	=SUMXMY2($B$7:$B$26,C7:C26)/COUNT(C7:C26)	D28

the moving average technique tends to average out the peaks and valleys occurring in the original data. Thus, the moving average technique is sometimes referred to as a *smoothing* method. The larger the value of k (or the more past data points are averaged together), the smoother the moving average prediction will be.

We can evaluate the relative accuracy of the two moving average forecasting functions by comparing the MSE values for these two techniques shown in cells C28 and D28 in Figure 11.2. The following formula calculates these MSE values:

> Formula for cell C28:   =SUMXMY2($B$7:$B$26,C7:C26)/COUNT(C7:C26)
> (Copy to D28.)

Note that the SUMXMY2( ) function calculates the sum of squared differences between corresponding values in two different ranges. The COUNT( ) function returns the number of values in a range. Also note that the forecasts using the two-month moving average begin in time period 3 (cell C5), and the four-month moving average forecasts begin in time period 5 (cell D7). We are calculating the MSE values starting in time period 5 for both forecasting techniques so that a fair comparison between them can be made.

The MSE value describes the overall fit of the forecasting technique to the historical data. By comparing the MSE values for the two moving averages, we might conclude that the two-month moving average (with an MSE of 6.60) provides more accurate forecasts than the four-month moving average (with an MSE of 7.66). Note, however, that the MSE includes and weighs relatively old data with the same importance as the most recent data. Thus, selecting a forecast based on the total MSE of the forecasting functions might not be wise because a forecasting function might have achieved a lower total MSE by fitting older data points very well while being relatively inaccurate on more recent data.

Because we want to forecast *future* observations, we might be interested in how well the forecasting function performed on the most recent data. We can determine this by calculating other MSE values using only the most recent data. For example, if we calculate MSE values using only the last 12 time periods (periods 13 through 24), the four-month moving average produces an MSE of 6.01, and the two-month moving average produces an MSE of 6.02. These results are shown in the table below the graph in Figure 11.3. So an argument could be made that the four-month moving average model should be used to predict the future because it produced the most accurate predictions of the actual values observed during the past 12 time periods. Note, however, that there is no guarantee that the forecasting technique that has been most accurate recently will continue to be most accurate in the future.

11.4.1 FORECASTING WITH THE MOVING AVERAGE MODEL

Assuming (for simplicity) that the manager of Electra-City is satisfied with the accuracy of the two-month moving average model, the prediction of the number of DVRs to be sold in the next month (time period 25) is calculated as:

$$\hat{Y}_{25} = \frac{Y_{24} + Y_{23}}{2} = \frac{36 + 35}{2} = 35.5$$

To forecast *more* than one period into the future using the moving average technique, we must substitute forecasted values for unobserved actual values. For example, suppose that at the end of time period 24, we want to forecast the number of DVRs to be sold in time periods 25 *and* 26. Using a two-period moving average, the forecast for time period 26 is represented by:

$$\hat{Y}_{26} = \frac{Y_{25} + Y_{24}}{2}$$

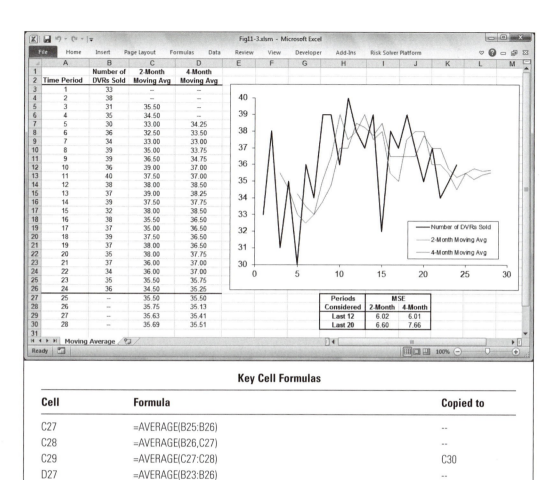

FIGURE 11.3

Forecasts of the DVR sales data

Key Cell Formulas

Cell	Formula	Copied to
C27	=AVERAGE(B25:B26)	--
C28	=AVERAGE(B26,C27)	--
C29	=AVERAGE(C27:C28)	C30
D27	=AVERAGE(B23:B26)	--
D28	=AVERAGE(B24:$B$26,$D$27:D27)	D29:D30
I29	=SUMXMY2($B$15:$B26,C15:C26)/COUNT(C15:C26)	J29
I30	=SUMXMY2($B$7:$B26,C7:C26)/COUNT(C7:C26)	J30

However, at time period 24, we do not know the actual value for Y_{25}. We have to substitute $\hat{Y}_{25}$ for Y_{25} in the previous equation to generate the forecast for time period 26. Therefore, at time period 24, our estimate of the number of DVRs to be sold in time period 26 is:

$$\hat{Y}_{26} = \frac{\hat{Y}_{25} + Y_{24}}{2} = \frac{35.5 + 36}{2} = 35.75$$

Similarly, at time period 24, forecasts for periods 27 and 28 would be calculated as follows:

$$\hat{Y}_{27} = \frac{\hat{Y}_{26} + \hat{Y}_{25}}{2} = \frac{35.75 + 35.5}{2} = 35.63$$

$$\hat{Y}_{28} = \frac{\hat{Y}_{27} + \hat{Y}_{26}}{2} = \frac{35.63 + 35.75}{2} = 35.69$$

Figure 11.3 shows forecasts made at time period 24 for periods 25, 26, 27, and 28 for both the two-month and four-month moving average techniques.

11.5 Weighted Moving Averages

One drawback of the moving average technique is that all the past data used in calculating the average are weighted equally. We can often obtain a more accurate forecast by assigning different weights to the data. The **weighted moving average** technique is a simple variation on the moving average technique that allows for weights to be assigned to the data being averaged. In the weighted moving average technique, the forecasting function is represented by:

$$\hat{Y}_{t+1} = w_1 Y_t + w_2 Y_{t-1} + \cdots + w_k Y_{t-k+1} \qquad \textbf{11.3}$$

where $0 \le w_i \le 1$, and $\sum_{i=1}^{k} w_i = 1$. Note that the simple moving average forecast in equation 11.2 is a special case of equation 11.3 where $w_1 = w_2 = \cdots = w_k = \frac{1}{k}$.

Although the weighted moving average offers greater flexibility than the moving average, it is also a bit more complicated. In addition to determining a value for k, we must also determine values for the weights w_i in equation 11.3. However, for a given value of k, we can use Solver to determine the values for w_i that minimize the MSE. The spreadsheet implementation of a two-month weighted moving average model for the Electra-City example is shown in Figure 11.4 (and in the file Fig11-4.xlsm that accompanies this book).

FIGURE 11.4 *Spreadsheet implementation of the weighted moving average model*

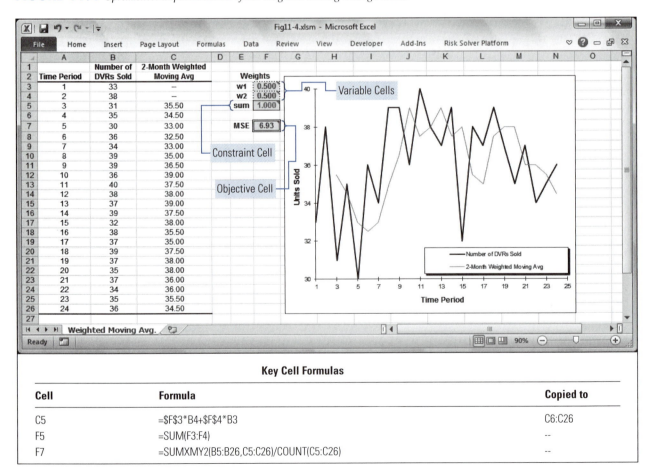

Key Cell Formulas

Cell	Formula	Copied to
C5	=$F$3*B4+$F$4*B3	C6:C26
F5	=SUM(F3:F4)	--
F7	=SUMXMY2(B5:B26,C5:C26)/COUNT(C5:C26)	--

Solver Settings:
Objective: F7 (Min)
Variable cells: F3:F4
Constraints:
F3:F4 <= 1
F3:F4 >= 0
F5 = 1
Solver Options:
Standard GRG Nonlinear Engine

FIGURE 11.5

Solver settings and options for the weighted moving average model

Cells F3 and F4 represent the weights w_1 and w_2, respectively. Cell F5 contains the sum of cells F3 and F4. The weighted average forecasting function is implemented in cell C5 with the following formula, which is copied to cells C6 through C26:

Formula for cell C5:   =$F$3*B4+$F$4*B3
(Copy to C6 through C26.)

Notice that with $w_1 = w_2 = 0.5$, the weighted average predictions are identical to those of the simple moving average method shown in Figure 11.2. The formula for the MSE is implemented in cell F7 as follows:

Formula for cell F7:   =SUMXMY2(B5:B26,C5:C26)/COUNT(C5:C26)

We can use the Solver settings and options shown in Figure 11.5 to identify the values for the weights in cells F3 and F4 that minimize the MSE. Notice that this is a nonlinear optimization problem because the MSE represents a nonlinear objective function. Figure 11.6 shows the solution to this problem.

Notice that the optimal weights of $w_1 = 0.291$ and $w_2 = 0.709$ reduce the value of the MSE only slightly, from 6.93 to 6.29.

11.5.1 FORECASTING WITH THE WEIGHTED MOVING AVERAGE MODEL

Using the weighted moving average technique, the predicted number of DVRs to be sold at Electra-City in the next month (time period 25) is calculated as:

$$\hat{Y}_{25} = w_1 Y_{24} + w_2 Y_{23} = 0.291 \times 36 + 0.709 \times 35 = 35.29$$

We can also use the weighted moving average technique to forecast more than one time period into the future. However, as with the moving average technique, we must substitute forecasted values for unobserved actual values where needed. For example, suppose that at the end of time period 24, we want to forecast the number of DVRs to be sold in time periods 25 *and* 26. The weighted moving average forecast for time period 26 is represented by:

$$\hat{Y}_{26} = w_1 Y_{25} + w_2 Y_{24}$$

However, at time period 24, we do not know the actual value for Y_{25}. As a result, we have to substitute $\hat{Y}_{25}$ for Y_{25} in the previous equation to generate the following forecast for time period 26:

$$\hat{Y}_{26} = w_1 \hat{Y}_{25} + w_2 Y_{24} = 0.291 \times 35.29 + 0.709 \times 36 = 35.79$$

FIGURE 11.6 *Optimal solution and forecasts with the weighted moving average model*

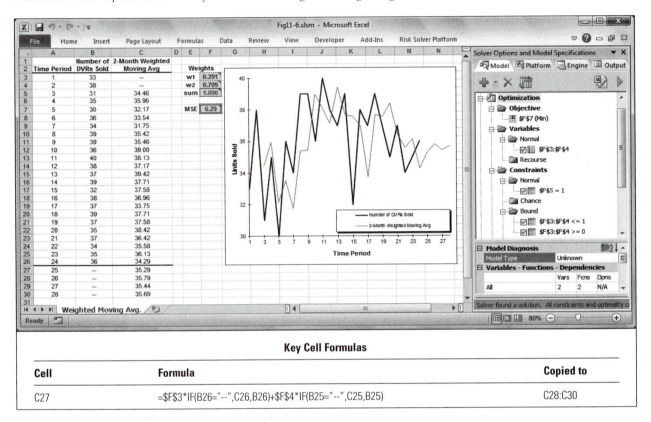

Key Cell Formulas

Cell	Formula	Copied to
C27	=$F$3*IF(B26="--",C26,B26)+$F$4*IF(B25="--",C25,B25)	C28:C30

Similarly, at time period 24, forecasts for time periods 27 and 28 would be computed as:

$$\hat{Y}_{27} = w_1\hat{Y}_{26} + w_2\hat{Y}_{25} = 0.291 \times 35.79 + 0.709 \times 35.29 = 35.44$$
$$\hat{Y}_{28} = w_1\hat{Y}_{27} + w_2\hat{Y}_{26} = 0.291 \times 35.44 + 0.709 \times 35.79 = 35.69$$

Figure 11.6 shows forecasts made at time period 24 for periods 25, 26, 27, and 28 for the two-month weighted average technique.

11.6 Exponential Smoothing

Exponential smoothing is another averaging technique for stationary data that allows weights to be assigned to past data. Exponential smoothing models assume the following form:

$$\hat{Y}_{t+1} = \hat{Y}_t + \alpha(Y_t - \hat{Y}_t) \qquad \textbf{11.4}$$

Equation 11.4 indicates that the predicted value for time period $t + 1$ ($\hat{Y}_{t+1}$) is equal to the predicted value for the previous period ($\hat{Y}_t$) plus an adjustment for the error made in predicting the previous period's value ($\alpha(Y_t - \hat{Y}_t)$). The parameter α in equation 11.4 can assume any value between 0 and 1 ($0 \leq \alpha \leq 1$).

It can be shown that the exponential smoothing formula in equation 11.4 is equivalent to:

$$\hat{Y}_{t+1} = \alpha Y_t + \alpha(1 - \alpha)Y_{t-1} + \alpha(1 - \alpha)^2 Y_{t-2} + \cdots + \alpha(1 - \alpha)^n Y_{t-n} + \cdots$$

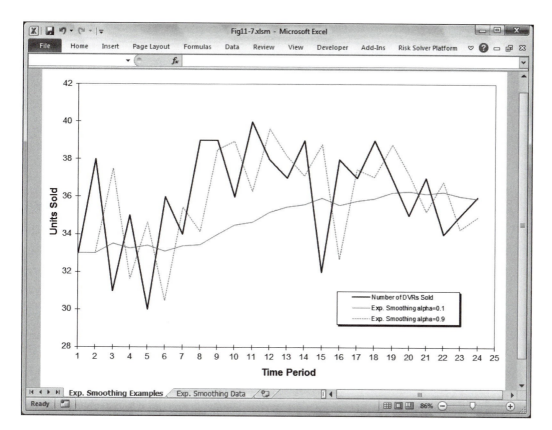

FIGURE 11.7

Two exponential smoothing models of the DVR sales data

As shown in the previous equation, the forecast $\hat{Y}_{t+1}$ in exponential smoothing is a weighted combination of all previous values in the time series where the most recent observation Y_t receives the heaviest weight (α), the next most recent observation Y_{t-1} receives the next heaviest weight ($\alpha(1 - \alpha)$), and so on.

In an exponential smoothing model, small values of α tend to produce sluggish forecasts that do not react quickly to changes in the data. A value of α near 1 produces a forecast that reacts more quickly to changes in the data. Figure 11.7 (and file Fig11-7.xlsm that accompanies this book) illustrates these relationships, showing the results of two exponential smoothing models for the DVR sales data with α-values of 0.1 and 0.9.

We can use Solver to determine the optimal value for α when building an exponential smoothing forecasting model for a particular data set. The spreadsheet implementation of the exponential smoothing forecasting model for the Electra-City example is shown in Figure 11.8 (and in the file Fig11-8.xlsm that accompanies this book).

In Figure 11.8, cell F3 represents α. In an exponential smoothing forecasting model, it is customary to assume that $\hat{Y}_1 = Y_1$. Thus, in Figure 11.8, cell C3 contains the following formula:

Formula for cell C3:   =B3

The forecasting function in equation 11.4 begins for time period $t = 2$ with the following formula, which is implemented in cell C4 and copied to cells C5 through C26:

Formula for cell C4:   =C3+$F$3*(B3−C3)
(Copy to C5 through C26.)

FIGURE 11.8 *Spreadsheet implementation of the exponential smoothing model*

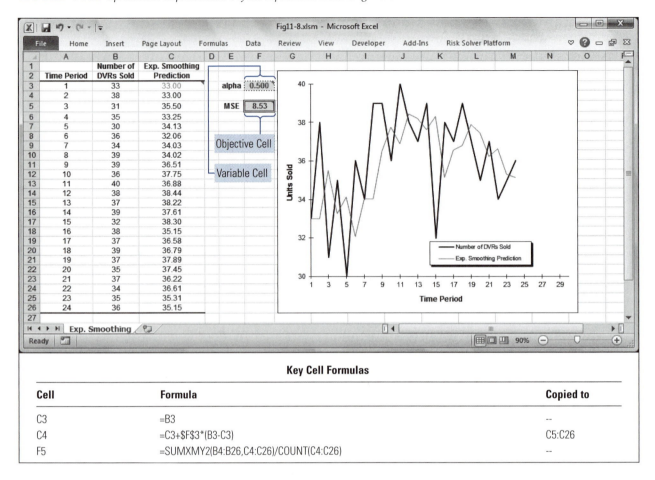

The formula in cell F5 calculates the MSE value as:

Formula for cell F5:   =SUMXMY2(B4:B26,C4:C26)/COUNT(C4:C26)

We can use the Solver settings and options shown in Figure 11.9 to identify the value for α that minimizes the MSE. Again, this is a nonlinear optimization problem because the MSE represents a nonlinear objective function. Figure 11.10 shows the solution to this problem. Notice that the optimal value for α is given in cell F3 as 0.268.

11.6.1 FORECASTING WITH THE EXPONENTIAL SMOOTHING MODEL

Using the exponential smoothing model, the predicted number of DVRs to be sold at Electra-City in the next month (time period 25) is calculated as:

$$\hat{Y}_{25} = \hat{Y}_{24} + \alpha(Y_{24} - \hat{Y}_{24}) = 35.74 + 0.268*(36 - 35.74) = 35.81$$

An interesting property of the exponential smoothing technique becomes apparent when we try to use it to forecast more than one time period into the future. For example,

Solver Settings:
Objective: F5 (Min)
Variable cells: F3
Constraints:
F3 <= 1
F3 >= 0
Solver Options:
Standard GRG Nonlinear Engine

FIGURE 11.9

Solver settings and options for the exponential smoothing model

FIGURE 11.10 *Optimal solution and forecasts for the exponential smoothing model*

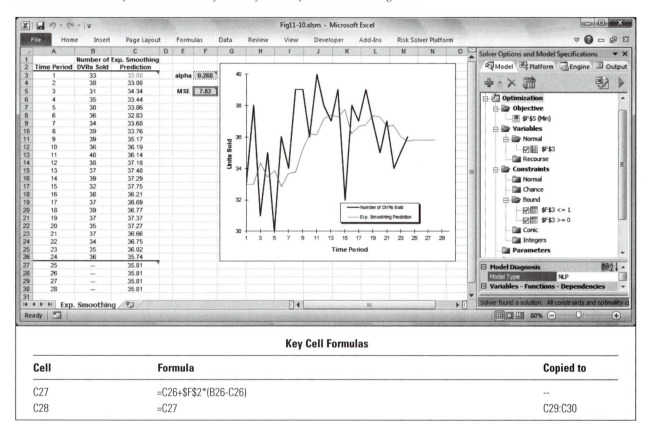

Key Cell Formulas		
Cell	**Formula**	**Copied to**
C27	=C26+$F$2*(B26-C26)	--
C28	=C27	C29:C30

suppose that at time period 24, we want to forecast the number of DVRs to be sold in time periods 25 *and* 26. The forecast for time period 26 is represented by:

$$\hat{Y}_{26} = \hat{Y}_{25} + \alpha(Y_{25} - \hat{Y}_{25})$$

Because Y_{25} is unknown at time period 24, we must substitute $\hat{Y}_{25}$ for Y_{25} in the previous equation. However, in that case we obtain $\hat{Y}_{26} = \hat{Y}_{25}$. In fact, the forecast for all future time periods would equal $\hat{Y}_{25}$. So when using exponential smoothing, the forecast for *all* future time periods equals the same value. This is consistent with the underlying idea of a stationary time series. If a time series is stationary (or has no trend), it is reasonable to assume that the forecast of the next time period and all future time periods should equal the same value. Thus, the exponential smoothing forecasting model for all future time periods in the Electra-City example is represented by $\hat{Y}_t = 35.81$ (for $t = 25, 26, 27, \ldots$).

A Word of Caution About Forecasting...

Although we can use the moving average or exponential smoothing technique to forecast a value for any future time period (or any value of $n \geq 1$), as the forecast horizon lengthens, our confidence in the accuracy of the forecast diminishes because there is no guarantee that the historical patterns on which the model is based will continue indefinitely into the future.

11.7 Seasonality

Many time series variables exhibit **seasonality**, or a regular, repeating pattern in the data. For example, in time series data for monthly fuel oil sales, we would expect to see regular jumps in the data during the winter months each year. Similarly, monthly or quarterly sales data for suntan lotion would likely show consistent peaks during the summer and valleys during the winter.

Two different types of seasonal effects are common in time series data: additive effects and multiplicative effects. Additive seasonal effects tend to be on the same order of magnitude each time a given season is encountered. Multiplicative seasonal effects tend to have an increasing effect each time a given season is encountered. Figure 11.11 (and

FIGURE 11.11

Examples of additive and multiplicative seasonal effects in stationary data

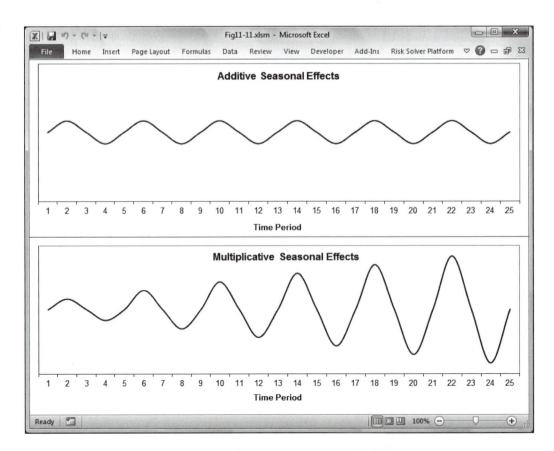

the file Fig11-11.xlsm that accompanies this book) illustrates the difference between these two types of seasonal effects for stationary data.

We will use the following example to illustrate two techniques for modeling additive and multiplicative seasonality in stationary time series data.

> Savannah Climate Control (SCC) sells and services residential heat pumps. Sales of heat pumps tend to be higher than average in the winter and summer quarters when temperatures are more extreme. Similarly, sales tend to be lower than average in the spring and fall quarters when temperatures are less extreme and homeowners can put off replacing inoperable heat pump units. The owner of SCC, Bill Cooter, has collected quarterly unit sales data for the past several years as shown in Figure 11.12 (and in file Fig11-12.xlsm that accompanies this book). He wants to analyze this data to create a model to estimate the number of units he will sell in each of the next four quarters.

FIGURE 11.12 *Historical heat pump sales data for Savannah Climate Control*

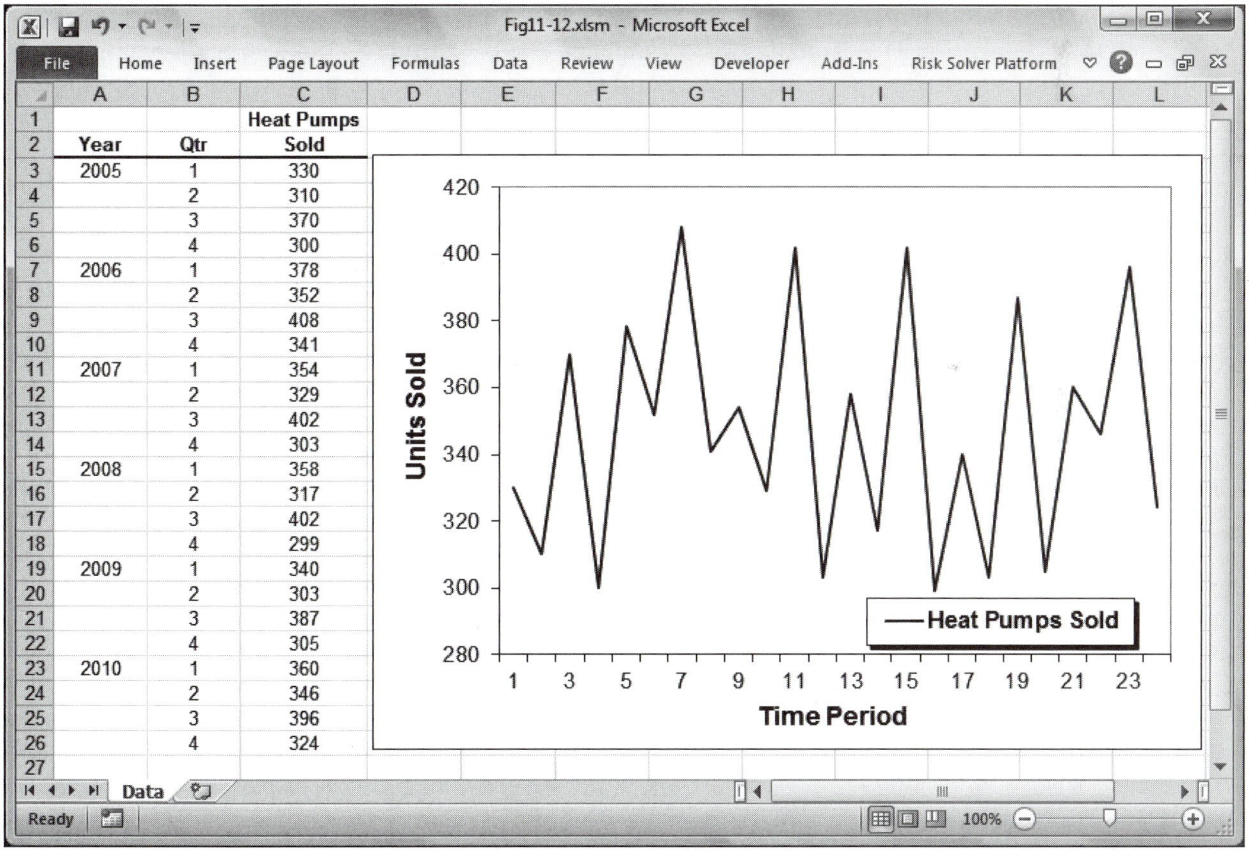

Year	Qtr	Heat Pumps Sold
2005	1	330
	2	310
	3	370
	4	300
2006	1	378
	2	352
	3	408
	4	341
2007	1	354
	2	329
	3	402
	4	303
2008	1	358
	2	317
	3	402
	4	299
2009	1	340
	2	303
	3	387
	4	305
2010	1	360
	2	346
	3	396
	4	324

11.8 Stationary Data with Additive Seasonal Effects

The data shown in Figure 11.12 indicate that unit sales tend to be high in quarters one and three (corresponding to the winter and summer months) and low in quarters two and four (corresponding to the spring and fall months). Thus, this data exhibits quarterly seasonal effects that likely can be modeled to make more accurate forecasts.

The following model is useful for modeling stationary time series data with additive seasonal effects:

$$\hat{Y}_{t+n} = E_t + S_{t+n-p} \qquad \textbf{11.5}$$

where

$$E_t = \alpha(Y_t - S_{t-p}) + (1 - \alpha)\,E_{t-1} \qquad \textbf{11.6}$$
$$S_t = \beta(Y_t - E_t) + (1 - \beta)S_{t-p} \qquad \textbf{11.7}$$
$$0 \le \alpha \le 1 \text{ and } 0 \le \beta \le 1$$

In this model, E_t represents the expected level of the time series in period t, and S_t represents the seasonal factor for period t. The constant p represents the number of seasonal periods in the data. Thus, for quarterly data $p = 4$, and for monthly data $p = 12$.

In equation 11.5, the forecast for time period $t + n$ is simply the expected level of the time series at period t adjusted upward or downward by the seasonal factor S_{t+n-p}. Equation 11.6 estimates the expected level for period t as a weighted average of the deseasonalized data for period t ($Y_t - S_{t-p}$) and the previous period's level (E_{t-1}). Equation 11.7 estimates the seasonal factor for period t as the weighted average of the estimated seasonal effect in period t ($Y_t - E_t$) and the previous seasonal factor for that same season (S_{t-p}).

In order to use equations 11.5 through 11.7, we must initialize the estimated levels and seasonal factors for the first p time periods. There are numerous ways to do this. However, for convenience we will do this as follows:

$$E_t = \sum_{i=1}^{p} \frac{Y_i}{p}, \quad t = 1, 2, \ldots, p$$
$$S_t = Y_t - E_t, \quad t = 1, 2, \ldots, p$$

That is, we will use the average value of the first p time periods as the initial expected levels for each of these time periods. We then use the difference between the actual values and expected levels as the initial seasonal factors for the first p time periods.

The spreadsheet implementation for this technique is shown in Figure 11.13 (and in file Fig11-13.xlsm that accompanies this book).

The initial expected level values for the first four time periods were entered into cells E3 through E6 as follows:

Formula for cell E3:   =AVERAGE($D$3:$D$6)
(Copy to cells E4 through E6.)

Next, the initial seasonal factors for the first four periods were entered into cells F3 through F6 as follows:

Formula for cell F3:   =D3-E3
(Copy to cells F4 through F6.)

Cells J3 and J4 represent the values of α and β, respectively. The remaining expected levels and seasonal factors defined by equations 11.6 and 11.7 were then entered in columns E and F, respectively, as follows:

Formula for cell E7:   =$J$3*(D7-F3)+(1-$J$3)*E6
(Copy to cells E8 through E26.)

Formula for cell F7:   =$J$4*(D7-E7)+(1-$J$4)*F3
(Copy to cells F8 through F26.)

FIGURE 11.13 *Spreadsheet implementation of model with additive seasonal effects*

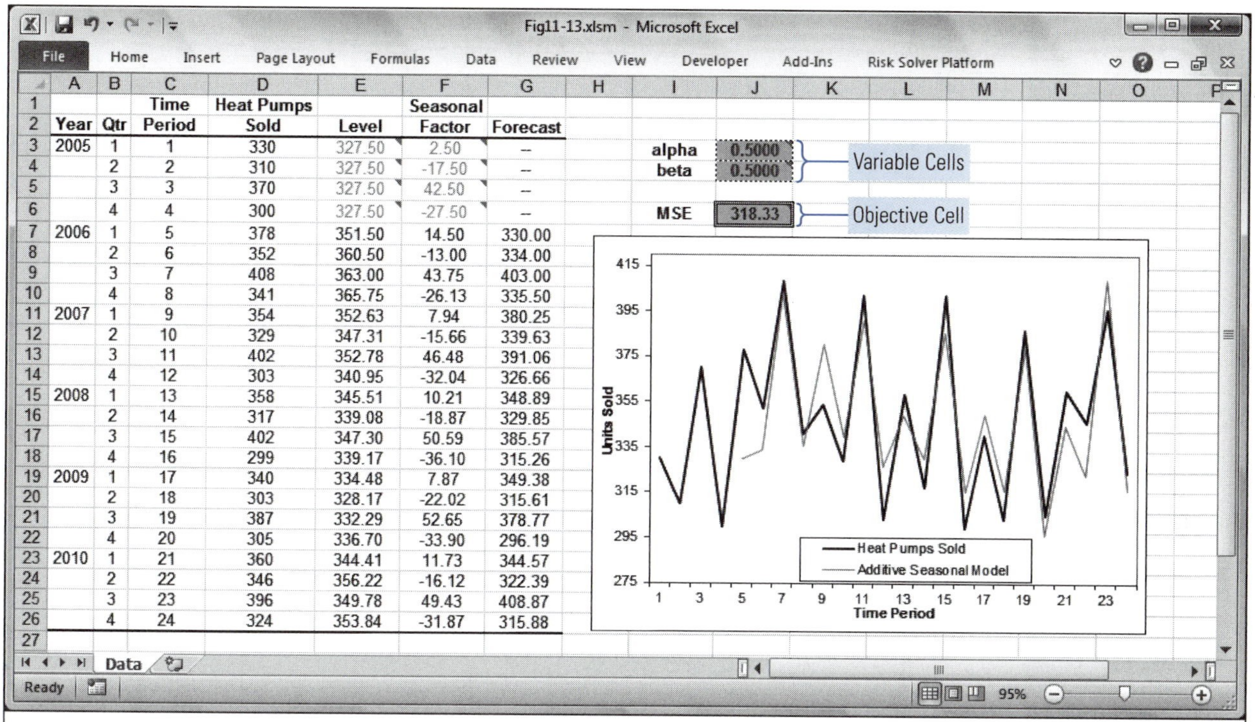

Year	Qtr	Time Period	Heat Pumps Sold	Level	Seasonal Factor	Forecast
2005	1	1	330	327.50	2.50	--
	2	2	310	327.50	-17.50	--
	3	3	370	327.50	42.50	--
	4	4	300	327.50	-27.50	--
2006	1	5	378	351.50	14.50	330.00
	2	6	352	360.50	-13.00	334.00
	3	7	408	363.00	43.75	403.00
	4	8	341	365.75	-26.13	335.50
2007	1	9	354	352.63	7.94	380.25
	2	10	329	347.31	-15.66	339.63
	3	11	402	352.78	46.48	391.06
	4	12	303	340.95	-32.04	326.66
2008	1	13	358	345.51	10.21	348.89
	2	14	317	339.08	-18.87	329.85
	3	15	402	347.30	50.59	385.57
	4	16	299	339.17	-36.10	315.26
2009	1	17	340	334.48	7.87	349.38
	2	18	303	328.17	-22.02	315.61
	3	19	387	332.29	52.65	378.77
	4	20	305	336.70	-33.90	296.19
2010	1	21	360	344.41	11.73	344.57
	2	22	346	356.22	-16.12	322.39
	3	23	396	349.78	49.43	408.87
	4	24	324	353.84	-31.87	315.88

Key Cell Formulas

Cell	Formula	Copied to
E3	=AVERAGE($D$3:$D$6)	E4:E6
E7	=$J$3*(D7-F3)+(1-$J$3)*E6	E8:E26
F3	=D3-E3	F4:F6
F7	=$J$4*(D7-E7)+(1-$J$4)*F3	F8:F26
G7	=E6+F3	G8:G26
J6	=SUMXMY2(G7:G26,D7:D26)/COUNT(G7:G26)	--

Now, according to equation 11.5, at any time period t, the prediction for time period $t + 1$ is given by:

$$\hat{Y}_{t+1} = E_t + S_{t+1-p}$$

Thus, at time period 4, we are able to calculate the prediction for time period 5 as follows:

Formula for cell G7: =E6+F3
(Copy to cells G8 through G26.)

This formula is then copied to cells G8 through G26 to complete the one period ahead predictions for the remaining observations.

We can use Solver options and settings shown in Figure 11.14 to determine the values of α and β that minimize the MSE for this problem, computed in cell J6 as follows:

Formula for cell J6: =SUMXMY2(G7:G26,D7:D26)/COUNT(G7:G26)

FIGURE 11.14

Solver settings and options for the heat pump sales problem with seasonal additive effects

Solver Settings:
Objective: J6 (Min)
Variable cells: J3:J4
Constraints:
J3:J4 <= 1
J3:J4 >= 0
Solver Options:
Standard GRG Nonlinear Engine

Figure 11.15 shows the optimal solution to this problem along with a graph showing the actual sales data plotted against the values predicted by our model. Note that the predicted values fit the actual data reasonably well.

11.8.1 FORECASTING WITH THE MODEL

We can use the results in Figure 11.15 to compute forecasts for any future time period. According to equation 11.5, at time period 24, the forecast for time period $24 + n$ is given by:

$$\hat{Y}_{24+n} = E_{24} + S_{24+n-4}$$

FIGURE 11.15 *Optimal solution and forecasts for the heat pump sales problem with additive seasonal effects*

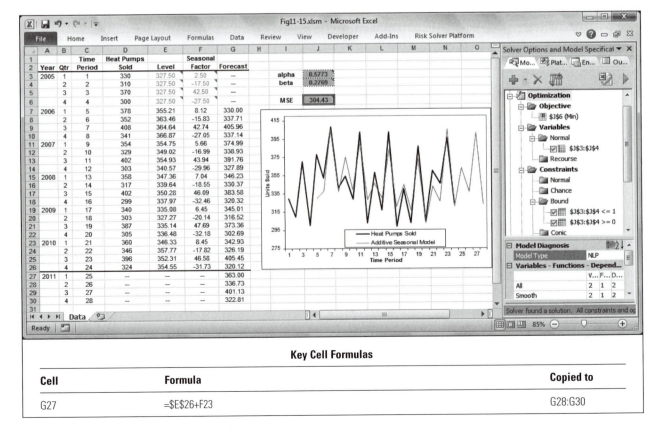

							Key Cell Formulas		

Cell	Formula	Copied to
G27	=$E$26+F23	G28:G30

Our forecasts for each quarter in the year 2006 would be calculated as follows:

$$\hat{Y}_{25} = E_{24} + S_{21} = 354.55 + 8.45 = 363.00$$
$$\hat{Y}_{26} = E_{24} + S_{22} = 354.55 - 17.82 = 336.73$$
$$\hat{Y}_{27} = E_{24} + S_{23} = 354.55 + 46.58 = 401.13$$
$$\hat{Y}_{28} = E_{24} + S_{24} = 354.55 - 31.73 = 322.81$$

Thus, each forecast is simply the expected level of the time series in period 24 adjusted by the relevant seasonal factor. The calculations for these forecasts were implemented in Figure 11.15 as follows:

Formula for cell G27:   =$E$26+F23

(Copy to cells G28 through G30.)

Initializing Forecasting Models

It is important to note that the other methods can be used to initialize the base level (E_t) and seasonality (S_t) values used in the previous model and those presented later in this chapter. For instance, we could have used Solver to determine optimal (minimum MSE) values for the level and seasonality parameters along with the smoothing constants α and β. However, even if Solver is used to determine "optimal" initial values, there is no guarantee that the resulting forecasts will be any more accurate than if the initial values were determined using an alternative technique. When the data set being modeled is large, minor differences in the initial values are likely to have little impact on your forecasts. But as the size of the data set decreases, the impact of difference in the initial values becomes more pronounced.

11.9 Stationary Data with Multiplicative Seasonal Effects

A slight modification to the previous model makes it appropriate for modeling stationary time series data with multiplicative seasonal effects. In particular, the forecasting function becomes:

$$\hat{Y}_{t+n} = E_t \times S_{t+n-p} \qquad \textbf{11.8}$$

where

$$E_t = \alpha \, (Y_t/S_{t-p}) + (1 - \alpha) \, E_{t-1} \qquad \textbf{11.9}$$
$$S_t = \beta \, (Y_t/E_t) + (1 - \beta)S_{t-p} \qquad \textbf{11.10}$$
$$0 \leq \alpha \leq 1 \text{ and } 0 \leq \beta \leq 1$$

In this model, E_t again represents the expected level of the time series in period t, and S_t represents the seasonal factor for period t. The constant p represents the number of seasonal periods in the data.

In equation 11.8, the forecast for time period $t + n$ is simply the expected level of the time series at period t multiplied by the seasonal factor S_{t+n-p}. Equation 11.9 estimates the expected level for period t as a weighted average of the deseasonalized data for period t (Y_t/S_{t-p}) and the previous period's level (E_{t-1}). Equation 11.10 estimates the seasonal factor for period t as the weighted average of the estimated seasonal effect in period t (Y_t/E_t) and the previous seasonal factor for that same season (S_{t-p}).

In order to use equations 11.8 through 11.10, we must initialize the estimated levels and seasonal factors for the first p time periods. One simple way to do this is as follows:

$$E_t = \sum_{i=1}^{p} \frac{Y_i}{p}, \quad t = 1, 2, \ldots, p$$

$$S_t = Y_t/E_t, \quad t = 1, 2, \ldots, p$$

That is, we will use the average value of the first p time periods as the initial expected levels for each of these time periods. We then use the ratio of the actual values to the expected levels as the initial seasonal factors for the first p time periods.

The spreadsheet implementation for this technique is shown in Figure 11.16 (and in file Fig11-16.xlsm that accompanies this book).

FIGURE 11.16 *Spreadsheet implementation of model with multiplicative seasonal effects*

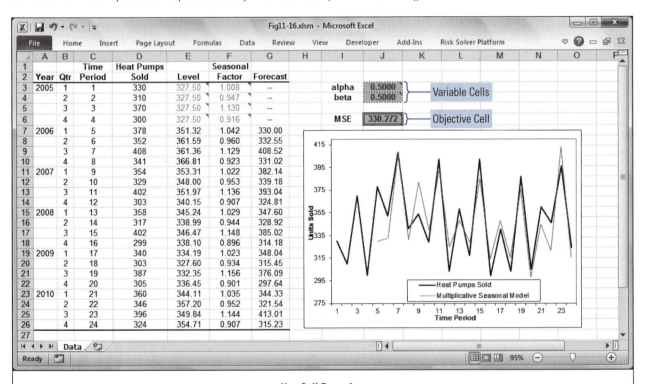

Key Cell Formulas

Cell	Formula	Copied to
E3	=AVERAGE($D$3:$D$6)	E4:E6
E7	=$J$3*(D7/F3)+(1-$J$3)*E6	E8:E26
F3	=D3/E3	F4:F6
F7	=$J$4*(D7/E7)+(1-$J$4)*F3	F8:F26
G7	=E6*F3	G8:G26
J6	=SUMXMY2(G7:G26,D7:D26)/COUNT(G7:G26)	--

The initial expected level values for the first four time periods were entered into cells E3 through E6 as follows:

Formula for cell E3:   =AVERAGE($D$3:$D$6)

(Copy to cells E4 through E6.)

Next, the initial seasonal factors for the first four periods were entered into cells F3 through F6 as follows:

Formula for cell F3:   =D3/E3

(Copy to cells F4 through F6.)

Cells J3 and J4 represent the values of α and β, respectively. The remaining expected levels and seasonal factors defined by equations 11.9 and 11.10 were then entered in columns E and F, respectively, as follows:

Formula for cell E7:   =$J$3*(D7/F3)+(1-$J$3)*E6

(Copy to cells E8 through E26.)

Formula for cell F7:   =$J$4*(D7/E7)+(1-$J$4)*F3

(Copy to cells F8 through F26.)

Now, according to equation 11.8, at any time period t, the prediction for time period $t + 1$ is given by:

$$\hat{Y}_{t+1} = E_t \times S_{t+1-p}$$

Thus, at time period 4, we are able to calculate the prediction for time period 5 as follows:

Formula for cell G7:   =E6*F3

(Copy to cells G8 through G26.)

This formula is then copied to cells G8 through G26 to complete the one period ahead predictions for the remaining observations.

We can use the Solver settings and options shown in Figure 11.17 to determine the values of α and β that minimize the MSE for this problem, computed in cell J6 as follows:

Formula for cell J6:   =SUMXMY2(G7:G26,D7:D26)/COUNT(G7:G26)

Solver Settings:
Objective: J6 (Min)
Variable cells: J3:J4
Constraints:
J3:J4 <= 1
J3:J4 >= 0
Solver Options:
Standard GRG Nonlinear Engine

FIGURE 11.17

Solver settings and options for the heat pump sales problem with multiplicative seasonal effects

Figure 11.18 shows the optimal solution to this problem along with a graph showing the actual sales data plotted against the values predicted by our model. Note that the predicted values fit the actual data reasonably well.

FIGURE 11.18 *Optimal solution to the heat pump sales problem with multiplicative seasonal effects*

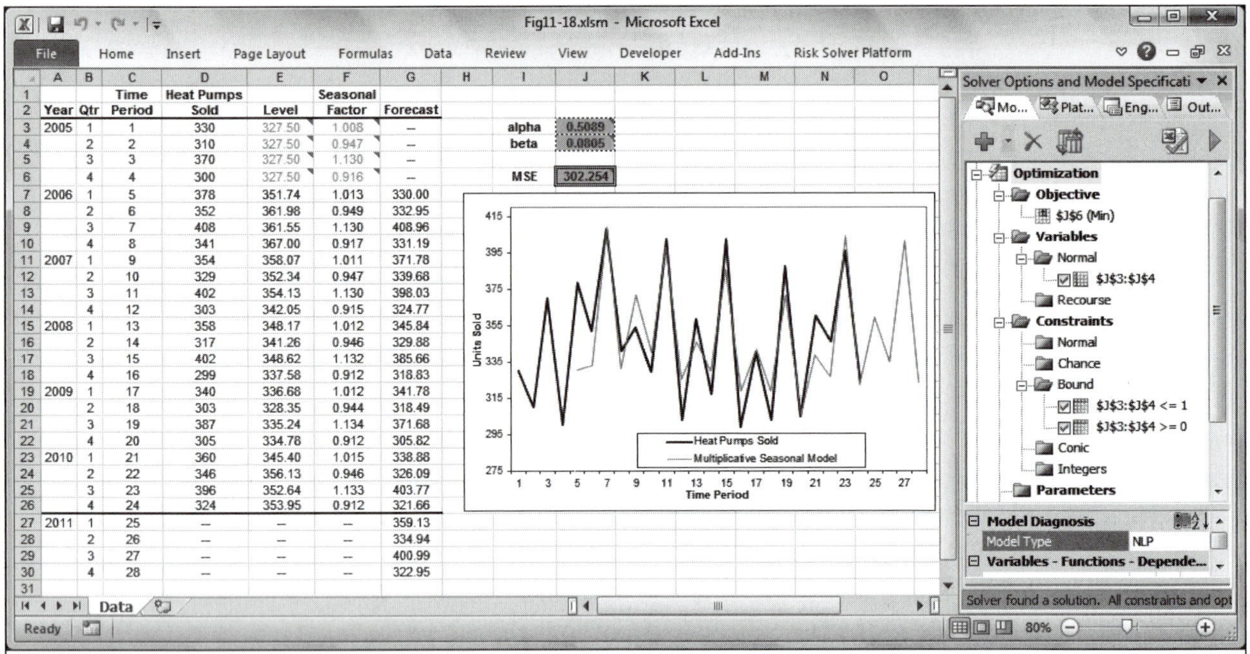

Year	Qtr	Time Period	Heat Pumps Sold	Level	Seasonal Factor	Forecast
2005	1	1	330	327.50	1.008	–
	2	2	310	327.50	0.947	–
	3	3	370	327.50	1.130	–
	4	4	300	327.50	0.916	–
2006	1	5	378	351.74	1.013	330.00
	2	6	352	361.98	0.949	332.95
	3	7	408	361.55	1.130	408.96
	4	8	341	367.00	0.917	331.19
2007	1	9	354	358.07	1.011	371.78
	2	10	329	352.34	0.947	339.68
	3	11	402	354.13	1.130	398.03
	4	12	303	342.05	0.915	324.77
2008	1	13	358	348.17	1.012	345.84
	2	14	317	341.26	0.946	329.88
	3	15	402	348.62	1.132	385.66
	4	16	299	337.58	0.912	318.83
2009	1	17	340	336.68	1.012	341.78
	2	18	303	328.35	0.944	318.49
	3	19	387	335.24	1.134	371.68
	4	20	305	334.78	0.912	305.82
2010	1	21	360	345.40	1.015	338.88
	2	22	346	356.13	0.946	326.09
	3	23	396	352.64	1.133	403.77
	4	24	324	353.95	0.912	321.66
2011	1	25	–	–	–	359.13
	2	26	–	–	–	334.94
	3	27	–	–	–	400.99
	4	28	–	–	–	322.95

Key Cell Formulas

Cell	Formula	Copied to
G27	=$E$26*F23	G28:G30

11.9.1 FORECASTING WITH THE MODEL

We can use the results in Figure 11.18 to compute forecasts for any future time period. According to equation 11.8, at time period 24, the forecast for time period 24 + n is given by:

$$\hat{Y}_{24+n} = E_{24} \times S_{24+n-4}$$

Our forecasts for each quarter in the year 2006 would then be calculated as follows:

$$\hat{Y}_{25} = E_{24} \times S_{21} = 353.95 \times 1.015 = 359.13$$
$$\hat{Y}_{26} = E_{24} \times S_{22} = 353.95 \times 0.946 = 334.94$$
$$\hat{Y}_{27} = E_{24} \times S_{23} = 353.95 \times 1.133 = 400.99$$
$$\hat{Y}_{28} = E_{24} \times S_{24} = 353.95 \times 0.912 = 322.95$$

Thus, each forecast is simply the expected level of the time series in period 24 multiplied by the relevant seasonal factor. The calculations for these forecasts were implemented in Figure 11.18 as follows:

Formula for cell G27: =$E$26*F23

(Copy to cells G28 through G30.)

11.10 Trend Models

The forecasting techniques presented so far are appropriate for stationary time series data in which there is no significant trend in the data over time. However, it is not unusual for time series data to exhibit some type of upward or downward trend over time. **Trend** is the long-term sweep or general direction of movement in a time series. It reflects the net influence of long-term factors that affect the time series in a fairly consistent and gradual way over time. In other words, the trend reflects changes in the data that occur with the passage of time.

Because the moving average, weighted moving average, and exponential smoothing techniques use some average of the previous values to forecast future values, they consistently *underestimate* the actual values if there is an upward trend in the data. For example, consider the time series data given by 2, 4, 6, 8, 10, 12, 14, 16, and 18. These data show a clear upward trend leading us to expect that the next value in the time series should be 20. However, the forecasting techniques discussed up to this point would forecast that the next value in the series is less than or equal to 18 because no weighted average of the given data could exceed 18. Similarly, if there is a downward trend in the data over time, all of the methods discussed so far would produce predictions that *overestimate* the actual values in the time series. In the following sections, we will consider several techniques that are appropriate for nonstationary time series involving an upward or downward trend in the data over time.

11.10.1 AN EXAMPLE

The following example will be used to illustrate a variety of techniques for modeling trends in time series data.

> WaterCraft, Inc. is a manufacturer of personal water crafts (also known as jet skis). Throughout its first five years of operation, the company has enjoyed a fairly steady growth in sales of its products. The officers of the company are preparing sales and manufacturing plans for the coming year. A critical input to these plans involves a forecast of the level of sales that the company expects to achieve. Quarterly sales data for the company during the past five years are given in Figure 11.19 (and in the file Fig11-19.xlsm that accompanies this book).

The plot of the data in Figure 11.19 suggests a fairly strong upward trend in the data over time. Thus, to forecast the value of this time series variable, we can use one of the forecasting techniques discussed in the following sections. These techniques account for a trend in the data.

11.11 Double Moving Average

As its name implies, the double moving average technique involves taking the average of averages. Let M_t be the moving average for the past k time periods (including t):

$$M_t = (Y_t + Y_{t-1} + \cdots + Y_{t-k+1})/k$$

The double moving average D_t for the last k time periods (including period t) is the average of the moving averages:

$$D_t = (M_t + M_{t-1} + \cdots + M_{t-k+1})/k$$

FIGURE 11.19 *Historical sales data for the WaterCraft sales forecasting problem*

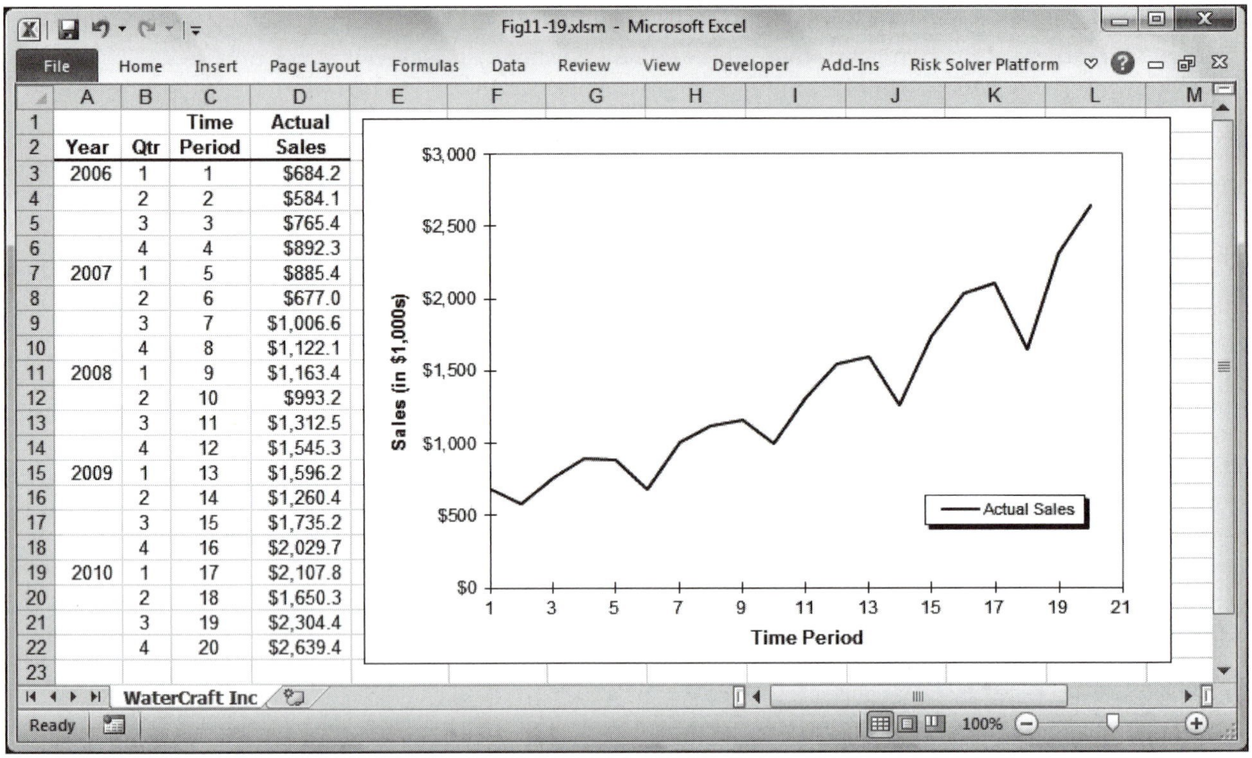

Year	Qtr	Time Period	Actual Sales
2006	1	1	$684.2
	2	2	$584.1
	3	3	$765.4
	4	4	$892.3
2007	1	5	$885.4
	2	6	$677.0
	3	7	$1,006.6
	4	8	$1,122.1
2008	1	9	$1,163.4
	2	10	$993.2
	3	11	$1,312.5
	4	12	$1,545.3
2009	1	13	$1,596.2
	2	14	$1,260.4
	3	15	$1,735.2
	4	16	$2,029.7
2010	1	17	$2,107.8
	2	18	$1,650.3
	3	19	$2,304.4
	4	20	$2,639.4

The double moving average forecasting function is then given by:

$$\hat{Y}_{t+n} = E_t + nT_t \tag{11.11}$$

where:

$$E_t = 2M_t - D_t$$
$$T_t = 2(M_t - D_t)/(k - 1)$$

The values of E_t and T_t are basically derived by minimizing the sum of squared errors using the last k periods of data. Note that E_t represents the estimated level of the time series at period t, and T_t represents the estimated trend. Thus, at period t, the forecast n periods into the future would be $E_t + nT_t$ as indicated in equation 11.11.

Figure 11.20 (and file Fig11-20.xlsm that accompanies this book) shows how the double moving average technique with $k = 4$ can be applied to the sales data for WaterCraft, Inc.

First, the four period moving averages (M_t) and double moving averages (D_t) are calculated in columns E and F, respectively, as follows:

Formula for cell E6: =AVERAGE(D3:D6)
(Copy to cells E7 through E22.)

Formula for cell F9: =AVERAGE(E6:E9)
(Copy to cells F10 through F22.)

FIGURE 11.20

Spreadsheet implementation of the double moving average technique

Fig11-20.xlsm - Microsoft Excel

	Year	Qtr	Time Period	Actual Sales	Moving Avg	Dbl Moving Avg	Level	Trend	Forecast
3	2006	1	1	$684.2	–	–	–	–	–
4		2	2	$584.1	–	–	–	–	–
5		3	3	$765.4	–	–	–	–	–
6		4	4	$892.3	731.49	–	–	–	–
7	2007	1	5	$885.4	781.79	–	–	–	–
8		2	6	$677.0	805.02	–	–	–	–
9		3	7	$1,006.6	865.33	795.91	934.75	46.28	–
10		4	8	$1,122.1	922.78	843.73	1001.82	52.70	981.04
11	2008	1	9	$1,163.4	992.27	896.35	1088.20	63.95	1054.52
12		2	10	$993.2	1071.32	962.92	1179.71	72.26	1152.15
13		3	11	$1,312.5	1147.78	1033.54	1262.02	76.16	1251.97
14		4	12	$1,545.3	1253.59	1116.24	1390.94	91.57	1338.18
15	2009	1	13	$1,596.2	1361.79	1208.62	1514.97	102.12	1482.51
16		2	14	$1,260.4	1428.60	1297.94	1559.25	87.10	1617.08
17		3	15	$1,735.2	1534.27	1394.56	1673.98	93.14	1646.36
18		4	16	$2,029.7	1655.36	1495.00	1815.71	106.90	1767.11
19	2010	1	17	$2,107.8	1783.25	1600.37	1966.14	121.92	1922.61
20		2	18	$1,650.3	1880.73	1713.40	2048.05	111.55	2088.06
21		3	19	$2,304.4	2023.04	1835.59	2210.48	124.96	2159.60
22		4	20	$2,639.4	2175.48	1965.62	2385.33	139.90	2335.44
23	2011	1	21	–	–	–	–	–	2525.23
24		2	22	–	–	–	–	–	2665.13
25		3	23	–	–	–	–	–	2805.03
26		4	24	–	–	–	–	–	2944.94

Data / Graph

Ready   100%

Key Cell Formulas

Cell	Formula	Copied to
E6	=AVERAGE(D3:D6)	E7:E22
F9	=AVERAGE(E6:E9)	F10:F22
G9	=2*E9-F9	G10:G22
H9	=2*(E9-F9)/(4-1)	H10:H22
I10	=G9+H9	I11:I22
I23	=$G$22+B23*$H$22	I24:I26

The estimated level (E_t) and trend (T_t) values for each period are calculated in columns G and H, respectively, as follows:

Formula for cell G9:   =2*E9-F9

(Copy to cells G10 through G22.)

Formula for cell H9:   =2*(E9-F9)/(4-1)

(Copy to cells H10 through H22.)

The predicted values for time periods 8 through 20 are then calculated in column I as follows:

Formula for cell I10:   =G9+H9

(Copy to cells I11 through I22.)

Figure 11.21 graphs the actual sales data against the values predicted by our model. Note that the predicted values seem to follow the upward trend in the actual data reasonably well.

FIGURE 11.21

Plot of double moving average predictions versus actual WaterCraft sales data

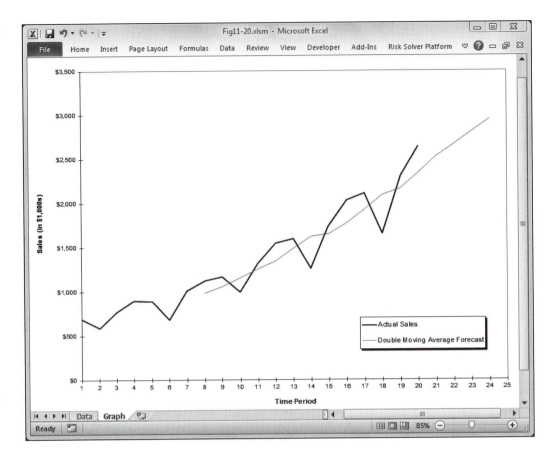

11.11.1 FORECASTING WITH THE MODEL

We can use the results in Figure 11.20 to compute trend forecasts for any future time period. According to equation 11.11, at time period 20, the forecast for time period $20 + n$ is given by:

$$\hat{Y}_{20+n} = E_{20} + nT_{20}$$

The values of E_{20} and T_{20} are given in Figure 11.20 in cells G22 and H22, respectively ($E_{20} = 2{,}385.33$, and $T_{20} = 139.9$). So at time period 20, trend forecasts for time periods 21, 22, 23, and 24 are computed as:

$$\hat{Y}_{21} = E_{20} + 1 \times T_{20} = 2{,}385.33 + 1 \times 139.9 = 2{,}525.23$$
$$\hat{Y}_{22} = E_{20} + 2 \times T_{20} = 2{,}385.33 + 2 \times 139.9 = 2{,}665.13$$
$$\hat{Y}_{23} = E_{20} + 3 \times T_{20} = 2{,}385.33 + 3 \times 139.9 = 2{,}805.03$$
$$\hat{Y}_{24} = E_{20} + 4 \times T_{20} = 2{,}385.33 + 4 \times 139.9 = 2{,}944.94$$

The calculations for these forecasts were implemented in Figure 11.20 as follows:

Formula for cell I23:   =$G$22+B23*$H$22

(Copy to cells I24 through I26.)

11.12 Double Exponential Smoothing (Holt's Method)

Double exponential smoothing (also known as Holt's method) is often an effective forecasting tool for time series data that exhibits a linear trend. After observing the value of the time series at period t (Y_t), Holt's method computes an estimate of the base, or expected, level of the time series (E_t) and the expected rate of increase or decrease (trend) per period (T_t). The forecasting function in Holt's method is represented by:

$$\hat{Y}_{t+n} = E_t + nT_t \tag{11.12}$$

where:

$$E_t = \alpha Y_t + (1 - \alpha)(E_{t-1} + T_{t-1}) \tag{11.13}$$

$$T_t = \beta(E_t - E_{t-1}) + (1 - \beta)T_{t-1} \tag{11.14}$$

We can use the forecasting function in equation 11.12 to obtain forecasts n time periods into the future where $n = 1, 2, 3$, and so on. The forecast for time period $t + n$ (or $\hat{Y}_{t+n}$) is the base level at time period t (given by E_t) plus the expected influence of the trend during the next n time periods (given by nT_t).

The smoothing parameters α and β in equations 11.13 and 11.14 can assume any value between 0 and 1 ($0 \leq \alpha \leq 1$, $0 \leq \beta \leq 1$). If there is an upward trend in the data, E_t tends to be larger than E_{t-1}, making the quantity $E_t - E_{t-1}$ in equation 11.14 positive. This tends to increase the value of the trend adjustment factor T_t. Alternatively, if there is a downward trend in the data, E_t tends to be smaller than E_{t-1}, making the quantity $E_t - E_{t-1}$ in equation 11.14 negative. This tends to decrease the value of the trend adjustment factor T_t.

Although Holt's method might appear to be more complicated than the techniques discussed earlier, it is a simple three-step process:

1. Compute the base level E_t for time period t using equation 11.13.
2. Compute the expected trend value T_t for time period t using equation 11.14.
3. Compute the final forecast $\hat{Y}_{t+n}$ for time period $t + n$ using equation 11.12.

The spreadsheet implementation of Holt's method for the WaterCraft problem is shown in Figure 11.22 (and in the file Fig11-22.xlsm that accompanies this book).

Cells J3 and J4 represent the values of α and β, respectively. Column E implements the base levels for each time period as required in step 1 (that is, this column contains the E_t values). Equation 11.6 assumes that for any time period t, the base level for the previous time period (E_{t-1}) is known. It is customary to assume that $E_1 = Y_1$, as reflected by the formula in cell E3:

Formula for cell E3:   =D3

The remaining E_t values are calculated using equation 11.13 in cells E4 through E22 as:

Formula for cell E4:   =$J$3*D4+(1−$J$3)*(E3+F3)
(Copy to E5 through E22.)

Column F implements the expected trend values for each time period as required in step 2 (that is, this column contains the T_t values). Equation 11.14 assumes that for any time period t, the expected trend value at the previous time period (T_{t-1}) is known. So, we assume as an initial trend estimate that $T_t = 0$ (although any other initial trend estimate could be used), as reflected by the formula in cell F3:

Formula for cell F3:   =0

FIGURE 11.22 *Spreadsheet implementation of Holt's method*

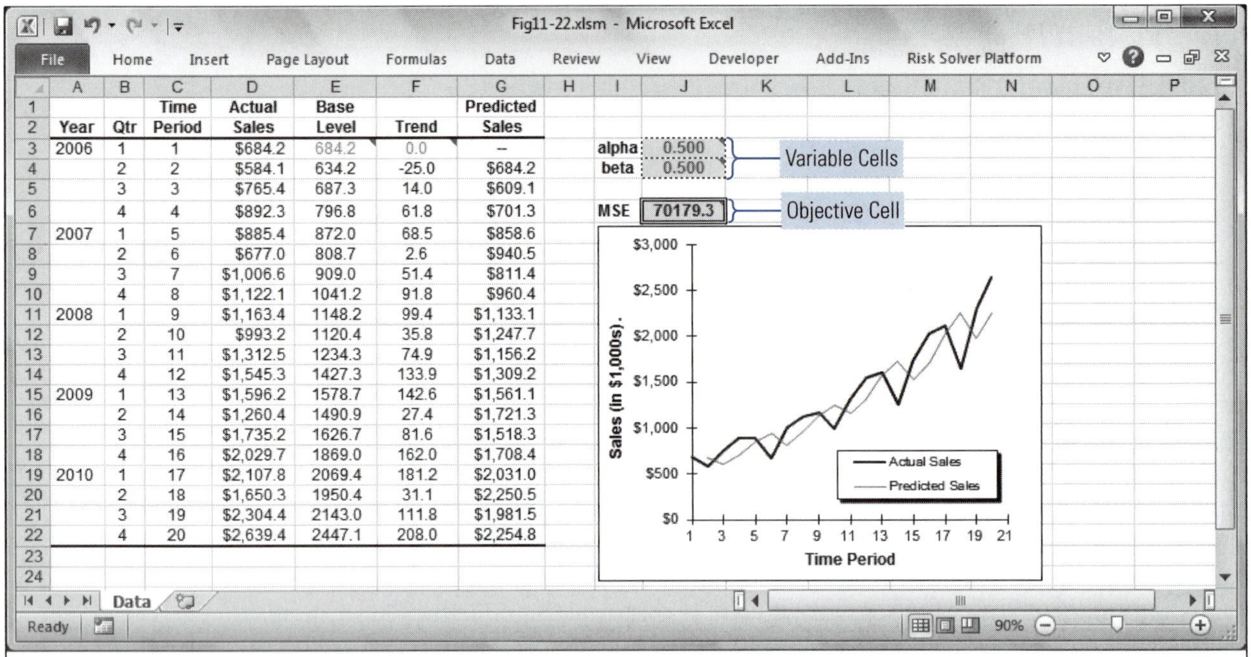

Year	Qtr	Time Period	Actual Sales	Base Level	Trend	Predicted Sales
2006	1	1	$684.2	684.2	0.0	--
	2	2	$584.1	634.2	-25.0	$684.2
	3	3	$765.4	687.3	14.0	$609.1
	4	4	$892.3	796.8	61.8	$701.3
2007	1	5	$885.4	872.0	68.5	$858.6
	2	6	$677.0	808.7	2.6	$940.5
	3	7	$1,006.6	909.0	51.4	$811.4
	4	8	$1,122.1	1041.2	91.8	$960.4
2008	1	9	$1,163.4	1148.2	99.4	$1,133.1
	2	10	$993.2	1120.4	35.8	$1,247.7
	3	11	$1,312.5	1234.3	74.9	$1,156.2
	4	12	$1,545.3	1427.3	133.9	$1,309.2
2009	1	13	$1,596.2	1578.7	142.6	$1,561.1
	2	14	$1,260.4	1490.9	27.4	$1,721.3
	3	15	$1,735.2	1626.7	81.6	$1,518.3
	4	16	$2,029.7	1869.0	162.0	$1,708.4
2010	1	17	$2,107.8	2069.4	181.2	$2,031.0
	2	18	$1,650.3	1950.4	31.1	$2,250.5
	3	19	$2,304.4	2143.0	111.8	$1,981.5
	4	20	$2,639.4	2447.1	208.0	$2,254.8

Key Cell Formulas

Cell	Formula	Copied to
E3	=D3	--
E4	=$J$3*D4+(1-$J$3)*(E3+F3)	E5:E22
F3	=0	--
F4	=$J$4*(E4-E3)+(1-$J$4)*F3	F5:F22
G4	=SUM(E3:F3)	G5:G22
J6	=SUMXMY2(D4:D22,G4:G22)/COUNT(G4:G22)	--

The remaining T_t values are calculated using equation 11.14 in cells F4 through F22 as:

Formula for cell F4: =$J$4*(E4−E3)+(1−$J$4)*F3

(Copy to F5 through F22.)

According to equation 11.12, at any time period t, the forecast for time period $t + 1$ is represented by:

$$\hat{Y}_{t+1} = E_t + 1 \times T_t$$

At time period $t = 1$ shown in Figure 11.22, the forecast for time period $t = 2$ (shown in cell G4) is obtained by summing the values in cells E3 and F3, which correspond to E_1 and T_1, respectively. Thus, the forecast for time period $t = 2$ is implemented in cell G4 as:

Formula for cell G4: =SUM(E3:F3)

(Copy to G5 through G22.)

This formula is copied to cells G5 through G22 to compute the predictions made using Holt's method for the remaining time periods.

We can again use Solver to determine the values for α and β that minimize the MSE. The MSE for the predicted values is calculated in cell J6 as:

Formula for cell J6:   =SUMXMY2(D4:D22,G4:G22)/COUNT(G4:G22)

We can use the Solver settings and options shown in Figure 11.23 to identify the values for α and β that minimize the nonlinear MSE objective. Figure 11.24 shows the solution to

Solver Settings:

Objective: J6 (Min)
Variable cells: J3:J4
Constraints:
    J3:J4 <= 1
    J3:J4 >= 0

Solver Options:
    Standard GRG Nonlinear Engine

FIGURE 11.23

Solver settings and options for Holt's method

FIGURE 11.24 *Optimal solution and forecasts using Holt's method*

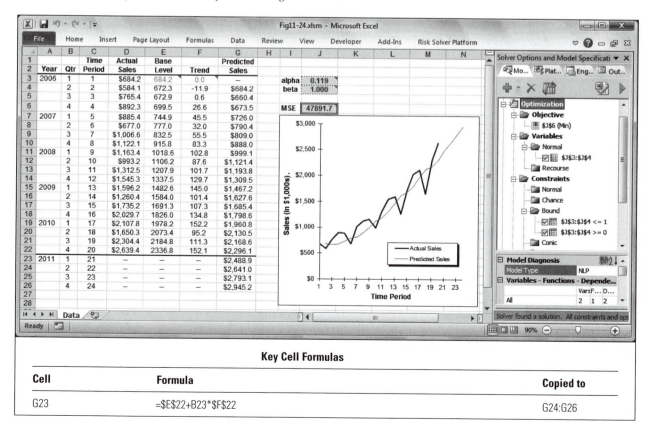

Key Cell Formulas

Cell	Formula	Copied to
G23	=$E$22+B23*$F$22	G24:G26

this problem. The graph in Figure 11.24 indicates that the predictions obtained using Holt's method follow the trend in the data quite well.

11.12.1 FORECASTING WITH HOLT'S METHOD

We can use the results in Figure 11.24 to compute forecasts for any future time period. According to equation 11.12, at time period 20, the forecast for time period $20 + n$ is represented by:

$$\hat{Y}_{20+n} = E_{20} + nT_{20}$$

The values of E_{20} and T_{20} are given in Figure 11.24 in cells E22 and F22, respectively ($E_{20} = 2{,}336.8$ and $T_{20} = 152.1$). So at time period 20, forecasts for time periods 21, 22, 23, and 24 are computed as:

$$\hat{Y}_{21} = E_{20} + 1 \times T_{20} = 2{,}336.8 + 1 \times 152.1 = 2{,}488.9$$
$$\hat{Y}_{22} = E_{20} + 2 \times T_{20} = 2{,}336.8 + 2 \times 152.1 = 2{,}641.0$$
$$\hat{Y}_{23} = E_{20} + 3 \times T_{20} = 2{,}336.8 + 3 \times 152.1 = 2{,}793.1$$
$$\hat{Y}_{24} = E_{20} + 4 \times T_{20} = 2{,}336.8 + 4 \times 152.1 = 2{,}945.2$$

The calculations for these forecasts were implemented in Figure 11.24 as follows:

Formula for cell G23:   =$E$22+B23*$F$22

(Copy to cells G24 through G26.)

11.13 Holt-Winter's Method for Additive Seasonal Effects

In addition to having an upward or downward trend, nonstationary data may also exhibit seasonal effects. Here again, the seasonal effects may be additive or multiplicative in nature. Holt-Winter's method is another forecasting technique that we can apply to time series exhibiting trend and seasonality. We discuss the Holt-Winter's method for *additive* seasonal effects in this section.

To demonstrate Holt-Winter's method for additive seasonal effects, let p represent the number of seasons in the time series (for quarterly data, $p = 4$; for monthly data, $p = 12$). The forecasting function is then given by:

$$\hat{Y}_{t+n} = E_t + nT_t + S_{t+n-p} \qquad\qquad \textbf{11.15}$$

where:

$$E_t = \alpha(Y_t - S_{t-p}) + (1 - \alpha)(E_{t-1} + T_{t-1}) \qquad\qquad \textbf{11.16}$$
$$T_t = \beta(E_t - E_{t-1}) + (1 - \beta)T_{t-1} \qquad\qquad \textbf{11.17}$$
$$S_t = \gamma(Y_t - E_t) + (1 - \gamma)S_{t-p} \qquad\qquad \textbf{11.18}$$

We can use the forecasting function in equation 11.15 to obtain forecasts n time periods into the future, where $n = 1, 2, \ldots, p$. The forecast for time period $t + n$ ($\hat{Y}_{t+n}$) is obtained in equation 11.15 by adjusting the expected base level at time period $t + n$ (given by $E_t + nT_t$) by the most recent estimate of the seasonality associated with this time period (given by S_{t+n-p}). The smoothing parameters α, β, and γ (gamma) in equations 11.16, 11.17, and 11.18 can assume any value between 0 and 1 ($0 \le \alpha \le 1, 0 \le \beta \le 1, 0 \le \gamma \le 1$).

The expected base level of the time series in time period t (E_t) is updated in equation 11.16, which takes a weighted average of the following two values:

- $E_{t-1} + T_{t-1}$, which represents the expected base level of the time series at time period t before observing the actual value at time period t (given by Y_t)
- $Y_t - S_{t-p}$, which represents the deseasonalized estimate of the base level of the time series at time period t after observing Y_t

The estimated per-period trend factor T_t is updated using equation 11.17, which is identical to the procedure in equation 11.14 used in Holt's method. The estimated seasonal adjustment factor for each time period is calculated using equation 11.18, which takes a weighted average of the following two quantities:

- S_{t-p}, which represents the most recent seasonal index for the season in which time period t occurs
- $Y_t - E_t$, which represents an estimate of the seasonality associated with time period t after observing Y_t

Holt-Winter's method is basically a four-step process:

1. Compute the base level E_t for time period t using equation 11.16.
2. Compute the estimated trend value T_t for time period t using equation 11.17.
3. Compute the estimated seasonal factor S_t for time period t using equation 11.18.
4. Compute the final forecast $\hat{Y}_{t+n}$ for time period $t + n$ using equation 11.15.

The spreadsheet implementation of Holt-Winter's method for the WaterCraft data is shown in Figure 11.25 (and in the file Fig11-25.xlsm that accompanies this book). Cells K3, K4, and K5 represent the values of α, β, and γ, respectively.

Equations 11.16 and 11.18 assume that at time period t, an estimate of the seasonal factor from time period $t - p$ exists or that there is a value for S_{t-p}. Thus, our first task in implementing this method is to estimate values for $S_1, S_2, \ldots, S_p$ (or, in this case, S_1, S_2, S_3, and S_4). One easy way to make these initial estimates is to let:

$$S_t = Y_t - \sum_{i=1}^{p} \frac{Y_i}{p}, \quad t = 1, 2, \ldots, p \qquad \textbf{11.19}$$

Equation 11.19 indicates that the initial seasonal estimate S_t for each of the first p time periods is the difference between the observed value in time period Y_t and the average value observed during the first p periods. In our example, the first four seasonal factors shown in column G in Figure 11.25 are calculated using equation 11.19 as:

> Formula for cell G3:   =D3-AVERAGE($D$3:$D$6)
>
> (Copy to G4 through G6.)

The first E_t value that can be computed using equation 11.16 occurs at time period $p + 1$ (in our example, time period 5) because this is the first time period for which S_{t-p} is known. However, to compute E_5 using equation 11.16, we also need to know E_4 (which cannot be computed using equation 11.16 because S_0 is undefined) and T_4 (which cannot be computed using equation 11.17 because E_4 and E_3 are undefined). Thus, we assume $E_4 = Y_4 - S_4$ (so that $E_4 + S_4 = Y_4$) and $T_4 = 0$, as reflected by placing the following formulas in cells E6 and F6:

> Formula for cell E6:   =D6−G6
>
> Formula for cell F6:   =0

FIGURE 11.25 *Spreadsheet implementation of Holt-Winter's method for additive seasonal effects*

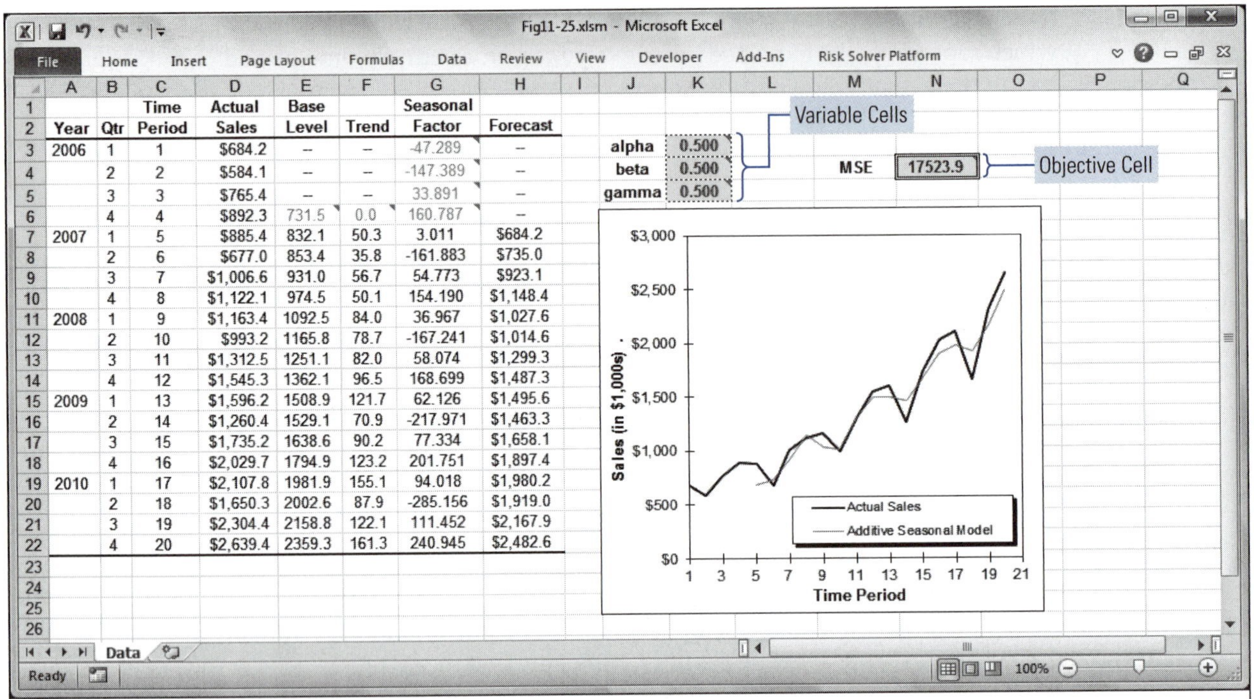

Year	Qtr	Time Period	Actual Sales	Base Level	Trend	Seasonal Factor	Forecast
2006	1	1	$684.2	--	--	-47.289	--
	2	2	$584.1	--	--	-147.389	--
	3	3	$765.4	--	--	33.891	--
	4	4	$892.3	731.5	0.0	160.787	--
2007	1	5	$885.4	832.1	50.3	3.011	$684.2
	2	6	$677.0	853.4	35.8	-161.883	$735.0
	3	7	$1,006.6	931.0	56.7	54.773	$923.1
	4	8	$1,122.1	974.5	50.1	154.190	$1,148.4
2008	1	9	$1,163.4	1092.5	84.0	36.967	$1,027.6
	2	10	$993.2	1165.8	78.7	-167.241	$1,014.6
	3	11	$1,312.5	1251.1	82.0	58.074	$1,299.3
	4	12	$1,545.3	1362.1	96.5	168.699	$1,487.3
2009	1	13	$1,596.2	1508.9	121.7	62.126	$1,495.6
	2	14	$1,260.4	1529.1	70.9	-217.971	$1,463.3
	3	15	$1,735.2	1638.6	90.2	77.334	$1,658.1
	4	16	$2,029.7	1794.9	123.2	201.751	$1,897.4
2010	1	17	$2,107.8	1981.9	155.1	94.018	$1,980.2
	2	18	$1,650.3	2002.6	87.9	-285.156	$1,919.0
	3	19	$2,304.4	2158.8	122.1	111.452	$2,167.9
	4	20	$2,639.4	2359.3	161.3	240.945	$2,482.6

alpha 0.500 beta 0.500 gamma 0.500 MSE 17523.9

Key Cell Formulas

Cell	Formula	Copied to
G3	=D3-AVERAGE($D$3:$D$6)	G4:G6
E6	=D6-G6	--
E7	=$K$3*(D7-G3)+(1-$K$3)*(E6+F6)	E8:E22
F6	=0	--
F7	=$K$4*(E7-E6)+(1-$K$4)*F6	F8:F22
G7	=$K$5*(D7-E7)+(1-$K$5)*G3	G8:G22
H7	=E6+F6+G3	H8:H22
N4	=SUMXMY2(H7:H22,D7:D22)/COUNT(H7:H22)	--

We generated the remaining E_t values using equation 11.16, which is implemented in Figure 11.25 as:

Formula for cell E7: $= \$K\$3*(D7-G3)+(1-\$K\$3)*(E6+F6)$
(Copy to E8 through E22.)

We generated the remaining T_t values using equation 11.17, which is implemented in Figure 11.25 as:

Formula for cell F7: $=\$K\$4*(E7-E6)+(1-\$K\$4)*F6$
(Copy to F8 through F22.)

We used equation 11.18 to generate the remaining S_t values in Figure 11.25 as:

Formula for cell G7: $=\$K\$5*(D7-E7)+(1-\$K\$5)*G3$
(Copy to G8 through G22.)

Finally, at time period 4, we can use the forecasting function in equation 11.15 to predict one period ahead for time period 5. This is implemented in Figure 11.25 as:

Formula for cell H7: $=E6+F6+G3$

(Copy to H8 through H22.)

Before making predictions using this method, we want to identify optimal values for α, β, and γ. We can use Solver to determine the values for α, β, and γ that minimize the MSE. The MSE for the predicted values is calculated in cell N4 as:

Formula for cell N4: $=\text{SUMXMY2}(H7:H22, D7:D22)/\text{COUNT}(H7:H22)$

We can use the Solver settings and options shown in Figure 11.26 to identify the values for α, β, and γ that minimize the nonlinear MSE objective. Figure 11.27 shows the solution to this problem.

Solver Settings:

Objective: N4 (Min)
Variable cells: K3:K5
Constraints:
    K3:K5 <= 1
    K3:K5 >= 0

Solver Options:
    Standard GRG Nonlinear Engine

FIGURE 11.26

Solver settings and options for Holt-Winter's method

FIGURE 11.27 *Optimal solution for Holt-Winter's method for additive seasonal effects*

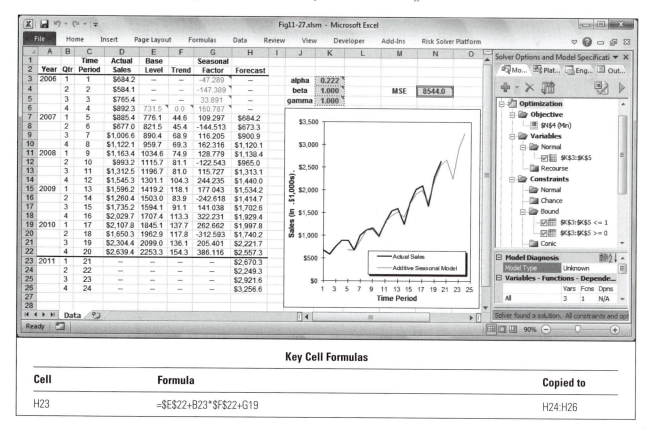

Key Cell Formulas

Cell	Formula	Copied to
H23	=$E$22+B23*$F$22+G19	H24:H26

Figure 11.27 displays a graph of the predictions obtained using Holt-Winter's method and the actual data. This graph indicates the forecasting function fits the data reasonably well. However, it does appear that the seasonal effects in the data may be becoming more pronounced over time, suggesting a model with multiplicative seasonal effects may be more appropriate in this case.

11.13.1 FORECASTING WITH HOLT-WINTER'S ADDITIVE METHOD

We can use the results in Figure 11.27 to compute forecasts for any future time period. According to equation 11.15, at time period 20, the forecast for time period $20 + n$ is represented by:

$$\hat{Y}_{20+n} = E_{20} + nT_{20} + S_{20+m-p}$$

Figure 11.27 shows the values of E_{20} and T_{20} in cells E22 and F22, respectively ($E_{20} = 2253.3$ and $T_{20} = 154.3$). At time period 20, forecasts for time periods 21, 22, 23, and 24 are computed as:

$$\hat{Y}_{21} = E_{20} + 1 \times T_{20} + S_{17} = 2{,}253.3 + 1 \times 154.3 + 262.662 = 2{,}670.3$$
$$\hat{Y}_{22} = E_{20} + 2 \times T_{20} + S_{18} = 2{,}253.3 + 2 \times 154.3 - 312.593 = 2{,}249.3$$
$$\hat{Y}_{23} = E_{20} + 3 \times T_{20} + S_{19} = 2{,}253.3 + 3 \times 154.3 + 205.401 = 2{,}921.6$$
$$\hat{Y}_{24} = E_{20} + 4 \times T_{20} + S_{20} = 2{,}253.3 + 4 \times 154.3 + 386.116 = 3{,}256.6$$

The calculations for these forecasts were implemented in Figure 11.27 as follows:

Formula for cell H23:   =$E$22+B23*$F$22+G19

(Copy to cells H24 through H26.)

11.14 Holt-Winter's Method for Multiplicative Seasonal Effects

As noted previously, the graph in Figure 11.27 indicates the seasonal effects in the data may be becoming more pronounced over time. As a result, it may be more appropriate to model this data with the Holt-Winter's method for *multiplicative* seasonal effects. Fortunately, this technique is very similar to Holt-Winter's method for additive seasonal effects.

To demonstrate Holt-Winter's method for multiplicative seasonal effects, we again let p represent the number of seasons in the time series (for quarterly data, $p = 4$; for monthly data, $p = 12$). The forecasting function is then given by:

$$\hat{Y}_{t+n} = (E_t + nT_t)S_{t+n-p} \qquad \text{11.20}$$

where:

$$E_t = \alpha \frac{Y_t}{S_{t-p}} + (1 - \alpha)(E_{t-1} + T_{t-1}) \qquad \text{11.21}$$

$$T_t = \beta(E_t - E_{t-1}) + (1 - \beta)T_{t-1} \qquad \text{11.22}$$

$$S_t = \gamma \frac{Y_t}{E_t} + (1 - \gamma)S_{t-p} \qquad \text{11.23}$$

Here, the forecast for time period $t + n$ ($\hat{Y}_{t+n}$) is obtained from equation 11.20 by *multiplying* the expected base level at time period $t + n$ (given by $E_t + nT_t$) by the most recent estimate of the seasonality associated with this time period (given by S_{t+n-p}). The smoothing parameters α, β, and γ (gamma) in equations 11.21, 11.22, and 11.23 again can assume any value between 0 and 1 ($0 \leq \alpha \leq 1$, $0 \leq \beta \leq 1$, $0 \leq \gamma \leq 1$).

The expected base level of the time series in time period t (E_t) is updated in equation 11.21, which takes a weighted average of the following two values:

- $E_{t-1} + T_{t-1}$, which represents the expected base level of the time series at time period t before observing the actual value at time period t (given by Y_t)
- $\frac{Y_t}{S_{t-p}}$, which represents the deseasonalized estimate of the base level of the time series at time period t after observing Y_t

The estimated seasonal adjustment factor for each time period is calculated using equation 11.23, which takes a weighted average of the following two quantities:

- S_{t-p}, which represents the most recent seasonal index for the season in which time period t occurs
- $\frac{Y_t}{E_t}$, which represents an estimate of the seasonality associated with time period t after observing Y_t

The spreadsheet implementation of Winter's method for the WaterCraft data is shown in Figure 11.28 (and in the file Fig11-28.xlsm that accompanies this book). Cells K3, K4, and K5 represent the values of α, β, and γ, respectively.

Equations 11.21 and 11.23 assume that at time period t, an estimate of the seasonal index from time period $t - p$ exists or that there is a value for S_{t-p}. Thus, we need to estimate values for $S_1, S_2, \ldots, S_p$. An easy way to do this is to let:

$$S_t = \frac{Y_t}{\sum_{i=1}^{p} \frac{Y_i}{p}}, \quad t = 1, 2, \ldots, p \qquad \textbf{11.24}$$

Equation 11.24 indicates that the initial seasonal estimate S_t for each of the first p time periods is the ratio of the observed value in time period Y_t divided by the average value observed during the first p periods. In our example, the first four seasonal factors shown in column G in Figure 11.28 are calculated using equation 11.19 as:

Formula for cell G3:   =D3/AVERAGE($D$3:$D$6)
(Copy to G4 through G6.)

The first E_t value that can be computed using equation 11.21 occurs at time period $p + 1$ (in our example, time period 5) because this is the first time period for which S_{t-p} is known. However, to compute E_5 using equation 11.21, we also need to know E_4 (which cannot be computed using equation 11.16 because S_0 is undefined) and T_4 (which cannot be computed using equation 11.22 because E_4 and E_3 are undefined). Thus, we assume $E_4 = Y_4/S_4$ (so that $E_4 \times S_4 = Y_4$) and $T_4 = 0$, as reflected by placing the following formulas in cells E6 and F6:

Formula for cell E6:   =D6/G6
Formula for cell F6:   =0

We generated the remaining E_t values using equation 11.21, which is implemented in Figure 11.28 as:

Formula for cell E7:   =$K$3*D7/G3+(1−$K$3)*(E6+F6)
(Copy to E8 through E22.)

FIGURE 11.28 *Spreadsheet implementation of Holt-Winter's method for multiplicative seasonal effects*

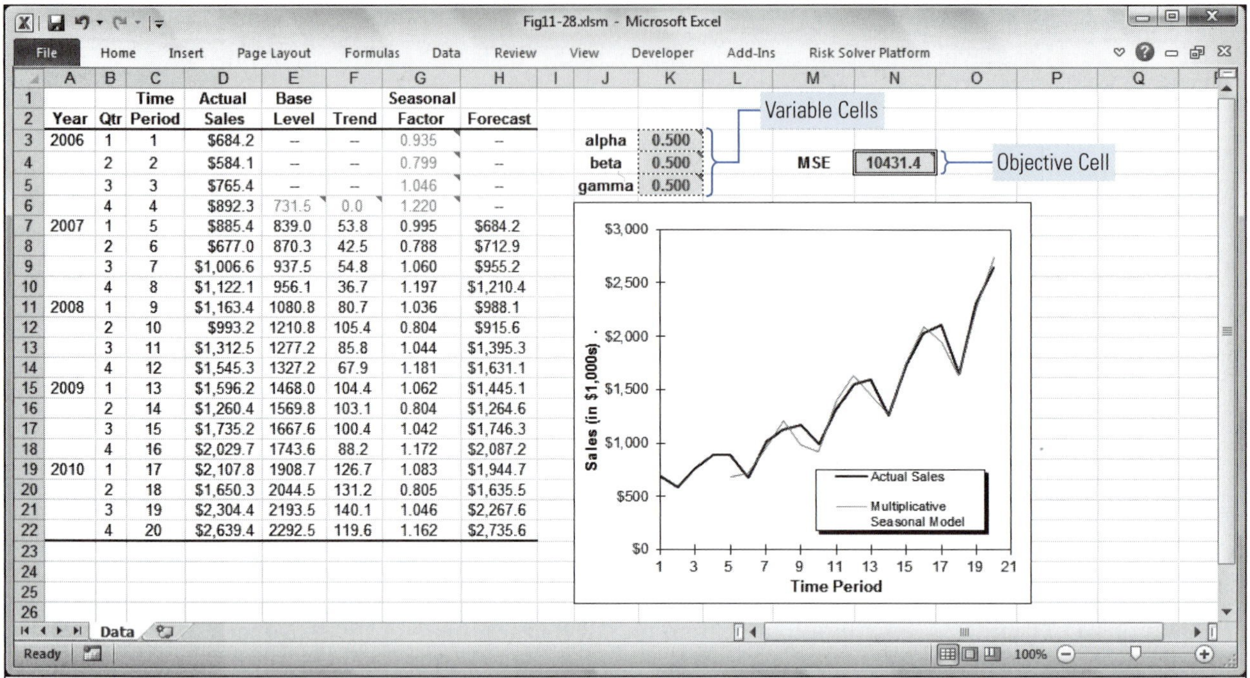

Year	Qtr	Time Period	Actual Sales	Base Level	Trend	Seasonal Factor	Forecast
2006	1	1	$684.2	--	--	0.935	--
	2	2	$584.1	--	--	0.799	--
	3	3	$765.4	--	--	1.046	--
	4	4	$892.3	731.5	0.0	1.220	--
2007	1	5	$885.4	839.0	53.8	0.995	$684.2
	2	6	$677.0	870.3	42.5	0.788	$712.9
	3	7	$1,006.6	937.5	54.8	1.060	$955.2
	4	8	$1,122.1	956.1	36.7	1.197	$1,210.4
2008	1	9	$1,163.4	1080.8	80.7	1.036	$988.1
	2	10	$993.2	1210.8	105.4	0.804	$915.6
	3	11	$1,312.5	1277.2	85.8	1.044	$1,395.3
	4	12	$1,545.3	1327.2	67.9	1.181	$1,631.1
2009	1	13	$1,596.2	1468.0	104.4	1.062	$1,445.1
	2	14	$1,260.4	1569.8	103.1	0.804	$1,264.6
	3	15	$1,735.2	1667.6	100.4	1.042	$1,746.3
	4	16	$2,029.7	1743.6	88.2	1.172	$2,087.2
2010	1	17	$2,107.8	1908.7	126.7	1.083	$1,944.7
	2	18	$1,650.3	2044.5	131.2	0.805	$1,635.5
	3	19	$2,304.4	2193.5	140.1	1.046	$2,267.6
	4	20	$2,639.4	2292.5	119.6	1.162	$2,735.6

Key Cell Formulas

Cell	Formula	Copied to
G3	=D3/AVERAGE($D$3:$D$6)	G4:G6
E6	=D6/G6	--
E7	=$K$3*D7/G3+(1-$K$3)*(E6+F6)	E8:E22
F6	=0	--
F7	=$K$4*(E7-E6)+(1-$K$4)*F6	F8:F22
G7	=$K$5*D7/E7+(1-$K$5)*G3	G8:G22
H7	=SUM(E6:F6)*G3	H8:H22
N4	=SUMXMY2(H7:H22,D7:D22)/COUNT(H7:H22)	--

We generated the remaining T_t values using equation 11.22, which is implemented as:

Formula for cell F7: =$K$4*(E7−E6)+(1−$K$4)*F6

(Copy to F8 through F22.)

We used equation 11.23 to generate the remaining S_t values as:

Formula for cell G7: =$K$5*D7/E7+(1−$K$5)*G3

(Copy to G8 through G22.)

Finally, at time period 4, we can use the forecasting function in equation 11.20 to predict one period ahead for time period 5. This is implemented as:

Formula for cell H7: =SUM(E6:F6)*G3

(Copy to H8 through H22.)

Before making predictions using this method, we want to identify optimal values for α, β, and γ. We can use Solver to determine the values for α, β, and γ that minimize the MSE. The MSE for the predicted values is calculated in cell N4 as:

Formula for cell N4:   =SUMXMY2(H7:H22,D7:D22)/COUNT(H7:H22)

We can use the Solver settings and options shown in Figure 11.29 to identify the values for α, β, and γ that minimize the nonlinear MSE objective. Figure 11.30 shows the solution to this problem.

Figure 11.30 displays a graph of the predictions obtained using Holt-Winter's multiplicative method and the actual data. Comparing this graph to the one in Figure 11.27, it seems the multiplicative model produces a forecasting function that may fit the data better.

FIGURE 11.29

Solver settings and options for Holt-Winter's multiplicative method

---

Solver Settings:

Objective: N4 (Min)

Variable cells: K3:K5

Constraints:

K3:K5 <= 1

K3:K5 >= 0

Solver Options:

Standard GRG Nonlinear Engine

FIGURE 11.30 *Optimal solution for Holt-Winter's method for multiplicative seasonal effects*

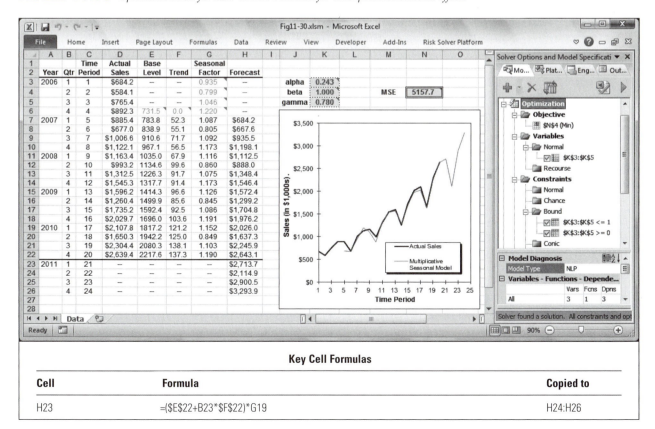

Key Cell Formulas

Cell	Formula	Copied to
H23	=($E$22+B23*$F$22)*G19	H24:H26

11.14.1 FORECASTING WITH HOLT-WINTER'S MULTIPLICATIVE METHOD

We can use the results in Figure 11.30 to compute forecasts for any future time period. According to equation 11.15, at time period 20, the forecast for time period $20 + n$ is represented by:

$$\hat{Y}_{20+n} = (E_{20} + nT_{20})S_{20+n-p}$$

Figure 11.30 shows the values of E_{20} and T_{20} in cells E22 and F22, respectively ($E_{20} = 2{,}217.6$ and $T_{20} = 137.3$). At time period 20, forecasts for time periods 21, 22, 23, and 24 are computed as:

$$\hat{Y}_{21} = (E_{20} + 1 \times T_{20})S_{17} = (2{,}217.6 + 1 \times 137.3)1.152 = 2{,}713.7$$
$$\hat{Y}_{22} = (E_{20} + 2 \times T_{20})S_{18} = (2{,}217.6 + 2 \times 137.3)0.849 = 2{,}114.9$$
$$\hat{Y}_{23} = (E_{20} + 3 \times T_{20})S_{19} = (2{,}217.6 + 3 \times 137.3)1.103 = 2{,}900.5$$
$$\hat{Y}_{24} = (E_{20} + 4 \times T_{20})S_{20} = (2{,}217.6 + 4 \times 137.3)1.190 = 3{,}293.9$$

The calculations for these forecasts were implemented in Figure 11.30 as follows:

Formula for cell H23:   =($E$22+B23*$F$22)*G19

(Copy to cells H24 through H26.)

11.15 Modeling Time Series Trends Using Regression

As mentioned in the introduction, we can build a regression model of a time series if data are available for one or more independent variables that account for the systematic movements in the time series. However, even if no independent variables have a *causal* relationship with the time series, some independent variables might have a *predictive* relationship with the time series. A predictor variable does not have a cause-and-effect relationship with the time series. Yet the behavior of a predictor variable might be correlated with that of the time series in a way that helps us forecast future values of the time series. In the following sections, we will consider how to use predictor variables as independent variables in regression models for time series data.

As mentioned earlier, trend is the long-term sweep or general direction of movement in a time series that reflects changes in the data over time. The mere passage of time does not cause the trend in the time series. But like the consistent passage of time, the trend of a time series reflects the steady upward or downward movement in the general direction of the series. Thus, time itself might represent a predictor variable that could be useful in accounting for the trend in a time series.

11.16 Linear Trend Model

To see how we might use time as an independent variable, consider the following linear regression model:

$$Y_t = \beta_0 + \beta_1 X_{1_t} + \varepsilon_t \qquad\qquad \textbf{11.25}$$

where $X_{1_t} = t$. That is, the independent variable X_{1_t} represents the time period t ($X_{1_1} = 1$, $X_{1_2} = 2$, $X_{1_3} = 3$, and so on). The regression model in equation 11.25 assumes that the *systematic* variation in the time series (Y_t) can be described by the regression function $\beta_0 + \beta_1 X_{1_t}$ (which is a linear function of time). The error term ε_t in equation 11.25 represents the *unsystematic*, or random, variation in the time series not accounted for by our model. Because the values of Y_t are assumed to vary randomly around (above and below) the regression function $\beta_0 + \beta_1 X_{1_t}$, the average (or expected) value of ε_t is 0. Thus, if we use ordinary least squares to estimate the parameters in equation 11.25, our best estimate of Y_t for any time period t is:

$$\hat{Y}_t = b_0 + b_1 X_{1_t} \qquad\qquad \textbf{11.26}$$

In equation 11.26, the estimated value of the time series at time period t ($\hat{Y}_t$) is a linear function of the independent variable, which is coded to represent time. Thus, equation 11.26 represents the equation of the line passing through the time series that minimizes the sum of squared differences between the actual values (Y_t) and the estimated values ($\hat{Y}_t$). We might interpret this line to represent the linear trend in the data.

An example of this technique is shown in Figure 11.31 (and in the file Fig11-31.xlsm that accompanies this book) for the quarterly sales data for WaterCraft. We can use the Time Period values in cells C3 through C22 as the values for the independent variable X_1 in our regression model. Thus, we can use the Regression command settings shown in Figure 11.32 to obtain the values for b_0 and b_1 required for the estimated regression function for these data.

FIGURE 11.31 *Spreadsheet implementation of the linear trend model*

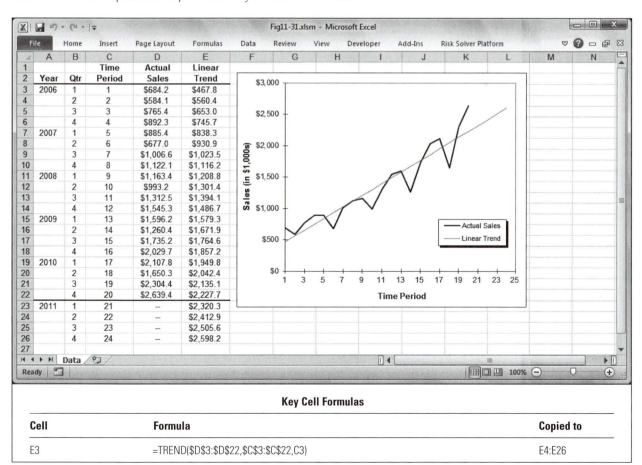

Key Cell Formulas

Cell	Formula	Copied to
E3	=TREND($D$3:$D$22,$C$3:$C$22,C3)	E4:E26

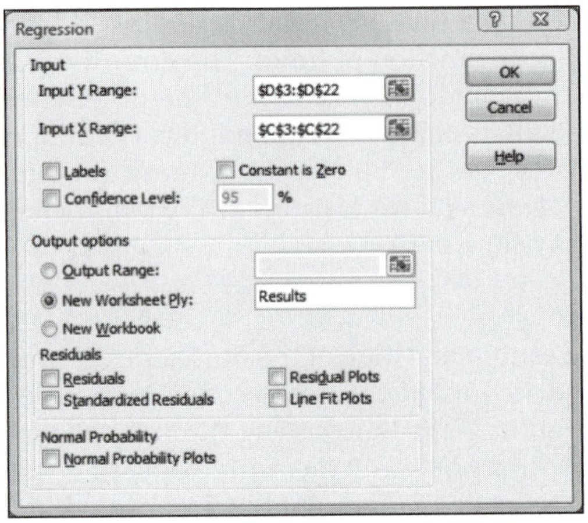

FIGURE 11.32

Regression command settings for the linear trend model

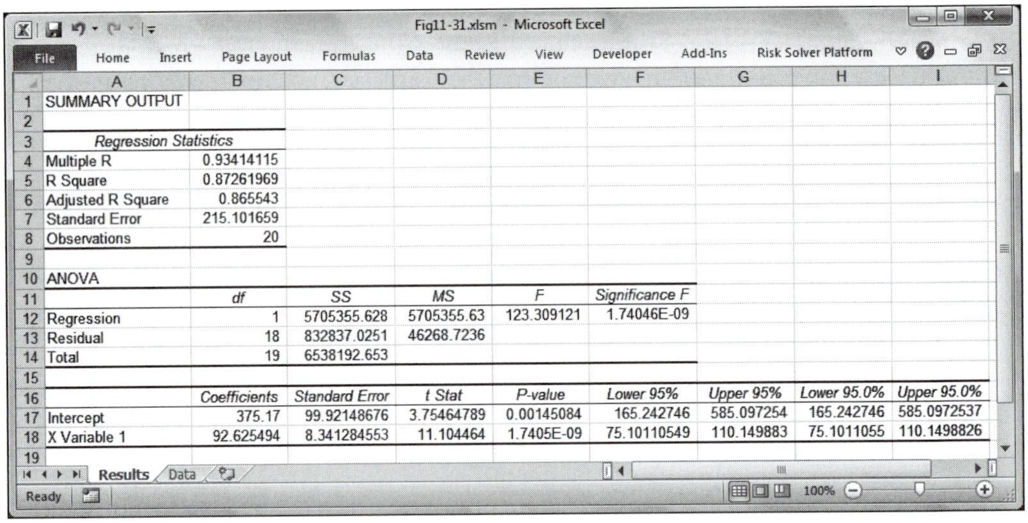

	A	B	C	D	E	F	G	H	I
1	SUMMARY OUTPUT								
2									
3	*Regression Statistics*								
4	Multiple R	0.93414115							
5	R Square	0.87261969							
6	Adjusted R Square	0.865543							
7	Standard Error	215.101659							
8	Observations	20							
9									
10	ANOVA								
11		*df*	*SS*	*MS*	*F*	*Significance F*			
12	Regression	1	5705355.628	5705355.63	123.309121	1.74046E-09			
13	Residual	18	832837.0251	46268.7236					
14	Total	19	6538192.653						
15									
16		*Coefficients*	*Standard Error*	*t Stat*	*P-value*	*Lower 95%*	*Upper 95%*	*Lower 95.0%*	*Upper 95.0%*
17	Intercept	375.17	99.92148676	3.75464789	0.00145084	165.242746	585.097254	165.242746	585.0972537
18	X Variable 1	92.625494	8.341284553	11.104464	1.7405E-09	75.10110549	110.149883	75.1011055	110.1498826
19									

FIGURE 11.33

Regression results for the linear trend model

Figure 11.33 shows the results of the Regression command, which indicate that the estimated regression function is:

$$\hat{Y}_t = 375.17 + 92.6255X_{1_t} \qquad \textbf{11.27}$$

Figure 11.31 shows the predicted sales level for each time period in column E (labeled Linear Trend) where the following formula is entered in cell E3 and copied to cells E4 through E26:

Formula for cell E3: =TREND($D$3:$D$22,$C$3:$C$22,C3)
(Copy to E4 through E26.)

11.16.1 FORECASTING WITH THE LINEAR TREND MODEL

We can use equation 11.27 to generate forecasts of sales for any future time period t by setting $X_{1_t} = t$. For example, forecasts for time periods 21, 22, 23, and 24 are computed as:

$$\hat{Y}_{21} = 375.17 + 92.6255 \times 21 = 2{,}320.3$$
$$\hat{Y}_{22} = 375.17 + 92.6255 \times 22 = 2{,}412.9$$

$$\hat{Y}_{23} = 375.17 + 92.6255 \times 23 = 2{,}505.6$$
$$\hat{Y}_{24} = 375.17 + 92.6255 \times 24 = 2{,}598.2$$

Note that these forecasts were calculated using the TREND( ) function in cells E23 through E26 in Figure 11.31.

Again, as the forecast horizon lengthens, our confidence in the accuracy of the forecasts diminishes because there is no guarantee that the historical trends on which the model is based will continue indefinitely into the future.

The TREND( ) Function

The TREND( ) function can be used to calculate the estimated values for linear regression models. The format of the TREND( ) function is as follows:

TREND(Y-Range, X-Range, X-value for prediction)

where Y-Range is the range in the spreadsheet containing the dependent Y variable, X-Range is the range in the spreadsheet containing the independent X variable(s), and X-value for prediction is a cell (or cells) containing the values for the independent X variable(s) for which we want an estimated value of Y. The TREND( ) function has an advantage over the regression tool in that it is dynamically updated whenever any inputs to the function change. However, it does not provide the statistical information provided by the regression tool. It is best to use these two different approaches to doing regression in conjunction with one another.

11.17 Quadratic Trend Model

Although the graph of the estimated linear regression function shown in Figure 11.31 accounts for the upward trend in the data, the actual values do not appear to be scattered randomly around the trend line, as was assumed by our regression model in equation 11.25. An observation is more likely to be substantially below the line or only slightly above the line. This suggests that the linear trend model might not be appropriate for this data.

As an alternative, we might try fitting a curved trend line to the data using the following quadratic model:

$$Y_t = \beta_0 + \beta_1 X_{1_t} + \beta_2 X_{2_t} + \varepsilon_t \qquad\qquad \textbf{11.28}$$

where $X_{1_t} = t$ and $X_{2_t} = t^2$. The resulting *estimated* regression function for this model is:

$$\hat{Y}_t = b_0 + b_1 X_{1_t} + b_2 X_{2_t} \qquad\qquad \textbf{11.29}$$

To estimate the quadratic trend function, we must add a column to the spreadsheet to represent the additional independent variable $X_{2_t} = t^2$. This can be accomplished as shown in Figure 11.34 (and in the file Fig11-34.xlsm that accompanies this book) by inserting a new column D and placing the values t^2 in this column. Thus, the following formula is entered in cell D3 and copied to cells D4 through D26:

Formula for cell D3:   =C3^2
(Copy to D4 through D26.)

FIGURE 11.34 *Spreadsheet implementation of the quadratic trend model*

Year	Qtr	Time Period	Time^2	Actual Sales	Quadratic Trend
2006	1	1	1	$684.2	$674.0
	2	2	4	$584.1	$701.5
	3	3	9	$765.4	$736.2
	4	4	16	$892.3	$778.2
2007	1	5	25	$885.4	$827.4
	2	6	36	$677.0	$883.9
	3	7	49	$1,006.6	$947.6
	4	8	64	$1,122.1	$1,018.5
2008	1	9	81	$1,163.4	$1,096.7
	2	10	100	$993.2	$1,182.1
	3	11	121	$1,312.5	$1,274.7
	4	12	144	$1,545.3	$1,374.6
2009	1	13	169	$1,596.2	$1,481.6
	2	14	196	$1,260.4	$1,596.0
	3	15	225	$1,735.2	$1,717.5
	4	16	256	$2,029.7	$1,846.3
2010	1	17	289	$2,107.8	$1,982.4
	2	18	324	$1,650.3	$2,125.6
	3	19	361	$2,304.4	$2,276.1
	4	20	400	$2,639.4	$2,433.8
2011	1	21	441	--	$2,598.8
	2	22	484	--	$2,771.0
	3	23	529	--	$2,950.4
	4	24	576	--	$3,137.1

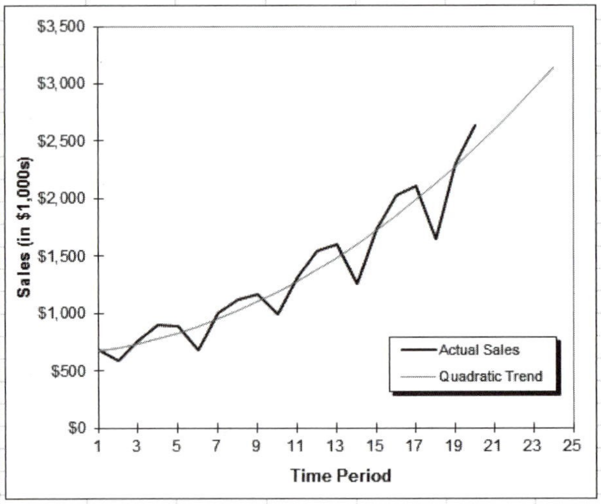

Key Cell Formulas

Cell	Formula	Copied to
D3	C3^2	D4:D22
F3	=TREND($E$3:$E$22,$C$3:$D$22,C3:D3)	F4:F26

We can obtain the values of b_0, b_1, and b_2 required for the estimated regression function for this data using the Regression command settings shown in Figure 11.35.

Figure 11.36 shows the results of the Regression command, which indicate that the estimated regression function is:

$$\hat{Y}_t = 653.67 + 16.671\,X_{1_t} + 3.617\,X_{2_t} \quad \textbf{11.30}$$

Figure 11.34 shows the estimated sales level for each time period in column F (labeled Quadratic Trend) where the following formula is entered in cell F3 and copied to cells F4 through F26:

Formula for cell F3: =TREND($E$3:$E$22,$C$3:$D$22,C3:D3)
(Copy to F4 through F26.)

Figure 11.34 also shows a graph of the sales levels predicted by the quadratic trend model versus the actual data. Notice that the quadratic trend curve fits the data better than the straight trend line shown in Figure 11.31. In particular, the deviations of the actual values above and below this curve are now more balanced.

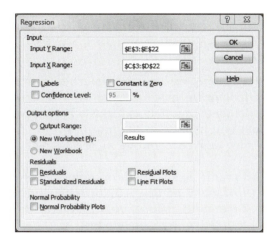

FIGURE 11.35

Regression command settings for the quadratic trend model

FIGURE 11.36

Regression results for the quadratic trend model

11.17.1 FORECASTING WITH THE QUADRATIC TREND MODEL

We can use equation 11.30 to generate forecasts of sales for any future time period t by setting $X_{1t} = t$ and $X_{2t} = t^2$. For example, forecasts for time periods 21, 22, 23, and 24 are computed as:

$$\hat{Y}_{21} = 653.67 + 16.671 \times 21 + 3.617 \times (21)^2 = 2{,}598.8$$
$$\hat{Y}_{22} = 653.67 + 16.671 \times 22 + 3.617 \times (22)^2 = 2{,}771.0$$
$$\hat{Y}_{23} = 653.67 + 16.671 \times 23 + 3.617 \times (23)^2 = 2{,}950.4$$
$$\hat{Y}_{24} = 653.67 + 16.671 \times 24 + 3.617 \times (24)^2 = 3{,}137.1$$

Note that these forecasts were calculated using the TREND( ) function in cells F23 through F26 in Figure 11.34.

As with earlier models, as the forecast horizon lengthens, our confidence in the accuracy of the forecasts diminishes because there is no guarantee that the historical trends on which the model is based will continue indefinitely into the future.

11.18 Modeling Seasonality with Regression Models

The goal of any forecasting procedure is to develop a model that accounts for as much of the systematic variation in the past behavior of a time series as possible. The assumption is that a model that accurately explains what happened in the past will be useful in predicting what will happen in the future. Do the trend models shown in Figures 11.31 and 11.34 adequately account for all the systematic variation in the time series data?

All these graphs show a fairly regular pattern of fluctuation around the trend line. Notice that each point below the trend line is followed by three points at or above the trend line. This suggests some additional *systematic* (or predictable) variation in the time series exists that is not accounted for by these models.

Figures 11.31 and 11.34 suggest that the data in the graphs include seasonal effects. In the second quarter of each year, sales drop well below the trend lines, whereas sales in the remaining quarters are at or above the trend line. Forecasts of future values for this time series would be more accurate if they reflected these systematic seasonal effects. The following sections discuss several techniques for modeling seasonal effects in time series data.

11.19 Adjusting Trend Predictions with Seasonal Indices

A simple and effective way of modeling multiplicative seasonal effects in a time series is to develop seasonal indices that reflect the average percentage by which observations in each season differ from their projected trend values. In the WaterCraft example, observations occurring in the second quarter fall below the values predicted using a trend model. Similarly, observations in the first, third, and fourth quarters are at or above the values predicted using a trend model. Thus, if we can determine seasonal indices representing the average amount by which the observations in a given quarter fall above or below the trend line, we could multiply our trend projections by these amounts and increase the accuracy of our forecasts.

We will demonstrate the calculation of multiplicative seasonal indices for the quadratic trend model developed earlier. However, we could also use this technique with any of the other trend or smoothing models discussed in this chapter. In Figure 11.37 (and in the file Fig11-37.xlsm that accompanies this book), columns A through F repeat the calculations for the quadratic trend model discussed earlier.

11.19.1 COMPUTING SEASONAL INDICES

The goal in developing seasonal indices is to determine the average percentage by which observations in each season differ from the values projected for them using the trend model. To accomplish this, in column G of Figure 11.37, we calculated the ratio of each actual value in column E to its corresponding projected trend value shown in column F as:

> Formula for cell G3:   =E3/F3
> (Copy to G4 through G22.)

	A	B	C	D	E	F	G	H	I	J	K	L
1			Time		Actual	Quadratic	Actual as a	Seasonal			Seasonal	
2	Year	Qtr	Period	Time^2	Sales	Trend	% of Trend	Forecast		Qtr	Index	
3	2006	1	1	1	$684.2	$674.0	102%	$712.6		1	105.7%	
4		2	2	4	$584.1	$701.5	83%	$561.9		2	80.1%	
5		3	3	9	$765.4	$736.2	104%	$758.9		3	103.1%	
6		4	4	16	$892.3	$778.2	115%	$864.8		4	111.1%	
7	2007	1	5	25	$885.4	$827.4	107%	$874.9				
8		2	6	36	$677.0	$883.9	77%	$708.0				
9		3	7	49	$1,006.6	$947.6	106%	$976.8				
10		4	8	64	$1,122.1	$1,018.5	110%	$1,131.8				
11	2008	1	9	81	$1,163.4	$1,096.7	106%	$1,159.6				
12		2	10	100	$993.2	$1,182.1	84%	$946.8				
13		3	11	121	$1,312.5	$1,274.7	103%	$1,314.0				
14		4	12	144	$1,545.3	$1,374.6	112%	$1,527.5				
15	2009	1	13	169	$1,596.2	$1,481.6	108%	$1,566.6				
16		2	14	196	$1,260.4	$1,596.0	79%	$1,278.4				
17		3	15	225	$1,735.2	$1,717.5	101%	$1,770.5				
18		4	16	256	$2,029.7	$1,846.3	110%	$2,051.7				
19	2010	1	17	289	$2,107.8	$1,982.4	106%	$2,096.0				
20		2	18	324	$1,650.3	$2,125.6	78%	$1,702.6				
21		3	19	361	$2,304.4	$2,276.1	101%	$2,346.3				
22		4	20	400	$2,639.4	$2,433.8	108%	$2,704.6				
23	2011	1	21	441	--	$2,598.8	--	$2,747.8				
24		2	22	484	--	$2,771.0	--	$2,219.6				
25		3	23	529	--	$2,950.4	--	$3,041.4				
26		4	24	576	--	$3,137.1	--	$3,486.1				
27												

Key Cell Formulas

Cell	Formula	Copied to
D3	=C3^2	D4:D26
F3	=TREND($E$3:$E$22,$C$3:$D$22,C3:D3)	F4:F26
G3	=E3/F3	G4:G22
K3	=AVERAGEIF($B$3:$B$22,J3,$G$3:$G$22)	K4:K6
H3	=F3*VLOOKUP(B3,$J$3:$K$6,2)	H4:H26

The value in cell G3 indicates that the actual value in time period 1 was 102% of (or approximately 2% larger than) its estimated trend value. The value in cell G4 indicates that the actual value in time period 2 was 83% of (or approximately 17% smaller than) its estimated trend value. The remaining values in column G have similar interpretations.

We obtain the seasonal index for each quarter by computing the average of the values in column G on a quarter-by-quarter basis. For example, the seasonal index for quarter 1 equals the average of the values in cells G3, G7, G11, G15, and G19. The seasonal index for quarter 2 equals the average of the values in cells G4, G8, G12, G16, and G20. Similar computations are required to calculate seasonal indices for quarters 3 and 4. We can use separate AVERAGE( ) functions for each quarter to compute these averages. However, for large data sets, such an approach would be tedious and prone to error. Thus, the averages shown in cells K3 through K6 are calculated as:

> Formula for cell K3:   =AVERAGEIF($B$3:$B$22,J3,$G$3:$G$22)
> (Copy to K4 through K6.)

The AVERAGEIF( ) function in cell K3 compares the values in the range B3 through B22 to the value in J3 and, when a match occurs, averages the corresponding values in the range G3 through G22. Thus, the number displayed by the formula in cell K3 represents the seasonal index value for observations in quarter 1. The values computed in cells K4, K5 and K6 have similar interpretations for the seasonal indices for quarters 2, 3 and 4, respectively.

The seasonal index for quarter 1 shown in cell K3 indicates that, on average, the actual sales value in the first quarter of any given year will be 105.7% of (or 5.7% larger than) the estimated trend value for the same time period. Similarly, the seasonal index for quarter 2 shown in cell K4 indicates that, on average, the actual sales value in the second quarter of any given year will be 80.1% of (or approximately 20% less than) the estimated trend value for the same time period. The seasonal indices for the third and fourth quarters have similar interpretations.

We can use the calculated seasonal indices to refine or adjust the trend estimates. This is accomplished in column H of Figure 11.37 as:

Formula for cell H3:   =F3*VLOOKUP(B3,$J$3:$K$6,2)
(Copy to H4 through H26.)

This formula takes the estimated trend value for each time period and multiplies it by the appropriate seasonal index for the quarter in which the time period occurs. The trend estimates for quarter 1 observations are multiplied by 105.7%, the trend estimates for quarter 2 observations are multiplied by 80.1%, and so on for quarters 3 and 4 observations.

Figure 11.38 shows a graph of the actual sales data versus the seasonal forecast calculated in column H of Figure 11.37. As this graph illustrates, the use of seasonal indices is very effective on this particular data set.

FIGURE 11.38

Plots of the predictions obtained using seasonal indices versus the actual WaterCraft sales data

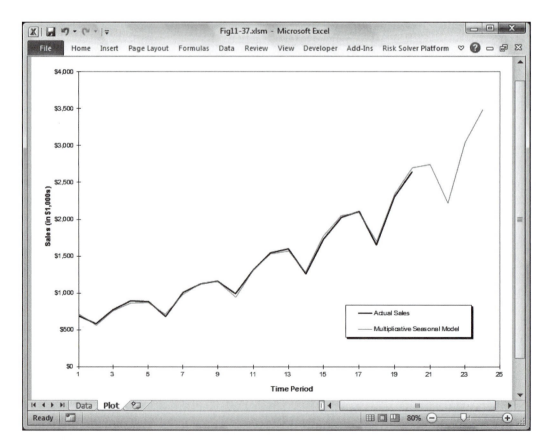

11.19.2 FORECASTING WITH SEASONAL INDICES

We can use the seasonal indices to adjust trend projections of future time periods for the expected effects of seasonality. Earlier, we used the quadratic trend model to obtain the following forecasts of the expected level of sales in time periods 21, 22, 23, and 24:

$$\hat{Y}_{21} = 653.67 + 16.671 \times 21 + 3.617 \times (21)^2 = 2{,}598.8$$
$$\hat{Y}_{22} = 653.67 + 16.671 \times 22 + 3.617 \times (22)^2 = 2{,}771.0$$
$$\hat{Y}_{23} = 653.67 + 16.671 \times 23 + 3.617 \times (23)^2 = 2{,}950.4$$
$$\hat{Y}_{24} = 653.67 + 16.671 \times 24 + 3.617 \times (24)^2 = 3{,}137.1$$

To adjust these trend forecasts for the expected effects of seasonality, we multiply each of them by the appropriate seasonal index. Because time periods 21, 22, 23, and 24 occur in quarters 1, 2, 3, and 4, respectively, the seasonal forecasts are computed as:

Seasonal forecast for time period 21 = 2,598.9 × 105.7% = 2,747.8

Seasonal forecast for time period 22 = 2,771.1 × 80.1% = 2,219.6

Seasonal forecast for time period 23 = 2,950.5 × 103.1% = 3,041.4

Seasonal forecast for time period 24 = 3,137.2 × 111.1% = 3,486.1

These forecasts are also calculated in Figure 11.37. Note that although we demonstrated the calculation of multiplicative seasonal indices, additive seasonal indices could easily be obtained in a very similar manner.

> # Summary of the Calculation and Use of Seasonal Indices
>
> 1. Create a trend model and calculate the estimated value ($\hat{Y}_t$) for each observation in the sample.
> 2. For each observation, calculate the ratio of the actual value to the predicted trend value: $Y_t/\hat{Y}_t$. (For additive seasonal effects, compute the difference: $Y_t - \hat{Y}_t$.)
> 3. For each season, compute the average of the values calculated in step 2. These are the seasonal indices.
> 4. Multiply any forecast produced by the trend model by the appropriate seasonal index calculated in step 3. (For additive seasonal effects, add the appropriate seasonal index to the trend model's forecast.)

11.19.3 REFINING THE SEASONAL INDICES

Although the approach for calculating seasonal indices illustrated in Figure 11.37 has considerable intuitive appeal, it is important to note that these seasonal adjustment factors are not necessarily optimal. Figure 11.39 (and file Fig11-39.xlsm that accompanies this book) shows a very similar approach to calculating seasonal indices that uses Solver to simultaneously determine the optimal values of the seasonal indices and the parameters of the quadratic trend model.

FIGURE 11.39 *Spreadsheet implementation to calculate refined seasonal indices and quadratic trend parameter estimates*

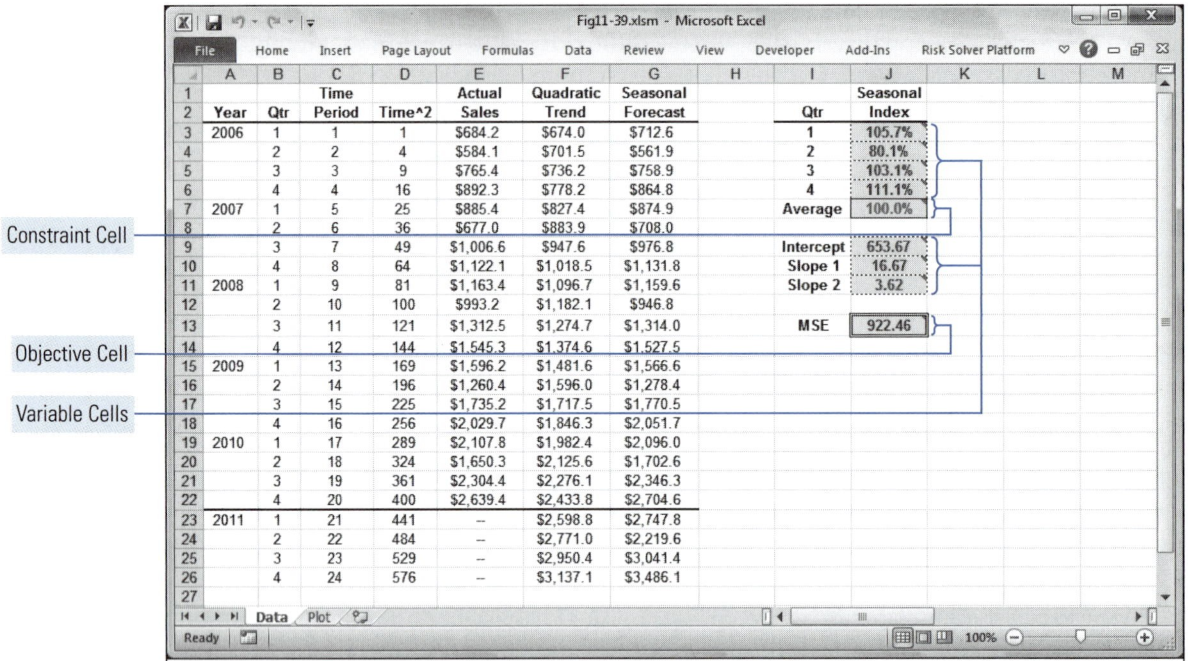

	A	B	C	D	E	F	G	H	I	J
1			Time		Actual	Quadratic	Seasonal			Seasonal
2	Year	Qtr	Period	Time^2	Sales	Trend	Forecast		Qtr	Index
3	2006	1	1	1	$684.2	$674.0	$712.6		1	105.7%
4		2	2	4	$584.1	$701.5	$561.9		2	80.1%
5		3	3	9	$765.4	$736.2	$758.9		3	103.1%
6		4	4	16	$892.3	$778.2	$864.8		4	111.1%
7	2007	1	5	25	$885.4	$827.4	$874.9		Average	100.0%
8		2	6	36	$677.0	$883.9	$708.0			
9		3	7	49	$1,006.6	$947.6	$976.8		Intercept	653.67
10		4	8	64	$1,122.1	$1,018.5	$1,131.8		Slope 1	16.67
11	2008	1	9	81	$1,163.4	$1,096.7	$1,159.6		Slope 2	3.62
12		2	10	100	$993.2	$1,182.1	$946.8			
13		3	11	121	$1,312.5	$1,274.7	$1,314.0		MSE	922.46
14		4	12	144	$1,545.3	$1,374.6	$1,527.5			
15	2009	1	13	169	$1,596.2	$1,481.6	$1,566.6			
16		2	14	196	$1,260.4	$1,596.0	$1,278.4			
17		3	15	225	$1,735.2	$1,717.5	$1,770.5			
18		4	16	256	$2,029.7	$1,846.3	$2,051.7			
19	2010	1	17	289	$2,107.8	$1,982.4	$2,096.0			
20		2	18	324	$1,650.3	$2,125.6	$1,702.6			
21		3	19	361	$2,304.4	$2,276.1	$2,346.3			
22		4	20	400	$2,639.4	$2,433.8	$2,704.6			
23	2011	1	21	441	--	$2,598.8	$2,747.8			
24		2	22	484	--	$2,771.0	$2,219.6			
25		3	23	529	--	$2,950.4	$3,041.4			
26		4	24	576	--	$3,137.1	$3,486.1			
27										

Key Cell Formulas

Cell	Formula	Copied to
D3	=C3^2	D4:D26
F3	=$J$9+$J$10*C3+$J$11*D3	F4:F26
G3	=F3*VLOOKUP(B3,$I$3:$J$6,2)	G4:G26
J13	=SUMXMY2(G3:G22,E3:E22)/COUNT(G3:G22)	--
J7	=AVERAGE(J3:J6)	--

In Figure 11.39, cells J9, J10, and J11 are used to represent, respectively, the estimated values of b_0, b_1, and b_2 in the following quadratic trend model (where $X_{1_t} = t$ and $X_{2_t} = t^2$):

$$\hat{Y}_t = b_0 + b_1 X_{1_t} + b_2 X_{2_t}.$$

Note that the values shown in cells J9, J10, and J11 correspond to the least square estimates shown in Figure 11.36.

The quadratic trend estimates are then calculated in column F as follows:

Formula for cell F3: =$J$9+$J$10*C3+$J$11*D3
(Copy to F4 through F22.)

Cells J3 through J6 represent the seasonal adjustment factors for each quarter. Note that the values shown in these cells correspond to the average seasonal adjustment values shown in Figure 11.37. Thus, the seasonal forecasts shown in column G of Figure 11.39 are computed as follows:

Formula for cell G3: =F3*VLOOKUP(B3,$I$3:$J$6,2)
(Copy to G4 through G22.)

The forecasts shown in Figure 11.39 are exactly the same as those in Figure 11.37 and result in an MSE of 922.46 as shown in cell J13. However, we can use the Solver settings and options shown in Figure 11.40 to determine values for the trend and seasonal parameters that minimize the MSE.

Figure 11.41 shows the optimal solution to this problem. By using Solver to fine-tune the parameters for the model, we are able to reduce the MSE to approximately 400.

Note that the Solver settings used to solve this problem includes a constraint that requires the average of the seasonal indices in cell J7 to equal one (or 100%). To understand the reason for this, suppose the seasonal indices average to something other than one, for example 105%. This suggests that the trend estimate is, on average, about 5% too low. Thus, if the seasonal indices do not average to 100%, there is some upward or downward bias in the trend component of the model. (Similarly, if the model included additive seasonal effects, they should be constrained to average to zero.)

FIGURE 11.40

Solver settings and options for calculating refined seasonal indices and quadratic trend parameter estimates

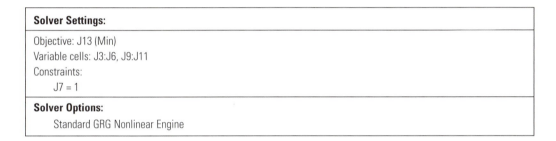

Solver Settings:

Objective: J13 (Min)

Variable cells: J3:J6, J9:J11

Constraints:

    J7 = 1

Solver Options:

    Standard GRG Nonlinear Engine

FIGURE 11.41 *Optimal solution for calculating refined seasonal indices and quadratic trend parameter estimates*

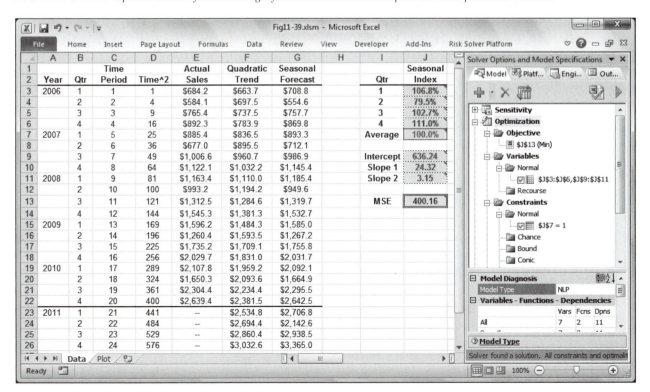

11.20 Seasonal Regression Models

As discussed in Chapter 9, an indicator variable is a binary variable that assumes a value of 0 or 1 to indicate whether or not a certain condition is true. To model additive seasonal effects in a time series, we might set up several indicator variables to indicate which season each observation represents. In general, if there are p seasons, we need $p - 1$ indicator variables in our model. For example, the WaterCraft sales data were collected on a quarterly basis. Because we have four seasons to model ($p = 4$), we need three indicator variables, which we define as:

$$X_{3_t} = \begin{cases} 1, \text{ if } Y_t \text{ is from quarter 1} \\ 0, \text{ otherwise} \end{cases}$$

$$X_{4_t} = \begin{cases} 1, \text{ if } Y_t \text{ is from quarter 2} \\ 0, \text{ otherwise} \end{cases}$$

$$X_{5_t} = \begin{cases} 1, \text{ if } Y_t \text{ is from quarter 3} \\ 0, \text{ otherwise} \end{cases}$$

Notice that the definitions of X_{3_t}, X_{4_t}, and X_{5_t} assign a unique coding for the variables to each quarter in our data. These codings are summarized in the following table:

Quarter	Value of		
	X_{3_t}	X_{4_t}	X_{5_t}
1	1	0	0
2	0	1	0
3	0	0	1
4	0	0	0

Together, the values of X_{3_t}, X_{4_t}, and X_{5_t} indicate in which quarter observation Y_t occurs.

11.20.1 THE SEASONAL MODEL

We might expect that the following regression function would be appropriate for the time series data in our example:

$$Y_t = \beta_0 + \beta_1 X_{1_t} + \beta_2 X_{2_t} + \beta_3 X_{3_t} + \beta_4 X_{4_t} + \beta_5 X_{5_t} + \varepsilon_t \qquad \textbf{11.31}$$

where $X_{1_t} = t$, and $X_{2_t} = t^2$. This regression model combines the variables that account for a quadratic trend in the data with additional indicator variables discussed earlier to account for any additive systematic seasonal differences.

To better understand the effect of the indicator variables, notice that for observations occurring in the fourth quarter, the model in equation 11.31 reduces to:

$$Y_t = \beta_0 + \beta_1 X_{1_t} + \beta_2 X_{2_t} + \varepsilon_t \qquad \textbf{11.32}$$

because in the fourth quarter $X_{3_t} = X_{4_t} = X_{5_t} = 0$. For observations occurring in the first quarter, we can express equation 11.31 as:

$$Y_t = (\beta_0 + \beta_3) + \beta_1 X_{1_t} + \beta_2 X_{2_t} + \varepsilon_t \qquad \textbf{11.33}$$

because, by definition, in the first quarter $X_{3_t} = 1$ and $X_{4_t} = X_{5_t} = 0$. Similarly, for observations in the second and third quarters, the model in equation 11.31 reduces to:

For the second quarter: $\quad Y_t = (\beta_0 + \beta_4) + \beta_1 X_{1_t} + \beta_2 X_{2_t} + \varepsilon_t \qquad \textbf{11.34}$

For the third quarter: $\quad Y_t = (\beta_0 + \beta_5) + \beta_1 X_{1_t} + \beta_2 X_{2_t} + \varepsilon_t \qquad \textbf{11.35}$

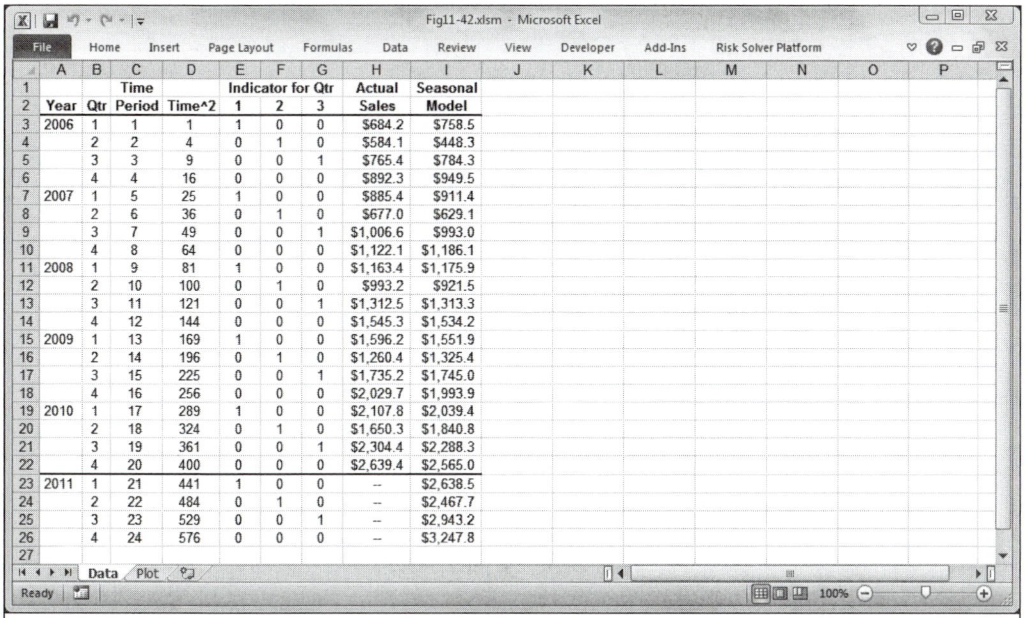

FIGURE 11.42

Spreadsheet implementation of the seasonal regression model

	A	B	C	D	E	F	G	H	I
1			Time		Indicator for Qtr			Actual	Seasonal
2	Year	Qtr	Period	Time^2	1	2	3	Sales	Model
3	2006	1	1	1	1	0	0	$684.2	$758.5
4		2	2	4	0	1	0	$584.1	$448.3
5		3	3	9	0	0	1	$765.4	$784.3
6		4	4	16	0	0	0	$892.3	$949.5
7	2007	1	5	25	1	0	0	$885.4	$911.4
8		2	6	36	0	1	0	$677.0	$629.1
9		3	7	49	0	0	1	$1,006.6	$993.0
10		4	8	64	0	0	0	$1,122.1	$1,186.1
11	2008	1	9	81	1	0	0	$1,163.4	$1,175.9
12		2	10	100	0	1	0	$993.2	$921.5
13		3	11	121	0	0	1	$1,312.5	$1,313.3
14		4	12	144	0	0	0	$1,545.3	$1,534.2
15	2009	1	13	169	1	0	0	$1,596.2	$1,551.9
16		2	14	196	0	1	0	$1,260.4	$1,325.4
17		3	15	225	0	0	1	$1,735.2	$1,745.0
18		4	16	256	0	0	0	$2,029.7	$1,993.9
19	2010	1	17	289	1	0	0	$2,107.8	$2,039.4
20		2	18	324	0	1	0	$1,650.3	$1,840.8
21		3	19	361	0	0	1	$2,304.4	$2,288.3
22		4	20	400	0	0	0	$2,639.4	$2,565.0
23	2011	1	21	441	1	0	0	--	$2,638.5
24		2	22	484	0	1	0	--	$2,467.7
25		3	23	529	0	0	1	--	$2,943.2
26		4	24	576	0	0	0	--	$3,247.8
27									

Key Cell Formulas

Cell	Formula	Copied to
D3	=C3^2	D4:D26
E3	=IF($B3=E$2,1,0)	E4:E26
I3	=TREND($H$3:$H$22,$C$3:$G$22,C3:G3)	I4:I26

Equations 11.32 through 11.35 show that the values β_3, β_4, and β_5 in equation 11.31 indicate the average amounts by which the values of observations in the first, second, and third quarters are expected to differ from observations in the fourth quarter. That is, β_3, β_4, and β_5 indicate the expected effects of seasonality in the first, second, and third quarters, respectively, relative to the fourth quarter.

An example of the seasonal regression function in equation 11.31 is given in Figure 11.42 (and in the file Fig11-42.xlsm that accompanies this book).

The major difference between Figures 11.37 and 11.42 is the addition of the data in columns E, F, and G in Figure 11.42. These columns represent the indicator values for the independent variables X_{3_t}, X_{4_t}, and X_{5_t}, respectively. We created these values by entering the following formula in cell E3 and copying it to E4 through G22:

Formula for cell E3:　　　=IF($B3=E$2,1,0)

(Copy to E4 through E26.)

In Figure 11.42, column I (labeled Seasonal Model) shows the predicted sales level for each time period where the following formula is entered in cell I3 and copied to cells I4 through I22:

Formula for cell I3:　　　=TREND($H$3:$H$22,$C$3:$G$22,C3:G3)

(Copy to I4 through I26.)

We can obtain the values of b_0, b_1, b_2, b_3, b_4, and b_5 required for the estimated regression function using the Regression command settings shown in Figure 11.43. Figure 11.44 shows the results of this command, which indicate that the estimated regression function is:

$$\hat{Y}_t = 824.472 + 17.319X_{1_t} + 3.485X_{2_t} - 86.805X_{3_t} - 424.736X_{4_t} - 123.453X_{5_t} \qquad \textbf{11.36}$$

FIGURE 11.43

Regression command settings for the seasonal regression model

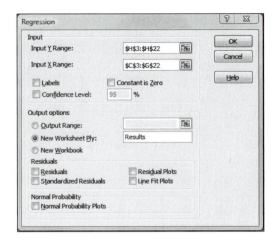

FIGURE 11.44

Regression results for the seasonal regression model

	A	B	C	D	E	F	G	H	I
1	SUMMARY OUTPUT								
2									
3	*Regression Statistics*								
4	Multiple R	0.992740856							
5	R Square	0.985534407							
6	Adjusted R Square	0.980368124							
7	Standard Error	82.19264615							
8	Observations	20							
9									
10	ANOVA								
11		*df*	*SS*	*MS*	*F*	*Significance F*			
12	Regression	5	6443613.818	1288722.764	190.76275	2.31527E-12			
13	Residual	14	94578.83513	6755.631081					
14	Total	19	6538192.653						
15									
16		*Coefficients*	*Standard Error*	*t Stat*	*P-value*	*Lower 95%*	*Upper 95%*	*Lower 95.0%*	*Upper 95.0%*
17	Intercept	824.4727144	71.38844455	11.54910601	1.5268E-08	671.3597288	977.5856999	671.359729	977.5856999
18	X Variable 1	17.3188557	13.43309658	1.289267563	0.21819982	-11.49227103	46.12998243	-11.492271	46.12998243
19	X Variable 2	3.48547572	0.620679918	5.615576755	6.3681E-05	2.154249695	4.816701746	2.15424969	4.816701746
20	X Variable 3	-86.8050143	52.88906781	-1.64126573	0.12300747	-200.2407829	26.63075425	-200.240783	26.63075425
21	X Variable 4	-424.73674	52.40244365	-8.105285	1.1757E-06	-537.128804	-312.344677	-537.128804	-312.344677
22	X Variable 5	-123.453356	52.09941535	-2.36957278	0.03271855	-235.1954888	-11.7112238	-235.195489	-11.7112238
23									

The coefficients for the indicator variables are given by $b_3 = -86.805$, $b_4 = -424.736$, and $b_5 = -123.453$. Because X_{3t} is the indicator variable for quarter 1 observations, the value of b_3 indicates that, on average, the sales level in quarter 1 of any year is expected to be approximately \$86,805 lower than the level expected for quarter 4. The value of b_4 indicates that the typical sales value in quarter 2 of any given year is expected to be approximately \$424,736 less than the level expected in quarter 4. Finally, the value of b_5 indicates that the typical sales value in quarter 3 is expected to be approximately \$123,453 less than the level expected in quarter 4.

In Figure 11.44, notice that $R^2 = 0.986$, suggesting that the estimated regression function fits the data very well. This is also evident from the graph in Figure 11.45, which shows the actual data versus the predictions of the seasonal forecasting model.

FIGURE 11.45

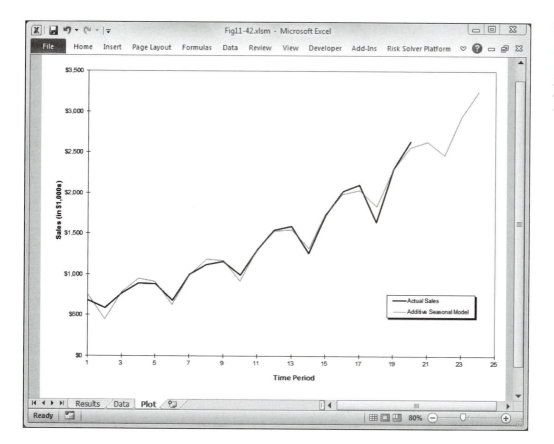

Plot of seasonal regression model predictions versus actual WaterCraft sales data

11.20.2 FORECASTING WITH THE SEASONAL REGRESSION MODEL

We can use the estimated regression function in equation 11.36 to forecast an expected level of sales for any future time period by assigning appropriate values to the independent variables. For example, forecasts of WaterCraft's sales in the next four quarters are represented by:

$$\hat{Y}_{21} = 824.472 + 17.319(21) + 3.485(21^2) - 86.805(1) - 424.736(0) - 123.453(0) = 2{,}638.5$$
$$\hat{Y}_{22} = 824.472 + 17.319(22) + 3.485(22^2) - 86.805(0) - 424.736(1) - 123.453(0) = 2{,}467.7$$
$$\hat{Y}_{23} = 824.472 + 17.319(23) + 3.485(23^2) - 86.805(0) - 424.736(0) - 123.453(1) = 2{,}943.2$$
$$\hat{Y}_{24} = 824.472 + 17.319(24) + 3.485(24^2) - 86.805(0) - 424.736(0) - 123.453(0) = 3{,}247.8$$

Note that these forecasts were calculated using the TREND( ) function in Figure 11.42.

11.21 Combining Forecasts

Given the number and variety of forecasting techniques available, it can be a challenge to settle on a *single* method to use in predicting future values of a time series variable. Indeed, the state-of-the-art research in time series forecasting suggests that we should *not* use a single forecasting method. Rather, we can obtain more accurate forecasts by combining the forecasts from several methods into a composite forecast.

For example, suppose that we used three methods to build forecasting models of the same time series variable. We denote the predicted value for time period t using each of these methods as F_{1_t}, F_{2_t}, and F_{3_t}, respectively. One simple approach to combining these forecasts into a composite forecast $\hat{Y}_t$ might involve taking a linear combination of the individual forecasts as:

$$\hat{Y}_t = b_0 + b_1 F_{1_t} + b_2 F_{2_t} + b_3 F_{3_t} \qquad \textbf{11.37}$$

We could determine the values for the b_i using Solver or least squares regression to minimize the MSE between the combined forecast $\hat{Y}_t$ and the actual data. The combined forecast $\hat{Y}_t$ in equation 11.37 will be at least as accurate as any of the individual forecasting techniques. To see this, suppose that F_{1_t} is the most accurate of the individual forecasting techniques. If $b_1 = 1$, and $b_0 = b_2 = b_3 = 0$, then our combined forecast would be $\hat{Y}_t = F_{1_t}$. Thus, b_0, b_2, and b_3 would be assigned nonzero values only if this helps to reduce the MSE and produce more accurate predictions.

In Chapter 9, we noted that adding independent variables to a regression model can never decrease the value of the R^2 statistic. Therefore, it is important to ensure that each independent variable in a multiple regression model accounts for a significant portion of the variation in the dependent variable and does not simply inflate the value of R^2. Similarly, combining forecasts can never increase the value of the MSE. Thus, when combining forecasts, we must ensure that each forecasting technique plays a significant role in accounting for the behavior of the dependent time series variable. The adjusted-R^2 statistic (described in Chapter 9) can also be applied to the problem of selecting forecasting techniques to combine in time series analysis.

11.22 Summary

This chapter presented several methods for forecasting future values of a time series variable. The chapter discussed time series methods for stationary data (without a strong upward or downward trend), nonstationary data (with a strong upward or downward linear or nonlinear trend), and data with repeating seasonal patterns. In each case, the goal is to fit models to the past behavior of a time series and use the models to project future values.

Because time series vary in nature (for example, with and without trend, with and without seasonality), it is helpful to be aware of the different forecasting techniques and the types of problems for which they are intended. There are many other time series modeling techniques besides those discussed in this chapter. Descriptions of these other techniques can be found in texts devoted to time series analysis.

In modeling time series data, it is often useful to try several techniques and then compare them based on measures of forecast accuracy, including a graphical inspection of how well the model fits the historical data. If no one procedure is clearly better than the others, it might be wise to combine the forecasts from the different procedures using a weighted average or some other method.

11.23 References

Clemen, R. T. "Combining Forecasts: A Review and Annotated Bibliography." *International Journal of Forecasting*, vol. 5, 1989.

Clements, D., and R. Reid. "Analytical MS/OR Tools Applied to a Plant Closure." *Interfaces*, vol. 24, no. 2, 1994.

Gardner, E. "Exponential Smoothing: The State of the Art." *Journal of Forecasting*, vol. 4, no. 1, 1985.

Georgoff, D., and R. Murdick. "Managers Guide to Forecasting." *Harvard Business Review*, vol. 64, no. 1, 1986.

Makridakis, S., and S. Wheelwright. *Forecasting: Methods and Applications*. New York: Wiley, 1986.

Pindyck, R., and D. Rubinfeld. *Econometric Models and Economic Forecasts*. New York: McGraw-Hill, 1989.

Chemical Bank of New York employs more than 500 people to process checks averaging $2 billion per day. Scheduling shifts for these employees requires accurate predictions of check flows. This is done with a regression model that forecasts daily check volume using independent variables that represent calendar effects. The regression model used by Ohio National Bank (see "Better Predictions Create Cost Savings for Ohio National Bank" in Chapter 9) is based on this Chemical Bank model.

The binary independent variables in the regression model represent months, days of the month, weekdays, and holidays. Of 54 possible variables, 29 were used in the model to yield a coefficient of determination (R^2) of 0.83 and a standard deviation of 142.6.

The forecast errors, or residuals, were examined for patterns that would suggest the possibility of improving the model. Analysts noticed a tendency for overpredictions to follow one another and underpredictions to follow one another, implying that check volumes could be predicted not only by calendar effects but also by the recent history of prediction errors.

An exponential smoothing model was used to forecast the residuals. The regression model combined with the exponential smoothing model then became the complete model for predicting check volumes. Fine-tuning was accomplished by investigating different values of the smoothing constant (α) from 0.05 to 0.50. A smoothing constant of 0.2 produced the best results, reducing the standard deviation from 142.6 to 131.8. Examination of the residuals for the complete model showed nothing but random variations, indicating that the exponential smoothing procedure was working as well as could be expected.

Although the complete model provides better forecasts on the average, it occasionally overreacts and increases the error for some periods. Nevertheless, the complete model is considered to be preferable to regression alone.

Source: Kevin Boyd and Vincent A. Mabert. "A Two Stage Forecasting Approach at Chemical Bank of New York for Check Processing." *Journal of Bank Research*, vol. 8, no. 2, Summer 1977, pages 101–107.

Questions and Problems

1. What is the result of using regression analysis to estimate a linear trend model for a stationary time series?
2. A manufacturing company uses a certain type of steel rod in one of its products. The design specifications for this rod indicate that it must be between 0.353 to 0.357 inches in diameter. The machine that manufactures these rods is set up to produce them at 0.355 inches in diameter, but there is some variation in its output. Provided that the machine is producing rods within 0.353 to 0.357 inches in diameter, its output is considered acceptable or within control limits. Management uses a control chart to track the diameter of the rods being produced by the machine over time so

FIGURE 11.46

Graph for rod manufacturing problem

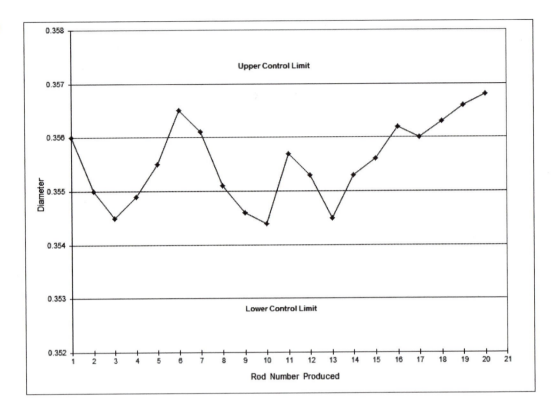

that remedial measures can be taken if the machine begins to produce unacceptable rods. Figure 11.46 shows an example of this type of chart.

Unacceptable rods represent waste. Thus, management wants to develop a procedure to predict when the machine will start producing rods that are outside the control limits, so that appropriate actions can be taken to prevent the production of rods that must be scrapped. Of the time series models discussed in this chapter, which is the most appropriate tool for this problem? Explain your answer.

3. Each month, Joe's Auto Parts uses exponential smoothing (with $\alpha = 0.25$) to predict the number of cans of brake fluid that will be sold during the next month. In June, Joe forecast that he would sell 37 cans of brake fluid during July. Joe actually sold 43 cans in July.
   a. What is Joe's forecast for brake fluid sales in August and September?
   b. Suppose that Joe sells 32 cans of brake fluid in August. What is the revised forecast for September?

(Questions 4 through 10 refer to the data in the file that accompanies this book named SmallBusiness.xls representing annual sales (in $1000s) for a small business.)

4. Prepare a line graph of these data. Do the data appear to be stationary or nonstationary?
5. Compute the two-period and four-period moving average predictions for the data set.
   a. Prepare a line graph comparing the moving average predictions against the original data.
   b. Do the moving averages tend to overestimate or underestimate the actual data? Why?
   c. Compute forecasts for the next two years using the two-period and four-period moving average techniques.

6. Use Solver to determine the weights for a three-period weighted moving average that minimizes the MSE for the data set.
   a. What are the optimal values for the weights?
   b. Prepare a line graph comparing the weighted moving average predictions against the original data.
   c. What are the forecasts for the next two years using this technique?
7. Create a double moving average model (with $k = 4$) for the data set.
   a. Prepare a line graph comparing the double moving average predictions against the original data.
   b. What are the forecasts for the next two years using this technique?
8. Create an exponential smoothing model that minimizes the MSE for the data set. Use Solver to determine the optimal value of α.
   a. What is the optimal value of α?
   b. Prepare a line graph comparing the exponential smoothing predictions against the original data.
   c. What are the forecasts for the next two years using this technique?
9. Use Holt's method to create a model that minimizes the MSE for the data set. Use Solver to determine the optimal values of α and β.
   a. What are the optimal values of α and β?
   b. Prepare a line graph comparing the predictions from Holt's method versus the original data.
   c. What are the forecasts for the next two years using this technique?
10. Use regression analysis to fit a linear trend model to the data set.
   a. What is the estimated regression function?
   b. Interpret the R^2 value for your model.
   c. Prepare a line graph comparing the linear trend predictions against the original data.
   d. What are the forecasts for the next two years using this technique?
   e. Fit a quadratic trend model to these data. What is the estimated regression function?
   f. Compare the adjusted-R^2 value for this model to that of the linear trend model. What is implied by this comparison?
   g. Prepare a line graph comparing the quadratic trend predictions against the original data.
   h. What are the forecasts for the next two years using this technique?
   i. If you had to choose between the linear and quadratic trend models, which would you use? Why?

(Questions 11 through 14 refer to the data in the file that accompanies this book named FamilyHomePrices.xls representing actual average sales prices of existing single family homes in the United States over a number of years.)

11. Prepare a line graph of these data. Do the data appear to be stationary or nonstationary?
12. Create a double moving average model (with $k = 2$) for the data set.
   a. Prepare a line graph comparing the double moving average predictions against the original data.
   b. What are the forecasts for the next two years using this technique?
13. Use Holt's method to create a model that minimizes the MSE for the data set. Use Solver to determine the optimal values of α and β.
   a. What are the optimal values of α and β?
   b. Prepare a line graph comparing the predictions from Holt's method versus the original data.
   c. What are the forecasts for the next two years using this technique?

14. Use regression analysis to answer the following questions.
   a. Fit a linear trend model to the data set. What is the estimated regression function?
   b. Interpret the R^2 value for your model.
   c. Prepare a line graph comparing the linear trend predictions against the original data.
   d. What are the forecasts for the next two years using this technique?
   e. Fit a quadratic trend model to these data. What is the estimated regression function?
   f. Compare the adjusted-R^2 value for this model to that of the linear trend model. What is implied by this comparison?
   g. Prepare a line graph comparing the quadratic trend predictions against the original data.
   h. What are the forecasts for the next two years using this technique?
   i. If you had to choose between the linear and quadratic trend models, which would you use? Why?

(Questions 15 through 22 refer to the data in the file that accompanies this book named SUVSales.xls representing quarterly data on the number of four-wheel drive, sport utility vehicles sold by a local car dealer during the past three years.)

15. Use regression analysis to fit a linear trend model to the data set.
   a. What is the estimated regression function?
   b. Interpret the R^2 value for your model.
   c. Prepare a line graph comparing the linear trend predictions against the original data.
   d. What are the forecasts for each quarter in 2011 using this technique?
   e. Calculate seasonal indices for each quarter using the results of the linear trend model.
   f. Use these seasonal indices to compute seasonal forecasts for each quarter in 2011.
16. Use regression analysis to fit a quadratic trend model to the data set.
   a. What is the estimated regression function?
   b. Compare the adjusted-R^2 value for this model to that of the linear trend model. What is implied by this comparison?
   c. Prepare a line graph comparing the quadratic trend predictions against the original data.
   d. What are the forecasts for each quarter in 2011 using this technique?
   e. Calculate seasonal indices for each quarter using the results of the quadratic trend model.
   f. Use these seasonal indices to compute seasonal forecasts for each quarter in 2011.
17. Use the additive seasonal technique for stationary data to model the data. Use Solver to determine the optimal values of α and β.
   a. What are the optimal values of α and β?
   b. Prepare a line graph comparing the predictions from this method against the original data.
   c. What are the forecasts for each quarter in 2011 using this technique?
18. Use the multiplicative seasonal technique for stationary data to model the data. Use Solver to determine the optimal values of α and β.
   a. What are the optimal values of α and β?
   b. Prepare a line graph comparing the predictions from this method against the original data.
   c. What are the forecasts for each quarter in 2011 using this technique?

19. Use Holt's method to create a model that minimizes the MSE for the data set. Use Solver to determine the optimal values of α and β.
    a. What are the optimal values of α and β?
    b. Prepare a line graph comparing the predictions from Holt's method against the original data.
    c. What are the forecasts for each quarter in 2011 using this technique?
    d. Calculate multiplicative seasonal indices for each quarter using the results of Holt's method.
    e. Use these seasonal indices to compute seasonal forecasts for each quarter in 2011.
20. Use Holt-Winter's additive method to create a seasonal model that minimizes the MSE for the data set. Use Solver to determine the optimal values of α, β, and γ.
    a. What are the optimal values of α, β, and γ?
    b. Prepare a line graph comparing the predictions from this method against the original data.
    c. What are the forecasts for each quarter in 2011 using this technique?
21. Use Holt-Winter's multiplicative method to create a seasonal model that minimizes the MSE for the data set. Use Solver to determine the optimal values of α, β, and γ.
    a. What are the optimal values of α, β, and γ?
    b. Prepare a line graph comparing the predictions from this method against the original data.
    c. What are the forecasts for each quarter in 2011 using this technique?
22. Use regression analysis to fit an additive seasonal model with linear trend to the data set.
    a. What is the estimated regression function?
    b. Interpret the R^2 value for your model.
    c. Interpret the parameter estimates corresponding to the indicator variables in your model.
    d. Prepare a line graph comparing the linear trend predictions against the original data.
    e. What are the forecasts for each quarter in 2011 using this technique?

(Questions 23 through 27 refer to the data in the file that accompanies this book named CalfPrices.xls representing the selling price of three-month-old calves at a livestock auction during the past 22 weeks.)

23. Prepare a line graph of these data. Do the data appear to be stationary or nonstationary?
24. Compute the two-period and four-period moving average predictions for the data set.
    a. Prepare a line graph comparing the moving average predictions against the original data.
    b. Compute the MSE for each of the two moving averages. Which appears to provide the best fit for this data set?
    c. Compute forecasts for the next two weeks using the two-period and four-period moving average techniques.
25. Use Solver to determine the weights for a four-period weighted moving average on the data set that minimizes the MSE.
    a. What are the optimal values for the weights?
    b. Prepare a line graph comparing the weighted moving average predictions against the original data.
    c. What are the forecasts for weeks 23 and 24 using this technique?

26. Create an exponential smoothing model that minimizes the MSE for the data set. Use Solver to estimate the optimal value of α.
    a. What is the optimal value of α?
    b. Prepare a line graph comparing the exponential smoothing predictions against the original data.
    c. What are the forecasts for weeks 23 and 24 using this technique?
27. Use Holt's method to create a model that minimizes the MSE for the data set. Use Solver to estimate the optimal values of α and β.
    a. What are the optimal values of α and β?
    b. Are these values surprising? Why or why not?

(Questions 28 through 32 refer to the data in the file that accompanies this book named HealthClaims.xls representing two years of monthly health insurance claims for a self-insured company.)

28. Use regression analysis to fit a linear trend model to the data set.
    a. What is the estimated regression function?
    b. Interpret the R^2 value for your model.
    c. Prepare a line graph comparing the linear trend predictions against the original data.
    d. What are the forecasts for each of the first six months in 2011 using this technique?
    e. Calculate multiplicative seasonal indices for each month using the results of the linear trend model.
    f. Use these seasonal indices to compute seasonal forecasts for the first six months in 2011.
    g. Calculate additive seasonal indices for each month using the results of the linear trend model.
    h. Use these seasonal indices to compute seasonal forecasts for the first six months in 2011.
29. Use regression analysis to fit a quadratic trend model to the data set.
    a. What is the estimated regression function?
    b. Compare the adjusted-R^2 value for this model to that of the linear trend model. What is implied by this comparison?
    c. Prepare a line graph comparing the quadratic trend predictions against the original data.
    d. What are the forecasts for each of the first six months in 2011 using this technique?
    e. Calculate multiplicative seasonal indices for each month using the results of the quadratic trend model.
    f. Use these seasonal indices to compute seasonal forecasts for each of the first six months in 2011.
    g. Calculate additive seasonal indices for each month using the results of the quadratic trend model.
    h. Use these seasonal indices to compute seasonal forecasts for each of the first six months in 2011.
30. Use Holt's method to create a model that minimizes the MSE for the data set. Use Solver to determine the optimal values of α and β.
    a. What are the optimal values of α and β?
    b. Prepare a line graph comparing the predictions from Holt's method against the original data.
    c. What are the forecasts for each of the first six months in 2011 using this technique?
    d. Calculate multiplicative seasonal indices for each month using the results of Holt's method.

e. Use these seasonal indices to compute seasonal forecasts for each of the first six months in 2011.

f. Calculate additive seasonal indices for each month using the results of Holt's method.

g. Use these seasonal indices to compute seasonal forecasts for each of the first six months in 2011.

31. Use Holt-Winter's additive method to create a seasonal model that minimizes the MSE for the data set. Use Solver to determine the optimal values of α, β, and γ.

a. What are the optimal values of α, β, and γ?

b. Prepare a line graph comparing the predictions from this method against the original data.

c. What are the forecasts for each of the first six months in 2011 using this technique?

32. Use Holt-Winter's multiplicative method to create a seasonal model that minimizes the MSE for the data set. Use Solver to determine the optimal values of α, β, and γ.

a. What are the optimal values of α, β, and γ?

b. Prepare a line graph comparing the predictions from this method against the original data.

c. What are the forecasts for each of the first six months in 2011 using this technique?

(Questions 33 through 36 refer to the data in the file that accompanies this book named LaborForce.xls containing monthly data on the number of workers in the U.S. civilian labor force [in 1,000s] over 94 consecutive months.)

33. Prepare a line graph of these data. Do the data appear to be stationary or nonstationary?

34. Create a double moving average model (with $k = 4$) for the data set.

a. Prepare a line graph comparing the double moving average predictions against the original data.

b. What are the forecasts for the next four months using this technique?

35. Use Holt's method to create a model that minimizes the MSE for the data set. Use Solver to estimate the optimal values of α and β.

a. What are the optimal values of α and β?

b. Prepare a line graph comparing the predictions from Holt's method against the original data.

c. What are the forecasts for the next four months using this technique?

36. Use regression analysis to answer the following questions.

a. Fit a linear trend model to the data set. What is the estimated regression function?

b. Interpret the R^2 value for your model.

c. Prepare a line graph comparing the linear trend predictions against the original data.

d. What are the forecasts for the next two years using this technique?

e. Fit a quadratic trend model to these data. What is the estimated regression function?

f. Compare the adjusted-R^2 value for this model to that of the linear trend model. What is implied by this comparison?

g. Prepare a line graph comparing the quadratic trend predictions against the original data.

h. What are the forecasts for the next two years using this technique?

i. If you had to choose between the linear and quadratic trend models, which would you use? Why?

(Questions 37 through 43 refer to the data in the file that accompanies this book named MortgageRates.xls containing average monthly 30-year mortgage rates over 94 consecutive months.)

37. Prepare a line graph of these data. Do the data appear to be stationary or nonstationary?

38. Compute the two-period and four-period moving average predictions for the data set.
    a. Prepare a line graph comparing the moving average predictions against the original data.
    b. Compute the MSE for each of the two moving averages. Which appears to provide the best fit for this data set?
    c. Compute forecasts for the next two months using the two-period and four-period moving average techniques.

39. Use Solver to determine the weights for a four-period weighted moving average on the data set that minimizes the MSE.
    a. What are the optimal values for the weights?
    b. Prepare a line graph comparing the weighted moving average predictions against the original data.
    c. What are the forecasts for the next two months using this technique?

40. Create an exponential smoothing model that minimizes the MSE for the data set. Use Solver to estimate the optimal value of α.
    a. What is the optimal value of α?
    b. Prepare a line graph comparing the exponential smoothing predictions against the original data.
    c. What are the forecasts for the next two months using this technique?

41. Create a double moving average model (with $k = 4$) for the data set.
    a. Prepare a line graph comparing the double moving average predictions against the original data.
    b. What are the forecasts for the next two months using this technique?

42. Use Holt's method to create a model that minimizes the MSE for the data set. Use Solver to estimate the optimal values of α and β.
    a. What are the optimal values of α and β?
    b. Prepare a line graph comparing the predictions from Holt's method against the original data.
    c. What are the forecasts for the next two months using this technique?

43. Use regression analysis to estimate the parameters of a 6th-order polynomial model for this data. That is, estimate the least squares estimates for the parameters in the following estimated regression equation:

$$\hat{Y}_t = b_0 + b_1 t + b_2 t^2 + b_3 t^3 + b_4 t^4 + b_5 t^5 + b_6 t^6$$

    a. What are the optimal values of $b_0, b_1, \ldots, b_6$?
    b. What are the forecasts for the next two months using this technique?
    c. Comment on the appropriateness of this technique.

(Questions 44 through 48 refer to the data in the file that accompanies this book named ChemicalDemand.xls containing monthly data on the demand for a chemical product over a two year period.)

44. Prepare a line graph of these data. Do the data appear to be stationary or nonstationary?

45. Use the additive seasonal technique for stationary data to model the data. Use Solver to determine the optimal values of α and β.
    a. What are the optimal values of α and β?
    b. Prepare a line graph comparing the predictions from this method against the original data.
    c. What are the forecasts for the next four months using this technique?

46. Use the multiplicative seasonal technique for stationary data to model the data. Use Solver to determine the optimal values of α and β.
    a. What are the optimal values of α and β?
    b. Prepare a line graph comparing the predictions from this method against the original data.
    c. What are the forecasts for the next four months using this technique?

47. Use Holt-Winter's additive method to create a seasonal model that minimizes the MSE for the data set. Use Solver to determine the optimal values of α, β, and γ.
    a. What are the optimal values of α, β, and γ?
    b. Prepare a line graph comparing the predictions from this method against the original data.
    c. What are the forecasts for the next four months using this technique?

48. Use Holt-Winter's multiplicative method to create a seasonal model that minimizes the MSE for the data set. Use Solver to determine the optimal values of α, β, and γ.
    a. What are the optimal values of α, β, and γ?
    b. Prepare a line graph comparing the predictions from this method against the original data.
    c. What are the forecasts for the next four months using this technique?

(Questions 49 through 53 refer to the data in the file that accompanies this book named ProductionHours.xls containing monthly data on the average number of hours worked each week by production workers in the United States over 94 consecutive months.)

49. Prepare a line graph of these data. Do the data appear to be stationary or non-stationary?

50. Use the additive seasonal technique for stationary data to model the data. Use Solver to determine the optimal values of α and β.
    a. What are the optimal values of α and β?
    b. Prepare a line graph comparing the predictions from this method against the original data.
    c. What are the forecasts for the next four months using this technique?

51. Use the multiplicative seasonal technique for stationary data to model the data. Use Solver to determine the optimal values of α and β.
    a. What are the optimal values of α and β?
    b. Prepare a line graph comparing the predictions from this method against the original data.
    c. What are the forecasts for the next four months using this technique?

52. Use Holt-Winter's additive method to create a seasonal model that minimizes the MSE for the data set. Use Solver to determine the optimal values of α, β, and γ.
    a. What are the optimal values of α, β, and γ?
    b. Prepare a line graph comparing the predictions from this method against the original data.
    c. What are the forecasts for the next four months using this technique?

53. Use Holt-Winter's multiplicative method to create a seasonal model that minimizes the MSE for the data set. Use Solver to determine the optimal values of α, β, and γ.
    a. What are the optimal values of α, β, and γ?
    b. Prepare a line graph comparing the predictions from this method against the original data.
    c. What are the forecasts for the next four months using this technique?

(Questions 54 through 58 refer to the data in the file that accompanies this book named QtrlySales.xls containing quarterly sales data for a Norwegian export company over 13 consecutive years.)

54. Prepare a line graph of these data. Do the data appear to be stationary or nonstationary?
55. Use the additive seasonal technique for stationary data to model the data. Use Solver to determine the optimal values of α and β.
    a. What are the optimal values of α and β?
    b. Prepare a line graph comparing the predictions from this method against the original data.
    c. What are the forecasts for the next four quarters using this technique?
56. Use the multiplicative seasonal technique for stationary data to model the data. Use Solver to determine the optimal values of α and β.
    a. What are the optimal values of α and β?
    b. Prepare a line graph comparing the predictions from this method against the original data.
    c. What are the forecasts for the next four quarters using this technique?
57. Use Holt-Winter's additive method to create a seasonal model that minimizes the MSE for the data set. Use Solver to determine the optimal values of α, β, and γ.
    a. What are the optimal values of α, β, and γ?
    b. Prepare a line graph comparing the predictions from this method against the original data.
    c. What are the forecasts for the next four quarters using this technique?
58. Use Holt-Winter's multiplicative method to create a seasonal model that minimizes the MSE for the data set. Use Solver to determine the optimal values of α, β, and γ.
    a. What are the optimal values of α, β, and γ?
    b. Prepare a line graph comparing the predictions from this method against the original data.
    c. What are the forecasts for the next four quarters using this technique?

CASE 11.1   PB Chemical Corporation

Mac Brown knew something had to change. As the new vice president of sales & marketing for the PB Chemical Company, Mac understood that when you sell a commodity product, where there is minimal difference between the quality and price, customer service and proactive selling effort usually are the difference between success and failure. Unfortunately, PB's sales staff was using a fairly random method of soliciting sales, where they would work through an alphabetical list of customers, making phone calls to those who had not placed any orders that month. Often, the difference between whether PB or a competitor got an order simply boiled down to who called at the time the customer needed materials. If the BP salesperson called too soon, they didn't get an order. And if they waited too long for a customer to call, they often lost business to a competitor.

Mac decided it was time for PB to be a bit more proactive and sophisticated in its sales efforts. He first convinced his counterparts at PB's largest customers that they could create a more efficient supply chain if they shared their monthly usage data of various chemicals with PB. That way, PB could better anticipate its customers' needs for various products. This, in turn, would reduce PB's need to hold inventory as safety stock, allow PB to operate more efficiently, and allow PB to pass some of these cost savings on to its customers.

PB's five largest customers (that account for 85% of PB's sales) agreed to share their monthly product use data. Now it was up to Mac to decide what to do with this data. It has been quite a while since Mac actually did any demand forecasting on his own, and he is far too busy with PB's strategic planning committee to be bothered by such details anyway. So Mac called one of the firm's top business analysts, Dee Hamrick, and dumped the problem in her lap. Specifically, Mac asked her to come up with a plan for forecasting demand for BP's products and using these forecasts for maximum advantage.

1. What issues should Dee consider in coming up with forecasts for BP's various products? How would you suggest she go about creating forecasts for each product?
2. Should Dee try to forecast aggregate monthly product demand for all customers or individual monthly product demand for each customer? Which of these forecasts would be more accurate? Which of these forecasts would be more useful (and to whom)?
3. Given the available data, how might Dee and Mac judge or gauge the accuracy of each product forecast?
4. Suppose Dee's technical staff could come up with a way of accurately forecasting monthly demand for BP's products. How should PB use this information for strategic advantage?
5. What other information should Dee suggest Mac try to get from BP's customers?

Forecasting COLAs

Tarrows, Pearson, Foster and Zuligar (TPF&Z) is one of the largest actuarial consulting firms in the United States. In addition to providing its clients with expert advice on executive compensation programs and employee benefits programs, TPF&Z also helps its clients determine the amounts of money they must contribute annually to defined benefit retirement programs.

Most companies offer two different types of retirement programs to their employees: defined contribution plans and defined benefit plans. Under a **defined contribution plan**, the company contributes a fixed percentage of an employee's earning to fund the employee's retirement. Individual employees covered by this type of plan determine how their money is to be invested (for example, stocks, bonds, or fixed-income securities), and whatever the employees are able to accumulate over the years constitutes their retirement fund. In a **defined benefit plan**, the company provides covered employees with retirement benefits that are usually calculated as a percentage of the employee's final salary (or sometimes an average of the employee's highest five years of earnings). Thus, under a defined benefit plan, the company is obligated to make payments to retired employees, but the company must determine how much of its earnings to set aside each year to cover these future obligations. Actuarial firms such as TPF&Z assist companies in making this determination.

Several of TPF&Z's clients offer employees defined benefit retirement plans that allow for cost of living adjustments (COLAs). Here, an employee's retirement benefit is still based on some measure of his or her final earnings, but these benefits are increased over time as the cost of living rises. These COLAs are often tied to the national consumer price index (CPI), which tracks the cost of a fixed-market basket of items over time. Each month, the Federal government calculates and publishes the CPI. Monthly CPI data from January 1991 through May 2010 is given in the file CPIData.xls that accompanies this book).

To assist their clients in determining the amount of money to accrue during a year for their annual contribution to their defined benefit programs, TPF&Z must forecast the value of the CPI one year into the future. Pension assets represent the largest single source of investment funds in the world. As a result, small changes or differences in

TPF&Z's CPI forecast translate into hundreds of millions of dollars in corporate earnings being diverted from the bottom line into pension reserves. Needless to say, the partners of TPF&Z want their CPI forecasts to be as accurate as possible.

1. Prepare a plot of the CPI data. Based on this plot, which of the time series forecasting techniques covered in this chapter would *not* be appropriate for forecasting this time series?

2. Apply Holt's method to this data set, and use Solver to find the values of α (alpha) and β (beta) that minimize the MSE between the actual and predicted CPI values. What is the MSE using this technique? What is the forecasted CPI value for June 2010 and June 2011 using this technique?

3. Apply linear regression to model the CPI as a function of time. What is the MSE using this technique? What is the forecasted CPI value for June 2010 and June 2011 using this technique?

4. Create a graph showing the actual CPI values plotted along with the predicted values obtained using Holt's method and the linear regression model. Which forecasting technique seems to fit the actual CPI data the best?

   Based on this graph, do you think it is appropriate to use linear regression on this data set? Explain your answer.

5. A partner of the firm has looked at your graph and asked you to repeat your analysis excluding the data prior to 2002. What MSE do you obtain using Holt's method? What MSE do you obtain using linear regression? What is the forecasted CPI value for June 2010 and June 2011 using each technique?

6. Graph your results again. Which forecasting technique seems to fit the actual CPI data the best? Based on this graph, do you think it is appropriate to use linear regression on this data set? Explain your answer.

7. The same partner has one final request. She wants to consider if it is possible to combine the predictions obtained using Holt's method and linear regression to obtain a composite forecast that is more accurate than either technique used in isolation. The partner wants you to combine the predictions in the following manner:

$$\text{Combined Prediction} = \mathbf{w} \times H + (1 - \mathbf{w}) \times R$$

   where H represents the predictions from Holt's method, R represents the predictions obtained using the linear regression model, and $\mathbf{w}$ is a weighting parameter between 0 and 1. Use Solver to determine the value of $\mathbf{w}$ that minimizes the MSE between the actual CPI values and the combined predictions. What is the optimal value of $\mathbf{w}$ and what is the associated MSE? What is the forecasted CPI value for June 2010 and June 2011 using this technique?

8. What CPI forecast for June 2010 and June 2011 would you recommend TPF&Z actually use?

CASE 11.3   Strategic Planning at Fysco Foods

Fysco Foods, Inc. is one of the largest suppliers of institutional and commercial food products in the United States. Fortunately for Fysco, the demand for "food away from home" has been growing steadily over the past 22 years as shown in the following table (and the file FyscoFoods.xls that accompanies this book). Note that this table breaks the total expenditures on food away from home (shown in the final column) into six component parts (for example, eating & drinking places, hotels & motels, and so on).

Total Food Away From Home Expenditures (in millions)

Year	Eating & Drinking Places[1]	Hotels & Motels[1]	Retail Stores, Direct Selling[2]	Recreational Places[3]	Schools & Colleges[4]	All Other[5]	Total[6]
1	75,883	5,906	8,158	3,040	11,115	16,194	120,296
2	83,358	6,639	8,830	2,979	11,357	17,751	130,914
3	90,390	6,888	9,256	2,887	11,692	18,663	139,776
4	98,710	7,660	9,827	3,271	12,338	19,077	150,883
5	105,836	8,409	10,315	3,489	12,950	20,047	161,046
6	111,760	9,168	10,499	3,737	13,534	20,133	168,831
7	121,699	9,665	11,116	4,059	14,401	20,755	181,695
8	146,194	11,117	12,063	4,331	14,300	21,122	209,127
9	160,855	11,905	13,211	5,144	14,929	22,887	228,930
10	171,157	12,179	14,440	6,151	15,728	24,581	244,236
11	183,484	12,508	16,053	7,316	16,767	26,198	262,326
12	188,228	12,460	16,750	8,079	17,959	27,108	270,584
13	183,014	13,204	13,588	8,602	18,983	27,946	265,338
14	195,835	13,362	13,777	9,275	19,844	28,031	280,124
15	205,768	13,880	14,210	9,791	21,086	28,208	292,943
16	214,274	14,195	14,333	10,574	22,093	28,597	304,066
17	221,735	14,504	14,475	11,354	22,993	28,981	314,043
18	235,597	15,469	14,407	8,290	24,071	30,926	328,760
19	248,716	15,800	15,198	9,750	25,141	31,926	346,530
20	260,495	16,623	16,397	10,400	26,256	33,560	363,730
21	275,695	17,440	16,591	11,177	27,016	34,508	382,427
22	290,655	17,899	16,881	11,809	28,012	35,004	400,259

Notes:

[1] Includes tips.

[2] Includes vending machine operators but not vending machines operated by organization.

[3] Motion picture theaters, bowling alleys, pool parlors, sports arenas, camps, amusement parks, golf and country clubs.

[4] Includes school food subsidies.

[5] Military exchanges and clubs; railroad dining cars; airlines; food service in manufacturing plants, institutions, hospitals, boarding houses, fraternities and sororities, and civic and social organizations; and food supplied to military forces.

[6] Computed from unrounded data.

As part of its strategic planning process, each year Fsyco generates forecasts of the total market demand in each of the six food away from home expenditure categories. This assists the company in allocating its marketing resources among the various customers represented in each category.

1. Prepare line graphs of each of the six expenditure categories. Indicate whether each category appears to be stationary or nonstationary.
2. Use Holt's method to create models for each expenditure category. Use Solver to estimate the values of α and β that minimize the MSE. What are the optimal values of α and β and the MSE for each model? What is the forecast for next year for each expenditure category?
3. Estimate linear regression models for each expenditure category. What is the estimated regression equation and MSE for each model? What is the forecast for next year for each expenditure category?

4. Fysco's vice president of marketing has a new idea for forecasting market demand. For each expenditure category, she wants you to estimate the growth rate represented by g in the following equation: $\hat{Y}_{t+1} = Y_t(1 + g)$. That is, the estimated value for time period $t + 1$ is equal to the actual value in the previous time period (t) multiplied by one plus the growth rate g. Use Solver to identify the optimal (minimum MSE) growth rate for each expenditure category. What is the growth rate for each category? What is the forecast for next year for each expenditure category?

5. Which of the three forecasting techniques considered here would you recommend Fysco use for each expenditure category?

Chapter 12

Introduction to Simulation Using Risk Solver Platform

12.0 Introduction

Chapter 1 discussed how the calculations in a spreadsheet can be viewed as a mathematical model that defines a functional relationship between various input variables (or independent variables) and one or more bottom-line performance measures (or dependent variables). The following equation expresses this relationship:

$$Y = f(X_1, X_2, \ldots, X_k)$$

In many spreadsheets, the values of various input cells are determined by the person using the spreadsheet. These input cells correspond to the independent variables $X_1, X_2, \ldots, X_k$ in the previous equation. Various formulas (represented by $f(\,)$ above) are entered in other cells of the spreadsheet to transform the values of the input cells into some bottom-line output (denoted by Y in the preceding equation). Simulation is a technique that is helpful in analyzing models in which the value to be assumed by one or more independent variables is uncertain. This chapter discusses how to perform simulation using a popular commercial spreadsheet add-in called Risk Solver Platform, created and distributed by Frontline Systems.

12.1 Random Variables and Risk

In order to compute a value for the bottom-line performance measure of a spreadsheet model, each input cell must be assigned a specific value so that all the related calculations can be performed. However, some uncertainty often exists regarding the value that should be assumed by one or more independent variables (or input cells) in the spreadsheet. This is particularly true in spreadsheet models that represent future conditions. A **random variable** is any variable whose value cannot be predicted or set with certainty. Thus, many input variables in a spreadsheet model represent random variables whose actual values cannot be predicted with certainty.

For example, projections of the cost of raw materials, future interest rates, future numbers of employees, and expected product demand are random variables because their true values are unknown and will be determined in the future. If we cannot say with certainty what value one or more input variables in a model will assume, we also cannot say with certainty what value the dependent variable will assume. This uncertainty associated with the value of the dependent variable introduces an element of risk to the decision-making problem. Specifically, if the dependent variable represents some bottom-line performance measure that managers use to make decisions, and its value is uncertain, any decisions made on the basis of this value are based on uncertain (or incomplete) information. When such a decision is made, some chance exists that the decision will not produce the intended results. This chance, or uncertainty, represents an element of **risk** in the decision-making problem.

The term "risk" also implies the *potential* for loss. The fact that a decision's outcome is uncertain does not mean that the decision is particularly risky. For example, whenever we put money into a soft drink machine, there is a chance the machine will take our money and not deliver the product. However, most of us would not consider this risk to be particularly great. From past experience, we know that the chance of not receiving the product is small. But even if the machine takes our money and does not deliver the product, most of us would not consider this to be a tremendous loss. Thus, the amount of risk involved in a given decision-making situation is a function of the uncertainty in the outcome of the decision and the magnitude of the potential loss. A proper assessment of the risk present in a decision-making situation should address both of these issues, as the examples in this chapter will demonstrate.

12.2 Why Analyze Risk?

Many spreadsheets built by business people contain *estimated* values for the uncertain input variables in their models. If a manager cannot say with certainty what value a particular cell in a spreadsheet will assume, this cell most likely represents a random variable. Ordinarily, the manager will attempt to make an informed guess about the values such cells will assume. The manager hopes that inserting the expected, or most likely, values for all the uncertain cells in a spreadsheet will provide the most likely value for the cell containing the bottom-line performance measure (Y). The problem with this type of analysis is that it tells the decision maker nothing about the variability of the performance measure.

For example, in analyzing a particular investment opportunity, we might determine that the expected return on a \$1,000 investment is \$10,000 within two years. But how much variability exists in the possible outcomes? If all the potential outcomes are scattered closely around \$10,000 (say from \$9,000 to \$11,000), then the investment opportunity might still be attractive. If, on the other hand, the potential outcomes are scattered widely around \$10,000 (say from −\$30,000 up to +\$50,000), then the investment opportunity might be unattractive. Although these two scenarios might have the same expected or average value, the risks involved are quite different. Thus, even if we can determine the expected outcome of a decision using a spreadsheet, it is just as important, if not more so, to consider the risk involved in the decision.

12.3 Methods of Risk Analysis

Several techniques are available to help managers analyze risk. Three of the most common are best-case/worst-case analysis, what-if analysis, and simulation. Of these methods, simulation is the most powerful and, therefore, is the technique that we will focus on in this chapter. Although the other techniques might not be completely effective in risk analysis, they are probably used more often than simulation by most managers in business today. This is largely because most managers are unaware of the spreadsheet's ability to perform simulation and of the benefits provided by this technique. So before discussing simulation, let's first briefly look at the other methods of risk analysis to understand their strengths and weaknesses.

12.3.1 BEST-CASE/WORST-CASE ANALYSIS

If we don't know what value a particular cell in a spreadsheet will assume, we could enter a number that we think is the most likely value for the uncertain cell. If we enter such numbers for all the uncertain cells in the spreadsheet, we can easily calculate the most likely value of the bottom-line performance measure. This is also called the **base-case** scenario. However, this scenario gives us no information about how far away the actual outcome might be from this expected, or most likely, value.

One simple solution to this problem is to calculate the value of the bottom-line performance measure using the **best-case**, or most optimistic, and **worst-case**, or most pessimistic, values for the uncertain input cells. These additional scenarios show the range of possible values that might be assumed by the bottom-line performance measure. As indicated in the earlier example about the $1,000 investment, knowing the range of possible outcomes is very helpful in assessing the risk involved in different alternatives. However, simply knowing the best-case and worst-case outcomes tells us nothing about the distribution of possible values within this range, nor does it tell us the probability of either scenario occurring.

Figure 12.1 displays several probability distributions that might be associated with the value of a bottom-line performance measure within a given range. Each of these distributions describes variables that have identical ranges and similar average values. But each distribution is very different in terms of the risk it represents to the decision maker. The appeal of best-case/worst-case analysis is that it is easy to do. Its weakness is that it tells us nothing about the shape of the distribution associated with the bottom-line performance measure. As we will see later, knowing the shape of the distribution of the bottom-line performance measure can be critically important in helping us answer a number of managerial questions.

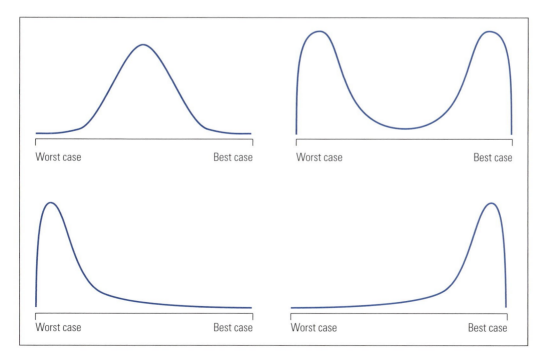

FIGURE 12.1

Possible distributions of performance measure values within a given range

12.3.2 WHAT-IF ANALYSIS

Prior to the introduction of electronic spreadsheets in the early 1980s, the use of best-case/worst-case analysis was often the only feasible way for a manager to analyze the risk associated with a decision. This process was extremely time-consuming, error prone, and tedious, using only a piece of paper, pencil, and calculator to recalculate the performance measure of a model using different values for the uncertain inputs. The arrival of personal computers and electronic spreadsheets made it much easier for a manager to play out a large number of scenarios in addition to the best and worst cases—which is the essence of what-if analysis.

In **what-if analysis**, a manager changes the values of the uncertain input variables to see what happens to the bottom-line performance measure. By making a series of such changes, a manager can gain some insight into how sensitive the performance measure is to changes to the input variables. Although many managers perform this type of manual what-if analysis, it has three major flaws.

First, if the values selected for the independent variables are based only on the manager's judgment, the resulting sample values of the performance measure are likely to be biased. That is, if several uncertain variables can each assume some range of values, it would be difficult to ensure that the manager tests a fair, or representative, sample of all possible combinations of these values. To select values for the uncertain variables that correctly reflect their random variations, the values must be randomly selected from a distribution, or pool, of values that reflects the appropriate range of possible values, as well as the appropriate relative frequencies of these variables.

Second, hundreds or thousands of what-if scenarios might be required to create a valid representation of the underlying variability in the bottom-line performance measure. No one would want to perform these scenarios manually nor would anyone be able to make sense of the resulting stream of numbers that would flash on the screen.

The third problem with what-if analysis is that the insight the manager might gain from playing out various scenarios is of little value when recommending a decision to top management. What-if analysis simply does not supply the manager with the tangible evidence (facts and figures) needed to justify why a given decision was made or recommended. Additionally, what-if analysis does not address the problem identified in our earlier discussion of best-case/worst-case analysis—it does not allow us to estimate the distribution of the performance measure in a formal enough manner. Thus, what-if analysis is a step in the right direction, but it is not quite a large enough step to allow managers to analyze risk effectively in the decisions they face.

12.3.3 SIMULATION

Simulation is a technique that measures and describes various characteristics of the bottom-line performance measure of a model when one or more values for the independent variables are uncertain. If any independent variables in a model are random variables, the dependent variable (Y) also represents a random variable. The objective in simulation is to describe the distribution and characteristics of the possible values of the bottom-line performance measure Y, given the possible values and behavior of the independent variables $X_1, X_2, \ldots, X_k$.

The idea behind simulation is similar to the notion of playing out many what-if scenarios. The difference is that the process of assigning values to the cells in the spreadsheet that represent random variables is automated so that (1) the values are assigned in a nonbiased way, and (2) the spreadsheet user is relieved of the burden of determining these values. With simulation, we repeatedly and randomly generate sample values for each uncertain input variable ($X_1, X_2, \ldots, X_k$) in our model and then compute the resulting value of our bottom-line performance measure (Y). We can then use the sample values of Y to estimate the true distribution and other characteristics of the performance measure Y. For example, we can use the sample observations to construct a frequency distribution of the performance measure, to estimate the range of values over which the performance measure might vary, to estimate its mean and variance, and to estimate the probability that the actual value of the performance measure will be greater than (or less than) a particular value. All these measures provide greater insight into the risk associated with a given decision than a single value calculated based on the expected values for the uncertain independent variables.

On Uncertainty and Decision-Making...

"Uncertainty is the most difficult thing about decision making. In the face of uncertainty, some people react with paralysis, or they do exhaustive research to avoid making a decision. The best decision making happens when the mental environment is focused. In a physical environment, you focus on something physical. In tennis, that might be the spinning seams of the ball. In a mental environment, you focus on the facts at hand. That fined-tuned focus doesn't leave room for fears and doubts to enter. Doubts knock at the door of our consciousness, but you don't have to have them in for tea and crumpets."—Timothy Gallwey, author of *The Inner Game of Tennis* and *The Inner Game of Work*

12.4 A Corporate Health Insurance Example

The following example demonstrates the mechanics of preparing a spreadsheet model for risk analysis using simulation. The example presents a fairly simple model to illustrate the process and give a sense of the amount of effort involved. However, the process for performing simulation is basically the same regardless of the size of the model.

Lisa Pon has just been hired as an analyst in the corporate planning department of Hungry Dawg Restaurants. Her first assignment is to determine how much money the company needs to accrue in the coming year to pay for its employees' health insurance claims. Hungry Dawg is a large, growing chain of restaurants that specializes in traditional southern foods. The company has become large enough that it no longer buys insurance from a private insurance company. The company is now self-insured, meaning that it pays health insurance claims with its own money (although it contracts with an outside company to handle the administrative details of processing claims and writing checks).

The money the company uses to pay claims comes from two sources: employee contributions (or premiums deducted from employees' paychecks), and company funds (the company must pay whatever costs are not covered by employee contributions). Each employee covered by the health plan contributes $125 per month.

However, the number of employees covered by the plan changes from month to month as employees are hired and fired, quit, or simply add or drop health insurance coverage. A total of 18,533 employees were covered by the plan last month. The average monthly health claim per covered employee was $250 last month.

An example of how most analysts would model this problem is shown in Figure 12.2 (and in the file Fig12-2.xlsm that accompanies this book). The spreadsheet begins with a listing of the initial conditions and assumptions for the problem. For example, cell D5 indicates that 18,533 employees are currently covered by the health plan, and cell D6 indicates that the average monthly claim per covered employee is $250. The average monthly contribution per employee is $125, as shown in cell D7. The values in cells D5 and D6 are unlikely to stay the same for the entire year. Thus, we need to make some assumptions about the rate at which these values are likely to increase during the year. For example, we might assume that the number of covered employees will increase by about 2% per month and that the average claim per employee will increase at a rate of 1% per month. These assumptions are reflected in cells F5 and F6. The average contribution per employee is assumed to be constant over the coming year.

Using the assumed rate of increase in the number of covered employees (cell F5), we can create formulas for cells B11 through B22 that cause the number of covered employees to increase by the assumed amount each month. (The details of these formulas are covered later.) The expected monthly employee contributions shown in column C are calculated as $125 times the number of employees in each month. We can use the assumed rate of increase in average monthly claims (cell F6) to create formulas for cells D11 through D22 that cause the average claim per employee to increase at the assumed rate. The total claims for each month (shown in column E) are calculated as the average claim figures in column D times the number of employees for each month in column B. Because the company must pay for any claims that are not covered by the employee

FIGURE 12.2

Original corporate health insurance model with expected values for uncertain variables

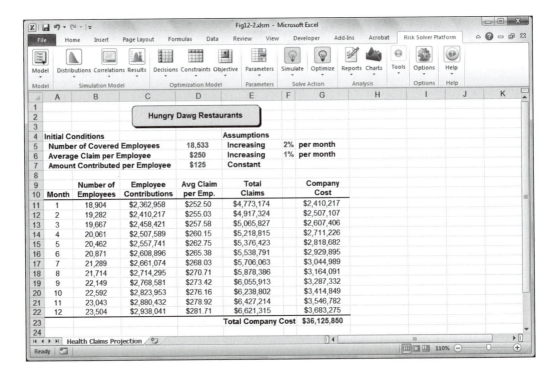

contributions, the monthly company cost figures in column G are calculated as the total claims minus the employee contributions (column E minus column C). Finally, cell G23 sums the monthly company cost figures listed in column G and shows that the company can expect to contribute $36,125,850 of its revenues toward paying the health insurance claims of its employees in the coming year.

12.4.1 A CRITIQUE OF THE BASE CASE MODEL

Now, let's consider the model we just described. The example model assumes that the number of covered employees will increase by *exactly* 2% each month and that the average claim per covered employee will increase by *exactly* 1% each month. Although these values might be reasonable approximations of what might happen, they are unlikely to reflect exactly what will happen. In fact, the number of employees covered by the health plan each month is likely to vary randomly around the average increase per month—that is, the number might decrease in some months and increase by more than 2% in others. Similarly, the average claim per covered employee might be lower than expected in certain months and higher than expected in others.

Both of these figures are likely to exhibit some uncertainty or random behavior, even if they do move in the general upward direction assumed throughout the year. So, we cannot say with certainty that the total cost figure of $36,125,850 is exactly what the company will have to contribute toward health claims in the coming year. It is simply a prediction of what might happen. The actual outcome could be smaller or larger than this estimate. Using the original model, we have no idea how much larger or smaller the actual result could be—nor do we have any idea of how the actual values are distributed around this estimate. We do not know if there is a 10%, 50%, or 90% chance of the actual total costs exceeding this estimate. To determine the variability or risk inherent in the bottom-line performance measure of total company costs, we will apply the technique of simulation to our model.

12.5 Spreadsheet Simulation Using Risk Solver Platform

To perform simulation in a spreadsheet, we must first place a **random number generator** (RNG) formula in each cell that represents a random, or uncertain, independent variable. Each RNG provides a sample observation from an appropriate distribution that represents the range and frequency of possible values for the variable. After the RNGs are in place, new sample values are provided automatically each time the spreadsheet is recalculated. We can recalculate the spreadsheet n times, where n is the desired number of replications or scenarios, and the value of the bottom-line performance measure will be stored after each replication. We can analyze these stored observations to gain insights into the behavior and characteristics of the performance measure.

The process of simulation involves a lot of work but, fortunately, the spreadsheet can do most of the work for us fairly easily. In particular, the spreadsheet add-in package Risk Solver Platform is designed specifically to make spreadsheet simulation a simple process. Risk Solver Platform provides the following capabilities, which are not otherwise available while working in Excel: additional functions that are helpful in generating the random numbers needed in simulation; additional commands that are helpful in setting up and running the simulation; and graphical and statistical summaries of the simulation data. As we shall see, these capabilities make simulation a relatively easy technique to apply in spreadsheets.

12.5.1 STARTING RISK SOLVER PLATFORM

If you are running Risk Solver Platform from a local area network (LAN) or in a computer lab, your instructor or LAN coordinator should give you directions on how to access this software. If you have installed Risk Solver Platform on your own computer, the Risk Solver Platform tab should automatically appear on the ribbon as shown in Figure 12.2. You can also load (or unload) Risk Solver Platform manually from within Excel as follows:

1. Click File, Options, Add-Ins.
2. Select Excel Add-Ins and click Go.
3. Select (or unselect) Risk Solver Platform and click OK.
4. Click File, Options, Add-Ins.
5. Select COM Add-Ins and click Go.
6. Select (or unselect) Risk Solver Platform Add-in and click OK.

The Risk Solver Platform tab contains the custom ribbon shown in Figure 12.2. We will refer to the various icons on this ribbon throughout this chapter.

12.6 Random Number Generators

As mentioned earlier, the first step in spreadsheet simulation is to place an RNG formula in each cell that contains an uncertain value. Each of these formulas will generate (or return) a number that represents a randomly selected value from a distribution, or pool, of values. The distributions that these samples are taken from should be representative of the underlying pool of values expected to occur in each uncertain cell.

Risk Solver Platform provides several "Psi" functions that can be used to create the RNGs required for simulating a model. (The "Psi" prefix on these functions stands for Polymorphic Spreadsheet Interpreter, which is the technology Frontline Systems developed and uses in Risk Solver Platform to recalculate Excel workbooks extremely quickly.) Figure 12.3 describes some of the most common RNGs. These functions allow us to generate a variety of random numbers easily. For example, if we think that the behavior of an uncertain cell could be modeled as a normally distributed random variable with a mean of 125 and standard deviation of 10, then according to Figure 12.3, we could enter the formula =PsiNormal(125,10) in this cell. (The arguments in this function could also be formulas and could refer to other cells in the spreadsheet.) After this formula is entered, Risk Solver Platform will randomly generate or select a value from a normal distribution with a mean of 125 and standard deviation of 10 for this cell whenever the spreadsheet is recalculated.

Similarly, a cell in our spreadsheet might have a 30% chance of assuming the value 10, a 50% chance of assuming the value 20, and a 20% chance of assuming the value 30. As noted in Figure 12.3, we could use the formula =PsiDiscrete({10,20,30}, {0.3,0.5,0.2}) to model the behavior of this random variable. If we recalculated the spreadsheet many times, this formula would return the value 10 approximately 30% of the time, the value 20 approximately 50% of the time, and the value 30 approximately 20% of the time.

FIGURE 12.3 *Commonly used RNGs supplied with Risk Solver Platform*

Distribution	RNG	Description
Binomial	PsiBinomial(n,p)	Returns the number of "successes" in a sample of size n where each trial has a probability p of "success."
Discrete	PsiDiscrete($\{x_1, x_2, \ldots x_n\}$, $\{p_1, p_2, \ldots p_n\}$)	Returns one of the n values represented by the x_1. The value x_i occurs with probability p_i.
Discrete	PsiDisUniform ($\{x_1, x_2, \ldots, x_n\}$)	Returns one of the n values represented by the x_i. Each value x_i is equally likely to occur.
Poisson	PsiPoisson(λ)	Returns a random number of events occurring per some unit of measure (for example, arrivals per hour, defects per yard, and so on). The parameter λ represents the average number of events occurring per unit of measure.
Chi-square	PsiChisquare(λ)	Returns a value from a chi-square distribution with mean λ.
Continuous	PsiUniform(*min, max*)	Returns a value in the range from a minimum (*min*) to a maximum (*max*). Each value in this range is equally likely to occur.
Exponential	PsiExponential(λ)	Returns a value from an exponential distribution with mean λ. Often used to model the time between events or the lifetime of a device with a constant probability of failure.
Normal	PsiNormal(μ,σ)	Returns a value from a normal distribution with mean μ and standard deviation σ.
Truncated Normal	PsiNormal(μ ,σ, PsiTruncate(*min*,*max*))	Same as PsiNormal except the distribution is truncated to the range specified by a minimum (*min*) and a maximum (*max*).
Triangular	PsiTriangular(*min, most likely, max*)	Returns a value from a triangular distribution covering the range specified by a minimum (*min*) and a maximum (*max*). The shape of the distribution is then determined by the size of the *most likely* value relative to *min* and *max*.

The arguments, or parameters, required by the RNG functions allow us to generate random numbers from distributions with a wide variety of shapes. Figures 12.4 and 12.5 illustrate some example distributions. Additional information about these and other RNGs provided by Risk Solver Platform is available in the Risk Solver Platform user manual and in the online Help facility in Risk Solver Platform.

> # Risk Solver RNG Functions
>
> A listing of all the available Risk Solver Platform RNG functions is available in Excel. To view this listing, follow these steps:
>
> 1. Select an empty cell in a worksheet.
> 2. Click Formulas, Insert Function.
> 3. Select the Psi Distribution function category.

FIGURE 12.4

Examples of distributions associated with selected discrete RNGs

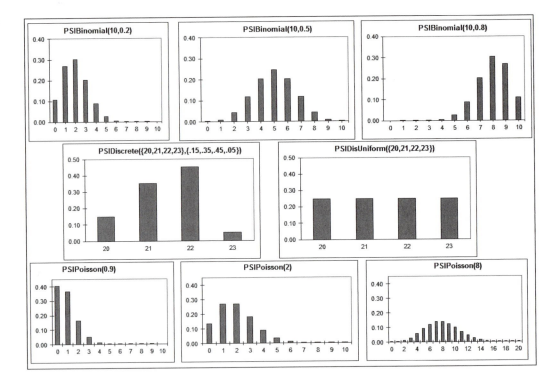

12.6.1 DISCRETE VS. CONTINUOUS RANDOM VARIABLES

An important distinction exists between the graphs in Figures 12.4 and 12.5. In particular, the RNGs depicted in Figure 12.4 generate *discrete* outcomes, whereas those represented in Figure 12.5 generate *continuous* outcomes. That is, some of the RNGs listed in Figure 12.3 can return only a distinct set of individual values, whereas the other RNGs can return any value from an infinite set of values. The distinction between discrete and continuous random variables is very important.

For example, the number of defective tires on a new car is a discrete random variable because it can assume only one of five distinct values: 0, 1, 2, 3, or 4. On the other hand, the amount of fuel in a new car is a continuous random variable because it can assume

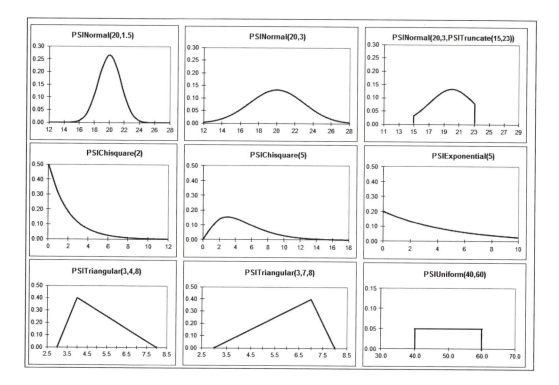

FIGURE 12.5

*Examples of
distributions
associated with
selected
continuous RNGs*

any value between 0 and the maximum capacity of the fuel tank. Thus, when selecting an RNG for an uncertain variable in a model, it is important to consider whether the variable can assume discrete or continuous values.

12.7 Preparing the Model for Simulation

To apply simulation to the model for Hungry Dawg Restaurants described earlier, we must first select appropriate RNGs for the uncertain variables in the model. If available, historical data on the uncertain variables could be analyzed to determine appropriate RNGs for these variables. Alternatively, the historical data itself can be sampled from using Risk Solver Platform's PsiDisUniform( ), PsiResample( ), PsiSip( ), or PsiSlurp( ) functions. (Refer to the Risk Solver Platform user manual for more information about these topics.) Risk Solver Platform also has the ability to identify probability distributions automatically that fit your historical data reasonably well. However, if past data are not available, or if we have some reason to expect the future behavior of a variable to be significantly different from the past, then we must use judgment in selecting appropriate RNGs to model the random behavior of the uncertain variables.

For our example problem, assume that by analyzing historical data, we determined that the change in the number of covered employees from one month to the next is expected to vary uniformly between a 3% decrease and a 7% increase. (Note that this should cause the average change in the number of employees to be a 2% increase because 0.02 is the midpoint between -0.03 and $+0.07$.) Further, assume that we can model the

FIGURE 12.6

Modified corporate health insurance model with RNGs replacing expected values for uncertain variables

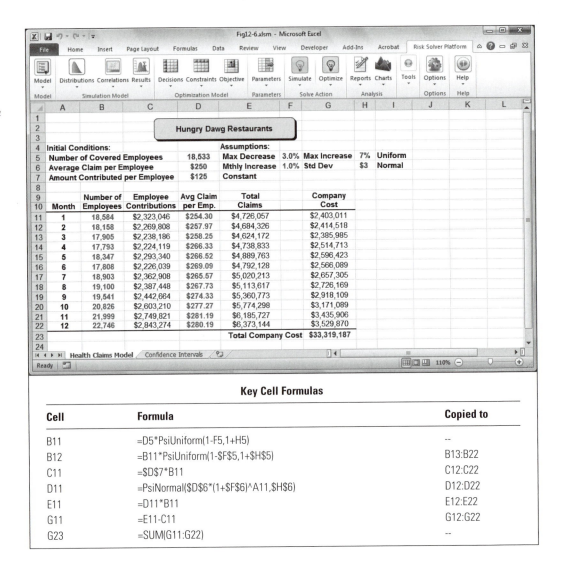

Key Cell Formulas

Cell	Formula	Copied to
B11	=D5*PsiUniform(1-F5,1+H5)	--
B12	=B11*PsiUniform(1-$F$5,1+$H$5)	B13:B22
C11	=$D$7*B11	C12:C22
D11	=PsiNormal($D$6*(1+$F$6)^A11,$H$6)	D12:D22
E11	=D11*B11	E12:E22
G11	=E11-C11	G12:G22
G23	=SUM(G11:G22)	--

average monthly claim per covered employee as a normally distributed random variable with the mean (μ) increasing by 1% per month and a standard deviation (σ) of approximately $3. (Note that this will cause the *average* increase in claims per covered employee from one month to the next to be approximately 1%.) These assumptions are reflected in cells F5 through H6 at the top of Figure 12.6 (and in the file Fig12-6.xlsm that accompanies this book).

To implement the formula to generate a random number of employees covered by the health plan, we will use the PsiUniform( ) function described in Figure 12.3. Because the change in the number of employees from one month to the next can vary between a 3% decrease and a 7% increase, in general, the number of employees in the current month is equal to the number of employees in the previous month multiplied by the sum of 1 plus the percentage change. Applying this logic, we obtain the following equation for the number of employees in a given month:

$$\text{Number of employees in current month} = \text{Number of employees in previous month} \times \text{PsiUniform}(0.97, 1.07)$$

If the PsiUniform( ) function returns the value 0.97, this formula causes the number of employees in the current month to equal 97% of the number in the previous month (a 3% decrease). Alternatively, if the PsiUniform( ) function returns the value 1.07, this formula causes the number of employees in the current month to equal 107% of the number in the previous month (a 7% increase). All the values between these two extremes (between 0.97 and 1.07) are also possible and equally likely to occur. The following formulas were used to create formulas that randomly generate the number of employees in each month in Figure 12.6:

Formula for cell B11:   =D5*PsiUniform(1−F5,1+H5)

Formula for cell B12:   =B11*PsiUniform(1−$F$5,1+$H$5)

(Copy to B13 through B22.)

Note that the terms "1 − $F$5" and "1 + $H$5" in the preceding formulas generate the values 0.97 and 1.07, respectively.

To implement the formula to generate the average claims per covered employee in each month, we will use the PsiNormal( ) function described earlier in Figure 12.3. This formula requires that we supply the value of the mean (μ) and standard deviation (σ) of the distribution from which we want to sample. The assumed $3 standard deviation ($\sigma$) for the average monthly claim, shown in cell H6 in Figure 12.6, is constant from month to month. Thus, the only remaining problem is to determine the proper mean value (μ) for each month.

In this case, the mean for any given month should be 1% larger than the mean in the previous month. For example, the mean for month 1 is:

$$\text{Mean in month } 1 = (\text{original mean}) \times 1.01$$

and the mean for month 2 is:

$$\text{Mean in month } 2 = (\text{mean in month } 1) \times 1.01$$

If we substitute the previous definition of the mean in month 1 into the previous equation, we obtain:

$$\text{Mean in month } 2 = (\text{original mean}) \times (1.01)^2$$

Similarly, the mean in month 3 is:

$$\text{Mean in month } 3 = (\text{mean in month } 2) \times 1.01 = (\text{original mean}) \times (1.01)^3$$

So in general, the mean (μ) for month n is:

$$\text{Mean in month } n = (\text{original mean}) \times (1.01)^n$$

Thus, to generate the average claim per covered employee in each month, we use the following formula:

Formula for cell D11:   =PsiNormal($D$6*(1+$F$6)^A11,$H$6)

(Copy to D12 through D22.)

The term "$D$6*(1 + $F$6)^A11" in this formula implements the general definition of the mean (μ) in month n.

After entering the appropriate RNGs, each time we press the recalculate key (the function key [F9]), the RNGs automatically select new values for all the cells in the spreadsheet that represent uncertain (or random) variables. Similarly, with each recalculation, a new value for the bottom-line performance measure (total company cost) appears in cell G23. Thus, by pressing the recalculate key several times, we can observe representative values of the company's total cost for health claims. This also helps to verify that we implemented the RNGs correctly and that they are generating appropriate values for each uncertain cell.

12.7.1 ALTERNATE RNG ENTRY

Risk Solver Platform also offers an alternate way of entering RNGs in spreadsheet models. If you select a worksheet cell and then click any of the icons in the Distributions icon on the Risk Solver Platform ribbon shown in Figure 12.6, a Distribution dialog appears similar to the one shown in Figure 12.7 (for the normal probability distribution with the dialog's panels expanded). Double-clicking any cell containing a Psi distribution function also launches the dialog shown in Figure 12.7. This dialog allows you to select any of the available probability distributions and see its shape as you vary the value of the various parameters. It also shows you the Psi function required to implement the RNG for the displayed probability distribution. Risk Solver Platform then automatically implements in your model the appropriate formula for the RNG you select. While this is a very useful feature of Risk Solver Platform, the RNG formula created by Risk Solver Platform often requires some manual editing to make it work correctly with the rest of the model you are building, particularly if you intend to copy this RNG formula to other cells in your workbook.

FIGURE 12.7 *Risk Solver Platform's Uncertain Variable dialog*

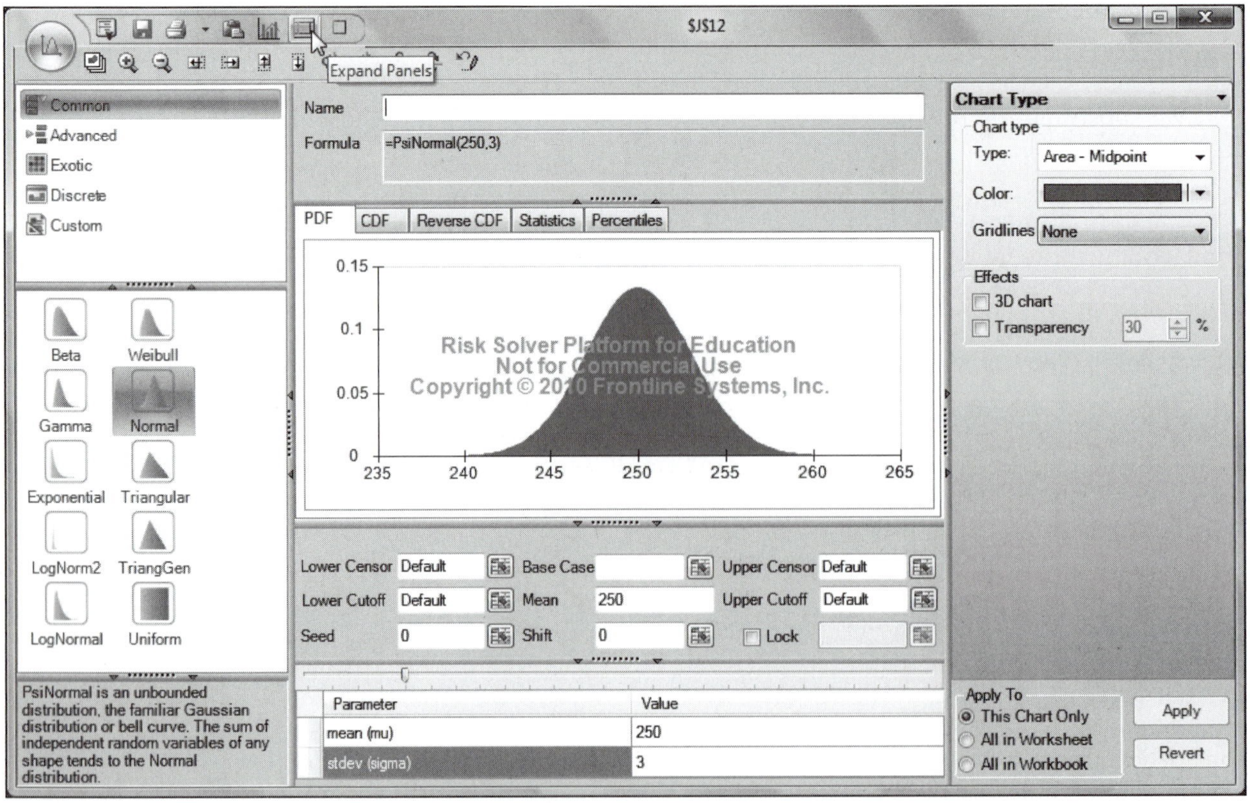

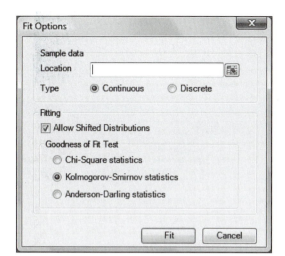

FIGURE 12.8

*Risk Solver
Platform's Fit
Options dialog*

Fitting a Distribution to Sample Data...

Note that the Fit Distribution icon (resembling a bar chart, immediately to the left of the Expand Panels icon) at the top of Figure 12.7 launches the Fit Options dialog shown in Figure 12.8. If you have historical data for any of the random variables in your model, you can use this dialog to instruct Risk Solver Platform to automatically fit a probability distribution to your data.

12.8 Running the Simulation

The next step in performing the simulation involves recalculating the spreadsheet several hundred or several thousand times and recording the resulting values generated for the output cell(s), or bottom-line performance measure(s). Fortunately, Risk Solver Platform can do this for us very easily if we indicate how many times we want it to replicate the model (or how many trials we want it to perform) and which cell(s) in the spreadsheet we want to track.

12.8.1 SELECTING THE OUTPUT CELLS TO TRACK

We can use the Add Output button on the Risk Solver Platform menu to indicate the output cell (or cells) that we want Risk Solver Platform to track during the simulation. In the current example, cell G23 represents the output cell we want Risk Solver Platform to track. To indicate this, follow these steps:

1. Click cell G23.
2. Click the Results icon on the Risk Solver Platform menu.
3. Click the Output option.
4. Click the In Cell option.

FIGURE 12.9

*Selecting the
output cell to track*

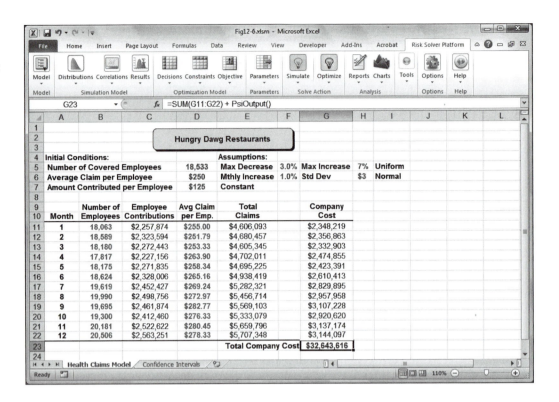

If you now look at the formula in cell G23, as shown in Figure 12.9, you will observe that it has been changed to:

Formula for cell G23:   =SUM(G11:G22) + PsiOutput( )

Clicking Risk Solver Platform's Results, Output, In Cell command with cell G23 selected caused the PsiOutput( ) function to be added to the original formula in cell G23. This is how Risk Solver Platform identifies output cells for our model. If you prefer, you can also manually add the PsiOutput( ) function to the contents of any numeric cell in your workbook to designate it as an output cell to Risk Solver. Alternatively, in any empty cell in the worksheet, we could enter the formula =PsiOutput(G23), and Risk Solver Platform would then know that cell G23 is an output cell. (This is also what happens if you choose the Referred Cell option rather than the In Cell option when using the Results, Output command.)

12.8.2 SELECTING THE NUMBER OF REPLICATIONS

If we click the Options icon on the Risk Solver Platform menu shown in Figure 12.9, the Risk Solver Platform Options dialog box shown in Figure 12.10 appears. This dialog allows you to control several aspects of the simulation analysis. The Trials per Simulation option allows you to specify the number of trials or replications of your model Risk Solver Platform will generate when performing a simulation. All the examples in this book will use 5,000 trials per simulation.

You might wonder why we selected 5,000 trials. Why not 1,000, or 10,000? Unfortunately, there is no easy answer to this question. Remember that the goal in simulation is to estimate various characteristics about the bottom-line performance measure(s) under consideration. For example, we might want to estimate the mean value of the performance

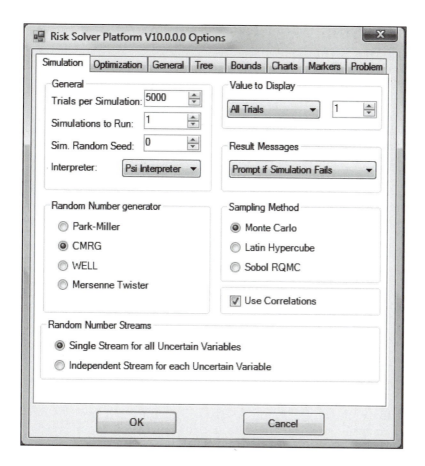

FIGURE 12.10

*The Risk Solver
Platform Options
dialog box*

measure and the shape of its probability distribution. However, a different value of the bottom-line performance measure occurs each time we manually recalculate the model in Figure 12.9. Thus, there is an infinite number of possibilities—or an **infinite population**— of total company cost values associated with this model.

We cannot analyze all of these infinite possibilities. But by taking a large enough sample from this infinite population, we can make reasonably accurate estimates about the characteristics of the underlying infinite population of values. The larger the sample we take (that is, the more replications we do), the more accurate our final results will be. Although Risk Solver Platform is extremely fast, performing many replications takes time (especially for large models), so we must make a trade-off in terms of estimation accuracy versus convenience. Thus, there is no simple answer to the question of how many replications to perform, but, as a bare minimum, you should always perform at least 1,000 replications, and more as time permits or accuracy demands.

The Maximum Number of Trials

The educational version of Risk Solver Platform allows for 10,000 trials per simulation. The commercial version of this product removes this restriction and allows for as many trials as you desire.

12.8.3 SELECTING WHAT GETS DISPLAYED ON THE WORKSHEET

When Risk Solver Platform carries out our simulation, it generates 5,000 replications or trials of our model. So for each Psi distribution and Psi output cell, Risk Solver Platform will compute and store 5,000 values; but it can display only one value in any particular cell. So which of the 5,000 values do we want it to display? Or might we prefer Risk Solver Platform to display the mean (average) of the 5,000 values? Our answers to these questions can be communicated to Risk Solver Platform via the Value to Display setting on the Risk Solver Platform Options dialog shown earlier in Figure 12.10 (or via the trial display counter immediately below the Thaw icon in the Tools section of the Risk Solver Platform ribbon shown earlier in Figure 12.9). Using this option, we can instruct Risk Solver Platform to display the value of one particular trial (the default setting) or have it display the mean of the sample of our replications.

It is important to note that if you select the sample mean option, Risk Solver Platform returns the sample mean for each Psi distribution cell and the resulting *computed* values for any Psi output cells. These computed values *may* or *may not* be the mean value of the Psi output cells depending on the nature of the functional relationship between the Psi distribution cells and the Psi output cells.

It is also important to note that if you ask Risk Solver Platform to display the values associated with one particular trial, the numbers displayed on the worksheet represent one random replication of your model that is no more special or important than any of the other replications in the simulation. Of course, any one random trial might be very unrepresentative of the typical values for the cells in the worksheet. As mentioned earlier, what we are really interested in is the **distribution** of outcomes associated with our output cells. As we will see, Risk Solver Platform offers a very elegant yet simple way to look at and answer questions about the distribution of outcomes associated with the output cells in a spreadsheet model.

12.8.4 RUNNING THE SIMULATION

Having identified the output cells to track and the number of replications to perform, we now need to instruct Risk Solver Platform to perform the simulation. This can be done in two different ways. The Simulate dropdown on the Risk Solver Platform ribbon has options for Interactive and Run Once. The Run Once option does just that—it runs one simulation consisting of the currently specified number of trials. Alternatively, you can select the Interactive option—or simply click the Simulate icon (that looks like a light bulb) in the Risk Solver Platform menu. When the Simulate icon is on (or the light bulb is illuminated), Risk Solver Platform is in **interactive simulation** mode. In this mode, anytime you make a change to your workbook that requires the spreadsheet to be recalculated (or manually recalculate the spreadsheet by pressing the [F9] key), Risk Solver Platform performs a complete simulation of your model—generating however many trials you specified per simulation in the Risk Solver Platform Options dialog in Figure 12.10. So while in interactive simulation mode, manually recalculating your workbook may actually cause your model to be replicated 5,000 times. If this sounds like a lot of computational work, it is. However, if you use Risk Solver Platform's internal spreadsheet interpreter (by choosing the PSI Interpreter option in the Risk Solver Platform Options dialog shown earlier in Figure 12.10), these trials will usually be executed very quickly. The first time Risk

Solver Platform performs a simulation for a given workbook, it must parse or interpret the formulas in the spreadsheet, which sometimes takes a few seconds. However, after this is accomplished once, Risk Solver Platform performs future simulations with impressive speed.

12.9 Data Analysis

As mentioned earlier, the objective of performing a simulation is to estimate various characteristics of the outputs or bottom-line performance measures that are influenced by uncertainty in some or all of the input variables. While in interactive simulation mode, simply double-click on any of the output cells in your model (identified using the PsiOutput( ) function as described earlier), and Risk Solver Platform opens a dialog that allows you to summarize the output data for that cell in a variety of ways. Figure 12.11 shows the Risk Solver Platform Statistics window, created by double-clicking cell G23 (representing the total company cost) in Figure 12.9.

12.9.1 THE BEST CASE AND THE WORST CASE

As shown in Figure 12.11, the average (or mean) value for cell G23 is approximately $36.1 million. (If you are working through this example on a computer, the results you generate may be somewhat different from the results shown here because you may be working with a different sample of 5,000 observations.) However, decision makers usually want to know the best-case and worst-case scenarios to get an idea of

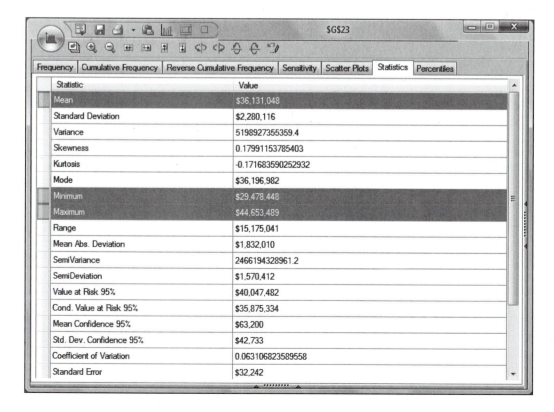

FIGURE 12.11

Summary statistics for the simulation trials

Statistic	Value
Mean	$36,131,048
Standard Deviation	$2,280,116
Variance	5198927355359.4
Skewness	0.17991153785403
Kurtosis	-0.171683590252932
Mode	$36,196,982
Minimum	$29,478,448
Maximum	$44,653,489
Range	$15,175,041
Mean Abs. Deviation	$1,832,010
SemiVariance	2466194328961.2
SemiDeviation	$1,570,412
Value at Risk 95%	$40,047,482
Cond. Value at Risk 95%	$35,875,334
Mean Confidence 95%	$63,200
Std. Dev. Confidence 95%	$42,733
Coefficient of Variation	0.063106823589558
Standard Error	$32,242

Tabs: Frequency | Cumulative Frequency | Reverse Cumulative Frequency | Sensitivity | Scatter Plots | Statistics | Percentiles

$G$23

the range of possible outcomes they might face. This information is available from the simulation results, as shown by the Minimum and Maximum values listed in Figure 12.11.

Although the average total cost value observed in the 5,000 replications is $36.1 million, in one case, the total cost is approximately $29.4 million (representing the minimum or best case), and, in another case, the total cost is approximately $44.6 million (representing the maximum or worst case). These figures should give the decision maker a good idea about the range of possible cost values that might occur. Note that these values might be difficult to determine manually (without simulation) in a complex model with many uncertain independent variables.

12.9.2 VIEWING THE DISTRIBUTION OF THE OUTPUT CELLS

The best- and worst-case scenarios are the most extreme outcomes and might not be likely to occur. To determine the likelihood of these outcomes requires that we know something about the shape of the distribution of our bottom-line performance measure. To view a graph of the distribution of the results of the 5,000 replications generated for the output cell in our model, we can switch to the Frequency tab on the simulation results dialog for cell G23 as shown in Figure 12.12.

Figure 12.12 provides a visual summary of the approximate shape of the probability distribution associated with the output cell tracked by Risk Solver Platform during the simulation. In this case, the shape of the distribution associated with the total cost variable is somewhat bell-shaped, with a maximum value around $44 million and a minimum value around $29 million. Thus, we now have a clear idea of the shape of the distribution associated with our bottom-line performance measure—one of the goals in simulation. You can right-click on the frequency graphs like the one shown in Figure 12.12 to add upper and lower markers to the graph and then click and drag these markers to identify the probability associated with different ranges of outcomes.

FIGURE 12.12

Frequency distribution of the sampled total company costs

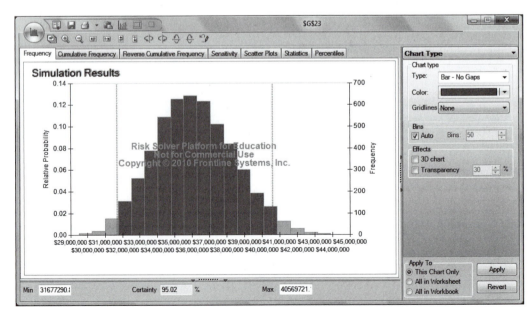

In Figure 12.12, we see that approximately 95% of our trials resulted in outcomes with total cost values between $31.7 million and $40.6 million.

In this example, cell G23 (representing total company cost) is the only output cell that we identified (via the PsiOutput( ) function as discussed in Section 12.8.1). However, it is important to note that if we tracked more than one output cell during the simulation (using multiple PsiOuput( ) functions), we could display summary statistics and histograms of the values occurring in these other output cells in a similar manner.

Working with Frequency Graphs

You can right-click on the frequency graphs like the one shown in Figure 12.12 to add upper and lower markers to the graph. You may then click and drag these markers to identify the probability associated with different ranges of outcomes.

12.9.3 VIEWING THE CUMULATIVE DISTRIBUTION OF THE OUTPUT CELLS

At times, we might want to view a graph of the cumulative probability distribution associated with one of the output cells tracked during a simulation. For example, suppose that the chief financial officer (CFO) for Hungry Dawg would rather accrue an excess amount of money to pay health claims than not accrue enough money. The CFO might want to know what amount the company should accrue so that there is only a 10% chance of coming up short of funds at the end of the year. So, how much money would you recommend be accrued?

Figure 12.13 shows a graph of the cumulative probability distribution of the values that occurred in cell G23 during the simulation. This graph could help us ascertain and explain the answer to the preceding question.

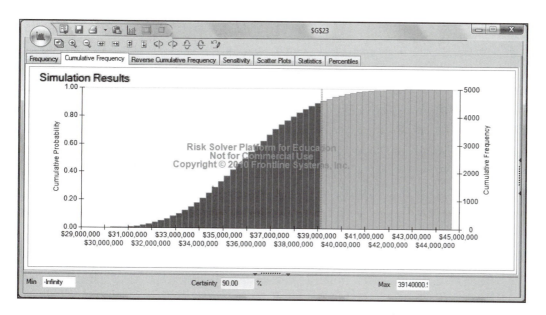

FIGURE 12.13

Cumulative frequency distribution of sampled total company costs

This graph displays the probability of the selected output cell taking on a value smaller than each value on the X-axis. For example, this graph indicates that approximately a 20% chance exists of the output cell assuming a value smaller than approximately $34 million. Similarly, this graph indicates that roughly an 80% chance exists of total costs being less than approximately $38 million (or a 20% chance of total costs exceeding approximately $38 million). Thus, from this graph, we would estimate that roughly a 10% chance exists of the company's costs exceeding approximately $39 million.

12.9.4 OBTAINING OTHER CUMULATIVE PROBABILITIES

We can also answer the CFO's question from information in the Percentiles tab shown in Figure 12.14. This window reveals a number of percentile values for the output cell G23. For example, the 75th percentile of the values generated for the output cell is $37,642,736—or 75% of the 5,000 values generated for cell G23 are less than or equal to this value. Similarly, the 90th percentile of the distribution of values is $39,139,854. Thus, based on these results, if the company accrues $39 million, we would expect that only about a 10% chance exists of the actual company costs exceeding this amount.

The ability to perform this type of analysis highlights the power and value of simulation and Risk Solver Platform. For example, how could we have answered the CFO's question about how much money to accrue using best-case/worst-case analysis or what-if analysis? The fact is, we could not answer the question with any degree of accuracy without using simulation.

FIGURE 12.14

Percentiles of the distribution of possible total company costs

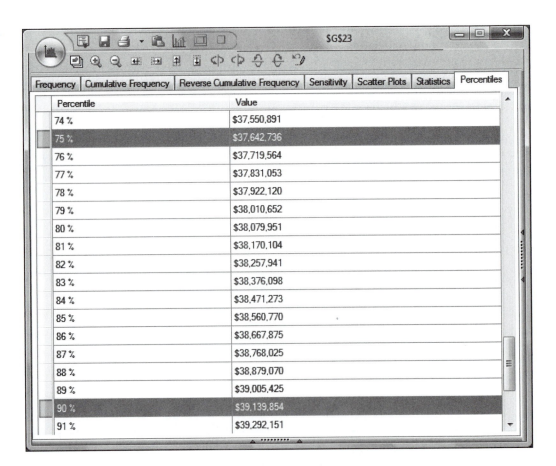

Percentile	Value
74 %	$37,550,891
75 %	$37,642,736
76 %	$37,719,564
77 %	$37,831,053
78 %	$37,922,120
79 %	$38,010,652
80 %	$38,079,951
81 %	$38,170,104
82 %	$38,257,941
83 %	$38,376,098
84 %	$38,471,273
85 %	$38,560,770
86 %	$38,667,875
87 %	$38,768,025
88 %	$38,879,070
89 %	$39,005,425
90 %	$39,139,854
91 %	$39,292,151

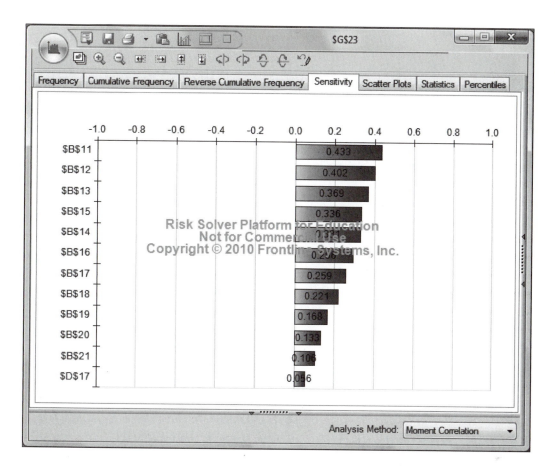

FIGURE 12.15

Sensitivity chart of the simulation results

12.9.5 SENSITIVITY ANALYSIS

At times, you may be interested in examining how sensitive the simulation output results are to various uncertain input cells in the model. This helps us determine which uncertain input cells are most influential in effecting the bottom-line output performance measure in the model. Such information can help direct our efforts to ensure that the most influential input cells are modeled accurately. In some cases, it can also help managers control (or reduce the variability of) the output variable by taking steps to reduce the variability in the most influential input variables.

Figure 12.15 shows how a Sensitivity chart identifies and summarizes the uncertain input cells in our model that are most significantly correlated (linearly) with the total company cost values generated for cell G23. As this graph shows, the number of covered employees each month (in column B in our spreadsheet model) tends to have the largest impact on the total company cost.

12.10 The Uncertainty of Sampling

To this point, we have used simulation to generate 5,000 observations on our bottom-line performance measure and then calculated various statistics to describe the characteristics and behavior of the performance measure. For example, Figure 12.11 indicates that the mean company cost value in our sample is $36,131,048, and Figure 12.14 shows that a 90% chance exists of this performance measure assuming a value less than $39,139,854. But what if we repeat this process and generate another 5,000 observations? Would the sample mean for the new 5,000 observations also be exactly $36,131,048? Or would exactly 90% of the observations in the new sample be less than $39,139,854?

The answer to both these questions is "probably not." The sample of 5,000 observations used in our analysis was taken from a population of values that is theoretically infinite in size. That is, if we had enough time and our computer had enough memory, we could generate an infinite number of values for our bottom-line performance measure. Theoretically, we could then analyze this infinite population of values to determine its true mean value, its true standard deviation, and the true probability of the performance measure being less than $39,139,854. Unfortunately, we do not have the time or computer resources to determine these true characteristics (or parameters) of the population. The best we can do is take a sample from this population and, based on our sample, make estimates about the true characteristics of the underlying population. Our estimates will differ depending on the sample we choose and the size of the sample.

So, the mean of the sample we take is probably not equal to the true mean we would observe if we could analyze the entire population of values for our performance measure. The sample mean we calculate is just an estimate of the true population mean. In our example problem, we estimated that a 90% chance exists for our output variable to assume a value less than $39,139,854. However, this most likely is not equal to the true probability we would calculate if we could analyze the entire population. Thus, there is some element of uncertainty surrounding the statistical estimates resulting from simulation because we are using a sample to make inferences about the population. Fortunately, there are ways of measuring and describing the amount of uncertainty present in some of the estimates we make about the population under study. This is typically done by constructing confidence intervals for the population parameters being estimated.

12.10.1 CONSTRUCTING A CONFIDENCE INTERVAL FOR THE TRUE POPULATION MEAN

Constructing a confidence interval for the true population mean is a simple process. If $\bar{y}$ and s represent, respectively, the mean and standard deviation of a sample of size n from any population, then assuming n is sufficiently large ($n \geq 30$), the Central Limit Theorem tells us that the lower and upper limits of a 95% confidence interval for the true mean of the population are represented by:

$$95\% \text{ Lower Confidence Limit} = \bar{y} - 1.96 \times \frac{s}{\sqrt{n}}$$

$$95\% \text{ Upper Confidence Limit} = \bar{y} + 1.96 \times \frac{s}{\sqrt{n}}$$

Although we can be fairly certain that the sample mean we calculate from our sample data is not equal to the true population mean, we can be 95% confident that the true mean of the population falls between the lower and upper limits given previously. If we want a 90% or 99% confidence interval, we must change the value 1.96 in the previous equation to 1.645 or 2.575, respectively. The values 1.645, 1.96, and 2.575 represent, respectively, the 95, 97.5, and 99.5 percentiles of the standard normal distribution. Any percentile of the standard normal distribution can be obtained using Excel's NORMSINV( ) function.

For our example, the lower and upper limits of a 95% confidence interval for the true mean of the population of total company cost values can be calculated easily, as shown in cells B9 and B10 in Figure 12.16.

Formula for cell B9:   =B4−NORMSINV(1−B7/2)*B5/SQRT(B6)
Formula for cell B10:   =B4+NORMSINV(1−B7/2)*B5/SQRT(B6)

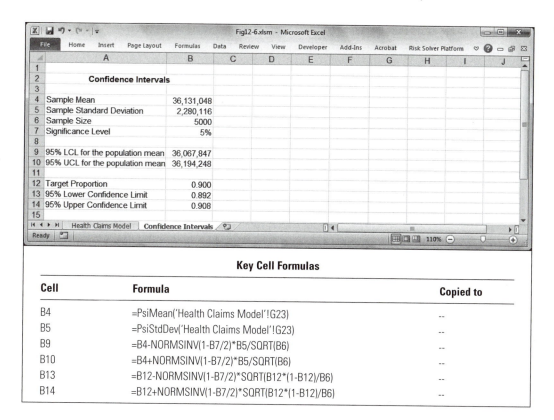

Key Cell Formulas

Cell	Formula	Copied to
B4	=PsiMean('Health Claims Model'!G23)	--
B5	=PsiStdDev('Health Claims Model'!G23)	--
B9	=B4-NORMSINV(1-B7/2)*B5/SQRT(B6)	--
B10	=B4+NORMSINV(1-B7/2)*B5/SQRT(B6)	--
B13	=B12-NORMSINV(1-B7/2)*SQRT(B12*(1-B12)/B6)	--
B14	=B12+NORMSINV(1-B7/2)*SQRT(B12*(1-B12)/B6)	--

Thus, we can be 95% confident that the true mean of the population of total company cost values falls somewhere in the interval from \$36,067,847 to \$36,194,248.

Notice that the sample mean and standard deviation shown in cells B4 and B5 of Figure 12.16 can be obtained directly from the simulation results using two of Risk Solver Platform's Psi statistics functions.

Formula for cell B4:   =PsiMean('Health Claims Model'!G23)

Formula for cell B5:   =PsiStdDev('Health Claims Model'!G23)

These formulas, respectively, return the mean and standard deviation of the 5,000 numbers that Risk Solver Platform has stored for cell G23. The Statistic, Measure, and Range icons on the Risk Solver menu provide galleries of several other Psi functions that can be used in a similar way to calculate and report simulation results directly on a spreadsheet. These functions can be extremely helpful in summarizing simulation results. However, it is also important to note that these functions work only while Risk Solver Platform is in interactive simulation mode.

12.10.2 CONSTRUCTING A CONFIDENCE INTERVAL FOR A POPULATION PROPORTION

In our example, we estimated that 90% of the population of total company cost values fall below \$39,139,854 based on our sample of 5,000 observations. However, if we could evaluate the entire population of total cost values, we might find that only 80% of these values fall below \$39,139,854. Or, we might find that 99% of the entire population falls below this mark. It would be helpful to determine how accurate the 90% value is. So, at times, we might want to construct a confidence interval for the true proportion of a population that falls below (or above) some value, for example Y_p.

To see how this is done, let $\bar{p}$ denote the proportion of observations in a sample of size n that falls below some value Y_p. Assuming that n is sufficiently large ($n \geq 30$), the Central Limit Theorem tells us that the lower and upper limits of a 95% confidence interval for the true proportion of the population falling below Y_p are represented by:

$$95\% \text{ Lower Confidence Limit} = \bar{p} - 1.96 \times \sqrt{\frac{\bar{p}(1 - \bar{p})}{n}}$$

$$95\% \text{ Upper Confidence Limit} = \bar{p} + 1.96 \times \sqrt{\frac{\bar{p}(1 - \bar{p})}{n}}$$

Although we can be fairly certain that the proportion of observations falling below Y_p in our sample is not equal to the true proportion of the population falling below Y_p, we can be 95% confident that the true proportion of the population falling below Y_p is contained within the lower and upper limits given previously. Again, if we want a 90% or 99% confidence interval, we must change the value 1.96 in the previous equations to 1.645 or 2.575, respectively.

Using these formulas, we can calculate the lower and upper limits of a 95% confidence interval for the true proportion of the population falling below \$39,139,854. From our simulation results, we know that 90% of the observations in our sample are less than \$39,139,854. Thus, our estimated value of $\bar{p}$ is 0.90. This value was entered into cell B12 in Figure 12.16. The lower and upper limits of a 95% confidence interval for the true proportion of the population falling below \$39,139,854 are calculated in cells B13 and B14 of Figure 12.16 using the following formulas:

Formula for cell B13:   =B12−NORMSINV(1−B7/2)*SQRT(B12*(1−B12)/B6)

Formula for cell B14:   =B12+NORMSINV(1−B7/2)*SQRT(B12*(1−B12)/B6)

We can be 95% confident that the true proportion of the population of total cost values falling below \$39,139,854 is between 0.892 and 0.908. Because this interval is fairly tight around the value 0.90, we can be reasonably certain that the \$39,139,854 figure quoted to the CFO has approximately a 10% chance of being exceeded.

12.10.3 SAMPLE SIZES AND CONFIDENCE INTERVAL WIDTHS

The formulas for the confidence intervals in the previous section depend on the number of replications (n) in the simulation. As the number of replications (n) increases, the width of the confidence interval decreases (or becomes more precise). Thus, for a given level of confidence (for example, 95%), the only way to make the upper and lower limits of the interval closer together (or tighter) is to make n larger—that is, use a larger sample size. A larger sample should provide more information about the population and, therefore, allow us to be more accurate in estimating the true parameters of the population.

12.11 Interactive Simulation

One of Risk Solver Platform's amazing capabilities is performing interactive simulation. As mentioned earlier, when the Simulate icon on the Risk Solver Platform tab is on (or the light bulb is illuminated), Risk Solver Platform is in interactive simulation mode. (You can turn interactive simulation mode on or off simply by clicking the Simulate icon.) In interactive simulation mode, anytime you make a change to your workbook that requires the spreadsheet to be recalculated (or manually recalculate the spreadsheet by pressing the [F9] key), Risk Solver Platform performs a complete simulation of your model.

To understand why this is useful, recall that Figures 12.13 and 12.14 suggest there is approximately a 90% chance of the total company cost being less than $39 million—or, equivalently, approximately a 10% chance of the total company cost exceeding $39 million. Now suppose the executives at Hungry Dawg Restaurants feel that this exposes the company to too much risk. In particular, they would like there to be only a 2% chance of the total company cost exceeding $39 million. One way to reduce the costs the company might incur is by increasing the amount of money employees must contribute each month—currently set at $125 per employee each month. Essentially, this shifts some of the costs for the health insurance plan from the company to its employees. But how much should the amount contributed per employee each month increase in order for there to only be a 2% chance of the company's liability exceeding $39 million?

We can answer this question easily using Risk Solver Platform in interactive simulation mode as shown in Figure 12.17 (and the file Fig12-17.xlsm that accompanies this book). In interactive simulation mode (that is, when the Simulate icon is illuminated), if you change the amount contributed per employee each month (in cell D7), Risk Solver Platform instantly performs 5,000 replications of the model and summarizes the results

FIGURE 12.17 *Using interactive simulation*

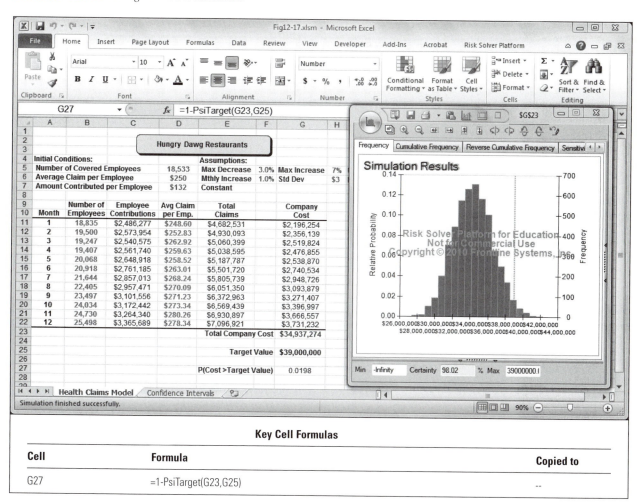

			Key Cell Formulas		
Cell		**Formula**			**Copied to**
G27		=1-PsiTarget(G23,G25)			--

in the frequency chart. So an analyst can quickly see how changes to the amount the company charges its employees for health insurance coverage affects the distribution of costs for which the company is liable. In this case, we can quickly determine that if employees pay $132 per month for health insurance coverage, there is only about a 2% chance that the company's liability will exceed $39 million.

In Figure 12.17, also note the use of the PsiTarget( ) function in cell G27 that computes the probability of the total company cost (in cell G23) exceeding $39 million (in cell G25).

Formula for cell G27:   =1−PsiTarget(G23,G25)

In general, PsiTarget(*cell, target value*) returns the cumulative probability of a specified distribution or output *cell* being less than or equal to a given *target value*. In the case shown in Figure 12.17, there is a 98.02% chance of the total company cost being less than $39 million. So there is a 1 − .9802 = 0.0198 probability of the total company cost exceeding $39 million.

The PsiTarget( ) Function

The function PsiTarget(*cell, target value*) returns the cumulative probability of a specified distribution or output *cell* being less than or equal to a given *target value*. This function is very useful in calculating various probabilities associated with simulation results.

12.12 The Benefits of Simulation

So what have we accomplished through simulation? Are we really better off than if we had just used the results of the original model proposed in Figure 12.2? The estimated value for the expected total cost to the company in Figure 12.2 is comparable to that obtained through simulation (although this might not always be the case). But remember that the goal of modeling is to give us greater insight into a problem to help us make more informed decisions.

The results of our simulation do give us greater insight into the problem. In particular, we now have some idea of the best- and worst-case total cost outcomes for the company. We have a better idea of the distribution and variability of the possible outcomes and a more precise idea about where the mean of the distribution is located. We also now have a way of determining how likely it is for the actual outcome to fall above or below some value. Thus, in addition to our greater insight and understanding of the problem, we also have solid empirical evidence (the facts and figures) to support our recommendations.

Applying Simulation in Personal Financial Planning

A recent article in the *Wall Street Journal* highlighted the importance of simulation in evaluating the risk in personal financial investments. "Many people are taking a lot more risk than they realize. They are walking around with a false sense of security," said Christopher Cordaro, an investment advisor at Bugen Stuart Korn & Cordaro of Chatman, NJ. "Using one online retirement calculator, after entering information about your finances and assumptions about investment gains, the screen shows a green or red light indicating whether you have saved enough to

(Continued)

retire. What is doesn't tell you is whether there is a 95% chance or just a 60% chance that your plan will succeed."

Although any planning is better than nothing, traditional planning models spit out answers that create "the illusion that the number is a certainty, when it isn't," said Ross Levin, a Minneapolis investment advisor who uses simulation. Mutual-fund firm T. Rowe Price applied simulation to its recently launched Retirement Income Manager, a personalized consultation service that helps retirees understand how much income they can afford without outliving their assets or depleting funds they want to leave to heirs. A number of independent financial planning companies are now also using simulation software.

In the face of widely divergent possibilities, the number crunching involved in simulation can bring some peace of mind. Steven Haas, of Randolph, NJ, was not sure whether he had saved enough to accept an early retirement package from AT&T at age 53. After his financial advisor used simulation to determine he had a 95% probability that his money would last until he reached age 110, Mr. Haas took the package and retired, reporting "I found that even under significantly negative scenarios, we could live comfortably. It relieved a lot of anxiety."

12.13 Additional Uses of Simulation

Earlier, we indicated that simulation is a technique that *describes* the behavior or characteristics of a bottom-line performance measure. The next several examples show how describing the behavior of a performance measure gives a manager a useful tool in determining the optimal value for one or more controllable parameters in a decision problem. These examples reinforce the mechanics of using simulation and also demonstrate some additional capabilities of Risk Solver Platform.

12.14 A Reservation Management Example

Businesses that allow customers to make reservations for services (such as airlines, hotels, and car rental companies) know that some percentage of the reservations made will not be used for one reason or another, leaving these companies with a difficult decision problem. If they accept reservations for only the number of customers that can actually be served, then a portion of the company's assets will be underutilized when some customers with reservations fail to arrive. On the other hand, if they overbook (or accept more reservations than can be handled), then at times, more customers will arrive than can actually be served. This typically results in additional financial costs to the company and often generates ill will among those customers who cannot be served. The following example illustrates how simulation might be used to help a company determine the optimal number of reservations to accept.

Marty Ford is an operations analyst for Piedmont Commuter Airlines (PCA). Recently, Marty was asked to make a recommendation on how many reservations PCA should book on Flight 343—a flight from a small regional airport in New England to a major hub at Boston's Logan airport. The plane used on Flight 343 is a small twin-engine turbo-prop with 19 passenger seats available. PCA sells nonrefundable tickets for Flight 343 for $150 per seat.

Industry statistics show that for every ticket sold for a commuter flight, a 0.10 probability exists that the ticket holder will not be on the flight. Thus, if PCA sells 19 tickets for this flight, there is a fairly good chance that one or more seats on the plane will be empty. Of course, empty seats represent lost potential revenue to the company. On the other hand, if PCA overbooks this flight, and more than 19 passengers show up, some of them will have to be bumped to a later flight.

To compensate for the inconvenience of being bumped, PCA gives these passengers vouchers for a free meal, a free flight at a later date, and sometimes also pays for them to stay overnight in a hotel near the airport. PCA pays an average of $325 (including the cost of lost goodwill) for each passenger that gets bumped. Marty wants to determine if PCA can increase profits by overbooking this flight, and, if so, how many reservations should be accepted to produce the maximum average profit. To assist in the analysis, Marty analyzed market research data for this flight that reveals the following probability distribution of demand for this flight:

Seats Demanded	14	15	16	17	18	19	20	21	22	23	24	25
Probability	0.03	0.05	0.07	0.09	0.11	0.15	0.18	0.14	0.08	0.05	0.03	0.02

12.14.1 IMPLEMENTING THE MODEL

A spreadsheet model for this problem is shown in Figure 12.18 (and in the file Fig12-18.xlsm that accompanies this book). The spreadsheet begins by listing the relevant data from the problem, including the number of seats available on the plane, the price PCA charges for each seat, the probability of a no-show (a ticketed passenger not arriving in time for the flight), the cost of bumping passengers, and the number of reservations that will be accepted.

The distribution of demand for seats on the flight is summarized in columns E and F. Using this data, the number of seats demanded for a particular flight is randomly generated in cell C10 as follows:

Formula for cell C10:   =PsiDiscrete(E5:E16, F5:F16)

The number of tickets actually sold for a flight cannot exceed the number of reservations the company is willing to accept. Thus, the number of tickets sold is calculated in cell C11 as follows:

Formula for cell C11:   =MIN(C10,C8)

Because each ticketed passenger has a 0.10 probability of being a no-show, a 0.9 probability exists that each ticketed passenger will arrive in time to board the flight. The PsiBinomial( ) function (described earlier in Figure 12.3) is used in cell C12 to model the number of ticketed passengers for the flight:

Formula for cell C12:   =PsiBinomial(C11,1–C6)

Cell C14 represents the ticket revenue PCA earns based on the number of tickets it sells for each flight. The formula for this cell is:

Formula for cell C14:   =C11*C5

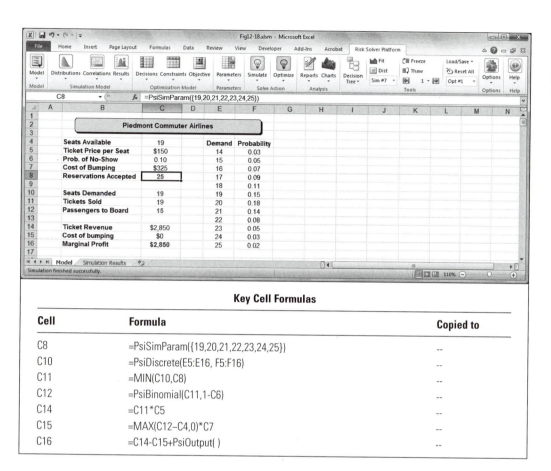

FIGURE 12.18

Spreadsheet model for the overbooking problem

Key Cell Formulas

Cell	Formula	Copied to
C8	=PsiSimParam({19,20,21,22,23,24,25})	--
C10	=PsiDiscrete(E5:E16, F5:F16)	--
C11	=MIN(C10,C8)	--
C12	=PsiBinomial(C11,1-C6)	--
C14	=C11*C5	--
C15	=MAX(C12-C4,0)*C7	--
C16	=C14-C15+PsiOutput( )	--

Cell C15 computes the costs PCA incurs when passengers must be bumped (i.e., when the number of passengers wanting to board exceeds the number of available seats).

Formula for cell C15:   =MAX(C12−C4,0)*C7

Finally, cell C16 computes the marginal profit PCA earns on each flight. This is also the output cell to be tracked when simulating this model.

Formula for cell C16:   =C14−C15+ PsiOutput( )

12.14.2 DETAILS FOR MULTIPLE SIMULATIONS

Marty wants to determine the number of reservations to accept that, on average, will result in the highest marginal profit. To do so, he needs to use the PsiSimParam( ) function to simulate what would happen if 19, 20, 21, 22, 23, 24, and 25 reservations are accepted. Cell C8 contains the following formula:

Formula for cell C8:   =PsiSimParam({19,20,21,22,23,24,25})

This formula, along with the Simulations to Run setting shown in the Risk Solver Platform Options dialog in Figure 12.19, instructs Risk Solver Platform to use seven different values in cell C8 and simulate what will happen with each value.

When comparing different values for one or more decision variables, it is best if each possible value is evaluated in a simulation using exactly the same series of random numbers. In this way, any difference in the performance of two possible solutions can be

FIGURE 12.19

*Risk Solver
Platform options
for the overbooking
problem*

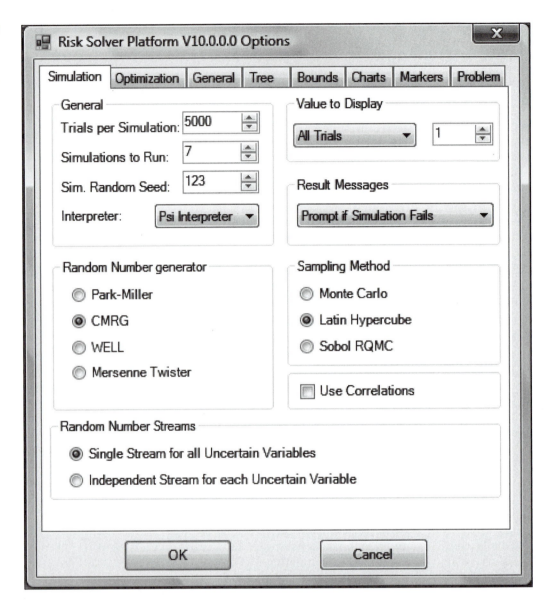

attributed to the decision variables' values and not the result of a more favorable set of random numbers for one of the simulations. The Sim. Random Seed option shown in Figure 12.19 controls this behavior in Risk Solver Platform. By default, Risk Solver Platform will use a randomly chosen seed value to initialize its RNG when performing multiple simulations using the PsiSimParam( ) function. Alternatively, you may override Risk Solver Platform's default behavior and instruct it to use a seed value you specify when it performs multiple simulations. Choosing your own seed allows you to repeat the same simulation again in the future if needed.

It is worth noting that the Sampling Method options shown in Figure 12.19 also have an impact on the accuracy of the results of a simulation run. Using the Monte Carlo option, Risk Solver Platform is free to select any value for a particular RNG during each replication of the model. For example, Risk Solver Platform might repeatedly generate several very extreme (and rare!) values from the upper tail of a normal distribution. The Latin Hypercube option guards against this by ensuring that a fair representation of values is generated from the entire distribution for each RNG. As you might imagine, the Latin Hypercube sampling option requires a bit more work during each replication of the model, but it tends to generate more accurate simulation results in a fewer number of trials. Refer to Risk Solver Platform's user manual for additional information about its supported sampling methods.

12.14.3 RUNNING THE SIMULATIONS

In Figure 12.18, we included the PsiOutput( ) function in our formula for cell C16 (representing marginal profit) to indicate it is the output cell we want Risk Solver Platform to track. In Figure 12.19, we indicated Risk Solver Platform should perform 7 simulations (one for each value from 19 to 25 indicated by the PsiSimParam( ) function in cell C8) and run a simulation consisting of 5,000 replications for each possible value for C8. If Risk Solver Platform is in interactive simulation mode, it will automatically carry out each of the desired 7 simulations (involving 35,000 replications of our model).

12.14.4 DATA ANALYSIS

Risk Solver Platform provides a number of ways for us to look at the results of the seven simulations. If we double-click on cell C16 (which includes the PsiOutput( ) function), we can look at the marginal profit results for each of the seven simulations. Figure 12.20 shows how Risk Solver Platform allows us to view the statistics associated with any of the seven simulations.

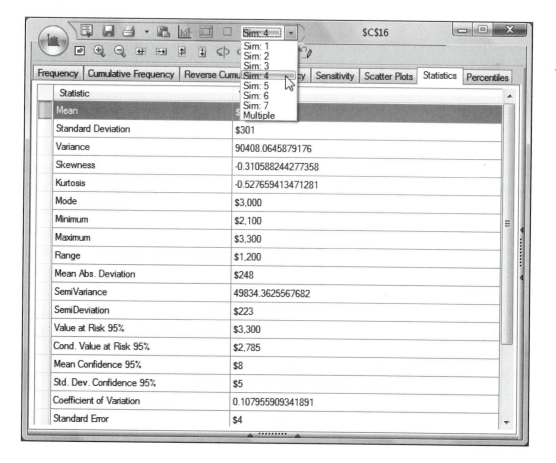

FIGURE 12.20

Viewing statistics for any of the seven simulations

FIGURE 12.21

Viewing the cumu-lative frequency distribution of each simulation

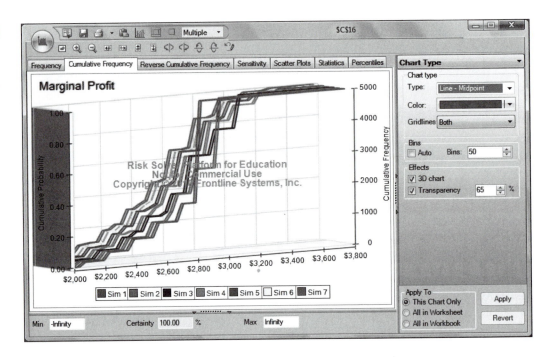

Using the Frequency tab, we can also simultaneously chart the cumulative frequency distribution of the marginal profit values associated with each of the seven simulations as shown in Figure 12.21.

Of course, we can also use Psi statistic functions to create a custom summary of the simulation results directly in a worksheet (see Figure 12.22). In the case of multiple simulations, note that the last argument of each Psi statistic function indicates to which set of simulation data the function applies. For example, the formula =PsiMean(Model!C16,1) would return the mean marginal profit from simulation one (where 19 reservations were accepted), whereas =PsiMean(Model!C16,5) would return the mean marginal profit from simulation five (where 23 reservations were accepted). This data makes it clear that if PCA wants to maximize its expected (or average) marginal profit, it should accept 21 reservations per flight. Accepting more than 21 reservations makes it possible to achieve higher levels of profit on some flights but, on average (over a large number of flights), accepting more than 21 reservations would result in less profit for the company if the assumptions in our model are correct.

12.15 An Inventory Control Example

According to the *Wall Street Journal*, U.S. businesses recently had a combined inventory worth $884.77 billion dollars. Because so much money is tied up in inventories, businesses face many important decisions regarding the management of these assets. Frequently asked questions regarding inventory include the following:

- What's the best level of inventory for a business to maintain?
- When should goods be reordered (or manufactured)?
- How much safety stock should be held in inventory?

The study of inventory control principles is split into two distinct areas—one assumes that demand is known (or deterministic), and the other assumes that demand is random (or stochastic). If demand is known, various formulas can be derived that provide answers

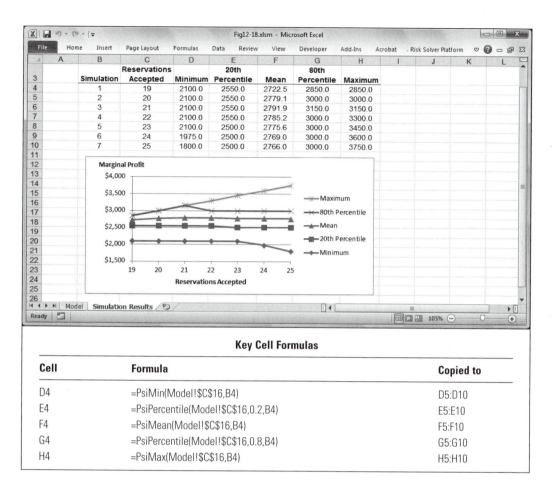

FIGURE 12.22

Summary of results from all seven simulations

Key Cell Formulas

Cell	Formula	Copied to
D4	=PsiMin(Model!$C$16,B4)	D5:D10
E4	=PsiPercentile(Model!$C$16,0.2,B4)	E5:E10
F4	=PsiMean(Model!$C$16,B4)	F5:F10
G4	=PsiPercentile(Model!$C$16,0.8,B4)	G5:G10
H4	=PsiMax(Model!$C$16,B4)	H5:H10

to the previous questions (an example of one such formula is given in the discussion of the EOQ model in Chapter 8). However, when demand for a product is uncertain or random, answers to the previous questions cannot be expressed in terms of a simple formula. In these situations, the technique of simulation proves to be a useful tool, as illustrated in the following example.

Laura Tanner is the owner of Millennium Computer Corporation (MCC), a retail computer store in Austin, Texas. Competition in retail computer sales is fierce—in terms of both price and service. Laura is concerned about the number of stockouts occurring on a popular type of computer monitor. Stockouts are very costly to the business because when customers cannot buy this item at MCC, they simply buy it from a competing store, and MCC loses the sale (there are no backorders). Laura measures the effects of stockouts on her business in terms of service level, or the percentage of total demand that can be satisfied from inventory.

Laura has been following the policy of ordering 50 monitors whenever her daily ending inventory position (defined as ending inventory on hand plus outstanding orders) falls below her reorder point of 28 units. Laura places the order at the beginning of the next day. Orders are delivered at the beginning of the day and, therefore, can be used to satisfy demand on that day. For example, if the ending inventory position on day 2 is less than 28, Laura places the order at the beginning of day 3. If the actual time between order and delivery, or lead time, turns out to be four days, then the order arrives at the start of day 7. The current level of on-hand inventory is 50 units, and no orders are pending.

MCC sells an average of six monitors per day. However, the actual number sold on any given day can vary. By reviewing her sales records for the past several months, Laura determined that the actual daily demand for this monitor is a random variable that can be described by the following probability distribution:

Units Demanded	0	1	2	3	4	5	6	7	8	9	10
Probability	0.01	0.02	0.04	0.06	0.09	0.14	0.18	0.22	0.16	0.06	0.02

The manufacturer of this computer monitor is located in California. Although it takes an average of four days for MCC to receive an order from this company, Laura has determined that the lead time of a shipment of monitors is also a random variable that can be described by the following probability distribution:

Lead Time (days)	3	4	5
Probability	0.2	0.6	0.2

One way to guard against stockouts and improve the service level is to increase the reorder point for the item so that more inventory is on hand to meet the demand occurring during the lead time. However, there are holding costs associated with keeping more inventory on hand. Laura wants to evaluate her current ordering policy for this item and determine if it might be possible to improve the service level without increasing the average amount of inventory on hand.

12.15.1 CREATING THE RNGs

To solve this problem, we need to build a model to represent the inventory of computer monitors during an average month of 30 days. This model must account for the random daily demands that can occur and the random lead times encountered when orders are placed. First, we will consider how to create RNGs to model the daily demands and order lead times. The data for these variables are entered in the spreadsheet as shown in Figure 12.23 (and in the file Fig12-23.xlsm that accompanies this book).

FIGURE 12.23

RNG data for MCC's inventory problem

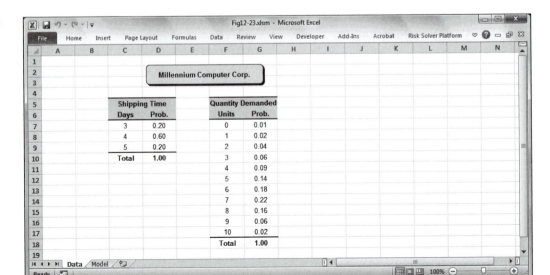

The order lead time and daily demand variables are both examples of *general, discrete* random variables because the possible outcomes they assume consist solely of integers, and the probabilities associated with each outcome are not equal (or not uniform). Thus, using the PsiDiscrete( ) function described in Figure 12.5, the RNGs for each variable are:

RNG for order lead time: =PsiDiscrete(Data!$C$7:$C$9,Data!$D$7:$D$9)

RNG for daily demand: =PsiDiscrete(Data!$F$7:$F$17,Data!$G$7:$G$17)

12.15.2 IMPLEMENTING THE MODEL

Now that we have a way of generating the random numbers needed in this problem, we can consider how the model should be built. Figure 12.24 shows the model representing 30 days of inventory activity. Notice that cells M5 and M6 have been reserved to represent, respectively, the reorder point and order quantity for the model.

The inventory on hand at the beginning of each day is calculated in column B in Figure 12.24. The beginning inventory for each day is simply the ending inventory from the previous day. The formulas in column B are:

Formula for cell B6:   =50

Formula for cell B7:   =F6

(Copy to B8 through B35.)

Column C represents the number of units scheduled to be received each day. We will discuss the formulas in column C after we discuss columns H, I, and J, which relate to ordering and order lead times.

In column D, we use the technique described earlier to generate random daily demands, as:

Formula for cell D6:   =PsiDiscrete(Data!$F$7:$F$17,Data!$G$7:$G$17)

(Copy to D7 through D35.)

Because it is possible for demand to exceed the available supply, column E indicates how much of the daily demand can be met. If the beginning inventory (in column B) plus the ordered units received (in column C) is greater than or equal to the actual demand, then all the demand can be satisfied; otherwise, MCC can sell only as many units as are available. This condition is modeled as:

Formula for cell E6:   =MIN(D6,B6+C6)

(Copy to E7 through E35.)

The values in column F represent the on-hand inventory at the end of each day and are calculated as:

Formula for cell F6:   =B6+C6−E6

(Copy to F7 through F35.)

To determine whether to place an order, we first must calculate the inventory position, which was defined earlier as the ending inventory plus any outstanding orders. This is implemented in column G as:

Formula for cell G6:   =F6

Formula for cell G7:   =G6−E7+IF(H6=1,$M$6,0)

(Copy to G8 through G35.)

FIGURE 12.24

Spreadsheet for MCC's inventory problem

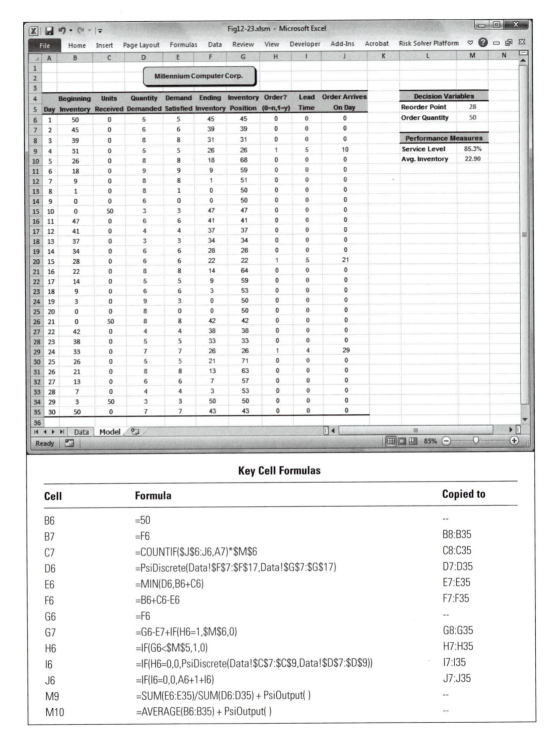

Key Cell Formulas

Cell	Formula	Copied to
B6	=50	--
B7	=F6	B8:B35
C7	=COUNTIF($J$6:J6,A7)*$M$6	C8:C35
D6	=PsiDiscrete(Data!$F$7:$F$17,Data!$G$7:$G$17)	D7:D35
E6	=MIN(D6,B6+C6)	E7:E35
F6	=B6+C6-E6	F7:F35
G6	=F6	--
G7	=G6-E7+IF(H6=1,$M$6,0)	G8:G35
H6	=IF(G6<$M$5,1,0)	H7:H35
I6	=IF(H6=0,0,PsiDiscrete(Data!$C$7:$C$9,Data!$D$7:$D$9))	I7:I35
J6	=IF(I6=0,0,A6+1+I6)	J7:J35
M9	=SUM(E6:E35)/SUM(D6:D35) + PsiOutput( )	--
M10	=AVERAGE(B6:B35) + PsiOutput( )	--

Column H indicates if an order should be placed based on the inventory position and reorder point, as:

Formula for cell H6:   =IF(G6<$M$5,1,0)

(Copy to H7 through H35.)

If an order is placed, then we must generate the random lead time required to receive the order. This is done in column I as:

Formula for cell I6:   =IF(H6=0,0,PsiDiscrete(Data!$C$7:$C$9,
(Copy to I7 through I35.)   Data!$D$7:$D$9))

This formula returns the value 0 if no order was placed (if H6 = 0); otherwise, it returns a random lead time value (if H6 = 1).

If an order is placed, column J indicates the day on which the order will be received based on its random lead time in column I. This is done as:

Formula for cell J6:   =IF(I6=0,0,A6+1+I6)
(Copy to J7 through J35.)

The values in column C are coordinated with those in column J. The nonzero values in column J indicate the days on which orders will be received. For example, cell J9 indicates that an order will be received on day 10. The actual receipt of this order is reflected by the value of 50 in cell C15, which represents the receipt of an order at the beginning of day 10. The formula in cell C15 that achieves this is:

Formula for cell C15:   =COUNTIF($J$6:J14,A15)*$M$6

This formula counts how many times the value in cell A15 (representing day 10) appears as a scheduled receipt day between days 1 through 9 in column J. This represents the number of orders scheduled to be received on day 10. We then multiply this by the order quantity (50), given in cell M6 to determine the total units to be received on day 10. Thus, the values in column C are generated as:

Formula for cell C6:   =0
Formula for cell C7:   =COUNTIF($J$6:J6,A7)*$M$6
(Copy to C8 through C35.)

The service level for the model is calculated in cell M9 using the values in columns D and E as:

Formula for cell M9:   =SUM(E6:E35)/SUM(D6:D35) + PsiOutput( )

Again, the service level represents the proportion of total demand that can be satisfied from inventory and is one of the output cells we want Risk Solver Platform to track as we simulate this inventory system. The value in cell M9 indicates that in the scenario shown, 85.3% of the total demand is satisfied.

The average inventory level is also an output we want Risk Solver Platform to track. It is calculated in cell M10 by averaging the values in column B. This is accomplished as follows:

Formula for cell M10:   =AVERAGE(B6:B35) + PsiOutput( )

12.15.3 REPLICATING THE MODEL

The model in Figure 12.24 indicates one possible scenario that could occur if Laura uses a reorder point of 28 units for the computer monitor. Figures 12.25 and 12.26 show the results of using Risk Solver Platform to replicate this model 5,000 times, tracking the values in cells M9 (service level) and M10 (average inventory) as output cells.

FIGURE 12.25

Service level results of 1,000 replications of the MCC model

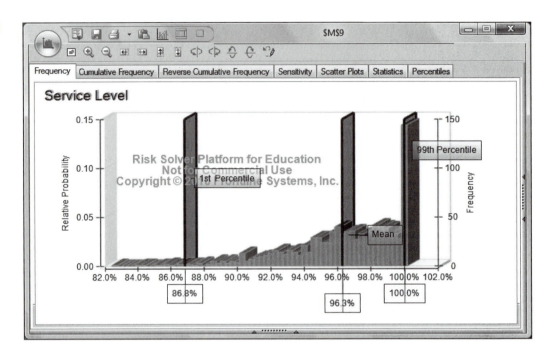

FIGURE 12.26

Inventory results of 1,000 replications of the MCC model

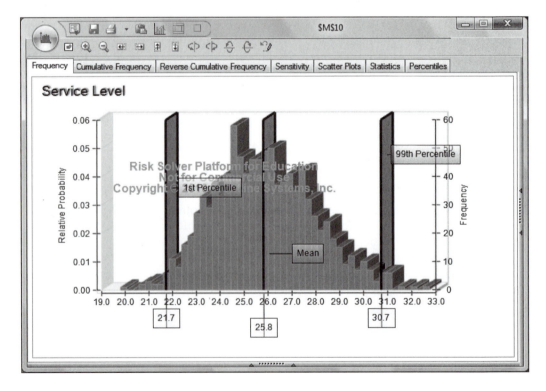

Figures 12.25 and 12.26 indicate that MCC's current reorder point (28 units) and order quantity (50 units) results in an average service level of approximately 96% (with a minimum value around 82% and a maximum value of 100%) and an average inventory level of almost 26 monitors (with a minimum value around 20 and a maximum value near 33).

12.15.4 OPTIMIZING THE MODEL

Now suppose Laura wants to determine a reorder point and order quantity that provides an average service level of 98% while keeping the average inventory level as low as possible. One way to do this is to run additional simulations at various reorder point and inventory level combinations trying to find the combination of settings that produce the desired behavior. However, as you might imagine, this could be very time-consuming. Fortunately, Risk Solver Platform can solve this type of problem for us.

Risk Solver Platform allows us to maximize or minimize a value associated with some target or objective cell in a worksheet by changing the values of other cells (representing controllable decision variables) while satisfying various constraints. However, because the worksheet contains RNGs in various cells, Risk Solver Platform must simulate (or run multiple replications of) the model at each solution it considers to evaluate the behavior or quality of a particular solution. Although this is very computationally intensive, Risk Solver Platform's interactive simulation abilities allow these computations to be done quite rapidly.

When attempting to optimize a simulation model (also known as **simulation optimization**), we typically want to maximize or minimize the *average* value of (or some other statistic describing) the cell representing the objective or bottom-line performance measure. Again, this is because no single definite or certain outcome is associated with a particular solution in a simulation model; rather, there is a distribution of possible outcomes. Similarly, constraints are typically expressed as some statistical measure (for example, average, percentile, standard deviation) of the constraint cell in question. So, in simulation optimization, the goal is to automatically identify a solution (values for the decision variables) that causes a model of a process containing randomness (or uncertainty) to behave in the most desirable way possible.

Figure 12.27 (and the file Fig12-27.xlsm that accompanies this book) shows how the spreadsheet was changed to find the optimal solution to MCC's inventory problem. Recall that Laura wants to determine the reorder point and order quantity that will keep the average inventory level as low as possible while achieving an average service level of 98%. To do this, we added formulas in cells M13 and M14 that compute, respectively, the average service level and average inventory level for the entire simulation as follows,

Formula for cell M13:	=PsiMean(M9)
Formula for cell M14:	=PsiMean(M10)

Let's take a moment to make sure you understand the difference between the values in cells M9 and M13 and also between M10 and M14. In Figure 12.27, cells M9 and M10 are displaying, respectively, the service level and average inventory for the *single* replication of the model that is displayed. However, because each of these cells serve as output cells for the simulation (via the PsiOutput( ) functions shown in their formula definitions in Figure 12.24), when Risk Solver Platform is in interactive simulation mode (with the Simulate light bulb illuminated), there are actually 5,000 values saved for cells M9 and M10, corresponding to 5,000 trials of a simulation. So, in interactive simulation mode, the PsiMean( ) functions in cells M13 and M14 compute, respectively, the averages of the 5,000 trial values associated with cells M9 and M10. (The PsiMean( ) functions in cells M13 and M14 return the value "#N/A" if a simulation has not been run.) The values in cells M13 and M14 are the ones of interest from an optimization perspective because Laura is interested in the average service level and average inventory level over an entire 5,000 trial simulation—not the average service level and average inventory level for any one particular trial. (The point being made in this paragraph is key to understanding simulation optimization, so be sure you understand this before proceeding.)

Clicking the Model icon on the Risk Solver Platform ribbon causes the Risk Solver task pane to appear, as shown in Figure 12.27. This pane provides an integrated

FIGURE 12.27 *Revised spreadsheet for MCC's inventory problem*

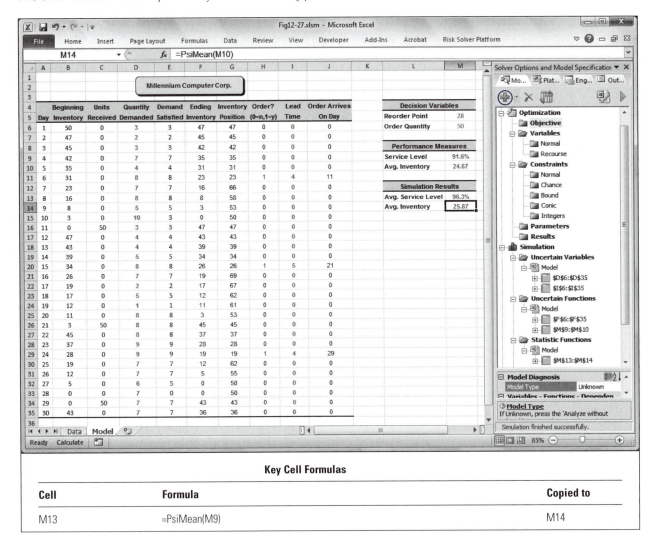

		Key Cell Formulas	
Cell	**Formula**		**Copied to**
M13	=PsiMean(M9)		M14

approach to optimization and simulation. Note that the Simulation section of this pane summarizes everything that Risk Solver Platform understands about the model in this spreadsheet: that cells D6 through D35 and I6 through I35 are uncertain (or random) variables, cells M9 and M10 are uncertain functions (outputs), and M13 and M14 are statistic functions (computing descriptive statistics about the simulation). (Note that in Figure 12.17, we have also identified the ending inventory cells in F6 through F35 as PsiOutput( ) cells to facilitate the creation of trend charts, which will be covered shortly.)

The Optimization section of the task pane allows us to specify the objective, variables, and constraints for our model. In this case, we want to instruct Risk Solver Platform to minimize the average inventory in the simulation (in cell M14) by changing the values of the reorder point and order quantity (decision variables) in cells M5 and M6, respectively, while simultaneously keeping the simulation's average service level (in cell M13) at or above 98%.

To specify the objective for this problem, follow these steps:

1. Select cell M14 (representing the average inventory for the simulation).
2. Select Objective in the Risk Solver task pane.
3. Click on the green plus (+) symbol (indicated by the blue circle in Figure 12.27).

FIGURE 12.28 *Defining the objective for the optimization model*

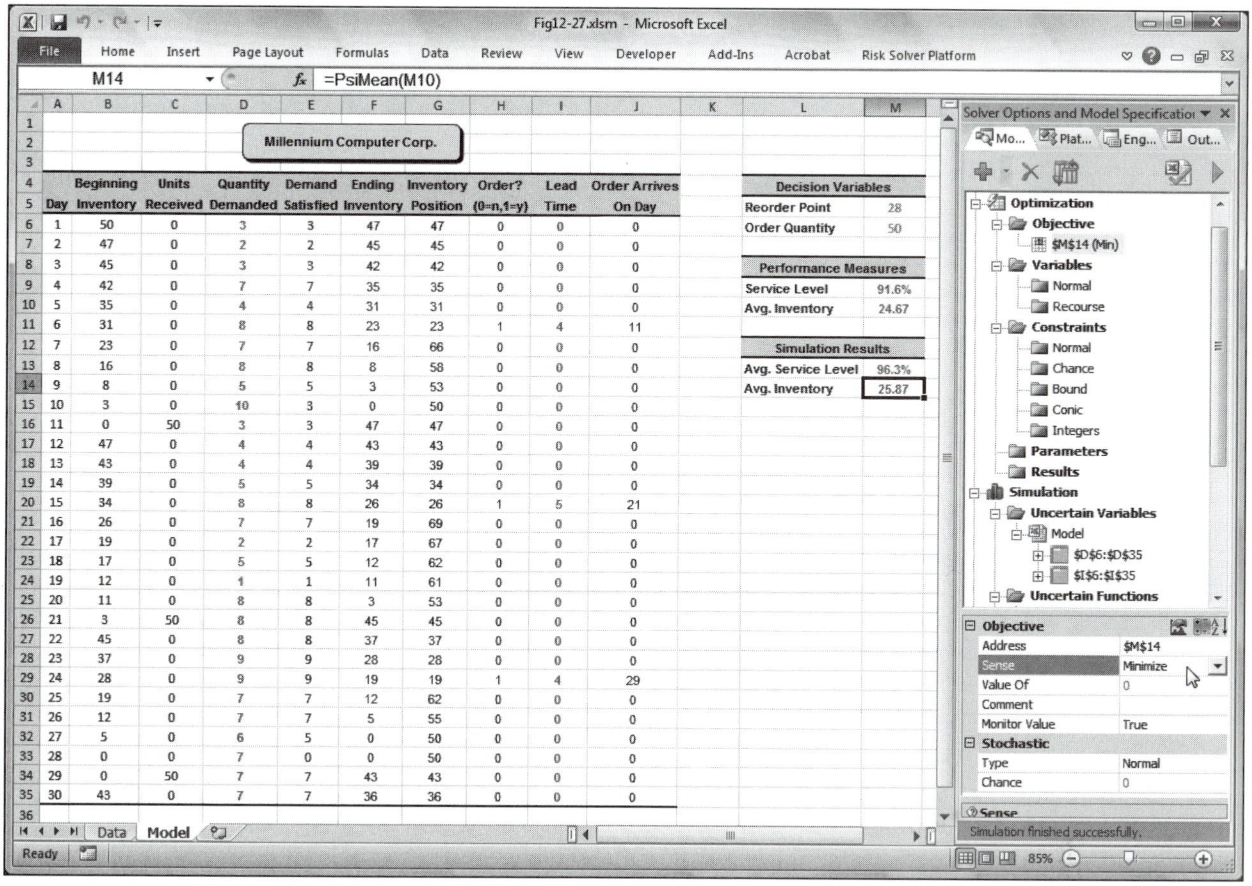

The results of these steps are shown in Figure 12.28. Note that after the objective is added, the bottom of the Risk Solver Platform pane displays various options associated with our action, and we can indicate our desire to minimize the objective.

Next, we specify the variable (or adjustable) cells representing the decisions about the reorder point and order quantity. To do this, follow these steps:

1. Select cells M5 and M6 (representing the reorder point and order quantity, respectively).
2. Select Variables in the Risk Solver task pane.
3. Click on the green plus (+) symbol.

The results of these steps are shown in Figure 12.29. Note that additional variables (when needed) would be added in a similar manner. And after variables are added, the bottom of the Risk Solver task pane displays various options associated with the selected variables.

Next, we need to specify any constraints that apply to the problem. One such constraint relates to Laura's desire to achieve at least a 98% average service level. To do this, follow these steps:

1. Select cell M13 (representing the average service level for the simulation).
2. Select Constraints in the Risk Solver task pane.
3. Click on the green plus (+) symbol.

FIGURE 12.29 *Defining the decision variables for the optimization model*

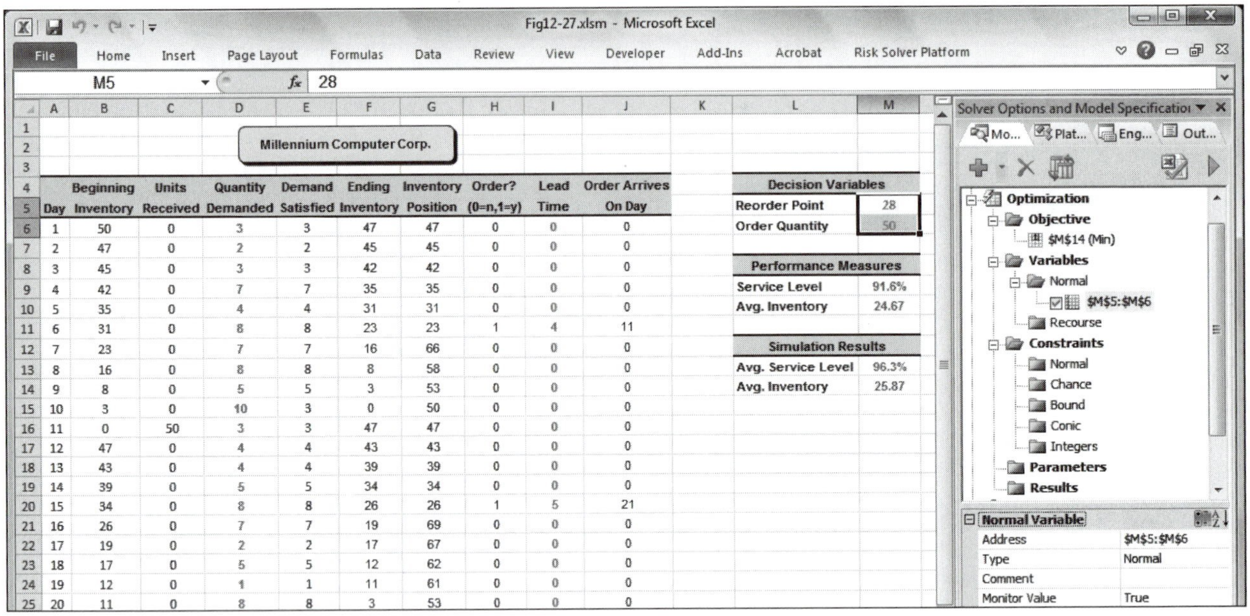

This results in the dialog shown in Figure 12.30 where we can indicate that cell M13 must be greater than or equal to 98% (or 0.98).

After clicking OK in the Add Constraint dialog shown in Figure 12.30, we also need to add upper and lower bounds on the decision variables for this problem. We will assume that Laura is interested in considering values between 10 and 70 for both

FIGURE 12.30 *Defining the service level constraint for the optimization model*

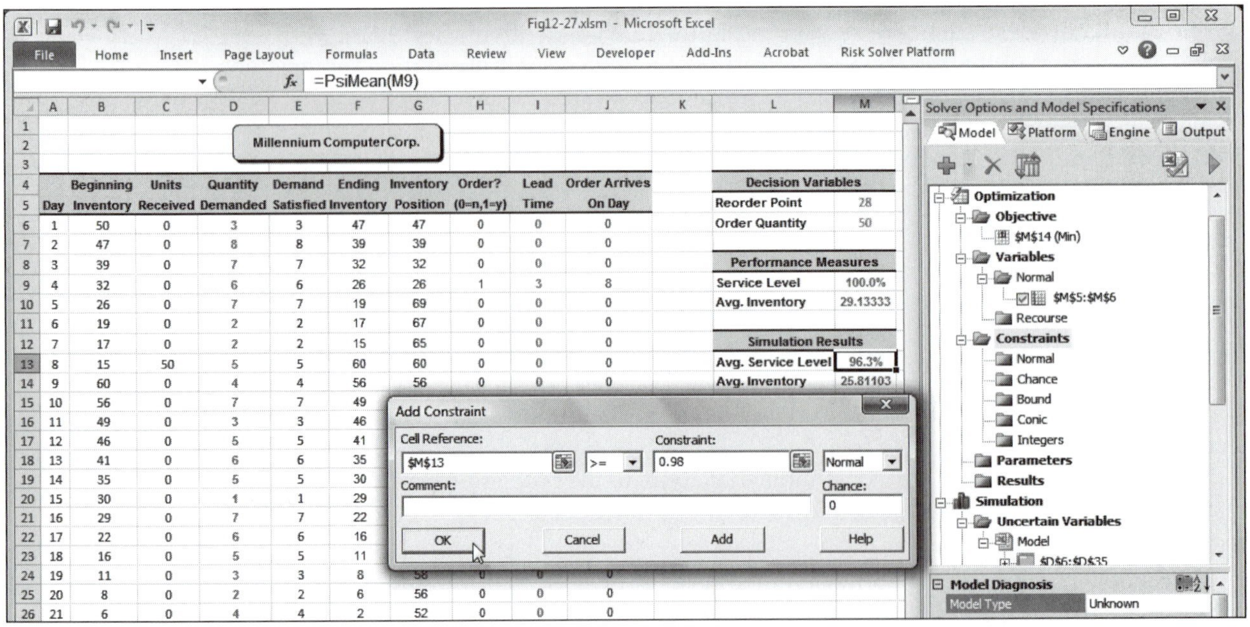

the reorder point and order quantity variables (cells M5 and M6). To create this constraint, follow these steps:

1. Select cells M5 and M6 (representing the reorder point and order quantity, respectively).
2. Select Constraints in the Risk Solver task pane.
3. Click on the green plus (+) symbol.

Figure 12.31 shows the resulting dialog and settings to specify a lower bound of 10 for the decision variables. The same step of steps can be used to define an upper bound of 70, as shown in Figure 12.32.

FIGURE 12.31 *Defining a lower bound for the decision variables*

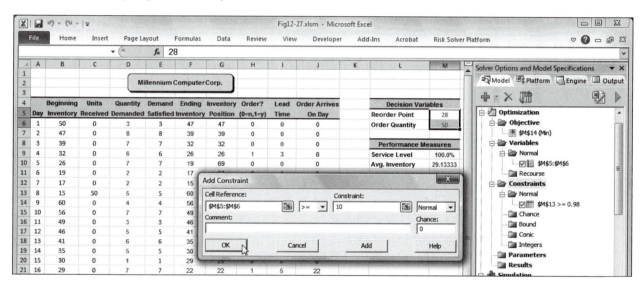

FIGURE 12.32 *Defining an upper bound for the decision variables*

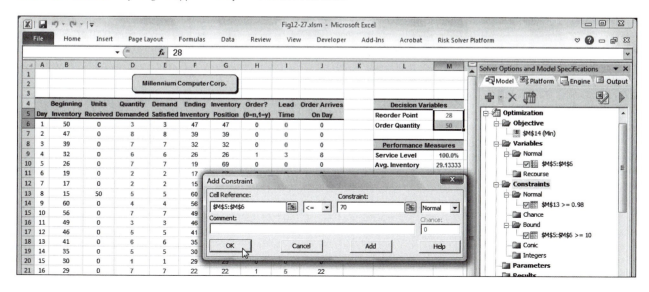

Finally, we need to indicate that the decision variables may only take on integer values. To do this, follow these steps:

1. Select cells M5 and M6 (representing the reorder point and order quantity, respectively).
2. Select Constraints in the Risk Solver task pane.
3. Click on the green plus (+) symbol.

Figure 12.33 shows the resulting dialog where we select the "int" option from the dropdown list to indicate that cells M5 and M6 must be integers.

FIGURE 12.33 *Defining integer conditions for the decision variables*

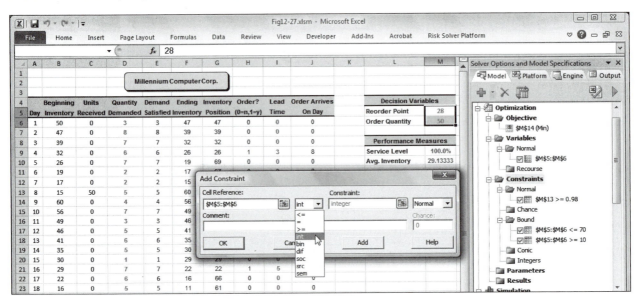

Figure 12.34 shows a summary of the Risk Solver Platform settings required for the MCC problem. Clicking the Solve icon (the green triangle) in the Risk Solver task pane causes Risk Solver Platform to solve the problem.

Remember that a separate simulation must be run for each combination of the decision variables that Risk Solver Platform chooses. Risk Solver Platform uses a number of heuristics to search intelligently for the best combination of decision variables. However, this is still inherently a very computationally intensive and time-consuming process, and very complicated models could take hours (or days) of solution time.

As shown in Figure 12.35, Risk Solver Platform ultimately found a reorder point of 35 and an order quantity of 10. Because Risk Solver Platform is using a heuristic search algorithm, it might not find the same solution each time it solves a problem, and it might stop at a local (rather than global) optimal solution. Thus, on difficult problems, it is wise to run Risk Solver Platform several times to see if it can improve upon the solution it finds. Using a reorder point of 35 and an order quantity of 10, 5,000 replications were

FIGURE 12.34 *Summary of Risk Solver Platform settings*

Day	Beginning Inventory	Units Received	Quantity Demanded	Demand Satisfied	Ending Inventory	Inventory Position	Order? (0=n,1=y)	Lead Time	Order Arrives On Day
1	50	0	3	3	47	47	0	0	0
2	47	0	8	8	39	39	0	0	0
3	39	0	7	7	32	32	0	0	0
4	32	0	6	6	26	26	1	3	8
5	26	0	7	7	19	69	0	0	0
6	19	0	2	2	17	67	0	0	0
7	17	0	2	2	15	65	0	0	0
8	15	50	5	5	60	60	0	0	0
9	60	0	4	4	56	56	0	0	0
10	56	0	7	7	49	49	0	0	0
11	49	0	3	3	46	46	0	0	0
12	46	0	5	5	41	41	0	0	0
13	41	0	6	6	35	35	0	0	0
14	35	0	5	5	30	30	0	0	0
15	30	0	1	1	29	29	0	0	0
16	29	0	7	7	22	22	1	5	22
17	22	0	6	6	16	66	0	0	0
18	16	0	5	5	11	61	0	0	0
19	11	0	3	3	8	58	0	0	0
20	8	0	2	2	6	56	0	0	0
21	6	0	4	4	2	52	0	0	0
22	2	50	4	4	48	48	0	0	0
23	48	0	4	4	44	44	0	0	0
24	44	0	7	7	37	37	0	0	0
25	37	0	5	5	32	32	0	0	0
26	32	0	8	8	24	24	1	3	30
27	24	0	6	6	18	68	0	0	0
28	18	0	7	7	11	61	0	0	0
29	11	0	7	7	4	54	0	0	0
30	4	50	4	4	50	50	0	0	0

Decision Variables

Reorder Point	28
Order Quantity	50

Performance Measures

Service Level	100.0%
Avg. Inventory	29.13333

Simulation Results

Avg. Service Level	96.3%
Avg. Inventory	25.81103

run resulting in an average service level of 98.2% and an average inventory of approximately 15.3 units per month.

12.15.5 ANALYZING THE SOLUTION

Comparing the solution shown in Figure 12.35 to the original solution in Figure 12.27, we see that by using a reorder point of 35 and an order quantity of 10, MCC can simultaneously increase its average service level from 96.3% to 98.2% and reduce its average inventory level from approximately 26 units to 15 units. Another advantage of the optimal solution becomes apparent if we compare the behavior of the daily ending inventory balance under the original and optimal scenarios as shown in Figure 12.36.

In Figure 12.36, note that under the original policy (reorder point 28, order quantity 50), there are fairly wide swings in the amount of inventory MCC would be carrying for this product. Under the optimal policy (reorder point 35, order quantity 10), there is less volatility in the amount of inventory being held, which offers operational advantages from a warehousing and logistics perspective.

FIGURE 12.35 *Optimal solution to the MCC problem*

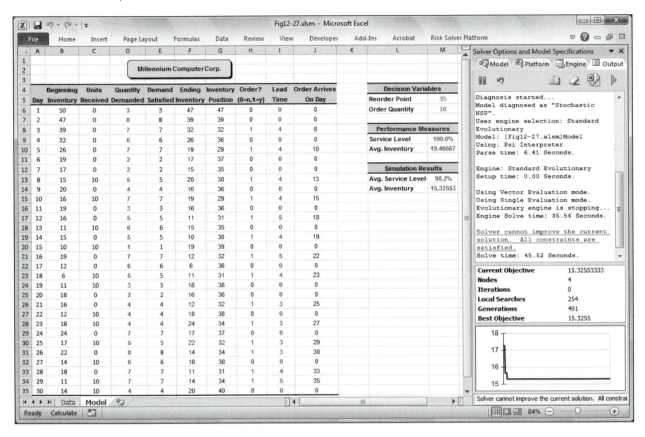

FIGURE 12.36 *Trend charts of the daily inventory balances*

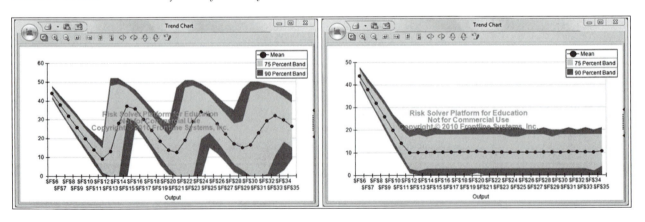

Creating Trend Charts

To create a trend chart like the ones in Figure 12.36, add PsiOutput( ) functions to whatever cells you want to include in the chart cells (cells F6 through F35 in the MCC example). Then select Charts, Multiple Outputs, Trend on the Risk Solver Platform ribbon. In the resulting dialog, select the outputs you want to chart and click OK.

12.15.6 OTHER MEASURES OF RISK

In the MCC example, Laura wanted to identify an inventory policy that would provide a 98% service level on average. While that might be a very reasonable goal, it would be wise to more carefully consider the downside risk associated with such a goal. Figure 12.37 displays the average service level distribution associated with the "optimal" solution to the MCC inventory problem.

Recall that Laura wanted a solution that provided an average service level of 98%. The mean of the distribution shown in Figure 12.37 is 98.2% and therefore satisfies Laura's requirement. However, approximately 41.1% (or 2,055 out of 5,000) of the trials in this simulation actually resulted in service levels that were less than 98%, with some as low as 89%. So if Laura uses a reorder point of 35 and an order quantity of 10, then in any month, there is approximately a 41% chance that the actual service level will be below her desired average service level of 98%.

This discussion highlights the purpose of two other types of constraints available in Risk Solver Platform: the **value at risk constraint** and the **conditional value at risk constraint**. A value at risk (VaR) constraint allows you to specify the percentage of trials in a simulation that must satisfy a constraint. For example, Laura might want a solution where at least 90% of the trials have a service level of at least 98%. (Clearly, the solution in Figure 12.37 violates such a VaR constraint.)

A VaR constraint only limits the percentage of trials that violate the constraint— counting a small violation the same as a large violation. In contrast, the conditional value at risk (CVaR) constraint places a bound on the average magnitude of the violations that may occur. Thus, the (CVaR) constraint is a more conservative version of the VaR constraint.

To illustrate the use of a VaR constraint, suppose that Laura would like only a 10% chance of any particular trial's average service level falling below 98%. This additional

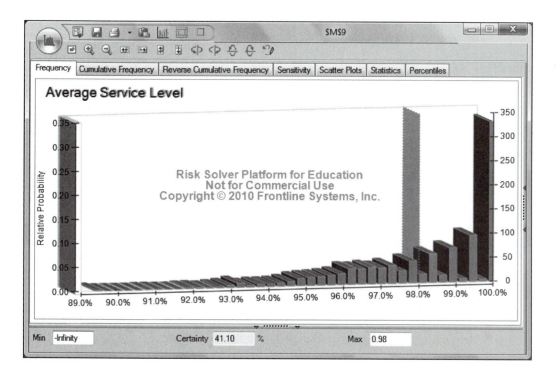

FIGURE 12.37

Service level distribution for the "optimal" solution

FIGURE 12.38 *Revised MCC problem solution with VaR constraint*

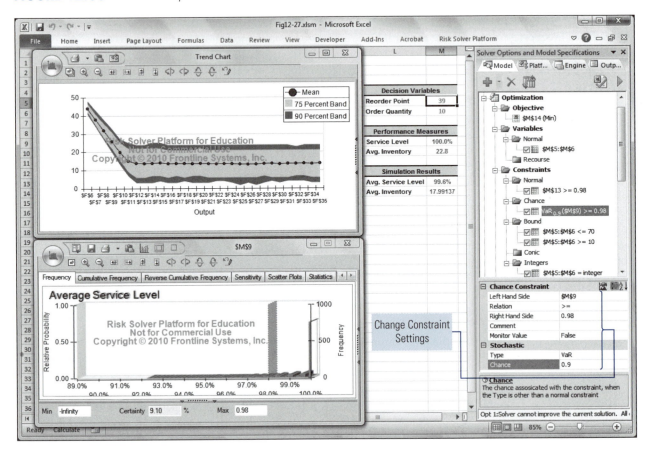

constraint and the resulting solution are summarized in Figure 12.38. Note that a *chance* constraint was added to the model. You create a chance constraint in the same way that our other constraints were created and then adjust its properties as indicated in Figure 12.38. This constraint is of the VaR type and requires a 0.9 chance of the average service level (in cell M9) being at least 98%. This constraint will be satisfied if no more than 10% of the trials in a simulation have a service level less than 98%.

Rerunning the optimization with this additional constraint resulted in a solution with a reorder point of 39 and an order quantity of 10. The frequency chart at the bottom of Figure 12.38 indicates that, as desired, approximately 10% of the simulation trials had average service levels of less than 98%.

12.16 A Project Selection Example

In Chapter 6, we saw how Solver can be used in project selection problems in which the payoff for each project is assumed to be known with certainty. In many cases, a great deal of uncertainty exists with respect to the ultimate payoff that will be received if a particular project is undertaken. In these situations, Risk Solver Platform is a powerful aid in deciding which project(s) to undertake. Consider the following example.

TRC Technologies has $2 million to invest in new R&D projects. The following table summarizes the initial cost, probability of success, and revenue potential for each of the projects.

			Revenue Potential ($1,000s)		
Project	Initial Cost ($1,000s)	Probability of Success	Min.	Most Likely	Max.
1	$250.0	90%	$ 600	$ 750	$ 900
2	$650.0	70%	$1,250	$1,500	$1,600
3	$250.0	60%	$ 500	$ 600	$ 750
4	$500.0	40%	$1,600	$1,800	$1,900
5	$700.0	80%	$1,150	$1,200	$1,400
6	$ 30.0	60%	$ 150	$ 180	$ 250
7	$350.0	70%	$ 750	$ 900	$1,000
8	$ 70.0	90%	$ 220	$ 250	$ 320

TRC's management wants to determine what set of projects should be selected.

12.16.1 A SPREADSHEET MODEL

A spreadsheet model for this problem is shown in Figure 12.39 (and the file Fig12-39.xlsm that accompanies this book). Cells C6 through C13 in this spreadsheet indicate which

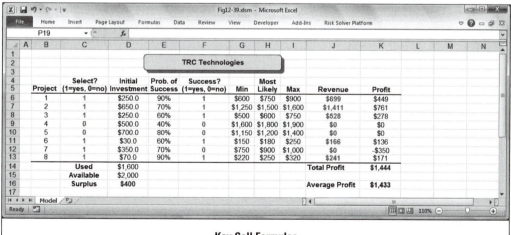

FIGURE 12.39

Spreadsheet model for TRC Technologies' project selection problem

Key Cell Formulas

Cell	Formula	Copied to
D14	=SUMPRODUCT(D6:D13,C6:C13)	--
D16	=D15–D14	--
F6	=IF(C6=1,PsiBinomial(1,E6),0)	F7:F13
J6	=IF(F6=1,PsiTriangular(G6,H6,I6),0)	J7:J13
K6	=J6–C6*D6	K7:K13
K14	=SUM(K6:K13)+PsiOutput( )	--
K16	=PsiMean(K14)	--

projects will be selected. Using Risk Solver Platform, we can define these cells to be decision variables that must take on discrete values between zero and one—or operate as binary variables. The values shown in cells C6 though C13 were assigned arbitrarily. We will use Risk Solver Platform to determine the optimal values for these variables.

In cell D14 , we compute the total initial investment required by the selected projects as follows:

> Formula for cell D14:   =SUMPRODUCT(D6:D13,C6:C13)

In cell D16, we calculate the amount of unused or surplus investment funds. Using Risk Solver Platform, we can place a lower bound constraint of zero on the value of this cell to ensure that the projects selected do not require more than $2 million in initial investment funds.

> Formula for cell D16:   =D15 − D14

A project has the potential to be successful only if it is selected. The success or failure of each project may be modeled using a binomial random variable using a single trial and the probability of success given in column E. Thus, we model the potential success of selected projects in column F as follows:

> Formula for cell F6:   =IF(C6=1,PsiBinomial(1,E6),0)
> (Copy to cells F7 through F13.)

If a project is selected and successful, there is uncertainty about the revenue that it will generate. Because we have estimates of the minimum, most likely, and maximum possible revenue for each project, we will model the revenues for selected, successful projects using a triangular distribution. This is accomplished in column J as follows:

> Formula for cell J6:   =IF(F6=1,PsiTriangular(G6,H6,I6),0)
> (Copy to cells J7 through J13.)

The profit associated with each project is computed in column K as follows:

> Formula for cell K6:   =J6−C6*D6
> (Copy to cells K7 through K13.)

Cell K14 computes the total profit for each replication of the model. We will define this as an output cell using a PsiOutput( ) function.

> Formula for cell K14:   =SUM(K6:K13)+PsiOutput( )

Finally, cell K16 computes the average (or expected) simulated total profit associated with cell K14. We will attempt to find the set of projects that maximizes this value using Risk Solver Platform. (Note that this formula will return the error value "#N/A" until a simulation has been run or interactive simulation mode has been turned on.)

> Formula for cell K16:   =PsiMean(K14)

12.16.2 SOLVING AND ANALYZING THE PROBLEM WITH RISK SOLVER PLATFORM

The Risk Solver Platform settings and options used to solve this problem are shown in Figure 12.40. The best solution found is shown in Figure 12.41 along with some additional statistics describing this solution. Risk Solver Platform identified a solution that

FIGURE 12.40

*Solver settings and
options for TRC
Technologies'
project selection
problem*

Solver Settings:

Objective: K16 (Max)
Variable cells: C6:C13
Constraints:
    D16 >= 0
    C6:C16 = binary

Solver Options:
    Standard Evolutionary Engine (Simplex LP)

FIGURE 12.41 *Solution maximizing average profit*

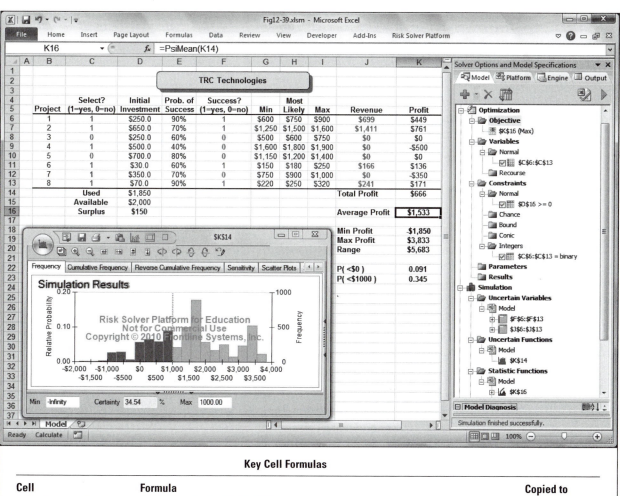

Key Cell Formulas

Cell	Formula	Copied to
K18	=PsiMin(K14)	--
K19	=PsiMax(K14)	--
K20	=PsiRange(K14)	--
K22	=PsiTarget(K14,0)	--
K23	=PsiTarget(K14,1000)	--

involves selecting projects 1, 2, 4, 6, 7, and 8, requiring an initial investment of $1.85 million, and resulting in an expected profit of approximately $1.533 million.

The frequency chart in Figure 12.41 shows the distribution of possible profit values that might occur if TRC adopts this solution. Although the expected (mean) profit associated with this solution is approximately $1.53 million, the range of the possible outcomes is fairly wide at approximately $5.683 million (computed in cell K20 via =PsiRange(K14)). The worst-case outcome observed with this solution resulted in approximately a $1.85million loss (computed in cell K18 via =PsiMin(K14)), whereas the best-case outcome resulted in approximately a $3.833 million profit (computed in cell K19 via =PsiMax(K14)). Also in Figure 12.41, we see in cell K22 (labeled P(<$0)) that there is about a 0.091 probability of losing money if this solution is implemented. This probability was computed using the PsiTarget( ) function as follows,

$$\text{Formula for cell K22:} \qquad = \text{PsiTarget(K14,0)}$$

In general, the PsiTarget(*cell*, *target value*) function returns the cumulative probability of the specified output *cell* taking on a value less than or equal to the specified *target value*. Thus, the formula in cell K22 computes the probability of the profit distribution in cell K14 taking on a value of less than $0.

Similarly, as shown in cell K23, there is about a .345 probability of making less than $1 million (or roughly a 65.5% chance of making more than $1 million). Thus, there are significant risks associated with this solution that are not apparent if one simply looks at its expected profit level of $1.53 million.

12.16.3 CONSIDERING ANOTHER SOLUTION

Because each of the projects is a one-time occurrence that can either succeed or fail, the decision makers in this problem do not have the luxury of repeatedly selecting this set of projects over and over and realizing the average profit level of $1.53 million over time. As an alternative objective, TRC's management might want to find a solution that minimizes the probability of having outcomes with profits below $1 million (or equivalently, maximizing the probability of having an outcome of $1 million or more).

To pursue this new objective, we can simply optimize the model again with an objective of minimizing the value of cell K23. The solution to this problem is shown in Figure 12.42.

In Figure 12.42, notice that the expected (mean) profit for this solution is about $1.45 million, representing a decrease of approximately $80,000 from the earlier solution. The range of possible outcomes has also decreased to about $4.9 million, with a worst-case outcome of a $1.98 million loss, and a best-case outcome of almost $2.93 million profit. This solution *reduces* the chances of realizing a loss to approximately 8.1% and *increases* the chances of making at least $1 million to almost 71%. Thus, although the best possible outcome realized under this solution ($2.9 million) is not as large as that of the earlier solution ($3.8 million), it reduces the downside risk in the problem and makes it more likely for the company to earn at least $1 million; however, it also requires a larger initial investment. It is also interesting to note that the probability of *all* the selected projects being successful under this solution is 0.2116 (that is, $0.2116 = .9 \times .7 \times .8 \times .6 \times .7$), whereas the probability of all selected projects being successful under the first solution is only 0.0953 (that is, $0.0953 = .9 \times .7 \times .4 \times .6 \times .7 \times .9$).

So, what is the best solution to this problem? It depends on the risk attitudes and preferences of the decision makers at TRC. However, the simulation techniques we have described clearly provide valuable insights into the risks associated with various solutions.

FIGURE 12.42 *Solution minimizing the probability of outcomes below $1 million*

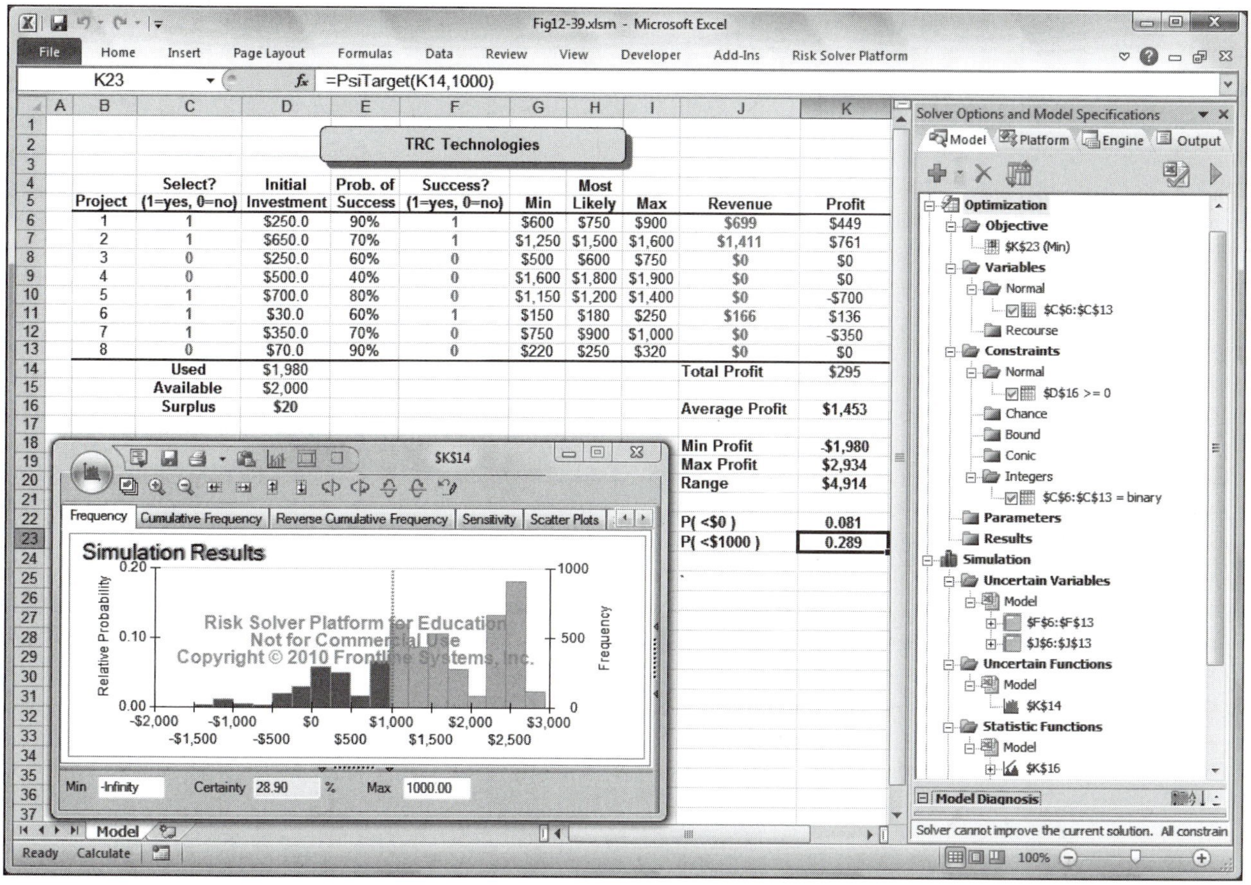

12.17 A Portfolio Optimization Example

In Chapter 8, we saw how Solver can be used to analyze potential trade-offs between risk and return for a given set of stocks using the idea of an **efficient frontier**. The efficient frontier represents the highest level of return a portfolio can achieve for any given level of risk. While portfolio optimization and efficient frontier analysis are most commonly associated with financial instruments such as stocks and bonds, they can be applied to physical assets as well. This will be illustrated using Risk Solver Platform with the following example.

> In recent years, a fundamental shift occurred in power plant asset ownership. Traditionally, a single regulated utility would own a given power plant. Today, more and more power plants are owned by merchant generators that provide power to a competitive wholesale marketplace. This makes it possible for an investor to buy, for example, 10% of 10 different generating assets rather than 100% of a single power plant. As a result, nontraditional power plant owners have emerged in the form of investment groups, private equity funds, and energy hedge funds.
>
> The McDaniel Group is a private investment company in Richmond, VA that currently has a total of $1 billion that it wants to invest in power-generation assets. Five different types of investments are possible: natural gas, oil, coal, nuclear, and

wind-powered plants. The following table summarizes the megawatts (MW) of generation capacity that can be purchased per each $1 million investment in the various types of power plants.

	Generation Capacity per $1 Million Invested				
Fuel Type	**Gas**	**Coal**	**Oil**	**Nuclear**	**Wind**
MWs	2.0	1.2	3.5	1.0	0.5

The return on each type of investment varies randomly and is determined primarily by fluctuations in fuel prices and the spot price (or current market value) of electricity. Assume the McDaniel Group analyzed historical data to determine that the return per MW produced by each type of plant can be modeled as normally distributed random variables with the following means and standard deviations.

	Normal Distribution Return Parameters by Fuel Type				
	Gas	**Coal**	**Oil**	**Nuclear**	**Wind**
Mean	16%	12%	10%	9%	8%
Std Dev	12%	6%	4%	3%	1%

Additionally, while analyzing the historical data on operating costs, it was observed that many of the returns are correlated. For example, when the returns from plants fueled by natural gas are high (due to low gas prices), returns from plants fueled by coal and oil tend to be low. So there is a negative correlation between the returns from gas plants and the returns from coal and oil plants. The following table summarizes all the pairwise correlations between the returns from different types of power plants.

	Correlations Between Returns by Fuel Type				
	Gas	**Coal**	**Oil**	**Nuclear**	**Wind**
Gas	1	−0.49	−0.31	0.16	0.12
Coal	−0.49	1	−0.41	0.11	0.07
Oil	−0.31	−0.41	1	0.13	0.09
Nuclear	0.16	0.11	0.13	1	0.04
Wind	0.12	0.07	0.09	0.04	1

The McDaniel Group would like to determine the efficient frontier for its investment options in power-generation assets.

12.17.1 A SPREADSHEET MODEL

A spreadsheet model for this problem is shown in Figure 12.43 (and the file Fig12-43.xlsm that accompanies this book). Cells D5 through D9 in this spreadsheet indicate how much money (in millions) will be invested in each type of generation asset. The values shown in cells D5 though D9 were assigned arbitrarily. Notice in the Risk Solver task pane that we have defined these cells to be decision variables that must take on values between $0 and $1,000. We have also created a constraint that requires the sum of these values (computed in cell D10) to equal $1,000 (or $1 billion).

Formula for cell D10:   =SUM(D5:D9)

FIGURE 12.43 *Settings and solution for maximizing average profit*

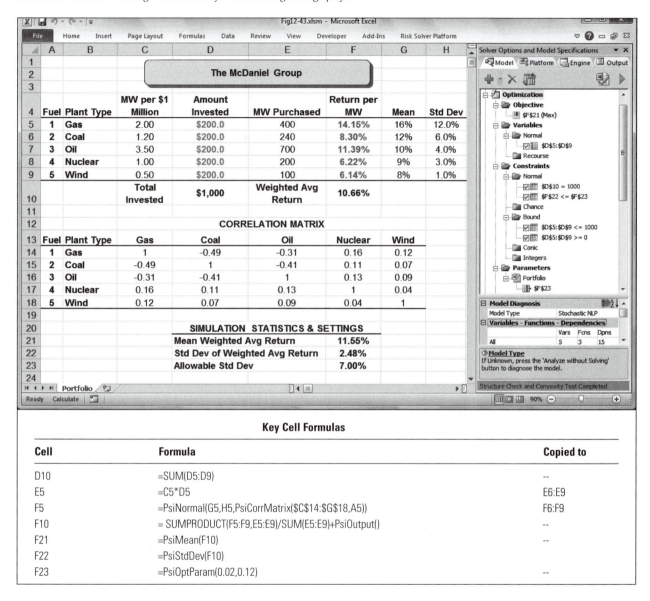

Key Cell Formulas

Cell	Formula	Copied to
D10	=SUM(D5:D9)	--
E5	=C5*D5	E6:E9
F5	=PsiNormal(G5,H5,PsiCorrMatrix($C$14:$G$18,A5))	F6:F9
F10	= SUMPRODUCT(F5:F9,E5:E9)/SUM(E5:E9)+PsiOutput()	--
F21	=PsiMean(F10)	--
F22	=PsiStdDev(F10)	--
F23	=PsiOptParam(0.02,0.12)	--

In column E, we compute the MW of generation capacity purchased in each asset category as follows:

Formula for cell E5:   =C5*D5

(Copy to cells E6 through E9.)

The cells representing random returns for each asset category are implemented in column F. Recall that we are assuming that correlations exist between these returns. Risk Solver Platform offers a number of different ways of dealing with correlations among variables. In this case, we model the correlations by including an appropriate PsiCorrMatrix( ) function as a third argument in the PsiNormal( ) function as shown below for investments in gas fueled plants in cell F5.

Formula for cell F5:   =PsiNormal(G5,H5,PsiCorrMatrix($C$14:$G$18,A5))

(Copy to cells F6 through F9.)

Note that the PsiCorrMatrix( ) function requires a (rank order) correlation matrix (C14 through G18 in our example) and an integer indicating which column (or row) in the matrix corresponds to the random variable being sampled (the value 1 in cell A5 in this example).

Correlation

Any correlation matrix used in a Risk Solver Platform simulation must exhibit the mathematical property of being positive definite. The details of this property are beyond the scope of this book; however, it has to do with ensuring that the correlations are internally consistent with one another. For instance, if variables A and B have a high positive correlation, and variables B and C have a high positive correlation, then variables A and C should have a fairly high positive correlation. The Correlations icon on the Risk Solver Platform ribbon offers a tool for checking if a correlation matrix is positive definite.

Also, it is important to note that, statistically speaking, correlation measures the strength of *linear* relationship between two variables. Sometimes variables are related in a *nonlinear* fashion. These nonlinear relationships cannot be summarized accurately in a correlation matrix. Risk Solver Platform supports the modeling of nonlinear relationships between variables using its PsiSip( ) and PsiSlurp( ) functions that are described in the Risk Solver Platform user guide.

In cell F10, we calculate the weighted average return on the chosen investments in generating assets. This will also be the output cell that drives much of our analysis in this problem.

Formula for cell F10:   =SUMPRODUCT(F5:F9,E5:E9)/SUM(E5:E9)+PsiOutput( )

In cells F21 and F22, we compute, respectively, the mean and standard deviation of the weighted average return in F10 for each simulation that is performed.

Formula for cell F21:   =PsiMean(F10)

Formula for cell F22:   =PsiStdDev(F10)

12.17.2 SOLVING THE PROBLEM WITH RISK SOLVER PLATFORM

Recall that the McDaniel Group is interested in examining solutions on the efficient frontier of its possible investment options for these power-generation assets. This requires determining the portfolios that provide the maximum expected (or average) return at a variety of different risk levels. In this case, we will define risk to be the standard deviation of a portfolio's weighted average return. The Risk Solver task pane in Figure 12.43 indicates that our objective is to maximize the mean value of the weighted average return calculated in cell F21 in our spreadsheet.

We also specify a variable requirement on the allowable upper bound of the standard deviation of the weighted average return (in cell F22). To do this, we use a

PsiOptParam( ) function in cell F23 to identify a range of risk levels we want to use in constructing an efficient frontier for this problem.

Formula for cell F23:   =PsiOptParam(0.02,0.12)

In Figure 12.43, note that we also have defined a constraint requiring cell F22 (the standard deviation of the weighted average return) to be less than or equal to the value in cell F23. The PsiOptParam( ) function specifies a parameter that will be varied as multiple optimizations are performed. The number of optimizations to be performed is indicated on the Risk Solver Platform Options dialog shown in Figure 12.44. (This dialog is displayed by clicking the Options icon on the Risk Solver Platform ribbon.) When the Solve icon in the task pane is pressed, Risk Solver Platform performs six optimization runs, automatically

FIGURE 12.44 *Specifying the number of optimizations to perform*

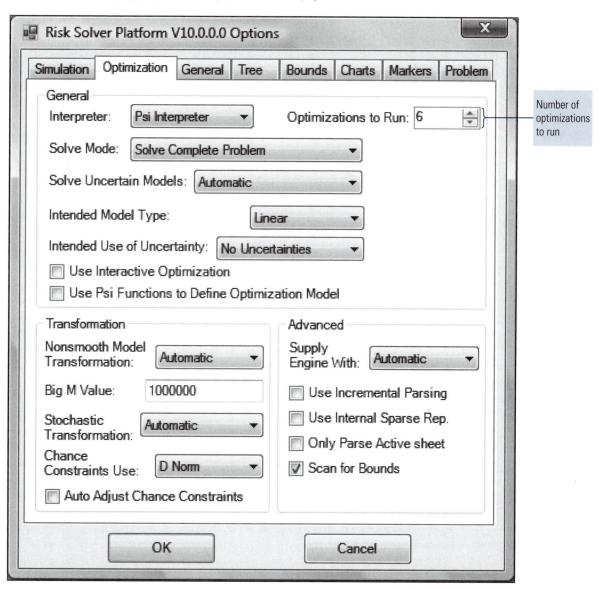

FIGURE 12.45

Solver settings and parameters for the McDaniel Group

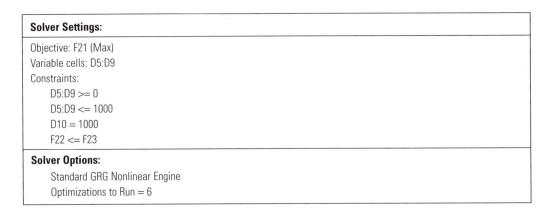

Solver Settings:

Objective: F21 (Max)
Variable cells: D5:D9
Constraints:
    D5:D9 >= 0
    D5:D9 <= 1000
    D10 = 1000
    F22 <= F23

Solver Options:

    Standard GRG Nonlinear Engine
    Optimizations to Run = 6

varying the value in cell F23 to six different values equally spaced between 2% and 12%. The Solver settings and options for this problem are summarized in Figure 12.45.

Figure 12.46 displays a chart summarizing the maximum weighted average return found for each of the six optimizations. To create this chart, follow these steps:

1. On the Risk Solver Platform tab, click Charts, Multiple Optimizations, Monitored Cells.
2. Select the objective cell (F21), and move it to the pane in the right side of the dialog.
3. Click OK.

This chart corresponds to the efficient frontier for the McDaniel Group's asset investment decision, summarizing the six portfolios it found and their relative trade-offs in

FIGURE 12.46 *Efficient frontier for the McDaniel Group's investment problem*

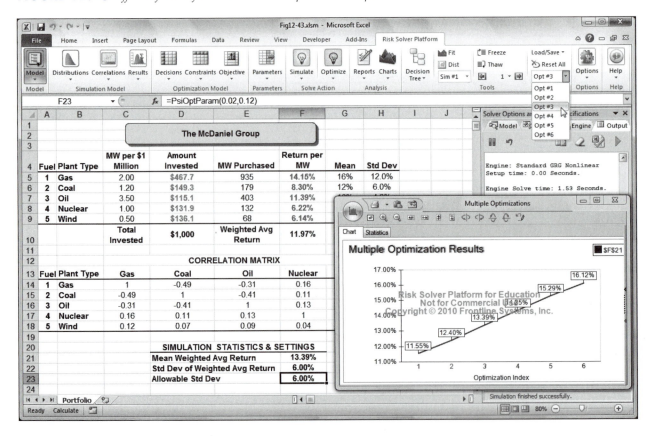

terms of risk and return. The expected returns on these portfolios vary from 11.55% to 16.12% with standard deviations varying from 2% to 12% with higher expected returns being associated with higher levels of risk. Any of the six solutions can be inspected in detail on the spreadsheet by selecting the appropriate optimization from the Opt # drop-down in Figure 12.46. Risk Solver Platform's PsiOptValue( ) function can also be used to retrieve specific values of interest from the various optimization runs.

The result of optimization #3 is shown in Figure 12.46, representing a portfolio with a standard deviation of 6% and an expected return of 13.39%. Note that the return on coal-fired plants also has a standard deviation of 6% but only an expected return of 12%. So by allocating investments funds in several different types of plants, the McDaniel Group can earn higher levels of returns for the same levels of risk as offered by individual investment types. Which portfolio is optimal for the McDaniel Group depends on the firm's preferences for risk versus return. But this analysis should help the firm select a portfolio that provides the maximum return for the desired level of risk—or the minimum level of risk for the desired level of return.

12.18 Summary

This chapter introduced the concept of risk analysis and simulation. Many of the input cells in a spreadsheet represent random variables whose values cannot be determined with certainty. Any uncertainty in the input cells flows through the spreadsheet model to create a related uncertainty in the value of the output cell(s). Decisions made on the basis of these uncertain values involve some degree of risk.

Various methods of risk analysis are available, including best-case/worst-case analysis, what-if analysis, and simulation. Of these three methods, simulation is the only technique that provides hard evidence (facts and figures) that can be used objectively in making decisions. This chapter introduced the use of the Risk Solver Platform add-in to perform spreadsheet simulation and optimization. To simulate a model, RNGs are used to select representative values for each uncertain independent variable in the model. This process is repeated over and over to generate a sample of representative values for the dependent variable(s) in the model. The variability and distribution of the sample values for the dependent variable(s) can then be analyzed to gain insight into the possible outcomes that might occur. We also illustrated the use of Risk Solver Platform in determining the optimal value of controllable parameters or decision variables in simulation models.

12.19 References

Banks, J., and J. Carson. *Discrete-Event Simulation*. Englewood Cliffs, NJ: Prentice Hall, 1984.
Evans, J., and D. Olson, *Introduction to Simulation and Risk Analysis*. Upper Saddle River, NJ: Prentice Hall, 1998.
Hamzawi, S. "Management and Planning of Airport Gate Capacity: A Microcomputer-Based Gate Assignment Simulation Model." *Transportation Planning and Technology*, vol. 11, 1986.
Kaplan, A., and S. Frazza. "Empirical Inventory Simulation: A Case Study." *Decision Sciences*, vol. 14, January 1983.
Khoshnevis, B. *Discrete Systems Simulation*. New York: McGraw-Hill, 1994.
Law, A., and W. Kelton. *Simulation Modeling and Analysis*. New York: McGraw-Hill, 1990.
Marcus, A. "The Magellan Fund and Market Efficiency." *Journal of Portfolio Management*, Fall 1990.
Risk Solver Platform v10.0 User Manual. Incline Village, NV: Frontline Systems, Inc., 2010.
Russell, R., and R. Hickle. "Simulation of a CD Portfolio." *Interfaces*, vol. 16, no. 3, 1986.
Savage, Sam L. "The Flaw of Averages." *Harvard Business Review*, November 2002.
Savage, S., S. Scholtes, and D. Zweidler. "Probability Management." *OR/MS Today*, February 2006.
Savage, S., S. Scholtes, and D. Zweidler. "Probability Management-Part II." *OR/MS Today*, April 2006.
Watson, H. *Computer Simulation in Business*. New York: Wiley, 1981.

THE WORLD OF MANAGEMENT SCIENCE

The U.S. Postal Service Moves to the Fast Lane

Mail flows into the U.S. Postal Service at the rate of 500 million pieces per day, and it comes in many forms. There are standard-sized letters with nine-digit ZIP codes (with or without imprinted bar codes), five-digit ZIP codes, typed addresses that can be read by optical character readers, handwritten addresses that are barely decipherable, Christmas cards in red envelopes addressed in red ink, and so on. The enormous task of sorting all these pieces at the sending post office and at the destination has caused postal management to consider and adopt many new forms of technology. These include operator-assisted mechanized sorters, optical character readers (last-line and multiple-line), and bar code sorters. Implementation of new technology brings with it associated policy decisions, such as rate discounts for bar coding by the customer, finer sorting at the origin, and so on.

A simulation model called META (model for evaluating technology alternatives) assists management in evaluating new technologies, configurations, and operating plans. Using distributions based on experience or projections of the effects of new policies, META simulates a random stream of mail of different types; routes the mail through the system configuration being tested; and prints reports detailing total pieces handled, capacity utilization, work hours required, space requirements, and cost.

META has been used on several projects associated with the Postal Service corporate automation plan. These include facilities planning, benefits of alternative sorting plans, justification of efforts to enhance address readability, planning studies for reducing the time carriers spend sorting vs. delivering, and identification of mail types that offer the greatest potential for cost savings.

According to the Associate Postmaster General, ". . . META became the vehicle to help steer our organization on an entirely new course at a speed we had never before experienced."

Source: Cebry, M., A. deSilva, and F. DiLisio, "Management Science in Automating Postal Operations: Facility and Equipment Planning in the United States Postal Service," *Interfaces*, vol. 22, no. 1, 1992, pp. 110–130.

Questions and Problems

1. Under what condition(s) is it appropriate to use simulation to analyze a model? That is, what characteristics should a model possess in order for simulation to be used?
2. The graph of the probability distribution of a normally distributed random variable with a mean of 20 and standard deviation of 1.5 is shown in Figure 12.5. The Excel function =NORMINV(Rand( ),20,1.5) also returns randomly generated observations from this distribution.
   a. Use Excel's NORMINV( ) function to generate 100 sample values from this distribution.
   b. Produce a histogram of the 100 sample values you generated. Does your histogram look like the graph for this distribution shown earlier in Figure 12.5?
   c. Repeat this experiment with 1,000 sample values.

d. Produce a histogram for the 1,000 sample values you generated. Does the histogram now more closely resemble the graph in Figure 12.5 for this distribution?

e. Why does your second histogram look more "normal" than the first one?

3. Refer to the Hungry Dawg Restaurant example presented in this chapter. Health claim costs actually tend to be seasonal, with higher levels of claims occurring during the summer months (when kids are out of school and more likely to injure themselves) and during December (when people schedule elective procedures before the next year's deductible must be paid). The following table summarizes the seasonal adjustment factors that apply to RNGs for average claims in the Hungry Dawg problem. For instance, the average claim for month 6 should be multiplied by 115%, and claims for month 1 should be multiplied by 80%.

Month	1	2	3	4	5	6	7	8	9	10	11	12
Seasonal Factor	0.80	0.85	0.87	0.92	0.93	1.15	1.20	1.18	1.03	0.95	0.98	1.14

Suppose the company maintains an account from which it pays health insurance claims. Assume there is $2.5 million in the account at the beginning of month 1. Each month, employee contributions are deposited into this account and claims are paid from the account.

a. Modify the spreadsheet shown in Figure 12.9 to include the cash flows in this account. If the company deposits $3 million in this account every month, what is the probability that the account will have insufficient funds to pay claims at some point during the year? (*Hint*: You can use the COUNTIF( ) function to count the number of months in a year in which the ending balance in the account is below 0.)

b. If the company wants to deposit an equal amount of money in this account each month, what should this amount be if they want there to only be a 5% chance of having insufficient funds?

4. One of the examples in this chapter dealt with determining the optimal reorder point for a computer monitor sold by Millennium Computer Corp. Suppose that it costs MCC $0.30 per day in holding costs for each monitor in beginning inventory, and it costs $20 to place an order. Each monitor sold generates a profit of $45, and each lost sale results in an opportunity cost of $65 (including the lost profit of $45 and $20 in lost goodwill). Modify the spreadsheet shown in Figure 12.23 to determine the reorder point and order quantity that maximize the average monthly profit associated with this monitor.

5. A debate recently erupted about the optimal strategy for playing a game on the TV show called "Let's Make a Deal." In one of the games on this show, the contestant would be given the choice of prizes behind three closed doors. A valuable prize was behind one door and worthless prizes were behind the other two doors. After the contestant selected a door, the host would open one of the two remaining doors to reveal one of the worthless prizes. Then, before opening the selected door, the host would give the contestant the opportunity to switch his or her selection to the other door that had not been opened. The question is, should the contestant switch?

a. Suppose a contestant is allowed to play this game 500 times, always picks door number 1, and never switches when given the option. If the valuable prize is equally likely to be behind each door at the beginning of each play, how many times would the contestant win the valuable prize? Use simulation to answer this question.

b. Now suppose the contestant is allowed to play this game another 500 times. This time the player always selects door number 1 initially and switches when given the option. Using simulation, how many times would the contestant win the valuable prize?

c. If you were a contestant on this show, what would you do if given the option of switching doors?

6. Suppose a product must go through an assembly line made up of five sequential operations. The time it takes to complete each operation is normally distributed with a mean of 180 seconds and standard deviation of 5 seconds. Let X denote the cycle time for the line, so that after X seconds, each operation is supposed to be finished and ready to pass the product to the next operation in the assembly line.

a. If the cycle time X = 180 seconds, what is the probability that all five operations will be completed?

b. What cycle time will ensure that all operations are finished 98% of the time?

7. Suppose a product must go through an assembly line made up of five sequential operations. The time it takes to complete each operation is normally distributed with a mean of 180 seconds and standard deviation of 5 seconds. Define the flow time to be the total time it takes a product to go through the assembly line from start to finish.

a. What is the mean and standard deviation of the flow time? What is the probability that the total time will be less than 920 seconds?

b. Now assume that the time required to complete each operation has a 0.40 correlation with the operation time immediately preceding it. What is the mean and standard deviation of the flow time? What is the probability that the total time will be less than 920 seconds?

c. Now assume that the time required to complete each operation has a −0.40 correlation with the operation time immediately preceding it. What is the mean and standard deviation of the flow time? What is the probability that the total time will be less than 920 seconds?

d. Explain the effects of positive and negative correlations on the previous results.

8. Hometown Insurance sells 10-year annuities to retirees who are looking for stable sources of investment income. Hometown invests the annuity funds it receives in an equity index fund with annual returns that are normally distributed with a mean of 9% and standard deviation of 3%. It guarantees investors a minimum annual return of 6% and a maximum return (or rate cap) of 8.5%. This limits both the retirees' down-side risk and up-side return potential. Of course, Hometown makes its money on these contracts when the actual return exceeds the rate cap. Suppose a retiree invests $50,000 in such an annuity contract. Assume investment earnings are credited at the end of the year and are reinvested.

a. Build a spreadsheet model for this problem that computes the profit Hometown would make on the contract.

b. How much money can Hometown expect to make on average on the contract?

c. What is the probability that Hometown would lose money on the contract?

d. Suppose that Hometown wants to identify the minimum guaranteed annual rate of return that provides a 2% chance of the company losing money on the contract. What should the minimum guaranteed annual rate of return be?

9. WVTU is a television station that has 20 thirty-second advertising slots during its regularly scheduled programming each evening. The station is now selling advertising for the first few days in November. The station could sell all the slots immediately for $4,500 each, but because November 7 will be an election day, the station manager knows she may be able to sell slots at the last minute to political candidates

in tight races for a price of $8,000 each. The demand for these last-minute slots is estimated as follows:

					Demand						
8	9	10	11	12	13	14	15	16	17	18	19
Probability	0.03	0.05	0.10	0.15	0.20	0.15	0.10	0.05	0.05	0.05	0.05	0.02

Slots not sold in advance and not sold to political candidates at the last minute can be sold to local advertisers at a price of $2,000.

a. If the station manager sells all the advertising slots in advance, how much revenue will the station receive?

b. How many advertising slots should be sold in advance if the station manager wants to maximize expected revenue?

c. If the station manager sells in advance the number of slots identified in the previous question, what is the probability that the total revenue received will exceed the amount identified in part a where all slots are sold in advance?

10. The owner of a ski apparel store in Winter Park, Colorado must make a decision in July regarding the number of ski jackets to order for the following ski season. Each ski jacket costs $54 each and can be sold during the ski season for $145. Any unsold jackets at the end of the season are sold for $45. The demand for jackets is expected to follow a Poisson distribution with an average rate of 80. The store owner can order jackets in lot sizes of 10 units.

a. How many jackets should the store owner order if she wants to maximize her expected profit?

b. What are the best-case and worst-case outcomes the owner may face on this product if she implements your suggestion?

c. How likely is it that the store owner will make at least $7,000 if she implements your suggestion?

d. How likely is it that the store owner will make between $6,000 and $7,000 if she implements your suggestion?

11. The owner of a golf shop in Myrtle Beach, SC must decide how many sets of beginner golf clubs to order for the coming tourist season. Demand for golf clubs is random but follows a Poisson distribution with the average demand rates indicated in the following table for each month. The expected selling price of the clubs is also shown for each month.

	May	**June**	**July**	**August**	**September**	**October**
Average Demand	60	90	70	50	30	40
Selling Price	$145	$140	$130	$110	$80	$60

In May, each set of clubs can be ordered at a cost of $75. This price is expected to drop 5% a month during the remainder of the season. Each month, the owner of the shop also gives away a free set of clubs to anyone who makes a hole-in-one from a short practice tee next to the shop. The number of people making a hole-in-one on this tee each month follows a Poisson distribution with a mean of 3. Any sets of clubs left over at the end of October are sold for $45 per set.

a. How many sets of clubs should the shop owner order if he wants to maximize the expected profit on this product?

b. What are the best-case and worst-case outcomes the owner may face on this product if he implements your suggestion?

    c. How likely is it that the store owner will make at least $17,000 if he implements your suggestion?

    d. How likely is it that the store owner will make between $12,000 and $14,000 if he implements your suggestion?

    e. What percentage of the total demand for this product (excluding the free give-aways) will the owner be able to meet if he implements your suggestion?

12. Large Lots is planning a seven-day promotion on a discontinued model of 31″ flatscreen TVs. At a price of $575 per TV, the daily demand for this type of TV has been estimated as follows:

	Units Demanded per Day					
	0	**1**	**2**	**3**	**4**	**5**
Probability	0.15	0.20	0.30	0.20	0.10	0.05

Large Lots can order up to 50 of these TVs from a surplus dealer at a cost of $325. This dealer has offered to buy back any unsold TVs at the end of the promotion for $250 each.

    a. How many TVs should Large Lots order if it wants to maximize the expected profit on this promotion?

    b. What is the expected level of profit?

    c. Suppose the surplus dealer will only buy back a maximum of four TVs at the end of the promotion. Would this change your answer? If so, how?

13. The monthly demand for the latest computer at Newland Computers follows a normal distribution with a mean of 350 and a standard deviation of 75. Newland purchases these computers for $1,200 and sells them for $2,300. It costs the company $100 to place an order and $12 for every computer held in inventory at the end of each month. Currently, the company places an order for 1,000 computers whenever the inventory at the end of a month falls below 100 units. Assume the beginning inventory is 400 units, unmet demand in any month is lost to competitors, and orders placed at the end of one month arrive at the beginning of the next month.

    a. Create a spreadsheet model to simulate the profit the company will earn on this product over the next two years. What is the average level of profit the company will earn?

    b. Suppose the company wants to determine the optimum reorder point and order quantity. Which combination of reorder point and order quantity will provide the highest average profit over the next two years?

14. The manager of Moore's Catalog Showroom is trying to predict how much revenue will be generated by each major department in the store during 2011. The manager has estimated the minimum and maximum growth rates possible for revenues in each department. The manager believes that any of the possible growth rates between the minimum and maximum values are equally likely to occur. These estimates are summarized in the following table:

		Growth Rates	
Department	**2010 Revenues**	**Minimum**	**Maximum**
Electronics	$6,342,213	2%	10%
Garden Supplies	$1,203,231	−4%	5%
Jewelry	$4,367,342	−2%	6%
Sporting Goods	$3,543,532	−1%	8%
Toys	$4,342,132	4%	15%

Create a spreadsheet to simulate the total revenues that could occur in the coming year.

   a. Construct a 95% confidence interval for the average level of revenues the manager could expect for 2011.

   b. According to your model, what are the chances that total revenues in 2011 will be more than 5% larger than those in 2010?

15. The Harriet Hotel in downtown Boston has 100 rooms that rent for $150 per night. It costs the hotel $30 per room in variable costs (cleaning, bathroom items, and so on) each night a room is occupied. For each reservation accepted, there is a 5% chance that the guest will not arrive. If the hotel overbooks, it costs $200 to compensate guests whose reservations cannot be honored.

   a. How many reservations should the hotel accept if it wants to maximize the average daily profit?

16. Lynn Price recently completed her MBA and accepted a job with an electronics manufacturing company. Although she likes her job, she is also looking forward to retiring one day. To ensure that her retirement is comfortable, Lynn intends to invest $3,000 of her salary into a tax-sheltered retirement fund at the end of each year. Lynn is not certain what rate of return this investment will earn each year, but she expects each year's rate of return could be modeled appropriately as a normally distributed random variable with a mean of 12.5% and standard deviation of 2%.

   a. If Lynn is 30 years old, how much money should she expect to have in her retirement fund at age 60?

   b. Construct a 95% confidence interval for the average amount Lynn will have at age 60.

   c. What is the probability that Lynn will have more than $1 million in her retirement fund when she reaches age 60?

   d. How much should Lynn invest each year if she wants there to be a 90% chance of having at least $1 million in her retirement fund at age 60?

   e. Suppose that Lynn contributes $3,000 annually to her retirement fund for eight years and then terminates these annual contributions. How much of her salary would she have contributed to this retirement plan and how much money could she expect to have accumulated at age 60?

   f. Now suppose that Lynn contributes nothing to her retirement fund for eight years and then begins contributing $3,000 annually until age 60. How much of her salary would she have contributed to this retirement plan, and how much money could she expect to have accumulated at age 60?

   g. What should Lynn (and you) learn from the answers to questions e and f?

17. Employees of Georgia-Atlantic are permitted to contribute a portion of their earnings (in increments of $500) to a flexible spending account from which they can pay medical expenses not covered by the company's health insurance program. Contributions to employees' "flex" accounts are not subject to income taxes. However, the employee forfeits any amount contributed to the "flex" account that is not spent during the year. Suppose Greg Davis makes $60,000 per year from Georgia-Atlantic and pays a marginal tax rate of 33%. Greg and his wife estimate that in the coming year, their normal medical expenses not covered by the health insurance program could be as small as $500, as large as $5,000, and most likely about $1,300. However, Greg also believes there is a 5% chance that an abnormal medical event could occur that might add $10,000 to the normal expenses paid from their flex account. If their uncovered medical claims exceed their contribution to their "flex" account, they will have to cover these expenses with the after-tax money Greg brings home.

   a. Use simulation to determine the amount of money Greg should contribute to his flexible spending account in the coming year if he wants to maximize his disposable income (after taxes and all medical expenses are paid).

18. Acme Equipment Company is considering the development of a new machine that would be marketed to tire manufacturers. Research and development costs for the project are expected to be about $4 million but could vary between $3 and $6 million. The market life for the product is estimated to be 3 to 8 years with all intervening possibilities being equally likely. The company thinks it will sell 250 units per year but acknowledges that this figure could be as low as 50 or as high as 350. The company will sell the machine for about $23,000. Finally, the cost of manufacturing the machine is expected to be $14,000 but could be as low as $12,000 or as high as $18,000. The company's cost of capital is 15%.
    a. Use appropriate RNGs to create a spreadsheet to calculate the possible NPVs that could result from taking on this project.
    b. What is the expected NPV for this project?
    c. What is the probability of this project generating a positive NPV for the company?

19. Representatives from the American Heart Association are planning to go door-to-door throughout a community, soliciting contributions. From past experience, they know that when someone answers the door, 80% of the time it is a female, and 20% of the time it is a male. They also know that 70% of the females who answer the door make a donation, whereas only 40% of the males who answer the door make donations. The amount of money that females contribute follows a normal distribution with a mean of $20 and standard deviation of $3. The amount of money males contribute follows a normal distribution with a mean of $10 and standard deviation of $2.
    a. Create a spreadsheet model that simulates what might happen whenever a representative of the American Heart Association knocks on a door and someone answers.
    b. What is the average contribution the Heart Association can expect to receive when someone answers the door?
    c. Suppose that the Heart Association plans to visit 300 homes on a given Saturday. If no one is home at 25% of the residences, what is the total amount that the Heart Association can expect to receive in donations?

20. Techsburg, Inc. uses a stamping machine to manufacturer aluminum bodies for lightweight, miniature aircraft used for military reconnaissance. Currently, forms in the stamping machine are changed after every 65 hours of operation or whenever a form breaks, whichever happens first. The lifetime of each form follows a Weibull distribution modeled as PsiWeibull(2, 25) + 50. The machine is operated 480 hours per month. It costs $800 to replace the stamping forms. If a form breaks before its scheduled replacement time (or in less than 65 hours of use), the shop loses 8 hours of production time. However, if a form lasts until its scheduled replacement after 65 hours of use, the shop only loses 2 hours of production time. The company estimates that each hour of lost production time costs $1,000.
    a. On average, how much does Techsburg spend maintaining this stamping machine over 6 months?
    b. Suppose Techsburg wanted to minimize its total maintenance cost for the stamping machine. How often should the company plan on changing the stamping forms, and how much money would it save?
    c. Suppose the cost to replace the stamping forms is expected to increase. What impact should this have on the optimal planned replacement time of the forms? Explain.
    d. Suppose the cost of lost production time is increased. What impact should this have on the optimal planned replacement time of the forms? Explain.

21. After spending 10 years as an assistant manager for a large restaurant chain, Ray Clark has decided to become his own boss. The owner of a local submarine sandwich store

wants to sell the store to Ray for $65,000 to be paid in installments of $13,000 in each of the next five years. According to the current owner, the store brings in revenue of about $110,000 per year and incurs operating costs of about 63% of sales. Thus, after the store is paid for, Ray should make about $35,000 − $40,000 per year before taxes. Until the store is paid for, he will make substantially less—but he will be his own boss. Realizing that some uncertainty is involved in this decision, Ray wants to simulate what level of net income he can expect to earn during the next five years as he operates and pays for the store. In particular, he wants to see what could happen if sales are allowed to vary uniformly between $90,000 and $120,000, and if operating costs are allowed to vary uniformly between 60% and 65% of sales. Assume that Ray's payments for the store are not deductible for tax purposes and that he is in the 28% tax bracket.

a. Create a spreadsheet model to simulate the annual net income Ray would receive during each of the next five years if he decides to buy the store.

b. Given the money he has in savings, Ray thinks he can get by for the next five years if he can make at least $12,000 from the store each year.

c. What is the probability that Ray will make at least $12,000 in each of the next five years?

d. What is the probability that Ray will make at least $60,000 total over the next five years?

22. Road Racer Sports, Inc. is a mail-order business dedicated to the running enthusiast. The company sends out full-color catalogs several times a year to several hundred thousand people on its mailing list. Production and mailing costs are fairly expensive for direct mail advertising, averaging about $3.25 per catalog. As a result, management does not want to continue sending catalogs to persons who do not buy enough to cover the costs of the catalogs they receive. Currently, the company removes a customer from their mailing list if they receive six consecutive catalogs without placing an order. The following table summarizes the probability of a customer placing an order.

Last Order	Prob. of Order
1 catalog ago	0.40
2 catalogs ago	0.34
3 catalogs ago	0.25
4 catalogs ago	0.17
5 catalogs ago	0.09
6 catalogs ago	0.03

According to the first row in this table, if a customer receives a catalog and places an order, there is a 40% chance he will place another order when he receives his next catalog. The second row indicates there is a 34% chance a customer will receive a catalog, place an order, and then not order again until they receive two more catalogs. The remaining rows in this table have similar interpretations.

a. How much profit must the company earn on an average order to cover the cost of printing and distributing the catalogs?

b. Approximately what percentage of the names on the mailing list will be purged before each catalog mailing?

23. Sammy Slick works for a company that allows him to contribute up to 10% of his earnings into a tax-deferred savings plan. The company matches a portion of the contributions its employees make based on the organization's financial performance. Although the minimum match is 25% of the employee's contributions, and the maximum match is 100%, the company match is about 50% in most years.

Sammy is currently 30 years old and makes $35,000. He wants to retire at age 60. He expects his salary to increase in any given year to be at least 2% per year, at most 6%, and most likely 3%. The funds contributed by Sammy and his employer are invested in mutual funds. Sammy expects the annual return on his investments to vary according to a normal distribution with a mean of 12.5% and standard deviation of 2%.

  a.   If Sammy contributes 10% of his income to this plan, how much money could he expect to have at age 60?

  b.   Suppose Sammy makes 10% contributions to this plan for eight years, from age 30 to 37, and then stops contributing. How much of his own money would he have invested, and how much money could he expect to have at age 60?

  c.   Now suppose Sammy contributes nothing to the plan his first 8 years and then contributes 10% for 23 years from age 38 to age 60. How much of his own money would he have invested, and how much money could he expect to have at age 60?

  d.   What do you learn from Sammy's example?

24. Podcessories manufactures several accessories for a popular digital music player. The company is trying to decide whether to discontinue one of the items in this product line. Discontinuing the item would save the company $600,000 in fixed costs (comprised of leases on building and machinery) during the coming year. However, the company is anticipating that it might receive an order for 60,000 units from a large discount retailer that could prove to be very profitable. Unfortunately, the company is being forced to make a decision about renewing the leases required to continue this item before it will know if it will receive the large order from the discount retailer. The variable cost per unit for this item is $6. The regular selling price of the item is $12 per unit. However, the company has offered the discount retailer a price of $10.50 per unit due to the size of its potential order. Podcessories believes there is a 60% chance it will receive the order from the discount retailer. Additionally, it believes general demand for this product (apart from the discount retailer's order) will vary between 45,000 to 115,000 units with a most likely outcome of 75,000 units.

  a.   Create a spreadsheet model for this problem.

  b.   How much money might the company lose next year (worst case) if they continue this line?

  c.   How much money might the company make next year (best case) if they continue this line?

  d.   If the company loses money, on average how much could they expect to lose?

  e.   If the company makes money, on average how much could they expect to make?

  f.   What other actions might you suggest this company take to improve its chance of making a decision with a good outcome?

25. Bob Davidson owns a newsstand outside the Waterstone office building complex in Atlanta, near Hartsfield International Airport. He buys his papers wholesale at $0.50 per paper and sells them for $0.75. Bob wonders what is the optimal number of papers to order each day. Based on history, he has found that demand (even though it is discrete) can be modeled by a normal distribution with a mean of 50 and standard deviation of 5. When he has more papers than customers, he can recycle all the extra papers the next day and receive $0.05 per paper. On the other hand, if he has more customers than papers, he loses some goodwill in addition to the lost profit on the potential sale of $0.25. Bob estimates the incremental lost goodwill costs five days' worth of business (that is, dissatisfied customers will go to a competitor the next week but come back to him the week after that).

  a.   Create a spreadsheet model to determine the optimal number of papers to order each day. Round the demand values generated by the normal RNG to the closest integer value.

b. Construct a 95% confidence interval for the expected payoff from the optimal decision.

26. Vinton Auto Insurance is trying to decide how much money to keep in liquid assets to cover insurance claims. In the past, the company held some of the premiums it received in interest-bearing checking accounts and put the rest into investments that are not quite as liquid but tend to generate a higher investment return. The company wants to study cash flows to determine how much money it should keep in liquid assets to pay claims. After reviewing historical data, the company determined that the average repair bill per claim is normally distributed with a mean of $1,700 and standard deviation of $400. It also determined that the number of repair claims filed each week is a random variable that follows the probability distribution shown in the following table:

Number of Claims	1	2	3	4	5	6	7	8	9
Probability	0.05	0.06	0.10	0.17	0.28	0.14	0.08	0.07	0.05

In addition to repair claims, the company also receives claims for cars that have been "totaled" and cannot be repaired. A 20% chance of receiving this type of claim exists in any week. These claims for "totaled" cars typically cost anywhere from $2,000 to $35,000, with $13,000 being the most common cost.

a. Create a spreadsheet model of the total claims cost incurred by the company in any week.

b. Create a histogram of the distribution of total cost values that were generated.

c. What is the average cost the company should expect to pay each week?

d. Suppose that the company decides to keep $20,000 cash on hand to pay claims. What is the probability that this amount would not be adequate to cover claims in any week?

e. Create a 95% confidence interval for the true probability of claims exceeding $20,000 in a given week.

27. Executives at Meds-R-Us have decided to build a new production facility for the company's best-selling high blood pressure drug. The problem they now face is determining the size of the facility (in terms of production capacity). Last year, the company sold 1,085,000 units of this drug at a price of $13 per unit. They expect the demand for the drug to be normally distributed with a mean increasing by approximately 59,000 units per year over the next 10 years with a standard deviation of 30,000 units. They expect the price of the drug to increasing with inflation at a rate of 3% per year. Variable production costs are currently $9 per unit and are also expected to increase in future years at the rate of inflation. Other operating costs are expected to be $1.50 per unit of capacity in the first year of operation and increasing at the rate of inflation in subsequent years. The plant construction cost is expected to be $18 million for 1 million units of annual production capacity. The company can increase the annual production capacity above this level at a cost of $12 per unit of additional capacity. Assume the company must pay for the plant when it is completed and all other cash flows occur at the end of each year. The company uses a 10% discount rate on cash flows for financial decisions.

a. Create a spreadsheet model to compute the NPV for this decision.

b. What is the expected NPV for a plant with a production capacity of 1.2 million units per year?

c. What is the expected NPV for a plant with a production capacity of 1.4 million units per year?

d. How large a plant should the company build if they want to be 90% certain of obtaining a positive NPV for this project?

28. The owner of a local car dealership has just received a call from a regional distributor stating that a $5,000 bonus will be awarded if the owner's dealership sells at least 10 new cars next Saturday. On an average Saturday, this dealership has 75 potential customers look at new cars, but there is no way to determine exactly how many customers will come this particular Saturday. The owner is fairly certain that the number would not be less than 40 but also thinks it would be unrealistic to expect more than 120 (which is the largest number of customers to ever show up in one day). The owner determined that, on average, about 1 out of 10 customers who look at cars at the dealership actually purchase a car—or, a 0.10 probability (or 10% chance) exists that any given customer will buy a new car.
   a. Create a spreadsheet model for the number of cars the dealership might sell next Saturday.
   b. What is the probability that the dealership will earn the $5,000 bonus?
   c. If you were this dealer, what is the maximum amount of money you would be willing to spend on sales incentives to try to earn this bonus?

29. Dr. Sarah Benson is an ophthalmologist who, in addition to prescribing glasses and contact lenses, performs optical laser surgery to correct nearsightedness. This surgery is fairly easy and inexpensive to perform. Thus, it represents a potential gold mine for her practice. To inform the public about this procedure, Dr. Benson advertises in the local paper and holds information sessions in her office one night a week at which she shows a videotape about the procedure and answers any questions potential patients might have. The room where these meetings are held can seat 10 people, and reservations are required. The number of people attending each session varies from week to week. Dr. Benson cancels the meeting if two or fewer people have made reservations. Using data from the previous year, Dr. Benson determined that the distribution of reservations is as follows:

Number of Reservations	0	1	2	3	4	5	6	7	8	9	10
Probability	0.02	0.05	0.08	0.16	0.26	0.18	0.11	0.07	0.05	0.01	0.01

Using data from the past year, Dr. Benson determined that each person who attends an information session has a 0.25 probability of electing to have the surgery. Of those who do not, most cite the cost of the procedure—$2,000—as their major concern.
   a. On average, how much revenue does Dr. Benson's practice in laser surgery generate each week?
   b. On average, how much revenue would the laser surgery generate each week if Dr. Benson did not cancel sessions with two or fewer reservations?
   c. Dr. Benson believes that 40% of the people attending the information sessions would have the surgery if she reduced the price to $1,500. Under this scenario, how much revenue could Dr. Benson expect to realize per week from laser surgery?

30. Calls to the 24-hour customer support line for Richman Financial Services occur randomly following a Poisson distribution with the following average rates during different hours of the day:

Time Period	Avg. Calls Per Hour	Time Period	Avg. Calls Per Hour
Midnight–1 am	2	Noon–1 pm	35
1 am–2 am	2	1 pm–2 pm	20
2 am–3 am	2	2 pm–3 pm	20
3 am–4 am	4	3 pm–4 pm	20

(Continued)

4 am–5 am	4	4 pm–5 pm	18
5 am–6 am	8	5 pm–6 pm	18
6 am–7 am	12	6 pm–7 pm	15
7 am–8 am	18	7 pm–8 pm	10
8 am–9 am	25	8 pm–9 pm	6
9 am–10 am	30	9 pm–10 pm	5
10 am–11 am	25	10 pm–11 pm	4
11 am–Noon	20	11 pm–Midnight	2

Richman's customer service representatives spend approximately seven minutes on each call and are assigned to work eight-hour shifts that begin at the top of each hour. Richman wants to ensure that, on average, they can provide a 98% service level.

a. Determine the customer service schedule that allows Richman to achieve their service level objective using the fewest number of employees.

b. According to your solution, how many customer service representatives should Richman employ and how should they be scheduled?

31. A European call option gives a person the right to buy a particular stock at a given price (the strike price) on a specific date in the future (the expiration date). This type of call option is typically sold at the NPV of the expected value of the option on its expiration date. Suppose you own a call option with a strike price of $54. If the stock is worth $59 on the expiration date, you would exercise your option and buy the stock, making a $5 profit. On the other hand, if the stock is worth $47 on the expiration date, you would not exercise your option, and you would make $0 profit. Researchers have suggested the following model for simulating the movement of stock prices:

$$P_{k+1} = P_k (1 + (\mu t + z\sigma\sqrt{t}))$$

where:

P_k = price of the stock at time period k

$\mu = v + 0.5\sigma^2$

v = the stock's expected annual growth rate

σ = the standard deviation on the stock's annual growth rate

t = time period interval (expressed in years)

z = a random observation from a normal distribution with mean 0 and standard deviation of 1.

Suppose a stock has an initial price (P_0) of $80, an expected annual growth rate (v) of 15%, and a standard deviation (σ) of 25%.

a. Create a spreadsheet model to simulate this stock's price behavior for the next 13 weeks (note $t = 1/52$ because the time period is weekly).

b. Suppose you are interested in purchasing a call option with a strike price of $75 and an expiration date at week 13. On average, how much profit would you earn with this option?

c. Assume a risk-free discount rate is 6%. How much should you be willing to pay for this option today? (*Hint*: Use Excel's NPV function.)

d. If you purchase the option, what is the probability that you will make a profit?

32. Refer to the previous question. Another type of option is the Asian option. Its payoff is not based on the price of the stock on the expiration date but, instead, on the average price of the stock over the lifetime of the option.

Suppose a stock has an initial price (P_0) of $80, an expected annual growth rate (v) of 15%, and a standard deviation (σ) of 25%.

a. Create a spreadsheet model to simulate this stock's price behavior for the next 13 weeks (note $t = 1/52$ because the time period is weekly).

b. Suppose you are interested in purchasing a call option with a strike price of $75 and an expiration date at week 13. On average, how much profit would you earn with this option?

c. Assume a risk-free discount rate is 6%. How much should you be willing to pay for this option today? (*Hint*: Use Excel's NPV function.)

d. If you purchase the option, what is the probability that you will make a profit?

33. Amanda Green is interested in investing in the following set of mutual funds whose returns are all normally distributed with the indicated means and standard deviations:

	Windsor	Columbus	Vanguard	Integrity	Nottingham
Mean	17.0%	14.0%	11.0%	8.0%	5.0%
Std Dev	9.0%	6.5%	5.0%	3.5%	2.0%

The correlations between the mutual funds are as follows:

	Windsor	Columbus	Vanguard	Integrity	Nottingham
Windsor	1	0.1	0.05	0.3	0.6
Columbus		1	0.2	0.15	0.1
Vanguard			1	0.1	0.2
Integrity				1	0.4
Nottingham					1

a. What is the expected return and standard deviation on a portfolio where Amanda invests her money equally in all five mutual funds?

b. Suppose Amanda is willing to assume the risk associated with a 5% standard deviation in returns on her portfolio. What portfolio will give her the greatest expected return for this level of risk?

c. Construct the efficient frontier for this portfolio. How would you explain this graph to Amanda?

34. Michael Abrams runs a specialty clothing store that sells collegiate sports apparel. One of his primary business opportunities involves selling custom screen-printed sweatshirts for college football bowl games. He is trying to determine how many sweatshirts to produce for the upcoming Tangerine Bowl game. During the month before the game, Michael plans to sell his sweatshirts for $25 a piece. At this price, he believes the demand for sweatshirts will be triangularly distributed with a minimum demand of 10,000, maximum demand of 30,000, and a most likely demand of 18,000. During the month after the game, Michael plans to sell any remaining sweatshirts for $12 a piece. At this price, he believes the demand for sweatshirts will be triangularly distributed with a minimum demand of 2,000, maximum demand of 7,000, and a most likely demand of 5,000. Two months after the game, Michael plans to sell any remaining sweatshirts to a surplus store that has agreed to buy up to 2,000 sweatshirts for a price of $3 per shirt. Michael can order custom screen-printed sweatshirts for $8 a piece in lot sizes of 3,000.

a. On average, how much profit would Michael earn if he orders 18,000 sweatshirts?

b. How many sweatshirts should he order if he wants to maximize his expected profit?

35. The Major Motors Corporation is trying to decide whether to introduce a new midsize car. The directors of the company only want to produce the car if it has at least an 80% chance of generating a positive NPV over the next 10 years. If the company decides to produce the car, it will have to pay an uncertain initial startup cost that is estimated to follow a triangular distribution with a minimum value of $2 billion, maximum value of $2.4 billion, and a most likely value of $2.1 billion. In the first year, the company would produce 100,000 units. Demand during the first year is uncertain but expected to be normally distributed with a mean of 95,000 and standard deviation of 7,000. For any year in which the demand exceeds production, production will be increased by 5% in the following year. For any year in which the production exceeds demand, production will be decreased by 5% in the next year, and the excess cars will be sold to a rental car company at a 20% discount. After the first year, the demand in any year will be modeled as a normally distributed random variable with a mean equal to the actual demand in the previous year and standard deviation of 7,000. In the first year, the sales price of the car will be $13,000, and the total variable cost per car is expected to be $9,500. Both the selling price and variable cost is expected to increase each year at the rate of inflation, which is assumed to be uniformly distributed between 2% and 7%. The company uses a discount rate of 9% to discount future cash flows.

   a. Create a spreadsheet model for this problem. What is the minimum, average, and maximum NPV Major Motors can expect if it decides to produce this car? (*Hint*: Consider using the NPV( ) function to discount the profits Major Motors would earn each year.)

   b. What is the probability of Major Motors earning a positive NPV over the next 10 years?

   c. Should Major Motors produce this car?

36. Each year, the Schriber Corporation must determine how much to contribute to the company's pension plan. The company uses a 10-year planning horizon to determine the contribution, which, if made annually in each of the next 10 years, would allow for only a 10% chance of the fund running short of money. The company then makes that contribution in the current year and repeats this process in each subsequent year to determine the specific amount to contribute each year. (Last year, the company contributed $23 million to the plan.) The pension plan covers two types of employees: hourly and salaried. In the current year, there will be 6,000 former hourly employees and 3,000 former salaried employees receiving benefits from the plan. The change in the number of retired hourly employees from one year to the next is expected to vary according to a normal distribution with a mean of 4% and standard deviation of 1%. The change in the number of retired salaried employees from one year to the next is expected to vary between 1% and 4% according to a truncated normal distribution with a mean of 2% and standard deviation of 1%. Currently, hourly retirees receive an average benefit of $15,000 per year, whereas salaried retirees receive an average annual benefit of $40,000. Both of these averages are expected to increase annually with the rate of inflation, which is assumed to vary between 2% and 7% according to a triangular distribution with a most likely value of 3.5%. The current balance in the company's pension fund is $1.5 billion. Investments in this fund earn an annual return that is assumed to be normally distributed with a mean of 12% and standard deviation of 2%. Create a spreadsheet model for this problem, and use simulation to determine the pension fund contribution the company should make in the current year. What is your recommendation?

Live Well, Die Broke

(Inspired by a presentation given by Dr. John Charnes)

For investment advisors, a major consideration in planning for a client in retirement is the determination of a withdrawal amount that will provide the client to with the funds necessary to maintain his or her desired standard of living throughout the client's remaining lifetime. If a client withdraws too much or if investment returns fall below expectations, there is a danger of either running out of funds or reducing the desired standard of living. A sustainable retirement withdrawal is the inflation-adjusted monetary amount a client can withdraw periodically from his or her retirement funds for an assumed planning horizon. This amount cannot be determined with complete certainty because of the random nature of investment returns. Usually, the sustainable retirement withdrawal is determined by limiting the probability of running out of funds to some specified level, such as 5%. The sustainable retirement withdrawal amount is typically expressed as a percentage of the initial value of the assets in the retirement portfolio but is actually the inflation-adjusted monetary amount that the client would like each year for living expenses.

Assume an investment advisor, Roy Dodson, is assisting a widowed client in determining a sustainable retirement withdrawal. The client is a 59 year-old woman who turns 60 in two months. She has $1,000,000 in a tax-deferred retirement account that will be the primary source of her retirement income. Roy has designed a portfolio for his client with returns he expects to be normally distributed with a mean of 8% and standard deviation of 2%. Withdrawals will be made at the beginning of each year on the client's birthday.

Roy assumes that the inflation rate will be 3%, based on long-term historic data. So if her withdrawal at the beginning of the first year is $40,000, her inflation-adjusted withdrawal at the beginning of the second year will be $41,200, and third year's withdrawal will be $42,436, and so on.

For his initial analysis, Roy wants to assume his client will live until age 90. In consultation with his client, he also wants to limit the chance that she will run out of money before her death to a maximum of 5%.

1. What is the maximum amount Roy should advise his client to withdraw on her 60th birthday? If she lives until age 90, how much should the client expect to leave to her heirs?

2. Roy is now concerned about basing his analysis on the assumption that his client will live to age 90. After all, she is healthy and might live to be 110, or she could be in a car accident and die at age 62. To account for this uncertainty in the client's age at death, Roy would like to model the client's remaining life expectancy as a random variable between 0 and 50 years that follows a lognormal distribution with a mean of 20 and standard deviation of 10 (rounded to the nearest integer). Under this assumption, what is the maximum amount Roy should advise his client to withdraw on her 60th birthday, and how much should the client expect to leave to her heirs? Hint: Modify your spreadsheet to accommodate ages up to 110, and use a VLOOKUP( ) function to return the client's ending balance in her randomly determined year of death.)

3. Roy is pleased to now be modeling the uncertainty in his client's life expectancy. But he is now curious about limiting to 5% the chance that his client will run out of money before her death. In particular, he is wondering how sensitive the sustainable withdrawal amount is to changes in this 5% assumption. To answer this question, create an efficient frontier showing the maximum sustainable withdrawal amount as

the chance of running out of money is varied from 1% to 10%. How should Roy explain the meaning of this chart to his client?

4. Suppose Roy's client has three children and wants there to be a 95% chance that they will each inherit at least $250,000 when she dies. Under this assumption, what is the maximum amount Roy should advise his client to withdraw on her 60th birthday, and how much should the client expect to leave to her heirs?

Death and Taxes

CASE 12.2

Benjamin Franklin once said, "In this world nothing is certain but death and taxes." Although that may be true, there is often great uncertainty involved in when one will encounter death and how much one must pay in taxes before arriving there. Another Benjamin made a very significant contribution toward assessing the uncertainty associated with both death and taxes. Benjamin Gompertz (1779-1865) was a British mathematician who, by studying Mediterranean fruit flies, theorized that mortality rates increase at an exponential rate as age increases (that is, as an organism gets older, its chance of dying per unit of time increases exponentially). Gompertz's Law of Mortality has since become a cornerstone of actuarial and financial planning activities.

In a group of people of a given age (for example, 65), some proportion of those people will not live another year. Let q_x represent the proportion of people of age x who will die before reaching age $x + 1$. The value q_x is sometimes referred to as the **mortality rate** at age x. The following formula, based on Gompertz's Law, is sometimes used to model mortality rates.

$$q_x = 1 - \text{EXP}\left(\frac{(\text{LN}(1-q_{x-1}))^2}{\text{LN}(1-q_{x-2})}\right)$$

Mortality rates play an important role in numerous financial planning and retirement decisions. For instance, most individuals do not want to retire unless they are reasonably certain they have enough assets to sustain themselves financially for the rest of their life. The uncertainties associated with this sort of decision create a perfect application for spreadsheet simulation.

The following questions give you the opportunity to explore several issues that actuaries and financial planners face on a daily basis. Assume the mortality rates for males at ages 63 and 64 are $q_{63} = 0.0235$ and $q_{64} = 0.0262$, respectively, and those of females at ages 63 and 64 are $q_{63} = 0.0208$ and $q_{64} = 0.0225$, respectively. (Remember the Risk Solver Platform for Education limits you to 100 uncertain [RNG] cells per workbook. So you might need to build models for questions 8, 9, and 10 in separate workbooks.)

1. On average, to what age should a 65-year-old male expect to live?
2. What is the probability of a 65-year-old male living to at least age 80?
3. What is the probability of a 65-year-old male living to exactly age 80?
4. On average, to what age should a 70-year-old male expect to live?
5. What is the probability of a 70-year-old male living to at least age 80?
6. What is the probability of a 70-year-old male living to exactly age 80?
7. Suppose a 65-year-old male has $1,200,000 in retirement investments earning an 8% interest rate. Assume he intends to withdraw $100,000 in his first year of retirement and 3% more in subsequent years to adjust for inflation. Annual interest earnings are credited on the beginning balance less one half the amount withdrawn. For example, in the first year, interest earnings would be 0.08 × ($1,200,000 + $100,000/2) = $92,000. What is the probability that this individual would outlive his retirement assets (assuming he spends all he withdraws each year)?

8. Refer to the previous question. Suppose the interest rate each year can be modeled as a normally distributed random variable with a mean of 8% and standard deviation of 1.5%. Further suppose the rate of inflation each year can be described as a random variable following a triangular distribution with minimum, most likely, and maximum values of 2%, 3%, and 5%, respectively. Under these conditions, what is the probability that this individual would outlive his retirement assets (assuming he spends all he withdraws each year)?

9. Suppose the person described in the previous question has a 65-year-old wife who is joint owner of the retirement assets described earlier. What is the probability that the retirement assets would be depleted before both spouses die (assuming they spend all they withdraw each year)?

10. Refer to the previous question. How much money should this couple plan on withdrawing in the first year if they want there to be a maximum of a 5% chance of depleting their retirement assets before they both die?

CASE 12.3 The Sound's Alive Company

(Contributed by Dr. Jack Yurkiewicz, Lubin School of Business, Pace University)

Marissa Jones is the president and CEO of Sound's Alive, a company that manufactures and sells a line of speakers, CD players, receivers, high-definition televisions, and other items geared for the home entertainment market. Respected throughout the industry for bringing many high-quality, innovative products to market, Marissa is considering adding a speaker system to her product line.

The speaker market has changed dramatically during the past several years. Originally, high-fidelity aficionados knew that to reproduce sound covering the fullest range of frequencies—from the lowest kettle drum to the highest violin—a speaker system had to be large and heavy. The speaker had various drivers: a woofer to reproduce the low notes, a tweeter for the high notes, and a mid-range driver for the broad spectrum of frequencies in between. Many speaker systems had a minimum of three drivers, but some had even more. The trouble was that such a system was too large for anything but the biggest rooms, and consumers were reluctant to spend thousands of dollars and give up valuable wall space to get the excellent sound these speakers could reproduce.

The trend has changed during the past several years. Consumers still want good sound, but they want it from smaller boxes. Therefore, the satellite system became popular. Consisting of two small boxes that house either one driver (to cover the mid-range and high frequencies) or two (a mid-range and tweeter), a satellite system can easily be mounted on walls or shelves. To reproduce the low notes, a separate subwoofer that is approximately the size of a cube 18 inches on a side is also needed. This subwoofer can be placed anywhere in the room. Taking up less space than a typical large speaker system and sounding almost as good, yet costing hundreds of dollars less, these satellite systems are hot items in the high-fidelity market.

Recently, the separate wings of home entertainment—high fidelity (receivers, speakers, CD players, CDs, and so on), television (large screen monitors, DVD players, Blue-Ray disc players, laser players), and computers (games with sounds, virtual reality software, and so on)—have merged into the home theater concept. To simulate the movie environment, a home theater system requires the traditional stereo speaker system plus additional speakers placed in the rear of the room so that viewers are literally surrounded with sound. Although the rear speakers do not have to match the high quality of the front speakers and, therefore, can be less expensive, most consumers choose a system in which the front and rear speakers are of equal quality, reproducing the full range of frequencies with equal fidelity.

It is this speaker market that Marissa wants to enter. She is considering having Sound's Alive manufacture and sell a home theater system that consists of seven speakers. Three small speakers—each with one dome tweeter that could reproduce the frequency range of 200 Hertz to 20,000 Hertz (upper-low frequencies to the highest frequencies)—would be placed in front, and three similar speakers would be placed strategically around the sides and back of the room. To reproduce the lowest frequencies (from 35 Hertz to 200 Hertz), a single subwoofer would also be part of the system. This subwoofer is revolutionary because it is smaller than the ordinary subwoofer, only 10 inches per side, and it has a built-in amplifier to power it. Consumers and critics are thrilled with the music from early prototype systems, claiming that these speakers have the best balance of sound and size. Marissa is extremely encouraged by these early reviews, and although her company has never produced a product with its house label on it (having always sold systems from established high-fidelity companies), she believes that Sound's Alive should enter the home theater market with this product.

Phase One: Projecting Profits

Marissa decides to create a spreadsheet that will project profits over the next several years. After consulting with economists, market analysts, employees in her own company, and employees from other companies that sell house brand components, Marissa is confident that the gross revenues for these speakers in 2010 would be around $6 million. She must also figure that a small percentage of speakers will be damaged in transit, or some will be returned by dissatisfied customers shortly after the sales. These returns and allowances (R&As) are usually calculated as 2% of the gross revenues. Hence, the net revenues are simply the gross revenues minus the R&As. Marissa believes that the 2010 labor costs for these speakers will be $995,100. The cost of materials (including boxes to ship the speakers) should be $915,350 for 2010. Finally, her overhead costs (rent, lighting, heating in winter, air conditioning in summer, security, and so on) for 2010 should be $1,536,120. Thus, the cost of goods sold is the sum of labor, material, and overhead costs. Marissa figures the gross profit as the difference between the net revenues and the cost of goods sold. In addition, she must consider the selling, general, and administrative (SG&A) expenses. These expenses are more difficult to estimate, but the standard industry practice is to use 18% of the net revenues as the nominal percentage value for these expenses. Therefore, Marissa's profit *before taxes* is the gross profit minus the SG&A value. To calculate taxes, Marissa multiplies her profits before taxes times the tax rate, currently 30%. If her company is operating at a loss, however, no taxes would have to be paid. Finally, Marissa's net (or after tax) profit is simply the difference between the profit before taxes and the actual taxes paid.

To determine the numbers for 2011 through 2013, Marissa assumes that gross revenues, labor costs, material costs, and overhead costs will increase over the years. Although the rates of increase for these items are difficult to estimate, Marissa figures that gross revenues will increase by 9% per year, labor costs will increase by 4% per year, material costs will increase by 6% per year, and overhead costs will increase by 3% per year. She figures that the tax rate will not change from the 30% mark, and she assumes that the SG&A value will remain at 18%.

The basic layout of the spreadsheet that Marissa creates is shown in Figure 12.47 (and in the file Fig12-47.xlsm that accompanies this book). (Ignore the Competitive Assumptions section for now; we will consider it later.) Construct the spreadsheet,

FIGURE 12.47

Spreadsheet template for the Sound's Alive case

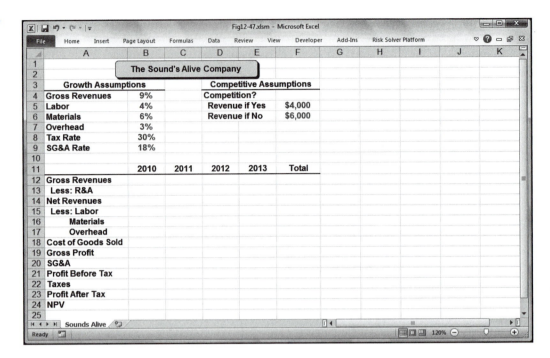

determine the values for the years 2010 through 2013, and then determine the totals for the four years.

Marissa not only wants to determine her net profits for 2010 through 2013, she also must justify her decisions to the company's Board of Trustees. Should she even consider entering this market, from a financial point of view? One way to answer this question is to find the NPV of the net profits for 2010 through 2013. Use Excel's NPV capability to find the NPV, at the current interest rate of 5%, of the profit values for 2010 through 2013.

To avoid large values in the spreadsheet, enter all dollar calculations in thousands. For example, enter labor costs as 995.10 and overhead costs as 1,536.12.

Phase Two: Bringing Competition into the Model

With her spreadsheet complete, Marissa is confident that entering the home theater speaker market would be lucrative for Sound's Alive. However, she has not considered one factor in her calculations—competition. The current market leader and company she is most concerned about is the Bose Corporation. Bose pioneered the concept of a satellite speaker system, and its AMT series is very successful. Marissa is concerned that Bose will enter the home market, cutting into her gross revenues. If Bose does enter the market, Marissa believes that Sound's Alive would still make money; however, she would have to revise her gross revenues estimate from $6 million to $4 million for 2010.

To account for the competition factor, Marissa revises her spreadsheet by adding a Competitive Assumptions section. Cell F4 will contain either a 0 (no competition) or a 1 (if Bose enters the market). Cells F5 and F6 provide the gross revenue estimates (in thousands of dollars) for the two possibilities. Modify your spreadsheet to take these options into account. Use the IF( ) function for the gross revenues for 2010 (cell B12). If Bose does enter the market, not only would Marissa's gross revenues be lower, but the labor, materials, and overhead costs would also be lower because Sound's Alive would be making and selling fewer speakers. Marissa thinks that if Bose enters the market, her 2010 labor costs would be $859,170; 2010 material costs would be $702,950; and 2010 overhead costs would be $1,288,750. She believes that her growth rate assumptions would stay the same whether or not Bose enters the market. Add these possible values to your spreadsheet using the IF( ) function in the appropriate cells.

Look at the net profits for 2010 through 2013. In particular, examine the NPV for the two scenarios: Bose does or does not enter the home theater speaker market.

Phase Three: Bringing Uncertainty into the Model

Jim Allison, the chief of operations at Sound's Alive and a quantitative methods special-ist, plays a key role in providing Marissa with estimates for the various revenues and costs. He is uneasy about the basic estimates for the growth rates. For example, although market research indicates that a 9% gross revenue increase per year is reasonable, Jim knows that if this value is 7%, for example, the profit values and the NPV would be quite different. Even more troublesome is a potential tax increase, which would hit Sound's Alive hard. Jim believes that the tax rate could vary around the expected 30% figure. Finally, Jim is uncomfortable with the industry's standard estimate of 18% for the SG&A rate. Jim thinks that this value could be higher or even lower.

The Sound's Alive problem is too complicated for solving with what-if analysis be-cause seven assumed values could change: the growth rates for gross revenues, labor, materials, overhead costs, tax rate, SG&A percent, and whether or not Bose enters the market. Jim believes that a Monte Carlo simulation would be a better approach. Jim thinks that the behavior of these variables can be modeled as follows:

Gross Revenues (%): normally distributed, mean = 9.9, std dev = 1.4

Labor Growth (%): normally distributed, mean = 3.45, std dev = 1.0

Materials (%)	Probability		Overhead (%)	Probability
4	0.10		2	0.20
5	0.15		3	0.35
6	0.15		4	0.25
7	0.25		5	0.20
8	0.25			
9	0.10			

Tax Rate (%)	Probability		SG&A (%)	Probability
30	0.15		15	0.05
32	0.30		16	0.10
34	0.30		17	0.20
36	0.25		18	0.25
			19	0.20
			20	0.20

Finally, Jim and Marissa agree that there is a 50/50 chance that Bose will enter the market.

1. Use simulation to analyze the Sound's Alive problem. Based on your results, what is the expected net profit for the years 2010 through 2013, and what is the expected NPV for this business venture?
2. The Board of Trustees told Marissa that the stockholders would feel comfortable with this business venture if its NPV is at least $5 million. What are the chances that Sound's Alive home theater venture will result in an NPV of $5 million or more?

CASE 12.4   The Foxridge Investment Group

(Inspired by a case written by MBA students Fred Hirsch and Ray Rogers for Professor Larry Weatherford at the University of Wyoming)

The Foxridge Investment Group buys and sells rental income properties in southwest Virginia. Bill Hunter, president of Foxridge, has asked for your assistance in analyzing a small apartment building the group is interested in purchasing.

The property in question is a small two-story structure with three rental units on each floor. The purchase price of the property is $170,000 representing $30,000 in land value and $140,000 in buildings and improvements. Foxridge will depreciate the buildings and improvements value on a straight-line basis over 27.5 years. The Foxridge Group will make a down payment of $40,000 to acquire the property and finance the remainder of the purchase price over 20 years with an 11% fixed-rate loan with payments due annually. Figure 12.48 (and the file Fig12-48.xlsm that accompanies this book) summarizes this and other pertinent information.

If all units are fully occupied, Mr. Hunter expects the property to generate rental income of $35,000 in the first year and expects to increase the rent at the rate of inflation (currently 4%). Because vacancies occur and some residents may not always be able to

FIGURE 12.48

Assumptions for the Foxridge Investment Group case

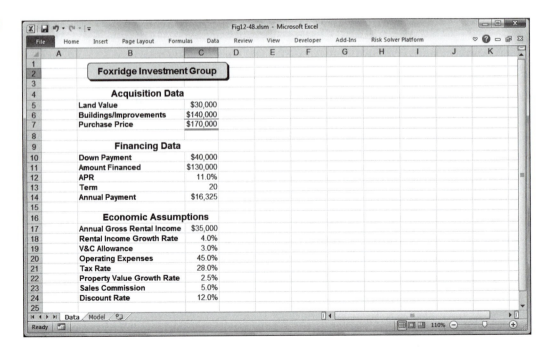

pay their rent, Mr. Hunter factors in a 3% vacancy & collection (V&C) allowance against rental income. Operating expenses are expected to be approximately 45% of rental income. The group's marginal tax rate is 28%.

If the group decides to purchase this property, their plan is to hold it for five years and then sell it to another investor. Presently, property values in this area are increasing at a rate of approximately 2.5% per year. The group will have to pay a sales commission of 5% of the gross selling price when they sell the property.

Figure 12.49 shows a spreadsheet model Mr. Hunter developed to analyze this problem. This model first uses the data and assumptions given in Figure 12.48 to generate the expected net cash flows in each of the next five years. It then provides a final summary of the proceeds expected from selling the property at the end of five years. The total NPV of the project is then calculated in cell I18 using the discount rate of 12% in cell C24 of Figure 12.47. Thus, after discounting all the future cash flows associated with this investment by 12% per year, the investment still generates an NPV of $2,007.

Although the group has been using this type of analysis for many years to make investment decisions, one of Mr. Hunter's investment partners recently read an article in the *Wall Street Journal* about risk analysis and simulation using spreadsheets. As a result, the partner realizes there is quite a bit of uncertainty associated with many of the economic assumptions shown in Figure 12.48. After explaining the potential problem to Mr. Hunter, the two have decided to apply simulation to this model before making a decision. Because neither of them know how to do simulation, they have asked for your assistance.

To model the uncertainty in this decision problem, Mr. Hunter and his partner have decided that the growth in rental income from one year to the next could vary uniformly from 2% to 6% in years 2 through 5. Similarly, they believe the V&C allowance in any year could be as low as 1% and as high as 5%, with 3% being the most likely outcome. They think the operating expenses in each year should be normally distributed with a mean of 45% and standard deviation of 2% but should never be less than 40% and never greater than 50% of gross income. Finally, they believe the property value growth rate could be as small as 1% or as large as 5%, with 2.5% being the most likely outcome.

1. Revise the spreadsheets shown in Figures 12.48 and 12.49 to reflect the uncertainties outlined.
2. Construct a 95% confidence interval for the average total NPV the Foxridge Investment Group can expect if they undertake this project. Interpret this confidence interval.

FIGURE 12.49

Cash flow and financial summary for the Foxridge Investment Group case

	1	2	3	4	5			
			Cash Flows in Year				Financial Summary	
	1	2	3	4	5		Sales price @ year 5	$192,339
Gross Income	$35,000	$36,400	$37,856	$39,370	$40,945		Less:	
Less:							Selling expense	$9,617
V&C Allowance	$1,050	$1,092	$1,136	$1,181	$1,228		Tax basis	$144,545
Operating Exp.	$15,750	$16,380	$17,035	$17,717	$18,425		Taxable gain	$38,177
Net Operating Income	$18,200	$18,928	$19,685	$20,473	$21,291			
Less:							Proceeds from sale	$182,722
Depreciation	$5,091	$5,091	$5,091	$5,091	$5,091		Less:	
Interest	$14,300	$14,077	$13,830	$13,556	$13,251		Taxes	$10,690
Taxable Income	($1,191)	($240)	$764	$1,826	$2,950		Loan payoff	$117,390
							Net cash from sale	$54,643
Taxes Paid (Saved)	($333)	($67)	$214	$511	$826			
							PV of sale proceeds	$31,006
Principal Paid	$2,025	$2,248	$2,495	$2,769	$3,074		PV of cash flows	$11,001
							Less: Original Equity	$40,000
Net Cash Flow	$2,209	$2,670	$3,146	$3,636	$4,141		Total NPV	$2,007

3. Based on your analysis, what is the probability of this project generating a positive total NPV if the group uses a 12% discount rate?
4. Suppose the investors are willing to buy the property if the expected total NPV is greater than zero. Based on your analysis, should they buy this property?
5. Assume the investors decide to increase the discount rate to 14% and repeat questions 2, 3, and 4.
6. What discount rate results in a 90% chance of the project generating a positive total NPV?

Chapter 13

Queuing Theory

13.0 Introduction

Sometimes it seems as if we spend most of our lives waiting in lines. We wait in lines at grocery stores, banks, airports, hotels, restaurants, theaters, theme parks, post offices, and traffic lights. At home, we are likely to spend time waiting in an "electronic line" if we use the telephone to order merchandise from mail-order firms, or to call the customer service number of most computer hardware or software companies.

Some reports indicate that Americans spend 37 *billion* hours a year waiting in lines. Much of this time represents a loss of a limited resource (time) that can never be recovered. Add the frustration and irritation many people experience while waiting in lines, and it is easy to see why businesses should be interested in reducing or eliminating the amount of time their customers spend waiting in lines.

Waiting lines do not always contain people. In a manufacturing company, subassemblies often wait in a line at machining centers to have the next operation performed on them. At a movie rental store, returned DVDs often wait to be placed on shelves so they can be rented again. Electronic messages on the Internet sometimes wait at intermediate computing centers before they are sent to their final destinations. Costs could be reduced, or customer service improved, by reducing the amount of time that the subassemblies, DVDs or electronic messages spend waiting in line.

In management science the term **queuing theory** refers to the body of knowledge dealing with waiting lines. Queuing theory was conceived in the early 1900s when a Danish telephone engineer named A. K. Erlang began studying the congestion and waiting times occurring in the completion of telephone calls. Since then, a number of quantitative models have been developed to help business people understand waiting lines and make better decisions about how to manage them. This chapter introduces some of these models and discusses other issues involved in queuing theory.

13.1 The Purpose of Queuing Models

Most queuing problems focus on determining the level of service that a company should provide. For example, grocery stores must determine how many cash registers to operate at a given time of day so that customers do not have to wait too long to check out. Banks must determine how many tellers to schedule at various times of day to maintain an acceptable level of service. Companies that lease copying machines must determine the number of technicians to employ so that repairs can be made in a timely manner.

In many queuing problems, management has some control over the level of service provided. In the examples just mentioned, customer waiting times could be kept to a

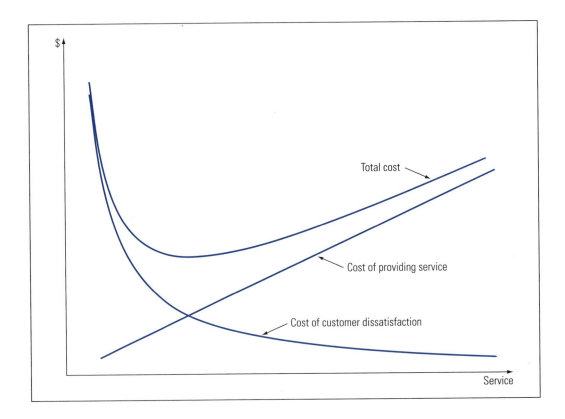

minimum by employing a large number of servers (in the form of cashiers, tellers, and technicians). However, this can be expensive, or actually wasteful, if an excessive number of idle servers is maintained. On the other hand, employing a small number of servers keeps the cost of providing service low but is likely to result in longer customer waiting times and greater customer dissatisfaction. Thus, a trade-off exists between the cost of providing service and the cost of having dissatisfied customers if service is lacking. The nature of this trade-off is illustrated in Figure 13.1.

Figure 13.1 indicates that as service levels increase, the cost of providing service also increases, but the cost of customer dissatisfaction decreases (as does the length of time customers must wait for service). As service levels decrease, the cost of providing service also decreases, but the cost of customer dissatisfaction increases. The objective in many queuing problems is to find the optimal service level that achieves an acceptable balance between the cost of providing service and customer satisfaction.

13.2 Queuing System Configurations

The queuing systems we encounter in everyday life are configured in a variety of ways. Three typical configurations are illustrated in Figure 13.2.

The first configuration in Figure 13.2 represents a single-queue, single-server system. In this configuration, customers enter the system and wait in line on a first-in, first-out (FIFO) basis until they receive service; then they exit the system. This type of queuing system is employed at most Wendy's and Taco Bell restaurants. You might also encounter this type of queuing system at some automatic teller machines (ATMs).

The second configuration in Figure 13.2 represents a single-queue, multiserver system. Here again, customers enter the system and join a FIFO queue. Upon reaching the front

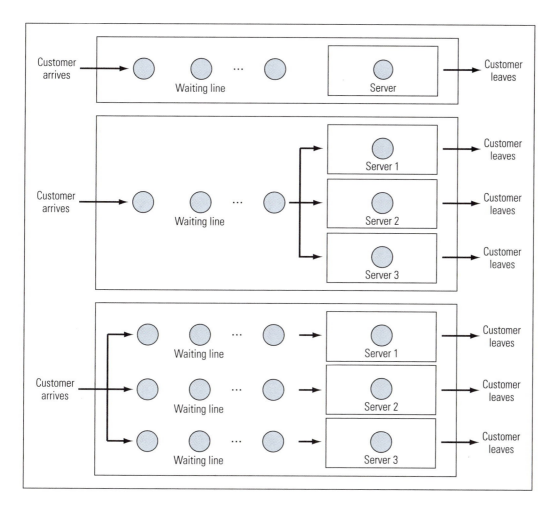

FIGURE 13.2

Examples of different queuing system configurations

of the line, a customer is serviced by the next available server. The example shows three servers, but there could be more or fewer servers depending on the problem at hand. This type of queuing system is found at most airport check-in counters, post offices, and banks.

The third configuration in Figure 13.2 represents a collection of single-queue, single-server systems. In this type of arrangement, when customers arrive, they must choose one of the queues and then wait in that line to receive service. This type of system is found at most grocery stores and most Burger King and McDonald's restaurants.

This chapter discusses queuing models that can be used to analyze the first two types of configurations shown in Figure 13.2. In some cases, the individual queues in the third configuration in Figure 13.2 can be analyzed as independent, single-queue, single-server systems. Thus, the results presented for the first type of configuration can sometimes be generalized to analyze the third configuration also.

13.3 Characteristics of Queuing Systems

To create and analyze mathematical models of the queuing configurations shown in Figure 13.2, we must make some assumptions about the way in which customers arrive to the system and the amount of time it takes for them to receive service.

13.3.1 ARRIVAL RATE

In most queuing systems, customers (or jobs in a manufacturing environment) arrive in a somewhat random fashion. That is, the number of arrivals that occurs in a given time period represents a random variable. It is often appropriate to model the arrival process in a queuing system as a Poisson random variable. To use the Poisson probability distribution, we must specify a value for the **arrival rate**, denoted as λ, representing the average number of arrivals per time period. (For a Poisson random variable, the variance of the number of arrivals per time period is also λ.) The probability of x arrivals in a specific time period is represented by

$$P(x) = \frac{\lambda^x e^{-\lambda}}{x!} \quad \text{for } x = 0, 1, 2, \ldots \qquad \textbf{13.1}$$

where e represents the base of the natural logarithm ($e = 2.71828$) and $x! = (x)(x - 1)(x - 2) \cdots (2)(1)$. (The expression $x!$ is referred to as x factorial and can be calculated using the FACT ( ) function in Excel.)

For example, suppose that calls to the customer service hotline of a computer retailer occur at a rate of five per hour and follow a Poisson probability distribution ($\lambda = 5$). The probability distribution associated with the number of calls arriving in a given hour is illustrated in Figure 13.3 (and in the file Fig13-3.xlsm that accompanies this book).

In Figure 13.3, the values in column B represent the probabilities associated with each value in column A. For example, the value in cell B5 indicates that a 0.0067 probability exists of 0 calls arriving in a given hour; cell B6 indicates that a 0.0337 probability exists of 1 call arriving; and so on. The histogram of the probability distribution indicates that, on average, we can expect approximately 5 calls to arrive in one hour. However,

FIGURE 13.3

Example of a Poisson probability distribution with mean $\lambda = 5$

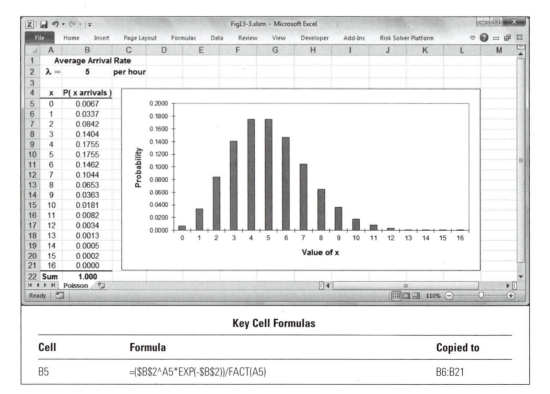

Key Cell Formulas		
Cell	**Formula**	**Copied to**
B5	=($B$2^A5*EXP(-$B$2))/FACT(A5)	B6:B21

because the Poisson distribution is skewed to the right, a significantly larger number of calls (in this case, 13 or more) could arrive in some one-hour time periods.

Figure 13.3 indicates that the probability of six calls occurring in a given hour is 0.1462. However, the six calls probably will not occur all at the same time. Some random amount of time is likely to transpire between arriving calls. This time between arrivals is known as the **interarrival time**. If the number of arrivals in a given period of time follows a Poisson distribution with mean λ, it can be shown that the interarrival times follow an exponential probability distribution with mean $1/\lambda$.

For example, if calls to the computer retailer's hotline follow a Poisson distribution and occur at an average rate of $\lambda = 5$ per hour, the interarrival times follow an exponential distribution with an average interarrival time of $1/5 = 0.2$ hours. That is, calls occur once every 12 minutes on average (because there are 60 minutes in an hour and 0.2×60 minutes $= 12$ minutes).

The exponential distribution plays a key role in queuing models. It is one of the few probability distributions that exhibits the **memoryless** (or lack of memory) property. An arrival process is memoryless if the time until the next arrival occurs does not depend on how much time has elapsed since the last arrival. The Russian mathematician Markov was the first to recognize the memoryless property of certain random variables. Therefore, the memoryless property is also sometimes referred to as the Markov or Markovian property.

All the queuing models presented in this chapter assume that arrivals follow a Poisson distribution (or, equivalently, that interarrival times follow an exponential distribution). To use these models, it is important to verify that this assumption is valid for the queuing system being modeled. One way to verify that arrivals can be approximated by the Poisson distribution is to collect data on the number of arrivals occurring per time period for several hours, days, or weeks. The average number of arrivals per time period can be calculated from these data and used as an estimate of λ. A histogram of the actual data can be constructed and compared to a histogram of the actual probabilities expected of a Poisson random variable with mean λ. If the histograms are similar, it is reasonable to assume that the arrival process is approximately Poisson. (Additional goodness-of-fit tests can be found in most texts on queuing and simulation.)

13.3.2 SERVICE RATE

A customer who arrives at a service facility spends some amount of time (possibly 0) waiting in line for service to begin. We refer to this time as **queue time**. **Service time** is the amount of time a customer spends at a service facility once the actual performance of service begins. (So service time *does not* include queue time.)

It is often appropriate to model the service times in a queuing system as an exponential random variable. To use the exponential probability distribution for this purpose, we must specify a value for the **service rate**, denoted by μ, representing the average number of customers (or jobs) that can be served per time period. The average service time per customer is $1/\mu$ time periods (and the variance of the service time per customer is $(1/\mu)^2$ time periods). Because the exponential distribution is continuous, the probability of an exponential random variable equaling any specific value is zero. Thus, probabilities associated with an exponential random variable must be defined in terms of intervals. If the distribution of service times follows an exponential distribution, the probability that the service time T of a given customer will be between t_1 and t_2 time periods is defined by:

$$P(t_1 \leq T \leq t_2) = \int_{t_1}^{t_2} \mu e^{-\mu x} dx = e^{-\mu t_1} - e^{-\mu t_2}, \quad \text{for } t_1 \leq t_2 \qquad \textbf{13.2}$$

For example, suppose that the operator on the customer service hotline can service calls at a rate of seven per hour, on average, and that the service times follow an exponential distribution ($\mu = 7$). Figure 13.4 (and the file Fig13-4.xlsm that accompanies this book) shows the probability of the service time falling within several time intervals.

In Figure 13.4, the value in cell D5 indicates that a 0.295 probability exists that it will take from 0 to 0.05 hours (or 3 minutes) to service any call. Similarly, the value in cell D9 indicates that a 0.073 probability exists that it will take between 0.2 and 0.25 hours (or from 12 to 15 minutes) to service any call.

The data and graph in Figure 13.4 indicate that for exponential distributions, shorter service times have the largest relative probability of occurring. In reality, some minimal amount of time is usually required to provide most services. This might lead us to believe that the exponential distribution would tend to underestimate the actual service time required by most customers. However, the exponential distribution also assumes that some very long service times will occur (though very infrequently). The possibility of these very long (but infrequent) service times provides a balance to the very short (but frequent) service times so that, on average, the exponential distribution provides a reasonably accurate description of the behavior of service times in many real-world problems. But keep in mind that the exponential distribution is not an adequate model of service times in all applications.

One way to verify that the service rate can be modeled using the exponential distribution is to collect data on the service times occurring per time period for several hours, days, or weeks. The average number of customers serviced per time period can be calculated from these data and used as an estimate of the service rate μ. Using actual data, a relative frequency distribution of the service times falling within various intervals can be constructed and compared to the distribution of the actual probabilities

FIGURE 13.4

Example of an exponential distribution with $\mu = 7$

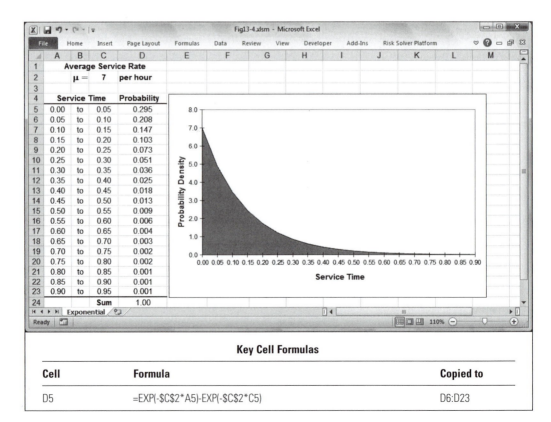

	Cell	Formula	Copied to
		Key Cell Formulas	
	D5	=EXP(-$C$2*A5)-EXP(-$C$2*C5)	D6:D23

expected for each interval for an exponential random variable with a service rate of μ (like the one shown in Figure 13.4). If the distributions are similar, it is reasonable to assume that the distribution of service times is approximately exponential. (Again, additional goodness-of-fit tests can be found in most texts on queuing and simulation.)

13.4 Kendall Notation

Given the variety of queuing models that exist, a system known as **Kendall notation** was developed to allow the key characteristics of a specific queuing model to be described in an efficient manner. With Kendall notation, simple queuing models can be described by three characteristics in the following general format:

$$1/2/3$$

The first characteristic identifies the nature of the arrival process using the following standard abbreviations:

M = Markovian interarrival times (following an exponential distribution)

D = deterministic interarrival times (not random)

The second characteristic identifies the nature of the service times using the following standard abbreviations:

M = Markovian service times (following an exponential distribution)

G = general service times (following a nonexponential distribution)

D = deterministic service times (not random)

Finally, the third characteristic indicates the number of servers available. So, using Kendall notation, an M/M/1 queue refers to a queuing model in which the time between arrivals follows an exponential distribution, the service times follow an exponential distribution, and there is one server. An M/G/3 queue refers to a model in which the interarrival times are assumed to be exponential, the service times follow some general distribution, and three servers are present.

An expanded version of Kendall notation involves specifying six (rather than three) queue characteristics. A more complete description of this notation can be found in advanced management science or queuing texts.

13.5 Queuing Models

Numerous queuing models are available to evaluate different combinations of arrival distributions, service time distributions, and other queuing characteristics. This chapter discusses only a few of these models. Typical operating characteristics of interest include the following:

Characteristic	Description
U	Utilization factor, or the percentage of time that all servers are busy
P_0	Probability that there are no units in the system
L_q	Average number of units in line waiting for service
L	Average number of units in the system (in line and being served)
W_q	Average time a unit spends in line waiting for service
W	Average time a unit spends in the system (in line and being served)
P_w	Probability that an arriving unit has to wait for service
P_n	Probability of n units in the system

Information about these operating characteristics can be helpful to managers who need to make decisions about the trade-offs between the costs of providing different levels of service and the associated impact on customers' experiences in the queuing system. Where possible, researchers have derived closed-form equations to calculate various operating characteristics of a particular queuing model. For instance, for the M/M/1 queuing model it can be shown that:

$$W = \frac{1}{\mu - \lambda}$$

$$L = \lambda W$$

$$W_q = W - \frac{1}{\mu}$$

$$L_q = \lambda W_q$$

This chapter does not show the derivation of the equations used to calculate operating characteristics. Rather, it simply states the equations for several common queuing models and shows how they can be used. The equations for the queuing models we will consider are implemented in spreadsheet templates in the file Q.xlsx that accompanies this book. Figure 13.5 shows the introduction screen for these templates.

As Figure 13.5 indicates, the templates in this file can be used to analyze four types of queuing models: the M/M/s model, the M/M/s model with finite queue length, the M/M/s model with finite arrival population, and the M/G/1 model.

FIGURE 13.5

Introductory screen for Q.xlsx queuing template file

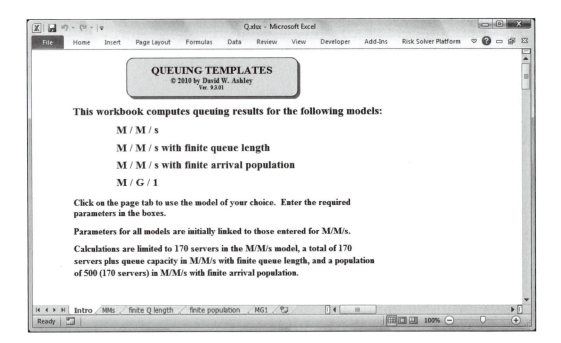

13.6 The M/M/s Model

The M/M/s model is appropriate for analyzing queuing problems where the following assumptions are met:

- There are s servers, where s is a positive integer.
- Arrivals follow a Poisson distribution and occur at an average rate of λ per time period.
- Each server provides service at an average rate of μ per time period, and actual service times follow an exponential distribution.
- Arrivals wait in a single FIFO queue and are serviced by the first available server.
- $\lambda < s\mu$

The final assumption indicates that the total service capacity of the system, $s\mu$, must be strictly greater than the rate at which arrivals occur λ. If the arrival rate exceeds the system's total service capacity, the system would fill up over time, and the queue would become infinitely long. In fact, the queue becomes infinitely long even if the average arrival rate λ is equal to the average service rate $s\mu$. To see why, note that individual arrival times and service times vary in an unpredictable manner (even though their averages may be constant). So there will be times when the servers are idle. This idle time is lost forever, and the servers will not be able to make up for this at other times when the demand for service is heavy. (Note that demand is never lost forever but is assumed to wait patiently in the queue.) This causes the servers to fall hopelessly behind if $\lambda \geq s\mu$.

The formulas describing the operating characteristics of the M/M/s model are given in Figure 13.6. Although these formulas might seem somewhat daunting, they are easy to use when implemented in a spreadsheet template.

$$U = \lambda / (s\mu)$$

$$P_0 = \left(\sum_{n=0}^{s-1} \frac{(\lambda/\mu)^n}{n!} + \frac{(\lambda/\mu)^s}{s!} \left(\frac{s\mu}{s\mu - \lambda} \right) \right)^{-1}$$

$$L_q = \frac{P_0(\lambda/\mu)^{s+1}}{(s-1)!(s - \lambda/\mu)^2}$$

$$L = L_q + \frac{\lambda}{\mu}$$

$$W_q = \frac{L_q}{\lambda}$$

$$W = W_q + \frac{1}{\mu}$$

$$P_w = \frac{1}{s!} \left(\frac{\lambda}{\mu} \right)^s \left(\frac{s\mu}{s\mu - \lambda} \right) P_0$$

$$P_n = \begin{cases} \dfrac{(\lambda/\mu)^n}{n!} P_0, & \text{for } n \leq s \\ \dfrac{(\lambda/\mu)^n}{s! s^{(n-s)}} P_0, & \text{for } n > s \end{cases}$$

FIGURE 13.6

Formulas describing the operating characteristics of an M/M/s queue

13.6.1 AN EXAMPLE

The following example illustrates how the M/M/s model might be used.

> The customer support hotline for Bitway Computers is currently staffed by a single technician. Calls arrive randomly at a rate of five per hour and follow a Poisson distribution. The technician can service calls at an average rate of seven per hour, but the actual time required to handle a given call is an exponential random variable. The president of Bitway, Rod Taylor, has received numerous complaints from customers about the length of time they must wait "on hold" for service when calling the hotline. Rod wants to determine the average length of time customers currently wait before the technician answers their calls. If the average waiting time is more than five minutes, he wants to determine how many technicians would be required to reduce the average waiting time to two minutes or less.

13.6.2 THE CURRENT SITUATION

Because only one technician (or server) currently staffs Bitway's customer service hotline, we can calculate the operating characteristics for the hotline using an M/M/1 queuing model. Figure 13.7 shows the results of this model for Bitway's current configuration.

Cells E2, E3, and E4 contain the values for the arrival rate, service rate, and number of servers in our example problem, respectively. The various operating characteristics of this model are calculated automatically in column F.

The value in cell F12 indicates that a 0.7143 probability exists that callers to Bitway's customer service hotline must wait on hold before receiving service from the technician. The value in cell F10 indicates that the average length of this wait is 0.3571 hours (or approximately 21.42 minutes). The value in cell F11 indicates that, on average, a caller

FIGURE 13.7

Results of the M/M/1 model for Bitway's customer service model

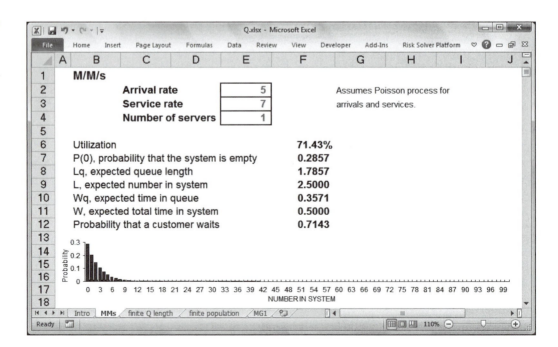

spends a total of 0.5 hours (or 30 minutes) waiting for service and being served under Bitway's current hotline configuration. Thus, it appears that the customer complaints to Bitway's president are justifiable.

13.6.3 ADDING A SERVER

To improve the level of service on the hotline, Bitway could investigate how the operating characteristics of the system would change if two technicians were assigned to answer calls. That is, incoming calls could be handled by either one of two equally capable technicians. We can calculate the operating characteristics for this configuration using an M/M/2 queuing model, as shown in Figure 13.8.

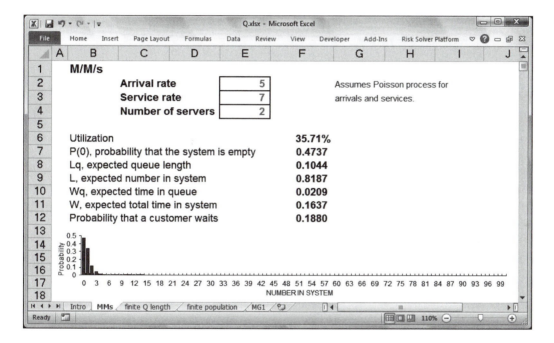

FIGURE 13.8

Results of the M/M/2 model for Bitway's customer service hotline

The value in cell F12 indicates that with two servers, the probability that a caller must wait before receiving service drops significantly from 0.7143 to 0.1880. Similarly, cell F10 indicates that the average amount of time a caller must wait before service begins drops to 0.0209 hours (or approximately 1.25 minutes). Thus, it seems that adding a second technician to the customer service hotline would achieve the two-minute average waiting time objective Rod wants.

Although the addition of a second server greatly reduces the average time hotline callers spend waiting for service to begin, it does not reduce the expected *service time*. For the M/M/1 model in Figure 13.7, which includes only one server, the expected total time in the system is 0.5 hours, and the expected queue time is 0.3571 hours. This implies that the expected service time is 0.5 − 0.3571 = 0.1429 hours. For the M/M/2 model in Figure 13.8, which includes two servers, the expected total time in the system is 0.1637 hours, and the expected queue time is 0.0209 hours. This implies an expected service time of 0.1637 − 0.0209 = 0.1429 hours (allowing for a slight rounding error). The M/M/2 model assumes that both servers can provide service at the same rate—in this case, an average of seven calls per hour. Therefore, the average service time per call should be $1/7 = 0.1429$ hours, which is consistent with the observed results.

13.6.4 ECONOMIC ANALYSIS

Bitway will undoubtedly incur some additional costs in going from one to two customer support technicians. This might include the cost of salary and benefits for the additional technician and perhaps an additional telephone line. However, the improved service level provided by the two-server system should reduce the number of customer complaints and perhaps lead to favorable word-of-mouth advertising and increased business for the company. Rod could attempt to quantify these benefits and compare them to the cost of adding a customer support technician. Alternatively, Rod may simply view the addition of the customer support technician as a competitive necessity.

13.7 The M/M/s Model with Finite Queue Length

The results for the M/M/s models in Figures 13.7 and 13.8 assume that the size or capacity of the waiting area is infinite, so that all arrivals to the system join the queue and wait for service. In some situations, however, the size or capacity of the waiting area might be restricted—in other words, there might be a finite queue length. The formulas describing the operating characteristics of an M/M/s queue with a finite queue length of K are summarized in Figure 13.9.

FIGURE 13.9

Formulas describing the operating characteristics of an M/M/s queue with a finite queue length of K

$$U = (L - L_q)/s$$

$$P_0 = \left(1 + \sum_{n=1}^{s} \frac{(\lambda/\mu)^n}{n!} + \frac{(\lambda/\mu)^s}{s!} \sum_{n=s+1}^{K} \left(\frac{\lambda}{s\mu}\right)^{n-s}\right)^{-1}$$

$$P_n = \frac{(\lambda/\mu)^n}{n!} P_0, \text{ for } n = 1, 2, \ldots, s$$

$$P_n = \frac{(\lambda/\mu)^n}{s!s^{n-s}} P_0, \text{ for } n = s+1, s+2, \ldots, K+s$$

$$P_n = 0, \text{ for } n > K + s$$

$$L_q = \frac{P_0(\lambda/\mu)^s \rho}{s!(1-\rho)^2} (1 - \rho^{K-s} - (K-s)\rho^{K-s}(1-\rho)), \text{ where } \rho = \lambda/(s\mu)$$

$$L = \sum_{n=0}^{s-1} nP_n + L_q + s\left(1 - \sum_{n=0}^{s-1} P_n\right)$$

$$W_q = \frac{L_q}{\lambda(1 - P_K)}$$

$$W = \frac{L}{\lambda(1 - P_K)}$$

To see how this queuing model might be used, suppose that Bitway's telephone system can keep a maximum of five calls on hold at any point in time. If a new call is made to the hotline when five calls are already in the queue, the new call receives a busy signal. One way to reduce the number of calls encountering busy signals is to increase the number of calls that can be put on hold. However, if a call is answered only to be put on hold for a long time, the caller might find this more annoying than receiving a busy signal. Thus, Rod might want to investigate what effect adding a second technician to answer hotline calls would have on the number of calls receiving busy signals and on the average time callers must wait before receiving service.

13.7.1 THE CURRENT SITUATION

Because only one technician (or server) currently staffs Bitway's customer service hotline, we can calculate the current operating characteristics for the hotline using an M/M/1 queuing model with a finite queue length of 5. Figure 13.10 shows the results of this model for Bitway's current configuration.

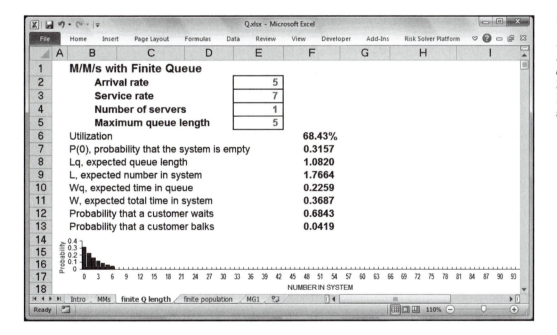

FIGURE 13.10

Results of the M/M/1 model with a finite queue length of five for Bitway's customer service hotline

Cells E2, E3, and E4 contain the values for the arrival rate, service rate, and number of servers in our example problem, respectively. Cell E5 contains the maximum queue length of five.

The value in cell F13 indicates that a 0.0419 probability exists that callers to Bitway's customer service hotline will balk (or, in this case, receive a busy signal). A **balk** refers to an arrival that does not join the queue because the queue is full or too long. The value in cell F10 indicates that the average length of this wait is 0.2259 hours (or approximately 13.55 minutes). The value in cell F11 indicates that, on average, a caller spends a total of 0.3687 hours (or 22.12 minutes) either waiting for service or being served under Bitway's current hotline configuration.

FIGURE 13.11

Results of the M/M/2 model with a finite queue length of five for Bitway's customer service hotline

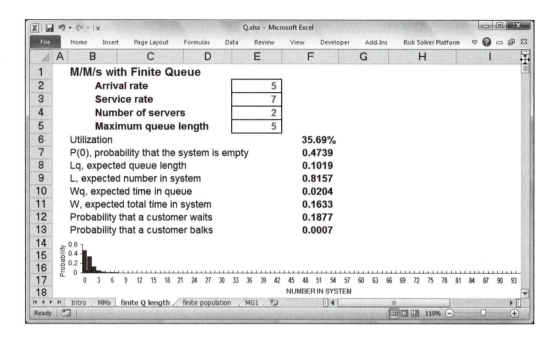

13.7.2 ADDING A SERVER

To improve the level of service on the hotline, Bitway could investigate how the operating characteristics of the system would change if two technicians were assigned to answer calls. We can calculate the operating characteristics for this configuration using an M/M/2 queuing model with a finite queue length of five, as shown in Figure 13.11.

The value in cell F13 indicates that, with two servers, the probability that a caller receives a busy signal drops to 0.0007. Similarly, cell F10 indicates that the average amount of time a caller must wait before service begins drops to 0.0204 hours (or approximately 1.22 minutes). Thus, it seems that adding a second technician to the customer service hotline would achieve the two-minute average waiting time objective Rod wants and would virtually eliminate any chance of a customer receiving a busy signal. Here again, Rod should consider weighing the costs of adding the additional support technician against the benefits of eliminating the chances of customers receiving busy signals when they call the customer support hotline.

13.8 The M/M/s Model with Finite Population

The previous queuing models assume that the customers (or calls) arriving at the queuing system come from a population of potential customers that is infinite, or extremely large. Under this assumption, the mean arrival rate, λ, remains constant regardless of the number of calls in the system.

In some queuing problems, however, the possible number of arriving customers is finite. In other words, these queuing models have a finite arrival (or calling) population. In such a model, the average arrival rate for the system changes depending on the number of customers in the queue. The M/M/s model for finite arrival populations is appropriate for analyzing queuing problems where the following assumptions are met:

- There are s servers, where s is a positive integer.
- There are N potential customers in the arrival population.
- The arrival pattern of *each customer* follows a Poisson distribution with a mean arrival rate of λ per time period.
- Each server provides service at an average rate of μ per time period, and actual service times follow an exponential distribution.
- Arrivals wait in a single FIFO queue and are serviced by the first available server.

Note that the average arrival rate for this model (λ) is defined in terms of the rate at which *each customer* arrives. The formulas describing the operating characteristics for an M/M/s queue with a finite arrival population of size N are summarized in Figure 13.12.

$$P_0 = \left(\sum_{n=0}^{s-1} \frac{N!}{(N-n)!n!} \left(\frac{\lambda}{\mu}\right)^n + \sum_{n=s}^{N} \frac{N!}{(N-n)!s!s^{n-s}} \left(\frac{\lambda}{\mu}\right)^n \right)^{-1}$$

$$P_n = \frac{N!}{(N-n)!n!} \left(\frac{\lambda}{\mu}\right)^n P_0, \text{ if } 0 \leq n \leq s$$

$$P_n = \frac{N!}{(N-n)!s!s^{n-s}} \left(\frac{\lambda}{\mu}\right)^n P_0, \text{ if } s < n \leq N$$

$$P_n = 0, \text{ if } n > N$$

$$L_q = \sum_{n=s}^{N} (n-s)P_n$$

$$L = \sum_{n=0}^{s-1} nP_n + L_q + s\left(1 - \sum_{n=0}^{s-1} P_n\right)$$

$$W_q = \frac{L_q}{\lambda(N-L)}$$

$$W = \frac{L}{\lambda(N-L)}$$

FIGURE 13.12

Formulas describing the operating characteristics of an M/M/s queue with a finite arrival population of size N

13.8.1 AN EXAMPLE

One of the most common applications for the M/M/s model with a finite arrival population is the machine repair problem, as illustrated in the following example.

The Miller Manufacturing Company owns 10 identical machines that it uses in the production of colored nylon thread for the textile industry. Machine breakdowns occur following a Poisson distribution with an average of 0.01 breakdowns occurring per operating hour per machine. The company loses $100 each hour a machine is inoperable. The company employs one technician to fix these machines when they break down. Service times to repair the machines are exponentially distributed with an average of eight hours per repair. Thus, service is performed at a rate of 1/8 machines per hour. Management wants to analyze what impact adding another service technician would have on the average length of time required to fix a machine when it breaks down. Service technicians are paid $20 per hour.

13.8.2 THE CURRENT SITUATION

The 10 machines in this problem represent a finite set of objects that can break down. Therefore, the M/M/s model for a finite calling operation is appropriate to use for analyzing this problem. The current operating characteristics for Miller Manufacturing's machine repair problem are summarized in Figure 13.13.

FIGURE 13.13

Results of an M/M/1 model with a finite population of 10 machines for Miller Manufacturing's machine repair problem

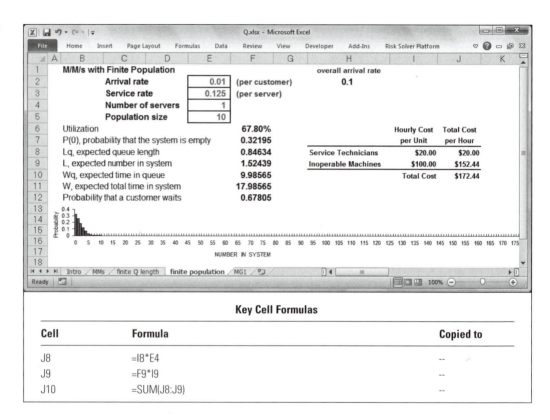

Key Cell Formulas

Cell	Formula	Copied to
J8	=I8*E4	--
J9	=F9*I9	--
J10	=SUM(J8:J9)	--

Because the individual machines break down at a rate of 0.01 per hour, this is the rate at which individual machines "arrive" for repair. Thus, cell E2 contains the value 0.01 to represent the arrival rate per customer (machine). The technician can service broken machines at an average rate of $1/8 = 0.125$ machines per hour, as indicated in cell E3. The number of servers (or technicians) is shown in cell E4. Because there are 10 machines that can break down, cell E5 contains a population size of 10. The spreadsheet calculates the overall arrival rate shown in cell H2. Because there are 10 machines, each with a 0.01 probability of breaking down each hour, the overall arrival rate of broken machines is $10 \times 0.01 = 0.1$, as indicated in cell H2.

The operating characteristics for this system are calculated in cells F6 through F12. According to cell F11, whenever a machine breaks down, it is out of operation for an average of 17.98 hours. Of this total down time, cell F10 indicates that the machine spends approximately 10 hours waiting for service to begin. Cell F9 indicates that approximately 1.524 machines are out of operation at any point in time.

We used columns H through J of the worksheet to calculate the economic consequences of the current situation. There is one server (or service technician) in this problem who is paid $20 per hour. According to cell F9, an average of approximately 1.524 machines are broken in any given hour. Because the company loses $100 each hour a machine is inoperable, cell J9 indicates the company is presently losing about $152.44 per hour due to machine down time. Thus, with a single service technician, the company is incurring costs at the rate of $172.44 per hour.

Software Note

The Q.xlsx file comes "protected" so that you will not inadvertently write over or delete important formulas in this template. Sometimes, you may want to turn off this protection on a sheet so you can do your own calculations off to the side or format your results (as shown in Figure 13.13). To do this, follow these steps:

1. Click Review.
2. Click Unprotect Sheet.

If you unprotect a sheet, you should take special care not to alter any of the formulas on the sheet.

13.8.3 ADDING SERVERS

Figure 13.14 shows the expected operation of this system if Miller Manufacturing adds another service technician.

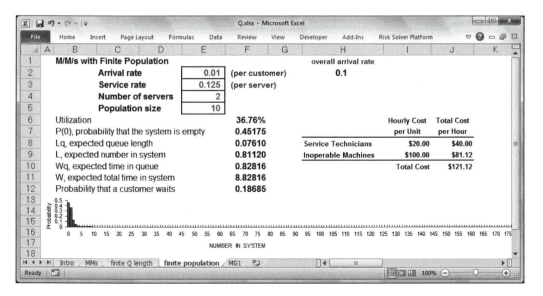

FIGURE 13.14

Results of an M/M/2 model with a finite population of 10 machines for Miller Manufacturing's machine repair problem

Cell F10 indicates that when a machine breaks down, repairs start, on average, in only 0.82 hours (or approximately 49 minutes), in comparison to the 10-hour waiting time with only one technician. Similarly, cell F9 indicates that with two technicians, an average of only 0.81 machines are out of operation at any point in time. Thus, by adding another repair technician, Miller Manufacturing can keep approximately one more machine in operation at all times. While the additional service technician increases the total hourly cost to $40, the decrease in the average number of machines in the system saves the company $71.32 per hour (that is, 152.44 − 81.12 = 71.32). The net effect is a cost savings of $51.32 as the total hourly cost in cell J10 drops to $121.12.

Figure 13.15 shows the results of adding a third service technician for this problem. Notice that this has the effect of increasing labor costs by $20 per hour over the solution shown in Figure 13.14 while reducing the losses due to idle machines by only $6.36. So, as we go from two to three service technicians, the total hourly cost increases from $121.12 to $134.76 per hour. Thus, the optimal solution is for Miller Manufacturing to employ two service technicians because this results in the smallest total hourly cost.

FIGURE 13.15

Results of an M/M/3 model with a finite population of 10 machines for Miller Manufacturing's machine repair problem

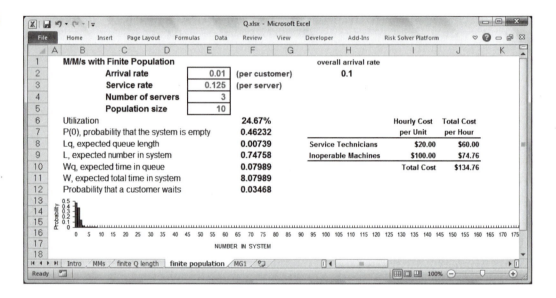

13.9 The M/G/1 Model

All the models presented so far assume that service times follow an exponential distribution. As noted earlier in Figure 13.4, random service times from an exponential distribution can assume *any* positive value. However, in some situations, this assumption is unrealistic. For example, consider the time required to change the oil in a car at an auto service center. This service probably requires *at least* 10 minutes and might require up to 30, 45, or even 60 minutes, depending on the service being performed. The M/G/1 queuing model enables us to analyze queuing problems in which service times cannot be modeled accurately using an exponential distribution. The formulas describing the operating characteristics of an M/G/1 queue are summarized in Figure 13.16.

The M/G/1 queuing model is quite remarkable because it can be used to compute the operating characteristics for *any* one-server queuing system where arrivals follow a Poisson distribution, and the mean μ and standard deviation σ of the service times are known. That is, the formulas in Figure 13.16 do not require that service times follow one

$$P_0 = 1 - \lambda/\mu$$

$$L_q = \frac{\lambda^2\sigma^2 + (\lambda/\mu)^2}{2(1 - \lambda/\mu)}$$

$$L = L_q + \lambda/\mu$$

$$W_q = L_q/\lambda$$

$$W = W_q + 1/\mu$$

$$P_w = \lambda/\mu$$

FIGURE 13.16

Formulas describing the operating characteristics of an M/G/1 queue

specific probability distribution. The following example illustrates the use of the M/G/1 queuing model.

> Zippy-Lube is a drive-through automotive oil change business that operates 10 hours a day, 6 days a week. The profit margin on an oil change at Zippy-Lube is $15. Cars arrive randomly at the Zippy-Lube oil change center following a Poisson distribution at an average rate of 3.5 cars per hour. After reviewing the historical data on operations at this business, the owner of Zippy-Lube, Olie Boe, has determined that the average service time per car is 15 minutes (or 0.25 hours) with a standard deviation of 2 minutes (or 0.0333 hours). Olie has the opportunity to purchase a new automated oil dispensing device that costs $5,000. The manufacturer's representative claims this device will reduce the average service time by 3 minutes per car. (Currently, Olie's employees manually open and pour individual cans of oil.) Olie wants to analyze the impact the new automated device would have on his business and determine the payback period for this device.

13.9.1 THE CURRENT SITUATION

We can model Olie's current service facility as an M/G/1 queue. The operating characteristics of this facility are shown in Figure 13.17.

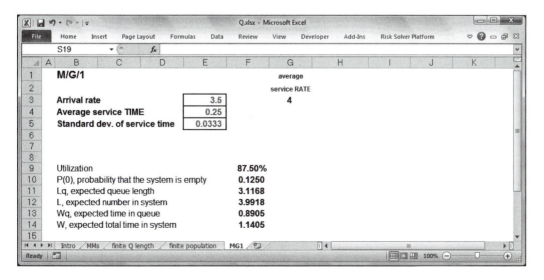

FIGURE 13.17

Results of an M/G/1 model for the original Zippy-Lube problem

Cell E3 contains the average arrival rate of 3.5 cars per hour. The average service time per car (also in hours) is indicated in cell E4, and the standard deviation of the service time (in hours) is indicated in cell E5.

Cell F11 shows that an average of about 3.12 cars wait for service at any given point in time. Cell F14 indicates that, on average, 1.14 hours (or about 68 minutes) elapse between the time a car arrives and leaves the system.

13.9.2 ADDING THE AUTOMATED DISPENSING DEVICE

If Olie purchases the automated oil dispensing device, the average service time per car should drop to 12 minutes (or 0.20 hours). Figure 13.18 show the impact this would have if the arrival rate remained constant at 3.5 cars per hour.

FIGURE 13.18

Results of an M/G/1 model for the Zippy-Lube problem after purchasing the automatic oil dispensing machine and assuming an increase in arrivals

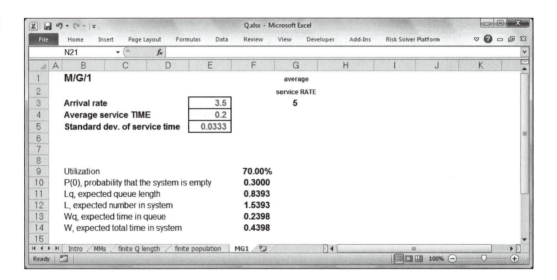

The value in cell F14 indicates that going to the automated oil dispensing device reduces the amount of time a car spends in the system from 1.14 hours to 0.4398 hours (or about 26 minutes). Cell F11 indicates that the expected queue in front of the service bay consists of only 0.8393 cars, on average. Thus, the addition of a new oil dispensing device would significantly improve customer service.

The shorter queue at Zippy-Lube resulting from the acquisition of the automated dispensing device would likely result in an increase in the arrival rate because customers who previously balked when confronted with a lengthy queue might now consider stopping for service. Thus, Olie might be interested in determining just how much the arrival rate could increase before the average queue length returned to its original level of about 3.12 shown in Figure 13.17. We can use the Goal Seek tool to answer this question by following these steps:

1. Click Data, What-If Analysis.
2. Click Goal Seek.
3. Fill in the Goal Seek dialog box as shown in Figure 13.19.
4. Click OK.

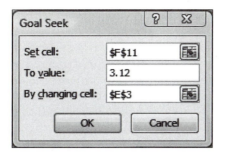

FIGURE 13.19

Goal Seek settings to determine the arrival rate that produces an average queue length of 3.12 cars

The results of this Goal Seek analysis are shown in Figure 13.20. Here, we see that if the arrival rate increases to 4.37 cars per hour, the average length of the queue will return to approximately 3.12. Thus, by purchasing the automatic oil dispensing machine, it is reasonable to expect that the average number of cars arriving for service at Zippy-Lube might increase from 3.5 per hour to approximately 4.371.

Column I in Figure 13.20 summarizes the financial impact of purchasing the new oil dispensing machine. Because the arrival rate may be expected to increase by approximately 0.871 cars per hour, weekly profits should increase by approximately $783.63 per week. If this increase in profits occurs, the payback period for the new machine will be approximately 6.38 weeks.

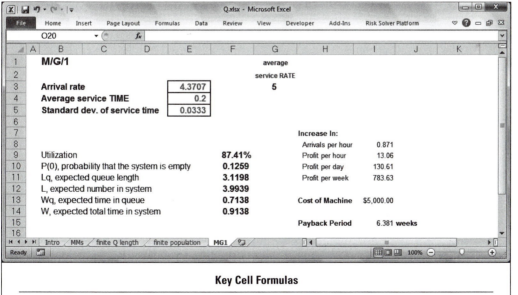

FIGURE 13.20

Results of an M/G/1 model for the Zippy-Lube problem after purchasing the automatic oil dispensing machine and assuming arrival rate will increase

Key Cell Formulas

Cell	Formula	Copied to
I8	=E3-3.5	--
I9	=I8*15	--
I10	=I9*10	--
I11	=I10*6	--
I13	=5000	--
I15	=I13/I11	--

13.10 The M/D/1 Model

The M/G/1 model can be used when service times are random with known mean and standard deviation. However, service times might not be random in some queuing systems. For example, in a manufacturing environment, it is not unusual to have a queue of material or subassemblies waiting to be serviced by a certain machine. The machine time required to perform the service might be very predictable—such as exactly 10 seconds of machine time per piece. Similarly, an automatic car wash might spend exactly the same amount of time on each car it services. The M/D/1 model can be used in these types of situations in which the service times are deterministic (not random).

The results for an M/D/1 model can be obtained using the M/G/1 model by setting the standard deviation of the service time to 0 ($\sigma = 0$). Setting $\sigma = 0$ indicates that no variability exists in the service times, and, therefore, the service time for each unit is equal to the average service time μ.

13.11 Simulating Queues and the Steady-state Assumption

Queuing theory is one of the oldest and most well-researched areas of management science. Discussions of other types of queuing models can be found in advanced texts on management science and in texts devoted solely to queuing theory. However, keep in mind that the technique of simulation can also be used to analyze virtually any queuing problem you might encounter. Indeed, not all queuing models have closed-form equations to describe their operating characteristics. So, simulation is often the only means available for analyzing complex queuing systems where customers **balk** (don't join a queue upon arrival), **renege** (leave a queue before being served), or **jockey** (switch from one queue to another).

The formulas used in this chapter describe the *steady-state* operations of the various queuing systems presented. At the beginning of each day, most queuing systems start in an "empty and idle" condition and go through a **transient** period as business activity gradually builds up to reach the normal, or **steady-state**, level of operation. The queuing models presented describe only the behavior of the system in its steady-state level of operation. A queuing system can have different levels of steady-state operations at different times throughout the day. For example, a restaurant might have one steady-state level of operation for breakfast and different steady-state levels at lunch and dinner. So, before using the models in this chapter, it is important to identify the arrival rate and service rate for the specific steady-state level of operation you want to study. If an analysis of the transient phase is needed or if you want to model the operation of the system across different steady-state levels, you should use simulation.

Figure 13.21 (and the file Fig13-21.xlsm that accompanies this book) contains a spreadsheet model that simulates the operation of a single server (M/M/1) queue and plots several graphs associated with different operating characteristics of the system. (If you open this file, your graph may not match the one in Figure 13.21 because the random numbers used in the simulation will change.) The graph in Figure 13.21 shows a plot of the average waiting time per customer (W_q) for 500 customers. The horizontal line indicates the steady-state value of W_q. Note that several hundred customers are processed in the system in this transient period before the observed average waiting time begins to converge on its steady-state value.

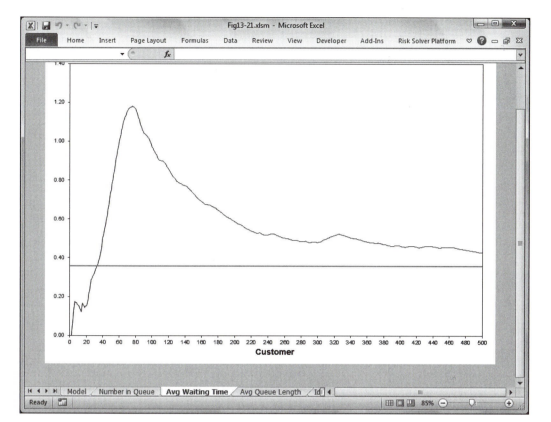

FIGURE 13.21

Graph of the average waiting time in the simulation of a single-server queuing system

13.12 Summary

Waiting lines, or queues, are a common occurrence in many types of businesses. The study of the operating characteristics of waiting lines is known as queuing theory. Numerous mathematical models are available to represent and study the behavior of different types of queues. These models have different assumptions about the nature of the arrival process to the queuing system, the allowable size and nature of the queuing discipline, and the service process within the system. For many models, closed-form equations have been developed to describe various operating characteristics of the system. When closed-form solutions are not possible, the technique of simulation must be used to analyze the behavior of the system.

13.13 References

Gilliam, R. "An Application of Queueing Theory to Airport Passenger Security Screening." *Interfaces*, vol. 9, 1979.

Gross, D., and C. Harris. *Fundamentals of Queueing Theory*. New York: Wiley, 1985.

Hall, R. *Queueing Methods for Service and Manufacturing*. Englewood Cliffs, NJ: Prentice Hall, 1991.

Kolesar, P. "A Quick and Dirty Response to the Quick and Dirty Crowd: Particularly to Jack Byrd's 'The Value of Queueing Theory'." *Interfaces*, vol. 9, 1979.

Mann, L. "Queue Culture: The Waiting Line as a Social System." *American Journal of Sociology*, vol. 75, 1969.

Quinn, P., et al. "Allocating Telecommunications Resources at LL Bean, Inc." *Interfaces*, vol. 21, 1991.

THE WORLD OF MANAGEMENT SCIENCE

"Wait Watchers" Try to Take Stress Out of Standing in Line

Standing in line—at the bank, the market, the movies—is the time-waster everyone loves to hate. Stand in just one 15-minute line a day, every day, and kiss goodbye four days of idle time by year's end.

While we've been waiting and grumbling, researchers have been analyzing lines with an eye to making them, if not shorter, at least less stressful.

The field of line analysis—more scientifically known as queuing theory—began in the early 1900s when a Danish telephone engineer devised a mathematical approach to help design phone switches. Researchers found that the principles developed through that system, which helped process calls more efficiently, could be applied to help move people through lines more efficiently.

The concept has spread from the communications and computer industries to other fields, helping modern researchers predict such things as how long customers might wait for a restaurant lunch or how many customers might visit a bank ATM at noon on Saturday. Now, some researchers have gone beyond a mere mathematical analysis of lines, focusing as well on our psychological reactions.

In one recent study, Richard Larson, a professor of electrical engineering at the Massachusetts Institute of Technology, wanted to determine which of two approaches would be more tolerable to Bank of Boston customers. As Larson's researchers filmed the customers, one group watched an electronic news board while waiting in line; the other group was advised via an electric clock how long the wait would be before each one entered the line. About 300 customers, nearly a third of those filmed, were interviewed after they finished their transactions. The findings, published in the *Sloan Management Review*, an MIT publication circulated to corporate managers, showed the following:

- Customers in both lines overestimated their waits by nearly a minute; those who watched the news board overestimated the most. On average, customers thought they waited 5.1 minutes to see a teller but actually waited 4.2 minutes.
- Watching the news board did not change customers' perceptions of their waiting time, but it did make the time spent more palatable, customers reported. (After the bank removed the news board, many customers asked that it be reinstalled.)
- The news board also seemed to make customers less fidgety. Without it, they touched their faces and played with their hair. With the news board in view, they stood still with their arms at their sides.
- Customers who were advised of the length of the line via an electronic clock at the entry did not find the experience less stressful than those not told the expected waiting time, much to Larson's surprise. Nor were they more satisfied than the other group with the service. The electronic clock's display of waiting time may backfire, Larson speculates, by making respondents even more aware of time wasted standing in line.

(Continued)

- Customers in the lines with the clock tended to play "beat the clock." They felt they had "won" if they spent less time in line than predicted. The clock also seemed to make more customers balk at joining the line if the predicted delay was lengthy.
- In both lines, customers altered their definition of a "reasonable" wait depending on their time of arrival. They were willing to wait longer during lunch time than during other times of day.

Larson's recent findings bear out a formula published in 1984 by David Maister, a former Harvard Business School faculty member and now a business consultant. When it comes to lines, Maister said, satisfaction is tied to both perception and expectation.

"Nowhere in that [equation] does reality appear," Maister said with a laugh during a telephone interview. Giving a personal example of how perception influences reaction, he said he would wait "40 minutes for a performance by a world-class musician but less than 30 seconds for a hamburger."

Larson, a professional "wait watcher" for 20 years, puts it a bit differently: "When it comes to customer satisfaction, perception is reality."

If those concepts are true, taming customer unrest does not necessarily mean a business must beef up its staff to eliminate lines, Larson and Maister contend. It's much more a matter of "perception management," they say. "People in the service industries who think they have a line problem may be able to virtually erase customer dissatisfaction and customer complaints not by changing the statistic of the wait but by changing the environment of it," Larson said.

He points to a number of companies already actively wooing waiters. Some companies use a "queue delay guarantee," giving customers free dessert or money if the wait exceeds a preset time period.

Larson predicts customers can expect lines that segment them by personality type. Impatient souls may have the option of paying more to join an automated express line; "people watchers" could opt to wait for less expensive, friendlier human service.

Source: Kathleen Doheny, "Wait Watchers Try to Take Stress Out of Standing in Line," *Los Angeles Times*, 7/15/91, p. B3. Copyright © Kathleen Doheny. Reprinted with permission from Kathleen Doheny.

Questions and Problems

1. Consider the three queuing configurations shown in Figure 13.2. For each configuration, describe a situation (besides the examples mentioned in the chapter) in which you have encountered or observed the same type of queuing system.
2. Of the queuing configurations shown in Figure 13.2, which would you prefer to wait in? Explain your response.
3. This chapter implies that customers find waiting in line to be an unpleasant experience. In addition to reducing the length of the wait itself, what other steps could a business take to reduce the frustration customers experience while waiting? Give specific examples.
4. Describe a situation in which a business might want customers to wait some amount of time before receiving service.

5. The day after a snow storm, cars arrive at Mel's Auto-Wash at an average rate of 10 per hour according to a Poisson process. The automated car washing process takes exactly 5 minutes from start to finish.
   a. What is the probability that an arriving car will find the car wash empty?
   b. On average, how many cars are waiting for service?
   c. On average, what is the total length of time (from arrival to departure) cars will spend at the car wash?
6. Tri-Cities Bank has a single drive-in teller window. On Friday mornings, customers arrive at the drive-in window randomly, following a Poisson distribution at an average rate of 30 per hour.
   a. How many customers arrive per minute, on average?
   b. How many customers would you expect to arrive in a 10-minute interval?
   c. Use equation 13.1 to determine the probability of exactly 0, 1, 2, and 3 arrivals in a 10-minute interval. (You can verify your answers using the POISSON( ) function in Excel.)
   d. What is the probability of more than three arrivals occurring in a 10-minute interval?
7. Refer to question 6. Suppose that service at the drive-in window is provided at a rate of 40 customers per hour and follows an exponential distribution.
   a. What is the expected service time per customer?
   b. Use equation 13.2 to determine the probability that a customer's service time is one minute or less. (Verify your answer using the EXPONDIST( ) function in Excel.)
   c. Compute the probabilities that the customer's service time is between two and five minutes, less than four minutes, and more than three minutes.
8. Refer to questions 6 and 7 and answer the following questions:
   a. What is the probability that the drive-in window is empty?
   b. What is the probability that a customer must wait for service?
   c. On average, how many cars wait for service?
   d. On average, what is the total length of time a customer spends in the system?
   e. On average, what is the total length of time a customer spends in the queue?
   f. What service rate would be required to reduce the average total time in the system to two minutes? (*Hint*: You can use Solver or simple what-if analysis to answer this question.)
9. On Friday nights, patients arrive at the emergency room at Mercy Hospital following a Poisson distribution at an average rate of seven per hour. Assume that an emergency-room physician can treat an average of three patients per hour, and that the treatment times follow an exponential distribution. The board of directors for Mercy Hospital wants patients arriving at the emergency room to wait no more than five minutes before seeing a doctor.
   a. How many emergency-room doctors should be scheduled on Friday nights to achieve the hospital's objective?
10. Seabreeze Furniture in Orlando maintains a large, central warehouse where it stores items until they are sold or needed by the company's many stores in the central Florida area. A four-person crew works at the warehouse to load or unload trucks that arrive at the warehouse at a rate of one per hour (with exponentially distributed interarrival times). The time it takes the crew to unload each truck follows an exponential distribution with a mean service rate of four trucks per hour. Each worker costs the company $21 per hour in wages and benefits. Seabreeze's management is currently trying to cut costs and is considering reducing the number of workers on this warehouse crew. They believe three workers would be able to provide a service

rate of three trucks per hour, two workers a service rate of two trucks per hour, and one worker a service rate of one truck per hour. The company estimates it costs $35 for each hour a truck spends at the loading dock (whether it is waiting for service or being loaded or unloaded).

a. Should Seabreeze ever consider having just one worker on the crew? Explain your answer.

b. For each possible crew size, determine the expected queue length, expected total time in the system, the probability that a customer waits, and the total hourly cost.

c. What crew size would you recommend?

11. The Madrid Mist outlet store at Chiswell Mills sells discount luggage and does most of its daily business in the evening between the hours of 6 and 9 pm. During this time, customers arrive at the checkout desk at a rate of one every two minutes following a Poisson distribution. The check-out operation takes an average of three minutes per customer and can be approximated well by an exponential distribution. Madrid Mist's corporate policy is that customers should not have to wait longer than one minute to begin the check out operation.

a. What is the average service rate per minute?

b. What is the average arrival rate per minute?

c. What would happen if the store operated a single check-out station during the time period in question?

d. How many check-out stations should the store plan to operate during this time period to stay within the corporate policy on check-out operations?

12. Customers checking out at Food Tiger arrive in a single-line queue served by two cashiers at a rate of eight per hour according to a Poisson distribution. Each cashier processes customers at a rate of eight per hour according to an exponential distribution.

a. If, on average, customers spend 30 minutes shopping before getting in the check-out line, what is the average time a customer spends in the store?

b. What is the average number of customers waiting for service in the check-out line?

c. What is the probability that a customer must wait?

d. What assumption did you make to answer this question?

13. The manager of the Radford Credit Union (RCU) wants to determine how many part-time tellers to employ to cover the peak demand time in its lobby from 11:00 am to 2:00 pm. RCU currently has three full-time tellers that handle the demand during the rest of the day, but during this peak demand time, customers have been complaining that the wait time for service is too long. The manager at RCU has determined that customers arrive according to a Poisson distribution with an average of 60 arrivals per hour during the peak period. Each teller services customers at a rate of 24 per hour, with service times following an exponential distribution.

a. On average, how long must customers wait in line before service begins?

b. Once service begins for a customer, how long does it take to complete the transaction, on average?

c. If one part-time teller is hired to work during the peak time period, what effect would this have on the average amount of time a customer spends waiting in the queue?

d. If one part-time teller is hired to work during the peak time period, what effect would this have on the average amount of time it takes to serve a customer?

14. The Westland Title Insurance Company leases one copying machine for $45 per day that is used by all individuals at their office. An average of five persons per hour arrive to use this machine, with each person using it for an average of eight

minutes. Assume the interarrival times and copying times are exponentially distributed.

   a. What is the probability that a person arriving to use the machine will find it idle?

   b. On average, how long will a person have to wait before getting to use the machine?

   c. On average, how many people will be using or waiting to use the copy machine?

   d. Suppose that the people who use the copy machine are paid an average of $9 per hour. On average, how much does the company spend in wages during each eight-hour day paying the people who are using or waiting to use the copy machine?

   e. If the company can lease another copying machine for $45 per day, should they do it?

15. The Orange Blossom Marathon takes place in Orlando, Florida, each December. The organizers of this race are trying to solve a problem that occurs at the finish line each year. Thousands of runners take part in this race. The fastest runners finish the 26-mile course in just over two hours, but the majority of the runners finish about 1 1/2 hours later. After runners enter the finish area, they go through one of four finish chutes where their times and places are recorded. (Each chute has its own queue.) During the time in which the majority of the runners finish the race, the chutes become backlogged, and significant delays occur. The race organizers want to determine how many chutes should be added to eliminate this problem. At the time in question, runners arrive at the finish area at a rate of 50 per minute according to a Poisson distribution, and they randomly select one of the four chutes. The time required to record the necessary information for each finishing runner at any chute is an exponentially distributed random variable with a mean of four seconds.

   a. On average, how many runners arrive at each chute per minute?

   b. Under the current arrangement with four chutes, what is the expected length of the queue at each chute?

   c. Under the current arrangement, what is the average length of time a runner waits before being processed?

   d. How many chutes should be added if the race organizers want to reduce the queue time at each chute to an average of five seconds?

16. State University allows students and faculty to access its supercomputer by high-speed proxy servers. The university has 15 proxy server connections that can be used to access the supercomputers. When all of the connections are in use, the system can keep up to 10 users in a queue waiting for a connection to become available. If all 15 connections are in use, and 10 users are already holding, any new users are rejected. Requests to the proxy server pool follow a Poisson distribution and occur at an average rate of 60 per hour. The length of each session with the supercomputer is an exponential random variable with a mean of 15 minutes—therefore, each proxy server services an average of four users per hour.

   a. On average, how many users are in the queue waiting for a connection?

   b. On average, how long is a user kept in the queue before receiving a connection?

   c. What is the probability that a user is rejected?

   d. How many connections would the university need to add to its server pool in order for there to be no more than a 1% chance of a user being rejected?

17. During tax season, the IRS hires seasonal workers to help answer the questions of taxpayers who call a special 800 telephone number for tax information. Suppose that calls to this line occur at a rate of 60 per hour and follow a Poisson distribution. The IRS workers manning the phone lines can answer an average of 5 calls per hour with

the actual service times following an exponential distribution. Assume that 10 IRS workers are available and, when they are all busy, the phone system can keep 5 additional callers on hold.

a. What is the probability that a caller receives a busy signal?
b. What is the probability that a caller is put on hold before receiving service?
c. On average, how long must a caller wait before speaking with an IRS agent?
d. How many additional workers would be required if the IRS wants no more than a 5% chance of a caller receiving a busy signal?

18. Road Rambler sells specialty running shoes and apparel through catalogs and the Web. Customers can phone in orders at any time day or night, seven days a week. During the 4 am to 8 am shift, a single sales rep handles all calls. During this time, calls arrive at a rate of 14 per hour following a Poisson distribution. It takes the sales rep an average of four minutes to process each call. The variability in service times is approximately exponentially distributed. All calls received while the sales rep is busy are placed in a queue.

a. On average, how long (in minutes) must callers wait before talking to the sales rep?
b. On average, how many customers are on hold?
c. What is the probability that the customer will be placed on hold?
d. What is the sales rep's utilization rate?
e. Suppose Road Rambler wants there to be no more than a 10% chance that a customer will be placed on hold. How many sales reps should the company employ?

19. Refer to the previous question. Suppose that Road Rambler's phone system can only keep four calls on hold at any time, the average profit margin of each call is $55, and sales reps cost the company $12 per hour.

a. If callers who receive a busy signal take their business elsewhere, how much money is the company losing per hour (on average) if it employs a single sales rep?
b. What is the net effect on average hourly profits if the company employs two sales reps instead of one?
c. What is the net effect on average hourly profits if the company employs three sales reps instead of one?
d. How many sales reps should the company employ if it wants to maximize profit?

20. Several hundred PCs are in use at the corporate headquarters for National Insurance Corporation. The pattern of breakdowns for these PCs follows a Poisson distribution with an average rate of 4.5 breakdowns per five-day work week. The company has a repair technician on staff to repair the PCs. The average time required to repair a PC varies somewhat, but takes an average of one day with a standard deviation of 0.5 days.

a. What is the average service time in terms of a five-day work week?
b. What is the standard deviation of the service times in terms of a five-day work week?
c. On average, how many PCs are either being repaired or waiting to be repaired?
d. On average, how much time transpires from the time a PC breaks down to the time it is repaired?
e. Suppose that National Insurance estimates it loses $40 a day in productivity and efficiency for each PC that is out of service. How much should the company be willing to pay to increase service capacity to the point where an average of seven PCs a week could be repaired?

21. Interstate 81 through southwest Virginia is heavily traveled by long-distance truckers. To cut down on accidents, The Virginia State Patrol carries out random inspections of a truck's weight and the condition of its brakes. On Fridays, trucks approach the inspection station at a rate of one every 45 seconds following a Poisson process.

The time required to check a truck's weight and brakes follows an exponential distribution with an average inspection time of 5 minutes. The state troopers only pull over trucks when at least one of their three portable inspection units is available.

    a. What is the probability that all three inspection units will be idle at the same time?

    b. What proportion of trucks traveling this section of Interstate 81 will be inspected?

    c. On average, how many trucks will be pulled over for inspection each hour?

22. The drive-thru window at Hokie Burger requires 2.5 minutes on average to process an order with a standard deviation of 3 minutes. Cars arrive at the window at a rate of 20 per hour.

    a. On average, how many cars are waiting to be served?

    b. On average, how long will a car spend in the service process?

    c. Suppose Hokie Burger can install an automated drink-dispensing device that would reduce the standard deviation of the service time to 1 minute. How would your answers to the previous questions change?

23. A manufacturer of engine belts uses multipurpose manufacturing equipment to produce a variety of products. A technician is employed to perform the setup operations needed to change the machines over from one product to the next. The amount of time required to set up the machines is a random variable that follows an exponential distribution with a mean of 20 minutes. The number of machines requiring a new setup is a Poisson random variable with an average of two machines per hour requiring setup. The technician is responsible for setups on five machines.

    a. What percentage of time is the technician idle, or not involved in setting up a machine?

    b. What should the technician do during this idle time?

    c. On average, how long is a machine out of operation while waiting for the next setup to be completed?

    d. If the company hires another, equally capable technician to perform setups on these machines, how long on average would a machine be out of operation while waiting for the next setup to be completed?

24. DeColores Paint Company owns 10 trucks that it uses to deliver paint and decorating supplies to builders. On average, each truck returns to the company's single loading dock at a rate of three times per eight-hour day (or at a rate of $3/8 = 0.375$ times per hour). The times between arrivals at the dock follow an exponential distribution. The loading dock can service an average of 4 trucks per hour with actual service times following an exponential distribution.

    a. What is the probability that a truck must wait for service to begin?

    b. On average, how many trucks wait for service to begin at any point in time?

    c. On average, how long must a truck wait before service begins?

    d. If the company builds and staffs another loading dock, how would your answers to parts a, b, and c change?

    e. The capitalized cost of adding a loading dock is $5.40 per hour. The hourly cost of having a truck idle is $50. What is the optimal number of loading docks that will minimize the sum of dock cost and idle truck cost?

25. Suppose that arrivals to a queuing system with one server follow a Poisson distribution with an average of $\lambda = 5$ per time period, and that service times follow an exponential distribution with an average service rate of $\mu = 6$ per time period.

    a. Compute the operating characteristics for this system using the M/M/s model with $s = 1$.

    b. Compute the operating characteristics for this system using the M/G/1 model. (Note that the average service time for the exponential random variable is $1/\mu$, and the standard deviation of the service time is also $1/\mu$.)

c. Compare the results obtained from the M/M/1 and M/G/1 models. (They should be the same.) Explain why they are the same.

26. Calls arrive at a rate of 150 per hour to the 800 number for the Land's Beginning mail-order catalog company. The company currently employs 20 operators who are paid $10 per hour in wages and benefits and can each handle an average of 6 calls per hour. Assume that interarrival times and service times follow the exponential distribution. A maximum of 20 calls can be placed on hold when all the operators are busy. The company estimates that it costs $25 in lost sales whenever a customer calls and receives a busy signal.

    a. On average, how many customers are waiting on hold at any point in time?
    b. What is the probability that a customer will receive a busy signal?
    c. If the number of operators plus the number of calls placed on hold cannot exceed 40, how many operators should the company employ?
    d. If the company implements your answer to part c, on average, how many customers will be waiting on hold at any point in time, and what is the probability that a customer will receive a busy signal?

May the (Police) Force Be with You   `CASE 13.1`

"I hope this goes better than last time," thought Craig Rooney as he thought about having to walk into the city council's chambers next week. Craig is the assistant chief of police in Newport, VA, and, each September, he has to provide the city council with a report on the effectiveness of the city's police force. This report immediately precedes the council's discussion of the police department's budget. So Craig often feels like a tightrope artist trying to find the right balance in his presentation to both convince the council that the department is being run well and also persuade them to increase the department's budget for new officers.

The city of Newport has a total of 19 police officers assigned to 5 precincts. Currently, precinct A has 3 officers assigned to it while the others each have 4 officers. One of the town council's primary concerns each year is the amount of time it takes for an officer to begin responding when a 911 emergency call is received. Unfortunately, the city's information system does not track this data exactly, but it does keep track of the number of calls received in each precinct each hour and the amount of time that elapses between when an officer first begins responding to a call and the time he or she reports being available again to respond to other calls (this is also known as the service time for each call).

A student intern from a local university worked for Craig last summer and collected data shown in the file named CallData.xls that accompanies this book. One of the sheets in this workbook (named Calls Per Hour) shows the number of 911 calls received during 500 randomly chosen hours of operation in each precinct. Another sheet (named Service Times) shows the services time required for each of these calls.

The student intern also set up a worksheet (based on the formulas in Figure 13.6) to calculate operating characteristics of an M/M/s queue for each of the Newport's five precincts. Unfortunately, the student interim had to return to school before finishing this project. But Craig believes with a little work, he can use the data collected to figure out appropriate arrival and service rates for each precinct and complete the analysis. More importantly, he feels sure the queuing model will allow him to quickly answer many of the questions he expects the city council to ask.

1. What are the arrival rate of 911 calls and the service rates for each precinct?
2. Does the arrival rate of calls for each precinct appear to follow a Poisson distribution?

3. Does the service rate for each precinct appear to follow an exponential distribution?
4. Using an M/M/s queue, on average, how many minutes must a 911 caller in each precinct wait before a police officer begins responding?
5. Suppose Craig wants to redistribute officers among precincts so as to reduce the maximum amount of time callers in any one precinct have to wait for a police response. What should he do, and what impact would this have?
6. How many additional police officers would Newport have to hire in order for the average response time in each precinct to be less than two minutes?

CASE 13.2   Call Center Staffing at Vacations Inc.

Vacations Inc. (VI) markets time-share condominiums throughout North America. One way the company generates sales leads is by offering a chance to win a free mini-vacation to anyone who fills out an information card and places it in boxes VI has distributed at various restaurants and shopping malls. All those who fill out the card and indicate an adequate income level subsequently receive a letter from VI indicating they have indeed won the mini-vacation. To claim their prize, all the "winner" needs to do is call VI's toll-free number. When the "winner" calls the number, they learn that their mini-vacation consists of a free dinner, entertainment, and two-night stay at one of VI's time-share properties; but they must agree to sit through a two-hour property tour and sales presentation.

About half the people who call VI's toll-free number to claim their prize wind up rejecting the offer after they learn about the two-hour property tour. About 40% of those who call accept the mini-vacation and do the property tour but don't buy anything. The remaining 10% of those who call the toll-free number accept the mini-vacation and ultimately purchase a time-share. Each mini-vacation that VI awards costs the company about $250. Each sale of a time-share generates a net profit of $7,000 for VI after all commissions and other costs (including the $250 for the buyer's mini-vacation) have been paid.

VI's call center operates from 10 am to 10 pm daily with four sales representatives and receives calls at a rate of 50 per hour following a Poisson distribution. It takes an average of 4 minutes to handle each call with actual times being exponentially distributed. The phone system VI uses can keep up to 10 callers on hold at any time. Assume those who receive a busy signal don't call back.

1. On average, how many customers per hour does each salesperson process?
2. What is the expected value of each call to VI's toll-free line?
3. Suppose VI pays its phone reps $12 per hour. How many phone reps should it employ if it wants to maximize profit?

CASE 13.3   Bullseye Department Store

Bullseye Department store is a discount retailer of general merchandise in the southeastern United States. The company owns more than 50 stores in Florida, Georgia, South Carolina, and Tennessee that are serviced by the company's main warehouse near Statesboro, GA. Most of the merchandise received at the warehouse arrives in trucks from ports in Jacksonville, FL, and Savannah, GA.

Trucks arrive at the warehouse following a Poisson process with a rate of once every 7 minutes. Eight loading docks are available at the warehouse. A single worker mans each dock and is able to unload a truck in approximately 30 minutes on average. When all the docks are occupied, arriving trucks wait in a queue until one becomes available.

Bullseye has received complaints from some of the trucking firms that deliveries are taking too long at the warehouse. In response, Bullseye is considering a number of options to try to reduce the time trucks must spend at the warehouse. One option is to hire an extra worker for each of the loading docks. This is expected to reduce the average time it takes to unload a truck to 18 minutes. It costs approximately $17 per hour in salary and benefits to employ each additional worker.

Alternatively, the company can continue to use a single worker at each loading dock but upgrade the forklift equipment workers use to unload trucks. The company can replace the existing forklift equipment with a new model that can be leased for $6 per hour and is expected to reduce the average time required to unload a truck to 23 minutes.

Finally, the company can build two new loading docks for a capitalized cost of $6 per hour and hire two additional workers at a rate of $17 per hour to man these locations. Bullseye estimates it costs $60 in goodwill for each hour a truck spends at the warehouse. Which, if any, of the three alternatives would you recommend Bullseye implement?

Chapter 14

Decision Analysis

14.0 Introduction

The previous chapters in this book describe a variety of modeling techniques that can help managers gain insight and understanding about the decision problems they face. But models do not make decisions—people do. Although the insight and understanding gained by modeling problems can be helpful, decision making often remains a difficult task. The two primary causes for this difficulty are uncertainty regarding the future and conflicting values or objectives.

For example, suppose that when you graduate from college you receive job offers from two companies. One company (company A) is in a relatively new industry that offers potential for spectacular growth—or rapid bankruptcy. The salary offered by this company is somewhat lower than you would like, but it would increase rapidly if the company grows. This company is located in the city that is home to your favorite professional sports team and close to your friends and family.

The other job offer is from an established company (company B) that is known for its financial strength and long-term commitment to its employees. It has offered you a starting salary that is 10% more than you asked, but you suspect it would take longer for you to advance in this organization. Also, if you work for this company, you would have to move to a distant part of the country that offers few of the cultural and sporting activities that you enjoy.

Which offer would you accept? Or would you reject both offers and continue looking for employment with other companies? For many, this might be a difficult decision. If you accept the job with company A, you might be promoted twice within a year—or you could be unemployed in six months. With company B, you can be reasonably sure of having a secure job for the foreseeable future. But if you accept the job with company B and then company A grows rapidly, you might regret not accepting the position with company A. Thus, the uncertainty associated with the future of company A makes this decision difficult.

To further complicate the decision, company A offers a more desirable location than company B, but the starting salary with company A is lower. How can you assess the trade-offs between starting salary, location, job security, and potential for advancement in order to make a good decision? There is no easy answer to this question, but this chapter describes a number of techniques that can help you structure and analyze difficult decision problems in a logical manner.

14.1 Good Decisions vs. Good Outcomes

The goal of decision analysis is to help individuals make good decisions. But good decisions do not always result in good outcomes. For example, suppose that after carefully considering all the factors involved in the two job offers, you decide to accept the position with company B. After working for this company for nine months, it suddenly announces that, in an effort to cut costs, it is closing the office in which you work and eliminating your job. Did you make a bad decision? Probably not. Unforeseeable circumstances beyond your control caused you to experience a bad outcome, but it would be unfair to say that you made a bad decision. Good decisions sometimes result in bad outcomes.

The techniques for decision analysis presented in this chapter can help you make good decisions, but they cannot guarantee that good outcomes will always occur as a result of those decisions. Even when a good decision is made, luck often plays a role in determining whether a good or bad outcome occurs. However, using a structured approach to make decisions should give us enhanced insight and sharper intuition about the decision problems we face. As a result, it is reasonable to expect good outcomes to occur more frequently when using a structured approach to decision making than if we make decisions in a more haphazard manner.

14.2 Characteristics of Decision Problems

Although all decision problems are somewhat different, they share certain characteristics. For example, a decision must involve at least two alternatives for addressing or solving a problem. An **alternative** is a course of action intended to solve a problem. The job selection example described earlier involves three alternatives: You could accept the offer from company A, accept the offer from company B, or reject both offers and continue searching for a better one.

Alternatives are evaluated on the basis of the value they add to one or more decision criteria. The **criteria** in a decision problem represent various factors that are important to the decision maker and influenced by the alternatives. For example, the criteria used to evaluate the job offer alternatives might include starting salary, expected salary growth, desirability of job location, opportunity for promotion and career advancement, and so on. The impact of the alternatives on the criteria is of primary importance to the decision maker. Note that not all criteria can be expressed in terms of monetary value, making comparisons of the alternatives more difficult.

Finally, the values assumed by the various decision criteria under each alternative depend on the different states of nature that can occur. The **states of nature** in a decision problem correspond to future events that are not under the decision maker's control. For example, company A could experience spectacular growth, or it might go bankrupt. Each of these contingencies represents a possible state of nature for the problem. Many other states of nature are possible for the company; for example, it could grow slowly or not grow at all. Thus, an infinite number of possible states of nature could exist in this and many other decision problems. However, in decision analysis, we often use a relatively small, discrete set of representative states of nature to summarize the future events that might occur.

14.3 An Example

The following example illustrates some of the issues and difficulties that arise in decision problems.

> Hartsfield International Airport in Atlanta, Georgia, is one of the busiest airports in the world. During the past 30 years, the airport has expanded again and again to accommodate the increasing number of flights being routed through Atlanta. Analysts project that this increase will continue well into the future. However, commercial development around the airport prevents it from building additional

FIGURE 14.1

Data for the Magnolia Inns decision problem

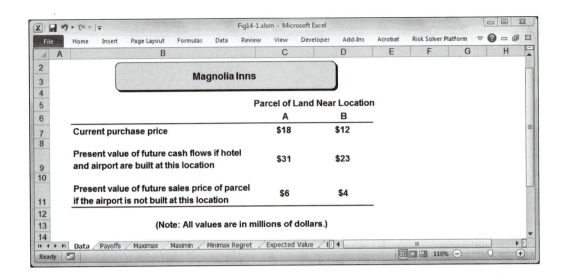

runways to handle the future air-traffic demands. As a solution to this problem, plans are being developed to build another airport outside the city limits. Two possible locations for the new airport have been identified, but a final decision on the new location is not expected to be made for another year.

The Magnolia Inns hotel chain intends to build a new facility near the new airport after its site is determined. Barbara Monroe is responsible for real estate acquisition for the company, and she faces a difficult decision about where to buy land. Currently, land values around the two possible sites for the new airport are increasing as investors speculate that property values will increase greatly in the vicinity of the new airport. The spreadsheet in Figure 14.1 (and in the file Fig14-1.xlsm that accompanies this book) summarizes the current price of each parcel of land, the estimated present value of the future cash flows that a hotel would generate at each site if the airport is ultimately located at the site, and the present value of the amount for which the company believes it can resell each parcel if the airport is not built at the site.

The company can buy either site, both sites, or neither site. Barbara must decide which sites, if any, the company should purchase.

14.4 The Payoff Matrix

A common way of analyzing this type of decision problem is to construct a payoff matrix. A **payoff matrix** is a table that summarizes the final outcome (or payoff) for each decision alternative under each possible state of nature. To construct a payoff matrix, we need to identify each decision alternative and each possible state of nature. The following four decision alternatives are available to the decision maker in our example problem:

14.4.1 DECISION ALTERNATIVES

The possible decision alternatives are listed here:

1. Buy the parcel at location A.
2. Buy the parcel at location B.
3. Buy the parcels at locations A and B.
4. Buy nothing.

Regardless of which parcel or parcels Magnolia Inns decides to purchase, two possible states of nature can occur.

14.4.2 STATES OF NATURE

The two states of nature are the following:

1. The new airport is built at location A.
2. The new airport is built at location B.

Figure 14.2 shows the payoff matrix for this problem. The rows in this spreadsheet represent the possible decision alternatives, and the columns correspond to the states of nature that might occur. Each value in this table indicates the financial payoff (in millions of dollars) expected for each possible decision under each state of nature.

14.4.3 THE PAYOFF VALUES

The value in cell B5 in Figure 14.2 indicates that if the company buys the parcel of land near location A, and the airport is built in this area, Magnolia Inns can expect to receive a payoff of $13 million. This figure of $13 million is computed from the data shown in Figure 14.1 as:

	Present value of future cash flows if hotel and airport are built at location A	$31,000,000
minus:	Current purchase price of hotel site at location A	−$18,000,000
		$13,000,000

The value in cell C5 in Figure 14.2 indicates that if Magnolia Inns buys the parcel of land at location A (for $18 million), and the airport is built at location B, the company would later resell the parcel at location A for only $6 million, incurring a loss of $12 million.

The calculations of the payoffs for the parcel near location B are computed using similar logic. The value in cell C6 in Figure 14.2 indicates that if the company buys the parcel of land near location B, and the airport is built in this area, Magnolia Inns can expect to receive a payoff of $11 million. The value in cell B6 in Figure 14.2 indicates that if Magnolia Inns buys the parcel of land at location B (for $12 million), and the airport is built at location A, the company would later resell the parcel at location B for only $4 million, incurring a loss of $8 million.

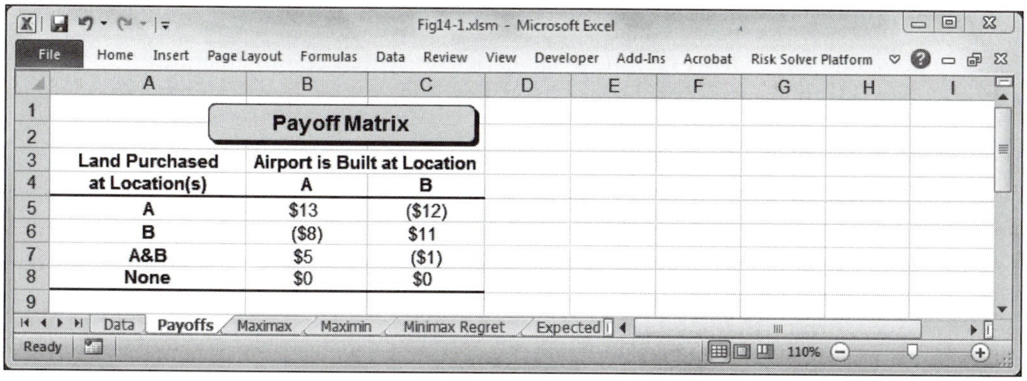

Land Purchased at Location(s)	Airport is Built at Location A	B
A	$13	($12)
B	($8)	$11
A&B	$5	($1)
None	$0	$0

FIGURE 14.2

Payoff matrix for the Magnolia Inns decision problem

Let's now consider the payoffs if the parcels at both locations A and B are purchased. The value in cell B7 in Figure 14.2 indicates that a payoff of $5 million will result if both parcels are purchased, and the airport is built at location A. This payoff value is computed as:

	Present value of future cash flows if hotel and airport are built at location A	$31,000,000
plus:	Present value of future sales price for the unused parcel at location B	+$ 4,000,000
minus:	Current purchase price of hotel site at location A	−$18,000,000
minus:	Current purchase price of hotel site at location B	−$12,000,000
		$ 5,000,000

The value in cell C7 indicates that a loss of $1 million will occur if the parcels at both locations A and B are purchased, and the airport is built at location B.

The final alternative available to Magnolia Inns is to not buy either property at this point in time. This alternative guarantees that the company will neither gain nor lose anything, regardless of where the airport is located. Thus, cells B8 and C8 indicate that this alternative has a payoff of $0 regardless of which state of nature occurs.

14.5 Decision Rules

Now that the payoffs for each alternative under each state of nature have been determined, if Barbara knew with certainty where the airport was going to be built, it would be a simple matter for her to select the most desirable alternative. For example, if she knew the airport was going to be built at location A, a maximum payoff of $13 million could be obtained by purchasing the parcel of land at that location. Similarly, if she knew the airport was going to be built at location B, Magnolia Inns could achieve the maximum payoff of $11 million by purchasing the parcel at that location. The problem is that Barbara does not know where the airport is going to be built.

Several decision rules can be used to help a decision maker choose the best alternative. No one of these decision rules works best in all situations and, as you will see, each has some weaknesses. However, these rules help to enhance our insight and sharpen our intuition about decision problems so that we can make more informed decisions.

14.6 Nonprobabilistic Methods

The decision rules we will discuss can be divided into two categories: those that assume that probabilities of occurrence can be assigned to the states of nature in a decision problem **(probabilistic methods)**, and those that do not **(nonprobabilistic methods)**. We will discuss the nonprobabilistic methods first.

14.6.1 THE MAXIMAX DECISION RULE

As shown in Figure 14.2, the largest possible payoff will occur if Magnolia Inns buys the parcel at location A, and the airport is built at this location. Thus, if the company optimistically believes that nature will always be "on its side" regardless of the decision it makes, the company should buy the parcel at location A because it leads to the largest possible payoff. This type of reasoning is reflected in the **maximax decision rule**, which determines the maximum payoff for each alternative and then selects the alternative associated with the largest payoff. Figure 14.3 illustrates the results of the maximax decision rule on our example problem.

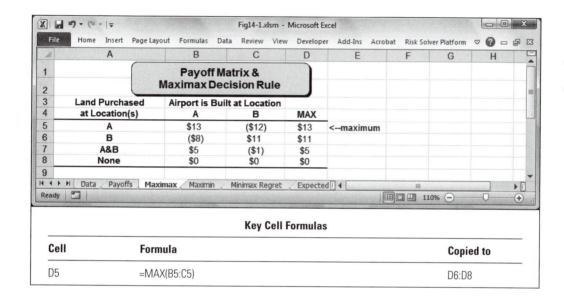

FIGURE 14.3

The maximax decision rule for the Magnolia Inns decision problem

	Key Cell Formulas	
Cell	**Formula**	**Copied to**
D5	=MAX(B5:C5)	D6:D8

Although the alternative suggested by the maximax decision rule enables Magnolia Inns to realize the best possible payoff, it does not guarantee that this payoff will occur. The actual payoff depends on where the airport is ultimately located. If we follow the maximax decision rule, and the airport is built at location A, the company would receive $13 million; but if the airport is built at location B, the company would lose $12 million.

In some situations, the maximax decision rule leads to poor decisions. For example, consider the following payoff matrix:

	State of Nature		
Decision	**1**	**2**	**MAX**
A	30	−10,000	30 ← maximum
B	29	29	29

In this problem, alternative A would be selected using the maximax decision rule. However, many decision makers would prefer alternative B because its guaranteed payoff is only slightly less than the maximum possible payoff, and it avoids the potential large loss involved with alternative A if the second state of nature occurs.

FIGURE 14.4

The maximin decision rule for the Magnolia Inns decision problem

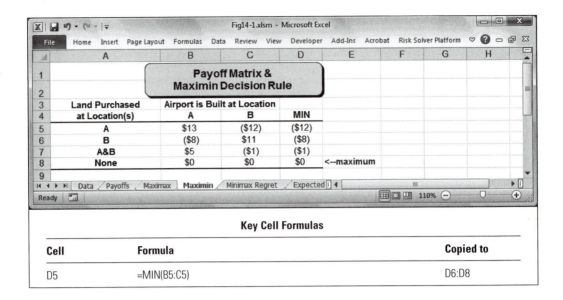

	Key Cell Formulas	
Cell	**Formula**	**Copied to**
D5	=MIN(B5:C5)	D6:D8

14.6.2 THE MAXIMIN DECISION RULE

A more conservative approach to decision making is given by the **maximin decision rule**, which pessimistically assumes that nature will always be "against us" regardless of the decision we make. This decision rule can be used to hedge against the worst possible outcome of a decision. Figure 14.4 illustrates the effect of the maximin decision rule on our example problem.

To apply the maximin decision rule, we first determine the minimum possible payoff for each alternative and then select the alternative with the largest minimum payoff (or the maximum of the minimum payoffs—hence the term "maximin"). Column D in Figure 14.4 lists the minimum payoff for each alternative. The largest (maximum) value in column D is the payoff of $0 associated with not buying any land. Thus, the maximin decision rule suggests that Magnolia Inns should not buy either parcel because, in the worst case, the other alternatives result in losses, whereas this alternative does not.

The maximin decision rule can also lead to poor decision making. For example, consider the following payoff matrix:

	State of Nature			
Decision	**1**	**2**	**MIN**	
A	1,000	28	28	
B	29	29	29	← maximum

In this problem, alternative B would be selected using the maximin decision rule. However, many decision makers would prefer alternative A because its worst-case payoff is only slightly less than that of alternative B, and it provides the potential for a much larger payoff if the first state of nature occurs.

14.6.3 THE MINIMAX REGRET DECISION RULE

Another way of approaching decision problems involves the concept of **regret**, or opportunity loss. For example, suppose that Magnolia Inns decides to buy the parcel of land at location A as suggested by the maximax decision rule. If the airport is built at location A, the company will not regret this decision at all because it provides the largest possible payoff under the state of nature that occurred. However, what if the company buys the parcel at location A and the airport is built at location B? In this case, the company would experience a regret, or opportunity loss, of $23 million. If Magnolia Inns had bought the parcel at location B, it would have earned a payoff of $11 million, and the decision to buy the parcel at location A resulted in a loss of $12 million. Thus, there is a difference of $23 million in the payoffs between these two alternatives under this state of nature.

To use the minimax regret decision rule, we must first convert our payoff matrix into a regret matrix that summarizes the possible opportunity losses that could result from each decision alternative under each state of nature. Figure 14.5 shows the regret matrix for our example problem.

The entries in the regret matrix are generated from the payoff matrix as:

Formula for cell B5: =MAX(Payoffs!B$5:B$8) – Payoffs!B5

(Copy to B5 through C8.)

Each entry in the regret matrix shows the difference between the maximum payoff that can occur under a given state of nature and the payoff that would be realized from each alternative under the same state of nature. For example, if Magnolia Inns buys the parcel of land at location A and the airport is built at this location, cell B5 indicates that the company experiences 0 regret. However, if the company buys the parcel at location B, and the airport is built at location A, the company experiences an opportunity loss (or regret) of $21 million ($13 - (-8) = 21$).

Column D in Figure 14.5 summarizes the maximum regret that could be experienced with each decision alternative. The minimax regret decision corresponds to the alternative with the smallest (or minimum) maximum regret. As indicated in Figure 14.5, the minimax regret decision in our example problem is to buy the parcels at both sites. The maximum regret that could be experienced by implementing this decision is $12 million, whereas all other decisions could cause a larger regret.

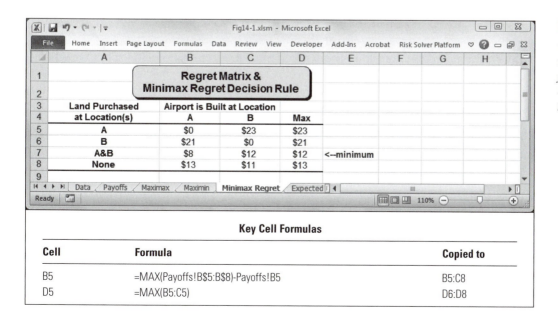

FIGURE 14.5

The maximax regret decision rule for the Magnolia Inns decision problem

The minimax regret decision rule can lead to peculiar decision making. For example, consider the following payoff matrix:

	State of Nature	
Decision	**1**	**2**
A	9	2
B	4	6

The regret matrix and minimax regret decision for this problem are represented by:

	State of Nature			
Decision	**1**	**2**	**MAX**	
A	0	4	4	← minimum
B	5	0	5	

Thus, if the alternatives are given by A and B, the minimax regret decision rule would select alternative A. Now, suppose that we add a new alternative to this decision problem to obtain the following payoff matrix:

	State of Nature	
Decision	**1**	**2**
A	9	2
B	4	6
C	3	9

Notice that the payoffs for alternatives A and B have not changed—we simply added a new alternative (C). The regret matrix and minimax regret decision for the revised problem are represented by:

	State of Nature			
Decision	**1**	**2**	**MAX**	
A	0	7	7	
B	5	3	5	← minimum
C	6	0	6	

The minimax regret decision is now given by alternative B. Some decision makers are troubled that the addition of a new alternative, which is not selected as the final decision, can change the relative preferences of the original alternatives. For example, suppose that a person prefers apples to oranges, but would prefer oranges if given the options of apples, oranges, and bananas. This person's reasoning is somewhat inconsistent or incoherent. But such reversals in preferences are a natural consequence of the minimax regret decision rule.

14.7 Probabilistic Methods

Probabilistic decision rules can be used if the states of nature in a decision problem can be assigned probabilities that represent their likelihood of occurrence. For decision problems that occur more than once, it is often possible to estimate these probabilities from historical data. However, many decision problems (such as the Magnolia Inns problem) represent one-time decisions for which historical data for estimating probabilities are unlikely to exist. In these cases, probabilities are often assigned subjectively based on interviews with one or more domain experts. Highly structured interviewing techniques exist to solicit probability estimates that are reasonably accurate and free of the unconscious biases that may impact an expert's opinions. These interviewing techniques are described in several of the references at the end of this chapter. Here, we will focus on the techniques that can be used once appropriate probability estimates have been obtained either from historical data or expert interviews.

14.7.1 EXPECTED MONETARY VALUE

The **expected monetary value decision rule** selects the decision alternative with the largest expected monetary value (EMV). The EMV of alternative i in a decision problem is defined as:

$$\text{EMV}_i = \sum_j r_{ij} p_j$$

where:

$$r_{ij} = \text{the payoff for alternative } i \text{ under the } j^{th} \text{ state of nature}$$
$$p_j = \text{the probability of the } j^{th} \text{ state of nature}$$

Figure 14.6 illustrates the EMV decision rule for our example problem. In this case, Magnolia Inns estimates a 40% chance that the airport will be built at location A and a 60% chance that it will be built at location B.

The probabilities for each state of nature are computed in cells B10 and C10, respectively. Using these probabilities, the EMV for each decision alternative is calculated in column D as:

Formula for cell D5:   =SUMPRODUCT(B5:C5,$B$10:$C$10)
(Copy to D6 through D8.)

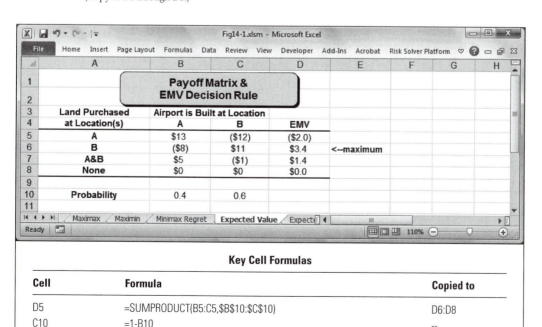

FIGURE 14.6

The expected monetary value decision rule for the Magnolia Inns decision problem

The largest EMV is associated with the decision to purchase the parcel of land at location B. Thus, this is the decision suggested according to the EMV decision rule.

Let's consider the meaning of the figures in the EMV column in Figure 14.6. For example, the decision to purchase the parcel at location B has an EMV of $3.4 million. What does this figure represent? The payoff table indicates that Magnolia Inns will receive a payoff of $11 million if it buys this land and the airport is built there, or it will lose $8 million if it buys this land and the airport is built at the other location. So, there does not appear to be any way for the company to receive a payoff of $3.4 million if it buys the land at location B. However, imagine that Magnolia Inns faces this same decision not just once but over and over again (perhaps on a weekly basis). If the company always decides to purchase the land at location B, we would expect it to receive a payoff of $11 million 60% of the time and incur a loss of $8 million 40% of the time. Over the long run, then, the decision to purchase land at location B results in an average payoff of $3.4 million.

The EMV for a given decision alternative indicates the average payoff we would receive if we encounter the identical decision problem repeatedly and always select this alternative. Selecting the alternative with the highest EMV makes sense in situations where the identical decision problem will be faced repeatedly, and we can "play the averages." However, this decision rule can be very risky in decision problems encountered only once (such as our example problem). For example, consider the following problem:

	State of Nature			
Decision	**1**	**2**	**EMV**	
A	15,000	−5,000	5,000	← maximum
B	5,000	4,000	4,500	
Probability	0.5	0.5		

If we face a decision with these payoffs and probabilities repeatedly and always select decision A, the payoff over the long run would average to $5,000. Because this is larger than decision B's average long-run payoff of $4,500, it would be best to always select decision A. But what if we face this decision problem only once? If we select decision A, we are equally likely to receive $15,000 or lose $5,000. If we select decision B, we are equally likely to receive payoffs of $5,000 or $4,000. In this case, decision A is more risky. Yet this type of risk is ignored completely by the EMV decision rule. Later, we will discuss a technique—known as the utility theory—that allows us to account for this type of risk in our decision making.

14.7.2 EXPECTED REGRET

We can also use the probability of the states of nature to compute the **expected regret**, or **expected opportunity loss** (EOL), for each alternative in a decision problem. Figure 14.7 illustrates this process for our example problem.

The calculations in Figure 14.7 are identical to those used in computing the EMVs, only here we substitute regret values (or opportunity losses) for the payoffs. As shown in Figure 14.7, the decision to purchase the parcel at location B results in the smallest EOL. It is not a coincidence that this same decision also resulted in the largest EMV in Figure 14.6. The decision with the smallest EOL will also have the largest EMV. Thus, the EMV and EOL decision rules always result in the selection of the same decision alternative.

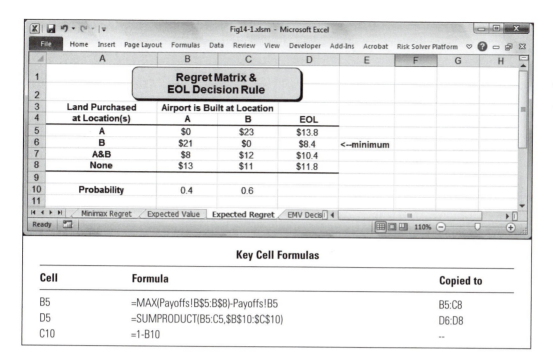

FIGURE 14.7

The expected regret decision rule for the Magnolia Inns decision problem

Key Cell Formulas

Cell	Formula	Copied to
B5	=MAX(Payoffs!B$5:B$8)-Payoffs!B5	B5:C8
D5	=SUMPRODUCT(B5:C5,$B$10:$C$10)	D6:D8
C10	=1-B10	--

EMV and EOL

The expected monetary value (EMV) and expected opportunity loss (EOL) decision rules always result in the selection of the same decision alternative.

14.7.3 SENSITIVITY ANALYSIS

When using probabilistic decision rules, one should always consider how sensitive the recommended decision is to the estimated probabilities. For instance, the EMV decision rule shown in Figure 14.6 indicates that if there is a 60% probability of the new airport being built at location B, the best decision is to purchase the land at location B. However, what if this probability is 55%? Or 50%? Or 45%? Would it still be best to purchase the land at location B?

We can answer this by building a data table that summarizes the EMVs for each alternative as we vary the probabilities. Figure 14.8 shows how to set up a data table for this problem.

First, in cells A14 through A24, we entered the values from 0 to 1 representing different probabilities for the airport being built at location A. Next, in cells B13 through E13, we entered formulas that link back to the EMVs for each of the decision alternatives. To finish the data table, follow these steps:

1. Select cells A13 through E24.
2. Click Data, What-If Analysis, Data Table.
3. Specify a Column Input Cell of B10 (as shown in Figure 14.8).
4. Click OK.

FIGURE 14.8

Creating a data table of EMVs for the various alternatives as the probabilities change

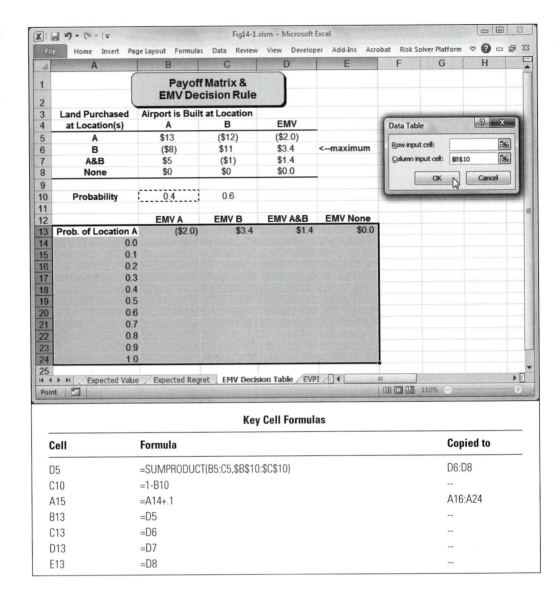

Key Cell Formulas

Cell	Formula	Copied to
D5	=SUMPRODUCT(B5:C5,$B$10:$C$10)	D6:D8
C10	=1-B10	--
A15	=A14+.1	A16:A24
B13	=D5	--
C13	=D6	--
D13	=D7	--
E13	=D8	--

This causes Excel to plug each of the values in cells A14 through A24 into cell B10, recalculate the spreadsheet, and then record the resulting EMVs for each decision alternative in our table. (Note that the formula in cell C10 makes the probability of the airport being built at location B dependent on the value in cell B10.) The resulting data table is shown in Figure 14.9.

The data table in Figure 14.9 indicates that if the probability of the airport being built at location A is 0.4 or less, then purchasing the land at location B has the highest EMV. However, if the airport is equally likely to be built at either location, then the decision to purchase land at both locations A and B has the highest EMV. If the airport is more likely to be built at location A, then purchasing the land at location A becomes the preferred decision.

The graph of the possible payoffs shown in Figure 14.9 makes it clear that buying the land at both locations A and B is a less risky alternative than buying either location individually. If there is much uncertainty in the probability estimates, the preferred alternative may well be to buy both pieces of property. For probability values between 0.4 and 0.6, the

FIGURE 14.9 *Data table for the Magnolia Inns decision problem*

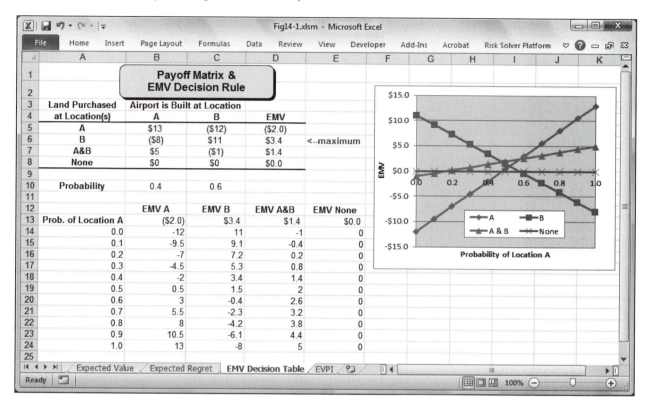

EMV of buying land at both locations A and B is always positive and varies from $1.4 million to $2.6 million. Within this same range of probabilities, a decision to buy at location A individually or location B individually poses a risk of a negative EMV.

14.8 The Expected Value of Perfect Information

One of the primary difficulties in decision making is that we usually do not know which state of nature will occur. As we have seen, estimates of the probability of each state of nature can be used to calculate the EMV of various decision alternatives. However, probabilities do not tell us which state of nature will occur—they only indicate the likelihood of the various states of nature.

Suppose that we could hire a consultant who could tell us in advance and with 100% accuracy which state of nature will occur. If our example problem were a repeatable decision problem, 40% of the time, the consultant would indicate that the airport will be built at location A, and the company would buy the parcel of land at location A and receive a payoff of $13 million. Similarly, 60% of the time, the consultant would indicate that the airport will be built at location B, and the company would buy the parcel at location B and receive a payoff of $11 million. Thus, with advance perfect information about where the airport is going to be built, the average payoff would be the following:

Expected value *with* perfect information = 0.40 × $13 + 0.60 × $11 = $11.8 (in millions)

So, how much should Magnolia Inns be willing to pay this consultant for such information? From Figure 14.6, we know that *without* the services of this consultant, the best decision identified results in an EMV of $3.4 million. Therefore, the information provided by the consultant would enable the company to make decisions that increase the EMV by $8.4 million ($11.8 − $3.4 = $8.4). Thus, the company should be willing to pay the consultant up to $8.4 million for providing perfect information.

The **expected value of perfect information** (EVPI) is the expected value obtained with perfect information minus the expected value obtained without perfect information (which is given by the maximum EMV), that is:

$$\begin{matrix} \text{Expected value } of \\ \text{perfect information} \end{matrix} = \begin{matrix} \text{Expected value } with \\ \text{perfect information} \end{matrix} - \text{maximum EMV}$$

Figure 14.10 summarizes the EVPI calculation for our example problem. Cell D6 in Figure 14.10 shows the calculation of the maximum EMV of $3.4 million, which was described earlier in our discussion of the EMV decision rule. The payoffs of the decisions made under each state of nature with perfect information are calculated in cells B12 and C12 as:

Formula for cell B12:   =MAX(B5:B8)

(Copy to C12.)

The expected value *with* perfect information is calculated in cell D12 as:

Formula for cell D12:   =SUMPRODUCT(B12:C12,B10:C10)

Finally, the expected value *of* perfect information is computed in cell D14 as:

Formula for cell D14:   =D12−MAX(D5:D8)

FIGURE 14.10

The expected value of perfect information for the Magnolia Inns decision problem

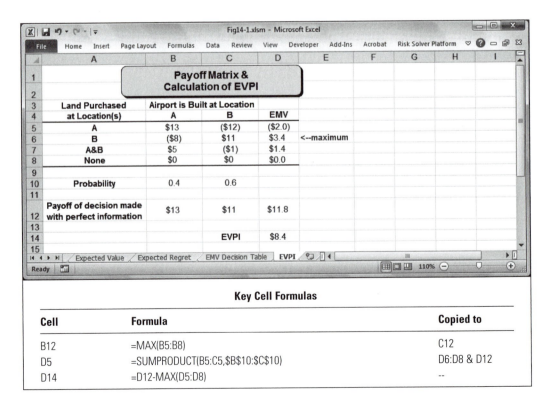

Cell	Formula	Copied to
B12	=MAX(B5:B8)	C12
D5	=SUMPRODUCT(B5:C5,$B$10:$C$10)	D6:D8 & D12
D14	=D12-MAX(D5:D8)	--

Notice that the $8.4 million EVPI figure in cell D14 is identical to the minimum EOL shown earlier in Figure 14.7. This is *not* just a coincidence. The minimum EOL in a decision problem will always equal the EVPI.

K e y   P o i n t

The expected value of perfect information (EVPI) is equivalent to the minimum expected opportunity loss (EOL).

14.9 Decision Trees

Although some decision problems can be represented and analyzed effectively using payoff tables, we can also represent decision problems in a graphical form known as a **decision tree**. Figure 14.11 shows the decision problem for Magnolia Inns represented in this format.

As shown in Figure 14.11, a decision tree is composed of a collection of nodes (represented by circles and squares) interconnected by branches (represented by lines). A square node is called a **decision node** because it represents a decision. Branches emanating from a decision node represent the different alternatives for a particular decision. In Figure 14.11, a single square decision node represents the decision Magnolia Inns faces about where to buy land. The four branches coming out of this decision node represent the four alternatives under consideration. The cash flow associated with each alternative is also listed. For example, the value −18 below the alternative labeled "Buy A" indicates that if the company purchases the parcel at location A, it must pay $18 million.

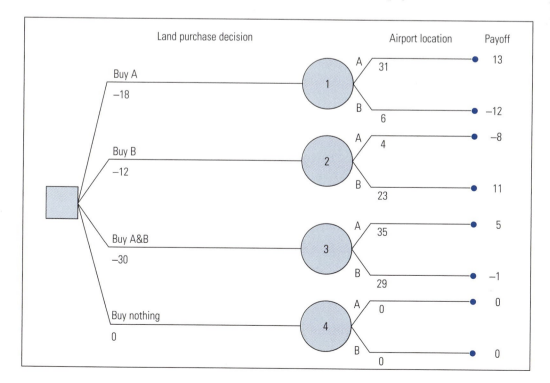

FIGURE 14.11

The decision tree representation of the Magnolia Inns problem

The circular nodes in a decision tree are called **event nodes** because they represent uncertain events. The branches emanating from event nodes (called **event branches**) correspond to the possible states of nature or the possible outcomes of an uncertain event. Figure 14.11 shows that each decision alternative emanating from the decision node is followed by an uncertain event represented by the event nodes 1, 2, 3, and 4. The branches from each event node represent a possible location of the new airport. In each case, the airport can be built at location A or B. The value beneath each branch from the event nodes indicates the cash flow that will occur for that decision/event combination. For example, at node 1, the value 31 below the first event branch indicates that if the company buys the parcel at location A, and the airport is built at this location, a cash flow of $31 million will occur.

The various branches in a decision tree end at objects called **leaves**. Because each leaf corresponds to one way in which the decision problem can terminate, leaves are also referred to as **terminal nodes**. Each terminal node in Figure 14.11 corresponds to an entry in the payoff table in Figure 14.2. The payoff occurring at each terminal node is computed by summing the cash flows along the set of branches leading to each leaf. For example, following the uppermost branches through the tree, a payoff of $13 million results if the decision to buy the parcel at location A is followed by the new airport being built at this location ($-18 + 31 = 13$). You should verify the cash-flow values on each branch and at each leaf before continuing.

14.9.1 ROLLING BACK A DECISION TREE

After computing the payoffs at each terminal node, we can apply any of the decision rules described earlier. For example, we could identify the maximum possible payoff for each decision and apply the maximax decision rule. However, decision trees are used most often to implement the EMV decision rule—that is, to identify the decision with the largest EMV.

We can apply a process known as **rolling back** to a decision tree to determine the decision with the largest EMV. Figure 14.12 illustrates this process for our example problem.

Because the EMV decision rule is a probabilistic method, Figure 14.12 indicates the probabilities associated with each event branch emanating from each event node (that is, a 0.4 probability exists of the new airport being built at location A, and a 0.6 probability exists of it being built at location B). To roll back this decision tree, we start with the payoffs and work our way from right to left, back through the decision tree, computing the expected values for each node. For example, the event represented by node 1 has a 0.4 probability of resulting in a payoff of $13 million, and a 0.6 probability of resulting in a loss of $12 million. Thus, the EMV at node 1 is calculated as:

$$\text{EMV at node 1} = 0.4 \times 13 + 0.6 \times -12 = -2.0$$

The expected value calculations for the remaining event nodes in Figure 14.12 are summarized as:

$$\text{EMV at node 2} = 0.4 \times -8 + 0.6 \times 11 = 3.4$$
$$\text{EMV at node 3} = 0.4 \times 5 + 0.6 \times -1 = 1.4$$
$$\text{EMV at node 4} = 0.4 \times 0 + 0.6 \times 0 = 0.0$$

The EMV for a decision node is computed in a different way. For example, at the (square) decision node, we face a decision among four alternatives that lead to events

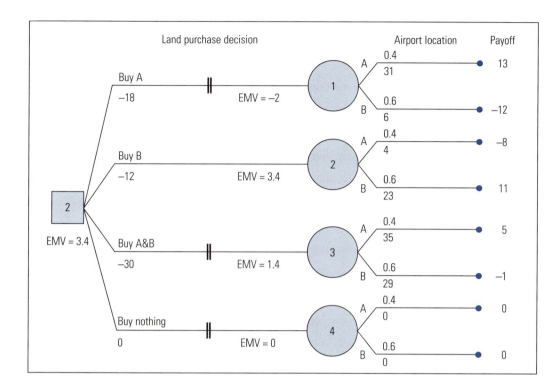

FIGURE 14.12

Rolling back the decision tree for the Magnolia Inns decision problem

with EMVs of −2, 3.4, 1.4, and 0, respectively. At a decision node, we always select the alternative that leads to the best EMV. Thus, the EMV at the decision node is 3.4, which corresponds to the EMV resulting from the decision to buy land at location B. (This decision is represented by the number 2 in the decision node because the decision to buy land at location B is the second decision alternative at this decision node.) The optimal alternative at a decision node is sometimes indicated by "pruning" the suboptimal branches. The pruned branches in Figure 14.12 are indicated by the double vertical lines (‖) shown on the suboptimal alternatives emanating from the decision node.

The relationship between the decision tree in Figure 14.12 and the payoff table in Figure 14.2 should now be clear. However, you might wonder if it is necessary to include event node 4 in the tree shown in Figure 14.12. If Magnolia Inns decides not to buy either property, the payoff it receives does not depend on where the airport is ultimately built—regardless of where the airport is built, the company will receive a payoff of 0.

Figure 14.13 shows an alternative, and perhaps more efficient, way of representing this problem as a decision tree in which it is clear that the decision not to purchase either parcel leads to a definite payoff of $0.

14.10 Creating Decision Trees with Risk Solver Platform

Risk Solver Platform includes a tool that can help us create and analyze decision trees in Excel. We will illustrate how to use this tool to implement the decision tree shown in Figure 14.13 in Excel.

FIGURE 14.13

Alternative decision tree representation of the Magnolia Inns decision problem

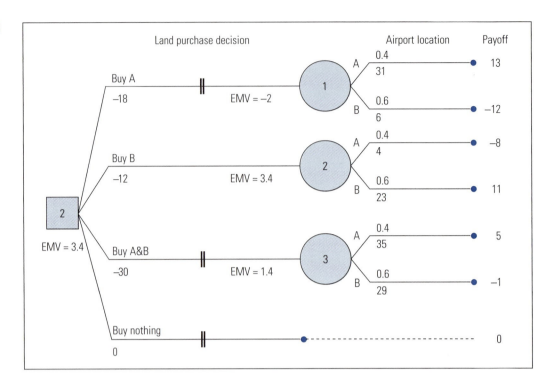

To create a decision tree, open a new workbook, and follow these steps:

1. Select cell A1.
2. Click the Risk Solver Platform tab.
3. Click Decision Tree, Node, Add Node.

In response, Risk Solver Platform displays the Decision Tree dialog box as shown in Figure 14.14. (Alternatively, you can also display the Decision Tree dialog box by selecting Decision Tree in the Risk Solver task pane and clicking the green plus sign icon in the task pane.)

In Figure 14.14, we filled in the entries shown for the Node Name and supplied names and values (cash flows) for each of the four branches that should emanate from the initial decision node (as shown in Figure 14.13). When you click OK on the Decision Tree dialog, an initial decision tree is created in Excel as shown in Figure 14.15.

In Figure 14.15, note that a representation of the decision tree is also created in the Decision Tree section of the Risk Solver task pane. If you click the different elements of the tree in the task pane, various properties associated with the selected element appear in the lower part of the task pane.

14.10.1 ADDING EVENT NODES

Each of the first three decision branches in Figure 14.13 leads to an event node with two event branches. Thus, we need to add similar event nodes to the decision tree shown in Figure 14.15. To add the first event node, follow these steps:

1. Select the terminal node for the branch labeled Buy A (cell F3).
2. Click Decision Tree, Node, Change Node.

FIGURE 14.14 *Initial Decision Tree dialog box*

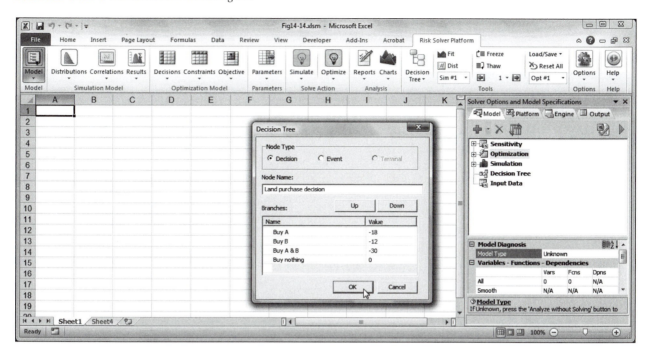

FIGURE 14.15 *Initial tree with four decision branches*

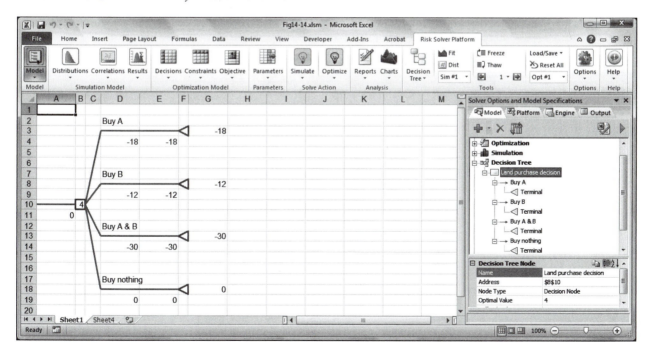

This causes the Decision Tree dialog to appear again. However, as shown in Figure 14.16, this time we select the Event option and provide the name, value (or cash flows), and chance (probability) information associated with the event node we want to add to the tree. The resulting spreadsheet is shown in Figure 14.17.

FIGURE 14.16 *Adding an event node*

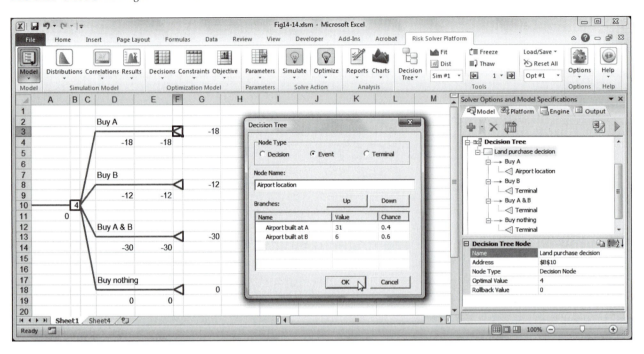

FIGURE 14.17 *Modified decision tree with an event node*

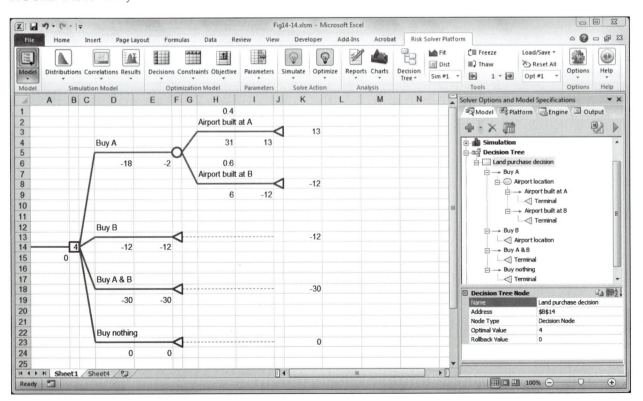

The procedure used to create the event node for the Buy A decision could be repeated to create event nodes for the decisions corresponding to Buy B and Buy A & B. However, because all of the event nodes are identical in this problem (except for the values on the branches), we could also simply copy the existing event node two times. You might be tempted to copy and paste the existing event node using the standard Excel commands—but if you do, Risk Solver cannot update the formulas in the tree properly. Thus, it is important to copy and paste portions of the decision tree using Risk Solver's Copy Node and Paste Node commands. To create a copy of the event node:

1. Select the node you want to copy (cell F5).
2. Click Decision Tree, Node, Copy Node.

This creates a copy of the selected event node in your computer's memory. To paste a copy of this subtree onto the next branch in the decision tree:

1. Select the target cell location (cell F13).
2. Click Decision Tree, Node, Paste Node.

The resulting decision tree is shown in Figure 14.18. We can repeat this copy-and-paste procedure to create the third event node needed for the decision to buy the parcels at both locations A and B. Figure 14.19 shows the resulting spreadsheet after the cash flow values have been updated on the branches from the newly added event nodes.

FIGURE 14.18 *Decision tree with three event nodes*

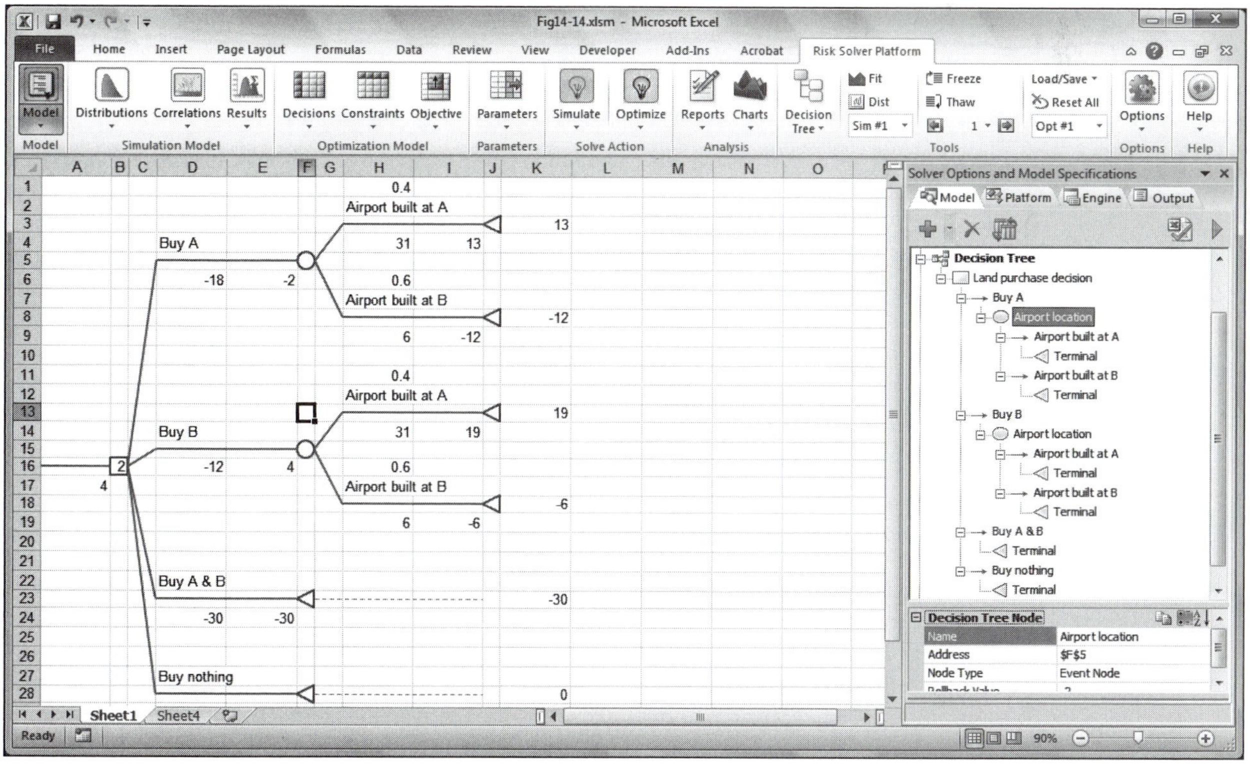

FIGURE 14.19 *Completed decision tree for the Magnolia Inns decision problem*

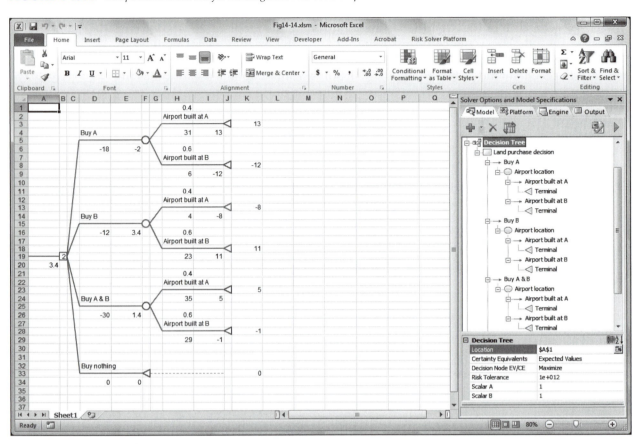

14.10.2 DETERMINING THE PAYOFFS AND EMVs

Next to each terminal node, the Decision Tree tool automatically created a formula that sums the payoffs along the branches leading to that node. For example, cell K3 in Figure 14.19 contains the formula =SUM(H4,D6). Thus, when we enter or change the cash flows for the branches in the decision tree, the payoffs are updated automatically.

Immediately below and to the left of each node, the Decision Tree tool created formulas that compute the EMV at each node in the same way as described earlier in our discussion of rolling back a decision tree. Thus, cell A20 in Figure 14.19 indicates that the largest EMV at the decision node is $3.4 million. The value 2 in the decision node (cell B19) indicates that this maximum EMV is obtained by selecting the second decision alternative (that is, by purchasing the parcel at location B).

14.10.3 OTHER FEATURES

The preceding discussion was intended to give you an overview of how the Decision Tree tool operates and some of its capabilities and options. Many of its other capabilities are self-explanatory.

By default, the Decision Tree tool assumes that the EMVs it calculates represent profit values and that we want to identify the decision with the largest EMV. However, in some decision trees, the expected values could represent costs that we want to minimize. In Figure 14.19, note that when the Decision Tree component is selected on the Model tab in the Risk Solver task pane, a number of properties are displayed in the lower portion of the task pane. The Decision Node EV/CE option allows you to specify whether you are using values that should be maximized or minimized.

Also by default, the Decision Tree tool assumes that we want to analyze the decision tree using expected values. However, another technique (described later) uses exponential utility functions in place of expected values. Thus, the Certainty Equivalents property controls whether the Decision Tree tool uses expected values or exponential utility functions while evaluating the alternatives in a decision tree.

14.11 Multistage Decision Problems

To this point, our discussion of decision analysis has considered only **single-stage** decision problems—that is, problems in which a single decision must be made. However, most decisions that we face lead to other decisions. As a simple example, consider the decision of whether to go out to dinner. If you decide to go out to dinner, you must then decide how much to spend, where to go, and how to get there. Thus, before you actually decide to go out to dinner, you'll probably consider the other issues and decisions that must be made if you choose that alternative. These types of problems are called **multistage** decision problems. The following example illustrates how a multistage decision problem can be modeled and analyzed using a decision tree.

The Occupational Safety and Health Administration (OSHA) has recently announced it will award an $85,000 research grant to the person or company submitting the best proposal for using wireless communications technology to enhance safety in the coal-mining industry. Steve Hinton, the owner of COM-TECH, a small communications research firm located just outside of Raleigh, North Carolina, is considering whether or not to apply for this grant. Steve estimates he would spend approximately $5,000 preparing his grant proposal and that he has about a 50-50 chance of actually receiving the grant. If he is awarded the grant, he would then need to decide whether to use microwave, cellular, or infrared communications technology. He has some experience in all three areas but would need to acquire some new equipment depending on which technology is used. The cost of the equipment needed for each technology is summarized as:

Technology	Equipment Cost
Microwave	$4,000
Cellular	$5,000
Infrared	$4,000

In addition to the equipment costs, Steve knows he will spend money in research and development (R&D) to carry out the research proposal, but he does not know exactly what the R&D costs will be. For simplicity, Steve estimates the following best-case and worst-case R&D costs associated with using each technology, and he assigns probabilities to each outcome based on his degree of expertise in each area.

	Possible R&D Costs			
	Best Case		Worst Case	
	Cost	Prob.	Cost	Prob.
Microwave	$30,000	0.4	$60,000	0.6
Cellular	$40,000	0.8	$70,000	0.2
Infrared	$40,000	0.9	$80,000	0.1

Steve needs to synthesize all the factors in this problem to decide whether or not to submit a grant proposal to OSHA.

14.11.1 A MULTISTAGE DECISION TREE

The immediate decision in this example problem is whether or not to submit a grant proposal. To make this decision, Steve must also consider the technology selection decision that he will face if he receives the grant. So, this is a multistage decision problem. Figure 14.20 (and the file Fig14-20.xlsm that accompanies this book) shows the decision tree representation of this problem.

This decision tree clearly shows that the first decision Steve faces is whether or not to submit a proposal, and that submitting the proposal will cost $5,000. If a proposal is submitted, we then encounter an event node showing a 0.5 probability of receiving the grant (and a payoff of $85,000) and a 0.5 probability of not receiving the grant (leading to a net loss of $5,000). If the grant is received, we then encounter a decision about which technology to pursue. Each of the three technology options has an event node representing the best-case (lowest) and worst-case (highest) R&D costs that might be incurred. The final (terminal) payoffs associated with each set of decisions and outcomes are listed next to each terminal node. For example, if Steve submits a proposal, receives the grant, employs cellular technology, and encounters low R&D costs, he will receive a net payoff of $35,000.

According to this decision tree, Steve should submit a proposal because the expected value of this decision is $13,500, and the expected value of not submitting a proposal is $0. The decision tree also indicates that if Steve receives the grant, he should pursue the

FIGURE 14.20

Multistage decision tree for COM-TECH's grant proposal problem

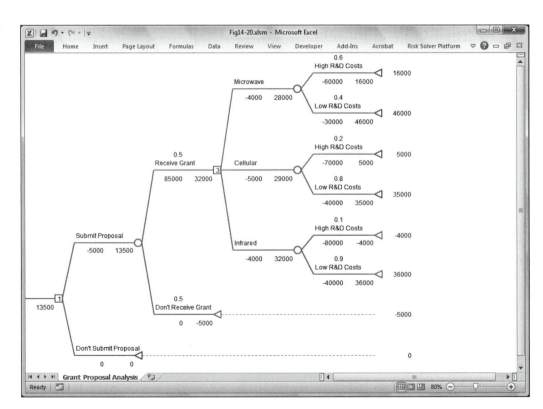

infrared communications technology because the expected value of this decision ($32,000) is larger than the expected values for the other technologies.

In Figure 14.20, note that the probabilities on the branches at any event node must always sum to 1 because these branches represent all the events that could occur. The R&D costs that would actually occur using a given technology could assume an infinite number of values. Some might argue that these costs could be modeled more accurately by some continuous random variable. However, our aim is to estimate the expected value of this random variable. Most decision makers probably would find it easier to assign subjective probabilities to a small, discrete set of representative outcomes for a variable such as R&D costs rather than try to identify an appropriate probability distribution for this variable.

14.11.2 DEVELOPING A RISK PROFILE

When using decision trees to analyze one-time decision problems, it is particularly helpful to develop a risk profile to make sure the decision maker understands all the possible outcomes that might occur. A **risk profile** is simply a graph or tree that shows the chances associated with possible outcomes. Figure 14.21 shows the risk profile associated with not submitting the proposal and that of the optimal EMV decision-making strategy (submitting the proposal and using infrared technology) identified from Figure 14.20.

From Figure 14.21, it is clear that if the proposal is not submitted, the payoff will be $0. If the proposal is submitted, there is a 0.50 chance of not receiving the grant and incurring a loss of $5,000. If the proposal is submitted, there is a 0.05 chance ($0.5 \times 0.1 = 0.05$) of receiving the grant but incurring high R&D costs with the infrared technology and suffering a $4,000 loss. Finally, if the proposal is submitted, there is a 0.45 chance ($0.5 \times 0.9 = 0.45$) of enjoying small R&D costs with the infrared technology and making a $36,000 profit.

A risk profile is an effective tool for breaking an EMV into its component parts and communicating information about the actual outcomes that can occur as the result of various decisions. By looking at Figure 14.21, a decision maker could reasonably decide that the risks (or chances) of losing money if a proposal is submitted are not worth the

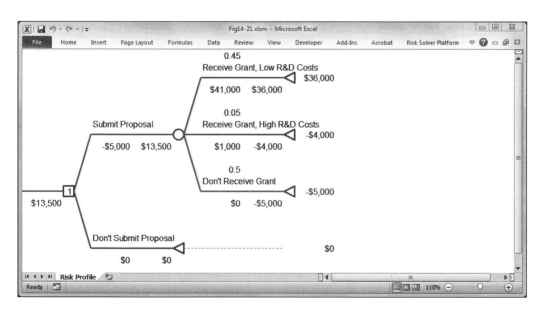

FIGURE 14.21

A risk profile for the alternatives of submitting or not submitting the proposal

potential benefit to be gained if the proposal is accepted and low R&D costs occur. These risks would not be apparent if the decision maker was provided only with information about the EMV of each decision.

14.12 Sensitivity Analysis

Before implementing the decision to submit a grant proposal as suggested by the previous analysis, Steve would be wise to consider how sensitive the recommended decision is to changes in values in the decision tree. For example, Steve estimated that a 50-50 chance exists that he will receive the grant if he submits a proposal. But what if that probability assessment is wrong? What if only a 30%, 20%, or 10% chance exists of receiving the grant? Should he still submit the proposal?

Using a decision tree implemented in a spreadsheet, it is fairly easy to determine how much any of the values in the decision tree can change before the indicated decision would change. For example, Figure 14.22 (and the file Fig14-22.xlsm that accompanies this book) shows how we can use optimization to determine how small the probability of receiving the grant would need to be before it would no longer be wise to submit the grant proposal (according to the EMV decision rule).

FIGURE 14.22 *Using optimization to determine the sensitivity of a decision to changes in probabilities*

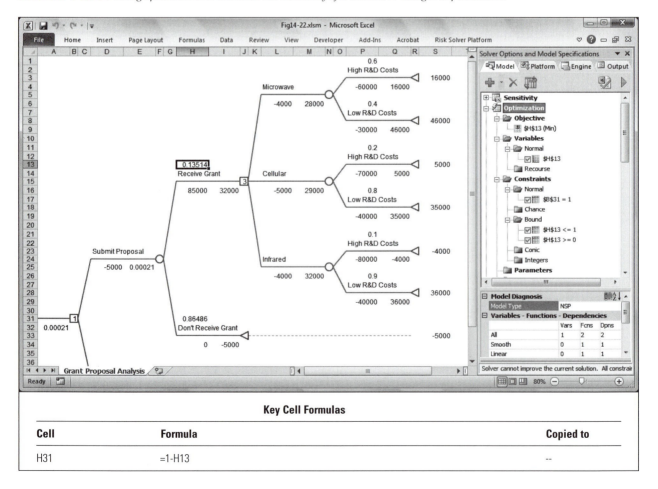

Key Cell Formulas		
Cell	**Formula**	**Copied to**
H31	=1-H13	--

In this spreadsheet, we are using cell H13 (the probability of receiving the grant) as both our objective cell and our variable cell. In cell H31, we entered the following formula to compute the probability of not receiving the grant:

Formula for cell H31:   =1−H13

Minimizing the value in cell H13 (using Risk Solver Platform's GRG nonlinear engine) while constraining the value of B31 to equal 1 determines the probability of receiving the grant that makes the EMV of submitting the grant equal to zero. The resulting probability (that is, approximately 0.1351) gives the decision maker some idea of how sensitive the decision is to changes in the value of cell H13.

If the EMV of submitting the grant is $0, most decision makers would probably not want to submit the grant proposal. Indeed, even with an EMV of $13,500 (as shown in Figure 14.22), some decision makers would still not want to submit the grant proposal because there is still a risk that the proposal would be turned down and a $5,000 loss incurred. As mentioned earlier, the EMV decision rule is most appropriately applied when we face a decision that will be made repeatedly and the results of bad outcomes can be balanced or averaged with good outcomes.

14.12.1 TORNADO CHARTS

As shown in the previous section, optimization can be used to determine the amount by which almost any value in a decision tree can be changed before a recommended decision (based of EMV) would change. However, given the number of probability and financial estimates used as inputs to a decision tree, it is often helpful to use tornado charts to identify the inputs that, if changed, have the greatest impact on the EMV. This helps to identify the areas where sensitivity analysis is most important and prioritize where time and resources should be applied in refining probability and financial estimates represented in the decision tree.

Risk Solver Platform provides a simple way to create tornado charts. This tool allows you to specify an output cell of interest, and then it automatically identifies the input cells that have the greatest impact on the value of the output cell. (The tornado chart refers to the identified input cells as **candidate cells**.) The tornado chart tool incrementally changes the value of each input cell from its base case value (while holding the other input cells constant) within a specified percentage range (±10% by default) and records the effect of each change on the output cell's value.

As an example, suppose we are interested in identifying the input cells in COMTECH's decision tree shown in Figure 14.20 that have the greatest influence on the EMV shown in cell A32. The tornado chart in Figure 14.23 summarizes the impact on the decision tree's EMV of each input cell being set at +10% and −10% of its original (base case) value. The input cell with the largest impact on the EMV's range is shown first, the input cell with the next largest impact is shown second, and so on, creating the tornado-shaped appearance in the chart. To create the tornado chart shown in Figure 14.23 (using file Fig14-23.xlsm that accompanies this book), follow these steps:

1. Select the output cell of interest (cell A32).
2. On the Risk Solver Platform tab, click Parameters, Identify.

At the top of the tornado chart we readily see that cell H16 (the grant award amount of $85,000) has the largest impact on the EMV as it is adjusted from −10% to +10% of its original value. Cell H13 (the probability of receiving the grant) has the next largest influence, followed by cell P29 (the best case R&D costs for infrared technology), and so on. Thus, the tornado chart quickly gives us a good sense for which

FIGURE 14.23 *An automatic tornado chart for the COM-TECH decision problem*

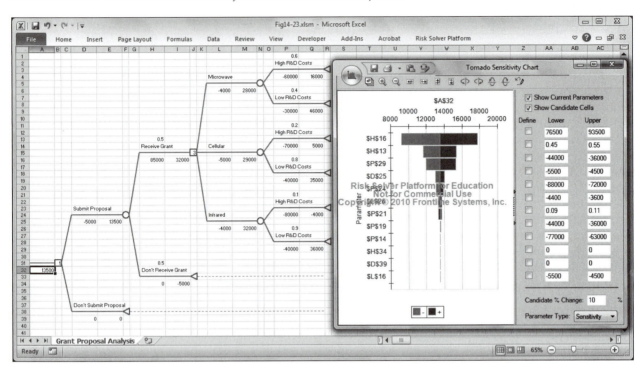

input cells have the most significant impact on the EMV and the associated recommended decision.

In Figure 14.23, note that Risk Solver identified *all* the input cells that affect the output cell and summarized the most significant ones in the tornado chart. However, it is unlikely that the amount of the grant award (the "most significant" input cell) is actually going to differ from the stated value of $85,000. As a result, instead of having Risk Solver automatically identify the input cells that, if changed, have the most significant impact on the output cell, we might want to consider only the input cells whose values are most uncertain and/or subject to change. Fortunately, it is possible to specify the input cells of interest and only include those in the tornado chart. This is done by defining those cells as sensitivity parameter cells using the PsiSenParam(A, B) function, where A and B represent, respectively, lower- and upper limits on the range of possible values for each cell.

For example, suppose we are only interested in considering the output cell's (cell A32) sensitivity to changes of up to 20% in the best-case and worst-case R&D costs for each of the possible technology choices (that is, cells P4, P9, P14, P19, P24, and P29). We would first replace the values in each of the cells representing R&D costs with PsiSenParam( ) functions that allow their cells to be varied within plus or minus 20% of their original values as shown in Figure 14.24 (and the file Fig14-24 that accompanies this book). If you then create a new tornado chart and uncheck the Show Candidate Cells checkbox, the chart shows change in the output cell as each of the parameter cells (that is, those cells containing PsiSenParam( ) functions) are varied from their lower limits to their upper limits.

FIGURE 14.24 *A customized tornado chart for the COM-TECH decision problem*

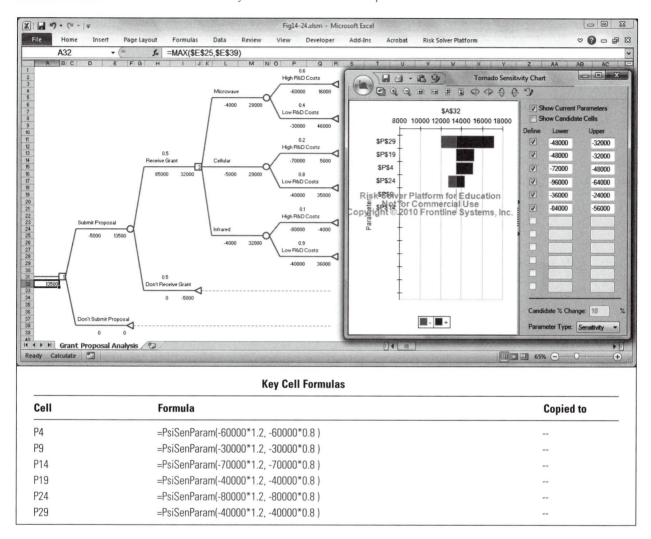

Key Cell Formulas

Cell	Formula	Copied to
P4	=PsiSenParam(-60000*1.2, -60000*0.8)	--
P9	=PsiSenParam(-30000*1.2, -30000*0.8)	--
P14	=PsiSenParam(-70000*1.2, -70000*0.8)	--
P19	=PsiSenParam(-40000*1.2, -40000*0.8)	--
P24	=PsiSenParam(-80000*1.2, -80000*0.8)	--
P29	=PsiSenParam(-40000*1.2, -40000*0.8)	--

Software Note

The results plotted in a tornado chart can consist of two different types of input cells: those that Risk Solver identifies automatically (referred to as candidate cells), and those that we manually identify as sensitivity parameter (via PsiSenParam( ) functions). The Candidate % Change option in the lower section of the tornado chart (see Figure 14.24) only applies to the candidate cells; it will *not* effect the cells containing PsiSenParam( ) functions. As a result, it is possible for a tornado chart to simultaneously display results where, for instance, candidate cells are varied from ±10% from their base case values, and sensitivity parameters are varied a different amount, such as ±20% from their base case values.

14.12.2 STRATEGY TABLES

A **strategy table** is another sensitivity analysis technique that allows a decision maker to analyze how the optimal decision strategy changes in response to two simultaneous changes in probability estimates. For example, the optimal strategy in Figure 14.20 is to submit the proposal and use infrared technology. However, suppose there is uncertainty about the probability of receiving the grant and the probability of encountering high R&D costs while carrying out the research proposal. Specifically, suppose the decision maker wants to see how the optimal strategy changes as the probability of receiving the grant varies from 0.0 to 1.0 and the probability of encountering high infrared R&D costs varies from 0.0 to 0.5. As shown in Figure 14.25 (and file Fig14-25.xlsm that accompanies this book), a two-way data table can be used to analyze this situation.

In Figure 14.25, cells W12 through W22 represent different probabilities of receiving the grant. Using the Data Table command, we will instruct Excel to plug each of these values into cell H13, representing the probability of receiving the grant. The following formula was entered in cell H31 to calculate the complementary probability of not receiving the grant.

Formula for cell H31:   =1−H13

FIGURE 14.25 *Setting up a strategy table for the COM-TECH decision problem*

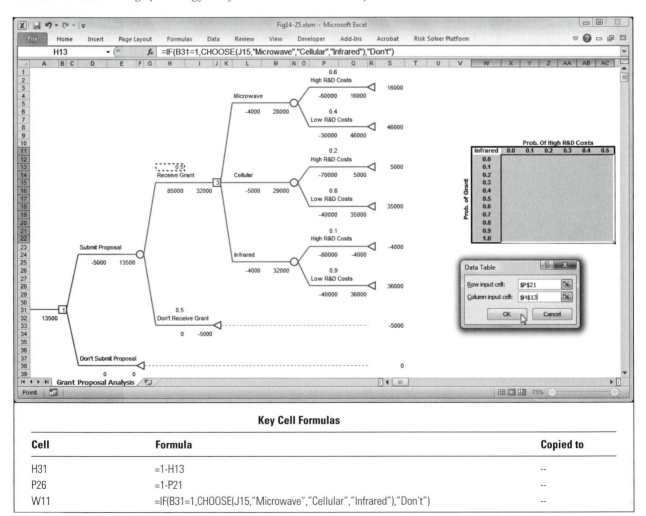

Key Cell Formulas		
Cell	Formula	Copied to
H31	=1-H13	--
P26	=1-P21	--
W11	=IF(B31=1,CHOOSE(J15,"Microwave","Cellular","Infrared"),"Don't")	--

Cells X11 through AC11 represent different probabilities of encountering high R&D costs. Using the Data Table command, we will instruct Excel to plug each of these values into cell P21, representing the probability of receiving the grant. The following formula was entered in cell P26 to calculate the complementary probability of not receiving the grant.

Formula for cell P26:   =1–P21

As these different probabilities are changed, the spreadsheet will be recalculated, and the value returned by the formula in cell W11 will be recorded in the appropriate cell in the data table.

Formula for cell W11:   =IF(B31=1,CHOOSE
(J15,"Microwave","Cellular","Infrared"),"Don't")

This formula first inspects the value of cell B31; which equals 1 if the EMV of submitting the proposal is positive. Thus, if B31 is equal to 1, the formula then returns (chooses) the label "Microwave", "Cellular", or "Infrared" depending on whether the value in cell J15 is 1, 2, or 3, respectively. Otherwise, the previous formula returns the label "Don't" indicating that the proposal should not be submitted. The results of executing the Data Table command are shown in Figure 14.26.

Figure 14.26 summarizes the optimal strategy for the various probability combinations. For instance, if the probability of receiving the grant is 0.10 or less, the company should not submit a proposal. Note that cell Y17 corresponds to the base case solution shown earlier in Figure 14.20. The strategy table makes it clear that this solution is relatively insensitive to changes in the probability of receiving the grant. However, if the probability of encountering high infrared R&D costs increases, the preferred strategy

FIGURE 14.26 *Completed strategy table for the COM-TECH decision problem*

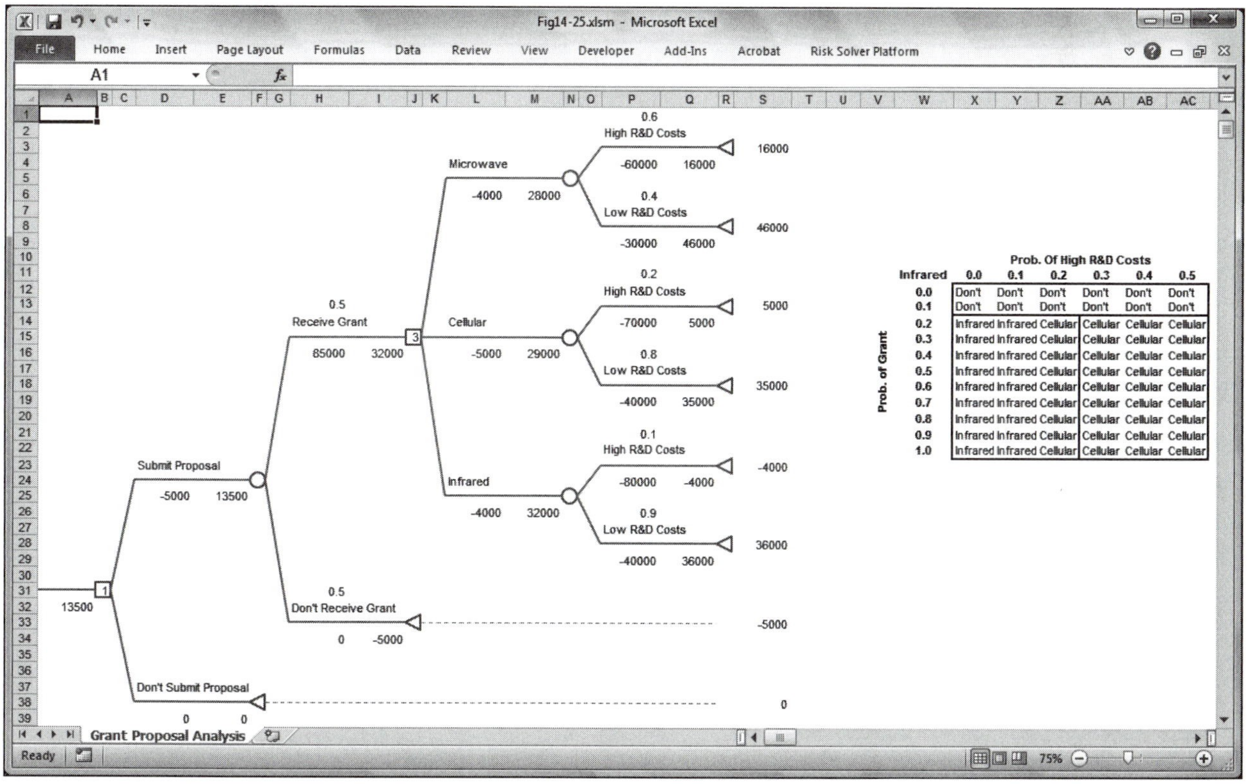

quickly switches to the cellular technology alternative. Thus, the decision maker might want to give closer attention to the risks of encountering high infrared R&D costs before implementing this strategy.

14.12.3 STRATEGY CHARTS

Similar to strategy tables, a **strategy chart** is a technique to graphically show how the optimal decision strategy changes in response to two simultaneous changes in probability estimates. Again, suppose there is uncertainty about the probability of receiving the grant and the probability of encountering high R&D costs while carrying out the research proposal. Specifically, assume the decision maker wants to see how the optimal strategy changes as the probability of receiving the grant varies from 0.0 to 1.0 and the probability of encountering high infrared R&D costs varies from 0.0 to 0.5. To create a strategy chart for this situation using Risk Solver Platform, we first change cells P21 and H13 in Figure 14.27

FIGURE 14.27 *Setting up a strategy chart for the COM-TECH decision problem*

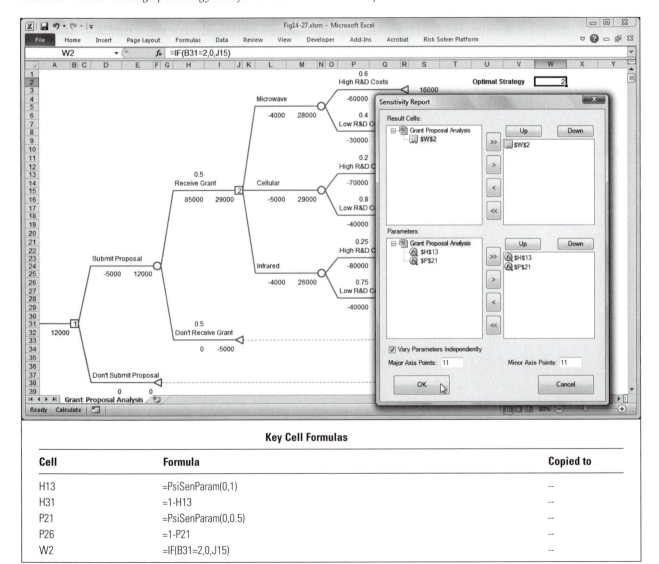

Key Cell Formulas

Cell	Formula	Copied to
H13	=PsiSenParam(0,1)	--
H31	=1-H13	--
P21	=PsiSenParam(0,0.5)	--
P26	=1-P21	--
W2	=IF(B31=2,0,J15)	--

(and the file Fig14-27.xlsm that accompanies this book) to sensitivity parameter cells as follows:

Formula for cell P21:   =PsiSenParam(0,0.5)
Formula for cell H13:   =PsiSenParam(0,1)

We must also create an output cell that assigns a unique numeric value to each decision strategy. This is done in cell W2 as follows:

Formula for cell W2:   =IF(B31=2,0,J15)

Note that the formula in cell W2 returns the value 0 if the optimal strategy is to not submit a proposal (that is, if B31 = 2) and otherwise returns the value of 1, 2, or 3 (from cell J15) if the optimal decision is to submit a proposal and use microwave, cellular, or infrared technology, respectively.

We can then create a strategy chart for our problem as follows:

1. Select cell W2.
2. On the Risk Solver ribbon, click Sensitivity Analysis, Parameter Analysis.
3. Complete the Sensitivity Report dialog as shown Figure 14.27.
4. Click OK.

Risk Solver Platform then creates the 3D area chart shown in Figure 14.28. This chart shows how the optimal decision strategy changes for different combinations of probability values in cells P21 and H13. Note that the decision chart provides a graphical summary of the results in the strategy table shown in Figure 14.26.

FIGURE 14.28 *Completed strategy chart for the COM-TECH decision problem*

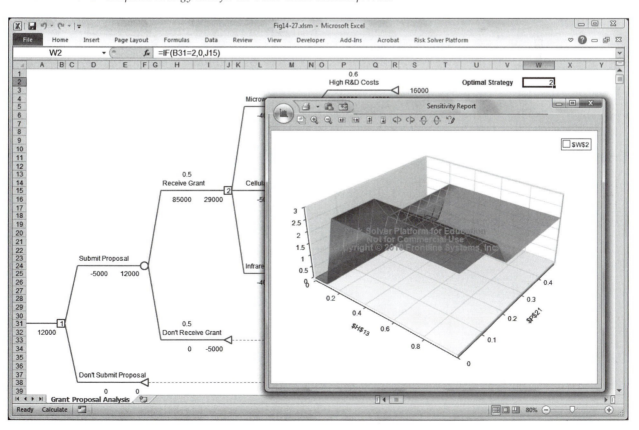

14.13 Using Sample Information in Decision Making

In many decision problems, we have the opportunity to obtain additional information about the decision before we actually make the decision. For example, in the Magnolia Inns decision problem, the company could have hired a consultant to study the economic, environmental, and political issues surrounding the site selection process and predict which site will be selected for the new airport by the planning council. This information might help Magnolia Inns make a better (or more informed) decision. The potential for using this type of additional sample information in decision making raises a number of interesting issues that are illustrated using the following example.

> Colonial Motors (CM) is trying to determine what size of manufacturing plant to build for a new car it is developing. Only two plant sizes are under consideration: large and small. The cost of constructing a large plant is $25 million, and the cost of constructing a small plant is $15 million. CM believes there is a 70% chance that the demand for this new car will be high and a 30% chance that it will be low. The following table summarizes the payoffs (in millions of dollars) the company expects to receive for each factory size and demand combination (not counting the cost of the factory).

	Demand	
Factory Size	**High**	**Low**
Large	$175	$ 95
Small	$125	$105

A decision tree for this problem is shown in Figure 14.29 (and in the file Fig14-29.xlsm that accompanies this book). The decision tree indicates that the optimal decision is to build the large plant and that this alternative has an EMV of $126 million.

Now suppose that before making the plant size decision, CM conducts a survey to assess consumer attitudes about the new car. For simplicity, we will assume that the results

FIGURE 14.29

Decision tree for the CM plant size problem

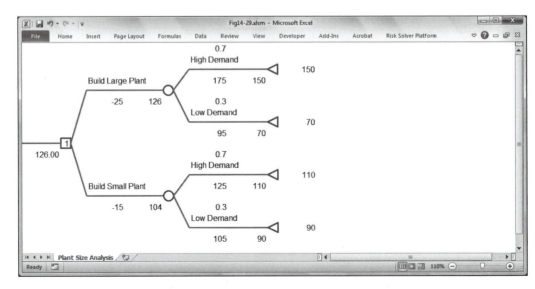

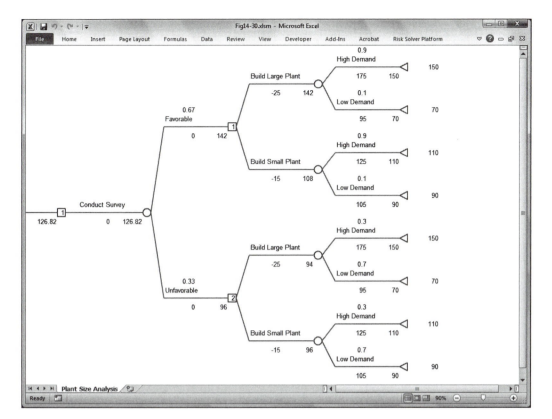

FIGURE 14.30

Decision tree if consumer survey is conducted before CM makes a plant size decision

of this survey indicate either a favorable or unfavorable attitude about the new car. A revised decision tree for this problem is shown in Figure 14.30 (and in the file Fig14-30.xlsm that accompanies this book).

The decision tree in Figure 14.30 begins with a decision node with a single branch representing the decision to conduct the market survey. For now, assume that this survey can be done at no cost. An event node follows, corresponding to the outcome of the market survey, which can indicate either favorable or unfavorable attitudes about the new car. We assume that CM believes that the probability of a favorable response is 0.67 and the probability of an unfavorable response is 0.33.

14.13.1 CONDITIONAL PROBABILITIES

After the survey results are known, the decision nodes in the tree indicate that a decision must be made about whether to build a large plant or a small plant. Following each decision branch, event nodes occur with branches representing the market demands for the car that could occur. Four event nodes represent the market demand that might occur for this car. However, the probabilities we assign to the branches of these nodes are likely to differ depending on the results of the market survey.

Earlier, we indicated that CM believed a 0.70 probability exists that demand for the new car will be high, expressed mathematically as:

$$P(\text{high demand}) = 0.7$$

In this formula, $P(A) = X$ is read, "the probability of A is X." If the market survey indicates that consumers have a favorable impression of the new car, this will raise expectations that demand will be high for the car. Thus, given a favorable survey response, we might increase the probability assessment for a high-market demand to 0.90. This is expressed mathematically as the following *conditional* probability:

$$P(\text{high demand} \mid \text{favorable response}) = 0.90$$

In this formula $P(A \mid B) = X$ is read, "the probability of A given B is X."

As noted earlier, the probabilities on the branches at any event node must always sum to 1. If the favorable survey response increases the probability assessment of a high demand occurring, it must decrease the probability assessment of a low demand given this survey result. Thus, the probability of a low demand given a favorable response on the survey is:

$$P(\text{low demand} \mid \text{favorable response}) = 1 - P(\text{high demand} \mid \text{favorable response})$$
$$= 1 - 0.90 = 0.10$$

These conditional probabilities are shown in Figure 14.30 on the first four event branches representing high and low demands given a favorable survey response.

If the market survey indicates consumers have an unfavorable response to the new car, this will lower expectations for high-market demand. Thus, given an unfavorable survey response, we might reduce the probability assessment of a high-market demand to 0.30:

$$P(\text{high demand} \mid \text{unfavorable response}) = 0.30$$

We must also revise the probability assessment for a low-market demand given an unfavorable market response as:

$$P(\text{low demand} \mid \text{unfavorable response}) = 1 - P(\text{high demand} \mid \text{unfavorable response})$$
$$= 1 - 0.3 = 0.70$$

These conditional probabilities are shown on the last four demand branches in Figure 14.30. Later, we will discuss a more objective method for determining these types of conditional probabilities.

14.13.2 THE EXPECTED VALUE OF SAMPLE INFORMATION

The additional information made available by the market survey allows us to make more precise estimates of the probabilities associated with the uncertain market demand. This, in turn, allows us to make more precise decisions. For example, Figure 14.30 indicates that if the survey results are favorable, CM should build a large plant; and if the survey results are unfavorable, it should build a small plant. The expected value of this decision-making strategy is $126.82 million, assuming that the survey can be done at no cost—which is unlikely. So, how much should CM be willing to pay to perform this survey? The answer to this question is provided by the expected value of sample information (EVSI), which is defined as:

$$EVSI = \begin{pmatrix} \text{Expected value of the best} \\ \text{decision with sample infor-} \\ \text{mation (obtained at no cost)} \end{pmatrix} - \begin{pmatrix} \text{Expected value of the best} \\ \text{decision without sample} \\ \text{information} \end{pmatrix}$$

The EVSI represents the *maximum* amount we should be willing to pay to obtain sample information. From Figure 14.30, we know that the expected value of the best decision *with* sample information for our example problem is $126.82 million. From Figure 14.29, we know that the expected value of the best decision *without* sample information is $126 million. So for our example problem, the EVSI is determined as:

$$\text{EVSI} = \$126.82 \text{ million} - \$126 \text{ million} = \$0.82 \text{ million}$$

Thus, CM should be willing to spend up to $820,000 to perform the market survey.

14.14 Computing Conditional Probabilities

In our example problem, we assumed that the values of the conditional probabilities were assigned subjectively by the decision makers at CM. However, a company often has data available from which it can compute these probabilities. We will illustrate this process for the CM example. To simplify our notation, we will use the following abbreviations:

H	=	high demand
L	=	low demand
F	=	favorable response
U	=	unfavorable response

To complete the decision tree in Figure 14.30, we determined values for the following six probabilities:

$$P(F)$$
$$P(U)$$
$$P(H \mid F)$$
$$P(L \mid F)$$
$$P(L \mid U)$$
$$P(H \mid U)$$

Assuming that CM has been in the auto business for some time, it undoubtedly has performed other market surveys prior to introducing other new models. Some of these models probably achieved high consumer demand, whereas others achieved only low demand. Thus, CM can use historical data to construct the joint probability table shown at the top of Figure 14.31 (and in the file Fig14-31.xlsm that accompanies this book).

The value in cell B4 indicates that of all the new car models CM developed and performed market surveys on, 60% received a favorable survey response and subsequently enjoyed high demand. This is expressed mathematically as:

$$P(F \cap H) = 0.60$$

In this formula, $P(A \cap B) = X$ is read, "the probability of A *and* B is X." Similarly, in the joint probability table we see that:

$$P(F \cap L) = 0.067$$
$$P(U \cap H) = 0.10$$
$$P(U \cap L) = 0.233$$

The column totals in cells B6 and C6 represent, respectively, the estimated probabilities of high and low demands as:

$$P(H) = 0.70$$
$$P(L) = 0.30$$

FIGURE 14.31

The calculation of conditional probabilities for the CM decision problem

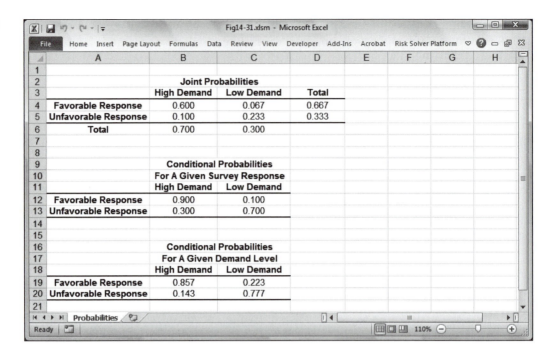

The row totals in cells D4 and D5 represent, respectively, the estimated probabilities of a favorable and unfavorable response. These values correspond to the first two of the six probability values listed earlier; that is:

$$P(F) = 0.667$$
$$P(U) = 0.333$$

With these values, we are now ready to compute the necessary conditional probabilities. One general definition of a conditional probability is:

$$P(A|B) = \frac{P(A \cap B)}{P(B)}$$

We can use this definition, along with the values in the joint probability table, to compute the conditional probabilities required for Figure 14.30 as:

$$P(H|F) = \frac{P(H \cap F)}{P(F)} = \frac{0.60}{0.667} = 0.90$$

$$P(L|F) = \frac{P(L \cap F)}{P(F)} = \frac{0.067}{0.667} = 0.10$$

$$P(H|U) = \frac{P(H \cap U)}{P(U)} = \frac{0.10}{0.333} = 0.30$$

$$P(L|U) = \frac{P(L \cap U)}{P(U)} = \frac{0.233}{0.333} = 0.70$$

We can calculate these conditional probabilities of the demand levels for a given survey response in the spreadsheet. This is done in the second table in Figure 14.31 using the following formula:

$$\text{Formula for cell B12:} \quad =B4/\$D4$$

(Copy to B12 through C13.)

Although not required for Figure 14.30, we can also compute the conditional probabilities of the survey responses for a given level of demand as:

$$P(F|H) = \frac{P(H \cap F)}{P(H)} = \frac{0.60}{0.70} = 0.857$$

$$P(U|H) = \frac{P(H \cap U)}{P(H)} = \frac{0.10}{0.70} = 0.143$$

$$P(F|L) = \frac{P(L \cap F)}{P(L)} = \frac{0.067}{0.30} = 0.223$$

$$P(U|L) = \frac{P(L \cap U)}{P(L)} = \frac{0.233}{0.30} = 0.777$$

The third table in Figure 14.31 calculates conditional probabilities of the survey responses for a given level of demand using the following formula:

$$\text{Formula for cell B19:} \quad =B4/B\$6$$

(Copy to B20 through C20.)

14.14.1 BAYES'S THEOREM

Bayes's Theorem provides another definition of conditional probability that is sometimes useful. This definition is:

$$P(A \mid B) = \frac{P(B|A)P(A)}{P(B|A)P(A) + P(B|\overline{A})P(\overline{A})}$$

In this formula, A and B represent any two events, and $\overline{A}$ is the complement of A. To see how this formula might be used, suppose that we want to determine $P(H \mid F)$ but we do not have accecc to the joint probability table and Figure 14 31. According to Bayes's Theorem, we know that:

$$P(H \mid F) = \frac{P(F|H)P(H)}{P(F|H)P(H) + P(F|L)P(L)}$$

If we know the values for the various quantities on the RHS of this equation, we can compute $P(H \mid F)$ as in the following example:

$$P(H \mid F) = \frac{P(F|H)P(H)}{P(F|H)P(H) + P(F|L)P(L)} = \frac{(0.857)(0.70)}{(0.857)(0.70) + (0.223)(0.30)} = 0.90$$

This result is consistent with the value of $P(H|F)$ shown in cell B12 in Figure 14.31.

14.15 Utility Theory

Although the EMV decision rule is widely used, sometimes the decision alternative with the highest EMV is not the most desirable or most preferred alternative by the decision maker. For example, suppose that we could buy either of the two companies listed in the following payoff table for exactly the same price:

Company	State of Nature 1	State of Nature 2	EMV	
A	150,000	−30,000	60,000	← maximum
B	70,000	40,000	55,000	
Probability	0.5	0.5		

The payoff values listed in this table represent the annual profits expected from this business. Thus, in any year, a 50% chance exists that company A will generate a profit of $150,000 and a 50% chance that it will generate a loss of $30,000. On the other hand, in each year, a 50% chance exists that company B will generate a profit of $70,000 and a 50% chance that it will generate a profit of $40,000.

According to the EMV decision rule, we should buy company A because it has the highest EMV. However, company A represents a far more risky investment than company B. Although company A would generate the highest EMV over the long run, we might not have the financial resources to withstand the potential losses of $30,000 per year that could occur in the short run with this alternative. With company B, we can be sure of making at least $40,000 each year. Although company B's EMV over the long run might not be as great as that of company A, for many decision makers, this is more than offset by the increased peace of mind associated with company B's relatively stable profit level. However, other decision makers might be willing to accept the greater risk associated with company A in hopes of achieving the higher potential payoffs this alternative provides.

As this example illustrates, the EMVs of different decision alternatives do not necessarily reflect the relative attractiveness of the alternatives to a particular decision maker. **Utility theory** provides a way to incorporate the decision maker's attitudes and preferences toward risk and return in the decision-analysis process so that the most desirable decision alternative is identified.

14.15.1 UTILITY FUNCTIONS

Utility theory assumes that every decision maker uses a **utility function** that translates each of the possible payoffs in a decision problem into a nonmonetary measure known as a utility. The **utility** of a payoff represents the total worth, value, or desirability of the outcome of a decision alternative to the decision maker. For convenience, we will begin by representing utilities on a scale from 0 to 1, where 0 represents the least value, and 1 represents the most.

Different decision makers have different attitudes and preferences toward risk and return. Those who are "risk neutral" tend to make decisions using the maximum EMV decision rule. However, some decision makers are risk avoiders (or "risk averse"), and others look for risk (or are "risk seekers"). The utility functions typically associated with these three types of decision makers are shown in Figure 14.32.

Figure 14.32 illustrates how the same monetary payoff might produce different levels of utility for three different decision makers. A "risk averse" decision maker assigns the

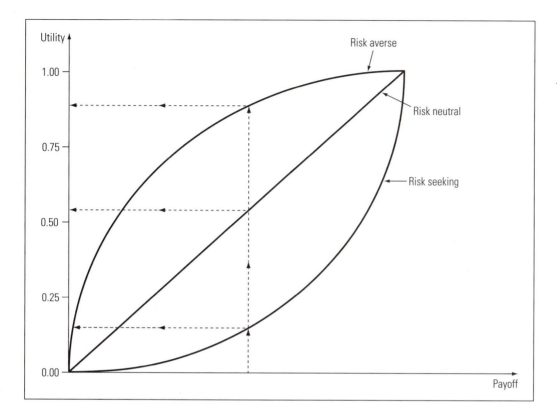

FIGURE 14.32

Three common types of utility functions

largest relative utility to any payoff but has a diminishing marginal utility for increased payoffs (that is, every additional dollar in payoff results in smaller increases in utility). The "risk seeking" decision maker assigns the smallest utility to any payoff but has an increasing marginal utility for increased payoffs (that is, every additional dollar in payoff results in larger increases in utility). The "risk neutral" decision maker (who follows the EMV decision rule) falls in between these two extremes and has a constant marginal utility for increased payoffs (that is, every additional dollar in payoff results in the same amount of increase in utility). The utility curves in Figure 14.32 are not the only ones that can occur. In general, utility curves can assume virtually any form depending on the preferences of the decision maker.

14.15.2 CONSTRUCTING UTILITY FUNCTIONS

Assuming that decision makers use utility functions (perhaps at a subconscious level) to make decisions, how can we determine what a given decision maker's utility function looks like? One approach involves assigning a utility value of 0 to the worst outcome in a decision problem and a utility value of 1 to the best outcome. All other payoffs are assigned utility values between 0 and 1. (Although it is convenient to use endpoint values of 0 and 1, we can use any values provided that the utility value assigned to the worst payoff is less than the utility value assigned to the best payoff.)

We will let $U(x)$ represent the utility associated with a payoff of x. Thus, for the decision about whether to buy company A or B, described earlier, we have:

$$U(-30,000) = 0$$
$$U(150,000) = 1$$

Now suppose that we want to find the utility associated with the payoff of $70,000 in our example. To do this, we must identify the probability p at which the decision maker is indifferent between the following two alternatives:

Alternative 1:   Receive $70,000 with certainty.

Alternative 2:   Receive $150,000 with probability p and lose $30,000 with probability $(1 - p)$

If $p = 0$, most decision makers would choose alternative 1 because they would prefer to receive a payoff of $70,000 rather than lose $30,000. On the other hand, if $p = 1$, most decision makers would choose alternative 2 because they would prefer to receive a payoff of $150,000 rather than $70,000. So as p increases from 0 to 1, it reaches a point—p^*—at which the decision maker is indifferent between the two alternatives. That is, if $p < p^*$, the decision maker prefers alternative 1, and if $p > p^*$, the decision maker prefers alternative 2. The point of indifference, p^*, varies from one decision maker to another, depending on the decision maker's attitude toward risk and according to his or her ability to sustain a loss of $30,000.

In our example, suppose that the decision maker is indifferent between alternative 1 and 2 when $p = 0.8$ (so that $p^* = 0.8$). The utility of the $70,000 payoff for this decision maker is computed as:

$$U(70,000) = U(150,000)\, p^* + U(-30,000)(1 - p^*) = 1\, p^* + 0(1 - p^*) = p^* = 0.8$$

Notice that when $p = 0.8$, the expected value of alternative 2 is:

$$\$150,000 \times 0.8 - \$30,000 \times 0.2 = \$114,000$$

Because the decision maker is indifferent between a risky decision (alternative 2) that has an EMV of $114,000 and a nonrisky decision (alternative 1) that has a certain payoff of $70,000, this decision maker is "risk averse." That is, the decision maker is willing to accept only $70,000 to avoid the risk associated with a decision that has an EMV of $114,000.

The term **certainty equivalent** refers to the amount of money that is equivalent in a decision maker's mind to a situation that involves uncertainty. For example, $70,000 is the decision maker's certainty equivalent for the uncertain situation represented by alternative 2 when $p = 0.8$. A closely related term, **risk premium**, refers to the EMV that a decision maker is willing to give up (or pay) in order to avoid a risky decision. In our example, the risk premium is $114,000 - $70,000 = $44,000; that is:

$$\text{Risk premium} = \begin{pmatrix} \text{EMV of an} \\ \text{uncertain situation} \end{pmatrix} - \begin{pmatrix} \text{certainty equivalent of} \\ \text{the same uncertain situation} \end{pmatrix}$$

To find the utility associated with the $40,000 payoff in our example, we must identify the probability p at which the decision maker is indifferent between the following two alternatives:

Alternative 1:   Receive $40,000 with certainty.

Alternative 2:   Receive $150,000 with probability p and lose $30,000 with probability $(1 - p)$.

Because we reduced the payoff amount listed in alternative 1 from its earlier value of $70,000, we expect that the value of p at which the decision maker is indifferent would also be reduced. In this case, suppose that the decision maker is indifferent between the two alternatives when $p = 0.65$ (so that $p^* = 0.65$). The utility associated with a payoff of $40,000 is:

$$U(40,000) = U(150,000) \, p^* + U(-30,000)(1 - p^*) = 1 \, p^* + 0(1 - p^*) = p^* = 0.65$$

Again, the utility associated with the amount given in alternative 1 is equivalent to the decision maker's indifference point p^*. This is not a coincidence.

K e y   P o i n t

When utilities are expressed on a scale from 0 to 1, the probability p^* at which the decision maker is indifferent between alternatives 1 and 2 always corresponds to the decision maker's utility for the amount listed in alternative 1.

Notice that when $p = 0.65$, the expected value of alternative 2 is:

$$\$150,000 \times 0.65 - \$30,000 \times 0.35 = \$87,000$$

Again, this is "risk averse" behavior because the decision maker is willing to accept only $40,000 (or pay a risk premium of $47,000) to avoid the risk associated with a decision that has an EMV of $87,000.

For our example, the utilities associated with payoffs of $-\$30,000$, $40,000, $70,000, and $150,000 are 0.0, 0.65, 0.80, and 1.0, respectively. If we plot these values on a graph and connect the points with straight lines, we can estimate the shape of the decision maker's utility function for this decision problem, as shown in Figure 14.33. Note that the shape of this utility function is consistent with the general shape of the utility function for a "risk averse" decision maker given in Figure 14.32.

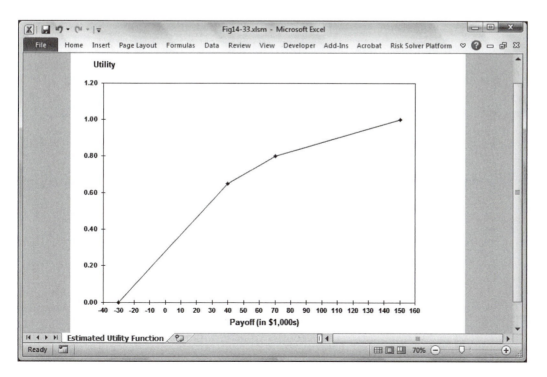

FIGURE 14.33

An estimated utility function for the example problem

14.15.3 USING UTILITIES TO MAKE DECISIONS

After determining the utility value of each possible monetary payoff, we can apply the standard tools of decision analysis to determine the alternative that provides the highest expected utility. We do so using utility values in place of monetary values in payoff tables or decision trees. For our current example, we substitute the appropriate utilities in the payoff table and compute the expected utility for each decision alternative as:

	State of Nature		
Company	1	2	Expected Utility
A	1.00	0.00	0.500
B	0.80	0.65	0.725 ← maximum
Probability	0.5	0.5	

In this case, the decision to purchase company B provides the greatest expected level of utility to this decision maker—even though our earlier analysis indicated that its EMV of $55,000 is less than company A's EMV of $60,000. Thus, by using utilities, decision makers can identify the alternative that is most attractive given their personal attitudes about risk and return.

14.15.4 THE EXPONENTIAL UTILITY FUNCTION

In a complicated decision problem with numerous possible payoff values, it might be difficult and time-consuming for a decision maker to determine the different values for p^* that are required to determine the utility for each payoff. However, if the decision maker is "risk averse," the **exponential utility function** can be used as an approximation of the decision maker's actual utility function. The general form of the exponential utility function is:

$$U(x) = 1 - e^{-x/R}$$

In this formula, e is the base of the natural logarithm ($e = 2.718281 \ldots$), and R is a parameter that controls the shape of the utility function according to a decision maker's risk tolerance. Figure 14.34 shows examples of the graph of this function for several values of R. Note that as R increases, the shape of the utility curve becomes flatter (or less "risk averse"). Also note that as x becomes large, $U(x)$ approaches 1; when $x = 0$, then $U(x) = 0$; and if x is less than 0, then $U(x) < 0$.

To use the exponential utility function, we must determine a reasonable value for the risk tolerance parameter R. One method for doing so involves determining the maximum value of Y for which the decision maker is willing to participate in a game of chance with the following possible outcomes:

Win $Y with probability 0.5

Lose $Y/2 with probability 0.5

The maximum value of Y for which the decision maker would accept this gamble should give us a reasonable estimate of R. Note that a decision maker willing to accept this gamble only at very small values of Y is "risk averse," whereas a decision maker willing to play for larger values of Y is less "risk averse." This corresponds with the relationship between the utility curves and values of R shown in Figure 14.34. (As a rule of thumb, anecdotal evidence suggests that many firms exhibit risk tolerances of approximately one-sixth of equity or 125% of net yearly income.)

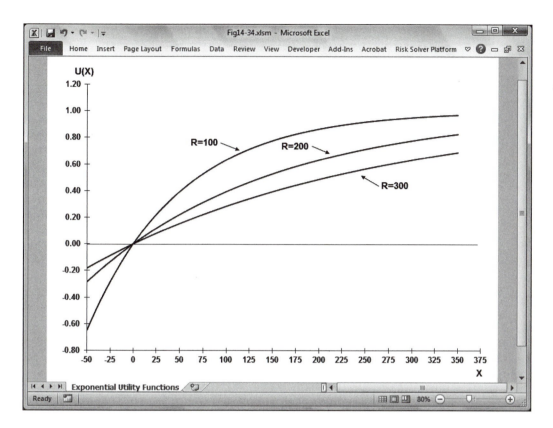

FIGURE 14.34

Examples of the exponential utility function

14.15.5 INCORPORATING UTILITIES IN DECISION TREES

Risk Solver Platform's Decision Tree tool provides a simple way to use the exponential utility function to model "risk averse" decision preferences in a decision tree. We will illustrate this using the decision tree developed earlier for Magnolia Inns, where Barbara needs to decide which parcel of land to purchase. The decision tree developed for this problem is shown again in Figure 14.35 (and in the file Fig14-35.xlsm that accompanies this book).

To use the exponential utility function, we first construct a decision tree in the usual way. We then determine the risk tolerance value of R for the decision maker using the technique described earlier. Because Barbara is making this decision on behalf of Magnolia Inns, it is important that she provide an estimated value of R based on the acceptable risk levels of the corporation—not her own personal risk tolerance level.

In this case, let's assume that $4 million is the maximum value of Y for which Barbara believes Magnolia Inns is willing to gamble winning $Y with probability 0.5 and losing $Y/2 with probability 0.5. Therefore, $R = Y = 4$. (Note that the value of R should be expressed in the same units as the payoffs in the decision tree.)

We can now instruct the Decision Tree tool to use an exponential utility function to determine the optimal decision by following these steps:

1. Select the Decision Tree element in the Risk Solver task pane.
2. Change the Risk Tolerance property to 4.
3. Change the Certainty Equivalents property to Exponential Utility Function.

FIGURE 14.35 *Decision tree for the Magnolia Inns land purchase problem*

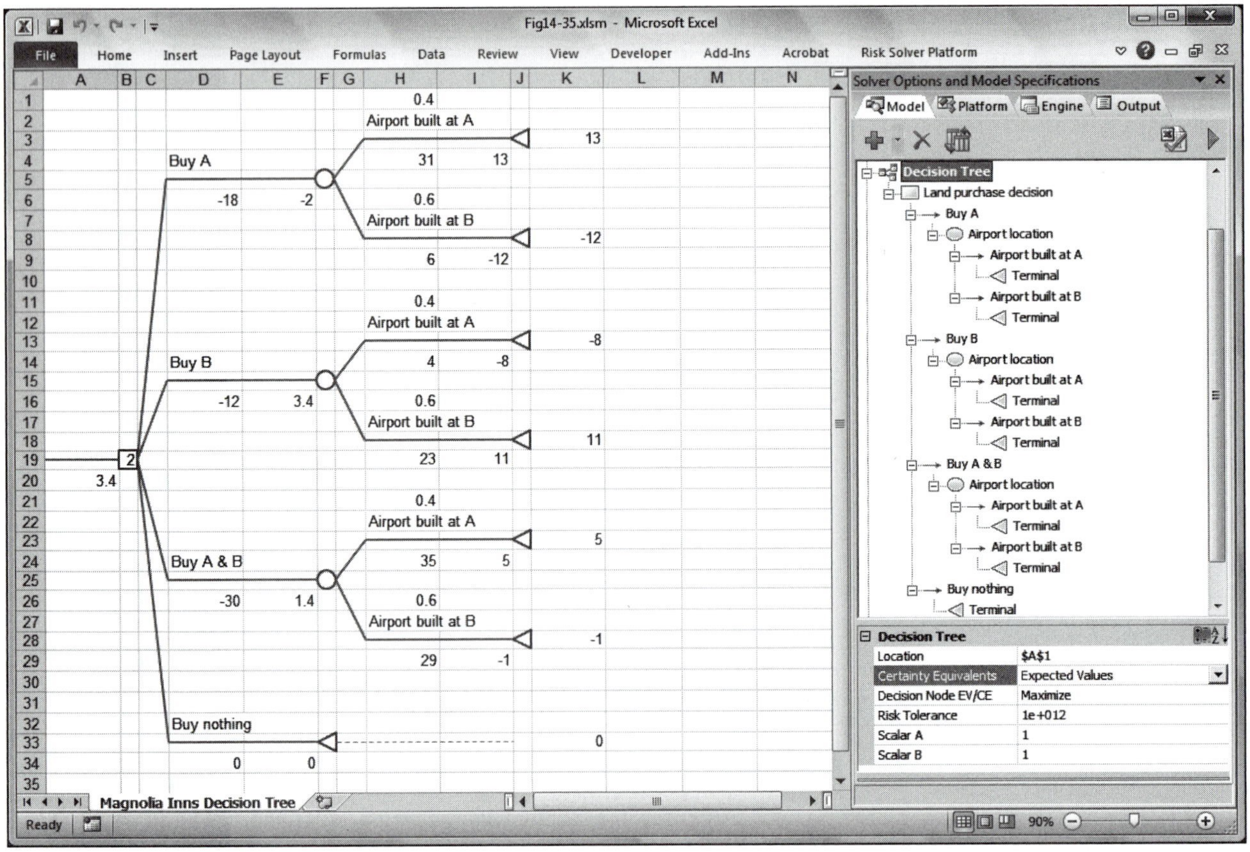

The decision tree is then automatically converted so that the rollback operation is performed using expected utilities rather than EMVs. The resulting tree is shown in Figure 14.36. The certainty equivalent at each node appears in the cell directly below and to the left of each node (previously the location of the EMVs). The expected utility at each node appears immediately below the certainty equivalents. According to this tree, the decision to buy the parcels at locations A and B provides the highest expected utility for Magnolia Inns. Here again, it might be wise to investigate how the recommended decision might change if we had used a different risk tolerance value and/or different probabilities.

14.16 Multicriteria Decision Making

A decision maker often uses more than one criterion or objective to evaluate the alternatives in a decision problem. Sometimes, these criteria conflict with one another. For example, consider again the criteria of risk and return. Most decision makers desire high levels of return and low levels of risk. But high returns are usually accompanied by high risks, and low levels of return are associated with low risk levels. In making investment decisions, a decision maker must assess the trade-offs between risk and return to identify the decision that achieves the most satisfying balance of these two criteria. As we have seen, utility theory represents one approach to assessing the trade-offs between the criteria of risk and return.

FIGURE 14.36 *Analysis of the Magnolia Inns decision tree using an exponential utility function*

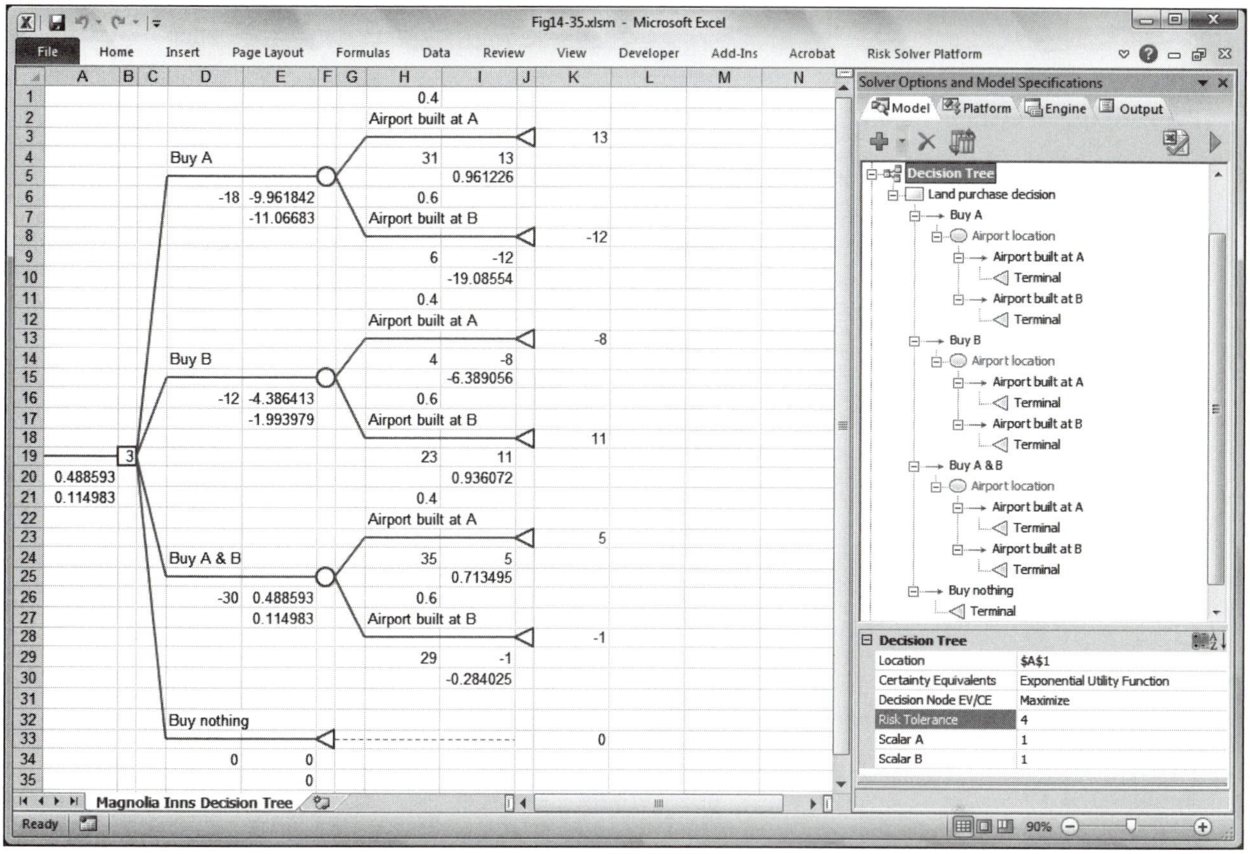

Many other types of decision problems involve multiple conflicting criteria. For example, in choosing between two or more different job offers, you must evaluate the alternatives on the basis of starting salary, opportunity for advancement, job security, location, and so on. If you purchase a video camcorder, you must evaluate a number of different models based on the manufacturer's reputation, price, warranty, size, weight, zoom capability, lighting requirements, and a host of other features. If you must decide whom to hire to fill a vacancy in your organization, you will likely have to evaluate a number of candidates on the basis of education, experience, references, and personality. This section presents two techniques that can be used in decision problems that involve multiple criteria.

14.17 The Multicriteria Scoring Model

The **multicriteria scoring model** is a simple procedure in which we score (or rate) each alternative in a decision problem based on each criterion. The score for alternative j on criterion i is denoted by s_{ij}. Weights (denoted by w_i) are assigned to each criterion indicating its relative importance to the decision maker. For each alternative, we then compute a weighted average score as:

$$\text{Weighted average score for alternative } j = \sum_i w_i s_{ij}$$

FIGURE 14.37

A multicriteria scoring model

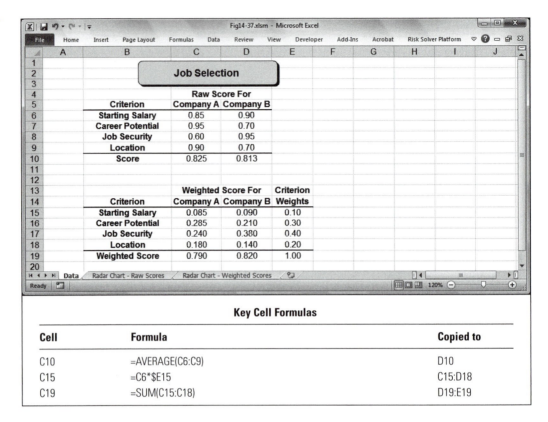

	Key Cell Formulas	
Cell	**Formula**	**Copied to**
C10	=AVERAGE(C6:C9)	D10
C15	=C6*$E15	C15:D18
C19	=SUM(C15:C18)	D19:E19

We then select the alternative with the largest weighted average score.

The beginning of this chapter described a situation that many students face when they graduate from college—choosing between two job offers. The spreadsheet in Figure 14.37 (and in the file Fig14-37.xlsm that accompanies this book) illustrates how we might use a multicriteria scoring model to help in this problem.

In choosing between two (or more) job offers, we would evaluate criteria for each alternative, such as the starting salary, potential for career development, job security, location of the job, and perhaps other factors as well. The idea in a scoring model is to assign a value from 0 to 1 to each decision alternative that reflects its relative worth on each criterion. These values can be thought of as subjective assessments of the utility that each alternative provides on the various criteria.

In Figure 14.37, scores for each criterion were entered in cells C6 through D9. These scores indicate the starting salary offered by company B provides the greatest value, but the salary offered by company A is not much worse. (Note that these scores do not necessarily mean that the starting salary offered by company B was the highest. These scores reflect the *value* of the salaries to the decision maker, taking into account such factors as the cost of living in the different locations.) The remaining scores in the table indicate that company A provides the greatest potential for career advancement and is in the most attractive location but provides considerably less job security than that offered by company B. The average scores associated with each job offer are calculated in cells C10 and D10 as follows:

Formula for cell C10:   =AVERAGE(C6:C9)

(Copy to D10.)

Notice that the offer from company A has a higher average score than that of company B. However, this implicitly assumes that all the criteria are of equal importance to the decision maker, which is not often the case.

Next, the decision maker specifies weights that indicate the relative importance of each criterion. Again, this is done subjectively. Hypothetical weights for each criterion in this example are shown in cells E15 through E18 in Figure 14.37. Note that these weights must sum to 1. The weighted scores for each criterion and alternative are calculated in cells C15 through D18 as:

> Formula for cell C15:   =C6*$E15
> (Copy to C15 to D18.)

We can then sum these values to calculate the weighted average score for each alternative as:

> Formula for cell C19:   =SUM(C15:C18)
> (Copy to E19.)

In this case, the total weighted average scores for company A and B are 0.79 and 0.82, respectively. Thus, when the importance of each criterion is accounted for via weights, the model indicates that the decision maker should accept the job with company B because it has the largest weighted average score.

Radar charts provide an effective way of graphically summarizing numerous alternatives in a multicriteria scoring model. Figure 14.38 shows the raw scores associated with each of the alternatives in our job selection example. A glance at this chart makes it clear that the offers from both companies offer very similar values in terms of salary,

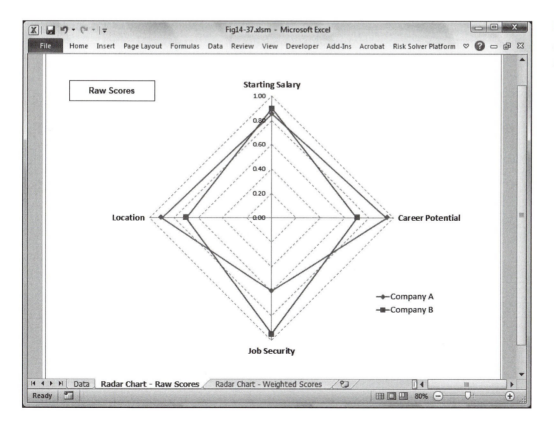

FIGURE 14.38

Radar chart of the raw scores

FIGURE 14.39

Radar chart of the weighted scores

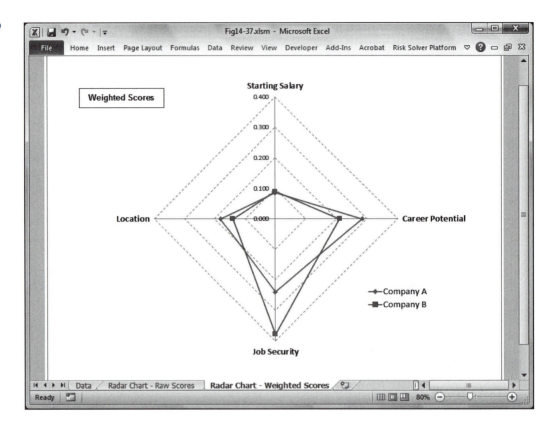

company A is somewhat more desirable in terms of career potential and location, and company B is quite a bit more desirable in terms of job security.

Figure 14.39 shows another radar chart of the weighted scores for each of the alternatives. Using the weighted scores, the radar chart tends to accentuate the differences on criteria that were heavily weighted. For instance, here the offers from the two companies are very similar in terms of salary and location and are most different with respect to career potential and job security. The radar chart's capability to graphically portray the differences in the alternatives can be quite helpful—particularly for decision makers that do not relate well to tables of numbers.

Creating a Radar Chart

To create a radar chart like the one shown in Figure 14.39:

1. Select cells B14 through D18.
2. Click the Insert menu.
3. Click Other Charts.
4. Click Radar with Markers.

Excel then creates a basic chart that you can customize in many ways. Right-clicking a chart element displays a dialog box with options for modifying the appearance of the element.

14.18 The Analytic Hierarchy Process

Sometimes, a decision maker finds it difficult to subjectively determine the criterion scores and weights needed in the multicriteria scoring model. In this case, the analytic hierarchy process (AHP) can be helpful. AHP provides a more structured approach for determining the scores and weights for the multicriteria scoring model described earlier. This can be especially helpful in focusing attention and discussion on the important aspects of a problem in group decision-making environments. However, the validity of AHP is not universally accepted. As with any structured decision-making process, the recommendations of AHP should not be followed blindly but should be carefully considered and evaluated by the decision maker(s).

To illustrate AHP, suppose that a company wants to purchase a new payroll and personnel records information system and is considering three systems, identified as X, Y, and Z. The systems differ with respect to three key criteria: price, user support, and ease of use.

14.18.1 PAIRWISE COMPARISONS

The first step in AHP is to create a pairwise comparison matrix for each alternative on each criterion. We will illustrate the details of this process for the price criterion. The values shown in Figure 14.40 are used in AHP to describe the decision maker's preferences between two alternatives on a given criterion.

FIGURE 14.40

Scale for pairwise comparisons in AHP

Value	Preference
1	Equally Preferred
2	Equally to Moderately Preferred
3	Moderately Preferred
4	Moderately to Strongly Preferred
5	Strongly Preferred
6	Strongly to Very Strongly Preferred
7	Very Strongly Preferred
8	Very Strongly to Extremely Preferred
9	Extremely Preferred

To create a pairwise comparison matrix for the price criterion, we must perform pairwise comparisons of the prices of systems X, Y, and Z using the values shown in Figure 14.40. Let P_{ij} denote the extent to which we prefer alternative i to alternative j on a given criterion. For example, suppose that when comparing system X to Y, the decision maker strongly prefers the price of X. In this case, $P_{XY} = 5$. Similarly, suppose that when comparing system X to Z, the decision maker very strongly prefers the price of X, and when comparing Y to Z, the decision maker moderately prefers the price of Y. In this case, $P_{XZ} = 7$, and $P_{YZ} = 3$. We used the values of these pairwise comparisons to create the pairwise comparison matrix shown in Figure 14.41 (and file Fig14-41.xlsm that accompanies this book).

The values of P_{XY}, P_{XZ}, and P_{YZ} are shown in cells D4, E4, and E5 in Figure 14.41. We entered the value 1 along the main diagonal in Figure 14.41 to indicate that if an alternative is compared against itself, the decision maker should equally prefer either alternative (because they are the same).

FIGURE 14.41

*Pairwise
comparisons of the
price criterion for
the three systems*

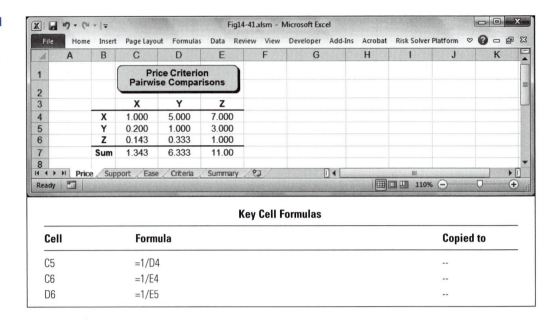

Key Cell Formulas

Cell	Formula	Copied to
C5	=1/D4	--
C6	=1/E4	--
D6	=1/E5	--

The entries in cells C5, C6, and D6 correspond to P_{YX}, P_{ZX}, and P_{ZY}, respectively. To determine these values, we could obtain the decision maker's preferences between Y and X, Z and X, and Z and Y. However, if we already know the decision maker's preference between X and Y (P_{XY}), we can conclude that the decision maker's preference between Y and X (P_{YX}) is the reciprocal of the preference between X and Y; that is, $P_{YX} = 1/P_{XY}$. So, in general, we have:

$$P_{ji} = \frac{1}{P_{ij}}$$

Thus, the values in cells C5, C6, and D6 are computed as:

Formula for cell C5:   =1/D4
Formula for cell C6:   =1/E4
Formula for cell D6:   =1/E5

14.18.2 NORMALIZING THE COMPARISONS

The next step in AHP is to normalize the matrix of pairwise comparisons. To do this, we first calculate the sum of each column in the pairwise comparison matrix. We then divide each entry in the matrix by its column sum. Figure 14.42 shows the resulting normalized matrix.

We will use the average of each row in the normalized matrix as the score for each alternative on the criterion under consideration. For example, cells F11, F12, and F13 indicate that the average scores on the price criterion for X, Y, and Z are 0.724, 0.193, and 0.083, respectively. These scores indicate the relative desirability of the three alternatives to the decision maker with respect to price. The score for X indicates that this is by far the most attractive alternative with respect to price, and alternative Y is somewhat more attractive than Z. Note that these scores reflect the preferences expressed by the decision maker in the pairwise comparison matrix.

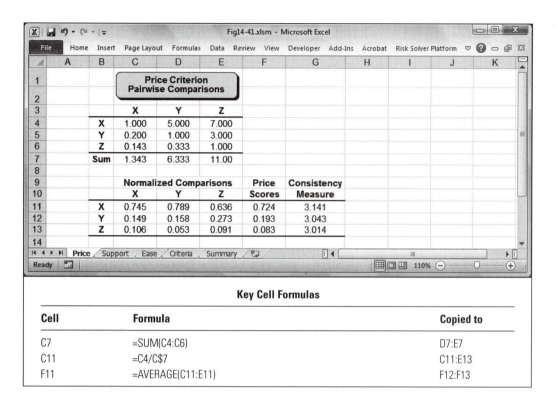

FIGURE 14.42

*Price scores
obtained from
the normalized
comparison matrix*

14.18.3 CONSISTENCY

In applying AHP, the decision maker should be consistent in the preference ratings given in the pairwise comparison matrix. For example, if the decision maker strongly prefers the price of X to that of Y, and strongly prefers the price of Y to that of Z, it would be inconsistent for the decision maker to indicate indifference (or equal preference) regarding the price of X and Z. Thus, before using the scores derived from the normalized comparison matrix, the preferences indicated in the original pairwise comparison matrix should be checked for consistency.

A consistency measure for each alternative is obtained as:

$$\text{Consistency measure for X} = \frac{0.724 \times 1 + 0.193 \times 5 + 0.083 \times 7}{0.724} = 3.141$$

$$\text{Consistency measure for Y} = \frac{0.724 \times 0.2 + 0.193 \times 1 + 0.083 \times 3}{0.193} = 3.043$$

$$\text{Consistency measure for Z} = \frac{0.724 \times 0.143 + 0.193 \times 0.333 + 0.083 \times 1}{0.083} = 3.014$$

The numerator in each of these calculations multiplies the scores obtained from the normalized matrix by the preferences given in one of the rows of the original pairwise comparison matrix. The products are summed and then divided by the score for the alternative in question. These consistency measures are shown in Figure 14.43 in cells G11 through G13.

If the decision maker is perfectly consistent in stating preferences, each consistency measure will equal the number of alternatives in the problem (which, in this case, is three). So, there appears to be some amount of inconsistency in the preferences given in

FIGURE 14.43

Checking the consistency of the pairwise comparisons

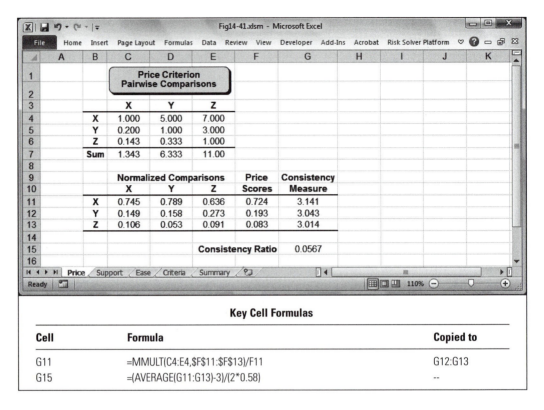

			Price Criterion **Pairwise Comparisons**				
		X	**Y**	**Z**			
	X	1.000	5.000	7.000			
	Y	0.200	1.000	3.000			
	Z	0.143	0.333	1.000			
	Sum	1.343	6.333	11.00			
		Normalized Comparisons			**Price**	**Consistency**	
		X	**Y**	**Z**	**Scores**	**Measure**	
	X	0.745	0.789	0.636	0.724	3.141	
	Y	0.149	0.158	0.273	0.193	3.043	
	Z	0.106	0.053	0.091	0.083	3.014	
					Consistency Ratio	0.0567	

Key Cell Formulas

Cell	Formula	Copied to
G11	=MMULT(C4:E4,$F$11:$F$13)/F11	G12:G13
G15	=(AVERAGE(G11:G13)-3)/(2*0.58)	--

the pairwise comparison matrix. This is not unusual. It is difficult for a decision maker to be perfectly consistent in stating preferences between a large number of pairwise comparisons. Provided that the amount of inconsistency is not excessive, the scores obtained from the normalized matrix will be reasonably accurate. To determine whether the inconsistency is excessive, we compute the following quantities:

$$\text{Consistency Index (CI)} = \frac{\lambda - n}{n - 1}$$

$$\text{Consistency Ratio (CR)} = \frac{\text{CI}}{\text{RI}}$$

where:

λ = the average consistency measure for all alternatives

n = the number of alternatives

RI = the appropriate random index from Figure 14.44

FIGURE 14.44

Values of RI for use in AHP

n	RI
2	0.00
3	0.58
4	0.90
5	1.12
6	1.24
7	1.32
8	1.41

If the pairwise comparison matrix is perfectly consistent, then $\lambda = n$, and the consistency ratio is 0. The values of RI in Figure 14.44 give the average value of CI if all the entries in the pairwise comparison matrix were chosen at random, given that all the diagonal entries equal 1, and $P_{ij} = 1/P_{ji}$. If $CR \leq 0.10$, the degree of consistency in the pairwise comparison matrix is satisfactory. However, if $CR > 0.10$, serious inconsistencies might exist and AHP might not yield meaningful results. The value for CR shown in cell G15 in Figure 14.43 indicates that the pairwise comparison matrix for the price criterion is reasonably consistent. Therefore, we can assume that the scores for the price criterion obtained from the normalized matrix are reasonably accurate.

14.18.4 OBTAINING SCORES FOR THE REMAINING CRITERIA

We can repeat the process for obtaining the price criterion scores to obtain scores for the user support and ease-of-use criteria. Hypothetical results for these criteria are shown in Figures 14.45 and 14.46, respectively.

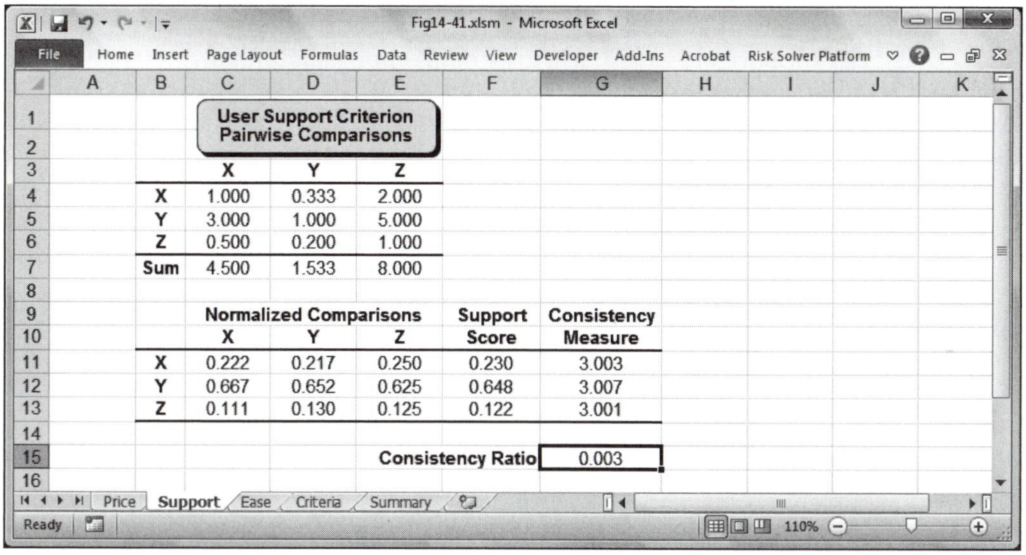

	X	Y	Z
X	1.000	0.333	2.000
Y	3.000	1.000	5.000
Z	0.500	0.200	1.000
Sum	4.500	1.533	8.000

	Normalized Comparisons X	Y	Z	Support Score	Consistency Measure
X	0.222	0.217	0.250	0.230	3.003
Y	0.667	0.652	0.625	0.648	3.007
Z	0.111	0.130	0.125	0.122	3.001
				Consistency Ratio	0.003

FIGURE 14.45

Spreadsheet used to calculate scores for the user support criterion

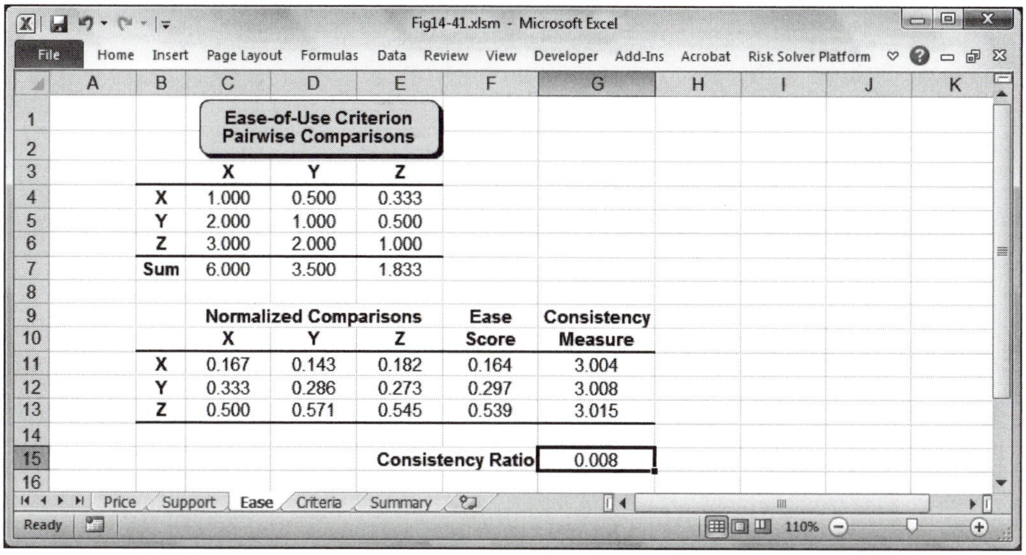

	X	Y	Z
X	1.000	0.500	0.333
Y	2.000	1.000	0.500
Z	3.000	2.000	1.000
Sum	6.000	3.500	1.833

	Normalized Comparisons X	Y	Z	Ease Score	Consistency Measure
X	0.167	0.143	0.182	0.164	3.004
Y	0.333	0.286	0.273	0.297	3.008
Z	0.500	0.571	0.545	0.539	3.015
				Consistency Ratio	0.008

FIGURE 14.46

Spreadsheet used to calculate scores for the ease-of-use criterion

We can create these two spreadsheets easily by copying the spreadsheet for the price criterion (shown in Figure 14.43) and having the decision maker fill in the pairwise comparison matrices with preferences related to the user support and ease-of-use criteria. Notice that the preferences given in Figures 14.45 and 14.46 appear to be consistent.

14.18.5 OBTAINING CRITERION WEIGHTS

The scores shown in Figures 14.43, 14.45, and 14.46 indicate how the alternatives compare with respect to the price, user support, and ease-of-use criteria. Before we can use these values in a scoring model, we must also determine weights that indicate the relative importance of the three criteria to the decision maker. The pairwise comparison process used earlier to generate scores for the alternatives on each criterion can also be used to generate criterion weights.

The pairwise comparison matrix in Figure 14.47 shows the decision maker's preferences for the three criteria. The values in cells C5 and C6 indicate that the decision maker finds user support and ease of use to be more important (or more preferred) than price, and cell D6 indicates that ease of use is somewhat more important than user support. These relative preferences are reflected in the criterion weights shown in cells F11 through F13.

FIGURE 14.47

Spreadsheet used to determine the criterion weights

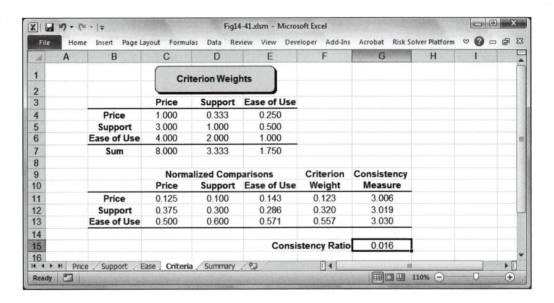

14.18.6 IMPLEMENTING THE SCORING MODEL

We now have all the elements required to analyze this decision problem using a scoring model. Thus, the last step in AHP is to calculate the weighted average scores for each decision alternative. The weighted average scores are shown in cells C8 through E8 in Figure 14.48. According to these scores, alternative Y should be selected.

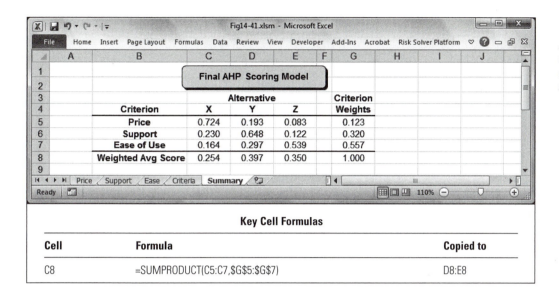

FIGURE 14.48

Final scoring model for selecting the information system

14.19 Summary

This chapter presented a number of techniques for analyzing a variety of decision problems. First, it discussed how a payoff table can be used to summarize the alternatives in a single-stage decision problem. Then, a number of nonprobabilistic and probabilistic decision rules were presented. No one decision rule works best in all situations, but together, the rules help to highlight different aspects of a problem and can help develop and sharpen a decision maker's insight and intuition about a problem so that better decisions can be made. When probabilities of occurrence can be estimated for the alternatives in a problem, the EMV decision rule is the most commonly used technique.

Decision trees are particularly helpful in expressing multistage decision problems in which a series of decisions must be considered. Each terminal node in a decision tree is associated with the net payoff that results from each possible sequence of decisions. A rollback technique determines the alternative that results in the highest EMV. Because different decision makers derive different levels of value from the same monetary payoff, the chapter also discussed how utility theory can be applied to decision problems to account for these differences.

Finally, the chapter discussed two procedures for dealing with decision problems that involve multiple conflicting decision criteria. The multicriteria scoring model requires the decision maker to assign a score for each alternative on each criterion. Weights are then assigned to represent the relative importance of the criteria, and a weighted average score is computed for each alternative. The alternative with the highest score is the recommended alternative. AHP provides a structured approach to determining the scores and weights used in a multicriteria scoring model if the decision maker has difficulty specifying these values.

14.20 References

Bodin, L., and S. Gass. "On Teaching the Analytic Hierarchy Process." *Computers & Operations Research*, vol. 30, pp. 1487–1497, 2003.

Clemen, R. *Making Hard Decisions: An Introduction to Decision Analysis.* Duxbury Press, 1997.

Corner, J., and C. Kirkwood. "Decision Analysis Applications in the Operations Research Literature 1970–1989." *Operations Research*, vol. 39, no. 2, 1991.

Coyle, R. *Decision Analysis.* London: Nelson, 1972.

Hastie, R., and R. Dawes. *Rational Choice in an Uncertain World: The Psychology of Judgment and Decision Making.* Thousand Oaks, CA: Sage Publications, Inc., 2001.

Heian, B., and J. Gale. "Mortgage Selection Using a Decision-Tree Approach: An Extension." *Interfaces*, vol. 18, July-August 1988.

Howard, R. A., "Decision Analysis: Practice and Promise." *Management Science*, vol. 34, pp. 679–695, 1988.

Keeney, R. *Value-Focused Thinking.* Cambridge, MA: Harvard University Press, 1992.

Keeney, R., and H. Raiffa. *Decision With Multiple Objectives.* New York: Wiley, 1976.

Merkhofer, M. W. "Quantifying Judgmental Uncertainty: Methodology, Experiences & Insights." *IEEE Transactions on Systems, Man, and Cybernetics*, vol. 17, pp. 741–752, 1987.

Skinner, D. *Introduction to Decision Analysis: A Practitioner's Guide to Improving Decision Quality.* Gainesville, FL: Probabilistic Publishing, 2001.

Wenstop, F., and A. Carlsen. "Ranking Hydroelectric Power Projects with Multicriteria Decision Analysis." *Interfaces*, vol. 18, no. 4, 1988.

Zahedi, F. "The Analytic Hierarchy Process—A Survey of the Method and Its Applications." *Interfaces*, vol. 16, no. 4, 1986.

THE WORLD OF MANAGEMENT SCIENCE

Decision Theory Helps Hallmark Trim Discards

Many items distributed by Hallmark Cards, Incorporated can be sold only during a single season. Leftovers, or discards, must then be disposed of outside normal dealer channels. For example, table items such as napkins can be used in the company's cafeteria, donated to charity, or sold without the brand name to volume discounters. Other items have no salvage value at all.

A product manager deciding the size of a production run or quantity to purchase from a supplier faces two risks. First is the consequence of choosing a quantity that is larger than the eventual demand for the product. Products that have been paid for must be discarded, and the salvage value (if any) might not make up for the cost. The second risk is that the quantity might be less than demand, in which case, revenues are lost.

A substantial increase in the dollar volume of discards prompted Hallmark management to initiate a training program for product managers and inventory controllers. They were taught to use product cost and selling price together with a probability distribution of demand to make order quantity decisions. The format for conducting the analysis was a payoff matrix in which rows represented order quantities, and columns represented demand levels. Each cell in the payoff matrix contained a computed contribution to profit.

Salvage values and shortage costs were not included in the values of the payoff matrix cells. Instead, sensitivity analysis provided ranges of values within which the order quantity was still optimal.

Although some probability distributions could be estimated from sales data for previous years, it was sometimes necessary to use subjective probabilities. This was especially true for special promotions that had no relevant product history. For this reason, product managers were trained in specifying subjective probabilities. Although direct assessment of a cumulative distribution function would have tied into the order quantity decision more efficiently, it turned out that the managers became more adept at estimating a discrete probability function.

Enough managers adopted the payoff matrix technique, with positive results, that the training program has been continued and expanded within the company.

Source: F. Hutton Barron. "Payoff Matrices Pay Off at Hallmark." *Interfaces*, vol. 15, no. 4, August 1985, pp. 20–25.

Questions and Problems

1. This chapter presented the problem of having to decide between two job offers. The decision maker could accept the job with company A, accept the job with company B, or reject both offers and hope for a better one. What other alternatives can you think of for this problem?

2. Give an example of a national business, political, or military leader who made a good decision that resulted in a bad outcome, or a bad decision that resulted in a good outcome.

3. Consider the following payoff matrix:

	State of Nature		
Decision	**1**	**2**	**3**
A	50	75	35
B	40	50	60
C	40	35	30

   Should a decision maker ever select decision alternative C? Explain your answer.

4. Brenda Kelley runs a specialty ski clothing shop outside of Boone, North Carolina. She must place her order for ski parkas well in advance of ski season because the manufacturer produces them in the summer months. Brenda needs to determine whether to place a large, medium, or small order for parkas. The number sold will depend largely on whether the area receives a heavy, normal, or light amount of snow during the ski season. The following table summarizes the payoffs Brenda expects to receive under each scenario.

	Amount of Snow		
Size of Order	**Heavy**	**Normal**	**Light**
Large	10	7	3
Medium	8	8	6
Small	4	4	4

   Payoffs (in $1,000s)

   Brenda estimates the probability of heavy, normal, and light snowfalls as 0.25, 0.6, and 0.15, respectively.
   a. What decision should be made according to the maximax decision rule?
   b. What decision should be made according to the maximin decision rule?
   c. What decision should be made according to the minimax regret decision rule?
   d. What decision should be made according to the EMV decision rule?
   e. What decision should be made according to the EOL decision rule?

5. One of Philip Mahn's investments is going to mature, and he wants to determine how to invest the proceeds of $30,000. Philip is considering two new investments: a stock mutual fund and a one-year certificate of deposit (CD). The CD is guaranteed to pay an 8% return. Philip estimates the return on the stock mutual fund as 16%, 9%, or −2%, depending on whether market conditions are good, average, or poor, respectively. Philip estimates the probability of a good, average, and poor market to be 0.1, 0.85, and 0.05, respectively.
   a. Construct a payoff matrix for this problem.
   b. What decision should be made according to the maximax decision rule?
   c. What decision should be made according to the maximin decision rule?
   d. What decision should be made according to the minimax regret decision rule?

e. What decision should be made according to the EMV decision rule?
f. What decision should be made according to the EOL decision rule?
g. How much should Philip be willing to pay to obtain a market forecast that is 100% accurate?

6. A car dealer is offering the following three two-year leasing options:

Plan	Fixed Monthly Payment	Additional Cost Per Mile
I	$200	$0.095 per mile.
II	$300	$0.061 for the first 6,000 miles; $0.050 thereafter.
III	$170	$0.000 for the first 6,000 miles; $0.14 per mile thereafter.

Assume a customer expects to drive between 15,000 and 35,000 miles during the next two years according to the following probability distribution:

$$P(\text{driving } 15{,}000 \text{ miles}) = 0.1$$
$$P(\text{driving } 20{,}000 \text{ miles}) = 0.2$$
$$P(\text{driving } 25{,}000 \text{ miles}) = 0.2$$
$$P(\text{driving } 30{,}000 \text{ miles}) = 0.3$$
$$P(\text{driving } 35{,}000 \text{ miles}) = 0.2$$

a. Construct a payoff matrix for this problem.
b. What decision should be made according to the maximax decision rule? (Keep in mind that the "payoffs" here are costs, where less is better.)
c. What decision should be made according to the maximin decision rule?
d. What decision should be made according to the minimax regret decision rule?
e. What decision should be made according to the EMV decision rule?
f. What decision should be made according to the EOL decision rule?

7. The Fish House (TFH) in Norfolk, Virginia, sells fresh fish and seafood. TFH receives daily shipments of farm-raised trout from a nearby supplier. Each trout costs $2.45 and is sold for $3.95. To maintain its reputation for freshness, at the end of the day, TFH sells any leftover trout to a local pet food manufacturer for $1.25 each. The owner of TFH wants to determine how many trout to order each day. Historically, the daily demand for trout is:

Demand	10	11	12	13	14	15	16	17	18	19	20
Probability	0.02	0.06	0.09	0.11	0.13	0.15	0.18	0.11	0.07	0.05	0.03

a. Construct a payoff matrix for this problem.
b. What decision should be made according to the maximax decision rule?
c. What decision should be made according to the maximin decision rule?
d. What decision should be made according to the minimax regret decision rule?
e. What decision should be made according to the EMV decision rule?
f. What decision should be made according to the EOL decision rule?
g. How much should the owner of TFH be willing to pay to obtain a demand forecast that is 100% accurate?
h. Which decision rule would you recommend TFH use in this case? Why?
i. Suppose that TFH receives a quantity discount that reduces the price to $2.25 per trout if it purchases 15 or more. How many trout would you recommend TFH order each day in this case?

8. Bob Farrell, owner of Farrell Motors, is trying to decide whether to buy an insurance policy to cover hail damage on his inventory of more than 200 cars and trucks. Thunderstorms occur frequently, and they sometimes produce hail the size of golf balls that can severely damage automobiles. Bob estimates the potential damage from hail in the next year as:

Hail Damage (in 1,000s)	0	15	30	45	60	75	90	105
Probability	0.25	0.08	0.10	0.12	0.15	0.12	0.10	0.08

- Bob can buy an insurance policy for $47,000 that would cover 100% of any losses that occur.
- Bob can buy an insurance policy for $25,000 that would cover all losses in excess of $35,000.
- Bob can choose to self-insure, in which case he will not have to pay any insurance premium but will pay for any losses that occur.
   a. Construct a payoff matrix for this problem.
   b. What decision should be made according to the maximax decision rule?
   c. What decision should be made according to the maximin decision rule?
   d. What decision should be made according to the minimax regret decision rule?
   e. What decision should be made according to the EMV decision rule?
   f. What decision should be made according to the EOL decision rule?

9. Morley Properties is planning to build a condominium development on St. Simons Island, Georgia. The company is trying to decide between building a small, medium, or large development. The payoffs received for each size of development will depend on the market demand for condominiums in the area, which could be low, medium, or high. The payoff matrix for this decision problem is:

	Market Demand		
Size of Development	Low	Medium	High
Small	400	400	400
Medium	200	500	500
Large	−400	300	800

(Payoffs in 1,000s)

The owner of the company estimates a 21.75% chance that market demand will be low, a 35.5% chance that it will be medium, and a 42.75% chance that it will be high.
   a. What decision should be made according to the maximax decision rule?
   b. What decision should be made according to the maximin decision rule?
   c. What decision should be made according to the minimax regret decision rule?
   d. What decision should be made according to the EMV decision rule?
   e. What decision should be made according to the EOL decision rule?

10. Refer to the previous question. Morley Properties can hire a consultant to predict the most likely level of demand for this project. This consultant has done many similar studies and has provided Morley Properties with the following joint probability table summarizing the accuracy of the results:

	Actual Demand		
Forecasted Demand	Low	Medium	High
Low	0.1600	0.0300	0.0100
Medium	0.0350	0.2800	0.0350
High	0.0225	0.0450	0.3825

The sum of the entries on the main diagonal of this table indicates that the consultant's forecast is correct about 82.25% of the time, overall.

a. Construct the conditional probability table showing the probabilities of the various actual demands given each of the forecasted demands.

b. What is the EMV of the optimal decision without the consultant's assistance?

c. Construct a decision tree Morley Properties would use to analyze the decision problem if the consultant is hired at a cost of $0.

d. What is the EMV of the optimal decision with the consultant's free assistance?

e. What is the maximum price Morley Properties should be willing to pay the consultant?

11. Refer to question 9. Suppose that the utility function for the owner of Morley Properties can be approximated by the exponential utility function:

$$U(x) = 1 - e^{-x/R}$$

where the risk tolerance value $R = 100$ (in $1,000s).

a. Convert the payoff matrix to utility values.

b. What decision provides the owner of the company with the largest expected utility?

12. Refer to question 10. Suppose that the consultant's fee is $5,000, and the utility function for the owner of Morley Properties can be approximated by the exponential utility function:

$$U(x) = 1 - e^{-x/R}$$

where the risk tolerance value $R = 100$ (in $1,000s).

a. What expected level of utility is realized if Morley Properties hires the consultant?

b. What expected level of utility is realized if Morley Properties does not hire the consultant?

c. Based on this analysis, should Morley Properties hire the consultant?

13. The Tall Oaks Wood Products Company is considering purchasing timberland for $5 million that would provide a future source of timber supply for the company's operations over the next 10 years. Alternatively, for $5 million, the company could also buy timber as needed on the open market. The future cash flows from using the timber are estimated to have a present value of $6 million regardless of whether the company buys the timberland today or waits to purchase its timber as needed over the next 10 years. This means there is a $1 million net present value (NPV) of either buying the timberland now or buying the timber as needed. In other words, from a financial standpoint, the two alternative timber acquisition strategies would be equal. Now suppose, that the company believes there is only a 60% chance that the environmental regulations affecting timber supply will remain unchanged. Furthermore, the company believes that there is a 30% chance these regulations will become stricter during the next 10 years and only a 10% chance that these regulations will be relaxed. A reduction in timber supply should cause an increase in both the present value of future cash flows from using the timber due to higher sales prices and an increase in the present value of the cost of purchasing the timber as needed. (Of course, the change in selling price and buying cost may not be equal.) Should regulations become stricter, the company believes the NPV from buying the timberland now would increase to $1.5 million while an NPV of buying the timber as needed would decrease to −$0.50 million. Increases in the timber supply should have the opposite effects. Thus, should regulations become less strict, the company believes the NPV from buying the timberland now would decrease to −$0.5 million while an NPV of buying the timber as needed would increase to $1.50 million.

a. Construct a payoff matrix for this problem.
b. What decision should be made according to the maximax decision rule?
c. What decision should be made according to the maximin decision rule?
d. What decision should be made according to the minimax regret decision rule?
e. What decision should be made according to the EMV decision rule?
f. What decision should be made according to the EOL decision rule?
g. Construct a decision tree for this problem.

14. MicroProducts, Incorporated (MPI) manufactures printed circuit boards for a major PC manufacturer. Before a board is sent to the customer, three key components must be tested. These components can be tested in any order. If any of the components fail, the entire board must be scrapped. The costs of testing the three components are provided in the following table, along with the probability of each component failing the test:

Component	Cost of Test	Probability of Failure
X	$1.75	0.125
Y	$2.00	0.075
Z	$2.40	0.140

a. Create a decision tree for this problem that could be used to determine the order in which the components should be tested to minimize the expected cost of performing the tests.
b. In which order should the components be tested?
c. What is the expected cost of performing the tests in this sequence?

15. Refer to the previous question. A manufacturing engineer for MPI collected the following data on the failure rates of components X, Y, and Z in a random sample of 1,000 circuit boards:

X	Y	Z	Number of Boards
p	p	p	710
p	f	p	45
p	p	f	110
p	f	f	10
f	p	p	95
f	f	p	10
f	p	f	10
f	f	f	10
	Total:		1,000

(p = pass, f = fail)

For example, the first row in this table indicates that components X, Y, and Z all passed their inspections in 710 out of the 1,000 boards checked. The second row indicates that 45 boards passed inspection on components X and Z but failed on component Y. The remaining rows can be interpreted similarly.

a. Using this data, compute conditional probabilities for the decision tree you developed in question 13. (Note that $P(A|B) = P(A \cap B)/P(B)$ and $P(A|B \cap C) = P(A \cap B \cap C)/P(B \cap C)$.)
b. According to the revised probabilities, in which order should the components be tested?
c. What is the expected cost of performing the tests in this sequence?

16. Bill and Ted are going to the beach with hopes of having an excellent adventure. Before going, they read a report by the world's leading authority on tiger shark behavior indicating that when a tiger shark is in the vicinity of swimmers at the beach, there is a 0.20 probability of the shark biting a swimmer. Shortly after arriving at the beach and getting in the water, Bill and Ted spot the unmistakable dorsal fin of a tiger shark on the surface of the water in the vicinity of where they are swimming. Bill says to Ted, "Dude, let's get out of the water, there's a 0.20 probability someone is going to get bitten by that shark." Ted replies to Bill, "You are *way* wrong man! That probability *could* be zero. Chill out and enjoy the surf, dude."
    a. Show that Ted is correct about the probability. (*Hint*: Consider that $P(A) = P(A \cap B) + P(A \cap \bar{B})$.)
    b. Suppose Bill and Ted decide to stay in the water and are bitten by the shark. Was staying in the water a good decision? Was the outcome of the decision good or bad?
    c. Suppose Bill and Ted decide to stay in the water and are not bitten by the shark. Was staying in the water a good decision? Was the outcome of the decision good or bad?

17. The Banisco Corporation is negotiating a contract to borrow $300,000 to be repaid in a lump sum at the end of nine years. Interest payments will be made on the loan at the end of each year. The company is considering the following three financing arrangements:
    • The company can borrow the money using a fixed rate loan (FRL) that requires interest payments of 9% per year.
    • The company can borrow the money using an adjustable rate loan (ARL) that requires interest payments of 6% at the end of each of the first five years. At the beginning of the sixth year, the interest rate on the loan could change to 7%, 9%, or 11% with probabilities of 0.1, 0.25, and 0.65, respectively.
    • The company can borrow the money using an ARL that requires interest payments of 4% at the end of each of the first three years. At the beginning of the fourth year, the interest rate on the loan could change to 6%, 8%, or 10% with probabilities of 0.05, 0.30, and 0.65, respectively. At the beginning of the seventh year, the interest rate could decrease by 1 percentage point with a probability of 0.1, increase by 1 percentage point with a probability of 0.2, or increase by 3 percentage points with a probability of 0.7.
    a. Create a decision tree for this problem, computing the total interest paid under each possible scenario.
    b. Which decision should the company make if it wants to minimize its expected total interest payments?

18. Refer to the previous question. The present value (PV) of a future cash-flow value (FV) is defined as:

$$PV = \frac{FV}{(1 + r)^n}$$

where n is the number of years into the future in which the cash flow occurs, and r is the discount rate. Suppose that the discount rate for Banisco is 10% ($r = 0.1$).
    a. Create a decision tree for this problem, computing the PV of the total interest paid under each possible scenario.
    b. Which decision should the company make if it wants to minimize the expected PV of its total interest payments?

19. Southern Gas Company (SGC) is preparing to make a bid for oil and gas leasing right in a newly opened drilling area in the Gulf of Mexico. SGC is trying to decide whether to place a high bid of $16 million or a low bid of $7 million. SGC expects to be bidding against its major competitor, Northern Gas Company (NGC) and predicts

NGC to place a bid of $10 million with probability 0.4 or a bid of $6 million with probability 0.6. Geological data collected at the drilling site indicates a 0.15 probability of the reserves at the site being large, a 0.35 probability of being average, and a 0.50 probability of being unusable. A large or average reserve would most likely represent a net asset value of $120 million or $28 million, respectively, after all drilling and extraction costs are paid. The company that wins the bid will drill an exploration well at the site for a cost of $5 million.

   a. Develop a decision tree for this problem.

   b. What is the optimal decision according to the EMV criterion?

   c. Create a sensitivity table showing how the optimal decision would change if the probability of the NGC bidding $10 million varies from 0% to 100% in steps of 10%.

   d. Create a sensitivity table showing how the optimal decision would change if the net asset value of a large reserve varies from $100 million to $140 million in $5 million increments and the net asset value of an average reserve varies from $20 million to $36 million in increments of $2 million.

20. Bulloch County has never allowed liquor to be sold in restaurants. However, in three months, county residents are scheduled to vote on a referendum to allow liquor to be sold by the drink. Currently, polls indicate there is a 60% chance that the referendum will be passed by voters. Phil Jackson is a local real estate speculator who is eyeing a closed restaurant building that is scheduled to be sold at a sealed bid auction. Phil estimates that if he bids $1.25 million, there is a 25% chance he will obtain the property; if he bids $1.45 million, there is a 45% chance he will obtain the property; and if he bids $1.85 million, there is an 85% chance he will obtain the property. If he acquires the property and the referendum passes, Phil believes he could then sell the restaurant for $2.2 million. However, if the referendum fails, he believes he could sell the property for only $1.15 million.

   a. Develop a decision tree for this problem.

   b. What is the optimal decision according to the EMV criterion?

   c. Create a sensitivity table showing how the optimal decision might change if the probability of the referendum passing varies from 0% to 100% in steps of 10%.

   d. To which financial estimate in the decision tree is the EMV most sensitive?

21. Medical studies have shown that 10 out of 100 adults have heart disease. When a person with heart disease is given an EKG test, a 0.9 probability exists that the test will indicate the presence of heart disease. When a person without heart disease is given an EKG test, a 0.95 probability exists that the test will indicate the person does not have heart disease. Suppose that a person arrives at an emergency room complaining of chest pains. An EKG is given and indicates that the person has heart disease. What is the probability that the person actually has heart disease?

22. The Mobile Oil company has recently acquired oil rights to a new potential source of natural oil in Alaska. The current market value of these rights is $90,000. If there is natural oil at the site, it is estimated to be worth $800,000; however, the company would have to pay $100,000 in drilling costs to extract the oil. The company believes there is a 0.25 probability that the proposed drilling site actually would hit the natural oil reserve. Alternatively, the company can pay $30,000 to first carry out a seismic survey at the proposed drilling site. Historically, if the seismic survey produces a favorable result, there is a 0.50 chance of hitting oil at the drilling site. However, if the seismic survey produces an unfavorable result, there is only a 0.14285 probability of hitting oil. The probability of a favorable seismic survey when oil is present at the drilling site is 0.6. The probability of an unfavorable seismic survey when no oil is present is 0.80.

   a. What is the probability of a favorable seismic survey?

   b. What is the probability of an unfavorable seismic survey?

   c. Construct a decision tree for this problem.

   d. What is the optimal decision strategy using the EMV criterion?

   e. To which financial estimate in the decision tree is the EMV most sensitive?

23. Johnstone & Johnstone (J&J) has developed a new type of hand lotion with a distinctive fragrance. Before distributing it nationally, J&J will test market the new product. The joint probability of a successful test market and high sales upon national distribution is 0.5. The joint probability of a successful test market and low sales nationally is 0.1. The joint probabilities of an unsuccessful test market and either high or low sales are both 0.2.

   a. Use this data to construct a joint probability table.

   b. What is the marginal probability of a successful test market?

   c. What is the conditional probability of high sales given a successful test market?

   d. What is the conditional probability of a successful test market given that the product is destined for high sales nationally?

24. Eagle Credit Union (ECU) has experienced a 10% default rate with its commercial loan customers (that is, 90% of commercial loan customers pay back their loans). ECU has developed a statistical test to assist in predicting which commercial loan customers will default. The test assigns either a rating of "Approve" or "Reject" to each loan applicant. When applied to recent commercial loan customers who paid their loans, the test gave an "Approve" rating in 80% of the cases examined. When applied to recent commercial loan customers who defaulted, it gave a "Reject" rating in 70% of the cases examined.

   a. Use this data to construct a joint probability table.

   b. What is the conditional probability of a "Reject" rating given that the customer defaulted?

   c. What is the conditional probability of an "Approve" rating given that the customer defaulted?

   d. Suppose a new customer receives a "Reject" rating. If they are given the loan anyway, what is the probability that they will default?

25. From industry statistics, a credit card company knows that 0.8 of its potential card holders are good credit risks, and 0.2 are bad credit risks. The company uses discriminant analysis to screen credit card applicants and determine which ones should receive credit cards. The company awards credit cards to 70% of those who apply. The company has found that of those awarded credit cards, 95% turn out to be good credit risks. What is the probability that an applicant who is a bad credit risk will be denied a credit card?

26. Thom DeBusk, an architect, is considering buying, restoring, and reselling a home in the Draper-Preston historic district of Blacksburg, VA. The cost of the home is $240,000 and Thom believes it can be sold for $450,000 after being restored. Thom expects he can sell the house as soon as the restoration is completed and expects to pay $1500 a month in finance charges from the time he purchases the house until it is sold. Thom has developed two sets of plans for the restoration. Plan A will cost $125,000 and require three months to complete. This plan does not require changes to the front of the house. Plan B is expected to cost $85,000 and require four months of work. This plan does involve changes to the front of the house, which will require the approval of the town's historic preservation committee. Thom expects the approval process for plan B to take two months and cost about $5,000. Thom thinks there is a 40% chance the historic preservation committee will approve this design. Thom plans to buy the home immediately but cannot decide what he should do next. He could immediately proceed with restoration plan A, or he could start immediately with restoration plan B. Of course, if he starts immediately with plan B, he

will not know for two months whether the historic preservation committee approves of this plan. If they do not approve it, he will have to start over and implement plan A instead. Starting over with plan A would cost an additional $20,000 over plan A's normal cost and add an additional month to plan A's normal completion schedule. Alternatively, Thom can hold off implementing either plan until he knows the outcome of the historic planning committee's decision.

a. Create a decision tree for this problem.
b. What set of decisions should Thom make if he follows the maximum EMV criterion?

27. Suppose that you are given the following two alternatives:

Alternative 1: Receive $200 with certainty.
Alternative 2: Receive $1,000 with probability p or

lose $250 with probability $1 - p$.

a. At what value of p would you be indifferent between these two alternatives?
b. Given your response to part a, would you be classified as risk averse, risk neutral, or risk seeking?
c. Suppose that alternative 2 changed so that you would receive $1,000 with probability p or lose $0 with probability $(1 - p)$. At what value of p would you now be indifferent between these alternatives?
d. Given your response to part c, would you be classified as risk averse, risk neutral, or risk seeking?

28. Rusty Reiker is looking for a location to build a new restaurant. He has narrowed the options down to three possible locations. The following table summarizes how he rates each location on the criteria that are most important to his business.

Criterion	Location 1	Location 2	Location 3
Price	0.9	0.7	0.4
Accessibility	0.6	0.7	0.8
Traffic Growth	0.9	0.8	0.7
Competition	0.4	0.5	0.8

Upon reflection, Rusty decides that the weights he would assign to each criterion are as follows: Price 20%, Accessibility 30%, Traffic Growth 20%, and Competition 30%.

a. Create a multicriteria scoring model for this problem.
b. Create a radar chart showing the weighted scores for each location on each of the criteria.
c. According to this model, which location should Rusty purchase?

29. Hiro Tanaka is going to purchase a new car and has narrowed the decision down to three different sedans. The following table summarizes how he rates each sedan on the criteria that are most important to him.

Criterion	Sedan 1	Sedan 2	Sedan 3
Economy	0.9	0.7	0.4
Safety	0.6	0.7	0.8
Reliability	0.9	0.8	0.7
Style	0.4	0.5	0.8
Comfort	0.5	0.8	0.9

Upon reflection, Hiro decides that the weights he would assign to each criteria are as follows: Economy 30%, Safety 15%, Reliability 15%, Style 15%, and Comfort 25%.

a. Create a multicriteria scoring model for this problem.
b. Create a radar chart showing the weighted scores for each car on each of the criteria.
c. According to this model, which car should Hiro purchase?
d. Suppose Hiro is uncertain about the weights he assigned to the comfort and safety criteria. If he is willing to trade comfort for safety, how would the solution change?
e. Suppose Hiro is uncertain about the weights he assigned to the economy and safety criteria. If he is willing to trade economy for safety, how would the solution change?

30. The president of Pegasus Corporation is trying to decide which of three candidates (denoted as candidates A, B, and C) to hire as the firm's new vice president of marketing. The primary criteria the president is considering are each candidate's leadership ability, interpersonal skills, and administrative ability. After carefully considering their qualifications, the president used AHP to create the following pairwise comparison matrices for the three candidates on the various criteria:

Leadership Ability

	A	B	C
A	1	3	4
B	1/3	1	2
C	1/4	1/2	1

Interpersonal Skills

	A	B	C
A	1	1/2	3
B	2	1	8
C	1/3	1/8	1

Administrative Ability

	A	B	C
A	1	1/5	1/8
B	5	1	1/3
C	8	3	1

Next, the president of Pegasus considered the relative importance of the three criteria. This resulted in the following pairwise comparison matrix:

Criteria

	Leadership Ability	Interpersonal Skills	Administrative Ability
Leadership Ability	1	1/3	1/4
Interpersonal Skills	3	1	1/2
Administrative Ability	4	2	1

a. Use AHP to compute scores for each candidate on each of the three criteria and to compute weights for each of the criteria.
b. Was the president consistent in making pairwise comparisons?
c. Compute the weighted average score for each candidate. Which candidate should be selected according to your results?

31. Kathy Jones is planning to buy a new minivan, but after narrowing her choices down to three models (X, Y, and Z) within her price range, she is having difficulty

deciding which one to buy. Kathy has compared each model against the others on the basis of four criteria: price, safety, economy, and comfort. Her comparisons are summarized as:

Price

	X	Y	Z
X	1	1/4	3
Y	4	1	7
Z	1/3	1/7	1

Safety

	X	Y	Z
X	1	1/2	3
Y	2	1	8
Z	1/3	1/8	1

Economy

	X	Y	Z
X	1	1/3	1/6
Y	3	1	1/3
Z	6	3	1

Comfort

	X	Y	Z
X	1	1/4	1/8
Y	4	1	1/3
Z	8	3	1

Kathy wants to incorporate all of these criteria into her final decision, but not all of the criteria are equally important. The following matrix summarizes Kathy's comparisons of the importance of the criteria:

Criteria

	Price	Safety	Economy	Comfort
Price	1	1/7	1/2	1/5
Safety	7	1	4	2
Economy	2	1/4	1	1/2
Comfort	5	1/2	2	1

a. Use AHP to compute scores for each minivan on each of the four criteria and to compute weights for each of the criteria.
b. Was Kathy consistent in making pairwise comparisons?
c. Compute the weighted average score for each minivan. Based on this analysis, which minivan should Kathy buy?
32. Identify a consumer electronics product that you want to purchase (for example, a TV, VCR, camcorder, PC, and so on). Identify at least three models of this product that you would consider purchasing. Identify at least three criteria on which these models differ (for example, price, quality, warranty, options).
a. Create a multicriteria scoring model and radar charts for this decision problem. Using this model, which product would you choose?
b. Use AHP to determine scores for each model on each of the criteria and to determine weights for the criteria. Which model should you choose according to the AHP results?

Hang On or Give Up?   CASE 14.1

Success or failure as a farmer depends in large part of the uncertainties of the weather during the growing seasons. Consider the following quote from a recent news article:

"... In a summer plagued by drought and heat, many Southern crops are withering in the fields, taking farmers' profits down with them. Some farmers are fighting to break *even. But others have had to give up hope that this year's crop will survive to harvest. 'Farmers must decide if they're going to continue to nurture that crop or give up and plow it under,' said George Shumaker, an Extension Service economist with the University of Georgia College of Agricultural and Environmental Sciences. Making that decision takes courage and careful calculation."*

Assume that you are a farmer facing the decision of whether or not to plow under your crops. Suppose you have already invested $50 per acre in seed, water, fertilizer, and labor. You estimate it will require another $15 per acre to produce and harvest a marketable crop. If the weather remains favorable, you estimate your crop will bring a market price of $26 per acre. However, if the weather becomes unfavorable, you estimate your crop will bring a market price of $12 per acre. Currently, the weather forecasters are predicting favorable weather conditions with a probability of 0.70. The owner of the farm next to yours (who is growing the same product and has made the same $50 per acre investment) has just decided to plow his fields under because the additional $15 per acre to produce a marketable crop would just be "throwing good money after bad."

1. Develop a decision tree for your decision problem.
2. What is the EMV of harvesting and bringing the crop to market?
3. Would you bring this crop to market or plow it under like your neighbor?
4. By how much would the probability of favorable weather have to change before your answer to the question in part c would change?
5. By how much would the $15 per acre cost of bringing the crop to market have to change before your answer to the question in part c would change?
6. What other factors might you want to consider in making this decision?

Should Larry Junior Go to Court or Settle?

CASE 14.2

In the mid-1990s, DHL was the world's largest shipping company, with $5.7 billion in revenue and 60,000 employees. Larry Hillblom was the "H" in DHL and founder of the company. DHL started on a shoestring budget in 1969 with a business plan to deliver shipping documents by air courier to ports of call days before cargo ships arrived, so that vessels could be unloaded quickly upon arrival and be on their way. The company grew into an international air courier, making Hillblom a millionaire before he turned 30. While not as famous in the United States as Federal Express, overseas DHL is so ubiquitous that its name is synonymous with next-day-air shipping in the same manner that the word "Coke" is used to mean "soft drink."

To avoid U.S. income taxes, Hillblom moved from the San Francisco Bay area to Saipan, a tropical tax haven a thousand miles off the southeast coast of Japan. He became a Micronesian kingpin, launching dozens of businesses and financing land development projects in the Philippines, Hawaii, and Vietnam. He owned European castles and hotels, a Chinese jet, an airline called Continental Micronesia and, in addition to his mansion in Saipan, maintained residences in Manila, Hawaii, and Half Moon Bay. His hobbies included high-end stereo equipment, boats, airplanes, fancy cars and, reportedly, illicit relationships with young Asian girls.

On May 21, 1995, Hillblom and two business associates took off for Saipan in Hillblom's twin-engine seaplane from nearby Pagan Island for a short business trip. Bad weather turned the travelers back and, soon thereafter, dispatchers lost track of the plane. The next morning a search party located parts of the plane and the sodden bodies of Hillblom's companions. Hillblom's body was never found.

Larry Hillblom never married and had no legitimate children. Unfortunately for the Hillblom estate, his will did not contain a clause disinheriting any illegitimate children. Under the prevailing laws, he could have written his children out of the will, but since he didn't, anyone who could prove to be his child would be entitled to an inheritance. Shortly after Hillblom's death, one such child, Larry Junior (age 12), filed suit claiming a share of the estate. (Months after Hillblom's death, several young women emerged from Vietnam, the Philippines, and the Islands of Micronesia claiming that Hillblom had taken up with them briefly and left them with children. See http://dna-view.com/sfstory.htm for additional sordid details.)

Several possible impediments stood in the way of Larry Junior's claim to the Hillblom estate. First, Larry Junior and his attorneys must await the outcome of a proposed law (known as the Hillblom Law) written under serious financial pressure from attorneys for the Hilbloom estate. If passed by the legislature and signed by the governor, the proposed law would retroactively invalidate the claims of illegitimate heirs not specifically mentioned in a will. Larry Junior's advisers estimate a 0.60 probability of the proposed law passing. If the law passes, Larry Junior's attorneys plan to challenge its constitutionality and assign a 0.7 probability to this challenge being successful.

If the Hillblom Law does not pass (or passes and is later deemed unconstitutional) Larry Junior will still have to present evidence that he is the son of the deceased Larry Hillblom. Such claims of paternity are routinely proven or disproven using DNA matching. However, Hillblom disappeared without leaving a physical trace. (Twelve gallons of muriatic acid were delivered to Hillblom's house shortly after his death, and by the time Larry Junior's attorney's got there, the house was antiseptically clean.) However, during facial reconstruction surgery following another plane crash that Larry Hillblom had been in and survived, a mole was removed from his face. That mole could be used for DNA testing if Larry Junior's attorney's can gain access to it. But the mole is in possession of a medical center that is the primary beneficiary of the estate under the contested will. Without DNA evidence, the case cannot go forward. Larry Junior's attorney's estimate a 0.8 probability of being able to obtain appropriate DNA evidence in one way or another. If they are able to obtain a DNA sample, the attorneys estimate a 0.7 probability of it proving a biological relation between Larry Junior and the decedent.

If DNA proof of Larry Junior's claimed parentage is established, his attorney's believe the Hillblom estate will offer a settlement of approximately $40 million to avoid going to court. If this settlement offer is rejected, Larry Junior's legal team faces an uncertain outcome in court. His attorney's believe there is a 0.20 chance that their claim could be dismissed by the court (in which case Larry Junior would receive $0). However, even if they are successful in court, the amount of the award to Larry Junior would depends on how many other illegitimate children make successful claims against the estate. Larry Junior's advisors estimate a 0.04 probability that he would win $338 million, a 0.16 probability that he would receive $68 million, a 0.40 probability that he would receive $34 million, and a 0.20 probability that he would receive $17 million.

While vehemently denying that Larry Junior was Mr. Hillblom's son, in early 1996 (and prior to the outcome of the Hillblom Law), the trustees of the Hillblom estate offered Larry Junior a settlement worth approximately $12 million if he would relinquish all his claims to the Hillblom estate. So Larry Junior and his attorneys face a difficult decision. Do they accept the estate's settlement offer or hope the Hillblom Law doesn't pass and that DNA evidence will establish Larry Junior's rightful claim to the Hillblom estate?

1. Create a decision tree for this problem.
2. What decision should Larry Junior make according to the EMV criterion?

3. What is the minimum settlement offer Larry Junior should accept according to the EMV criterion?
4. What would you do if you were Larry Junior?
5. If you were advising Larry Junior, what other issues might you want to consider in making this decision?

CASE 14.3   # The Spreadsheet Wars

Contributed by Jack Yurkiewicz, Lubin School of Business, Pace University, New York.

Sam Ellis is worried. As president and CEO of Forward Software, Sam introduced a new spreadsheet product, Cinco, to the market last year. Forward Software has been developing and marketing high-quality software packages for more than five years, but these products are mostly computer software language interpreters, similar to Pascal, FORTRAN, and C. These products received excellent critical reviews, and because of Forward's aggressive pricing and marketing, the company quickly captured a major share of that software market. Buoyed by its wide acceptance, last year Forward decided to enter the applications arena for the IBM and compatible audience, leading off with Cinco and following up with a word-processing application, Fast.

The spreadsheet market is dominated by Focus Software, whose product—Focus A-B-C—has an 80% market share. Focus A-B-C was released in 1981, shortly after the IBM PC was introduced, and the two products had an immediate symbiotic effect. The spreadsheet was a major advance over what was available at the time but required the extra 16-bit processing power that the IBM PC offered. IBM, on the other hand, needed an application that would make its PC a "must buy." Sales of Focus A-B-C and the IBM PC took off as a result of their near-simultaneous release.

At the time of its release, Focus A-B-C was a superb product, but it did have flaws. For example, because the software was copy-protected, it could be installed on a hard disk, but the original floppy disk had to be inserted each time before the software could run. Many users found this step an annoyance. Another problem with A-B-C was printing graphs. In order to print a graph, users had to exit the software and load a new program, called Printgraf, which would then print the graph. Finally, the product had a list price of $495, and the best discounted price available was approximately $300.

However, Focus A-B-C had a unique menu system that was intuitive and easy to use. Pressing the slash key (/) displayed the menu system at the top of the spreadsheet. The menu allowed the user to make choices and provided a one-line explanation of each menu option. Compared to the cryptic commands or keystrokes users had to enter in other products, the Focus A-B-C menu system was a model of simplicity and clarity. Millions of users became accustomed to the menu system and hailed its use.

Another advantage of Focus A-B-C was its ability to let users write their own macros. Literally a program, a macro allowed a user to automate spreadsheet tasks and then run them with a keystroke or two.

In 1985, a small company named Discount Software introduced its own spreadsheet to the market. Called VIP Scheduler, the product looked and worked exactly the same as Focus A-B-C. Pressing the slash key displayed the identical menu as found in Focus A-B-C, and the product could read any macros developed with Focus A-B-C. VIP Scheduler was designed to look and work exactly as Focus A-B-C so that users would not have to learn a new system and could start productive work immediately. VIP Scheduler also offered two advantages over Focus A-B-C: its list price was $99, and the software was not copy-protected. Sales for VIP Scheduler were strong, but many consumers, perhaps feeling safer with the Focus name, did not buy the product, even though critical reviews were positive. VIP Scheduler did find a receptive market in academia.

When Forward released its first spreadsheet product, Cinco, it was hailed by critics as a better all-around product than Focus A-B-C. It had better graphics, allowed users to print graphs from within Cinco, and was 100% compatible with Focus A-B-C. Cinco had its own menu system, which was as flexible as the Focus A-B-C system, but the menus and options were arranged more intuitively. For users who did not want to invest the time to learn a new menu system, Cinco could emulate the Focus A-B-C menu system. Both menus were activated by pressing the slash key, and users could specify easily which menu system they wanted. All macros written for Focus A-B-C ran perfectly on Cinco, provided that the Focus A-B-C menu system was being used. Because of favorable reviews and aggressive marketing by Forward, Cinco quickly gained market share.

In a move that surprised the industry, Focus recently sued Discount Software, publisher of VIP Scheduler, for copyright infringement. Focus claimed that its menu system was an original work, and that VIP Scheduler, by incorporating that menu system in its product, had violated copyright laws. Focus claimed that the look and feel of its menu system could not be used in another product without permission. Sam is certain that Focus initiated this lawsuit because Cinco has made such dramatic progress in gaining a share of the spreadsheet market. Sam also is sure that Focus's target is not really VIP Scheduler because it has such a small market share, but Cinco.

After discussions with Forward's attorneys, Sam thinks that if he makes a quiet overture to Focus to settle out of court, Focus would be amenable to such a proposal. This would stave off potential negative publicity if Focus wins its suit against Discount Software and then follows up with a lawsuit against Forward. Based on projections of Cinco's sales, Forward's attorneys think that Focus could ask for $5, $8, or as much as $15 million in damages. Sam believes that the probability of Focus agreeing to $5 million is 50%, $8 million is 30%, and $15 million is 20%.

Sam knows that settling now means an immediate loss of income, in the amount of one of the three estimates given, plus an admission of defeat and guilt for Forward. On the other hand, Sam could wait for the outcome of the Focus versus Discount Software unit. Forward's attorneys believe that Focus has a 40% chance of winning its lawsuit against Discount Software. With a win, Focus would have its legal precedent to sue Forward. It is by no means certain that Focus would institute a lawsuit against Forward because Forward is a much larger company than Discount Software and could afford a vigorous legal defense. Also the case against Forward is not as clear cut because Cinco has its own menu system as the primary mode of operation and offers the Focus A-B-C menu system for those who want to use it. VIP Scheduler provides only the Focus A-B-C menu system. However, Forward's attorneys believe there is an 80% chance that Focus would initiate a lawsuit against Forward if Focus wins its suit against Discount Software.

Sam believes that even if Focus sues Forward, he could still try to settle the case out of court at that time or decide to go to trial. An attempt to settle out of court at that time would be more expensive for Forward because Focus would feel secure that it would win its case against Forward, having already won its lawsuit against Discount Software. Thus, Forward's attorneys think that Focus would settle for no less than $7 million, possibly asking for $10 million or even $12 million. The respective probabilities that Focus would settle for these amounts ($7, $10, and $12 million) are estimated to be 30%, 40%, and 30%. Also, Forward would have to pay its attorneys roughly $1 million to go through the settling process.

However, if Focus sues Forward and Forward decides to go to trial instead of initiating settlement proceedings, Forward could lose the case. Forward's attorneys estimate there is an 80% chance that Forward would lose the trial, resulting in a judgment of $10 million, $12 million, or $18 million against Forward, with probabilities of 10%, 20%, and 70%, respectively. The attorneys also estimate that their fees for a trial could run as high as $1.5 million.

Use decision analysis to determine what Sam's optimal strategy should be. Create the decision tree for this problem, including all costs and probabilities, and find the optimal decision strategy / and expected cost for that strategy. Consider Sam to be "risk neutral" in this analysis.

Index